CONTENTS

HOW TO USE OCCUPATIONS...

COLOUR VISION AND EMPLOYMENT

Occupations '97 is a comprehensive reference book containing details of around 600 jobs and careers of all types, from manual to professional work.

The book has an article about colour vision and employment; a list of the jobs included in Occupations '97 in Careers Library Classification Index (CLCI) order; the occupational articles and the alphabetical index.

Most career practitioners will be familiar with CLCI, which has 18 major occupational groups, each identified by an index letter. For example, group R is Engineering and group N is Finance and Related Work.

Each group is subdivided into smaller occupational areas identified by a further two or three-letter classification, such as RAL Electronic Engineering or NAD Banking. As far as possible, we have used the CLCI. However, on occasion, we have departed from it for the sake of clarity. Hotel receptionist, for example, is under Catering and Other Services in group I, rather than under its usual classification with clerical work, in group C.

Users of Occupations '97 can find information about occupations either by using the CLCI listing or through the alphabetical index.

The CLCI listing is useful because it groups jobs and careers with similar backgrounds together. Readers without a specific occupation in mind, but with a broad idea of their chosen career area (say engineering or social work) are presented with a range of related careers.

However, if a reader wants information about a specific job, the relevant page can readily be found using the alphabetical index.

Each career article contains the following details: background information, the work, work environment, skills and interests, entry requirements, training, late entry, opportunities, pay and conditions, prospects and related occupations.

There is also a list of addresses and publications for further information. These address lists are of professional and other bodies which should be able to provide information over and above that contained in the relevant article.

Every effort is made to ensure that the information contained in Occupations is accurate at the time of going to print.

However, if we have got something wrong then please let us know by writing to Judy Leavesley (Editor), Occupations '97, COIC, Room West 4B, Moorfoot, Sheffield S1 4PQ.

Normal colour vision is useful or important to a wide range of jobs that involve any kind of visual judgement.

In the case of a small number of occupations – notably those where colour recognition is critical to health and safety – perfect colour vision may be required as a condition for training or employment.

Serious defects in colour vision are usually diagnosed early on in childhood and those affected should seek detailed advice from their local careers service about the implications for them individually. For jobs or training in which perfect colour vision is essential, a sight test will normally form part of the selection procedure.

What is defective colour vision?

Defective colour vision (colour-blindness) occurs in about 8 per cent of men and 0.4 per cent of women in Western Europe and America and is caused by a defect or abnormality in the light-sensitive pigments (photopigments) contained in the cone-shaped cells that form part of the retina (the layer of sensory cells at the back of the eye).

It is usually inherited, does not change with age and cannot be treated. However, the level of defect is often only moderate and still allows people to recognize or distinguish between colours to a greater or lesser extent. In these cases it may not represent any serious disability in terms of employment.

Types of defect

There are three main types of defective colour vision:

1. Total or partial loss of sensitivity to red light. This affects two per cent of men and four in every ten thousand women.

2. Total or partial loss of sensitivity to green light. This affects six per cent of men and 36 women in every ten thousand.

3. Total or partial loss of sensitivity to blue light affects about one person in every ten thousand. It occurs equally in men and women.

Only about three people in every hundred thousand are totally colour-blind and see the world exclusively in monochrome. In most cases these individuals have poor sight in general.

In addition there are some people who lose some degree of colour vision in later life due to injury, illness or adverse reaction to prescribed drugs. Their symptoms are different from those of people who have inherited defective colour vision and, according to individual circumstances, they may have other sight problems as well.

Testing for colour vision

As defective colour vision is usually spotted early in life, it can be tested at school. In addition, the following university departments can provide testing services (for which, in some cases, there may be a fee): Cardiff, Glasgow Caledonian, City (London), Leeds, and University of Manchester Institute of Science and Technology (UMIST).

Certain employers may also administer colour vision tests as part of the recruitment process.

A number of tests are available, including the Ishihara test (one of the most commonly used) and the City University test.

Tests check both the presence, type and degree of defective colour vision (for example, whether different shades can be recognized).

Implications for career choice

Some occupations are not suitable for people with defective colour vision. For instance, people who lack sensitivity to red light may have difficulty recognizing signals and would be unsuited to certain careers in transport. However, in some jobs, it is possible to predict where problems may occur and take steps to avoid them. It may also be possible to redesign a job so that a person with defective colour vision can do it satisfactorily.

Occupations where good colour vision is an entry requirement

Armed Forces – certain trades. Check with the appropriate Forces careers information office

Carpet manufacture – certain jobs. Check with your local careers office

Civil aviation – air traffic control, flight crew

Colour matcher – in dyeing, textiles, paints, inks, coloured paper, ceramics, cosmetics

Electrical/electronic technician

Merchant Navy deck officer

Motor mechanic

Police officer

Railway worker – train driver, signals/telecoms technician, track worker, station assistant

Radio and telecommunications – telecoms technician

Typical occupations where defective colour vision is a handicap, though not an absolute bar, to entry

Note: this is *not* an exhaustive list. Cartography

Design

Horticulture

Merchant Navy engineering officer

Pharmacy

There are many other occupations where normal colour vision may be helpful, but defective colour vision is not a serious handicap. If you have problems with your colour vision it is advisable to discuss your choice of occupation with your local careers service. The Health and Safety Executive's Employment Medical Advisory Service may advise on occupational placements and suggest agencies which can provide testing facilities.

Further information and further reading

NB: The following publications are primarily technical and aimed primarily at professionals in the field.

Diagnosis of Defective Colour Vision – Jennifer Birch – Oxford University Press (1993) – (Senior lecturer in Clinical Optometry, City University), contains a checklist of occupations where normal colour vision is required or in which defective colour vision is a handicap.

The Public Enquiry Point, Information Centre, Health and Safety Executive, Broad Lane, Sheffield S3 7HQ, 0114 2892345 (can supply a list of references).

Thanks are due to the City University Optometry Department for their help in preparing this information.

**For Alphabetical Index
see page 653**

LIST OF OCCUPATIONAL ARTICLES IN CLCI ORDER

LIST OF OCCUPATIONAL ARTICLES IN CLCI ORDER

x

LIST OF OCCUPATIONAL ARTICLES IN CLCI ORDER

SELF-EMPLOYMENT

The 1980s saw a phenomenal growth in self-employment. From just under two million self-employed people at the end of 1979, by 1990 the number had risen to over three million, around twelve per cent of the workforce.

The increase in self-employment during the 1980s was actively promoted by government policy. This operated in two ways – first, the government aimed to make the general business environment more favourable for the self-employed, for instance by removing red tape in the form of unnecessary regulations; second, a number of direct measures of assistance to the self-employed and owners of small businesses were introduced.

The boom years came to an end in 1990. As business failures mounted, and many of those who had chosen self-employment in the 1980s faltered or went under, the risks of working for oneself were highlighted. At the same time, however, there were still people who were prepared to take these risks: the National Westminster Bank estimates that 460,000 businesses were started in 1991 – only a slight drop from the 500,000 which were started up in 1989 and 1990.

Why self-employment?

To explain why people become self-employed, despite the obvious difficulties, one has to look at the powerful appeal of working for oneself. One of the main attractions of self-employment is that it gives the individual a degree of control over his or her own work. The self-employed person can decide, within limits, what type of work to do, when to do it, what standards to achieve and at what pace. The self-employed can set their own targets and decide when and where to work. Any successes and achievements are their own, with no risk of others claiming credit for them.

Financial rewards are also an attraction, but anyone who is considering self-employment purely for financial gain should think carefully – it is quite possible to make a lot of money by working for oneself, but on the whole a more realistic target – after the start-up period – is a standard of living comparable with, or slightly lower than, previous earnings from employment, but with the freedom and sense of achievement of working independently.

Many of us probably consider the idea of becoming self-employed at some stage in our lives, but the number of people who dream about working for themselves far exceeds the number who actually start up on their own. It requires a lot of confidence to give up a full-time job to face years of financial insecurity and long hours, with no guarantee of success. Some of the self-employed are true entrepreneurs, but in many cases, the decision to go it alone is triggered by external events – like unemployment, failure to achieve an expected promotion, relocation of the employer's business, or personality clashes at work.

Businesses set up in response to external events may well succeed. But with around one in three new businesses failing to survive their first three years, it is essential to assess one's suitability for self-employment, to take advantage of advice and training (which reduces the failure rate to around one in six) and to discuss the idea with family and friends – their support again improves the odds against failure.

Unlike a job, there is no application form or interview for self-employment. It is open to anyone. This puts the burden of deciding whether to go ahead fairly and squarely on the shoulders of the individual concerned. It is important to think about whether one has the necessary personal qualities – resilience, self-motivation, confidence, ability to cope with stress, flexibility, organizational skills and willingness to take advice. Completing a self-assessment questionnaire (often included in books on self-employment) is a useful aid to deciding whether to go ahead.

Finding a business idea

The standard advice is to find a 'gap in the market' – a product or service that no one else is providing, either in the local area or nationally. The proposal need not necessarily be original; for example, there may be no local desk-top publisher, jobbing gardener or window cleaner – and it is worth investigating whether there is potential demand for such services.

On the other hand, plenty of businesses are started up in direct competition with others, and competition may, in fact, stimulate trade. Customers may not bother to make a special trip to visit one clothing store in a shopping area – but half-a-dozen gives sufficient choice to make the expedition worthwhile. However, there still needs to be a good reason – high quality, for instance, or a particular line of speciality goods – to attract customers.

Many people start up businesses based around the skills they have gained in employment, or through training courses, or spare-time interests and hobbies. It is likely that something that excites one's own interest and enthusiasm will be more successful than an activity undertaken solely for financial gain.

An alternative to starting a new business from scratch is to buy a franchise – in other words, the right to use a recognized and established name, trade mark and business system. Well-known franchises include Burger King, Dyno-Rod and Pizza Express. In return for a fee, the company selling the franchise provides a blueprint for running the business, training and back-up support such as assistance with raising finance, national advertising and promotion, and management expertise.

Franchising is a relatively safe way of starting up on one's own – the failure rate is lower than for other small businesses. On the other hand, it is expensive. The franchisee (the person running the business) is not totally independent, but must follow guidelines laid down by the parent company. However, if the parent company runs into difficulties, franchisees can also be badly affected.

It is also possible to buy an existing business, although it is important to look at the reasons for its sale. For example, the owner may be selling because profits are falling, or because he/she anticipates that profits will fall in the future. As with new businesses, professional advice and careful market research are essential.

Market research

Having settled on a business idea, it is then necessary to devote some time to market research, in order to decide whether the proposed business is going to be viable. Ways of tackling this task will depend on the type of business proposed, but could include:

– contacting potential customers, by phone or in person, to test out whether they would buy the proposed product or service, and if so, how much they would be prepared to spend;

– visiting the local library, to consult the specialist trade press and trade directories for information on potential customers, suppliers and competitors;

– discussing the proposal with your nearest Business Link or at a Local Enterprise Agency;

– test marketing – if it is possible to sell a small number of items, or to provide a service to customers on a 'trial run' basis, then this can be a valuable way of assessing whether there is a market and whether the product or service satisfies customer needs. Customers can be followed up, and if they suggest modifications to the product/service, these can be made before the business gets fully under way.

Selling and pricing

Market research will establish whether anyone will buy the product or service. The next question is how to sell. There are a number of choices, including: direct selling – face-to-face or by telephone; advertisements; brochures and leaflets; or via an agent. Many businesses use a mixture of methods. For individuals without any sales experience, some training in direct selling skills may be beneficial.

Pricing is a complex question. If prices are too high, projected sales may not be achieved, but if prices are too low, little or no profit will be made. A price has to take into account a realistic rate for the labour involved, as well as both fixed costs – those which have to be paid for all the time, irrespective of how much work is done, like rent, heating and insurance – and variable costs, like materials, which are related to a particular job. It is also important to remember that no self-employed person spends all their time producing goods or services. Part of the time has to be spent selling, quoting for work which does not materialize, keeping accounts and other business records. It is a common mistake to set a price for one's labour that does not take these time-consuming but necessary tasks into account.

Advice and training

It is in the early stages, when the business is still an idea or plan rather than a reality, that advice and training can be most useful. Sadly, the self-employed often fail to seek help until things go wrong.

Business Links provide information, training, financial advice etc.

Young people

Apart from local advice, counselling and training offered by TECs/LECs and Enterprise Agencies/Trusts, there are also a number of national schemes aimed at helping young people to start up their own businesses. They include:

1. Youth Enterprise Centres, which specialize in giving advice and providing starter premises, mainly for people under 26 years. They are sometimes part of Local Enterprise Agencies.

2. The Prince's Youth Business Trust and the Prince's Scottish Youth Business Trust, which offer business advice, bursaries or loans, and arrange training for young people between the ages of 18 and 25 years (30 in the case of those with disabilities).

3. Livewire. An initiative sponsored by Shell, to provide free business advice and practical help to young people (16 to 25 years) anywhere in the UK. Cash awards are made to those applicants who submit the best business plans each year (as part of an annual competition) – the plans are judged by local panels.

Advice and information is also available from banks, many of which have small business advisers. Then there are specialist bodies, such as the Rural Development Commission, which assists businesses in rural counties in England, or Instant Muscle, which provides 'training, counselling and help with business plans, mainly in areas of high unemployment (London, South Wales, Scotland, the North West, Yorkshire and East Anglia). Some advisory bodies specialize in working with particular groups of people – the Small Business Bureau and the Ethnic Minority Career Development Unit are examples.

The organizations already described provide free advice and counselling on general business matters. More specialist advice may also be necessary, depending on the size and scope of the intended business. Most will need the services of an accountant; in certain circumstances it will be necessary to consult a solicitor; in appropriate cases, other professionals such as insurance brokers, designers and surveyors may be needed. These advisers operate on a fee-paying basis (although an initial consultation may sometimes be free); it is important to get an estimate of charges in advance, and to choose an appropriate adviser – a one-person business, for instance, would probably be wasting money by going to a large, city-based firm of chartered accountants – a small practice or self-employed accountant would be cheaper and more suitable.

Raising money

Even for a very simple idea for self-employment, with modest equipment costs, some capital is needed to get the business under way. Sales take a while to build up, stationery and other supplies need to be bought, and there is usually a gap between selling an item, or completing a piece of work, and being paid by the customer. However, the self-employed person needs money to live on in the meantime. If business premises or substantial purchases of stock are required, then of course the start-up costs will be much greater.

There are a number of ways of raising money to start up a new enterprise. First of all, there is the simple expedient of using one's own money – savings or redundancy payments, for example. Another simple way of raising money is to borrow from other family members – although this has its drawbacks, particularly if there are any problems about repaying the loan later on, or if the lender feels that investing in the business gives him or her a say in how it is run.

The most common source of borrowing is from the bank, usually in the form of an overdraft facility or, for the purchase of equipment, a loan over a specified term of years. Bank managers are generally sympathetic to a well-thought-out case for borrowing, but do need written information on which to assess the business proposal.

In order to borrow from the bank and, perhaps more importantly, to clarify one's own ideas and intentions, it is usual to draw up a written business plan. The length of the plan and the amount of detail it contains will vary according to the size of the business, but it should certainly contain personal information about the owner, a clear description of the product or service being offered, the market, and future prospects, backed up by detailed financial forecasts. Help with drawing up a business plan is available from the advice agencies described above.

Business Links will be able to supply information about other sources of business finance such as local authority grants and the Government's Loan Guarantee Scheme for small businesses.

The structure of the business

Another choice to make before starting up is the form of business structure. Most self-employed people start off as sole traders. This simply means that the individual is running an independent business and is treated by the Inland Revenue as being self-employed. Despite the name, a sole trader doesn't necessarily work alone – he or she can employ others, but is solely responsible for the business. In terms of paperwork, there are few obligations involved in this type of business structure, apart from keeping records for tax purposes. On the other hand, sole traders are personally liable for all debts they incur.

A second option is to go into business with a partner or partners. Ideally, these should be individuals with complementary skills; for instance, someone whose skills are purely practical might seek out a partner with a liking for paperwork, to run the administrative side of the business.

A partnership can be a difficult structure to work within, and it is important to think through the implications before making a commitment. All members of a partnership are personally liable for the debts of the business, even if those debts are incurred without their knowledge.

A third possibility is to form a limited company, but for a very small new business this is not generally advisable, although it may be worth considering in certain circumstances. A limited company does have the advantage of limited liability – creditors' claims are limited to the assets of the company – but there are tax advantages in starting as a sole trader or partner. It is always possible to change to limited company status later, as the business grows.

The fourth possibility is a co-operative – a business owned and controlled by all the people who work in it. In a co-op, decisions are usually made by democratic majority vote. There are many examples of successful co-operatives, although there is always a danger of the democratic process involving too many meetings and unnecessary delay in making operational decisions.

Other matters

There are a number of other points to take into consideration before starting trading:

– Where to work. The self-employed often start by working from home, in order to save on costs. It may be necessary to check whether planning permission is required and whether the landlord or mortgagee will allow the premises to be used for business. An inexpensive alternative is to rent a 'starter unit' for small businesses – these are often available through Local Enterprise Agencies (LEAs).

– Tax. The local tax inspector should be notified as soon as trading begins. Sole traders and partners pay tax in arrears, in two lump sums a year.

– National Insurance. The self-employed must pay a regular National Insurance contribution (the rates vary from year to year), by direct debit from a bank account. There are exemptions for low earners. Additional contributions are made, and collected along with income tax, by those making a profit over a certain level.

– Financial records. Accountants will advise on the most appropriate form of book-keeping for the business.

– Insurance. It is important to check the insurance needs of the business and to make sure that existing insurers are notified where necessary (for example, if a car is to be used for business, the motor insurers should be informed).

In conclusion

Self-employment is no easy option, and it demands careful planning, research and assessment of the business idea. Perhaps most important, however, are self-discipline and self-knowledge – an understanding of one's own strengths and weaknesses, self-motivation, and the ability to keep going in bad times as well as good. It is also essential to be able to accept and act upon advice; together with appropriate training, this can considerably reduce the risks involved in starting up a new business venture.

FURTHER INFORMATION

Association of Enterprise Agencies, New Enterprise House, St Helen's Street, Derby DE1 3GY

The Ethnic Minority Career Development Unit, London Guildhall University, Calcutta House, Old Castle Street, London E1 7NT, 0171 320 1201

Instant Muscle, Springside House, 84 North End Road, London W14 9ES, 0171 603 2604

Livewire, Hawthorn House, Forth Banks, Newcastle-upon-Tyne NE1 3SG, 0191 261 5584

National Federation of Enterprise Agencies*, c/o Cadbury Schweppes plc, Bournville D24, Birmingham B30 2LU, 0121 458 2000, ext 3955

The Prince's Youth Business Trust*, 18 Park Square East, London NW1 4LH, 0171 543 1234

Rural Development Commission, 141 Castle Street, Salisbury, Wiltshire SP1 3TP, 01722 336255

Small Business Bureau, Curzon House, Church Road, Windlesham, Surrey GU20 6BH, 01276 452010

FURTHER READING

Leaflets/booklets are available from the addresses marked* and from Business Link – Signpost 0345 567765.

Lloyds Bank Small Business Guide – Penguin
Taking up a Franchise – Kogan Page
Working for Yourself – The Daily Telegraph Guide to Self-Employment – Kogan Page.

In the careers library classified under AP.

GROUP B – ARMED FORCES

1. RN/QARNNS OFFICER CLCI:BAB
2. RN RATING CLCI:BAB
3. ROYAL MARINES OFFICER CLCI:BAB
4. ROYAL MARINES – OTHER RANKS
   CLCI:BAB

BACKGROUND INFORMATION

The Naval Service is made up of three branches: The Royal Navy (RN), The Royal Marines (RM), and Queen Alexandra's Royal Naval Nursing Service (QARNNS). It provides Britain with a maritime defence force and plays an important role in NATO and worldwide.

The Royal Navy operates warships, submarines and ship-borne aircraft. The fleet at sea is supported by communications centres, training establishments and other installations ashore.

The Royal Navy is divided into six teams: Warfare, Engineering, Supply and Secretariat, Medical, Fleet Air Arm and the Submarine Service. Women work alongside men in almost all jobs. The exceptions are jobs in submarines (Deep Navy) and some smaller ships such as minesweepers, which are only available to men.

The Royal Marines is a specialist force of amphibious commandos. It operates from Royal Navy ships and assault/landing craft. Commando units may specialize as Air or Special Boat Squadrons, Ship's Detachment, Embarked Force or in Jungle, Mountain and Arctic Warfare. The Royal Marines is not open to women with the exception of the Royal Marines Band Service.

Queen Alexandra's Royal Naval Nursing Service cares for Service personnel and their families in land-based Naval hospitals in Britain and abroad. QARNNS is open to men and women. All QARNNS have a liability to serve at sea.

Entry to the Naval Service is as an officer or rating. All entrants undergo basic training as an officer or rating before beginning specialist training in one of the wide range of jobs. Some posts are open to those who have qualified in their specialization in civilian life (eg nursing officer).

1. RN/QARNNS OFFICER (BAB)

THE WORK

Officers manage and lead the many personnel who make up the Royal Navy. As well as specializing in a particular area, officers are responsible for looking after the welfare, career advancement and discipline of the ratings under their command.

Seaman officer

Seaman officers are responsible for 'working' and 'fighting' the ship; in other words, making sure the ship is handled safely and efficiently and to the best tactical advantage. Their first appointment is usually as officer of the watch, responsible for the safety of the ship and the ship's company during their watch on the bridge. This involves controlling the ship's course and speed, using information from charts, sensors, the weather and the sea. Most seaman officers then go on to a second watchkeeping job, but it is also possible to sub-specialize in a number of areas.

Aircraft Control. Aircraft controllers are responsible for the guidance and control of various aircraft, using radar and computer systems. Fighter controllers control fighter aircraft to carry out interception of enemy aircraft.

Aviation. Pilots fly naval helicopters or Sea Harrier 'jump jets' to locate and attack enemy vessels or to provide air defence. Observers co-ordinate warfare from the air. Aircrew officers (pilots and observers) also take part in amphibious warfare, search and rescue operations, casualty evacuation, communications work and reconnaissance. There are also opportunities as air traffic controllers.

Mine Warfare and Clearance Diving (MCD). MCD officers qualify as diving officers before learning how to handle and dispose of explosives, and the techniques of minehunting and minesweeping;

Submarines. Submariners are specially trained to serve in the Submarine Service.

Hydrographic Surveying Service. Hydrographic surveyors carry out hydrographic and oceanographic surveying to obtain information for navigational charts.

Later, seaman officers can become principal warfare officers, specializing in Anti-Air Warfare or Anti-Submarine Warfare. They are responsible for 'fighting' the ship and working with the captain to direct fighting operations.

Engineer officer

The Royal Navy Service uses advanced technology in all areas and engineer officers are responsible for monitoring the equipment and ensuring it works properly. Engineer officers specialize in one of five areas.

Weapon engineer officer (surface ships). Surface ships WEOs are responsible for the ship's weapon systems including gun, torpedo and missile systems. This work also covers all aspects of the weapons' sensor and communications systems.

Weapon engineer officer (submarines). Submarines WEOs have similar responsibilities to WEOs on surface ships, but also act as control room watchkeepers.

Marine engineer officer (surface ships). Surface ships MEOs are responsible for everything that keeps the ship afloat, including the structure of the ship, the engines, electricity, air conditioning, heating, ventilation, etc.

Marine engineer officer (submarines). In addition to the responsibilities of MEOs in surface ships, those in submarines are also concerned with nuclear reactors and the specialized submarine hull equipment.

Air engineer officer (mechanical and electrical). AEOs deal with the maintenance and repair of aircraft systems. They also look after the electrical systems and electronics associated with flight control radar and weapons systems.

Supply and secretariat officer

Supply and secretariat officers look after administration and the organization of equipment, food, money, etc. They may serve at sea or on land. When at sea they must also perform operational duties. The work of a supply and secretariat officer falls into four main areas.

Captain's secretary. The Captain's secretary deals with official correspondence, administrative, welfare and personnel matters on land or at sea.

Naval stores. Supply officers in naval stores are responsible for ensuring that any piece of equipment is in the right place at the right time.

Catering. Supply officers in catering handle the long-term ordering of food and provisions, and supervise meal preparation on a daily basis.

Pay and cash. Officers deal with pay and with special allowances, foreign currency and accounts.

Specialist officer

Specialist officers carry out their profession within service life. They include:

Medical officers who care for Naval Service personnel and their families. They may also be involved in providing medical aid during crises or natural disasters. When serving at sea they have additional duties such as watchkeeping, organizing entertainments, acting as wardroom treasurer or secretary, publishing newsletters or public relations. They may also have responsibility for the welfare of a division of ten to fourteen staff;

Dental officers look after the dental health of Naval Service personnel. On some postings they may also care for service families. Preventative dentistry is a large part of the work. Like medical officers they also carry out additional duties whilst at sea;

Nursing officers in The Queen Alexandra's Royal Naval Nursing Service care for service personnel and their families, and patients in both hospitals and medical centres. They have a liability to serve at sea both during peacetime and conflict.

Naval chaplains from many denominations, both male and female, serve ashore and afloat. They minister to service personnel and their families.

WORK ENVIRONMENT

RN officers serve at sea on a variety of ships (eg aircraft carriers, destroyers, frigates), or in a shore installation in Britain or abroad. Shore installations include training establishments, hospitals, air stations and base ports. RN (male) officers may also serve on submarines. Their immediate work environment depends on the job they do. Their social life, both at sea and ashore, revolves around the wardroom (officers' mess). They must be prepared to move abroad and within the UK.

SKILLS AND INTERESTS

Officers need leadership qualities and the ability to work effectively as part of a team. They must be able to think and react quickly. They must be ready to accept responsibility, make decisions and manage other personnel. They should be able to communicate with people of all abilities, explain ideas, give spoken and written instructions, and motivate others. Officers must be interested in the people they supervise, and be able to listen to, guide and discipline them. All officers must be physically fit and prepared to work in combat. An interest in science/technology is important in many of the jobs.

Each specialization has its own requirements. For example, aircraft controllers must be able to stay calm, think quickly and concentrate for long periods. Supply and secretariat officers must be methodical and have a flair for organization. Engineer officers need technological ability and the skills to find solutions to problems. Aviators must have initiative and the ability to react quickly.

ENTRY REQUIREMENTS

The minimum entry requirements for RN officers are five subjects – three GCSEs/two S grades (A-C/1-3) and two A levels/three H grades or equivalent, including English and maths at either level. Entry is normally by Naval College Entry (NCE) or Direct Graduate Entry for those who have a degree. Naval college entrants begin as Midshipmen,

graduates as Sub-Lieutenants. Officers join the Naval Service on a full, medium or short-career commission (FCC, MCC, SCC).

NB: After 1 April 1997 career structures are altering. Entrants will be offered an Initial Commission of twelve years, with the possibility of a career commission to follow.

More entry requirements for these types of commission are given below.

FCC/MCC/SCC seaman and FCC/SCC supply and secretariat officers need the minimum entry requirements as should those who want an MCC/SCC as a pilot or observer or in air traffic control. They should be aged at least 17 years. FCC/MCC/SCC seaman and FCC/SCC supply and secretariat direct graduate entrants must have a degree in addition to the minimum requirements.

NB: An FCC is not available for flying duties.

FCC/MCC/SCC engineer officer direct graduate entrants need a degree in mechanical, aeronautical, electrical or electronic engineering or equivalent which gives exemption from parts I and II of the Engineering Council Examination, plus GCSEs/S grades (A-C/1-3) in English.

Medical officers can enter at all levels from student (on a bursary) to post-registration, initially on an SCC, with the opportunity to apply for an FCC after two years. Dental officers can join at any stage from obtaining 2nd BDS (Bachelor of Dental Surgery degree) or equivalent, to post-qualifications. They start on an SCC with the opportunity to apply for an MCC or FCC after a year. Nursing officers (QARNNS) must have proof of registration plus a minimum of two years' post-registration nursing experience in a hospital. They take an SCC, with the right to apply for an MCC. Chaplains must be ordained, be recommended by their church authorities and, normally, have had three or more years' experience of parish work.

There are a number of opportunities for sponsorship. The Scholarship/Reserved Place Scheme is available for seaman and engineer officers in the RN to enable them to study for A levels. Financial assistance during the A level course is given to the parents of those who are awarded scholarships. University cadetships provide a salary to students who are officers on an FCC/MCC, whilst bursaries are available to those who wish to remain civilians during their studies. Holders of bursaries may apply for an SCC, MCC or FCC.

To become an RN officer, candidates must pass a series of selection tests held at the Admiralty Interview Board at HMS Sultan, Gosport. These include aptitude tests, practical initiative tests and an interview, and last around two-and-a-half days.

The minimum height for an officer is 1.57m (5 feet 2 inches), and weight must be in proportion to height. There are strict eyesight standards, and all candidates must pass a medical.

All officers must meet the RN nationality and residence requirements. Armed Forces careers offices will give guidance on eligibility.

TRAINING

All new officers begin with Naval General Training at the Britannia Royal Naval College at Dartmouth. The length of this training varies from two to five terms, depending on qualifications and type of entry. It includes experience at sea. Specialist training for the officer's chosen branch begins at the end of this course.

Seaman officer

Seaman officers complete the last part of their Naval General Training with up to twelve months at sea before moving on to further professional training, such as the 16-week Officer of the Watch (OOW) course. Six months' satisfactory service leads to the Bridge Watchkeeping Certificate, and officers can take the Ocean Navigation Certificate at the same time. Those who wish to specialize then take appropriate courses:

Aircraft controllers take a five-month training course on the guidance and tactical control of a range of aircraft, using radar and computer systems, immediately after the completion of Naval General Training.

Aviation trainee pilots follow a practical training, initially in a dual-control Bulldog, then in a Gazelle helicopter, together with a theoretical course covering theory of flight, meteorology, navigation and air engineering. Observers have 100 hours flying in a Jetstream as well as learning the theory of airmanship, navigation, radar, navigation aids, air engineering, oceanography, etc. Both pilots and observers then prepare for the aircraft they will operate in active duty. Sea Harrier pilots follow a 47-week Basic Flying Training course in Jet Provosts, followed by 23 weeks on Advanced Flying Training in Hawks and a further 16 weeks on Tactical Weapons Training, before converting to Sea Harriers.

Mine warfare and clearance divers take a four-week course to qualify as ship's diving officer. They then serve as an SDO for at least one year, before following a seven-month course which includes diving to 180 feet, handling and disposing of explosives, and minehunting and minesweeping.

Submariners begin training immediately after they complete their Officer of the Watch course. They learn about the systems to be found on board a submarine, escaping methods and the specific equipment carried on their first submarine. They then go to sea and gain the experience to qualify as an officer of the watch before taking up a junior appointment, or further training in tactical operations.

Hydrographic surveyors spend six months on a surveying ship before following a 14-week course at the Royal Naval Hydrographic School. After this they are appointed to a surveying ship.

FCC seaman officers may take a 42-week Principal Warfare Officer course. After serving as a PWO, specialists may return to their specialization.

Engineer officer

Engineer officers either join with a relevant degree acceptable to the Ministry of Defence, or are sponsored to take a degree in engineering at the University of Southampton. All engineer officers then take an application course appropriate to their sub-specialization. They may also undertake advanced courses in control engineering, guided weapons, etc.

Supply and secretariat officer, instructor officer

After general naval training, supply and secretariat officers follow supply courses to learn the organizational and administrative techniques required. Courses include specialist training, such as naval law. They may also take additional courses necessary to the operational role they will undertake at sea.

Instructor officers receive a short period of teacher training after basic naval training. Those who go to sea also train in sub-specialist tasks required at sea.

Medical and dental officers

Medical officers spend four weeks at Dartmouth before following a five-week post-registration course to become familiar with maritime medicine.

Dental officers also spend four weeks at Dartmouth, followed by a week's course to learn about the Naval Dental Services.

LATE ENTRY

Upper age limits vary according to the job (all ages apply to the first day of the month of entry):

FCC naval college entrants should be under 23 and direct graduate entrants under 26. University cadets must be under 22 and those on the Scholarship/Reserved Place Scheme may not have a break between GCSEs/S grades and A levels/H grades.

MCC/SCC entrants should be under 26. However, instructor officer direct graduate entrants may be considered up to the age of 34.

Engineers with experience may enter up to age 32, and chaplains under 39.

Medical and dental officers who are training should, preferably, be under 25, pre-registration medical officers under 33 and post-registration medical officers under 44. Post-qualification dental officers are preferred under 32. QARNNS nursing officers must be under 34.

There is normally a delay between being accepted for a commission and the start of training, so candidates are advised to apply at least a year in advance of age limits. Very rarely, upper age limits will be waived for exceptional candidates.

OPPORTUNITIES

The number of officers recruited each year varies, but was 182 during 1994-95. Cutbacks in the Armed Forces are expected to have a slight effect on officer recruitment. Competition is fierce. Those not accepted can re-apply, with a minimum of twelve months between applications. An individual can go before the Admiralty Interview Board up to three times.

PAY AND CONDITIONS

Short-career commissions are usually eight years (twelve for Aviation/Aircraft Control), depending on the job. Medium-career commissions are for 16 years or to the age of 38, whichever is later. A full-career commission is for 22 years or to age 50.

On entry a Midshipman would receive £9,774, rising to £12,150 after one year. Sub-Lieutenants are appointed on £13,932 and Lieutenants earn £23,462 to £27,258. Lieutenant-Commanders receive up to £35,667 and Commanders up to £46,289. Captains with more than six years' seniority earn £59,681. Additional flying pay and submarine pay are available for suitably qualified staff, and special allowances are paid to those serving at sea. An officer's point of entry would depend on the type of commission and, possibly, on professional or academic qualifications and past experience. Officers receive six weeks paid leave a year, usually taken in periods of a fortnight.

Officers are on-call 24 hours a day, but basically work eight-hour turns of duty. This can include shifts and irregular hours. During exercises, hours can be long and unpredictable. Whilst serving at sea, officers can be separated from their families for several months at a time.

PROSPECTS

RN officers can expect new appointments every two or three years.

Promotion is through a structured system from Midshipman (aged 17-26), through Sub-Lieutenant (aged 19-26), Lieutenant (aged 22- 34), Lieutenant-Commander (aged 30-36) Commander (aged 33-40), Captain (aged around 45), to Admiral (aged around 52). Speed of promotion depends on a number of factors, including ability, qualifications and training. Officers on full-career commissions receive automatic promotion to Lieutenant-Commander. Beyond this, advancement is by selection based on merit and performance.

Only seaman officers can become Ship's Captains.

RELATED OCCUPATIONS

Royal Marines officer, RN rating, Army officer, RAF officer, Merchant Navy officer, pilot, air traffic controller, training officer.

FURTHER INFORMATION AND READING

Please see article 4. ROYAL MARINES – OTHER RANKS.

2. RN RATING (BAB)

THE WORK

RN ratings work in a wide variety of jobs needed to run an efficient Naval Service. They may serve on a number of different kinds of ships or in shore establishments. Each has a skill or trade essential to the Navy, and they work closely in teams to keep ships, communications and weapons systems and other equipment ready for action. They work in one of six teams.

Warfare Branch

The Warfare Branch team comprises the people who operate and maintain ship and submarine weapon systems; they also carry out seamanship tasks to sustain operations at sea.

The Warfare Branch includes:

Above-water Warfare OM (AW)

Operates the sensors and weapons that protect the ships from air and surface attacks.

Underwater Warfare OM (UW)

Detects enemy submarines and torpedoes using powerful, modern sonars.

Electronic Warfare OM (EW)

Listens in at long range to enemy electronic equipment and missiles in flight, and provide early warning of danger.

Communications OM (C)

Deals with the incoming and outgoing signals from and to ships and shore establishments.

Communications technicians specialize as linguists, concentrating on voice communications, or as analysts, concerned with naval and air weaponry, radar and communications systems.

Mine Warfare OM (MW)

Keeps shipping lanes clear of mines, around the UK's coastline and other major sea channels.

Survey Recorder OM (SR)

Survey recorders chart coastlines and sea-beds.

Communication Submarine OM (CSM)

Experts in the special communications system that submarines use.

Weapons Submarine OM (SSM)

Operates and looks after the submarine's weapons, torpedoes and missiles and their launch systems.

Tactical Submarine OM (TSM)

Involved in navigation, computer-assisted plotting, and compiling the tactical picture.

Sensors Submarine OM (SSM)

Sonar operators rely on sonar to detect submarines and surface vessels.

Engineering

The Engineering team is responsible for the maintenance and repair of the wide range of highly technical equipment used by the Royal Navy.

Engineering technicians (artificers) are highly skilled personnel, responsible for repairing and maintaining all types of equipment including flight systems (air), missiles (weapons) and propulsion plants (marine). They also manage teams of experts.

Air engineering mechanics help to service and repair the Navy's aircraft. They specialize in servicing the airframe, engine and major mechanical systems (mechanical), looking after avionic systems (radio) and weapons systems (electrical).

Marine engineering mechanics are concerned with the ship's power. MEMs (mechanical) look after the main propulsion and auxiliary systems. MEMs (electrical) work with generators, power distribution systems, electrical switchgear and other heavy electrical plant.

Supply and Secretariat

The Supply and Secretariat team is responsible for the administrative side, including catering, office work and stores.

Stewards run the wardroom (the officers' mess), preparing and serving food, working the bar and looking after officers' accommodation.

Chefs produce food of all types, and maintain financial and stock control records.

Stores accountants ensure that all necessary equipment is available, properly controlled and accounted for.

Writers carry out a range of accounting and clerical duties in personnel, cash and administrative sections.

Medical

The Medical team is responsible for the health of the Navy's personnel.

Medical assistants are paramedics caring for patients either alone or as part of a team.

Medical technicians specialize as:

– physiotherapists, helping people regain their strength and fitness after injury or illness;

– naval health inspectors, responsible for hygiene and safety standards;

– radiographers, using X-ray and other scanning equipment to diagnose and treat;

– pharmacy dispensers, mixing and dispensing medicines;

– laboratory technicians, analysing and identifying samples;

– registered mental nurses, caring for personnel who are suffering from mental illness, including combat stress.

Fleet Air Arm

The Fleet Air Arm ensures that the Navy's aircraft are always ready for action.

Naval airmen (aircraft handling) make sure that aircraft take off and land correctly and that they are kept in the right position. They are also responsible for firefighting duties.

Naval airmen (survival equipment) keep all the life-saving equipment on the aircraft and ships in working order and ensure that it is correctly stored.

Naval airmen (meteorology and oceanography) observe and record the weather details to provide information for use by the whole ship.

Deep Navy

Men in the Deep Navy carry out their specialisms on submarines. The following jobs are available: sonar (submarine), tactical (submarine), weapon (submarine), communication (submarine), marine engineering artificer, weapon engineering artificer, marine engineering mechanic, cook, steward, stores accountant, writer, medical assistant.

Women do not serve on submarines at the moment.

WORK ENVIRONMENT

Please see article 1. RN OFFICER.

SKILLS AND INTERESTS

Ratings must be able to form part of a team, living and working closely with other people. Self-discipline and the ability to live in a small, closed environment are particularly important for those who serve on submarines. Ratings must be able to follow orders. Senior ratings should be able to supervise others. The ability to accept responsibility, make decisions and react quickly under pressure is important. Physical fitness is essential. Ratings must be prepared to work anywhere in the world, and those who go to sea must be ready for long separations from their families. They must also be prepared to work in combat, if necessary.

Practical and technical skills are needed to deal with the advanced equipment used in the Navy, and an interest in science and technology is useful. Good communication skills are also important. In addition, each specialization has its own requirements. For example, some communications technicians must be fluent in another language, whilst stores accountants need to be methodical and have a good memory. Operator mechanics must have good co-ordination, common sense and the ability to stay calm.

ENTRY REQUIREMENTS

All candidates must pass a selection test (reasoning, English, numeracy and mechanical comprehension), interview and medical examination. In addition:

Naval airmen (meteorology and oceanography) need one GCSE/S grade (A-C/1-3) in maths, meteorology, geography or a science subject.

Communications technicians need two GCSEs/S grades (A-C/1-3), including English. They must also pass aptitude tests. Artificer apprentices (the usual entry route for artificers) must pass aptitude tests and a written examination. Exemption from the written examination is available to those with GCSEs/S grades (A-C/1-3) in physics or a physics-based science, maths and English, or who have passed an appropriate BTEC/SCOTVEC course and have GCSE/S grade (A-C/1-3) English.

Medical technicians are members of the Royal Navy's medical team who have very specialized tasks. They include physiotherapists, radiographers, pharmacy dispensers, laboratory technicians, naval health inspectors and registered mental nurses. Entry requirements are five GCSEs/S grades (A-C/1-3) and possibly up to three A levels/four H grades in academic and science subjects. Fully qualified medical technicians may join as direct entrants.

Probationary student nurses need five GCSEs/S grades (A-C/1-3), including English, maths and a science subject (four must have been obtained in one sitting), and direct entrant naval nurses must have proof of registration.

Entry is possible from age 16 years except in the cases of medical assistant and medical technician (17 years), communications technicians and student naval nurses (18½ years), and direct entry registered general nurse (21 years).

The minimum height for all entrants is 1.57m (5 feet 2 inches). Weight must be in proportion to height. There are strict eyesight standards and, for some jobs, good colour vision is essential.

All entrants must meet the RN nationality and residence requirements. Armed Forces careers offices will give guidance on eligibility.

TRAINING

All new entrants spend eight weeks undergoing basic training at HMS Raleigh at Torpoint in Cornwall. This includes practical exercises, drill, PE, personal weapons test, swimming test, naval general training and the Naval Mathematics and English Test. Specialist training for the recruit's chosen trade begins at the end of this course. Some trade training involves working for nationally recognized qualifications, including BTEC and City and Guilds certificates. Ratings may be encouraged to take other advanced qualifications as their careers progress.

The amount of time before a trainee is drafted to a ship varies according to the trade, but training often includes short periods at sea.

Warfare Branch

Above-water warfare training lasts eight weeks, with the emphasis on the setting up and operating of operations room equipment, data processing, and practising the skills required on board ship.

Underwater warfare training lasts for seven weeks. This practical course involves learning how to operate sonar in realistic simulators.

Mine warfare training lasts for eight weeks and covers all aspects of mining (laying and recovery), minesweeping and minehunting.

Electronic warfare training lasts eleven weeks and covers audio and radar training, voice procedure and radar/platform/threat skills.

Communications training covers work with a wide variety of modern equipment, including satellite communications, and lasts for 18 weeks.

Sensors submarine training lasts for eight weeks. The course concentrates on the use of submarine sonar and the detection of both surface ships and submarines.

Weapons submarine training lasts for five weeks. Training includes the operation and maintenance of submarine weapons, torpedoes, missiles and their launch systems.

Tactical submarine training lasts for seven weeks and includes the use of navigation equipment and computer-assisted plotting, and compiling the tactical picture from various sensors.

Communications submarine training lasts for 20 weeks and covers many types of communications including morse code, radio, radio teletype, satellite and telex.

All submariners carry out additional special training to prepare them for life on board a submarine (including a simulated escape from 100 feet underwater in a training tank).

Communications technician training lasts for 150 weeks (including 52 weeks at sea). The linguist concentrates on voice communications, whilst the analyst is concerned with naval and air weaponry, radar and communications systems.

Survey recorders take a six-week course in the recording of data and the use and maintenance of survey instruments.

Engineering

Engineering artificers follow a four-year training course to become skilled in air engineering, weapons engineering or marine engineering.

Engineering artificers follow a common 14-week course before training in their specialism.

Air engineering mechanics take a 20-week basic engineering course covering work on a wide range of airframes, hydraulics, flying controls, fuel systems, radio equipment, weapons and electrical systems.

Marine engineering mechanics (MEM) have a common eight-week course covering basic tools and the equipment they will maintain at sea. MEM (mechanical) then receive two weeks further training on ship main propulsion and auxiliary systems.

MEM (electrical) take a nine-week course which includes electrical principles, test equipment, various types of generators and power distribution systems, electrical switchgear and other heavy electrical plant.

Supply and Secretariat

Stewards spend six weeks learning the professional ways of serving food and drinks, some basic cookery, wardroom organization and the duties of a wine steward.

Cooks follow a 14-week course to learn basic culinary skills, accounting, field cookery and cooking for large numbers.

Stores accountants learn stores accounting, storekeeping, typing and keyboarding during a nine-week course.

Writers have a nine-week course which covers pay accounting, staff records, letter writing, office procedure and word processing.

Medical

Medical assistants follow a nine-week theory course covering anatomy, physiology, first aid, nursing, administration and storekeeping, followed by 29 weeks gaining practical experience in the wards and medical departments.

Medical technicians spend four weeks on a medical training course before following specialized training in their chosen profession. Training takes place in Service hospitals and/or civilian universities and lasts over three years.

Fleet Air Arm

All naval airmen take a seven-week course covering fire fighting, first aid, air traffic control, flight safety and how a naval air station works. After this:

Naval airmen (aircraft handling) have a 15-week course on flight deck procedures, launching of aircraft and aircrew rescue. Rescue handlers are also responsible for firefighting duties.

Naval airmen (survival equipment) have a six-week introduction to aircraft engineering followed by an 18-week safety equipment course.

Naval airmen (meteorology and oceanography) spend eleven weeks learning how to use and maintain basic instruments, how to observe wind, weather, clouds and visibility, and how to code and plot these on weather charts.

Deep Navy

Everyone who serves on submarines undergoes specialist training to accustom them to the conditions and systems on submarines, the escape procedures, etc.

LATE ENTRY

The upper age limit for communications technicians and artificer apprentices is 28 years. For all other trades it is 33 years.

There is normally a delay between being accepted and the start of the training, so candidates are advised to apply at least six months in advance of age limits. Very rarely, upper age limits will be waived for exceptional candidates.

OPPORTUNITIES

The number recruited into different jobs can vary. Cutbacks in the Armed Forces have caused some areas to be closed temporarily to new entrants. Individuals who are not accepted may apply a second time after a twelve-month gap.

PAY AND CONDITIONS

RN ratings enter for a period of 22 years from age 18 years or date of entry, whichever is later. They can leave on 18 months' notice after two-and-a-half years' (technicians and student naval nurses three-and-a-half years') service or after completion of training, whichever is the later. Premature release is available under certain conditions to those who are not suited to Naval Service. Pregnant women have the choice of confinement leave and returning after a given period or of leaving the service. (If the option to remain is taken, the same conditions of service apply.)

Junior Ratings earn £447 a month under the age of 17 and £542 aged 17 to 17 years and 6 months. Ordinary ratings, aged over 17 years and 6 months, get £717 to £802, Able Ratings £932 to £1,164 and Leading Ratings £1,330 to £1,400. Petty Officers earn up to £1,612, Chief Petty Officers up to £1,731 and Warrant Officers up to £2,069. After training, artificers, communications technicians and medical technicians receive higher rates. Additional pay is available for those on submarines or in the Survey Service, divers and anyone required to fly. Ratings receive 36 days paid leave each year.

Ratings work eight-hour turns of duty. This can include shifts and irregular hours. During exercises, hours can be long and unpredictable. Whilst serving at sea, ratings can be separated from their families for several months at a time.

PROSPECTS

Promotion is through a structured system. Those under 17 years and 6 months join as Junior Ratings and get automatic advancement to Ordinary Rating at 17 years and 6 months. New entrants over this age join as Ordinary Ratings. After this, promotion is to Able Rating, Leading Rating, Petty Officer, Chief Petty Officer and Warrant Officer. Promotion to Naval Officer rank is possible for those with the necessary qualifications and potential. Around 25 per cent of Naval Officers began their careers as an Ordinary Rating.

Engineering and operator mechanics may be selected to train as artificers.

RELATED OCCUPATIONS

RN officer, Army NCO/private, RAF airman/woman, Merchant Navy rating, Royal Marines – other ranks.

FURTHER INFORMATION AND READING

Please see article 4. ROYAL MARINES – OTHER RANKS.

3. ROYAL MARINES OFFICER (BAB)

THE WORK

Officers lead and manage the commando units that make up the small, highly trained corps of the Royal Marines. The Royal Marines is primarily a security combat force on hand for any emergency, anywhere in the world, so officers' main duties involve organizing and controlling men in a wide variety of fighting situations. Each officer has his own specialist area of work, but each unit trains in all of the activities with which the Corps as a whole is involved. Main areas are:

Air Squadron which involves working on the five flights of aircraft and also the Royal Navy's Sea King aircraft.

Jungle Warfare which includes carrying out such missions as clearing villages, dismantling booby traps and maintaining jungle camouflage.

Mountain and Arctic Warfare which is developed to defend NATO's territory inside the Arctic Circle and involves skills from rock climbing and skiing to basic medical work.

Special Boat Squadron which deals with the whole range of secret operations, so a wide variety of skills is needed, from explosives techniques to navigation and photography.

Ships Detachment which involves serving on Royal Navy ships, providing landing parties and taking part in operations at sea.

Embarked Force which works at sea and forms part of the amphibious Task Force.

After basic training, Royal Marines officers choose, in negotiation with their trainers, to work in one of ten specializations.

Landing craft officers plan and lead beach assaults and supervise the maintenance and development of all landing craft and raiding boats. Landing craft officers are appointed to an Assault Squadron or to an Assault Ship, and are involved in navigation, seamanship and operational planning.

Signals officers plan and oversee all radio communications across the Corps.

Heavy weapons officers work in the support company of a commando with responsibility for up to 80 men. Officers work with weapons such as anti-tank missiles or mortars and are also responsible for transporting and installing weapons and for the men in their command.

Weapons training officers advise on the use of small arms and snipers. Officers are responsible for training men in the use of these arms; they also supervise firing ranges.

Special boat services officers supervise and organize special reconnaissance projects from both ships and aircraft.

Mountain leaders advise and instruct companies on mountain exercises and lead the reconnaissance troops in a commando. All aspects of mountaineering are involved in the work, including route finding and low-temperature survival.

Intelligence officers collect and co-ordinate information and circulate it to the appropriate people. Analysis and interpretation are important aspects of this job.

Helicopter pilots fly the full range of helicopters used by the Royal Navy and Marines, after initial work on fixed wing aircraft.

Physical training and sports officers are responsible for the development and supervision of all physical training, and work either within a commando or at a training centre.

Staff duties officers cover a wide range of specialist areas and could be located at the Ministry of Defence, in a commando unit or one of the larger headquarters. Jobs include training, personnel and logistics work.

WORK ENVIRONMENT

Royal Marines officers have to work in a very wide range of conditions, from jungle heat to arctic mountains. They are engaged in action in Northern Ireland, and have to be prepared to move at short notice to any areas in the world where crises occur. As specialist leaders, they operate from air or sea craft as well as on the land, and are required to undergo some of the most physically demanding tasks in the Royal Navy.

Their social life is based around colleagues in the commando units.

SKILLS AND INTERESTS

Please see article 1. RN OFFICER.

Each specialization has its own requirements. Officers in the Special Boat Squadron, for example, must become very good swimmers, canoeists, divers and parachutists as well as experts in reconnaissance, navigation and demolition techniques.

ENTRY REQUIREMENTS

The minimum entry requirements for short-career entry are five subjects – three GCSEs/two S grades (A-C/1-3) and two A levels/three H grades including English and maths at either level. Applicants should be aged between 17 years and 6 months and 23 years on the first day of the month of their entry.

For full-career entrants, two A levels and three GCSEs (A-C), or three H grades plus two S grades (1-3) or equivalent are required. Age limits are 17 years and 6 months to 22 years.

Direct graduate entrants must have a UK degree or equivalent and English and maths at GCSE/S grade (A-C/1-3). They should be under 25 years on the first day of the month of their entry.

Details of scholarships and bursaries are available from Armed Forces careers offices, as are nationality and residence requirements.

All applicants must pass the three stages in the recruitment process as well as a medical screening.

1. Potential officers course. This is a three-day course held at the Commando Training Centre at Lympstone in Devon. Candidates are tested on physical ability, mental attitude and leadership potential.

2. Admiralty interview board. This takes place over three days at HMS Sultan in Gosport, Hampshire, and is designed to assess motives, personality and suitability for training.

3. Final selection board. The Ministry of Defence makes a final decision based on the first two stages and the number of places available.

Candidates are normally notified of their success four weeks before their start date. Those not accepted may reapply after one year. Three applications are allowed.

TRAINING

The first 15 months of Young Officer training is based at CTCRM, Lympstone. This training phase is similar to that taken by commando trainees, but officers are expected to receive a higher standard than other ranks. About 40 per cent of the course is classroom based.

There are five parts to the training.

1. Initial training consists of ten weeks of general basic instruction. Among the areas covered are general fitness, drill and weapon handling, and the role and history of the Royal Marines.

2. Part one military training takes twelve weeks and for this, trainees work in small groups on more realistic exercises, putting their own plans into practice, and using more advanced weapons. Classroom work includes military law, information technology and current affairs.

3. Part two military training lasts for twelve weeks and is organized around troops and companies. Practical work covers, for example, advanced tactical skills, field engineering, counter-revolutionary operations and fighting in built-up areas.

4. Commando course consists of four weeks preparation for the commando tests, and a week spent on the tests. Much of the preparation concentrates on amphibious training as well as survival techniques and unarmed combat. There is an emphasis on long-distance endurance work.

5. Part three military training is the final 15-week stage. Much of this part covers management technique, particularly leadership skills. The final two weeks are spent on Sea Training in Western Scotland.

After this 15-month phase, trainee officers are given command of a troop or other sub-unit, consisting of up to 28 men, including a sergeant and three corporals. After nine months working in one of the specialist activity areas of the Royal Marines, they are fully qualified.

Officers can expect their education and training to continue throughout their careers. Courses, which may be taken with the Navy or the Army, can be in preparation for standard promotion examinations or to enhance ability in their own specialist area.

LATE ENTRY

Entry is described above. All graduate entrants must be aged under 25 years. Other full career entrants must be under 22 years. The naval services favour applications from the lower end of the age scales.

OPPORTUNITIES

The number of officers recruited each year varies. The Royal Marines is a relatively small force, and competition is extremely fierce.

PAY AND CONDITIONS

Officers join the Royal Marines as either full or short-career officers. Short-career officers serve for five years with the opportunity to extend for eight years, and can apply at any stage for a full-career commission. Full-career officers will normally work until the age of 50.

Pay rates on appointment vary according to an officer's type of commission, experience, and in some cases, academic or professional qualifications. A Royal Marines Second Lieutenant is appointed at £12,150 for example, and an Acting Lieutenant entering the Corps as a graduate would earn £13,932

Men who are married and work away from their families for any length of time are given extra daily payments. Travel warrants are available to cover the cost of visits home, and officers normally take six weeks paid holiday annually.

Officers are on-call at all times, but usually work eight-hour shifts. During exercises, hours are long and irregular.

PROSPECTS

Royal Marines officers can expect new appointments on a frequent basis.

Promotion for full-career officers is through a clearly structured system. After seven years' development as a Lieutenant, officers can expect promotion to Captain. Subsequent promotion is awarded by selection based on performance record, qualifications and aptitude. It is possible to become a Major by the age of 35, a Lieutenant-Colonel by 45, and opportunities exist to achieve the rank of Colonel and higher.

Short-career officers are only eligible for promotion if they extend their commission.

RELATED OCCUPATIONS

Royal Navy officer, Army officer , RAF officer, Royal Marines – other ranks, police officer, physical education teacher.

FURTHER INFORMATION AND READING

Please see article 4. ROYAL MARINES – OTHER RANKS.

4. ROYAL MARINES – OTHER RANKS (BAB)

THE WORK

All Royal Marines have some specialization in their work, as in other parts of the Navy. Commando troops, however, are all primarily trained for combat and their daily duties and the operations and exercises in which they take part all reflect this. The only exceptions are those who join as musicians or buglers – these men serve only with the Royal Marines Band Service.

After training, Royal Marines can enter the same six areas of work as officers, that is: **Ships Detachment, Air Squadron, Special Boat Squadron, Jungle Warfare, Mountain and Arctic Warfare** and the **Embarked Force.** Please see article 3. ROYAL MARINES OFFICER.

The majority of Royal Marines work as riflemen in one of the above areas, but specialist trades are available for men to enter after commando training, or after spending some time as riflemen.

Armourers are responsible for inspecting and repairing all weapons and optical instruments.

Assault engineers provide immediate engineering support in a range of areas which may include mine warfare or demolition work.

Physical training instructors work on all areas of fitness training and sports coaching.

Landing craft specialists pilot, navigate and maintain all types of water-borne assault vessels.

Heavy weapons specialists are expert in all large weapons, such as mortars and anti-tank missiles.

Platoon weapons specialists train troops to use personal weapons.

Cooks provide troops with vital nutrition in battle conditions and in extreme weather conditions.

Clerks provide an efficient administrative system, so that all areas function smoothly.

Mountain leaders are expert in long-range patrols and reconnaissance work in mountainous country.

Signallers use all forms of communication equipment.

Telecoms technicians maintain and keep radio equipment working.

Drivers drive, service and administer all motor vehicles, including large goods vehicles.

Metalsmiths work on vehicle body repairs including panel beating and welding.

Carpenters and joiners are responsible for all forms of repair on wooden constructions, including making portable buildings.

Illustrators work on all graphics, map making, aerial photography interpretation and making briefing models.

WORK ENVIRONMENT

Please see article 3. ROYAL MARINES OFFICER.

SKILLS AND INTERESTS

All Royal Marines must be able to work as part of a team, living and working closely with other people. They must be able to follow orders and supervise others. The ability to accept responsibility, make decisions and react quickly is important.

Practical and technical skills are important, as a wide range of equipment and advanced weaponry is used in all areas of the work.

Physical fitness and stamina are crucial. Marines must be prepared to work anywhere in the world at short notice and be separated from their families for long periods of time. All must be prepared to work in combat.

Each specialism has its own requirements. For example, those involved in the Special Boat Squadron must be strong swimmers, while those who work in Mountain and Arctic Warfare must be skilled at skiing and rock climbing. Fluency in foreign languages is useful for those who wish to work in communications and telecommunications.

ENTRY REQUIREMENTS

All candidates must pass a selection test involving reasoning, English language, numeracy and mechanical comprehension. An interview and medical check are also given. The minimum height requirement for all Royal Marines is 1.65m (5 feet 5 inches), and weight must be in proportion to height.

Those entering as musicians and junior musicians will have to audition and take a musical aptitude test.

Junior Marines and Junior Musicians must be aged between 16 and 17 years and 6 months. Others must be aged between 17 years and 6 months and 28 years.

All entrants must meet the RN nationality and residence requirements. Armed Forces careers offices will give guidance on eligibility.

All non-musicians must pass the Potential Recruits Course, which consists of three days of written tests, physical exercises and a personal interview.

Those not accepted at their first attempt may apply again after one year.

TRAINING

For commandos, initial training lasts for 30 weeks and is based at the Commando Training Centre, Royal Marines at Lympstone in Devon.

The first 15 weeks of training includes care of equipment, drill, assault courses, survival training, weapons training and one week spent gaining amphibious warfare skills at Royal Marines Poole, in Dorset. This part of training concentrates mainly on individual fitness and skills.

Part two of training is spent working in small groups consolidating team work. Work includes endurance tests, heavy weapons training and the use of live ammunition. Classroom studies are also an important part of Stage Two training, as all men must understand, for example, how weapons work and the strategies and techniques of modern warfare.

All aspects of training are used in the final three-day exercise on Dartmoor, after which trainees become full commandos and are entitled to wear the green beret.

Those who have completed this training period may choose to train further for one of the specialist trades, and are encouraged to take City and Guilds or BTEC certificates appropriate to their trade and their qualifications on entry.

Musicians and buglers train at the Royal Marines School of Music in Kent.

LATE ENTRY

The upper age limit for entrants is their 28th birthday.

OPPORTUNITIES

Competition is extremely fierce for places in the Royal Marines, which is a comparatively small force.

PAY AND CONDITIONS

Please see article 2. ROYAL NAVY RATING – pay and service requirements are the same as for Navy entrants, both for Junior Marines and those who enter later.

PROSPECTS

People who do well in training and exercises have good prospects for promotion. The rank of Corporal can be reached after five years, and Sergeant after seven or eight years. It is possible to gain commissions from the ranks.

Commandos who wish to find civilian work may attend Naval vocational training centres for six months in order to train for a new trade, or to study supervisory and management techniques. Many Royal Marines however, have obtained qualifications and experience as part of their work which are acceptable to civilian employers.

RELATED OCCUPATIONS

Royal Marines officer, Royal Navy rating, Army NCO/private, RAF airman/woman, Merchant Navy rating, police officer.

FURTHER INFORMATION

Free leaflets and advice are available from all local Armed Forces careers offices. The addresses of these can be found in telephone directories.

FURTHER READING

Job Outlines – Armed Services – COIC
Working in The Armed Services – COIC

In the careers library classified under BAB.

THE ARMY: BAF

1. ARMY OFFICER CLCI:BAF
2. ARMY NON-COMMISSIONED OFFICER/PRIVATE CLCI:BAF

BACKGROUND INFORMATION

The British Army defends Britain and its allies both in this country and abroad, and plays an important part in NATO. It provides the commander and much of the headquarters of NATO's new Allied Command Europe Rapid Reaction Corps (ARRC), as well as 1st UK Armoured Division, three UK Division and 24 Airmobile Brigade, together with their support elements.

The Army is made up of regiments and corps, each of which has a specific military function. New recruits join a regiment of corps which will train them in the skills necessary to carry out their chosen employment trade, as well as encouraging them to develop their particular interests and abilities.

Regiments and corps are either an Arm or a Service. The Arms are actively involved in fighting, or providing close support to those fighting (eg engineering, communications, flying). The Service provides a range of essential support services to the Arms (eg transport, catering, medical care).

Entry to the Army is by joining a specific regiment or corps. Both men and women can join all corps except the Household Cavalry, the Royal Armoured Corps and the Infantry, which are open to men only. Entrants go through basic training at officer or private level before going on to train with their chosen regiment or corps. Some jobs are open to those who have trained in their specialism in civilian life, eg registered general nurses, accountants, engineers, and who meet the eligibility requirements.

1. ARMY OFFICER (BAF)

THE WORK

Officers lead and manage teams of trained soldiers. They are responsible for both personnel and equipment, and for making decisions about their deployment. They must understand how weapons and equipment work(s), as well as the skills and tactics necessary in battle. All officers follow two alternating career development paths – regimental duty and staff administration – and must, therefore, develop administrative as well as leadership skills. In addition, they are responsible for the training and welfare of the men and women under their command.

Officers develop their expertise according to the regiment or corps they are in.

The Arms
Household Cavalry

The Household Cavalry consists of the two senior regiments of the British Army – the Life Guards and the Blues and Royals. Between them they provide an armoured reconnaissance regiment and the Mounted Regiment, which is well known for its ceremonial duties.

Royal Armoured Corps (RAC)

The RAC consists of armoured regiments equipped with the main battle tank, and armoured reconnaissance regiments equipped with light but fast armoured reconnaissance vehicles. The role of the armoured regiments is to fight the armoured battle, whilst the reconnaissance regiments obtain information about the ground and the enemy, as well as guarding the flanks and countering any enemy air or heli-borne assaults.

Infantry

The Infantry is made up of a large number of regiments and forms around 25 per cent of the Army. It takes a major role in the Army's peace-keeping tasks. It is also responsible for fighting the enemy on foot, using machine guns, rifles, anti-tank weapons and mortars.

Special Air Service Regiment (SAS)

The SAS undertakes special, often top secret, operations. It consists of highly skilled personnel who have proved themselves in other regiments and corps. They volunteer for the SAS and, if selected, are seconded to it.

Royal Artillery

The Royal Artillery provides both ground fire support and air defence for the Army. In the ground fire support role, the Royal Artillery has a number of indirect fire weapons. In the air defence role there is a variety of surface-to-air missile systems. In both roles the Royal Artillery works closely with the other combat arms, and provides forward observation officers to RAC and Infantry units.

Corps of Royal Engineers

Engineers have a wide range of responsibilities. In combat they build bridges, lay minefields, create obstacles, and destroy enemy bridges, minefields and obstacles. Behind the combat area they build bridges, roads and airfields, construct camps, ports and bulk fuel installations, and generate and distribute electric power. They also provide support for the Royal Air Force by constructing airstrips and helicopter pads, repairing airfields and maintaining essential services. They carry out military survey work and explosive ordnance disposal for all three Armed Forces.

Royal Corps of Signals

The Royal Corps of Signals is responsible for providing, operating and maintaining the field communication system of the Army, using both voice and data transmissions. It also provides satellite communications to facilitate worldwide contact between the UK and elements of the Armed Forces wherever they are deployed. In addition, it is responsible for electronic warfare.

Army Air Corps (AAC)

The AAC has a variety of roles, including reconnaissance, directing artillery fire, controlling ground attack aircraft, evacuating casualties, and their main task of launching missile attacks on enemy armour. They may also transport troops, stores or equipment or act as an airborne command post. Officers in the AAC are all qualified helicopter pilots.

Intelligence Corps

The Intelligence Corps collects, analyses and interprets information to form a picture of the enemy and what it is likely to do. In addition to providing combat intelligence, the Corps is responsible for providing security intelligence and protective security to counter espionage, subversion and sabotage; signal intelligence; specialist intelligence; and photographic interpretation. Languages are an important part of the Corps' activities.

The Services
Royal Logistics Corps (RLC)

The RLC is responsible for providing, storing and distributing all stores and equipment used by the Army; for the transportation of men and freight by rail, road, sea and air; for all catering and food supplies; and for providing postal and courier facilities for all three Services. These operations are worldwide.

Officers will specialize in one particular area to start with, but will broaden their knowledge of the Corps' activities as they progress up the promotion ladder. Specializations include transport, supply, ammunition, petroleum, catering, postal, and civil labour.

Royal Electrical and Mechanical Engineers (REME)

REME is the Equipment Support Corps of the Army. It is concerned with the maintenance and availability of all technical equipment including vehicles, weapons, radio, etc. It is divided into three categories: Mechanical, Electrical/Electronic and Aeronautical, and makes up around ten per cent of the Army.

Adjutant General's Corps

The Adjutant General's Corps consists of four Branches, through which it provides a range of administrative services to the Army:

Education Training Services Branch (ETS)

The ETS is an all-officer branch that provides education for all Army personnel. It prepares candidates for promotional examinations, carries out language training (including English as a foreign language) and advises on the Army's training systems. It also provides guidance for those about to leave the Army.

Provost Branch (RMP)

In peacetime the RMP is responsible for preventing and detecting crime and helping to maintain discipline. In war, it additionally controls traffic moving to and from the battle area. It has a separate detective force, the Special Investigation Branch (SIB), and also has specially trained personnel who protect Royalty and diplomatic/military VIPs abroad.

Army Legal Services Branch (ALS)

The ALS is an all-officer branch consisting of barristers, advocates and solicitors who advise on military law, prepare for and prosecute at courts martial, lecture in military law, and provide legal aid for Army personnel and their families.

Staff and Personnel Support Branch (SPS)

The SPS Branch is responsible for providing all the personnel administration in the Army, including pay and allowances. SPS officers specialize in personnel management, management accountancy and information technology.

Royal Army Chaplains' Department (RAChD)

The Department is responsible for the spiritual and moral needs of the Army. It has chaplains of a number of denominations who minister to both soldiers and their families.

Royal Army Medical Corps (RAMC)

The RAMC provides a medical health care service to the Army, in both peace and war, ranging from general practice to consultancy and specialist facilities within military hospitals.

Royal Army Dental Corps (RADC)

The RADC is responsible for the dental health of Army personnel. It also looks after Service families abroad.

Queen Alexandra's Royal Army Nursing Corps (QARANC)

The QARANC provides a complete nursing service to the Army, and works closely with the RAMC.

Royal Army Veterinary Corps (RAVC)

The RAVC is responsible for the provision, care and training of the Army's animals – mainly dogs and horses.

WORK ENVIRONMENT

Army officers are likely to be stationed in the United Kingdom or Germany, but there are also forces elsewhere, including other parts of Europe, the Falkland Islands, Brunei, Cyprus, Gibraltar, Belize and Hong Kong. Exercise locations include Australasia, North America, the Middle East and several African countries. Officers may be expected to work in climates from desert to Arctic, but their immediate work environment depends on the job they do.

SKILLS AND INTERESTS

Officers need leadership qualities and the ability to work effectively as part of a team. They must be able to think and react quickly. They must be ready to accept responsibility, make decisions and manage other personnel. Officers must be able to lead their soldiers and earn their respect. They should be able to communicate with people of all abilities, explain ideas, give spoken and written instructions and motivate others. Officers must be interested in the people they supervise, and be able to listen to, guide and discipline them when necessary. All officers must be physically fit and prepared to work in combat. An interest and ability in science/technology is important for many of the jobs.

As well as having the general leadership and management qualities required of an Army Officer, officers in particular corps and Regiments need to have the skills and attributes required by that corps or regiment.

ENTRY REQUIREMENTS

Officer candidates must first decide which regiment or corps they wish to join, and then apply to that regiment or corps for sponsorship through the selection process. (The final choice of regiment or corps – and subsequent acceptance – is made during the latter stage of the Sandhurst commissioning course.)

To become an officer, candidates must pass a medical board and a series of selection tests at the Regular Commissions Board (RCB). These last three-and-a-half days, and include computer tests, written tests, outdoor tasks and interviews.

There are two main types of commission in the Army:

The Regular Commission (REG C) is for men and women over the age of 17 years and 9 months but under the age of 25, who wish to make the Army their career. Applicants should have a minimum of five GCSEs/S grades (A-C/1-3) with two A levels/three H grades. These qualifications should be in approved subjects, and must include English and maths, and either a science subject or a foreign language. Graduates should have a recognized UK degree, although some BTEC/SCOTVEC higher national diploma or DipHE qualifications may also be acceptable, as may membership of certain professional institutions. REME and the ETS Branch of the Adjutant General's Corps only accept graduates with appropriate degrees. The RAMC, RADC, RAChD, RAVC, ALS Branch of the AG Corps and QARANC only accept those who are professionally qualified. Some of these Corps accept candidates of a higher age.

The Short Service Commission (SSC) is for three years after completing the Sandhurst course, and is extendible, if mutually agreed, to eight years. Non-graduates require five

GCSEs/S grades (A-C/1-3) normally including English and mathematics, though some corps require much higher qualifications. Graduates should have a recognized UK degree, although some BTEC/SCOTVEC higher national diploma or DipHE qualifications may also be acceptable, as may membership of certain professional institutions. REME and the ETS Branch of the Adjutant General's Corps only accept graduates with appropriate degrees. The RAMC, RADC, RAChD, RAVC, ALS Branch of the AG Corps and QARANC only accept those who are professionally qualified. Candidates must be at least 17 years and 9 months and under the age of 25. Some of the technical/professional corps accept candidates of a higher age. After two years' service an SSC officer may apply for a REG C provided they are recommended and a vacancy is confirmed. (Note: SSCs are not available in the Intelligence Corps.)

A third type of commission:

The Short Service Limited Commission (SSLC) is available to people aged between 18 and 20 years who have a firm place at university. They must be recommended by their Headteacher, be unmarried, pass an Army Medical Board and pass the Regular Commissions Board (RCB) with a special recommendation for SSLC. (Note: not all corps accept SSLC Officers.)

Appropriate qualifications are required for certain corps. Graduate clergy applying for a commission in the Royal Army Chaplains' Department should have served at least one curacy. Candidates for the Royal Army Medical Corps can join as fully qualified medical practitioners, as qualified doctors in their pre-registration year, or as Medical Cadets if they have passed the second MB and are within three years of qualifying. Entry to the Royal Army Dental Corps is open to qualified dental practitioners or to those within two years of completing their studies, who may be awarded Dental Cadetships. The Royal Army Veterinary Corps requires applicants to be qualified veterinary graduates. The Army Legal Services employs qualified barristers, advocates and solicitors who are aged at least 25 years. Those who have reached the final year of a law degree and have at least one year's full professional training to complete may apply for an Army Legal Cadetship or Bursary. Queen Alexandra's Royal Army Nursing Corps is open to qualified Registered General Nurses aged over 21 years with at least one year's post-registration experience.

Those who are already professionally qualified may apply to the corps which is appropriate to their qualifications.

Various forms of sponsorship are available for undergraduates and A level/H grade students. There are two types of undergraduate awards: Cadetship and Bursary. The Cadetship is designed for young men and women who decide, before entering university, or early in their degree course, to make a career as an Army officer. Cadetship officers serve for a minimum of five years after completing their training at the Royal Military Academy Sandhurst (RMAS) (44 weeks). Whilst at university they receive a special rate of pay. The Bursary is for men and women who wish to commit themselves to a minimum of three years' service after the end of their training at RMAS. Bursary holders receive financial support which supplements the Local Education Authority grant. The Army Scholarship Scheme is for the last two A level years at school, and assures entry to Sandhurst with a commitment to serve a minimum of three years after commissioning, on a REG C (providing that at least two A levels were achieved). Candidates should have the GCSE academic requirements for a REG C, and be aged between 16 and 16 years 6 months. Financial assistance during the A level/H grade course is given to the parents or guardians of those who are awarded scholarships.

Welbeck College, the Army's sixth-form college, provides a residential sixth-form education. Candidates should have at least five GCSEs/S grades (A-C/1-3), including English, maths, physics (or a subject involving physics) and, preferably, chemistry. All students take A levels in maths and a science subject (usually physics), a third subject (science or arts) and, often, general studies. Candidates must be under 17 years and 6 months on entry. After the A level course most go on to RMAS, although some go to university first. Welbeck students are normally commissioned into a technical corps.

Officers must be physically fit and capable of strenuous work and of working long hours. Height and weight should be within the limits for the candidate's age and build. There are strict hearing and visual standards, and candidates must be able to distinguish accurately white, signal red and signal green.

All candidates must meet the Army nationality and residence requirements. Further guidance is available from Army university and schools liaison officers. Contact the appropriate liaison officer through your university or school careers staff; contact can also be made with local Army careers information offices or Armed Forces careers offices.

TRAINING

All officers, except those listed below, follow a 44-week (three-term) Commissioning Course (CC) at Royal Military Academy Sandhurst (RMAS). The aim of the course is to develop qualities of leadership and to provide the basic knowledge required by an officer, regardless of their corps. The CC includes tactics and weapon training, Army organization and administration, lessons from military history, leadership, military law, physical fitness and adventure training (eg climbing, parachuting, sailing, etc).

Professionally qualified officers joining the Royal Army Chaplains' Department, the Royal Army Medical Corps, the Royal Army Dental Corps, the Royal Army Veterinary Corps and the Army Legal Services Branch follow a four-week course of basic training and general information about the Army. Professionally qualified officers joining the QARANC follow a nine-week course at the Army Medical Services Training Centre. The Short Service Limited Commission Officers follow a three-week course of basic training at Sandhurst before joining the regiment or corps for SSLC commission. Undergraduate Cadets also attend a three-week course at Sandhurst before taking up Cadetship and proceeding to university.

After leaving Sandhurst at the end of the commissioning course, officers join their regiments or corps to learn their necessary skills, putting into practice the leadership and management skills that they learnt at Sandhurst. Many then complete the Young Officers course run by their regiment or corps; others will carry out a short tour of regimental duty before attending the course.

Throughout their career, REG C officers attend a variety of courses which may be specific to their own particular cap badge, or common across the Army. Many of these courses are associated with preparation for promotion to the next higher rank.

LATE ENTRY

The age limits for entry to the Army on either a REG C or SSC are over 17 years nine months and under 25 years on entry to the Royal Military Academy Sandhurst. There are some exceptions: graduate candidates for the Royal Engineers, Royal Signals, REME and the Educational Training Services Branch of the Adjutant General's Corps who hold a degree in a relevant discipline may be considered up to age 27; graduate clergy for the RAChD up to age 34; veterinary surgeons for the RAVC up to age 42; qualified solicitors and barristers for the Army Legal Services Branch up to age 30. Professionally qualified officers for the RAMC, RADC and QARANC who are over the age of 25 need to apply to the appropriate corps headquarters for consideration.

As the selection procedure can take some time, candidates are advised to apply well before they reach the upper age limit.

OPPORTUNITIES

There are approximately 13,000 officers in the Army. Around 700 are recruited each year for the CC.

Approximately 40 per cent of candidates pass the Regular Commissions Board. Those not accepted may be able to reapply, depending on the recommendations made by the RCB. If the recommendation is that the candidate should reapply, the RCB will also state when this should be. An RCB pass remains valid for four years.

PAY AND CONDITIONS

Those who join the Army on REG C can reasonably expect a career to age 55. They must serve three years after completion of their officer training at RMAS. They may then apply to leave at any time (unless there are exceptional circumstances such as a national emergency), giving seven months' notice. There are certain time bars of between two and five years from the completion of some courses. On retirement they must transfer to the Regular Army Reserve of Officers. SSC is for a period of three years (six years for Army Air Corps) from the date of leaving RMAS, extendible to a maximum of eight years. SSC officers may apply for a REG C after completing two years. On leaving they have a reserve liability until eight years after their commissioning. SSLC officers serve for between four and eighteen months and must give six weeks' notice prior to leaving. (SSLCs are only available to individuals from 18 to 20 between school and university.)

On entry, Second Lieutenants earn £13,352. Lieutenants receive £17,649 to £19,508, Captains £22,571 to £26,239 and Majors £28,543 to £34,323. Lieutenant-Colonels are paid £40,381 to £44,626 and Colonels £47,020 to £51,968. Brigadiers receive £57,736. Those on SSLC are paid £10,001 to £10,694 and Cadetship Officers £7,657 to £10,771. Bursary holders receive £1,500 (£500 a term). Doctors' and dentists' pay is allied to NHS pay scales.

Officers can be called upon to work 24 hours a day, but in barracks usually work a normal office-hours day and five-day week. However, they remain on-call and will be required to work the occasional weekend. On exercises and operations they work throughout, taking breaks for sleep and meals when conditions permit.

Officers who become pregnant are granted maternity leave at the end of which they may resume their commissions. Those who have completed the minimum service for their commission may leave; those who have not will need to negotiate with the appropriate department on how their commission may be either fulfilled or terminated.

PROSPECTS

Promotion is through a structured system from Second Lieutenant through Lieutenant, Captain, Major, Lieutenant-Colonel and beyond. Promotion exams have to be passed for promotion from Lieutenant to Captain, and from Captain to Major. Promotion beyond major is on selection and merit. All officers start as Second Lieutenants, though professionally qualified officers (eg for the RAChD, RAMC, RADC, RAVC, ALS and QARANC) are commissioned as Lieutenants or Captains, depending on their qualifications and experience. Graduate officer entrants on commissioning are given an antedate of seniority for their degree which usually results in promotion to Lieutenant. All candidates attend the commissioning course at Sandhurst as officer cadets.

Before being promoted, officers are trained for the next level of responsibility. Successful candidates can expect to become Captains at about age 26, and Majors at about age 33. Promotion beyond Major is on selection and merit, and is subject to vacancies. Majors will be considered for promotion to Lieutenant-Colonel between the ages of 36 and 45 years.

RELATED OCCUPATIONS

Army NCO/private, Royal Navy officer, Royal Marines officer, RAF officer, police officer.

FURTHER INFORMATION AND READING

Please see article 2. ARMY NON-COMMISSIONED OFFICER/PRIVATE.

2. ARMY NON-COMMISSIONED OFFICER/PRIVATE (BAF)

THE WORK

All soldiers are trained firstly for combat. This means that each person in the Army must keep very fit, maintain a high level of combat skills and awareness of battle strategy, and be able to use an increasingly sophisticated range of weapons and equipment. They must also go on exercises from time to time, both near to their base and in other countries, so that they can test out their battle skills in a realistic, simulated situation.

There are over 150 different employments available in the Army. They range from pure soldiering as an infantryman to a skilled technician or craftsman/woman.

The regiments and corps that make up the Army are either an Arm or a Service. The Arms are those actively involved in the fighting, and the Services provide the necessary support, both administrative and practical.

Although women may not be enlisted into the three most active elements of the Combat Arms (the Household Cavalry, Royal Armoured Corps and the Infantry), and therefore will not be involved in front-line fighting, they may join any other part of the Army, and could find themselves deployed in a combat zone.

The Arms

The Household Cavalry – (male only) provides an armoured reconnaissance regiment and the mounted regiment. Jobs include armoured vehicle crewman and mounted dutyman.

The Royal Armoured Corps – (male only) consists of armoured regiments equipped with the main battle tank, and armoured reconnaissance vehicles. The role of the armoured regiments is to fight the armoured battle; whilst the reconnaissance regiments obtain information about the ground and the enemy, as well as guarding the flanks and countering any enemy air or heli-borne assaults. Everyone starts by learning to drive an armoured vehicle before progressing to crewman.

The Infantry – (male only) forms about 25 percent of the Army. The role of the Infantry is to close with and defeat the enemy. They are trained to operate on their feet. The Infantry usually take a major role in the Army's peace-keeping task. The footguards and parachute regiment are part of the Infantry.

The Royal Artillery – provides ground fire support and air defence for the Army. In both roles the Royal Artillery works closely with the Infantry and Royal Armoured Corps. Jobs include gunner technical (covering surveyor, meteorologist, command post assistant and artillery intelligence operator, radar operator and range assistant), gunner, signaller/driver, mounted gunner and gunner weapons. There are also units serving with commando and parachute forces.

The Corps of Royal Engineers – provides engineering support to the Army and particularly to the Combat Arms. Engineers carry out building projects such as making bridges, roads and airfields. The Corps also produces the maps for the Army, the Royal Navy and the Royal Air Force. Jobs include a variety of engineering trades such as surveyor, draughtsman, plant operator, carpenter, blacksmith, etc.

The Royal Corps of Signals – is responsible for all communications and electronic warfare. Jobs include telecoms technician, telecoms mechanic, and telecoms operator.

The Army Air Corps – operates the Army's fleet of helicopters which are tasked with carrying out reconnaissance, attacking enemy armour with air-to-air missiles, or with lifting troops, casualties, equipment or stores. Soldiers in the AAC carry out a variety of ground crew duties but may progress to aircrew, including pilot.

The Intelligence Corps – collects and analyses information about the enemy so that successful operations can be carried out. It is responsible for security and counter-intelligence. Jobs include intelligence and security operator and special intelligence operator (analyst or linguist).

The Services

The Royal Logistics Corps – is responsible for providing, storing and distributing all stores equipment used by the Army; for the transportation of men and freight by rail, road, sea and air; for all catering and food supplies; and for providing postal and courier facilities for all three Services. Jobs include movement controller, railwayman/woman, seaman/woman, driver, supply controller, supply specialist, chef, postal and courier operator, pioneer, ammunition technician, air despatcher and petroleum operative.

The Corps of Royal Electrical and Mechanical Engineers – organizes the maintenance, repair and recovery of all technical equipment. The Corps divides into three sections: mechanical, electrical/electronic and aeronautical. Jobs include aircraft technician, avionics technician, telecoms technician, radar technician, control equipment technician, instrument technician, armourer, gun fitter, metalsmith, vehicle electrician, vehicle mechanic, technical storeperson, recovery mechanic and shipwright.

The Adjutant General's Corps – provides a range of administrative services for the Army. Branches of this corps that soldiers may join are:

Provost Branch (RMP) – prevent and detect crime, maintain discipline and control the traffic. All soldiers in this group are known as Military Policemen/women.

Staff and Personnel Support Branch (SPS) – is responsible for providing all the personnel administration in the Army, including pay and allowances. All soldiers in this Branch are military clerks but may specialise further in the clerical aspects, including accountancy and information technology.

The Royal Army Medical Corps – provides a medical health care service to the Army, in both peace and war, ranging from general practice to consultancy. Jobs in this corps include radiographer, laboratory technician, physiological measurement technician, pharmacy technician, physiotherapist, operating theatre technician, environmental health technician, and combat medical technician.

The Queen Alexandra's Royal Army Nursing Corps – provides a nursing service to the Army and works closely with the RAMC. Jobs include registered general nurse, registered mental nurse and health care assistant.

The Royal Army Dental Corps – is responsible for the dental health of the Army. Jobs include dental support specialist, dental hygienist and dental technician.

The Royal Army Veterinary Corps – provides, trains and cares for the Army's animals – mainly horses and dogs. Soldiers join the corps as animal technical assistants.

The Corps of Army Music – provides the Army's State and Staff Bands. In addition to their musical skills, musicians also have an operational role, usually as medical assistants. Soldiers join this corps as musicians.

WORK ENVIRONMENT

Please see article 1. ARMY OFFICER.

SKILLS AND INTERESTS

All soldiers must be able to form part of a team, living and working closely with their colleagues. They must be able to follow orders without question on some occasions, while at other times be able to accept responsibility, make decisions quickly and use their initiative.

The ability to act promptly and remain calm under pressure is important.

Practical and technical skills are essential, as all soldiers are expected to use a wide range of equipment, advanced weaponry and vehicles.

Physical fitness and stamina are vital as soldiers could be required to work in extremes of climate after strenuous physical exertion, when tired and when under stress. Army staff must be prepared to be sent anywhere in the world at short notice, and be separated from their families for long periods of time. Every soldier may be called upon to work in hostile combat conditions when necessary.

Each specialism has its own additional requirements. For example, fluency in foreign languages is useful for those wishing to work in telecommunications and intelligence, and a methodical approach to paperwork is required for administrative posts. Those involved in particularly dangerous jobs such as bomb disposal must be absolutely calm and steady at all times and have very high levels of manual dexterity.

ENTRY REQUIREMENTS

All candidates must pass the Army Entrance Test and do well at interview to be sent to the Recruit Selection Centre. Here candidates must pass a medical examination, the Physical Assessment test and an interview with an Army personnel selection officer.

For the majority of jobs, no particular academic qualifications are needed, but those who have taken some GCSEs/S grades and have a good school report have a better chance of being selected. In general, personal qualities and good motivation are more important than exam passes.

For the more technical trades, however, candidates are preferred with GCSEs/S grades (A-C/1-3) in subjects appropriate to the trade they are seeking. Entry qualifications for these technical trades are available from Armed Forces careers offices.

Those entering the Corps of Army Music will have to undertake a two-day audition.

All entrants must meet Army nationality and residence requirements. Those not accepted at their first attempt will be advised about further applications. The possibility and timing of subsequent applications will depend on the reasons for an individual's rejection.

TRAINING

All new entrants to the Army take an initial ten-week training course, known as the Common Military Syllabus for Recruits.

The first few days of the course are taken up with administration, documentation, a full medical examination and a general introduction. The course continues with instruction in drill, weapon training, fieldcraft, map reading, first aid, defensive measures in nuclear, biological and chemical warfare, military history and physical fitness. The training is also designed to develop self-discipline, teamwork and fitness.

The course ends with a passing out parade, and the recruit then leaves the Army Training Regiment. Recruits then move to their Arm or Service for training in their chosen employment.

Army Apprentices - are encouraged in those technical corps where a lengthy employment training is involved. These are:

The Royal Engineers; The Royal Signals; The Royal Logistic Corps (Chefs and Marine Engineers); The Royal Electrical and Mechanical Engineers.

Apprentices join the Apprentice Training establishment of their corps (except for RLC Marine Engineers who join in with Royal Engineer Apprentices) for a foundation course which includes the ten-week Common Military Syllabus for Recruits, as well as character and leadership training, and instruction in the theory principles of their chosen trade.

Apprentices then move on to the appropriate Army School for training in their specific trade up to Class 2 standard. This is then followed by on-the-job experience in an operational unit before returning to further training at the appropriate Army School up to Class 1 standard. Depending on their chosen trade, Apprentices will earn BTEC or City and Guilds qualifications at an early stage of their career.

An Army Apprenticeship, therefore, is a fast-track sandwich course designed both to produce Class 1 tradespeople at an early age, and to prepare suitable candidates for early promotion to middle management.

Apprentices may join the Army at the age of 16 years (the upper limit is 17 years 6 months), and may apply to Armed Forces careers offices from the age of 15. These offices can give up-to-date details of the apprenticeships available.

LATE ENTRY

The upper age limit for the majority of trades is 26 years. Some sections will take recruits aged up to 30 years, and for certain employments in RAMC, RADC and QARANC the upper age limit is 33 years.

Armed Forces careers offices will give precise details of age limits. The Army normally prefers candidates at the lower end of the age ranges.

OPPORTUNITIES

There is a constant need for new recruits to the Army, despite the current restructuring. To maintain staff levels of about 117,000 soldiers and officers, approximately 15,000 adult entrants are taken each year of which about 1,100 are Apprentices. Information on the present situation is available from Armed Forces careers office.

PAY AND CONDITIONS

All recruits are enlisted on an Open Engagement, which is for a period of 22 years' service from the age of 18 or the date of entry, whichever is later. All soldiers have the right to leave on completion of three years' service from the age of 18. One year's notice is required. The exception to this is in the case of pregnancy, when women may choose either to resign or take maternity leave.

A recruit who is under the age of 17 years 6 months on enlistment may leave at any time after the end of 28 days and before the end of six months. A recruit who is enlisted between 17 years 6 months and 18 years may also leave, but with repayment, and, for those 18 years or over, on payment, at an early stage of their training.

Salaries are reviewed every year, and pay depends on age, profession and qualifications and rank held. An entrant aged 16 to 17 years will earn a minimum of £99.88 a week, while an untrained Private aged over 17 years 6 months on entry will initially earn a minimum of £160.31 a week. Rates of pay are the same for men and women.

Additions to pay are made in certain circumstances. For example, extra money is given to those serving overseas, and a separation allowance can be made to those living away from their families. Certain specialists, such as parachutists, receive additional pay.

Charges are made for accommodation and where appropriate, for meals.

Soldiers are on-call at all times, but usually work a normal office- hours day and five-day week. However, they remain on-call and will be required to work the occasional evening and weekend.

Four weeks annual holiday is normal, but this rises to six weeks when serving overseas.

PROSPECTS

Those who do well in training and exercises have good prospects of promotion, and a planned promotional structure exists. The route is from Private to Lance-Corporal, to Corporal to Sergeant, then Staff Sergeant. Warrant Officer Class 2 and Class 1 are the following rank and at this level, soldiers may be considered for a commission. In some trades, soldiers may become non-commissioned officers as soon as they qualify.

About five per cent of those entering Sandhurst for officer training are taken from the ranks.

RELATED OCCUPATIONS

Army officer, Royal Navy rating, Royal Air Force airman/air woman, police officer.

FURTHER INFORMATION

Free leaflets and information on all aspects of work and training are available from the Army's university and schools liaison officers (details available from university or school careers staff), from an Armed Forces careers office, or by phoning 0345 300111.

FURTHER READING

Job Outlines – The Armed Services – COIC
Working in The Armed Services – COIC

In the careers library classified under BAF.

1. RAF OFFICER CLCI:BAL
2. RAF AIRMAN/AIRWOMAN CLCI:BAL

BACKGROUND INFORMATION

The Royal Air Force patrols and defends the United Kingdom from the air, and plays an important role in NATO.

It has a force of around 70,000 men and women, comprising more than 90 trades and branches, and is organized into three commands: Strike Command, Logistics Command and Personnel and Training Command. Strike Command is directly concerned with flying and operating missile systems. Logistics Command is responsible for supply and maintenance, and Personnel and Training Command looks after careers and training. Organizational changes and force reductions will take place between 1996 and 1999 in order to reduce RAF strength to around 52,500.

The commands are made up of stations which are divided into wings. The number of wings depends on the size and role of the station, but is likely to include operations, engineering and administrative wings. The wings are divided into squadrons and the squadrons into flights. Stations are communities made up of RAF personnel and their families.

Entry to the Royal Air Force is either at officer, sergeant aircrew or airman/airwoman level. All entrants have initial training at officer, sergeant or airman/airwoman level before beginning specialist training in one of the wide range of jobs. Some posts are open to those who have qualified in their specialism in civilian life, such as legal officer, nursing officer. All branches are open to both sexes, except that women cannot join as RAF Regiment officers.

1. RAF OFFICER (BAL)

THE WORK

Officers manage and lead the many personnel who make up the RAF. Their specific roles vary according to the branch in which they work. In addition to their primary duty, most officers have secondary duties to contribute to the welfare of the RAF community. This may mean organizing such things as sports teams or a station social club. Their specific roles vary according to the branch in which they work.

Pilots and navigators

They are employed almost exclusively in flying during the early part of their careers, although later they may combine flying with ground duties.

Pilots usually specialize in one type of aircraft – fast jets, multi-engine aircraft or helicopters. All pilots plan flights and fly training exercises. Fast jet pilots learn many techniques, including battle formation flying and low-level fighting formations. Pilots flying multi-engine aircraft carry out maritime patrol, transport duties and air-to-air refuelling. Helicopter pilots supply support for Army exercises and may specialize in search and rescue services.

Navigators guide pilots by map reading and operating radar and navigational equipment. They are involved in planning routes and sorties. Additionally, they watch for enemy action and co-ordinate evasive action.

Fighter controllers

There are two types of fighter controllers: systems controllers who keep a constant watch on the airspace using radar, and report and identify objects within it, and interception controllers who use radar to detect aircraft. They direct RAF fighters to intercept suspect aircraft, giving them information about the direction, speed and height of the possible intruder aircraft. Some fighter controllers now fly as mission crew on airborne early-warning aircraft. In war, fighter controllers co-ordinate the air battles.

Air traffic controllers

Air traffic controllers work in one of two areas: terminal controllers are responsible for aircraft on the ground and within about 30 miles of the airfield. They use radar equipment and radio contact to help aircraft take off and land safely. Area controllers cover hundreds of square miles, providing pilots with flight information, navigational assistance and a position-fixing service to help them fly safely through airspace.

Intelligence

Intelligence officers use a variety of photographic and electronic equipment to analyse defence-related and civil installations. They interpret images received from reconnaissance aircraft and advise other staff on the development and implementation of plans.

Engineers

Engineer officers work in one of two areas: aerosystems engineers are concerned with keeping as many aircraft in operation as possible – this includes looking after aircraft, weapons and air-to-ground communications systems; communications/electronics engineers work with computer networks, defence radar systems and radio and air security systems – they are involved with planning, operating and maintaining battle management systems.

Security

RAF Regiment officers lead teams of men who defend RAF airfields and other installations from ground and low-level air attacks, using specialist ground defence units and surface-to-air missiles.

Provost officers manage the RAF police force that protects personnel, aircraft and other equipment as well as investigating criminal and security offences. They may also maintain discipline.

Suppliers

Suppliers are responsible for providing equipment, using a large automated stock-control system. They deal with all goods ranging from complete aircraft, weapons, fuel and gases to clothing and furniture. Technical supply officers liaise with engineer and other officers, and set up supply systems in the field. Movements officers specialize in moving freight, mail and people, usually by air but often by land and sea. Other specialisms include fuels, explosives, data processing and systems design.

Administrators

The administrative branch is responsible for the smooth running of RAF bases and includes a wide range of jobs.

Catering officers have similar duties to civilian catering managers – food purchase and accounting, food preparation and service, bar service and accommodation, and personnel management. They may organize catering for a banquet or a disco or arrange in-flight meals for aircrew and meals for those on exercise.

Secretarial officers may work in accounts dealing with pay instructions, budget forecasts and fund administration. They may also be estates officers, responsible for organizing the construction and maintenance of all RAF buildings from hangars to housing. Other secretarial officers work in personnel and may have responsibility for over 1,000 people, helping with their work and personal problems, advising on RAF careers and attending courts martial.

Education and training officers advise on the implementation and development of training schemes for RAF personnel.

Physical education officers administer and manage a wide variety of sports, promote a healthy lifestyle and assess fitness, as well as providing specialist training in military parachuting, survival techniques, leadership and adventurous activities.

Specialist officers

They carry out their profession within service life.

Medical officers provide medical care for RAF personnel and their families, advise on occupational and community medicine and assist in the aeromedical evacuation of patients.

Nursing officers in Princess Mary's Royal Air Force Nursing Service care for patients whilst helping to manage a ward. They nurse service personnel and their families.

Dental officers work in dental centres on RAF stations, looking after the dental health of RAF personnel. Those abroad also take care of the families of service personnel.

Legal officers advise on evidence for courts martial, drafting charges and conducting prosecutions. They also provide general legal advice to staff.

Chaplains from a number of denominations work in RAF stations to minister to service personnel and their families.

WORK ENVIRONMENT

An RAF station usually consists of around 1,000 staff, including 100 to 150 officers. Officers can be posted to RAF bases in the UK or abroad; they may also go on exercises anywhere in the world. Their social life focuses around the officers' mess but their immediate work environment depends on the job they do.

SKILLS AND INTERESTS

Officers need leadership qualities and the ability to work as part of a team. They must be able to accept responsibility, make decisions and manage large groups of personnel. Officers should be able to communicate with people of all abilities, explain ideas, give spoken and written instructions and motivate others. They must be interested in the people they supervise, able to listen, guide and discipline them. All officers must be physically fit and prepared for combat.

Each branch has its own requirements. The ability to think and react quickly is particularly important for pilots, navigators, fighter controllers and air traffic controllers, as are skills and aptitude for operating advanced equipment.

Ground intelligence officers need analytical skills and a wide general knowledge to understand what an image represents. Engineer officers must be logical, analytical and practically minded. Supply officers need to be methodical and have a flair for organization. Regiment officers must enjoy being outdoors and active; they should be able to think and react quickly to situations.

ENTRY REQUIREMENTS

Basic entry

Candidates for entry to branches that do not require specialist qualifications should possess, as a minimum, two A levels/three H grades, plus five GCSEs/S grades (A-C/1-3) including English language and maths or equivalent qualifications.

Qualified entry

Candidates should hold acceptable professional qualifications (contact RAF Careers Information Offices for details). For example, a candidate for the administrative secretarial branch who holds a BTEC/SCOTVEC Higher National Certificate in Business Studies would meet the qualified entry standard for that branch and would enjoy special terms of entry. Qualified entry is not available in all branches.

Graduate entry

Special enhanced terms of entry are available for those with recognized degrees.

Nationality

All candidates must meet the strict nationality and residence requirements. RAF Careers Information Offices will give guidance on eligibility.

Sponsorship

The RAF operates a number of sponsorship schemes, most of which require individuals to commit themselves to some future form of RAF service. Contact the RAF Careers Information Offices for details.

TRAINING

All new officer recruits begin with an intensive 24-week training course which includes physical fitness, classroom learning and practical exercises to develop operational and leadership skills. Specialist training in the chosen branch begins at the end of this course.

Pilots

Entrants with no flying experience spend time on elementary flying training. Those with university air squadron flying experience begin with six weeks at ground school, covering aerodynamics, radar, air traffic control and cockpit training. This is then followed by basic flying training with an instructor before pilots are streamed as fast jet, multi-engine or helicopter pilots. They then receive training according to the type of aircraft they may be flying. Pilot training takes around three years.

Navigators

Basic navigator training is lengthy and includes study at ground school covering subjects such as maths, meteorology, radar and basic navigational techniques. Trainees also experience flight simulations and sorties in various aircraft. They are then trained in fast-jet, multi-engine or support helicopters.

Fighter controllers

Fighter controllers begin training with an Air Defence Foundation course in which their speed, reactions and technical abilities are tested. Simulators are used to allow fighter controllers to talk 'pilots' into contact positions.

Systems controllers then undertake an Identification and Recognition course, whilst interception controllers take an Interception Control course followed by further training at a front-line unit.

Air traffic controllers

Student air traffic controllers attend a course covering: division of air space, meteorology, navigation and air traffic regulation, as well as practical training in a variety of simulators. Further training in the relevant control positions then follows.

Ground intelligence

Ground intelligence officers follow a course at the Joint School of Photographic Interpretation. Here they are trained to analyse what photographic and electronic images represent and to use this information to advise on strategies. Training involves many aspects of intelligence and security and it is important that ground intelligence officers keep up to date with changes in technology.

Engineers

All engineer officers undergo Engineering Officer Training – Phase 1 which involves management training as well as practical experience of technical problems. After a brief pre-employment course on the aircraft or equipment, a first tour of duty is followed by the Phase 2 course. The first part is completed by all engineer officers and covers the work of engineering staff and the applications of computers. Students are then streamed to follow aerosystems or communications and electronics modules. There are further courses, if the work requires it, on weapons, computers, propulsion, etc.

Security

RAF Regiment officers complete a course that concentrates on command skills, weapon training and field combat exercises. Depending on the squadron to which they are posted, officers then receive further instruction about the specific equipment used by that squadron. Additional training on specialist courses usually follows.

Provost officers attend a course at the RAF Police School where they learn about criminal law, security and counter-intelligence. Later they may be selected for specialist training in criminal detection or computer security. There are opportunities to attend the civil police staff college at Bramshill. After some 18 months' service all officers follow an advanced course, leading to opportunities with the RAF's specialist criminal and investigation and counter-intelligence service.

Suppliers

Suppliers follow a Supply Training course during which they learn about the RAF's computerized supply system. They may undertake further specialist training in areas such as movements, storing fuels and explosives, or advanced data processing systems.

Administrative officers

Secretarial officers follow a course covering office management, personnel management, Service accountancy, military law, housing management and welfare matters.

Catering officers follow a course that introduces them to the RAF's catering management and accounting systems.

Physical education officers attend a course to familiarize them with the RAF's physical education requirements, followed by a parachute course.

Education and training officers have a four-week introductory course at the Training Development Support Unit, and other specialist training is given as required by new postings.

Medical officer

Fully registered medical practitioners undertake general service training and courses in community and occupational and aviation medicine. Provisionally registered house officers attend the RAF Institute of Community and Occupational Medicine for a short stay and then follow the RAF medical training described above.

LATE ENTRY

Upper age limits vary according to the job:

Pilots should be under 24 years, and navigators and RAF Regiment candidates under 26 years.

Fighter controllers, air traffic controllers and ground intelligence, provost and engineer officers should be under 30 years.

Supply, catering and secretarial officers should be under 27 years and education training officers should be under 30 years. Physical education officers should be under 29 years.

Medical officers should be under 39 years if fully registered and under 38 if house officers. Dental officers should be under 33 years, and nursing officers under 34 years. Legal officers should be aged up to 32 years, and Chaplains to 36 years, but older candidates will be considered in both cases.

There is normally a delay between being accepted for a commission and the start of training, so candidates are advised to apply at least a year in advance of age limits.

NB: Age limits are subject to continual review.

OPPORTUNITIES

The numbers of officers recruited varies from year to year. About 40 per cent are graduates. Competition is fierce. Candidates not accepted may be able to reapply. The RAF may recommend a one or two-year gap between applications, depending on the reason for non-selection.

PAY AND CONDITIONS

Pilot officers receive approximately £13,932, and Flying Officers from £18,414 to £20,352. The maximum for a Flight Lieutenant is £27,258 and for a Squadron Leader £35,667. Wing Commanders can earn up to £46,289. Pilots and navigators are entitled to flying pay in addition to basic salary. An officer's rank and starting salary depend on the type of entry to the service and on qualifications. Various allowances are also available. Officers receive six weeks holiday a year plus bank holidays. They are on-call 24 hours a day but basically work a minimum of eight hours. This can include shifts and irregular hours. During exercises and detachments, hours can be long and unpredictable.

Officers enter the RAF on either permanent or short-service commission. A permanent commission means serving as an officer either to the age of 38 years, or for 16 years in total, whichever is the later. A short-service commission is usually six years (twelve years for pilots and navigators). Women can be released early from their commission if pregnant or may take a maternity break.

PROSPECTS

Non-graduate entrants may spend about a year as an Acting Pilot Officer followed by a year as a Pilot Officer and up to four years as a Flying Officer before being promoted to Flight Lieutenant, subject to satisfactory service. Graduates are normally eligible for a faster promotion system up to the rank of Flight Lieutenant.

Promotion beyond Flight Lieutenant to Squadron Leader, Wing Commander, Group Captain and above is usually competitive and depends on merit, performance and quotas.

RELATED OCCUPATIONS

Royal Navy officer, Royal Marines officer, Army officer, RAF airman/woman, airline pilot, air traffic control officer, police officer, engineer, aircraft engineer.

FURTHER INFORMATION AND READING

Please see article 2. RAF AIRMAN/AIRWOMAN.

2. RAF AIRMAN/AIRWOMAN (BAL)

THE WORK

All non-commissioned staff who join the RAF are referred to as airmen or airwomen.

Airmen and airwomen are employed in a wide range of trades. They are all expected to carry out other essential duties, such as taking part in military exercises and training sessions.

All trades are open to both sexes except for the RAF Regiment.

The RAF divides the work into two areas: non-commissioned officer (NCO) aircrew and specialist ground trades. About 70 separate job categories are available.

NCO aircrew fly on multi-engined aircraft and helicopters. They consist of: air engineers, who are responsible for the operation of all aircraft systems; air electronics operators, who use electronic communications equipment such as radar or underwater detection systems on air-sea rescue missions and on-water and below-water surveillance; and air loadmasters, who supervise the despatch of parachute troops, aircraft loading and cabin services in passenger aircraft, together with tasks on air-sea rescue helicopters (female air electronic operators and loadmasters are not employed on air-sea rescue helicopters).

The majority of airmen and airwomen are employed in the ground trades, which are:

Aircraft engineering

Airmen/airwomen in this group maintain and repair RAF aircraft and missiles and propulsion systems. They carry out checks on RAF aircraft before and after flight, and do regular routine services. They also work in specialist maintenance units making major repairs, or on restructuring work.

Avionics

Personnel in this group maintain all airborne electrical, electronic, radar, navigation and flight systems, aircraft cameras, and communications and recording equipment in aircraft, airborne missiles and flight simulators.

Ground electronic engineering

Staff in this specialization are responsible for ground-based telecommunications, air defence radar and airfield navigation systems.

General engineering

This group looks after aircraft ground support equipment, and ground electrical equipment, including aerials. It involves machine tool work, metalworking and welding. Work done by this section is divided into four areas – ground support equipment, workshops, electrical work and aerial erecting.

Mechanical transport

This group comprises drivers who drive and operate the vehicles, and mechanics and technicians who maintain vehicles in an operational and roadworthy condition.

Air traffic control

Staff in air traffic control monitor aircraft transmissions, help plan flights and control aircraft access to runways from airfield control towers. They may also be employed at area radar units, where they may work alongside civilian controllers. Duties for airmen and airwomen in this group include updating essential information displays, setting up airfield signals, recording aircraft movement, operation of switchboards.

General service

The work of this group involves welfare and discipline of personnel, normally connected with station guardroom duties on stations. This includes organizing disciplinary actions, staff training and ceremonial events. Physical training instructors are also employed in this group.

Telecommunications

The telecommunications section operate and control all land and radio communications, often using computerized systems. This is a 24-hour operation. Employed in this group are: telecommunications operators, who send and receive messages, and systems analysts, who work with both telegraphic and voice communications.

Aerospace operations

Using advanced radar systems, aerospace systems operators help monitor and report the air situation. They provide warning of aircraft and missile attack using information from radars. They help to provide a recognized air picture for the United Kingdom airspace and its approaches.

Aerospace systems operators also man mobile radar convoys, and suitably qualified operators form part of the E3D airborne early-warning mission crews.

Safety equipment

This trade group consists of survival equipment fitters who maintain and repair equipment such as parachutes, ejection seats, liferafts and life-preservers.

Photography

Staff take photographs, operate and service ground cameras, carry out film processing work, print and copy photographs and assist with the interpretation of both ground and aerial photographs. Air cartographers are also part of this group.

Medical

The medical trade group is concerned with providing an essential medical service to the RAF at home and overseas. Highly trained staff are engaged in the clerical, nursing and medical administrative work at stations, hospitals, medical units and command headquarters.

This group includes personnel of the Princess Mary's Royal Air Force Nursing Service which provides all staff nurses in the Royal Air Force medical service.

Dental

A dental service is provided to all RAF personnel. Jobs include dental surgery assistants, dental hygienists and dental technicians.

Accounting and secretarial

This group provides the accounting, personnel administration, administrative, computer and statistical support for the RAF.

Supply and movements

Staff in this group are responsible for the storage of all sorts of RAF materials, as well as organizing the transportation of passengers, equipment, supplies and vehicles.

Catering

This trade group orders, prepares and serves food for all RAF institutions, including hospitals, temporary bases, and officers', sergeants' and airmens' messes.

Musician

Work is in established bands, ranging from marching and concert bands to the RAF salon orchestras and wind ensembles. Selected airmen and airwomen may also work as music instructors.

Security

This group is made up of three separate specialisms.

The RAF police carries out criminal investigations and counter-intelligence work, and is responsible for base security and dog handling.

The RAF Regiment provides a wide variety of jobs, all closely related to the support of flying operations. The Regiment provides field squadrons and Rapier squadrons. The Regiment also includes instructors for training all RAF personnel in all aspects of ground defence.

The RAF Fire Service is responsible for aircraft crash rescue.

WORK ENVIRONMENT

An RAF station may consist of from 300 to 1,500+ staff. Airmen/airwomen can be posted to RAF bases in the UK or abroad; they may also go on exercises anywhere in the world. Communal living and close team work are an important part of RAF life.

SKILLS AND INTERESTS

All airmen/airwomen require initiative, good communication skills and the ability to work as part of a team. They must be prepared to spend much of their free time with colleagues and, in most cases, live in RAF accommodation. It is important to be able to follow orders, and all personnel must appreciate the main function of the RAF and be prepared to work in combat. Airmen/airwomen must be prepared to work under pressure and maintain security at all times.

Each trade has its own particular requirements, but the ability to organize work and pay attention to detail are important in all trades.

NCO aircrew and those working in engineering and transport need practical and technical aptitudes.

Clear speech and verbal skills are necessary in aerospace and telecommunications, and the ability to speak foreign languages is also an asset in any communications-based trade.

Trades involved in the interpretation of data (eg photographic interpretation, ground electronics and data analysis) require the ability to write clear reports.

ENTRY REQUIREMENTS

There are no minimum educational qualifications needed for many jobs but the following personnel require academic qualification. Technical or vocational qualifications may be considered.

Aircraft mechanics (technician stream): three GCSEs/S grades (A-C/1-3) including maths and a physical science.

Other engineering mechanics (technician stream): three GCSEs/S grades (A-C/1-3) in maths and a physical science.

Air engineer, air loadmaster and air electronics operator: aged under 31 years, GCSEs/S grades (A-C/1-3) in English, maths and one other subject plus a background in a science subject (normally physics).

Operating theatre technician: three GCSEs/S grades (A-C/1-3) including English, maths, and one science subject, preferably biology/human biology.

Electrophysiological technician, laboratory technician, pharmacy technician: five academic GCSEs/S grades (A-C/1-3) including English, maths, physics (or approved physics-based science) and chemistry (or approved chemistry-based subject).

Environmental health technician: five GCSEs/S grades (A-C/1-3) including English, maths, biology (or human biology), chemistry and physics.

Mental nurse: civilian qualified on Part 3 of UKCC Register.

Radiographer: between three and five GCSEs/S grades (A-C/1-3) and two A levels or three H grades. Subjects should include English, maths/physics and a science subject. For exact requirements contact an Armed Forces careers office.

Physiotherapist: members of the Chartered Institute of Physiotherapists.

Staff nurse: RGN/UKCC registration.

Dental hygienist: General Dental Council Diploma of Proficiency in Oral Hygiene.

Dental technician: City and Guilds Dental Technician Certificate (Final) or BTEC/SCOTVEC National Diploma in Dental Technology.

Musician: grade 8 of the Associated Board or a Degree/Diploma in Music and passing an audition.

The minimum age for entry varies according to the trade.

All candidates must meet the RAF's nationality and residence requirements, and must sit aptitude tests in arithmetic, English vocabulary and general knowledge, as well as mechanical and electrical aptitude.

A complete medical check has to be passed before applicants can go on to the interview stage.

Good colour vision is needed by photography staff, movements operators, most security workers, engineers and those in safety and surface and aerospace systems. Perfect vision is a requirement for firefighters but, in other security services, glasses for reading are allowed.

Good hearing is necessary for firefighters, gunners and all staff in the telecommunications group.

TRAINING

All entrants to ground trades attend a seven-week recruit training course at RAF Halton, which includes physical fitness and military weapons training for all staff. An increasing proportion of trades training now involves working for nationally recognized qualifications, such as

NVQ/SVQ, BTEC/SCOTVEC or City and Guilds qualifications, and the RAF encourages airmen and airwomen to take advanced vocational qualifications as their careers progress.

Most entrants receive specialist training, for example:

Engineering Mechanics (technicians stream) and mechanics take courses in different engineering skills, which are a combination of theory and practical work. Initial engineering training takes place at RAF stations Cosford, Locking and St Athan.

Air engineers, air loadmasters and air electronics operators

take a twelve-week basic training course followed by a specialist training course. Trainees then do more detailed training to develop their expertise on particular aircraft.

Motor transport drivers are taught to drive light vehicles, and after experience can be selected for LGV training.

Policemen/women are given a three-week driving course if necessary. This is followed by an eight-and-a-half week basic police course, covering activities such as crowd control and vehicle search procedures. Further training can lead to dog handling, security services work or counter-intelligence duty.

Gunners take a 16-week course. This includes weapons training, survival, navigation and fieldcraft. The course is practical training done outdoors. Most gunners then take specialist courses in either light armour or Rapiers.

Assistant air traffic controllers are trained at the Central Air Traffic Control school. Tests are taken in signalling, meteorology, navigation, air traffic procedures and aircraft control regulations.

Physical training instructors that require specialist training take a 23-week course at RAF Cosford and a two-week parachuting course.

Telecommunications operators are taught typing, message handing, and how to work by computer, radio, telegraph and facsimile. Morse code is taught at a later stage.

Communications systems analysts are initially trained in a combination of office skills and languages. This is followed by operational techniques and RAF aircraft operations theory. Training is usually consolidated by work in an operational unit overseas.

Aerospace systems operators are trained on an induction course at the RAF School of Fighter Control. This includes keyboard skills training, basic radio principles, radar and computer systems, radar interpretation, meteorology and navigation.

Survival equipment fitters train in parachute maintenance and packing as well as learning about liferafts, flying clothing and all types of aircrew safety equipment.

Photographic trades – photographers, photographic interpreters' assistants and air cartographers all have separate courses.

Medical trades for which recruits can receive full training from the RAF include radiographer, laboratory technician, electrophysiology technician, operating theatre technician, pharmacy technician and environmental health technician. Courses are similar to those available in civilian life.

Dental technicians are trained at the Institute of Dental Health and Training at RAF Cosford. Students are fully qualified after a three-year course has been successfully completed.

Dental hygienists' training lasts for a year, and includes the study of anatomy, physiology and pathology, as well as practical work on model mouths for the first stage of the training.

Personnel and administrative clerks' training includes work on typing, filing and data transmission and postal procedures, as well as personnel management skills such as disciplinary procedures and document administration.

Data analysts take a short course which includes computer appreciation, statistics and the interpretation of aircraft records.

Suppliers take a course which covers all aspects of receiving, storing and issuing a whole range of equipment. Training covers both administration, which includes computerized accounting techniques, and practical work. Further specialist courses are available for work within, for example, explosives and fuels.

Movements operators – training lasts for eight weeks and is a combination of practical and theoretical work, covering air, road, rail and sea transport.

Caterers take a general catering course lasting four months, before returning to RAF bases where they may choose to take advanced or specialist training.

Musicians train at the RAF School of Music, studying the theory of music and band drill, and developing their playing ability in two musical instruments. The initial training course lasts up to a year, and is followed by more specialized work with one of the RAF bands.

Command and management training is provided for those who show potential, so that they may be promoted to non-commissioned status.

LATE ENTRY

The normal upper age limit for entry to the RAF is 24 years. Some trades, however, specify different limits.

NB: Age limits are subject to continual review.

OPPORTUNITIES

The number of vacancies available depends on particular trades, some of which are more competitive than others.

PAY AND CONDITIONS

Pay is reviewed annually, and the rates vary according to length of service and rank. The rates are higher for the skilled trades. Extra allowances are given to all staff working abroad. Armed Forces careers offices (AFCOs) can supply full details.

Airmen/airwomen aircrew appointments are for a fixed twelve-year engagement, but recruits for the RAF ground trades enlist for a period of nine years for regular service, followed by six years in the Reserve Force. For most trades, notice can be given after a minimum of three years training, or after the age of 18 years, if this is later. Airwomen can leave early if they are pregnant or they may continue their engagement in the RAF. Those who join under the age of 17 years and 6 months can have 'free discharge' up to six months after starting, but must work at least 28 days.

Most trades have fairly standard working hours, except when on exercises. Some workers, such as those involved in telecommunications, aerospace systems and security services, need to take part in 24-hour watch, which means that shift work is a regular feature. Catering staff and aircrew often work flexible hours and shifts, while medical and dental staff are on-call as normal routine.

PROSPECTS

Promotion for all airmen and airwomen is generally awarded for good individual performance. Examination results and Trade Ability Test marks are used to assess trade knowledge and skills. A high standard of personal conduct is also needed.

Some non-commissioned officer positions are reached only after prescribed training courses have been completed.

Airmen/women are promoted to Leading Aircraftmen/women on completion of basic training, and to Senior Aircraftmen/women after a minimum of one year's service.

Technicians are promoted to Junior Technician after appropriate technician training.

The ranks of Corporal and Sergeant are normally achieved by selection to fill vacancies, apart from some medical and dental trades, where time and qualifications are the criteria. Warrant Officer is the highest rank a non-commissioned officer can achieve.

Commissions and cadetships are available to airmen/women who satisfy the various conditions of eligibility – most types of commission are open to serving personnel.

RELATED OCCUPATIONS

Army non-commissioned officer, Royal Navy rating, Royal Marines–other ranks, aircraft maintenance engineer, RAF officer, police constable.

FURTHER INFORMATION

Information on all aspects of work and training is available from Armed Forces careers offices. The addresses of these offices can be found in telephone directories.

FURTHER READING

Job Outlines – The Armed Services – COIC
Working in The Armed Services – COIC
Working in Geography – COIC

In the careers library classified under BAL.

GROUP C – ADMIN, BUSINESS, CLERICAL AND MANAGEMENT

1. ADMINISTRATIVE STAFF CLCI:CAB
2. SUPPORT STAFF CLCI:CAB
3. SPECIALIST STAFF CLCI:CAB

BACKGROUND INFORMATION

It is the job of the Civil Service to put the policies of the elected government into practice. Civil servants work in all departments and agencies of central government. These range from large departments with a network of regional offices, such as the Department of Trade and Industry, to smaller units with more limited responsibilities and fewer staff, like the Department of National Heritage.

The Civil Service is non-political, and civil servants are expected to remain impartial, working for successive governments formed by different political parties.

There are approximately 500,000 civil servants. Although the headquarters of most departments are in London, larger departments and agencies have offices throughout the country; 80 per cent of civil servants now work outside London.

The main government departments and agencies, and their responsibilities, are:

Advisory, Conciliation and Arbitration Service: employment advice, conciliation in industrial disputes and arbitration.

Ministry of Agriculture, Fisheries and Food: farming, fishing and food production.

Audit Commission for Local Authorities and the National Health Service in England and Wales: auditing and advisory services; value for money.

Cabinet Office: Civil Service management, recruitment and assessment; science and technology.

Central Communications and Telecommunications Agency: government communications – an executive agency of the Cabinet Office.

Central Office of Information: information and publicity services – an executive agency of the Office of Public Services and Science.

Charity Commission: registering, advising and monitoring charities.

Commission for Racial Equality: elimination of racial discrimination; promotion of good race relations – a fringe body of the Civil Service.

Crown Prosecution Service: prosecution of offenders on behalf of the police.

HM Customs and Excise: collection of VAT and duties on tobacco, drink and petrol.

Office of the Data Protection Registrar: administering of the Data Protection Act – a fringe body of the Civil Service.

Ministry of Defence: Navy, Army and Air Services policy and support, procurement research and development.

Department for Education and Employment: primary, secondary, further and higher education; employment and training.

Department of the Environment: local government; housing and construction.

Equal Opportunities Commission: elimination of sexual discrimination at work – a fringe body of the Civil Service.

Export Credit Guarantee Department: insuring businesses against non-payment by overseas customers.

Office of Fair Trading: protecting the public and businesses from unfair trading practices.

Foreign and Commonwealth Office: foreign policy; representing business interests overseas.

Department of Health: administration of the National Health Service.

Health and Safety Executive: advice and enforcement of health and safety legislation – an executive agency of the Department of the Environment.

Home Office: law and order administration; immigration.

Inland Revenue: collection of income, capital gains and corporation tax; valuation of properties.

Lord Chancellor's Department: government legal services.

Meteorological Office: weather forecasting and information services.

Department of National Heritage: the arts, sport, heritage and the media.

National Rivers Authority: controlling pollution and improving the quality of inland and coastal waterways – a fringe body of the Civil Service.

Office for National Statistics: government statistical services, including registration of births, marriages and deaths, population census and national surveys.

Northern Ireland Office: policy and legislation relevant to Northern Ireland.

Ordnance Survey: mapping, charting and surveying.

Overseas Development Administration: overseas aid to developing countries.

Patent Office: patents, trade marks, registered designs and copyright.

Radiocommunications Agency: the national radio frequency spectrum – an executive agency of the Department of Trade and Industry.

Scottish Office: policy and legislation relevant to Scotland.

Department of Social Security: social security benefits and welfare services.

HM Stationery Office: publisher for government and Parliament – an executive agency of the Office of Public Service and Science.

Department of Trade and Industry: international trade policy, industrial liaison, consumer protection, insurance, radio and patent regulations.

Department of Transport and Highways Agency: aviation, shipping, roads and railways.

HM Treasury: economic policy and public spending.

Welsh Office: policy and legislation relevant to Wales.

It is possible to start work in the Civil Service at a number of different levels, depending on qualifications and experience, and there are opportunities to develop a successful career in general administrative roles as well as in many different specialisms.

It is also possible for civil servants to work on secondment for statutory bodies such as English Nature, the Rural Development Commission or the Arts Council.

THE WORK

There is a massive range of employment opportunities for civil servants in hundreds of different fields, from developing policy for the National Health Service to map making, from running a Jobcentre to translating technical information.

1. Administrative staff

Administrative assistants are basically junior clerks. Their work can include keeping records, either manually or on computer, sorting and filing papers, simple figurework, writing basic letters and dealing with enquiries.

Administrative officers work with administrative assistants, but have a higher level of responsibility. Their work can include handling incoming correspondence, writing or drafting letters, assessing charges or grants, checking accounts, maintaining records, either manually or on computer, and assisting the public.

Executive Officers fill junior and middle management positions. They could be responsible for managing a section of administrative officers and assistants, assisting a senior civil servant with policy work, external liaison or general administration. The work varies enormously from running a section in a local office to dealing with major domestic or international issues. About a third of executive officers take up specialized work in areas such as customs and excise or immigration.

Higher executive and senior executive officers are more senior management posts available to experienced staff. Success in these posts can lead to promotion to the most senior posts – from grade 7 to grade 1, a permanent secretary.

Fast-stream and development programme administrators and managers take part in an accelerated promotion scheme for high-calibre graduate entrants. The work could include working in a minister's office, providing support to an agency chief executive, or as part of a management team on a special project or inquiry. The work could involve researching and analysing policy options, working with specialists transforming policy objectives into the delivery of services, dealing with parliamentary business or in the many current international or national political issues. The Government Communications Headquarters also operates a graduate management training scheme. This fast-track scheme provides work experience and development training to prepare those involved for early promotion. Some of the work is technical, some administrative. Other departments also operate management development schemes for graduates.

2. Support staff

The Civil Service requires many different types of support staff to function effectively. These include personal secretaries, typists, telephonists, reprographics and photocopier operators, paperkeepers, messengers, cleaners, car drivers and security officers.

3. Specialist staff

As well as administrative staff, the Civil Service recruits for a variety of specialists.

Accountants are employed throughout the Civil Service to audit, analyse and verify their department's accounts. They also pay creditors' invoices, collect debts, provide financial accounts, and supply financial advice and information to managers.

Actuaries are employed by the Government Actuary's Department. The work involves acting as a financial services consultant to the public sector in the areas of social security, pensions and insurance. This could include costing of benefit provision, developing national pensions policy or monitoring insurance companies.

Agricultural development and advisory service consultants provide services to agriculture, horticulture and a wide range of public and private sector customers concerned with the countryside. The Service is also responsible for technical work arising from a number of statutory schemes.

Architects are employed in very limited numbers by the Department of the Environment, the Department of Transport and the Building Research Establishment, primarily on policy work.

Cartographic staff are recruited by the Ordnance Survey and several other departments to carry out mapping and charting work. As well as the traditional geographic maps, air and sea charts, many map production techniques and processes are now automated and mapping information is frequently provided in digital form. Mapping and charting officers work in jobs requiring specialist knowledge in a particular aspect of cartography, hydrography, topographic surveying, map and chart production or an associated function.

Computing staff work in a wide range of government departments and agencies in a variety of information technology roles, from data processing to systems analysis. The work centres on developing and updating systems and providing administrative support. Computer scientists, normally entering as assistant scientific officers, are employed by government research establishments, laboratories and organizations such as the Meteorological Office.

Diplomatic Service Staff are employed to protect and promote British interests abroad, and advise and support ministers as they formulate Britain's foreign policy. The work is divided between the Foreign and Commonwealth Office in London and diplomatic missions overseas. In Commonwealth countries these missions are known as High Commissions and in other countries as Embassies. In addition, Britain maintains missions to a number of international organizations, including the United Nations and the European Commission. The work of diplomatic missions is divided into five sections: political, commercial, information, consular/immigration and management.

Those starting in mainstream Diplomatic Service posts at grade 9 can expect to spend their first two years in London. A first overseas post is likely to involve consular, immigration or management work in a mission. With experience, it is possible to progress to more senior posts.

The Diplomatic Service also operates a fast-stream programme for high-calibre graduates.

Economists are employed in the Government Economic Service to provide ministers and senior administrators in all major departments with expert advice on economic matters. The work includes the analysis of current trends, the development of forecasting models and the preparation of forecasts, the development and evaluation of economic policy, and application of economic principles and techniques to industrial, social and institutional problems. There are also opportunities for research. It is possible to join as an economic assistant or senior economic assistant and to progress to economic adviser.

Engineers and *engineering technicians* work on a wide variety of different projects, from costing a new weapons system to advising on field drainage, from investigating aircraft accidents to developing computer systems. The main areas of employment are in the Ministry of Defence, the Government Communications Headquarters, the Department of Transport and the Radiocommunications Agency. Much of the work involves the most advanced technologies, and there are opportunities for engineers to be attached to industry and research establishments. There is a science and engineering fast-stream scheme for high-calibre graduates.

Health and safety inspectors are responsible for the well-being of the UK's workforce and those who may be affected by its activities. Most of their time is spent visiting workplaces to ensure that conditions, machinery and safeguards comply with health and safety legislation. They also advise employers, staff and suppliers and investigate accidents at work. Factory inspectors work in all industrial sectors and agricultural inspectors work mainly in farming, horticulture and forestry. Please see article HEALTH AND SAFETY INSPECTOR (COT).

Immigration Service staff are employed by the Home Office. Those who are recruited at executive officer level can choose to specialize in this area of activity. The work includes office-based activities, such as processing immigration applications and dealing with appeals, as well as work at airports and seaports, which includes checking passports and visas.

Information officers are employed by the Government Information Service to explain government policy and action. They work in every department. Press officers keep the media informed and may accompany ministers on official visits. Publicity officers are responsible for marketing and the organization of publicity campaigns, conferences and exhibitions. Information specialists provide the creative input and include graphic and exhibition designers, journalists, writers, illustrators and film producers.

Lawyers are employed by both the Government Legal Service and the Crown Prosecution Service. Within the Government Legal Service, lawyers work in all departments and some agencies, covering virtually every aspect of the law dealt with by private practice. They also have additional responsibilities for drafting legislation, advising ministers and, increasingly, with EU law. The Crown Prosecution Service prosecutes criminal cases instituted by the police in magistrates' courts and the Crown Court. It is possible to specialize in areas, such as juvenile law or fraud investigation.

Librarians work in all major government departments and agencies. Areas of work include cataloguing, classifying and indexing, database and computer systems, editorial work, literature searches, supervision of readers' services and clerical staff, and general library duties.

Linguists work for the Joint Technical Language Service, which is part of the Government Communications Headquarters, on transcription, translation and linguistic research for a number of government departments. The Ministry of Defence also employs linguists who initially carry out written translation, largely of a technical nature, and research into publications in a foreign language. More senior staff can work on advanced and specialized translation, foreign document research and simultaneous translation at conferences.

Museum staff are responsible for the vast and richly varied collections housed in Britain's museums and galleries. As well as having the opportunity to pursue studies in a particular area of interest, graduate curators are occupied in organizing exhibitions, managing technical staff, assisting with administrative work, helping to prepare publications and answering enquiries from the public. The type of work varies as greatly as the collections themselves – from computerizing records to supervising the care of antiquities. Some posts have a significant research element and some a requirement for public speaking.

Patent staff blend scientific, technical and legal work in the field of patents, designs, technical information and other intellectual property rights. Patent examiners work in the Patent Office to evaluate patent applications, to check that the requirements of patent law are met and that the public interest and the rights of other investors are protected. Patent officers are employed by either the Ministry of Defence or the Defence Research Agency and are involved in all aspects of intellectual property rights related to research, development and production.

Photographers are employed by the Central Office of Information and can work on a wide variety of projects from taking black-and-white news shots of a government press conference to shooting a series of transparencies of equipment for use in an information booklet. The work frequently involves working away from the office.

Psychologists in the Civil Service are involved in both research and casework. Those working for the Department for Education and Employment may work across a broad range of occupational psychology, assessing, guiding and counselling special-needs clients in order to help them into employment. Psychologists are also employed in the Prison Service, the Research and Planning Unit of the Home Office, and by the Ministry of Defence and the Defence Research Agency.

Research officers study the impact of government policies and provide information on which future policy decisions will be based. The Resource and Planning Research Group deals with policies relating to resource allocation and the environment. Staff normally have a degree in geography, economics, agricultural economics or economic history. The Social Sciences Research Group looks at patterns of behaviour among people in contemporary society, with staff usually having a social science degree.

Scientists and **technicians** are employed in various government departments and agencies, including the Meteorological Office, the National Physical Laboratory, and the Forensic Science Service. Their work covers a broad range, including fundamental research, technical administration, operational research, providing advisory services and contributing to the development of government policy. Half of the scientists in the Civil Service are engaged in research and development, the rest in advisory, management and policy activities. There is a science and engineering fast-stream scheme for high-calibre graduates.

Statisticians collect and process data of national importance and interest. Areas of work include the economy, employment, education, environment, crime, education and health. It is possible to join as a trainee statistician, assistant statistician or senior assistant statistician.

Surveyors are employed in a number of departments, including the Valuation Office Agency, the Ministry of Defence, the Ministry of Agriculture, Fisheries and Food, and by the Mapping and Charting Group. Areas of work include general practice, rural practice, quantity, building, land and mineral surveying.

Tax inspectors are concerned with determining the tax liability of individuals and companies. The work includes assessing whether accounts submitted are accurate, further investigation when this is considered necessary, reaching fair settlements and, on occasions, defending judgements at an independent tribunal. District inspectors, who head local offices, must also be managers. It is possible to specialize in areas such as serious fraud, tax avoidance, international taxation and oil taxation.

WORK ENVIRONMENT

Administrative staff are normally office-based. Specialist staff, such as scientists, engineers and graphic designers may work in research laboratories, test centres or design studios. Engineers, surveyors and architects may be involved in outdoor site visits. Some staff work in offices which are open to the public.

The work of many civil servants, particularly those in more senior grades, involves travel to external meetings, conferences or exhibitions. This can involve long days and periods spent away from home. The growing importance of the EU is resulting in more European travel for some administrative staff.

Members of the Diplomatic Service must be prepared to work anywhere in the world. Postings can include locations in tropical climates or in cities where living conditions are difficult. In the course of a full career, those working in the Diplomatic Service are likely to spend up to two-thirds of their time abroad.

SKILLS AND INTERESTS

The Civil Service is dependent on team work, and staff at all levels must be able to work well with others. Effective communication – in writing, face-to-face and on the telephone – is essential to the smooth running of government departments, and civil servants are therefore expected to be able to communicate well with their colleagues, representatives of external organizations and members of the public.

Good organizational abilities and a methodical and accurate approach to work are important at all levels. A responsible approach to confidential information is necessary for many civil servants. A high standard of numeracy is required for some posts.

Those recruited at executive officer level and above require the potential to lead and motivate other staff. They require an ability to act on their own initiative, to work without close supervision and to deliver results within agreed deadlines.

Fast-stream entrants must be able to work quickly and under pressure, to think creatively, to exercise sound judgement and achieve results. Those wishing to enter the Diplomatic Service or participate in the European fast-stream programme must also have an interest in international affairs.

Many specialist posts require specific abilities. For example, a high level of mathematical ability is essential for government actuaries and statisticians.

ENTRY REQUIREMENTS

It is possible to enter the Civil Service at a number of different levels, depending on qualifications and previous experience.

1. Administrative staff

Administrative assistant/officer

Selection for administrative assistant/officer posts is by competitive interview. Candidates for administrative assistant posts must normally possess two GCSEs/S grades (A-C/1-3) including English or equivalent. NVQs/SVQs may also be accepted. Administrative officers require five GCSEs/S grades (A-C/1-3) including English. Where necessary, departments may also recruit clerical staff by means of written tests for which no specific educational qualifications are required, or occasionally on the basis of previous relevant experience. Registered disabled persons who do not possess these qualifications may take written tests instead.

Executive officer

The minimum qualifications for entry as an executive officer (grade 9) are normally two A levels/three H grades and three GCSEs/S grades (A-C/1-3).

Equivalent qualifications including BTEC/SCOTVEC awards and GNVQs/GSVQs may also be acceptable. However, competition for entry to the Civil Service at executive officer level is fierce, and half of all recruits are graduates. Selection processes vary from department to department.

Fast-stream administrators

Around 100 graduate entrants are accepted each year to the Administrative fast-stream, after a rigorous selection procedure that is designed to test both intellectual and other abilities including personal and leadership qualities. It is also possible to enter the Diplomatic Service fast-stream. There is now a European fast-stream, which offers a route to a career in the European Union. It is specifically designed to help British candidates compete for administrative posts in EU institutions. A first or second-class honours degree or equivalent in any discipline is required for fast-stream entry.

2. Support staff

Typists recruited without a recognized typing qualification are required to pass a 30 wpm test. Personal secretaries, who are normally promoted from the typing grades, should have the same skill, and be capable of 100 wpm shorthand or 360-word audio transcription in 20 minutes. Secretaries also need three GCSEs/S grades (A-C/1-3) including English or the equivalent.

Entry requirements for other support staff vary depending on the nature of the post and may include academic qualifications or previous relevant experience.

3. Specialist staff

Accountants

Accountancy trainees require five GCSEs/S grades (A-C/1-3) and two A levels/three H grades or equivalent, including English and Maths.

Actuaries

The Government Actuary's Department requires actuaries to possess a first or second-class honours degree, and a good A level/H grade in maths if the degree is not in a mathematically-based subject.

Agricultural development and advisory service consultants

Agricultural development and advisory service consultants require a degree or equivalent qualification, preferably with honours, in a relevant science, engineering or surveying subject.

Architects

Architects require a recognized diploma in architecture. However, as the Civil Service employs very few architects and numbers are expected to fall in the near future, opportunities for new recruits are extremely limited.

Cartographic staff

Entrants as mapping and charting technicians grade 2 must have two GCSEs/S grades (A-C/1-3) in relevant subjects. Entry at grade 1 requires three GCSEs/S grades (A-C/1-3) or a BTEC national award in a relevant subject. NVQs/SVQs at the appropriate level in a relevant subject may also be accepted. Mapping and charting officer trainees require five GCSEs/S grades (A-C/1-3), including English and maths, and two A levels/three H grades.

Computing staff

Computing staff are recruited at a number of different levels. Executive officers normally require a minimum of two A levels, although many are graduates. Qualified and experienced staff are also recruited for many senior posts in systems development and administrative support. Research establishments and government laboratories also recruit graduates with relevant degrees, such as computer studies or maths, for assistant scientific officer posts.

Diplomatic staff

Mainstream Diplomatic Service officers require a minimum of two A levels, but many are graduates. Entry to the Diplomatic fast-stream requires entrants to hold at least a second-class honours degree in any subject. An aptitude for languages is an asset but not a prerequisite.

Economists

A first or good second-class honours degree or a postgraduate degree in economics or in a related subject with around 50 per cent economics content is required for entry as an economist. Cadet economists require a first or good second-class honours degree, plus the ability to complete a master's degree in economics.

Engineers and engineering technicians

Technician apprentices require four GCSEs/S grades (A-C/1-3) including maths, an appropriate science subject and, preferably, English. Engineers entering the Defence Engineering Service require an honours degree in a relevant engineering discipline. GCHQ or the Radiocommunications Agency require entrants to hold a first or second-class degree in electrical/electronic engineering, physics or computing. Entry to the Department of Transport and Highways Agency requires a first or second-class honours degree and an appropriate engineering qualification accredited by a professional engineering body.

Health and safety inspectors

Trainee health and safety inspectors require a first or second-class honours degree or equivalent in any subject and GCSE/S grade (A-C/1-3) in maths. They must hold a valid driving licence.

Immigration service staff

Entry at executive officer level requires a minimum of two A levels/three H grades and three GCSEs (A-C) or two S grades (1-3). However, many recruits are graduates.

Information specialists

For press and publicity officer posts, a high standard of education and excellent communication skills are required. Entry is with a relevant professional qualification.

Lawyers

Although the majority of government lawyers enter after completing their articles or pupillage, both the Government Legal Service and the Crown Prosecution Service offer salaried articles and pupillage. Applicants must have passed the Legal Practice Course or Bar Finals.

Librarians

Assistant librarians require professional qualifications and some practical experience of librarianship.

Linguists

The Joint Technical Language Service requires entrants to possess a first or second-class honours degree or a substantial working knowledge of a foreign language. Linguist officers require a degree or equivalent in at least one modern foreign language. Translators require a degree or equivalent in a modern foreign language with a sound knowledge of at least one other language.

Museum staff

Minimum entry requirements for curatorial staff are four GCSEs/S grades (A-C/1-3) including English. Conservation staff require two GCSEs/S grades (A-C/1-3) including English. Graduate entry requires a degree in an appropriate subject or equivalent qualification. However, competition for curatorial posts is intense and many entrants have postgraduate qualifications and research or other relevant experience.

Patent examiner

Patent examiners require a first or second-class honours degree or equivalent qualification in engineering, science or maths, or an equivalent qualification, such as corporate membership of one of the major professional institutions.

Photographers

Photographers are recruited with a relevant qualification or experience.

Psychologists

Psychologists require a first or second-class honours degree in psychology or an equivalent qualification that is acceptable for registration with the British Psychological Society. A postgraduate qualification is desirable, and experience in a relevant field is valued.

Research officers

Entry as a research officer requires a first or second-class degree or equivalent in an appropriate subject, such as geography, economics, agricultural economics or economic history.

Scientists and technicians

Assistant scientific offers require at least four GCSEs/S grades (A-C/1-3) including English, maths and a science subject. Scientific officers require a relevant degree or equivalent. Higher scientific officers require a relevant first or upper-second-class degree plus at least two years' postgraduate experience. Senior scientific officers require a relevant first or upper-second-class degree and at least four years' postgraduate experience. More specialized qualifications or abilities may be desirable for some posts.

Entry to the science and engineering fast-stream and most research posts require a first or upper-second-class honours degree in an engineering or science-related subject.

Statisticians

Entry as an assistant or senior assistant statistician requires a first or second-class honours degree with a minimum of 25 per cent theoretical statistics. Trainee statisticians require at least a second-class honours degree with a good maths A level or equivalent.

Surveyors

Surveyors must have passed or gained exemption from the written examinations of the Royal Institution of Chartered Surveyors or the Incorporated Society for Valuers and Auctioneers. Some training posts are open to graduates in other disciplines.

Tax inspectors

Entry to the Tax Inspectorate requires a first or second-class degree or equivalent in any subject.

To join the Civil Service, you must be a British citizen, a Commonwealth citizen or a citizen of the Republic of Ireland. For posts in the Cabinet Office (or its agencies) and the Ministry of Defence, at least one of your parents must also have been born a citizen of a Commonwealth country or the Republic of Ireland.

For posts in HM Diplomatic Service, at least one of your parents must have been a Commonwealth citizen or a citizen of the Republic of Ireland from a date 30 years or more before your appointment. If they have died, they should have been a Commonwealth citizen or citizen of the Irish Republic continuously from a date 30 years or more before your appointment. Applicants must have close affiliations with the UK in terms of upbringing and residence. All members of the Diplomatic Service and the Government Communications Headquarters must undergo enquiries, known as positive vetting, to ensure that they have the right temperament and attitudes to handle confidential work. A medical test is also required before entering the Diplomatic Service.

TRAINING

Training opportunities are available throughout the Civil Service including day release for those under 18 years, block release, college and university sponsorship, distance learning, in-house and on-the-job training, assistance with study for professional qualifications and attachment to external organizations.

There is a well-structured system for regular staff appraisal; identifying training needs and development opportunities is a key element of this. Fully structured management training development programmes ensure that staff with potential are encouraged to enhance their knowledge and skills.

The Civil Service College provides residential training both in specialist subjects, such as accountancy, personnel and finance, and in general management skills such as communication and negotiation. Its courses are available to all civil servants.

1. Administrative staff

Administrative officers and assistants

Training is provided to develop knowledge and skills and to prepare administrative staff for promotion. NVQs/SVQs may be available. These vary depending on the post held and the employing department or agency. Those who are under the age of 18 years can apply for day release to attend further education courses.

Executive officers

Most departments organize a management development programme aimed at improving the effectiveness of middle management. Specialist training is given to accountancy trainees, those in the automatic data processing field, to tax officers and examiners in insolvency.

A range of NVQs/SVQs are available – these vary depending on the post held.

For mainstream entrants to the Diplomatic Service, training in the first two years includes professional, developmental and management courses. Training for a first posting can include both specific skills and foreign languages.

Fast-stream administrators

Fast-stream administrators and managers are provided with extensive training opportunities, demanding work and early responsibility to develop their skills.

European fast-stream administrators receive additional training to prepare them for Europe, including language tuition, courses and tutorials on European issues and coaching to prepare them for the EC competitions.

2. Support staff

Relevant training is provided for support staff to equip them with the knowledge and skills to perform effectively. This can range from secretarial skills courses to programmes on the use of office equipment.

3. Specialist staff

Accountants

Accountancy trainees are trained under sponsored schemes for a professional accountancy qualification (eg the Chartered Association of Certified Accountants, The Institute of Cost and Management Accountants, The Institute of Chartered Accountants and the Chartered Institute of Public Finance and Accountancy). Trainees have time off on full pay for block or day release tuition, pre-examination study and attendance at examinations.

Actuaries

Trainees are given the opportunity to gain experience in all three main areas of work in the Government Actuary's Department (social security, pensions and insurance). They are prepared for the professional examinations of the Institute of Actuaries.

Agricultural development and advisory services consultants

New recruits to ADAS receive training – this covers technical expertise and communication skills, including personal development, writing, selling and presentation skills. Training may also be provided to allow individuals to obtain professional qualifications.

Cartographic staff

Training is provided in a particular aspect of cartography, hydrography, topographic surveying or map and chart production.

Computing staff

Executive officers specializing in automatic data processing receive training to equip them for their first post in computing, followed by further training which may lead to qualifications for membership of the British Computer Society.

Diplomatic Service staff

For mainstream and fast-stream entrants to the Diplomatic Service, training in the first two years includes professional, developmental and management courses. Recruits are also expected to acquire information technology and keyboard skills. Training for a first overseas posting can include both specific skills and foreign languages.

Some posts in the Diplomatic Service carry a language requirement and, if necessary, training to the required standard is provided. Certain postings carry with them a language requirement, such as Russian, Japanese or

Arabic. For these languages, two years intensive tuition is provided, split between London and living with a family in the host country. For overseas posts that do not have a language requirement, 100 hours tuition is available to officers and their spouses.

Economists

Economists receive both professional and administrative training, as all staff are encouraged to develop their economic skills and managerial abilities. This includes courses at the Civil Service College and other external seminars. Cadet economists undertake a postgraduate university course in economics.

Engineers and engineering technicians

GCHQ provides special project manager training schemes which lead to Institution of Electrical Engineers chartered status (Graduate Electronic Engineer scheme). The Radiocommunications Agency offers a two-year Institution of Electrical Engineers accredited training programme, followed by opportunities to gain experience for corporate membership.

The Highway's Agency's graduate training scheme for civil engineers provides experience throughout the highways engineering industry and enables young graduates to gain early chartered status with the Institution of Civil Engineers.

A range of training opportunities is provided by the Defence Evaluation Research Agency (DERA).

Health and safety inspectors

Training begins with two probationary years of hands-on inspection work in the company of more senior inspectors, combined with training. Trainees also undertake a modular, residential postgraduate diploma course.

Immigration service staff

Training is provided both to develop management skills and in specific skills related to the Immigration Service.

Information specialists

Assistant information officers receive training in various information subjects in each of their first two years, with additional training thereafter. Information officers are offered a similar but slightly reduced training package.

Lawyers

Pupil barristers with the Crown Prosecution Service spend their first six months in chambers in a non-practising role, followed by six months' practical placement with an experienced CPS pupil master.

Trainee solicitors serve their training through a two-year modular programme. During this, two of the required topics – criminal litigation and magisterial law – are covered by the CPS, while others are covered in sabbatical periods of six to eight months spent in local authorities, private practice or industry.

Librarians

Qualified librarians may undertake both management development and specialist training programmes.

Linguists

Graduate entrants may be given additional linguistic training, which may involve full-time study of a new language. Further training is provided for those moving on to advanced and specialized translation, foreign document research or simultaneous interpretation at conferences.

Museum staff

A range of NVQs for curatorial and conservation staff have been developed by the Museums Training Institute, and junior staff are encouraged to undertake training leading to these qualifications.

Graduate entrants are given the opportunity both to develop specialist research interests relevant to the collections with which they are working, as well as undertaking management development programmes.

Patent examiner

Newly-appointed patent examiners are assigned to an experienced examiner for a period of training – usually twelve months. They receive instructions and gain experience in all aspects of Patent Law and the various skills required of an examiner. Many documents searched by examiners are published in French or German and training is given in these languages.

Psychologists

Psychologists receive professional training leading to chartered status. Those joining the Prison Service receive two years' part-time training leading to an MSc in Applied Criminological Psychology.

Research officers

Training is provided in areas such as research techniques and project management as well as more general topics such as communication skills and staff management.

Scientists and technicians

Training is provided in specialist scientific disciplines and recruits are encouraged to develop their professional and management skills. Scientists are encouraged to publish and present reports and papers related to their research activities.

Statisticians

Trainee statisticians receive a six-month course in statistics. Those starting as an assistant statistician or senior assistant statistician initially spend some time in two or three different departments or agencies to gain experience. All recruits are encouraged to develop their management, administrative and communication skills.

Surveyors

Training is given in general practice, rural practice, quantity, building, land and mineral surveying, and to qualify for full membership of the Royal institution of Chartered Surveyors or the Incorporated Society of Valuers and Auctioneers.

Tax inspectors

Entrants receive two to three years' training, leading to two sets of examinations comparable to those of other professions. In addition to one day a week spent at a training centre, ten hours a week of office time are set aside for this training.

LATE ENTRY

It is possible for mature entrants to take up careers in the Civil Service and to return to work after a career break. There are no age limits for administrative assistants and officers or executive officers except for the European Fast Stream.

OPPORTUNITIES

Departments and agencies are now responsible for recruiting all their own personnel, excluding senior appointments at grade 7 and above, and appointments to the graduate entry fast-stream schemes. They either undertake this recruitment themselves or via a recruitment company or organization, often the Recruitment and Assessment Services Agency.

There is no longer any service-wide vacancy information. Vacancies are advertised in Jobcentres and sometimes in the national or local press. Specialist posts may be advertised in trade or professional publications. For example, vacancies for librarians are advertised in the *Library Association Record* and for psychologists in the *British Psychological Society Appointment Memorandum*. It is also possible to write directly to the department or agency in which applicants are interested in working.

Recruitment to the Civil Service is now far more limited than in the past, and competition for entry in many areas is highly intense.

PAY AND CONDITIONS

There are variations in pay and conditions between different jobs, grades and locations, although there are many common factors. Starting salaries are linked to skills and experience, and there is a system of annual increments.

Most civil servants work normal office hours from Monday to Friday. However, longer hours and weekend work may be required during busy periods and in more senior posts. Shift work may be required for a limited number of posts where it is essential for services to be provided on a 24-hour basis, for example, in the Government Information Service or in the Immigration Service.

Civil Servants have between 22 and 30 days holiday according to grade and length of service.

Employees working at executive officer level and above are appointed as mobile staff and must be prepared to work anywhere in the country.

Salary scales are no longer set for the Civil Service as a whole, but by individual departments. Performance-related pay has been introduced in most areas and there may be additional allowances for those working in London.

Part-time work and job-share opportunities are available.

Those working in the Diplomatic Service overseas receive allowances to ensure that their standard of living is maintained wherever they are serving in the world. These include cost-of-living allowances based on local living conditions, family size and grade, hardship allowances in posts where living conditions are difficult, rent-free accommodation overseas, free removal of personal effects, an education allowance for dependent children and fare-paid journeys for children at school in the UK, and overseas additions to basic leave with one or more fare-paid journeys to and from the UK.

PROSPECTS

Promotion for staff throughout the Civil Service is based on merit, regardless of level or method of entry. All employees are set targets, and performance is assessed against these goals.

Promotion to the highest grades is very competitive and only the most talented staff could expect to reach these positions.

RELATED OCCUPATIONS

Local authority administrator, local authority clerk, health service manager, medical records clerk, clerk.

FURTHER INFORMATION

Government Actuary's Department, Personnel Section, 22 Kingsway, London WC2B 6LE, 0171 242 6828

Personnel Division, MAFF, Victory House, 30-34 Kingsway, London WC2B 6TU, 0171 413 2767

Cabinet Office, Room 127/2, Horseguard Road, London SW1P 3AL, 0171 270 5713

Crown Prosecution Service, Personnel Branch 2*, 50 Ludgate Hill, London EC4M 3EX, 0171 273 8000

Defence Engineering and Science Group, Room 136, Pinesgate East, Lower Bristol Road, Bath BA1 5AB, 01225 449136

Economist Group Management Unit, HM Treasury, Room 105/G, Parliament Street, London SW1P 3AG, 0171 270 5000

Department for Education and Employment, Group Management Development Unit, Area C, Ground Floor, Castle View House, East Lane, Runcorn WA7 2DN, 01928 794345

Foreign and Commonwealth Office*, Personnel Policy Department, 4 Matthew Parker Street, London SW1H 9NL, 0171 210 0417

Government Communications Headquarters Recruitment Office, Room A/1108, Priors Road, Cheltenham, Gloucestershire GL52 5AJ, 01242 232912/3

Government Information Service, IOMU, Cabinet Office (OPS), Ashley House (Room 205), 2 Monck Street, London SW1P 2BQ, 0171 276 2717

Health and Safety Executive*, Room 321, HRM POSU, St Hugh's House, Stanley Precinct, Bootle, Merseyside L20 3QY, 0151 951 4425

Personnel Section 2, Hydrographic Office, Ministry of Defence, Taunton, Somerset TA1 2DN, 01823 337900, ext 3460

Inland Revenue Personnel Division, R and ER, Fast-Stream Recruitment Section, PO Box 55, Mowbray House, Castle Meadow Road, Nottingham NG2 1BE, 0115 9740603

Recruitment Office, Joint Technical Language Service, Room A/1108, Priors Road, Cheltenham, Gloucestershire GL52 5AJ

Government Legal Service Recruitment Team, Queen Anne's Chambers, 28 Broadway, London SW1H 9JS, 0171 210 3304

Military Survey, Personnel Section, Elmwood Avenue, Feltham, Middlesex TW13 7AF, 0181 890 3622

Office of Public Service*, Fastream and European Staffing Division, Graduate and Schools Liaison Branch, Horse Guards Road, London SW1P 3AL, 0171 270 5697

Ordnance Survey, Recruitment Officer, Romsey Road, Maybush, Southampton SO9 4DH, 01703 792665

The Principal Examiner (Admin), Patent Office, Concept House, Cardiff Road, Newport NP9 1RH

HM Prison Service Headquarters, Cleland House, Page Street, London SW1P 4LN, 0171 217 3000

Radiocommunications Agency, South Quay Three, 189 Marsh Wall, London E14 9SX, 0171 211 0528

Recruitment and Assessment Services, (Application helpdesk/general enquiries) Alengon Link, Basingstoke, Hampshire RG21 1JB, 01256 29222

GSS Personnel (Government Statistical Service), Room 613, Millbank Tower, Millbank, London SW1P 4QQ

Department of Transport, Recruitment Section (PD1F), Floor 4/02, Great Minster House, 76 Marsham Street, London SW1P 4DR, 0171 271 5346/5351

Valuation Office Agency, New Court, Carey Street, London WC2E 2JE

FURTHER READING

Leaflets/booklets are available from the addresses marked*.
Working in the Civil Service – COIC
In the careers library classified under CAB.

1. LOCAL GOVERNMENT ADMINISTRATOR CLCI:CAG
2. LOCAL GOVERNMENT CLERK CLCI:CAG

BACKGROUND INFORMATION

Local government is one of the UK's largest employers, with about two million people working in local authorities in England and Wales. The authorities vary in structure: in England there are a variety of authorities providing all services, whereas in Scotland 'all purpose' authorities each provide a full range of services. These include education, social services, emergency services, leisure services, housing and engineering.

1. LOCAL GOVERNMENT ADMINISTRATOR (CAG)

THE WORK

Administrators work in most departments in a local authority, from engineering to education, tourism, public relations, environmental health and housing, implementing decisions made by the council. Administrators plan, control, organize and maintain systems, procedures and practices to implement these decisions in the most efficient way.

Administrative work includes dealing with people – managing staff, personnel administration, servicing committees (preparing agendas and minutes of meetings); dealing with enquiries and providing advice; dealing with data – information gathering, storage and retrieval, and processing statistics; dealing with finance – budgeting, purchasing and supply, and processing invoices. The particular mix of activities depends largely on the level of job and the department in which the administrator is employed.

Whatever department administrators work in, they usually work in close contact with other people. These include colleagues from the same and different departments, elected councillors and often the public. Administrators are responsible, for instance, for preparing reports on available council housing for use by councillors and other departments, such as planning. This involves information retrieval and processing of statistics (for instance numbers and types of housing available by ward), liaison with colleagues from different departments and elected councillors and tenants.

Recent changes in local government structure have led to some services being contracted out, so that for instance, private contractors may provide catering services or refuse collection. This has changed the emphasis of administrators' work more towards managing client/contractor relationships and monitoring their performance to ensure it is of a high enough quality.

WORK ENVIRONMENT

Administrators work mainly in offices. At a more senior level, they may be required to travel to attend conferences and meetings in other regions.

SKILLS AND INTERESTS

Local government administration suits people who are well-organized and like organizing things. They monitor performance and must be methodical and pay close attention to detail.

A numerical aptitude certainly helps for some types of administrative work. An ability to analyse figures is vital when producing statistical reports. It is also useful for checking invoices and setting, implementing and monitoring budgets.

As a large part of any administrative role involves liaison with other people, it is essential to get on with people from a wide variety of backgrounds. This is particularly true for administrators who have any personnel or management responsibilities. Good communications skills are essential both verbally and in writing. Administrators must be able to elicit information from other people and provide easy-to-understand advice to others.

ENTRY REQUIREMENTS

Normal entry requirements for junior administrators are one A level or equivalent; an Advanced GNVQ/GSVQ Level III in Business; an NVQ/SVQ in Administration. An increasing number of councils are recruiting graduates to administrative posts, and some require non-graduate entrants to have a BTEC/SCOTVEC higher national certificate. Other councils have less stringent entry requirements, so individual authorities should be contacted. This is particularly true in the Scottish Authorities, which often take entrants with GCSEs/S grades (A-C/1-3) in English and maths.

An alternative route into administrative work is by starting with clerical work at a local authority. With experience and/or training such as NVQs/SVQs it is possible to be promoted to administrative level.

TRAINING

New administrators receive a great deal of on-the-job training in their council, department and particular duties. Some councils offer in-house training courses in particular areas, such as computer applications. In addition, administrative staff may study and train for additional qualifications – many councils offer day or block release for this study, or correspondence courses may be possible. Most local authorities are firmly committed to training, so release for study to specific qualifications as well as actual job training is not unusual.

Increasingly, training for local government administrators is leading to the award of NVQs/SVQs Level 3. These awards are usually in Administration, showing competence in such areas as researching and retrieving information, preparing and administrating meetings, maintenance of health and safety standards, banking procedures and a wide range of office duties. Other awards that a local government administrator can train towards include: the professional qualification of the Institute of Chartered Secretaries and Administrators (ICSA) which takes four to five years to complete (two years for candidates with degrees); higher national diplomas; membership of some other professional bodies; and the Certificate or Diploma in Management Studies (CMS or DMS) awarded by the Council for National Academic Awards (CNAA), taking one and two years respectively to complete. Study concentrates on subjects such as finance, law and personnel.

LATE ENTRY

Age is no barrier to starting work as a local government administrator.

Adults can gain recognition of their skills and experience by working towards NVQs/SVQs. There is open access to NVQs/SVQs – no academic qualifications are required, and there are no age limits. NVQs/SVQs are based on competence, and it does not matter how that competence has been gained – through experience, company training programmes, college courses or open learning. Past experience can be put forward as evidence of competence, via Accreditation of Prior Learning (APL).

There may be specific training opportunities directed at adults available in some areas for this type of work. Candidates may have to satisfy certain conditions to be eligible. Contact your local Jobcentre, careers office or TEC/LEC for details.

OPPORTUNITIES

Opportunities for administrators are available in almost every department. A large number of local government jobs have an administrative element, and it has been estimated that nearly half the workforce employed by local government work in administrative jobs of one type or another.

Administrative jobs are equally widespread geographically. Local government operates in every area of the UK, so opportunities are fairly evenly distributed around the country. However, competition for these posts can be fierce.

Both part-time and temporary work opportunities for local government administrators are available.

PAY AND CONDITIONS

Exact salaries are determined locally by each council, but most administrative staff are paid in a salary range within a national pay framework negotiated by the National Joint Council for Administrative, Professional, Technical and Clerical Staffs. The range is usually revised each year. In the year 1995/1996 the range was £6,692 to £28,798 with 49 levels. The range in Scottish authorities was the same but with a separate pay spine and grading structure. Salaries reflect differences between jobs, local grading policies, labour market forces and size of council. They are usually higher in London and the South East – London locations and those adjoining London attract an additional allowance (£360 and £522 for outer and inner fringes, and £1,052 and £2,163 for outer and inner London). More senior administrative managers (such as chief executives and chief officers) have different agreements.

Administrators usually work office hours. Salary scales are based on a 37-hour week, although some authorities operate a 35-hour week. At more senior levels flexibility regarding working hours may be required.

PROSPECTS

Ambitious administrators can progress all the way up the local government hierarchy. Obviously, to go this far requires the right experience, particularly managerial, as well as plenty of motivation. Administrators with sufficient motivation to progress to the upper levels of management may wish to add further qualifications along the way such as NVQs/SVQs at Levels 4 and 5 (currently being piloted and developed). Other options might include a general management qualification, such as a Master of Business Administration (MBA).

For those with ambitions to move out of local government, the experience and skills gained in the work of administrators are highly transferable to business, commerce and other concerns. Local government experience is useful for many general management jobs.

RELATED OCCUPATIONS

Company secretary, health service manager, Civil Service executive officer, personnel officer, local government clerk.

FURTHER INFORMATION AND READING

Please see article 2. LOCAL GOVERNMENT CLERK.

2. LOCAL GOVERNMENT CLERK (CAG)

THE WORK

There is a wide variety of clerical work available in most departments in a local authority from trading standards to town planning or leisure services.

Clerical work is essential to local government, to help administrators implement decisions and policies of the authority. Clerks deal with paperwork, telephone and other enquiries. Some clerks are given more responsibility, including supervisory duties, where more personal initiative is required.

Clerical assistants work for supervisors and administrators in virtually every sphere of local government work. Their duties often include filing documents and retrieving information as required. Some clerks write letters in response to enquiries from other departments, organizations and the public. Some process statistical information, inputting data for invoices, budgets, etc.

Much of a clerk's work involves dealing with standard enquiries. These can be from colleagues, outside bodies or the public. Often these are dealt with on the telephone, but they can be written enquiries. Clerks either respond to these themselves, finding out the information if necessary, or refer the query on to an administrator or other colleague.

Clerks use a range of office equipment, such as: word processors, typewriters, or computers; telephones and switchboards, fax and telex machines; calculators and photocopiers.

Clerical work also includes openings for typists, word processor operators, telephonists and receptionists.

WORK ENVIRONMENT

Clerks generally work in an office environment. The work often involves using office equipment such as work processor or telephone switchboard.

SKILLS AND INTERESTS

Clerks need good written and spoken communication skills. They must be able to convey information back to the enquirer equally clearly. They need to be able to understand and follow instructions and work without constant supervision. A certain amount of initiative is required, in that if the clerk does not know the answer to a particular query they need to know where to find it out, or to whom they should refer it.

Clerical staff who work on telephones and in reception are often the first point of contact for the public, so it is very important that they are helpful and can provide the correct information or directions. They need to be able to get on well with other people, because their job includes a great deal of contact with colleagues, the public and others.

ENTRY REQUIREMENTS

For many local authorities, skills and interests are just as important entry requirements as more formal qualifications. Specific requirements vary, so individual authorities should be contacted for exact details.

Many local authorities prefer candidates with three GCSEs/S grades (A-C/1-3). English, maths and keyboard skills are useful.

For people with few or no qualifications, a few authorities offer trainee posts, where they can learn the necessary skills on the job.

People with keyboard skills, who are applying for clerical work with a typing element, will need to demonstrate speed and accuracy. Jobs requiring keyboard skills range from copy and audio typing to word processing and computer work. Specific qualifications are not usually stipulated, but an aptitude test is normally given.

Entry may be possible for young people through Modern Apprenticeships leading to at least an NVQ/SVQ Level 3. Contact your local careers office, TEC/LEC for details.

TRAINING

Most local government clerks receive extensive on-the-job training in their particular duties, department and council structure. Some councils offer in-house training courses in particular subjects or job areas, to help clerks progress in their local government career. In addition, clerical staff can often study and train for further qualifications – many councils offer day or block release or correspondence courses may be possible. Most local authorities are firmly committed to training, so release to study for specific qualifications as well as actual job training is not unusual.

Increasingly, training in local government is leading to the award of NVQs/SVQs at Level 2 and 3, which for clerical staff would usually be in Administration, covering subjects such as the operation and maintenance of office equipment, processing and retrieving information and organizing office supplies and travel and accommodation. Alternatively, for clerical staff who wish to add other keyboard or administrative qualifications to their skills base, opportunities to study for RSA, Pitman, LCCI or BTEC/ SCOTVEC awards may be available.

It is possible to start work as a local government clerk via a training scheme for young people. This can be done either by getting day release from an existing employer to go to college, or by going directly to a college to study and being sent to employers for work experience. Contact your local careers office or TEC/LEC for further details.

LATE ENTRY

There are no barriers for mature applicants to start work as a local government clerk.

Adults can gain recognition of their skills and experience by working towards NVQs/SVQs. There is open access to NVQs/SVQs – no academic qualifications are required, and there are no age limits. NVQs/SVQs are based on competence, and it does not matter how that competence has been gained – through experience, company training programmes, college courses or open learning. Past experience can be put forward as evidence of competence, via Accreditation of Prior Learning (APL).

There may be specific training opportunities directed at adults available in some areas for this type of work. Candidates may have to satisfy certain conditions to be eligible. Contact your local Jobcentre, careers office or TEC/LEC for details.

OPPORTUNITIES

Opportunities for clerks are available in almost every department in a local government. It has been estimated that about half of the workforce employed by local government work in administrative roles, of whom many are at clerical level.

Clerical jobs are equally widespread geographically. Local government operates in every area of the UK, so opportunities are fairly evenly distributed around the country. Although vacancies are available, entry is quite competitive.

There are plenty of opportunities for both part-time and temporary work as a local government clerk.

PAY AND CONDITIONS

Exact salaries are determined locally by each council, but most clerical staff are paid in a salary range within a national pay framework negotiated by the National Joint Council for Administrative, Professional, Technical and Clerical Staffs. The range is usually revised each year. In the year 1994/1995 the range was £6,504 to £11,319, although more responsible or supervisory posts attract higher salaries. The range in Scottish authorities was the same but with a separate pay spine and grading structure. Salaries reflect differences between jobs, local grading policies, labour market forces and the size of the council. They are usually higher in London and the South East – London locations and those adjoining London attract an additional allowance (from £360 for the outer fringe to £2,163 for inner London).

Clerks usually work office hours. Salary scales are based on a 37-hour week, although some authorities operate a 35-hour week.

PROSPECTS

With motivation and experience, clerks can move to more responsible and supervisory posts. It is possible to be promoted to administrator and beyond, though it is likely that further training and qualifications would be required, such as BTEC/SCOTVEC national awards, NVQs/SVQs at Level 3, in administration or subjects relevant for the employing department.

The experience and skills gained as a local government clerk are easily transferred into other areas. Clerical work is available for instance in the Civil Service and the National Health Service. It is also possible to move out of the public sector altogether, and move into private industry and commerce. Clerks with good typing skills, and the necessary organizational aptitude could look for secretarial work. They may wish to add a secretarial certificate or diploma to their qualifications if they choose this route, such as those of the Royal Society of Arts (RSA) or the London Chamber of Commerce and Industry (LCCI). Alternatively, they may choose to take NVQs/SVQs in Administration.

RELATED OCCUPATIONS

Civil service administrative officer, medical records clerk, general/finance/accounts clerk, secretary, typist/word processor operator, local government administrator.

FURTHER INFORMATION

Business and Technology Education Council (BTEC)*, Central House, Upper Woburn Place, London WC1H 0HH, 0171 413 8400

Convention of Scottish Local Authorities (COSLA)*, Rosebery House, 9 Haymarket Terrace, Edinburgh EH12 5XZ, 0131 346 1222

Institute of Administrative Management*, 40 Chatsworth Parade, Petts Wood, Orpington, Kent BR5 1RW, 01689 875555

Institute of Chartered Secretaries and Administrators (ICSA)*, 16 Park Crescent, London W1N 4AH, 0171 580 4741

Local Government Opportunities (LGO), Local Government Management Board*, Layden House, 76-76 Turnmill Street, London EC1M 5QU, 0171 296 6600

LCCI Examinations Board*, Marlowe House, Station Road, Sidcup DA15 7BJ, 0181 302 0261

National Council for Vocational Qualifications (NCVQ)*, 222 Euston Road, London NW1 2BZ, 0171 387 9898

Pitman Qualifications*, 1 Giltspur Street, London EC1A 9DD, 0171 294 2471

RSA Examinations Board, Westwood Way, Coventry CV4 8HS, 01203 470033

Scottish Vocational Education Council (SCOTVEC)*, Hanover House, 24 Douglas Street, Glasgow G2 7NQ, 0141 248 7900

FURTHER READING

Leaflets/booklets are available from the addresses marked*.

Careers and Training in Local Government (CATLOG) – CRAC
Working in Local Government – COIC
Job Outlines – Local Government Administration – COIC

In the careers library classified under CAG.

1. HEALTH SERVICE MANAGER CLCI:CAL
2. MEDICAL RECORDS CLERK CLCI:CAL

1. HEALTH SERVICE MANAGER (CAL)

BACKGROUND INFORMATION

The National Health Service is the largest organisation in the UK, with around 1.2 million staff. The service is organized, in England, into district health authorities and regional authorities. The district is the main operational division – regional authorities are larger management groupings. Each district administers a number of units; a unit may be a hospital or a group of community services such as day centres or clinics.

In Scotland and Northern Ireland, the structure of the NHS is similar, but instead of districts there are health boards. Wales is a single region, with nine districts.

The health service is currently undergoing major changes. To improve the quality of service, make best use of resources and provide value for money, there is now a clear distinction between 'purchasers' and 'providers' of health care services.

'Purchasers' of health care are district health authorities or health boards, regional health authorities and some GPs with large practices, who have opted to become 'budget or fund holders', with responsibility for buying services for their own patients.

'Providers' of health care fall into two main categories: hospitals and community units. The latter include facilities such as day centres for the mentally ill, or sheltered homes for the disabled. As a result of recent changes, providers now sell their services to both local and more distant purchaser organizations.

A related development has been the creation of self-governing trusts within the NHS. These organizations (which are mainly hospitals) have opted for a greater degree of independence than other health care providers. Trust status allows them to decide which services to offer, to seek out new opportunities and to organize their services to respond to these.

Health service managers are employed both by purchaser organizations (in district or regional centres) and by providers – ie, community units and self-governing trusts.

Managers face a major challenge in terms of implementing and coping with these changes. Managing such a large organisation, particularly at a time of rapid development, is a demanding and sometimes difficult task.

THE WORK

Most general managers are involved in the provision or purchasing of services at district and unit level, and concern for quality and cost of services is a major focus of their work. Increasingly, managerial roles in the health service involve decision making on matters such as marketing, provision of services, resources and budgeting.

However, the work varies considerably in different settings. Broadly, a general manager may be responsible for some or all of the following.

Supervision: of clerical and secretarial staff.

Operational management: day-to-day management of a unit or a service within a unit.

Financial management: maintaining cash limits, setting budgets, working with health care professionals to decide on the best use of resources, staying within budgets.

Planning: setting objectives and deciding, with health care professionals, on the resources that will be needed to meet those objectives. Planning the implementation of changes.

Working with people: creating effective working relationships with teams of health professionals, eg medical staff within a particular clinical speciality. Working with personnel specialists to draw up job descriptions.

Information management: using information collected by medical records departments to make informed decisions, for instance on the provision of a specific service or the recruitment of staff, and determining the costs of providing or purchasing health care.

Most jobs involve negotiating with health care staff, attending committee meetings, using computers, analysing numerical data and writing reports, job descriptions, etc. Some managers liaise with the press.

There are also several specialist areas, and it is quite common for a managerial career to start in one of the specialist areas, with transfer to general management later on. The main specialisms are:

Finance: the work is broadly similar to that of other public finance accountants, and involves the management of financial systems, auditing, responsibility for proposing and assessing cost-effective projects, issuing and paying invoices, paying salaries, etc. Financial specialists usually study for accountancy qualifications.

Human resources: human resource managers are responsible for recruitment, selection and training of staff, for industrial relations, manpower planning and associated functions.

Purchasing and supply: this involves the organization and management of stores (except drugs), purchase of equipment, and advice to other departments on supply matters.

Hotel services: a new function that involves managing services such as catering, cleaning, linen and laundry, portering, security, telephones, hairdressing and sterile services.

There are also opportunities for IT specialists and for statisticians. The management of information, and its use to identify health care costs and future demand for services, is growing in importance.

WORK ENVIRONMENT

The work is office-based. At junior levels, managers usually share offices; more senior managers normally have their own private offices.

The amount of travel involved in the work varies according to the manager's seniority. Most jobs involve some travel – for instance, to different sites, and to attend training courses. The more responsible posts are likely to involve more extensive travel. For some positions, a driving licence is an advantage.

Most health service management posts involve a considerable degree of contact with medical, nursing and clerical staff and with representatives of other organizations.

SKILLS AND INTERESTS

Although the main objective of the work is the provision of health care, the manager's contribution is to run the organization efficiently. Management skills, rather than medical knowledge or an interest in helping people, are the main requirement. Managers need adaptability, drive and determination, with the ability to lead others and to implement and manage change. It is essential that they should be capable of working under pressure.

Excellent spoken and written communication skills are required. Managers need to persuade and influence others and to convince people of their case. It is also important to listen to other people's views.

Intellectual ability – including the capacity to analyse complex issues and to understand numerical data – is important. Managers need to be resourceful and creative, able to innovate and find imaginative solutions to problems.

ENTRY REQUIREMENTS

Applicants from outside the Health Service, applying for general-management training schemes (national, regional or local), need a degree in any subject or an equivalent qualification, or an acceptable professional qualification.

Internal applicants for general-management training schemes need to be over 21 years, with at least one year's experience in the NHS or related employment. Two A levels or equivalent, or a pass in the intermediate examination of an acceptable professional qualification, are required.

Applicants without these qualifications may enter the NHS at clerical or secretarial level and can apply for management training after gaining relevant experience and qualifications within the service. Nurses and other health service staff may also move into management posts, after gaining appropriate experience and qualifications.

For the Managing Health Services Programme there are no specific academic entry requirements.

TRAINING

There are two main entry and training routes for school and college leavers: (1) via national, regional or local training schemes, (2) via entry into other branches of the health service, followed by in-service training.

1. National, regional and local training schemes

National Schemes

The NHS Management Training Scheme (England) combines work experience, formal management courses, projects and investigations, and study for a professional qualification. The scheme lasts 22 months and involves approximately:

—twelve weeks introductory training in a district, with experience of patient care in varied setting and work with NHS staff in different departments;

—six months in a management post with responsibility for staff and resources;

—four months elective allowing development of management skills;

—time spent throughout the scheme at a management education centre.

For further details contact the Management Training Scheme Office.

The Financial Management Scheme (Scotland) lasts 40 months. It covers planned instruction/practice within a health board, intensive management modules and study for the CIPFA training programme. Please see article PUBLIC SERVICE ACCOUNTANT (NAB).

The Business and Operations Management and *Human*

Resource Management Scheme. Entrants to both schemes are given 24-month contracts and training includes a common induction programme, two or three different placements and 16 one-week residential blocks for the MSc in Health Care Management.

Regional and local schemes

Other regional management training schemes may be available in certain areas, but not necessarily every year.

These schemes are designed to attract candidates who wish to make a commitment to a career in that particular area. Entry requirements, length and content of training are similar to the general-management training schemes.

Local schemes may be run in different areas according to need; the entry requirements and length of training vary according to local demand. Further information about local and regional schemes may be obtained from Regional or District Health Authorities.

Training schemes for specialists in finance, personnel, purchasing and supply and hotel services are run, according to need, by Regional Health Authorities (except in Scotland, where the financial management scheme is run on a national basis).

2. In-service training

Individuals who are already employed by the NHS – for instance, in clerical or secretarial roles – may apply for management training. With the appropriate entry qualifications, they may apply for general-management training schemes or other regional or local schemes.

The Managing Health Services Programme (MHS) is an alternative training route for those employed in the NHS to study via open/distance learning or college courses for the Managing Health Services programme. This programme has been developed by the Institute of Health Record Information and Management (IHRIM) and the Open University (OU). It is offered via: (1) distance learning, available through the OU; (2) open learning programmes, provided by some health authorities/boards; or (3) courses at some institutions of higher education. The MHS normally takes approximately 400 hours of study over a twelve-month period; students may gain one of the following qualifications: the IHRIM Certificate in Managing Health Services (CHRIM), an Open University Certificate in Management Studies or NVQ Level 4.

Diploma in Health Services Management courses normally involve two to three years' part-time study. Further details of this and other IHRIM qualifications are available from the Institute.

LATE ENTRY

There is no upper age limit for entry to health service management. Applicants with previous experience in the NHS (in any capacity) are particularly welcome. The Managing Health Services programme is appropriate pre-entry training for mature applicants, particularly if they have health service experience.

Individuals who have obtained professional qualifications outside the NHS may apply for management posts. Appropriate qualifications may be in professions such as accountancy, personnel, purchasing and supply, or information technology. Applicants may be selected for management development programmes.

OPPORTUNITIES

The vast majority of health service managers are employed by the NHS. Small numbers work for private hospitals and

HM Forces. Experienced managers with Institute of Health Services Management qualifications can work abroad; one of the main areas in which health service managers work is the Middle East.

In the short term, the demand for managers is expected to increase, to cope with the implementation of recent NHS reforms. In the following years, demand is expected to decrease.

Entry to the Management Training Scheme is highly competitive. It may be easier to enter as a trainee financial manager.

PAY AND CONDITIONS

The salary scale ranges from £15,490 to £48,340, covering 30 spine points. It is also possible to increase the salary ranges with performance-related pay.

Hours of work are 37 a week, Monday to Friday. There are 20 working days holiday entitlement a year, plus public holidays. The NHS runs a contributory pension scheme.

PROSPECTS

After training, it is usual to gain experience in operational management, working towards unit general manager level. Beyond that, there are opportunities to reach the most senior posts at district or regional level. Willingness to relocate to different areas of the country is likely to improve promotion prospects.

There are opportunities for experienced managers to study for qualifications such as the Master of Business Administration (MBA) or the Diploma in Management Studies (DMS). Such qualifications may be particularly useful for specialists who wish to move into general management.

RELATED OCCUPATIONS

Civil Service executive officer/administration trainee, local government administrator, industrial relations officer, public finance accountant, personnel officer, purchasing officer, medical records clerk.

FURTHER INFORMATION

The Institute of Health Services Management, Registry, 39 Chalton Street, London NW1 1JD, 0171 388 2626

Management Development Group, Scottish Health Service Centre*, Crewe Road South, Edinburgh EH4 2LF, 0131 332 2335

NHS Training Division*, St Bartholomew's Court, 18 Christmas Street, Bristol BS1 5BT, 0117 929 1029

Management Training Scheme Office, NHS Executive Trust, Lodge Moor Conference Centre, 29 Lodge Moor Complex, Redmires Road, Sheffield S10 4LH

Provider Support Unit*, Central Services Agency, The Beeches, 12 Hampton Manor Drive, Belfast BT2 3EN, 01232 644811

FURTHER READING

Leaflets/booklets are available from the addresses marked*.

Working in Hospitals – COIC

In the careers library classified under CAL

2. MEDICAL RECORDS CLERK (CAL)

BACKGROUND INFORMATION

Medical records clerks play an essential role in the management of the NHS. They provide a reception service for the public, maintain links between GPs and consultants and provide administrative support for the treatment and care of patients. They also process statistical information which is vital for the Health Service's effective management.

THE WORK

The work involves filing, maintaining and compiling all the documents relating to hospital patients, making sure medical records are available to hospital staff, receiving patients, arranging appointments, and directing patients to wards or clinics.

There are several areas of work; clerks may rotate between these different areas, or may be concerned with only one aspect. The specialist areas are:

Filing and administration. Every hospital has a Master Patient Index (usually a computerized system), with details of every patient who has had contact with the hospital – either as an inpatient or outpatient – at any time. When a patient registers with the hospital, clerks check the Master Patient Index to see if that person has previously attended – if not, they allocate a unit number to the patient and start a new case record containing details of treatment, operations, etc.

Clerks are also responsible for filing and retrieving case records. For outpatient clinics, they work from a list of patients due to attend, pulling out the case records, checking them off against clinic lists, making sure that the records are ready for use in clinics and that the results of tests have been correctly filed.

Other duties include retrieving case records for waiting lists and admissions, compiling and updating waiting lists, and tracing any files or documents that go missing.

Outpatient reception, admissions and ward clerks. These jobs involve contact with patients, as well as administration and telephone work.

Outpatient receptionists deal with correspondence from GPs, book appointments, receive patients and direct them to clinics, arrange follow-up appointments and, where necessary, book ambulance transport.

Admissions clerks may work either in planned admissions or in accident/emergency departments; in smaller hospitals, these functions are combined in a single department. Clerks dealing with planned admissions keep records of all patients to be admitted to the hospital, direct patients to wards, maintain a register of patients who have been admitted, and circulate patient details to telephonists, ward staff and hospital chaplains. They also keep records of patient transfers, discharges and deaths. Emergency admissions work involves taking patient details, recording attendances, and keeping records of children attending the hospital and of patients who have been in specific types of accidents (eg road traffic accidents).

Ward clerks provide clerical assistance to nursing staff. They are based in hospital wards, where they receive patients, carry out clerical duties and answer telephone enquiries.

Other duties may include support to patients and their relatives who need to claim travelling expenses, and dealing sensitively with administrative matters – issuing relevant documents, for example, when patients die.

Clinical coding. This type of work involves adding a distinguishing code, which shows the type of disease the patient is suffering from or the operation performed. Clinical coding clerks use doctors' notes and medical reference books to select the correct codes. The coded data is then input on to the computer and sent to a central point where it is used for planning, statistical analysis, etc.

Clinical coding has become increasingly important since the NHS reforms, because, with the current emphasis on best use of resources, accurate information about the diagnosis and cost of treating each patient is essential.

The information processed by clinical coding clerks is also important for the collection of statistics for epidemiology, for research purposes and for the Department of Health's statistical records.

Other statistical work. Clerks are also involved in gathering statistics for various other purposes. For example, each day they check the number of beds available; this involves keeping a record of the patients admitted and discharged from each ward within the previous 24 hours. They also gather information about the number of referrals to the hospital and the number of patients attending clinics. On a monthly basis, they complete forms showing the pattern of activity in the hospital – including outpatient attendances, admissions, discharges, and the number of patients on the waiting list.

Most jobs now involve the use of computers.

WORK ENVIRONMENT

Filing clerks generally work in the medical records library, which can be the size of a hospital ward. Records are stored on metal or wooden racks, or mobile filing units. Clerks need reasonable agility, they may have to bend to reach lower racks, or climb on ladders or kickstools (running on castors) to reach the upper tiers. The passages between the racks may be narrow, and some agility is required for manoeuvring. Occasionally, when clerks need to retrieve older records from secondary storage areas (eg in basements), the work environment may be dusty.

Outpatient and admissions receptionists work at reception desks in outpatient clinics, admissions departments or accident/emergency departments. Admissions work may also take place in separate offices.

Ward clerks work behind main nursing stations on wards, or in separate offices Statistical clerks are office-based. Coding clerks are based in separate offices within the medical records department, or sometimes on wards or adjacent to doctor's offices.

Most jobs involve some movement in and around the hospital – fetching and delivering case records, messages and other documents.

SKILLS AND INTERESTS

A methodical and efficient approach to administrative tasks is essential.

Clerks who deal directly with patients – in admissions, reception and on wards – need good spoken communication skills, together with a pleasant, reassuring manner. They have to be able to cope tactfully with patients and relatives who are anxious or apprehensive.

Flexibility about tackling a range of tasks is an important requirement. Clerks also need to be able to work well with others, as members of a team.

It is essential to respect the confidentiality of patient records, and not to mention details of patients or their treatment to outsiders, or to colleagues within the hospital (unless the colleagues are involved in the patient's treatment or care).

Clerks specializing in statistical work need an aptitude for figures. Clinical coding clerks need an interest in biology and human anatomy.

ENTRY REQUIREMENTS

There are no minimum educational entry requirements. However, those who wish to take the Institute of Health Record Information and Management (IHRIM-UK) Certificate need five GCSEs/S grades (A-C/1-3), including English language and one of: arithmetic, maths or statistics. Candidates for the IHRIM Diploma need either the IHRIM Certificate or an equivalent qualification which grants exemption from the Certificate (such as associateship of the Institute of Health Services Management).

Keyboard skills are an advantage for most posts.

TRAINING

Training varies in different hospitals, but is mainly on-the-job.

One-day induction courses, introducing new staff to the NHS, are usually available. Additionally, there may be an introduction to medical records work, lasting one week to one month, typically involving short attachments to each department within medical records. Trainees learn how to use computers, and how the hospital's administrative systems operate. Further on-the-job training, under supervision, continues until clerks are fully proficient – this can take about six months.

The IHRIM Certificates of Technical Competence (CTCs) in Basic Medical Records Practice offer work-based assessment. These certificates are awarded for demonstrable knowledge and skills in health records practice. The IHRIM produces study material for the Certificate Examination.

Career prospects are improved for those who take the IHRIM Certificate and Diploma qualifications. It may be possible to study at a college, on day release (usually over one year), but it is more common to study at home, over one to two years. The Certificate may be followed by the Diploma, which usually involves a further one year's study on day release or one to two years at home. The qualifying letters CHRIM for Certificate exam success or AHRIM (associate) for Diploma success are awarded.

For clerks who wish to specialize in diagnostic coding, the specialist AHRIM diagnostic coding qualification is desirable. Day release courses for this qualification may be available in some areas.

In some areas of the country, training opportunities for young people may be available. Contact local careers offices, TECs, LECs or Jobcentres for further details.

LATE ENTRY

There are good opportunities for adult entrants. Maturity is an advantage for receptionists, admissions and ward clerks, for whom dealing tactfully with patients, relatives and other visitors is an important part of the work.

For those over 21 years wishing to take the IHRIM certificate, entry requirements are two CGSEs/S grades (A-C/1-3) including English language.

There may be specific training opportunities directed at adults available in some areas for this type of work. Candidates may have to satisfy certain conditions to be eligible. Contact your local Jobcentre, careers office or TEC/LEC for details.

OPPORTUNITIES

Opportunities are increasing because NHS reforms have created more administrative/information processing work and therefore a greater need for clerical staff.

Every hospital employs medical records clerks. The availability of vacancies, and the degree of competition for jobs, varies in different parts of the country. There is more competition for vacancies in areas of high unemployment.

The principal employer is the NHS, but there are also opportunities in private hospitals and HM Forces.

Local hospital personnel departments may give advice about vacancies.

Medical records clerks with IHRIM qualifications may work abroad; one of the main countries in which medical records clerks work is Saudi Arabia.

PAY AND CONDITIONS

In the basic clerical grade 2, 16-year-olds start on about £5,544 rising to £6,596 at 17 years. At the age of 18 years and over, the basic salary range is from £7,687 to £8,815. Basic hours for full-time staff are 37 a week; for any additional hours, paid overtime or time off in lieu is available. Some hospitals now operate flexitime systems.

In the supervisory grades, salaries range from Grade 3 £8,815 to Grade 6 £15,104. Managers' salaries depend on the size of the hospital and range of duties.

Most medical records clerks work days. Some filing clerks and receptionists in accident and emergency departments work shifts, including nights, weekends and bank holidays.

Part-time work is widely available, and opportunities for job sharing are increasing.

PROSPECTS

Experienced medical records clerks may progress to supervisory and management posts. Supervisors are typically responsible for between four and ten staff, for instance in the medical records library. Assistant managers are responsible for the work of supervisors; managers oversee the whole medical records department, and in a large hospital this means taking responsibility for several hundred staff. There are further opportunities to move into general NHS management.

Staff who are aiming for promotion usually take the IHRIM qualifications (see TRAINING). Good interpersonal skills are also required for promotion, as supervisory and managerial posts in medical records are very much orientated towards the management of people.

There are opportunities for clerks to move into other types of clerical/administrative/information technology work, for instance in banking, insurance or solicitors' offices. Some clerks train as medical secretaries.

RELATED OCCUPATIONS

Medical secretary, receptionist, Civil Service administrative officer/assistant, local government clerk, health service manager.

FURTHER INFORMATION

Institute of Health Record Information and Management (IHRIM-UK) Headquarters*, c/o Warrington Community Healthcare NHS Trust, Winwick Hospital, Warrington, Cheshire WA2 8RR, 01925 639772

FURTHER READING

Leaflets/booklets are available from the address marked*.

Job Outlines – Hospital Support Staff – COIC
Working in Hospitals – COIC

In the careers library classified under CAL.

1. POSTMAN/WOMAN CLCI:YAT/CAM
2. POST OFFICE COUNTER CLERK
CLCI:CAM

BACKGROUND INFORMATION

The Post Office provides postal and retail services to the public and business community. It is among the top 30 businesses in the UK, with a turnover of more than £5 billion, and one of the country's largest employers, with over 197,000 employees. The Post Office is organized into three main businesses:

Royal Mail, which is responsible for the collection, sorting and delivery of letters in the UK and overseas. It delivers over 60 million letters a day in the UK and is the largest part of the Post Office;

Parcelforce, which collects, sorts and delivers parcels to business customers and private individuals;

Post Office Counters Ltd, which operates around 20,000 Crown, franchise and sub-post offices. Apart from postage items, TV and other licenses and passport applications are available in these retail outlets, as well as a variety of financial services.

The Post Office's delivery work means it has an extensive transport network, including road, rail and air. In addition, the Post Office Group Centre offers headquarters services across the business, such as specialist finance, planning, legal services, welfare, purchasing, public relations and training and development. Under the same umbrella comes Subscription Services Ltd, which is a wholly-owned subsidiary including the TV Licence Records Office.

The government has announced a review of the Post Office which may affect its structure and opportunities within it in the near future. At present, apart from the jobs of postman/postwoman and counter clerk, each Post Office business offers a variety of opportunities for specialist managers (sometimes recruited at graduate level) in such fields as finance, personnel, marketing, operations, engineering, transport, estates management and information technology. Candidates are recruited to specific jobs, for which they must have the appropriate specialist expertise or potential.

1. POSTMAN/WOMAN (YAT/CAM)

THE WORK

Postmen/women collect, sort and deliver mail to homes and workplaces. Their work covers every stage of the journey of letters and small packets from sender to receiver.

Postmen/women collect mail from pillar boxes, businesses and post offices, transporting mail by van to sorting offices. Mail is sorted there for despatch to its destination, into towns, cities, counties and countries. Although unusual-sized letters and those without postcodes sometimes have to be sorted by hand, increasingly sorting is done by high speed automatic sorting machines. The mail is prepared for these machines by postmen/women using a keyboard to convert the postcodes into dots on the envelopes.

Next, the mail moves through a vast transport network, including road, rail and air. Postmen/women work at stations, airports and road depots loading and unloading mailbags. Others drive a variety of vehicles including vans and large goods vehicles, and some sort mail on travelling post offices (trains that have sorting offices). Postmen/women then sort incoming mail by areas and roads, and deliver it by van, bicycle or on foot.

Parcelforce has its own network of sorting and delivery offices where staff work as parcel handlers, sorters and drivers. Like Royal Mail postmen/women, their work also involves collection, sorting, transporting and final delivery. Parcelforce sorting is highly automated, so very little sorting is done by hand.

WORK ENVIRONMENT

Making postal collections and deliveries is outdoor work. It has to be done in all weather conditions: working in the summer heat can be as difficult as working in the rain, or in the winter cold and ice. Delivery and collection rounds in some country areas involve a great deal of driving.

Sorting all the incoming and outgoing mail, and preparing mail for machine sorting are indoor jobs. Sorting offices can be large and very busy places. Automatic sorting equipment can be very noisy.

Some jobs involve high physical demands, lifting and carrying, while others are mainly sedentary, working at a keyboard for example.

SKILLS AND INTERESTS

Postmen/women have a responsible job in ensuring the safe delivery of all mail. They must be honest and trustworthy. They often have direct contact with customers, either collecting or delivering, and must be comfortable with this personal contact. The ability to read addresses and carry out clerical tasks is required, eg resorting and redirecting mail.

While carrying out sorting duties, postmen/women need to be able to work accurately, quickly and carefully. They must also work as part of a team. Sorting mail ready for final delivery on a 'walk' needs a good memory and detailed local knowledge.

Postmen/women need to be fit and active; postbags are heavy at the start of a round, and the work can involve a great deal of walking. They also need to be able to work on their own, as well as in a team, and to be both reliable and adaptable.

ENTRY REQUIREMENTS

There are no formal academic qualifications required for entry as a postman/woman with Royal Mail, or as a parcel handler and sorter with Parcelforce.

Selection is by aptitude test and interview. The aptitude test is based on some of the skills used in the day-to-day work of postmen/women, such as checking for errors in lists of names and addresses.

Postmen/women may also be required to attend a medical examination. For some jobs, applicants must be willing to ride a bicycle.

TRAINING

New entrants at postman/woman grade with Royal Mail attend a variety of off-the-job short courses introducing them to their various duties during their first two weeks. Most of the basic delivery and sorting skills are taught on the job by more experienced colleagues. Further courses are given as staff take on more senior duties. An NVQ/SVQ for postmen/women is being developed.

New entrants with Parcelforce attend an introductory

course, and then work alongside experienced staff while they learn the basic skills. All new entrants also have the opportunity to attend off-the-job training courses at regional training schools. Courses lead to the City and Guilds Certificate in Parcel Distribution. There is also further on-the-job training during the first year.

Parcelforce collection, sorting and distribution staff can work towards the Certificate in Parcel Distribution awarded by City and Guilds. Staff over the age of 21 with a driving licence may apply for Large Goods Vehicles (Class 1) driver training.

LATE ENTRY

Adult entry is common. The upper age limit for recruiting is 57 years. Entry for older candidates is by successfully completing the short test and passing the interview.

OPPORTUNITIES

The majority of Royal Mail's staff work as postmen/women in the district offices and local sorting offices. Parcelforce has its own network of sorting and delivery centres.

At present, opportunities to join royal Mail are limited and are expected to remain so for some time to come. The number of postmen and postwomen is falling, so recruitment has stopped in some cases and is restricted to temporary contracts in others. Competition for jobs can be strong. Christmas is usually a very busy period for Royal Mail and extra postmen/women are often employed for the season.

Parcelforce has increased the number of staff employed as collection and delivery staff and drivers, while reducing its administrative staff. Opportunities for depot staff and drivers are likely to remain steady.

PAY AND CONDITIONS

Royal Mail

The basic rate of pay for a postman/postwoman at 16 years is £111.51 a week, rising to £175.19 a week at 18 years. The basic rate of pay for adult recruits is £175.19 a week, rising to a maximum of £183.10 a week. Higher grade postmen/women and supervisors are paid on a different scale.

There is a bonus scheme, linked to the performance of each sorting office. This leads to minimum additional payments after twelve months' satisfactory service.

The business is moving towards a fixed shift with an emphasis on team working. Shifts start at 5 or 6am, 1.30pm and 9 or 10pm. The early shift generally prepares and makes the morning deliveries of mail, while the late shift normally collects and sorts mail and the night shift sorts and despatches it. Some Sunday work is required.

A shift allowance of time-and-a-third is paid for normal duties between 7pm and 6am. There are additional payments for Saturday working, for overtime and for driving.

Postmen/women get four weeks holiday a year, rising to five weeks a year after 30 years' service. This is in addition to two-and-a-half 'occasional' days

Other benefits include free uniform, subsidized meals and a contributory pension scheme.

Parcelforce

The basic rate of pay is £119.08 week. The basic rate for adult recruits is £167.37 a week rising to a maximum of

£174.50. There is a bonus scheme at sorting offices linked to group performance, whilst at delivery offices bonus payments depend on the performance of each driver.

Most staff work Monday to Friday. Holiday entitlement is four weeks a year.

PROSPECTS

Postmen/women recruited at 18 years or over work on trial for the first six months. After one year of satisfactory service, promotion is possible to higher-grade postman/women, with greater responsibility, such as operating the range of automatic sorting equipment, or directly to management positions. Mobility is an advantage. At Parcelforce, staff can progress from Level 1 (recruitment grade) to Level 5 or directly to a supervisory post.

RELATED OCCUPATIONS

Post office counter clerk, warehouse worker, mail order clerk, car/van driver, messenger, courier, despatch rider, station assistant.

FURTHER INFORMATION

For more information, contact your local delivery office. Addresses are in the local phone book, or available from the nearest post office.

FURTHER READING

Job Outlines – Post Office – COIC

In the careers library classified under YAT; CAM.

2. POST OFFICE COUNTER CLERK (CAM)

THE WORK

As well as dealing with postage, such as selling stamps, taking parcels and registered documents on behalf of Royal Mail and Parcelforce, Post Office Counters Ltd provides services on behalf of the Benefits Agency, Driver and Vehicle Licensing Agency, Girobank and the Department for National Savings. These include paying pensions and social security benefits, taking deposits and providing vehicle tax discs. Counter clerks also sell TV licences on behalf of the BBC, and provide a revenue collection service for a variety of services, such as home help and meals on wheels, on behalf of about 60 local authorities. Other bodies for which counter clerks collect revenue include a number of utility companies, such as electricity, gas and water.

In all, clerks can provide up to about 150 different services, including a wide variety of banking and information services as well as the more usual ones associated with retail operations. They keep records of their transactions and balance their own accounts. Many post offices have introduced computer terminals for counter clerks to manage their sales and accounting systems, capturing many transactions electronically and producing receipts.

The work of counter clerks involves an enormous amount of direct contact with the public, each of whom may require a completely different service from the last person. Clerks can come under pressure to work quickly to reduce waiting times for the public, while needing to retain accuracy in every transaction they make.

Post office counter clerks work at main post offices, while

people who work for post office counters at postal outlets in supermarkets, village shops and so on are agents, ie not direct employees.

WORK ENVIRONMENT

The work of a post office counter clerk is conducted inside the particular branch. Many post offices have gone through a refurbishment in the early 1990s to make them brighter and smarter. The job is mainly sedentary, as most clerks sit at the actual counter dealing with the public. Clerks are provided with standard post office 'career wear' (uniforms).

SKILLS AND INTERESTS

As clerks have a high level of contact with the public, it is essential that they feel at ease dealing with a wide variety of people. Clerks need friendly, helpful personalities. They should be responsible and trustworthy, interested in helping other people and providing them with a service. Sometimes their work may involve dealing with people who are in a hurry and may have had to wait. In this type of situation, an ability to keep calm under pressure is needed. As well as dealing with the public, clerks work in a team, so good communication skills are essential.

Clerks provide a wide range of different services, so good clerical skills, a good memory and the initiative to find out information not to hand are needed. It is essential that clerks are numerate and are able to balance their own stock and cash. They need to be able to handle money efficiently and accurately.

ENTRY REQUIREMENTS

Post office counter clerks do not need formal qualifications, although GCSEs/S grades (A-C/1-3) are preferred, especially in English and maths, which demonstrate the communications and numeracy skills the job requires. More importantly, applicants need to pass the Post Office Counters Ltd aptitude test. These tests check numerical skills and accuracy in copying. Once the aptitude test has been passed, candidates are then interviewed.

Previous retail work experience – in a bank, building society or shop – is useful for applicants for counter clerk posts. Retail assistants at post offices that have post shops selling stationery and other items are sometimes promoted to counter clerk posts, but they must still sit the aptitude test first. Clerks should be generally fit and healthy, although physical disabilities are not necessarily a bar and the Post Office actively makes provision wherever possible.

It is possible to become a post office counter clerk via training schemes for young people in some parts of the country. Contact regional post offices for further information (see below for addresses).

TRAINING

New recruits to the job of post office counter clerk complete a six-week training course on full pay. The course includes periods at a post office training school and practical experience. Apart from learning about the wide variety of transactions they will perform, trainees also do courses in customer care, accounting and security. Trainee clerks who are joining a computerized post office receive additional coaching in the post office computer system. The final two weeks of the course are spent at their particular branch and their line manager gives them further training in the Post Office Counters Quality Management Scheme.

LATE ENTRY

The upper age limit for applicants for post office counter clerk jobs is 55 years. Relevant previous work experience, especially in the retail or financial sector, is an asset.

OPPORTUNITIES

Post office clerks work for Europe's largest retail chain. Vacancies for counter clerks vary from region to region and from year to year. Contact the relevant regional Post Office Counters headquarters for the current situation in their region.

About 7,500 counter clerks are employed at around 850 main post offices around the UK. Main post offices are found in towns and cities, and so are spread through the country at all the major population centres. Rural postal outlets are usually sub-post offices run in conjunction with other retail concerns.

As well as full-time posts, there are plenty of opportunities to work part-time as a counter clerk, and to work temporary contracts too. Self-employed opportunities exist for sub-postmasters and sub-postmistresses, although counter clerks at main post offices are always employees.

PAY AND CONDITIONS

Post office counter clerks earn a starting salary of £10,281 at 18 years and over. There are annual increments to a maximum of £13,169, plus London weighting. Clerks work a 42-hour week, including an hour a day for set meal breaks. Those entitled to London weighting work a 41-hour week. The week includes Saturday mornings and late evening (up to about 7.45pm) on Wednesdays to balance accounts. Clerks have a day off during the week to balance for these extra times.

The holiday entitlement for a post office counter clerk is 25 days a year plus bank holidays, rising to a maximum of 30 days a year with long service.

PROSPECTS

Once counter clerks have completed their one-year trial period, they can apply for promotion for jobs that are advertised internally. Clerks can move into supervisory and managerial posts in the same field. Alternatively, there are limited opportunities to progress into administrative duties at a regional office or at post office headquarters. These opportunities depend on individual skills and aptitudes, but include work in such areas as finance, personnel, marketing or operational services.

There are a wide range of training courses available to develop management and other skills, including outward bound courses. Clerks with management potential being groomed for assistant branch manager posts can study for the management skills diploma, or perhaps a qualification from the Institute of Personnel Management, while those with financial potential may take accountancy qualifications.

RELATED OCCUPATIONS

Retail assistant, accounts clerk, bank/building society clerk, local government clerk, postman/women, post office branch manager.

FURTHER INFORMATION

Post Office Counters Ltd*, Midlands Regional Office, 86 Lionel Street, Birmingham B3 1HQ

Post Office Counters Ltd, North East Regional Office, Post Office House, 3 Infirmary Street, Leeds LS1 1AJ

Post Office Counters Ltd*, North Thames and East Anglia Region, Verulam Point, Station Way, St Albans, Hertfordshire AL1 5HE

Post Office Counters Ltd*, North Wales and North West Regional Office, Capstan House, Chandler's Point, 35 the Broadway, Salford Quays, Salford, M5 2YY

Post Office Counters Ltd*, Scotland and Northern Ireland Regional Office, The Athenaeum, Nelson Mandela Place, Glasgow G2 1BT

Post Office Counters Ltd*, South East Regional Office, Brockbourne House, 77 Mount Ephraim, Royal Tunbridge Wells, Kent TN4 8AB

Post Office Counters Ltd*, South Wales and South West Regional Office, Network House, The Quadrant, Aztec West, Almondsbury, Bristol BS12 4QX

FURTHER READING

Leaflets/booklets are available from the addresses marked*.

Job Outlines – Post Office – COIC

In the careers library classified under CAM.

CHARTERED SECRETARY CLCI:CAP

BACKGROUND INFORMATION

Chartered secretaries are professional administrators. Their job is to make sure that their organization runs efficiently and economically within the law.

This calls for understanding and judgement. In order to improve efficiency it is necessary to understand how every part of the organization works and integrates – its finances, business activities, the people who work there and what they do.

Chartered secretaries may perform a variety of administrative roles, such as legal adviser, financial administrator or office manager. They are ideally qualified to work as company secretaries, the chief administrative officers of their organization. Associateship of the Chartered Institute of Secretaries is recognized in company law as a suitable professional qualification for this job.

THE WORK

A chartered secretary working as a company secretary has a very wide range of responsibilities. Some of these are defined by law.

Secretaries maintain the statutory company records – its Memorandum and Articles of Association, lists of directors and shareholders, annual accounts – and send annual returns based on these to the Company Registry. This involves making sure that the company reports and accounts are produced and distributed on time each year. They also keep records of acquisitions and dispersals, which can range from car fleets and office blocks to shares in other companies. Secretaries of public companies – those in which members of the public can buy shares – are required to supply details about their company to the Stock Exchange.

The memorandum and articles define how a company is governed and financed and the nature of its business. The company secretary makes sure that none of the company's activities infringes either its own memorandum and articles or the Companies Act, and advises the directors on what they can legally do within these terms.

The company secretary is the company's named representative on legal documents and has charge of the company seal, authorizing and signing the official stamp on share certificates and other documents.

Company secretaries organize board and general meetings. At the meetings they take minutes and advise the directors on legal points. They act as a link between shareholders and directors, monitoring share ownership, keeping shareholders and the public informed about new issues and keeping the directors informed about the take-up of shares.

Besides these statutory duties, company secretaries may have a range of other administrative duties: many are involved in accounting and finance, including responsibility for the payroll, the annual budget, internal audit, credit control and financial or management accounting.

Other responsibilities may include personnel management, pension schemes, office management, insurance or computer systems. They may also assist the general management team in planning and in liaising with professional advisers.

WORK ENVIRONMENT

The work is office-based, with some travelling to meetings. There may be frequent discussions and meetings with departmental managers and other members of staff throughout the organization, and also with bankers, accountants, lawyers and other professional advisers.

SKILLS AND INTERESTS

Chartered secretaries need the ability to understand the details and implications of complex legal and financial affairs. As there are often several matters in hand at once, they should be quick to assess priorities and methodical in dealing with them.

They work alongside managers and policymakers, and must be familiar with all that goes on in the organization. Chartered secretaries require tact and good powers of judgement in solving problems. Tact, discretion and absolute integrity are vital.

Chartered secretaries require an excellent command of written and spoken English. They have to write up the minutes of board and other meetings, so have to be able to express themselves accurately. They have to explain complex business and technical matters to experts and non-experts in a clear, balanced way. They are involved in negotiations with lawyers, auditors and other professional advisers. As they deal with accounts, insurance and other financial matters, competence with figures is essential.

ENTRY REQUIREMENTS

To achieve membership of the Institute of Chartered Secretaries and Administrators, it is necessary to:

– successfully complete the ICSA Qualifying Examination;

– gain appropriate work experience, normally three years for graduates, six years for others;

– be recognized as a fit and proper person by two referees.

The Qualifying Examination Scheme has three stages: Foundation, Pre-professional, Professional. The minimum age for entry is 17 years. Through the ICSA's open access policy, there are no formal academic requirements for the Foundation programme.

Graduates who already hold recognized first degrees or postgraduate diplomas are normally exempt from the Foundation and Pre-professional stages and register directly onto the Professional programme. Students holding BTEC/SCOTVEC higher national awards or certain professional qualifications may be exempt from at least the Foundation stage.

TRAINING

The ICSA scheme of study is based on the themes of administration, management, corporate law and corporate finance. It also aims to qualify students for a wide range of careers in administration and management across both public and private sectors.

The Foundation stage introduces business subjects: business economics, information systems, organization and the human resource, quantitative techniques, introduction to English and European Union law.

The Pre-Professional stage prepares for positions of responsibility: managing information systems, management principles, business law, introduction to accounting.

The Professional stage covers the eight modules:

management accounting; financial accounting; company secretarial practice; professional administration; corporate finance, regulation and taxation; management practice; corporate law; administration of corporate affairs.

Success in the qualifying examinations confers graduateship for the ICSA. To become an associate member (ACIS) it is also necessary to gain six years' appropriate work experience. This may be reduced by up to three years for time spent in full-time study. Associates should be at least 21 years. Fellows of the Institute (FCIS) should be at least 25 years with a minimum of eight years' experience, of which some should be in a position of seniority.

The courses may be studied full-time, part-time in the evening, or by distance learning. On average it takes three to four years to complete the three programmes by part-time study. Several universities and colleges offer collaborative qualifying programmes developed and assessed jointly with the ICSA. These lead to graduate membership of the ICSA as well as a degree or postgraduate diploma. Full details are available from the ICSA.

LATE ENTRY

The ICSA's open access policy enables anyone over 17 years, with or without formal academic qualifications, to register on the Foundation Programme. There is no upper age limit.

Access courses for adults who wish to qualify for a degree but do not have the necessary qualifications are available in many parts of the county.

A chartered secretary's job carries a high level of responsibility and demands such organisational skill that maturity and experience can be an advantage. Many job advertisements state a preference for applicants over 30 years.

It is usual to spend several years gaining experience in different kinds of administrative work before becoming a company secretary. Up to six years' relevant experience is in any case required for full associate membership of the ICSA.

OPPORTUNITIES

Every company in the UK is required by law to have a company secretary, who should hold a suitable professional qualification either in law or accountancy, or as a member of the ICSA. Besides company secretarial work, chartered secretaries are well qualified for a wide variety of administrative jobs in all sectors of the economy. Their roles range from financial or personnel management to computing services or corporate planning. They may work in public or private companies, financial services, utilities

such as gas or water supply, central and local government, health service, trade and professional associations, charities and educational administration.

The ICSA internationally has about 45,000 members and 28,000 students in the United Kingdom and around 100 other countries. The ICSA qualification is recognized under the European Community Professional Qualifications Directive, enabling chartered secretaries to work in all EU states.

Vacancies are advertised in the national and local press and in Administrator, the journal of the ICSA.

PAY AND CONDITIONS

Salaries vary widely. A typical starting figure for a newly qualified associate member might be £20,000 rising to over £60,000 with experience.

Chartered secretaries generally work 36 to 40 hours a week, Monday to Friday. Hours may vary, according to the demands of the job. They may have to attend evening meetings. Part-time work may be available in some companies.

PROSPECTS

Most company secretarial departments are small and offer limited prospects for internal promotion. It is usual to change jobs and change companies in order to gain experience and responsibility. Some chartered secretaries specialize in, for example, pensions, office administration, financial management or personnel management.

Experience as a company secretary can lead to positions in general management, or to partnerships in other firms.

Administrators in the Civil Service or local government have a more structured career ladder than in industry, but it is increasingly common to move from one sector to another.

RELATED OCCUPATIONS

Accountant, solicitor, advocate/barrister, Civil Service administrator, local government administrator, health service manager, personnel officer, bank manager, stockbroker, office manager.

FURTHER INFORMATION

Education Help Desk, The Institute of Chartered Secretaries and Administrators (ICSA)*, 16 Park Crescent, London W1N 4AH, 0171 580 4741

FURTHER READING

Leaflets/booklets are available from the address marked*.

Information pack available from the ICSA.

In the careers library classified under CAP.

1. PERSONNEL OFFICER CLCI:CAS
2. TRAINING OFFICER CLCI:FAP

BACKGROUND INFORMATION

An organization's workforce is extremely important in determining whether it is successful. Personnel officers are specialist members of the management team who help to make the most effective use of the workforce. They help to recruit suitable people, arrange for training and help to keep the people the organization require. They also make sure that an organization deals with its employees consistently, fairly and within employment law.

Training of staff is vital as it helps people to acquire the knowledge and skills needed to do their jobs successfully. Developing staff helps to prepare them for more responsibility in the future. Some personnel officers are responsible for staff training but, in many organizations, specialist training officers are employed for this important area of work.

1. PERSONNEL OFFICER (CAS)

THE WORK

Personnel officers, often called human resources officers, are responsible for selecting the right people for an organization and helping to make sure that they are managed effectively.

The work of personnel officers can differ considerably from organization to organization but the following are the main areas of work:

Recruitment and selection, which includes drawing up job descriptions and personnel specifications, preparing advertisements, checking application forms, interviewing and sometimes testing applicants, obtaining references and selecting or rejecting candidates. Personnel officers work closely with other departments of the organization and with Jobcentres and careers offices.

Training and development is concerned with providing training programmes for employees, including induction and skills training for new employees. Personnel officers consult line managers (those with direct authority over some people in a work area) to analyse training needs. They may deliver some training themselves and arrange training by other staff and with outside training organizations, such as local colleges. They also monitor the effectiveness of training.

Industrial and employee relations includes meeting trade union representatives to negotiate pay and conditions or advising the managers who conduct these negotiations. Personnel officers also deal with disciplinary matters and disputes, grievances and redundancy procedures. This area can include responsibility for equal-opportunities policy, recruitment literature, employee handbooks and house magazines.

Employee services work is concerned with matters of health and safety. It can include responsibility for medical, sports and social facilities, maintaining staff records, personal counselling, community relations and other welfare related activities.

Reward management involves setting up and running a pay policy that is appropriate to the staff, meets legal requirements and can be afforded by the employer. It also includes reviewing, introducing and administering company benefits, such as share ownership and incentive schemes.

Human resource planning is about assessing an organization's future staffing needs and measuring them against current availability. A human resources plan indicates how much an organization needs to recruit, train, retrain, transfer or reduce staff.

Personnel officers in some organizations are responsible for just one of the above areas, while in other organizations they are responsible for all areas of work for one type of staff, eg production workers. Personnel officers are increasingly becoming an important part of management groups as organizations recognize the value of human resources.

WORK ENVIRONMENT

Personnel officers spend most of their time working in an office but are mobile within their place of work to attend meetings and to see individual members of staff.

They may travel locally, eg to visit a local college. They also travel to other sites for which they are responsible, such as branch offices.

SKILLS AND INTERESTS

Personnel officers should like working with people. They must be able to get on well with many different people and have good social skills including tact, patience, understanding and persuasiveness.

Communication skills are important, both written and spoken: personnel officers should be able to write reports accurately; listening and spoken skills are essential for interviewing, discussions with staff, negotiations and delivery of training.

It is essential that personnel officers have a commercial awareness and see things from the employer's as well as the employee's perspective.

Ability with figures is necessary, as work involves making financial calculations and producing statistics on, for example, labour turnover, absence rates and salary budgets.

Personnel officers need analytical and problem-solving skills to help them create policies, plan and forecast future staffing needs. Good organizational ability is required, for example, when planning and arranging recruitment interviews.

Personnel officers should be able to work in a team, as they work closely with other personnel and management staff, line managers, training personnel and employees.

ENTRY REQUIREMENTS

There are no minimum entry requirements. In practice, however, the majority of personnel officers enter with degrees or higher national diplomas. The minimum entry requirements for degree courses is two A levels/three H grades plus five GCSEs/S grades (A-C/1-3), or equivalent. Entry to a higher national diploma course is normally with a minimum of one A level/two H grades plus three GCSEs/S grades (A-C/1-3), or equivalent.

It is possible to become a personnel officer following experience in a personnel department in a clerical or secretarial post. Such posts often need several GCSEs/S grades (A-C/1-3). Progression to personnel officer is normally only possible if part-time study has led to the Institute of Personnel and Development (IPD) Certificate in Personnel Practice, which does not require specific entry qualifications, or an NVQ/SVQ in Personnel Support at Level 3.

There are some postgraduate personnel management courses. They require a degree for entry.

Many personnel officers have had experience of other work before entering personnel.

TRAINING

Pre-entry

BTEC/SCOTVEC Higher National Diplomas in Business and Finance (two years full-time or three years sandwich) and degrees (three years full-time or four years sandwich) in such subjects as economics, business studies, law, industrial psychology or sociology and public administration are useful preparation for personnel work. They are offered at many universities and colleges. Some degree courses are accredited by the IPD and other relevant courses may be considered for IPD membership through the Assessment of Prior Certificated Learning (APCL) – details from IPD.

Postgraduate courses in personnel management that enable students to prepare for the IPD examinations are offered at over 30 universities and colleges, mostly one year full-time.

On entry

Training for personnel officers is provided in-house but many employers expect staff to become professionally qualified by working for IPD qualifications.

The IPD's Certificate in Personnel Practice is designed to provide a wide range of practical personnel skills. It includes interpersonal and interviewing skills, employment law, personnel records and optional subjects. Courses are normally day release for one year and are held at over 100 colleges and universities.

Details of the IPD's new Professional Qualification Scheme starting in September 1996 are available from the IPD.

NVQ/SVQ in Personnel Support at Level 3, Personnel Management at Level 4 and Personnel Strategy at Level 5 are available.

LATE ENTRY

There are no age restrictions on entry to personnel work. Many personnel officers have had experience of other work such as marketing, production, sales or public administration.

Those seeking entry to personnel work should be willing to study for IPD qualifications.

OPPORTUNITIES

Personnel officers are employed throughout the UK by all but the smallest organizations. Employers include manufacturers, retailers, banks, insurance companies and other commercial companies, transport companies, local authorities, the Civil Service, the National Health Service, educational institutions, and those in the leisure and hotel catering industries.

Competition for vacancies is very keen. Vacancies may be advertised in the local and national press and in specialist journals such as *Personnel Management* and *PM Plus*.

Increasingly, organizations are seeking to recruit graduates with IPD qualifications. Relatively few organizations, however, recruit graduates direct into personnel work. Instead, they tend to recruit them into general management training schemes that include personnel experience and that may later lead to specialization in personnel work.

Opportunities for those in clerical and secretarial posts to move into professional personnel work are decreasing.

PAY AND CONDITIONS

Starting salaries paid to graduates entering personnel traineeships immediately after a first degree are very similar to those entering other trainee posts.

Personnel officers earn between £12,716 and £23,790. Personnel directors earn between £35,000 and £82,200. Salaries paid by local authorities and smaller retailers tend to be lower than those paid by large manufacturing firms and public authorities.

Personnel officers work standard office hours Monday to Friday with pressure of work leading, on occasion, to work outside those hours.

PROSPECTS

Promotion is dependent largely on achievement and potential, although it is helpful to have IPD qualifications. Promotion possibilities are greater in larger organizations, where there may be a structure that includes a personnel manager and personnel director. It is common for personnel staff to move from employer to employer in order to progress.

It is possible for those who have specialized in one area of personnel work to achieve promotion, although it is perhaps easier for those who have had experience of several areas.

Some experienced personnel officers set up their own consultancies offering specialist services, such as recruitment.

There are some opportunities to work abroad for multinational organizations.

RELATED OCCUPATIONS

Careers officer, retail manager, training officer, employment agency consultant/interviewer, occupational psychologist, Civil Service executive officer.

FURTHER INFORMATION AND READING

Please see article 2. TRAINING OFFICER.

2. TRAINING OFFICER (FAP)

THE WORK

Training officers identify the training needs of employees, then plan and organize appropriate training programmes for them.

The work of individual training officers can differ greatly between organizations but the following are the main activities:

Analysing training needs. Training officers seek to identify the training gap (the difference between what employees can do and what they need to be capable of to perform their jobs successfully). This involves discussions with line managers and personnel officers, and reference to job descriptions.

Meeting training needs. Training officers have to advise on the most effective methods of training to meet the identified needs, eg in-house courses, on-the-job instruction, coaching, distance learning, external courses. An important consideration is the cost of training.

Clarifying learning objectives. Before recommending a training activity, training officers need to clarify with the line manager exactly what is required. A clear statement is agreed on what skills people should be able to perform after training and within what time scale.

Designing training programmes. Training officers need a good knowledge of available training provision. Cost of training is important and they must be aware of any government financial assistance that may be available. If it is decided to use external training, eg at colleges, universities or by using consultancies, the training officer makes the necessary arrangements. In-house training may be delivered by training officers or they may negotiate with other staff to deliver it. Training officers choose or recommend appropriate methods of training delivery, eg lectures, discussion groups, role playing, videos.

Evaluating effectiveness. Training must be evaluated to make sure it has achieved what was required. Training officers use questionnaires, interviews and discussions with line managers to achieve this.

In some organizations a training officer is responsible for all these tasks, either for the whole staff or for a particular category, eg technical staff. In others, responsibilities are divided laterally so that training officers are responsible for different activities, eg designing training courses, delivering training, liaison with external training providers and associated administration.

WORK ENVIRONMENT

Training officers spend most of their time working indoors in an office or training centre. They are mobile within their place of work to attend meetings and to liaise with line managers, personnel officers and employees. They may visit training providers and employees in training.

SKILLS AND INTERESTS

Training officers must be interested in people as individuals and in their development.

They need a good standard of English and strong communication skills, both spoken and written. Verbal skills are necessary in discussions with line managers, training providers and others and for presenting training sessions. Written skills are needed for writing reports and keeping records.

Social skills are important. Training officers must be able to work well with a variety of people, which needs tact, patience and understanding. Negotiation skills are required in their contacts with line managers, employees, training providers and others. Identifying training needs and designing training programmes requires the ability to analyse problems and consider possible solutions.

Organizational ability is necessary. Training officers have to plan ahead, meet deadlines and keep accurate records. They work within a training budget so need numerical ability to control the budget. Judgement is required to weigh the cost-effectiveness of different methods of training available.

Commitment to training is essential. Training officers have to keep up-to-date with changes in vocational training, financial assistance and legal requirements affecting training. They do this by reading and by attending meetings and courses.

ENTRY REQUIREMENTS

No formal educational qualifications are required for entry as a training officer, but numeracy and a high standard of written and spoken English are necessary.

Although most entrants have qualified in another area of work before entering training, some begin as a trainee in a personnel or training department. There is no standard entry requirement for trainees but such posts often need several GCSEs/S grades (A-C/1-3).

There are professional qualifications available through the Institute of Personnel and Development. The Certificate in Training Practice is a foundation qualification designed for those wishing to move into training.

Training modules are included in the existing Institute of Personnel and Development's Certificate in Personnel Practice. The IPD's new professional standards increase the choice of specialist modules in the new professional qualification, available from July 1996, enabling those who wish to specialize in training and development to do so.

NVQs/SVQs in Training and Development are available at Levels 3, 4 and 5, with Training and Development at Level 3, Training and Development (Human Resource Development) at Level 4, Training and Development (Learning Development) at Level 4 and Training and Development Strategy at Level 5.

TRAINING

Training officers may receive in-house training from their employers. Some attend short external introductory courses and/or seminars and courses on particular topics. Such courses rarely last longer than a few days and are run by private training organizations.

Those engaged in personnel and training activities may study for IPD qualifications. The new Professional Qualification Scheme, available from September 1996, has a wider choice of specialist modules suitable for trainers.

LATE ENTRY

There is no upper age limit for entry, and the maturity that late entrants bring to the training role is valuable. Most training officers come to training following experience in another area of work, eg personnel, teaching, supervisory and management posts.

OPPORTUNITIES

Training officers are employed throughout the UK by many different kinds of organizations including commercial firms, eg banks and building societies and retailers, manufacturers, voluntary bodies, local authorities and other public sector organizations, and by local and national training agencies. The number of training consultancies is increasing, as is the number of trainers working freelance.

The number of training officers employed was increasing until the late 1980s. That growth has since stopped and the number is now stable.

Competition is keen when vacancies arise. Some vacancies are advertised in *People Management; Personnel Today* and in the local and national press.

PAY AND CONDITIONS

There are no set salary scales but a training officer may expect to earn between £12,000 and £24,000 depending on experience, responsibilities and the type of employing organization. A training manager may expect to earn between £20,492 and £31,798 and a training director between £34,250 and £43,235.

Training officers normally work standard office hours, Monday to Friday. Pressure of work can involve additional hours. Some training officers with organizations that have shift work may have to work outside normal office hours to liaise with staff and to conduct training. Some part-time work is available, particularly with training consultancies.

PROSPECTS

It may be possible in a large organization to gain promotion from training officer to training manager and training director. Small organizations do not offer that possibility. It is common for training officers to move from employer to employer for advancement.

Some training officers regard training as just one of a number of management skills they wish to acquire. They may seek promotion into personnel or general management.

It is possible for British-trained training officers to work abroad. It is particularly helpful if they have previous experience of the country in which they wish to work.

Experienced training officers may join training consultancies or set up a consultancy themselves.

RELATED OCCUPATIONS

Personnel officer, careers officer, employment agency consultant/interviewer, safety officer, further education/tertiary college lecturer, teacher, training manager, training instructor.

FURTHER INFORMATION

Institute of Personnel and Development*, IPD House, 35 Camp Road, London SW19 4UX, 0181 971 9000

FURTHER READING

Leaflets/booklets are available from the address marked*.

Careers in Personnel and Development – IPD
Job Outlines – Personnel Work – COIC
Personnel – The Department at Work – IPD
Personnel Work – AGCAS

In the careers library classified under CAS; FAP.

1. EXECUTIVE SECRETARY/PERSONAL ASSISTANT CLCI:CAT
2. SPECIALIST SECRETARY CLCI:CAT

BACKGROUND INFORMATION

Businesses of every type employ secretaries to undertake administrative work. Secretarial roles are called by a variety of job titles, sometimes reflecting work of different levels, but sometimes as an anomaly of the particular business or sector providing the employment. Job titles include secretary, senior secretary, administrative assistant, personal assistant and executive secretary. While PA and executive secretary are viewed as the most senior of these job titles, job titles vary between employers.

1. EXECUTIVE SECRETARY/PERSONAL ASSISTANT (CAT)

THE WORK

Secretaries/PAs take care of many administrative tasks for executives. They follow office procedures as laid down by superiors, or at a more senior level may decide upon and implement them themselves. Key duties include the efficient flow in and out of documents, and being the first point of contact for their manager with colleagues and people from outside organizations. The main tools of a secretarial job include typewriter, word processor or computer; dictaphone for audio work; telephone; fax; telex machine; telephone.

At more junior levels, a secretary spends time doing general typing for one or more executives or managers. Typing may be done from handwritten notes, shorthand or audio (when the secretary listens to a dictated tape). Typing is likely to include documents such as invoices, business forms and correspondence. Other duties at this level may include sorting and opening incoming mail, franking outgoing mail, photocopying, filing, maintaining stationery and other supplies, and providing refreshments. Another key element of the job will be answering the telephone, routing calls and taking messages. Some diary management may be needed at this level, to organize internal or external meetings.

Senior secretaries usually have only one executive or manager and would be expected to use more of their own initiative. They may have a junior for the photocopying, filing and some of the typing or they may do all of the duties themselves. Senior secretaries may type and file confidential documents. Filing procedures and other systems for record management may well be initiated and arranged by senior secretaries. They open all the manager's and their own mail and deal with or respond to routine mail without consultation, but would not be involved in franking of outgoing mail. Senior secretaries also organize all aspects of functions, conferences, meetings and travel arrangements without supervision. This work can include the preparation of agendas, taking of minutes and distribution to participants.

At the most senior level of personal assistant or executive secretary, a great deal of personal initiative is required. Indeed, in some jobs, there is a certain amount of job crossover between the executive or director and the personal assistant. While some PAs may do all of the above duties, many supervise more junior secretaries and only perform confidential typing or filing. They may be responsible for recruiting and training these staff. PAs often screen their executive's or director's incoming telephone calls and mail, dealing with it themselves if they do not consider it necessary to pass on to their boss. They collate, organize and edit material for inclusion in reports to be written by their executive, and research and pricis information and other materials for meetings. Many PAs are responsible for preparing budget or other financial or statistical records, and may be responsible for purchasing equipment and supplies. The most senior PAs stand in for their bosses, greeting or having preliminary meetings with clients or suppliers, liaising with clients and senior management, delegating tasks to appropriate departments or making decisions in the absence of their boss. PAs also have a responsibility for ensuring office procedures are updated in line with new equipment and personnel, and to keep abreast of developments in office automation. They should be aware of new legislation, such as Health and Safety or Data Protection laws, and ensure their requirements are implemented.

WORK ENVIRONMENT

Secretarial work is sedentary. Secretaries of every level work mainly in offices, whatever the nature of business of their employer. The more senior they become, the more likely they are to have their own office. At senior levels, secretaries/PAs may be expected to travel on business with their boss.

SKILLS AND INTERESTS

Secretarial work requires a well-organized and orderly approach. Attention to detail, accuracy and a conscientious attitude are needed for this type of work. Clear speaking and writing, as well as a good grasp of the English language – spelling, grammar, punctuation and sentence construction – are also useful. Employers also look for people who are well-presented and smart.

It is a career for people who enjoy working closely with others – both colleagues and a wide variety of other people. It is essential to enjoy contact with people from different backgrounds and to have the communications skills this requires. Tact and diplomacy may be called for when putting off would-be callers whom the secretary knows their boss does not wish to speak to or see. At more senior levels, an aptitude for judging characters may be required, both for recruitment purposes and deciding whether to put through calls or arrange meetings for the executive or director.

ENTRY REQUIREMENTS

There are a variety of ways to start work as a fully-qualified secretary. The Royal Society of Arts (RSA) offers a Higher Diploma in Administrative and Secretarial Procedures (HDASP), while the London Chamber of Commerce and Industry (LCCI) offers a Private Secretary's Certificate (PSC) and a Private and Executive Secretary's Diploma (PESD). The equivalent to the Certificate is an NVQ/SVQ in Administration at Level 3.

Formal entrance requirements for these courses are not stipulated, but the LCCI certificate is intended as a post-GCSE/S grades qualification and both diplomas are intended as a post-A level/H grade qualification. Individual colleges should be contacted directly, as they may have specific entry requirements, such as four GCSEs/S grades, including English. GNVQs/GSVQs in Business are useful backgrounds for these courses. An equivalent-level qualification is a BTEC/SCOTVEC Higher National

Diploma in Business and Finance combined with RSA, LCCI or Pitman typing, shorthand, audio and word processing awards.

An alternative entry route to secretarial work is to get basic RSA, Pitman or LCCI qualifications in typing, audio or shorthand and to start work as a shorthand or audio typist. With the right experience and motivation, it may be possible to be promoted to secretarial work. This may require additional study or attaining NVQ/SVQ awards while at work.

TRAINING

The courses mentioned above last one to two years on a full-time basis or may be studied on a modular scheme whilst working. They cover shorthand, typing/word processing, audio, general office procedures, business structures, finance and human resource management. Once qualified, secretaries are most likely to receive additional training that is specific to their work on the job. Training may include the office procedures of the particular business, or additional computing applications, such as the spreadsheet or word processing packages used by the company. Secretaries with the LCCI certificate may be encouraged to study for the diploma. Those without NVQs/SVQs may be encouraged to train for NVQ/SVQ in Administration at Level 3 and 4. Senior secretaries and PAs may be encouraged to do specific short courses such as time management or budget control.

It is possible to enter secretarial work via training schemes for young people. This can be done either by getting day release from an existing employer to go to college, or by going directly to a college to study and being sent to employers for work experience. Contact local careers offices for further details.

LATE ENTRY

Age is not a barrier for starting secretarial work. Some employers prefer more mature secretaries, although others do not. Training for work schemes are available for suitably qualified unemployed adults in some areas. Contact TECs/LECs for more information.

OPPORTUNITIES

As every type of business and industry needs people to work in secretarial roles, opportunities for secretaries tend to reflect the general economic mix and state of the particular region or times. Opportunities are immensely varied, reflecting the whole range of businesses. At the end of 1993, an industry spokesperson claimed that opportunities for secretaries are better and will become better than they have ever been. This is particularly true for people with a range of qualifications and skills, such as in desktop publishing, spreadsheets and databases. While vacancies are reasonably plentiful, competition can be fierce, so extra skills can improve employment prospects.

Self-employment is possible for those who wish to concentrate on the typing/word processing side. Work can be done with a home typewriter or computer, or more ambitious secretaries could set up word processing bureaux employing several people.

PAY AND CONDITIONS

According to the IQPS, a typical starting salary for a secretary is about £8,713. For more senior secretaries £15,000 is typical, while for top PAs in London £20,000 to £25,000 is the accepted range. Salaries vary according to company, business sector and region, with those in central London usually being higher than elsewhere.

Most secretaries work a five-day week for office hours only (usually 9/9.30am to 5/5.30pm). More senior secretaries and PAs are expected to be flexible about their working hours, especially if travelling on business. Part-time work and temping opportunities are usually plentiful, especially for holiday cover.

PROSPECTS

The most direct route up the career ladder for a secretary is to work for increasingly senior executives, managers and directors. A managing director's PA is often an extremely senior and responsible job. For those who wish to go into more general administration, it is possible to be promoted to office or operations manager and possibly eventually operations director. For secretaries in the right type of department, it is possible to cross over to executive work in the same department. This type of move occurs most often in sales or marketing departments, although it may also be possible in market research and customer training. Further training specific to the department may be needed.

RELATED OCCUPATIONS

Administrative assistant, specialist secretary, telephonist/receptionist, customer care officer, hotel receptionist, office manager, operations manager/director.

FURTHER INFORMATION AND READING

Please see article 2. SPECIALIST SECRETARY.

2. SPECIALIST SECRETARY (CAT)

THE WORK

Medical

The medical secretary practises secretarial duties in a variety of medical places of work, including general practice (GP) surgeries, a wide variety of departments in hospitals (general, teaching, psychiatry, etc) and research laboratories. Much of the work is similar to that of general secretaries, except that correspondence and documents are about medical matters and are full of medical terminology.

In general practice, medical secretaries work a great deal on their own initiative. They make patient appointments and arrange home visits; establish priorities and emergencies; keep records and deal with telephone enquiries. The administration of a practice may be run by the secretary, including financial affairs. Medical secretaries in consultant practice often work on their own for much of the time, acting as receptionist too.

Legal

Legal secretaries work in solicitors' offices and in the legal departments of a wide range of other businesses, from local government to manufacturers, financial services companies and media owners. Their work is similar to that of general secretaries, but they must use and understand the use of legal terminology (often in Latin) and abbreviations. In addition, they must know what type of documents are required in different types of cases. In particular, legal secretaries must be especially accurate in their work, as the exact wording of contracts can make all the difference to their legal interpretation.

Bi/multilingual

In addition to the duties of a general secretary (see article 1. EXECUTIVE SECRETARY/PERSONAL ASSISTANT), bi/multilingual secretaries also translate documents. Their duties often involve a great deal of client liaison as well: the bi/multilingual secretary communicates with overseas clients and suppliers, both in writing and on the telephone; may participate in social or cultural occasions for overseas visitors; and may serve as an interpreter at business meetings.

Farm

Farm secretaries do the administrative work of farms. They are responsible for keeping records, particularly financial ones. Farm secretaries record livestock or crops, income and expenditure and deal with the Inland Revenue, Customs and Excise and the Department of Social Security. They are responsible for the farm's payroll and contracts of employment. For this work, an understanding of the technical side of farming and law relating to rural business is needed, such as food and environment protection and hazardous substances laws. Experienced secretaries form part of the farm's management team, providing budgets and draft accounts, as well as researching new enterprises. This side of the work can involve a good deal of liaison with bank managers, accountants and consultants.

WORK ENVIRONMENT

Specialist secretaries still tend to work in offices, mainly sitting at office equipment, whatever the general location (hospital department, GP practice, solicitors' offices, import/export office). Farm secretaries are the exception. As well as working in farm offices, they may work outdoors or in farm buildings during stock taking and may spend time travelling between farms and bank managers and other advisers. Mobile farm secretaries and farm bureaux operate their own offices/office equipment.

SKILLS AND INTERESTS

Apart from the skills and interests mentioned in article 1. EXECUTIVE SECRETARY/PERSONAL ASSISTANT, specialist secretaries require in addition:

Medical

A demonstrable keen interest in medicine, medical matters and people in general is essential. The ability to be sympathetic and helpful to patients who may be distressed is vital, to inspire confidence and allay anxiety. Employers look for people who are well organized and can deal with a large number of tasks simultaneously, keeping calm through numerous interruptions and possible emergencies. Medical secretaries need to be confident enough to work on their own initiative. They also need tact, to serve the patients' needs as well as the doctors', even if these may sometimes be in conflict.

Legal

An interest in legal matters and a careful, conscientious approach are important. People who wish to be legal secretaries need to take pride in the end product of their work and be perfectionist in terms of accuracy. Employers look for legal secretaries who are already excellent at legal secretarial work, but flexibility is required to adapt to different companies' systems and facilities.

Bi/multilingual

An aptitude for languages and excellent communications skills are a prerequisite for this job. Since it tends to involve an unusual amount of client, supplier and overseas colleagues contact, a particularly good ability to get on with other people is needed.

Farm

Self-motivation and an ability to work alone, with the confidence of working on your own initiative is essential for this job. However, getting on with other people is important, as the farm secretary is often the liaison point between a number of different people. The work is not routine and calls for an investigative approach. An organized mind helps to run the administrative and financial systems. Common sense and hard work are needed too.

ENTRY REQUIREMENTS

Medical

To work as a medical secretary, it is necessary to gain the certificate or diploma from the Association of Medical Secretaries, Practice Administrators and Receptionists Ltd (AMSPAR). The entry requirements for AMSPAR qualifications are four GCSEs/S grades (A-C/1-3), of which one must be English. An Intermediate GNVQ/GSVQ Level II in Business together with a GCSE/S grade (A-C/1-3) in English is an acceptable alternative. A numerical aptitude is also required. Mature students will be accepted at the discretion of each college.

Legal

To start work as a legal secretary it is necessary to have a diploma or certificate from the Institute of Paralegal Training (IPT – formerly the Association of Legal Secretaries) or the equivalent in NVQs/SVQs. To enter the certificate course four GCSEs/S grades (A-C/1-3) are required, or equivalent, such as an Intermediate GNVQ/GSVQ Level II in Business. For the diploma, one A level/two H grades are required.

Bi/multilingual

A certificate or diploma from a further education or private college in bi/multilingual secretarial work is needed. Entry requirements for courses vary, but are typically a GCSE/S grade (A-C/1-3) in English, plus an A level/two H grades or degree in a second language.

Farm

The two main entry routes to start work as a farm secretary. There is a one-year BTEC/SCOTVEC National Certificate for Farm Secretaries and a two-year BTEC/SCOTVEC diploma course. Entry requirements for both courses vary, but include evidence of competence in English and numeracy. Contact individual colleges for details.

TRAINING

Medical

The AMSPAR Medical Secretarial Diploma qualification includes two skills from a choice of three – medical shorthand (RSA or Pitman), medical audio transcription (RSA) and Medical word processing (RSA), plus three administrative papers. The syllabus covers administration and legal aspects relating to the National Health Service and social services, communications and medical secretarial practice and medical aspects of secretarial work. Study for these qualifications normally takes one to two years (four terms in the case of students with A levels/highers).

Once qualified to start work, medical secretaries receive mainly on-the-job training in the procedures of the particular practice or department where they are employed.

It is sometimes possible to become a medical secretary via training schemes for young people. Contact local careers offices, TECs/LECs for further details.

Legal

The IPT certificate lasts one year, covering general principles of English law, office practice, legal typewriting, legal shorthand or legal audio, and word processing. The IPT diploma takes two years full-time, covering the same subjects at a higher level (and secretarial practice replaces office practice). It is possible to study for the diploma part-time, but it must be completed in three years.

Once work has been started, on-the-job training is normally provided mainly on the particular procedures of the employer. At more senior levels, legal secretaries may go on refresher courses to update them on law.

It is possible to enter legal secretarial work via training schemes for young people. Contact local careers offices, TECs/LECs for further details.

Bi/multilingual

Bi/multilingual secretarial courses cover English secretarial syllabuses, plus tuition in the second (or more) language(s), including typing, audio and perhaps shorthand. Commercial terminology and business studies in the foreign language are often included too. Most colleges offer work experience either in the UK or abroad. Language qualifications, such as foreign languages at work, are currently being incorporated into the NVQ/ SVQ scheme.

Once bi/multilingual secretaries have started work, they receive on-the-job induction training on employer procedures and on new computer packages.

Farm

BTEC/SCOTVEC training in agricultural administration covers agricultural and secretarial subjects, with specializations in different sectors available. NVQs/SVQs for agricultural secretaries and administrators are expected to be introduced during the late 1990s.

Once work has been started, the job of farm secretary requires fairly continuous learning. Although farm secretaries are fully qualified when they start work, they need to keep updating their knowledge, particularly on the legal and technical side. New computer applications for agriculture are just one example of the constant updating that a farm secretary requires. This study is done more often by reading, practical experience and questioning other secretaries, farmers and advisers, than through formal structures or courses.

Entry to farm secretarial work is possible via a training scheme for young people. This can be done either by getting day release from an existing employer to go to college, or by going directly to a college to study and being sent to employers for work experience. Contact local careers offices, TECs/LECs for further details.

LATE ENTRY

There is no age limit for starting work as a specialist secretary. For medical and farm secretaries, some employers actually prefer more mature candidates. Mature candidates for legal secretarial work often enter by cross-training on the legal side. Training for work schemes for specialist secretarial work are available for suitably qualified unemployed adults in some areas. Contact local TECs/LECs for more information.

OPPORTUNITIES

Medical

Opportunities exist in numerous specialities, such as general medicine, general surgery, paediatrics, dermatology, psychiatry, cardiology, ophthalmics, X-ray department, and research. Other options include the World Health Organization (WHO), the medical corps of the Armed Forces, and pharmaceutical companies. Competition for vacancies is often fierce.

Legal

There are just under 14,000 companies with legal departments and nearly 10,000 private legal practices. Vacancies for legal secretaries occur in the vast majority of these employers but competition can be quite fierce. Most openings are in large cities, with competition being fiercest in London. Opportunities for temporary work are quite good and part-time work may be available.

Bi/multilingual

The number of jobs available in the UK is usually greater than the number of students qualified to fill them. Opportunities are found mainly in large cities. In addition, bi/multilingual secretaries can pursue openings in countries that speak their second language.

In the UK, the language with the largest call for secretaries is French, with German, Spanish and Italian having some importance too. Other European languages and those of more geographically remote countries are not in much demand.

Farm

Opportunities are available for resident farm secretaries, who work on one farm or estate, for mobile farm secretaries who work for a number of businesses, and in farm secretarial bureaux, which also work for several farms. Mobile farm secretaries are usually self-employed, and may have their own office, while farm secretarial bureaux offer part-time and temporary opportunities as well as full-time work. Bureaux sometimes offer work for secretaries in agricultural accountants and consultants. Changes in agricultural technology and legislation have increased the demand for trained agricultural administrators. Competition for the relatively scarce full-time jobs for college leavers can be fierce, and so newly qualified applicants often start at bureaux or in administrative jobs at accountants or land agents specializing in agriculture.

PAY AND CONDITIONS

Medical

Starting salaries for newly qualified medical secretaries are in the region of £8,076 with London weighting (about £1,225 to £2,060) available on top. Salaries are based on a 36-hour week in the London area and 37 hours elsewhere. Normal office hours are usually worked, although flexibility may be required to fit in with clinic hours, such as evenings and Saturday mornings.

Legal

The average salary for a legal secretary in London is £16,000 to £18,000, although pay is generally lower outside the capital. Legal secretaries normally work office hours, but they are expected to be flexible if work occurs late in the day.

Bi/multilingual

Starting salaries for bi/multilingual secretaries are in the region of £11,000 to £12,000 in London. Pay varies by company, business sector and region, with salaries normally being higher in London than elsewhere. Office hours are normally worked, though at more senior levels secretaries are expected to work longer hours.

Farm

Typical starting salaries for full-time farm secretaries are £8,500 to £9,000 although many farm secretaries work only part-time. Office hours are usually worked, although flexibility is necessary. For a resident farm secretary, accommodation is sometimes provided, which may be reflected in the salary.

PROSPECTS

Medical

Medical secretaries with the right motivation and experience can gain promotion in the health service. Within general practice, this could lead to practice management, but managerial and further financial training will be required. AMSPAR offers both a Diploma and Certificate in Practice Management. Secretaries wishing to leave the medical profession find their skills and experience can be translated into other business contexts.

Legal

Legal secretaries can work their way up the company, perhaps aiming for the job of personal assistant to the most senior partner. Alternatively, they can become legal executives, with a more managerial role, running the office. For this move, they may require additional paralegal qualifications from IPT or the Institute of Legal Executives.

Bi/multilingual

Bi/multilingual secretaries often use their job as an entry point to a particular industry or type of work in which they are interested. With the right motivation and ability, it is not uncommon for them to move into an executive role, such as in sales, personnel or even stockbroking. To pursue the language element of the work, it is possible to become a translator, especially if a secretary has a particular expertise, for instance in computer terminology.

Farm

Farm secretaries can move into larger farms or from bureaux to farms, or set up as a self-employed mobile farm secretary or open a bureau. Areas other than farm estate management, into which farm secretaries move, include forestry, land agency, agricultural marketing, food processing and retailing, veterinary practice management, conservation and countryside management, rural tourism, and auctioneering. Some farm secretaries take further accountancy qualifications to work in these and other areas.

RELATED OCCUPATIONS

Executive Secretary/PA, hotel receptionist, dental/medical receptionist, translator, legal executive, medical practice manager, farm manager, agricultural accountant.

FURTHER INFORMATION

AMSPAR*, Tavistock House North, Tavistock Square, London WC1H 9LN, 0171 387 6005

Business and Technology Education Council (BTEC)*, Central House, Upper Woburn Place, London WC1H 0HH, 0171 413 8400

Institute of Qualified Private Secretaries (IQPS)*, 68 Longmoor Road, Long Eaton, Nottingham NG10 4FP, 0115 9733235

Institute of Paralegal Training*, The Mill, Clymping Street, Clymping, Littlehampton, West Sussex BN17 5RN, 01903 714276

Institut Francais*, Bilingual College, 14 Cromwell Place, London SW7 2JR, 0171 581 2701

Institute of Agricultural Secretaries and Administrators*, NAC, Stoneleigh, Kenilworth, Warwickshire CV8 2LZ, 01203 696592

Law Society, Legal Education Information Unit, Berrington Close, Redditch, Worcestershire B98 0TD, 01527 517141 ext 3088

London Chamber of Commerce and Industry (LCCI)*, Marlowe House, Station Road, Sidcup DA15 7BJ, 0181 302 0261

National Council for Vocational Qualifications (NCVQ)*, 222 Euston Road, London NW1 2BZ, 0171 387 9898

Pitman Qualifications*, 1 Giltspur Street, London EC1A 9DD, 0171 294 2471

RSA Examinations Board, Westwood Way, Coventry CV4 8HS, 01203 470033

Scottish Vocational Education Council (SCOTVEC)*, Hanover House, 24 Douglas Street, Glasgow G2 7NQ, 0141 248 7900

FURTHER READING

Leaflets/booklets are available from the addresses marked*.

Working in Medicine and Surgery – COIC
Working in Hospitals – COIC
Working in Law – COIC
Working in Languages – COIC
Working in Agriculture and Horticulture – COIC

In the careers library classified under CAT.

1. CLERK CLCI:CAT
2. RECEPTIONIST CLCI:CAT
3. TYPIST/WORD PROCESSOR
OPERATOR CLCI:CAT

BACKGROUND INFORMATION

Clerks are employed by many different types of employer to record, update, amend and store information relating to their employer's business. They may work with general, factual, scientific, technical, financial or other specialist information. They usually work under the guidance of a supervisor. Other clerical grade workers are receptionists, telephonists and counter clerks, who all deal with members of the public, and typists/word processor operators, who need specialist skills.

1. CLERK (CAT)

THE WORK

Clerks manage all the information that is generated by their organizations and the additional information that comes into the company from other sources.

The main functions of any clerical job are:

Recording information. This may be done by hand, either by filling in forms or by writing notes; by typing the information, using a typewriter; or increasingly, by keying it into a computer. If any information is missing or is incorrect, the clerk searches files and records and may have to telephone customers or other departments within the company to obtain the correct facts. These are then recorded and notes are made cross-referring to other files and sources of information where necessary.

Filing. It is the clerk's responsibility to make sure that all information can be easily retrieved. It may be stored on computer or by using a manual system in filing cabinets. Filing clerks may have total responsibility for this aspect of the work. General clerks may do certain amounts of filing among their duties. Filing is also a duty often given to the newest entrants or trainees. This helps them to learn about the company, its organization and its products.

Communicating information. Clerks sort all the incoming mail and distribute it to the appropriate staff. They may also be responsible for photocopying documents, addressing envelopes, writing some letters and sending all these to the relevant people. They may also communicate and pass on information by telephone. Travel booking clerks, for instance, usually work with a VDU at their desk and, as a customer phones to make a reservation, they are able to call up details of vacancies and key in the booking information while talking with the client.

In addition to their general duties, clerks have specialist tasks, which vary according to their employer's business. They could include: in a personnel department – looking after staff records, sending out application forms and subsequently letters inviting applicants for interview, maintaining records on staff contributions to pension schemes; in a sales office – dealing with accounts, keeping records of sales made by individual salesmen/women, recording details of items ordered, sending invoices to customers; in an accounts office – checking figures using adding machines and calculators, book-keeping, preparing balance sheets, carrying out calculations for qualified accountants; in a wages office – calculating the amount of pay due to every employee, using records showing the number of hours worked and the number of these worked at overtime rates, deducting income tax and contributions for national insurance, pension funds, medical insurance, etc, producing a pay slip itemizing all these facts and either sending one of these to all staff, showing that the salary has been paid into their bank accounts or putting cash into pay packets and issuing these to employees; in an export department – processing documents for goods to be exported, recording the fact that customs clearance and insurance cover have been obtained, making transport arrangements with shipping or airline companies, sending out invoices; in the central reservations office of a hotel chain, travel company or with a transport operator (airline, road, rail or ferry company) – making bookings for clients, checking availability of seats or rooms, quoting a price, taking credit card details for payment or sending an invoice to the client, sending written confirmation of the reservation.

Some clerks are known as clerk typists. They combine general clerical duties with copy or audio typing and may do administrative work for several people working in their departments.

In some jobs, clerks spend some of their time working directly with members of the public. If they work for an organization that receives enquiries in person they may have to leave their office to go to the reception or information desk and answer the query.

WORK ENVIRONMENT

Offices vary in size and age but are usually clean and comfortable. Small companies tend to have older furniture and equipment and make less use of modern technology, such as word processors and computers. Large organizations usually have more modern furnishings and sophisticated office machinery. Some clerks work in small offices of two or three people; others work in large open-plan offices that are divided into sections by screens.

Most clerks work in sections managed by a supervisor who allocates work. They may or may not have contact with other employees and with managers depending on the size of their firm and the nature of the work. Many clerks remain seated all day. Those dealing with the post or responsible for distributing documents around the building, however, may be on their feet for a large part of the day.

They normally have contact with the public only by telephone – the exception being counter clerks.

SKILLS AND INTERESTS

Clerks should be well organized, tidy and able to work accurately and neatly. Some of the tasks may be repetitive, but must all be completed to the same standard. They need to be able to spell and have a knowledge of grammar. In many jobs clear handwriting is essential; in others a liking for basic arithmetic is needed, as is the ability to work with figures.

Clerks increasingly use computers and word processors. In some jobs they are also expected to use calculators, adding machines and typewriters.

Some clerks need a good telephone manner; others may need to deal with personal enquirers helpfully and efficiently. Although they work under the general direction of a supervisor or office manager, they should be capable of using their initiative and of working without constant supervision.

They must be willing to observe their employer's dress

code. Most companies expect clerks to wear smart and conventional clothes.

ENTRY REQUIREMENTS

There are no minimum entry requirements but many employers expect new entrants to have some GCSEs/S grades (A-C/1-3). The most useful subjects are English and maths. Other useful subjects are business studies and accounts.

Additional qualifications in word processing, typing and information technology may be advantageous. Alternative qualifications such as NVQ, and an Intermediate GNVQ/GSVQ Level II award in Business, are usually acceptable.

TRAINING

Most training for clerical work is given by employers on-the-job. Clerks may learn by watching and working with experienced colleagues or may be given initial training by their supervisors. Many begin by working as office juniors and do the more routine tasks such as opening and distributing the post, simple filing and operating fax, franking and photocopying machines.

Employers may expect clerks to obtain work-based NVQs/SVQs that are available at Levels 1, 2, 3 and 4. Modules are available in: filing, communicating information, data processing, processing petty cash and invoicing, mail handling, reprographics, stock handling, storing and supplying information, liaising with customers and colleagues, maintaining financial records, processing business documents, telecommunications, processing payments, processing payroll, reception, maintaining financial records, and servicing meetings. (Not all modules are available at all levels.)

There is no set time limit for obtaining NVQs/SVQs. Employees may work at their own pace and take modules as and when appropriate.

Some employers may give their clerical staff day release to a college of further education to study for single subject examinations in: typing, word processing, information technology, office practice and secretarial duties.

Some may give day release for an Intermediate/Advanced GNVQ/GSVQ Level II/III award in Business.

The above contain core units in general business procedures, and optional or additional units that are chosen according to the employee's place of work. Examples include: marketing, business law, personnel policy, financial planning and control.

These methods are less likely however, since the above awards are more normally studied on a full-time basis. Length of courses varies – from one to three years.

BTEC/SCOTVEC higher national diplomas and certificates may also be taken. These are useful for clerical staff with management potential. Courses usually take two years of part-time study.

Specific training opportunities for young people, including Modern Apprenticeships, may be available – contact your local careers office, TEC/LEC for details.

LATE ENTRY

There is no upper age limit for entering clerical work. In many areas colleges run refresher courses for adults who have been away from employment for some time. Other training opportunities specifically geared to adults may be available.

There may be specific training opportunities directed at adults available in some areas for this type of work. Candidates may have to satisfy certain conditions to be eligible. Contact your local Jobcentre, careers office or TEC/LEC for details.

OPPORTUNITIES

There are openings for clerks in all parts of the country. Almost every type of organization in industry, commerce and the public sector employs them. Although the number of jobs has decreased due to office technology, there is still a steady demand, particularly for those with, or prepared to gain, qualifications, usually in keyboarding and IT.

Smaller companies usually employ general clerks who are expected to carry out a range of clerical tasks. In the bigger companies it is more usual to specialize.

PAY AND CONDITIONS

Salaries vary considerably according to employer and location. They could be anywhere between £5,000 and £16,000 with the highest salaries being paid in London and the South East. Most clerks work 35 to 37 hours a week with opportunities for paid overtime. Some companies work from 9am to 5pm or 8.30am to 5.30pm. Others operate a flexitime system with staff being permitted to choose their hours outside core time (stipulated hours, during which all staff must be present).

There are often opportunities for part-time work and job sharing.

Some firms give a range of benefits such as subsidized canteens, pension schemes and life assurance.

PROSPECTS

There may be opportunities to change departments within a company and move to a different type of clerical work, or to gain promotion to section head, supervisor or office manager.

Promotion is more likely to come to those who have studied for recognized qualifications in business or office administration. It is also possible to obtain promotion or higher salaries by changing employer.

RELATED OCCUPATIONS

Accounting technician, bank officer, building society clerk, Civil Service administrative assistant/officer, insurance clerk, local government clerk, medical records clerk, receptionist, travel consultant/travel agency clerk.

FURTHER INFORMATION AND READING

Please see article 3. TYPIST/WORD PROCESSOR OPERATOR

2. RECEPTIONIST (CAT)

THE WORK

Receptionists have a very important job. They are the first representative of their organization to meet visitors. As such they must present a good image, greeting people in an efficient and friendly manner. The impression visitors gain of a company or organization is often due to the receptionist.

They must find out whom the visitor has come to see and

whether they have an appointment. If not, they may have to turn people away or make an appointment for a future date. If the visitor does have an appointment, receptionists phone through to check the person they have come to see is available, and then give the visitor directions to the appropriate office or ask them to wait until someone from that office comes to escort them. They often have to ask the visitor to sign a visitors' book on entering and leaving the building and to give details of their vehicle registration number for security purposes. (This must be done meticulously. It is not purely for the company's security: if there is a fire or other emergency it is essential that there is a list of people known to be in the building.) They may also issue the visitor with a badge bearing his or her name to be worn for the duration of the visit. If the person the visitor has come to see is unavoidably delayed it is the receptionist's duty to explain this, apologize, show them to a waiting area and sometimes offer a drink and magazines to read while they are waiting.

Receptionists also receive incoming goods and parcels and sign receipts for them, and take messages for colleagues who are out of the office. It is important that receptionists know who is in the building and who is not on the premises, which meetings are being held and where, and who in the organization deals with which matters. They must make sure that they keep in constant touch with other members of staff and often have to encourage people firmly but politely to make their movements, meetings, etc, known to reception.

Receptionists may be asked many questions that are not directly connected with their own employer but, in order to provide a service to visitors, they may keep a selection of useful telephone numbers, street maps and so on in order to be able to advise on booking taxis and accommodation, contacting emergency services, suggesting restaurants and giving general directions.

Receptionists may work in many different types of organization and, according to the type of work that they do, may need specialist skills and be willing to do additional duties.

Medical receptionists for example, need particular knowledge of the health service and of how a doctors' practice or hospital department is run; dental receptionists may also act as surgery assistants; hotel receptionists must be competent in accommodation operations and sometimes do other jobs within the hotel. Please see article HOTEL RECEPTIONIST CLCI:IC.

Many receptionists also operate the company's switchboard and fax machine and deal with telephone enquiries.

In some jobs receptionists may be expected to make out bills and make small sales (hairdressing salons, garages); make up pay packets and pay wages; send faxes; sort and distribute the post and frank outgoing mail (small companies); and quite often do some copy typing for various members of staff. These tasks are often done in quiet moments, since reception work can involve very busy periods of work followed by periods of inactivity.

WORK ENVIRONMENT

Receptionists work in the reception areas of all kinds of buildings. Many work in very pleasant and comfortable surroundings. In other premises however, the reception area may be very small and cramped – and sometimes noisy.

SKILLS AND INTERESTS

Receptionists should be confident, have a pleasant, outgoing disposition and enjoy working with people. They should have good communication skills, and in particular, clear speech.

They must not get upset if people are unpleasant. Frequently, visitors who have come to the wrong building or who have to be told that they cannot be seen without an appointment are aggressive and are rude to the receptionist. Telephone enquirers may be impatient.

They should be able to work under pressure. Often they are expected to deal with several personal callers and telephone calls at the same time. A good memory is an advantage since regular visitors like to be remembered and greeted by name. Patience is an essential quality.

Receptionists should have a smart appearance. They are often expected to dress in a certain way by their employers. Most of their time is spent sitting behind a desk.

ENTRY REQUIREMENTS

There are no minimum entry requirements, but employers may want receptionists who can type and have previous experience as a telephonist or in operating a switchboard. Many employers expect a good standard of general education which may include possession of several GCSEs/S grades (A-C/1-3) or equivalent qualifications. English is a desirable subject.

Useful pre-employment courses include: Intermediate GNVQ/GSVQ Level II awards in Business/Business Administration, which contain core units in general business procedures; single subject examinations in typing, word processing, office practice and secretarial duties, or AMSPAR Health Service Reception Diploma.

TRAINING

Training once in employment is on-the-job.

Employers may encourage receptionists to obtain work-based NVQs/SVQs, which include modules in: communicating information, mail handling, reprographics, liaising with customers and colleagues and reception duties. NVQs are available at Levels 1 and 2 specifically for receptionists working in the hospitality industry.

There is no set time limit for obtaining NVQs/SVQs. Employees may work at their own pace and take units as and when appropriate. The Association of Medical Secretaries, Practice Administrators and Receptionists (AMSPAR) runs courses for people who wish to specialize in medical reception. (Contact AMSPAR for further details.)

The above courses include the following subjects:

– reception duties: social skills; dealing with people; using the telephone; operating a switchboard; confidentiality; hygiene and grooming; inter-office communication;

– background information: business organization; banking, insurance and postal services;

– communication skills: verbal, written and numerical skills; typing; book-keeping; completion of documents; recording and filing systems.

LATE ENTRY

This is quite usual. Many employers in fact prefer older employees with previous experience of office work or dealing with the public.

OPPORTUNITIES

All types of organization employ receptionists. There are openings in the public and private sectors: in industry, commerce, medical services, education, the health service and in local government.

PAY AND CONDITIONS

Salaries vary considerably according to employer and location.

They could be anywhere between £6,500 and £14,500, with the highest salaries being paid in London and the South East.

Most receptionists work 35 to 37 hours a week, Monday to Friday. Receptionists employed in hairdressing establishments, airports, garages and hotels may have to work at weekends with time off during the week to compensate. There are often opportunities for part-time work and job sharing.

Some firms give a range of benefits, such as subsidized canteens, pension schemes and life assurance.

A few very large employers may give a dress or grooming allowance.

PROSPECTS

In general, there are few opportunities to progress, other than in large firms, particularly hotels where there is the possibility of promotion to head receptionist posts. Alternatively, it is often possible to obtain higher salaries by changing employer.

RELATED OCCUPATIONS

Hotel receptionist, medical secretary, telephonist, travel consultant/agency clerk.

FURTHER INFORMATION AND READING

Please see article 3. TYPIST/WORD PROCESSOR OPERATOR

3. TYPIST/WORD PROCESSOR OPERATOR (CAT)

THE WORK

Typists and word processor operators produce all kinds of typed material – letters, documents, reports, minutes of meetings, memos, invoices, forms, sheets of technical and statistical data and more lengthy texts and manuscripts. There are three main kinds of typist, who specialize in different types of work.

Copy typists type directly from handwritten drafts and documents, or from previously typed material. They may sometimes have to include statistical information, which may mean including data and figures from different documents. They may be expected to check their own work or it may be done by a supervisor.

Audio typists work from previously dictated material, using headphones and foot controls to stop and re-play the tape as necessary.

Shorthand typists first take down material to be typed in a one-to-one dictation session with the manager or other member of staff for whom the work is to be done, using one of the accepted systems such as Pitmans or Teeline. They then type it up reading back their own notes and transcribing it into English as they work. They may be expected to do some copy or audio typing or other office duties, as shorthand work does not always take up all their time.

Word processor operators do very similar work to copy typists, but by using a word processor that incorporates a keyboard and a VDU (visual display unit). They are able to correct mistakes as they appear on the screen and to recall text from the word processor's memory and update, amend or amalgamate documents as necessary.

Copy, audio and shorthand typists may also use word processors in their work, rather than typewriters.

All typists and word processor operators select the correct layout for their work, following their employers' methods, and may correct spelling and grammar.

Some people are employed as clerk typists. They combine typing with general clerical duties. Please see article 1. CLERK.

WORK ENVIRONMENT

Typists and word processor operators work in offices that vary in size and age, but are usually clean and comfortable. They may very occasionally use manual typewriters, but more usually, electronic typewriters or word processors. Small companies tend to have older furniture and equipment and make less use of modern technology. Large organizations usually have more modern furnishings and train their staff to use word processors.

Most typists and word processor operators work as part of a team. They may work in a large section, known as a typing pool, with other typists, doing work for many different people within the company as allocated by their supervisor. Others work in smaller sections and some may be members of a company's departmental team – as the sole typist or word processor operator working for several executives.

Audio typists may share the work dictated on to one tape with other typists. If the office is busy it may be necessary to stop working on one tape in order to complete a more urgent piece of work. By the time they have finished that, the original tape may have been given to another typist to complete. Shorthand typists, however, must finish typing all the work they took down as they can generally transcribe only their own shorthand.

Typists and word processor operators spend most of their time working seated.

SKILLS AND INTERESTS

Typists and word processor operators must be careful, accurate and methodical, with an eye for detail when correcting work or calling up and changing text. They should understand correct layout procedures and be able in many cases to plan the presentation of a piece of work.

They should not object to doing routine work when this is required, but should also be prepared to adapt to working on their own initiative when work needs to be altered, or if they are expected to work from draft notes and produce a final version without going back to the person who originated the work.

They should be prepared to correct grammar, spelling and punctuation. Audio typists, in particular, need a good grasp of grammar and spelling, since they never work from written drafts.

Word processor operators must be willing to learn

additional skills, such as moving blocks of text around on the VDU and how to store and recall documents.

All typists and word processor operators should be able to work without supervision.

ENTRY REQUIREMENTS

There is no minimum general educational requirement, but many employers expect entrants to have GCSEs/S grades (A-C/1-3) in one or two subjects, including English.

They are also normally expected to have obtained minimum typing and/or shorthand speeds and hold certificates from one of the nationally recognized examining bodies.

Minimum speeds vary with different employers but are usually 30-40 words per minute (wpm) for general typing work, 40 wpm or the ability to transcribe a tape in a given amount of time for audio typists, and 80-100 wpm for shorthand typists.

TRAINING

It is usual for typists and word processor operators to have completed a full-time course at a college of further education or private college and to have obtained recognized qualifications before they apply for employment. Some may have learned to type on a part-time day release basis while employed as general clerks, or by attending evening classes while working in clerical or other forms of employment.

Once in employment they may take further examinations in single subjects (eg typing at stages 1 to 3 and shorthand at varying speeds), or may take certificates or diplomas in office skills. They may also choose to take qualifications in related subjects, like commercial arithmetic or business law. They may be given day release by their employers or be encouraged to attend evening classes.

Word processor operators must first be competent typists.

The main examining bodies offering single subject examinations are Pitman, the London Chamber of Commerce and Industry and the Royal Society of Arts (typing, audio transcription, shorthand, information technology, word processing and office practice). They also offer group awards that combine several of the subjects.

Units in office practice, preparing and producing documents, keyboarding, shorthand plus transcription and audio typing plus transcription are also included in NVQs in Administration. Please see article 1. CLERK.

Training for word processor operators is also provided by employers, by private colleges and training organizations, and by equipment manufacturers who offer cross-training in different word processing systems.

Organizations train their own employees in the techniques of layout and style.

Specific training opportunities for young people, including Modern Apprenticeships, may be available – contact your local careers office, TEC/LEC for details.

LATE ENTRY

There is no upper age limit for entering this work. In many areas colleges run refresher courses for adults who have been away from employment for some time and need to re-train to use new office technology.

Adults can gain recognition of their skills and experience by working towards NVQs/SVQs. There is open access to NVQs/SVQs – no academic qualifications are required, and there are no age limits. NVQs/SVQs are based on competence, and it does not matter how that competence has been gained – through experience, company training programmes, college courses or open learning. Past experience can be put forward as evidence of competence, via Accreditation of Prior Learning (APL).

There may be specific training opportunities, directed at adults, available in some areas for this type of work. Candidates may have to satisfy certain conditions to be eligible. Contact your local Jobcentre, careers office or TEC/LEC for details.

OPPORTUNITIES

There are openings for typists and word processor operators in all parts of the country and with every size and type of employer, including central and local government, the Armed Forces, the health service, industry, commerce, banks and financial institutions, etc.

There are opportunities for part-time work and job sharing. Many typists work as 'temps' for employment agencies who send them to work for different employers. Some typists are self-employed, working from home and offering a typing service to individuals and small businesses.

There are some opportunities to work overseas with British companies and for government departments such as the Foreign and Commonwealth Office and the Ministry of Defence.

Opportunities for copy typists are decreasing, since most documents can be reproduced using photocopiers. This is balanced, however, by an increase in demand for word processor operators. Shorthand typists are being replaced by audio typists in many companies, as audio typing gives greater flexibility. Shorthand is still an important skill, however, for typists hoping to become senior secretaries.

PAY AND CONDITIONS

Salaries vary considerably according to employer, location and individual's level of skills. They could be anywhere between £7,200 and £15,000, with the highest salaries being paid in London and the South East.

Most typists and word processor operators work 35 to 37 hours a week with opportunities for paid overtime. Some companies work from 9am to 5pm or 8.30am to 5.30pm. Flexitime is sometimes available.

Some firms give a range of benefits, such as subsidized canteens, pension schemes and life assurance.

PROSPECTS

There are good opportunities to become supervisors in large organizations. In some companies it is possible to progress from typing/word processing to secretarial work, although this normally involves gaining further qualifications. (In the Civil Service for example, it is possible to join as a typist and apply to become a secretary once qualified at 30 wpm in typing and 100 wpm shorthand/360-word audio transcription in 20 minutes.)

Prospects are more limited in smaller organizations, but it is possible to obtain promotion or higher salaries by changing employer.

RELATED OCCUPATIONS

Civil Service administrative assistant/officer, clerk, medical records clerk, receptionist, executive secretary/personal assistant, specialist secretary.

FURTHER INFORMATION

Business and Technology Education Council*, Central House, Upper Woburn Place, London WC1H 0HH, 0171 413 8400

City and Guilds (C&G)*, 1 Giltspur Street, London EC1A 9DD, 0171 294 2468

London Chamber of Commerce and Industry Commercial Education Trust Examination Board*, Marlowe House, Station Road, Sidcup, Kent DA15 7BJ, 0181 302 0261

Pitman Qualifications*, 1 Giltspur Street, London EC1A 9DD, 0171 294 2471

RSA Examinations Board, Westwood Way, Coventry CV4 8HS, 01203 470033

Scottish Vocational Education Council*, Hanover House, 24 Douglas Street, Glasgow G2 7NQ, 0141 248 7900

FURTHER READING

Leaflets/booklets are available from the addresses marked*.

In the careers library classified under CAT.

1. MICRO-ELECTRONICS ENGINEER CLCI:CAV/RAL
2. SYSTEMS PROGRAMMER/SOFTWARE ENGINEER CLCI:CAV
3. SYSTEMS ANALYST CLCI:CAV
4. APPLICATIONS PROGRAMMER CLCI:CAV
5. COMPUTER SERVICE TECHNICIAN CLCI:CAV/RAL

BACKGROUND INFORMATION

Developments in electronic systems occur at a very rapid rate and new applications are frequently found for existing technology. The use of computers and micro-electronic circuits is no longer restricted to industry and commerce – they can be found in domestic appliances, in school classrooms, and in hospitals.

To research, design, manufacture, install and service such complex equipment requires a large number of highly qualified personnel and, on average, between 5,000 and 10,000 people enter the industry each year. There are many different jobs available and a variety of ways to qualify for careers in the computing industry. Job titles vary considerably and many staff combine a number of different roles in one job, especially in some companies. Key occupations include:

Micro-electronics engineers research, design, develop, fabricate and test new electronic components and circuitry;

Hardware engineers create and produce new system architectures and equipment using micro-electronic devices and other components;

Programmers/software engineers write, test, maintain and update computer programs and packages for electronic systems. They can also develop new computing languages; software engineers design large systems using 'library' routines;

Systems analysts assess and specify the computing requirements of an organization and plan systems to ensure that work is undertaken more effectively;

Applications programmers write programs to enable computer systems to undertake specific tasks (usually business applications) but may also undertake similar work to a software engineer;

Computer service technicians install, service and repair computer hardware and software systems.

1. MICRO-ELECTRONICS ENGINEER (CAV/RAL)

THE WORK

Micro-electronics engineers are involved in the design, development, fabrication and testing of new electronic circuitry. Modern electronic circuits are built on printed circuit or hybrid boards carrying the latest in chip technology, both analogue and digital, in standard and customized form. Microprocessors are often employed with software playing an ever more important role.

The design and development of a new electronic circuit is carried out by teams of engineers. Each engineer has a specific area of responsibility, but makes sure that, when it is finished, their work is compatible with that of the rest of the team.

Micro-electronics engineers undertaking the logic design often work together with software engineers, who write the software. This process needs careful planning to decide which function will be achieved through the hardware, which through the software, and how they will interact. Often, a microprocessor is embedded in order to achieve flexibility. Senior engineers may be responsible for projects, supervising the work of other engineers and technicians and making decisions about the design of the overall system, rather than the individual circuit boards and software modules that the system contains. Some micro-electronics engineers may have a wider range of responsibilities than just design, development and testing. They may have direct contact with customers, and their work could cover everything from the design of a prototype and liaison with suppliers to the testing of the final product.

The main areas of work include:

– aerospace, including aircraft, satellites, space systems and guided weapons;

– computers, information technology and telecommunications;

– consumer electronics, such as washing machines and microwave ovens;

– sound and vision systems for home entertainment, the recording and film industry;

– defence contractors developing surveillance equipment, weapons and communications hardware;

– instruments, measurement and control systems;

– medical electronics for use in diagnosis, monitoring and caring for patients;

– automobile electronics for cars and specialist vehicles.

WORK ENVIRONMENT

Some engineers, who are device developers and are involved in the development or manufacture of semiconductors or other components, work in clean rooms for at least part of the time. These are dust-free, temperature-controlled, air-conditioned environments where no eating, drinking or smoking is permitted. Special clothes are often required. The majority of electronic design is now done by CAD (computer-aided design) and so a great deal of time is spent either at a workstation or in testing assembled equipment (although the latter can also be done via a computer). Engineers involved in design, test or applications may also be based in laboratories or workshops, and project managers would normally have a separate office. Those with responsibility for customer liaison may be required to travel.

SKILLS AND INTERESTS

Micro-electronic engineers must be highly numerate. A logical and enquiring mind and a willingness to tackle challenging problems is essential. Design and development requires creativity and imagination, and the ability to combine intellectual and practical skills. Attention to detail is also required. It is very important for engineers to keep up-to-date with the rapid developments in micro-electronics.

Most engineers work as part of a team, so it is important to work effectively with other people. Good communication skills are vital, and employers look for engineering staff able to express themselves well in writing and in face-to-face presentations. There is an increasing emphasis on the ability to present highly technical information to non-specialist audiences.

Multinational companies welcome staff with foreign language skills.

ENTRY REQUIREMENTS

Entry to micro-electronics requires a degree in a relevant subject, such as electronic engineering, micro-electronics, mathematics, physics or computer science.

Degrees. The minimum entry requirement for degree courses is: two A levels/three H grades with five GCSEs/S grades (A-C/1-3), or equivalent. Some courses demand either good grades in three A levels or four H grades, with one or more subjects specified (eg maths or physics).

Postgraduate courses. Entry is with first or upper second-class honours in a relevant degree. A postgraduate qualification, however, is not essential to enter micro-electronics engineering.

TRAINING

Degrees. Electronic engineering, micro-electronics, maths, physics and computer science degree courses are offered at many universities and colleges of higher education throughout the UK. Courses usually last three years full-time (four years in Scotland) or four years on a sandwich basis (four or five years in Scotland).

Sandwich courses combine full-time study with periods of work experience. Some employers offer sponsorship to students, which can involve employers specifying the institutions students should attend.

Postgraduate courses. These are available at universities and colleges of higher education, mostly one year full-time.

Employers usually offer training programmes to new entrants, which may include both technical and business management topics. Training may be provided through in-house courses, external short courses or distance learning programmes. The National Computing Centre, for example, offers a wide range of specialized courses.

Employers often offer opportunities for staff to update their knowledge and acquire new skills. Many engineers participate in the activities of relevant professional bodies, such as seminars and conferences, to keep abreast of new developments in their field.

Suitably qualified and experienced engineers may apply for membership of a professional body, such as the Institution of Electrical Engineers or British Computer Society, and registration with the Engineering Council as a chartered engineer. This can lead to the title of European engineer (Eur Ing), recognized in Europe.

LATE ENTRY

Late entry may be possible for those with an appropriate background in maths and physical science, or relevant experience. Employers are keen to welcome back people returning to work after a career break. There are also opportunities in the public sector, particularly in research centres, universities and the Ministry of Defence.

OPPORTUNITIES

As the applications of information technology and computing systems expand to meet new requirements in industry and commerce, the demand for qualified micro-electronics engineers is also increasing. Many micro-electronics engineers are employed by large private sector manufacturing companies, such as British Aerospace, IBM, Northern Telecom and GEC. Small high-tech companies may also employ engineers in specialized areas such as computing, telecommunications and aerospace.

There are also good opportunities for work overseas, particularly in Europe and North America. Vacancies are advertised in *Computer Weekly; Computing; Data Processing; Electronics Weekly* and the journals of professional bodies, such as the Institution of Electrical Engineers.

PAY AND CONDITIONS

Micro-electronics engineers normally work office hours from Monday to Friday. However, evening and weekend work may be required to meet project deadlines.

New graduates could expect a starting salary of approximately £15,000, rising to £20,000+ for more experienced staff. Senior staff and those with supervisory and management responsibilities could command far higher salaries.

PROSPECTS

Promotion prospects are good for graduate engineers with professional qualifications. It is possible to progress to supervisory and management positions, such as project management, with responsibility for a team of technical staff.

Exceptionally talented individuals may gain promotion to senior management and director level posts relatively quickly. Engineers can transfer to other related areas of work, such as lecturing and research in universities, or marketing and manufacturing positions.

RELATED OCCUPATIONS

Engineer, systems programmer/software engineer, systems analyst, materials scientist/technologist, scientist.

FURTHER INFORMATION AND READING

Please see article 5. COMPUTER SERVICE TECHNICIAN.

2. SYSTEMS PROGRAMMER/SOFTWARE ENGINEER (CAV)

THE WORK

Systems programmers research, design, develop and adapt application programs for computer systems. They may also be responsible for the maintenance and updating of programs. These direct the computer and tell it what to do and how to function. Software engineers usually create new programs and, perhaps, new languages. However, these two jobs can overlap and sometimes one individual will be responsible for both areas.

Systems programmers/software engineers are employed by software houses, computer manufacturers, large companies who use computers and develop their own programs, such as BT, and research departments in universities.

Systems programmers/software engineers work in a variety of ways – as an individual writing their own program for one particular task, or as part of a team to produce a more complex and sophisticated program. When a team is producing such complex software, it is important to ensure that all components are compatible. This necessitates quality testing against appropriate pre-defined standards to ensure the program functions correctly.

Systems programmers/software engineers use a variety of languages to create and adapt software, such as COBOL (Common Business Oriented Language), C, CORAL, or low-level languages, such as Assembler. However, the trend is towards using 4GLs (fourth-generation languages) and code generators for well-defined application areas.

Computer programs are increasingly being compiled from libraries of sub-programs, which will eventually make up a complete systems program rather than develop the whole program from scratch. This method of producing software saves a great deal of time and enables the software to retail at a lower cost.

Computer programs can be applied to many different tasks, from direct business applications to design assistance for production systems. The main ones are:

Computer-aided design (CAD). CAD is a tool to aid the design process and it is an increasingly important area, especially for architecture, product design, engineering and software development itself. CAD software can be used to design and specify buildings, engineering systems, or even for clothing.

Computer-aided manufacture (CAM). The main areas of application are robotics, process and quality control. Products can now be designed, produced and packaged all in one process using both CAD and CAM. Programs can be written for the whole process or divided into separate operations. Anything from a pair of shoes to an aircraft can be produced using CAM.

Business tools and applications. This includes software for office equipment, such as word processors and desktop publishing microcomputers. Some companies may require tailor-made software for certain operations, such as accounting, billing and customer services.

Computer games. These are an increasingly popular form of entertainment, and manufacturers require software engineers to update or write new programs.

Networking. Computers can be linked together to form a network where they can 'talk' to each other. Software specialists must ensure that different systems can interact.

Fifth-generation computers. These computers are very advanced and require sophisticated software. Such computers may be able to respond to a human voice or even touch. They may also undertake similar thought processes to the human brain, such as reasoning and logic.

WORK ENVIRONMENT

Systems programmers/software engineers work from offices and spend much of their time at workstations developing software and detailing systems design, where there are numerous built-in facilities. It may be necessary for programmers/engineers to visit clients' offices to discuss project work or to explain how a piece of software functions.

Most systems programmers/software engineers work as part of a team contributing individual work to complete a project.

SKILLS AND INTERESTS

Individuals in software engineering and programming work very much as part of a team, so it is necessary to be able to get on well with other people.

Systems programmers/software engineers are problem solvers and need to approach problems systematically and logically to provide effective solutions. Patience and determination are important, so that the job can be carried through to a successful result. A high level of intellectual ability is required, together with excellent mathematical skills and technical knowledge.

Creativity, imagination and resourcefulness are vital. Relevant management skills are necessary for those in supervisory positions. It is increasingly important for such professionals to be articulate and to appreciate the users' environment and problems.

ENTRY REQUIREMENTS

Most entrants to this work have been educated to degree level. Many companies require computer science or maths graduates or electronics engineers with good A levels/H grades including maths and/or physics or previous experience in a related field, such as programming. Please see article 4. APPLICATIONS PROGRAMMER. Most employers require applicants to take aptitude tests.

Degree courses. The minimum entry requirement for degree courses is two A levels/three H grades with five GCSEs/S grades (A-C/1-3), or equivalent. Some courses demand either good grades in three A levels or four H grades, with one or more subjects specified (eg maths or physics), or the achievement of merits or distinctions in a BTEC national award.

Postgraduate courses. Entry is with a good honours degree, but not necessarily in a relevant subject.

BTEC/SCOTVEC. The minimum entry requirement for higher national awards is either one A level/two H grades with four GCSEs/S grades (A-C/1-3), or equivalent.

Institute of Data Processing Management's (IDPM) higher diploma. Entry requires either: five GCSEs (A-C) including maths and English and two A levels including one in a computing subject; or three S grades (1-3) and four H grades including one in a computing subject; or a BTEC national award in a computing or computer-related subject; or successful completion of the IDPM's diploma examinations; or four years' experience relevant to computing. Minimum age is 21 years.

TRAINING

Degrees. Courses in computer science, maths, electronic and electrical engineering are offered at many universities and colleges of higher education throughout the UK. Courses usually last three years full-time (four years in Scotland) or four years on a sandwich basis (four or five years in Scotland). Sandwich courses combine full-time study with periods of work experience. Some employers offer sponsorships to students, which can involve employers specifying the institution students should attend.

Postgraduate courses. These are available at universities and colleges of higher education, mostly one year full-time. There are a number of courses designed for graduates of any discipline to convert their expertise into the information technology field.

BTEC/SCOTVEC. Software engineering higher national courses are offered at over 20 universities, colleges of higher education and colleges of further education throughout the UK. Many such institutions also offer higher national courses in computer studies, electrical and electronic engineering. Higher national diploma courses usually last two years full-time or three years on a sandwich basis. Higher national certificate courses usually last two or three years on a day release or evening basis, except in Scotland where they are one year full-time.

The Institute of Data Processing Management's (IDPM) higher diploma course is available at over 20 centres, either full-time (usually one year), part-time (two to four years), by self-study or by correspondence course.

Employers usually offer training programmes to new entrants. Training may be provided through in-house courses, external short courses or distance learning programmes. The National Computing Centre, for example, offers a number of courses including a two-day course leading to the Software Engineering Certificate.

A number of NVQs/SVQs are available. These include Software Production at Level 2, Multi-User Computer System Investigation and Installation at Level 3, Computer Network System Investigation and Installation at Level 3, Multi-User Computer System Selection and Installation Support at Level 4, and Computer Network System Selection and Installation Supervision at Level 4.

Suitably qualified and experienced personnel may apply to join the British Computer Society (BCS) or other appropriate body.

LATE ENTRY

Late entry into systems programming/software engineering can be difficult unless the individual has some relevant experience in a computer-related field. As computer technology moves so quickly, it is important to keep up-to-date.

Institutions of higher education accept older students on the basis of previous experience and qualifications.

OPPORTUNITIES

As the computer industry is still expanding, opportunities for systems programmers/software engineers are very good. Many employers are experiencing skill shortages in this area, as candidates need to be highly qualified and are in short supply. Experienced programmers/engineers are greatly prized.

Computer technology advances so rapidly that software is continually being improved and updated to match hardware developments. There are an increasing number of jobs available in software houses, computer manufacturers such as IBM and large user companies, such as British Airways, Marconi and BT, who require in-house systems programmers/software engineers. With such highly specialized knowledge, systems programmers/software engineers may find opportunities to work in North America and Europe.

Vacancies are advertised in various journals. Please see article 1. MICRO-ELECTRONICS ENGINEER.

PAY AND CONDITIONS

Trainee systems programmers/software engineers can expect a starting salary of £9,000 rising to £13,500, whereas experienced programmers/engineers can earn £17,500+. Senior personnel and managers can earn approximately £25,000+, depending on location and type of employer.

Systems programmers/software engineers work normal office hours, Monday to Friday, although project deadlines may mean working in the evenings or at weekends in highly motivated teams to produce the system on time and within a budget.

PROSPECTS

As systems programmers/software engineers develop specialized knowledge, they usually remain in this particular field. Progress to managerial posts can be fast for qualified and talented individuals, and some candidates may move into information systems management, where project planning is essential to ensure successful results.

Some systems programmers/software engineers are self-employed, or run consultancies with a small number of staff.

Opportunities also exist in investigation and experimental work, where research is carried out to develop control systems, fifth-generation computers and robotics.

RELATED OCCUPATIONS

Micro-electronics engineer, applications programmer, technical author, operational research officer.

FURTHER INFORMATION AND READING

Please see article 5. COMPUTER SERVICE ENGINEER.

3. SYSTEMS ANALYST (CAV)

THE WORK

Systems analysis is the understanding and documenting of the way in which an organization controls its work. This information can then be used to decide which procedures are best carried out by computer. Once the analysis stage is complete, then the systems design can commence. This may be undertaken by the systems analyst or by a systems designer. The aim is to improve the information available for managing the business and carrying out existing procedures more effectively, if possible.

This would typically lead to the development of an information system, together with its database. Alternatively, existing systems might need to be evaluated as to their suitability and efficiency. Sometimes the systems analyst may design a new system entirely, including the design of print and VDU layouts.

The job can be divided into two broad categories: firstly, analysing and understanding the company's needs and the nature of the work involved; and secondly, providing a cost-effective solution through outlining and developing a new system. After the analysis has been carried out, the systems analyst or systems designer can devise a practical computer system with the appropriate hardware and software.

Systems analysts require an excellent understanding of business methods and a good knowledge of the availability of computer hardware and software when it comes to the design stage. It is usually the larger computer-using organizations who have specific analysis and design requirements, whereas smaller companies can buy and use 'off-the-shelf' systems to carry out everyday tasks, such as accounting.

The majority of systems analysts follow a routine on each project:

Feasibility study. This is undertaken to assess whether or not a new (or perhaps an updated) system is viable for the company, and what the client hopes to achieve.

Investigating the user. On all projects, a systems analyst looks at the end-users of the proposed system. This might involve spending days or weeks studying existing working methods and interviewing personnel, especially those at operational level. Such work requires a great deal of tact, as staff may be irritated by such a presence, the necessary questioning, and the prospect of change.

Systems design. A systems analyst may also have to design and develop the computer system. With the help of the report and the customer, a systems analyst is able to draw up specifications of how each job is to be carried out by particular computers and how they are to be linked to develop a complete system. The analyst has to ensure that the device is user-friendly, as well as considering constraints such as physical size. A good knowledge of both hardware and software is needed.

The report. Once the actual analysis and design has been completed, the systems analyst prepares a full report that gives details of costs, software/hardware required, time-scales and the end results. It also includes details of system testing, how the project is to be controlled, and the requirements for staff training. The systems analyst may very well suggest more than one scheme for systems implementation. The report is circulated for comments to users such as project team members. It is at this stage that revisions are made, if any are needed.

Programming. At this point the systems analyst collaborates with the designer or programmer (if there is one). If problems arise when tests are carried out, then further work may be needed by the systems analyst to find solutions. Please see article 4. APPLICATIONS PROGRAMMER.

Implementation. Systems analysts usually oversee the introduction of their systems, and this could involve the use of various planning and control techniques to ensure that the system is in place to meet customer deadlines.

Systems analysts are employed by a range of firms, such as user organizations, software houses, computer manufacturers and consultancy companies. The scale of work depends on the employer. For example, work for microcomputer users does not necessarily require such intense and time-consuming analysis, since standard 'off-the-shelf' software/hardware can be used. However, in-depth analysis work may be required where large local area networks or micro-to-mainframe links are involved.

Many organizations employ analysts/programmers, who combine analysis and programming skills and are able to implement a project entirely. Please see article 4. APPLICATIONS PROGRAMMER.

WORK ENVIRONMENT

Analysts employed by large users are usually based at one office, although the work may also require travel to other locations.

Consultant systems analysts would be required to travel to the customer's site, either in this country or overseas.

SKILLS AND INTERESTS

Systems analysis is very much a people job, and success depends on the ability to form good working relationships with clients as well as other colleagues. As systems analysis involves investigation and questioning, candidates must be patient and diplomatic in extracting information. Excellent communication skills are important, as analysts may have to sell a system to a client. A good analytical mind, as well as project management skills, are necessary. Systems analysts should also be imaginative and creative in providing solutions.

Such work requires precision and the ability to work methodically, with meticulous attention to detail, as inaccurate work can cost the client money and result in on-going problems.

ENTRY REQUIREMENTS

Entry requirements vary between employers. Most entrants are educated to degree level. Although computing and business are the most relevant degree subjects, they are not essential. Some graduates are able to enter this work direct but many move into it following experience of programming or business. It is also possible for some with experience of programming to enter this work without formal qualifications.

Degree. The minimum entry requirement for a degree course is either two A levels/three H grades with five GCSEs/S grades (A-C/1-3), or equivalent. Some courses require three A levels/four H grades. GCSE/S grade (A-C/1-3) maths is essential for most computer-related degree courses, with A level/H grade maths being required for some.

Postgraduate study. Entry is with good honours in a relevant degree. A postgraduate qualification, however, is not essential to become a systems analyst.

BTEC/SCOTVEC. The minimum entry requirement for higher national awards is either one A level/two H grades with four GCSEs/S grades (A-C/1-3), or equivalent.

Institute of Data Processing Management's (IDPM) higher diploma. Entry requires either: five GCSEs (A-C) including maths and English and two A levels including one in a computing subject; or three S grades (1-3) and four H grades including one in a computing subject; or successful completion of the IDPM's diploma examinations; or four years' experience relevant to computing and minimum age 21.

TRAINING

Degrees. Computer science and computing for business degree courses are offered at many universities and colleges of higher education throughout the UK. Courses usually last three years full-time (four years in Scotland) or four years on a sandwich basis (four or five years in Scotland).

Postgraduate study. Courses are available at universities and colleges of higher education, mostly one year full-time.

BTEC/SCOTVEC. Computer studies higher national courses are offered at many universities, colleges of higher education and colleges of further education throughout the UK. Higher national diplomas usually last two years full-time or three years on a sandwich basis. Higher national certificates usually last two or three years on a day release or evening basis, except in Scotland where they are one year full-time.

Institute of Data Processing Management's (IDPM) higher diploma. The IDPM diploma course is available at over 20 centres, either full-time (usually one year), part-time (two to four years), by self-study or by correspondence course.

Most large employers provide in-house training. In addition, systems analysts may study for the National Computing Centre's Certificate in Systems Analysis and Design (six weeks full-time).

NVQs/SVQs are available at Levels 3 and 4. They include Information Systems Analysis and Design at Level 3 and Information Systems Analysis at Level 4.

Suitably qualified and experienced personnel may apply to

join the British Computer Society (BCS) or other appropriate body.

LATE ENTRY

Entry to systems analysis is no longer confined to those with computer experience. Adult entrants are welcomed, but need some previous experience in business or administration. Professional qualifications or in-house training are the most likely routes for those wanting to gain entry.

OPPORTUNITIES

As more companies rely on computers to carry out a wider range of tasks, so the demand for qualified systems analysts rises. In most cases, it is unlikely that school-leavers would have the necessary experience or qualifications required for such work. A great number of employers do look for candidates with previous experience. Analysis is often an avenue for career progression from programming and design. However, the number of graduates entering this field has risen with some companies offering in-house training programmes.

Opportunities exist within a wide spectrum of organizations, ranging from large user organizations, such as insurance and telecommunication firms, to software houses and small consultancies. Systems analysts employed by larger companies may have the opportunity to work on overseas projects.

In the past, systems analysts were mainly computer specialists, but a growing number are experienced users, who are often known as business systems analysts.

Vacancies are advertised in the press. Please see article 1. MICRO-ELECTRONICS ENGINEER.

PAY AND CONDITIONS

Salaries vary according to experience and geographical location, but a recent survey carried out by The National Computing Centre and the journal *Computer Weekly* suggests that newly appointed systems analysts could expect a salary of between £13,000 and £15,000, whereas an analyst with three years' experience could command £18,000. Salaries for senior personnel may be £30,000+.

Working hours vary, especially for those systems analysts working at clients' offices. Analysts would be required to fit in with the customer, and time-scale pressures may demand unsocial hours.

PROSPECTS

There are opportunities within this field for qualified systems analysts to work freelance or set up their own small consultancies.

Systems analysts can gain promotion from junior analyst to senior analyst and project manager. However, job titles and career progression varies from company to company.

Working as a systems analyst can also prove to be a springboard to other careers in management services and information technology.

RELATED OCCUPATIONS

Work study officer, operational research officer, applications programmer, researcher.

FURTHER INFORMATION AND READING

Please see article 5. COMPUTER SERVICE TECHNICIAN.

4. APPLICATIONS PROGRAMMER (CAV)

THE WORK

Applications programmers design and write specific applications that tell the computer what to do. Some programs are tailored to a specific task and function, while others involve large systems which may be interlinked. Applications programmers take their brief from a systems analyst/designer and they may work together for part of a project as a team, or these roles may be combined into a systems analyst-programmer role.

The applications programmer must follow or interpret the designers' instructions so as to allow the computer system to operate effectively. In order to write an application for a computer, the applications programmer uses certain computer languages. A variety of third and fourth-generation computer languages (or codes) are normally used. COBOL (Common Business Oriented Language) is the most common third-generation programming language for business. Small PC (personal computer)-based systems are written in a wide variety of user-friendly languages, and several new 'windows-based' languages are currently emerging for PCs. Some languages are specialized for scientific computer applications.

New tools or support environments are being developed to help programmers work more efficiently, often called CASE (computer assisted software engineering), or IPSE (integrated project support environment). Some extremely fast programming tasks require the use of low-level assembly languages, which enable the program to run faster, but often take longer to write than when using higher-level languages.

On larger projects, the programming is broken into smaller manageable tasks, and each job is given to a different applications programmer. This requires efficient team work and co-ordination, so CASE tools are used to ensure consistency and that no duplication takes place.

All this work needs to be carefully monitored to ensure quality and effectiveness. Some tools generate the code automatically; therefore the programmer can concentrate on design. Once the coding is complete, the applications programmer tests the software to ensure that the program functions correctly and that there are no faults. This can prove a time-consuming process. Reprogramming and changes may be necessary at this stage.

Programmers can specialize in applications for mainframes, minicomputers or PCs.

WORK ENVIRONMENT

Please see article 3. SYSTEMS ANALYST.

SKILLS AND INTERESTS

Like other personnel working in the information technology industry, applications programmers must be numerate, methodical, logical and clear-minded. Applications programmers need to be able to work systematically through programs, especially when running tests or carrying out modifications.

Programmers may be involved with customers as the end-users, and therefore need to be able to communicate effectively and to be able to explain computer systems to non-specialist staff. Applications programmers work as part of a team and so it is important to be able to get along with other people and work to prescribed deadlines.

ENTRY REQUIREMENTS

There is no standard entry requirement. Some employers accept applicants with A levels/H grades, a BTEC/SCOTVEC national award or equivalent, while others require a BTEC/SCOTVEC higher national award or a degree. It is also possible for some applicants with relevant experience, for example, in computer operating, to enter without formal qualifications. It is common for applicants to undergo an aptitude test.

Degrees. Some employers require a computer-related degree, while others accept degrees unrelated to computing. The minimum entry requirement for a degree course is two A levels/three H grades with five GCSEs/S grades (A-C/1-3), or equivalent. Some courses require three A levels/four H grades. GCSE/S grade (A-C/1-3) maths is essential for most computer-related degree courses, with A level/H grade maths being required for some.

Postgraduate courses. Entry is with a good honours degree, but not necessarily in a relevant subject.

BTEC/SCOTVEC. The minimum entry requirement for BTEC national award courses is either four GCSEs/S grades (A-C/1-3) or a BTEC first award. Entry requirements for SCOTVEC national certificate courses vary. For many modules, no minimum educational qualifications are specified.

The minimum entry requirement for higher national awards is one A level/two H grades with four GCSEs/S grades (A-C/1-3), or equivalent.

City and Guilds. Entry to the Preliminary Certificate in Applications Programming does not require specific qualifications, although City and Guilds advises that it is desirable to have four GCSEs/S grades (A-C/1-3) and a good standard of English, or similar qualifications. Entry to the Applications Programming Certificate requires: a pass in the Preliminary Certificate; or four GCSEs/S grades (A-C/1-3); or passing a selection test.

Institute of Data Processing Management's (IDPM) Applications Programming Certificate. Entry requires: four GCSEs/S grades (A-C/1-3) including English and a numerate subject; or two years' relevant work experience and minimum age 21; or completion of the core and mandatory modules of the IDPM Foundation Course; or minimum age 19 and judged capable of benefiting from the course.

TRAINING

Degree. Relevant degree courses, eg computer science, maths, electronic engineering and computing for business, are offered at many universities and colleges of higher education throughout the UK. Courses usually last three years full-time (four years in Scotland) or four years on a sandwich basis (four or five years in Scotland). Some employers sponsor students through their degree.

Postgraduate courses. These are available at universities and colleges of higher education, mostly one year full-time. There are a number of courses designed for graduates of any discipline to convert their expertise into the information technology field.

BTEC/SCOTVEC. BTEC national diploma courses in computer studies are offered at many colleges in England, Wales and Northern Ireland, mostly two years full-time. BTEC national certificate courses are also offered at many colleges on a day release or evening basis, usually for three years.

SCOTVEC national certificate modules in computing and computer studies are offered at over 20 colleges in Scotland, mainly full-time but also on a block, day release or evening basis.

Many universities and colleges of higher education offer higher national awards in computer studies. Higher national diploma courses usually last two years full-time or three years on a sandwich basis. Higher national certificate courses usually last two or three years on a day release or evening basis, except in Scotland where they are one year full-time.

City and Guilds. The Preliminary Certificate in Applications Programming is offered at many colleges of further education, mainly part-time on a day release or evening basis. The Applications Programming Certificate is offered at approximately 20 colleges of further education full-time, usually for six months, or part-time for a year.

Institute of Data Processing Management's (IDPM) Applications Programming Certificate. The IDPM course can be studied full-time, part-time or by correspondence course for varying lengths of time.

Most large employers provide in-house training, but applications programmers may study for the professional examination of the British Computer Society (BCS). The examination is designed for those without a degree or higher national qualification to satisfy the educational requirements of the BCS at a professional level. Tuition is offered at approximately 25 centres (universities, colleges of higher education, colleges of further education and private colleges), on a block release, day release or evening basis, usually for two or three years. Study is also possible by correspondence course.

A number of NVQs/SVQs are available: Software Production at Level 2, Information Systems and Design and Production at Level 3, Information Systems Delivery and Support Supervision at Level 3, and Information Systems Production Supervision at Level 4.

Specific training opportunities for young people, including Modern Apprenticeships, may be available – contact your local careers office, TEC/LEC for details.

Suitably qualified and experienced personnel may apply to join the BCS or other appropriate body.

LATE ENTRY

The information technology industry welcomes older entrants, although it is harder for individuals in their mid-thirties and above who have no previous computing experience. Employers look for candidates with previous business or computing experience, as well as those with a logical and methodical mind.

Individuals already employed in a business/computing environment may be able to move into applications programming through in-house training schemes or promotion.

OPPORTUNITIES

Many computer manufacturers, computer bureaux, software houses, user organizations and consultancies employ applications programmers. Many organizations, however, combine systems analysis and applications programming into one single job. There is a steady demand for experienced and qualified programmers although there are more opportunities within the large user companies, who are keen to attract trainees.

Information technology is very much a growth area, as software and hardware is becoming more user-friendly and less costly. However, many non-computer specialists now write their own computer applications using generic packages, such as spreadsheets, and the amount of work carried out by applications programmers is therefore declining, whereas software engineering is increasing. Please see article 2. SYSTEMS PROGRAMMER/ SOFTWARE ENGINEER.

PAY AND CONDITIONS

An applications programmer with three years' experience or more can expect to earn a salary of approximately £12,000 to £15,000, while newly qualified programmers may expect a salary of £10,500 to £13,000. Graduate salaries can start at £13,500. Senior programmers may earn a salary in excess of £20,000. Those working in specialist areas, such as scientific programming, or those working abroad, may command higher salaries.

Programmers who combine the work of a systems analyst and an applications programmer can also expect higher salaries. Please see article 3. SYSTEMS ANALYST for hours of work.

PROSPECTS

Applications programmers can progress from trainee to junior positions, through to senior programmers or team leaders with project management and supervisory responsibilities. Team leaders/project managers may be responsible for anything up to twelve programmers and would be expected to prepare schedules and ensure that deadlines are met. Programmers can also move into systems analysis, or more commonly combine analysis and programming to become an analyst programmer.

Applications programmers can also progress into areas such as systems programming, which involves the creation and development of software tools and programming languages. Programmers may also move into systems analysis and design. Please see articles 2. SYSTEMS PROGRAMMER/SOFTWARE ENGINEER and 3. SYSTEMS ANALYST.

RELATED OCCUPATIONS

Systems analyst, systems programmer/software engineer, data processing manager.

FURTHER INFORMATION AND READING

Please see article 5. COMPUTER SERVICE TECHNICIAN.

5. COMPUTER SERVICE TECHNICIAN (CAV/RAL)

THE WORK

In most areas of business and the public sector, computers play a vital role. Many organizations now employ a range of computer systems, all of which need careful servicing and maintenance.

Large computer companies are continually developing and manufacturing new and sophisticated hardware and software, which need installing and maintaining, while older computers may need replacing, upgrading or reconditioning.

As computer hardware and software is now much less expensive than in the past, and the functions of such equipment are continually being enhanced, users tend to replace and update computers rather than pay the high costs of repair work. A service technician spends most of the time installing and servicing equipment, rather than carrying out lengthy repairs.

Hardware service technicians maintain a firm's computer products at the customer's office and respond to requests for installations, servicing, upgrading and, perhaps, emergency repair work. This could range from installing a new disk drive for a word processor to repairing a visual display unit, or connecting additional equipment to an existing desktop publishing system. Very large mainframe computers may also need service attention, especially in emergencies. This can include diagnosing problems when systems break down, running programs through the computer and interpreting the resulting data, locating problems and deciding how to rectify them. Equipment used includes multimeters, earth loop testers and oscilloscopes.

This work requires liaison with computer users, and testing to ensure that the equipment functions effectively. If the hardware cannot be repaired on site, the service technician arranges for spare parts to be ordered or for the equipment to be transferred to a workshop. Some systems are so sophisticated that the computer itself can detect a fault and immediately send a message to a technician to order a spare part.

Software service technicians are on-call to help customers solve software problems and provide technical support. This may involve explaining a certain program function or locating and eradicating a computer virus. Many problems can be solved over the telephone, with the service technician diagnosing the fault and the customer correcting it him or herself. However, if the technician cannot provide a solution, the customer can be referred to a support centre or the manufacturers, where more experienced software technicians are available for the more complex problems.

Engineers are expected to keep up-to-date records of customers, their equipment and work carried out.

WORK ENVIRONMENT

Computer service technicians may spend a great deal of time at customers' premises servicing and installing equipment. However, service technicians are also needed at their own sites to provide technical support and advice over the telephone. Technicians are also employed in technical workshops repairing and reconditioning equipment.

Some jobs require frequent travel, and the service technician may therefore be provided with a car or van, which may be used for private use, depending on employer.

SKILLS AND INTERESTS

It is vital that computer service technicians operate logically, methodically and as quickly as possible. A systematic approach, together with a great deal of patience, is required. They must have a good understanding of electronics and computer science.

Technicians visiting clients are representatives of their company and must therefore dress neatly and behave in a friendly manner. Good communication skills are also essential.

A full clean driving licence is desirable and/or required for some jobs.

ENTRY REQUIREMENTS

Many employers require previous experience in a related area, or a relevant qualification. Most entrants have qualifications at BTEC/SCOTVEC national or higher national level. Some entrants have degrees in relevant subjects. Smaller employers often prefer applicants with experience, as they cannot provide lengthy training. Many employers require candidates to sit an aptitude test as part of the selection process.

BTEC/SCOTVEC. The minimum entry requirement for BTEC national award courses is either four GCSEs/S grades (A-C/1-3), or a BTEC first award. Entry requirements for SCOTVEC national certificate courses vary. For many modules, no minimum educational qualifications are specified.

The minimum entry requirement for higher national awards is one A level/two H grades with four GCSEs/S grades (A-C/1-3), or equivalent.

Degree. The minimum entry requirement for a degree course is two A levels/three H grades with five GCSEs/S grades (A-C/1-3), or equivalent. Some courses require three A levels/four H grades. GCSE/S grade (A-C/1-3) maths is essential for most computer-related degree courses, with A level/H grade maths being required for some.

TRAINING

BTEC/SCOTVEC. BTEC national diploma courses in computer studies are offered at many colleges in England, Wales and Northern Ireland, mostly two years full-time. BTEC national certificate courses are also offered at many colleges on a day release or evening basis, usually for three years.

SCOTVEC national certificate modules in computing and computer studies are offered at over 20 colleges in Scotland, mainly full-time but also on a block, day release or evening basis.

Many universities and colleges of higher education offer higher national awards in software engineering, computing and electrical and electronic engineering. Higher national diploma courses usually last two years full-time or three years on a sandwich basis. Higher national certificate courses usually last two or three years on a day release or evening basis, except in Scotland where they are one year full-time.

Degrees. Relevant degree courses, eg computer science, maths, electronic engineering and computing for business, are offered at many universities and colleges of higher education throughout the UK. Courses usually last three years full-time (four years in Scotland) or four years on a sandwich basis (four or five years in Scotland). Some employers sponsor students through their degree.

Employers usually offer training programmes to new entrants. Training may be provided through in-house courses, external short courses or distance learning programmes.

Computer service technicians may attend courses run by the National Computing Centre. They may study for the professional examination of the British Computer Society (BCS). The examination is designed for those without a degree or higher national qualification to satisfy the educational requirements of the BCS at a professional level. Tuition is offered at approximately 25 centres (universities, colleges of higher education, colleges of further education and private colleges), on a block release,

day release or evening basis, usually for two or three years. Study is also possible by correspondence course.

Suitably qualified and experienced personnel may apply to join the BCS or other appropriate body. This can lead to registration with the Engineering Council as IEng (incorporated engineer), CEng (chartered engineer) and the status of Eur Ing (recognized in Europe).

Specific training opportunities for young people, including Modern Apprenticeships, may be available – contact your local careers office, TEC/LEC for details.

NVQs in Servicing Office Information Technology Equipment and Systems are available at Levels 1, 2 and 3.

LATE ENTRY

Adult entrants must have similar qualifications or/and experience to younger trainees. It is important, however, to keep abreast of new developments.

OPPORTUNITIES

As the use of computers and other hardware products expands, there is a steady demand for experienced staff to provide technical back-up and support. Computer service technicians are usually employed either by servicing companies, computer manufacturers or large users, such as BT and the Ministry of Defence, who require 24-hour 'in-house' servicing for large hardware systems and software.

Vacancies are advertised in the national newspapers and specialist journals such as *Computer Weekly; Computing.*

PAY AND CONDITIONS

Although salaries vary, computer service technicians could expect to earn between £12,000 and £18,000 after training.

The hours worked depend entirely on the customer. Very often a technician will only be able to service the computer when it is not in use. Overtime may therefore be required. Companies offering a 24-hour service would operate a rota or shift system.

PROSPECTS

Promotion opportunities vary, but there is greater scope in larger companies where qualified technicians may become supervisors and managers, directing and scheduling a team of technicians.

Service technicians may also move into work in technical sales and marketing.

RELATED OCCUPATIONS

Business machine service technician, engineer, applications programmer, technician (schools), electrician.

FURTHER INFORMATION

The British Computer Society, 1 Sandford Street, Swindon SN1 1HG, 01793 417 417

The Engineering Council, 10 Maltravers Street, London WC2R 3ER, 0171 240 7891

Federation of Electronics Industry, Russell Square House, 10-12 Russell Square, London WC1B 5EE, 0171 331 2000

Information Technology Industry Training Organization, 16 Berners Street, London W1P 3DD, 0171 580 6677

Institute of Data Processing Management, IDPM House, Edgington Way, Ruxley Corner, Sidcup, Kent DA14 5HR, 0181 308 0747

Institute of Management Services*, 1 Cecil Court, London Road, Enfield, Middlesex EN2 6DD, 0181 363 7452

The National Computing Centre Ltd, Oxford House, Oxford Road, Manchester M1 7ED, 0161 228 6333

FURTHER READING

Leaflets/booklets are available from the addresses marked*.

Job Outlines – Computers – COIC
Working in Computing – COIC
In the careers library classified under CAV; RAL.

1. OPERATIONAL RESEARCHER CLCI:COF
2. ORGANIZATION AND METHODS/ WORK STUDY OFFICER CLCI:COD

BACKGROUND INFORMATION

Industry, commerce and the public sector are able to call on the services of a range of professionals whose specialist skills are used to advise managers and executives on how to make the best use of the resources available to them.

Such experts – sometimes known under the umbrella title of management services consultants – advise on problems of resource allocation and use (finance, staff and equipment) and on the effectiveness of methods and procedures, recommend and design new systems, and advise on long-term strategy.

Historically, work study or industrial engineering was the first management service. It developed from time-and-motion study techniques originating in the USA at the beginning of the century and was based firmly in factory and other manual workplaces, measuring work output. Organization and methods (O&M) came next. Similar techniques for measuring the efficiency of clerical workers began to be applied in the 1920s.

Strictly speaking, work study is still concerned with work measurement: observing and assessing tasks in order to set standard times and skill levels to complete them – information that can be used in determining staffing levels and pay structures – and method study: examining the stages of a manufacturing process and the mechanical and technical equipment used, in order to suggest more efficient ways of carrying out the process.

O&M uses a similar process of analysis and review in relation to clerical and administrative work. It examines working structures, systems, procedures and tasks in order to advise more effective or efficient working practices through the reorganization, rescheduling and reshaping of a system or job, including the introduction of appropriate information and communication technologies.

Since they use similar and overlapping techniques, O&M and work study have to all intents and purposes become a single profession.

Operational research (OR) was used during the Second World War, when it began as part of the UK defence effort. Government scientists started to analyse the campaign against U-boats to establish why it was proving less successful than hoped, and to use mathematical modelling techniques ultimately to plan better air and sea defences. After the war, experts returned to peace-time employment and began to apply their techniques to analysing all types of work-related problems. OR became established in manufacturing industry and, for a while, remained linked with that. Today it is used throughout industry and commerce.

OR originally used computational, statistical and mathematical techniques. These are still an important part of the work, but other techniques are now used. Hard OR makes much use of mathematical modelling, including visually interactive models, on which the effects of altering the speed of machinery or substituting pieces of equipment can be simulated on a computer screen. Soft OR refers to various techniques (usually of a graphical nature, using diagrams, flip charts, etc, though computer-based methods are emerging) that help people understand or structure problems, rather than necessarily pointing towards a solution. Visual models built for managers to experiment with as decision support systems come under the heading of soft OR.

Operational research is concerned with more complex situations than are work study/O&M. It is used in all kinds of situations, but particularly where large-scale problems of logistics are concerned – in oil extraction, defence planning or large-scale manufacturing.

1. OPERATIONAL RESEARCHER (COF)

THE WORK

Operational researchers support and advise the managers and executives who take the key decisions in an organization by using a broadly-based scientific or logical approach to examine managerial problems.

They may be consulted about decisions as varied as where to build a new factory, how to estimate the profitability of a new crop on a typical farm, how to lay out shelves to maximize profit in a supermarket, how to improve economy and efficiency in health authorities or local councils, or where to re-route a local bus service. They may be concerned with strategic or immediate problems.

Working alone or as part of a small team, operational researchers first establish what the problem is and what solution is hoped for. They then gather information, finding out how the present system works, what inefficiencies must be changed and what is worth retaining.

They often interview a wide range of people, for example directors, managers and workers at all levels, about the nature of the problem.

When they have completed the initial research they represent the system being examined with a model. Models can produce erroneous outputs, since assumptions have to be made. To guard against this possibility, accuracy is tested against already known data (known as validating the model). The model is used to compare various solutions.

Finally they present the results, often suggesting several different solutions and their recommendations to the managers who asked for their assistance. Often they produce a computer 'decision support' system, designed to help managers in making decisions in similar future situations.

WORK ENVIRONMENT

Operational researchers are based in offices, but the work involves interacting with people at their places of work. Depending on the projects they are engaged on, they visit different business and industrial environments: factories, offices, shops, and building sites and processing plants. Some projects require a considerable amount of travel, long periods away from home and possibly travel overseas.

SKILLS AND INTERESTS

Operational researchers must be capable of analysing technical and complex problems, handling large amounts of data and using computers. They need the ability to use the data they have acquired to get to the core of the problem, and they need logical and creative minds to produce potential solutions. They must be accurate and attentive to detail. While a solid grounding in maths is essential, not all problems require a high level of mathematical techniques. Many require a greater emphasis on numerical ability.

Communication skills are equally important, as operational

researchers spend approximately one third of their time in analysing problems, and two thirds in discussing, interviewing, writing reports and giving verbal presentations to clients in meetings.

They must be able to talk easily to a variety of people when conducting the early stages of research during a project, and discuss the results confidently with senior managers and directors.

The ability to write clear, concise reports and explain technical matters to non-experts in easily understood language is essential.

Persuasive skills are important, since they are, in effect, selling their solutions.

Operational researchers should also be flexible – able to work on very different types of project according to the needs of their clients.

ENTRY REQUIREMENTS

Most entrants are graduates and hold a master's degree in Operational Research. Although entry with A levels or equivalent qualifications is possible in theory, in practice it is almost impossible to find a traineeship.

Minimum entry requirements to a degree course are five GCSEs/S grades (A-C/1-3) plus two A level/three H grades or equivalent. Normal requirements are three A levels at grade C and above/four to five H grades at grade B.

There are some first degrees that include OR, although it is not necessary to have taken one. Other preferred subjects are maths, statistics, sciences, economics, business studies or computer studies.

An A level/H grade standard in a maths-related subject is the usual minimum requirement for those whose degree is not in a similar subject. Most people with a degree in a non-related subject may choose to take a one or two-year full-time postgraduate course in Operational Research, Management Science or Management Systems. A list is available from the Operational Research Society.

TRAINING

Training is on-the-job, usually supplemented by postgraduate training for entrants at first-degree level. Employers with large OR departments run graduate training programmes which assign new entrants to OR teams and permit them to work on projects under supervision, gradually giving them more responsibility. These programmes often include the opportunity to take a part-time MSc course.

Most employers also provide training in communication, presentation, business and management skills.

LATE ENTRY

Although late entry is by no means impossible, the majority of entrants come straight from university.

OPPORTUNITIES

There are opportunities throughout industry, commerce, local and central government, in the Health Service and in independent management consultancies. The Operational Research Society estimates that over 250 organizations employ OR staff.

Major employers include manufacturers, the oil industry, large retailers, banks, building societies, local authorities and central government departments including the Treasury, Ministry of Defence, the Inland Revenue, Customs and Excise, the Department of Health and the Home Office.

There are also increasing opportunities to work in consultancies, which are retained on a fee-paying basis by organizations that do not have their own departments, or sometimes by those that do have their own OR staff, to work on specialized assignments. It is quite possible, during the course of an OR career, to work for several different types of employer. Opportunities for self-employment and part-time work are good.

Vacancies appear in the national press and in the OR newsletter, supplied to members of the OR Society. The Society can also provide a list of organizations that intend to recruit new people to work in OR in the current year.

PAY AND CONDITIONS

Newly qualified operational researchers can expect to earn from £13,000 to £17,000. Those entering with an MSc can expect £15,000 to £22,000. With experience, high salaries can be expected. OR managers earn at least £40,000, but salaries can exceed £70,000.

Hours of work vary with the project being undertaken. It is often necessary to work in the evenings or to take work home, particularly when the deadline for the end of the project and the presentation of a report is approaching.

PROSPECTS

Prospects for promotion or advancement are very good. Within OR departments there are prospects of promotion to project and team leader, then to department manager.

There are opportunities to set up one's own consultancy business.

Promotion into general management within a company is becoming very usual. Operational researchers gain a thorough knowledge and overview of the workings of their organizations and are therefore well placed to move into management in other departments, such as marketing or production. Many senior managers and company directors have OR backgrounds.

RELATED OCCUPATIONS

Computer systems programmer, actuary, organization and methods officer, statistician, systems analyst, operations manager.

FURTHER INFORMATION

Operational Research Society*, Seymour House, 12 Edward Street, Birmingham B1 2RX, 0121 233 9300

FURTHER READING

Leaflets/booklets are available from the address marked*.

In the careers library classified under COF.

2. ORGANIZATION AND METHODS/ WORK STUDY OFFICER (COD)

THE WORK

O&M/work study takes place in almost all large organizations, which normally have their own work study/O&M teams.

Like operational researchers, O&M/work study officers are often called in by managers and requested to solve a problem. Alternatively, the management services department or section may have a brief to monitor performance levels and identify problems or opportunities for investigation. The need is usually to improve working practices in order to achieve greater productivity, efficiency or economy, to improve quality or to improve workers' health and safety.

They record (using a variety of charts and other recording techniques), examine and critically analyse the way in which a series of tasks is performed, in order to identify parts of the work that can be eliminated, combined, simplified or made more efficient by the introduction of new tools or equipment.

The projects they work on could range from reorganizing a company's post room – by such simple tasks as restructuring the work, changing the work flow, redesigning workstations or rescheduling activities to reduce the amount of walking, sorting and carrying – to investigating the implications of closing a local authority's public enquiry office in a small town and moving the workload to an office in another.

O&M officers/work study officers visit employees at their workplace to interview them in depth about their work. They observe them and possibly use work measurement to obtain times for the completion of certain tasks. Such observation and measurement sometimes makes use of sampling techniques to obtain data quickly, reliably and economically. Their observations may include the tasks that are performed, the persons doing the work, the sequence of the work, the physical layout, the tools and equipment and the conditions. Each of these are then examined to see if improvement can be made. O&M officers/workstudy officers usually write a detailed report showing their observations and making recommendations for the change.

WORK ENVIRONMENT

Please see article 1. OPERATIONAL RESEARCHER.

SKILLS AND INTERESTS

Personal qualities are very important in work study/O&M work. Employees are often anxious or hostile, since they may be worried about the implications for their jobs. Good communication and interview skills are necessary to put people at ease, reassure them about the purpose of a survey and win their co-operation. Persuasive powers are needed to convince managers of the need for a survey and to sell the recommendations when the investigation is completed.

Work study/O&M officers must also be able to liaise with other experts, who explain to them some of the technical features of the production processes being investigated.

A logical and orderly mind is essential, with the ability to grasp the core of a problem, research it, discard irrelevant material and produce a solution.

Work study/O&M officers must also be able to express themselves clearly in writing, since the end result of a survey is usually a written report.

Most of their work is carried out in teams. The ability to work well with colleagues is important.

ENTRY REQUIREMENTS

There are no formal entry requirements but an increasing number of practitioners have degrees.

Although employers consider personal qualities more important than degree subject, some may give preference to entrants with degrees in business studies, computing, engineering or economics.

The minimum qualifications required for entry to a degree course, or to take the examinations of the Institute of Management Services (which is the professional body for work study/O&M officers), are five GCSEs/S grades (A-C/1-3) plus two at A level/three at H grade or equivalent.

School-leavers with A levels/H grades either join an organization as work study/O&M or general management trainees, study part-time for qualifications of the Institute of Management Services and move into O&M/work study later.

Graduates/higher national diploma holders may be recruited to O&M/work study directly or join companies' general graduate trainee management programmes.

TRAINING

Most organizations put trainees through a planned training programme which involves working on real projects under the guidance of senior staff.

Some companies give graduate entrants the opportunity to study for an MBA.

Most employers expect trainees to obtain membership of the Institute of Management Services by obtaining appropriate qualifications from the Institute, or qualifications recognized by the Institute as equivalent.

The Institute offers a Certificate in Management Services which may be studied on a part-time basis over one year or through distance learning. The certificate may be followed by study for the Institute's diploma.

People with suitable qualifications may be given subject-for-subject exemptions at diploma level.

LATE ENTRY

This is frequently a second career, often not entered before the mid-twenties. People with relevant experience in commerce or industry are particularly welcome.

OPPORTUNITIES

The Institute of Management Services has approximately 7,000 members, the majority of whom are engaged in the promotion and development of productivity and quality through techniques such as workstudy, O&M and similar analytical methodologies. The incorporation of such approaches into mainstream management education and practice means the demand for specialist practitioners is decreasing slightly.

Most practitioners work in teams within organizations, but some are employed by management consultancies that work on a freelance basis for employers who do not have their own in-house teams.

There are opportunities nation-wide in large commercial companies, with banks, retailers and in manufacturing industry. There are also some in local authorities, central government departments and the health service, although these organizations now tend to use outside consultancies as and when necessary.

Job vacancies are advertised in the national and local press and in *Management Services,* the journal of the Institute of Management Services.

PAY AND CONDITIONS

Salaries vary between employers, but a new entrant could expect a salary of approximately £12,000. Experienced practitioners may earn between £16,000 and £25,000, while senior posts carry salaries of up to £40,000.

Hours are normally 9am to 5pm, Monday to Friday, but will vary according to the job being studied.

PROSPECTS

There are prospects of promotion to team leader and on to department head within the profession itself. Many practitioners use the experience and skills they have gained to move into general management.

RELATED OCCUPATIONS

Please see article 1. OPERATIONAL RESEARCHER.

FURTHER INFORMATION

Institute of Management Services*, 1 Cecil Court, London Road, Enfield, Middlesex EN12 6DD, 0181 363 7452

FURTHER READING

Leaflets/booklets are available from the address marked*.

In the careers library classified under COD.

TRADING STANDARDS OFFICER
CLCI:COP

BACKGROUND INFORMATION

Local authorities have a statutory duty to enforce standards of fairness and safety that are laid down by law for the protection of consumers and traders. The Trading Standards Service puts into effect the large and growing range of legislation on consumer affairs.

The most important measures include the Trade Description Act, Weights and Measures Act, Food Safety Act and laws on consumer credit and consumer protection. Product Safety and Fair Trading legislation encompasses a vast area of commercial activity. Other regulations concern prices, road traffic and animal health. Under the Weights and Measures Act, trading standards officers (TSOs) have the right to enter trade premises to carry out inspections. The Citizens' Charter sets out quality standards and, from 1994, TSOs have been obliged to grade and monitor all businesses in their areas.

THE WORK

Trading standards officers visit traders in their area to check on fair practice and give advice on the legislation that applies to them. Some visits are pre-arranged, some unannounced. Many are routine inspections, but others are made in response to complaints.

All sorts of businesses are covered: shops, street-markets, garages, factories, dairies, night clubs, finance companies and many others. Officers test and certify the weighing machines in shops and the petrol pumps at filling stations. They take samples of goods such as bread, meat pies, paint or fabric for analysis in the laboratory. TSOs check that information on labels is accurate and that advertisements do not mislead. Cases of fraud can involve them in long, complex investigations.

Duties vary to some extent from one place to another. In rural areas, TSOs may spend part of the time visiting farms to take milk samples or attending markets to oversee the loading of cattle trucks. In cities, there may be problems with milometers at used-car showrooms, with counterfeit goods in street-markets, or with inadequate packaging at a factory. At ports and airports, TSOs work with customs officers to inspect imported goods. They watch constantly for safety hazards such as small parts in toys or inflammable material in furniture.

A trader who refuses to comply with the law can be taken to court. Here, the case is conducted by a solicitor or a senior TSO, but the officer bringing the case compiles the evidence and may act as a witness in court.

In the office, TSOs may take turns as duty officers, receiving complaints and enquiries and advising people on their legal position.

To gain the co-operation of business and industry and to educate the public on their rights as consumers, trading standards officers give talks to trade associations, schools and other community groups.

Officers write reports on all cases and keep statistics on the problems they encounter. They plan their own work, in liaison with the police, environmental health officers, laboratory scientists and others. They attend meetings and may supervise assistants and trainees who help with scientific, technical or legal work.

WORK ENVIRONMENT

Trading standards officers are based at an office, but spend much of their time out visiting traders and suppliers, and sometimes interviewing consumers at home. Usually, they go out alone, sometimes taking an assistant, but a major investigation would involve a team of officers. Court attendance is regularly required. Officers enter all sorts of premises, some of them dirty and smelly. Protective clothing is provided.

SKILLS AND INTERESTS

Initiative, determination and resilience are demanded in organizing and carrying out inspections and investigations. Trading standards officers need the ability to take a clear, impartial view of a situation, and should be able to justify their decisions.

Good communication skills are essential. They have to talk to people from a variety of backgrounds – interviewing, advising or persuading. Trading standards officers should be good listeners and very observant. A firm but tactful manner is required. They also need the ability to write clear, concise reports and the confidence to present them in court. Team work is important, as they work in co-operation with colleagues and other professionals.

The job demands interest and aptitude in both technology and law.

ENTRY REQUIREMENTS

The minimum requirements for trainee TSOs are five GCSEs/S grades (A-C/1-3) and two A levels/three H grades, including English, maths and physics at either level, or equivalent qualifications. Many new entrants hold a degree. Maths, science, technology and business subjects are all relevant to some extent, but a wide range of degrees is acceptable.

These qualifications enable a trainee to enrol for the in-service course leading to the Diploma in Trading Standards, the statutory qualification for trading standards officers.

A driving licence is generally required after qualification.

An alternative means of qualification is the BA (Hons) Degree in Consumer Protection at Manchester Metropolitan University. Entry requirements are five GCSEs/S grades (A-C/1-3) in English language, maths and a science, and two A levels/three H grades, or equivalent. Similar courses are being developed at other centres.

TRAINING

The Diploma in Trading Standards (DTS) is administered by the Local Government Management Board. The course lasts three years and combines supervised work experience with block release to college in London, Glasgow or Weston-Super-Mare. The two-part examination covers civil and criminal consumer law, metrology, statistics, trading practice, quality assurance, enforcement and advice.

The degree course in Consumer Protection lasts three years full-time. It covers all the academic material from the DTS and, in addition, information technology, management studies, quality management and consumer protection. To qualify as a trading standards officer, students undertake a further period of practical training in the Trading Standards Service after completing their degree.

LATE ENTRY

There are no upper age limits. Applications are welcome from adults with relevant work experience, for example in health and safety, food hygiene, laboratory work or citizens' advice.

However, there are no exemptions from the DTS course and all applicants are expected to hold the minimum entry qualifications of three GCSEs/S grades and two A levels/ three H grades.

Adults are welcome to apply for the degree in consumer protection at Manchester Metropolitan University. There may be some flexibility over normal entry requirements for those with relevant experience.

OPPORTUNITIES

The Trading Standards Service is run by local authorities – county, regional or islands councils, metropolitan and borough councils. The department may also be named Consumer Protection, Consumer Services or Public Protection.

There are about 1,500 trading standards officers in the UK, and a shortage of qualified staff. However, it can be difficult to find training places and competition is fierce.

There is an increasing demand for qualified TSOs in private industry. They work in businesses such as retailing or food manufacture, as advisers on consumer law or in quality control and management.

PAY AND CONDITIONS

Salary scales vary widely. Newly qualified TSOs normally earn between £16,000 and £17,000.

A 37-hour week is normal. This may include working at night and at weekends, for example inspecting pubs and nightclubs or checking on Sunday trading.

PROSPECTS

The promotion structure leads through the grades of senior officer, section head and divisional officer to deputy and chief TSO. There are usually good opportunities for advancement, although it often means relocation. An increasing number of TSOs join the private sector.

It is possible to specialize in particular aspects of the job, such as safety, consumer credit, animal health or advertising standards. Short in-service courses on these special topics are run by the Institute of Trading Standards Administration, the professional organization for trading standards officers. Part-time management courses, such as the Diploma in Management Studies, are available for senior staff.

The ITSA offers various grades of membership from studentship to retirement.

RELATED OCCUPATIONS

Environmental health officer, consumer adviser, HM factory inspector, quality controller, police officer, scientist/ technician.

FURTHER INFORMATION

The Institute of Trading Standards Administration*, 3-5 Hadleigh Business Centre, 351 London Road, Hadleigh, Essex SS7 2BT, 01702 559922

Anyone wishing to find out more about this work is advised to contact their local trading standards department.

FURTHER READING

Leaflets/booklets are available from the address marked*.

Working in Local Government – COIC

In the careers library classified under COP.

1. ENVIRONMENTAL HEALTH OFFICER
CLCI:COP
2. HEALTH AND SAFETY INSPECTOR
CLCI:COT

1. ENVIRONMENTAL HEALTH OFFICER (COP)

BACKGROUND INFORMATION

The care and protection of the environment and its inhabitants are major modern issues. People are much more aware of environmental damage and the possible risks it presents in terms of health and well-being. Public concern about industrial pollution and disease has led to an increase in demand for protection and prevention.

Environmental health officers work to protect people from the risks and dangers resulting from all types of environmental hazard. Legislation covers many aspects of their work including food safety, noise, industrial waste, housing, occupational health and safety, pollution control and control of infectious disease. They use their statutory powers to enforce regulations, improve the environment and reduce pollution. Much of their work is advisory.

THE WORK

Environmental health officers have a wide range of responsibilities. These include food safety, public health, and the control and notification of infectious disease, housing, workplace conditions and safety. The work involves inspecting premises, monitoring conditions, and carrying out investigations by collecting and evaluating evidence. Typical incidents include pollution and outbreaks of infections like typhoid, salmonella and hepatitis. They give help and advice whenever necessary.

Officers visit homes, shops, abattoirs, factories, catering outlets, rubbish dumps, air or sea ports and other places in order to check food safety, hygiene, pests, working conditions, pollution emissions, etc. They collect samples and specimens for laboratory testing and take account of the results in decision making. This part of the work involves close liaison with experts like scientists, microbiologists and building surveyors, who can offer specialized support.

A report is usually written about every visit. Ongoing problems are regularly followed up and monitored. They attend meetings and give talks to consumers, producers and other interested parties. A major part of the job involves bringing changes in legislation to the attention of those affected and educating them so that they are aware of their responsibilities.

An important aspect of the work is prosecuting offenders on behalf of the local authority. When it becomes necessary to prosecute a case, the officer involved collects and prepares the evidence. This is presented at a court hearing and the officer may have to give evidence under oath. In many cases environmental health officers are able to give a warning and encourage those who have broken the law to avoid the problem in the future.

WORK ENVIRONMENT

Officers spend most of their time working alone outside the office. They may visit unpleasant, dirty places and wear protective clothing including hats, masks, boots and overalls.

SKILLS AND INTERESTS

The work requires investigative and decision-making abilities. It suits those who are interested in the quality of life and the well-being of other people and who enjoy solving problems. An interest in social problems and helping others to solve them is useful. Environmental health officers need a methodical, careful approach to gathering facts and assessing evidence.

A good standard of written and spoken communication skills is required, because environmental health officers deal with a wide range of people and prepare reports. It is important to be able to discuss problems with the public and colleagues. Negotiating skills and a patient, diplomatic manner are assets; environmental health officers must remain polite at all times.

A high level of scientific and technical understanding is necessary when checking pollution, safety and industrial processes, and interpreting rules like building regulations. Officers must be able to use their own judgement when examining and assessing hazards and to apply scientific principles.

It is important to be thorough, persistent and self-confident in order to make enquiries successfully; some of the people they meet may resent their work. Some site visits require a certain amount of physical agility and occasionally involve working at heights and in confined spaces.

ENTRY REQUIREMENTS

The minimum entry requirements in England and Wales are five GCSEs (A-C) with two A levels, or equivalents. One A level must be a science, and the GCSEs must include English, maths and another science. Many new entrants are graduates; entry to a degree course requires a minimum of five GCSEs (A-C), with two A levels. As much of the work has a scientific bias, people with qualifications in biology, food science, physics or biochemistry are preferred.

In Scotland, entrants must complete a four-year BSc in Environmental Health at the University of Strathclyde; entry is with four H grade passes (at B level) in maths, chemistry, and one other science subject. A pass in English at H grade or S grade is also required. Students who study for this degree are advised to obtain an appointment as a student environmental health officer with a local authority that is prepared to offer sponsorship.

A driving licence is usually required.

TRAINING

England and Wales

Training is via a four-year sandwich degree in Environmental Health/Science or a two-year MSc sandwich course for those who already have a degree in a natural science. The Institute keeps a list of approved courses that lead to the award of the Certificate of Registration of the Environmental Health Officers Registration Board.

Scotland

The recognized qualification for environmental health officers in Scotland is the Diploma in Environmental Health of the Royal Environmental Health Institute of Scotland. Candidates for the Diploma must hold an honours degree in Environmental Health.

Most trainees are appointed as student environmental health officers with a district council before starting a degree course. To gain the Diploma in Environmental Health, students are required to undertake 48 weeks of practical training, followed by a professional interview aimed at assessing their practical skills.

The courses that trainees undertake cover the full range of their duties. Topics include chemistry, microbiology, food science and hygiene, statistics, law, housing, public health, occupational health and safety, and pollution. There is a high scientific content, as much of the work relates to the identification and control of problems that can often only be identified in the laboratory.

LATE ENTRY

There are no age restrictions on entry to this occupation. For those with relevant work experience, the usual entry requirements may be waived.

OPPORTUNITIES

Environmental health services are provided at district levels of local government. There are around 6,000 qualified environmental health officers employed by local authorities throughout the country.

There is a steady demand for qualified staff, though applicants may have to move to find a suitable vacancy. Cutbacks in local authority spending have led to a decline in the number of training places available. This has led to fierce competition for trainee posts. The situation may change, depending on local and national government policy and funding.

A growing number are employed by hotel and retail companies and food manufacturers. Others work as self-employed consultants to industry and commerce.

PAY AND CONDITIONS

Salaries vary between individual local authorities. Newly qualified environmental health officers may earn from £17,055 to £21,351. Those working in the London area are paid additional allowances.

The work is 35 to 39 hours a week, with a rota covering occasional weekend and night duties. It may be necessary to make visits outside the normal hours, in the early mornings and evenings. Flexitime and part-time work may be available.

In Scotland, newly qualified environmental health officers enter on a salary scale starting at £17,000 rising to £21,000.

PROSPECTS

There is a clear promotion path into management, becoming a chief environmental health officer, or section leader, after gaining experience and proving managerial ability. It is usual to obtain further qualifications and specialize in certain aspects of the work.

RELATED OCCUPATIONS

Trading standards officer, health and safety inspector, quality controller, safety officer, forensic scientist, meat inspector.

FURTHER INFORMATION

Chartered Institute of Environmental Health*, Chadwick Court, 15 Hatfields, London SE1 8DJ, 0171 928 6006

The Royal Environmental Health Institute of Scotland*, 3 Manor Place, Edinburgh EH3 7DH, 0131 225 6999

The Local Government Management Board*, 4th Floor, Arndale House, Arndale Centre, Luton LU1 2TS, 01582 451166

FURTHER READING

Leaflets/booklets are available from the addresses marked*.

Working in Local Government – COIC

Careers in Local Government – Kogan Page

In the careers library classified under COP.

2. HEALTH AND SAFETY INSPECTOR (COT)

BACKGROUND INFORMATION

Health and safety inspectors are civil servants, employed by the Health and Safety Executive, a part of the Department of the Environment. The Executive is responsible for ensuring the health and safety of workers and members of the public who may be affected by work activities, and for minimizing injuries caused by unsafe working practices. Through its inspectors it is responsible for enforcing all health and safety legislation and may prosecute offenders where necessary.

The Executive is divided into a number of divisions, the largest of which is the Field Operations Division. This is made up of the Factory, Agricultural and Quarries Inspectorates, plus the Field Consultant Groups and the Employment Medical Advisory Service.

Despite the name, factory inspectors do not only visit industrial premises. They are also responsible for hospitals, docks, construction sites, sports grounds, fairgrounds, and commercial premises other than shops, which are the responsibility of environmental health officers. Specialist inspectors in the Field Consultant Groups cover technical aspects, such as mechanical engineering, chemicals, construction, electrical matters and explosives. The Agricultural Inspectorate looks after agricultural, horticultural and forestry establishments. Other Inspectorates deal with Railways, Offshore Safety, Mines, Nuclear Installations, and Chemicals and Explosives.

This article deals mainly with the more general work and training of the factory inspectors and, to some degree, of agricultural inspectors.

THE WORK

Health and safety inspectors work from area offices within one of seven regions and are responsible for the inspection of all workplaces within that area. They work in groups of three or four inspectors, reporting to a principal inspector. National Interest Groups have responsibility for the policy relating to different sectors of industry. Within limitations, inspectors have much freedom in planning their own work. Divisional Headquarters gives guidelines on work targets, but much is left to the discretion of local offices, which know the needs of their own areas.

A principal inspector may allocate a number of premises to each inspector, who must then draw up their own plans for the year's work. Not all premises can be visited annually, but inspectors must know which are 'high risk', or have proved unsatisfactory on previous visits, as against those which can safely be inspected less regularly.

Inspectors usually give no advance warning of their visits.

They are mainly concerned with the management's or employer's strategies for controlling risks to health and safety. On arrival, they ask to see the person in charge and are taken on a tour of the premises. They check machinery, equipment, substances and working methods. Among the things they are looking for might be unguarded machinery, toxic or inflammable materials not stored correctly, workers taking short cuts to increase speed but ignoring safety regulations, and excessive levels of dust or fumes. If they see any evidence of unsafe practices, they first try to persuade the owner or manager to remedy the situation. If verbal advice is ignored they may take several legal steps, from issuing a written 'improvement' notice, which gives an employer a certain period of time to put matters right, a 'prohibition' order, ordering work to cease until the required improvement is made, to making a prosecution. Inspectors use prosecution as a last resort and prefer to achieve their objectives by persuasion and diplomacy.

After each visit, inspectors write a full report.

About 35 per cent of inspections are routine assessments. Inspectors carry out the rest in response to complaints, accidents or disasters.

If inspectors feel in need of more technical help, they can obtain this by calling in an expert from a regional team of specialist inspectors. They may also use the services of the Health and Safety Executive's own research and analytical laboratories, or ask advice from the Employment Medical Advisory Service.

Inspectors in England and Wales conduct their own prosecutions in the magistrates' courts or, if a case goes to a higher court, they provide the necessary information for lawyers conducting the case and appear as witnesses. In Scotland, inspectors refer cases for prosecution to the Procurator Fiscal. If a case goes to trial the inspector may be called as a witness.

WORK ENVIRONMENT

Inspectors are based in offices, but spend at least 50 percent of their time visiting a wide variety of workplaces, both indoors and outside. Conditions may be noisy, dirty, smelly or dangerous. They may have to work outdoors in all weathers, at height or in confined spaces, for example crawling under road tunnels to examine air ducts. When necessary, they wear protective clothing.

SKILLS AND INTERESTS

Health and safety inspectors need to be observant, able to pay attention to detail, and make accurate assessments of potential safety hazards. They must be capable of absorbing a large amount of information, continually updating their knowledge, keeping abreast both of new technology in the various work places, and changes to health and safety legislation.

They must enjoy working on their own, be willing to make their own decisions and accept responsibility for them. However, they must also know when to ask colleagues for advice, or when to call on the expertise of a specialist inspector for technical help.

They must be able to plan their own work, and be sufficiently flexible to change their plans in response to a sudden emergency that requires an immediate visit.

Inspectors must be good communicators, as they need to establish relationships with a wide range of people: employers, managers, workers and those in other government departments. Since they rely heavily on advice and persuasion in their work they must be tactful and diplomatic, yet forceful when necessary.

Public speaking skills are important. If they do decide to bring a prosecution they must be able to present facts clearly when presenting the case in court. Senior inspectors sometimes have to give press and television interviews, either following an incident or as part of a particular publicity campaign.

Written communication skills are also important, since inspectors have to write reports on investigations and inspections they carry out.

ENTRY REQUIREMENTS

Factory and agricultural inspectors must have: an honours degree in any discipline, plus a GCSE/S grade (A-C/1-3) in maths; or an ordinary degree or BTEC/SCOTVEC higher award in a scientific or technological subject, with GCSE/S grade (A-C/1-3) in maths; plus appropriate industrial or managerial experience.

Entry requirements for degree and higher diploma courses vary according to the subject of study and the university or college chosen.

Minimum entry requirements for a degree course are usually: two A levels/three H grades plus five GCSEs/S grades (A-C/1-3); or Advanced GNVQ/GSVQ III; or a BTEC/SCOTVEC national award; or equivalent.

Entry to higher national diploma courses is usually with a minimum of: one A level/two H grades plus GCSEs and S grades; or Advanced GNVQ/GSVQ III; or a BTEC/SCOTVEC national award; or equivalent.

Inspectors working in the inspectorates for nuclear installations, mines and quarries, industrial air pollution, and specialist inspectors, must have appropriate first degrees followed by postgraduate training or experience.

All entrants must meet Civil Service nationality requirements and possess a full driving licence.

TRAINING

Factory and agricultural inspectors have a two year training period, the first year of which is probationary.

Practical training is conducted on-the-job. Trainees usually work in a number of different industry groups during the training period. At first they accompany and observe experienced inspectors, then gradually carry out site visits under supervision as they gain in confidence, writing reports which they discuss with a senior inspector.

They also attend a number of short, in-house specialist courses, including a one-week course in communication skills.

In the second year of training they attend modular training courses that lead to the award of a postgraduate diploma in Occupational Health and Safety developed by the Health and Safety Executive in conjunction with Aston, Birmingham and Loughborough Universities. Specialist inspectors receive on-the-job training, but are not required to take the postgraduate qualification.

An NVQ/SVQ Level 4 relevant to health and safety inspectors is being developed.

During the course of their careers, health and safety inspectors attend frequent courses to update their knowledge. They are expected to acquire a good understanding of legal and technical matters.

HEALTH AND SAFETY: COP/COT

LATE ENTRY

Applicants are welcome up to the age of 55 years. All entrants must, however, possess the normal entry requirements to become health and safety inspectors.

Adults applying for degree and higher national diploma courses may find that they are accepted without the normal entry requirements. They can prepare for applications to such courses by undertaking an approved higher education access course. Access courses are offered at local colleges and are usually one year full-time or one to two years part-time with daytime and/or evening attendance.

OPPORTUNITIES

There are approximately 660 factory inspectors, working in 20 area offices. The number is slowly increasing to meet a target figure of 675. A total of 170 agricultural inspectors are employed. Numbers of specialist inspectors are much smaller.

There are opportunities to work in different industry groups as an individual inspector's interests develop, to move to the head office on Merseyside and to work in branches concerned with policy-making in London.

PAY AND CONDITIONS

A new entrant is paid on a scale ranging from £15,363 to £23,009. On promotion, the next post carries a salary between £17,485 and £31,492. Annual increments are dependent on performance.

Health and safety inspectors work a standard five-day week, Monday to Friday, of 37 hours nationally except in London (36), but must be prepared to make some visits at unsocial hours or at weekends in the case of emergencies.

Inspectors are expected to take up appointment in any part of the country and they must also expect to be transferred at intervals during their service to other field posts, to headquarters in Merseyside or to a policy branch in London, although personal preferences are taken into account.

Job sharing, part-time work and work during the school terms only are quite common.

PROSPECTS

Inspectors are recruited as Inspectors Class 2. They should gain promotion to Class 1B after two years, subject to satisfactory performance.

There are possibilities of promotion to senior posts of Principal Inspector and above, with corresponding levels of responsibility.

RELATED OCCUPATIONS

Environmental health officer, health and safety consultant, occupational hygienist, safety officer, trading standards officer.

FURTHER INFORMATION

Health and Safety Executive*, St Hugh's House, Stanley Precinct, Bootle L20 3QY, 0151 951 4000

Office of Public Service and Science (OPSS)*, Cabinet Office, Fastream and European Staffing Division, Room 127/2, Horse Guards Road, London SW1P 3AL, 0171 270 5697

FURTHER READING

Leaflets/booklets are available from the addresses marked*.

Working in The Civil Service – COIC

In the careers library classified under COT.

1. **GRAPHIC DESIGNER CLCI:ED**
2. **ILLUSTRATOR/ARTIST CLCI:ED**
3. **THREE-DIMENSIONAL DESIGNER CLCI:EG**
4. **FASHION DESIGNER CLCI:EJ**
5. **TEXTILE DESIGNER CLCI:EP**
6. **INTERIOR DESIGNER CLCI:ET**

BACKGROUND INFORMATION

There are very few areas of modern living that are not influenced by the work of artists and designers. Every item in the sitting room of a house is produced using art and design skills – furniture, carpets, wall coverings, curtains, television sets, telephones, ornaments and paintings have all been professionally designed or painted. Design techniques also extend to every other room from kitchen to bathroom, and in the wider environment to advertisements, books, exhibitions, buildings like schools, hospitals, shops, offices and factories, and transport systems.

The distinction between art and design is not clear-cut, but in general it is accepted that artists are concerned purely with self-expression. They create pieces of work that people will eventually buy because they like them. Designers could be described as applied artists. They use a combination of creativity and technical knowledge to produce designs for products that serve a specific purpose while at the same time are pleasing to look at.

Designers have to accept limits on their creativity, since articles have to be produced within set time limits and to stipulated budgets; the clients commissioning the work will usually have their own ideas and requirements. Depending on their specialism, they may produce a design for selling and promotional purposes that must have a sharp impact on consumers, as in advertising and marketing. Alternatively, they may design a product or a piece of equipment that has to be reliable and safe to use.

Whilst some design work is concerned with totally new products, the majority is concerned with modifications or improvements to existing ones.

Two-dimensional design communicates ideas through illustration, colour and, often, words, on flat surfaces. It includes graphic, textile and surface pattern design (for furnishing fabrics, china and pottery).

Three-dimensional design is concerned with the effective use of form and space and embraces many specialisms: fashion, glass, ceramics, furniture, interior exhibition, industrial, theatre design, and jewellery and silversmithing.

Graphic design is part of the communications industry. Graphic designers have to know how to put across a message for information or publicity purposes, using illustration, line and colour. They work closely with copy writers or advertising writers who produce the text of an advertisement, leaflet, etc.

Illustration is concerned with the paintings and drawings that stand alongside written text, eg representing a scene from a novel or illustrating a technical process that the author has described.

Three-dimensional (3D) design is the broadest category of design. 3D designers work with a range of materials including metal, plastics, wood and glass. They design the exterior of a product, which may or may not contain moving parts. (Strictly speaking, design for products containing working parts forms another subdivision – **manufacturing** or **engineering design.)**

Fashion designers design garments and accessories while **textile designers** produce designs for the fabrics from which clothes, household linens and furnishings are made.

Interior or **spatial design** is another broad area, which contains its own subdivisions of exhibition/display/retail design and theatre/set/stage design. Interior designers are responsible for effective and attractive use of space – whether it is a small stage set for a production or a large national exhibition centre.

Whatever their specialism, all designers share similar working practices. If working on a project, designers first receive a brief, or detailed specification, from the client or person/company paying for the work, discuss this with the client, study the requirements, carry out research, and present ideas to the client – which are often modified several times – before producing the final design. If they work as freelances, they assess the market for different types of work, make up sample designs and are then responsible for finding buyers through their own efforts.

1. GRAPHIC DESIGNER (ED)

THE WORK

Graphic designers convey ideas and information through the appropriate use of images and words.

Designers receive the brief for the project together with the results of any market research already completed on the target audience and discuss it thoroughly with the client, clarifying the aim of the project and the media to be used. They are also given a time-scale to work to and are informed of the limit on cost.

Examples of graphic design projects include: a promotional cover for a book jacket or record sleeve; stationery for a company selling a particular product or service, which is to be suggested by the letter heading; designs for a retailer, which will be used on labels, carrier bags and signs throughout the store and which will have a common logo and colour scheme; a coloured signing scheme for a hospital which could include carpet stripes and wall designs in the same colour to lead patients easily to one department; brochures for a small company to be mailed out, promoting its services; a major advertising campaign incorporating posters, leaflets, brochures and TV advertisements.

After discussing the brief with the client, graphic designers do any necessary research, including looking at previous related projects and comparing costs of using different processes. They also consult the copywriter, if any new text is to be written, and make sure that both understand the aims of the project.

They next make rough sketches as a base for a series of visuals, or mock-ups, that they produce to show to the client. Depending on where they are employed, or whether they are self-employed, they may liaise directly with the client. In large studios, a senior designer or design manager is responsible for all liaison work with clients, attending all necessary meetings and then briefing the design team.

Visuals may be rough or simple sketches and sample black-and-white or colour layouts showing the spacing of the text, size of illustrations, type of lettering and headings, or they may be highly finished, closely resembling the intended finished design.

After discussion with clients, designs often have to be changed and re-submitted. Later, when the words are incorporated, the graphic designer may have to make further alterations if the text is now longer than at first proposed.

When the final layout is approved, the designer prepares detailed instructions for the printer, specifying typefaces and sizes, and produces either a full-colour layout, or one in black and white, with every colour to be used at each point clearly indicated with marker pen.

Much design work can now be created and manipulated via electronic systems, the whole page being designed using desktop publishing, altering wording and layout on the computer screen. In some cases the disk is sent direct to the printer. Hand skills are still used, however, at least in the early sketching stages. Graphic designers therefore work with a range of equipment – computer or drawing board and layout paper, using pencils, crayons, water colours and marker pens in the exact shade of the printer's ink colours.

WORK ENVIRONMENT

Graphic designers spend most of their time working in studios. They also, however, visit clients at their premises and also travel to see printers and possibly to visit exhibitions or libraries when doing research. Some stages of their work are done alone, but many work in teams. In addition, they work closely with colleagues such as account executives, copywriters and marketing or public relations professionals.

SKILLS AND INTERESTS

Graphic designers must possess creative talent and imagination and be able to visualize the end result of a project. At the same time they must understand the technical processes through which their work will be put. They must also be able to analyse problems and suggest solutions.

All need a thorough understanding of the technicalities of printing processes, surfaces, inks and colours. Some use hand drawing skills more than others, but the following skills are still essential.

They must be able to use computers. A basic understanding of photography techniques is also important.

They must be able to manage their time well and accept the discipline of working to tight deadlines very often, putting in long hours, if necessary, in order to finish a project on schedule.

As they work with colour, defective colour vision could present a handicap in this career.

Communication skills are necessary, when working with clients, in order to put forward their own ideas and explain why a certain idea might not work.

They need an understanding of business skills, budgets and costing.

They also need to be able to accept criticism and rejection of work on which they may have spent considerable time.

ENTRY REQUIREMENTS

These vary according to the level of training course chosen. (It is very difficult now to get a job as a junior in a studio and work up, although it may be possible in some parts of the country; day release courses still exist.)

Most graphic designers have completed one or more of the full-time courses listed below. There are no minimum entry requirements; students may be accepted on the basis of a good portfolio of work and interview. However, most colleges expect academic qualifications in addition. Requirements vary from college to college and must always be checked individually. The most usual entry requirements are given below.

An Intermediate GNVQ/GSVQ Level II Diploma or Certificate in Art and Design.

There is no minimum entry requirement.

Foundation course: two years for students aged 16 years with five GCSEs/S grades (A-C/1-3) or one year for students aged 17 years with the same qualifications. However, colleges may ask for higher qualifications for the one-year route, including A levels or H grades.

An Advanced GNVQ/GSVQ Level III in Art and Design (General) can be an alternative to a foundation course. GNVQ/GSVQ courses are available in general art and design only. When students begin a specialist course (in this case for graphic design) they take one of the following:

BTEC/SCOTVEC national diploma or certificate. Entry is usually with a minimum of four GCSEs/S grades (A-C/1-3).

BTEC/SCOTVEC higher diploma or certificate. These normally require successful completion of a national-level programme, a foundation course or, exceptionally, four GCSEs/S grades (A-C/1-3) plus one A level/two H grades.

Degree course. In England and Wales the entry requirements are usually a minimum of five GCSEs/S grades (A-C/1-3) plus two A levels/three H grades and, often, successful completion of a foundation course.

In Scotland, completion of a foundation course is not required, but entry requirements are higher. Applicants must have: five S grades (1-3) plus three H grades including English; or five GCSEs (A-C) plus two A levels with English being included at either level; or a BTEC national award plus A level English/SCOTVEC national award plus H grade English.

TRAINING

Foundation and general art and design courses act as a preparation for a higher-level specialist course. Students are introduced to a wide range of techniques and specialisms and are helped by tutors to decide on the branch of design in which they wish to specialize.

Students who are sure of their career intentions and are able to convince admissions staff, through their portfolio of work and by interview, that they are ready for a specialized course, may apply for direct entry to a relevant higher diploma or degree course. (It is, however, rare to gain admission without having completed a foundation course.)

Some students choose to take a postgraduate course of one to three years before entering employment.

Intermediate and Level II diploma courses last one year; Advanced and Level III/national diploma courses, two years; higher national courses take two years full-time. Degrees in Scotland take four years, with the first year acting as a diagnostic year similar to a foundation course. In England and Wales most degree courses take three years. (Four-year sandwich courses are occasionally available.) Recently introduced are some four-year design 'pathways' which include a 'year zero' diagnostic course.

The content of graphic design courses varies with different aspects being given greater emphasis by different institutions, so syllabuses must be carefully checked.

After completing a course, many designers join a company or agency, where they must carry out routine tasks or work on small parts of projects before being assigned greater responsibility. At this stage they may work for higher qualifications through part-time study or open learning.

NVQs/SVQs in Design are available at Levels 3 and 4.

LATE ENTRY

Mature students may be accepted on to courses with fewer than usual, or no qualifications, if they possess a good portfolio of work.

OPPORTUNITIES

There are more openings in graphic design than in many other areas. More than 50 per cent of designers working in commerce and industry are in graphics. It is still a very competitive field, however, with new designers leaving colleges each year, and it can be difficult to find a first job or to become established as a freelance designer.

Many graphic designers opt for freelance work, which means they must constantly promote themselves to prospective clients by showing their portfolios or sending samples of work. When established, they will get commissions from previous clients or by word of mouth. Their reputation always depends on the quality of the last project they completed for a client.

Salaried graphic designers work for particular employers, such as advertising agencies, TV companies, publishers, or for design groups and consultancies that gain commissions from a wide variety of clients.

PAY AND CONDITIONS

Salaries vary according to ability, experience and the type of employer. Salaried designers could expect a starting salary of £10,700 to £12,000. Experienced designers could expect to earn an average of £20,000, with design managers earning from £20,000 to £30,000 (more in London).

The salary of freelance graphic designers depends very much on their reputation, the effort put into marketing their work and seeking out new clients, and the number of hours they choose to work. Successful designers could earn over £30,000 and very well-established designers might earn up to £60,000, but initially work may be slow to come in and earnings low.

Graphic designers often work normal office hours, five days a week, with considerable overtime required when working to deadlines. Freelance designers choose their own hours. There are opportunities for part-time employment and to work from home.

PROSPECTS

Salaried graphic designers often work for agencies or companies that have a promotion structure. Progress to senior designer or design manager – who direct the work of teams – is possible, or to art director – who is responsible for creating new ideas, liaising with clients and bringing in new work. Alternatively, designers change employers in order to achieve higher salaries. It is, in fact, quite acceptable to change employers frequently in order to acquire a range of experience.

RELATED OCCUPATIONS

Art director, advertising account executive, copywriter, marketing manager, photographer, signwriter.

FURTHER INFORMATION AND READING

Please see article 6. INTERIOR DESIGNER.

2. ILLUSTRATOR/ARTIST (ED)

THE WORK

Illustrators

Illustrators combine elements of fine art and graphic design in their work, producing drawings and paintings for illustrations to accompany text in books, magazines and posters.

They discuss a brief with an editor or designer who describes the editorial content and the style required. They may read the whole text in order to get the 'feel' of it and may also consult the author.

First, designs are prepared and shown to the client. Following discussion, designs may have to be changed, and later, when the words are incorporated and the page layout finalized, the illustrator may have to make more alterations if the text is longer than at first intended.

General illustration includes all types of pictorial material but, in practice, many illustrators specialize and receive commissions from art editors who know of their work and its appropriateness for the publication in question.

Scientific, medical and technical illustration are three particular specialisms that cover the illustration of buildings, products, processes, illustrations for scientific textbooks, and, in the case of medical illustration, can include illustrating the stages of a new surgical technique.

Artists

Artists have very similar skills to those of the illustrator, in that they draw and paint. However, their work is not produced with any commercial constraints but for purely aesthetic reasons. They have usually studied fine art.

Since they rely on selling their work for a living, they must be able to promote their art, approaching managers of galleries and exhibitions to persuade them to display pieces. They must also develop business skills and be able to price work realistically. They may sell paintings for anything from a few pounds to several thousand pounds.

Very few artists make a living from selling work alone. Many combine it with teaching while others undertake some commercial art commissions – eg illustration work, signwriting or occasionally, scenic artist work, painting the 'flats' or backgrounds for theatre sets.

WORK ENVIRONMENT

Illustrators spend most of their time working in studios. They also spend considerable time taking their portfolios to art directors and editors in order to get work, may travel to see printers and visit libraries when doing research.

SKILLS AND INTERESTS

Illustrators must possess creative talent and imagination. Communication skills are also necessary. They must be able to grasp exactly what it is a client has in mind so as to make their own suggestions for suitable illustrations to accompany text.

Like graphic designers, they must understand the technicalities of printing processes. Most of their work consists of drawing and painting by hand, but they must also be willing to learn computer-aided design techniques.

Most illustrators are freelance. Therefore, they need self discipline and time-management ability plus business and marketing skills. They must be prepared to take their portfolios to potential clients and negotiate contracts and fees.

They must be able to accept criticism and rejection of work on which they have spent considerable time.

As they work with colour, defective colour vision could cause difficulties.

ENTRY REQUIREMENTS

Please see article 1. GRAPHIC DESIGNER.

TRAINING

This is largely described under article 1. GRAPHIC DESIGNER.

There are some courses in general illustration and others in the specialist branches: technical illustration; scientific and technical graphics; and industrial, scientific and technical illustration. There is one evening course in wildlife technical illustration (Bournemouth and Poole College).

Illustration may also be studied jointly with graphic design and, at some colleges, with animation.

LATE ENTRY

Mature entrants may be accepted on to courses with fewer than usual, or no qualifications, if they possess a good portfolio of work.

OPPORTUNITIES

Most illustrators are self-employed. It can be very difficult to become established. They must constantly market their work by showing their portfolios to possible clients. When established they may get commissions from previous clients or by word of mouth.

A very few work for design consultancies or in-house design departments.

PAY AND CONDITIONS

Please see article 1. GRAPHIC DESIGNER.

Salaries vary according to ability, experience, the effort put into marketing their work and seeking out new clients, and the number of hours they choose to work.

PROSPECTS

Salaried illustrators could become design managers or art directors.

RELATED OCCUPATIONS

Art director, advertising account executive, copywriter, graphic designer, marketing manager, photographer, signwriter.

FURTHER INFORMATION AND READING

Please see article 6. INTERIOR DESIGNER.

3. THREE-DIMENSIONAL DESIGNER (EG)

THE WORK

Three-dimensional (3D) designers are concerned with making a product look attractive and at the same time functional, and easy to use and maintain.

3D designers usually choose to specialize in either industrial or craft-based design and follow appropriate training courses.

Since many products contain internal working parts, industrial designers work closely with the engineers who design these and must themselves have an understanding of engineering principles.

Craft-based designers mainly design static objects – such as ornaments, pieces of jewellery and furniture. Their designs may be for mass-production in factories or for production by individual craftworkers, using traditional methods. Some produce their own designs and are more properly called designer/craftworkers.

The work of 3D designers has similarities wherever they work, but varies in detail in different industries, companies and in self-employment.

Designers examine their brief carefully and make notes of any problems they can foresee. They then discuss it thoroughly with everyone who will be involved in production and sales: production managers, design engineers and marketing staff, taking into account factors like safety, availability of materials, and whether the product can be manufactured using available machinery and equipment.

The next stage is to produce the design. Designers begin by selecting materials, colours and possible shapes for the product, bearing in mind the intended market.

Technical or price constraints often change designers' first ideas. Often, they are working to a tight schedule – and on several products simultaneously – and must produce new ideas within a specified time.

When a design has been approved, designers prepare detailed working designs. They may do this themselves, or it may be done by specialist draughtsmen/women. In either case, much of the design is likely to be done using a computer.

A full-size working test model or prototype of the product may then be made and if this is seen to work satisfactorily, full-scale production begins. The designer is normally expected to be available to help to solve any problems that might arise during manufacture.

WORK ENVIRONMENT

This is similar to that of the graphic designer with the exception that 3D designers' colleagues include engineers, production managers and technical experts, in addition to marketing managers. Please see article 1. GRAPHIC DESIGNER.

SKILLS AND INTERESTS

3D designers should be creative and imaginative, and possess the ability to think logically and solve problems. They must also be able to visualize and think in three dimensions.

They must be able to sketch, in order to demonstrate their ideas, and to produce very detailed drawings and specifications for production workers to follow. Increasingly, they must be able to make use of computer-aided design.

They need some mathematical ability and scientific knowledge (usually of physics and engineering principles, although some chemistry may also be necessary when working with different materials and their properties).

Craft-based designers need less engineering knowledge,

but must understand all the hand processes involved in manufacturing the objects they design: carving, decorating, firing, glazing, engraving, etc.

3D designers should be good communicators. They must be capable of presenting their ideas and justifying a point of view when necessary. Persuasive skills are often useful.

They need an understanding of business skills, budgets and costing.

Poor colour vision could be a handicap.

Like all designers, they must be willing to accept criticism and rejection of work on which they may have spent considerable time.

ENTRY REQUIREMENTS

Please see article 1. GRAPHIC DESIGNER.

Some colleges specify passes in maths, technology or science.

TRAINING

This is largely described in article 1. GRAPHIC DESIGNER.

3D design courses may be broad-based or specialize in either industrial or craft-based design.

Industrial design courses often have titles such as product design, industrial design or 3D design. They are predominantly available at higher diploma and degree level, with a small number offered at national diploma level. National diploma courses are available at: Bournemouth and Poole College of Art and Design; Cardonald College, Glasgow; Coventry Technical College; Dunstable College.

Craft-based design courses are available at all levels and may also be known as 3D design or as design crafts. There is usually the opportunity to specialize, for example, in wood, metals and plastics.

Competition for places on 3D design courses is not as severe as in other branches of art and design.

LATE ENTRY

Please see article 1. GRAPHIC DESIGNER.

OPPORTUNITIES

Traditionally, engineers designed the exterior of a product in addition to its internal components. In some companies this is still the case. However, there has been a growing awareness of the need for designers with creative skills who can combine these with an understanding of technology. The openings for 3D designers are therefore increasing.

Industrial designers may be employed as staff designers by manufacturers, or work for design consultancies, or in partnerships of consulting design engineers.

Some craft-based designers work for manufacturers. Others are self-employed, either as freelance designers, submitting their designs to manufacturers, or making the products they have designed. Opportunities for this type of employment depend on the market for their work and how easily they can afford the equipment required.

PAY AND CONDITIONS

Please see article 1. GRAPHIC DESIGNER.

PROSPECTS

Newly qualified 3D designers may begin work in a design team in either a manufacturing company or in a design consultancy. Promotion to senior designer or design manager is possible.

Prospects in self-employment depend on the designer's ability to find outlets for work and also on business skills.

Some 3D designers move into marketing, sales or technical writing.

RELATED OCCUPATIONS

Architect, craftworker, engineering craftsman/woman, engineer, interior designer, model maker, packaging designer, potter.

FURTHER INFORMATION AND READING

Please see article 6. INTERIOR DESIGNER.

4. FASHION DESIGNER (EJ)

THE WORK

Designers usually work in one of three main fields: haute couture; designer ready-to-wear; or high-street fashion. They may also specialize in various types of clothing: outerwear, lingerie, swimwear, knitwear or theatrical costumes. The majority work in clothing, but some specialize in hats and other accessories.

Haute couture involves the design of garments for individual customers, who pay for original clothes and attend the designer's workroom for fittings.

Most designers also design ready-to-wear clothes. These are produced in fairly small numbers and sold under the designer's label.

Mass market work involves the design of clothes and accessories that will be sold in large quantities through shops.

Ranges are designed and produced by wholesale manufacturers who sell them to retailers for resale.

Designs are produced well in advance of clothes appearing in the shops – often a year ahead. Designers do not work alone on this, but in close co-operation with fashion buyers from retail companies and fashion forecasters, whose job is to predict what customers will want two seasons ahead.

The first design stage takes the form of sketches, done by hand or using a computer. Fabrics and trimmings are then selected. At this stage, designers usually try out their ideas by pinning fabrics on to a dummy.

Then comes the making-up stage. Designers and their assistants make a pattern and cut sample garments, noting the number of different operations needed to make the garment and taking steps to reduce these, if necessary, to keep in line with budgeted costs.

Some designers cut the patterns themselves and make up the samples. Large manufacturers normally employ specialist pattern cutters and sample machinists. When the garment goes into production, the designer remains on hand to assist with any problems that arise.

WORK ENVIRONMENT

Fashion designers spend some of their time working alone, or with one or two other people in studios. They also attend meetings with textile designers, fashion buyers, production managers and individual clients. Most also have to work closely with sample machinists and pattern cutters.

They may travel extensively in this country and abroad to attend shows and sell their work.

SKILLS AND INTERESTS

Fashion designers must be artistic, creative and know how to use textiles effectively. They need an eye for tone and colour. Poor colour vision could be a handicap.

They should be able to explain their ideas through sketches, but do not need outstanding drawing ability. In developing a design, computer-aided design techniques may be used.

Communication and persuasive skills are important. Much of their time may be spent in persuading buyers from large retailers to accept their ideas.

Designers need a thorough understanding of how garments are made and should have a sound training in hand and machine sewing and in pattern cutting. They must be able to calculate the costs of producing garments.

Freelance designers need business and marketing skills. They must be prepared to take their portfolios to potential clients and negotiate contracts and fees.

Last, they need to be able to accept criticism and rejection of their ideas.

ENTRY REQUIREMENTS

Please see article 1. GRAPHIC DESIGNER.

TRAINING

This is largely described in article 1. GRAPHIC DESIGNER.

Most designers have some formal design training. Although, in theory, it is possible to train in a designer's studio, openings are almost non-existent.

Fashion design courses may concentrate solely on design, or may combine this with management, marketing or technology. (A certain amount of technology is included on all courses.) A growing number of courses include tuition in a European language.

Many have specialist options such as knitwear, footwear or accessory design.

Some courses have the title 'clothing technology'. They usually concentrate on garment production and management, but if they include design, they can be a suitable preparation for work in mass-market design.

LATE ENTRY

Please see article 1. GRAPHIC DESIGNER.

OPPORTUNITIES

Very few designers become well-known names. The largest number work in the mass-market sector with very few finding openings as assistants to couture designers.

New graduates from British higher education institutions often spend a period working abroad, particularly in Italy and France, to gain further experience in an international environment before looking for a job at home.

There are opportunities to work in design studios within manufacturing companies. A new graduate is likely to begin here as the junior in the design team and must be prepared to do the more routine tasks, initially. Some begin as pattern cutters.

Other fashion designers work in specialist design studios that produce designs for a number of manufacturers, and others opt for self-employment.

Designers who have specialized in costume design are sometimes employed by theatrical costumiers, or more usually work on a contract basis with film and TV companies.

PAY AND CONDITIONS

Please see article 1. GRAPHIC DESIGNER.

PROSPECTS

In a manufacturer's design studio there are prospects of promotion to senior designer or to move into design management, which is less concerned with producing designs and more with acting as the link between designers, production managers and workers in mass-market production companies.

Alternatively, designers change employers in order to achieve higher salaries.

There are possibilities to move into associated jobs such as marketing, buying, production management and, occasionally, into fashion forecasting.

RELATED OCCUPATIONS

Clothing production manager, fashion buyer, pattern cutter, quality controller, sample machinist, tailor, textile designer.

FURTHER INFORMATION AND READING

Please see article 6. INTERIOR DESIGNER.

5. TEXTILE DESIGNER (EP)

THE WORK

Designers usually specialize in printed, woven or knitted textiles. They may also specialize in designs for one particular type of product, for example furnishing fabrics, men's or women's clothing, or in designs for other surface patterns – not strictly textiles, but those decorated with a pattern repeat – like wallpaper or wrapping paper.

Before starting work on a design, textile designers research the market. They must be aware of fashions in colour, design trends and the popularity of different fabrics. They may analyse previous sales figures, and work with fashion designers and buyers in anticipating trends.

Every design must take into account the way in which the fabric is produced and the eventual cost. If the design is to be woven in, the designer has to consider the quality of the yarn and the dyes and colours available. If it is to be printed, the number of different colours each requiring a separate screen for printing will affect the final cost.

The first, rough sketches are produced on paper. Next the designer works out the construction of the design to very accurate measurements, using squared paper or computer, and specifying the colours of different parts of the thread and the position of the design on the fabric.

The sample stage involves the designer in working with technicians to produce a sample of cloth. Samples are then chosen by the marketing staff of a design company, or used by the designer in person to present to clients.

When the design goes into production the designer is expected to assist with any problems that arise during manufacture, or modify the design according to customers' requirements.

WORK ENVIRONMENT

Textile designers employed by manufacturers for the mass market often work in studios attached to the factories where the cloth is produced. Those who produce designs for printed fabrics or other surfaces sometimes work in design studios – the designs are then printed in a factory at another site.

They frequently work in small teams of no more than five designers, but also attend meetings with fashion designers, buyers, production managers and individual clients. This can involve them in a considerable amount of travel.

Self-employed textile designers have to travel to see agents and manufacturers and attend exhibitions, sometimes abroad, in order to get commissions.

SKILLS AND INTERESTS

Textile designers must be artistic and creative with a good eye for colour. Poor colour vision could be a handicap. They must also be capable of working in fine detail.

The amount of creativity required depends very much on where they work. Many popular designs are reproductions of traditional patterns or repeats of designs that have sold well in the past. Designers may be asked to reproduce a pattern making slight modifications, or to reproduce it using different colourways, rather than always create an original.

An understanding of the technical processes involved is essential. Weave designers must know what dyeing and weaving processes are used and what can be done on looms or knitting machines. Printed pattern designers need to know about printing processes. Their skills are similar to those of a graphic designer.

Communication and persuasive skills are important. They must be able to sell their ideas and must spend time getting feedback from customers. Freelance designers, in particular, need business and marketing skills. They must be prepared to take their portfolios to potential clients and negotiate contracts and fees.

ENTRY REQUIREMENTS

Please see article 1. GRAPHIC DESIGNER.

TRAINING

This is largely described in article 1. GRAPHIC DESIGNER.

Some courses are joint courses in fashion and textile design. On such courses, students normally eventually specialize in one or the other. A number of courses exist in surface pattern design. These include training for design on fabrics, paper, china, plastic, laminate and other materials.

LATE ENTRY

Please see article 1. GRAPHIC DESIGNER.

OPPORTUNITIES

This is a very competitive area in which to find work. There are some openings for trained junior designers with in-house design units at textile manufacturers' premises and in specialist studios that work for a number of manufacturers, but opportunities for newcomers are limited with both.

Some designers work on a freelance basis, from home or sharing a studio with other designers, and many find more success if they also produce their own work and sell it at craft fairs or direct to shops.

There are frequently more opportunities to sell designs to foreign markets than in Britain.

PAY AND CONDITIONS

Please see article 1. GRAPHIC DESIGNER.

PROSPECTS

In a design studio there are prospects of promotion to senior designer but, since studios are small, these opportunities are limited.

Alternatively, designers change employers in order to achieve higher salaries, and it is quite usual to do so.

Some designers change employers frequently, in order to acquire a range of experience before setting up their own businesses.

There are possibilities to move out of design work and into associated jobs such as marketing, buying, sales, and, occasionally, into textile conservation and museum work.

RELATED OCCUPATIONS

Fashion buyer, graphic designer, photographer, production manager, quality controller, textile technician.

FURTHER INFORMATION AND READING

Please see article 6. INTERIOR DESIGNER.

6. INTERIOR DESIGNER (ET)

THE WORK

Interior designers are concerned with the organization of space and the decoration of the interiors of many kinds of structures: buildings (shops, hotels, office blocks and sometimes private houses), ships, and aircraft.

Like other designers, they are initially briefed by a client, then work through the brief thoroughly to ensure that they understand all the requirements.

They then produce their first sketches and turn these into designs that are presented to the client. They normally produce several sets of designs for the client to compare.

Interior designers work bearing several factors in mind. They have to consider what image the client wishes to convey. If it is a hotel for example, the owners may want it to follow the style of a particular period. They must also consider the purpose of the building – the number of people who will be working in an office for instance, and limitations imposed by fittings and equipment. Shops need storage space as well as counters and display areas; aircraft interiors are particularly small, yet sufficient space must be allowed for passengers, luggage and working quarters for cabin crew.

Every interior has to include services, like electricity and heating. The designer has to incorporate radiators and even power points into the design.

Interior designers also recommend the materials, furniture, fabrics and fittings to be used, from cupboards and shelving down to door handles. They also plan colour schemes. (Some interior designers who specialize in advising on furnishings and colour schemes only, are usually known as interior decorators.)

Interior designers prepare detailed working drawings for the workmen/women who will be carrying out the work. This may be done using a computer. Some designers do this themselves; others employ draughtsmen/women.

Interior designers are expected to make frequent visits to the site while work is in progress, to check that everything is being done according to plan. Some are responsible for contracting out the work and choosing the firm of carpenters/joiners, decorators, shopfitters, etc.

Theatre/set design

This is a specialist branch of interior design. The work is very similar, with the client being a theatre, television or film director. Designers are responsible for everything on the set from scenery to furniture. They have to read the script, know how many changes of set there will be and, if it is a period play or film, do some historical research in order to make all the details accurate.

If designing a stage set, they must design sets that can be moved without difficulty by scene-shifters between acts. Television sets may be in small studios and allowances must be made for camera positions and angles. If working on a film or a television programme that requires outside shots, they are responsible for finding suitable locations.

Exhibition or display design

This is another specialism. Designers may plan a whole exhibition or one or more stands inside it for a client. They have limited space in which to work and must be able to plan the display around available power points and sometimes water supply. They need to make a stand look attractive, contain all the information an exhibitor wishes to display, and allow sufficient space within the area of floor space rented for customers to circulate.

WORK ENVIRONMENT

Interior designers are based in studios, but spend considerable time visiting sites. They also spend time travelling to meet prospective clients and making presentations in order to win contracts.

In order to keep abreast of the latest trends in materials and furnishings they may travel abroad to visit trade fairs and exhibitions.

SKILLS AND INTERESTS

Interior designers need creative talent and imagination and must be able to think three-dimensionally. They must also be capable of understanding building and safety regulations.

Drawing ability is important, from being able to convey their ideas in sketches to producing detailed working drawings. Increasingly, they need to work with computers.

Communication skills are extremely important. They may be working for clients who know exactly what they require or who have only a hazy idea. In both cases, they must translate those ideas into workable designs, and often explain why modifications are necessary. As they work with colour, defective colour vision could cause a problem.

They need an understanding of business skills, budgets and costing.

Selling skills are important. They spend much time in presenting ideas to prospective clients and bidding for business.

Willingness to work in a team is important. Interior designers work very closely throughout with architects, while the later stages of a project require them to liaise with contractors and, sometimes, directly supervise craftsmen/women.

They need to be able to accept criticism and rejection of work on which they may have spent considerable time.

ENTRY REQUIREMENTS

Please see article 1. GRAPHIC DESIGNER.

TRAINING

This is largely described in article 1. GRAPHIC DESIGNER.

It is also possible to train for interior design through private distance learning tuition. Courses are offered by Rhodec International and the Regent Academy.

LATE ENTRY

Please see article 1. GRAPHIC DESIGNER.

OPPORTUNITIES

This is not an easy branch of art and design in which to find employment. There are some openings with large organizations, like retail chains or hotel groups, but most interior designers work in interior design consultancies. Some are employed in architects' practices and others work on a freelance basis.

Theatre design is a particularly competitive area and there is very little salaried employment here, especially since the BBC, which used to employ its own designers, has now changed largely to using freelances.

PAY AND CONDITIONS

Please see article 1. GRAPHIC DESIGNER.

PROSPECTS

Most qualified interior designers first work assisting experienced designers. If they are in salaried positions they may then become designers. There are limited opportunities for promotion to the job of design manager, supervising the work of a number of designers and dealing with clients.

Many aim to become self-employed and may become partners in design consultancies.

RELATED OCCUPATIONS

Textile designer, graphic designer, fashion designer, illustrator/artist.

FURTHER INFORMATION

The Design Council, which was set up to encourage improvements in training and to promote British design, offers advice and provides a range of leaflets. Its Young Designers' Centre also has a resources and information centre open to visitors, and staff who will give telephone or written advice on choosing a course and finding a job.

The Association of Illustrators, 1st Floor, 32-38 Saffron Hill, London EC1N 8FH, 0171 636 4100

The Crafts Council, 44A Pentonville Road, Islington, London N1 9BY, 0171 278 7700

The Design Council*, 1 Oxendon Street, London SW1Y 4EE, 0171 208 2121

Institute of Packaging*, Sysonby Lodge, Nottingham Road, Melton Mowbray, Leicestershire LE1 0NU, 0116 250 0055

Institute of Printing*, 8A Lonsdale Gardens, Tunbridge Wells, Kent TN1 1NU, 01892 538118

National Society for Education in Art and Design (NSEAD)*, The Gatehouse, Corsham Court, Corsham, Wiltshire SN13 0BZ, 01249 714825

Regent Academy of Fine Arts, 153-155 Regent Street, London W1R 8PX, 0800 378281

Rhodec International College of Interior Design, 35 East Street, Brighton, East Sussex BN1 1HL, 01273 327476

University and Colleges Admissions Service, UCAS*, Fulton House, Jessop Avenue, Cheltenham, Glos GL50 3SH, 01242 227788

FURTHER READING

Leaflets/booklets are available from the addresses marked*.

Guide to Courses and Careers in Art, Craft and Design – NSEAD
Working in Art and Design – COIC
Working in Fashion – COIC

In the careers library classified under ED; EG; EJ; EP; ET.

PHOTOGRAPHY: EV

1. PHOTOGRAPHER CLCI:EV
2. PHOTOGRAPHIC TECHNICIAN CLCI:EV/SOZ

1. PHOTOGRAPHER (EV)

BACKGROUND INFORMATION

Photography is a highly competitive career and is not always as glamorous as it might appear. Photography students are often attracted to areas like fashion and advertising, which offer relatively few jobs; there are far greater opportunities in the more mundane areas, such as wedding photography, portraiture and industrial or scientific work.

Many college courses in photography are available, but there is no clear progression from formal training to employment. Most industry sources agree that there is an over-supply of photography graduates, relative to the number of jobs available.

Job opportunities in professional photography may be affected in future by the growing use of electronic imaging. With a computer, a designer can now manipulate photographs, merging them and adding special effects to create new images. The extent to which these techniques will affect the demand for original photographs is not yet clear, but they will certainly have an increasing impact on professional photography.

It is much easier to find a job as a photographic technician than as a professional photographer. However, working as a photographic technician should be seen as an interesting career in its own right, and not a second-best option for failed photographers.

Technicians work in photographic laboratories, which fall into two main categories:

Photofinishing laboratories provide developing and printing services for amateur photographers. Some are very large processing plants, with hundreds of employees; others are 'mini-labs', generally found in town centres, which provide a quick processing service.

Professional processing laboratories provide a range of services to professional photographers.

THE WORK

Professional photographers make permanent records of visual images – which may be of anything, from new-born babies to scientific processes.

Photography involves choosing and preparing locations, setting up lighting, selecting appropriate cameras, film, lenses and accessories, and composition of pictures.

A professional photographer usually works to a brief, set by the client or employer. The brief may be very detailed, or it may allow the photographer scope for creative interpretation of the client's ideas, after appropriate discussion and negotiation.

It is usual to specialize in one particular area of work. The main specializations are:

General practice photographers provide a service for the local community. The majority of their work is social photography – mainly portraits and weddings. They may also work for local businesses and advertising agencies, producing shots for brochures, posters and other promotional material. Some general practice photographers freelance for local newspapers.

Advertising, fashion and editorial photography. Advertising photographers tend to specialize in a particular area, such as cars or food, although some do a variety of work. Fashion photographers are also concerned with advertising, but of clothes, make-up and fashion accessories. Editorial photographers produce illustrations for magazine articles. Photographers in these fields often work with a team, including models, stylists, lighting technicians and photographers' assistants.

Most **press photographers** work for provincial or local newspapers, and much of their work involves recording local events and news stories. On the national newspapers they often specialize, for instance, in sports photography or political coverage. Photo-journalists provide words as well as pictures, and they generally work for magazines rather than newspapers.

Medical photographers make records used in hospitals for educational, diagnostic and scientific purposes. They use specialized techniques such as microphotography (photographing images of very small objects). Medical work may involve taking photographs on the wards, in theatres, research laboratories or post-mortem rooms.

Industrial photographers record industrial processes and similar subjects. They may also take photographs for company brochures and publicity material.

Scientific photographers are concerned with recording experiments or providing research data, often for purposes of measurement. They use special techniques, such as ultra-violet light or high-speed photography.

Police photographers may be concerned with forensic work – photographing scenes of crime – or with other types of police photography, including press and public relations, training material, or photographing accident victims.

The majority of photographers are self-employed and have to cope with all the problems of running a small business. Typically, they devote far more time – perhaps 85 per cent of their working hours – to running their businesses, rather than taking photographs.

Many photographers also make videos – for instance, of weddings or promotional events.

WORK ENVIRONMENT

Some photographers are studio-based, particularly those working in advertising and portraiture. Others work in a variety of locations, both indoors and out.

Location work involves travel and spending periods away from home.

SKILLS AND INTERESTS

Photographers have to be well-organized and practical, as well as creative. Business skills are essential. Strong motivation and self-confidence are needed to find work and survive in a competitive and overcrowded profession.

Artistic ability, with an understanding of the principles of composition and an appreciation of shape, form, colour and tone are required. It is also important to be able to master different techniques and to understand technical processes.

Photographers need to be able to deal with people – for instance, when taking wedding pictures or working with professional models. They also need negotiating skills for dealing with clients. Patience is important – in press photography they may wait for hours to get the right shot, or any kind of outdoor work may depend on waiting for the right weather conditions.

Medical and scientific photographers should have an interest in science and be capable of working to a high degree of accuracy.

ENTRY REQUIREMENTS

No set academic qualifications are required to work as a photographer or photographer's assistant. It is not always necessary to take a formal training course in photography. However, a keen amateur interest in the subject is absolutely essential. Employers and colleges assume a considerable knowledge of the subject prior to entry.

A portfolio of the candidate's photographic work is essential for applying for jobs and courses. The portfolio should be relevant, neatly presented and not too long – between ten and 15 photographs is sufficient.

A driving licence is a great advantage for those applying for posts as photographers' assistants.

College courses: there are no set entry requirements for courses leading to C&G, NVQ/SVQ or SCOTVEC national awards.

Entry to BTEC national certificate/diploma courses is with four GCSEs/S grades (A-C/1-3). Entry to BTEC/SCOTVEC higher national certificate/diploma courses is with one or two A levels/H grades and supporting GCSEs/S grades (A-C/1-3) or a national certificate/ diploma, Advanced GNVQ/GSVQ Level III or completion of a foundation course in Art and Design.

Entry to courses leading to the BIPP professional qualifying examinations is with a higher national diploma.

Entry to degree courses is with five GCSEs/S grades (A-C/1-3) with two A levels/three H grades, a BTEC/SCOTVEC national award, foundation course in Art and Design or equivalent.

Some specialist areas have particular requirements:

Press photographers: minimum educational requirements for direct entry to a newspaper as a trainee are: five GCSEs/S grades (A-C/1-3) including English; or two years' relevant experience in photography; or a further education course in photography. For the full-time pre-entry course at Sheffield College, minimum entry requirements are one A level/H grade and four other subjects at GCSE/S grade (A-C/1-3).

Medical photographers: for trainee posts, employers tend to prefer candidates with five GCSEs/S grades (A-C/1-3) including English, maths and a science subject. Some entrants have photography qualifications.

TRAINING

There is no set training pattern for most types of professional photography. Many training courses are available, but there is no direct link between formal training and employment, and it is possible to become a successful photographer by learning on-the-job.

In fields such as general practice, advertising, fashion and editorial photography, entrants usually start as a photographer's assistant. Assistants help with shoots, making sure that the set or location is prepared, loading film, setting up lighting. They organize transport of people and equipment, check supplies and deal with paperwork. They are also responsible for the day-to-day running of the studio, dealing with all the necessary mundane tasks, like making coffee, answering the telephone, making deliveries and cleaning.

It is not always necessary to have a formal qualification in photography to find a post as a photographer's assistant, and some photographers prefer to take untrained staff with a keen interest in photography, rather than college leavers.

Assistants may be granted day release to take college courses – until recently, the most usual course for assistants and trainees has been City and Guilds 747, Photography Competencies. This qualification is still currently available, but may have been replaced by NVQs or SVQs in Photography. Colleges may run courses leading to NVQs/SVQs; employers and other training providers may also be able to act as assessment centres.

NVQs/SVQs in Photography accredited to date are at Levels 3 and 4.

Other qualifications include:

BTEC/SCOTVEC national awards or GNVQs/GSVQs in Art and Design are mainly full-time courses, lasting two years, although a few part-time courses are available. Higher national diploma courses normally last two years, full-time.

Degree courses in photography normally last three years. There are specialist degree and higher national diploma courses in areas such as medical, industrial, scientific and advertising photography.

The Professional Qualifying Examination (PQE) of the British Institute of Professional Photography is a qualification with a good reputation with employers. Some colleges link the PQE to their higher national diploma courses, enabling students to take a third year of study and obtain both a PQE and a degree.

There is no guarantee that a formal qualification will lead to employment as a photographer or assistant. However, a photography course does provide a technical grounding and the opportunity for students to test their commitment to photography and make contacts in the industry – particularly if the course includes a period of industrial release. It is important to research courses thoroughly, finding out about their equipment, contacts in the industry and the record of past students in finding appropriate employment.

Two specialist areas of photography have a more standard pattern of training.

Press photography. There are two main schemes of training:

1. Direct entry to a training contract with a local or provincial newspaper. Direct entrants receive on-the-job training, supplemented by block release courses at Sheffield College.

2. A one-year full-time pre-entry course in Photo-Journalism/Press Photography at Sheffield College, followed by on-the-job training with a newspaper.

Both routes lead to qualifications of the National Council for the Training of Journalists (NCTJ), from whom further details are available.

It is not necessary to gain NCTJ qualifications to work as a freelance press photographer.

Medical photography. Trainees in hospitals gain experience on-the-job and usually study for the medical photography examinations of the British Institute of Professional Photography or the Institute of Medical Illustrators. It is also possible to enter after taking a specialist full-time course.

LATE ENTRY

There are no upper age limits and adults with a strong amateur interest in photography may be able to sell their work and develop a freelance business or small studio. They are most likely to succeed in general practice, taking wedding photographs and portraits – maturity can be an asset for this type of photography.

People in their twenties may have an advantage over school-leavers when applying for work as photographer's assistants. However, starting pay is likely to be low – this may be a deterrent.

Colleges may waive their normal academic entry requirements for mature applicants.

OPPORTUNITIES

Photography is a very competitive area, and considerable determination is needed to find work.

In fields like advertising, fashion and general practice photography, posts for assistants are sometimes advertised in the photographic press, but they are often found through word-of-mouth – informal contacts are important in photography. Would-be assistants can make speculative approaches to individual photographers or studios – probably the best way is to send a letter and cv, followed up by a telephone call. It is important that applicants can be easily contacted. A home telephone number is essential, and an answering machine, mobile phone or pager is an advantage.

Assistants may work full-time for one photographer or (in London and other large cities) as freelances, working for many different photographers as and when required. There is no set career pattern, although the work of a full-time assistant is more straightforward and therefore easier for a beginner. After gaining sufficient experience they usually leave to set up their own photographic practices.

Advice on finding employment in advertising, fashion and editorial photography is available from the Association of Photographers, who hold regular careers talks and supply details of current vacancies.

Entry to press photography is also highly competitive. Applicants can approach local or regional newspapers or apply to the full-time course at Sheffield College. The national newspapers only employ experienced photographers.

Entry to other areas, such as medical or police photography, is slightly less competitive and advertisements may be found in the local press, Jobcentres and the British Journal of Photography.

According to the Photography and Photographic Processing Industry Training Organization, there are about 17,000 people employed in professional photography.

About half of all professional photographers work in general practice. They are usually self-employed, although some larger practices employ photographers.

Most photographers working in advertising, fashion and editorial photography are also self-employed.

Full-time employment is the norm in police and medical photography. Some police photographers are uniformed officers, but the trend is towards employment of civilians for this type of work.

The Civil Service employs photographers in a number of departments, particularly in the Ministry of Defence, Central Office of Information (COI) and the Department of the Environment. There are also opportunities in HM Forces. Some large industrial firms have their own photographic departments. There are also opportunities for stills photographers with television and film companies.

PAY AND CONDITIONS

Because many photographers are self-employed, there is a great variation in earnings. Those with a good reputation in the more creative areas, such as advertising, fashion or press photography, can earn high incomes, but this is unusual. A more realistic figure for experienced photographers would be about £12,000 plus, with assistants or trainees earning from about £5,500 to £7,000.

Those on a fixed salary scale, such as medical photographers, may earn more during training and the early years of their careers, but do not have the opportunity of reaching the level of income sometimes achieved in the more creative areas.

Most self-employed photographers work long hours, including evenings and weekends. Wedding photography always involves weekend work.

Press photographers often work very irregular hours, to cover news stories and other events.

Police photographers should be prepared to work shifts.

PROSPECTS

Success for a self-employed photographer consists of building up a business and steadily gaining more prestige and higher fees.

Organizations that employ photographers, such as the police or Civil Service, have a formal promotion structure, but prospects are likely to be limited, as photographic departments are usually quite small.

RELATED OCCUPATIONS

Illustrator/artist, graphic designer, fashion designer, stage/set designer, camera operator, picture editor, photographic technician

FURTHER INFORMATION

British Institute of Professional Photography*, Fox Talbot House, 2 Amwell End, Ware, Herts SG12 9HN, 01920 464011 (Please send A4 sae, with 29p stamp)

The Association of Photographers*, 9-10 Domingo Street, London EC1Y 0TA, 0171 608 0598

National Council for the Training of Journalists*, Latton Bush Centre, Southern Way, Harlow, Essex CM18 7BL, 01279 430009 (please include sae)

The Royal Photographic Society*, The Octagon, Milsom Street, Bath BA1 1DN, 01225 462841

Photography and Photographic Processing Industry Training Organization, 44 St Georges Street, Reading RG3 2RL, 01734 590816

FURTHER READING

Leaflets/booklets are available from the addresses marked*.

Job Outlines – Photography – COIC
Where to Study – Photography, film, video and television – The British Journal of Photography
Design Courses – The Design Council
Beyond the Lens – Rights, Ethics and Business in Professional Photography – The Association of Photographers
Periodicals: The British Journal of Photography
In the careers library classified under EV.

2. PHOTOGRAPHIC TECHNICIAN (EV/ SOZ)

THE WORK

There is a wide range of different types of work, both in photofinishing and professional laboratories. Technicians may specialize in one area, or carry out a variety of different tasks. Some jobs are routine, involving machine operating; others are highly skilled.

All laboratories work to highly accurate, controlled standards, with fast turn-around times. However, targets vary in different parts of the processing industry. In labs processing films for the amateur market, the aim is to produce prints in large quantities, whereas the professional laboratories cater for more specialist needs. In terms of tasks, however, there is considerable overlap between the different types of lab.

Technicians' work can include:

Chemical mixing: photographic laboratories use large quantities of chemicals and these have to be combined in the correct order, following manufacturers' instructions and health and safety procedures.

Processing: is automatically controlled, although technicians are responsible for setting and adjusting the machines. Films are loaded into the machines, processed in total darkness and inspected as they emerge. Quality control is extremely important and test films are checked against control standards set by the manufacturers.

Negatives can be graded on a video analyser or by a colour-and-density scanner, to adjust colour and density.

Printing: mainly by machine, but also by hand. Most amateur prints, and many professional ones, are printed by sophisticated electronic machinery. The technician is responsible for setting up the machine, making adjustments and fault-finding.

Hand printing: is used when the photographer has specific requirements – for instance, for an unusual size, or for enlargement of part of the picture.

Finishing: prints can be mounted on hardboard, card or canvas. They can be laminated or given a variety of different surface textures.

Other specialist techniques include:

Re-touching: removing blemishes on prints and transparencies by hand, using a brush and dye;

Copying photographs or artwork, when no negative is available, by photographing them and producing a negative or transparency;

Duplicating or 'duping' – copying transparencies and negatives;

Reverse printing: making prints from transparencies;

Electronic imaging: mainly used for manipulating images, for instance merging two photographs, or re-touching. A print, transparency or negative is converted into a computer image, which can be manipulated on screen. The new image is then converted back into photographic form;

Electronic imaging is developing rapidly, and is likely to replace some of the traditional skills – particularly re-touching – in the next few years.

WORK ENVIRONMENT

Technicians spend most of their time in the laboratory, in clean and comfortable conditions. With modern technology, very little time is spent in total darkness.

When dealing with chemicals, technicians wear rubber gloves, goggles and laboratory coats.

SKILLS AND INTERESTS

Photographic technicians need patience, meticulous accuracy and must pay close attention to detail. An eye for colour, shade and tone is important. Re-touching work requires some artistic aptitude.

A responsible attitude is important, as technicians may be handling valuable negatives and transparencies. If they are processing film in large quantities, a small error in machine setting could cost thousands of pounds.

They may work under pressure to meet deadlines.

Manual dexterity and some mechanical aptitude, for operating machinery, are necessary.

ENTRY REQUIREMENTS

There are no set entry requirements for employment as a photographic technician. GCSEs/S grades, particularly in sciences, are useful.

Entry to the BTEC National Diploma in Photography and Photographic Laboratory Practice course at Kingsway College, London, is with four GCSEs/S grades (A-C/1-3) or equivalent, and a portfolio of photographic work.

TRAINING

The usual method of training is on-the-job. Entrants start as juniors or trainees, usually starting on the more routine and repetitive work, such as machine operating. Depending on the employer, they may be able to gain experience in different departments and attend short courses run by equipment manufacturers.

It is likely that trainees will work towards full NVQs/SVQs (or individual units of competence), which are expected to become available through companies, colleges and other training providers.

The following NVQs/SVQs are available: Supporting Photographic Processing Operations, Level 2; Processing Photographic Material, Level 3; Printing Photographic Material, Level 3. An NVQ/SVQ in Electronic Imaging is under development.

There is no fixed training period, but it is likely to take two to three years to become proficient as a technician. Technicians will need to take further training courses throughout their careers (eg equipment manufacturers' courses) to keep pace with new technology.

It is also possible to enter after taking the following full-time course:

The BTEC National Diploma in Photography and Photographic Laboratory Practice at Kingsway College, London. The course includes training in professional laboratory work and photography. It lasts two years, full-time, and can also be taken part-time over a longer period.

There is a considerable demand from employers for more training facilities for photographic processing skills, and it is likely that more courses will be established in the future.

LATE ENTRY

Adult entry is possible, although it tends to be school-leavers or young people aged about 18-21 years who are trained by employers in a range of skills. Older entrants are more likely to be taken on by the very large photofinishing laboratories to carry out less-skilled work.

PHOTOGRAPHY: EV

OPPORTUNITIES

Laboratories have expanded rapidly in the past 15-20 years and there is a shortage of qualified staff.

Photofinishing laboratories include a small number of very large firms and several hundred 'mini-labs'. Professional photographic laboratories number about 600 and are found in every major town or city. Many professional labs specialize.

Some photographic technicians are employed by hospitals and colleges.

About 12,000 people are employed in photographic laboratories, according to estimates by the Photography and Photographic Processing Industry Training Organization.

It is possible for experienced technicians to become self-employed, running their own photographic labs.

PAY AND CONDITIONS

Most technicians work a five-day week, Monday to Friday. In a few large laboratories they work shifts. Overtime may be available. It is possible to work part-time.

Pay varies with different employers and in different parts of the country. Young people, carrying out basic tasks, are likely to earn between £7,000 and £10,000. Top rates for the most skilled and experienced technicians can be up to £25,000.

PROSPECTS

Promotion prospects vary according to the size of the firm. It is possible to progress to senior technician level, and then into management.

It may be necessary to move to another firm to gain experience or improve chances of promotion.

RELATED OCCUPATIONS

Photographer, laboratory technician, textile dyeing technician, sound technician/operator, cameraman/woman/camera operator, cinema projectionist

FURTHER INFORMATION

Professional Photographic Laboratories Association, 35 Chine Walk, West Parley, Ferndown, Dorset BH22 8PR

British Institute of Professional Photography*, Fox Talbot House, 2 Amwell End, Ware, Herts SG12 9HN, 01920 464011 (Please send A4 size sae, with 29p stamp)

Photography and Photographic Processing Industry Training Organization, PO Box 2270, Reading RG1 4YG, 01734 590816

Blackpool and the Fylde College, Ashfield Road, Bispham, Blackpool, Lancashire FY2 0HB, 01253 352352

Kingsway College, The Gray's Inn Centre, Sidmouth Street, London WC1H 8JB, 0171 306 5700

FURTHER READING

Leaflets/booklets are available from the address marked*.

In the careers library classified under EV; SOZ.

1. **SCHOOL TEACHER – ENGLAND AND WALES CLCI:FAB**
2. **SCHOOL TEACHER – SCOTLAND CLCI:FAB**
3. **SPECIAL EDUCATIONAL NEEDS TEACHER CLCI:FAB**
4. **FURTHER EDUCATION/TERTIARY COLLEGE LECTURER CLCI:FAB**
5. **HIGHER EDUCATION LECTURER CLCI:FAB**

1. SCHOOL TEACHER – ENGLAND AND WALES (FAB)

BACKGROUND INFORMATION

Most schools are run by local authorities or are grant-maintained, though there are increasing numbers of independent schools. In the state system, children attend primary school from four or five to eleven or twelve years, and secondary school until 16 or 18 years. Some primary schools have a nursery unit or nursery school attached for three- to five-year-olds. Provision for 16 to 19-year-olds includes sixth-form, further education and tertiary colleges.

The 1988 Education Reform Act is now having a major effect. The most radical measure is the introduction of a prescribed National Curriculum made up of core and foundation subjects. Children's work is assessed continuously and tested at key stages.

The Act also brought in grant-maintained schools, City Technology Colleges, Colleges of technology and languages; and Local Management of Schools (LMS), devolving financial responsibility from local education authorities to school governors and head teachers.

Another potential major force for change is the single European market, which is broadening educational perspectives and offering teachers new challenges and openings.

THE WORK

Teachers aim to build a relationship with their pupils that brings out the best in them and makes them receptive to ideas and knowledge.

Teaching methods vary enormously. Lessons may be given based on text books, or may take the form of a demonstration, an experiment, a discussion, a field trip or a workplace visit. Pupils are encouraged to take an active role in their learning, and sometimes discovering facts for themselves rather than relying on teachers to present them; teachers direct pupils' research, provide resources, arrange group projects and periods of practical experience, and help pupils collate information.

Whether teachers plan lessons informally or formally, they must devise balanced learning programmes that develop pupils' academic, practical, creative and social skills. Teachers draw up a syllabus related to the National Curriculum, when appropriate, for the 39-week school year, liaising with colleagues when themes are chosen for cross-curricular study.

Outside the classroom, teachers spend many hours preparing lessons. This could entail practical preparation, from drawing letter shapes for first-year primary writing practice to setting up complicated apparatus for an A level chemistry class. Teachers also set and mark homework appropriate to the age of their pupils, which could cover a range of supplementary exercises and activities, for example essays, mathematical problems and project research. They are required to assess pupils' work continuously, testing them at specified ages in National Curriculum subjects. Further evaluation takes place in other tests and examinations, which must also be set and marked. At the end of each year, subject and general progress reports are written.

Teachers' resources vary, but a wide range of materials and teaching aids is available. In nursery and primary schools, where the emphasis is on learning through doing, resources may include paints and pens, scissors and glue, modelling clay, sewing materials, musical instruments, building blocks, dressing-up clothes, simple woodworking tools, water and sand, and gardening tools.

Technology teachers train young pupils to handle simple tools, such as chisels and soldering irons, and older ones to use precision tools. Information technology teachers show pupils how to use sophisticated design software. Language and music tapes and video cassettes are widely used, and computer skills are taught from the early primary years.

Teachers have extra administrative duties, managing resources, taking registers etc. They also attend different types of meeting, such as departmental and staff meetings and parents evenings.

Teachers have a pastoral or caring role, guiding pupils and advising them on personal problems. Year or form tutors have special responsibilities of this kind, and boarding school teachers often care for pupils outside school hours. Many teachers organize extracurricular activities such as concerts, outings and adventure holidays; there is a particular emphasis on these in residential independent schools.

As well as working closely with colleagues, teachers come into contact with parents, social workers, counsellors and many other members of the community.

Nursery/primary school teacher

Teachers specializing in the 'early years' (three to seven or eight years) work in nursery, infant or first schools. Those opting for the later years work in junior and middle schools. Most primary teachers cover every curriculum subject but have a specialism – for example, science, maths, technology, language development – which they help develop through the school as curriculum leaders and advisers to other members of staff. Unless the school is very small, they teach children of a particular age group, taking sole charge of a class or working with several other teachers. A small but growing number of schools are employing specialist teachers to teach their own subject to a number of classes across an age group, particularly in the upper years of primary school.

Teachers are responsible for teaching the basic skills of reading, language and numeracy. They teach science and technology, history, geography and creative performing arts. Creative play is used widely for younger children, while lessons for older ones are generally structured more formally and may involve tests and homework.

Secondary school teacher

Teachers specialize in one or two subjects, but commonly teach them to all age groups and abilities. They may only see each class for 40 minutes a day. Pupils are prepared for GCSE, Advanced Supplementary (AS) and A level examinations, GNVQs and other qualifications.

TEACHING: FAB

Secondary schools have introduced Records of Achievement and these are prepared jointly by teachers and pupils, and give prospective employers a profile of the student's attainments, such as positions of responsibility, yearly reports, extra-curricular and sporting activities, etc.

Teachers make contacts in local industry and arrange work experience for their pupils.

WORK ENVIRONMENT

Teachers may work in many different types of school of varying sizes, from large comprehensives with 1000 pupils, to village schools with 20 children and two teachers. Large urban schools, particularly, often cater for children from many different ethnic cultures. Most state schools are co-educational, and many independent schools are becoming mixed.

Most teachers work in classrooms, but they may teach in workshops, laboratories, and gyms. They are on their feet much of the day and must be fit and mobile. Teachers may work outside, or away from, the school when involved in walks, games and playground duty, the school farm or garden, sports matches, adventure holidays, and outings.

Boarding school teachers may live on the premises or nearby, working in residential and recreational areas as well as in classrooms. Other teachers tutor children in their homes, in hospitals, in centres for young offenders, and on film sets.

SKILLS AND INTERESTS

Teachers have to be caring and fair. They must respect, as well as like, children and want to help them realize their potential.

They need detailed knowledge of a subject and an enthusiasm for it. They also need the confidence and imagination to hold pupils' attention, stimulate their interest and creativity, and maintain order.

They must be able to explain ideas clearly, adapting their teaching methods to the requirements of different age groups and abilities.

Teachers have to be good listeners and encourage pupils to express themselves. Patience and a sense of humour are essential.

Teachers need the flexibility to adapt to new approaches and keep up to date with educational developments, engage in research and contribute to initial teacher training.

Teachers have to be highly motivated and able to organize their time properly, as they work on their own, without supervision. They must be effective managers and must build trusting relationships with pupils, colleagues and parents.

The work offers variety and the satisfaction of promoting children's academic and social development, but it is often stressful and requires mental and physical stamina and resilience.

ENTRY REQUIREMENTS

Teachers in state-maintained and grant-maintained schools in England and Wales must have Qualified Teacher Status (QTS). Independent schools also prefer their staff to be qualified.

QTS is obtained by taking an approved course of initial teacher training (ITT). The two main routes available are:
– a degree course, mainly a four-year BEd or BA/BSc with QTS (Three-year courses are being introduced)
– a postgraduate course, usually for one year and normally leading to the Postgraduate Certificate in Education (PGCE) at a teacher training institution or school consortium (SCITT). An 18-month part-time PGCE is also run by the Open University.

All applicants to ITT must have attained GCSE (A-C), or equivalent, in English language and maths. (Those born after 1 September 1979, who enter primary ITT after September 1998, should also hold GCSE (A-C), or equivalent, in science.)

The undergraduate is the main route for primary teaching. Secondary-level courses are available, but mainly in maths, the sciences, design/technology, modern foreign languages, business studies and PE. Courses are offered at universities and colleges and institutes of higher education.

The minimum entry requirements for the BEd and BA/BSc with QTS are five GCSEs (A-C) with two A levels, or equivalent.

The postgraduate route is mainly for secondary teaching. The entry requirement is a degree appropriate to the secondary curriculum, plus English language and maths at GCSE (A-C), or equivalent. Courses are offered at universities (including the Open University), colleges and institutes of higher education and consortia of schools or city technology colleges (School-centred initial teacher training – SCITT).

Preference may be given to teacher training applicants who have experience working with children – perhaps through a holiday play-scheme or local church. Students usually have to be 18 years old in the year they start a degree course and must be mentally and physically fit to teach. Any previous criminal convictions should be declared.

Applicants with disabilities are encouraged to enter teaching, provided the disability does not inhibit the applicants ability to teach. For further information refer to the institutions or DfEE Circular 13/93.

TRAINING

An emphasis is increasingly being placed on student teachers gaining classroom experience.

Course guides and handbooks are also available from the application clearing houses: the Universities and Colleges Admissions Service (UCAS) for undergraduates, or the Graduate Teacher Training Registry (GTTR) for graduates. The National Association of Teachers in Further and Higher Education (NATFHE) publishes a handbook listing all initial teacher training courses in England and Wales (see FURTHER READING). Detailed course prospectuses are available from individual institutions.

Undergraduate courses

Course content usually includes the study of specialist subjects (usually one main and a secondary subject) and their application to teaching; training in the teaching and assessment of National Curriculum subjects; educational and professional studies – teaching methods, classroom discipline, information technology, pastoral responsibilities, etc, and school experience. Teaching practice will account for a minimum of 32 weeks in school for four-year courses, 24 weeks for three-year courses and 18 weeks for part-time courses.

Postgraduate courses

PGCE courses are offered in universities, colleges of higher education and consortia of schools or city technology colleges. These full-time courses last about 36 weeks and concentrate on educational and professional studies rather than subject study. They include at least 24 weeks' school experience for secondary and 18 weeks' for primary, during which trainee teachers watch others at work, teach individuals and small groups, plan class work and gain experience in class management and control. A few PGCE courses include additional options, such as special needs or youth work. An 18-month distance learning PGCE is also offered by the Open University.

Religious education teaching

Catholic school teachers – particularly those teaching RE – may need the Catholic Teachers Certificate. They can qualify for this while taking a PGCE course at a Catholic college or on a part-time in-service course. Details from diocesan religious education advisers.

Anglican colleges of higher education offer a Certificate in Religious Studies course for teachers of RE in Church of England schools.

In-service training

Schools, institutions, LEAs and HMI run day release, evening and intensive full-time courses through which teachers may keep up with developments in their field, learn about new initiatives and teaching methods, and develop technical or management skills. In-service training includes five days a year for school-based continuing professional development.

LATE ENTRY

There is no upper age limit for entry to teacher training. Older entrants are encouraged and advised to consult teacher trainers about course details.

Many colleges offer access courses to adults over 21 years without conventional qualifications, to prepare them for entry to higher education.

Some institutions offer two-year BEd courses, in some subjects, for those with technical and professional qualifications (eg HNC/HND) and appropriate experience.

Licensed Teacher Scheme

School governing bodies may apply to the Teacher Training Agency (TTA) for a teaching licence for suitable applicants. They must be over 24 years, have GCSEs/S grades (A-C/1-3) in maths and English language (or equivalent) and have successfully completed two years in higher education (or part-time equivalent). Licensed teachers undertake a two-year initial teacher training course within a school, during which they must achieve a range of prescribed competences. A licensee may be recommended for QTS after only one year if they have previous teaching experience.

OPPORTUNITIES

More than 400,000 teachers work in state schools in England and Wales. There are 4,200 secondary schools and 19,000 primaries, catering for more than seven million pupils. The independent sector has about 2,500 schools.

There are shortages of teachers in some parts of the country. Secondary schools are particularly short of teachers in maths, science, modern languages and technology and, in primary education, there is a shortage in the early years. In Wales there is a demand for Welsh-language teachers and those who can teach in the Welsh language.

Opportunities arise in the city technology colleges, funded by the Government and industry. These follow the National Curriculum, but have a technological bias, offering a broad education across the ability range.

There are also openings in HM Forces schools, in young offender institutions, in private tuition, and in hospitals.

The lifting of EU controls offers prospects for language teachers. It also opens up the field for teachers with linguistic skills to work in Europe. Teachers without foreign languages may still find work abroad in company-run and other British schools, and in those run by missionary and other religious or charitable organizations. Details are available from the British Council.

Teaching posts are advertised in internal newsletters carrying details of posts available with the authority, *The Times Educational Supplement; The Teacher,*local papers, Jobcentres and national daily newspapers such as *The Guardian.*

PAY AND CONDITIONS

Teachers with QTS are paid according to a nationally agreed pay spine. Salaries for good honours graduates start from £14,001. Teachers progress up the scale to a designated limit. Additional points may be awarded for excellent performance, recruitment and retention and special educational needs. Head teachers and deputy head teachers are paid on a pay spine ranging from £23,676 to £53,559. Their salaries depend on the size of the school and the ages of the pupils. Teaching in the London area attracts London weighting.

Salaries vary enormously in the independent schools. Many independent schools link their scales to the state scale, others pay higher or lower salaries. Boarding schools may have a separate scale for those living in school accommodation.

State school teachers work 195 days (39 weeks) in the year. They must be available to work under the direction of the head teacher for 1,265 hours during those days – roughly six-and-a-half hours a day. In addition, they plan and prepare courses and lessons, prepare and mark tests and assignments, and attend meetings, sometimes having to work for three or four hours after school.

Opportunities also exist for part-time work, job share and supply teaching.

PROSPECTS

In most schools, there are opportunities for promotion to positions of responsibility. In primary schools, there is a strong demand for head teachers, deputy head teachers and curriculum leaders. Secondary teachers may become head of a subject department or head of year by their late twenties. The new pay structure also encourages those who wish to pursue a career as an expert classroom teacher.

In-service training, geographical mobility, and a willingness to take added responsibility – helping with timetabling or curriculum development, tutoring new teachers, becoming a teacher-governor, etc – increase prospects of promotion.

Some teachers branch into special needs, teacher training or educational administration, become education advisers for local authorities, or work for OFSTED (Office for Standards in Education).

RELATED OCCUPATIONS

Social worker, educational welfare officer, youth and community worker, nursery nurse, careers officer, educational psychologist, outdoor education leader.

FURTHER INFORMATION AND READING

Please see article 5. HIGHER EDUCATION LECTURER.

2. SCHOOL TEACHER – SCOTLAND (FAB)

BACKGROUND INFORMATION

Most Scottish schools belong to the state system – only 4 per cent are grant-aided or independent. The Scottish Office Education and Industry Department (SOEID) and the 32 unitary authorities are responsible for state education, and most authorities have both non-denominational and Roman Catholic state schools. Children attend state primaries from five to twelve years, then move without selection to a comprehensive, where they stay for four to six years. There is nursery provision for some three to five-year-olds. Scotland has its own curriculum guidelines and national assessment of primary children in English and maths.

THE WORK

Teachers aim to build a relationship with their pupils that brings out the best in them and makes them receptive to ideas and knowledge.

Teaching methods vary enormously. Lessons may be delivered from a prepared text or may take the form of a demonstration, an experiment, a discussion, a field trip or a workplace visit. Pupils are encouraged to take an active role in their learning, discovering facts for themselves rather than relying on teachers to present them; teachers direct pupils' research, provide resources, arrange group projects and periods of practical experience, and help pupils collate information.

Whether teachers structure lessons informally or formally, they must devise balanced learning programmes that develop pupils' academic, practical, creative, and social skills. Teachers draw up a syllabus for the 38-week school year, liaising with colleagues when themes are chosen for cross-curriculum study.

Outside the classroom, many hours are spent preparing lessons. This could entail drawing letter shapes for infants' writing practice, or setting up complicated apparatus for an H grade chemistry class. Teachers also set and mark homework, which takes many forms, including essays, lists of questions, mathematical problems, etc. They make continuous assessments of pupils' work and evaluate it through tests and examinations, which must also be set and marked. At the end of each year, subject and general progress reports are written.

Teachers' resources vary, but a wide range of materials and teaching aids is available. In nursery and primary schools, for instance, these may include paints and pens, scissors and glue, modelling clay, sewing materials, musical instruments, building blocks, dressing-up clothes, simple woodworking tools, water and sand, and gardening tools.

Technological education teachers train young pupils to handle simple tools; such as chisels and soldering irons, older ones to use precision tools and sophisticated design software. Language and music tapes and video cassettes are widely used, and computer skills are taught from the early primary years.

All teachers have administrative duties, such as collecting dinner money and ordering stationery. They may also become involved in more general administration and have to attend departmental, curriculum, and parent-teacher meetings.

Teachers have a pastoral or caring role, guiding pupils and advising them on personal problems. Guidance teachers have special responsibilities of this kind and boarding school teachers often care for pupils outside school hours. Many teachers organize extracurricular activities such as concerts, outings, and adventure holidays.

As well as working closely with colleagues, teachers come into contact with parents, social workers, counsellors and many other members of the community.

Nursery/primary school teacher

Nursery/primary teachers will usually have opportunities to teach all ages from three to twelve years, perhaps teaching one age group for a year and another the next. They teach all subjects at primary level and must include maths, language, science and technology, environmental studies, work with computers, art, music, drama, PE, and religious and moral education. Specialist help is available in a number of these areas.

Secondary school teacher

Secondary school teachers work with children of different age groups and levels of ability, specializing in one or two subjects.

In the first and second years, subject study is broad. In years three and four teachers prepare pupils for Scottish Certificate of Education (SCE) standard (S grade) examinations, taken at the end of the fourth year. They tutor fifth and sixth-year pupils for SCE Highers (H grade), and for Certificates of Sixth-Year Studies in special subjects. Fifth and sixth-year pupils may also undertake short courses leading to Scottish Vocational Education Council (SCOTVEC) qualifications in communications, keyboarding, German, etc.

Guidance teachers help pupils choose SCE subjects and give them advice on careers and personal problems. They work as part of a team and may have fewer teaching duties.

WORK ENVIRONMENT

Most primary schools have 100-200 pupils, though in remote districts there may be only 20 pupils and one or two teachers. Most secondary schools have 800-900 pupils. All Scottish state schools are co-educational.

Most teachers work in classrooms, but they may teach in workshops, laboratories, and gyms. They are on their feet much of the day and must be fit and mobile. They may walk long distances between classes or between sites, and often carry heavy loads of books and other equipment. Teachers may work outside, or away from, the school when involved in walks, games and playground duty, the school farm or garden, sports matches, field trips, and outings.

Boarding school teachers may live on the premises or nearby, working in residential and recreational areas as well as in classrooms. Other teachers tutor children in their homes or in hospital.

SKILLS AND INTERESTS

Please see article 1. SCHOOL TEACHER – ENGLAND AND WALES.

ENTRY REQUIREMENTS

Teachers in state and grant-aided schools, and some independent schools, have to register with the General

Teaching Council for Scotland (GTC). To be eligible they must have a teaching qualification (TQ). Primary teachers need a BEd degree in teaching or a Postgraduate Certificate in Education (PGCE). Secondary teachers need a Postgraduate Certificate in Education or a BEd degree in music, technological education, or PE.

Primary – minimum entry requirements are:

1. BEd in Primary Education – three H grades, including English (A-C) and two S grades (1-3) including maths if not offered as an H grade, or equivalent. These will be assessed by the teacher education institution.

2. Postgraduate Certificate in Education – degree plus H grade English and S grade (1-3) maths, or equivalents.

Secondary – minimum entry requirements are:

1. Postgraduate Certificate in Education – degree including at least 80 SCOTCAT points (of which at least 40 must be at second-year level) in the subject to be taught, and H grade English, or equivalents.

Some secondary subjects have more specific individual degree requirements. Details are available from the teacher education institutions, the SOEID or the GTC.

2. BEd in Music, Technological Education or PE – teacher education institutions will assess applications for admissions in terms of their own requirements. These will include H grade English, or equivalent.

SCOTVEC/BTEC and other qualifications may be acceptable. Further details on entry requirements are available from individual teacher education institutions, from the Teacher Education Admissions Clearing House (TEACH), and in the SOEID's annual Memorandum on Entry Requirements for Admission to Courses of Teacher Education in Scotland (from Her Majesty's Stationery Office).

Applications for entry to the postgraduate course are handled centrally by TEACH and the undergraduate courses by the Universities and Colleges Admissions Service (UCAS). All entrants must pass a medical examination before starting a course.

TRAINING

Primary

1. BEd in Primary Education – four-year courses are run at all the Scottish teacher education institutions: University of Paisley Craigie Campus (Ayr), University of Strathclyde Jordanhill Campus (Glasgow), Moray House Institute (Edinburgh), Northern College (Aberdeen/Dundee), and St Andrews College (Glasgow) – Scotland's national Catholic college. Students increase their knowledge of curriculum subjects and study the theory and practice of teaching. Topics include child development, teaching methods, and learning resources. Day and block placements allow students to watch teachers at work and gain classroom experience at nursery and all primary stages.

2. Postgraduate Certificate in Primary Education – one-year courses are run at all the TEIs. The course includes the theory and practice of teaching, curriculum study and analysis, and school placements.

Secondary training

1. Postgraduate Certificate in Secondary Education – one-year courses are run at: University of Paisley (Craigie Campus), University of Strathclyde (Jordanhill Campus), Moray House Institute, Northern College (Aberdeen), and St Andrews College. Applicants are advised to choose courses in two subjects if possible. Courses include subject study, studies in education, psychology, sociology, and educational administration. Half the course is spent on school placement.

2. BEd in Music – four-year courses are run at: University of Strathclyde (Jordanhill), St Andrews College, Royal Scottish Academy of Music and Drama, and at Northern College (Aberdeen). Courses combine specialist musical studies with a thorough grounding in teaching and practical experience in schools.

3. BEd in Technological Education – four-year courses are run at the University of Strathclyde (Jordanhill) and Moray House Institute/Napier University (Edinburgh). These qualify graduates to teach craft and design, technological studies and graphic communication. Courses combine acquisition of technological skills with problem solving, theoretical studies, and placements in schools, colleges and industry.

4. BEd in PE – four-year course run at Moray House includes studies of teaching and learning and of the nature and practice of physical activities, plus four school placements.

5. The University of Stirling offers a concurrent degree obtained over a minimum of seven semesters, which includes the study of education and school experience as part of its curriculum.

Registration

Once qualified, it is necessary to register with the General Teaching Council for Scotland (GTC) before teaching in an education authority school. New teachers undertake a two-year probationary period, before being eligible for full registration.

Students undertaking their probationary period outside Scotland should consult the GTC regarding probation arrangements. Teachers trained outside Scotland should write to the GTC to ensure that they qualify for 'exceptional' admission to the register. The GTC welcomes applications from qualified teachers from outside Scotland.

In-service training, staff development and appraisal

All education authorities are introducing staff development and appraisal schemes on a phased basis. These provide opportunities to review teachers and identify staff development needs. These needs are met through a combination of school-based and externally provided in-service training.

LATE ENTRY

There is no upper age limit for entry to teacher training. Entry requirements may be reduced for applicants of 23 years and over. Teacher education institutions run access courses for mature students who lack conventional qualifications.

OPPORTUNITIES

The state system employs more than 22,000 nursery/primary school teachers and nearly 24,000 secondary school teachers.

There may be opportunities for employment in all 32 education authorities.

There is a continuing demand for teachers who are Gaelic speakers, particularly at primary level. At secondary level, there are opportunities for teachers in maths, physics, computing, business studies, technological education, religious education, modern languages, and music.

Part-time work is available and job-sharing schemes are run in some areas.

There are openings outside the state education sector for teachers to work in independent schools, to give one-to-one tuition, to teach forces children overseas, to teach in hospitals and community homes, and to work voluntarily on short-term contracts overseas.

Teaching posts are advertised in *The Times Educational Supplement (Scottish edition)*, *The Scotsman* (Wednesdays) and *The Herald* (Tuesdays). Lists of vacancies should be available from the 32 education authorities and from governing bodies of independent schools.

PAY AND CONDITIONS

Salaries are paid on an incremental scale ranging from £12,510 to £20,796. The scale entry point for ordinary graduates and equivalents is £12,981; for Honours graduates, £13,605. Additional allowances are paid to teachers in remote schools and distant islands. Late entrants are paid half a scale point extra for every year over 24, up to a maximum of eight increments (subject to certain adjustments).

Head teachers' salaries vary according to number of pupils. They range from £26,376 to £35,532 in primary schools; £30,687 to £48,858 in secondary schools.

Independent school salaries are generally comparable or higher than those in the state sector.

State school teachers work 195 days a year, five of which are pupil-free (190 of them within the 39-week school year). The school day is usually 9am to 3.30pm or 4pm. Teachers work 27½ hours in school with maximum class contact of 25 hours in primary schools, and 23½ hours in secondary schools. In addition, up to 30 hours a year may be required for a maximum of six parents' meetings, along with an annual maximum of 50 hours for planned activities (eg staff meetings, professional developments).

PROSPECTS

Large primary schools may have one or more assistant head teachers, as well as a head. Assistant heads are responsible for an area such as early-stage education or curriculum development.

More than 50 per cent of secondary teachers are in promoted posts.

Promotion to senior teacher depends on expertise and experience. A senior teacher might, for instance, be responsible for helping probationer teachers. Other promoted posts include principal teacher – in charge of a subject department or working in guidance – and assistant principal teacher, assistant head, deputy head and head (rector).

There are opportunities for experienced teachers to move into special needs, work as advisers or administrators for an education authority, or join the schools inspectorate. Overseas work is possible, particularly for experienced teachers.

RELATED OCCUPATIONS

Please see article 1. SCHOOL TEACHER – ENGLAND AND WALES.

FURTHER INFORMATION AND READING

Please see article 5. HIGHER EDUCATION LECTURER.

3. SPECIAL EDUCATIONAL NEEDS TEACHER (FAB)

BACKGROUND INFORMATION

About 20 per cent of school-age children have special educational needs at some time during their school career, although only around two per cent have a long-term need requiring special provision to be made for them. It is this two per cent of children that have statements of special educational needs, and that make up the vast majority of the special school population. All children with impairments are entitled to an appropriate education, regardless of the nature or severity of their difficulty. Most go to ordinary schools. Others attend special schools or units for all or part of their school days, sometimes moving in and out of mainstream schooling as their needs change.

In common with all pupils in the state sector, children with special educational needs, receive – under the National Curriculum – a broad and balanced curriculum.

Over the past decade, increasing numbers of children with severe learning difficulties have been integrated successfully into mainstream schools. Integration policies vary from authority to authority and from school to school.

THE WORK

Teaching methods and curricula vary according to the children's individual requirements. Some children are taught mainstream curriculum subjects with the help of special equipment and resources. Teachers may also devise individual learning programmes or follow programmes designed for children with a particular impairment.

Helping children become more confident and independent is an important part of the work. Severely impaired children may have to be taught to speak or sign, and to dress themselves. Communication-impaired children have individual curriculum programmes or adapted programmes that bring out their strengths, helping them, for example, to understand the written and spoken word. Pupils with emotional and behavioural problems are taught to cope with stress and to manage feelings of anger, fear, or frustration. The teacher's work includes helping children to gain self-confidence, which will enable them to make the best of their abilities.

Pupils with mild learning difficulties are taught in remedial classes, or given extra help in an ordinary class. Some need special assistance across the curriculum, while others receive additional help in only one or two subjects.

Teachers of the deaf or hearing-impaired may use signing, finger spelling and other methods to communicate with children and encourage and develop their language skills.

Blind or partially-sighted children are taught to make the maximum use of residual vision and their other senses. Teaching aids include closed-circuit television, Braille and Moon (methods of reading by touch), cassettes, light-rooms, and computer touch screens.

Children in special schools may require constant medical care and teachers work alongside doctors, nurses, and therapists. Teachers may also liaise with educational psychologists, social workers, advisers and parents.

In residential schools, they help care for and counsel the

children, run hobbies and clubs, and organize games and outings. These extracurricular activities are used to improve skills and social training, as well as provide recreation.

Advisory and peripatetic teachers provide specialist services for schools and units. They teach and supply learning support, ensuring children have the correct lighting, seating position, equipment and resources, etc.

Special educational needs teachers have to carry out administrative duties, write detailed assessments and evaluations, prepare lessons, correct assignments, and attend meetings. Lesson preparation may involve the production of special resources, such as Braille copy.

WORK ENVIRONMENT

Teachers work with small groups of children and occasionally with individuals.

Mainstream schools may have a special unit attached, which draws pupils from a wide radius. Some schools have a classroom, or a quiet room, where teachers give one-to-one assistance. Advisory and peripatetic teachers travel extensively, seeing children at many schools and units. They also visit pre-school children in their homes. Special schools are smaller than most mainstream schools. Many take residential pupils, who are housed in family-style units.

SKILLS AND INTERESTS

The work is physically and emotionally demanding, requiring exceptional maturity and resilience and the ability to remain calm under stress.

Children with special educational needs have a wide range of impairments and behavioural problems. It may take a long time to win their confidence and build individual relationships. They must be treated firmly, but always fairly.

Teachers have to be enthusiastic, sympathetic, patient and persistent. They must remain encouraging and positive, despite setbacks or apparent lack of progress. They need to be able to communicate well by whatever means is most suitable, and have a cheerful and optimistic nature and a good sense of humour. Certain impairments require certain qualities in the teacher. Teachers of the deaf, for instance, need an interest in communication and an open mind on the method used, eg signing, oral communication.

All special educational needs teachers require the organizational skills to allocate their time effectively and make full use of equipment and resources. They work as part of a broad-based team and must relate well to other professionals and support staff. It is also particularly important for special educational needs teachers to build good relationships with parents.

ENTRY REQUIREMENTS

Only qualified school teachers may teach children with special educational needs. Please see articles 1. and 2. SCHOOL TEACHER – ENGLAND AND WALES/ SCOTLAND for initial teacher training entry requirements.

Deaf candidates for initial teacher training must satisfy Department for Education and Employment requirements regarding speech and understanding of speech. Details from the Royal National Institute for Deaf People.

TRAINING

Candidates for specialist training courses must have qualified as a school teacher (via a teaching degree or a subject degree and Postgraduate Certificate in Education) and had at least two years' teaching experience.

In England and Wales, specialist training is recommended for all teachers hoping to move into special educational needs, and is compulsory for those wishing to teach children with impaired vision or hearing.

In Scotland, all teachers of deaf or mentally impaired children, and primary teachers of blind or physically impaired children, need special qualifications.

In-service training courses are run at institutes of higher education throughout the UK. The Department for Education and Employment and local authorities also organize short courses, conferences and other training activities. A limited number of secondments to full-time training are available. Details in *Short Courses for Teachers* from the Department for Education and Employment and from individual colleges.

Training to teach the hearing-impaired – one-year full-time diploma and advanced certificate courses are run at: Birmingham University, Leeds University, Manchester University, University of Hertfordshire, and the Scottish Centre for the Education of the Deaf (c/o Moray House College, Edinburgh). Two-year part-time in-service diploma courses are run at: Birmingham University, Leeds University, Manchester University, Northumbria University and Oxford Brookes University and University College, Wales. Qualified, hearing-impaired teachers wishing to train to teach the deaf may obtain information on the most suitable institutions from the Co-ordinator, The Hearing-Impaired Teacher's Group, c/o RNID and the Director, The National Deaf Children's Society.

Training to teach the vision-impaired – one-year full-time diploma courses are run at: Birmingham University, Gwent College of Higher Education, London University (Institute of Education), Manchester Metropolitan University, Moray House College, Edinburgh and University College Swansea. Two-year part-time diploma courses are run at: Birmingham University (distance learning), the Cambridge Institute of Education, and London University.

More broadly based training includes the one-year full-time and two-year part-time courses run at The Institute of Education, London University, which lead to a Diploma in the Education and Psychology of Children with Special Needs. The course includes modules in severe and moderate learning difficulties, visual impairment, language and communication difficulty, special needs in the ordinary school, emotional and behavioural difficulty, plus advanced training in staff and curriculum development.

LATE ENTRY

Please see articles 1. and 2. SCHOOL TEACHER – ENGLAND AND WALES/SCOTLAND. The work may be suitable for someone returning to teaching after a career break or for someone who gained experience in an area related to special educational needs, before qualifying as a school teacher.

OPPORTUNITIES

Most special educational needs teachers work for local education authorities in special schools and units, in peripatetic services, in mainstream schools, in community homes, and in youth custody centres. Some are employed by the Royal National Institute for the Blind, Barnardo's, National Children's Homes and other voluntary organizations. They work in NHS hospitals and in clinics providing audiological and advisory services.

There are nearly 1,350 local authority special schools in the UK, employing about 16,300 full-time equivalent teachers in England, 680 in Wales, and about 1,900 in Scotland.

The number of special schools is declining, partly because more children are being taught in ordinary schools. Vacant posts tend to be filled by those already employed in special schools. More posts may be created to cope with the increasing number of special educational needs children attending mainstream schools.

There are six grant-aided residential schools in Scotland, run by charities, which cater for sensory-impaired and physically impaired children.

Demand is increasing for teachers to work with children who are language-impaired, with children who have mild learning difficulties, and with children who have social and behavioural difficulties.

Teachers may need to move location in order to obtain work, particularly those who specialize in a certain impairment. There are limited opportunities for part-time and supply teaching.

Vacancies are advertised in *The Times Educational Supplement; The Scottish Educational Journal; The Guardian* and *The Journal of the British Association of Teachers of the Deaf.*

PAY AND CONDITIONS

Most special educational needs teachers are paid on a national 18-point pay spine. (Please see articles 1 and 2. SCHOOL TEACHER – ENGLAND AND WALES/ SCOTLAND). Pupils have regular school hours, but teachers work extra hours for lesson and resource preparation, assessments, etc.

An additional spine point is paid to teachers in special schools and to teachers in mainstream schools who teach pupils with statements of special educational needs. Teachers will also be entitled to an additional point if they take charge of the classes for the hearing-impaired or visually impaired, even if these children do not have statements.

PROSPECTS

Special schools offer limited prospects for promotion because of their declining number. Teachers with relevant experience are sometimes able to move into special schools from other areas of special educational needs. In-service training is widely available to provide advanced specialist qualifications.

There are opportunities for experienced special educational needs teachers to become local education authority advisers, join HM Inspectorate, or move into teacher training.

RELATED OCCUPATIONS

Special support assistant, child care assistant, occupational therapist, youth leader, teacher, social worker.

FURTHER INFORMATION AND READING

Please see article 5. HIGHER EDUCATION LECTURER.

4. FURTHER EDUCATION/TERTIARY COLLEGE LECTURER (FAB)

BACKGROUND INFORMATION

Further education is provided in a wide range of colleges, adult education institutes and other institutions.

The further education sector has close links with commerce and industry, and course provision reflects local and national needs. Increasing emphasis is placed on meeting the educational and personal development requirements of whole communities. Many institutions provide a balanced and comprehensive range of vocational, non-vocational, and academic courses for young people and adults of all ages. Others specialize in an area such as art and design, agriculture and horticulture or hotel and catering, but still ensure that course provision remains broad. A growing number of tertiary colleges offer full-time academic and vocational courses for 16 to 19-year-olds, plus part-time courses for young people and adults. (Post-16 education is also provided in schools and sixth-form colleges.)

THE WORK

Further education/tertiary college lecturers may teach vocational or academic subjects. A few teach recreational or hobby interest subjects. Teaching methods include lectures, seminars, tutorials, demonstrations and practical sessions. Lecturers give advice on background reading and other methods of research, and stimulate analysis and discussion.

Many courses equip students for a particular occupation, trade or profession such as farming, horticulture, light engineering, building, librarianship, catering, hairdressing, textile manufacture, or printing. Courses often have a high practical content, requiring the lecturer to demonstrate skills, operate equipment and supervise workshop practice. Lecturers may also have to arrange and monitor students' work projects and industrial or commercial placements.

Lecturers teach full-time, sandwich, part-time, and short courses. They prepare students for City and Guilds, Royal Society of Arts, BTEC/SCOTVEC and GNVQ/GSVQ qualifications and NVQs/SVQs, and for A levels/H grades in academic subjects. They also teach 'access to higher education' courses. Lecturers in private tutorial colleges coach students for A levels and university entrance. In some colleges of further education, lecturers also prepare students for degrees and higher national certificates and diplomas. Increasingly, lecturers are providing courses on an outreach basis at the workplace or in the community.

Recent school-leavers and unemployed young people are taught skills to help them obtain work, eg job application and interview techniques, operation of computers and other office machinery.

Lecturers' duties also include designing the curriculum, preparing lectures and practical sessions, setting and marking assignments, tests and examinations, carrying out continuous assessments, and performing administrative duties associated with the planning and delivery of courses. Many agricultural and horticultural colleges are residential and lecturers may be involved in sports and other extracurricular activities.

When vocational courses are linked to local employment needs, lecturers spend a substantial amount of time making and maintaining contacts in industry and commerce. They may have to determine the training requirements of individual employers and design appropriate courses.

Lecturers have to keep up with the latest developments in their subjects, through extensive reading or other research.

Some lecturers teach evening and other classes in subjects or skills that do not lead to a particular qualification, eg painting or sculpture as a hobby, or a language for holiday or business purposes. These classes are sometimes referred to as 'informal further education' (as opposed to 'formal further education' that leads to a qualification). Lecturers have to make their subjects accessible to students of widely differing abilities.

WORK ENVIRONMENT

Further education colleges vary greatly in size. A small college may have 50 or fewer staff, while larger establishments could have up to 500 full-time staff.

Lecturers work in class-rooms, laboratories, demonstration rooms, home economics departments, studios, workshops, etc. These may be purpose-built or consist of facilities shared with a school or other centre.

Specialist colleges – those teaching agriculture and horticulture, for instance – have land and buildings attached where practical work is supervised.

SKILLS AND INTERESTS

Lecturers in further/tertiary education must have an interest in their subject and like teaching and training others. They must be able to deliver an appropriate curriculum, based on particular course requirements.

They have to express themselves concisely, and to present and explain ideas clearly to people of differing levels of ability and understanding. They need tact and patience and should be able to gain the respect of others. They must be able to lead and motivate others to develop high standards of work and study.

Lecturers in vocational subjects must have relevant skills and work experience, to enable them to run demonstrations and practical workshops and laboratory classes efficiently and safely.

Lecturers need to be able to manage their workloads efficiently.

ENTRY REQUIREMENTS

England and Wales

A degree; or BTEC/SCOTVEC higher certificate/diploma; or professional qualification; or full City and Guilds Technological Certificate; or advanced RSA certificate; and relevant work experience. Part-time lecturers, particularly in adult education classes, may be accepted on the basis of their work experience alone.

A teaching qualification is not compulsory, but is advisable, and about 50 per cent of FE teachers hold one. Entry requirements for the Certificate in Education (Further Education) are as above; non-graduate applicants should usually be over 24 years.

Scotland

To be eligible for permanent appointments in further education, candidates need one of the following: UK degree; associateship or diploma of a Scottish college of education or other central institution (or equivalent); SCOTVEC/BTEC higher diploma or certificate; full City and Guilds Technological Certificate. Candidates must also have reached an appropriate level in communication and numeracy (usually GCSEs/S grades (A-C/1-3) in English and maths).

A teaching qualification is not compulsory but is highly desirable; promotion within the further education service is difficult without one. About 80 per cent of lecturers have a teaching qualification. Lecturers who enter the service without a teaching qualification are seconded by their employers for professional training to the Scottish School of Further Education (University of Strathclyde).

A medical examination may be requested for full-time posts.

TRAINING

England and Wales

1. One-year full-time pre-service or in-service courses leading to the Certificate in Education (Further Education) are run at: Bolton Institute of Higher Education; The University of Huddersfield; University of Greenwich; and University of Wolverhampton. Courses are offered in business studies, engineering general studies, maths and science, and include study of teaching theory and methods and eleven weeks' teaching practice.

2. Part-time and day release pre-service or in-service courses, leading to a Certificate in Education are more widely available in some of the new universities, in addition to the four establishments mentioned above.

3. Some one-year, full-time Postgraduate Certificate in Education (PGCE) initial teacher training courses contain further education options.

4. The one or two-year part-time City and Guilds Course (7307/7306) leads to a Further and Adult Education Teachers Certificate. City and Guilds also runs an in-service course for further education teachers in special needs. Other courses include the RSA Teachers' Certificate and Diploma in Office Studies.

Further details are in *The NATFHE Handbook of Initial Teacher Training* and *The Directory of Further Education,* published by the Careers Research Advisory Centre.

Scotland

The Scottish School of Further Education Certificate in Education (Further Education) course spans two years and consists of two four-week and two one-week periods of block release combined with distance teaching between the blocks. This course is open to lecturers in further and higher education who are in permanent employment. Course details available from the SSFE at Jordanhill Campus, Glasgow. Post-experience courses are also offered by the SSFE, for career development purposes, to lecturers employed in post-16 education. These are part-time courses that lead to certificate, diploma, first and higher degree awards of the University of Strathclyde, and are open to those who already possess a recognized teaching qualification.

LATE ENTRY

There is no upper age limit to teaching in further/tertiary education, though the need to be up to date in developments and current working practice in a given field may preclude entrants who have had a lengthy career break.

Further education teaching is often a second career, and the mature entrant with appropriate experience is more likely to obtain a lectureship than a young graduate. Qualified adults often start by teaching evening classes. These also provide openings for adults without formal qualifications to teach in a wide range of art and leisure-based subjects.

OPPORTUNITIES

There are about 400 further education colleges in England and Wales and about 55 tertiary colleges, employing a total of about 55,000 full-time and 80,000 part-time teachers. There are about 43 further education colleges in Scotland offering further/higher education and employing about 6,000 full-time and 1,500 part-time lecturers.

The majority of openings arise in local colleges and adult education centres. Colleges may specialize in a particular field, or offer a variety of vocational and academic subjects and general interest courses.

Opportunities arise in tutorial colleges and in private industrial/commercial training establishments. There are also openings in the Prison Service. The Armed Forces employ lecturers (details from their careers offices), and organizations, such as the British Council, recruit lecturers to work in developing countries.

Demand varies locally, but competition is intense for many posts. In vocational subjects, appointments depend largely on work experience, while in more academic subjects, a teaching qualification and secondary school teaching experience may be an advantage.

There are widespread opportunities for part-time lecturing. Full-time lectureships often go to those who have worked part-time for the same local college, though many lecturers prefer to retain their original career and continue to teach part-time.

Positions are advertised in the national press, including *The Times Educational Supplement; The Times Higher Education Supplement; The Guardian; The Herald* and *The Scotsman,* in trade and professional magazines, and locally.

PAY AND CONDITIONS

In England and Wales, local authority incremental pay scales pay within the following ranges: lecturers £11,613 to £21,051; senior lecturers £20,325 to £25,410; management spine £21,111 to £48,507. London weighting is paid in addition.

Rates of pay are similar in Scotland.

NB: Pay and conditions of service in England, Wales and Scotland are under review.

PROSPECTS

In England and Wales, highly qualified candidates are sometimes appointed directly to the post of senior lecturer, but it is usually a promoted position that carries a fair amount of managerial responsibility.

Prospects of promotion to senior lecturer, head of department, etc, are enhanced for those who have teaching qualifications and experience, keep up with developments in their field, have management skills, and are willing to move location. For most promoted posts in Scotland, a teaching qualification is essential.

Many colleges run their own in-service training courses and many have staff development officers who advise other colleges and individuals. Management training is available at the Further Education Development Agency (FEDA), Bristol, and elsewhere. In Scotland, the national centre for such courses is the Scottish School of Further Education at the University of Strathclyde.

RELATED OCCUPATIONS

School teacher, youth and community worker, training officer, higher education lecturer.

FURTHER INFORMATION AND READING

Please see article 5. HIGHER EDUCATION LECTURER.

5. HIGHER EDUCATION LECTURER (FAB)

BACKGROUND INFORMATION

In Britain, higher education is provided in a variety of establishments – universities, colleges of education, etc. Lecturers prepare students for a wide range of first and higher degrees, professional and other qualifications. Courses may be purely academic, or may provide pre-employment training, or specialist training for professionals already in employment.

THE WORK

Lecturers spend many hours researching and preparing for lectures and practicals, setting and marking assignments and exams, carrying out continuous assessment, evaluating research, and monitoring work projects and placements.

Much of the teaching takes the form of lectures on a particular topic or course option. As well as providing information and suggesting areas for further research, lecturers aim to develop students' powers of interpretation, analysis and original thought.

Lectures last for about 50 minutes and may be attended by up to 100 students. Less formal teaching takes place in seminars or tutorials for small groups of students; lecturers may deliver prepared material, but also lead discussions and give comments on students' essays or other work.

In subjects such as science and engineering, lecturers supervise sessions of practical work or experiment lasting up to three hours. Lecturers also lead field trips and arrange work projects and placements.

Increasing numbers of higher education institutions are adapting curricula and teaching methods so that students can take more responsibility for their learning. Lecturers help students plan learning programmes based on their interests and talents and encourage them to acquire skills, such as word processing, management techniques, etc. They may arrange work experience for students who would not normally require it, and link courses more closely to regional and community needs.

Many full-time lecturers act as personal tutors to individual students, advising them on their study, careers and personal problems. They may specialize in student counselling, or become wardens of residential halls.

They also have many administrative duties, whether helping with student admissions, serving on curriculum development and departmental committees, or acting as external examiners for other colleges.

Lecturers have to keep up to date with their subject, through extensive reading and through following developments outside higher education. In the traditional universities, most staff are required to undertake research. Those engaged in research aim to publish their findings or contribute them to relevant companies or associations. The proportion of time devoted to teaching and to research varies between posts and institutions.

WORK ENVIRONMENT

Higher education institutions vary greatly in size and may have up to 1,000 full and part-time staff.

Depending on their subject, teachers work in lecture halls, seminar and tutorial rooms, laboratories and workshops, hospital wards and clinics. Field trips, work project placements, and visits to employer contacts, all take lecturers off-campus.

Research takes place in libraries, laboratories, and in the field. Many science and technical projects are team efforts, but research in the arts, for instance, may be undertaken alone.

SKILLS AND INTERESTS

Lecturers need an extensive knowledge of their subject. They are likely to specialize within their field, and must be able to produce a well-balanced programme of lectures based on course requirements.

They must be interested in teaching and be able to explain facts and theories clearly and imaginatively. This requires self-confidence and good written and spoken communication skills.

Lecturers should be able to encourage the development of intellectual skills in others and motivate them to achieve course objectives and deadlines. It is important to be flexible and to be able to work both with large numbers of students, and in one-to-one situations. Lecturers, especially those who are personal tutors, must be interested in the welfare of their students. Tact, patience, and the ability to get on with all kinds of people are essential.

Lecturers in vocational subjects must have relevant work experience and be able to set their teaching in an appropriate professional or industrial context.

All higher education teachers need to manage their work schedules efficiently.

ENTRY REQUIREMENTS

New entrants need a good honours first degree, usually a first-class or upper second. They may also need a postgraduate qualification, such as an MA, MSc, PhD, or equivalent professional qualification. In universities, increasingly, many new entrants spend some time working on short-term research or hourly paid teaching contracts.

Those teaching applied or vocational subjects also need professional and industrial experience, as well as academic qualifications, particularly in fields such as engineering, management, journalism, or art and design.

A medical is usually needed for permanent full-time positions.

TRAINING

There is no specific training for this kind of lecturing. Many college lecturers have a Postgraduate Certificate in Education (PGCE) – see article 1. SCHOOL TEACHER – ENGLAND AND WALES. Most institutions of higher education run their own training schemes.

LATE ENTRY

There is no upper age limit to teaching in higher education and late entry is common. Breadth of knowledge and experience determine teaching appointments and, in vocational subjects, particularly, lecturers are rarely younger than 28 years.

Entry to teacher training courses is usually relaxed, for mature entrants lacking conventional qualifications.

OPPORTUNITIES

There are over 100 institutions of higher education, employing around 60,000 lecturers on a part-time or full-time basis.

The institutions include universities, colleges, institutes of education and higher education. These are found throughout the United Kingdom, and are based in most major towns and cities.

Posts in higher education are generally scarce and go to those who have excellent academic or professional qualifications, plus substantial work experience, where applicable. In the universities, there are openings for young researchers, particularly in the sciences.

Competition is intense, although vacancies may be easier to find in shortage subjects, such as maths and science. The availability of vacancies also depends on student numbers and funding.

Some lecturers work abroad, teaching in English-speaking colleges or universities, or training teachers in developing countries. American universities have openings for highly qualified and experienced lecturers. The Overseas Development Administration and Voluntary Service Overseas recruit teacher-training staff.

Positions are advertised in *The Times Higher Education Supplement* and in national newspapers.

PAY AND CONDITIONS

Old universities in England, Wales, and Scotland

The pay scales are: lecturer A £15,154 to £19,848; lecturer B £20,677 to £26,430 (discretionary to £29,532); senior lecturer £27,747 to £31,357 (discretionary to £33,898); professor, minimum £28,742. The incremental scale includes discretionary points beyond standard maximum earnings. Rates above professor minimum are negotiated individually. Clinical teachers are paid higher salaries negotiated by the British Medical Association.

New universities in England and Wales

The incremental pay scale for new universities and colleges: lecturer £13,100 to £21,838; senior lecturer £26,381 to £26,931; principal lecturer £25,474 to £32,030; head of department, minimum £26,304; the part-time hourly rate for the work is £23.30 an hour. London weighting may also be paid.

Scotland

The incremental pay scale for centrally funded institutions: lecturer £12,897 to £23,145; senior lecturer £21,228 to £27,444; department head £28,305 to £37,764. Salaries of principals and other senior management staff are determined by individual governing boards.

Lecturers employed by local authorities are paid on the same scale as further education lecturers. Please see article 4. FURTHER EDUCATION/TERTIARY COLLEGE LECTURER.

Universities and colleges have ten to twelve-week terms, but working hours vary enormously according to subject, research commitments, etc.

PROSPECTS

In the old universities, academic ability is usually considered more important than teaching skill. This is less true in new universities and colleges. Promotion prospects are enhanced by published research or a doctorate, and through evidence of administrative skill. In recent years, promotional prospects have declined because of reduced funding.

In other higher education institutions, publication of work, acquisition of specialist professional qualifications, and proof of management ability enhance promotion prospects. Promotion usually leads to more consultancy work and more administration.

Specialists and recognized scholars are frequently offered work outside the institution where they teach. They may act as consultants, edit or annotate texts, contribute to magazines and newspapers, take part in radio and television broadcasts, and run or address conferences.

RELATED OCCUPATIONS

Training manager, further education/tertiary college lecturer, training officer, management consultant.

FURTHER INFORMATION

Association of University Teachers (AUT), United House, 9 Pembridge Road, Notting Hill, London W11 3JY, 0171 221 4370

The British Council*, Corporate Personnel (Recruitment), 10 Spring Gardens, London SW1A 2BN, 0171 930 8466

General Teaching Council for Scotland*, 5 Royal Terrace, Edinburgh EH7 5AF, 0131 556 0072

Graduate Teacher Training Registry*, Fulton House, Jessop Avenue, Cheltenham, Glos GL50 3SH, 01242 225868

National Association of Teachers in Further and Higher Education (NATFHE), 27 Britannia Street, London WC1X 9JP, 0171 837 3636

The National Deaf Children's Society, 15 Dufferin Street, London EC1Y 8PD

The Open University, PO Box 200, Milton Keynes MK7 6YZ, 01908 653231

University and College Lecturers' Union*, 27 Britannia Street, London WC1X 9JP, 0171 837 3636

Physical Education Association of the United Kingdom*, Suite 5, 10 Churchill Square, Kings Hill, West Malling, Kent ME19 4DU, 01732 875588

Royal National Institute for the Blind*, Physiotherapy Support Service, 224 Great Portland Street, London W1N 6AA, 0171 388 1266 (please send sae)

Royal National Institute for Deaf People*, 19-23 Featherstone Street, London EC1Y 8SL, 0171 296 8000 (please send sae)

The Scottish School of Further Education*, University of Strathclyde, Jordanhill Campus, 76 Southbrae Drive, Glasgow G13 1PP, 0141 950 3143

Further Education Development Agency (FEDA), Coombe Lodge, Blagdon, Bristol BS18 6RG, 01761 462503

The Teacher Training Agency (TTA)*, Communication Centre, PO Box 3210, Chelmsford, Essex CM1 3WA, 01245 454454

Teacher Education Admissions Clearing House (TEACH)*, Holyrood Road, PO Box 165, Edinburgh EH8 8AQ

Universities and Colleges Admissions Service, UCAS*, Fulton House, Jessop Avenue, Cheltenham, Glos GL50 3SH, 01242 227788

The Welsh Office*, Education Department, Cathays Park, Cardiff CF1 3NQ

FURTHER READING

Leaflets/booklets are available from the addresses marked* above, including a wide selection of literature from TTA, and videos from TEACH and GTC.

Working in Teaching – COIC
Secondary Teaching – The Challenge and the Reward – DfEE Publications Centre

NATFHE Handbook of Initial Teacher Training available in libraries and careers advisory departments. Or buy from Linneys (NATFHE), 121 Newgate Lane, Mansfield, Notts NG18 2PA.

In the careers library classified under FAB.

1. JOURNALIST CLCI:FAC
2. TECHNICAL AUTHOR CLCI:FAC

1. JOURNALIST (FAC)

BACKGROUND INFORMATION

Journalists keep people informed about events around them by researching, writing and presenting news stories and feature articles in newspapers, magazines, on radio and television and in other media.

THE WORK

Newspaper journalists may work for local and regional newspapers, where everyday activities form much of the reported news. Their reporters gather news of fetes, council meetings, court sittings and local crime. Stories reported in the larger national newspapers may be very different, but the work of all journalists brings them into contact with people, events and places.

Research methods, often aided by shorthand notes, include face-to-face and telephone interviews (with or without sophisticated recording equipment), visits and library research. The news story, or 'copy' is then written and typed by the journalist, often using a word processor or computer terminal in a newspaper newsroom. The completed copy, together with a carefully worded introduction and headline, then passes to a sub-editor who edits the work, and possibly returns some of the work for rewriting.

Magazine journalists may work for consumer magazines, or for business and trade magazines. There are many similarities with newspaper journalism – research, interviews, checking facts, writing-up copy and sub-editing, but magazines are usually produced to weekly or monthly deadlines. Many magazine publishers employ specialist freelance writers in addition to staff journalists.

Broadcast journalists work for national and independent radio and television companies. Many experienced press journalists hoping to move into this type of work start by working as a local radio reporter.

When employed as programme assistants, journalists may have to operate broadcast studio equipment as well as reading the news or presenting programmes. Most television newsreaders are also experienced journalists. Journalists also work on documentary programmes as researchers.

Press agency journalists supply news stories, features and photographs to newspaper and magazine publishers. Some press agencies, such as Reuters, specialize in supplying international news. Other journalists work as press or public relations officers for major companies and other commercial organizations. They prepare press releases of information about the organization, and provide information to their press and broadcasting colleagues.

WORK ENVIRONMENT

Many journalists are office-based, in conditions that vary considerably. Some offices are modern and well equipped, but others may be small and cramped. Working on an assignment may involve anything from interviewing on location and in the street, to using the full range of facilities provided in the press room at a major event.

While some reporters use the latest satellite links for the instant transmission of a news story back to a distant newsroom, others are still using a traditional notebook and pencil.

There are opportunities to travel locally while covering news stories. Journalists working on national newspapers may be expected to travel widely in the UK, often staying overnight in hotels. A small number of press and broadcast journalists travel abroad. The work environment may be pressured and hectic, particularly when publication deadlines are close.

SKILLS AND INTERESTS

Successful journalists need to be interested and inquisitive communicators: they must be interested in local and current affairs, able to discover the relevant facts of any story and to have the ability to communicate their interest and enthusiasm in clear and concise writing, or through broadcasting.

Some journalists have a detailed knowledge of one particular technical field, and work closely with people sharing the specialization. Information technology skills can be important, and include the ability to use different computer software systems and a knowledge of how information can be transferred electronically.

Self confidence, attention to detail, the ability to face criticism, the ability to work in a team and a willingness to work unsociable hours are important. A driving licence is an asset.

ENTRY REQUIREMENTS

This is an occupation without standard formal entry requirements, although the majority of journalists now enter as graduates – but not necessarily with degrees in journalism. Good communication skills are essential and appropriate technical knowledge of computer systems may be required.

Entry to degree courses: minimum entry requirements to a degree course are usually two A levels/three H grades plus five GCSEs/S grades (A-C/1-3), or equivalent. English is an essential requirement at GCSE/S grade level, but may not be required at A level/H grade. Appropriate work experience is essential for entry to some degree courses.

Entry requirements for a postgraduate diploma are usually a BTEC/SCOTVEC higher award, or a first degree, together with at least three years appropriate employment experience. A good first degree, or a postgraduate diploma, is usually required for entry to a higher degree.

Entry to BTEC and SCOTVEC higher awards: usual entry requirements are usually one pass at A level/H grade, plus five GCSEs/S grades (A-C/1-3). Appropriate industrial experience, or alternative qualifications, may also be acceptable.

Direct entry: minimum entry qualifications are five GCSEs/S grades (A-C/1-3) including English, or an equivalent. The majority of entrants have at least two A levels/three H grades. More than half of all recruits to training schemes now enter as graduates.

Entry to City and Guilds courses: no specific academic qualifications are required for entry to the Certificate in Media Techniques (Journalism and Radio), although this course is often provided with appropriate A level courses to create a full-time two-year course, for which entry requirements may be at least four GCSEs/S grades (A-C/1-3).

Entry to pre-entry courses: applicants are usually expected to have at least two A levels/three H grades, or equivalent qualifications.

TRAINING

There are many ways of training for a career in journalism. Degree courses in Journalism are available at: Bell College, Hamilton; Bournemouth University; University of Central Lancashire; City University; Darlington College; University of Wales College of Cardiff; London College of Printing; Napier University; Nottingham Trent University and West Surrey College of Art and Design. These courses usually last for three years.

Full-time postgraduate diploma courses in various aspects of journalism are available at: University of Central Lancashire; City University; University of Wales College of Cardiff; Falmouth School of Art and Design; Glasgow Caledonian University; London College of Printing; Trinity and All Saints College; University of Central England and University of Westminster. These courses usually last for one academic year.

Postgraduate higher degrees in Journalism can be studied at: University of Wales College Cardiff; City University; Westminster University and Bournemouth University.

BTEC and SCOTVEC higher national courses in journalism are available at: Harlow College; London College of Printing and Middlesex University. These courses usually last for two years.

A small number of school and college-leavers, and some graduates, are recruited directly by newspaper groups as journalist trainees. Most training schemes are linked to the National Council for the Training of Journalists (NCTJ). Trainees usually sit NCTJ examinations after two years, but may be entered for other qualifications. Some of the larger groups operate their own in-house training schemes.

Pre-entry and other certificate courses in journalism are available at: Cornwall College; Darlington College; Gloucestershire College of Arts and Technology; Gwent Tertiary College; University of Central Lancashire; Highbury College; Lambeth College; Sheffield College (Stradbroke) and South East Essex College of Art And Technology. These courses usually last for up to one year. Some courses start in January, and run for one calendar year. City and Guilds certificate courses in Journalism are available at some colleges of further education. These one-year part-time courses lead to a Level 2 C&G Certificate in Media Techniques – Journalism and Radio (7790). The course may be combined with A level courses as a full-time two-year foundation course in journalism that may be taken as preparation for direct-entry schemes or for further training and degree courses.

NVQs/SVQs in Journalism are available at Level 4.

For further details about training in journalism contact NCTJ Training Ltd.

LATE ENTRY

There are no formal upper age limits for entry to this occupation, but some newspaper groups may restrict training scheme entry to applicants under 25 years. Many adults develop a career in freelance journalism after previous career experience in another field.

Access-to-journalism courses are available at: Lambeth College; Handsworth Technical College; Sheffield College; Highbury College; Swansea College and City of Liverpool Community College.

OPPORTUNITIES

With the large numbers of national and regional newspapers, consumer and business magazines, local and national broadcasting stations and news agencies, the range of opportunities in journalism is broad. More than 130 daily and Sunday newspapers are published in the UK, plus almost 800 weekly newspapers and more than 1,000 local free papers. More than 2,000 consumer magazine titles are currently in publication, plus a further 4,500 business and professional titles. There has been considerable recent growth in the number of business and professional magazines, with an increase from 2,800 to the present figure in the past ten years. The expansion of satellite broadcasting may offer further opportunities in the future.

Approximately 700 places are taken by trainee journalists each year. More than half of these are direct entrants, who attend block release courses at college. The remainder train through one-year pre-entry or postgraduate courses. Opportunities are available throughout the country, but there is a concentration of national newspaper and magazines publishers in London and the South East. There is also a concentration of broadcasting and press agency opportunities in London, and many regional newspapers have London offices. Freelance journalists work on a self-employed basis, often for a variety of newspaper or magazine publishers. Estimates of the total number of journalists vary. The largest organization, the National Union of Journalists, currently has approximately 26,000 members. Some of these work as press or information officers. Job advertisements are found in the *UK Press Gazette, Media Week* and *The Guardian.*

PAY AND CONDITIONS

The basic rates for trainee journalists can start at between £7,000 and £8,000 for those working in provincial newspapers, or more than £10,000 for those working in radio or television journalism. The pay and working conditions of more experienced journalists vary considerably. Salaries are usually higher in national newspapers and in television journalism: experienced reporters can earn up to £30,000, but a small number of senior journalists earn considerably more.

Freelance journalists usually negotiate and agree a set fee for each piece of work. These rates vary considerably, according to the newspaper or magazine publisher. Some publishers pay freelance journalists at a rate for every 1,000 words.

'Stringers' are journalists working on a freelance basis for a number of publishers. Very few journalists work a routine 9-5 day and Monday-to-Friday week.

Newspaper journalists can be expected to work long and irregular hours, including some evenings and weekends spent reporting on events or writing up copy in time to reach a deadline.

Magazine journalists may work more regular hours, although they usually have some very long working days as publication deadlines approach.

National newspaper and broadcast journalists may work shifts, perhaps of eight hours, and be on call to cover any major news stories.

PROSPECTS

Promotion is based solely on merit. Many newspaper journalists spend at least two or three years working on a local paper, perhaps then progressing to a regional morning or evening daily.

Competition for national newspapers and broadcasting work is severe; many gain the necessary experience by working 'shifts' on a freelance basis. In this way, journalists become known for their style of work, and improve their chances of finding a permanent or 'staff' job. Experienced staff may have the opportunity to become specialist correspondents, providing regular contributions, for example, on arts, sports or education topics.

Examples of more senior jobs include: sub-editor, with responsibility for copy accuracy, headlines and page layout; news editor; features editor; editor; and chief editor (of a group of newspapers).

Each post involves an increasing level of responsibility for the nature of the editorial items included in the publication. Some journalists, often with a specialist background, move from newspapers to magazine journalism, with occasional opportunities for promotion to editor, publisher and director posts. Other experienced journalists move into broadcast journalism, news agency work and public relations.

Many large companies employ experienced journalists as press officers, with the responsibility for all communications between that company and the media.

RELATED OCCUPATIONS

Public relations officer, press officer, information officer, editor, advertising copywriter, writer, photojournalist, researcher.

FURTHER INFORMATION

British Broadcasting Corporation, PO Box 7000, London W5 2WY, 0181 849 0849

National Council for the Training of Journalists, Latton Bush Centre, Southern Way, Harlow, Essex CM18 7BL, 01279 430009 (please include sae)

National Union of Journalists, 314-320 Gray's Inn Road, London WC1X 8DP, 0171 837 8143 (please send sae)

Newspaper Society*, Bloomsbury House, Bloomsbury Square, 74-77 Great Russell Street, London WC1B 3DA, 0171 636 7014

Periodicals Training Council*, Imperial House, 15-19 Kingsway, London WC2B 6UN, 0171 836 8798

Scottish Newspaper Publishers' Association, 48 Palmerston Place, Edinburgh EH12 5DE, 0131 220 4353

FURTHER READING

Leaflets/booklets are available from the addresses marked*.

Job Outlines – Journalism – COIC
Working in Journalism – COIC
Working in TV and Video – COIC
Careers in Journalism – Kogan Page
Benn's UK Media Directory (Annual) – Benn Business Ltd

In the careers library classified under FAC.

2. TECHNICAL AUTHOR (FAC)

BACKGROUND INFORMATION

As technological equipment and commercial processes have become increasingly complex, and the demand for published information has continued to expand, this occupation has developed to deal with the preparation of technical documents, reports and instruction manuals.

There are various fields of technical authorship: writing manuals and user guides for computer software systems; writing technical reports for scientific, engineering and various commercial operations; preparing technical documents for publication; preparing technical catalogues and indexes; producing 'executive summaries' from longer documents and reports; writing instruction manuals for those using or maintaining technical equipment – from consumer products to large-scale manufacturing plant.

THE WORK

The list of organizations producing technical publications is very long, and includes engineering companies, software publishers, computer manufacturers, scientific research organizations, financial companies and other commercial firms.

Technical authors have to plan each new project to find out what information is needed, who will be using the publication and how the information will need to be presented. They collect necessary information by a variety of research methods, including tape-recorded interviews, 'on-site' visits, frequent meetings, telephone interviews, library work and using computer databases.

Much of the information needs to be carefully checked before it can be used. Once all the data is collected and prepared, the publication can be written in the most appropriate style for the intended readers. An instruction manual for someone without technical knowledge is written in a completely different way to a technical report intended only for experts in that field.

If illustrations are required, the technical author may need to work with a technical illustrator or a photographer. Before any technical publication can be published, the first draft version has to be carefully studied by other experts in that particular field. A second draft version is produced once everything has been checked and all corrections and alterations made.

The text is then produced in a style ready for publication. This may be done by the technical author, using word processing or desktop publishing software, by a professional typesetter, or by the printing company. The final responsibility of a technical author is to check and correct the printer's proof copy before printing and final publication.

Writers frequently have to work on several projects at once, with each at a different stage of production. Most projects have to be completed and checked by a particular deadline. Freelance authors have to spend some of their time finding new projects.

WORK ENVIRONMENT

Technical authors employed directly by industrial or research organizations may be based in offices close to production or laboratory areas; alternatively they may work in well-lit and well-equipped offices. Freelance technical authors may work at home, or from their own small office, but often make visits to the organizations for whom they are doing a particular project.

SKILLS AND INTERESTS

All technical authors must be able to write clearly and concisely. Those involved in the production of instruction manuals or summaries of detailed reports must be able to explain technical terms in straightforward language.

The work involves a great deal of research, cataloguing,

cross-referencing and filing; technical authors need an enquiring mind and the ability to work methodically. They frequently have a detailed knowledge of one particular technical field, and work closely with people sharing the specialization. They also need the ability to work with a wide variety of other people, including publishers and editors, technical specialists from other fields, and those who do not share their technical background.

Information technology skills are important for most technical authors. These include the ability to use different personal computer software systems, and a knowledge of how information can be transferred between computer systems. They also need to know about print production processes to be able to prepare text for publication.

ENTRY REQUIREMENTS

There are no standard formal entry requirements, but the majority of technical authors have previous qualifications and experience in specialist scientific, engineering, technical or commercial fields; many technical authors are graduates.

Good communication skills and appropriate technical knowledge are essential. It is possible for a school and college-leaver to train specifically in technical authorship, but the majority of students taking City and Guilds training courses are studying by day release or by distance learning, and are already employed in an engineering or other technical field.

Entry to City and Guilds courses: no specific academic qualifications are required for entry to the Level 1 course in Technical Communication. Applicants are usually expected to have technical qualifications and experience appropriate to their particular specialization. Applicants for the Level 2 course in Technical Authorship are usually expected to have a pass in the Level 1 course.

Entry to BTEC/SCOTVEC higher awards – minimum entry requirements are one A level/two H grades plus five GCSEs/S grades (A-C/1-3). Preferred examination subjects include English language, maths, and science or technical subjects. Appropriate industrial experience, or alternative qualifications, may also be acceptable.

Entry to degree courses – minimum entry requirements are two A levels/three H grades plus five GCSEs/S grades (A-C/1-3), or equivalent. Preferred examination subjects include languages, sciences or technical subjects.

Entry to postgraduate courses – usual entry requirements for a postgraduate diploma are a BTEC/SCOTVEC higher award, or a first degree, together with appropriate employment experience, such as working experience as a practising engineer for at least three years. A good first degree, or a postgraduate diploma, is usually required for entry to a higher degree.

TRAINING

City and Guilds courses in The Communication of Technical Information are available at: Chippenham Technical College; Cleveland College of Further Education and Highbury College. These one and two-year part-time evening or day release courses lead to a Level 1 C&G Certificate in Technical Communications Techniques (5361) and to a Level 2 C&G certificate in Technical Authorship (5362).

On completion of C&G 5361, students should be able to: have an outline appreciation of the communication process; match information to different users' needs; collect and sort information; prepare and present information; understand special factors in international communication; understand methods of communicating. On completion of C&G 5362, students should be able to: appreciate the role of the technical author; plan an assignment; gather information; establish the technical content; prepare draft information; commission technical illustrators; prepare work for reproduction and distribution; understand supporting equipment and processes.

Commercial training organizations, including BDC Limited, Tutortex Services and the College of Technical Authorship, offer tuition programmes by distance learning leading to certificate qualifications, and to the City and Guilds awards. These distance learning courses are available to individuals working as freelance technical authors, and to companies that offer them as in-house training provision for their employed technical authors. BTEC/SCOTVEC higher national courses in Communication Studies are available for students with an appropriate BTEC/SCOTVEC national diploma or with A level/H grade qualifications. The Higher National Diploma in Design (Publications) at Blackpool and the Fylde College is specifically related to technical authorship. This two-year course includes a practical project, and is suitable for people with a technical background.

A degree course in Technical Communication is available at Coventry University for students with a subject background in languages, technology or science. This is the only first-degree course specifically related to technical authorship, but many universities offer other degree courses in communication and information studies.

Full-time postgraduate diploma courses in Technical Authorship and Technical Communication are available at: Humberside University; Northumbria University at Newcastle and Sheffield Hallam University. These courses usually last for one academic year. Postgraduate higher degrees in Multilingual Professional Communication and Science Communication can be studied at Aston University and Imperial College of Science and Technology.

Other training opportunities for adults are available in some areas for this type of work. Contact your local Jobcentre, careers office or TEC/LEC for details.

LATE ENTRY

There are no formal upper age limits for entry to this occupation. Many technical authors undertake the work after previous technical career experience.

OPPORTUNITIES

The principal opportunities for technical authors are working as salaried employees of a company, or working as self-employed freelance writers. Employed technical writers typically work for the publications departments of major engineering and scientific companies, or for computer software publishers, where they produce a wide range of technical literature. There are also employed opportunities with professional bodies, research organizations and government departments.

Some technical authors are employed by technical publications contractors. These companies specialize in technical writing, and provide services for smaller companies that do not have their own publications departments.

There are full-time and part-time opportunities for employed technical authors. Freelance technical authors work on a self-employed basis. They often have considerable experience of technical authorship within a company or other organization, before setting up their own business. Some freelance writers work on projects for one main company, or for a technical publications contractor, while others work for a variety of clients.

Opportunities are available throughout the country. There is currently a shortage of skilled and experienced technical authors with an appropriate technical background.

PAY AND CONDITIONS

There are no standard pay scales for this occupation. Actual rates of pay within companies vary considerably, according to the level of previous technical experience, writing experience, qualifications, complexity of the project and the type of employer. Technical authors in training may earn less than £6,000; those with experience may earn in excess of £20,000.

Freelance technical authors either charge for their services at an hourly rate, or negotiate and agree a set fee for each piece of work. There are no standard fees; rates vary considerably according to the company involved and the degree of complexity of the particular project. Some freelance technical authors may charge £20 an hour or more, but others are paid considerably less. Employed technical authors usually work normal daytime office hours. Those who are self-employed are often expected to complete projects by a certain deadline, and therefore frequently work longer hours – sometimes including evenings and weekends.

PROSPECTS

There are few formal promotion routes with this type of work, although there are limited editorial and managerial opportunities in the publications departments of larger companies. With experience, many technical authors choose to set-up their own business and work on a freelance basis.

RELATED OCCUPATIONS

Engineer, scientist, journalist, editor, technical illustrator, computer programmer.

FURTHER INFORMATION

City and Guilds (C&G)*, 1 Giltspur Street, London EC1A 9DD, 0171 294 2468

Institute of Scientific and Technical Communicators*, Kings Court, 2-16 Goodge Street, London W1P 1FF, 0171 436 4425 (please include sae)

Eston Training, BDC Technical Services Limited, Slack Lane, Derby DE22 3FL, 01332 347123

Tutortex Services, 55 Lightburn Avenue, Ulverston, Cumbria LA12 0DL, 01229 586333

College of Technical Authorship, PO Box 7, Cheadle, Cheshire, SK8 3BY, 0161 437 4235

FURTHER READING

Leaflets/booklets are available from the address marked*.

In the careers library classified under FAC.

EDITOR CLCI:FAD

THE WORK

Editors control the process of newspaper, book and magazine publishing by deciding what to publish, finding the right person to research and write the copy, checking and making any necessary amendments to the completed copy, deciding the final page layout to be used, working with production staff and checking final proof copies immediately before printing. The work varies considerably with the type of publication, and with the type of editing to be done. Many different job titles are in use.

Newspaper publishing

Sub-editors receive items submitted by journalists and then check thoroughly for any spelling, grammatical or style errors that require amendment. Their work may also involve selection of suitable illustrations, liaison with production staff and a responsibility for checking the legality of printing particular items. Senior editors – with job titles such as features editor, political editor or sports editor – look after different sections of a national newspaper. Art editors, or picture editors, are responsible for the photographs and other illustrations used in each issue.

Book and magazine publishing

Copy-editors or desk-editors see each project through from first proposals and draft outline to final proofs. Once a completed manuscript has been submitted they have to check it carefully for any grammatical or factual errors. They may also need to amend the text to match a particular 'house-style', or sometimes request the author to make some alterations to style or length. Commissioning editors decide which titles will eventually be published. They gradually build-up a 'list' of titles by considering proposals or completed manuscripts submitted by authors, by suggesting topics to authors with whom they have worked previously, or by buying titles previously published by other publishing houses. They negotiate terms for payment with the author and produce some form of contract, usually a standard publishing agreement, and regularly discuss progress with the author.

Other jobs in editing

Some publishers employ specialist proofreaders to check manuscripts, and indexers to create the index to a technical book. Proofreaders and indexers, when required, are increasingly employed on a freelance basis for particular projects. Larger publishing houses may have senior posts, such as editorial managers or editorial directors, with overall responsibility for a team of editors, or for developing the list of that company.

WORK ENVIRONMENT

Many editors are office-based, in conditions that vary considerably. Some offices are modern and well equipped, but others may be small and cramped. Many editors work 'on-screen' using word processing computer software to edit the work of journalists or writers. Some editors produce final page layouts on-screen by using desktop publishing software. Book and magazine editors frequently attend meetings with writers, designers and production specialists, and with suppliers. The work environment is frequently pressured and hectic, particularly when publication deadlines are close.

SKILLS AND INTERESTS

Successful editors must have a good command of grammar and spelling, in order to locate and correct errors, and make essential checks for accuracy before final printing. They may also have to rewrite sections of copy. A knowledge of proof-correction marks, typography, in-house style guides and the requirements of various printing processes are all essential. Some book and technical magazine editors have a detailed knowledge of one particular field, and work closely with people sharing the specialization. Information technology skills can be important, including the ability to use different computer software systems and a knowledge of how information can be transferred electronically. Self confidence, attention to detail, the ability to face criticism, the ability to work in a team, and a willingness to work unsocial hours are important. A driving licence is an asset.

ENTRY REQUIREMENTS

There are no standard formal entry requirements, but a large proportion of editors are graduates. The majority of editors working in newspaper publishing and in broadcasting enter as experienced journalists. The majority of editors working for publishing houses enter as graduates, although people are increasingly entering with degrees specifically related to publishing.

Entry to degree courses is usually with a minimum of two A levels /three H grades, plus five GCSEs/S grades (A-C/1-3), or a BTEC/SCOTVEC national or higher award, or equivalent. Some courses may require additional examination passes at specific grades. Usual entry requirements for a postgraduate diploma are either a BTEC/SCOTVEC higher award, a first degree, or appropriate professional experience. A good first degree, or a postgraduate diploma is usually required for entry to a higher degree.

Entry to BTEC and SCOTVEC higher awards: usual entry requirements are one A level/two H grades, plus three GCSEs/S grades (A-C/1-3). Appropriate industrial experience, or alternative qualifications, may also be acceptable.

Publishers of specialist titles may recruit entrants with previous qualifications and experience in a particular field, perhaps legal, commercial scientific or teaching. Typing ability and word processing experience are often essential. Some editors are recruited with experience of particular desktop publishing computer systems, or with previous experience of preparation for various printing processes.

Entry to City and Guilds courses requires no specific academic qualifications, but applicants are usually already employed as editors.

TRAINING

Degree courses in aspects of publishing are available at: Loughborough University of Technology; Napier University; Robert Gordon University; and Thames Valley University. Degree courses in Graphic Media Studies, including publishing options, are available at Hertfordshire University and West Hertfordshire College. Multidisciplinary degree courses, including options in publishing, are available at: Middlesex University; Oxford Brookes University and Swansea Institute of Higher Education. Postgraduate diplomas in aspects of publishing are available at: London College of Printing; Middlesex University; Plymouth University; Stirling University and West Hertfordshire College. Postgraduate higher degrees in aspects of publishing are available at: Leeds University; Middlesex University; Plymouth University and Stirling University.

Short courses in a wide range of relevant topics, including copy-editing, production skills, proofreading, on-screen editing, computer skills, layout and print buying, are provided by various colleges, and by organizations such as the Book House Training Centre (the ITO for book and journal publishing – Book House Training Centre also offers distance learning courses in editing and proofreading). Participants are usually already employed in publishing companies. These courses are often provided 'in-house' by the larger publishing companies, who may use them as part of a training scheme. City and Guilds courses in information technology are available at many colleges. These part-time day release or one-year full-time courses lead to the C&G 7261 award, which is available at Levels 1,2,3 and 4. This is a modular scheme with wide variety of topics, but certain colleges offer particular modules to provide a qualification in desktop publishing. Other college courses lead to RSA awards in desktop publishing. (BTEC and SCOTVEC higher national courses in various aspects of publishing are available at: Farnborough College of Technology; Glasgow College of Building and Printing; London College of Printing and West Hertfordshire College.)

NVQs in various aspects of book, journal and magazine publishing are available at Levels 3 and 4.

LATE ENTRY

There are no formal upper age limits for entry to these occupations. Editors working in newspaper publishing usually undertake the work after previous career experience in journalism. Editors working in book or magazine publishing frequently have previous career experience in the specialist fields covered by the publications, or in journalism.

OPPORTUNITIES

Competition for the limited number of vacancies in all editing occupations can be intense. Newspaper reporters may progress to sub-editing and editing posts, but promotion is not automatic.

Recent mergers and take-overs in book publishing have led to some redundancies. Many magazine publishers employ freelance editors, often with knowledge of a specialist field. A small number of larger publishing houses have graduate recruitment schemes. There are magazine and book publishing houses in many major cities, but they are concentrated in London and the South East. Newspapers are published throughout the UK.

PAY AND CONDITIONS

Initial salaries for copy-editors and sub-editors may start at between £11,000 and £12,000 – even less on provincial newspapers. There are no agreed pay scales for these occupations, as most experienced editors negotiate their own salary. Experienced national newspaper sub-editors and book or magazine commissioning editors may earn up to £30,000. Salaries for more senior editors in large publishing companies can be higher.

Freelance editors usually negotiate a set fee for each commission, but may be paid at a daily rate. Fees for freelance editors vary considerably. Editors in all types of publishing rarely work a routine 9 to 5 day and Monday to Friday week. As publishing deadlines approach, working days can become longer, often including evening and occasional weekend work.

PROSPECTS

Experience is essential for promotion within these occupations. With some exceptions, newspaper publishers usually recruit only experienced journalists to editorial posts, and magazine and book publishers increasingly recruit those with previous experience. A first post in editing is frequently the most difficult to find.

Promotion prospects in all types of publishing are usually greater within the larger publishing houses. Experienced editors may move into senior management posts within larger publishing companies.

RELATED OCCUPATIONS

Journalist, proofreader, indexer, layout artist, publishing production controller, print buyer, researcher, bookseller.

FURTHER INFORMATION

Book House Training Centre*, 45 East Hill, Wandsworth, London SW18 2QZ, 0181 874 2718

IPC Magazines, Training and Development Department*, King's Reach Tower, Stamford Street, London SE1 9LS, 0171 261 5000

London College of Printing*, Elephant and Castle, London SE1 6SB, 0171 735 0810

National Council for the Training of Journalists, Latton Bush Centre, Southern Way, Harlow, Essex CM12 7BL, 01279 430009 (please include sae)

Newspaper Society*, Bloomsbury House, Bloomsbury Square, 74-77 Great Russell Street, London WC1B 3DA, 0171 636 7014

Periodical Training Council*, Imperial House, 15-19 Kingsway, London WC2B 6UN, 0171 836 8798

Publishers' Association*, 19 Bedford Square, London WC1B 3HJ, 0171 580 6321 (please include sae)

FURTHER READING

Leaflets/booklets are available from the addresses marked*.

Working in Journalism – COIC
Working in Publishing – COIC
Careers in Journalism – Kogan Page
Inside Book Publishing – Blueprint/Book House
The Bookseller – weekly

In the careers library classified under FAD.

MUSEUM AND ART GALLERY WORK: FAE

1. MUSEUM CURATOR/ART GALLERY KEEPER CLCI:FAE
2. CONSERVATOR/RESTORER CLCI:EZ/FAE

BACKGROUND INFORMATION

The world of museums and art galleries has changed considerably in recent years. The more traditional national and local government museums and art galleries have witnessed the rapid growth of heritage centres and independent, commercial museums. All museums and art galleries are now part of the leisure industry, increasingly concerned to entertain and inform the public and market themselves to attract increasing numbers of visitors. They have moved towards positive presentation of their objects and have developed educational, and other, services.

Many objects are seen as worth preserving because of their historical interest, or because they are collectors' items. Objects, though, are subject to long-term deterioration caused by exposure to humidity, heat, light, dirt or micro-organisms. They may also be damaged by fire, flood, accident and vandalism, etc.

Conservation has the aim of arresting decay in such objects and preventing further deterioration. Restoration shares that aim, but goes further by treating objects to restore them to their original appearance. Restoration is also concerned with making something work that has broken.

1. MUSEUM CURATOR/ART GALLERY KEEPER (FAE)

THE WORK

Museum curators and art gallery keepers manage collections of objects of artistic, archaeological, scientific, historical and general interest.

The work involved varies considerably, depending on the size and nature of the museum or art gallery. Curators tend to specialize if employed either by a specialist museum, eg natural history, or by a large general museum. In small, general museums, curators tend not to specialize.

Curators plan and mount displays and exhibitions. This involves choosing exhibits from the museum's or art gallery's stock, or buying or borrowing items. They label and arrange the exhibits, having designed the layout of the display. They arrange publicity and write the catalogue.

Curators and keepers are responsible for identifying objects, recording details (often using a computer), planning the cleaning and care of the objects, and arranging for restoration or conservation work if necessary.

Many curators and keepers are available to be consulted by visitors about the collection and to give talks to groups of visitors, including school parties. They may examine items brought in for identification.

Curators and keepers liaise with, and consult, colleagues in their own and other museums and art galleries, and with restorers and conservation experts.

Some curators and keepers in large national museums and art galleries are concerned solely with the management of collections, while others specialize in administration. Many combine both responsibilities. In smaller museums and art galleries, collection management and administration tend to be combined. Administration involves supervising staff – assistant curators, technicians and attendants – attending meetings, dealing with budgeting and fund raising.

Some curators and keepers research their specialist area and write books and articles for publication.

While the work of art gallery keeper is very similar to that of museum curator, in private galleries an important aspect of the work is selling art work to the public.

WORK ENVIRONMENT

Working conditions depend on the institution concerned. Exhibits must be kept in controlled conditions to preserve them, so most museums and art galleries tend to be warm and reasonably lit. Some museums, eg working farms and industrial sites, are based outdoors, so working conditions depend on the weather, which can be wet and cold and may lead to muddy conditions.

Jobs vary in the amount of heavy lifting and carrying involved.

SKILLS AND INTERESTS

The varied aspects of their work means that curators and keepers have to be versatile. They should have expertise, and a keen interest, in the subject matter they deal with. They need the ability to assess objects, to describe and record them accurately and in detail. They should understand the environmental conditions that exhibits need to prevent their deterioration.

Creative flair is important, together with the visual imagination to create exhibitions and displays that will attract the public. Many museums aim for visitor participation in their exhibitions, and curators need good imagination to make that possible.

Good communication skills are important – curators should be able to explain facts and ideas to visitors, give lectures and discuss matters with colleagues. Writing skills are necessary for the accurate recording of information and for writing catalogues, articles and papers.

A polite, pleasant manner is necessary, as contact with the public has become increasingly important.

Administration skills are essential for most curators. They should be capable of organizing staff and running a department or institution. Commercial interest is necessary too, as many curators are responsible for managing their department or institution within a fixed budget. Those working in private art galleries must have good selling ability.

In all but the smallest museums and art galleries, curators must be capable of working within a team, which may include other curators, restorers, conservation experts and attendants.

ENTRY REQUIREMENTS

There are no formal qualifications required for entry to curatorial work, but in practice over 85 per cent of curators and keepers have degrees and higher degrees.

The minimum entry requirement for degree courses is: five GCSEs/S grades (A-C/1-3) with two/three A levels or three/four/five H grades, or equivalent. Degrees relevant to museum work include: history, fine art, biology, botany, chemistry, anthropology, engineering, ceramics, textiles and any degree relevant to a specialist field of museum work. Degrees relevant to art gallery work include: fine art, art history and applied art. Applicants for degrees at art colleges are usually required to have completed a foundation art and design course.

Entry to postgraduate courses is with a relevant degree,

plus some evidence of commitment to the work, eg through voluntary work in a museum or art gallery. The National Association of Decorative and Fine Arts Societies (NADFAS) runs a volunteers scheme that offers such experience, or museums and art galleries may be approached direct.

Given the competition for vacancies in museum and art gallery work, it is recommended that applicants gain some relevant voluntary experience.

TRAINING

Pre-entry training

While there are no first degrees concerned solely with museum and art gallery studies, there are some that include museum studies and/or a period of study in museums, galleries or collections. They include the University of London/Courtauld Institute of Art's History of Art (three years full-time), the University of Leeds' History of Fine and Decorative Arts (four years full-time), the University of East Anglia's Art History (three years full-time) and De Montfort University's History of Art and Design (three years full-time).

Some first degrees include museum and heritage management, eg Heritage Conservation at Bournemouth University (three years full-time), Heritage Management at Cumbria College of Art and Design (three years full-time) and Social History and Heritage studies at the University of Kent (three years full-time).

There are a number of one-year full-time postgraduate courses that specifically train for museum or art gallery work. The University of Leicester offers a Diploma, MA or MSc, in Museum Studies, while the University of Manchester has a Diploma or MA in Art Gallery and Museum Studies, which emphasizes art gallery work. The Courtauld Institute of Art offers an MA in Art Museum Studies, the University of St. Andrews a Diploma in Museum/Gallery Studies, while University College London and The University of Newcastle-upon-Tyne both offer an MA in Museum Studies. Other postgraduate courses with some museum or art gallery relevance include those offered by the Victoria and Albert Museum/Royal College of Art, York Art Studies and the universities of Cambridge, Birmingham, Glasgow and Oxford.

Other relevant courses include: Sotheby's Works of Art course (nine months full-time), Christie's Fine Arts course (nine months full-time) and The Study Centre for the History of the Fine and Decorative Arts (one year full-time).

Post-entry training

Most training in museums and art galleries is on-the-job, with some organizations having formal training schemes.

There are a number of postgraduate courses that can be undertaken part-time while working, eg at University College London and at the universities of Leicester and Newcastle-upon-Tyne.

The Museum Training Institute has introduced NVQs/SVQs at Levels 3, 4 and 5 in Curatorial and Conservation Skills. Similarly, The Arts and Entertainment Training Council is working towards the introduction of NVQs/SVQs at Levels 2, 3 and 4 that have relevance for art gallery staff. NVQs/SVQs are based on demonstrating competence in the practical skills of a job.

LATE ENTRY

There is no upper age limit for entry to work as a museum curator or art gallery keeper.

Mature applicants need the same qualifications as described in ENTRY REQUIREMENTS. Voluntary experience of work in a museum or art gallery is extremely helpful.

There is a growing trend for museums and art galleries to recruit managers from outside the profession. This could provide some openings for those with experience in marketing, accountancy and administration, but for management rather than curatorial or keeping work.

OPPORTUNITIES

There are just over 3,000 museums in the UK, employing approximately 13,000 curators and managers. There are far fewer art galleries. Opportunities differ according to the type of museum or art gallery.

National museums and art galleries offer particular scope for specialist curators and keepers. While many of these institutions are based in London, there are around 35 throughout the rest of the UK.

Local authority museums and art galleries are to be found in most cities and towns in the UK and vary considerably. There are some large city museums and galleries that can offer specialist curatorial work. There are many more small local museums, including some that include a display of art, and opportunities in these tend to be for general curatorial work.

Independent museums are extremely varied, both in size and degree of specialization. There are many throughout the UK and they tend to offer general, rather than specialist, work to curators.

Opportunities in museums and art galleries grew in the 1980s, particularly as a considerable number of new independent museums opened. That growth has stopped. Turnover of staff is low and vacancies for museum curators and art gallery keepers are scarce. When vacancies arise, competition is very keen and applicants should be prepared to move to another location to find a job.

There are opportunities to work overseas, particularly in Australia, New Zealand and other Commonwealth countries. A small number of British curators work in Europe and the USA.

Vacancies for museum and art gallery work are advertised in *Museums Journal* (published by the Museums Association), the bi-monthly journal of the Association of Independent Museums (AIM), in the quality national newspapers and in the local press.

PAY AND CONDITIONS

Pay scales vary. The national museums and art galleries have similar terms of pay and conditions to the Civil Service. Many entrants start on trainee grade, with a starting salary of £7,623, or on curator grade G, with a salary scale from £8,679 to £11,766. Some graduates of 26 years or over start on curator grade F, with a salary scale from £11,138 to £16,813. A curator grade D is paid on a scale £16,813 to £24,167. Those working in London are paid extra. High standards of work performance can lead to considerable increases beyond these scales.

Local authority museums and art galleries pay local authority salary scales, which may be between £10,080 and £15,288, according to responsibilities and length of service. There are senior posts that attract over £17,500.

Independent museums have no standard salary scales, but they tend to pay similar salaries to local authorities.

Private art galleries often pay a basic salary with commission on sales.

Curators and art gallery keepers tend to work a 36 to 37-hour week, with a rota to include weekend opening times. Part-time work is possible.

PROSPECTS

Most entrants start as assistant curators or keepers and can move to curator or keeper posts. Beyond that level, advancement is difficult, as there are comparatively few posts.

In the national museums and art galleries there is a promotion structure from assistant curator to curator, department head and director. Many curators in these institutions tend to seek advancement within their department, rather than move elsewhere.

Promotion within individual local authority and independent museums and art galleries depends on the size of the institution. Many are too small for there to be a promotion structure and it is usual for curators and keepers to move for advancement.

There is some movement from the national museums and art galleries into academic posts in universities, and from local authority organizations into the leisure management field.

RELATED OCCUPATIONS

Conservator/restorer, information officer/scientist, archivist, archaeologist, leisure manager, antiques and fine arts dealer, teacher, further education/tertiary college lecturer, higher education lecturer, museum attendant/art gallery assistant.

FURTHER INFORMATION AND READING

Please see article 2. CONSERVATOR/RESTORER.

2. CONSERVATOR/RESTORER (EZ/FAE)

THE WORK

Conservators and restorers clean, repair and maintain works of art and objects of historic interest.

Many objects are the subject of conservation and restoration including: easel paintings, wall paintings, prints, ceramics, textiles, fossils, statues, monuments, arms and armour, natural history objects, furniture, machinery, metalwork and paper items. Conservators and restorers may work on a range of objects, although many specialize in one type.

Conservators and restorers first examine objects to assess the materials used in their creation. They diagnose the causes of damage or deterioration and decide on appropriate treatment. The conservator's purpose is to arrest objects' decay, although restorers may seek to restore them to their original condition. Both may need to estimate the time it will take to treat objects and the cost of treatment.

Having decided on treatment, conservators and restorers clean and treat objects appropriately. This may include: cleaning, support, repair, restoration, protection, or a combination of these. Tools used depend on the work involved and can include: microscopes, magnifying glasses, swabs, X-rays, scalpels, small brushes and carpentry hand-tools. Materials used include solvents and adhesives.

Treatment can involve undoing previous repair and restoration work. All modern treatment is designed to be reversible as far as possible. The work is very painstaking, and work on one object can take months. Careful recording of all treatment is important, both written and photographic.

An important part of conservators' and restorers' work is to survey collections and advise on the correct conditions needed to maintain the condition of objects, taking into account temperature, light and humidity. Those employed by museums and art galleries may help to set up exhibitions.

WORK ENVIRONMENT

Most conservation and restoration work takes place in laboratories or workshops, usually at a workbench or an easel. Much is done in laboratory conditions, which are clean, light and airy, but some work involves the use of chemicals, which can be inflammable or toxic. Some conservation and restoration work has to be undertaken on site, eg architectural stonemasonry.

Time is often spent in museums, art galleries and private homes, when advising on correct storage and monitoring environmental conditions.

Work involves much sitting or standing, depending on the subject of the work.

SKILLS AND INTERESTS

Conservators and restorers need a high level of hand skills for work that can be very intricate and painstaking. Good powers of concentration and infinite patience are required to work in detail on objects, possibly for weeks or months. Excellent colour vision is essential.

Conservators and restorers should have a scientific knowledge and understanding of materials used to create objects. This is necessary to determine when items were created, which materials were used, the causes of deterioration and the effect treatment may have. Aptitude for chemistry, artistic appreciation and interest in history are important in making those assessments. A strong regard for health and safety is important, as some processes are hazardous.

Conservators must be able to work as part of a team with other conservators, historians, museum and gallery staff, and have good communication skills in order to explain their work. Self-employed conservators need to communicate well with clients, who may include private collectors, museum and art gallery staff. Numerical skills are important in calculating the time and cost of treatment and for monitoring costs as projects progress.

Self-employed conservators and restorers need good commercial skills to run their businesses successfully.

Techniques of conservation are constantly improving and conservators need to keep up to date with such developments.

ENTRY REQUIREMENTS

There are no strict minimum entry qualifications for conservation and restoration work. Most entrants, though, have had full-time training before entering the work, many at degree and postgraduate level. Courses are available at different levels.

BTEC national diploma courses require: a minimum of four GCSEs/S grades (A-C/1-3); or a relevant BTEC first diploma; or appropriate SCOTVEC modules, or equivalent.

BTEC higher national diploma courses require: five GCSEs/S grades (A-C/1-3) with one A level/two H grades; or a relevant BTEC national diploma; or appropriate SCOTVEC modules, or equivalent.

Degree courses require: five GCSEs/S grades (A-C/1-3) with two or three A levels/three or four H grades; or a relevant BTEC national diploma; or appropriate SCOTVEC modules, or equivalent. Some courses require applicants to have completed a foundation art and design course.

Postgraduate courses require a relevant degree. Science, fine art and art history are extremely useful first degrees, while architecture, graphic art and archives studies degrees are accepted for some postgraduate courses.

There are some courses leading to certificates and diplomas awarded by individual colleges. Entry requirements for these vary.

It can be very helpful to have some voluntary experience before applying for entry to a course. This can be gained by joining the volunteers system organized by NADFAS – the National Association of Decorative and Fine Arts Societies.

TRAINING

Nearly all conservators and restorers undergo full-time training before entering work. There are approximately 35 full-time conservation and restoration courses offered at universities, colleges and private institutions. Details of the courses are in *Training in Conservation,* available from The Conservation Unit or the Scottish Conservation Bureau.

Most courses specialize in one type of object or material, eg sculpture, furniture, paintings, metalwork, archaeological objects, ceramics, textiles, stained and architectural glass, clocks, stonework, wood and paper objects. Not all subject areas have courses at all levels. Some courses are geared to the needs of the antiques and fine arts trades, while others are concerned more with museums' prime aim of preservation.

There are some broad-based courses that allow students to follow a variety of career paths. Lincolnshire College of Art and Design offers two courses in Conservation and Restoration: a BTEC national diploma (two years full-time) and a degree (three years full-time). Both are concerned with the treatment of a wide range of historical materials. The degree course allows students to specialize in the third year if they wish.

The City and Guilds of London Art School offers a Restoration and Conservation Studies course (three years full-time) that allows students to train as general object conservators, or to specialize, eg in ceramics or gilding.

Archaeological conservation degree courses are offered by University College London and University College Wales at Cardiff. They are concerned with training to conserve a broad range of archaeological materials.

The Area Museums Councils organize short post-entry training courses in aspects of conservation and restoration. The Museum Training Institute (MTI) has introduced NVQs/SVQs in Conservation Skills at Levels 4 and 5. NVQs/SVQs are based on demonstrating competence in the practical skills of a job.

The few who obtain apprenticeships in conservation and restoration are trained by their employer, or may have opportunities to study part-time for a relevant qualification.

LATE ENTRY

There is no upper age limit for entry to conservation or restoration work. Adults with relevant craft qualifications and experience may be able to enter the work, eg a cabinet maker into furniture restoration, or a stonemason into architectural stonework conservation. Adults seeking entry into full-time training courses may find that usual entry requirements are relaxed, particularly if they can offer relevant experience.

It can be helpful to have had some relevant voluntary experience.

OPPORTUNITIES

The majority of conservators and restorers work in the private sector for small firms, in partnerships or self-employed. They take on work contracted-out by museums and art galleries and work for private collectors, antiques dealers, auction houses, the National Trust and similar organizations.

There are a small number of apprenticeships or traineeships in the private sector, mainly concerned with furniture, textiles and stone and wood carving.

About a third of conservators and restorers work in the public sector. They work in national and local museums and art galleries, laboratories run by the nine Area Museums Councils, English Heritage and their Scottish and Welsh equivalents, Historic Scotland and Cadw. Some are employed by universities, archaeological units and government bodies. Some national museums have large conservation departments with sections for different kinds of materials, eg ceramics and prints.

The conservation and restoration field is small. Numbers employed in the private sector have grown over the past few years, while the number in the public sector has remained steady. Vacancies appear in the national press, *Museums Journal, Conservation News* and *Paper Conservation News.*

There are openings for trained conservators and restorers overseas, particularly in Canada, Australia and the USA.

PAY AND CONDITIONS

Conservators and restorers in the public sector tend to be paid similar salaries to museum curators, either based on Civil Service or local government pay scales. Salaries in national museums and art galleries range from £11,138 to £16,813, with more senior staff earning from £16,813 to £24,167. Those working in London are paid extra.

Those working for local authorities may earn between £10,080 and £15,288, with some senior staff earning over £17,500.

There are no set salary scales for conservators and restorers working in the private sector, particularly as many are self-employed. Salaries tend to range widely, some being below those in the public sector, others being above.

Those in the public sector work a 36 to 37-hour week, Monday to Friday, while hours worked in the private sector vary according to pressure of work.

PROSPECTS

Opportunities for promotion in conservation and restoration work are few. Only large national or regional museums and art galleries have a promotion structure – assistant conservation officer to conservation officer to senior keeper (conservation). These organizations may also have senior administrative and managerial posts. Small organizations are unlikely to have a career structure, so conservators and restorers seeking advancement in the public sector need to be willing to move to compete for scarce vacancies elsewhere.

In the private sector, organizations tend to be too small to have a career structure. Self-employment or entry into partnership is normal. Success is then measured in terms of expanding business and profit.

There are some opportunities for conservators and restorers to enter teaching, or become conservation scientists, seeking to develop new conservation techniques.

RELATED OCCUPATIONS

Fine artist, museum curator/art gallery keeper, archivist, taxidermist, archaeologist, cabinet maker.

FURTHER INFORMATION

The Arts and Entertainment Training Council, Glyde House, Glydegate, Bradford BD5 0BQ, 01274 738800

Association of British Picture Restorers*, Station Avenue, Kew, London TW9 3QA, 0181 948 5644

Association of Independent Museums (AIM)*, c/o Park Cottage, West Dean, Chichester, West Sussex PO18 0RX, 01452 318054

Institute of Field Archaeologists*, Ironbridge Institute, Ironbridge George Museum, Ironbridge, Telford, Shropshire TF8 7AW, 01952 432751

The Institute of Archaeology*, University College London, 31-34 Gordon Square, London WC1H 0PY, 0171 387 7050

Institute of Paper Conservation*, Leigh Lodge, Leigh, Worcestershire WR6 5LB, 01886 832323

Museums and Galleries Commission*, The Conservation Unit, 16 Queen Anne's Gate, London SW1H 9AA, 0171 233 4200

Museum Training Institute*, Glyde House, Glydegate, Bradford BD5 0UP, 01274 391 056

The Museums Association*, 42 Clerkenwell Close, London EC1R 0PA, 0171 250 1834 (please include sae)

National Association of Decorative and Fine Arts Societies (NADFAS)*, NADFAS House, 8 Guilford Street, London CW1N 1DT, 0171 430 0730

Recruitment and Assessment Services*, Alencon Link, Basingstoke, Hampshire RG21 1JB, 01256 846205

Scottish Conservation Bureau*, Historic Scotland, Longmore House, Salisbury Place, Edinburgh EH9 1SH, 0131 668 8668

The United Kingdom Institute for Conservation of Historic and Artistic Works (UKIC)*, 6 Whitehorse Mews, London SE1 7QD, 0171 620 3371

FURTHER READING

Leaflets/booklets are available from the addresses marked*.

Job Outlines – Archaeology – COIC
Job Outlines – Conservation (Arts) – COIC
Job Outlines – Museums and Art Galleries – COIC
Working In – Art and Design – COIC
Working In – History – COIC
Museums Yearbook – Museums Association
Heritage Management and Museum Work – AGCAS
Training in Conservation – The Conservation Unit/Scottish Conservation Bureau
Working in Conservation – The Conservation Unit/Scottish Conservation Bureau

In the careers library classified under EZ; FAE.

1. LIBRARIAN/INFORMATION OFFICER CLCI:FAF
2. LIBRARY/INFORMATION ASSISTANT CLCI:FAF
3. INFORMATION SCIENTIST CLCI:FAF

BACKGROUND INFORMATION

Information is increasingly important in all aspects of life, which makes information work very varied. Distinctions between librarians, information officers and information scientists are increasingly blurred, with the difference often being one of emphasis in their work, rather than one of their role.

In general terms librarians, information officers and information scientists acquire, organize and exploit information in printed form and other media. They have professional skills and either a broad-based general knowledge, or an in-depth subject knowledge, depending on where they work. Information technology (IT) developments have led to new ways of obtaining, storing, retrieving, exploiting and manipulating information, and everyone involved in this work must be familiar with computerized systems.

Librarians, information officers and information scientists may work alone or as part of a team. They are supported in their professional and managerial roles by library/information assistants.

1. LIBRARIAN/INFORMATION OFFICER (FAF)

THE WORK

Librarians/information officers handle information in a variety of media – books, journals, newspapers, leaflets, video, audio cassette, microfiche, multimedia CDs, computer databases, the Internet, etc. The emphasis of their work depends on their particular job but, in general, they are responsible for:

– being aware of new publications and materials and information sources, and deciding what to add to the library and which existing stock to update;

– cataloguing, classifying and indexing new material to make it available to library users;

– helping people access the information.

This may mean directing users to particular sources, or researching material, sometimes in depth, to answer enquiries. They may display new acquisitions or materials on a particular theme. Sometimes they produce bulletins listing new items, possibly with summaries of their contents as a current-awareness service. They can also obtain information held in other libraries by arranging inter-library loans or document retrieval.

Other tasks include budgeting and accounting, managing staff, stock, computer systems, buildings and fittings, and developing policy. Computers are heavily used both for internal management (keeping details of clients, stock, catalogues, etc) and to access information held elsewhere through on-line systems and on the Internet. Other equipment that is used may include microfiche readers, video recorders and photocopiers.

In a small library or information unit, the librarian/information officer may be responsible for all aspects of the work. In a larger organization, tasks are divided and one person may be responsible for a specific area, eg acquisitions (buying stock), cataloguing, on-line database enquiry work.

Other work is available in different types of library. For example, in a public library, where a wide range of services is provided, a librarian can specialize in working with a particular group such as the disabled, prisoners, the mentally ill, ethnic minorities, the elderly or children. Work with children involves organizing story readings or puppet shows and liaising with local schools. Some librarians/information officers are responsible for a particular collection, such as music, visual images, European Union information, local studies, foreign language materials. Public libraries usually have mobile facilities to take services to people who are house-bound, or do not live near a library.

Librarians in academic libraries (colleges, universities) may be in charge of a particular subject, and be involved in planning courses in that subject. They also provide information skills teaching to help students and lecturers make the most of library facilities. School librarians provide teachers with appropriate books and other teaching aids, encourage pupils to use libraries, assist with student-centred learning and help with curriculum development.

Librarians/information officers in industry, commerce, the NHS, local government, government departments, professional bodies and voluntary organisations provide information primarily for colleagues, but may also offer services to people outside the organization. Their work may involve research, information analysis, translating, report-writing, etc. There is the greatest overlap with information science work in this area. (Please see article 3. INFORMATION SCIENTIST.) In other kinds of special libraries, librarians/information officers may work only with media such as photographs, pictures, videos, philatelic collections, newspapers, etc.

WORK ENVIRONMENT

Librarians/information officers work indoors (except for the mobile service), often by artificial light. Some areas can be dusty. Libraries may be purpose-built or converted from other buildings. Some are very old, others new; some spacious and some cramped (eg a small room in a firm's offices).

Libraries that are open to the public are sometimes noisy. In busy libraries, continual enquiries can cause pressure on staff. Some librarians/information officers are responsible for more than one library and must travel regularly between them.

SKILLS AND INTERESTS

Librarians/information officers must be able to work with people of all ages and from a variety of backgrounds. They should have an outgoing personality, patience, tact, courtesy and stamina. They need good spoken and written communication skills. An interest in working with computers is essential, as information technology is widely used. Librarians/information officers should be methodical, organized and accurate. They need a good memory, an enquiring mind and the initiative to research information.

The job requires the ability to handle complex tasks, possibly with interruptions and whilst under pressure. Deadlines often have to be met. Flexibility is important, particularly as librarians/information officers often have to change roles (eg cataloguer to researcher to teacher to writer).

A willingness to take on responsibility and develop management skills is needed. Staff working in small units are often isolated from other colleagues and should be independent and resourceful.

Some jobs require specific skills. For example, some librarians/information officers need specialized subject knowledge; others need skills in a foreign language to deal with materials in that language. Those working with children must be able to relate to them, and librarians/information officers in academic and school libraries may need teaching ability.

ENTRY REQUIREMENTS

Entry to librarian/information officer work is by a Library Association-accredited first degree or postgraduate qualification, or NVQ/SVQ in Information and Library Services at Level 4. Either route is acceptable, although some academic libraries prefer applicants with postgraduate qualifications.

Entry to degree courses usually requires a minimum of two A levels/three H grades plus five GCSEs/S grades (A-C/1-3), or equivalent, such as a BTEC/SCOTVEC national diploma/certificate, or Advanced GNVQs/GSVQ Level III. Some courses specify particular subjects. Contact individual institutions for details. Entrants to full-time first degree courses do not need pre-course experience, although it can be required for part-time and distance learning courses.

Entry to postgraduate courses generally requires a degree in any subject or equivalent. Most postgraduate courses require applicants to have had around six to twelve months' appropriate work experience. This can be difficult to obtain, and students often have to apply to a good number of libraries or information services in both the public and private sectors. The Library Association publishes a list of graduate training opportunities offering fixed-term pre-postgraduate work experience. Other vacancies are advertised or placed with specialist recruitment agencies. Some graduates take posts as library/information assistants to gain the necessary experience.

Candidates should check with individual departments of library and information studies before making decisions.

TRAINING

First degree courses

First degree courses accredited by The Library Association are offered at 13 universities. They last three to four years full-time. Some are also available on a part-time basis over four to eight years. A distance learning BSc(Econ) Information and Library Studies lasting three to five years is also offered by The University of Wales, Aberystwyth.

Subjects studied include: management; training in information technology skills; information technology applications; on-line services; the Internet; organization and promotion of library and information services; what information is, where it comes from and who uses it; acquisition, organization, storage, retrieval and dissemination of information; information analysis; and the information needs of society. Optional subjects may include literature, archives, a foreign language or a specialist/technical subject.

Postgraduate courses

Courses accredited by The Library Association, leading to postgraduate diplomas or masters degrees, are offered by 17 universities. They usually last one year full-time or two to three years part-time. Some are available through distance learning for people with substantial experience in information work. Subjects studied include the same core subjects offered at first degree level, but some provide greater emphasis on information technology applications or specialist training, such as health information. It is important to check prospectuses, as course titles are not a complete guide to their content.

All departments of library and information studies also offer research degrees leading to PhD or MPhil.

Professional qualifications

The Library Association, which is the chartered professional body for librarians and information professionals, maintains a Register of chartered members. It awards professional qualifications (by admitting members to the Register as associates) to graduates who have met its requirements. Most candidates complete a Library Association-accredited course, followed by a minimum of a year's work experience and professional training. Candidates must submit an application that demonstrates their professional development and competence.

After at least five years as an associate, candidates who demonstrate appropriate continuing professional development may apply for the award of fellowship of The Library Association.

The Institute of Information Scientists also offers professional qualifications. Please see article 3. INFORMATION SCIENTIST.

NVQs/SVQs in Information and Library Services are available at Level 4. There is no prescribed training route, though training and open learning is available at a number of colleges and some universities.

LATE ENTRY

Mature entrants can develop successful careers in library and information work, but must still obtain professional qualifications (see ENTRY and TRAINING). Normal academic course entry requirements may be waived at the discretion of the academic institution. People with experience as library/information assistants, plus vocational qualifications, are often admitted to degree courses in librarianship/information studies. Successful completion of a one-year access course is an acceptable entry route to degree courses in librarianship and information studies. Candidates with degree, or equivalent, qualifications and/or experiential learning and, if required, appropriate pre-course experience, can enter a postgraduate course. Prospects for mature entrants depend on age, previous experience, knowledge and skills.

OPPORTUNITIES

Posts for librarians/information officers are found all over the country, primarily in towns and cities, with a majority of specialized posts in the South East. They are employed in the public sector in public libraries, academic libraries, government departments, the NHS, schools, museums, the four large national libraries, and in the private sector by, for example, banks, accountants', engineers', surveyors' or architects' practices, legal firms, the media, professional bodies, learned societies and publishers. There are some opportunities for work abroad, and both the British Council and Voluntary Service Overseas occasionally recruit for work overseas.

The largest number of Library Association members is found in public libraries (26.6 per cent), followed by further and higher education libraries (16 per cent), government, national, health, industry and commerce (16.7 per cent) and school libraries (five per cent) (1993/94 figures). Opportunities in the private sector are increasing, whereas those in the public sector, with the exception of technical libraries, are more static. Some graduate librarians/ information officers take paraprofessional (library/ information assistant) posts in order to make a start in the profession.

Librarians/information officers with a first degree in scientific/technical, business-related or computing subjects are particularly sought after.

Vacancy information is published by The Library Association, the Institute of Information Scientists and Aslib for their members, and vacancies are advertised in *TES, THES (Times Supplements), New Scientist,* quality national dailies and local or university/college careers services. There are also specialist recruitment agencies, such as INFOmatch (The Library Association), Aslib, TFPL, Instant Library, Informed Business Services and Access Information Recruitment.

PAY AND CONDITIONS

Salaries vary depending on the employer and the duties and responsibilities of the post. The Library Association publishes a series of salary guides. In local authority public libraries in England and Wales salaries for the main professional grades range from £11,874 to £19,818. Chartered members of The Library Association may start at £17,055. (Figures do not include London weighting.) Senior librarians/information officers with considerable responsibility for staff or departments receive higher salaries.

Salaries in other types of library (eg academic, industry, commerce) are broadly similar. They are sometimes lower in sectors such as schools and the NHS.

In many libraries, especially public and academic, librarians/ information officers work shifts, including evenings and weekends. In other library and information services, staff usually work office hours.

PROSPECTS

Larger libraries and information services often have a clearly defined structure for promotion to management positions, with responsibility for a specific subject, service or branch/site library. Promotion can be internal, but staff may have to change employers to progress in their career.

In small libraries and information units, an individual may be in charge very quickly, and will have to move for greater experience or promotion.

Some Chartered Librarians, who qualified before a degree was necessary, may now need an academic qualification for promotion in the current highly competitive job market.

It may be possible to become self-employed after several years of professional practice and take on consultancy work.

RELATED OCCUPATIONS

Museum/art gallery curator/keeper, archivist, public records officer, information scientist, library/information assistant.

FURTHER INFORMATION AND READING

Please see article 3. INFORMATION SCIENTIST.

2. LIBRARY/INFORMATION ASSISTANT (FAF)

THE WORK

Library/information assistants (often referred to as paraprofessionals) carry out work to support professionally qualified librarians/information officers and information scientists. The work is a mixture of routine administrative and library duties.

Assistants issue and take back materials (books, cassettes, journals, etc) and answer simple enquiries. They help people to find books and information and to use equipment such as photocopiers, microfiche readers, CD-ROM and computer terminals. They check returned materials for damage and arrange for repair. They re-shelve used books and other items and keep the library tidy. Assistants send out routine letters, and search computer databases to find out the numbers of photocopies made, inter-library loans, fines, book reservations, etc. They use computers to issue books, to update catalogues, to order new items and follow up orders, and to input and retrieve data.

Assistants also arrange for the purchase of new materials selected by professional staff. They check that materials have arrived and process them by recording their details in the catalogue and adding library details and classification codes where necessary. In public libraries, they may help librarians with story readings for children or community events. They may work in a mobile library, providing a service for people who can't get to a library.

Senior assistants supervise junior staff and may liaise with caretakers, cleaners and maintenance staff.

WORK ENVIRONMENT

Library/information assistants share the work environment of librarians/information officers. Please see article 1. LIBRARIAN/INFORMATION OFFICER. As they are responsible for re-shelving materials, the work can include a lot of bending, lifting, carrying and walking.

SKILLS AND INTERESTS

Library/information assistants often have regular contact with the public and should enjoy helping people of all ages and backgrounds. They need an outgoing personality, patience, tact, courtesy and stamina. They should have good communication skills. Assistants should be methodical and organized and have a good memory. An enquiring mind and initiative are essential to find information for people. An aptitude for work with computers is essential.

Some jobs require specific skills. For example, work with young children may make special demands on patience and ingenuity, and work with a collection of foreign language materials makes some knowledge of the language necessary.

ENTRY REQUIREMENTS

There are no minimum academic entry requirements, although many employers look for four GCSEs/S grades (A-C/1-3), including English. Some posts (for example, in academic or specialist libraries) require applicants to have

A level, or equivalent qualifications, such as BTEC/ SCOTVEC national certificates/diplomas or Advanced GNVQs/GSVQs Level III. Specialist knowledge (a foreign language or technical expertise, including word processing, for example) is necessary for some posts, particularly in specialist and industrial, or commercial, libraries. Senior library/information assistant posts are likely to require vocational qualifications. (See TRAINING).

Four GCSEs/S grades (A-C/1-3) are required to study for BTEC national awards. GCSE/S grade (A-C/1-3) in English is desirable for entry to the SCOTVEC national certificate. Colleges will usually only accept students who are in appropriate full-time or part-time employment on to these vocational courses.

TRAINING

Training is largely in the workplace, with supervision from a senior library/information assistant and/or a professional librarian. Trainees may study for the following qualifications, usually by day release to college, or through distance learning:

The City and Guilds 737 Certificate in Library and Information Competences is a one-year part-time or distance learning programme for those who are employed in library or information services. It is offered by a number of centres around the country on a day release basis, and by Sandwell College (West Midlands), Somerset College (Taunton) and Telford College (Edinburgh) through distance learning. Competences are assessed through practical coursework and examination.

The BTEC National Certificate of Achievement in Library and Information Work is a one-year course that may be taken as a stand-alone qualification, or as a module towards BTEC qualifications such as a national diploma. It is offered on a day release basis by some colleges and by distance learning from UNISON.

The SCOTVEC National Certificate in Library and Information Science is available at: Aberdeen College of Further Education (day release or evening classes); Central College of Commerce, Glasgow (day release) and Telford College of Further Education, Edinburgh (day release, full-time or distance learning). The SCOTVEC Higher National Certificate in Library and Information Science is offered by: Bell College, Hamilton (full or part-time); Napier University (distance learning) and Telford College, Edinburgh (full or part-time). The courses last one year full-time or two years part-time/distance learning.

In some areas, training opportunities are available for young people. Contact your local careers office, TEC/LEC for details.

NVQs/SVQs in Information and Library Services are available at Levels 2, 3 and 4.

LATE ENTRY

There are no age limits for entry. Specialist knowledge can be useful for some posts (eg in a technical library).

Many libraries are open in the evenings and at weekends. This can provide opportunities for flexible hours and part-time work. Some libraries employ assistants on a casual basis. These working patterns can be useful for older entrants with other responsibilities.

There may be specific training opportunities, directed at adults, available in some areas for this type of work. Candidates may have to satisfy certain conditions to be eligible. Contact your local Jobcentre, careers office, or TEC/LEC for details.

OPPORTUNITIES

Please see article 1. LIBRARIAN/INFORMATION OFFICER. Overall, there are far more library/information assistants than librarians/information officers, although some very small units do not employ any paraprofessional staff.

Some assistant posts are taken by graduates looking for pre-postgraduate course experience. Others are filled by people with library and information qualifications because of a shortage of professional posts in their area.

Vacancies are advertised in local and national newspapers and in local authority/college/university job bulletins.

PAY AND CONDITIONS

Salaries vary depending on the employer and the duties and responsibilities of the post and, in public libraries in England and Wales, can range from £6,693 to £11,646. Senior library assistants receive from £10,884 to £14,892, and those with considerable responsibility receive up to £16,404. (Figures do not include London weighting.)

Salaries in other types of library (eg academic, industrial, commercial) are broadly similar. They are sometimes lower in sectors such as schools and the NHS. The Library Association publishes a series of salary guides.

In many libraries, especially public and academic, library/ information assistants work shifts, including evenings and weekends. In other library and information services staff, usually work office hours.

PROSPECTS

Larger libraries and information units may have several paraprofessional grades, and assistants can progress to senior assistant posts. Some senior posts require vocational qualifications (see TRAINING). Organizations with a less formal structure may promote assistants by giving them more responsibility.

Library/information assistants cannot move into professional posts without taking professional qualifications, but experience in a post of this type may be acceptable for entry to courses in library and information work. Please see article 1. LIBRARIAN/INFORMATION OFFICER.

RELATED OCCUPATIONS

Museum/art gallery assistant, receptionist, research assistant, record keeper, librarian/information officer, information scientist, clerk.

FURTHER INFORMATION AND READING

Please see article 3. INFORMATION SCIENTIST.

3. INFORMATION SCIENTIST (FAF)

THE WORK

Information scientists research, obtain, produce, evaluate, organize and disseminate information. There is a lot of overlap with the work of librarians/information officers (please see article 1. LIBRARIAN/INFORMATION OFFICER), but information scientists' work often has a different emphasis. For example, information scientists frequently have a scientific or technical background and may be experts in a particular field (eg engineering, law, pharmaceuticals). They are often concerned with current information, rather than building a large collection of material for long-term use. They may also be involved in more retrieval and evaluation work than librarians/information officers (except those librarians/information officers employed in specialist and technical libraries), and tend to research information in greater depth. Some information scientists provide a service only to their colleagues. Others have regular contact with the public, either in person or by telephone or computer.

There are many jobs involved in information science work, but the most common tasks include:

– assessing the types of user and their information needs and providing appropriate materials and services;

– setting up and maintaining manual and computerized systems for efficient handling and storage of information;

– identifying relevant and useful information, which may involve searching on-line or CD-ROM databases, or printed versions of newspapers, abstracts, reports and other documents, and presenting the results to an enquirer;

– writing reports, abstracts of documents, information bulletins and so on.

Some information scientists are involved in press and publicity work and prepare and edit material for enquirers outside the organization. They may also arrange specialist displays or exhibitions, translate (or arrange for the translation of) material, produce technical manuals, participate in training, or be responsible for budgeting and accounting. Some supervise other staff.

WORK ENVIRONMENT

Information scientists work indoors in a wide range of organizations. Their immediate surroundings can vary from a spacious, purpose-built, highly computerized information base to a cramped back room. In larger organizations there may be a team of information professionals and support staff; in others, information scientists work alone.

The work is often done by artificial light, and conditions may be dusty, particularly where there are many paper-based resources.

SKILLS AND INTERESTS

Information scientists need good interpersonal skills. They have to be able to clarify exactly what users want from the information service and use imagination and initiative to develop it. They must be good communicators, and be able to write reports, abstracts and other documents. An ability and willingness to work with information technology is essential.

Information scientists should be organized, methodical and adaptable. A good memory is essential. They should display resourcefulness in researching information, and be able to evaluate the results to ensure they are appropriate to the needs of the user.

The job requires the ability to handle complex tasks, possibly with interruptions and whilst under pressure. Deadlines often have to be met. Information scientists must be able both to work closely with colleagues, and to motivate themselves when working alone. A willingness to take on responsibility and develop management skills is often needed.

Some jobs require specific skills. For example, those who work in specialized services may need subject knowledge, both to communicate with experts in the field and to evaluate technical information. Foreign language skills may also be useful for translating and abstracting (producing a summary of an article or book).

ENTRY REQUIREMENTS

Most professionally qualified information scientists are graduates and the most common routes into the profession are by relevant first degree or postgraduate qualification. Other pathways would be considered, including an NVQ/SVQ in Information and Library Services at Level 4. Please see article 1. LIBRARIAN/INFORMATION OFFICER for entry to degree and postgraduate courses.

TRAINING

First degree courses

First degree courses approved by the Institute of Information Scientists are offered at twelve universities. They last three to four years full-time. Some are also available on a part-time basis over four to eight years. Subjects studied include: what information is; providers and users of information; sources, storage, retrieval and dissemination of information; information analysis; information management and information technology.

Postgraduate courses

Courses approved by the Institute of Information Scientists, leading to postgraduate diplomas or masters degrees, are offered by 15 universities. They usually last one year full-time or two to three years part-time. Some are available through distance learning. Subjects studied include the same core subjects offered at first degree level. All departments of library and information studies also offer research degrees for qualified professionals.

Professional qualifications

Information scientists who hold a degree can apply for full professional membership of the Institute of Information Scientists after a minimum of five years' relevant experience. They must complete a detailed form demonstrating their experience and skills in information science. Exemptions from the period of work experience of one to three years apply if the candidate has a first degree or postgraduate qualification approved by the Institute.

Graduate information scientists can also gain professional qualifications awarding chartered status through The Library Association. Please see article 1. LIBRARIAN/INFORMATION OFFICER.

NVQs/SVQs in Information and Library Services are available at Levels 2, 3 and 4.

LATE ENTRY

Mature entrants can develop successful careers as information scientists. Normal entry requirements for courses approved by the Institute of Information Scientists may be waived at the discretion of the academic institution. Successful completion of a one-year access route is an acceptable entry route to degrees in information studies. Prospects for mature entrants depend on age, previous experience, knowledge and skills. Those with scientific/technical backgrounds or computing/management skills are most likely to find late entry possible.

OPPORTUNITIES

Information scientist posts occur all over the country, although the majority are found in the South East. There are jobs in industry (especially the pharmaceutical, energy, construction and chemical industries), libraries (particularly academic libraries), central and local government departments, business and finance, research associations, etc. Information posts are increasing in the private sector, although the public sector, with the exception of technical libraries, is static.

Twenty per cent of members of the Institute of Information Scientists work in industry, with more than twelve per cent employed in the information industry (including information technology, publishing, etc). Another eleven per cent work in academic libraries. There are some opportunities to work abroad, and the British Council occasionally recruits for overseas posts. Some information scientists work as self-employed brokers and consultants, designing and setting up information services.

Vacancy information is published by the Institute of Information Scientists, Aslib and The Library Association for their members, and vacancies are also advertised in *New Scientist,* quality national dailies, specialist computing, business or scientific journals and local authority or university/college careers services.

PAY AND CONDITIONS

Salaries vary depending on the employer and the duties and responsibilities of the post. In industry, the range starts at under £8,000, with the average being £21,660. Other averages range from £15,570 in local government to £23,474 in intergovernmental organizations. Those aged under 25 earn between £7,706 to £17,500.

In many information offices, staff work five days a week from 9am to 5pm. Where offices are open longer hours and at weekends, information scientists are likely to work shifts.

PROSPECTS

Most information departments are small and an individual may be in charge very quickly. Career progression is normally by changing job. Some organizations employ a number of information scientists and may have a formal promotion structure. Experienced information scientists may become consultants.

RELATED OCCUPATIONS

Museum/art gallery curator/keeper, technical author, computer database manager, researcher, patent agent, librarian/information officer, library/information assistant.

FURTHER INFORMATION

Aslib, The Association for Information Management*, Information House, 20-24 Old Street, London EC1V 9AP, 0171 253 4488

Information and Library Services Lead Body*, 7 Ridgmount Street, London WC1E 7AE, 0171 255 2271

The Institute of Information Scientists (IIS)*, 44-45 Museum Street, London WC1A 1LY, 0171 831 8003

The Library Association*, Information Services, 7 Ridgmount Street, London WC1E 7AE, 0171 636 7543 (please include sae)

Local Government Opportunities (LGO), Local Government Management Board*, 76-86 Turnmill Street, London

Specialist recruitment agencies for library and information work:

Aslib Professional Recruitment Ltd – address as above.

INFOmatch, c/o The Library Association, 7 Ridgmount Street, London WC1E 7AE, 0171 636 7543/0171 436 5843 (answerphone)

TFPL, 17-18 Britton Street, London EC1M 5NQ, 0171 251 5522

FURTHER READING

Leaflets/booklets are available from the addresses marked*.

Job Outlines – Library and Information Work – COIC
Working in Work with Children – COIC

In the careers library classified under FAF.

ARCHAEOLOGIST CLCI:FAH

BACKGROUND INFORMATION

Archaeology is the study of the human past through material remains. Evidence can range from buried cities to microscopic organisms. It provides us with the only source of information about many aspects of our development. Milestones such as the beginning of agriculture, the origins of towns, or the discovery of metals, can only be understood through the examination of physical evidence. Archaeology links with many subjects, including geography, history, social sciences, maths, physics, biology, chemistry, art, religion and technology.

Most professional archaeologists have an archaeology degree or postgraduate qualification.

THE WORK

Although its popular image is of site excavation, archaeology embraces many different kinds of work. Most jobs require a broad knowledge of archaeology, but most archaeologists specialize either geographically (Egypt, Britain, Europe, etc), chronologically (prehistory, Roman, Anglo-Saxon, etc) or technically (excavation, field survey, artefact study, etc), or, more usually, in a combination of these.

Field archaeology. Most excavation work is carried out by archaeological trusts or units, many of which operate over a wide geographical area. Archaeology units vary in size, the largest employing a director, field officers for excavation, field survey staff, conservators, finds researchers, environmental specialists, an editorial assistant, archivist, illustrators and graphic designers, a photographer and a team of professional excavators. Small units tend to employ specialist staff on a short-term or consultancy basis.

Field officers supervise evaluation of a site to assess its archaeological potential. Evaluation often begins with a desktop assessment of a site. If it is to proceed, decisions are made on methods of further evaluation, such as geophysical survey or trial trenching. Preservation of an archaeological site is preferable to excavation, but is not always possible where a site is to be developed. On-site earth moving is sometimes initially done by machine, but excavators use all kinds of equipment, ranging from pick and shovel to compressed air, trowel or toothpick, depending on circumstances.

The main objective of excavation is recovery of information. Although retrieval of objects is important, the recording of all kinds of accompanying features is of equal relevance. Such features may range from simple discolouration in the soil, to wells, burials, waterlogged timbers, deposits of seeds, pottery kilns and a huge range of traces of past activities.

Much work in archaeology takes place away from an excavation site and often takes much more time than the excavation. All finds from excavations are cleaned, catalogued and conserved, and all information recorded to form an archive for the site.

Archaeological science. A wide range of scientists is involved in the study of excavated materials. Specialisms include: radio-carbon dating of objects; the study of excavated environmental material, such as bones, teeth, wood, charcoal, seeds and grain, insect skeletons and pollen; the examination of excavated artefacts (man-made objects) to determine how they were made, the processes used and the exact composition of the materials; statistical study of the finds on-site; conservation of archaeological objects.

Geophysical survey of sites is increasingly important in field archaeology. All archaeological sites are built up from the accumulation of sediments. These may be naturally deposited, or a deliberate part of the site structure. They may result from the decay of buildings, or the development of soils and vegetation over parts of the site. Using the techniques of geology and soil science, study of these sediments forms a vital part of the unravelling of a site's history.

National agencies. Some archaeologists work for government agencies, principally English Heritage, Historic Scotland, Cadw (Welsh Historic Monuments) and the Department of the Environment for Northern Ireland. Inspectors of Ancient Monuments are responsible for the preservation and protection of sites and monuments, monitoring fieldwork projects and recommending grant aid. Historic Building Inspectors, who, in addition to an archaeology degree, need architecture or art history training, have a similar responsibility for buildings. Inspectors are assisted by a wide range of specialists, including architects, conservators, photographers, draughtsmen/women, illustrators and research assistants.

Archaeologists also work for The Royal Commissions on the Historic Monuments of England, Scotland and Wales. They are responsible for recording all ancient buildings and visible features of historical importance by carrying out detailed surveys (including aerial surveys) and publishing the results. A knowledge of surveying is essential for this work.

Archaeologists are employed by other national organizations, eg the National Trust, the National Trust for Scotland and the national parks to record, survey and, occasionally, excavate sites in their care. They also manage the archaeological resource and ensure its continued survival for future generations.

Local authorities. All counties, and most Scottish regions, have a sites and monuments officer responsible for the Sites and Monuments Record (SMR) – a database of the historic environment. The SMR officer and staff keep the record up to date and help the local authority to monitor the archaeological implications of planning applications.

Museums. Some archaeologists work in museums as keepers or assistant keepers of archaeology. Their responsibilities include management, conservation and care of collections, preparing exhibitions and dealing with enquiries from the public. The recent growth of heritage interpretation centres has led to the employment of some archaeologists, often for work that includes design and marketing. For further information please see the article on MUSEUM CURATOR.

Education. Some archaeologists are concerned mainly with education. Archaeology lecturers or technicians work in universities and colleges of higher education, while some archaeologists provide an education and information service on the archaeological concerns of museums and archaeology units, and organizations such as English Heritage and Cadw.

WORK ENVIRONMENT

As the jobs within archaeology vary, so do the types of workplace and working conditions.

Excavation work takes place outdoors at all times of the year in any weather. Work can be dirty and cold and involve bending, kneeling and working in cramped conditions. Field work and surveying involve travel over short or long distances to visit sites and attend meetings. The work may also include administration in offices.

Those in scientific archaeology may work outdoors on-site, but also in laboratory conditions that are clean, light and comfortable. Most work in museums is in warm, reasonably lit surroundings, although some museums are based outdoors and working conditions then depend on the weather. Some archaeological conservation work may take place outdoors on-site, but most is in laboratories or workshops, which are clean and light. Work involves much sitting.

Archaeologists in education spend most of their time indoors, except when taking students on field trips or carrying out field work in vacation periods.

Computer specialists, eg those responsible for keeping excavation records or national monuments records, work in clean, light and airy conditions and spend much time sitting.

SKILLS AND INTERESTS

Different jobs in archaeology demand different skills and interests, although some are common to all. Archaeologists should have a keen sense of curiosity about the past. Most archaeological activities involve team work, and individuals must be able to work as team members. Good communication skills are important in most jobs. Written skills are needed for recording purposes, while spoken communication is required when dealing with colleagues or members of other organizations. All archaeological work demands a methodical approach.

Those involved in excavation need to be capable of working fast to meet deadlines and prepared to work in all weather conditions. In common with archaeologists involved in conservation, they also need good practical ability to be able to use tools and instruments skilfully, as well as patience and an eye for detail.

Archaeologists concerned with field investigation should be physically fit. Archaeologists in museums and heritage centres need some artistic ability to design exhibitions. Tact is a requirement for inspectors, and others, who liaise with landowners, planners and other agencies.

Archaeologists involved in scientific investigation need to be capable of clear, logical thought, able to implement practical experiments and draw logical conclusions from their findings.

The use of computers in archaeology is widespread. Some organizations employ specialist computer officers, while others have many staff using computers in their work. It is desirable, therefore, that archaeologists should have a knowledge of computers.

Many archaeologists need management skills, as their work includes staff organization and financial planning.

ENTRY REQUIREMENTS

It is usual for entrants to archaeology to have a degree that includes archaeology, although there is scope for graduates in other disciplines to enter following relevant postgraduate training.

Entry to degree courses is usually with a minimum of five GCSEs/S grades (A-C/1-3) and two A levels/three H grades, or equivalent. Competition for entry to archaeology degrees is such that applicants normally need three A levels/three or four H grades, often with high grades.

Science-related and conservation courses often require science subjects at A level/H grade, particularly chemistry. Useful subjects at GCSE/S grade include English, maths, history, geography and foreign languages, plus sciences for archaeology courses with a scientific emphasis.

Given the competition for entry to degrees that include archaeology, it is desirable to have evidence of prior interest. That can be shown through membership of an archaeology society, and having helped voluntarily in a dig or in a museum. A supplement to *British Archaeological*, published by the Council for British Archaeology, gives information on excavations and fieldwork that volunteers can join.

The Higher National Diploma in Practical Archaeology requires one A level/two H grades, preferably in archaeology, history, geography, physical sciences or classical civilization, with GCSEs/S grades (A-C/1-3) in English and maths, or a science (not biology alone), or equivalent. Applicants are expected to have four weeks' excavation experience.

Those seeking to enter academic work in archaeology normally need a postgraduate research degree. Postgraduate training is also necessary for museum work and environmental archaeology. Entry to postgraduate courses is with a first degree.

TRAINING

Single-subject archaeology degrees are offered at 25 universities in the UK. Archaeology is also offered in some form at 32 universities and colleges. Most courses are full-time for three years.

The archaeological emphasis varies considerably between courses. Some courses offer a general approach with the opportunity to specialize as the course progresses. Some are concerned with particular periods or regions, while others specialize in conservation or archaeological science.

Courses include practical experience of excavations and field surveys, sometimes abroad. Methods and techniques, such as surveying, photography and conservation of finds are featured in most courses, particularly those with a scientific emphasis. Details of degree courses are given in *Degree Course Guide History (including Archaeology)*, published by CRAC.

The Higher National Diploma in Practical Archaeology is offered by Bournemouth University in conjunction with Yeovil College. It lasts for two years and includes archaeological skills and knowledge, non-destructive archaeological investigation, practical fieldwork, excavation, a field survey project and five weeks' archaeological experience. On completion of the course the majority of students transfer to a degree course in archaeology.

As with first degrees there are a wide range of postgraduate archaeology courses, eg archaeological sciences, aerial photography, conservation, heritage management, museum studies and period-based studies. Some courses are taught, others involve research.

Once in work, archaeologists receive in-service training. NVQs/SVQs in Archaeology are being developed at Levels 2, 3 and 4.

Seventeen University Continuing Education departments offer certificates and diplomas. They are studied part-time over one to three years and can be a method of entry to full-time undergraduate study.

LATE ENTRY

It is possible for late entrants to enter archaeology, but they need the qualifications described in ENTRY REQUIREMENTS. Those with relevant experience, eg in computing or science, may be more successful in entering the work.

Mature applicants may be accepted for the higher education courses without the normal entry requirements. As with applicants of any age, it is helpful to have evidence of interest in archaeology, eg membership of an archaeological society and practical experience of fieldwork.

OPPORTUNITIES

There are approximately 4,500 archaeologists in the UK, an estimated 2,000 of them working on short-term contracts.

Fieldwork opportunities are found mainly with archaeology units, some of which are independent trusts or charities, others being attached to museums, local authorities and universities. English Heritage also employs some archaeologists for fieldwork. Most fieldwork vacancies are short-term for the duration of a project, although employment may be extended as other projects are taken on. The number of these short-term opportunities increased rapidly until the early 1990s, when recession led to a contraction.

Some archaeologists are employed as Inspectors of Ancient Monuments and Historic Buildings Inspectors by English Heritage, Historic Scotland, Cadw (Welsh Historic Monuments) and the Department of the Environment for Northern Ireland.

Local authorities employ archaeologists in their planning departments, while some archaeologists are employed by organizations such as the National Trust, Ordnance Survey, the Forestry Commission, British Gas and Thames Water.

Some archaeologists work for national and local museums as curators or keepers. Archaeologists specializing in conservation are employed by museums, as well as by university departments and national agencies, such as English Heritage.

Jobs in science-based archaeology are found in university research projects, in laboratories – such as in the British Museum and English Heritage – in various dating services, and in environmental archaeology units.

Universities and colleges of higher education employ some archaeologists as lecturers and technicians, while some work as education officers for museums, archaeology units and the national agencies.

Organizations such as the Council for British Archaeology and Council for Scottish Archaeology employ some archaeologists. They act as a bridge between amateur and professional archaeologists, promoting the subject with emphases on information, education, conservation and publication. Competition for all vacancies in archaeology is fierce and applicants should be prepared to move to find a job. Vacancies are advertised in *The Guardian, The Independent* and *Museums Journal*. The Institute of Field Archaeologists runs a jobs information service.

Work abroad is possible, usually on a temporary basis. Information on overseas openings is given in *Archaeology Abroad*, published three times a year.

Freelance work is common in archaeology, particularly for site supervisors, post-excavation analysts, conservators, illustrators and computing officers. Working freelance is often undertaken by experienced specialists who wish to work on a consultancy or self-employed basis. It is also undertaken by the inexperienced as a means of gaining sufficient experience to apply for a permanent post.

PAY AND CONDITIONS

Salaries vary according to the employing organization and position held. The average starting salary for a graduate archaeologist is approximately £10,000. Those in senior posts may earn between £14,000 and £20,000, while some archaeologists with substantial managerial responsibility, and some involved in higher education lecturing earn considerably more.

Hours and patterns of work vary between employing organizations. Field archaeologists working on excavations often work variable hours depending on the location of the site and urgency of the project.

Archaeologists working for local authorities and national agencies, and those involved in laboratory work, usually work standard office hours, Monday to Friday, but may work outside normal hours because of pressure of work.

Those working in museums tend to work 36 to 37 hours a week, with a rota to include weekend opening times.

Part-time work is possible in many areas of archaeology.

PROSPECTS

Promotion in archaeology is difficult and usually very slow because of intense competition. Those with management and financial experience and ability may find it easier to progress. Moving geographically for promotion is often necessary.

Some archaeologists in fieldwork aim initially for permanent employment with a unit. Progression may then be to site supervisor, then director.

Some experienced archaeologists become self-employed. Progress is then measured in terms of expanding business and profit.

RELATED OCCUPATIONS

Museum/art gallery curator, conservator, archaeological surveyor, librarian/information officer, archivist, countryside/conservation officer, scientist, research assistant.

FURTHER INFORMATION

Council for British Archaeology*, Bowes Morrell House, 111 Walmgate, York YO1 2UA, 01904 671417

Institute of Field Archaeologists*, Ironbridge Institute, Ironbridge Gorge Museum, Ironbridge, Telford, Shropshire TF8 7AW, 01952 432751

Institute of Field Archaeologists, c/o The University of Manchester, Manchester M13 9PL, 0161 275 2304

Museums Association*, 42 Clerkenwell Close, London EC1R 0PA, 0171 608 2933

FURTHER READING

Leaflets/booklets are available from the addresses marked*.

Job Outlines – Archaeology – COIC
Working in History – COIC

In the careers library classified under FAH.

LANGUAGES: FAL

1. INTERPRETER CLCI:FAL
2. TRANSLATOR CLCI:FAL
3. TEACHER OF ENGLISH AS A FOREIGN OR SECOND LANGUAGE CLCI:FAL

BACKGROUND INFORMATION

There are a number of jobs where linguistic skills are an advantage and even an important attribute. However, in many of them, knowledge of foreign languages is secondary to other abilities, even though, for some, it may be a requirement. This is true of travel couriers and resort representatives, bilingual managers and secretaries, and diplomats.

The two occupations where linguistic skills are the dominant ones are interpreter and translator. Interpreters work with the spoken word, translating spoken statements in another language into their mother tongue (or vice versa) so that people who understand only the mother tongue can follow what is being said. Translators work with the written or printed word, converting documents originated in one language into the language of those who need to read them. Both jobs require detailed knowledge of foreign languages, but they call for very different skills and have different work situations, as the following articles show. They may also demand a knowledge of specialist terms in both languages, such as legal, business or medical.

Jobs where linguistic skills are essential to obtaining employment but where other skills or knowledge are equally important, include foreign language teacher, information scientist and tour guide. Teaching skills are as vital to the foreign language teacher as knowledge of science and engineering is to the information scientist, and knowledge of tourist sites and history is to the tour guide.

There are many jobs where conversational ability in a foreign language is useful, for instance travel couriers, resort representatives, hotel receptionists, and crew of ships or airlines. Languages are important in the diplomatic service, or for administrative posts with international organizations. Combined with knowledge of business expressions and practices, skills in a foreign language are a vital tool of bilingual managers and secretaries, and of sales and marketing staff selling to overseas customers. In these jobs, the work may involve an element of translating and interpreting, though the amount will vary.

In general, the increase in trade and tourism with other countries, and especially with other countries within the European Union, is making ability to converse in other languages a valuable asset in a whole range of occupations. It also opens up the possibility of employment abroad, whatever the occupation.

1. INTERPRETER (FAL)

THE WORK

Interpreting concerns the spoken word. The normal rule is that interpreters convert spoken statements from another language into their own mother tongue for people who know only that tongue. There are several forms of interpreting.

Simultaneous interpreting is used at multilanguage international conferences and meetings, at which the interpreter sits in a soundproof booth (one for each conference language). They listen via headphones to speeches in the source language and immediately speak the interpretation in the target language into a microphone feeding headphones worn by delegates who normally speak that language. A team of two works into one target language in each booth. They take it in turns to interpret for periods of 15 to 30 minutes.

Consecutive interpreting is for more formal speeches to an audience, where the speaker, using his/her own language, pauses at intervals and the interpreter presents, in the audience's language, what has just been said. Normally, it is used at conferences or meetings where only two languages are involved. Simultaneous and consecutive interpreting together are known as **conference interpreting.**

Liaison interpreting is for conversations between two or more politicians, engineers, etc who speak different languages. Here the interpreter works into and out of each language after each person speaks.

Community interpreting is used to enable officials to talk with foreigners or ethnic minority citizens, again with the interpreter working both ways.

Public service interpreting is the new title intended to cover both community interpreting and sections of liaison interpreting. It includes the interpreting needs of local authorities, law courts, immigration authorities, hospitals, etc.

WORK ENVIRONMENT

Places of work vary greatly. Simultaneous interpreting involves periods in the confines of a booth looking out on a conference or meeting through a glass partition. Consecutive interpreting puts the interpreter on the stage or rostrum with the speaker performing his/her address in another language. Both may require travel by air all over the world, associating with delegates at social occasions. Liaison and public service interpreting may involve work in local government offices, hospitals, immigration centres, law courts, prisons, factories, and industrial and commercial premises.

SKILLS AND INTERESTS

Interpreters have to present in their mother tongue, or target language, the equivalent of what was spoken in the source language, including tone of voice, jokes, ambiguities, colloquialisms. This calls for a sound command of the spoken mother tongue, together with a comparable understanding of the way the other language is used by an educated native speaker, including its cultural background. An ability to manipulate language in skilful ways is needed where exact equivalents are not available. It also demands a clear, non-hesitant speaking voice and, in certain contexts, a knowledge of the appropriate specialist vocabulary of politics, economics, trade, engineering, etc and willingness to research a topic and its vocabulary before a conference or meeting.

Interpreters should have stamina, a good memory and physical health. They need the ability to maintain intense concentration and to think rapidly. Coping with the pressures of speed and accuracy in close contact with colleagues and clients can be stressful.

Integrity is essential in interpreting for confidential or secret events. The confidence to speak in public and an ability to take rapid notes are needed for consecutive interpreting.

ENTRY REQUIREMENTS

These vary from organization to organization, but most require two other languages besides English. Different organizations have different official languages. For the EC it is the languages of each member country; for the UN it is Arabic, Chinese, English, French, Russian and Spanish.

Most interpreters hold a degree in languages or in translation and interpreting, or a combined degree of languages with business, law, engineering, etc. Normal entry for degree courses is five GCSEs/S grades (A-C/1-3) with two A levels/three H grades. A levels/H grades in a relevant foreign language and English may be required. Most interpreters hold postgraduate interpreting qualifications, and many live and work in the language's country to obtain normal usage and awareness of the culture.

Applicants for traineeships with international organizations normally have to take a highly competitive entry test and interview. Some international organizations require prior experience.

Full acceptance as a conference interpreter depends on membership of the International Association of Conference Interpreters (AIIC). This requires the completion of at least 200 days' total work as a freelance interpreter, which can take several years to achieve.

The Institute of Linguists (IOL) offers exams at several levels, for qualifications that validate language skills in a range of languages and may offer an alternative to a degree course or postgraduate qualification. These involve language tasks normally encountered in work situations. Its higher-level exams relate more to aspects of interpreting and translating, ie Intermediate Diploma (covering guided research, interviewing, summarizing and report-writing), and Diploma in Languages for International Communication (this tests language skills at degree-level in negotiating, translating, translation editing, and interpreting) plus the skills test at Intermediate Diploma Level.

Many candidates take IOL exams on the basis of work or life experience plus self-study, while many others attend part-time continuing education classes leading to the exams at FE colleges, universities or one of the few private language schools. Courses are usually one evening a week for one or two years. As the external examining body, the IOL asks for no formal qualifications to sit these exams but, makes the required level of language competence very clear. Some local colleges may ask for a GCSE/S grade in a language for entry to a course.

Familiarity with an ethnic minority language as mother tongue, together with good English and a general education is a good basis for public service interpreting. The IOL's Diploma in Public Service Interpreting is widely recognized as the required qualification. The exams for this are usually taken by people with the appropriate skills from past experience, or from taking short courses run by some local adult education institutes, FE colleges or universities. It is in three parts, including sight translation, written translation from and into English, as well as interpreting. Candidates can choose an area from public health, legal or local government.

TRAINING

Specific training in interpreting skills is provided on specialist interpreting degree and postgraduate courses. These include practice in simultaneous interpreting in a language laboratory, and in consecutive interpreting including the speed note-taking techniques needed while listening to a speech prior to interpreting. They also cover liaison interpreting. Some experience of specialist vocabularies – such as legal, financial, medical – may also be included. Some courses leading to the exams of the IOL may provide interpreting practice, as do public service interpreting courses leading to the IOL Diploma in Public Service Interpreting.

Those who gain employment with the EC as a trainee interpreter receive up to six months' training in simultaneous and consecutive interpreting. Some training is provided in Civil Service linguist posts, where duties may cover translating as well as interpreting. Other organizations recruiting trainees offer mainly on-the-job training.

Freelance interpreters aiming to become conference interpreters accumulate experience via liaison or public service interpreting.

LATE ENTRY

It is rare for people to enter interpreting later in life because of the special techniques and skills involved, though a few enter from language teaching or bilingual posts in industry. The exception is community interpreting, where life experience, ability in spoken English and an ethnic minority language are important factors. However, mature students can also take degree and postgraduate courses to qualify. The exams offered by the IOL test language ability and interpreting skills and enable those who have acquired these from life or work experience to obtain a qualification proving professional competence.

OPPORTUNITIES

There are about 500 conference interpreters in full-time posts with international organizations in all countries covering all official language combinations, and about 50-60 posts are advertised every year. Many of these are on short-term contracts. Membership of the AIIC is 2,000, including 120 members in Britain. On average about 50-60 new members qualify to join the AIIC each year. There are no figures available for public service and liaison interpreters, though the potential demand is quite high. The small number of openings and the stiff competition make this a difficult profession to succeed in.

The EC is the largest employer of interpreters, with each of its institutions recruiting separately and regularly, followed by the United Nations and its agencies. Other international organizations, such as NATO, and trade organizations employ a small number of each. All of these engage additional freelance interpreters for conferences, through the AIIC.

Interpreting and translating agencies normally fill the needs of their clients by hiring freelance interpreters. Due to the limited opportunities available, interpreters often do other work, such as translating or teaching, from which they can take days off to interpret when the opportunities arise.

Liaison and public service interpreters gradually build up contacts with clients. There are plans to create a national register of qualified and experienced public service interpreters to enable health or local authorities, police, etc, to find a suitable interpreter easily.

PAY AND CONDITIONS

The starting salary for recently qualified graduate interpreters at the European Commission is 1,641,216 Belgian francs (over £32,000) rising by increments and on promotion to a higher grade. The annual income of freelance interpreters depends on the rate (per day or hour) they agree with the clients and agencies who engage their services, and the number of engagements they get. For freelance conference interpreters, daily rates range from £200 to £300; for liaison interpreters, the rate is about £200 a day, though some areas pay much less, eg law courts.

Staff interpreters normally work a 35-hour week plus overtime but, like freelancers, they have to be available for conferences, meetings or interviews, and may be expected to travel in their own time. This work can be in the evenings and at weekends. It may include emergency meetings at short notice.

PROSPECTS

In the interpreting departments of international organizations there may be the possibility of promotion to senior interpreter or head of department. For freelance interpreters, advancement involves increasing the number of clients and the frequency of engagements, and commanding higher fees relating to increasing skill and experience. Some liaison interpreters move to conference interpreting as they accumulate enough days' experience to qualify for AIIC membership. Even well-established interpreters sometimes have a second earning activity, such as translating or language teaching. A small number move into teaching full-time on degree or postgraduate courses, or into administrative posts with international organizations.

Many interpreters add to their skills during their careers by learning additional languages and studying for extra qualifications. The ITI runs in-career training sessions for its members and offers professional development courses in conjunction with a number of new universities.

RELATED OCCUPATIONS

Translator, journalist/foreign correspondent, tourist guide, travel courier, resort representative, specialist secretary (bi/multilingual), teacher (languages).

FURTHER INFORMATION

Institute of Linguists (IOL)*, 24a Highbury Grove, London N5 2DQ, 0171 359 7445

Institute of Translation and Interpreting (ITI)*, 377 City Road, London EC1V 1NA, 0171 713 7600

FURTHER READING

Leaflets/booklets are available from the addresses marked*.

Useful information also from European Commission Information Office and from United Nations Information Office – see publications for addresses.

Job Outlines – Languages – COIC
Working in Languages – COIC
Careers Using Languages – Kogan Page
Languages and Your Career – IOL
Interpreters... What do they do? – ITI

In the careers library classified under FAL.

2. TRANSLATOR (FAL)

THE WORK

Translators work with the written word. They convert documents from the original or source language into the language of the people who need to know the content (the target language) and read the translation. Normally, they work into their mother tongue, or language of habitual use, from one or more other languages. The translated document should read as though originated in the target language.

The majority are concerned with scientific, technical or commercial material. Documents may include business letters, financial reports, legal communications, sales brochures, technical manuals, etc. Knowledge of fields such as finance, medicine, law or engineering and the technical terms they use can be important, and translators often specialize in one or more of these. In the course of translating, they refer to specialist dictionaries and reference books, type up translations on a word processor or personal computer, or dictate into a tape-recorder for later typing. A few large companies use computer programs to create a rough 'machine' translation which the translator then revises and edits.

Literary translation requires the translator to recreate the literary effects the original novelist, playwright or poet intended in another language.

WORK ENVIRONMENT

Translators normally work at a desk with a word processor and with reference books and specialist dictionaries to hand. They may visit clients, experts or specialist organizations, though most contact is by phone or mail, fax or modem.

SKILLS AND INTERESTS

Translators need ability in one or more foreign languages and also the skill of writing in clear and appropriate English, as the translated text should read as though written originally in English. They should be self-motivated and able to work at speed. Freelance translators have to cope with being on their own most of the time. A meticulous mind is needed to search for the correct word or phrase and to ensure they are themselves clear on complicated or ambiguous aspects. This may involve an element of problem solving.

Wide education and interests are important, as is sufficient interest in their specialist fields to keep up to date by reading magazines and books. Translators have to be discreet and trustworthy in translating secret and confidential documents. They must be neutral and free of bias, even if translating statements they disapprove of. Ability to use a word processor is important, though some translators speak their translation into a Dictaphone and pay someone else to type it up.

ENTRY REQUIREMENTS

Most translators firstly obtain a degree in:

– one or more modern foreign languages (preferably an applied language studies course, which offers some practice in translation and interpreting);

– a foreign language combined with a specialist subject, such as business, law, engineering, computer studies or European studies;

– translation and interpreting (including basic study of some specialist subjects and vocabulary).

It is increasingly common for translators to take a postgraduate diploma in translation by full-time or part-time study, or a master's degree. Often they take the Institute of Linguist's (IOL) Diploma in Translation.

Degree courses normally require a minimum of five GCSEs/S grades (A-C/1-3) with two A levels/three H grades. They may specify at least one relevant foreign language and English at A level/H grade for language and translation degrees. An appropriate specialist subject may be needed for a combined degree.

The Institute of Linguists (IOL) offers exams at several levels, for qualifications that validate language skills in a range of languages and may offer an alternative to a degree course.

Specifically for translators, the entry qualification is the IOL's Diploma in Translation (DipTrans IOL). Entry for this requires linguistic ability in the source language, at least equivalent to a good honours degree in languages.

Many candidates take IOL exams on the basis of work or life experience plus self-study, while others attend part-time adult education classes leading to the exams at colleges, universities and a few private language schools. Usually they are one evening a week for one or two years. The IOL asks for no formal qualifications to sit these exams, but sets out the required level of language competence. Content of these courses, as of degree courses, varies considerably.

TRAINING

Training is normally obtained during degree and postgraduate courses or by taking evening courses at colleges or universities, leading to qualifications of the IOL.

All IOL courses are based on practical language tasks normally encountered in work situations. At higher levels they cover translation and interviewing tasks, ie the Intermediate Diploma (covering guided research, interviewing, summarizing and report-writing), and the Diploma in Languages for International Communication (this tests language skills at professional level in negotiating, translating, translation editing, and interpreting). The Diploma in Translation involves a written exam with three papers covering general translation plus annotation of difficult points, and semi-specialized translation in one of the areas of technology, business, literature, and one of science or humanities. A pass in all three papers is required. DipTrans courses are available at a number of universities and HE colleges. Some language combinations have distance learning courses via National Extension College, etc.

Those recruited to trainee posts with international organizations or government departments have a period of training during which they learn the specialist practices and vocabulary involved and pick up accuracy and speed by doing increasingly more complex tasks.

Freelance translators have to practise to achieve a fast speed, together with accuracy of content and style.

LATE ENTRY

Because of the importance of detailed knowledge in a specialist field, people who have worked as lawyers, accountants, engineers, etc, who also have a second language and experience of reading and writing foreign texts may become a translator with no further training, or by taking the IOL's DipTrans. This, and other courses and exams the IOL runs, test language ability and translating skills and provide proof of professional competence. Mature students can also take degrees and postgraduate courses in languages and in translating.

Familiarity with an ethnic minority language, as well as good English, enables some mature people to obtain translation work at local level, sometimes starting as an unpaid volunteer. They go on to take training courses and aim for a relevant qualification.

OPPORTUNITIES

Full-time posts are few, so there is strong competition. Principal employers are international organizations, government departments, multinational companies and some large translation agencies. Some industrial and commercial companies with regular trade with other countries have staff translators to translate, eg technical manuals about their products.

Recruitment to United Nations organizations, EC institutions and government departments is by competitive examination and interview. Some are to trainee positions, but others require two years' experience. UN and EC jobs are based in New York, Brussels and other cities overseas.

However, many translators work on a freelance basis. They obtain individual translating tasks through translation agencies, or from personal contacts and mailings to companies, offering their services.

It is possible to make a full-time living from freelance translating, but some find it necessary to do teaching or interpreting work as well. Some freelance engagements are to work for a period in the offices of the employing organization.

Literary translation is a wholly freelance activity and few people rely on it solely for a living.

PAY AND CONDITIONS

The starting salary for a recently qualified graduate at the European Commission is about 1,641,216 Belgian francs (over £32,000), rising by increments and on promotion to a higher grade. Salaries in the UK range from £15,000 for full-time translators in smaller organizations to £30,000-£35,000 for senior, experienced staff in large ones. The annual income of freelance translators depends on the rate (per job or per thousand words) they agree with the clients and agencies who engage their services, the number of engagements they get, and the speed and accuracy with which they work. Rates can range from £48 per thousand words for translating into English from French, Spanish or Italian to £100 per thousand from Chinese. Translating from English into another language usually adds about 25 to 30 per cent to these fees, more for Japanese and Chinese. Additional charges are made for urgency and for areas of specialist knowledge.

Staff translators work normal office hours, around 35 hours a week, with occasional overtime for urgent tasks. Freelance translators working from home choose their own hours, but may have to work weekends to meet deadlines.

PROSPECTS

Promotion is to senior translator and to head of department for those employed in large translation departments or agencies. This may occasionally offer a route into management. Freelance translators who are successful, sometimes start their own translation agency. Progress for freelance translators usually takes the form of more jobs and clients, and higher fees. The European single market and the freeing of trade with Eastern Europe have increased the opportunities for translation work in other countries.

A small number of translators move into teaching full-time,

or into administrative posts with international organizations.

Many translators add to their skills during their careers by learning additional languages and studying for extra qualifications, often through the IOL. In addition, the ITI runs in-career training sessions for its members and offers professional development courses in conjunction with a number of new universities.

RELATED OCCUPATIONS

Interpreter, teacher (foreign languages), journalist/foreign correspondent, specialist secretary (bi/multilingual), information scientist.

FURTHER INFORMATION

Institute of Linguists (IOL)*, 24a Highbury Grove, London N5 2DQ, 0171 359 7445

Institute of Translation and Interpreting (ITI)*, 377 City Road, London EC1V 1NA, 0171 713 7600

Useful information also from European Commission Information Office and United Nations Information Centre – see publications below for addresses.

FURTHER READING

Leaflets/booklets are available from the addresses marked*.

Job Outlines – Languages – COIC
Working in Languages – COIC
Careers Using Languages – Kogan Page
Languages and Your Career – IOL
First Steps Up The Translating Ladder – IOL Translators' Information Pack – IOL
Thinking about being a Translator – ITI
Starting Up as a Freelance Translator – ITI
Career as a Staff Translator – ITI

In the careers library classified under FAL.

3. TEACHER OF ENGLISH AS A FOREIGN OR SECOND LANGUAGE (FAL)

THE WORK

Teaching English as a Foreign Language, known as TEFL, is often used as an umbrella title to cover several activities with somewhat different methods and requirements, though increasingly the title Teaching English to Speakers of Other Languages (TESOL) is used for this purpose.

Teaching English as a Foreign Language (TEFL), strictly speaking, involves teaching people in or from non-English-speaking countries how to understand, speak, read and write English. The students could be school pupils or adults in other countries, or foreigners (whether pupils, students or adults) visiting Britain to study. The emphasis in teaching is normally on spoken English, so teacher and pupils are expected to conduct classes in English. However, knowledge of the students' language may be useful, at times, to identify learner problems.

Teachers may follow a coursebook that ensures students gain practice in a balance of skills; they may use games, tasks and grammar exercises learnt on training courses, or prepare their own teaching materials, such as articles and photographs cut from newspapers and magazines, or pre-recorded audio-tapes. Teaching methods range from 'chalk and talk' using black/whiteboards, question-and-answer sessions and group conversation, to flash cards, videos and computers. Teachers plan and prepare lessons in advance, using textbooks and published materials, but also create their own teaching materials and exercises. They also mark tests, essays and exercises in non-teaching hours.

Teaching English as a Second Language (TESL or, sometimes, TE2L)

is concerned primarily with teaching groups of students who do not have English as their mother tongue and who settled, or intend to settle, in the UK. TESL also takes place in multilingual countries, such as Kenya or Singapore, which use English for administrative purposes, or in the education system. Students learn how to use English for everyday life, to shop, to get a job and to be able to successfully study other subjects at school or college in English.

All TESL teaching in UK schools, and much in colleges, is through giving language support to students' work on the National Curriculum, rather than in ESL classes. This may involve co-teaching with specialist teachers, or acting as an advisor to other teachers, running workshops with small groups, or teaching on a one-to-one basis. TESL teachers are likely to have a pastoral, as well as a teaching, role.

They use a range of teaching techniques – text books may be used but many classroom activities are based on materials prepared by the teacher, with topics often related to everyday life in the UK. Students may study for examinations such as C&G Communication Skills or GNVQ Core Skills in Communication.

Teaching English for Specific Purposes (TESP) consists of showing foreign managers, civil servants, lawyers, etc how to use English to do business, negotiate, or conduct themselves at special events. It includes courses to enable foreign students to study for degrees at British universities or colleges, ie English for Academic Purposes (EAP), and others to enable foreign nationals to teach English. Normally, the students know enough English already to be taught further in English only, so knowing the students' language is not an essential requirement.

Role-play simulations, possibly videotaped, of social or business situations can be an important part of the teaching, though, for some topics, formal explanation and learning of specialist vocabularies may predominate.

Some courses lead to exams for a certificate awarded by a range of bodies.

In different contexts, teaching aids may include: black/whiteboards, wallcharts, slide projectors, video players and cameras, tape recorders, and language laboratories.

WORK ENVIRONMENT

The normal place of work is a classroom in a school, college or private language school, though for TESL it may sometimes be a room in a community centre or evening institute. For TESP it may be a training centre attached to a large company's premises in another country. For many, the work involves living abroad, with wide variations in social environment and living/working conditions. It may involve travelling to several locations. Classes for adults are often in the evening.

In commercial language schools, a maximum class size of about twelve students is normal and in some contexts, eg English for executives, the numbers may be even fewer. Some commercial schools in the UK offer individual tuition.

SKILLS AND INTERESTS

Teachers need enthusiasm and energy. They have to be experienced and skilled in the way English is used in a wide range of situations. The ability to speak one or more foreign languages can be important in some areas, but not in all, and is not essential.

Clarity of diction is important. Ability to devise teaching exercises and activities to suit the level of the students and the course is needed. The teacher must be patient when pupils find it difficult to grasp a point and able to stay calm and think out other ways of getting the concept across.

A pleasant personality and the ability to get on with a wide range of character types, ages, abilities and cultures, are useful in the close relationships of small classes.

ENTRY REQUIREMENTS

To teach in schools within the state system in Britain requires a degree plus qualified teacher status (QTS). In England and Wales this is a Postgraduate Certificate in Education (PGCE) and in Scotland a one-year college of education course. A BEd degree also gives QTS. TEFL and TESL are no longer available as main subjects, though they may be a subsidiary option when taking modern languages as the main subject. Those hoping to teach TESL in schools should, therefore, aim for an additional specialist qualification, or go on to a specialist MA in TESL or Applied Linguistics.

Minimum entry requirements for degree courses are normally five GCSEs/S grades (A-C/1-3) with two A levels/three H grades, including at least GCSE/S grade English. An A level/H grade in the language to be studied may be needed, especially for French or German. For other languages, A levels/H grades should include a foreign language and English.

An appropriate degree gives entry to postgraduate courses leading to QTS. Prospective teachers in England and Wales must have GCSEs/S grades (A-C/1-3) in English and maths. In Scotland, they require H grade English and S grade maths.

No formal teaching qualifications are needed to teach in FE colleges and universities, but the usual minimum entry requirements are a degree plus a TEFL or TESL certificate.

Recognized commercial language schools in Britain (and most reputable commercial schools abroad) employing EFL teachers ask for graduates with at least the Royal Society of Arts/University of Cambridge Local Examinations Syndicate (RSA/UCLES) Certificate in the Teaching of English as a Foreign Language to Adults (CTEFLA) or the Trinity College London Certificate in Teaching English to Speakers of Other Languages (CTESOL). Though there is no standard international qualification, these are recognized in many countries. Entry to courses is normally with a degree or evidence of a good standard of education, for example A levels/H grades and minimum age of 20. Application forms for some schools also set pre-interview tasks to demonstrate language awareness. Most people take these courses after a degree, or after teaching experience in another discipline.

The British Council and larger language education organizations expect higher qualifications – usually a degree and an RSA/UCLES Diploma (DTEFLA), or a Trinity Licentiate Diploma in the Teaching of English as a Foreign or Second Language (TEFSL), or a Masters degree in Applied Linguistics or TEFL. Enrolling for most of these requires two years' experience of teaching EFL or ESL and, for some, a TEFL or TESL qualification and/or a degree.

For TESL, the most widely accepted qualifications are the RSA Certificate of Initial Training in English as a Second Language for Adults (CITESLA) and the RSA Diploma in ESL in Further, Adult and Continuing Education (FACE). For school-level teaching there is the RSA Diploma in Teaching of English across the Curriculum in Multilingual Schools, which is especially valuable for language support work.

Some universities offer their own postgraduate certificates and diplomas in TEFL and TESL and diplomas in linguistics or language education. These are not necessarily regarded as the equivalent of the RSA/UCLES and Trinity qualifications, because few have a practical teaching component.

A number of universities and independent colleges offer courses in TESP at Introductory, Certificate or Diploma levels, and in Business English. There is no course specifically in EAP, but ESP courses will normally cover this area. For entry, some colleges ask for a degree, most require two or three years' experience and a few want CTEFLA or CTESOL, so normally people take these courses after work in EFL, or part-time while working in it. Some people enter ESP from experience of working in business, engineering, the law, medicine, etc, with or without an ESP course.

Requirements for teaching English in overseas countries vary considerably and some are stringent. A detailed listing appears in the *EFL Guide.*

TRAINING

Modern-language degree courses are normally four years, with one year spent in the country of the language. An English degree is three years. PGCE and other courses leading to QTS are one year. Specialist TEFL and TESL certificate courses vary from four weeks full-time to twelve months part-time. Diploma courses are from eight weeks full-time to one year part-time. Fees vary for these courses. A list of training courses is issued by The British Council and details also appear in the *EFL Guide.*

The RSA/UCLES certificate course is very practical and covers, in lectures and seminars: principles underlying language teaching; analysis of English from a learner's viewpoint; teaching techniques, including drama and visual aids; classroom management and lesson planning. Students then have teacher practice under observation. It aims to qualify for teaching adults from beginner to First Certificate level (EFL students) or C&G Communication Skills (ESL students).

The Trinity certificate course covers similar areas, but varies from college to college within a set of syllabus requirements, so suitability should be checked. It includes techniques and practice of teaching children, an area that is not in the RSA course.

Courses are available at a wide range of universities, FE colleges and independent language schools around the country. To test one's aptitude for this field, it is possible to take a short introduction to EFL courses, one week full-time to ten weeks part-time. These do not count as qualifications, though two institutions regard their own introductory courses as stage one of certificate courses.

It is important to check that courses have a significant element of teaching practice and that this is with students, not fellow trainees. Some courses offer an element of distance learning but, because of the importance of practical aspects, none are wholly distance learning.

The ability to teach both EFL and ESL, or to teach other subjects as well as one of them, is likely to increase the chances of obtaining a post in further or adult education.

LATE ENTRY

As life experience is a distinct advantage, many people obtain TEFL/TESL qualifications and/or teaching qualifications and enter after work in teaching, training, or other industries, or after living and working abroad. Experience of business, for instance, is an asset for teaching in the ESP area.

OPPORTUNITIES

Employers for work in TEFL in Britain are mainly commercial language schools and FE colleges and, for TESL, local education authorities and FE colleges or adult education institutes. Some education authorities with high proportions of ethnic minority pupils employ specialist TESL teachers. Permanent full-time posts in TESL in FE colleges and adult education are few and teachers may be expected to act as 'language support' in classes in, for example, science, business studies or engineering taught by other lecturers. The easiest time to obtain initial TEFL engagements at commercial schools is the summer vacation, when parties of foreign school-children come over.

For work abroad in TEFL and TESP, employers include The British Council, local education authorities, private schools and language schools, large industrial concerns and government departments. A freelance teacher may obtain short-term engagements from some of these plus, in Britain, foreign embassies, cultural institutes, and branches of foreign companies situated in Britain. Some other regular employers are the Overseas Development Administration (ODA), Voluntary Service Overseas (VSO), and International House. There are a number of agencies that locate teachers for overseas posts.

In TESL, employment is possible with state education authorities and private language schools in other English-speaking countries, such as the USA, Australia and New Zealand, or countries that use English for administration and communication.

Private tuition may also be a possibility. Some schools in Europe and Japan have posts of language assistant, who support the teacher and provide conversation opportunities for pupils.

Advertisements for vacancies appear in national newspapers and, especially, the *Times Educational Supplement,* and in the *EL Gazette.* There is increasing competition for places, particularly in year-round jobs.

With English increasingly the dominant language of international trade and culture, there is growing demand for people equipped to teach it. The single European market and the EC's encouragement of languages, and the opening up of Eastern Europe and, to some extent, China have increased this demand. The increased training of their own nationals to teach English counters this trend somewhat. Continuing restrictions on immigration into Britain could mean the need for ESL teachers will decline.

PAY AND CONDITIONS

Salaries for posts within the UK state education system start at £12,500 with a degree and QTS. In the state education systems of other countries, pay is in line with normal levels for those countries, or with levels agreed by those countries with The British Council. Hours of work and other conditions also vary. Contracts for engagements overseas with The British Council and other British organizations are normally for one or two years; salaries are at the top end of local rates, and air fares and medical insurance are paid as well.

A full-time EFL teacher in a recognized commercial language school in the UK could expect anything from £10,000 to £17,000 for teaching 21 to 27 hours a week. Rates of £6 to £18 an hour apply to part-time and casual staff. Unrecognized schools pay less and are less likely to offer long-term contracts or paid holidays, and other conditions may be unfavourable. Similar variations apply to commercial language schools in other countries.

In Britain, most of the schools that are recognized by The British Council are members of the Association of Recognized English Language Services (ARELS), which insists on contracts, or of First Quality English Language Services (FIRST), which has charters regulating high standards for staff and students.

Fees paid by commercial language schools in other countries vary drastically depending on their status and financial soundness. In all situations, higher qualifications should win higher remuneration.

Teaching hours vary, but to these should be added time for preparation of teaching materials and lessons and marking of exercises. Teachers working with young people, especially on summer courses, may be expected to take parties sightseeing and oversee them in sporting and social activities outside teaching hours.

PROSPECTS

In Britain, some commercial schools and FE colleges may offer some promotion to senior or managerial posts, as may some overseas centres to staff on long-term contracts. However, the majority of teachers cannot expect this, though long experience and continued work for one establishment should bring increases in salaries or fees. A successful teacher may open their own private language school. A successful freelance should be able to demand higher fees as their reputation grows. Some teachers move into teacher training and others into writing books and articles about EFL. Experienced teachers add to their skills by taking additional courses, eg in ESP, or go on to an MA in TEFL, TESL, or linguistics in Britain or another country.

RELATED OCCUPATIONS

Teacher (foreign languages), teacher (English), community interpreter, resort representative, tour guide, bilingual secretary, bilingual manager.

FURTHER INFORMATION

Association of Recognized English Language Services (ARELS)*, 2 Pontypool Place, Valentine Place, London SE1 8QF, 0171 242 3136

The British Council, English Language Information Section*, Medlock Street, Manchester M15 4AA, 0161 957 7755

EFL Ltd, 10 Wrights Lane, Kensington, London W8 6TA

First Quality English Language Services (FIRST)*, 4 Russetts Drive, Fleet, Hants GU13 9QE, 01252 815 524

National Association for Teaching English and other Community Languages to Adults (NATECLA)*, South Birmingham College, 524 Stratford Road, Birmingham B11 4AJ, 0121 694 5070

International Association for Teachers of EFL (IATEFL), 3 Kingsdown Chambers, Kingsdown Park, Tankerton, Whitstable, Kent CT5 2DJ, 01227 276 528

FURTHER READING

Leaflets/booklets are available from the addresses marked*.

Job Outlines – Languages – COIC

Working in Languages – COIC
Careers Using Languages – Kogan Page
Languages and Your Career – IOL
Teaching English as a Foreign Language and Teaching Abroad – AGCAS
EFL Guide – EFL Ltd
How to Become a Teacher of English as a Foreign Language – The British Council

In the careers library classified under FAL.

GROUP G – ENTERTAINMENT AND LEISURE

1. ACTOR CLCI:GAB
2. MUSICIAN CLCI:GAD
3. MUSIC TEACHER CLCI:GAD/FAB
4. DANCER CLCI:GAF

1. ACTOR (GAB)

BACKGROUND INFORMATION

In this article the word 'actor' refers to both men and women. The title 'actress' is becoming less and less used in the profession.

Some people are attracted to the acting profession, believing it to be glamorous and well paid. The reality is that, at any one time, an estimated four out of five actors are without acting work, or 'resting'. During this time, they may have to rely for income on state benefits, or money from casual work, such as temping.

Actors may work either in live stage performances, or in recorded media, such as films, radio, television and video. Some actors prefer one of these to the other, and the techniques used differ. Most actors cover both in order to gain experience, improve their chances of obtaining regular work and reduce the risk of becoming 'type-cast'. Although film and television is often better paid, many actors find live theatre more challenging and stimulating.

When they are working, most actors work long, hard hours for relatively little pay. Even well-known names have periods when they are without work, and very few make a fortune from acting.

For many people, acting remains a pastime, which can be satisfied at any number of amateur theatre groups around the country.

THE WORK

Acting is a performance art, alongside music and dance. An actor's job is to assume a character created by a playwright or author, and communicate this to an audience, usually under the guidance of a director. The production may be anything from Shakespeare to street theatre, but, in each case, the actor must understand and interpret what the writer is trying to convey.

Actors use their own experience and emotions to help them portray characters. Communication is achieved through imaginative and creative use of the body and voice.

Much of an actor's time is spent learning parts and rehearsing plays. Acting is very much a group activity, in which each player is dependent upon others, including the director. Individual characters are developed by close co-operation between the actors and the director. The performance is the culmination of all the hard work, although it occupies only a small proportion of an actor's time.

The range and scope of acting is considerable. Some actors work mainly in the classical theatre, performing plays by Shakespeare and others; some specialize in more 'mainstream' theatre, including old and new plays; others work on comedy, musicals, community theatre, puppetry, mime, etc.

When they are out of work, actors spend as much time as possible auditioning for parts.

WORK ENVIRONMENT

Actors work mainly indoors in theatres and studios, though for films and TV, some scenes may be recorded on location.

Actors taking part in open air and street theatre obviously work outside, though rehearsals may take place under cover.

The temperatures in which actors work can vary widely, from cold and draughty rehearsal rooms to warm theatres and studios, where spotlights and (perhaps) heavy costumes may add to the overall heat.

Actors in the theatre have to work more or less continuously during the duration of the show, while in films and, to a lesser extent, television, there may be long breaks as sets are changed, lights and cameras re-angled, and so on. There can be a good deal of sitting around waiting for the next scene to be recorded.

While taking part in a show, actors may have to live away from their homes, in lodgings with other actors. If the show goes on tour, or a film or TV programme on location, they can spend lengthy periods away from home, perhaps even abroad.

SKILLS AND INTERESTS

Actors need to understand and interpret the roles they are given, and have a good memory, both for their lines and their moves. A clear speaking voice is important, and they also need empathy and imagination to understand and express the emotions of the characters they are asked to portray.

Actors must be mentally and physically tough, to cope with the demands of the job. They must be resilient and able to cope with the uncertainty of working in a profession where, at the end of a run or series, unemployment is always a prospect. Good general health is also important; actors are expected to turn up for rehearsals and performances even when unwell.

ENTRY REQUIREMENTS

There are no formal entry requirements for becoming an actor, and it is still possible for untrained people with talent and determination to enter the profession, perhaps via fringe or amateur theatre. The majority of actors today, however, have been through stage and/or drama school.

Drama schools take students from the age of 18 years (17 in one or two cases). Many do not set minimum academic entry requirements for performance courses, preferring to assess potential by audition and interview. Others specify five GCSEs/S grades (A-C/1-3), and a few require two A levels or three H grades. Competition is extremely intense, with some schools auditioning 20 or more people for each place.

Auditions vary, but often follow a two-tier system. For the first stage, candidates may be asked to prepare two contrasting pieces, one modern and one by Shakespeare, and perform them in front of a selection panel. They may then be required to read a piece at sight, improvise on a given subject, or sing. Those who succeed at this stage are invited back for a longer, more detailed, final audition. Selection panels are looking for evidence of talent, combined with absolute commitment to an acting career.

Degree courses in drama or theatre arts/studies usually ask for a minimum of five GCSEs/S grades (A-C/1-3) and two A levels or three H grades, or equivalent. The application procedure may include auditions and/or participation in workshops.

Stage schools are part of the private (fee-paying) education sector. They take children from the age of five upwards, and offer the usual National Curriculum subjects, but with extra training in drama, voice production, dance, mime, singing and so on. Nowadays, only a minority of new entrants to the acting profession have been through stage school. Young people who have not followed this path can gain acting experience in other ways, for example by taking part in school productions and/or joining a youth theatre group.

TRAINING

Although it is still possible to enter the acting profession without formal training, nowadays the National Council for Drama Training (NCDT) recommends that all intending actors should complete a course of recognized training. A list of courses is available from NCDT on receipt of an sae.

Professional acting courses

Nineteen drama schools throughout the UK run professional acting courses that have been accredited by the NCDT. Most of these are listed in the Conference of Drama Schools' prospectus. Courses vary widely, and students are recommended to read schools' prospectuses carefully before applying. Some courses are classically orientated, and concentrate on teaching students a range of skills in acting, movement, stage combat, etc. Other courses start from the student's own experience, emphasizing self-discovery and self-development, then move on to acquiring the necessary skills. At some colleges, students form a repertory company, performing a series of plays or musicals, and possibly touring. Professional acting courses are intensive. Most last three years, and often they involve working from early in the morning until late at night.

Although there is some variation between courses, the first year usually concentrates on the development of the actor's body and voice. Students learn how to breathe, project their voices and move, and may also study singing, mask work, stage fighting, improvisation and stage make-up. In the second year they may learn acrobatics, tumbling, and different styles of dance, such as tap and jazz. As students' skills develop, they spend more time working on set texts and rehearsing plays, culminating in public performances. Students also study social history and the history of drama and the visual arts.

Most professional acting courses do not attract mandatory grants. Students needing financial assistance with drama school fees and living expenses are often dependent on discretionary awards, which many local authorities are cutting back on. Check with your local education authority on the funding status of the various courses concerned, and, if appropriate, the availability of discretionary awards.

Other courses

There are other drama schools throughout the country, but graduates from non-accredited courses are likely to have more difficulty in obtaining an Equity card and beginning a career as an actor when they leave.

Many other courses, at all levels, include drama as part, or all, of their content. Colleges may offer A level drama or theatre studies, and the BTEC National Diploma in Performing Arts. These courses may be accepted as the academic part of the entry requirements for an acting course. The BTEC National Diploma in Performing Arts is vocationally based and provides practical experience in drama, music, dance and stagecraft, through workshops and performance. This experience can be invaluable when preparing for auditions.

A degree course in drama or performance arts is another option, and there are many courses to choose from. Some are academic, concentrating on the theoretical aspects of theatre, sometimes combining drama with an academic subject, such as English. Others offer a more practical training, perhaps alongside music and dance. The emphasis on most courses is not on training actors, though undoubtedly some graduates do go into the profession, perhaps after postgraduate training at drama school. A small, but increasing, number of drama schools are now themselves offering degree courses with NCDT accreditation.

Drama graduates can go into any field where a degree is a prerequisite, giving them an opportunity to pursue alternative careers should acting not work out.

LATE ENTRY

Experience of life outside the theatre can be of great benefit to an actor, and many drama schools are prepared to accept mature students. Some schools set an upper age limit of 25 or 26 years. Others accept students up to the age of 30, and, very occasionally, even older. Academic entry requirements, where specified, may be relaxed for mature students over a certain age; this varies between 21 and 25 years.

Once over the age of 30, opportunities to enter the acting profession are very limited.

OPPORTUNITIES

It is sometimes thought that opportunities for actors depend on their being accepted into Equity, the actors' trade union, and obtaining an Equity card. However, this is only true to a very limited extent. Equity negotiates pay and conditions for actors, but entry to acting jobs is dependent on selection by casting directors. This depends on the ability of an actor to impress at audition, which in turn depends on the talent of the actor.

Once an actor has been given a professional acting job in theatre, television, film or radio, they are eligible to join Equity. Newcomers receive provisional membership, and can apply for a full Equity card after completing 30 weeks of approved work (not necessarily consecutive). Actors who have successfully completed a drama school course accredited by the National Council for Drama Training can join Equity immediately as registered graduate members.

In films, radio and television, there are no restrictions on who can be employed. Within the theatre, Equity has agreements with employers limiting the number of newcomers to the profession who can be engaged in any one year. Even here, however, the requirement is not that the majority of people taken on should be Equity members, but rather that they should be 'people with previous professional experience', or registered graduates. Most experienced actors are members of Equity, but possession of an Equity card is, in itself, no guarantee of employment.

As already mentioned, even experienced actors face intense competition for jobs. Actors must therefore take every opportunity to bring themselves to the notice of producers and casting directors. Many advertise with a photograph in the actors' annual directory *Spotlight*.

Opportunities for actors are sometimes advertised in The Stage and Television Today, the weekly newspaper of the acting profession. Personal contacts and word-of-mouth are also important. Actors can find out who is currently casting for productions through publications such as *Production and Casting Report* and *Repertory Report.*

Many actors obtain work through agents, who negotiate their contracts and take a percentage of their earnings.

Good agents can greatly assist their clients' careers. Having an agent is not, however, essential.

Actors may work in the following areas:

Repertory companies

There are around 70 regional repertory companies, which may offer a starting point for newly-trained actors. Actors are engaged for a whole season, performing a different play on average every three weeks. Young actors are usually advised to gain varied experience in rep, before attempting to specialize in film, television or theatre work.

Commercial theatre companies

Several prominent commercial producers tour shows with a view to bringing them to the West End. Sometimes companies are set up to perform one particular play or show. Productions normally run for a specified period of weeks or months, though they may finish early if unsuccessful. Leading roles in such productions almost invariably go to experienced actors, but young actors may be taken on for juvenile or smaller parts.

Films

Actors are hired for a particular film. Although the whole production may take months, most are taken on for only a few days or weeks. Few films are made in Britain today, so opportunities for film actors in this country are limited.

Television

Television offers a growing number of opportunities, though starting work can be difficult. Actors are usually employed for one particular programme, though some may appear in long-running serials. Television work requires special skills for working to a camera.

Radio

Most radio work is on a one-off basis, although there are serials, and actors may also specialize in radio plays. Most work is with the BBC, and opportunities exist at both national and regional levels.

Commercials

Many actors work in commercials to boost their income, and such jobs can be well paid. Actors either appear in person in the commercials, or do 'voice-overs'.

Promotional and training videos

An increasing number of companies specialize in producing videos for commercial purposes. These may be to promote an organization and its products or services, or for staff training. Such companies offer a range of opportunities for actors.

Stunt work

Stunt performers need to have a range of skills, as well as acting. These might include driving, parachuting, riding, fencing, gymnastics, martial arts and diving. Equity operates a stunt register that film and television producers use. New applicants must be Equity members between 18 and 30 years and have recent qualifications in a range of skills.

Summer shows and pantomimes

Some actors specialize in this area, moving from one to the other, and thereby achieving regular work throughout the year.

Fringe theatre

There are many fringe theatre companies throughout the UK, whose aims are to put on productions that might not be viable in the commercial theatre, and to bring theatre to a wider than usual audience. They may perform in pubs, clubs, community centres, church halls, old people's homes, etc. Some try to raise awareness of issues, such as the environment or the role of women in society. Many have only a few members and operate on a low budget. Often, they are run as co-operatives with payment on a profit (or loss) sharing basis, rather than Equity rates. Occasionally, groups of out-of-work actors form themselves into a company, financing their own performances.

Community theatre

Community theatre companies aim to involve local people in productions reflecting local issues and concerns. Like fringe theatre, many such groups are unable to pay their members a living wage. However, working in a fringe or community theatre company provides valuable experience, and may give actors the chance of being 'spotted' by an agent or casting director.

Children's theatre

These companies perform work for children. A few large companies have their own theatre, but many smaller ones tour venues such as schools, parks and playgrounds. Many of the programmes demand a variety of skills, such as juggling, mime and puppetry, and often the children themselves are encouraged to participate.

Theatre-in-education

Like children's theatre companies, these companies bring theatre to children and young people. Working primarily in schools, they put on productions related to the curriculum, such as current set books and topics in history or science, as well as dramatizations of social issues. Theatre-in-education and children's theatre are most likely to appeal to actors who have an interest in the educational potential of drama.

Clubs and variety

Some actors perform speciality acts (for example, comedy, mime, conjuring), obtaining bookings in clubs, cabaret and variety shows, and perhaps going on to television, radio or films.

PAY AND CONDITIONS

The British Actors' Equity Association, or Equity, negotiates minimum wages and conditions for its members. Actors in the theatre may be employed on a once-nightly or, twice-daily/nightly rate. An actor on a once-nightly contract can be asked to perform a show on no more than six days a week (a total of eight performances). The basic minimum for an actor on a once-nightly contract at a West End theatre venue is £241.51 a week. In a provincial repertory theatre, the once-nightly minimum is £204.00 a week. If actors have to work away from home, they receive an additional allowance for lodgings.

The above are the minimum rates that would be paid to a newcomer to the profession. Agents can normally negotiate higher salaries for their clients. However, this must be set against the fact that many actors experience long periods of unemployment. Actors have to pay their Equity subscription whether or not they are working (although they pay less when they are not earning) and they often have to pay travelling expenses to auditions. Only a small minority of actors earn anything approaching a comfortable living from their profession.

While in employment, most actors work very long hours. Much of the work, particularly in live theatre, is performed in the evenings and at weekends, when most other people are at leisure. In addition, a considerable amount of time is spent rehearsing parts and learning lines. Actors working in television and film often start early in the morning, and may spend long periods waiting for their scenes to be shot.

PROSPECTS

An actor's prospects depend upon talent, good fortune and being in the right place at the right time. Many actors wait for as much as six months to a year after leaving college, before finding their first job. A tiny minority are 'spotted' by an agent or casting director while at college. Considerable numbers of actors leave the profession because of the insecurity and lack of a steady income. Some actors move into directing, while others become teachers. A number have found success as playwrights or novelists.

RELATED OCCUPATIONS

Dancer, musician, teacher, drama therapist, stage manager, director, theatre technician.

FURTHER INFORMATION

The Arts Council of Great Britain*, 14 Great Peter Street, London SW1P 3NQ, 0171 333 0100

British Actors' Equity Association, Guild House, Upper St Martin's Lane, London WC2 9EG, 0171 379 6000

Community Dance and Mime Foundation*, 13-15 Belvoir Street, Leicester LE1 6SL, 0116 275 5058

Conference of Drama Schools*, c/o Central School of Speech and Drama, Embassy Theatre, Eton Avenue, London NW3 3HY, 0171 722 8183 (enclose sae)

National Association of Youth Theatres, Unit 1304, The Custard Factory, Digbeth, Birmingham B9 4AA, 0121 608 2111

National Council for Drama Training, 5 Tavistock Place, London WC1H 9SN, 0171 387 3650

Production and Casting Report, PO Box 100, Broadstairs, Kent 01843 860885

The Spotlight, 1st Floor, Charles House, 7 Leicester Place, London WC2 7BP

FURTHER READING

Leaflets/booklets are available from the addresses marked*.

Job Outlines – The Performing Arts – COIC
Working in The Performing Arts – COIC
Acting Skills – A and C Black Ltd
Careers in the Theatre – Kogan Page

In the careers library classified under GAB.

2. MUSICIAN (GAD)

BACKGROUND INFORMATION

Many people are drawn to the idea of making music their profession, but few ever achieve that ambition. For those who do, the work is rarely glamorous or highly paid. When starting out, musicians have to take any work they can get while they build a reputation. They may also have to take work outside music, but must all the time keep on practising in case a music job arises.

Musicians produce music using an instrument, or, in the case of singers, their own voice. Musical instruments can be broadly divided into five main categories: keyboard, such as the organ or piano; woodwind, such as the flute or clarinet; brass, such as the trumpet or saxophone; strings, such as the guitar or violin; and percussion, such as the xylophone or drums. Some musicians play a number of instruments, but most concentrate their efforts on mastering just one. Performing music to a professional standard requires considerable talent allied with constant practice.

THE WORK

Music as a performing art can be divided into two main areas: classical and popular.

Classical music

Most classical musicians play in orchestras, ensembles or chamber groups, although they may also work as soloists. Singers may be part of a professional choir, and/or work as soloists or opera singers.

Classical music is probably more demanding, in terms of what is required of the performer, than other areas of music. Live performances occupy only a very small proportion of the musician's time, and are the culmination of many hours spent practising and rehearsing. Touring is also time-consuming and tiring. The highly developed skills of a violinist or classical pianist soon deteriorate without practice. Singers must take care of their voices, avoiding strain or overwork.

Classical musicians often make a living by working in several groups or orchestras. Some musicians feel that they can make more of an individual contribution in smaller groups. Some, especially soloists, may have agents, who help them get work.

Popular music

This includes rock and pop, jazz, blues, country and western, folk, light and brass band music. Some pop musicians combine playing an instrument, such as the guitar or piano, with singing. Pop or rock musicians either work as part of a group or band, or as solo artists. They usually work closely with a manager. Like classical musicians, their time is spent practising, rehearsing and performing.

In all areas of music, musicians sometimes make recordings, although it is far more common in the field of pop music. Some pop musicians rarely perform live to an audience, becoming well-known through recordings and videos. A tour often follows the release of an album, to ensure wide publicity. Some musicians, mainly in the popular field, write and perform their own music, and may also arrange musical scores for others to perform.

WORK ENVIRONMENT

Performance venues vary widely, from concert halls, theatres and arts centres to pubs, clubs, restaurants, schools, parks, sports grounds and street corners. They may be spacious and comfortable, or crowded and shabby. Pubs and clubs may be smoky and dark and, when full of people, hot and humid. Most recording studios have little natural light, and may be cramped. Classical musicians usually perform in more comfortable conditions, although premises such as church halls can be draughty and uncomfortable.

Rehearsal rooms can also be draughty and uncomfortable, with poor acoustics. Some rehearsal time is usually spent waiting, while other musicians work on their parts.

Musicians usually work indoors, although they may occasionally perform an outdoor concert. They often work as part of a team in a group or orchestra, although they also work at home while practising.

Classical concerts usually last for about two hours, during which time the musicians must remain fully alert.

Most musicians travel long distances and spend lengthy periods away from home, either for performances or while touring, in the UK or abroad. Although they usually work with a group of people, it can be a very lonely life.

SKILLS AND INTERESTS

Musicians must be talented and completely dedicated to a career as a performer. A high degree of self-discipline and motivation is essential to practise as much as required. Patience is also important while acquiring the necessary skills. For pop musicians, an attractive or striking appearance can be an asset.

Musicians must be prepared to work as part of a team, and be willing to accept constructive criticism and disappointment. They must be able to cope with insecurity and a variable income. Good general health is important, as is self-confidence.

ENTRY REQUIREMENTS

It is possible to become a musician without formal qualifications, although this is unlikely, particularly in classical music. The usual requirements for full-time music courses are as follows:

Performers' diploma courses

Entry requirements for these courses vary, and some do not specify traditional academic qualifications. Others look for five GCSEs/S grades (A-C/1-3), and possibly A level/H grade music. A high standard of musicianship is looked for, usually to grade 8 on the principal instrument, and grade 5 or 6 on the second. (Graded examinations are provided by organizations such as the Associated Board, Guildhall School of Music and Drama, etc.) Entry is by audition, which may include playing a number of pieces on first and second instruments, sight reading, written and aural tests, and an interview. Competition for places is intense, and experience gained playing in a school or local orchestra is an advantage.

Graduate diploma courses

These courses are equivalent to degrees. Entry requirements vary between schools of music, but most ask for five GCSEs/S grades (A-C/1-3) and two A levels or 3 H grades, usually including music. Most look for grade 8 on the principal instrument and grade 6 on the second, tested at audition. Most courses also require a reasonable standard of keyboard skills (at least grade 3-5).

Degree courses

Five GCSEs/S grades (A-C/1-3) are needed, together with two A levels or three H grades, usually including music. Auditions and interviews normally form part of the selection procedure.

Military bands

Entry requirements vary between the different services. Selection is by audition for musical ability, and in addition applicants are required to pass a medical examination and some entrance tests. For more information, contact the services that are of interest under FURTHER INFORMATION.

Grants

All students on degree and graduate diploma courses are normally eligible for mandatory awards. Performers' diploma courses at schools of music rate only discretionary awards. The availability of discretionary awards varies across the country, and students should contact their local education authority for more information.

TRAINING

In the field of classical music, most people start learning an instrument during childhood, by taking lessons either at school or privately. There are also a few specialist music schools that take musically gifted children, usually from around the age of eleven; they combine musical training with a traditional academic education. Choir schools take boys from the age of eight or nine years to train as choristers.

Performers' diploma courses

These courses are primarily aimed at training performers, and have limited academic content. They are run through specialist schools of music or conservatoires. Courses emphasize the development of performing skills, and students are expected to spend many hours practising. These courses usually lead to licentiate or associate qualifications, eg LRAM (Licentiate of the Royal Academy of Music).

Graduate diploma courses

These courses are also run through specialist schools of music or conservatoires, and are regarded as equivalent to degrees. They combine training for performance with academic study. Most such courses lead to qualifications with the word Graduate in their titles, eg GRSM (Graduate of the Royal Schools of Music).

Performers' courses last for three or four years. Although most time is devoted to a first study instrument, in most courses a second instrument must also be learned. Courses offer many opportunities to practise and perform in student groups and orchestras, and take classes with visiting professionals. There are many differences between courses, and applicants should check prospectuses carefully and visit institutions where possible.

Degree courses

Degree courses in music are also available at various colleges and universities. Many of these are academic, rather than strongly practical, and are not particularly aimed at training performers. Subjects studied may include history of music, musicology, methods of composition, musical analysis, etc. All degree courses in music do, however, offer some opportunities for performance. It is possible to complete a degree in music, then go on to a specialist music school to train for performance.

There are now a number of courses available offering training in popular music. Salford College of Technology offers a degree in popular music and recording, and a college higher certificate (access course) and degree in band musicianship. Perth College of Further Education offers SCOTVEC higher national certificate/ diploma courses in rock musicianship.

Training for Armed Forces' musicians varies according to the service they join. For example, the Army takes musicians aged 16 years and 3 months upwards. They start with ten weeks' basic military training, then go on to the Royal Military School of Music (RMSM) at Kneller Hall, Twickenham, for a foundation course of up to 44 weeks' instrumental training. They are then sent to join their bands. Military musicians are trained to a very high standard. They also receive military training, and may work as medical orderlies, signallers or LGV drivers in the event of a war or national emergency.

The *Music Education Directory* provides a list of courses in the contemporary music industry and is available from The British Phonographic Industry.

LATE ENTRY

It is very difficult for adults to train as musicians. Most adults who become professional musicians have already had considerable experience as amateurs. Most late opportunities are for singers, whose voices mature at a later age, and for those in the light music field, especially jazz, folk, country and western, etc. The usual upper age limits for Armed Forces' bands are as follows: RAF – 39 years; Royal Marines – 28 years; and Army – 30 years.

OPPORTUNITIES

Music is probably the most overcrowded of all the performing arts, and competition for jobs is therefore intense. The number of permanent full-time jobs is very small, and mainly in the classical field. Most musicians take whatever work they can find, trying to make a living from several sources, while building up a reputation. They are often self-employed. Opportunities exist in the following areas:

Orchestral players

Around 1,500 full-time jobs exist in British orchestras, with only a small number of new openings coming up each year. Many of these are in London with orchestras such as the London Symphony Orchestra (LSO). The remainder are in other major cities, such as Glasgow and Birmingham. The BBC has its own orchestras based in London, Manchester, Wales and Scotland. Vacancies are advertised in the press, with selection based on interview and audition.

Some orchestras offer occasional freelance work, which can sometimes lead into more regular jobs. A high standard of sight-reading is required. Opportunities also exist within smaller ensembles; these also use musicians on a freelance basis. Occasionally, groups of enterprising students from music colleges set up their own self-financing ensemble, which provides valuable experience, and sometimes leads on to paid bookings.

Soloists

There are even fewer opportunities for soloists than orchestral players, so it is even harder for them to make a living. Solo performers are generally engaged for a particular event or performance, and must have acquired a considerable reputation to be assured of regular work. Many soloists engage an agent who finds work and negotiates terms for them, in exchange for a percentage of their earnings.

Singers

A few opportunities exist for trained singers in opera, oratorio, sacred music, solo recitals and a variety of concert work, including light music and cabaret. Young singers often begin in a chorus, and can gain valuable experience with small touring companies. Many singers nowadays undergo training for musical theatre. Professional choirs, such as the BBC Singers, also recruit singers occasionally. Competition is fierce.

Pianists

Only the most outstanding performer can hope to make a career in solo recitals and concerts, and orchestras rarely use a full-time pianist. Some pianists find work in chamber groups or jazz ensembles, while others accompany dancers during rehearsals. A number are engaged by opera companies as repetiteurs, coaching singers and accompanying them on the piano during rehearsals.

Conductors

This is another extremely competitive field. In the past, conductors were usually also experienced performers, but nowadays some opportunities exist for younger people to enter this occupation directly. Regular competitions are held for young conductors (details in *Music Journal*), and some orchestras offer trainee conductorships with the chance to understudy experienced conductors.

Composers

Only a very few musicians make a full-time living from composing, and most are obliged to supplement their income by other work such as teaching. A fortunate few earn a living writing music for film, television, theatre, dance or TV commercials, but getting established is not easy, and luck, as well as talent, is needed. The Arts Council and regional arts associations provide some funds to commission new works.

Church music

Full-time paid opportunities are extremely limited, although the cathedrals employ organists and musical directors. Occasional work may be available with choral societies or by giving recitals.

Military bands

The Armed Forces (the Army, the RAF and the Royal Marines) offer musicians excellent training through their own schools of music. Military bandsmen and women are well paid, and travel overseas regularly. They perform all types of music, from pop to classical. String and woodwind players are in particular demand.

Session work

Experienced musicians may be able to supplement their income by working sessions in a studio. They record music for films, television programmes, commercials and jingles, or backing tracks for singles and albums. Sessions are often in the morning, to allow performers time to do other work. Much of the work is in London.

Pop music

Many successful bands start as a group of friends playing together, perhaps at school or college, and first building a reputation locally. Most bands have a manager to deal with their business affairs and negotiate bookings and recording deals. Only a tiny number ever achieve fame and fortune, and the great majority, after brief success, quickly slip back into obscurity. Many bands are part-time ventures, with the members also doing other jobs, often unrelated to music.

Vacancies for orchestral players and singers are advertised in *Classical Music, Church Music Quarterly, Melody Maker, The Stage and Television Today, The Daily Telegraph* and *Music Journal*.

PAY AND CONDITIONS

Musicians receive payment for recorded work, either through royalties (whereby the artist receives a percentage payment for each record sold), or in a single payment.

Musicians' pay, particularly at the start of their careers, may be very low.

For orchestral players in a 'continuing contract' orchestra such as the CBSO, Halle and RLPO, there are standard salary scales. Other symphony and chamber orchestras pay musicians on an ad hoc per-concert basis. The payments vary from £62.50 to £72.50. Musicians' Union casual engagement (gig) rates are a minimum of £6.25 per half hour, with a minimum payment of £28 for engagements up to two hours.

Rates for TV, radio and film performances are governed by often complex agreements. They depend on the length of time worked, and also on factors such as whether the performance is live. For example, rates for three hours of incidental music range from £98.95 to £140.00. Additional fees may be payable if the music is repeated over several episodes, or the programme repeated, or sold overseas.

Musicians in the Armed Forces generally enjoy greater job security than their civilian colleagues, and have a clear-cut career path that they can follow. An Army musician starts on a salary of around £10,000.

Most musicians work long, irregular hours. Performances are generally held during the evening and at weekends. While recording in a studio, musicians work very long hours; with pop musicians, in particular, this may be until midnight or later. Many musicians, particularly at the start of their careers, combine music with other jobs.

PROSPECTS

A musician's prospects depend on talent, good fortune and offering the public what they want. Being seen by the right people, and being in the right place at the right time, are also important. Competitions and prizes, such as those offered by the schools of music and the BBC, can greatly assist the winners' careers.

After further training, musicians can move into related fields, such as music therapy, teaching, or arts administration. Many people, having taken a degree in music, decide not to pursue a performing career.

Musicians in the Armed Forces may seek promotion within the service, or may elect to leave and further their career as civilians. According to the service, those wishing to leave early may be required to purchase their discharge at a price related to the length of time they have served. Musicians who have been on advanced training courses may be required to go on serving for a fixed period, after completing the course, to justify the expenditure that has been made on their musical education.

RELATED OCCUPATIONS

Music teacher, music therapist, dancer, actor, musical instrument tuner/technician, TV/radio producer, roadie.

FURTHER INFORMATION AND READING

Please see article 3. MUSIC TEACHER.

3. MUSIC TEACHER (GAD/FAB)

BACKGROUND INFORMATION

Music is increasingly recognized as having an important place in a well-rounded education. In schools, the availability of new technology, such as synthesizers, has contributed to a shift in music-teaching away from traditional history and theory of music to practical music-making and composition. School music teachers aim to foster children's creativity, as well as developing skills in areas such as communication and working as part of a team. They aim to develop in pupils greater discrimination in their appraisal of music, and introduce them to music of different times and cultures. Music is a foundation subject in the National Curriculum, which means it is taught to all children between the ages of 5 and 14 years.

Instrumental teachers are more concerned with developing performing skills on individual instruments to a high level. Many gain great satisfaction from passing on their skills and knowledge to a new generation of musicians.

THE WORK

Music teachers work in a variety of settings. They include the following:

School teaching

In nursery, infant and junior classes, music is often taught by the classroom teacher, but co-ordinated and led by a teacher responsible for music in the curriculum. Teachers (and particularly music co-ordinators) may also be involved in arranging school concerts, assemblies, recorder clubs, etc.

Secondary schools usually have one or more full-time specialist music teachers who, as well as teaching in the classroom, organize and encourage the musical life of the school. Their work may include conducting choirs and orchestras, supervising school concerts and productions, and organizing schedules for visiting instrumental teachers. Classroom duties include teaching National Curriculum to age 14, GCSEs/S grades to age 16, and, in some schools, A level/H grade examinations.

Some teachers work on a part-time basis in schools, youth and specialist music centres, adult education institutes and further education colleges. Instrumental teachers may work in a number of schools, teaching individuals or groups of pupils, and occasionally organizing orchestras.

Private teaching

Private teachers work with people of all ages and abilities. They give lessons individually, or in small groups, and generally charge by the hour for their services. Some have national reputations and take on only the most talented students; others take anyone who is interested. They may combine this work with part-time teaching in a school, performing or composing.

Other teaching

Teachers in music schools and colleges tend to be highly experienced and specialized, either in instrumental work or in the theoretical and historical aspects of music. Many are also accomplished performers and composers. Music is also taught at various levels in colleges and higher education institutions.

WORK ENVIRONMENT

Teachers work indoors in a variety of settings, including schools, colleges, higher education institutions, adult education institutes, youth clubs, arts centres, and many other places. The conditions are often, though not always, warm and comfortable. Since music teachers rarely work in purpose-designed accommodation, the acoustics are often poor. Many part-time and private teachers spend a lot of time travelling between pupils and schools.

SKILLS AND INTERESTS

A wish to share a love of music with other people is essential, combined with the desire to develop pupils' musical potential to the full. Patience is important to any teacher, and a broad appreciation of music in all its forms – popular and classical, European and other traditions – is essential. Because of their wide range of responsibilities, music teachers need to be well organized and good at managing their time. Good verbal communication skills are needed to work effectively with individual students and groups. Some music teachers are also performers, which gives a useful added dimension to their work.

Private teachers need to be self-motivated and resourceful, since they usually work alone. As most are self-employed, they need good business skills in areas such as budgeting, pricing and marketing their services.

ENTRY REQUIREMENTS

Music teachers working within state schools must have Qualified Teacher Status (QTS). Teachers in Scotland must be registered with the General Teaching Council for Scotland.

Private teachers working independently are not legally required to possess qualifications in teaching or music, although they are advised to have appropriate qualifications. The standard qualifications are the teaching diplomas awarded by the music colleges, though performers' diplomas, graduate diplomas and music degrees may be acceptable. (Please see article 2. MUSICIAN.) The Incorporated Society of Musicians accepts only professionally qualified and experienced teachers for its Register of Professional Private Music Teachers.

Intending school teachers normally require a minimum of five GCSEs/S grades (A-C/1-3) with two A levels or three H grades for entry to a first degree course (for exact details see School Teacher CLCI:FAB). Music teachers in England and Wales are normally expected to have an A level or equivalent in music. In Scotland, H grade English, or equivalent, is required, and H grade music normally expected.

Music teachers in higher education are usually required to hold a second degree, such as an MA, PhD in music. Requirements for applicants to further education teaching are variable, but similar to secondary teaching. A high standard of instrumental or vocal performance is normally required.

TRAINING

Full-time music teachers in state schools normally have followed a course of initial teacher training (ITT) leading to Qualified Teacher Status (QTS), or, in Scotland, Registration. The two most common ways of qualifying are as follows:

1. Completion of a three or four-year graduate diploma or degree in Music at a conservatoire or university (please see article 2. MUSICIAN for more information). This must be followed by a Postgraduate Certificate of Education (PGCE), which is usually taken on a one-year full-time basis, but is also offered by the Open University. PGCE courses are offered at a large number of universities and colleges in England and Wales and three institutions in Scotland. Institutions offering the PGCE may very occasionally (though not in Scotland) accept candidates holding non-graduate-level qualifications, provided they have at least two A levels and GCSEs (grade A-C) in maths and English. Such candidates are more likely to find employment as qualified instrumental teachers than as classroom teachers.

2. Completion of a four-year teaching degree course, either Bachelor of Education (BEd) or Bachelor of Arts (BA), with Qualified Teacher Status. Study of music at an advanced level is combined with the theory and practice of teaching. Courses such as these are generally seen as more suitable for people intending to make a career in primary school teaching. There are few institutions in the UK offering secondary school teacher training with music. At primary level, music is normally offered alongside other subjects.

The situation in Scotland differs from that above in a number of ways. Rather than QTS, intending teachers must gain a recognized Teaching Qualification (TQ). They must then complete two years' satisfactory service as probationary teachers before being granted full registration with the General Teaching Council for Scotland. Both one-year PGCE and four-year BEd courses are available in Scotland, but they are designated as qualifying the student to teach specifically in primary or secondary education. It is generally harder for teachers in Scotland to switch between primary and secondary school teaching.

Another means of entry to the teaching profession is the licensed teacher programme (not available in Scotland). This is open to people aged 24 or over, with two years' successful full-time higher education experience and GCSEs (grade A-C) in maths and English. Schools have the discretion to appoint people with suitable qualifications and experience on a licence normally lasting two years, during which they follow an individually tailored programme of training leading to Qualified Teacher Status. Not all employers operate the licensed teacher route, and many of those who do may only have a limited number of places available.

Teacher training courses are listed in the *British Music Education Yearbook.*

Music teachers in independent schools may not require QTS.

Instrumental and private teaching. The usual qualification for an instrumental teacher is a teaching diploma awarded by a conservatoire. These courses are similar to the performers' diploma courses described in article 2. MUSICIAN, but include modules in teaching, rather than performance. Most such teachers work as part-time instrumental teachers in schools, or as private teachers, and will have had a performance-biased main training.

LATE ENTRY

Some music schools and conservatoires are reluctant to take instrumentalists over the age of 20 years, while singers are often preferred between the ages of 20 and 24, as the voice matures later. Musical talent, apart from singing, often emerges early. Most institutions offering BEd or BA with QTS courses are willing to consider applications from adults without the normal entry requirements, since maturity is a definite asset in teaching. Some colleges offer a specially shortened two-year BEd course in music for people with substantial experience and advanced qualifications in music, or a related subject.

Colleges look for evidence of considerable musical ability, and may request graded examination passes. They also like to see evidence of recent study, which may be gained via an access course. These provide a bridge to higher education for people without the normal academic entry qualifications.

OPPORTUNITIES

Opportunities for school music teachers exist within both the state and independent sectors. A few posts are available for working with people with special needs, both in schools and other institutions. There is currently an acute shortage of music teachers in state schools. Vacancies are advertised in the *Times Educational Supplement* and other national newspapers, and the monthly magazines *Music Teacher* and *Music Journal.*

There are a small number of opportunities for music teachers in universities, colleges and music schools. As well as teaching, some research may be required. Competition for such vacancies is intense.

Anyone may set themselves up as a private music teacher, although those registered with the Incorporated Society of Musicians are required to meet certain professional standards.

PAY AND CONDITIONS

Rates of pay for full-time music teachers in schools and part-time instrumental teachers are generally governed by national regulations and recommendations, based on qualifications and types of employment. Visiting instrumental and singing teachers working in maintained and independent schools earn around £13 to £20 an hour, according to experience. The ISM recommends its registered private teachers to charge a minimum of £13.02 to £20.07 an hour for individual tuition. A shared lesson, with four pupils, earns a minimum fee of one-and-a-half times the individual rate. Private teachers set their own rates, and some charge considerably more than those quoted.

Teachers in maintained schools in England and Wales are paid on a unified 18-point pay spine ranging from £11,883. In Scotland, a new teacher earns a minimum starting salary of £12,603. Salaries within the private sector vary between schools.

Music teachers in schools work normal school hours, although they regularly give up time during lunch-breaks and after school to organize additional musical activities. In addition, they have to spend some time at evenings and weekends marking work, preparing lessons and writing arrangements. Private teachers often work during the evenings and weekends (outside normal school/working hours).

PROSPECTS

School music departments are generally small, so there are prospects of promotion to head of department within two to five years – twice as quickly as in other subjects. More senior jobs may involve a greater proportion of administration, with less time devoted solely to teaching. While continuing their work in school, some teachers develop their careers by conducting a local choir or orchestra. Experienced music teachers may become examiners for one of the main boards, or adjudicators in musical competitions. A few music teachers go on to become music advisers for local authorities. Others go on to become school headteachers and deputy heads – these are predominantly management posts, and may involve little actual teaching.

RELATED OCCUPATIONS

Teacher, musician, music therapist, actor, dancer, musical instrument technician, arts administrator.

FURTHER INFORMATION

Arts Council of Great Britain*, 14 Great Peter Street, London SW1P 3NQ, 0171 333 0100

British Actors' Equity Association*, Guild House, Upper St Martin's Lane, London WC2 9EG, 0171 379 6000

British Phonographic Industry Ltd (BPI)*, 25 Savile Row, London WIX 1AA

British Broadcasting Corporation*, PO Box 7000, London W5 2WY, 0181 849 0849

Department for Education and Employment, Sanctuary Buildings, Great Smith Street, Westminster, London SW1P 3BT, 0171 925 5000

Directorate of Naval Recruiting*, Royal Marines School of Music, HMS Nelson, Portsmouth, Hampshire PO1 3LS, 01705 727753

Incorporated Society of Musicians*, 10 Stratford Place, London W1N 9AE, 0171 629 4413

Musicians' Union*, 60-62 Clapham Road, London SW9 0JJ, 0171 582 5566 (please send sae)

National Music and Disability Information Service*, Foxhole, Dartington, Totnes, Devon TQ9 6EB, 01803 866701 (please include sae)

RAF School of Music*, Royal Air Force, Uxbridge, Middlesex UB10 0RZ, 01895 237144 ext 6345/6478

Rhinegold Publishing Ltd, 241 Shaftesbury Avenue, London WC2H 8EH, 0171 333 1700

Royal Military School of Music*, Careers Office, Kneller Hall, Kneller Road, Twickenham, Middlesex TW2 7DU, 0181 898 5533 ext. 38

Royal School of Church Music*, Addington Place, Gravel Hill, Croydon, Surrey CR9 5AD, 0181 654 7676

Career Development Edinburgh and Lothians, (formerly Scottish Department of Education), 17 Logie Mill, Edinburgh EH7 4HG, 0131 556 7384

The Teacher Training Agency, Information Section*, Portland House, Stag Place, London SW1E 5TT, 0171 925 5880/5882

FURTHER READING

Leaflets/booklets are available from the addresses marked*.

Job Outlines – Performing Arts – COIC
Working in Music – COIC
Working in Performing Arts – COIC
British Music Yearbook – Rhinegold
Music Teachers' Yearbook – Rhinegold
Degree Course Guide – Music – CRAC

Periodicals: Music Journal; Music Teacher.

In the careers library classified under GAD.

4. DANCER (GAF)

BACKGROUND INFORMATION

The life of a dancer can seem glamorous and exciting. While this may be true for a minority, the reality of gruelling daily exercise, combined with evening performances, is somewhat different. Although trained dancers may find it easier to get work than actors or musicians, the field is still highly competitive, and many dancers face periods of unemployment during their careers. At all times, however, dancers must keep their bodies in peak condition, exercising regularly and following a healthy eating plan. Few dancers make a fortune, and most face financial uncertainty throughout their lives. A dancer's working life is short: most retire from performing at around 35, or earlier if they suffer injury. Dancers need talent, stamina and a complete dedication to their art.

THE WORK

Dance is a performing art; dancers use their bodies to communicate creatively with an audience. The movements are usually directed by a choreographer, although they are occasionally devised by the dancers themselves. Dancers use their movements to portray a role without using words. In classical dance, the story is often obvious; in more modern work the story (if one exists) may not be immediately recognizable to an audience. Dancers spend only a small amount of their time actually performing; much more time is spent practising, exercising, taking classes and rehearsing. Even if they are unemployed, dancers must keep up with their exercise regime.

Classical ballet is one of the most demanding and precise forms of dance, and training generally begins at an early age, before the body is fully developed. Contemporary, or modern, dance is less formal and more experimental, with a wide and varying repertoire; it is often performed barefoot. Modern stage dance covers a wide range of dance styles, including tap. It originally developed in the variety theatre and stage musicals, and can also be seen today in television and films. Disco dancing is a more recent development, associated with modern pop music. A growing number of opportunities exist in night-clubs, films, promotional videos, etc, though mostly on part-time or short-term contracts. Social dance is performed mainly for the pleasure of those taking part, rather than for an audience. It includes the many forms of ballroom dancing, as well as folk and country dance.

Opportunities in social dance are mainly confined to teaching. Finally, non-western dance is an area of growing importance in the UK. It includes South Asian and African dance. South Asian dance, in particular, is very demanding, involving a wide range of formalized movements, which may take many years to learn and master.

The majority of dancers work in a group or company, such as a *corps de ballet,* chorus line or dance troupe. Members of the company support and depend on each other, and may enjoy a greater degree of stability in their working lives than their colleagues in the other performing arts. There are some opportunities to become a solo dancer, especially in non-western forms of dance.

Music is important in all forms of dance, and most dance is performed to it. In some areas, such as musical theatre, performers sing and act, as well as dance.

WORK ENVIRONMENT

Dancers work in a variety of settings, including theatres, film and TV studios, night-clubs, restaurants and hotels, summer shows at holiday resorts, circuses and Christmas pantomimes. The increase in community arts has extended dance beyond traditional venues, to places that offer access to a wider audience, including church and community halls, arts centres, art galleries, parks and schools.

Venues are usually warm, but dancers spend much of their time in rehearsal rooms, which may be cold and draughty. Dancers must make sure that cold conditions do not cause muscle strain, so they wear layers of clothing which may be discarded as they warm up.

Dancing places tremendous demands on the body, and these are probably greatest in ballet. Many dancers have painful feet from pointe work, and they may also suffer from orthopaedic problems.

Dancers work away from home when on tour, and the working hours may be longer than usual. While working, dancers' social lives can suffer, as performances are normally held in the evenings.

SKILLS AND INTERESTS

Talent is essential to succeed in a profession where competition is intense. In addition, dancers must have a well-proportioned body, strong legs and back, good general health and a high standard of physical fitness. They need stamina and resilience to cope with the mental and physical stresses of dancing, and a high degree of commitment and motivation.

Dancers must be tough, persistent and hard working, quick to learn, creative, intelligent and imaginative. They also need a retentive memory to learn and memorize complex sequences of movements, together with good powers of concentration. A good sense of rhythm and timing is important. Dancers with musical or acting skills may have improved job prospects. Those wishing to teach dance need patience and good verbal communication skills.

ENTRY REQUIREMENTS

There are no minimum academic entry requirements for most performers' courses in dance, though some require specific passes in relevant dance examinations. Entry to most courses is via audition, which normally involves participation in one or more classes, and sometimes the presentation of a solo piece. Some colleges give a music aural test, and candidates are given a medical examination.

Ballet dancers must be well-proportioned, with a good line, attractive appearance and a very high standard of fitness. Women should be from 1.52m to 1.65m (5 feet to 5 feet 5 inches), and men from 1.6m to 1.78m (5 feet 3 inches to 5 feet 10 inches). A background in ballet is useful for all dancers, although it is not essential for contemporary dance. Some contemporary schools look for potential and suitability for dancing, if the candidate has not had much chance to take lessons.

Teaching courses for the private sector do not generally require specific academic entry qualifications (though these are welcomed and encouraged, and will be introduced over the next couple of years). Candidates are expected to have achieved a high standard of performance, with passes in graded examinations in the case of theatre dance, or medals up to the third gold bar in the case of social dance.

Degree courses often ask for previous practical experience in dance, along with minimum educational requirements of five GCSEs/S grades (A-C/1-3) with two A levels or three H grades, or equivalent. The BTEC/SCOTVEC National Diploma in Performing Arts may be an acceptable alternative to A levels or H grades, although prospective students should check this with individual institutions. Applicants for degrees leading to Qualified Teacher Status (BEd or BA with QTS) must also have maths and English at GCSE/S grade (A-C/1-3). There is intense competition for most courses.

Most of the leading examining bodies in dance-teaching operate registration schemes. In order to be registered, dance teachers must be qualified, with passes in specific examinations covering practical, theoretical and historical aspects of dance. Only registered teachers are allowed to enter candidates for the major examination societies – these include the Royal Academy of Dancing, the Imperial Society of Teachers of Dancing, and the British Ballet Organization.

The Council for Dance Education and Training (CDET) is setting up a national register of dance teachers. As this becomes established, it will become increasingly difficult for unqualified dance teachers to find work.

TRAINING

Formal full-time training in dance is essential for anyone wishing to work as a performer, and is preferable for a teacher. Many dancers start their training by attending part-time classes as children, often taking a series of graded examinations. The ideal age to begin ballet training is around eight to ten years, since at this age the bones and joints are still flexible. Ballet dancers must normally have started to train by the age of twelve at the latest, for girls, and 14 for boys.

Several schools accept pupils from around the age of eleven, offering them a dance training alongside traditional academic subjects. It is also possible to learn dance at a stage or theatre school, often as part of a general theatre training that includes acting and music. Standards vary between schools, and it is advisable to check a school's standing with the Council for Dance Education and Training.

Most professional training for dancers takes place after leaving school. Performers' courses at independent vocational schools typically last three years, though a few are shorter. The Council for Dance Education and Training recognizes various courses as being of a suitably high standard for performers, and will supply a list on request. Most courses lead to a diploma or certificate awarded by the school, but three vocational schools offer CDET-accredited degree courses in dance: the Laban Centre for Movement and Dance (BA Honours Degree in Dance Theatre); the Northern School of Contemporary Dance (RAD BA Honours in the Art and Teaching of Ballet); and the London Contemporary Dance School (BA Ordinary and Honours Degrees in Contemporary Dance).

Course content varies between schools, but often includes ballet, modern theatre dance, jazz and contemporary dance, other dance forms from countries such as Greece, Spain, Africa and India, tap dance and choreography. Practical classes are supplemented by the theoretical study of anatomy, dance history and dance notation, as well as make-up and stagecraft. Music, drama and singing feature in many courses.

Courses specializing in contemporary dance often include choreography. In many schools, students stage a production at the end of the course, giving them experience in all aspects of dance administration and stage management, as well as the actual performing.

Degree courses, including dance, are available at over 30 colleges, institutions of higher education and universities across the UK (again, a list is available from CDET). Most courses lead to a BA honours degree, but they vary considerably in emphasis. This is reflected in the course names, which include dance, performing arts, human movement studies, creative arts, and others. Courses vary in the balance between practical work and academic study, though all include some practical dance. They are not, however, primarily aimed at training performers, and do not provide the intensive vocational training offered by the independent schools.

Those intending to teach dance in schools or colleges can study for a BEd degree or PGCE, specializing in dance at a number of colleges, institutions of higher education and universities.

Grants

Students on degree courses at universities receive mandatory grants, but those on non-degree and degree performers' courses are eligible only for discretionary awards. The two exceptions to this are students on the degree course at the Northern School of Contemporary Dance, and those students under 19 years of age at the Rambert School. Local education authorities are more likely to give grants to students on CDET-accredited courses, but many are cutting back and may offer only a limited number. In some cases LEAs may agree to pay tuition fees only, leaving the student to fund day-to-day expenses from other sources. It is advisable to contact your LEA early on to find out their position on discretionary awards for dance courses.

LATE ENTRY

Opportunities for mature students to train as professional dancers are almost non-existent, since dance training normally starts in the teens (and earlier for ballet). Adults up to the age of 30 may occasionally be accepted for contemporary dance training. It is possible for adults with some dance experience to train in dance therapy or community dance.

OPPORTUNITIES

Opportunities vary with the type of dancing and are often better for men than for women, because there are more parts for men and less competition. As with all the performing arts, dance is an extremely competitive field, and many dancers will face periods of unemployment during their careers. Many dancers are lowly paid, and may have to supplement their dancing with other, temporary, jobs or teaching. They may also have to move around the country, and even abroad, to find work. As with actors, most professional dancers belong to Equity, though this is not a prerequisite for obtaining work. Equity membership is discussed in more detail in article 1. ACTOR.

Opportunities for dancers exist in the following areas.

Dance teaching offers more employment opportunities than performing. Dance teachers working in state primary and secondary schools are qualified teachers who specialize in dance; most teach other subjects as well. Dance is now included as part of physical education within the National Curriculum, which may lead to some growth in demand for dance teachers in schools. Outside the state sector there are numerous dance schools and studios in the UK offering recreational classes as well as more formal training. Some teachers with sufficient financial resources set up their own schools, while others work in several locations, including adult education institutes and youth centres.

Ballet is a highly competitive area, with jobs in the Birmingham Royal Ballet and the Royal Ballet normally going to former students of the Royal Ballet Upper School. Opportunities also exist with the English National Ballet and Northern Ballet Theatre. There are a handful of other, smaller, ballet companies in the UK, and British-trained dancers may find work abroad, especially in continental Europe.

Contemporary dance is an expanding area, due partly to the recent growth in community dance. Because of the intense competition for jobs in established companies, dance schools encourage students to use their initiative and set up their own dance groups, either self-financing or occasionally grant-aided by the Arts Council or Regional Arts Boards. Such groups usually work for short seasons, after which the dancers must either find other work, or face periods of unemployment.

Musical theatre and cabaret is a major source of employment for dancers. Opportunities include working in night-clubs, on cruise ships, in circuses, in pantomimes and in West End musicals.

Non-western dance, including South Asian and African dance, is an area where opportunities are increasing. Employment is mainly in dance groups, though in South Asian dance, in particular, there are also opportunities for solo performers.

Ballroom dancing provides a few couples with the opportunity to make a living by giving dance demonstrations and appearing in cabaret. The majority of opportunities in this area, however, are in teaching.

Opera often employs choreographers and dancers, for example at the Royal Opera House, English National Opera and Scottish Opera. Employment is usually for one particular production.

Ice dancing combines dance with ice skating. In recent years it has become a popular form of mass entertainment. Ice dancing is a competitive amateur sport, and many competitors, once their competing days are over, make the move to ice dancing professionally. Ice dancers are sometimes required to perform in fancy dress.

Dance-in-education involves visits to schools and colleges by dance companies to encourage students to enjoy watching and performing dance. As well as dancers, some larger companies also employ education officers.

Community dance is a growing field: dancers are employed, usually by local authorities, to encourage the development of dance in specific areas. They sometimes teach classes themselves, and also organize workshops and classes for a variety of groups in the community, including children, adults, elderly people, and those with special needs.

Choreography is a difficult area to break into. Traditionally, it was the preserve of older, experienced dancers, but there is now a new breed of young choreographers who may combine this with an active performing career. There are several choreographer-led companies successfully touring the UK.

Notators/reconstructors use one of the two established systems of notation, Benesh or Labanotation, to record the movements of a dance so that it can be reconstructed by other dancers.

Dance/movement therapy is still relatively new to the UK. The therapeutic effects of dance are used to help people in need, due to physical disability, emotional disturbance, and so on.

PAY AND CONDITIONS

Minimum salaries for dancers are negotiated by Equity and depend on the type, length and location of the job. For example, a member of the *corps de ballet* at The Royal Ballet earns about £253.13 a week in the first year, rising to £408 in the fifth year. A soloist earns £417.66 a week, and a senior principal £711. All grades receive an additional £15.75 for classes. Salaries for most other companies are below Royal Ballet rates. Most contemporary dancers in subsidized productions earn £200-£300 a week.

Dancers in their own groups may be paid on a profit-share basis. Dancers with non-Equity jobs, such as working in some night-clubs, may have to live on a very low income. Dance teachers in schools and adult education are paid at standard teaching rates. Teachers at private dance schools may receive a low basic salary supplemented by commission on lessons taken.

Working hours are long and hard for dancers, and regularly include evenings and weekends. Dancers at The Royal Ballet spend at least 33 hours a week in rehearsals and performances, with a minimum of four additional hours in classes.

PROSPECTS

Even if dancers are fortunate enough to obtain a job with a top ballet company, they start at the bottom of the ladder and face keen competition for promotion. Most ballet dancers remain members of the *corps de ballet.* Only a minority go on to become soloists or principals. There are only a very few permanent ballet companies, and a number of ballet dancers move on to contemporary dance, which is a growth area.

The life of a performer in dance is a short one. Few go on beyond the age of 35, and only in very exceptional cases is there much chance of working as a performer after 40 years of age. Ex-dancers often move on to careers in teaching, lecturing, choreography, or arts administration. Performers and teachers can improve their prospects by further study, perhaps for a degree, or for a specialist diploma in choreography, notation, special education, teaching, community dance or dance therapy.

RELATED OCCUPATIONS

Choreographer, dance teacher, actor, singer, musician, dance therapist, health and fitness instructor.

FURTHER INFORMATION

ADiTi, The National Organization of South Asian Dance, Willowfield Street, Bradford BD7 2AH, 01274 522059

Arts Council of Great Britain*, 14 Great Peter Street, London SW1P 3NQ, 0171 333 0100

British Actors' Equity Association, Guild House, Upper St Martin's Lane, London WC2 9EG, 0171 379 6000

British Ballet Organization*, Woolborough House, 39 Lonsdale Road, Barnes, London SW13 9JP, 0181 748 1241

British Council of Ballroom Dancing, 240 Merton Road, South Wimbledon, London SW19 1EQ, 0181 545 0085

Council for Dance Education and Training (UK)*, Riverside Studios, Crisp Road, London W6 9RL, 0181 741 5084 (please include sae)

Dance UK, 23 Crisp Road, London W6 9RL, 0181 741 1932

Imperial Society of Teachers of Dancing*, Imperial House, 22-26 Paul Street, London EC2A 4QE, 0171 377 1577

International Dance Teachers Association*, 76 Bennett Road, Brighton BN2 5JL, 01273 685652

National Resource Centre for Dance*, University of Surrey, Guildford, Surrey GU2 5XH, 01483 259316

Royal Academy of Dancing*, 36 Battersea Square, London SW11 3RA, 0171 223 0091

Stage Dance Council International, 113 Braemar Road, Fallowfield, Manchester M14 6PQ, 0161 224 5231

FURTHER READING

Leaflets/booklets are available from the addresses marked*.

Job Outlines – The Performing Arts – COIC

Working In Performing Arts – COIC

Periodicals: Ballroom Dancing Times; Dance and Dancers; Dance News; Dance Theatre Journal; Dancing Times.

A wide range of resource packs, videos, catalogues and directories is available from the National Resource Centre for Dance.

In the careers library classified under GAF.

1. SPORTS COACH/INSTRUCTOR CLCI:GAG
2. PROFESSIONAL SPORTSMAN/WOMAN CLCI:GAG
3. SPORTS AND LEISURE CENTRE MANAGER CLCI:GAJ
4. SPORTS AND LEISURE CENTRE ASSISTANT CLCI:GAJ

1. SPORTS COACH/INSTRUCTOR (GAG)

BACKGROUND INFORMATION

Leisure is a growth industry. In Britain it now employs over 400,000 people, making it a larger source of employment than many traditional industries, such as chemicals or agriculture.

The leisure industry caters for the entire population, offering a wide range of sports and other forms of recreation. In recent years there has been a big increase in the demand for leisure facilities.

Sport is part of the leisure industry, but professional sportsmen/women make up only a tiny proportion of those working in leisure. Many more work as sports coaches/instructors, or as assistants and managers at sports and leisure centres. These have undergone a boom over the last 20 years or so. In 1970, for example, there were barely 20 sports centres in the whole country; now there are over 1,500. The Sports Council estimates that more than 500 sports halls and 200 swimming pools need to be built just to cope with current demand. Many centres are operated by local councils as a service for the community; many others have been opened as commercial enterprises by companies seeking to profit from the leisure boom. All these centres need managers and assistants to run them, and coaches and instructors to take classes and supervise activities.

Millions of people take part regularly in sport. Some are professionals who are paid for what they do, but many more are amateurs who are involved in sport purely as a recreation. Whether amateur or professional, most participants need the help of coaches and instructors to learn the sport, improve their skills and perform to the best of their ability.

THE WORK

Large numbers of coaches and instructors are needed to assist the millions of people who regularly participate in sport. Everyone taking up a sport needs someone to show them the skills and techniques, and, if they prove to have an aptitude, to help them develop their talents. Even in professional sport, however, full-time jobs are scarce. Many coaches are self-employed or employed part-time, and may combine coaching with another part-time or full-time job. Many others are amateurs, working in their spare time for love of their sport. Coaches and instructors teach the skills and techniques of one particular sport, or a few related ones, to a wide range of people, from beginners to experts.

Coaches in professional sport

Coaches who work with professional sportsmen/women have to devise a training programme that develops individuals to the full and gets them in peak condition at the right moment. They monitor performance and technique carefully, and point out where and how further improvements may be made. When their charges are injured, they devise recovery programmes. Coaches may also become involved on the administrative side, sorting out problems with equipment, and arranging accommodation, transport, etc.

Team coaches have to mould their players into an effective team by developing individual skills to the full and teaching team tactics. They use videos to explain techniques and strategies, and to analyse the performance of the team and their opponents. They may also use blackboards or overhead projectors to illustrate points. Team coaches work closely with managers, for example in selecting the members of a team for a particular match or contest.

Coaches/instructors in amateur sport

Coaches and instructors in amateur sport may work with anyone, from a complete beginner to an Olympic athlete. It is very important that beginners, even those who see sport primarily as a form of recreation, are taught the right techniques from the start; bad habits are hard to break, and bad techniques can lead to injury. Coaches have to see that sportsmen/women train safely and know their own capabilities.

It is part of a coach's job to motivate sportsmen/women, and this can involve thinking up interesting and varied ways of practising the same activity over and over again. Those who coach top-level performers must devise training programmes that will have their sportsmen/women in top mental and physical condition on the right day. Sometimes they have to be prepared to pass their trainees on to another coach who can do more for them.

Every sport, amateur or professional, has its governing body and its own rules and regulations. Coaches must be familiar with these, so that they can teach them to competitors and ensure that they stay within the rules.

Health and fitness instructors

Health and fitness instructors deliver training in aerobics, keep fit, weight training and other forms of exercise at privately run health and fitness centres and local authority sports centres. Their work includes assessing clients' levels of fitness when they arrive at the centre, and devising a programme of training that is neither too easy for them nor too demanding. They must be aware of the health and safety aspects of different forms of exercise, and prevent clients from injuring themselves by working too hard or using faulty techniques.

A few health and fitness instructors work with clients on a one-to-one basis, visiting them in their homes and workplaces, and planning and monitoring a personal fitness schedule for them.

WORK ENVIRONMENT

Coaches and instructors may work in gymnasiums, sports centres, health clubs, outdoor pursuits centres, on playing fields, etc. They may have to work outside in all weathers and spend long hours at matches and training sessions. They are likely to have to stand for long periods, and may expend considerable amounts of energy when taking part in training sessions. Those involved in professional, or serious amateur sport, are likely to have to travel a great deal to specialist training facilities, competitions and matches all over the UK and abroad.

SKILLS AND INTERESTS

Coaches and instructors must be enthusiastic about their sport, and have an in-depth knowledge and understanding of it. They must want to help people achieve their full potential, and this means finding the right approach for each individual. They must understand how to motivate people and encourage them to persevere – not always easy when things are not going well. They need patience and tact when teaching new skills and techniques. Good verbal communication skills are required, for example, when explaining where a performer may be going wrong and how they can improve.

Coaches and instructors must be able to teach, but they need not be exceptional at the sport themselves. They should inspire confidence, so need considerable expertise in their speciality and should set a good example in their appearance and behaviour. Good organizational skills are also desirable, for example, when arranging visits to sporting events in other parts of the UK or the world.

ENTRY REQUIREMENTS

No formal academic qualifications are required, but individuals must have experience in their sport and relevant governing body coaching qualifications.

Applicants to go on coaching courses must normally be at least 18 years, and may be required to hold a first aid certificate.

It is also possible to obtain coaching qualifications as part of a broader programme of study (see TRAINING). The options here include: NEBSM (National Examining Board for Supervisory Management) courses; BTEC/SCOTVEC Higher National Certificate/Diploma courses in Leisure Studies, or the Diploma in Youth and Community work; and degree courses in subjects such as sports or movement science.

There are no specific academic entry requirements for NEBSM, though applicants are expected to show some evidence of previous academic achievement. For the BTEC/SCOTVEC Higher National Certificate/Diploma in Leisure Studies, applicants must hold four GCSEs/S grades (A-C/1-3), including one A level or two H grades, or equivalent.

Minimum entry requirements for a degree course are five GCSEs/S grades (A-C/1-3) with two A levels/three H grades, or equivalent. For a BEd or BA with Qualified Teacher Status, GCSEs/S grades (A-C/1-3) in English and maths are also required.

Entry requirements for a Diploma in Youth and Community Work (England and Wales) are age 23+, relevant experience, and five GCSEs/S grades (A-C/1-3), or equivalent.

Entry requirements for a Diploma in Youth and Community Work (Scotland) are age 18+, four S grades (1-3) and two H grades, including English.

Entry may be possible for young people through Modern Apprenticeships, leading to at least an NVQ/SVQ Level 3. Contact your local careers office, TEC/LEC for details.

TRAINING

To become a qualified coach or instructor in a particular sport it is necessary to take the coaching awards offered in that sport. These are administered by the national governing body of the sport, and are usually achieved through part-time study. Alternatively, it is possible to gain suitable qualifications by completing a college or university course, in which coaching awards have been incorporated within a broader programme of studies. Such courses include some NEBSM and BTEC/SCOTVEC Higher

National Certificate and Diploma courses in Leisure Studies, and degree courses in sports science, movement studies or physical education. The National Coaching Foundation (NCF) also runs a programme of coaching courses and workshops, at all levels from introductory to advanced.

Anyone who has a good practical record in coaching, either on a professional or amateur basis, can apply to take the one-year, full-time Diploma in Professional Studies (Sports Coaching) at Heriot-Watt University's Moray House Institute.

A number of new qualifications in sports coaching are currently being developed. These include The National Coaching Foundation Introductory Coach Education and Coaching Awards, and the Certificate in Sports Coaching. These qualifications are being offered at a limited number of colleges and institutes of further and higher education – further advice is available from the NCF.

The Introductory Coaching Award is equivalent to NVQ/SVQ Level 2, and the Certificate in Sports Coaching is equivalent to NVQ/SVQ Level 3.

A number of NVQs/SVQs are available in Sport and Recreation at Levels 2, 3 and 4. These include: Coaching Children; Coaching Adults and Coaching Participants with Disabilities.

The training for sports coaches and instructors varies widely from sport to sport, and according to the type of client worked with. The following is a representative selection.

Professional golf

Professional golfers usually coach for a club or are full-time competitors. Those who have been registered for three years with the Professional Golfers' Association (PGA) may follow a residential course and, on passing the PGA's tests, become members and apply for professional jobs.

Swimming

The Swimming Teachers' Association and Amateur Swimming Association (ASA) offer teaching and coaching qualifications. Student membership of the Swimming Teachers' Association requires a pass in the student examination for young people aged 16 to 18 years. Associate membership requires a pass in the Swimming Teachers' Certificate, and a Royal Life Saving Society bronze medallion. Candidates for this must be 18 years or over. There are further exams leading to qualified member and diploma member status. The ASA offers a preliminary teachers' certificate, teachers' certificate for swimming and advanced teachers' certificate for swimming.

Mountain leaders

Applicants to the certificate course must be over 18 years and hold a first aid certificate. To obtain the certificate, applicants must keep an expedition logbook, assist a qualified mountain leader and pass practical and written tests in map reading, rescue work and equipment selection. Certificate holders can go on to take the instructors' certificate or the advanced certificate.

Health and fitness instructors

Health and fitness instructors must hold recognized qualifications, such as the RSA/Sports Council-validated Basic Certificate in the Teaching of Exercise to Music, or the British Amateur Weightlifters' Association Instructors' Certificate. Qualifications in more traditional types of exercise are offered by The Keep Fit Association. The Physical Education Association offers a Certificate in

Exercise and Health Studies, and the YMCA a variety of modular courses in exercise and fitness.

Outdoor pursuits instructors

Outdoor pursuits instructors must have gained instructor awards in a range of sports such as climbing, canoeing and mountaineering. They must also have considerable practical experience.

Youth and community workers

Some coaches and instructors are qualified youth and community workers. In England and Wales, courses take two years; in Scotland they take three, though exemption from the first year is granted to those with relevant experience. Such courses may include the opportunity to take coaching qualifications – these include the Community Sports Leaders Award (CSLA), and the CCPR's Hanson Leadership Award and Basic Expedition Training Award.

PE teachers

Some BEd courses offer specialization in outdoor pursuits, or youth and community work.

Armed Forces

The awards offered by the Armed Forces are the same as those recognized by civilian sporting bodies. Only the RAF takes recruits to train as PT instructors. The Army and Royal Navy recruit instructors from their serving members.

LATE ENTRY

Most people who go into coaching are older entrants from professional, or serious amateur sport. Maturity is usually an asset in coaching and most sports bodies have a minimum age limit of 18 years or more. Opportunities depend on physical fitness and abilities, rather than academic qualifications. Entry requirements for the Diploma in Youth and Community Work course may be waived for mature applicants with relevant experience.

OPPORTUNITIES

Full-time paid jobs are very scarce. Professional sport is extremely competitive, and coaches tend to be judged by results. Many coaches and instructors also do administrative and other work. Many are self-employed, giving private lessons to individuals; many others are volunteers who work in sports clubs, with local and national teams, in amateur sports, etc. There are openings for paid part-timers who coach and instruct in the evenings and weekends. If they have several such jobs and build up a reputation, they may then become self-employed, or they may get full-time jobs, either just coaching, or doing other management or administrative work, for example in sports centres.

There are paid jobs as national coaches with the governing bodies of various sports, with professional football clubs, golf clubs and local authorities. The six national sports centres employ coaches who, in addition to their practical work, are often involved in management and administration. Holiday camps, private hotels, leisure centres, outward bound schools and large sports and leisure centres employ instructors and coaches to run sporting/ fitness events and classes, and give private tuition to individuals.

Instructors are needed by organizations such as the security services, to give training in areas such as personal fitness and self-defence. There is also an increasing demand for outdoor pursuits instructors, to cater for the growing number of people who are choosing to spend some of their leisure time in the countryside. There are now a number of outdoor pursuit or activity holiday centres in coastal and rural areas across the UK, offering a range of activities, such as mountaineering, climbing, walking, canoeing, skiing, orienteering and sailing.

Some sports goods manufacturers employ instructors and coaches for publicity and public relations work. All three of the Armed Forces have physical training instructors, but not all take on recruits to train specifically for these posts.

Opportunities vary between sports. Professional sports, like soccer and cricket, have a long tradition of employing coaches; and, among the recreational sports, coaches and instructors have for many years been employed to teach ice skating, riding and golf. More recently, there have been openings for coaches and instructors in swimming, squash, tennis, water sports, horse-riding, table tennis, badminton, and the martial arts.

Vacancies for sports coaches and instructors appear in *The Times Educational Supplement*. Vacancies for coaching jobs for different sports appear in specialist magazines devoted to the sports concerned, and are advertised by sports associations. A lot of vacancy information is passed on by word of mouth, and, not infrequently, employers with vacancies will directly approach the candidate they want.

PAY AND CONDITIONS

National governing bodies of sports employ coaches on fixed contracts and for fixed salaries. In professional sport, pay often depends on how much prize money is earned, how well a particular team or individual is doing, how popular a sport is with spectators, how much television coverage it gets, and so on. Coaches are likely to get a basic salary, with bonuses for good results. Earnings for the self-employed depend on how many people they coach or teach, at what level, and how successful their students are. Self-employed people normally charge by the hour, and coaches and instructors with good reputations can charge more.

Work in holiday resorts, leisure centres and the like, which is usually seasonal, is not particularly well paid, but there may be extra money from tips, and accommodation is often included. Most of the coaches and instructors in this area are young people.

Work in local authority sports centres and outdoor pursuits centres, among others, is paid on nationally agreed scales for instructors. Full-time recreational assistants' rates are around £5 an hour. Many youth club leaders are unpaid volunteers, but there are some paid posts and scales that are nationally agreed. Most coaches work on a voluntary basis.

Coaches and instructors tend to work unsocial hours, since most sports competitions and matches take place in the evenings and weekends. They may also have to work during the day, as training for professional and high-level amateur sport is virtually full-time. Coaches attend training sessions, competitions and matches and can therefore work very long hours during the season. They also work during the off-season, when much of the preparatory training is done. A lot of coaches and instructors work part-time and do another job during the day. In amateur sport, they may have to work with participants very early in the morning, or late at night. In outdoor sports, the amount of time spent training on-site varies with the season, but where floodlights and all-weather surfaces have been installed, only very severe conditions bring training to a halt. Some coaching and instruction is only seasonal, so those who coach a summer or winter sport may have to find other work in the off-season.

PROSPECTS

Coaches' and instructors' prospects usually depend on their results. Successful coaches in professional sport may be rewarded by higher fees and earnings. In amateur sport, success may be judged not merely by the number of medals won, but by the progress and the level of enjoyment of the participants. Most sports coaches and instructors are in their 20s and 30s. As they grow older, they may move into less physically demanding jobs in management or administration.

RELATED OCCUPATIONS

Professional sportsman/woman, PE teacher, sports physiotherapist, sports/leisure centre manager, sports/leisure centre assistant.

FURTHER INFORMATION

British Amateur Weight Lifters' Association, 131 Hurst Street, Oxford OX4 1HE, 01865 200339 (please include sae)

Central Council of Physical Recreation (CCPR)*, Francis House, Francis Street, London SW1P 1DE, 0171 828 3163/4

Institute of Sport and Recreation Management (ISRM)*, Giffard House, 36-38 Sherrard Street, Melton Mowbray, Leicestershire LE13 1XJ, 01664 65531

Institute of Leisure and Amenity Management (ILAM), Education and Training Unit, ILAM House, Lower Basildon, Reading, Berkshire RG8 9NE, 01491 874222

Keep Fit Association*, Francis House, Francis Street, London SW1P 1DE, 0171 233 8898

Local Government Opportunities (LGO), Local Government Management Board*, 76-86 Turnmill Street, London

National Coaching Foundation*, 114 Cardigan Road, Headingley, Leeds LS6 3BJ, 0113 274 4802

The Physical Education Association of the United Kingdom*, Francis House, Francis Street, London SW1P 1DE, 0171 828 9229

The Exercise Association of England, Unit 4, Angel Gate, City Road, London EC1V 2PT, 0171 278 0811

Recreation Managers Association of Great Britain*, Recreation House, 7 Burkinshaw Avenue, Rawmarsh, Rotherham, South Yorkshire S62 7QZ, 01709 522463

Scottish Sports Council*, Caledonia House, South Gyle, Edinburgh EH12 9DQ, 0131 317 7200

The Sports Council*, 16 Upper Woburn Place, London WC1H 0QP, 0171 388 1277

The Sports Council for Northern Ireland, House of Sport, Upper Malone Road, Belfast BT9 5LA, 01232 381222

The Sports Council for Wales, Information Centre, Welsh Institute of Sport, Sophia Gardens, Cardiff CF1 9SW, 01222 397571

London and Central YMCA, Training and Development Department, 112 Great Russell Street, London WC1B 3NQ, 0171 580 2989

FURTHER READING

Leaflets/booklets are available from the addresses marked*.

Job Outlines – Physical Education and Sport – COIC
Working in Leisure – COIC
Working in Outdoor Jobs – COIC
Careers in Sport and Recreation – CCPR
Careers in Sport – Kogan Page

In the careers library classified under GAG.

2. PROFESSIONAL SPORTSMAN/WOMAN (GAG)

BACKGROUND INFORMATION

While most people take part in sport as amateurs, professional sportsmen and women get paid for their efforts. Amateurs may take their sport very seriously and compete at the highest level. In general, however, they take part for their own pleasure, and pay all their own costs and expenses. They do not make any money from the sport itself.

Historically, the distinction between amateur and professional has been an important one, and even today turning professional can have wide-ranging implications. Some events (eg the Olympic Games) are, in theory at least, open only to amateurs. In many sports, however, the old distinctions between amateur and professional are breaking down. In tennis, for instance, no official distinction is now drawn between amateurs and professionals, and highly paid tennis stars have been allowed to compete at the Olympics.

This article covers sportsmen/women who get paid for competing in their chosen sport. Comparatively few are able to make a living from sport alone, and only a tiny number earn large sums. Most sports-people have to take other full or part-time jobs, and play professional sport at the weekends or in the evenings. They may have to take time off work, perhaps unpaid, to attend tournaments and competitions, and may depend on the goodwill of a sympathetic employer.

There are two types of sport: team games and sports for individuals. Among the most popular team games in this country are soccer, cricket, rugby, cycling (also an individual sport) and basketball. Among individual sports, the best known are golf, tennis, boxing, horse-racing and other equestrian sports, motor sports, darts and snooker. This article deals briefly with all of these.

Soccer. This is organized into clubs, with players also having the chance to join their national squads. There are several leagues and other competitions, and the clubs are placed in divisions according to their success. There are around 90 Football League clubs in England and Wales, and 40 in Scotland. Matches are played mid-week and at weekends (mostly Saturday afternoons). Professional footballers spend the rest of their working week in running, fitness and weight-training, practising skills such as ball control and tackling, planning and rehearsing moves and tactics, and generally building their stamina, skill and strength.

There are eleven players in a football team, together with three nominated substitutes, of which at most two may actually play. Even taking into account second teams, this means each club can offer only a limited number of opportunities for full-time professionals. In England and Wales there are an estimated 2,000 full-time footballers, with 1,000 part-timers and 250 youth trainees. The corresponding figures in Scotland are around 450 full-time and 550 part-time players.

The governing bodies in soccer are the Football Association, the Football League, the Scottish Football Association and the Scottish Football League. The Professional Footballers Association (PFA) looks after the interests of professional footballers. Although many women now play the game, there are as yet no opportunities for women to play professionally in this country.

Cricket. There are 18 county sides which play in a championship league and other competitions such as the Sunday league. There is also an English national side run from the Test and County Cricket Board at Lords. Members of the England team are selected on merit from the county sides.

There are eleven players on a cricket team, and a twelfth man who may substitute in certain situations, eg if one of the players is unwell. Each county club retains a squad of around 20 to 25 professionals, creating opportunities for around 450 full-time players. Minor Counties cricket, Scottish and local county leagues (eg the Lancashire League) offer some opportunities for part-time professionals, who may supplement their playing fees with coaching and instructing.

Cricket is played in the summer months between April and September, in matches lasting between one and five days. Most full-time professionals play or coach abroad, or have other jobs in the winter.

Most cricketers specialize in either batting or bowling, though it is useful if they can do both. The other specialist, the wicket-keeper, benefits from being able to bat. When they are not playing, they train for fitness and stamina, and practise fielding or batting/bowling in the nets. Cricketers must keep fit and agile, as they may spend long hours on the field. Teams are tactically picked, depending on the type of game, the weather and the state of the pitch.

Cricket is regulated by the Test and County Cricket Board and the International Cricket Conference.

Rugby League. There are some 1,600 professional rugby league players. They play in 36 professional clubs, most of which are based in Yorkshire, Lancashire or Cumbria.

There are 13 players, plus two substitutes in a rugby league team. Many teams are sponsored by breweries or tobacco companies, and the sport is regulated by the Rugby Football League. While the players are paid professionals, only a minority receive enough to make a full-time living from it. Many have a full-time job as well, and fit in playing and training at evenings and weekends.

Basketball. There is a national league, with over 60 clubs competing in men's, women's and junior men's divisions. There are also cup competitions. Each team has ten players, though only five are on the court at any one time. Matches are played indoors according to three basic rules: no contact, no running with the ball, and one continuous dribble. Basketball matches are played in two 20-minute halves with a 10-minute interval, although most matches last around an hour-and-a-quarter, as the clock is stopped every time the referee blows his or her whistle. There are only a handful of full-time paid professionals, and most players do other jobs to support themselves. The best players may be invited to study at American universities.

Cycling. There are some 70 full-time professional cyclists, most of whom have worked their way up from the amateur ranks. Professional cycle racing is a tough and highly competitive world. The sport divides into four broad categories: road racing, time trials, track racing and cyclo-cross (cross-country cycle racing). Except for major international races such as the Tour de France, the financial rewards in cycling are small. Only the very top names can support themselves entirely through the sport, and the great majority have other part or full-time jobs. Cycling in Britain is regulated by the British Cycling Federation and the Professional Cycling Association. Cycling is both a team and an individual sport.

Speedway. There are around 300 professional speedway riders who are contracted to one of the 26 clubs currently operating. Teams of seven riders contest home and away matches in a league with two divisions. Top riders also ride for clubs abroad, and hence have considerable earning power. New riders, in contrast, are likely to have to supplement their income by other work. The British governing body is the Speedway Control Board Limited. The riders' interests are protected by the Speedway Riders' Association, while the British Speedway Promoters' Association represents the promoters.

Golf. There are two types of professional. The first is the player on the national and international tournament circuit, whose income derives mainly from prize money and sponsorship. There are currently around 250 men and 100 women. Golfers wishing to become tournament players must first obtain a qualifying card, competition for which is intense.

The other type of golfer is the club professional, attached to a golf club. Club professionals' duties include teaching players at all levels, organizing competitions, and selling and repairing golf equipment. Club professionals also take part in competitions and tournaments. There are around 1,600 club professionals in the UK, of whom ten are female.

Professional golfers need to become members of the Professional Golfers Association (PGA). This requires considerable talent and dedication, and the ability to pass a set of rigorous examinations. Golf is currently undergoing a boom in Britain, and opportunities for club professionals, in particular, are increasing with the number of new courses being opened.

Tennis. Tennis is now played on four main types of surface: grass, clay, cement and indoor. Players compete on all types of surface, though many find their game better suited to some surfaces than others. In Britain, no distinctions are drawn between professional and amateur status, but only a very small number of players are able to make any sort of living from the game.

Tennis players are ranked world-wide according to their successes. High-ranking players gain direct entry to top tournaments such as Wimbledon, and may even be 'seeded', so that they do not meet other top players until the later stages. Those with more modest rankings, by contrast, play in less prestigious 'satellite' tournaments to raise their rankings. They may also gain entry to top tournaments by playing well in preliminary, qualifying events.

Professionals play singles and, to a lesser extent, doubles matches. The most successful players can make a great deal of money on the circuit, as they move from tournament to tournament. All tennis players spend a lot of time travelling and living away from home.

Boxing. Boxing is a popular sport with spectators, with huge audiences watching televised bouts. Rewards for top boxers can be correspondingly large, but those lower down the scale may need to supplement their purses (payments received per bout) with other work.

Matches take place at night or weekends, or at special times suited to world-wide television coverage. They last for a prescribed number of two or three-minute rounds or until one contestant is knocked out, or until the referee judges that one man has reached the limits of his endurance. The main regulatory body in this country is the British Boxing Board of Control (BBBC). The BBBC licences professional boxers, who are required to show a high level of skill, and to undergo rigorous medical tests to prove their fitness for the professional ring.

Horse-racing. Some 25,000 people work in the horse-racing industry; around 5,000 at the stables where the horses are kept and trained. Although many of those joining a stable hope to become jockeys, competition is intense and only a tiny proportion can be successful.

Jockeys ride for racehorse owners and trainers. They get rides depending on their past performance and their weight. There are two types of horse-racing: flat (March to November) and national hunt over jumps (August to May). Jockeys are paid a riding fee and a percentage of any winnings, and most make a steady living rather than a fortune. There are, however, a fair number of established jockeys who earn a good income from the industry. The top jockeys are usually contracted to ride for wealthy owners, and can command very high fees.

Equestrian sports. Apart from horse-racing, there are a number of other equestrian sports. They include horse trials, endurance riding, dressage and horse-driving trials. Riders' income comes from sponsorship and prize money. They travel from event to event and, when not competing, spend most of their time caring for and schooling their horses. The horses are graded A, B or C, and move into the higher categories as they improve their placings. Most equestrian sports are under the control of the British Horse Society.

Motor-racing. This includes car and motorbike racing. Motor-racing and speedway take place on purpose-built circuits. Rallying, motocross and motorcycle road racing take place on the open road or in country areas on trails and tracks. Although the top drivers can earn large sums, earnings fall away sharply further down the scale. The Royal Automobile Club (RAC) has overall responsibility for the standards in some of these sports.

Darts. This is a sport sponsored mainly by the brewing industry. Many of the players have a high level of showmanship, as well as considerable individual skills. Accuracy and a steady hand are more important than all-round physical fitness, but darts players still need to spend many hours practising.

Professional darts players compete in national and international competitions and championships. When not competing, they give exhibitions in clubs, holiday camps, hotels, etc. They spend a great deal of time travelling between venues and generally work in the evenings in pubs and clubs. The national governing body is the British Darts Organization.

Snooker. In recent years, with the help of widespread television coverage, snooker has become a very popular sport, and top players can earn large sums in sponsorship and prize money. Players also give exhibitions and visit clubs, where they are challenged by the best players. There are around 600 snooker professionals, but only a minority can support themselves entirely by playing, and most have other jobs elsewhere. Professional snooker is controlled by the World Professional Billiards and Snooker Association.

THE WORK

Professional sports people spend a great deal of time practising their event, exercising and looking after their

bodies. It is important for them to stay at peak skill and fitness, even when not playing, as there are always promising adults and youngsters waiting to fill any vacancy. It is common to train twice or more a day, building strength and stamina as well as sporting prowess. Physical fitness also helps protect against injury.

They have to look after clothing and equipment, mending it and keeping it clean. For most professional sportsmen/women, actual competing takes up only a small proportion of their time. Much more is spent preparing, practising and training.

Some sports, such as horse-racing and boxing, require competitors to maintain certain weights. Jockeys have to pay a great deal of attention to weight, as, if they get too heavy, they may not get rides in races. Boxers are divided into weight divisions according to their size. Matches are made at a particular weight, and if a boxer is above the prescribed limit on the morning of a fight he may have to attempt to lose weight quickly by strenuous exercise.

In sports that rely on a partnership with a horse, the riders or jockeys spend a great deal of time schooling, exercising and caring for their animals.

In most cases sportsmen/women do not work on their own. They rely on coaches and trainers to improve their skills, physiotherapists and doctors to care for their injuries, and agents or managers (if they have them) to look after travel, competition bookings and other administrative matters. Tournament golfers normally employ a caddie, who carries their clubs for them and may assist them in judging distances, deciding which club to use, and so on.

In darts and snooker, the competitors are sometimes considered to be entertainers, rather than athletes, but they still have to practise regularly to maintain their consistency.

WORK ENVIRONMENT

Professional sportsmen/women provide entertainment for spectators and fans when they compete. They therefore perform in venues that allow spectators to attend and watch the action. Many sports take place in the open air, at venues including stadia, sports grounds, race courses and so on. Professionals in sports such as soccer and rugby are expected to perform in almost all weathers; other sports, such as cricket, may only be practicable when conditions are fine.

Some sports, such as boxing and basketball, are performed indoors, in halls, clubs and arenas. Even in indoor sports, conditions are normally light and well-ventilated. The exceptions may be snooker and darts, which traditionally take place in pubs, clubs and theatres.

Professional sportsmen/women often have to travel long distances between competitions, perhaps driving themselves, going on team coaches or using public transport. This can necessitate overnight stays in hotels or bed and breakfasts. Those competing in international events overseas may spend lengthy periods away from home.

SKILLS AND INTERESTS

The two main characteristics required by a professional sportsman/woman are ability and commitment. At the highest level, talent on its own is not sufficient. Players must be committed to winning, and prepared to put in all the hard work required to achieve that.

Most professional sportsmen/women have good all-round sporting ability. They need to be physically fit and strong, well balanced and sure-footed; have good hand/eye co-ordination; and be quick-thinking and decisive.

With coaching and constant practise, they build their skills until they are at the peak of skill and stamina. They must look after their bodies, using the help of doctors and physiotherapists to correct injuries, and eating and resting properly. They have to follow a regular, demanding daily routine that often leaves no time for a social life and which requires them to go to bed early when not competing. They must accept the advice of coaches, and practise single-mindedly to correct any weaknesses.

Professional sportsmen and women must also be able to cope with the enormous pressures placed on them. These may come from colleagues and opponents, parents and managers, and, not least, the paying public who watch them perform. They must have faith in themselves and their talents, and when they lose must have the resilience and self-discipline to go on training.

They must have a competitive nature and want to win, or at least improve their personal best performance. While they must be committed to winning, they must also play fairly.

Those in team sports need to be friendly and able to get on with other team members. Apart from the importance of co-operating during matches, players also spend lengthy periods together, training, travelling to matches, and staying overnight in hotels.

ENTRY REQUIREMENTS

There are no academic requirements, though a good standard of education is useful, bearing in mind that sporting careers are generally short.

Sportsmen/women must have talent which, in the opinion of coaches or talent scouts, can be developed into a top-level skill. Age of entry varies from sport to sport, from as young as 14 in football's Associated Schoolboy Scheme, while entry to cricket is common in the early twenties. The one thing all sports have in common is that most professionals started playing them at a very early age.

Certain sports have very specific entry requirements. Boxing has divisions according to weight. It also runs regular checks on participants, including eye tests and brain scans, which boxers must pass to be allowed to go on competing. Horse-racing requires boys and girls weighing no more than 57 kilograms (9 stone). Professional basketball players are usually well over 1.83m (6 feet) tall.

Most sports professionals have well-proportioned bodies, and 100 per cent vision, with or without glasses/contact lenses.

TRAINING

Some sports have special schemes for training young people. Some of these are specific training schemes aimed at young people. Contact your local careers office, TEC/LEC for details. In others, one progresses through school into clubs, county and national events until reaching a standard that allows one to join the professional circuit. Progress after that depends on achieving good results in competition. Most clubs have coaches or senior members who coach and train club members.

Football. Most professional footballers begin at the age of 14 as Associated Schoolboys at a professional club, having been 'spotted' by one of the club's talent scouts. They attend evening training sessions at the club two or three nights a week. At 16 they may be invited to become full-time trainees on the club's training programme. As well as

playing and practising, trainees undertake a variety of chores within the club, such as cleaning and checking kit. They are also required to attend college part-time to gain further academic qualifications. At 17 or 18 years they are either offered full-time professional terms, or not retained. Even if they are not retained, there is still a chance they may be taken on by another club. Even so, only a minority of trainees make it into the ranks of full-time professionals.

A small number of 14 and 15-year-old boys identified as having exceptional talent are selected each year to attend the Football Association's School of Excellence at Lilleshall in Shropshire. Here they have the chance to develop their skills with the country's top coaches and facilities, while attending local schools to continue their academic studies. The boys are signed to clubs in the normal way, and with this 'fast track' approach have a good chance of going on to achieve success at the highest level.

Cricket. In cricket, all the counties have selectors who watch school and club matches and invite young players with ability to attend trials. Players may also be recommended by teachers or club coaches. The best such players may be invited to play a few matches for the county 2nd XI. At this stage they play part-time until they are offered a summer season contract and a place on the playing staff. Counties use the 2nd XI as a means of discovering whether players have the ability to perform at the highest level, and only a very few get regular second-team places, let alone joining the first.

The MCC operate a scheme offering three summer seasons of cricket, together with study for an Advanced GNVQ in Leisure and Tourism.

Rugby League. Players often begin by playing in school teams. All professional clubs have scouts, who go to school and amateur matches, seeking new talent. Many clubs run training schemes for apprentices, and it is possible to take up a professional contract from the age of 17. Training usually consists of intensive sessions two or three nights a week. Players are also required to maintain a strict personal fitness programme in their own time.

Basketball. Players also frequently begin playing at school. Many clubs operate junior or 'cadet' teams that provide a training ground for the best players to go on to join senior teams. In training, players practise individual skills, such as dribbling, shooting, passing, pivoting and protecting the ball, and also team tactics for attack and defence. Basketball players often train in pairs or in groups.

Tennis. Players who perform well in school or club competitions may be invited to join county and regional training courses. The best young players in each of three age groups (under-12, under-14 and under-16) are invited to join the national training squad and attend training weekends or summer school at the Bisham Abbey National Sports Centre in Buckinghamshire. This is run by the Lawn Tennis Association as a national tennis centre. Trainees here practise and play tennis under the guidance of top national coaches. At 16, tennis players are classed as adults, and can expect to find themselves matched in competition against older and much more experienced players.

Golf. Professionals begin as assistant professionals in golf clubs. They are contracted to the club professional, and work in the club shop, selling and repairing equipment, and helping with the paperwork and administration. They may also coach club members, and have to fit in their own playing and practise in their spare time. After a six-month probationary period they are eligible to join the PGA training scheme. This involves three to five years of on-the-job training, with residential courses at the National Recreation Centre in Shropshire. At the end of this, PGA final examinations are taken, which, if passed, allow election as a full member of the PGA.

Golfers wishing to compete in professional tournaments must first obtain a 'player's ticket'. This is obtained by achieving good results in local competitions, and applicants must also have a handicap of less than two. This allows entry to one of the two pre-qualifying events. From here, about 130 players go on to a larger tournament of 250 players in Spain; and from this, about 50 go on to the European circuit with their 'card'.

It is possible to become a member of the PGA by gaining a Higher National Diploma in Golf Studies (three-year sandwich) at Merrist Wood College in Guildford, Surrey.

Horse-racing. Training for the horse-racing industry is supervised by the Racing and Thoroughbred Breeding Training Board (RTBTB). The Board offers three separate NVQs/SVQs: in Horse Care at Level 1, Racehorse Care at Level 2, and Racehorse Care and Management at Level 3. Anyone joining the racing industry between the ages of 16 and 18 is registered on the industry's youth training programme. Most new entrants begin working in stables as 'lads' (a term used for both sexes), where their responsibilities include riding and caring for the horses, and cleaning and maintaining the stables and equipment. After a short period of work experience, all new entrants to the industry have to attend one of the two racing schools at Newmarket and Doncaster. The job of the racing schools is to train stable staff. The best riders may have the chance to become trainee jockeys (known as apprentice jockeys in flat racing, conditional jockeys in jump racing). Apprenticeship as a jockey in flat racing finishes at the age of 24, or when 75 winners have been ridden. The equivalent for jump jockeys is age 25, or 40 winners.

Other equestrian sports. Training in other equestrian sports varies. Physical fitness is always very important, and riders have to exercise regularly for strength and suppleness. They also have to learn the correct posture for riding. Riders in sports that involve jumping need regular practise at this. They start with low obstacles, and gradually, as horse and rider become more experienced, work up to full competition height. Plenty of practice helps develop a good understanding between horse and rider, and also helps riders learn to judge pace.

Cycling. Most cyclists begin by joining a local club. Clubs may be based in sports and leisure centres, or in parks with suitable facilities. Cycling in itself promotes fitness, but professional cyclists regularly exercise out of the saddle as well. Exercise such as running improves stamina, while weight training helps build physical strength. A professional cyclist may prepare for a long road race by means of a series of shorter rides. With the aid of a coach or trainer, they aim to reach peak physical condition for the start of the race.

Motor sports. They require strength and stamina, as events often take place over a long period. In most such sports, a licence grading system operates. Drivers have to compete in a specified number of events to achieve each grade, not necessarily winning every time but driving well and safely. It is not possible to become a professional driver without an International Rally and Racing Licence. Successful drivers may be invited to join teams run by manufacturers on a professional or semi-professional (part-time) basis. Apart from racing skills and techniques, they learn how to maintain their vehicles and how to get the best out of them.

Speedway riders over 16 have to hold an Auto-Cycle Union licence.

Boxing. Boxers have to join a club that can provide proper training to the high safety standards required. They can compete in youth matches from the age of twelve, but seniors must be at least 17. All boxers have to train regularly. They may go on runs for stamina, and do weight and circuit training to build up their physical strength. Boxers practise punching on a punch-ball. They also spend some time practising in the ring with a sparring partner.

Darts and snooker. Players are traditionally self-taught. Players work their way up from local pub and club teams by performing well in competitions and defeating highly rated players. Here they combine practising their sport with general duties such as cleaning and brushing the tables. Both sports require long hours of practice to reach the top and to remain there. Some coaching schemes to assist young players are being set up under the auspices of the World Professional Billiards and Snooker Association.

LATE ENTRY

Most professional sportsmen/women have been playing and training seriously in their sport from an early age. In many sports it would be unlikely for someone taking up the sport as an adult to be able to achieve the required standard to compete professionally. Those who are successful as amateurs may, however, decide to turn professional at any point.

Some sports offer more opportunities for late entrants than others. Some cricketers, for example, do not become full-time professionals until their twenties, having first completed a university degree or a training in some other profession. Golf and snooker are two sports that can be performed at a high level until well into middle age.

Nevertheless, the average length of time a professional sportsman/woman can expect to stay at the top is around eight years, and many careers are over by the age of 35; so the opportunities for anyone to become a professional, in many sports, decline rapidly from about the mid-twenties.

OPPORTUNITIES

Most of the sports mentioned have amateur associations and clubs, where promising newcomers can receive instruction and coaching, and compete against more experienced opponents. The most successful may be spotted by managers or scouts and invited to try out for teams. Playing as an amateur in county, national or international competitions improves the chances of gaining recognition. There is a list of the main sports governing bodies in FURTHER INFORMATION.

There are clubs all over the country covering most sports, but anyone wishing to join a professional circuit or team is likely to have to move away from home.

In the main, opportunities are governed by the number of competitions or tournaments, and by the popularity of the sport with the paying public and the mass media. Sports that attract large crowds and receive regular television coverage can attract business sponsors and advertisers keen to promote their products to the viewing public. This, in turn, brings money into the sport, which can provide prize money, finance for sporting venues, and support for the sport in general.

Many professional sportsmen/women are self-employed in their sporting capacities, though they may have other jobs to support themselves. Others have contracts that are reviewed annually – this can mean a pattern of short-term employment with a succession of different employers. For instance, footballers may be asked to go on the transfer list, have to change team and location, and move home and family.

PAY AND CONDITIONS

In most professional sports – apart from football, cricket, cycling and a few others – players support themselves on appearance fees, prize money and income from advertising and product endorsements.

Prize money varies greatly between sports. In high-profile sports, such as tennis, boxing and golf, the prize for a win in a major competition can easily run into six figures. Most players, however, never have a major win. They make a steady living rather than a fortune. Their income is not their own until they have paid for insurance, travel, accommodation, tournament entry fees and training expenses. Others need part or full-time jobs to support themselves. Many, in sports such as cricket, speedway, cycling and so on, work on annual or fixed-term contracts.

Most professional sports take place in front of an audience, which means sportsmen/women have to work when spectators are free to watch, usually at evenings and weekends. They may have to practise when the public, who use the facilities for leisure or recreation, have finished. This often means using running tracks, gyms and so on late at night or very early in the morning.

PROSPECTS

There is no promotional ladder as such, except for the captaincy in team sports. Status is measured by success in competition and income, including sponsorships. Professional sportsmen/women must be seen to succeed at national and international level, to enhance their status and increase their earning potential.

Most sporting careers are short. Many competitors, because of the wear and tear on their bodies, finish by the age of 35, or earlier still if they suffer a serious injury. In less physically demanding sports, it may be possible to go on playing longer. However, with professional careers, in general, so short, it is important for sportsmen/women to make the most of their earning potential while they can, and to plan and prepare for their later careers. In football, the PFA provides finance for all its members to continue vocational training for their post-playing careers.

It is not uncommon for sportsmen/women to move into coaching or team management. Some find jobs in sports and leisure centres, or with national sporting organizations such as The Sports Council. Modelling, public relations and promotional work are other possibilities. Many sports people make contacts during their years as competitors, which they follow up when they leave. They may also become radio or television sports commentators, or journalists. Some move into officiating in their sports (eg most cricket umpires in first-class matches are former players). Some join firms that develop and design sports clothing, footwear and equipment; some even design ranges of goods themselves; others open their own sports equipment shops. Many move away from sport, creating new careers for themselves while keeping up their sporting interests.

RELATED OCCUPATIONS

Sports coach/instructor, PE teacher, sports physiotherapist, sports administrator, sports journalist/photographer, groundsman, sports and leisure centre manager, sports and leisure centre assistant.

FURTHER INFORMATION

In the first instance contact the local or regional organizer of the sport that is of interest. The national governing bodies below can give you details of local clubs, and will also advise on the best way to progress in your chosen sport.

Sports national governing bodies

The British Boxing Board of Control, Jack Peterson House, 52a Borough High Street, London SE1 1XW (please include sae)

British Cycling Federation, c/o National Cycling Centre, Stuart Street, Manchester M11 4DQ, 0161 230 2301

British Darts Organization, 2 Pages Lane, Muswell Hill, London N10 1PS, 0181 883 5544

The British Horse Society, British Equestrian Centre, Stoneleigh Park, Kenilworth, Warwickshire CV8 2LR, 01203 696697 (please include sae)

English Basketball Association, 48 Bradford Road, Stanningley, Pudsey, West Yorkshire LS28 6DF, 0113 2361166

Football Association*, 16 Lancaster Gate, London W2 3LW, 0171 262 4542

Lawn Tennis Association, The Queens Club, Barons Court, Palliser Road, West Kensington, London W14 9EG, 0171 381 7000

Professional Golfers Association*, Apollo House, The Belfry, Sutton Coldfield, West Midlands B76 9PT, 01675 470333

Racing and Thoroughbred Breeding Training Board (RTBTB)*, Unit 8, Suite 16, Kings Court, Willie Snaith Road, Newmarket, Suffolk CB8 7SG, 01638 560743

RAC Motor Sports Association, Motor Sports House, Riverside Park, Colnbrook, Berkshire SL3 0HG, 01753 681736

Rugby Football League, Redhall House, Redhall Lane, Leeds LS17 8NB

Speedway Control Board Limited, ACU House, Wood Street, Rugby CV21 2YX, 01788 540096

World Professional Billiards and Snooker Association, 27 Oakfield Road, Clifton, Bristol BS8 2AT, 0117 974 4491

Other organizations

The Institute of Professional Sport, Francis House, Francis Street, London SW1P 1DE, 0171 828 3163

The Sports Council*, 16 Upper Woburn Place, London WC1H 0QP, 0171 388 1277

Scottish Sports Council*, Caledonia House, South Gyle, Edinburgh EH12 9DQ, 0131 317 7200

The Sports Council for Northern Ireland, House of Sport, Upper Malone Road, Belfast BT9 5LA, 01232 381222

The Sports Council for Wales, Information Centre, Welsh Institute of Sport, Sophia Gardens, Cardiff CF1 9SW, 01222 397571

FURTHER READING

Leaflets/booklets are available from the addresses marked*.

Job Outlines – Physical Education and Sport – COIC
Working in Leisure – COIC
Careers in Sport – Kogan Page

Playing at the Top: A Guide to Professional Sport – The Institute of Professional Sport

Numerous specialized books and periodicals cover every sport, including Wisden Cricket Monthly, Footballers World, Tennis World, Golf World, Rally Sport, Cycling Weekly, Sporting Life, Horse and Hound, Motor Sport, Match, Snooker Scene and Darts World.

In the careers library classified under GAG.

3. SPORTS AND LEISURE CENTRE MANAGER (GAJ)

THE WORK

Sports and leisure centre managers are responsible for the smooth and efficient running of the centres in which they work. Centres vary widely, but a typical one might include a gymnasium, swimming pool, weights room, dance studios, squash courts, sauna, solarium, bar and cafe.

Managers' duties are wide-ranging. They include financial planning and record-keeping; organizing events and tournaments; timetabling facilities for use by schools, clubs and the general public; arranging for specialist coaches such as aerobics and swimming instructors to work at the centre; ensuring health and safety requirements are met; and dealing with any complaints. They have a team of office staff who assist them in this work, and coaches, instructors and assistants who are responsible for the day-to-day activities of the centre. Managers must handle personnel matters, such as recruitment and staff training. In addition, as most centres are open long hours, they may have to arrange shift rotas for themselves and their staff. Although their role is primarily one of organizing other people, they may also spend some time coaching and instructing, checking and maintaining equipment, and helping out at reception.

Managers may promote their centres by giving talks at schools, colleges, clubs and so on, and may be involved in preparing brochures and other publicity materials. Publicizing the centre and increasing the use of its facilities is an important part of a manager's job. Centres operated by commercial organizations are run as money-making operations, and high on the list of managers' responsibilities is maintaining and improving profitability. Local authority and other centres, while not primarily profit-making, must still be run as efficiently as possible and be seen to provide value for money.

Centres cover a wide range of interests and activities. They may include popular sports and pastimes such as swimming and keep-fit, as well as more specialized ones like judo, archery, gymnastics or canoeing. Depending on the facilities, managers and their staff have to ensure that fuel for warming the premises, chemicals for the pool and equipment, such as badminton nets, mats and trampolines, are available and in good order.

Often the interests of the various user groups – eg schools, clubs and the public – may be in conflict, especially in a small centre. The manager has to balance all interests and try to arrive at a solution acceptable to everyone. Although managers have an executive role and are primarily responsible for organizing others, they must also be prepared to step in themselves when required – for example, to cover at reception or to take over a class when a coach or instructor fails to arrive.

Sports and leisure centres are also used for craft fairs, exhibitions, conferences and sports tournaments. These involve a great deal of work for managers and their staff. Competitive quotations for use of facilities and meals have to be provided and then, once accepted, everything has to be prepared. Managers must arrange for part-time security staff and stewards to be hired if necessary, and ensure that sufficient tables and chairs, and any other equipment required, are available. They must also be there on the day to handle any problems if and when they arise.

WORK ENVIRONMENT

Centres vary considerably, but all managers spend a good deal of time working in an office. They may visit schools and clubs to give talks, and local council offices for meetings. This is likely to involve driving.

Most of a centre manager's work is carried out indoors, though at centres with outdoor facilities some time may be spent outside, coaching or instructing. They may also be involved with some water sports.

SKILLS AND INTERESTS

Self-motivation, administrative ability and management skills are essential.

Attention to detail and the ability to plan one's own work and the work of others is important. Numeracy is required to cope with the financial aspects of the job, such as book-keeping and budgeting.

Managers need business acumen and flair, to develop ideas for attracting new customers, and for increasing the use of facilities by existing ones. Interpersonal skills are also important. Managers must be able to relate well with their staff, colleagues in other organizations and departments, centre management committees and the general public. They need sufficient authority to tell staff what to do and to take charge when necessary (eg in an emergency). On the other hand, they must also be able to deal with any personnel problems fairly and sympathetically. They must be good team workers, capable of delegating responsibility where possible, and able to enthuse staff and motivate them to perform at their best.

Managers need good verbal skills for giving instructions, talking to people (in groups or individually) and expressing their views and recommendations at meetings. They must be capable of tact and diplomacy when required, for example when handling complaints from the public. Good written skills are needed for preparing reports and letters.

They must be enthusiastic about sport and recreation, and, as this is a service business, enjoy working with and helping people. They must be able to see a task through, analyse statistics and plan a budget. They are responsible for the efficient day-to-day running of their centre, and for the health and safety of visitors and those working there.

ENTRY REQUIREMENTS

Employers increasingly require an applicant for sports and leisure centre management to have a recognized qualification. This can mean one of a number of awards, as there is no single clear-cut route to becoming a sports and leisure centre manager. Practical experience is also essential in applicants for senior posts. Those with purely academic qualifications should not expect to start any higher than middle management level (eg assistant manager).

Degree courses leading to qualifications in sports and leisure management are available. It is also possible to study for a first degree in another subject, then take a postgraduate course. The minimum qualifications needed for admission to a degree course are five GCSEs/S grades (A-C/1-3) with two A levels or three H grades, or equivalent.

There are also BTEC/SCOTVEC Higher National courses in Leisure Studies, and GNVQs/GSVQs in Leisure and Tourism. There are no entry requirements for GNVQs/GSVQs; however applicants need to prove they can successfully undertake the course and colleges may set their own requirements. Entry to a BTEC/SCOTVEC higher national course requires five GCSEs/S grades (A-C/1-3) with one A level or two H grade passes, or equivalent.

It is possible to enter sports and leisure centre management without educational qualifications, either by starting with a NVQ/SVQ in Sport and Recreation at Level 1, or by taking an award provided by one of the professional bodies, once relevant experience has been gained. A good standard of general education, including English and maths, is useful. Anyone wanting to take this route should already be employed in the industry (see article 4. SPORTS AND LEISURE CENTRE ASSISTANT).

The Recreation Managers Association of Great Britain runs a correspondence course aimed at people recently employed within clubs or leisure centres. There is also a Certificate (Recreation) course run by the National Examining Board for Supervisory Management (NEBSM).

Whatever educational standards are reached, anyone entering sports and leisure centre management would normally study toward the Institute of Leisure and Amenity Management (ILAM) or the Institute of Sport and Recreation Management (ISRM) qualifications and membership.

In many cases, sports and leisure centre managers need to be able to drive.

Where work at a centre involves looking after a swimming pool, a manager is expected to hold, or be capable of gaining, the Pool Lifeguard Bronze Medallion Award of the Royal Life Saving Society. Some employers ask for Red Cross or St John's Ambulance first aid qualifications. In some cases, ability in one or more sports can be a big advantage, as can coaching or instructing qualifications.

Entry may be possible for young people through Modern Apprenticeships, leading to at least an NVQ/SVQ Level 3. Contact your local careers office, TEC/LEC for details.

TRAINING

Training to become a sports and leisure centre manager can be done by either part-time or full-time study. It can also be a combination of both.

One way is to take a degree course in Leisure Studies or Recreation Management and then look for a job in a sports/leisure centre. There are now numerous such courses run at colleges and universities throughout the country. They last three years, and lead to either a BA or BSc honours degree. Courses have varying emphases. Courses may concentrate on business management, sports or movement science, physical education, sociology, etc. It is therefore important to study individual prospectuses carefully before making any application. Many courses include the opportunity to gain coaching qualifications in one or more sports, and this can be particularly useful for jobs in centres where managers are expected to be able to take coaching sessions.

It is also possible to take a first degree in another subject

and follow this up with a postgraduate qualification in sport or recreation. Most commonly these are MA or MSc, or the Diploma in Management Studies (DMS). Courses are available at many colleges and universities, including Bangor, Birmingham, Cardiff, Loughborough, Sheffield, Southampton and the Moray House Institute at Heriot-Watt University. Courses usually last for one or two years. They are well regarded by employers, and competition for places is intense.

BTEC Higher National Diplomas (full-time) and Certificates (part-time) in Leisure Studies and related subjects are available at colleges throughout England, Wales and Northern Ireland. SCOTVEC higher national certificate/higher national diplomas are available at Aberdeen, Falkirk, Fife, Motherwell and Stow. A higher national certificate takes two years full-time or three years part-time, a higher national diploma two years full-time or three years part-time.

A number of colleges and schools are offering the Advanced GNVQ/GSVQ Level III in Leisure and Tourism; this is normally a two-year full-time course.

It is unlikely that a holder of a degree, higher national diploma or even a postgraduate qualification would obtain a manager's job without experience. They would be most likely to start as a trainee or assistant manager and work their way up as they gain experience and further qualifications. During this stage of their careers, trainee managers would normally study for vocational qualifications, such as those offered by the Institute of Leisure and Amenity Management (ILAM) or the Institute of Sport and Recreation Management (ISRM).

ILAM operates a Qualification Scheme based on the completion of work-based projects. The ILAM Scheme is at four levels; it is not course-based and does not require attendance at college. For the ILAM First Award, candidates must complete a project of 1,500-2,000 words. For the ILAM Certificate in Leisure Operations, 3,000-4,000 words are required. For the ILAM Certificate in Leisure Management, the project must be 5,000-7,000 words, and for the ILAM Diploma in Leisure Management, 8,000-10,000 words. Projects are related to real practical issues and problems in the candidate's own place of work.

To enter the ILAM Awards at each level, candidates must have attained NVQs/SVQs in leisure-related competencies, or have completed an appropriate college-based award in a leisure-related area. People working in the industry, but without such qualifications, may apply to have their experience recognized under the Institute's Recognition of Prior Experience Scheme.

Courses for the Institute of Sport and Recreation Management's examinations are held in colleges across the country on a day release and evening basis, and a correspondence course is also available. The main qualification for managers is the ISRM Sport and Recreation Management Certificate. The examination for this consists of four modules: operational management; resource management and administration; sport and recreation facility planning, design and technology; and sport and recreation environment. Candidates with other qualifications recognized by the ISRM may be given exemptions from up to three of the modules. Holders of the Certificate are entitled to apply for full membership of the Institute (MInstSRM).

The ISRM also offers a Diploma Examination for experienced managers who already possess the Certificate. This is designed to provide sports and leisure centre managers with the knowledge and understanding to progress to senior management levels, and/or to manage major facilities. The ISRM Diploma consists of two modules: the management of people, finance, and information; and the management of recreation technology. Qualification at this level is recognized by diploma membership of the Institute (MInstSRM Dip).

Other categories of ISRM membership are available for those without the qualifications above. For example, candidates studying for the Sport and Recreation Management Certificate may become registered students. Associate membership is open to people with various qualifications, including the ISRM's own Sport and Recreation Technician's Certificate and Sport and Facility Supervisor's Certificate; NVQ in Sport and Recreation Facility Operation at Level 2; and NVQ in Sport and Facility Supervision at Level 3. Applicants for associate membership must also have suitable experience in the industry.

Associate membership of the ISRM is also open to those who have a recognized qualification and relevant experience in an area associated with recreation facilities or management, for example architects, engineers, or managers with other professional qualifications.

Sports and leisure centre management is increasingly becoming a graduate profession. It is, however, possible to become a manager without having a degree or higher national certificate/higher national diplomas, perhaps by starting at operative or technician level and working one's way up. (Please see article 4. SPORTS AND LEISURE CENTRE ASSISTANT.) One common approach is to do a part-time college course, then go on to study for ILAM or ISRM awards. Anyone considering a college course needs to check carefully whether it will suit their needs and whether the qualifications are acceptable to gain admission on to a vocational training course. To study for ILAM or ISRM management qualifications, for instance, candidates are recommended to have an NVQ/SVQ at Level 3 or 4, four GCSEs/S grades (A-C/1-3), including one A level or two H grades, an Advanced GNVQ/GSVQ Level III in Leisure and Tourism, or equivalent qualifications.

LATE ENTRY

Sports and leisure centre management is an area where employers do take on adults. Athletes, former athletes, coaches, and semi-professional or ex-professional sportsmen/women may have an advantage. Some colleges are prepared to relax their normal entry requirements in the case of adult students with relevant interests and/or experience.

Both the ILAM and ISRM are prepared to relax their normal academic entry requirements for management courses for candidates over the age of 23. They must have had at least three years' management or supervisory experience, or have worked for at least five years in the industry.

OPPORTUNITIES

Sports and leisure centre management is an area where opportunities have increased greatly in recent years, as people have had more time for leisure pursuits, and a growing awareness of the importance of physical fitness. As a luxury industry, however, leisure is also vulnerable to downturns in the economy.

Opportunities occur throughout the country, in rural as well as urban areas. Many centres are run by councils as a service to the local community, but an increasing number are being opened by commercial operators. Large employers, such as the health service and police, provide centres for the benefit of their staff. Educational institutions, such as universities, also run centres for staff and students, and there are some centres run by voluntary groups or trusts.

Five national centres are operated by The Sports Council. These are: Bisham Abbey, Lilleshall, Holme Pierrepont (water sports), Plas y Brenin (mountain activities) and Crystal Palace. There are a number of major sports centres in Scotland, including Inverclyde, Glenmore Lodge and Aviemore. Opportunities also exist to work in sports and leisure centres overseas.

PAY AND CONDITIONS

Salaries vary according to location, experience and responsibilities. Junior/trainee managers can expect to earn up to £12,000; middle managers from £15,000 to £20,000; and senior managers from £20,000 upwards. In local authority centres, payment is based on nationally or locally agreed scales; in commercial centres, payment may be negotiable, based on performance and the profitability of the centre.

Managers at local authority centres work a 37-hour, five-day week. Many centres are open from 7am until 10pm, making some antisocial hours necessary. Senior managers may have to work longer hours.

Managers employed by local authorities may be required to attend council meetings in the evenings. Evening and weekend work is usually done on a rota basis and shared between the manager and deputies or assistants.

PROSPECTS

Promotion prospects for sports and leisure centre managers are to more senior management positions in large centres, though to get such jobs, managers have to be prepared to move to another location. For managers who work in local authorities, there are also prospects of moving into administrative positions in the recreation department. Many authorities prefer sports and leisure administrators who have had experience of managing a centre.

RELATED OCCUPATIONS

Sports coach/instructor, professional sportsman/woman, retail manager, countryside/conservation officer, local authority administrator, sports and leisure centre assistant.

FURTHER INFORMATION AND READING

Please see article 4. SPORTS AND LEISURE CENTRE ASSISTANT.

4. SPORTS AND LEISURE CENTRE ASSISTANT (GAJ)

THE WORK

Sports and leisure centre assistants carry out a range of duties concerned with sport and recreation.

Their work varies according to the type of centre and the exact nature of their job. Many assistants spend some or all of their time working at reception. This may involve selling tickets and taking bookings or reservations, eg for use of squash courts; accepting payments and giving receipts; responding to personal and telephone enquiries; general clerical and administrative work; and handling complaints.

Other responsibilities may include keeping sports areas clean and tidy; looking after sports equipment; setting up equipment, such as badminton nets or table tennis tables; setting out tables and chairs for public events; and generally assisting other staff and users of the centre.

In centres with a swimming pool, assistants who are suitably qualified may work as swimming pool attendants. This involves keeping a close watch on people using the pool, especially children and beginners. The attendant usually sits in an elevated observation chair giving a good view across the pool. The attendant may have to rescue a swimmer in difficulty. In the event of an accident the attendant provides first aid, including resuscitation if required. Some attendants also give swimming instruction.

Some assistants have specific responsibility for the safe and hygienic operation of the pool and associated facilities, such as spa pools, Jacuzzis and showers. They ensure that heating, ventilation and filtration equipment is working correctly; treatment chemicals are maintained at the correct levels; and electrical equipment, such as pumps, is regularly maintained and operating safely and efficiently.

Assistants with coaching qualifications may run classes and give personal tuition and instruction in a wide range of sports and activities. These could include aerobics, keep-fit, dance, yoga, ta'i chi, squash, tennis, judo, weightlifting and many more. (Please see article 1. SPORTS COACH/ INSTRUCTOR).

Some assistants work in catering facilities or bars. Their duties include assisting customers, preparing and serving food and drinks, taking payments and giving change, washing up, and generally keeping the facilities clean and tidy.

Experienced sports and leisure centre assistants may have supervisory responsibilities, for example organizing duty rotas and arranging cover if other staff are off sick.

WORK ENVIRONMENT

Sports and leisure centre assistants work mainly indoors. Many centres do have some outdoor facilities, however, and assistants may spend some time working outside, coaching or supervising sports such as tennis or football.

Sports and leisure centres are mainly clean, light and airy. In swimming pools, however, the chlorine-based chemicals used to treat the water can cause breathing irritation in some people. Newer forms of water treatment are less prone to this.

For assistants whose jobs include coaching or instructing, the work may require considerable personal mobility. Catering and bar assistants may spend much of the time on their feet. Pool attendants, on the other hand, spend lengthy periods sitting in one place. Reception assistants may spend much of their time either sitting or standing.

Most assistants work on one site only, and they are rarely required to travel. They do, however, often have to work unsocial hours, including evenings and weekends. Many sports and leisure centre assistants work shifts.

SKILLS AND INTERESTS

Sports and leisure centre assistants must have an interest in sport. Some sporting ability is helpful, and essential if the job involves coaching or instructing.

Assistants need to be cheerful and outgoing, and enjoy working with the public. They should be courteous and helpful, and able to work as members of a team. Flexibility and adaptability are often required, for example in changing shifts to cover for a colleague who is off sick.

They must be conscientious and reliable. Assistants working as pool attendants need good powers of concentration, as they must watch events in the pool over a lengthy period and be prepared to intervene at a moment's notice if a swimmer appears to be getting into difficulties.

Good verbal communication skills are important, for example when coaching or giving classes. Sometimes assistants must be assertive, eg if some pool users are being rowdy or otherwise endangering the comfort and safety of other swimmers. They must also be tactful and diplomatic, for example when dealing with complaints from members of the public.

Assistants whose work involves handling money – such as reception and catering staff – must be trustworthy. They must be capable of adding up a bill and giving the correct change.

Assistants must have good general health and stamina to cope with the demands of the work and the variable, sometimes long hours.

ENTRY REQUIREMENTS

No formal academic qualifications are required to become a sports and leisure centre assistant. Personal qualities, such as self-motivation and a pleasant personality, are generally seen as more important. Some employers look for good GCSEs/S grades in English and maths. A good standard of general education is helpful, especially for those who hope to move on to supervisory and management positions.

Entry may be possible for young people through Modern Apprenticeships, leading to at least an NVQ/SVQ Level 3. Contact your local careers office, TEC/LEC for details.

According to the exact nature of the job, some specific qualifications may be required. Assistants whose work involves coaching or instructing require coaching qualifications in the sport concerned. These are normally acquired through part-time study, either in the candidate's own time or as part of a full-time course. For further information, please see article 1. SPORTS COACH/ INSTRUCTOR.

Swimming pool attendants must be good swimmers and are usually required to obtain life-saving qualifications, such as the Royal Life Saving Society's Pool Lifeguard Bronze Medallion.

Candidates for an Advanced GNVQ/GSVQ Level III in Leisure and Tourism need to prove that they can successfully undertake courses, and colleges may set their own requirements.

Candidates for a BTEC/SCOTVEC Higher National Diploma/Certificate in Leisure Studies require one A level or two H grades, with supporting GCSEs/S grades (A-C/1-3), or equivalent.

Assistants working in a licensed bar must be 18 years or over.

TRAINING

Many sports and leisure centre assistants begin on training schemes for young people, attending college part-time to study for further qualifications.

New assistants joining the industry may study for NVQs/

SVQs in Sports and Recreation. These qualifications are designed to provide a nationally comparable means of assessing and recognizing the skills and abilities of those working in leisure.

Full-time GNVQs are also being introduced for those who wish to study at school or college for a vocational qualification. The GNVQ in Leisure and Tourism – a broader-based qualification than the NVQs/SVQs mentioned above – is offered at a growing number of centres. GNVQs/GSVQs in Leisure and Tourism are available at three levels: Foundation, Intermediate/ Advanced Level I, II and III.

Assistants may also study for BTEC/SCOTVEC qualifications in Leisure Studies. The national certificate takes two years part-time and the national diploma three years part-time or two years full-time. Courses are available at colleges and institutes across the country.

Both ILAM and ISRM offer a wide range of short courses for sports and leisure centre assistants. The ISRM Sport and Recreation Technician's Scheme provides opportunities for staff to register with ISRM as Candidate Sport and Recreation Technicians. They may acquire modular qualifications over an open period of learning, and join the ISRM as associate members (AInstSRM). Training modules, normally studied over two or three days, include core skills, pool plant operations, customer care, reception work, operation of health and fitness suites and health/ fitness skills.

LATE ENTRY

Some opportunities exist for adults to enter this occupation, but they would normally have relevant qualifications or experience, eg in coaching.

Adults can gain recognition of their skills and experience by working towards NVQs/SVQs. There is open access to NVQs/SVQs – no academic qualifications are required, and there are no age limits. NVQs/SVQs are based on competence, and it does not matter how that competence has been gained – through experience, company training programmes, college courses or open learning. Past experience can be put forward as evidence of competence, via Accreditation of Prior Learning (APL).

OPPORTUNITIES

The last 20 years have seen a growth in interest in sports and leisure, and many new centres have been built. Opportunities occur throughout the country, in rural as well as urban areas.

Many centres are run by local councils as a service to the community, but an increasing number are being opened by commercial companies. These include private health clubs, gymnasiums, health and fitness centres, etc. There are also sports and leisure facilities in many hotels and holiday centres. Educational institutions, such as colleges and universities often run sports centres for staff and students. Large employers, such as the health service and police, also run centres for the benefit of their employees.

Competition to work in sports and leisure centres is intense, and those with relevant qualifications or experience have an advantage. As a luxury industry, leisure is vulnerable to downturns in the economy. In addition, many sports and leisure pursuits fluctuate in popularity.

PAY AND CONDITIONS

Salaries vary according to the job and the location. Assistants can expect to start on a salary of £7,000 to £9,000.

Assistants gaining qualifications may receive increments, and it may also be possible to augment income through part-time teaching and/or coaching work. Assistants at some centres may receive commission for enrolling new members.

Many centres are open from early in the morning until late at night, six or seven days a week, making some antisocial hours necessary. Many assistants are required to work shifts, for example 7am to 2.30pm one week, 2.30pm to 10pm the next. They also have to work some weekends.

Some part-time work may be available, especially for those with relevant experience.

PROSPECTS

Prospects exist for promotion initially to supervisory level. Pool attendants may be promoted to baths supervisor, where their responsibilities may include arranging duty rotas and organizing cover if a member of staff is off sick. Alternatively, they may be promoted to sports hall supervisor, with a wide range of duties and responsibilities. Courses for supervisors are run by a variety of organizations, including NEBSM, ILAM and ISRM.

For those with the ability and aptitude, there are also prospects for progression to sports and leisure centre management. To make the move to this level, a management qualification such as the Diploma of Management Studies (DMS) – available at many colleges and institutes – is a necessity. This normally requires two years' part-time study. The ladder of promotion varies from centre to centre; it is likely to involve progressing from the post of assistant manager, responsible for some specific area of operations, such as the gymnasium, to deputy manager and finally to manager.

RELATED OCCUPATIONS

Sports coach/instructor, professional sportsman/woman, retail assistant, receptionist, counter service assistant, tourist information centre assistant, groundsman/woman, sports and leisure centre manager

FURTHER INFORMATION

Central Council of Physical Recreation (CCPR)*, Francis House, Francis Street, London SW1P 1DE, 0171 828 3163/4

Institute of Sport and Recreation Management (ISRM)*, Giffard House, 36/38 Sherrard Street, Melton Mowbray, Leicestershire LE13 1XJ, 01664 65531

Institute of Leisure and Amenity Management (ILAM), ILAM House, Lower Basildon, Reading, Berkshire RG8 9NE, 01491 874222

Local Government Management Board*, 4th floor, The Arndale Centre, Arndale House, Luton, Bedfordshire LU1 2TS, 01582 451166

National Coaching Foundation*, Information Centre, 114 Cardigan Road, Headingley, Leeds LS6 3BJ, 0113 274 4802

Recreation Managers Association of Great Britain*, Recreation House, 7 Burkinshaw Avenue, Rawmarsh, Rotherham, South Yorkshire S62 7QZ, 01709 522463

Scottish Sports Council*, Caledonia House, South Gyle, Edinburgh EH12 9DQ, 0131 317 7200

The English Sports Council*, 16 Upper Woburn Place, London WC1H 0QP, 0171 388 1277

FURTHER READING

Leaflets/booklets are available from the addresses marked*.

Job Outlines – Physical Education and Sport – COIC
Working in Leisure – COIC
Careers in Sport and Recreation – CCPR
Careers in Sport – Kogan Page

Periodicals: Recreation; The Leisure Manager.

In the careers library classified under GAJ.

1. **PRODUCTION ASSISTANT CLCI:GAL**
2. **RESEARCHER CLCI:GAL**
3. **FLOOR/STAGE MANAGER/ASSISTANT DIRECTOR CLCI:GAL**
4. **CAMERAMAN/WOMAN/CAMERA OPERATOR CLCI:GAL**
5. **SOUND TECHNICIAN/OPERATOR CLCI:GAL**

BACKGROUND INFORMATION

This is a very complex industry with a range of jobs involved. On major projects, eg a feature film or TV drama, the structure would be roughly as follows:

Producers have overall responsibility for completion on time and within budget – they may make many early decisions on writer/script, the choice of director and performers and generally oversee the organizational and financial side. The director makes most of the creative decisions, directing the actors, and briefing the designers, camera team, sound crew, editors, etc on the effect they want to achieve. The producer may be assisted by a production manager who deals with the day-to-day organization, and a production accountant who keeps track of the financial aspects. In TV, a production assistant acts as the director's personal assistant. A set designer (or production designer/art director) and a costume designer design settings and costumes. During filming, an assistant director (in film) or floor manager (in TV) is responsible for ensuring that all the practical things needed are present and ready, either in the studio (or 'sound stage') or on location, and has a key role in shooting. After shooting/recording, especially if film is being used, a picture editor and sound editor assemble the material to make the finished product, and post-production may involve recording sound effects and specially composed music and mixing or dubbing the various soundtracks together (voice, music, sound effects). Many other people are involved from carpenters and electricians to stuntmen/women and drivers.

For documentary or news TV, the team is much smaller and many tasks are doubled up. A researcher gathers information on the subject, finds suitable people to be interviewed and places to be filmed, and writes a script or treatment. An independent video production company may have as few as four people on a shoot – director, camera operator, sound recordist and a camera assistant (or general assistant/runner).

Most feature films, many commercials, some pop promos and some films and dramas for TV are made on celluloid film that is processed and printed by a film laboratory. Other TV programmes and most corporate and non-broadcast videos are created on videotape using electronic cameras. The period of scripting and planning before filming is called 'pre-production'; the actual filming or recording is 'production'; and the process of editing the picture and soundtrack is known as 'post-production'.

A big theatre production (eg a West End play) will have a structure that is similar in many ways, though the stage manager takes the place of the floor manager and, to some extent, the production assistant, and the company manager that of the production manager. There are no camera people involved but there may be a sound technician/designer and a lighting designer. In theatre, the term 'company' often means the team of people brought together to mount a specific play or show.

Structure of the industry

Feature film production companies. Basically, these may be just a producer and a secretary, or producers, secretaries and management people in a larger company. Other staff are employed for their particular specialism on a freelance basis.

Broadcast TV companies. These include BBC TV at national and regional levels and the ITV network companies. They have their own studios and equipment, edit suites, etc. They employ some staff in all categories for the programmes they make themselves, though increasingly these are on fairly short-term (eg one-year) renewable contracts, and they take on additional freelances as required. They also buy ready-made programmes from other countries and commission independent production companies to make at least 25 per cent of their programmes for them. Channel 4 and S4C operate entirely on a commissioned-programme basis.

Satellite and cable TV companies. These put out mainly programmes and films bought from other sources, but create linking and promotional material and some programmes themselves, eg cable companies do local news. For this, they employ some production staff plus freelances.

Independent production companies. There are more than 1,000 of these; the vast majority with only a few permanent staff. They make commissioned TV programmes and TV films and/or corporate videos, commercials, pop promos, educational or training videos – including interactive videos – and videos for sale in bookshops. The larger ones have their own studio and post-production facilities and employ some production staff full-time but most hire in freelances or the services of facilities houses, as needed for each project.

In-house film/video/audio-visual units. Some major industrial and commercial concerns and non-business organizations have their own units or departments to create promotional and training videos for the company's own use. Some of these employ production technicians full-time, though many have a producer who hires in freelances and facilities for each project. The technicians may also look after closed-circuit TV and audio-visual aspects of sales and training activities. Some universities and colleges also employ multiskilled technicians to provide audio-visual services.

Facilities houses and suppliers. These range from film studios to post-production facilities, such as video editing suites and sound mixing (dubbing) studios, but also include companies that hire out camera, sound and lighting equipment, costumes and props, build scenery, search for suitable locations, create computer graphics sequences, etc. Some employ full-time staff to operate equipment and resources provided to clients; others have a list of technicians they call in to meet demand. Some of them also service theatre and radio/recording.

West End and touring theatre production companies. Some touring companies are subsidized and create a full company for at least a season. Commercial companies are more likely to put together a new company from freelance performers and technicians for each show they produce, though they may have some staff on retainers, moving them from show to show if they have a continuing programme of productions. Length of employment may depend on the success of a show in attracting audiences, determining the length of a West End run. Some fringe and small-scale touring companies are very small and performers and stage managers may act as technicians, too.

Subsidized national and regional repertory theatres. Companies like the National Theatre, Royal Opera House, and Bristol Old Vic maintain a permanent staff of technicians, including stage management, lighting and sound; and some performers will be under contract for a long period. Other staff may be recruited for specific productions or a season.

Theatrical venues. West End theatres in London and touring theatres in other cities are hired by theatre production companies wanting to present their show. The venues usually have front-of-house and technical staff that include technicians capable of setting up and operating the lighting and sound, though big productions may take their own people for these tasks. The same applies to small-scale and fringe touring venues, down to the cabaret circuit in pub rooms, though in some cases the venue manager may act as the technician.

Network radio. Network radio includes BBC Radios 1, 2, 3, 4 and 5 and the two independent channels. At both national and regional levels these have their own studio facilities and make many of their own news, drama, documentary, etc programmes for transmission. They are similar to BBC TV and ITV in their employment policies – most staff are on fixed-term or 'rolling' contracts.

Local radio stations. These include BBC local stations and Independent Local Radio (about 120 companies), which broadcast to specific geographic areas and/or ethnic/cultural communities. All employ multiskilled technicians to maintain and operate their equipment, though radio journalists, presenters and disc jockeys may prepare news items and programmes and do an element of operating themselves. Average staff of an ILR station is about twelve.

Independent radio/audio production companies: operate much like independent TV/video production companies, offering ideas to radio stations and making commissioned drama or documentary programmes, but may also create audio tapes on special topics, eg car maintenance or readings of novels for sale in newsagents and record shops, or make training tapes, audio-magazines or recordings of conferences for industrial and commercial concerns.

Closely associated with this field is the music and recording industry.

The film and TV industry has changed a lot in recent years and is still changing. Pressures from new technology, de-regulation, the ending of the union closed shop, and the drive to cut costs are resulting in, for instance, multiskilling, which in effect means the merging of several jobs into one, whereby a camera operator may handle lighting and sound and even some editing tasks. But it is still not clear how these mergers will work out. The changes also tend to mean that working hours are longer for less remuneration and with less favourable conditions. A much smaller proportion of the industry's workers are long-term employees and most are now freelance and 'casualized'. However, entry is more open, though this means that the competition for places in employment and on relevant education and training courses has intensified.

1. PRODUCTION ASSISTANT (GAL)

THE WORK

TV

The production assistant (PA) functions as personal assistant to the director or producer, giving organizational and secretarial support. In the planning stage of drama programmes, the director has meetings with the designers, lighting, camera, sound experts and leading performers to discuss how the play or show is going to be done. The PA attends, takes notes of any decisions and follows up with minutes or memos and phone calls to make sure everyone knows what they have to do and that it has been done, and receives messages back for the director. It may be possible to pass some of the typing work to a production secretary. The PA may arrange meetings, book rehearsal rooms and hotel accommodation, book or hire equipment, crews, catering facilities and other services, and type up and circulate the script, rehearsal schedule, shooting schedule and shotlist. They may also clear permission-to-film and copyright on, for example, the music used.

During rehearsals, often held in rooms outside the studios, or meetings with the scriptwriter or researcher, changes may be made to the script that have to be typed up and circulated. This can happen repeatedly. Other changes may be made, or requirements realized, that call for modifications of set, costumes, type of camera equipment needed, and so on, and these have to be passed on to the relevant department for action. During the final camera rehearsal and actual recording in the studio, the PA sits with the director in the control room. They call out cues over 'talk-back' systems to the camera operators and other technicians, pass messages to the floor manager, time each sequence with a stopwatch to make sure the finished programme will be the correct length (critical with TV to fit standard time-slots), advise the presenter to speed up or slow down, and take notes of any comments of the director that require action. During post-production, the PA's notes and timings are important to the picture and sound editors and they may refer to the PA to answer queries that arise. On completion, the PA makes sure the finished videotape reaches the transmission point on time.

On location, filming with a single camera, the PA also handles the functions of the continuity person in films, carefully noting the position of everything, especially actors' hands, to ensure everything matches up when the camera is moved to shoot from a different angle.

In short, the PA is the main co-ordinator of a programme or series and a key figure in bringing it in on time, to length and within budget.

Radio

PAs here do similar work in the assisting producer/director, booking studio space and facilities, keeping track of programme expenditure, etc. They may also make arrangements for guests and interviewees and look after them.

Film

There is no directly comparable role. The production manager or, sometimes, on feature films, a production co-ordinator does the work of arranging transport for crews and equipment, making location arrangements, booking facilities, catering, accommodation, etc.

Theatre

Some large theatre and opera companies have a production assistant who helps with administrative/organizational tasks, but it is not a clearly defined occupation, as in TV and radio.

WORK ENVIRONMENT

Much of the work is in a production office, but the PA also attends meetings in a variety of offices and meeting rooms, may have call to visit the camera, sound, lighting, set construction and wardrobe departments, sits with the director and vision mixer in the enclosed control room, checks that everything is ready on the studio floor and goes on location to whatever places are involved. Location work may involve travel to other parts of Britain or foreign countries, working in buildings, city streets, the depths of wild country, and being away from home for short or long periods.

SKILLS AND INTERESTS

Social and communication skills are needed to relate tactfully and confidently to technicians and professionals inside the company and suppliers and contacts outside. PAs must be able to work quickly and calmly under pressure but still need to be accurate, to analyse, organize and assess priorities, and to interpret instructions correctly. They should be able to split their attention, keeping an eye or ear on one activity while doing something else themselves. A methodical and orderly mind is needed to keep track of the different versions of the script and amendments, as well as of matters that await resolution.

Some financial awareness is important in handling budgets and spreadsheets. Stamina, a cheerful personality and sense of humour help the PA to cope with the pressure and long hours and get on easily with others in the production team. They also need initiative and self-reliance, normal eyesight and hearing, good colour vision (in TV) and a clear speaking voice. They need keyboard skills, and shorthand is an advantage.

ENTRY REQUIREMENTS

Basic educational requirements are a broad general education with three/four GCSEs/S grades (A-C/1-3) including English, but many PAs have A levels/H grades and some have degrees – usually in an arts subject; sometimes in media-related studies. Advanced and Intermediate GNVQs are available in Media, Communication and Production. GNVQs are intended to provide progression to higher education and industry. Other basics are speedy and accurate typing (about 40 wpm), reliable shorthand or speedwriting (about 100 wpm), and secretarial skills. Also required are previous secretarial and/ or organizing experience and familiarity with word processors/computers, gained in another job. Ability to talk knowledgeably about television, current affairs, theatre, music, films is an advantage, and experience in amateur dramatics, radio or film-making are useful.

TRAINING

After an initial short course, a trainee production assistant in TV or radio learns mainly on-the-job by working alongside and helping an experienced PA, usually with periods on different types of programme, and possibly with short courses to understand the more technical aspects. They are then given responsibility for segments or aspects of programmes, before handling PA duties on a programme on their own. However, they will be expected to have acquired some of their skills in earlier training and employment in secretarial or administrative work, before becoming a trainee PA.

There are few pre-entry training courses aimed specifically at this occupation. Film and Television Freelance Training (ft2) includes production assistant as one of its training areas. (Please see TRAINING in article 4.

CAMERAMAN/WOMAN/CAMERA OPERATOR.) A number of FE and HE courses will give an understanding of the production processes and techniques, so may be helpful (see course directories listed in FURTHER READING), but gaining secretarial skills may be more so. There are also a variety of short courses available in different aspects of film/TV/radio.

LATE ENTRY

This occupation is normally entered as an adult after experience in at least one job, often from within the TV or radio organization, with most PAs starting in their twenties. Later entry may be possible.

OPPORTUNITIES

The starting point with large TV companies is as a trainee production assistant. However, these posts are normally only advertised internally and are filled by people working in the company as a secretary, or in a clerical or administrative job. Competition for these posts is intense.

Independent production companies are likely to look for people with experience as a PA with a large TV company, though they may occasionally consider someone who has been a personal secretary or personal assistant in another industry, where organizing and co-ordinating was a significant part of the job.

When advertised publicly, job vacancies appear in *The Guardian, Broadcast, Screen International, The Stage* and *Television Today,* ethnic newspapers, some local newspapers. BBC external vacancies appear on CEEFAX page 696. Most smaller companies do not advertise, but appoint from people who contact them speculatively.

PAY AND CONDITIONS

A trainee with a regional TV company could expect a salary of about £12,000 and an experienced PA about £15,000. Senior PAs could earn £20,000 or more. Salaries in radio and in independent production companies are lower.

Working hours are unlikely to be regular, with early morning starts and late nights during busy periods being common. Some PAs work shifts. Overtime may be paid in some situations. PAs are more likely to be on permanent or renewable contracts, rather than freelance.

PROSPECTS

PAs progress from relatively straightforward programmes, eg local news and current affairs, to more complex and costly ones, and ultimately drama. The promotion line in major TV organizations is to senior PA, principal PA, senior principal PA, up to head of production assistants. These posts may give responsibility for all the PAs on a major series, in a department or in charge of all the PAs in a TV production company. The job gives a thorough understanding of the whole process of television production and transmission, with a knowledge of the different personnel and activities involved. This makes it a good training ground for future producers or production managers. PAs also move into positions as floor manager, vision mixer or researcher.

RELATED OCCUPATIONS

Production secretary, floor/stage manager/assistant director, assistant/associate producer, production manager, producer, director, continuity person, film/video editor.

FURTHER INFORMATION AND READING

Please see article 5. SOUND TECHNICIAN/ OPERATOR.

2. RESEARCHER (GAL)

THE WORK

TV

The work varies according to the nature of the programme involved. On a chat show, where a host interviews famous guests, the researcher provides the host with background notes on the life and career of each guest, suggestions for questions that may result in interesting anecdotes and possibly also photographs and film coverage of the guest when younger, for use in the programme. They may also put forward names of possible guests for the show's producer to decide on, research their availability and make the initial contacts with guests or their agent. On a quiz programme, the researcher has to find suitable people to take part, possibly selecting from hundreds of applicants responding to advertisements, provide information and opinions about them to enable the producer to select, and notes about amusing incidents in their lives and questions for the presenter.

On a current affairs programme, especially a local one, the researcher has to find suitable topics, incidents and people, possibly going out with a camera crew to film material for inserts or doing actual location interviews, either on or off-camera, themselves, and writing either a script or a treatment for the on-screen presenter in the studio. On a network current affairs programme, serious investigative journalism is involved, often on sensitive and controversial issues, which may incur personal risk.

On documentaries or arts programmes, the researcher may do library research into the subject, or interview visits to provide the producer, editor, director or scriptwriter with the information needed to compile the programme. This may also include finding suitable places and people to film, which could be in other countries, and locating and negotiating the use of old prints, paintings, photographs, newsreel/archive clips and appropriate music. They may write a script. When interviewees or participants come to the studio, the researcher may look after them, see that they are comfortable and at ease, explain what clothes they should wear, etc. The researcher would be expected to suggest ideas/topics for future programmes.

So the actual work may be reading or writing, looking through files of old photographs or screening old newsreels, phoning or writing to, or advertising for, potential subjects, dealing with agents or copyright holders of visual or audio material, going out to visit and assess possible locations and people, interviewing informally to gather information and provide cassette or photographic evidence of the suitability of a potential interviewee, typing up their findings, so the producer and director can make decisions, discussing these with them, setting up a schedule of visits/locations for reconnaissance or filming, or conducting filmed/recorded interviews. There will also be meetings and discussions with producer, director, editor, scriptwriter, presenter depending on the type of programme. Some researchers specialize, for example, in science, religion, or nature.

Radio

Broadly similar to TV, except that the title 'research assistant' is often used and the emphasis is more on research in books, newspapers and sound archives.

Film

Employment of researchers is not common. When it occurs, it is likely to be to provide information for historical movies (on costumes, customs, practices) or for scientific/technical plausibility on science fiction movies or those with a specialist basis, eg medical or legal. For these, people with specialist knowledge may be preferred to general researchers. Researchers may also be engaged for film documentaries, working in the same way as for TV documentaries.

Theatre

A researcher may be engaged occasionally (but very rarely) by the larger permanent theatres to research visual and textual material that will help designers, director and performers to achieve historical accuracy and/or to provide pictures and text for a programme booklet.

WORK ENVIRONMENT

Much is office-based: reading, at the keyboard, writing, or making phone calls. As many researchers are self-employed, freelances may work from home. Considerable time is spent in archives and libraries, and looking at possible locations, talking to possible subjects, taking notes, or recording on a pocket tape recorder. This could involve travel to many parts of the country or TV region and to other countries. During preparation for filming/recording, the researcher is present in the studio, dressing rooms and entertainment facilities, ensuring that subjects are briefed.

SKILLS AND INTERESTS

Communication and social skills are of prime importance. Researchers have to understand, and be understood by, a wide range of people, in different occupations and social classes, as well as communicating with their producer/ director/editor. They have to be able to get on friendly terms quickly and inspire trust, in order to draw out the information and co-operation required. They work alone and carry responsibility for their own work, so they need to be self-motivated, but also capable of relating and contributing as part of the production team. They should be open-minded and investigative, determined and resourceful.

Researchers should be logical and methodical in their approach and presentations, good at organizing themselves, able to think quickly and flexibly and to make decisions/recommendations. Intense concentration may be needed to sort out the essentials of a story that will make a good programme or item, plus the ability to then switch to a totally different topic. For magazine and news programmes, they may have to follow leads on several topics at the same time. They work under time pressure. Some programme series may have more than one researcher.

They need a clear speaking voice. Also important are keyboard skills, a good telephone manner, knowledge of reference/archive sources and production processes (to be able to reject subjects for filming/recording that cannot work for technical or logistical reasons). A driving licence and car may be essential for some projects.

ENTRY REQUIREMENTS

There are no minimum educational requirements, though about 75 per cent of researchers have a degree which, for many specialist researchers, is in their specialist subject.

However, staff vacancies tend to go to people already working in the organization, eg as production secretary or production assistant, or to applicants with experience in journalism. Their chances are increased if they have film, TV or radio experience as well. Those offering their skills as a freelance researcher also need a track record, usually in journalism, and knowledge of a specialist area helps. Fluency in one or more foreign languages opens up work on programmes about other countries, or possibly for production companies in other countries.

TRAINING

Most researchers have either gained experience in the research aspects of another job, as a journalist or editorial assistant on a newspaper or magazine, or production assistant in TV, or start on local current affairs programmes, learning on the job, and go on to more complex and specialist programmes. However, Film and Television Freelance Training (ft2) does include the research function and processes within its two-year new entrant training scheme.

An NVQ in Production Research is available at Level 3.

LATE ENTRY

Most researchers enter as adults after work in journalism, TV, radio or a specialist field. There is no maximum age limit.

OPPORTUNITIES

The BBC employs some full-time researchers on a permanent basis, though, even here, limited-term renewable contracts are becoming more usual. More common is a 'run-of-series' contract basis, though, in some cases, this can be quite long. Most researchers are employed on short fixed-term contracts for the pre-production and production period of, for example, a documentary series or quiz show. This may lead to a more established post, or they may find they go from contract to contract, but there are likely to be gaps. The work is usually on a freelance basis. In the corporate video and independent TV production area, contracts may be for only a few weeks, or even days, and may be on a daily-rate basis. They and film/theatre production companies engage researchers when a project requires one.

Local current affairs programmes sometimes provide a useful starting point with a local journalist suggesting topics to the producer or editor at a local radio or regional TV station, possibly topics the journalist has covered for a newspaper. Similarly, a national newspaper or magazine journalist, staff or freelance, may offer ideas in the special area they cover and be asked to follow through and so gain the necessary experience to become a regular freelance or contract researcher.

Some freelance researchers may do work in other fields, eg for magazine or book publishers, either as researchers or as writer/researchers.

Most companies and regional TV/radio stations that employ researchers are based in large cities. The majority of employers are in London and South East England, though there are centres in Edinburgh/Glasgow, Cardiff/Swansea and Manchester/Liverpool. Some independent production companies operate from a small town or rural situation.

Research posts on, for example, a major new documentary series are sometimes advertised externally. Job advertisements appear in *The Guardian* (Monday), *Broadcast, Screen International,* ethnic newspapers, some local newspapers. BBC external vacancies appear on CEEFAX page 696.

PAY AND CONDITIONS

Salaries for full-time posts for an experienced researcher may be from about £15,000 to £20,000 in TV, depending on size of the company, or £13,000 to £19,000 in radio. A researcher on salary with an independent production company has a minimum weekly rate of £368 and daily rate of £92. Freelance work could be based on a daily rate of from £100 to £400, depending on status of the project, experience and specialism, or, more usually, on an agreed fee for the whole project. Travel, accommodation and subsistence expenses will normally be paid for research visits away from base or home, and incidental expenses (eg phone and postage costs) when the production company's resources cannot be used. Overtime may be paid in some situations.

Some programmes may have a regular 9-5 work pattern, but most researchers have irregular hours that vary with the type of programme. It often involves evening and weekend work, as these are the times when people doing other jobs can be contacted, or because deadlines have to be met.

Freelancers may provide their own office space and equipment (eg word processor, tape recorder, camera).

PROSPECTS

There is no formal promotion ladder, though some companies promote to senior researcher and even associate producer. Researchers may move on to writing or journalism, to programme editor of documentary series, or to director or producer, for which the experience they gain of organizing the content of programmes is a good basis. Some join with one or more colleagues to start their own independent production companies. Some become presenters or newsreaders.

RELATED OCCUPATIONS

Journalist, screenwriter, production assistant, assistant producer, floor/stage manager, presenter.

FURTHER INFORMATION AND READING

Please see article 5. SOUND TECHNICIAN/OPERATOR.

3. FLOOR/STAGE MANAGER/ASSISTANT DIRECTOR (GAL)

THE WORK

These jobs relate to similar roles in different industries, but there are distinct differences.

Film

The assistant director (or first assistant director on a feature film) acts as the general foreman of the unit during filming in the studio or on location. On features, commercials and drama series created on film, this is a team activity with a first assistant director, second assistant director and third or even fourth assistant director. On documentaries, there may be one assistant director plus possibly a runner.

The first assistant director analyses the script with the

producer, director and production manager to break it down into scenes and arrive at a shooting schedule that will be most economical on time, both on different sets in the studio and on location, and can be divided into amounts of filming that can be achieved in a day's shoot (or night's in some cases). They make sure that the necessary equipment and props are ready and on-site and that the appropriate performers, crowd artists, hairdressers, make-up artists, and stuntpeople have been called. Having learnt from the director what the next camera position will be ('set-up') and the content of the picture (close-up, wide-shot, two-shot, etc), the first assistant director informs the camera and sound teams, so that they can get their equipment and the lighting ready. The first assistant director also tells the carpenters, painters, set-dressers, and so on to, for example, remove or replace a wall of a set if necessary, retouch paintwork or age a wall, or rearrange the props to suit the new camera angle.

When everyone is ready, the first assistant director calls a rehearsal, and performers and technicians practise to shoot the scene. Problems are spotted and adjustments may be made. When all is ready, the first assistant director calls for the studio doors to be shut, the red light switched on forbidding entry and everyone in the studio to be silent, for the lights to be switched on, for the camera motor to be started, and then tells the director all is ready for filming.

Because the first assistant director is tied to the shooting area, the second assistant director liaises with the producer and production manager off the set, and with the design and technical departments and prepares the call-sheet for the following day. The third and fourth assistant directors (sometimes called runners) call performers from their dressing rooms, run messages and fetch refreshments for leading technicians and performers and the director. The third assistant director usually gets the call-sheet copied and circulates it to everyone present – performers and technicians. This tells them if they are needed the following day and at what time. On location, the assistant directors could all be involved in cueing (eg a distant car not visible to the first assistant director to start and move into shot) by arm signals from one to another, or in requesting pedestrians or vehicles to stay out of an area where a shot is in progress. On a big crowd scene, they may each be involved in directing the action of the crowd artists ('extras') in sections of the set or location. If, for some reason, the first assistant director has to be away from the camera for a time, the second assistant director takes over, and so on down the line.

On documentary crews, there may be only one assistant director and a runner, or, on small video shoots, no assistant directors at all, with the director and possibly a researcher doing all the organizing and co-ordinating.

TV

The floor manager (FM) co-ordinates activity on the studio floor. The team includes assistant floor managers (much like the second assistant director above), who liaise between the production office and other departments and work out call times, and floor assistants, who call performers to make-up and set, run errands, deliver scripts, etc. With the director in the control room, the FM passes on instructions (relayed by the production assistant over headphones) to the performers, presenters, newscasters, celebrities and members of the public taking part in the programme. With studio audiences, safety and ready access to fire exits are major considerations of the FM. They may brief guests and audience on what is happening and how to relate to the cameras, microphones, etc. The FM thinks ahead to make sure everything is ready and everyone is in the right place at the right time. They may also book rehearsal rooms, mark out floorplans of the set (scenery) and act like a stage manager during rehearsals, though some TV companies have stage managers who handle this part of the production process. Floor management staff play similar roles on outside broadcasts (eg recording a pop concert) but, when film is used on location for a TV drama or programme, a film crew is used including assistant directors.

Theatre

The stage manager (SM) also co-ordinates during rehearsals and performances but, in this case, the director is not present during most of the performances, so that the SM carries full responsibility for ensuring that the show goes on at the right time and in the form and quality intended, with especial regard to safety.

Again, this is a team job, with a deputy stage manager (DSM) and one or more assistant stage managers (ASM). Tasks delegated to them vary from company to company, but often it is the DSM who runs performances from the prompt corner at the side of the stage and the ASM who has responsibility for obtaining and looking after hand props, arranging costume fittings, calling performers when needed, running messages to technical departments. Some tasks may be taken in turns.

With the director, the stage manager may prepare a rehearsal schedule and a production schedule for the main events: the design of sets and costumes, their construction and painting, the casting auditions if needed, the 'get in' (when the set is put up on stage and lighting and sound equipment are rigged/adjusted/focused), technical rehearsal, dress rehearsal, opening night, and the 'get out' if it is a short run (when the set and technical equipment are removed). They liaise with the technical departments to make sure everything is ready on time. They book rehearsal rooms and get them ready by marking out on the floor, with chalk or tape, the positions of the elements of scenery and furniture. They get together 'substitute props' to stand in for the furniture and for hand props such as guns, books, teacups, until these are obtained by the ASM or, in large companies, by the props department.

One of the team, usually the DSM, is present at all rehearsals, where they 'hold the book'. This is the prompt book, a specially pasted-up version of the acting script, with dialogue on one side and ruled-up sheets for notes on the other. They prompt the performers with any forgotten lines, but also note any changes to the dialogue, draw small sketches of the positions of the performers at key points and their moves, and note any special requirements of scenery, props, sound effects, and lighting changes as they are realized. The SM handles liaison and makes sure the relevant departments are informed.

When rehearsals are nearly complete, a final version of the prompt book is prepared, which becomes the company bible and contains all the sound and lighting cues and points to call performers from their dressing room in time for their entrance on stage. During performances, this is in the prompt corner at the side of the stage, as the guide for the DSM to call the performers and cue the lighting and sound operators either over headphones or by push buttons which operate red and green cue lights (though in large theatres the lighting is controlled by a computer program). From here they prompt performers with any forgotten lines. They also supervise the stagehands in any scene changes and may cue the fly gallery to raise or lower backcloths, or direct the person operating the revolving stage.

During a run, the SM is responsible for company discipline and, when the director has gone, if they feel aspects of the performance are slipping, they may call an extra rehearsal to get them right. If a performer is ill, they alert the stand-in/understudy and possibly rehearse them. If there is no stand-in, they may have to 'read-in' the part, going on stage and walking through the character's moves but reading the lines from a script. ASMs quite often do 'walk-on' and 'one-line' acting parts themselves.

In a small touring company, where there is no company manager, the SM may be responsible for organizing transport and accommodation, liaising with the management of the theatres they visit over get-ins, get-outs and rehearsals, briefing the resident technicians at these theatres, and even paying the performers at the end of each week.

Radio

The studio manager fills this role as well as some duties of a sound technician or recordist. Please see article 5. SOUND TECHNICIAN/OPERATOR for more details.

WORK ENVIRONMENT

Film and TV studios are specially built to ensure that everything needed is to hand and within reach of workshops and equipment stores. They are usually big enclosed spaces, with smooth floors and many lights suspended above or on scaffolding, and capable of being made completely sound and lightproof when the doors are closed. Many TV programmes involve a studio audience, who can watch the crew as they work.

Outside broadcasts could be in concert halls or cathedrals. Location filming, whether for feature films, TV dramas or documentaries, may be in city streets, on mountains, in caves, factories, dockyards, offices, or people's homes, with all the complications of being away from full resources, variable weather and sometimes very cramped working conditions. Facilities (including catering), equipment and personnel may all have to be brought. On location (or touring for theatre), travel to other parts of Britain and to other countries is involved, which may mean short or long periods away from home.

Radio studios are generally smaller than film or TV studios and are enclosed, with artificial light. Normally the soundproof studio with table, chair and microphones where presenter, guests, and performers sit or stand is separated by a glass partition from the control room where the director/producer sits, which contains tape decks, record turntables, CD players, sound mixing desk, etc.

In theatre, stage managers spend time in rehearsal rooms, on stage, in the theatre auditorium, and in offices and also visit backstage dressing rooms and departments (eg wardrobe) and workshops where scenery is built.

SKILLS AND INTERESTS

The ability to handle people tactfully but firmly is the main requirement. There are a lot of people working under pressure and depending on one another to achieve results. Assistant directors/floor managers/stage managers have to be able to resolve differences, smooth things over and keep the show on the road. They need a strong personality, a clear analytical mind to spot the real basis of a problem and devise a solution, and a methodical one to plan and organize very complex work processes, as well as calmness in a crisis, an ability to get on with everybody and to accept decisions made by the producer or director.

Leadership qualities, ability to work in a team, a commanding voice and manner and the ability to deal tactfully with the conflicting interests of different personalities and departments all help. Though often not technically expert themselves, they need to understand the technical aspects, because they have to relate to skilled technicians on a knowledgeable basis that wins respect. They need to be alert and keep a clear mind despite the high level of stress and long hours.

In film work, a driving licence is useful and a knowledge of one or more languages opens up employment on films being shot in other countries, possibly using some foreign technicians.

ENTRY REQUIREMENTS

Film

There are no minimum requirements, but some entrants now have C&G or BTEC/SCOTVEC certificates or diplomas and/or degrees in media-related subjects. Traditionally, many start as third or fourth AD (runner) and work their way up. Gaining experience as a runner or in a junior position within another area of the industry, eg post-production facilities house or film laboratory, may make it easier to obtain work as a third AD on a film production. Evidence of good work in an organizing capacity on student or amateur films/videos/theatre can help a lot, as well as indicating knowledge of the production process. It is possible for applicants with experience in student productions to be taken on as first or second AD on an independent feature or pop promo.

TV

Entry is usually post-experience, either from other jobs in TV, such as production assistant or camera assistant (from which they may be seconded for a period to discover aptitude), as a stage manager in theatre, or an assistant director in films. Floor assistants may be recruited from secretarial, clerical or administrative staff in the same TV company.

Theatre

Entry is usually as an ASM, for which there are no minimum requirements, but many applicants have done a drama school course in stage management or have a degree in drama or theatre studies. Practical experience in a stage management role on student or amateur theatre productions is advisable. Casual work in a local theatre, as, for example, stage hand or front-of-house manager is useful. For details of courses, refer to ABTT or Conference of Drama Schools directories listed in FURTHER READING in article 5. SOUND TECHNICIAN/OPERATOR.

Radio

Please see article 5. SOUND TECHNICIAN/OPERATOR.

Entry requirements for C&G courses vary, so check locally. For national certificate/diploma courses they are four GCSEs/S grades (A-C/1-3); for higher national courses one/two A levels/H grades and four GCSEs/S grades (A-C/1-3); for degree courses five GCSEs/S grades and two/three A levels/H grades. However, competition for places on media courses is high, so a keen interest in the arts, entertainment and current affairs and evidence of having gained some understanding of film/TV/theatre from work on school or amateur plays/films/videos may be vital.

TRAINING

Trainee floor managers learn mainly by working on the job alongside an experienced floor manager, possibly with short off-the-job courses. Otherwise, entrants in the most junior grade (floor assistant/third assistant director/assistant stage manager) learn the higher-level jobs by observing as they handle their own duties.

Faced with the changeover to freelance contracts, the industry has created traineeships, some of which relate to this area (eg ft2 Film and Television Freelance Training). Please see article 4. CAMERAMAN/WOMAN/CAMERA OPERATOR for more information.

Many people obtain training before entry by doing a BTEC/SCOTVEC national certificate/diploma or higher national certificate/diploma course or a degree or postgraduate course at an FE/HE college. Some people take short courses or evening classes in film/video/TV techniques or drama.

For suitable courses, consult the course directories listed in FURTHER INFORMATION AND READING in article 5. SOUND TECHNICIAN/OPERATOR. Courses with a higher practical content may be most useful when applying for jobs.

The NVQ in Production at Level 3 includes units relevant to floor managers and assistant directors.

LATE ENTRY

There is no upper age limit and FE and degree courses are open to mature students (sometimes on the basis of life experience and/or an access course). However, most adult entrants to these jobs are moving from other jobs in film/TV/theatre, eg as a junior technician or stagehand.

OPPORTUNITIES

Generally, competition for work is very intense and deregulation has resulted in a lot more experienced technicians (previously staff in TV and broadcasting studios) working on a freelance basis, making entry for newcomers extremely difficult.

Film

Assistant director is, in the main, a freelance occupation with production companies engaging individuals as needed. Work at any level is on a project basis – a few days for a commercial or pop promo; several months for a major feature film. The film industry fluctuates drastically and there are times when very few films are being made, and so there are few opportunities.

TV

BBC TV, ITV companies and the larger independent TV/video production companies employ full-time floor managers. A common entry route is as holiday relief during the summer, which may lead to further engagements or a staff job.

Theatre

All producing theatres and most theatrical production companies need SMs, DSMs and ASMs (small touring companies may just have an SM), but the number of permanent theatres and touring companies has been reducing, which cuts opportunities and increases competition for jobs.

Most studios, production companies and theatres are in major towns and cities, with the bulk of them in London and the South East of England.

When advertised externally, job vacancy advertisements appear in *The Guardian, Broadcast, Screen International, The Stage* and *Television Today,* ethnic newspapers, some local newspapers. BBC external vacancies are on CEEFAX page 696.

PAY AND CONDITIONS

In major TV studios, salaries vary from about £10,000 for a floor assistant to about £20,000 for an experienced or supervisory FM, with significant variations between companies. Minimum weekly rate for an ASM in a major repertory theatre is £158 and for a SM on a West End production £315 (but on a big musical it would be much more). Minimum weekly salary for a first AD on a feature film is £368.50 and £313 for a second AD. A freelance third AD earns £207.50 minimum a week with a daily rate of £51.87.

Hours are often irregular. In films, early starts and late finishes are common. In TV, shift-working enables maximum use to be made of studios. In repertory theatre, rehearsals may take place for one production during the day, while the previous one is performed in the theatre during the evenings, and the same stage management team may handle both, though they may rotate some duties to provide some days or evenings off. In major subsidized and West End theatres, when working on performances, SMs would start late afternoon to prepare, and finish after the show when all performers have left the theatre. Because of the importance of the senior positions, they may take work home to prepare for the next day, reading and analysing scripts, preparing shotlists, schedules, and so on. In TV, theatre and major feature films, overtime working may be paid at overtime rates but, in independent production, it is increasingly common to sign a contract that includes a percentage of overtime within the agreed fee.

PROSPECTS

The job structures listed in THE WORK traditionally serve as promotion ladders with TV companies, going up to senior and supervisory grades of FM. On documentary films, TV programmes or videos made by small production companies, or in fringe theatre companies, there may be only one assistant director or stage manager. By being in on the start of such a company with, perhaps, other ex-students, employment and increasing experience can sometimes be assured.

The logical next step is to production manager in films and TV, and company manager or production manager in theatre, but some go on to director or producer.

Some people use an ASM post as a stepping stone to an acting career.

RELATED OCCUPATIONS

Road manager, production assistant, production manager/co-ordinator, assistant producer, producer, director, company manager.

FURTHER INFORMATION AND READING

Please see article 5. SOUND TECHNICIAN/OPERATOR.

4. CAMERAMAN/WOMAN/CAMERA OPERATOR (GAL)

Feature films, documentaries, commercials and non-broadcast videos are normally filmed with one camera and one camera crew, whether created on film or videotape. TV shows made inside a studio, and also TV outside broadcasts (OBs), such as sporting events, are created on several cameras at once, each with its own operator, with the director in a control room selecting from the available pictures to broadcast live or to record on tape for future broadcasting, while a vision mixer ensures a neat flow from camera to camera. The film or videotape from one-camera shoots goes to a film editor or video editor for editing, or 'cutting', to assemble shots in the final sequence, working with the director.

There are different standards of film (70mm for widescreen, 35mm for feature films and many commercials, and 16mm for documentaries and some independent features) and videotape (from one-inch for TV studio work and Beta SP for TV documentaries and quality corporate videos, to VHS for recording weddings). These call for different sizes and complexities of camera and any one cameraman/woman or camera operator may have experience of, or specialize in, only a limited range of these, though many of the skills involved are similar.

THE WORK

Film

In feature films, and in TV when shooting drama or commercials on celluloid film, rather than videotape, the senior member of the camera team is the lighting cameraman/woman (called director of photography or DP on major feature film productions). Other members are the camera operator, focus puller and clapper-loader. The DP discusses with the director and the production designer/art director the effect required, decides on the filmstock and lenses to be used, instructs the gaffer (who controls the electricians) on how to place the lights, their intensity and colour, agrees with the director and camera operator the positioning of the camera, any camera or lens movement, and the framing of the picture. The DP also instructs the laboratories in any special treatment required during processing, assesses the results of each day's filming and decides if anything needs to be shot again for lighting or camera reasons, and plans ahead to the next day's shoot. The DP is responsible for the photography, creating the right mood with light, shade and colour, eliminating unwanted shadows, making sure all that should be visible is, to create a pleasing or striking picture on the screen.

Some aspects of this may be delegated to the camera operator. As well as operating the camera while looking through the viewfinder during filming, they usually decide the precise framing and composition of shots, and may settle the pace of camera movement, such as pans (sideways movement), tracks (forward and backward moving the whole camera) and zooms (forward and backward using only the lens). They also instruct the focus puller on lens and camera movement, the key grip on the laying of tracks or mounting the camera on dolly or crane, and the clapper-loader on assisting generally.

During shooting (and rehearsals to shoot) the focus puller turns the lens and/or the camera on its mount at the agreed speed and time, and otherwise assists the camera operator with preparing the camera with any special lenses, filters or mounts, and generally cleans and looks after the camera and accessories.

The clapper-loader is a camera assistant who writes up and operates the clapperboard to mark the beginning of each take, loads film into magazines and unloads used film and labels and packs it for sending to the laboratories for processing.

The key grip, though working closely with the camera crew, is regarded as leader of a separate team of grips or riggers who, as well as preparing tracks, cranes and dollies, erect scaffolding and platforms for the camera and lighting. On a modest feature, drama or documentary, this might be a grip and assistant grip.

On a small documentary unit using film, the cameraman/woman could be responsible for the lighting as well as camera aspects and have just a camera assistant to help with all tasks.

TV

In the TV studio, there are from three to six electronic cameras, each with its own electronic camera operator and one or more camera assistants or trainee camera operators. The most junior moves the cables out of the way as the camera moves around ('cable bashing'). If the camera is mounted on a motorized crane, one assistant is responsible for swinging the counterbalanced arm or jib and another drives the crane to positions marked on the studio floor. But most cameras are on pedestals on mobile mountings that the camera operator moves or drives into position. This is not always easy when other cameras, the sound boom and performers have to be avoided. During camera rehearsals, these movements are practised to a shotlist fixed to the camera and, during shooting, the production assistant reminds the camera operator over headphones of what is coming next.

The director decides most aspects of camera position, size of shot, and so on, possibly consulting with the lighting director, but the operator may offer up on the studio monitor the framing and composition they feel the director is after. On current affairs, quiz shows and other programmes which cannot be rehearsed in detail, the director will depend much more on the operator to obtain good shots, passing general instructions on position and size of shot over headphones via the production assistant. During shooting/recording, the director sits in a control room and selects from the pictures seen by different cameras displayed on a bank of monitors. For dramas and other rehearsed programmes, this selection may be decided in advance; for others, the director decides on the spot.

On outside broadcasts (sporting events, ceremonial occasions), the operator may have more say in the positioning of the camera and choice of picture (though still connected by a talkback system to the control room in a van). The camera may be supported on their shoulder or set up on a tripod or a specially installed mount (eg at a sports stadium) or on top of a moving vehicle (eg at a racetrack).

In the studio, lighting is controlled by a lighting director, who may have been a camera operator previously, but may also have come in by another route.

TV dramas, or the sections of them made on location, are often created with film rather than electronic cameras. In this case, a lighting camera operator functions like a lighting cameraman/woman in films, supervising lighting and camera teams.

Electronic news gathering (ENG) is increasingly done, using an electronic camera, by a lone camera operator, or a team of two who handle all aspects of camera, sound, lighting and basic maintenance of equipment and use communications links to play their material back to base.

They may work closely with a reporter/presenter or researcher, who goes with them.

Documentary filming may be handled by an exterior camera operator working with a camera assistant, handling all lighting and camera aspects.

Video

Independent production companies creating corporate videos or TV programmes on videotape may use large or small crews, depending on the video or programme and the size of the budget. However, in many cases, the cameraman/woman is likely to operate the camera as well as setting the lighting, with the aid of one or more camera assistants. Speed may be essential because of a limited shooting schedule and the short time people being filmed can spare from their normal duties or are prepared to give.

Theatre

There are no cameras in theatre, but lighting designers/technicians design and control the lighting aspects of the stage show, as the director of photography or lighting director does in films/TV. On a major West End musical or pop concert, they choose the types of lighting equipment to achieve the effects they and the director envisage, design how it will be rigged in the theatre, decide on colours of 'gels' in front of each light at different points, intensities and changes, and may prepare a lighting plot with diagrams, for use by technicians and operator, or for programming into a computer.

On pop concerts and some stage and promotional shows, lighting aspects may include laser beams and projected images, strobes and flashing/moving lights or reflectors, and dry ice for smoke effects. In smaller theatres, the chief electrician may design and operate the lighting. Touring pop groups may have a technical road manager who handles both lighting and sound aspects. Lighting designers/technicians may work on fashion shows, exhibitions, conferences and multi-media presentations for advertising/PR agencies and industrial clients to, for example, launch (promote) a new car, as well as on theatrical productions.

WORK ENVIRONMENT

See this section in article 3. FLOOR/STAGE MANAGER/ASSISTANT DIRECTOR for general characteristics of film, TV and radio studios and location work.

News gathering may involve competing with other camera crews and photographers for a position to catch an adequate view of a celebrity or event, and may involve personal danger and rough conditions when covering war, riot and natural disasters. Outside broadcasts could mean being in uncomfortable positions in the cold and rain. Travel to other parts of Britain and to other countries is often involved, which may mean short or long periods away from home.

SKILLS AND INTERESTS

A strong interest in photography, film and video, both artistically and technically, is important, as are a good sense of colour and composition and some knowledge of optics and electronics. All this implies creativity in interpreting the scriptwriter's/playwright's and director's ideas into visual form. Physical fitness and stamina are essential in coping with working long hours, carrying heavy equipment, and sometimes the camera, on the shoulder.

Normal eyesight and colour vision, a good head for heights,

and the ability to react quickly, are all attributes of a good cameraman/woman. Verbal cueing from actors' dialogue, or over headphones from the control room, calls for good hearing. In some situations, such as news gathering, personal initiative and the ability to work alone may be more important than the ability to work in a team. Ability to work at speed, take quick decisions and keep calm under pressure are all valuable.

A driving licence is essential for news gatherers and useful in many other types of camera work, as studios and locations are not always easily accessible.

ENTRY REQUIREMENTS

For direct entry to training posts with companies such as BBC TV and ITV, whether on the electronic or film sides, the minimum requirement is normally GCSEs/S grades (A-C/1-3) in English, maths and physics. But these openings are relatively rare, competition is fierce and successful applicants often have some A levels/H grades and have done a film/TV or photography course at FE or HE college leading to a City and Guilds (C&G), BTEC/SCOTVEC national certificate/diploma, or higher national certificate/diploma, or degree (see TRAINING below). Practical evidence of interest and ability in photography (a portfolio of still photographs or a videotape of film/video work) is important. An involvement in amateur dramatics, knowledge of lighting/optics/electronics, and an interest in current affairs, TV, film or theatre all help. Some applicants have experience in the industry, or in professional photography.

Entry as a freelance is difficult even with a BTEC/SCOTVEC qualification and usually requires significant experience on student/amateur films.

Entry requirements for C&G courses vary so check locally. For national certificate/diploma courses they are four GCSEs/S grades (A-C/1-3); for higher national courses one/two A levels/H grades and four GCSEs/S grades (A-C/1-3); for degree courses, five GCSEs/S grades and two/three A levels/H grades. However, competition for places on media courses is high and interests and knowledge, such as those cited above for entry to traineeships, may prove important.

Most entrants to theatre lighting have GCSEs/S grades, A levels/H grades and a college or drama school course to higher national diploma level, possibly entering as electrician or assistant electrician.

TRAINING

The number of traineeships offered by employers (BBC TV, ITV companies), which carry the likelihood of a job at the end, is very small and competition for them is fierce.

Traditionally, BBC TV and ITV have had an annual intake of trainees, with most training on the job over a number of years, together with periods off the job and/or in training centres. However, they are now tailoring training to meet specific requirements as they arise, covering shorter time-scales and, increasingly, training multiskilled technicians over a range of equipment and aspects (eg camera, sound, some editing techniques) rather than specialists.

Faced with the need to train technicians for a freelance career, the whole industry has developed the following schemes:

– ft2 (Film and Television Freelance Training). This takes about 20 trainees each year for a two-year scheme. In the first year, trainees are seconded to a range of different film and TV production situations to experience a variety of departments in feature films, drama series, commercials and documentaries. In the second year, their attachments relate to one discipline. Job areas offered currently include camera assistant/clapper-loader, sound assistant, third assistant director, production assistant, research assistant, art department assistant, grips and assistant editor/ videotape operations/post-production. This on-the-job training is backed up by practical and theoretical courses at colleges and training centres. Applications are accepted throughout the year, but selection usually begins in April/ May of each year. Completion brings eligibility for union membership (BECTU). A training allowance is paid and travel expenses to location shoots. This is seen as similar to an apprenticeship.

– CYFLE offers six to eight places on two-year courses to train Welsh-speaking technicians.

– Gaelic Television Training Trust offers up to eight grants each year to enable Gaelic-speakers to train with Scottish Television (STV) or Grampian TV on one-year attachments.

– Scottish Broadcast and Film Training has recently been established to co-ordinate and provide training in Scotland, but detailed plans are not yet available.

– Channel 4 finances two training schemes every two years for people with disabilities and those from ethnic backgrounds. These provide college training and placements with independent production companies.

Most traineeships are advertised.

Many people organize their own training by taking media-related diploma, degree and postgraduate courses at colleges and universities. Some of these offer students the possibility of hands-on experience and of gaining credits on student films, and can possibly be used in a showtape (a videotape of excerpts). However, it is important to analyse prospectuses carefully, as some courses in this area of study are primarily theoretical, with very little practical content. Another possibility is the many short courses available. Consult the course directories listed in FURTHER READING for details of courses.

NVQs/SVQs are available in Camera Assistance at Level 2, Camera Operation at Level 3 and Camera Direction at Level 4.

Drama school stage management courses include theatre lighting and sound (stage electrics). City of Westminster College offers one-year courses in lighting and in sound, evolved with the ABTT. Oldham College has two-year national diploma courses. Some degree courses in drama and theatre studies offer a chance to gain practical experience. Some larger theatres provide part-time college training for assistant electricians.

LATE ENTRY

There is no upper age limit, but most of the training schemes are intended primarily for people in their late teens or early twenties. Degree and diploma courses are open to mature students. However, most mature people moving into camerawork have experience in other jobs in the industry, such as lighting electrician/gaffer, or in professional photography.

OPPORTUNITIES

This is a very competitive industry, with more qualified people than jobs. The larger TV organizations sometimes advertise trainee camera posts in videotape or film.

Nowadays, this is usually to meet specific needs, rather than an annual intake, and the vacancies may be filled internally from people already working in secretarial, clerical or general assistant/runner jobs. Some cameramen/women are employed full-time on long or short contracts by BBC TV and ITV companies. The more successful independent production companies and facilities houses that provide crews, as well as equipment, employ cameramen/women or have a contractual or retainer relationship with them.

Most camera crew members are freelance and are hired on a fee-basis or daily/weekly rate for each film, or project, by film, TV or video production companies. Freelance cameramen/women may obtain work through specialist agencies or facilities houses, by entries in directories, advertising in the trade press, mailings to production companies or (more effective) personal phone calls and visits. Essential for enough bookings to earn a living is to establish and maintain contacts with a number of producers, production managers and lighting cameramen/ women or DPs. Some ex-students of film/TV courses join with others to form an independent production company of their own and try to set up film, TV or video projects together.

The number of theatres and theatre companies has been reducing, so there are few openings for theatre lighting specialists. Even if entry as an assistant electrician or electrician is achieved, it may be a long time before an opportunity to design the lighting for a show arrives.

PAY AND CONDITIONS

In the regional TV companies, on completion of training, a cameraman/woman can earn from £11,500 to £16,500, with news and features camera operators earning significantly more than studio-based ones. Senior cameramen/women may earn around £19,000 to £20,000. A freelance lighting cameraman/woman on feature films has a minimum weekly rate of £839 and a daily rate of about £210. A well-known director of photography on major feature films would expect a very much higher fee, as one of the most important technicians involved. The camera operator weekly minimum is £470, and for a focus puller £345. Some freelance camera operators supply their own camera equipment.

To work in the industry or gain essential experience, existing freelance technicians and new entrants find themselves working on 'deferred payment' on low-budget feature films, on the understanding that they will be paid at professional rates retrospectively if and when the film is sold and makes a profit. Normally expenses and sometimes 'per diem' payments are made.

In full-time posts, overtime is normally paid at overtime rates. This applies also for work in feature films/ commercials and the independent sector but, increasingly, agreements are reached allowing an extended working day or an agreed amount of overtime per week within the agreed fee. Shiftwork may be involved in TV.

PROSPECTS

The crew structures described in THE WORK for film and TV serve as promotion ladders from junior to more senior jobs. This works reasonably effectively in organizations that are producing regularly with established crews, like TV companies, where the ladder may include senior and supervisory posts up to, for example, head of production operation services.

Deregulation, multiskilling and the ending of the trade

union closed shop mean that entry is, in theory, easier, but that crews are smaller and more skills may have to be acquired so that a cameraman/woman, with or without an assistant, may handle lighting, camera and sound. This trend is likely to continue. Another development has been the opening up of television to independent production companies, which has increased the number of potential employers. But, at the same time, areas that once had permanent staff have been casualized by switching to hiring freelances on short-term contracts and releasing experienced cameramen/women onto the freelance market.

Some lighting cameramen/directors and DPs move on to become directors.

In theatre, the promotion route is assistant electrician, electrician, chief electrician, lighting designer. Achieving this may involve moving from smaller to larger theatre companies as opportunity arises. A small number of expert lighting designers have set up their own companies providing lighting design services for theatres, pop concerts, fashion shows, etc.

When externally advertised, job vacancy advertisements, including traineeships, appear in *The Guardian, Broadcast, Screen International, Televisual, The Stage* and *Television Today,* ethnic newspapers, some local newspapers. BBC external vacancies appear on CEEFAX page 696.

RELATED OCCUPATIONS

Photographer, vision mixer, sound technician/operator, film/TV director, film/video editor, lighting electrician/technician, telecine operator.

FURTHER INFORMATION AND READING

Please see article 5. SOUND TECHNICIAN/OPERATOR.

5. SOUND TECHNICIAN/OPERATOR (GAL)

THE WORK

Film

On feature films, the sound crew is headed by the sound mixer, who sits at a mobile mixing desk, or console, and adjusts the level, tone, and so on, of the sound of the actors' speech coming through his headphones. Other crew members are the boom operator and sound assistant. Sound reaches the sound mixer from fixed microphones within the set and/or radio microphones on the actor's person, but primarily from the movable microphone on the mechanical boom operated by the boom operator. The sound assistant helps them both and prepares blank audio tapes, labels recorded tapes to go for transfer to sprocketed magnetic tape for use by the sound editor or dialogue editor, and may keep a log of takes, noting any problem areas. Guided by the sound mixer, the boom operator sets up the microphones in the best positions available (so that they are not visible and do not cast a shadow) and runs cables to them.

During shooting, the boom operator's task is to swivel and move/raise/lower the microphone to catch the best possible speech from each of the performers. The sound mixer may switch between microphones, as performers move within the set, and adjust controls rapidly to compensate for any

drop in level as a performer turns their head. The sound mixer usually has the power to end a take if they hear a distant sound that could affect the recording, perhaps an aeroplane or train, or to declare sound quality unusable and requiring replacement dialogue-recording during post-production. The overall aim is to achieve 'perspective' sound, so that the performers' voices sound as though they are the distances from one another that the camera sees. The sound crew also record an 'atmos track' (ie the background sound when no-one is speaking) for use by the sound editor to fill any gaps in the edited soundtrack. They may record sound effects as well, such as vehicles braking or starting up, or may be sent out separately to obtain these for the sound editor.

On documentaries, all these tasks may be handled by one sound recordist who, when appropriate, holds the microphone on a boom (usually a long metal rod) while keeping an eye on the dials on a portable recorder or, for some video systems, a control panel slung round the neck and attached to the video camera by cable. They may mix between several microphones and control tone, volume, etc. On other units, a sound assistant or general assistant (to camera and sound) may assist with, for example, boom operation.

In post-production, specialist sound technicians and mixers work in sound studios on, for example, recording the narrator's voice for documentaries, sound effects, the music or replacement dialogue for feature films, and so on. Re-recording mixers (or dubbing mixers) and their assistants handle the tasks of 'cleaning up', 'equalizing' and 'levelling out' of all the dialogue, music and sound effects tracks to create the final balanced soundtrack.

TV

A similar structure applies in TV, but there could be more than one boom operator to allow for reaching other sets or distant areas of a large set, when performers move. In the studio, the sound mixer sits in the control room with the mixing console, in direct touch with the director and vision mixer, and communicates with boom operators over headphones (talkback). Microphones may also be suspended from the studio ceiling. On rehearsed shows, the boom operators work to a sound script that tells them when to move the mechanical boom to new positions, etc. On others, they work on their own initiative and guidance from the control room. In a studio discussion, possibly with audience participation, a lot can depend on their catching each speaker in turn and adequately receiving any interruptions.

On outside broadcasts, the control room is in a van and microphones and cables have to be rigged for the occasion (sports fixture, royal wedding, pop concert) and taken down afterwards. The sound crew also handles communications back to the studio.

Other sound jobs in TV include the grams operator. On cue from the director via the production assistant, they play music or sound effects chosen from a collection of audiotapes and CDs that the sound mixer mixes into the soundtrack.

Theatre

In large theatres and on West End and major touring productions, a sound designer, or technician or engineer, designs the sound aspects. For some productions and companies, this may mean only discussing with the director and stage manager the sound effects and music needed, obtaining these (sometimes recording them specially) and editing them onto one audiotape.

For a major musical, it could involve positioning microphones for instruments in the orchestra, as well as on stage for the performers (which could include radio microphones on individuals) and the loudspeakers for best coverage of the audience. During performances, a sound operator sits at a complex mixing console, switching between microphones and adjusting levels to get the required balance between singers and different instruments, working to a complex sound plot as the live sound is fed through the speakers.

In smaller theatres, the sound technician may design and operate, or the chief electrician may set up the sound, as well as the lights, and operate from the lighting box, or the stage manager may operate during performances from the prompt corner.

Radio

In most radio organizations, a studio manager (SM) runs each studio, handling bookings of studio time (received from producers or production assistants) for the succession of programmes that may use it during each day or week. The SM prepares for each user programme by setting up chairs, tables, stands to hold music and/or scripts, and microphones, which is more complex for a panel discussion or musical ensemble than for a talk, newscast or one-to-one interview. During recording, the studio manager operates tape recorders, mixing between microphones and adjusting volume, tone, and so on to their own creative/technical feeling and to instructions from the producer/director, who sits in the control room with them. They may mix in music, sound effects and previously recorded elements from tape, disc and CD players, which they also operate. Some sound effects may be created manually.

During rehearsals and run-throughs, the SM tests presenters, guests and performers for level, advises them on the use of microphones and adjusts the positions of microphones, and they mark up their own copy of the script with cues for effects, music, etc. Some elements of a documentary, arts, news or current affairs programme may be recorded in advance during another studio session, or by a radio journalist on location. The studio manager may edit these tapes, extracting selected statements from an interview and cutting out unnecessary words and pauses. All elements may be pre-mixed for broadcast from one tape, or mixed during broadcast.

Some studio managers go on location to set up equipment and microphones to record or broadcast, for example, sports fixtures, concerts, travelling discussion programmes, with all the problems of coping with extraneous sounds, wind, variable acoustics, and audience/crowd participation.

WORK ENVIRONMENT

See this section in article 3. FLOOR/STAGE MANAGER/ ASSISTANT DIRECTOR for general characteristics of film, TV and radio studios and location work.

News gathering may involve competing with other sound recordists, camera crews and photographers for a position to best catch the statements of a celebrity, or the live sounds of an event, and may involve personal danger and rough conditions when covering war, riot and natural disasters. Outside broadcasts could mean being in uncomfortable positions in the cold and rain. Travel to other parts of Britain and to other countries is often involved, which may mean short or long periods away from home.

Theatre sound technicians rig equipment on stage, in the orchestra pit and in the auditorium. They may have a workroom and equipment store backstage or outside the actual theatre building. During dress rehearsal and performances, they usually sit in a control box or open area at the back of the auditorium.

SKILLS AND INTERESTS

Sharp hearing is needed to catch faint sounds and to differentiate an unwanted sound from the intended sounds coming through the headphones. Good hand and ear/eye co-ordination and speedy reactions are important in responding to performer moves and changes of voice level. Sound technicians must be able to concentrate, hold one physical position for lengthy periods, and have steady arms and stamina. A methodical mind and close attention to detail will also help. They should be able to read music, and may possibly have studied it and play a musical instrument, gaining a sense of timing and rhythm. They have knowledge of electronics and computers and a strong interest in film, television, radio or recording and the current music scene. They need to be able to get on well with people, fit easily into a team and have good communication skills. In some situations they need to be able to take initiative and work alone.

For freelance work and work on location, a driving licence is important.

ENTRY REQUIREMENTS

For direct entry to training posts with companies such as the BBC and ITV, the minimum requirement is GCSEs/S grades (A-C/1-3) in English, maths and physics, but competition for these places is fierce, and successful applicants often have some A levels/H grades and have done a film/TV or electronics course at FE college leading to a BTEC/SCOTVEC certificate or diploma (see TRAINING, below). These courses also require the exam results mentioned above. Practical evidence of interest and ability in sound, recording and music is important. Having your own hi-fi rig and doing mixes (of which you can offer a tape as a portfolio), or helping out on a local, hospital, or university radio station, or with a pop group (amateur or professional) or disco, or working on student productions during a college course, provides this evidence. An involvement in amateur dramatics, playing a musical instrument, knowledge of electronics, and an interest in current affairs, TV, radio, film or theatre all help. Some applicants have experience in the industry or in recording in junior or ancillary roles, for example, as a runner, clerical assistant or secretary.

Entry as a freelance is difficult, even with a BTEC/ SCOTVEC qualification, and usually requires significant experience on student/amateur films or radio, on hospital radio or in DJ mixing, constituting a list of credits and providing an impressive showtape (and hopefully a few contacts with potential employers).

TRAINING

Please see TRAINING in article 4. CAMERAMAN/ WOMAN/CAMERA OPERATOR.

In addition, NVQs/SVQs are available in Sound Assistance at Level 2, Sound Operation at Level 3 and Sound Direction at Level 4.

LATE ENTRY

There is no upper age limit, but most of the training schemes are intended primarily for people in their late teens or early twenties. Degree and diploma courses are open to mature students. However, most mature people moving into sound work have experience in other jobs in the industry, or related industries.

OPPORTUNITIES

This is a very competitive industry, with more qualified people than jobs. The larger TV and radio organizations sometimes advertise for trainee sound operators, or audio assistants, or trainee studio managers, but there is no longer an annual intake, and these posts may be filled internally from people in secretarial, clerical or assistant jobs. Some sound technicians/operators are employed full-time on long or short contracts by BBC TV and ITV companies, post-production houses and established theatres. The more successful independent production companies and facilities houses that provide crews, as well as equipment, employ sound technicians/operators, or have a contractual, or retainer relationship with them that amounts to regular or near-regular employment. Most sound crew members are freelance and are hired on a fee-basis or daily/weekly rate for each film or project, by film, TV or video production companies. Freelance sound technicians/operators may obtain work through specialist agencies or facilities houses, by entries in directories, advertising in the trade press, mailings to production companies or (more effective) personal phone calls and visits.

The number of theatres and theatre companies has been declining, so openings are few. It may be easier to start in theatre as an electrician or assistant stage manager.

When advertised externally, job vacancy advertisements, including traineeships, appear in *The Guardian, Broadcast, Screen International, Televisual, The Stage* and *Television Today,* ethnic newspapers, some local newspapers. BBC external vacancies are on CEEFAX page 696.

PAY AND CONDITIONS

In a regional TV company, a trainee sound technician earns about £9,000, and, after training, goes onto a scale rising to over £17,000. An experienced electronic recordist could receive over £20,000. Union (BECTU) freelance weekly rates for feature film work are: sound assistant £207.50, boom operator £345, sound mixer £531.

A trainee studio manager in radio at the BBC would earn about £9,000, while an experienced studio manager receives £15,000, or more.

Some freelance sound recordists supply their own sound equipment.

To work in the industry or gain essential experience, existing freelance technicians and new entrants may work on low-budget feature films on the understanding that they will be paid at professional rates retrospectively if and when the film is sold and makes a profit. Normally expenses and sometimes 'per diem' payments are made.

In full-time posts, overtime is normally paid at overtime rates. This applies also for work in feature films/ commercials and the independent sector, but, increasingly, agreements are reached allowing an extended working day or an agreed amount of overtime per week within the agreed fee.

PROSPECTS

The crew structures described in THE WORK section for film and TV traditionally serve as promotion ladders from junior to more senior jobs. The heavily practical training courses and funding sometimes found for student films/ audio projects have made it possible for some individuals to demonstrate their technical and creative abilities early and so jump a few rungs.

In large TV and radio organizations, there may be progress to senior sound mixer or senior sound technician, or to sound engineer in charge of sound staff in a specific area or concern. Similarly, in radio, senior studio managers may specialize in, and be responsible for, a specific type of programme, a major studio or group of small studios. The largest theatres have a sound department with a promotion structure to head of sound or head of post-production sound services.

Deregulation, multiskilling and the ending of the trade union closed shop mean that entry is, in theory, easier, but that crews are smaller and more skills may have to be acquired so that a cameraman/woman may handle lighting, camera and sound, eliminating the need for a sound recordist. Another development has been the opening up of television to independent production companies, which has increased the number of potential employers. However, at the same time, areas that once had permanent staff now use freelances or people on short-term contracts.

Some sound mixers/recordists/technicians move on to become sound/dialogue/effects editors, or into the recording or pop music industries. Some radio studio managers graduate to producer or director, as do some senior sound staff in TV. Some sound technicians set up their own small company as a facilities house, servicing production or post-production. Work on pop concerts as a technical road manager is a related field that may offer openings, though it may be necessary to start as a non-technical roadie (humper) with a pop group.

RELATED OCCUPATIONS

Recording technician, audio/visual technician, sound maintenance engineer, sound editor, broadcasting engineer, electrical/electronics technician.

FURTHER INFORMATION

Association of British Theatre Technicians* (ABTT), 47 Bermondsey Street, London SE1 3XF, 0171 403 3778 (please enclose a large sae)

Association of Independent Radio Companies Ltd*, Radio House, 46 Westbourne Grove, London W2 5SH, 0171 727 2646 (sae required)

British Broadcasting Corporation*, PO Box 7000, London W5 2WY, 0181 849 0849

British Film Institute (BFI), BFI Publications, 21 Stephen Street, London W1P 2LN, 0171 636 3289

BKSTS – The Moving Image Society*, 63-71 Victoria House, Vernon Place, London WC1B 4DA, 0171 242 8400

Conference of Drama Schools, Honorary Secretary, c/o Central School of Speech and Drama, Embassy Theatre, Eton Avenue, London NW3 3HY

CYFLE*, Gronant, Penrallt Isaf, Caernarfon, Gwynedd LL55 1NW, 01286 671000

ft2 – Film and Television Freelance Training*, The Administrator, ft2, Fourth Floor, Warwick House, Warwick Street, London W1R 5RA, 0171 734 5141 (A4 sae required)

Gaelic Television Training Trust, Sabhal Mor Ostaig College, An Teanga, Isle of Skye IV44 8RQ, 01471 844373

ITV Careers Advisory Service*, c/o ITV Network, 200 Grays Inn Road, London WC1 8XZ, 0171 843 8000

North East Media Training Centre (NEMTC), Stonehills Studios, Stonehills, Shields Road, Pelaw, Gateshead, Tyne and Wear NE10 0HW, 0191 438 4044

Television and Radio Training Unit*, GWR Group plc, Granville House, Granville Road, Leicester LE1 7RW, 0116 255 1616

Scottish Film Council*, 212 Broomielaw, Glasgow G1, 0141 334 4445

SKILLSET* (The Industry Training Organization for Broadcast, Film and Video), 60 Charlotte Street, London W1P 2AX, 0171 927 8585

Stage Management Association* (SMA), Southbank House, Black Prince Road, London SE1 7SJ, 0171 587 1514

FURTHER READING

Leaflets/booklets are available from the addresses marked*.

Working in Performing Arts – COIC
Working in TV, Film and Radio – COIC
Careers in the Theatre – Kogan Page
Careers in Television and Radio (Fifth Edition) – Kogan Page
The Official ITV Careers Handbook – Hodder and Stoughton
Skillset Careers Information – Skillset Lights, Camera, Action – BFI
Media Courses UK 1996 (Third Edition) – BFI
A Guide to Short Courses – BFI
So You Want to Work in Theatre – ABTT
Directory of Drama and Theatre Courses – ABTT
Guide to Courses – Conference of Drama Schools Stage Management: A Career Guide – SMA
Changing Channels – A Guide to Working in Television, Film and Radio – BBC

In the careers library classified under GAL; RAL.

1. TOURIST INFORMATION CENTRE ASSISTANT CLCI:GAX
2. TRAVEL CONSULTANT/TRAVEL AGENCY CLERK CLCI:GAX
3. TRAVEL COURIER CLCI:GAX
4. TOUR MANAGER CLCI:GAX
5. RESORT REPRESENTATIVE CLCI:GAX

BACKGROUND INFORMATION

Travel and tourism is big business in the UK and very important to the economy. It employs 1.7 million people and is Britain's fastest growing industry.

Overseas visitors are attracted to Britain by its heritage, cultural attractions and beautiful countryside. It is very important that these visitors have help in identifying places of interest and in booking travel and accommodation. Tourist Information Centres (TICs) provide that help.

TICs also have an important job in relation to British tourists. An increasing number of people in Britain have short-break holidays. By attracting those people and helping them, TICs bring money into their localities and help provide jobs.

There have been a number of trends that have led to more Britons taking holidays abroad more frequently – increased leisure time, greater wealth, improved transport facilities and longer life expectancy. A large industry has developed to cater for travel abroad, particularly using package holidays. Travel agents are vital in selling package holidays and travel (both holiday and business) to the public. Travel couriers and resort representatives play an important part in ensuring the smooth running of these holidays.

1. TOURIST INFORMATION CENTRE ASSISTANT (GAX)

THE WORK

Tourist Information Centre (TIC) assistants aim to encourage people to spend time and money in a local area by providing information and help and promoting local facilities. The range of services offered by TICs varies according to their location and size, but many activities are common to them all.

The main task of assistants is to deal with enquiries by post, by telephone and from personal callers. They give information on places of local interest, eg museums, leisure parks, stately homes and country houses. This includes opening times, admission prices, etc.

They also provide information on local transport facilities, including bus and train timetables, and on local entertainments and facilities, eg theatres, cinemas, nightclubs, restaurants and sporting events. In addition to local information, TICs are required to hold detailed information for a 50-mile radius and less detailed information for the rest of the UK.

TIC assistants liaise with local guest-houses and hotels to keep a record of good quality accommodation. Most TICs offer callers an accommodation booking service both locally and nationally, known as the BABA (book-a-bed-ahead) Service. This involves working closely with other TICs to book accommodation in other parts of the UK. In some TICs, assistants use computers for information storage and for making reservations.

Assistants can also make reservations for sightseeing tours, theatres, sporting events and transport.

TIC assistants gather information by sending for leaflets, brochures, guidebooks and timetables, both for their own use and to give to customers. They regularly reorder and update stock, and display free material.

TIC staff also sell a range of retail goods, for example guidebooks, maps and souvenirs. Assistants have to order these items, display them, handle cash and keep accounts.

At times of the year when there are few callers, assistants often try to improve their knowledge of local attractions by making familiarization visits.

WORK ENVIRONMENT

TICs are located in a variety of premises, at council offices, in bus and railway stations, airports, libraries and museums. Other TICs occupy purpose-built shops or kiosks.

TIC assistants work indoors, usually in comfortable, pleasant conditions. Their work involves standing and sitting and occasional travel in the locality.

SKILLS AND INTERESTS

Much of TIC assistants' work is in direct contact with other people, in person or by telephone. It is important, therefore, that they enjoy dealing with people and can do so in a pleasant and friendly way. They need to be keen to help and have tact and patience.

Communication skills are important. Assistants should be good listeners, to find out what an enquiry is about and be able to answer enquiries clearly and accurately. Accuracy is also important when making reservations. Since much work is conducted by telephone, a good telephone manner is necessary.

In high season, TICs can be very busy, so assistants should be able to keep calm and work well under pressure. They need to be able to work well in a team.

Assistants should have an interest in, and good knowledge of, their local area – its history, geography and places of interest. The greater their knowledge, the more they are able to help clients.

As computers are used increasingly for information storage in TICs, keyboard skills are usually required and an interest in information technology is important.

The ability to communicate in one or more foreign languages is useful and, in some TICs, it is essential.

A smart, tidy appearance is required.

ENTRY REQUIREMENTS

Entry requirements vary, but employers usually prefer applicants with at least four GCSEs/S grades (A-C/1-3) or equivalent.

The ability to communicate in one or more foreign languages may be required for some posts. This is particularly the case in major tourist areas, such as London, and at sites frequented by many overseas visitors. In areas that tend to have few overseas visitors, a foreign language may not be required.

Many entrants are over 21 years.

TRAINING

There are no pre-entry courses to prepare specifically for TIC work, although some entrants have taken a travel and tourism college course – see article 2. TRAVEL CONSULTANT/TRAVEL AGENCY CLERK.

All TIC assistants receive training from their employers and regional tourist boards, and may also have the opportunity of going on familiarization visits within the UK.

Most TIC assistants were expected to study for the City and Guilds Certificate in Tourist Information Centre Competence (COTICC).

COTICC is being phased out in 1996/1997 and is being replaced with NVQs/SVQs in Tourist Information at Levels 2 and 3. Candidates must study a number of mandatory units and a further selection of optional units that are applicable to their work. Common units include providing an accommodation information and booking service, identifying and providing tourist information and maintaining a tourist information centre information system.

LATE ENTRY

Previous experience of work in dealing with people is useful, as is experience of clerical work. It can also be helpful to have lived in the TIC locality for some years and to have good local knowledge.

The part-time and/or seasonal nature of the work in some TICs may make the work attractive to adult entrants.

Adults may be able to enter travel and tourism courses without the usual educational qualifications.

OPPORTUNITIES

TIC assistants are employed by local authorities and regional tourist boards. They are employed in approximately 560 TICs in England, 170 in Scotland, 80 in Wales, 30 in Northern Ireland, six in the Isle of Man and six in the Channel Islands. TICs are located wherever tourism is actively encouraged. In England there are about 2,500 staff.

About one fifth of TICs in England open only from Easter to September, as do most TICs in other regions. Other TICs are open all year round.

Although a few TICs employ up to 20 staff, many have just one or two employees. Full-time permanent vacancies occur infrequently and, when they arise, competition for them is strong. Part-time and seasonal vacancies are more plentiful, but entry to them is also competitive.

PAY AND CONDITIONS

There are no nationally agreed rates of pay for TIC assistants. Salaries vary according to age, geographical location and employer. Some TIC assistants are on a salary scale that starts at £5,229 at age 16 and rises to £9,294 at age 21 and over. In London, salaries are considerably higher.

TICs in major cities and towns, and at particularly busy sites, are open seven days a week. Other TICs open from 9am to 5pm, Monday to Friday, but also open at weekends during the summer season and extend their opening hours to meet local requirements.

Assistants may work full-time or part-time, and some work in the summer season only. Some assistants work shifts.

PROSPECTS

TIC assistants who work part-time, or on a temporary basis, may seek full-time or permanent posts. Promotion possibilities with TICs are limited. All TICs have a manager and some larger employers have a structure of senior information assistant, supervisor and manager, but there are relatively few staff in TICs above assistant level.

There are some opportunities for TIC assistants to seek promotion with local authority tourism departments and regional tourist boards. TIC assistants may use their experience to enter the travel agency or tour operating fields.

RELATED OCCUPATIONS

Hotel receptionist, travel consultant/travel agency clerk, air passenger service assistant, reservations clerk, tourist guide, retail assistant, local authority tourism officer.

FURTHER INFORMATION AND READING

Please see article 5. RESORT REPRESENTATIVE.

2. TRAVEL CONSULTANT/TRAVEL AGENCY CLERK (GAX)

THE WORK

Travel agencies act as a link between travellers and companies selling holidays, transport and accommodation.

Much of a travel consultant/travel agency clerk's work takes place at the counter, dealing with clients wanting package holidays. Travel consultants talk to clients to find out what they require, then show them brochures containing suitable packages. If a client is interested in a particular holiday, the travel consultant checks its availability by telephone or computer. If the holiday is not available, the clerk suggests alternative holidays, usually using a computer to identify them. When the client chooses an available holiday, the travel consultant collects a deposit and makes a booking with the tour operator.

Travel consultants also advise clients about health requirements, visas, insurance and foreign currency, and arrange holiday excursions, passports and car hire and/or airport parking.

Travel consultants book holidays on a computerized system linked directly to tour operators. Tour operators usually send tickets and transport details to the travel agency, where they are checked and then passed to the client prior to departure.

When first working in a travel agency, a travel consultant normally stamps travel brochures and displays them, as well as undertaking administrative duties, such as writing out late availability cards and opening and sorting incoming mail.

Travel agencies also provide a service for 'independent travellers', who do not wish to use package holidays. Travel consultants may help the client work out an itinerary by consulting travel timetables, booking rail, sea or air tickets and accommodation.

Some travel agencies specialize in business travel. This involves making arrangements for travel abroad, often to very tight schedules. Nearly all business travel work is conducted with the client by telephone.

At least two large travel agency groups provide foreign exchange facilities. The work involves providing clients with foreign currency and travellers cheques, and arranging for money to be transferred abroad. Foreign exchange work is dealt with by specially trained travel consultants.

A large part of the travel consultant's work is spent dealing with clients and others in person and by telephone. Travel consultants are sales people and have to meet sales targets. They also complete forms, use computers, photocopiers and calculators and handle cash, debit and credit card payments.

WORK ENVIRONMENT

Travel consultants spend most of their time working indoors in comfortable surroundings. Travel agencies tend to be in modern shop premises.

Travel consultants spend most of their working day sitting behind a counter. They may go on one 'educational' visit a year, spending time at a resort, usually abroad, to learn about the accommodation and facilities at the resort. They may occasionally travel to short training courses in the UK. Some business travel clerks work in offices within large companies.

SKILLS AND INTERESTS

Travel consultants should like dealing with people and be polite and friendly. Communication skills are important. They should be good listeners, be able to find out what clients require and be able to give information clearly and accurately. A good telephone manner is important, as much work is conducted by telephone.

A knowledge of travel geography is essential for discussing travel and holiday resorts.

Travel agencies can be very busy, particularly at lunch-times and on Saturdays. Travel consultants should therefore be able to work under pressure, which includes being able to organize work to make sure that priorities are met.

Travel consultants need a smart and tidy appearance. As computers are used increasingly in travel agencies, both for information and for booking purposes, keyboard skills are required, and an interest in information technology is very useful.

Numeracy is important, as travel agency work includes some figure work, such as calculating holiday or travel costs and deposits.

ENTRY REQUIREMENTS

There are no set entry requirements, although a good standard of secondary education is necessary. Many employers prefer applicants with some GCSEs/S grades (A-C/1-3), particularly in English, maths and geography.

Most young people enter the work via The Travel Training Programme.

A number of entrants to travel agency work have previously taken a course relevant to travel and tourism. NVQs/SVQs in Travel Services are available at a number of colleges of further education. Contact The Travel Training Company for a list of approved centres. In addition, Intermediate and Advanced GNVQs/GSVQs Levels II and III in Leisure and Tourism are available.

While NVQs/SVQs and GNVQ/GSVQ courses do not necessarily need particular entry qualifications, educational institutes may specify entry requirements for such courses.

NVQs/SVQs are also available through The Travel Training Company's Approved Centre, and many large companies run NVQ/SVQ training programmes.

BTEC/SCOTVEC Higher National Certificate/Diploma in Tourism or Travel and Tourism, or Business and Finance or Business Studies with travel and tourism options, require a minimum of one A level/two H grades and three other

subjects at GCSE/S grade (A-C/1-3), including English and maths, or equivalent.

Degree courses in Travel and Tourism or in Business Studies with travel and tourism options, require a minimum of two A levels/three H grades and three other subjects at GCSE/S grade (A-C/1-3), usually including English and maths or equivalent

Postgraduate courses in tourism usually need a degree for entry.

TRAINING

All entrants to travel agencies start as a junior travel consultant and receive on-the-job training from their employers. Some clerks may be sent on short courses for telephone techniques and selling skills. They also attend 'educational' visits to hotels and resorts, organized by tour operators, and short courses in airline ticketing, held by airlines.

The Travel Training Programme. Most young people who enter travel agency work do so through The Travel Training Programme, organized by The Travel Training Company. The Travel Training Programme involves work experience and travel training lasting about 24 months, that leads to NVQs/SVQs Level 2 and 3 in Travel Services.

Modern Apprenticeships in Travel Services include on and off-the-job training, leading to an NVQ in Travel Services at Level 3. Contact your local careers office, TEC/LEC or the Travel Training Company for details.

BTEC Higher National Diploma in Tourism or Travel and Tourism – two years' full-time.

SCOTVEC Higher National Diploma in Tourism – two years' full-time.

Degree courses relating to travel and tourism are either three-year full-time or four-year sandwich courses. Sandwich courses include one year away from college, or university, gaining experience in one part of the travel and tourism industry.

Postgraduate courses last one year full-time.

ABTAC ABTA Travel Agents Council offer ABTAC at Primary and Advanced Levels. This qualification is relevant to the work of a retail travel agent and provides evidence of underpinning knowledge for NVQ/SVQ candidates.

LATE ENTRY

There is no maximum age limit for entry to travel agency work, although entry beyond age 35 is likely to be difficult.

Some agencies prefer mature adults, particularly if they have relevant experience, such as work with people, or in travel and tourism.

The increase in part-time work in travel agencies may be particularly helpful to adult applicants with family commitments.

It may be possible for adults to be accepted onto courses in travel and tourism without the usual minimum entry requirements.

There may be specific training opportunities directed at adults, in some areas, for this type of work. Candidates may have to satisfy certain conditions to be eligible. Contact your local Jobcentre, careers office or TEC/LEC for details.

OPPORTUNITIES

There are just over 7,300 travel agencies in the UK. They range from small, independent agencies to large agencies with branches in most cities and towns. Some specialize in arranging travel and holidays for one area – Australia, for example, but most offer a more general service. An average travel agency is staffed by five or six people.

The number of staff employed in travel agencies expanded until the late 1980s. This growth has stopped and the number employed is now stable. Entry to travel agency work is always competitive.

The main route into the work for young people is The Travel Training Programme. The percentage of trainees that progress into full-time work in travel agencies is very high (approximately 98%).

PAY AND CONDITIONS

Trainees on The Travel Training Programme are paid a training allowance plus travelling expenses.

Rates of pay for trained travel consultants vary between approximately £6,000 and £12,000. Experienced travel consultants dealing with foreign exchange work, or business travel, earn up to £14,000. Clerks may receive a discount on the cost of their own holidays.

Travel agencies normally open shop hours Monday to Saturday. Travel consultants usually work between 35 and 37½ hours a week over five days. Part-time work is available in some agencies and is increasingly used to cover busier periods, eg lunch-times and Saturdays.

PROSPECTS

Moving between agencies for promotion is common. Many small travel agencies have little or no promotion possibilities. Opportunities for progression are much greater in large agencies and can be from travel consultant to senior travel consultant, assistant manager, manager and area manager.

It may be possible to transfer to other branches of travel and tourism, such as tourist information centres and tour operators, including work as a travel courier or resort representative.

RELATED OCCUPATIONS

Tourist information centre assistant, tourist guide, tour operator, foreign exchange clerk, travel courier, resort representative, travel agency manager, retail assistant.

FURTHER INFORMATION AND READING

Please see article 5. RESORT REPRESENTATIVE.

3. TRAVEL COURIER (GAX)

THE WORK

Travel couriers represent tour operators and are responsible for ensuring that travel arrangements made for parties of holiday-makers run smoothly and as enjoyably as possible. This they do by accompanying holiday parties on their journey. Most couriers work with holiday-makers travelling by coach.

Couriers join the party at the start of a journey, welcome clients, check tickets and seat allocation, and announce details of the travel arrangements and stopover points. They commentate on places of interest during the journey and liaise with the coach driver to stop at appropriate times and places. Couriers also liaise with hotel staff, on arrival at stopover points, concerning meals and accommodation.

Couriers make sure, during changes of transport, that the full party and all luggage is successfully transferred. They are responsible for answering enquiries and helping their party with any problems they may have, such as mislaid luggage or illness.

There are different kinds of courier work:

Coach couriers escort parties from the UK to the continent, ensuring passengers and luggage all arrive safely via coach and ferry or channel tunnel. They may then meet a similar party returning from holiday and escort them from the continent to the starting point of their holiday in the UK.

Transfer couriers meet flights at airports and accompany a party to their hotel by coach. They give any help needed in passing through customs and immigration, making sure that the entire party and all luggage are aboard the coach. They make announcements about the holiday and resort. At the end of the holiday they escort the party from the hotel onto their flight home.

WORK ENVIRONMENT

Most travel couriers are concerned with travel overseas with British tourists, although some work in the UK with incoming tourists.

Coach couriers spend the majority of their time travelling – mostly by coach; sometimes by cross-channel ferry. Much of their time is spent sitting. Overnight stops are usually spent in hotels.

Transfer couriers work at airports and on coaches between airports and holiday resorts.

SKILLS AND INTERESTS

Couriers work in very close contact with their party of holiday-makers. They should, therefore, like dealing with people. They need to be outgoing, self-confident, polite and tolerant of others.

Couriers have to cope with any problems that may arise during a journey, such as lost luggage, travel delays and illness. This requires them to be adaptable, flexible and able to make decisions.

They are responsible for ensuring that travel arrangements run as smoothly as possible, without delays caused by any of the party. To achieve this, couriers have to be able to organize others in a tactful manner. Couriers must be well-organized and self-reliant as they work with little or no supervision.

Communication skills are important, since couriers deal with holidaymakers, coach drivers, customs and immigration officials, and so on. Communication often needs to be in a foreign language, so fluency in one or more foreign languages is important.

Travel couriers must be in good health to cope with the long hours and physical demands of the job.

Travel couriers need a smart and tidy appearance.

ENTRY REQUIREMENTS

No formal educational qualifications are required, but a good general education is necessary. Some employers prefer couriers to have some GCSEs/S grades (A-C/1-3). English, maths, geography and languages are useful. A background in travel agency work can also be useful.

Regardless of qualifications, a good working knowledge of foreign languages is important, except if working solely in the UK.

The minimum age of entry for most companies is 20-21 years, although most entrants are in their mid-twenties. Good health is essential.

Employers look for applicants who have previous experience of working with people. Experience of working abroad is particularly valuable.

Some entrants have previously taken a course relevant to travel and tourism – please see article 2. TRAVEL CONSULTANT/TRAVEL AGENCY CLERK.

TRAINING

Employers usually provide a short induction course for couriers, to familiarize them with the company and the work. Couriers must learn about the route they are to take and the places of interest they will pass through, so they can describe them to holiday-makers.

The main qualifications for couriers are NVQs/SVQs in Travel Services (Tour Operations or Commentaries and Interpretation for Tourism) at Levels 2 and 3.

LATE ENTRY

Entry after 35 years tends to be restricted largely to companies specializing in holidays for retired people.

Any kind of work that involves working with the public is valuable experience, with previous work abroad particularly useful.

OPPORTUNITIES

Travel couriers are mainly employed by tour operators that organize package holidays, particularly holidays that include coach transport. Employing companies range from large, international organizations to small specialist companies. The majority of couriers are freelance and work on fixed-term contracts.

The work is seasonal, and couriers are employed on a short-term basis. Vacancies arise every year, but competition for them is very strong. Vacancies are sometimes advertised, but many companies find that they do not need to advertise, as they receive a large number of speculative enquiries. Applications for summer season jobs should be made in the preceding autumn. For jobs in the winter season, applications are made in the preceding summer. When advertisements are used they appear in the quality newspapers and in *Overseas Jobs Express, Travel Trade Gazette* and *Travel Weekly*.

PAY AND CONDITIONS

Pay varies from company to company, but is within a range between £70 to £130 a week plus free board and lodgings, and expenses.

Hours of work depend on the job concerned:

Coach couriers have no set hours, as they are responsible for their party from the time they join the coach until the end of the journey.

Transfer couriers tend to work shifts, including nights, but travel delays can prolong their hours.

PROSPECTS

Inexperienced staff in some companies begin as transfer couriers and progress to coach couriers or tour managers.

It is possible for couriers employed by large companies to progress to supervising a team of couriers.

Couriers rarely see their work as a long-term career. Typically, they work as couriers for two or three years, although some work for much longer. If they wish to work abroad they may seek to become overseas resort representatives for tour operators. Those wishing to settle in the UK may seek permanent work with a travel company in administration, or promotions work. Some become tourist guides in the UK on a self-employed basis.

RELATED OCCUPATIONS

Tourist guide, air cabin crew, resort representative, travel consultant/travel agency clerk, travel agency manager, tourist information centre assistant, holiday centre worker, tour operator.

FURTHER INFORMATION AND READING

Please see article 5. RESORT REPRESENTATIVE.

4. TOUR MANAGER (GAX)

THE WORK

Tour managers represent tour operators and are responsible for ensuring that travel arrangements made for groups of tourists run according to the published itinerary. They also ensure that the standards and quality of all services are maintained, and care for the well-being of each individual in their group. This they do by accompanying the tour group throughout their entire journey. Most tour managers work with tourists travelling by coach. The duration of a tour can be as short as two or three nights, up to one month, or even longer.

Tour managers meet their group at the beginning of the tour, welcome clients and announce details of travel arrangements, stopover points, safety requirements, border procedures, etc. They provide background information on places of interest during the journey and liaise with the coach driver to stop at appropriate times and places. Tour managers also liaise with hotel staff on arrival, concerning meals and accommodation. They may organize optional excursions, to shops, restaurants, or places of entertainment.

Tour managers are responsible for answering enquiries and helping the group with any problems they may encounter, such as mislaid baggage, theft, local regulations, hospitalization, etc.

WORK ENVIRONMENT

Most tour managers accompany groups of clients on cross-border itineraries throughout Europe, though some work in the UK with incoming tourists.

SKILLS AND INTERESTS

Tour managers work in very close contact with their groups. They should, therefore, genuinely like people and be able to relate to people of all kinds and nationalities. They need to be outgoing, self-confident, polite and tolerant of others.

Tour managers have to be able to cope with any problems or emergencies which may arise during the tour, such as lost luggage, travel delays and illness. This requires them to be adaptable, flexible and able to make decisions.

They are responsible for ensuring that all arrangements run as published in the tour operator's brochure, without delays caused by any of the group. To achieve this, tour managers must be well-organized themselves and able to organize others in a tactful manner. Tour managers must be self-reliant as they work with little or no supervision.

Communication skills are important, both in dealing with tourists and with coach drivers, hoteliers, customs and immigration officials. A tour manager must be articulate and able to convey information and instruction clearly and confidently. Most communication needs to be in a foreign language, so a good working knowledge of one or more foreign languages is important.

Tour managers must be in good health to cope with the long hours and physical demands of the job.

Tour managers need a smart and tidy appearance.

ENTRY REQUIREMENTS

No formal educational qualifications are required, but a good general education is essential. Proficiency in English, and a sound knowledge of geography and history are important.

Regardless of qualifications, a good working knowledge of foreign languages is important, except if working solely in the UK.

Most tour operators prefer tour managers to be in their mid-twenties or older. Good health is essential.

As well as a good educational standard, employers look for applicants who are mature and caring. Personality and the ability to inspire confidence are major factors in the selection process.

TRAINING

Tour operators usually provide a short induction course for tour managers, to familiarize them with the company and the work. Tour managers must learn about the routes they are to take and the countries they will pass through, so they can describe them to tourists.

NVQs/SVQs in Travel Services (Tour Managing) are available at Level 4.

LATE ENTRY

The vast majority of tour managers are in their mid-twenties or older. Due to the long hours on duty, all tour managers need to be physically fit and in excellent health.

Any kind of work that involves working with the public is valuable, with previous experience of working abroad particularly useful, but personality and the ability to inspire confidence are equally important.

OPPORTUNITIES

Tour managers are employed by tour operators, which organize group package holidays, usually by coach. Employing companies range from large, international organizations to small specialist companies. The majority of tour managers are freelance and are hired from tour to tour.

The work is seasonal, and many tour operators invite tour managers they have used before to work successive seasons. Vacancies do arise each year, but competition for them is very strong. Vacancies are sometimes advertised, but most companies find they do not need to advertise as they receive a large number of speculative enquiries. Applications for work in the summer season should be made in the preceding autumn. When advertisements are used they appear in the quality newspapers and in *Overseas Job Express*, *Travel Trade Gazette* and *Travel Weekly*.

PAY AND CONDITIONS

Pay, and the means of payment, varies from company to company, but is usually based on a daily allowance and free board and lodgings for the duration of the tour, plus expenses.

Tour managers do not work set hours and are usually active from early morning until late evening.

PROSPECTS

Some tour managers are also tourist guides and may prefer to confine themselves to local tour guiding. Those wishing to settle in an office environment may sometimes be offered a position by their tour operator in a planning or quality control department.

RELATED OCCUPATIONS

Tourist guide, tour operator, travel agency manager.

FURTHER INFORMATION AND READING

Please see article 5. RESORT REPRESENTATIVE.

5. RESORT REPRESENTATIVE (GAX)

THE WORK

Resort representatives are responsible for representing a tour operator at a holiday resort, usually abroad, although some work in the UK. They normally spend a whole holiday season in the resort.

Representatives meet a party of holiday-makers on their arrival at a resort and help them settle into their accommodation. A common way for representatives to welcome holiday-makers and give them information is to host a party. They give details about the resort and its facilities and information on sightseeing trips. They may sell tickets for trips.

Representatives usually meet holiday-makers regularly to make announcements and are always on hand to answer enquiries, give advice and help with any problems. Problems may be minor, concerning difficulties about accommodation, lost passports or money, or may be more serious, for example dealing with holiday-makers who are ill, injured or who may have been arrested. This may involve representatives contacting the police or medical personnel.

Representatives liaise with staff in hotels, restaurants and coach companies and with tourist guides. They also keep any necessary records, including accounts.

Whilst most representatives are responsible for normal package tours, some are concerned with more specialist holidays. Winter sports representatives have similar responsibilities to those of other representatives, but also act as guides to ski trips and organize apres-ski activities.

Representatives can spend much of their time organizing and participating in entertainments for their holiday-makers.

Children's representatives are responsible particularly for looking after younger children and organizing activities and entertainment for them. Some may also provide evening patrols to allow parents to leave their children during the evenings.

There are other specialist representatives employed by some travel companies, for example, for caravan and tent campsites and for sports.

WORK ENVIRONMENT

Resort representatives work in holiday resorts, usually abroad, with conditions varying according to location and climate. Work is both indoors and outdoors. It involves travel within the locality to deal with holiday makers and to liaise with local people and officials.

Representatives in summer resorts typically are based abroad from April to October, while winter holiday representatives may be abroad from December to April.

Representatives usually live in hotels, villas or apartments. Those working for specialist camping holiday organizers live in tents.

SKILLS AND INTERESTS

Resort representatives should like dealing with a wide variety of people, including holiday-makers and local people and officials. They must be polite and tolerant of others.

It is essential that representatives are flexible and adaptable, as they must deal effectively with any problems or crises that arise. They must be able to organize their own work with little or no supervision.

Communication skills are important: advice and information must be given clearly and accurately. Listening skills are necessary, if representatives are to understand the exact nature of holiday-makers' queries and problems.

Good conversational ability in the language of the country concerned is necessary, as representatives have to liaise with local hoteliers, officials, police, medical personnel and others in their own language.

Good health, energy and great stamina are required, as representatives are on-call at all times and the work can be very demanding.

Basic literacy is needed for dealing with necessary paperwork. Numeracy is required, as money is collected for excursions and simple accounts have to be kept.

ENTRY REQUIREMENTS

No formal educational qualifications are required, but most employers prefer applicants with some GCSEs/S grades (A-C/1-3). English, maths, geography and foreign languages are useful.

Applicants should have a good working knowledge of one or more foreign languages and it is useful to have lived abroad. Employers usually expect resort representatives to be at least 20 to 21 years old and some companies require them to be single. Good health is essential.

Applicants' previous work experience is important, with experience of working with people being an asset. Specialist knowledge is required for specialist holidays, such as photography skills. Winter sports representatives must be able to ski to an advanced level.

Children's representatives may be accepted from age 18 or 19 years. They are usually expected to have a qualification in nursery nursing, nursing or teaching. Some companies require them to be single.

Some entrants have previously taken a course relevant to travel and tourism – see article 2. TRAVEL CONSULTANT/TRAVEL AGENCY CLERK.

TRAINING

There is no set pattern of training for resort representatives. Employers usually provide a few days' induction training in the UK. Experienced staff in the resort concerned then support newly appointed representatives. Some large tour operators have overseas offices where they provide additional training.

The main qualifications for resort representatives are NVQs/SVQs. These are available in Travel Services (Tour Operations) at Levels 2 and 3.

LATE ENTRY

Most entrants are over 19 years. Opportunities are limited for adults over 35 years, except for companies that specialize in holidays for mature clients.

Many different kinds of experience are valuable, such as retail, nursing, teaching, reception and other work within travel and tourism. Previous experience of working abroad is particularly useful.

OPPORTUNITIES

Resort representatives are employed by tour operators, which range from large, international organizations to small, specialist firms. The travel industry expanded until the late 1980s, with a consequent increase in the number of representatives employed. This growth has stopped and the number employed is now stable.

As the jobs are short-term, vacancies arise regularly. Competition for vacancies is very strong, although children's representatives posts tend to be less competitive.

Vacancies are sometimes advertised, but many companies find that they do not need to advertise, as they receive a large number of speculative enquiries. Applications for work as a representative during a summer season should be made in the preceding autumn. For winter season vacancies, applications should be made in the previous summer. When advertisements are used, they appear in the quality newspapers and in *Overseas Jobs Express; Travel Trade Gazette* and *Travel Weekly.*

PAY AND CONDITIONS

Pay varies considerably according to the employer and the responsibility a job involves. One national company pays its representatives between £86 and £145 a week, depending on experience. Another company pays between £95 and £125 a week. Representatives are provided with free accommodation, insurance and uniform, and can earn commission by selling excursions and arranging car hire.

Representatives have no set working hours. They are usually on-call 24 hours a day and are often active from early morning to late in the evening. It is usual for representatives to have free time each day and one day a week free, but they may lose part, or all, of this if they are needed.

Work is seasonal for a fixed term, although some representatives manage to work approximately ten months a year, with summer work being followed by winter sports or winter sun work.

PROSPECTS

Some resort representatives do not consider the work as a long-term career, but in large companies there is a promotion structure abroad. Typically this may be to senior representative, head representative or resort controller, area manager and regional manager.

Those wanting to settle in the UK may seek permanent

work with a tour operator in personnel, marketing or brochure production work. Experience of resort representative work is excellent preparation for entry to other branches of travel and tourism, such as local government, national and regional tourist boards and travel agencies. Some become tourist guides in the UK on a self-employed basis.

RELATED OCCUPATIONS

Tourist guide, hotel manager, travel courier, tourist information centre assistant, travel representative/travel agency clerk, travel agency manager, holiday centre worker.

FURTHER INFORMATION

The Travel Training Company*, The Cornerstone, The Broadway, Woking, Surrey GU21 5AR, 01483 727321 (please include sae)

British Tourist Authority/English Tourist Board, TIC Networking Unit, Thames Tower, Blacks Road, Hammersmith, London W6 9EL, 0181 846 9000 (please include sae)

Institute of Travel and Tourism*, 113 Victoria Street, St Albans, Hertfordshire AL1 3TJ, 01727 854395 (Please enclose £3 for a careers information pack)

Local Government Opportunities (LGO), Local Government Management Board*, 76-86 Turnmill Street, London

Northern Ireland Tourist Board, St Anne's Court, 59 North Street, Belfast BT1 1NB, 01232 231221

Scottish Tourist Board, 23 Ravelston Terrace, Edinburgh EH4 3EU, 0131 332 2433

Wales Tourist Board, Brunel House, 2 Fitzallan Road, Cardiff CF2 1UY, 01222 499909

FURTHER READING

Leaflets/booklets are available from the addresses marked*.

Job Outlines – Travel and Tourism – COIC
Working in Tourism – COIC
Working in Languages – COIC
Jobs in Travel and Tourism – Kogan Page
Careers in the Travel Industry – Kogan Page
How To... Get a Job in Travel and Tourism – How To Books

In the careers library classified under GAX.

1. **HOTEL MANAGER CLCI:IB**
2. **RESTAURANT/CATERING MANAGER CLCI:IB**
3. **HOUSEKEEPER/HOUSEKEEPING MANAGER CLCI:IB**
4. **CHEF/COOK CLCI:IC**
5. **KITCHEN ASSISTANT CLCI:IC**
6. **FOOD SERVICE ASSISTANT CLCI:IC**
7. **COUNTER SERVICE ASSISTANT CLCI:IC**
8. **HOTEL RECEPTIONIST CLCI:IC/CAT**
9. **HOTEL ROOM ATTENDANT CLCI:IC**
10. **HOTEL PORTER CLCI:IC**

BACKGROUND INFORMATION

The hotel and catering industry is one of Britain's largest growth industries, with the fastest growth in restaurants and contract catering. Nearly one in ten of the UK workforce (or 2.4 million people) is employed in this sector.

Employment opportunities are split between the commercial sector and the catering services sector. The commercial sector includes hotels, restaurants, holiday camps, leisure centres, pubs, wine bars, motorway services, take-away restaurants, and clubs, as well as contract catering to a wide range of establishments, from businesses in the City of London to sports stadia. The catering services sector covers schools and colleges, rail, airlines and cruises, hospitals, nursing homes, residential hostels and the Armed Forces.

The hospitality industry spans large international groups, competing in a world market, to small family-owned restaurants and guest-houses. This range can make a great difference to the nature of the work within the same job title, with small businesses often requiring involvement in all aspects of the operation.

1. HOTEL MANAGER (IB)

THE WORK

Hotel managers are responsible for the efficient provision of all hotel services for guests, that is, food, drink and accommodation. In large hotels, services may also include entertainment and conference facilities. Hotel managers have the final responsibility for customer satisfaction, ensuring guests enjoy their visit. If guests have any complaints, it is the manager's responsibility to rectify them and make amends to the guest.

The type of work depends, to an extent, on the size of the hotel and the number of its staff. Large hotels have departmental managers, such as food and beverage manager and housekeeping manager, each of whom is responsible for their own department and who reports to the hotel manager. The hotel manager's job is more to analyse financial and statistical data, set business targets and plan marketing and investment strategies to meet those targets. Hotel managers prepare budgets, control expenditure and keep accounts. They supervise hotel security and plan all aspects of the hotel's operation, from building work to daily operations, such as the time of staff shift changes or of meals provision. Managers spend a lot of time in meetings and dealing with key staff and VIP customers. In a smaller hotel, the manager is much more involved in the practical day-to-day running of the hotel's services, sometimes including making beds and serving drinks, and solving any problems that arise, which could include minor repairs.

Staff management is a major responsibility for hotel managers, and monitoring their performance is essential to ensure guests have a good impression of the hotel's services. Managers set the standard for hotel services provision, and it is their job to ensure other staff meet that standard. In addition, the manager is responsible for selling and marketing the hotel's services to new and previous customers, and ensuring the hotel is well run and makes a profit.

WORK ENVIRONMENT

The work environment of a hotel manager depends, again, on the size of hotel. Generally, in smaller establishments, a manager could be working in the dining room or bar, as well as doing the administrative tasks at the end of the day in the reception area or a back room. In a larger establishment, the manager would spend more time at a desk in an office, and in meetings. Managers with sales responsibilities may visit other businesses, such as tour operators, to sell their facilities. However, in larger establishments, the sales department would generally have this responsibility.

SKILLS AND INTERESTS

Hotel managers need a wide range of knowledge and skills, not just those of managing food, drink and accommodation services, but also in finance, marketing and staff management. They need leadership skills, such as the ability to make decisions and take action quickly. An ability to think quickly, come up with creative solutions to problems and have plenty of ideas, energy and enthusiasm are all qualities the hotel manager needs.

Hotel managers need an outgoing personality and a natural flair for dealing with people, both staff and customers. Good communication skills are vital for all aspects of this job. To deal with the financial, statistical and marketing side, a numerical aptitude is important. Good organizational skills are essential, whether dealing with few staff in a small establishment, or with dozens of staff in several different departments in a large hotel.

A smart appearance is an asset, and a knowledge of foreign languages is useful, especially in areas popular with overseas visitors.

ENTRY REQUIREMENTS

For entry to management trainee positions, it is usually necessary to have a degree, BTEC/SCOTVEC higher national diploma, or the Hotel and Catering International Management Association (HCIMA) Professional Diploma. Most degrees require at least two A levels/three H grades plus five GCSEs/S grades (A-C/1-3), or equivalent. Higher National Diplomas require one A level/ two H grades plus four GCSEs/S grades (A-C/1-3), or equivalent, such as Advanced GNVQ in Hospitality and Catering. Graduates in subjects other than hospitality management may take a one-year postgraduate hospitality conversion course, either through a university or the HCIMA. Normal entry requirements for the HCIMA professional diploma are a BTEC/SCOTVEC national award or equivalent, NVQ/SVQ Level 3 plus at least one year's work experience in the industry, or the HCIMA professional certificate, which requires industry experience, or four GCSEs (A-C), or equivalent.

Frequently, recruits to hotel manager jobs are promoted to their post on the basis of their experience in the industry, rather than coming through the full-time college/university route. Such experience is likely to be in a variety of departments, such as food and beverages, reception and bars. Such entrants have normally achieved supervisory or higher-level work experience equivalent to NVQs/SVQs in Catering and Hospitality at Level 3 or 4.

TRAINING

Most of the pre-entry training options listed above take between two and four years to complete. The HCIMA Diploma can be taken full-time in a year for those with substantial industry experience, but it is usually completed part-time in three years, or as a two-year sandwich course. Degrees and higher national diplomas are available in hospitality and hotel and catering management. Studies cover subjects such as management accounting, the industry's role in the economy, sales and marketing, food and operations management, accommodation management, interior furnishings and fittings, customer care and the management of staff and plant and premises in accommodation operations.

Management trainee schemes provide on-the-job training, giving trainees experience in a wide variety of departments, such as the kitchens, banqueting or reception, so that they understand the whole hotel operation. In hotel chains, this can include working in departments that deal with taking over new hotels. A management trainee programme may include day release to complete the HCIMA Certificate or Diploma, short courses (lasting one or more days) in such areas as the craft trainer award (so that the manager is qualified to train craft-level staff), or interviewing skills. Entrants may train towards nvqs/svqs in Catering and Hospitality at Levels 3 and 4, which may take two to three years to complete at each level.

Further information is available from HCIMA, Springboard (a one-stop job shop), and the Hospitality Training Foundation (HTF), the industry-led body jointly responsible for catering and hospitality NVQs/SVQs with the National Council for Vocational Qualifications (NCVQ) and the Scottish Vocational Educational Council (SCOTVEC).

LATE ENTRY

It is often possible to be promoted to a hotel manager position without coming through the standard training procedures, but on the basis of successful experience in the industry.

Adults can gain recognition of their skills and experience by working towards NVQs/SVQs. There is open access to NVQs/SVQs – no academic qualifications are required, and there are no age limits. NVQs/SVQs are based on competence, and it does not matter how that competence has been gained – through experience, company training programmes, college courses or open learning. Past experience can be put forward as evidence of competence, via Accreditation of Prior Learning (APL).

However, for a typical hotel management training scheme, an upper age limit of 25 or 30 years may apply. Contact individual hotel groups for details. Entry requirements may be waived by colleges/universities offering courses.

OPPORTUNITIES

Most of the UK hotel chains take about one hotel management trainee every year for every hotel in the chain.

Competition for these training schemes is very stiff. While there are more openings in London, there are correspondingly more applicants. Most trainees are moved all around the country during their training.

Hotel managers are employed in every type of establishment, whether it is a large luxury hotel, in one of a chain of mid-market hotels, a country house hotel, a small privately owned hotel or a budget-priced lodge. There are about 35,000 hotels and guest-houses in the UK, over half of which are small and are proprietor or partnership-run, and another 20 per cent or so employ ten staff or less. So there are plenty of opportunities for self-employment.

Competition for hotel manager positions is fierce. The hotel industry is quite mature, so opportunities are limited, as little growth is expected. The largest number of hotels (about 23 per cent) are located in the South East, with Scotland and the South West coming next. The three regions together account for 50 per cent of the total. However, hotels are spread over the whole of the UK. Some hotel chains provide opportunities to travel and work abroad.

Opportunities for similar work exist in catering management in the 70,000 catering establishments in the UK, and in contract catering. Please see article 2. RESTAURANT/CATERING MANAGER.

PAY AND CONDITIONS

The average salary for a hotel manager in a three-star hotel in central London is £32,000. The salary range for duty managers is £12,500 to £15,000 and for trainee managers £7,500 to £8,500. Salaries vary according to type and size of hotel and the location. Salaries in central London are normally higher than elsewhere.

Hotel managers work long hours, although they may arrange a shift system with deputy or assistant managers in larger hotels. Some hotel chains do not like their managers to live on the premises. In smaller establishments, the manager will often live on or very near the premises, and will always be on call in an emergency.

PROSPECTS

Promotion from management trainee to hotel manager requires successful experience in departmental management positions. Depending on the size of hotel, a typical route could be: assistant front-of-house manager, assistant conference and banqueting manager, food and beverage manager, deputy general manager, manager. This progression could easily take five to ten years.

It is then possible to be promoted to larger or more prestigious hotels. Within a chain, it is also possible to move into the corporate management side, perhaps working in acquisition departments, looking at possible new hotels to add to a chain, or working in a corporate sales or marketing department. Other possible developments could be in corporate training or personnel departments. To progress into these other fields, it may be necessary to gain additional qualifications, such as a Master of Business Administration (MBA), an Institute of Personnel and Development (IPD) qualification, or a marketing qualification. General management experience and training is also transferable to completely different areas in business, industry or public services.

RELATED OCCUPATIONS

Restaurant/catering manager, publican/licensee, holiday centre manager, personnel/training manager.

FURTHER INFORMATION AND READING.

Please see article 10. HOTEL PORTER.

2. RESTAURANT/CATERING MANAGER (IB)

THE WORK

Restaurant and catering managers are responsible for ensuring their customers are satisfied with the quality of food and service and that the restaurant or catering services operate efficiently and profitably. Restaurant managers are found in restaurants, hotels and fast-food outlets, while catering manager is the term often used for managers who provide catering for businesses, educational and welfare establishments, and the Armed Forces.

The restaurant manager's job involves dealing with people – both staff and customers. Managers often welcome guests and see them to their table, and organize table reservations. Catering managers may have less direct contact with their customers. For both, staff management duties include recruitment, training and motivating, as well as organizing and supervising shifts. Ultimate responsibility for quality control, hygiene, and health and safety falls to managers too, as it is their job to ensure high standards are kept. This includes the quality of the raw materials of the food, how staff handle it, and the state of the equipment used to store and prepare it. Ensuring this side of the operation works smoothly is an essential part of providing a service that will satisfy customers, whether they are guests, hospital patients or factory workers. If a customer is not satisfied with any aspect of the catering service, it is the manager's job to deal with complaints.

The restaurant manager also sets budgets, or agrees them with more senior management, and then implements them. It is the manager's job to keep costs down and profits up, while maintaining standards. Planning the efficient provision of supplies can be an important part of this. Some managers are responsible for planning and co-ordinating menus and ordering supplies, but others delegate this work to the head chef. This side of the job involves a certain amount of paperwork, especially for stock and cash control.

WORK ENVIRONMENT

Restaurant/catering managers are required in all styles of restaurants, fast-food outlets, hotels, sports and entertainment establishments, businesses, factories, schools, hospitals, department stores, yachts, airlines, etc. In small restaurants, the proprietor may act as manager. Managers are often on duty in the dining area as well as in the kitchen, if they are responsible for the whole operation. Some managers have use of an office for paperwork and meetings.

SKILLS AND INTERESTS

Leadership and management skills are important qualities for restaurant/catering managers, as it is their job to keep staff motivated so as to provide a quality service that attracts new, and retains existing, customers. Enjoying working with other people as part of a team is as important as being a leader. Good communication skills and an outgoing personality are assets, both in relation to staff and to customers. Managers are often in a dining area welcoming customers, or near at hand to deal with problems or complaints.

Organizational and planning skills are necessary, and an ability to keep calm under pressure when things are very busy. The fast pace of the catering business means problems can arise at any time, so a calm and creative mind helps the manager to find workable solutions.

Contract catering managers can work regular hours, though their counterparts in restaurants, fast-food outlets and hotels may work unsocial shifts. In both cases, a willingness to work beyond the set hours is often needed.

ENTRY REQUIREMENTS

There are several entry routes into restaurant or catering management. Those coming straight from education into trainee restaurant/catering management positions would normally need a degree, BTEC/SCOTVEC higher national diploma, or the Hotel and Catering International Management Association (HCIMA) Professional Diploma. For a degree, at least two A levels/three H grades plus five GCSEs/S grades (A-C/1-3), or equivalent, are normally required, while a BTEC/SCOTVEC higher national diploma normally requires one A level/two H grades and four GCSEs/S grades (A-C/1-3), or equivalent, such as an Advanced GNVQ in Hospitality and Catering. Non-catering graduates may take a one-year postgraduate catering conversion course, either through a university or the HCIMA. Normal entry requirements for the HCIMA Professional Diploma are a BTEC/SCOTVEC national award, Advanced GNVQ/GSVQ Level III, or equivalent, an NVQ/SVQ Level 3 and work experience in the industry, or the HCIMA Professional Certificate, which requires industry experience, or four GCSEs/S grades (A-C/1-3), or equivalent.

However, it is very common for restaurant/catering managers to be promoted to the job on the basis of their experience in the industry, for example as a chef manager with an NVQ Level 2 or 3 in Food Preparation and Cooking. Many restaurant/catering managers work their way up from posts such as a trainee chef, bar or waiting staff.

TRAINING

Most of the pre-entry training options listed above take between two and four years to complete. Degrees and higher national diplomas are available in hospitality, hotel and catering management and catering technology. Studies cover subjects such as catering technology, the industry's role in the economy, sales and marketing, gastronomy, customer care and the management of staff and equipment in food and beverage operations. The HCIMA diploma can be taken full-time in a year for those with industry experience, but it is usually completed part-time in three years, or as a two-year sandwich course.

Entrants without high-level qualifications, who have perhaps worked their way up the industry, may wish to train for NVQs/SVQs in Catering and Hospitality at Levels 3 and 4. This qualification is more readily available, especially with larger employers.

A number of restaurant chains recruit applicants with suitable personalities straight from school, and then train them for management positions. These employers provide on-the-job training, moving trainees through the different operations of the restaurant (the kitchen, the bar, waiting at tables, and so on), promoting them on the way, until they are judged to have adequate experience and skills to become managers. Some chains provide NVQ/SVQ qualifications.

LATE ENTRY

The flexibility of entry routes to the job of restaurant/catering manager means there are no formal set age limits to start training for the job. However, it should be remembered that catering is a young industry that depends on personality, to a large extent.

Entry requirements for many qualifications may be waived for adult candidates with experience in the industry – check with individual colleges for details.

OPPORTUNITIES

There are around 70,000 restaurants, cafis and snack bars in the UK, with a proprietor or manager in charge, while a significant proportion of the 35,000 hotels also have a restaurant requiring management. The mid-price sector of restaurants is a growth area, while the fast-food sector is increasing most rapidly. The licensed retailing sector has become increasingly important in recent years, with a very large number of pubs and wine bars offering restaurant facilities.

Contract catering remains fairly buoyant, with the greatest number of opportunities in industry and commerce, private education, the Ministry of Defence and health care. Recent privatization programmes have opened up new opportunities in the National Health Service, local government, schools and the Civil Service. Opportunities in the catering services sector are most likely to increase during the 1990s in education, the medical sector, retail, recreational and cultural establishments.

Self-employment opportunities are good – more than half of the UK's restaurants are proprietor or partnership-run. Contract catering attracts former managers who wish to set up on their own. As food and drink is often prepared on customers' own sites, large investment in property is often unnecessary.

Although catering opportunities are spread throughout the UK, the South East region dominates, with 36 per cent of restaurants and 37 per cent of contract catering companies. The next largest number of opportunities are in the North West (11 per cent of restaurants and 9 per cent of contract catering companies) and Yorkshire (10 per cent of restaurants).

PAY AND CONDITIONS

Salaries range from £15,000 to £35,000 for a restaurant or catering manager, as an average for three-star, four-star and five-star hotels in central London. Clearly, salaries vary according to the type of restaurant or establishment, and will tend to be higher in central London than elsewhere. In contract catering, average salaries would be at the lower end of these scales.

Restaurant and catering managers usually work long hours, although shifts can be arranged with deputies or assistants in large restaurants and hotels. Contract catering managers for commerce and industry often work regular hours, as lunch is usually the main focus of the day.

PROSPECTS

There are a number of routes by which to progress from the role of restaurant/catering manager. Opportunities to progress to regional/area management exist for managers in restaurant chains or large contract caterers. Managers wishing to run their own business often decide to open their own restaurant or catering company. Restaurant managers

at hotels could be promoted to hotel manager. Another option would be to move into pub management.

RELATED OCCUPATIONS

Hotel manager, publican/licensee, room service manager, banqueting and conference manager, head chef, head food service assistant.

FURTHER INFORMATION AND READING

Please see article 10. HOTEL PORTER.

3. HOUSEKEEPER/HOUSEKEEPING MANAGER (IB)

THE WORK

Housekeepers, or housekeeping managers, are responsible for the provision of accommodation services and sometimes for choosing furnishings and fittings in hotels. It is the housekeeper's responsibility to ensure that the bedrooms, bathrooms and public rooms look clean, tidy and attractive, creating a good impression with the hotel's customers. Housekeepers work in hotels and similar establishments, while domestic services managers and bursars are responsible for the catering and accommodation services at colleges, universities, hospitals and residential homes.

Housekeepers/housekeeping managers (sometimes called head housekeeper or executive housekeeper) supervise other staff, such as room attendants, cleaners, linen and laundry staff. They allocate daily cleaning duties, issue keys, linen and cleaning materials to the staff and inspect rooms to check they have been thoroughly cleaned. It is their duty to ensure that every detail is attended to, whether cleaning or repairs are required. They are responsible for replacing damaged items and, in some hotels, for arranging maintenance work. They liaise with other hotel departments, such as reception, to check availability of rooms or to ensure guests' requests are met quickly and efficiently. Housekeepers may be responsible for their own budget, preparing and implementing it and keeping records of expenditure. They may be responsible for buying supplies, and getting them at the best possible price.

In a large hotel, the housekeeping manager may manage several floor housekeepers, who all supervise room attendants on their floor. In smaller establishments there may be just one housekeeper/housekeeping manager in charge. In either case, the job involves team work, motivating and managing staff, and sometimes stepping in to do the actual cleaning and tidying work. In very small establishments, there may be only one or two people involved in cleaning duties, reporting directly to the manager or proprietor.

Domestic services managers and bursars are more concerned with organizing the provision of catering and accommodation services to students, tourists and conference delegates. They are responsible for the daily supervision of dining rooms and the allocation of rooms. They are usually responsible for their own budgets, often using contract caterers and cleaners, rather than permanent staff.

WORK ENVIRONMENT

Housekeepers are required in every type of hospitality establishment, from bed-and-breakfasts, to holiday centres and five-star hotels. In smaller establishments, the housekeeper is more often involved in the physically demanding work of cleaning and tidying rooms. In larger hotels, the housekeeper may spend more time liaising with management and suppliers, and checking that high standards of cleanliness are maintained.

Domestic services managers and bursars work in a wide variety of establishments, from private residential homes to large student halls of residence. Much of their work is office-based, especially when they are involved in letting accommodation for other uses, such as conferences.

SKILLS AND INTERESTS

Like any management position, the job of housekeeper/housekeeping manager requires leadership skills. The ability to recruit, train, motivate and lead staff is essential. Good communications are necessary for dealing with guests, management and staff, as well as liaising with other departments, such as maintenance and reception. Strong organizational skills are needed, both for arranging staff duties and keeping supplies well stocked. A practical approach and an eye for detail help the housekeeper provide a consistent environment for the hotel's guests. Housekeepers must be able to make decisions and to keep calm in a crisis.

As well as being a leader, though, housekeepers/housekeeping managers need to be part of a team. They are not only in the housekeeping team, but are also a key member of the team that runs the hotel, working with a variety of departments and other managers. Being a member of the housekeeping team means doing the actual cleaning sometimes, so it is essential to be physically fit and prepared to work hard.

The job of housekeeper entails unsocial hours, as accommodation needs to be available 24-hours a day. While people with day jobs sleep at night, airline crew for instance, may require a clean room to check into and go to bed in at 11am after flying all night. Housekeepers must be prepared to start work early in the morning, and often to work shifts. It is an active job, suitable for people who do not want to be tied to a desk or work from nine to five.

As well as leadership and organizational skills, housekeeping managers need skills to handle budgets. For domestic services managers and bursars, these can be in the order of several million pounds a year.

ENTRY REQUIREMENTS

Housekeeper/housekeeping manager entry requirements are NVQ/SVQ in Catering and Hospitality Management (Housekeeping) at Level 3, or the equivalent demonstrable experience and knowledge. The most common entry route is promotion from within the hotel after gaining NVQs/SVQs. It may be possible to gain an Advanced/Intermediate GNVQ/GSVQ at Level II/III in Hospitality and Catering, and join a hotel as a floor housekeeper or in a similar-level job. Candidates for these qualifications usually require four GCSEs/S grades (A-C/1-3) or equivalent, such as an Intermediate GNVQ/GSVQ in Hospitality and Catering at Level II. As a floor housekeeper, NVQ/SVQ in Catering and Hospitality (Housekeeping) at Level 3 could be achieved.

An alternative route would be to start straight from school as a cleaner, room attendant or similar. With the right combination of motivation and potential, it would be possible to then work up the ranks, adding experience and qualifications perhaps through part-time study. People management skills are extremely important in this job, as is physical fitness.

Entry may be possible for young people through Modern Apprenticeships, leading to at least an NVQ/SVQ Level 3. Contact your local careers office, TEC/LEC for details.

For domestic service managers or bursars, experience in managing budgets, catering or accommodation services is usually required. This could be gained during work, for example, as an assistant housekeeping manager.

TRAINING

The Advanced GNVQ/GSVQ in Hospitality and Catering trains students in accounting and finance as well as cleaning programmes and accommodation operations. Students learn subjects such as the safe use of hazardous cleaning substances and how beds should be made properly. Housekeepers training towards NVQ/SVQ Levels 3 and 4 learn similar subjects, as well as about the materials of different floorings and their appropriate cleaning agents, organizing cleaning systems and rotas and training other staff.

Once the position of housekeeper/housekeeping manager has been reached, formal qualifications and training would normally have been completed. A housekeeper without relevant qualifications in the personnel or training side of the job may wish to pursue further relevant training, such as with the Institute of Personnel and Development (IPD) or via organizations such as the Hospitality Training Foundation (HTF) or the Hotel and Catering International Management Association (HCIMA). This study could be done part-time or by distance learning. Some hotel chains may be able to organize relevant training via their own in-house training.

LATE ENTRY

Age is not a barrier for housekeeper/housekeeping management posts. Well-motivated and qualified housekeepers can be appointed to the post from as young as 20 to late middle age. As housekeepers are often promoted on the basis of experience, it is perfectly possible to start the job aged over 40 years.

Adults can gain recognition of their skills and experience by working towards NVQs/SVQs. There is open access to NVQs/SVQs – no academic qualifications are required, and there are no age limits. NVQs/SVQs are based on competence, and it does not matter how that competence has been gained – through experience, company training programmes, college courses or open learning. Past experience can be put forward as evidence of competence, via Accreditation of Prior Learning (APL).

OPPORTUNITIES

Housekeeper/housekeeping managers tend to stay in the job for extended periods once started, so opportunities at this level do not come up regularly. Opportunities at more junior housekeeping levels are more frequent, but competition is fairly strong. There are about 35,000 hotels and guest-houses spread across the UK, although many are small and do not employ housekeepers. The largest number of hotels (about 23 per cent) are located in the South East, with Scotland and the South West coming next. The three regions together account for 50 per cent of the total.

Openings for domestic services work at hospitals are spread across the country according to the density of population.

Competition for similar work at residential homes is fiercer, and opportunities for bursars at colleges and universities are almost exclusively for the more mature person, who already has industry experience. Few colleges have openings for younger staff at more junior levels, as they tend to use students or contracted-in services.

PAY AND CONDITIONS

The average salary for a head housekeeper in hotels in central London is £14,000 to £21,000. The range for assistant head housekeeper and floor housekeeper is £8,250 to £17,000. Salaries vary according to type and size of hotel and the location. Salaries in central London are normally higher than elsewhere.

Housekeepers usually work shift systems, often covering evenings and weekends, as well as early mornings, to ensure every day of the week is covered, and every part of every day.

PROSPECTS

Housekeepers/housekeeping managers often move into similar areas in other establishments, such as head of domestic services at a hospital, or facilities manager in businesses or schools. As the post involves all the management skills of other managerial posts, housekeepers have transferable skills. So if, for example, a housekeeper joined a contract cleaning company, it would be quite possible to progress to area manager. This move might require further qualifications, such as a Master of Business Administration (MBA).

Staying within the hotel world, possibilities include managing the front of house in a hotel, or pursuing personnel or training management positions, perhaps by taking additional qualifications, such as those of the Institute of Personnel and Development (IPD). In some cases, it might be possible to progress to hotel manager, or to open their own guest-house or hotel.

RELATED OCCUPATIONS

Domestic/school bursar, hospital domestic services manager, facilities manager, contract cleaning manager, front-of-house manager, room attendant/cleaner, head linen keeper, hotel manager.

FURTHER INFORMATION AND READING

Please see article 10. HOTEL PORTER.

4. CHEF/COOK (IC)

THE WORK

Chefs or cooks are responsible for preparing and cooking attractive food that is enjoyable and safe to eat, at a huge variety of restaurants and other eating establishments. Chef is the term normally used in kitchens at restaurants or hotels; cook is the word used in hospitals and schools. The same job is called short order cook or call order cook in some snack bars, cafis and fast-food outlets.

There are a number of different types of chef. Large kitchens in restaurants and hotels are divided into departments, each responsible for specific preparation and cooking activities, such as the pastry section, which makes all the desserts, pastries and breads. Trainee chefs, or *commis chefs*, work for three to six months in each section

to gain experience in every area of the kitchen. They learn, for instance, how to prepare and cook vegetables or make sauces, as well as doing general cleaning and washing up (although there may be kitchen porters or assistants to help with this). Hygiene is essential for the safe preparation of food, so this side of the work is very important. Each different section of the kitchen is run by a *chef de partie*. The next step up is *sous chef* or under-chef, who is skilled and experienced enough to run any section, and to take charge of the whole kitchen in the absence of the head chef. The head chef (sometimes called executive chef or *maitre chef de cuisine*) runs the whole kitchen, including planning menus, ordering supplies, managing staff and budgets, and ensuring food of a consistently high standard is produced.

In smaller establishments, the cook or chef could be doing everything: food preparation and cooking, cleaning up and even helping serve customers. In fast-food restaurants, staff often work on a rota system, sometimes serving, sometimes cooking.

Chefs/cooks use a wide variety of cooking utensils and equipment, and must learn the safe handling of sharp knives and hot apparatus. Protective uniforms and head coverings are worn. Some employers provide uniforms, but other chefs buy their own. For hygiene reasons, chefs/cooks are not allowed to wear jewellery (except for a plain wedding ring).

WORK ENVIRONMENT

Whether in a coffee shop, carvery, French or Japanese restaurant, the kitchen is likely to be hot, steamy and noisy. Cooking smells tend to get into clothes and hair. The kitchen atmosphere reflects the style of the head chef – some kitchens are calm, low-key and quiet; others are noisy and buzzing. Chefs/cooks spend most of their working day in this hot environment, almost continuously on their feet.

SKILLS AND INTERESTS

Working as a chef/cook is very demanding, with a lot of pressure at service time. Kitchens can get very hectic, especially when many dishes must be produced at the same time. So it is important to be able to deal with pressure and cope with several tasks at once. Equally important is to be able to get on with others in the kitchen and enjoy working in a team.

An interest in food preparation is a prerequisite, and those with creative flair and imagination, who enjoy learning a wide variety of skills, find the work rewarding. But organizational skills are vital too, to ensure correct timing of different dishes and to have the right ingredients and equipment available in the right quantities at the right time. A practical approach and an ability to plan methodically are useful qualities for this side of the work. The ability to stay calm in a crisis and to think of a practical solution can avert a potential problem.

Chefs need good communication, management and leadership skills to manage and train kitchen staff under them. Some chefs are responsible for budgets and negotiating with suppliers, so a head for figures helps.

ENTRY REQUIREMENTS

Formal qualifications are not required to start work as a trainee in a kitchen, but they are useful. From then on, good experience counts most.

It is possible to go on a full-time college-based course for one to two years and gain NVQs/SVQs in Catering and

Hospitality (Food Preparation and Cooking) at Levels 1 and 2, before starting a job. However, following this route usually means starting as a trainee or *commis chef*, especially in the more prestigious restaurants and hotels.

A number of private cookery schools offer a wide variety of short courses for fee-paying students. Courses usually last between a few weeks and a year, and lead to the school's own certificate. Students sometimes go into business catering (such as directors' dining rooms) or private dinner parties. Success there may lead to a career in the mainstream catering industry.

A popular route to work in a kitchen is via training schemes for young people. This can be done either by getting day release from an existing employer to go to a college or training centre, or by getting a traineeship at an organization such as the Hotel and Catering Training Company (HCTC) and getting them to send you to employers for work experience. For further details of schemes, contact local careers offices, TECs/LECs, HTF or Springboard.

Various employers offer chef training schemes, usually for 16 to 19-year-olds. These include a number of the luxury hotels and hotel chains, and some contract caterers.

Entry may be possible for young people through Modern Apprenticeships leading to at least an NVQ/SVQ Level 3. Contact your local careers office, TEC/LEC for details.

TRAINING

Working in a kitchen involves a great deal of on-the-job training and often off-the-job college study as well. To become a chef, it is necessary to learn different methods of food preparation and cooking. Training usually begins with the simpler (but often repetitive) preparation and cooking tasks. Hygiene and safety, including the safe handling of knives, are very important. Increasingly, employers provide on and off-the-job training and assessment support, enabling chefs to qualify with NVQs/SVQs in Catering and Hospitality (Food Preparation and Cooking) at Levels 1 and 2 for the basic skills, at Level 3 for Catering and Hospitality Supervisory Management (Food Preparation and Cooking), and at Level 4 for Catering and Hospitality Management (Food Preparation and Cooking).

Different cooking skills, such as carving or decorating, can be learned on the job. Some large employers let chefs experiment too, for example trying out new recipes or styles, such as Mexican or Japanese cooking. Differences between service styles are learned too – for instance, producing food to be presented on platters and trays for banquets and on individual plates, which must be done very quickly.

LATE ENTRY

Although there are few age limits on entering kitchen work, many employers in hotels and restaurants prefer to train chefs while they are young and adaptable. So applicants beyond their mid to late-twenties may find it easier to enter hospital or educational catering.

There may be specific training opportunities, directed at adults, available in some areas for this type of work. Candidates may have to satisfy certain conditions to be eligible. Contact your local Jobcentre, careers office or TEC/LEC for details.

OPPORTUNITIES

Opportunities are far greater for qualified chefs than for trainees, although more openings are expected as the 1990s progress. Please see article 2. RESTAURANT/CATERING MANAGER for more details on distribution of restaurants, catering companies and hotels.

PAY AND CONDITIONS

Salaries range from £7,000 to £8,500 for a *commis chef* and £16,750 to £37,500 for a head chef as an average for three-star, four-star and five-star hotels in central London. Salaries vary according to the type of establishment and are usually higher in central London than elsewhere.

Chefs/cooks usually work long, and hectic hours. In restaurants and hotels, shift work covering evenings and weekends is normal to cover all the hours the restaurant is open. Contract catering chefs for commerce and industry, and school cooks, often work regular hours, as lunch is usually the main focus of the day. However, for residential schools, colleges and hospitals, shifts are required.

PROSPECTS

With NVQs/SVQs at Levels 3 or 4, or the equivalent in work experience, a chef can be promoted to head chef. For those at smaller establishments, it is always possible to move to larger and more prestigious ones. From there it is possible to move more into management as a catering or food and beverages manager in a hotel, employing their own kitchen staff. Some chefs may open their own restaurant, often with a partner who focuses on service aspects. The management experience of running a busy kitchen could also lead to contract catering management, pub management or hotel management. Other opportunities lie in lecturing, becoming a nutritionist, or moving into food product development for commercial producers of tinned, chilled, frozen or other packaged foodstuffs.

RELATED OCCUPATIONS

Restaurant/catering manager, head chef, food and beverage manager, kitchen assistant, contract caterer, chef manager, food product development manager.

FURTHER INFORMATION AND READING

Please see article 10. HOTEL PORTER.

5. KITCHEN ASSISTANT (IC)

THE WORK

Kitchen assistants work for chefs in hotels, restaurants and other catering establishments and organizations. A large part of their job can be cleaning, but they also perform basic food preparation tasks. Some assistants get involved in organizing storerooms, and may help with unloading deliveries.

Kitchen assistants who help with the preparation of meals perform tasks related to the kitchen department in which they work (such as larder or pastry). Their work could include cleaning, peeling or slicing vegetables, dicing or chopping meat or skinning fish. Sometimes they may be responsible for simple cooking jobs, such as grilling bacon, making toast or tea and coffee. Using automatic equipment, such as chipping machines, can be part of the job too.

High standards of cleanliness and hygiene are essential in kitchens, so that food is safe to eat, as well as enjoyable.

Keeping the kitchen clean is often the kitchen assistant's major responsibility. Washing up is needed, even if there is a dishwasher for crockery and cutlery, as pots and pans may need to be scoured by hand. Equipment must be kept clean and shining too (fridges, ovens and so on) while surfaces, floors and walls must be kept free from grease and dirt. However, cleaning contractors may be used to do the heavier jobs.

Kitchen assistants use a variety of cleaning equipment and materials, many of which are hazardous or corrosive, as well as kitchen utensils. Protective uniforms, head coverings and, when appropriate, gloves are normally provided.

WORK ENVIRONMENT

Kitchen assistants spend most of their working day on their feet, in a hot and often steamy and noisy kitchen. Cooking smells may get into their clothes and hair. Assistants may need to reach into awkward spaces to clean them or stretch up to the top part of a wall to keep it clean. Handling heavy loads may also be required – such as carrying and unpacking deliveries of supplies.

SKILLS AND INTERESTS

A great deal of stamina and enthusiasm is needed for this job, as the kitchen assistant has to do a variety of jobs that keep them on their feet in a hot, and sometimes pressured, environment all day. They must be flexible and prepared to tackle a range of tasks – not always directly related to food preparation – including doing some fairly dirty jobs. It is a job for practical people, who can work quickly and efficiently under the direction of other people. It is important to be able to complete a number of different tasks in the time allocated, according to the chef's needs.

Kitchens are very much team-based environments, and it is essential that a kitchen assistant gets on well with people and enjoys working as part of a team. They should be able to communicate clearly with chefs and other kitchen staff and may need to do so with suppliers too. It is essential for assistants to understand the pressure that chefs come under at service time and to learn the protocol for when and how to ask questions so that they do not disturb the chef's concentration at a vital moment.

ENTRY REQUIREMENTS

Formal academic qualifications are not needed to start a job as a kitchen assistant. Employers are more interested in a basic interest in food preparation and a willingness to learn. A demonstrable ability to communicate well and participate in a team all help. Employers are also looking for people who are prepared to work hard, take a pride in their work and start at the bottom.

A kitchen assistant's job is a fairly active one, so a reasonable level of fitness is required. This is particularly true for jobs where lifting and carrying are required. Even if a kitchen assistant does not help with unloading deliveries, they are likely to be asked to carry supplies in the kitchen and storeroom and in between.

TRAINING

Kitchen assistants learn a great deal on the job. They also get on-the-job training, both in how to clean different materials and what to use, and in different food-preparation techniques. They are trained in hygiene, health and safety, the safe handling of dangerous equipment, such

as sharp knives, as well as the safe use of hazardous cleaning substances. Off-the-job college study may be available too, in basic food-preparation skills. This can be done at catering colleges or through organizations such as the Hotel and Catering Training Company (HCTC). Kitchen assistants may train towards nvqs/svqs in Catering and Hospitality (Preparing and Serving Food) at Levels 1 and 2 or Catering and Hospitality (Kitchen Portering) at Level 1.

It is possible to start working in a kitchen via a training scheme for young people. This can be done, either by getting day release from an existing employer to go to off-the-job training providers, or by taking a traineeship at a training provider and having them send you to employers for work experience. For further details of schemes, local careers offices, TECs/LECs, the HTF or Springboard should be consulted.

LATE ENTRY

There are no age restrictions on entering kitchen work, although those with ambition to progress may find it more difficult, the older they are before they start. Some employers favour more mature applicants in the belief that their standards may be higher.

There may be specific training opportunities, directed at adults, available in some areas for this type of work. Candidates may have to satisfy certain conditions to be eligible. Contact your local Jobcentre, careers office or TEC/LEC for details.

OPPORTUNITIES

Vacancies for kitchen assistants are usually fairly plentiful. Please see article 2. RESTAURANT/CATERING MANAGER for more details on the distribution of restaurants, catering companies and hotels.

PAY AND CONDITIONS

A kitchen assistant's salary ranges from £6,500 to £8,250 as an average for three-star, four-star and five-star hotels in central London. Salaries vary according to the type of establishment and are usually higher in central London than elsewhere.

In restaurants and hotels, kitchen assistants work shifts in the evenings and at weekends to cover all the hours the restaurant is open. Assistants with contract catering companies for commerce, industry and school often work regular hours, as lunch is usually the main focus of the day. However, for residential schools, colleges and hospitals, shifts are required.

PROSPECTS

Kitchen assistants with the right motivation may aim to become chefs. After gaining an NVQ/SVQ in Catering and Hospitality (Food Preparation and Cooking) at Level 1, or equivalent experience, they could be appointed trainee or *commis chef*. This move may be easier in smaller operations, where the kitchen assistant's job involves more food preparation. The employer may offer in-house training, or college study, or a combination. With further experience and qualifications, they could then work their way up the kitchen career ladder (please see article 4. Chef/Cook). Alternatively, they may prefer to move into food service, fast-food provision, banqueting provision, or to bar work, portering work or other cleaning work, such as a hotel room attendant, and then up the career ladder from any of those areas.

RELATED OCCUPATIONS

Hotel room attendant, contract cleaner, steward (cruise liners and trains), food service assistant, catering assistant, storeperson, *commis chef.*

FURTHER INFORMATION AND READING

Please see article 10. HOTEL PORTER.

6. FOOD SERVICE ASSISTANT (IC)

THE WORK

Food service assistants may also be known as waiters or waitresses. The duties of individual food service assistants differ according to their place of work, but generally the work includes three elements: preparation, serving and clearing away.

Preparation. Before a restaurant or dining room opens to the public, it must be made ready. Food service assistants may clean floors, dust, set tables with clean cloths (if cloths are used), cutlery and condiments, and generally make sure that the area is clean and tidy.

Serving. Assistants greet customers on arrival and show them to their tables. They discuss the menu and answer questions about the dishes on offer. In doing so, they may encourage customers to increase their spending. Orders are written down on a pad and taken to the kitchen for preparing. In some restaurants, orders for drinks are taken by specialist wine waiters/waitresses. In other outlets, the same food service assistants take orders for food and drink.

While food is being prepared in the kitchens, assistants set any additional cutlery that will be needed and bring items such as sauces to the table. They then serve the food. The main types of food service are plate service and silver service.

The majority of organizations now use plate service, where meals are put onto plates by kitchen staff and carried to tables in the dining area by food service assistants. In silver service, food is placed into dishes or tureens in the kitchen. Food service assistants then serve the food onto plates at the table by using a spoon and fork.

Other kinds of service include: gueridon service, where food service assistants cook dishes at the table; carvery/ buffet service, used especially for breakfasts, where guests help themselves to food, although a food service assistant may serve main dishes and carve meat and poultry.

Clearing away. When they see that diners have finished a course, food service assistants clear the table and take orders for the next course. At the end of the meal they may prepare the bill and take payment, using a cash register and dealing with credit cards. When diners have left, assistants clear the table and prepare it for the next customers.

In many catering outlets, food service assistants are responsible for all the activities described above. In more formal outlets, food service may be a team responsibility. A head waiter, who may be restaurant manager, oversees *chefs de rang.* These are senior waiters, responsible for a specific number of tables. They advise on menus, take orders and serve food. There are also *commis waiters*, who are learning the skills involved and, at this stage, are mostly involved in preparation work, fetching and carrying dishes and clearing away.

WORK ENVIRONMENT

Food service assistants work in the dining rooms of restaurants and other catering establishments, which tend to be clean, warm and comfortable. Some time is spent in kitchens, which can be hot, steamy and noisy. They are on their feet all day and may carry heavy loads.

SKILLS AND INTERESTS

The reputation of restaurants and other catering establishments is based as much on the quality of service as of the food. Food service assistants are the main contact with diners and need, therefore, to be interested in providing a service, and they need to be pleasant, polite and tactful. It is also important that they are neat and tidy in appearance, with high standards of personal hygiene and cleanliness.

Food service work can be very busy, so the ability to work well and remain calm under pressure is desirable. Good memory is needed to remember which diners at a table ordered which dishes. Good spoken English is required for dealing with customers, as is clear handwriting for noting orders. Ability with figures is necessary for making up bills and giving change.

Food service assistants need good knowledge of the food on the menu so they can answer diners' questions and advise them on their choices. A knowledge of wine and other drinks is also necessary, unless there is a specialist wine waiter.

Selling skills are required to advise diners of the range of products on offer, with the aim of increasing sales.

Silver service work requires good dexterity for serving food from dishes to plates.

Food service assistants work as part of a team, with kitchen staff and other food service staff, and should be capable of operating as team members.

Most food service assistants must be willing to work unsocial hours. Good health and fitness are essential, as food service is physically active and demanding.

ENTRY REQUIREMENTS

No formal qualifications are required for entry to food service, although a good standard of secondary education is desirable. In particular, GCSEs/S grades in English and maths are useful.

Entry to many full-time courses leading to GNVQ/GSVQ and NVQ/SVQ qualifications does not demand specific qualifications, but schools and colleges wish to be satisfied that students can benefit from the courses.

TRAINING

Pre-entry

GNVQs/GSVQs in Hospitality and Catering can provide useful preparation for entry to a wide range of work in the hotel and catering industry, including food service. GNVQ Foundation and Intermediate courses and GSVQ Level I and II courses, and Scottish national certificate courses, are offered by many schools and colleges of further education, mostly one year full-time. They do not provide specific training for jobs, but aim to give students knowledge and understanding of the industry and develop their communication, numeracy and information technology skills. They can lead to direct entry to work, or to further courses.

Full-time training

Many colleges of further education throughout the UK offer one-year or two-year full-time courses leading to

Catering and Hospitality NVQ/SVQ qualifications in serving food and drink. Courses include a large amount of practical work experience in colleges' own training kitchens and restaurants, and often in industry.

NVQ/SVQ qualifications are based on demonstrating competence (adequate ability) in the practical skills of the work. In food service, the relevant NVQs/SVQs are Level 1 Serving Food and Drink – Table and Counter/ Take-away and Level 2 Serving Food and Drink – Table.

Post-entry training

An increasing number of employers offer training leading to NVQs/SVQs. In some cases, this is provided with the help of a local college.

Training schemes for young people

It is possible to start work via a training scheme for young people. This can be done by getting day release from an existing employer to go to college, or by a traineeship/ Modern Apprenticeship. For further details of schemes, contact local careers offices, TECs/LECs, HCTC or Springboard.

LATE ENTRY

There is no upper age limit for entry to food service. Recruitment policy differs from company to company. Previous experience of work in hotel and catering is an advantage, as is experience of other work providing service to the public.

There may be specific training opportunities, directed at adults, available in some areas for this type of work. Candidates may have to satisfy certain conditions to be eligible. Contact your local Jobcentre, careers office or TEC/LEC for details.

OPPORTUNITIES

The number of food service assistants is increasing and there are approximately 100,000 employed throughout the UK. They work in hotels, restaurants, public houses, contract catering and industrial catering organizations, cafis, fast-food outlets, transport companies and roadside and motorway outlets.

Vacancies arise frequently as staff turnover in food service is high. Vacancies are advertised in *Caterer and Hotelkeeper, Catering, Scottish Licensed Trade News* and in local newspapers.

Work overseas is possible, both in the EU and elsewhere, providing the language of the country is spoken.

PAY AND CONDITIONS

Wages vary according to location and employer. For a 39-hour week, food service assistants may earn between £83 and £156 plus tips. Overtime may be available at enhanced rates.

Employers often provide a uniform or clothing.

Full-time work is usually 38 to 40 hours a week, but patterns of work vary. Some work split shifts, ie working at lunch-times and evenings with a rest period during the afternoons. Weekend work is usual. Where restaurants are open for very long hours, shift work is normal. Those working for contract caterers providing lunch-time service may work Mondays to Fridays only.

There are many opportunities for part-time work. Casual work, for special events, is also common, as is temporary or seasonal work – over the Christmas and summer holiday seasons, for instance.

PROSPECTS

Prospects for promotion depend to some extent on the size of organization. Most food service assistants work for small organizations that do not have a career structure, so those seeking advancement have to change employers. Large organizations often have a career structure allowing promotion from *commis* waiter/waitress to *chef de rang* to head waiter/waitress. Head waiters/waitresses often also act as restaurant managers, organizing and supervising restaurant staff.

Those aiming to advance to management positions can work towards NVQs/SVQs in Catering and Hospitality (Food and Drink Service) at Levels 3 and 4.

The turnover of staff in food service tends to be high, which means that prospects for promotion are good and rapid advancement is possible.

RELATED OCCUPATIONS

Barman/woman, sales assistant, airline steward/stewardess, merchant navy steward/stewardess, counter service assistant, cook, restaurant/catering manager, kitchen assistant.

FURTHER INFORMATION AND READING

Please see article 10. HOTEL PORTER.

7. COUNTER SERVICE ASSISTANT (IC)

THE WORK

Counter service assistants serve food to customers at catering establishments, where customers collect food from a counter or bar, rather than being served at their tables. Examples include: snack bars, canteens, cafes, coffee shops and self-service restaurants. Many work in fast-food outlets, where they are known as food service assistants.

In fast-food restaurants, staff rotate duties. In other organizations, duties differ according to the place of work but may include:

Preparation

Assistants make sure that the counter area is clean and tidy, and well stocked with crockery, cutlery, glasses and trays. They may fill hot and cold drinks machines.

Food is usually prepared by chefs or cooks, but counter service assistants may help with some tasks, such as preparing salads and mixing sauces. In smaller establishments, like snack bars, assistants may prepare all the food and drinks – make sandwiches and tea and coffee, for example. They may set out food in display cabinets.

Serving customers

In some establishments, such as canteens and self-service restaurants, assistants serve hot dishes selected by customers. That can involve cutting dishes, such as pies, into portions and serving a set amount of each dish on to plates, taking care to arrange the food attractively. They may use knives, ladles and scoops.

Assistants keep a watch for items of food and drink that are running low, and reorder them from the kitchen, or prepare more themselves.

Those working in snack bars and fast-food restaurants may also cook certain food items – pies, pizzas, hamburgers, chicken portions and chips, for example – that can involve using ovens, microwave cookers, grills or deep fat fryers. The cookery skills required are fairly easy to master.

In take-away restaurants, assistants may also cook food, or use food that has already been cooked and kept hot. They pack the food into trays or cartons for the customers to take away. With large chains of fast-food take-aways, there are carefully worked out set procedures for serving each customer.

Taking customers' money is part of many assistants' duties. Each item bought is rung in on a cash register that gives a total to be charged. Assistants take cash and may also process credit cards and/or luncheon vouchers. Some assistants cash up at the end of a work session, checking that the takings and cash register records agree.

Cleaning

Assistants keep the counter area clean and tidy throughout the serving session, which includes mopping up spilt food and drink and wiping over counter surfaces. They may clear tables, collect used crockery and cutlery, empty ashtrays and wipe tables. They may have to wash up, although most establishments have dishwashing machines, which the assistants stack and unload.

At the end of a session, assistants may sweep and wash the floor, clean out drinks machines, wash equipment and leave everything clean and tidy in readiness for the next session.

WORK ENVIRONMENT

Counter service assistants work in warm and light conditions. Some spend time in preparing food in kitchens or washing up, which can be hot and steamy. Clearing away used crockery and cutlery and cleaning food dishes can be messy. The work involves standing much of the time, with some bending and carrying.

SKILLS AND INTERESTS

Counter service assistants need to get on well with people. They should be able to cope with any difficult customers, and deal with complaints. With counter service, customers usually have to be served quickly, so assistants should be capable of working under pressure.

Assistants have to be able to work well in a team with other staff, cooks or supervisors.

Counter service work can be physically demanding, so it is necessary to be fit and capable of standing for long periods of time. Some skin complaints make this work unsuitable.

Appearance is important. Assistants should be clean and tidy and concerned with high standards of hygiene, health and safety. Assistants must be prepared to follow their employers rules that restrict the use of cosmetics and jewellery.

Practical skills are required for basic food preparation, such as sandwich making. An eye for presentation is useful for displaying and serving food attractively. Accuracy is important for portion control.

Assistants responsible for taking money and giving change should have the ability to use tills and deal with cash accurately.

ENTRY REQUIREMENTS

No formal qualifications are required for entry, although a good standard of education is desirable. Employers are more concerned with personal qualities, but look for some ability with figures if handling cash is involved.

Entry to GNVQ/GSVQ courses does not demand specific qualifications, but schools and colleges wish to be satisfied that students can benefit from the courses.

TRAINING

Pre-entry

GNVQs/GSVQs in Hospitality and Catering can provide useful preparation for entry to a wide range of work in the hotel and catering industry, including counter service. GNVQ Foundation and Intermediate courses and GSVQ Level I and II courses are offered by many schools and colleges of further education, mostly one year full-time. They do not provide specific training for jobs, but aim to give students knowledge and understanding of the industry and develop their communication, numeracy and information technology skills. They can lead to direct entry to work or to further courses.

Post-entry

Training for counter service work usually takes place on entry to a job. It varies between organizations, although assistants are usually trained by experienced assistants or supervisors.

Assistants may begin by learning simple jobs, such as preparing the counter and keeping cutlery containers filled, before progressing to serving food. Large organizations, especially the fast-food companies, have formal training programmes. New recruits learn about the company and its policies, conditions of employment and staff welfare matters. They are also instructed on matters such as health and safety, using the cash register and presenting food.

Assistants may be helped by their employer to work towards NVQ/SVQ qualifications, which are based on demonstrating competence (adequate ability) in the practical skills of the job. Counter service assistants can work for an NVQ/SVQ in Catering and Hospitality (Serving Food and Drink) at Level 1, which includes dealing with customers, effective working relationships, dealing with payments, preparing and cleaning areas for counter service, providing a counter service, plus hygiene, health and safety.

Training schemes for young people

There are opportunities for 16 and 17-year-olds to train for counter service. Experience and on-the-job training are combined with training at a local college, or training centre, to work towards NVQ/SVQ qualifications. Contact local careers offices, TECs/LECs for details.

LATE ENTRY

There is no upper age limit for entry to counter service work. Some fast-food outlets mainly employ people in their teens and twenties, but most catering organizations are happy to employ adults of varying ages.

The large amount of part-time work available may particularly attract adults with family commitments.

For this type of work, specific training opportunities, directed at adults, may be available. Candidates may have to satisfy certain conditions to be eligible. Contact your local Jobcentre, careers office or TEC/LEC for details.

OPPORTUNITIES

Counter service assistants work in a variety of catering establishments throughout the UK. They include: cafis, self-service restaurants, coffee shops, fast-food outlets, snack bars, cafeterias, staff restaurants in factories, schools, colleges and hospitals, and outside caterers specializing in functions.

The number employed in this work is increasing,

particularly as more fast-food outlets are opening, and vacancies arise frequently. Vacancies may be advertised in local newspapers, Jobcentres, careers offices, or may be found by direct approach to local catering establishments. There are no opportunities for self-employment.

PAY AND CONDITIONS

Wages vary according to location and employer. For a 39-hour week, counter service assistants may earn between £111 and £175, with extra for overtime.

Full-time work is usually between 38 and 40 hours a week, but patterns of work vary according to the place of work. Weekend work may be required, especially in fast-food restaurants. Where outlets are open for very long hours, shift work is normal. There are opportunities for permanent day and permanent night work in some outlets that open 24 hours a day, such as motorway service areas.

Seasonal work is common – working during the summer season in a tourist area, for example – and there are many opportunities for part-time work.

PROSPECTS

Some organizations have a career structure that allows promotion from counter service work to supervisor and then to manager. Assistants working for organizations where that possibility does not exist need to move to another employer for advancement. Capable workers can find that advancement in the catering industry is rapid. Prospects for promotion, particularly with large catering organizations, may be improved by achieving further NVQs/SVQs, for example, in Catering and Hospitality (Food Preparation and Cookery) or (Food Service) at Level 2 or above.

RELATED OCCUPATIONS

Fast-food cook, retail assistant, cash till/checkout operator, barman/woman, food service assistant, chef/cook, kitchen assistant.

FURTHER INFORMATION AND READING

Please see article 10. HOTEL PORTER.

8. HOTEL RECEPTIONIST (IC/CAT)

THE WORK

Hotel receptionists provide the first impression guests have of a hotel, and often the last one too, when they check out. The first impression may come across the telephone, when a booking is made, or face-to-face when guests first arrive at the beginning of their visit.

The job is not just about greeting and helping guests, though – a large part of reception work involves administration. This can include taking reservations and cancellations, allocating rooms, record-keeping (for instance use of the telephone or delivery of newspapers), taking and passing on messages, compiling bills and handling money (including foreign exchange), ordering room service and organizing the fulfilment of any special requirements guests have. In all but the smallest hotels, reservations will be handled by a computer system, on which the receptionist must update and check information. Receptionists often use word processors to write letters confirming reservations, as well as fax and telex machines and telephone switchboards.

Apart from checking guests in and out of the hotel, the receptionist has a great deal of other contact with guests. Questions about the local area and its amenities must be answered, valuables taken for safe keeping, and requests for taxis or theatre tickets must be dealt with. These queries and requests often provide constant interruptions to the receptionists' routine administrative tasks. Sometimes guests' requests must be referred on to other hotel departments, such as porters or restaurant staff. Receptionists must liaise constantly with the housekeeping department too, so that they know which rooms are occupied and which are not.

In large hotels, specialist teams may deal with certain aspects of reception work, for instance there may be an advance reservations telephone team and/or one handling guest accounts. In smaller hotels, the receptionist may handle a very large range of tasks, including carrying luggage or helping in the bar or restaurant.

WORK ENVIRONMENT

The nature of reception areas depends, to an extent, on the size and nature of hotel, but in general they are situated near the main hotel entrance behind a counter, often with office equipment. Receptionists work both standing at the counter and sitting at computer terminals and telephone switchboards. In smaller establishments, receptionists may also work in bars, restaurants and elsewhere.

SKILLS AND INTERESTS

This is a job where personality is of the utmost importance. Hotel reception work suits people who are friendly, outgoing and cheerful. It is essential to enjoy interacting with other people, guests and colleagues alike, and to have the good communications skills this entails. These skills include verbal and written communications, as well as body language. Receptionists must be willing to please and serve customers, and so the work suits people who enjoy a lot of contact with people and helping them to enjoy their visit. Sometimes receptionists find themselves being constantly interrupted, so they need to be patient and helpful, even with the occasional difficult guest.

Receptionists also need to be able to think on their feet, come up with creative solutions to problems, or be able to direct guests to another department or person who can. They need to be able to handle a wide variety of tasks at the same time and remain calm under the pressure this situation can cause.

Hotel reception work involves a good deal of administration too, so it suits people who are well organized and have an administrative flair. An aptitude for using office equipment is useful too.

ENTRY REQUIREMENTS

Personal qualities tend to be regarded by employers as more important requirements than specific qualifications. A good general education, good handwriting and reasonable levels of numeracy and literacy to deal with billing, record-keeping and letter writing all help. So, for example, GCSEs/S grades in English and maths are useful. Alternatively, a GNVQ/GSVQ in Hospitality and Catering at Foundation, Intermediate or Advanced level demonstrates an interest in, and understanding of, the industry.

An aptitude for languages is helpful for dealing with overseas guests and will enhance opportunities for working abroad. A demonstrable ability to communicate well with a wide variety of people and to enjoy helping them is sought by employers. Problem-solving skills and experience are of interest too. Employers look for people who have a smart appearance and pleasant personality and who can keep calm when under pressure.

TRAINING

Those who wish to study before starting full-time work can go on a full-time college course for one or two years, gaining NVQs/SVQs in Hospitality and Catering (Reception) at Levels 1 and 2. Alternatively, with four GCSEs/S grades (A-C/1-3), or equivalent, and the two-year Advanced GNVQ/GSVQ Level III in Hospitality and Catering is an option. From that route, work would still be started at the level of trainee receptionist, but promotion would be quicker. Training includes either realistic simulated work environments, or work experience, or both, and covers subjects such as reservations systems, telephone answering techniques, customer care, credit control, accounting and invoicing.

Trainee reception staff receive extensive on-the-job training in the technical side of the work, such as making and cancelling reservations and allocating rooms, how to calculate bills and how to use computers and the office equipment. They are also trained on information about the local area, places of interest and transport facilities. Training is provided in the all-important area of customer care too. Trainees without relevant qualifications are often given the opportunity to train towards NVQs/SVQs in Catering and Hospitality (Reception) at Levels 1 and 2. These qualifications are normally offered through in-house training, although some employers provide the opportunity to attend a part-time college course.

It is possible to start or develop work as a hotel receptionist via a training scheme for young people. This can be done either by getting day release from an existing employer to go to college, or by going on a traineeship at a centre such as the Hotel and Catering Training Company (HCTC) and being sent by them to employers for work experience. For further details of schemes, contact local careers offices, TECs/LECs, HCTC or Springboard.

LATE ENTRY

It can be harder to start work as a hotel receptionist over the age of 30, although some employers prefer more mature applicants, especially with good secretarial skills. Suitably qualified unemployed adults in some areas may be eligible for Training for Work schemes. Contact HCTC, local Jobcentre, careers office or TEC/LEC for more information.

OPPORTUNITIES

Vacancies for reception staff are usually plentiful, but competition is fierce. For further details on the numbers and distribution of hotels and other accommodation establishments, please see article 1. HOTEL MANAGER.

PAY AND CONDITIONS

Salaries range from £7,500 to £9,750 for a receptionist and £6,500 to £10,250 for hotel reservations clerks, cashiers and telephonists, as an average for three-star, four-star and five-star hotels in central London. Salaries vary according to the type of establishment and are usually higher in central London than elsewhere.

Reception desks operate from early morning to late at night, many for 24 hours a day, so receptionist staff usually work shifts, including evenings, overnight and weekends. Some hotels compensate for this by providing accommodation; others help with transport to and from home.

PROSPECTS

For receptionists at smaller establishments, it is always possible to move to larger and more prestigious hotels. From there, with appropriate experience and qualifications, such as an NVQ/SVQ in Catering and Hospitality (Hotel Reception Supervisory Management) at Level 3, receptionists can be promoted to shift leader or supervisor, and then on to head receptionist. Those with the right management potential and skills could be promoted to front office manager. For this level, further qualifications may be desired, such as an NVQ/SVQ in Catering and Hospitality (Reception Management) at Level 4, or more general hotel management qualifications, such as membership of the Hotel Catering and Institutional Management Association (HCIMA).

Alternatively, hotel receptionists may choose to try out other departments of the hotel, such as the bar, restaurant or banqueting services. Many large hotels operate schemes encouraging employees to work in different departments to develop their skills and so increase promotion prospects. Many receptionists choose to move into the sales or accounts departments, which, in turn, can lead up the management path. Some move into personnel or training, where a qualification from the Institute of Personnel and Development (IPD) is useful. Those who wish to try other environments, could take their skills to commerce and industry to take office jobs. Other options include customer care roles in the travel or leisure industry.

RELATED OCCUPATIONS

Secretary, bookkeeper, administrative assistant, air steward/hostess, information officer, hotel porter, reservations clerk, front office manager

FURTHER INFORMATION AND READING

Please see article 10. HOTEL PORTER.

9. HOTEL ROOM ATTENDANT (IC)

THE WORK

Hotel room attendants are responsible for keeping bedrooms, bathrooms and public rooms in hotels clean, tidy and pleasant. It is their job to ensure the hotel's appearance is clean, tidy, attractive and welcoming to guests.

Hotel room attendants are often allocated between six and 15 rooms to clean. The number depends on the type and size of hotel, the type and size of room and its furnishings, the number of cleaning staff available, and the standards expected. This work involves replacing used towels and linen, making the beds, emptying bins, dusting, vacuuming the floor and so on. Apart from cleaning the bedroom and bathroom, the attendant also tidies up and replenishes stocks of guest supplies, such as soap and shampoo, drinks in the mini-bar or coffee, tea and biscuits. Room attendants may also turn down beds before guests retire, and leave a good night message and chocolate on the pillow. Room attendants must take care not to disturb guests' possessions in occupied rooms, and to check unoccupied ones for left property.

Room attendants clean, polish and tidy public rooms too, and may arrange flowers or displays of tourist information and hotel sales leaflets and brochures. It is their job to make sure every detail of how a room looks is just right. If an item is damaged and needs to be repaired or replaced, the room attendant notifies the housekeeper, who will arrange for its repair or replacement.

Room attendants routinely use a vacuum cleaner, mop or both, and a variety of cleaning materials and substances. They learn to care for different types of surfaces, including wood, glass and fabrics. Some cleaning substances are hazardous or corrosive, and protective gloves and aprons, or overalls, should be worn.

Room attendants often work on their own as they perform the actual cleaning and tidying duties, but also work in a team. In large hotels, room attendants report to a floor housekeeper or assistant housekeeper. In smaller ones, they report directly to the housekeeper or housekeeping manager. In the smallest establishments, the room attendant may report directly to the manager or proprietor.

WORK ENVIRONMENT

Room attendants work in bedrooms, bathrooms, public rooms and supplies rooms (such as the linen room). They may need to access awkward spaces to clean, either bending down (for instance in bathrooms) or stretching up (perhaps to polish to the top of a mirror). The work can involve handling heavy loads of linen, or equipment such as vacuum cleaners.

SKILLS AND INTERESTS

Hotel room attendants need to be strong and physically fit. People with back, or other, physical problems would not be suitable for this work. Apart from moving heavy loads, and bending and stretching while making beds and cleaning bathrooms, they have to work hard, efficiently and quickly to complete all their rooms in the time allocated.

Attention to detail is very important in this job. The right number of towels should be left, the correct display of menus and stationery should be available and the flowers replaced if they are no longer fresh. It is the room attendant's job to notice these details (although, in most establishments, work is checked by supervisors or housekeepers). The work suits careful, practical people with an eye for detail, who like to see results quickly.

A hotel room attendant must be prepared to work on their own a lot of the time as they clean and tidy rooms. An ability to work on their own initiative is important, although equally important is working within the housekeeping team. This may involve liaising with supervisors, letting them know if items are damaged, or requesting replacement cleaning materials or fresh linen and reporting anything unusual or suspicious. So good communications and an ability to get on well with people are necessary. These characteristics will help with dealing with customers too. Hotel guests quite often ask room attendants for information or bring them problems or complaints.

ENTRY REQUIREMENTS

Formal qualifications are not usually required to start this job. Employers are looking for people who are reasonably strong and fit, to cope with the physical demands of the job. They also require people who are prepared to work hard

and for unsocial hours – hotel room attendants must fit in their work around guests, which usually means starting early in the morning and can involve working shifts in the evenings and weekends, so that services are provided seven days a week, whenever guests require them.

Applicants need to demonstrate an ability to work on their own initiative and in a team, and to get on with other people.

TRAINING

Hotel room attendants often start straight from school, or later in life, with few formal qualifications. Most employers offer them on-the-job training, combined with in-house training or sometimes part-time study at other colleges or commercial training centres, which would normally lead towards NVQs/SVQs in Catering and Hospitality (Housekeeping) at Levels 1 and 2.

Essential training for hotel room attendants includes the safe handling of hazardous substances for cleaning, which may be provided by the suppliers of the materials. Room attendants are also trained on the safe use of equipment, such as industrial vacuum cleaners and presses. Training on security issues, and general health and safety procedures is provided too. In addition, many employers offer hotel room attendants training in customer care to help them deal with guests.

It is also possible to train via a training scheme for young people. Contact local careers offices, TECs/LECs for further details.

LATE ENTRY

There are no age restrictions on entering the job of hotel room attendant, but it should be remembered that physical fitness and a degree of strength are needed for it. Room attendants with ambition for promotion may find opportunities limited if they start too late.

OPPORTUNITIES

Apart from the opportunities available in-house in hotels, guest-houses, holiday centres and the like, hotel room attendants can also work for agencies and contract cleaning companies. Those working for agencies can work in a variety of establishments, gaining experience in different systems. Many hotels use such agencies to vary their staff numbers, according to the different needs they have on different days. Generally, there are plenty of vacancies available.

For the numbers and distribution of hotels and accommodation establishments, please see article 1. HOTEL MANAGER.

PAY AND CONDITIONS

Average salaries for a hotel room attendant range from £7,300 to £9,000 in hotels in central London. Salaries vary according to type and size of hotel and the location. Salaries in central London are normally higher than elsewhere.

Hotel room attendants usually work shift systems, covering early mornings, evenings and weekends.

PROSPECTS

Hotel room attendants who demonstrate ability and management potential, and who are physically fit and well-motivated, can progress on to supervisory posts such as floor housekeeper. Increasingly, employers are offering the opportunity and training support to gain an NVQ/SVQ in Catering and Hospitality (Housekeeping) at Level 3. Another option would be to move to the linen room and perhaps become head linen keeper. Again, with the right qualities and training (for example, in training other people) floor managers and head linen keepers can progress on to housekeeper or housekeeping manager posts. Promotion to this level might offer the opportunity to gain further qualifications, such as an NVQ/SVQ in Catering and Hospitality (Housekeeping) at Level 4.

RELATED OCCUPATIONS

Contract (or other) cleaner, linen porter, hospital domestic services assistant, room steward (cruise liners and trains), head linen keeper, floor housekeeper, housekeeping manager.

FURTHER INFORMATION AND READING

Please see article 10. HOTEL PORTER.

10. HOTEL PORTER (IC)

THE WORK

Porters are often one of the first people guests meet when they arrive at a hotel, so they can make an enormous impact on the first impression guests have. Porters have a great deal of contact with people, and helping guests is their main function.

Apart from greeting guests, porters' duties include carrying luggage, directing people through the hotel, advising on hotel facilities (such as how to work the TV, when the restaurant serves dinner and where the fire exits are) and those of the local area, looking after keys, post and messages, calling or booking taxis, parking cars, arranging restaurant, theatre and travel reservations and running any other errands that guests require. Hotels with conference facilities may involve porters in organizing conference equipment, carrying it and setting it up in the right place. Porters on duty overnight may become involved in an even-wider range of tasks, including checking guests in and out if no other receptionist is on duty, preparing and serving snacks, drinks and breakfast trays and distributing morning newspapers.

In larger hotels, these tasks may be split among the different porters (or uniformed staff as they are also known). For instance, the doorman/woman is responsible for greeting guests, opening and closing car doors and hailing taxis; the luggage porter helps guests with carrying their bags; the hall porter answers queries and passes on post; while the bell hops locate guests and deliver messages. The head porter, or concierge, manages the team and arranges its shifts, recommends and books restaurants, shows and travel facilities. In smaller establishments, there may be only one or two porters to provide all these services.

WORK ENVIRONMENT

Whatever the size and nature of hotel, porters work mainly on their feet, standing or walking around the hotel. Depending on their particular job, a porter may stand near the hotel main entrance, or at the porter's desk, usually a counter in the main reception area, or lifting and carrying luggage, laundry, linen, housekeeping supplies, furniture or conference equipment all around the hotel.

SKILLS AND INTERESTS

As a porter's main function is to help guests, a friendly, pleasant and helpful personality will be a great asset in this job. It is a job for people who enjoy meeting and helping others. Good communications skills help with this side of the work. As part of the package of helping create a good impression with guests, porters are required to look their best, so employers look for people who have a smart appearance. People suited to portering work have an interest in the local area, for instance the different types of show available at different theatres and concert halls, the relative merits and prices of different restaurants, and the fastest, cheapest or most comfortable way to travel from one place to another.

Porters' jobs are active ones, so a reasonable degree of physical fitness helps. There is a lot of lifting and carrying work to be done, especially for new trainees, and so it is not a job for someone with a bad back. Even if a specific porter's job does not include much lifting and carrying, porters need to be comfortable with being on their feet most of the working day.

ENTRY REQUIREMENTS

Formal or academic qualifications are not usually required. A personality that is demonstrably friendly, cheerful and helpful is generally considered more important. Good communication skills are required, with employers often stipulating that porters have good spoken English, or are well spoken. An aptitude for and/or knowledge of other languages is useful too, for helping guests from overseas. Employers look for candidates with a smart appearance, and some ask for them to be over the age of 18, while others are prepared to take 16 or 17-year-olds.

Employers look for a reasonable degree of physical fitness too, particularly for those being considered for luggage or linen portering. Good local knowledge is important, especially for those working on the hall porters desk, or at reception.

TRAINING

Training for porters is generally provided on the job, including training in hotel services and local amenities. Security and fire procedures are covered, as well as health and safety and, often, first aid. Customer care training is provided too.

Porters who work overnight shifts are trained on procedures for checking guests in and out if they arrive late or depart early, and on preparing and serving refreshments. Occasionally, employers support this with off-the-job training, either through an in-house school (available in some hotel chains) or external·providers. In this way, porters can work towards gaining an NVQ/SVQ in Catering and Hospitality (Portering) at Level 1, learning subjects such as customer care, room service and making continental breakfasts. For those involved in a range of activities in the hotel, Catering and Hospitality (Guest Service) at Levels 1 and 2 may be appropriate.

It is possible to start or develop work as a hotel porter via a training scheme for young people. This can be done, either by getting day release from an existing employer to go to college or training centre, or by entering a traineeship with an organization such as the Hotel and Catering Training Company (HCTC) and being sent by them to employers for work experience. For further details of schemes, contact local careers offices, TECs/LECs, the HCTC or Springboard.

LATE ENTRY

Age is not a barrier to starting work as a hotel porter, but obviously the need for a degree of physical fitness and the ability to carry heavy loads should be borne in mind.

There may be specific training opportunities, directed at adults, available in some areas for this type of work. Candidates may have to satisfy certain conditions to be eligible. Contact your local Jobcentre, careers office or TEC/LEC for details.

OPPORTUNITIES

Vacancies for hotel porters are usually plentiful, but competition is quite strong. For further details of the number and distribution of hotels and other accommodation establishments, please see article 1. HOTEL MANAGER.

PAY AND CONDITIONS

Salaries range from £6,500 to £8,000 for a luggage porter, £7,250 to £9,250 for hall porters and £7,500 to £8,750 for doormen/women as an average for three-star, four-star and five-star hotels in central London. Salaries vary according to the type of establishment and are usually higher in central London than elsewhere. Generous tips can add to the salary. For head concierges in luxury city hotels, perks can include theatre tickets, restaurant meals and sightseeing tours, so that they can make informed recommendations to guests.

Portering services are usually available 18 to 24 hours a day, so porters work shifts, including evenings, overnight and weekends.

Porters are normally required to wear a uniform provided by the employer.

PROSPECTS

For porters at small establishments, it is always possible to move to larger and more prestigious hotels. From there, with further experience and qualifications, such as NVQs/SVQs at Levels 2, 3 and 4 in Reception Skills, porters can proceed up the career ladder to head porter – managing the team – or concierge. It is sometimes possible to proceed to jobs such as front-of-house manager.

Porters may choose to move across the hotel to the nearest department, reception, or some may prefer to try out other departments, such as working in the bar or food service in the restaurant, and proceed up the career ladders there. For those who wish to specialize in personnel or training, further qualifications may be required, from the Institute of Personnel and Development (IPD), for instance. Eventually general management is possible, with the right motivation and experience.

RELATED OCCUPATIONS

Security officer, hospital porter, receptionist, bartender, food service assistant, air steward/hostess, linen porter, front-of-house manager.

FURTHER INFORMATION

Business and Technology Education Council (BTEC)*, Central House, Upper Woburn Place, London WC1H 0HH, 0171 413 8400

City and Guilds (C&G)*, 1 Giltspur Street, London EC1A 9DD, 0171 294 2468

Hotel and Catering International Management Association (HCIMA)*, 191 Trinity Road, London SW17 7HN, 0181 672 4251

Hospitality Training Foundation (HTF)* – address as (HCTC)

Hotel and Catering Training Company (HCTC), International House, High Street, Ealing, London W5 5DB, 0181 579 2400

National Council for Vocational Qualifications (NCVQ)*, 222 Euston Road, London NW1 2BZ, 0171 387 9898

Scottish Vocational Education Council (SCOTVEC)*, Hanover House, 24 Douglas Street, Glasgow G2 7NQ, 0141 248 7900

Springboard*, 1 Denmark Street, London WC2H 8LP, 0171 497 8654 (please include sae)

FURTHER READING

Leaflets/booklets are available from the addresses marked*.

Working in Hotels and Catering – COIC
Working in Food and Drink – COIC
Working in Leisure – COIC
Working in Tourism – COIC
Careers and Training in Hotels, Catering and Tourism – Butterworth Heinemann
The Handbook of Tourism and Leisure – CRAC
Careers in Catering and Hospitality – HCTC
How To... Get a Job in Hotels and Catering – How To Books
Periodical: Caterer and Hotelkeeper (also publishes annual careers guide, available from HTF)
In the careers library classified under IB; IC.

1. PUBLICAN/LICENSEE CLCI:IB
2. BARMAN/WOMAN CLCI:IC

BACKGROUND INFORMATION

The on-licensed retail sector is a large and important part of the hospitality and catering industry. There are around 60,000 pubs in Britain employing about 500,000 staff.

The majority of British adults visit a pub on a regular basis and their demands, together with changes in legislation, have led to pubs changing considerably over the past few years. Many offer a much wider range of drinks, both alcoholic and non-alcoholic. The provision of food has become a very important part of pub business and an increasing number of pubs now offer food, ranging from bar snacks to full meals. Some pubs offer accommodation and, to compete with other leisure activities, many pubs offer a variety of types of entertainment.

1. PUBLICAN/LICENSEE (IB)

THE WORK

Publicans/licensees run pubs and other premises licensed to sell alcohol for consumption on the premises. They are concerned with running the business profitably, which involves buying in drink, food and other goods and pricing them to sell for a profit, as well as stock control and keeping accounts. Publicans/licensees must observe the laws governing the retail sale of intoxicating drink in the operation of licensed premises.

Many publicans/licensees employ bar staff, and they recruit, train and supervise those staff. They may also employ cellar and catering staff. Publicans/licensees often work alongside bar staff, making sure the pub is well stocked and prepared for opening, serving customers, re-stocking, collecting and washing glasses and keeping the bar areas clean. If pubs serve food, publicans/licensees supervise the catering operations; any entertainment is their responsibility too. After closing time publicans/licensees help to clean up.

Publicans/licensees are responsible for the health and safety of staff and customers and for maintaining hygienic conditions for food and drink service. They must deal with security, due to the large amounts of cash that go through the tills and the high value of alcoholic drinks.

The success of pubs is largely due to the publicans/licensees. They must make sure that their pub has a welcoming atmosphere and that the quality of service, food, drink and entertainment encourages customers to return.

WORK ENVIRONMENT

Pubs vary considerably in size and type but, when busy, most can be noisy and smoky. The work is physical, involving lifting and carrying crates and handling barrels. The hours are long and publicans/licensees spend most of their time standing.

SKILLS AND INTERESTS

Publicans/licensees must be able to get on well with people of all kinds. They should be polite and outgoing with good conversational and listening skills, so they can talk easily to customers, whether regulars or occasional visitors. They must, though, be capable of dealing with any trouble that may arise in the pub.

Publicans/licensees need managerial skills to be able to recruit, train and motivate staff, in order that they can work efficiently and well, while maintaining a friendly, welcoming atmosphere in the pub.

Good figurework skills are needed for cash handling, costing and the keeping of accounts. Good business sense is vital. They need to be capable of controlling spending, buying effectively, pricing goods realistically and careful stock control. New ways of attracting business need to be tried, which may involve trying different menus or different forms of entertainment.

Publicans/licensees must be able to learn and observe the legal aspects of their business relating to licensing, food provision and health and safety.

ENTRY REQUIREMENTS

No formal academic qualifications are required to become a publican/licensee, but personal qualities are considered important.

Previous business experience is very desirable, although not essential, and some experience of bar work is helpful.

Relevant qualifications include NVQs/SVQs in Catering and Hospitality (Serving Food and Drink – Bar) at Levels 1 and 2, On-Licensed Premises Supervisory Management at Level 3 and On-Licensed Premises Management at Level 4. Also relevant are the British Institute of Innkeeping's Certificate of Induction and Qualifying Examinations, the Degree in Licensed Retail Management awarded by the University of Wolverhampton, and higher diplomas or degrees including licensed retailing modules and catering management.

Running a pub is often seen as a job for a couple, but there are an increasing number of openings for individuals. There is no legal minimum age to become a publican/licensee, other than the requirement to be at least 18 years to serve behind a bar. The Brewers' Society, and Licensed Retailers Association, however, recommends 25 years to be a realistic lower age limit for a publican/licensee, with the occasional exception, and, increasingly, publicans/licencees require the National Licensee's Certificate awarded by the British Institute of Innkeeping.

Anyone considering becoming a publican/licensee ought to be in good health and be physically fit. A driving licence, while not essential, is useful.

TRAINING

Publicans/licensees can be managers, tenants or free traders (owners). See OPPORTUNITIES for the differences.

Managers can receive training from the employing brewer or pub owner, which can last from a few weeks to several months. Trainee managers may be sent to a training pub, followed by periods of relief management at different pubs, before being sent to manage their own. Many trainees take the British Institute of Innkeeping (BII) Qualifying Examination, which covers all aspects of running a public house.

Publicans/licensees may gain NVQs/SVQs, in Catering and Hospitality On-Licensed Premises Supervisory Management at Level 3 and On-Licensed Premises Management at Level 4.

Many pub owners provide training for potential tenants, which may lead to a BII qualification. Those considering becoming tenants or free traders can undertake a fee-paying five-day course run by the colleges and training companies. The course includes business planning and finances, cellar management, stock control, menu planning, food hygiene, health and safety, staff selection and recruitment, legislation, marketing and security. On completion of the course, the BII Qualifying Examination may be taken. The BII has also developed a new qualification aimed at those wishing to obtain a justice's licence for the first time. The exam: The National Licensee's Certificate, covers all aspects of licensing legislation and the social responsibilities of the licensee.

The HCTC also offers some one-day courses suitable for publicans/licensees.

The British Institute of Innkeeping admits those who have attained specific units of NVQs/SVQs in Catering and Hospitality On-Licensed Premises Management, or its own qualifications, in the various grades of membership.

LATE ENTRY

Pub owners tend to select trainee managers who are between 25 to 45 or 50 years. Their tenants tend to be selected between 25 to 50 or 55 years. People of any age can buy a free house, providing they have the necessary capital.

There may be specific training opportunities, directed at adults, available in some areas for this type of work. Candidates may have to satisfy certain conditions to be eligible. Contact your local Jobcentre, careers office or TEC/LEC for details.

OPPORTUNITIES

There are opportunities for publicans/licensees throughout the UK, either as managers, tenants or free traders. Entry is very competitive.

Managers are employed by a company that owns the pub; they are salaried staff. Applicants do not need to have capital to become managers.

Tenants (sometimes known as lessees) run pubs leased to them by a landlord – usually a brewer, a licensed retailer or a property company. They effectively operate their business independently although, if the pub is owned by a brewer, they may have to sell the beer of the brewer concerned. Tenants have to buy fixtures and fittings, and furnishings and stock, the cost of which varies according to the pub in question. In 1992 the Brewers' Society and Licensed Retail Association quoted a range of £10,000 to £40,000.

Free traders run pubs they have bought themselves and are independent of brewers. The cost of buying a pub varies, but averages over £250,000.

There are approximately 13,500 managed houses in Britain, 29,800 tenancies and over 22,000 free traders. The proportion of managed free houses is growing, while that of tenancies is declining. A feature of Scotland is that a larger proportion of pubs are privately owned, and managed pubs outnumber tenancies.

PAY AND CONDITIONS

Managers are paid a salary, either individually or as a couple, and may be able to earn bonuses, or participate in a profit sharing scheme. They usually have accommodation provided on the premises. There are no set earnings for tenants or managed free traders. Earnings vary considerably from pub to pub, according to turnover. Publicans'/licensees' annual earnings range from under £5,000 to over £40,000. Additional benefits may include profit-related pay, qualifications-related pay and bonus schemes.

Pubs are able to serve alcohol between 11am and 11pm Monday to Saturday and 12 noon to 10.30pm on Sundays. In Scotland, Sunday hours are 12.30 to 2.30pm and 6.30 to 11pm, although application can be made to open between 2.30 and 6.30pm.

Preparation takes place before opening time and clearing up after closing. While not necessarily working all those hours, publicans/licensees work very long hours, often seven days a week, with few holidays.

PROSPECTS

Successful managers may get promoted to run a larger pub, with an increased salary and larger bonuses.

There is no promotion as such for tenants or free traders. Success for them is measured in increased earnings through increased and more profitable business. Successful tenants may buy the tenancy of a larger pub or buy a free house. Free traders may buy larger free houses.

RELATED OCCUPATIONS

Hotel manager, catering/restaurant manager, off-licence manager, club steward, retail manager, barman/woman.

FURTHER INFORMATION AND READING

Please see article 2. BARMAN/WOMAN.

2. BARMAN/WOMAN (IC)

THE WORK

Bar staff work in licensed premises. They are responsible for selling drinks of all kinds, tobacco products like cigarettes and cigars, and food. Depending where they work, the food can range from crisps and peanuts to bar snacks and full meals.

An important part of the work is to talk to customers; to provide a welcoming, friendly atmosphere. They must, though, keep alert for any trouble that is developing and try to prevent it.

Duties begin before the bar opens. Bar staff prepare the bar by stocking it with bottles, putting out fresh beer mats and ashtrays and any small snacks, like bowls of peanuts and crisps. They stock up with ice and sundries, like sliced lemons and cherries. Bar staff may help to organize the cellar, where beer barrels and bottles of all kinds are stored. They may clean the beer pipes.

During opening time, they mix and serve a whole range of drinks, both alcoholic and non-alcoholic. They calculate customers' bills, collect the money and give change. This involves using cash registers. Some also deal with payments by cheque and credit card.

Apart from serving customers, bar staff collect empty glasses and wash them, often using a glass-washing machine, collect bottles, empty ashtrays and keep the bar and tables clean. When beer barrels are empty they may attach fresh barrels to the pumps. They stock up on any bottle shortages as they occur and change the optics on empty spirits bottles.

When the bar closes, bar staff make sure all glasses are washed and that the premises are left clean and tidy.

WORK ENVIRONMENT

Licensed premises can differ greatly. They can be old or modern. Some are large, some quite small. When busy, most can be noisy and smoky.

Bar staff spend most of their time standing. Their work is physically demanding as it involves lifting and carrying crates and handling barrels; bending and stretching to reach glasses and goods for sale.

SKILLS AND INTERESTS

It is important that bar staff get on well with people of all kinds. They should be cheerful and outgoing; polite and tactful.

Communication skills are important to gauge which customers wish to talk and which do not. Those skills are needed too when coping with difficult situations, like refusing to serve a customer who has had too much to drink or in asking a troublesome customer to leave.

Entrants to bar work must be able to gain a knowledge of the range of products sold, and of the licensing laws.

Bar work can be hectic, so an ability to work under pressure is desirable. A good memory is helpful for keeping track of orders and prices. Mental arithmetic ability is useful, as bills are often calculated in the head rather than on a till. As bar staff handle money, they must be honest and reliable.

Bar staff should have a clean and tidy appearance. Some may wear a uniform or standard clothing.

ENTRY REQUIREMENTS

No formal educational qualifications are required to enter bar work. Personal qualities are more important. Employers have a preference for entrants with some ability in mental arithmetic. The minimum age for bar work is, by law, 18 years.

TRAINING

Most bar staff are trained on the job by the publican/ licensee, bar manager or experienced bar staff, although some employers run formal training programmes. They learn the skills needed to dispense and serve drinks, serve food, stock the bar, clean glasses, handle cash and use the cash register. Staff are taught the legal aspects of work in licensed premises and their employer's policies concerning the running of the business.

Bar staff can work towards NVQs/SVQs in Catering and Hospitality (Serving Food and Drink – Bar) at Levels 1 and 2.

LATE ENTRY

There is no upper age limit. Providing the applicant is suitable, maturity can be a distinct advantage in bar work. The part-time nature of much bar work can be particularly suitable for adults with family responsibilities.

OPPORTUNITIES

Bar staff are employed at numerous licensed premises throughout the UK. There are many different kinds of public houses, including city centre, town, country, theme, disco, those offering accommodation and many specializing in food service. There are wine bars, hotels, restaurants, private clubs, holiday centres, leisure and sports centres, workplace social centres, and bars at airports, stations, on board trains and ships and in Armed Forces establishments.

The number of people employed in bar work has grown over the past few years.

It is comparatively easy for a suitable applicant to find work in a bar, as the turnover of bar staff is high. There are few opportunities to become self-employed. There are some possibilities of working abroad.

PAY AND CONDITIONS

Earnings vary according to the type of bar and its location. Hourly rates vary regionally and range between £2.50 and £5.00.

Pubs can serve alcohol from 11am to 11pm Monday to Saturday and 12 noon to 10.30pm on Sundays (12.30 to 2.30pm and 6.30 to 11pm on Sundays in Scotland, although application can be made to open between 2.30 and 6.30pm). Bar work can be full-time or part-time, with part-time work often used to cover the busiest times of evenings and weekends. In some areas, like holiday resorts, bar work can be seasonal. Full-time staff may work a 40-hour week on a shift basis, usually including lunch-times and evenings. Paid overtime may be available to full-time and part-time staff.

PROSPECTS

Bar staff can become bar managers or club stewards. They may become pub managers or, with capital, buy a tenancy or the freehold of a pub.

RELATED OCCUPATIONS

Food service assistant, counter service assistant, retail assistant, publican/licensee.

FURTHER INFORMATION

Brewers and Licensed Retailers Association*, 42 Portman Square, London W1H 0BB, 0171 486 4831

The British Institute of Innkeeping*, Wessex House, 80 Park Street, Camberley, Surrey GU15 3PT, 01276 684449

Hotel and Catering Training Company*, International House, High Street, Ealing, London W5 5DB, 0181 579 2400

The Scottish Licensed Trade Association*, 10 Walker Street, Edinburgh EH3 7LA, 0131 225 5169

FURTHER READING

Leaflets/booklets are available from the addresses marked*.

Job Outlines – The Licensed Trade – COIC
In the careers library classified under IB; IC.

HOME ECONOMIST CLCI:ID

BACKGROUND INFORMATION

The Institute of Home Economics defines a home economist as 'a professional adviser on food, clothing, home management and design, household services, and research related to the home and community.' Home economists are the link between producers and consumers of goods and services.

Home economics as a subject is very broad, and that is reflected in the fact that, after training, home economists work in a very wide range of jobs. Many of those jobs have titles other than 'home economist', such as consumer services adviser, home economics adviser, but each uses some of the numerous skills that home economics training provides.

THE WORK

There are a number of activities that are the concern of home economists. Individual home economists are not usually involved in all the activities.

Research and development, testing and assessment. Home economists in the food and retailing industries create new products in co-operation with food technologists. They develop a prototype, make up kitchen samples, and test and modify them until the product is ready for manufacture. Home economists in the domestic appliance industry work in co-operation with engineers, designers and marketing staff to develop new domestic appliances, like cookers and washing machines, or modify existing models. Their particular expertise is in representing the consumers' point of view, suggesting how best the product can suit consumers. Quality testing of both food and other products is part of home economists' work too.

Demonstrations and talks. These can be to audiences of all sizes and are an important part of the work of many home economists. In the fuel industries (gas, electricity), home economists demonstrate the use of appliances and talk to a variety of audiences about subjects such as energy conservation. Some home economists in the retail industry demonstrate new recipes or food products, while those working for health authorities give talks on health care and nutrition.

Marketing and promotion. This includes the preparation of products to be photographed for advertisements, presentations, leaflets and articles.

Advice. Home economists in the food, retail and domestic appliance industries advise customers about the use of their company's products and respond to any complaints. Those in the fuel industries may visit people who have difficulty using appliances, or advise disabled customers on the adaptation of appliances. Home economists in social services departments liaise with home helps and social workers.

Writing. Home economists in the food, retail and domestic appliance industries are concerned with writing technical reports, instructions for new recipes, food products or domestic appliances, pack instructions, recipe leaflets, cookery books, advertisements and press releases. Some home economists work for magazines, devising recipes and testing products, and write up their findings for publication. Those in the health field write leaflets concerned with health and nutrition advice.

Teaching. Some home economists work in schools, teaching within the design and technology team, in such areas as food and nutrition, health and safety, and textile studies. Others lecture in colleges within the home economics/consumer studies areas.

Some home economists work in the leisure industry, in recreational management.

WORK ENVIRONMENT

Home economists' surroundings vary considerably according to their job. They may be based in well-equipped kitchens, laboratories, offices, schools or colleges, or be working in stores, people's homes, or exhibition venues.

In some jobs, home economists travel to attend exhibitions and give demonstrations or talks; these may involve trips away from home.

SKILLS AND INTERESTS

The work of many home economists demands a confident, lively personality, for example when dealing with customers or giving talks to audiences.

Home economists should be able to communicate with a variety of people. Verbal skills are needed, both for public speaking and for liaison and individual advice. Those who work with the public need to present a good image, which includes a good standard of dress. Tact is important, particularly when dealing with customers.

Written skills are necessary to produce technical reports, product instructions and leaflets. Some ability with figures is needed to cope with statistical information.

All home economics jobs demand an interest in people, but different jobs demand it in different ways; for example, those working for local authorities need an interest in social care. Most home economists work as part of a team and need to be able to work with others.

Patience, a methodical approach and an eye for detail are required for many jobs, for example, when devising a new recipe or testing a product. Scientific ability is necessary, particularly for work involving research and development.

ENTRY REQUIREMENTS

City and Guilds Certificate for Family and Community Care course does not usually require any particular academic qualifications, but a good standard of general education is needed to cope with the course.

BTEC National Diploma in Home Economics/Consumer Studies – entry is with: at least four GCSEs/S grades (A-C/1-3), usually including English, with a science subject desirable; or a BTEC first award in a relevant subject; or successful completion of the Certificate for Family and Community Care; or an equivalent. (NVQs/SVQs in Food Preparation and Service may be considered as an alternative entry qualification.)

BTEC Higher National Diploma in Home Economics/Consumer Studies/Food and Consumer Studies – entry is with: at least one A level/two H grades, preferably including home economics, and three other GCSEs/S grades (A-C/1-3), usually including English and a science; or a BTEC national qualification in a relevant subject. Advanced GNVQs/GSVQs Level III in relevant subjects may also be accepted.

Degree courses – entry is with a minimum of two A levels/

three H grades, including home economics, and five GCSEs/S grades (A-C/1-3) or equivalent. Most courses require entrants to hold GCSEs/S grades in English and maths, and some ask for a science. (For courses leading to a teaching qualification, English and maths are essential.)

The work of many home economists is physically demanding, often requiring long periods of standing and talking, so stamina and good health are required.

TRAINING

City and Guilds Certificate for Family and Community Care is offered by many local colleges (usually two years full-time). The course combines theory and practice, subjects including nutrition, meal planning and special diets, home and accommodation, welfare and health services. Visits and work experience are part of the courses.

BTEC National Diploma in Home Economics/Consumer Studies is offered at some colleges in England and Wales, mostly as two-year full-time courses.

BTEC Higher National Diploma in Home Economics/ Consumer Studies/Food and Consumer Studies is usually two years full-time; it is offered at institutions in England: Birmingham College of Food, Tourism and Creative Studies; the University of North London; the University of Northumbria; University College Salford and Sheffield Hallam University.

Most BTEC courses include four main areas of study: food studies; technical studies of consumer products such as household equipment and detergents; behavioural studies, such as consumer studies and sociology; and business and management studies such as marketing and communications. With the introduction of modular courses, some optional subjects may be studied: resources and textile care, plus marketing and business studies. Higher national diploma courses involve study in more depth than the national courses. Both include work placements.

In Scotland, colleges offer a modular programme that can be tailored to home economics and lead to a SCOTVEC national certificate.

Degree courses – single-subject Home Economics/Consumer Studies/Consumer Science degree courses are offered at several institutions throughout the UK. The titles of courses vary: Applied Consumer Science; Food and Consumer Management; Consumer Services Management; Human Ecology and Consumer Health and Community Studies – titles give an indication of the emphasis of different courses. Home economics is also offered in combination with other subjects. Most degree courses include some work-based learning – usually a placement.

BEd degrees – (four years, full-time) are offered at several institutions and prepare students for teaching home economics/food technology/textile technology/home economics/design and technology. Those already holding a home economics degree can train for teaching by taking a Postgraduate Certificate in Education (one year, full-time). Please see TEACHING (FAB) articles.

Higher degrees – these are available in subjects such as technology and consumer science and consumer science/home economics.

LATE ENTRY

There are no special entry arrangements for adults. Older applicants may be accepted onto courses without the usual entry qualifications.

OPPORTUNITIES

Those completing the Certificate for Family and Community Care can enter community service in, for example, residential homes and day centres for the young and the elderly, the disabled, adult training centres and special schools.

Most other home economics jobs demand a BTEC national diploma, higher national diploma or degree qualification. The range of possible jobs is very wide and there has been considerable growth in home economics opportunities over the past few years.

Many openings are in business and industry, particularly the food industry, working for food manufacturers, national food boards and food retailers. There are opportunities in the domestic appliance and equipment industry. Openings are developing in the leisure industry, in recreational management.

Local authority work in the social services department is a small but growing area, as is work with health authorities on health promotion. Consumer advice work is available with some local authorities and with some retail organizations and magazines.

A number of home economists enter teaching in schools or colleges. A small number work for magazines, in radio and television, and in public relations.

PAY AND CONDITIONS

Newly qualified home economists in industry may begin on £10,500 to £12,000, depending on qualifications and experience. After two to six years' experience, salaries rise to £14,500 to £25,000. Those in senior positions earn more; top salaries exceed £42,000. Jobs in London may pay more. A car or travel allowance is provided with some jobs, as are meal and overnight expenses and uniform or clothing allowances.

Teachers are paid on the same scale as teachers of other subjects. Those employed by local authorities are paid on the local government scale.

Freelance charges very considerably. A cookery demonstrator may earn £20 to £35 an hour, while a home economist working on recipe and product development may earn £140 or more a day.

Most home economists work normal office hours, but demonstrations and talks can be in the evening, and exhibitions may involve weekend work.

PROSPECTS

There are promotion possibilities in all areas of home economics work. It may be possible to progress with a company, or to move to another employer in the same field. It is possible to switch from one area of work to another, because of the broad nature of home economics.

Some experienced home economists work freelance in private catering, demonstration work, product development and testing, writing and television.

RELATED OCCUPATIONS

Food scientist/technologist/technician, chef/cook, restaurant/catering manager, dietitian, environmental health officer, marketing manager, social worker, store demonstrator.

FURTHER INFORMATION

The Institute of Home Economics*, 21 Portland Place, London W1N 3AF, 0171 436 5677 (please include sae)

The National Association of Teachers of Home Economics and Technology*, Hamilton House, Mabledon Place, London WC1H 9BJ

FURTHER READING

Leaflets/booklets are available from the addresses marked*.

Job Outlines – Home Economics – COIC

In the careers library classified under ID.

DRY CLEANING/LAUNDRY WORKER
CLCI:IG

BACKGROUND INFORMATION

Dry cleaning and laundry workers are employed in the textile care industry. They meet individual, commercial and industrial needs for clean clothing, soft furnishings, workwear and linen. Launderettes are also regarded as part of the industry -- most launderettes now offer serviced washes and dry cleaning.

The washing machines in laundries use water and a cleansing agent such as a detergent. Dry cleaning machines use a solvent, commonly perchloroethylene, instead of water. The solvent removes the oil and fat that hold the dirt and is less likely than water to shrink or expand certain fibres, or cause dyes to run.

Many of the big cleaning firms offer, or specialize in, textile rental services. Businesses, factories, leisure facilities, and so on, pay rental for a weekly supply of items such as workwear, towels, linen, dust mats, and industrial wipers.

Specialist cleaning processes include dyeing, re-texturing, and flame-proofing. Retail outlets may also offer services such as repairs and alterations, carpet cleaning equipment rental, shoe repairs and photo-laboratory services.

THE WORK

Dry cleaning/laundry workers are usually trained in a number of skills, but their duties may vary according to the size of the operation, methods of cleaning, and where the cleaning takes place. Many laundries/dry cleaning plants are highly automated, but there may still be a considerable amount of repetitive, manual and sometimes heavy work involved in sorting soiled articles, loading machines, and pressing, folding, and packing clean articles.

Reception/collection

Staff in reception/collection are usually sales assistants/ managers. They take articles from individual customers over the counter. They discuss cleaning method, cost, time of collection and special requirements; draw the customer's attention to tears and holes, and check linings and pockets for coins, papers, etc. Then they tag the garment, or other articles, to be cleaned and issue a collection ticket. Articles to be cleaned or treated elsewhere are bagged ready for transportation to the plant.

Drivers collect laundry by van from private customers, textile rental customers, businesses, and public institutions.

Sorting

Dry cleaning workers sort articles for dry cleaning into light/medium/dark colours. They separate woollens, which might shed fibres, badly stained and oily items, and foreign items (those not intended for dry cleaning).

In a laundry, workers check each item against the customer's list and give it a serial number. They count textile rental articles to make sure numbers tally with the delivery note. Items for repair are ticketed. Workers separate white and coloured articles and sort linen into categories (towels, sheets, table linen, etc) – either by hand or by loading it into an automatic classifier.

Cleaning/washing

Before articles are dry cleaned, workers remove food particles with a steam gun and hand-spot chemical stains – tar, rust, paint, etc – with an appropriate agent. Any stains remaining after cleaning are re-spotted and the items re-cleaned if necessary. Spotting requires the skilled use of chemicals.

Workers weigh articles for dry cleaning, then hand-load them into machines that look like large domestic washing machines. They select the correct programme and the machines work automatically, tumbling the articles into solvent (twice, if badly soiled), rinsing them in clean solvent, and part-drying them by gentle tumbling in warm air. Workers add solvent to the machines, perhaps once a week, and carry out routine maintenance, including cleaning the button trap and fluff bag, checking temperature gauges, etc.

A different cleaning process is used for suede, leather and sheepskin garments. After being cleaned and dried, the garments are sprayed with oil, to which dye is sometimes added. Other specialist procedures include water proofing with wax silicone, which may be done in a standard dry cleaning machine, carpet cleaning and dyeing.

In the less automated laundries, workers weigh the dirty laundry, load it into automatic washing machines, select the programme to suit the fabric, and add detergent and bleach. Wet washing is unloaded into a laundry truck, and may need to be loaded into an extractor, which spins it before it is ready for drying. In other laundries, employees load the laundry – by hand or by operating a bag-handling system – into a computer-controlled tunnel batch washer that processes the washing through up to 20 phases.

Some workers operate and maintain the boilers that provide the steam heating for cleaning and finishing processes.

Finishing (drying, pressing, folding, etc)

Once they have been dry cleaned and checked again for stains, articles go through various finishing processes. Workers place garments on body-shaped formers and hang them in steam cabinets for crease removal and hot air drying. They may also use steam and vacuum presses – laying garments on the presses in a sequence of positions – and hand iron, for example, pockets and linings.

The work is skilled, and dry cleaning workers often specialize in, for instance, pressing a particular type of garment, or hand ironing pleats and delicate fabrics.

Finishing processes vary from laundry to laundry. For instance, workers may load and unload towels into/from a tumble drier; stack towels that have been folded automatically; load work-wear into a tunnel finisher for steam-conditioning and drying; feed sheets into a two-roller press known as a calender; or sort folded sheets into singles, doubles, etc.

Staff with machining/hand sewing skills replace buttons and carry out other minor repairs resulting from the cleaning process. They may also carry out alterations for customers: turn up hems, insert zip fasteners, etc.

Packing

Workers sort dry-cleaned articles according to number and hang them in polythene ready for the customer to collect.

In laundries, clean items are batched – by hand or automatically – then packed. This may involve wrapping linen in brown paper or film, then packing it in bags, cages or baskets; or hanging garments on dispatch rails for delivery by van.

Staff in textile rental services check that the same number of articles are returned to customers as was collected and that particular requirements have been met.

Customer services

Staff in the customer services departments of laundries take orders, dispatch invoices, promote services, deal with complaints, keep records, order stock and stationery, and carry out other administrative and clerical duties. Managers and sales assistants in unit shops perform some of the same tasks, and also receive payment from customers when they collect the cleaning.

WORK ENVIRONMENT

The unit shop has a counter where articles are handed in and rails nearby where cleaned articles are hung ready for collection. Unit shops are situated in high streets, shopping centres, and superstores. Most have only one dry cleaning machine and perhaps a washing machine, so only a small number of employees are on the premises at one time.

In dry cleaning plants/laundries, steam-heated cleaning and finishing processes may make the environment hot and humid. The noise from machines and from vacuum presses can be considerable. But, in larger laundries particularly, the environment is much better than it used to be. Laundry workers are not expected to handle infected or badly soiled linen; this is placed in water-soluble bags by staff wearing protective gloves and clothing, then processed at thermal disinfection temperatures. Employees may come into contact with solvent or stain-removing chemicals, but their use is strictly controlled, to minimize the risk of fume inhalation, burns, and so on. Workers are likely to spend much of the day on their feet.

SKILLS AND INTERESTS

Dry cleaning/laundry workers must be prepared to handle dirty clothing and undertake tiring, often repetitive work.

Workers require an eye for detail, whether they are treating stains or ironing in pleats. They have to work carefully and quickly, maintaining high standards when under pressure. Mistakes in sorting, for instance, can result in staining, discoloration, or delays.

As well as being literate and numerate, employees must have the technical aptitude and adaptability to learn new skills and operate different machines, computer systems, etc. They must be able to get on well with people, whether they are working as part of a large team in a laundry or attending to customers in a unit shop. Courtesy, tact and patience are required in dealing with customers.

Managers need a clear and detailed understanding of the many techniques used in the cleaning process, so they may give the correct advice to employees and customers. They must co-ordinate operations smoothly, communicate well with their staff and the public, handle complaints, and settle disputes fairly and firmly. They must be able to run promotions and generate new business.

ENTRY REQUIREMENTS

There are no set entry requirements, though a good standard of education is preferred; GCSEs/S grades in maths and/or chemistry, and in English, are an advantage. Candidates for managerial positions should preferably have four GCSEs/S grades (A-C/1-3) in subjects including maths, English, physics/chemistry. But those with suitable experience and no formal qualifications are still likely to be considered.

Some firms require applicants to take short tests to ensure they are literate and numerate and have the level of comprehension needed to operate machinery.

Candidates must be fit and strong, particularly those required to work on their feet all day and carry heavy bags of laundry. They may also need good eyesight, including normal colour vision.

Applicants with a particularly sensitive skin, or a tendency to allergies, may not be suitable for some aspects of the work involving solvents, washing powders, and so on.

TRAINING

All employees are given on-the-job training, enabling them to acquire a number of different skills. Many employees have the opportunity to take Guild of Cleaners and Launderers (GCL) examinations and NVQs/SVQs in Dry Cleaning at Levels 1 and 2; Laundering (Washing), Laundering (Finishing) Level 1 and Laundering Level 2.

The Fabric Care Research Association, GCL and City and Guilds form the awarding body that offers NVQs. In Scotland, the awarding body consists of FCRA, GCL and SCOTVEC. The FCRA runs a number of short in-service technical courses, as well as longer training and in-service training courses for managers and supervisors. Short dry-cleaning courses (two to four-and-a-half days) are available in: introduction to dry cleaning; stain removing; garment finishing; processing delicate garments; leather processing; customer care in retail dry cleaning; and dry cleaning technology. Short laundering courses (two to four-and-a-half days) are available in: washing technology; laundry finishing; laundering technology and operations management; achieving and maintaining quality in laundering; flowline costing for launderers; advanced washing technology.

These courses provide training in direct support of NVQs/SVQs.

Longer FCRA courses include an eight-month course in laundry management leading to the Certificate of the Institute for Supervision and Management. Four two-week residential modules at the FCRA cover subjects such as washing and textile technology, technical management of laundry processes and systems, advanced wash control methods, distribution requirements, and effective team work. Project work is undertaken between modules.

NVQs/SVQs are being developed at Levels 3 and 4.

LATE ENTRY

There is no upper age limit to entry, provided candidates are fit and strong enough to carry out the work.

OPPORTUNITIES

There are around 100,000 employees working in the dry cleaning and laundry industry. The textile rentals sector, particularly, is expanding.

Most employees work for one of the national or multinational chains. Their operations vary from area to area, but openings are available in shop units, in dry cleaning plants and in laundries. Independent dry cleaning outlets are often family partnerships offering fewer employment prospects.

Opportunities also exist in independent laundries, or small chains serving hotels, restaurants, factories, and private customers; in hotel laundries; and in hospital, prison service and other public sector laundries.

Part-time work is available.

PAY AND CONDITIONS

Laundry workers are usually paid around £3 an hour, or £130.00 for a 39-hour week. Rates of pay vary considerably throughout the industry. Employees may receive merit and skills payments, and bonuses.

A laundry production manager earns about £10,000 to £15,000 and a general manager, £20,000 to £25,000. Salaries are determined by the size of plants being managed, rather than the area of the country. In unit shops, managers' earnings are often linked to turnover.

Full-time employees work 38 to 40 hours a week, Monday to Friday. Many unit shops open on Saturday and employees have a day off during the week. Laundry and dry cleaning plant employees are expected to work overtime when required.

PROSPECTS

Unit shops have positions such as senior assistant, assistant branch manager, and branch manager. A branch manager can move to a larger branch and eventually become district manager, or obtain a head office appointment. In laundries, an assistant can be promoted to leading hand – in charge of a machine – or supervisor concerned with quality control. Management positions include: production manager, responsible for shop-floor productivity and quality; factory manager, controlling work sequence and flow, staff training, and so on; operations manager, in charge of transport, as well as performing factory management duties; and general manager, in charge overall.

Dry cleaning/laundry work allows those with a practical bias to advance rapidly, provided they take the necessary training and are willing to accept additional responsibility. Most senior managers in dry cleaning and laundry work entered the industry at shop-floor level.

There are also opportunities to move into customer services, personnel and training, marketing and sales, and research and development.

It may be possible for those with the necessary skills and administrative ability to open their own dry cleaning outlet.

RELATED OCCUPATIONS

Sterile supplies worker, shop assistant, garment examiner/quality controller, retail manager, housekeeper.

FURTHER INFORMATION

Fabric Care Research Association (FCRA) Ltd*, Forest House Laboratories, Knaresborough Road, Harrogate, North Yorkshire HG2 7LZ, 01423 885977

Textile Services Association Ltd*, 7 Churchill Court, 58 Station Road, North Harrow, Middlesex HA2 7SE, 0181 863 7755

FURTHER READING

Leaflets/booklets are available from the addresses marked*.

In the careers library classified under IG.

CLEANING SERVICES: IJ

1. WINDOW CLEANER CLCI:IJ
2. REFUSE COLLECTOR CLCI:IJ

1. WINDOW CLEANER (IJ)

THE WORK

When cleaning domestic or ground floor shop windows, the window cleaner usually works alone. On domestic rounds, window cleaners are able to arrange their working days to suit themselves. This type of window cleaning has the greatest amount of customer contact. Domestic and shop window cleaners usually work from ladders at low levels. Some companies may provide a barrow or a car/van to transport materials.

In addition to cleaning windows, larger companies clean and polish the glass in fanlights, skylights and glass partitions, both indoors and outdoors in domestic, commercial and industrial buildings. They also clean windows that are too high to be reached by ladder. This involves working from a cradle – a working platform operated by ropes and pulleys – or from a bosun's chair or scaffolding. Although the actual cleaning techniques are the same, this type of work carries greater responsibilities. All window cleaners involved in high-risk work must be familiar with the rigging of these devices and how to operate them, including the fixing and knotting of the ropes. When working on scaffolding, or from a cradle, it may be necessary to wear a safety harness.

Larger-contract window cleaners tend to work in gangs and are paid on a piece-rate basis. It is therefore important to be able to work quickly and efficiently, so as to keep up production without taking any safety risks.

These gangs of window cleaners usually move from job to job in a van. Very few gang-working window cleaners have any contact with the customer. One of them, usually the foreman/woman, must ensure that the gang's worksheet is signed to say that the work has been satisfactorily completed. There is not usually any cash handling involved in larger contract cleaning jobs.

WORK ENVIRONMENT

The major part of the work is outdoors in both cold and hot weather, though work may stop during rain. Cradle work on office and tower blocks can be particularly cold and windy. Contract window cleaners may also work indoors, cleaning the interior faces of windows.

SKILLS AND INTERESTS

Window cleaning is a job suited to someone interested in working outdoors in all weathers. Much of the work is carried out at heights, requiring a good sense of balance. The amount of carrying and climbing varies according to the type of building being cleaned, but it is an advantage to be physically fit and reasonably strong. Safety is an important aspect of the job, particularly when working at heights or dealing with the winching machinery for a cradle/ bosun's chair containing other workers. Window cleaners must follow workplace health safety and welfare regulations. When working they must also respect and care for other people's property. The self-employed window cleaner, or one working for a small company, must enjoy working alone. When cleaning domestic windows they may also collect money, and need a pleasant manner when dealing with customers. They should also be completely trustworthy.

Larger contract cleaning companies often send out their window cleaners in gangs. Gang workers must work effectively as a team and co-operate with each other.

ENTRY REQUIREMENTS

Window cleaners are seldom required to have any formal educational qualifications. Some employers may test basic literacy and numeracy to ensure that applicants are able to understand their worksheets.

Some companies may prefer applicants who hold a full UK driving licence. This tends to be desirable, rather than essential.

TRAINING

It is possible to set up as a self-employed window cleaner without any training at all, and many smaller companies do not offer any structured training programme.

Larger organizations usually insist that a trainee works alongside an experienced window cleaner or as a member of a gang. Initially they work on interior glass and partitions, possibly using a short ladder. They then progress to outside and long-ladder work, receiving instructions on the correct angle of ladders, footing and lashing them. They also learn how to clean outside glass from the inside of the building without taking unnecessary risks. Safety is always a vital component in training.

Becoming a 'cradle hand' is usually the final part of the training. The trainee must become familiar with the principles of cradle rigging, traversing the cradle, operating winches and electrical gear, tying off and generally handling the equipment in the correct and safe manner. The length of training varies according to the policy of the employer and how quickly the trainee is able to progress and accept increasing responsibility.

An NVQ/SVQ in Cleaning: Windows, Glass and Facade Surfaces is available at Level 2.

LATE ENTRY

Window cleaning is a responsible job and some employers prefer to recruit candidates with a more mature approach. The work can, however, be physically demanding, and older applicants must demonstrate that they are sufficiently agile to cope with the climbing and carrying that window cleaning involves.

OPPORTUNITIES

It is very difficult to be precise about the numbers of people employed as window cleaners.

There are two main types of employer offering opportunities to window cleaners: the small local concern dealing mainly with domestic windows, and the large commercial cleaning companies who deal with industrial and commercial buildings. Some small window cleaning companies also get contracts for cleaning local low-rise buildings where ladders give sufficient height. Larger organizations often obtain the contracts for cleaning the windows of high-rise multi-storey industrial and commercial buildings. In addition to providing window cleaners, these larger concerns are often able to provide a whole range of contract cleaning services.

PAY AND CONDITIONS

Self-employed window cleaners set their own rates of charges, often related to the numbers and size of windows to be cleaned. They therefore control their earnings by working additional hours as and when necessary. Window cleaning rates vary and range from around £2 to £6 for a house of average size. Contract window cleaners operate on a piecework basis, and earnings vary according to the type of work being done. Those working on high-rise buildings, using sophisticated equipment, earn more than those cleaning ground floor or interior windows only. Most experienced contract window cleaners can expect to earn about £120 to £180 a week. However, this varies from area to area.

Small businesses dealing with the windows of high street stores often need to work regular hours; many stores like to have their windows cleaned on the same day(s) of the week. This type of work often calls for an early start. Contract window cleaners usually work a 40-hour, five-day week. Starting and finishing times can be variable. Paid overtime may be available.

PROSPECTS

Window cleaning is a job with limited promotion prospects. When working for a large contract cleaning company it may be possible to progress from low-rise building work to multi-storey work. This requires the use of more equipment and the acceptance of increasing responsibility for safety. Multi-storey work usually attracts higher salaries. Opportunities also occur for promotion to foreman/woman responsible for a gang of workers. Many window cleaners leave contract cleaning companies in order to become self-employed.

Those working in small businesses may be offered partnerships.

RELATED OCCUPATIONS

Road sweeper, cleaner, forecourt attendant, carpet cleaner

FURTHER INFORMATION

British Institute of Cleaning Science, Whitworth Chambers, George Row, Northampton NN1 1DF, 01604 230075

Cleaning and Support Services Association Industry Training Organization (ITO), Suite 73/74 The Hop Exchange, 24 Southwark Street, London SE1 1TY, 0171 403 2747

Cleaning Industry Lead Body (CILB), Hill House, Wroxham, Norwich, NR12 8SJ, 01603 784547

National Federation of Master Window and General Cleaners, Summerfield House, Harrogate Road, Reddish, Stockport, Cheshire SK5 6HH, 0161 432 8754

FURTHER READING

Working in Outdoor Jobs – COIC

In the careers library classified under IJ.

2. REFUSE COLLECTOR (IJ)

THE WORK

The job involves emptying dustbins and large containers of rubbish, and taking it in a specially built vehicle (a dust cart or refuse wagon) to an official refuse tip or incinerator. Refuse collectors work in small teams, usually of two to five loaders and a driver. Covering a specified area each day and following a planned route, the team collect refuse from a variety of premises – household, commercial and industrial.

The bins, containers and plastic sacks are taken, either by hand or on a trolley, to the refuse vehicle. Refuse collectors may work ahead of the lorry, moving the rubbish to a point that is easily accessible. They empty the rubbish into the back of the vehicle by hand, or by attaching the bins to a mechanical or electrical lift and operating a tipping device. The team may return to the depot or dumping site several times with a full lorry, which they may help to unload.

Most vehicles are equipped with an automatic device for crushing and compressing the refuse, enabling large quantities to be collected and transported. The team follows safety regulations while this is in operation.

They return the empty bins, ensuring there is no spilt rubbish left on the road or pavement. They may also supply new bins to houses and provide plastic sacks for the following week's collection.

Refuse collectors can reject large items, such as furniture or excess garden rubbish, unless a special collection has been arranged. Private firms often undertake the removal of such items.

Some local authorities offer a service to collect waste material from large office buildings or industrial sites and they loan out containers or skips that are emptied at regular intervals. If waste or dust from industrial processes is a potential health hazard, employers provide special protective clothing, and washing facilities are usually provided for the refuse collectors at the depot.

WORK ENVIRONMENT

Refuse collection is an outdoor job. Daily schedules must be completed, regardless of weather conditions. Although a job in the open air has pleasant aspects, it also involves work in cold and wet conditions. A refuse collector is considerably hampered when it is icy, or if there is snow on the ground, making it hazardous underfoot.

The work is generally dirty, and in hot weather may also be smelly and dusty.

Specific working environments vary, depending on the location of an employer, or the route allocated to a team. They may work in city, suburban or rural areas. A lot of work is undertaken on busy roads; refuse collectors must remain aware of traffic.

Their work base is the depot, from where they receive instructions and route details, and to which they return each day. It is usually equipped with basic facilities for the convenience of staff, such as a cafeteria and showers.

The job involves being constantly mobile, both by lorry from district to district and by foot from house to house. Continual bending, lifting, carrying and walking is unavoidable.

SKILLS AND INTERESTS

Refuse collection is a manual job suited to someone who enjoys working outdoors regardless of weather conditions. The work is demanding, very active and may involve emptying around 1,100 dustbins a day, so good health and physical strength are essential. Applicants should not suffer from bad backs, chest complaints or allergies.

Refuse collectors need to be able to work quickly and for

long periods without a break. They must not mind dirt, unpleasant smells or occasionally encountering vermin.

The ability to work and co-operate as part of a team is important, and all workers must be reliable and able to carry out instructions.

Extreme care must be taken not to drop litter or damage people's property; the public should be treated with respect and courtesy.

Refuse collectors must also be aware of safety precautions at work. Slippery paths, steps and busy roads are all potentially dangerous and particular attention should be paid to safety regulations regarding the refuse vehicle.

ENTRY REQUIREMENTS

No formal educational qualifications are necessary, although some employers may prefer a good general education. Basic literacy and numeracy are needed, in order that instructions may be followed correctly and the work quota completed satisfactorily.

Applicants must be at least 18 years; older applicants are sometimes preferred. They must be fit and reasonably strong. A full UK driving licence may be an advantage, but is not essential.

TRAINING

Training is often provide by the employer and carried out on the job, alongside, and under the supervision, of experienced workers.

An introduction to the job may include being offered, or asked to attend, short courses lasting one or two days, covering subjects like health and safety at work.

NVQs/SVQs in waste collection are being developed by the Waste Management Industry Training and Advisory Board (WAMITAB).

LATE ENTRY

The work requires a mature, reliable and responsible attitude. Employers often prefer to recruit older candidates, providing they are able to meet the physical demands of the job.

OPPORTUNITIES

The majority of refuse collectors are employed by local authority cleansing departments and they deal mainly with domestic refuse collection.

There is usually competition for jobs and few advertised vacancies, since most authorities keep a waiting list of applicants. It is difficult to give details of the demand for workers, but a large city can, for example, employ around 300 refuse collectors.

Opportunities exist to work for private contract firms. They may operate in an area where a local authority has contracted out the work. Hired by a variety of individuals or bodies, they undertake daily domestic collections and/or specialize in collecting bulky items and large quantities of waste material, for instance, after demolition processes or house clearances. Similar work may be offered by waste disposal or food disposal firms and waste paper merchants. The job is open to both men and women.

PAY AND CONDITIONS

Refuse collectors employed by local authorities are paid according to manual worker grades that are set on an hourly scale. Basic wages range from around £142 to £160 a week. Additional bonus payments are payable.

Refuse collectors in London are paid an additional allowance.

Contract refuse collectors may be paid on a piece-rate basis, so earnings may vary according to the number of hours they work, or collections they complete.

Most refuse collectors work eight-hour shifts, five days a week. Work normally begins early in the morning, between 6 and 7am. Some employers operate a task-and-finish system, which enables workers to go home once their allocation of work has been completed; this may be by 1 or 2pm. Other employers require the team to return to the depot, where they must remain until the official clocking-off time, rarely later than 4pm.

At Christmas and Easter periods, workloads are heavier and hours are therefore longer.

Hours vary for refuse collectors employed by private contractors, depending on workloads. They may start and finish work at relatively later times.

Paid overtime may be available.

PROSPECTS

Promotion prospects for refuse collectors depend on ability. It may be possible to progress to being in charge of a team of collectors, with responsibility for their work, ensuring that daily tasks are completed and that the streets are left litter free.

Opportunities may exist for suitably qualified workers to become drivers, although drivers are generally recruited specifically for the job and are LGV licence holders.

Those with proven ability and suitable experience may move to a higher-level job, such as a depot superintendent or an inspector, but such openings are limited. After gaining experience working for a small, private firm, there may be an opportunity to move into management or partnership. Setting up a contract firm requires considerable business sense, management skills, and a lot of capital.

RELATED OCCUPATIONS

Industrial cleaner, road sweeper, building/construction operative, water/sewage worker, removalman/woman, groundsman/woman.

FURTHER INFORMATION

Job information and details of vacancies are available from the cleansing department of local authorities. The addresses and telephone numbers of private contractors are listed in Yellow Pages.

FURTHER READING

Working in Outdoor Jobs – COIC

In the careers library classified under IJ.

1. BEAUTY THERAPIST CLCI:IK
2. BEAUTY CONSULTANT CLCI:IK

BACKGROUND INFORMATION

Beauty consultants and beauty therapists are concerned with improving people's physical appearance, either through offering treatments for the face and body, or recommending special products. Beauty therapists and beauticians are primarily concerned with offering treatments in salons. A beauty therapist (sometimes called an aesthetician) is trained to be able to offer more extensive treatments than a beautician, who will have had a more basic training. In this context, the term beauty therapist is used to cover all beauty professions offering treatment in salons and similar environments.

Beauty consultants sell and demonstrate products in stores and do not offer treatments, although they may do make-up demonstrations and advise customers on skin care.

Most beauty therapist and beauty consultants are women. Most clients are also women, although there is a growing interest amongst males for skin and body care treatments and cosmetics.

Beauty salons can claim exemption from the Sex Discrimination Act, which normally requires all jobs to be open to both men and women applicants.

1. BEAUTY THERAPIST (IK)

THE WORK

Beauty therapists are trained to be able to offer a wide range of treatments for the face and body, including the hands and feet. Some of these treatments are designed to improve the texture and appearance of the skin; others are concerned with body shaping and fat reduction. All therapists must be able to perform facials, wax treatments, eye lash tinting, manicures and pedicures, and apply make-up. Some of these treatments involve the use of special machines.

Facials

A beauty therapist needs to be able to analyse a client's skin condition and offer appropriate treatment. The purpose of a facial differs according to the needs of each client. Some may need special treatment for acne; older clients and those with drier skins may need treatments which hydrate and nourish the skin. The classic facial starts with thorough cleansing of the skin. This may be followed by a steam treatment, which helps to bring impurities to the surface of the skin, then by facial massage with creams or oils and, finally, a face mask.

There are also a number of specialist facial treatments. Some involve the use of aromatherapy oils or other special products and techniques. Other treatments works by stimulating the facial muscles or the application of high frequency currents through vacuum electrodes, resulting in a 'mini face lift'. Separate training is needed before a therapist can administer these kinds of treatments, which all involve the use of special machines.

Make-up

All beauty therapists administer make-up to clients. This is often called a make-over. It may include make-up for photographic sessions, corrective make-up for blemishes, or make-up for special occasions, such as weddings.

Other facial treatments include eyebrow plucking and eyelash and eyebrow tinting. Some salons may also offer ear piercing.

Manicure and nail extensions

This involves filing and shaping fingernails, removal of cuticles and hard skin, the application of creams to make the hands more supple and the application of nail polish. Many salons now offer nail extensions and other special treatments.

Pedicure

This is similar to the manicure, but is concerned with the feet. The therapist may also offer foot massage.

Body treatments

A beauty therapist may be expected to carry out a number of body treatments. Body massage is normally carried out manually, although there are some treatments which use machines.

Special creams or oils (such as aromatherapy oils) are often used. The therapist needs to have a good understanding of anatomy and physiology and of the effect of massage on patients with high blood pressure or back problems. Some massage treatments are concerned with lymph drainage, which helps remove wastes and toxins from the body. Massage therapists are people who specialize in massage.

A range of slimming treatments, which use different types of machinery, are offered in many salons. These include faradic treatments, where pads are applied to areas of muscle to give physical contractions, and vibrating tables or bed bands, which help to remove stubborn fat. There are also treatments for cellulite (a condition which affects many women and makes the skin look like orange peel). These include machines that give a vigorous massage; machines with a vacuum suction device to help break down fat and various treatments using products containing seaweed or mud.

Hair removal

Depilation (hair removal) involves the use of wax or sugaring to remove hair from the legs, face and bikini line. Electrolysis (epilation) involves the insertion of a needle, through which an electric current is sent, into the hair follicle.

Other treatments

Some salons and health spas may offer hydrotherapy treatments (literally, any treatment using water) with whirlpool baths, spa pools or air baths, where jets of air are passed through water to massage the body. Many beauty salons also offer saunas and steam treatments, as well as tanning treatments, usually from a sun bed. These can be used by clients with minimal supervision. However, therapists must be able to advise clients on correct usage.

Other duties

Beauty therapists may also be required to book appointments, take telephone calls, work in reception, handle money, order new supplies and generally keep the salon clean and tidy. Beauty therapists may also be required to take down details of clients' medical history and advise on exercise, slimming, diet and nutrition.

WORK ENVIRONMENT

Most beauticians and beauty therapists work in high street salons, or in salons within department stores. Some work in health and fitness clubs, hotels, in holiday centres or on cruise ships; some self-employed beauty therapists visit clients in their homes.

Salons are usually divided up into small cubicles where the treatments take place. Beauty therapists spend most of the day on their feet in these cubicles, which are sometimes cramped, carrying out treatments on clients. There may not be a great deal of contact with other staff during the working day.

SKILLS AND INTERESTS

Clients may be nervous and shy about undergoing treatments. Beauty therapists must be sympathetic and able to put patients at their ease. They are dealing with the public in a most intimate sense. Beauty therapists should also be knowledgeable enough to be able to diagnose a client's skin condition, advise on treatments and recommend the best products. They may sometimes have to deal with difficult clients, or have to cope when things go wrong, such as when an eyelash tint may not have taken properly. Patience is important in these situations.

Beauty therapists must be clean, well groomed, wear suitable make-up and pay attention to personal hygiene. A perfect skin is not essential, but they must take care with their appearance. Stamina is also important, as the work involves long periods of standing. Massage, in particular, can be very tiring. There may be little time to rest or take breaks between clients.

An interest in science, particularly human biology, and the way that treatments affect the skin, is important. Therapists must be aware of the affect of treatments on the client and be able to answer probing questions.

ENTRY REQUIREMENTS

It is very unusual for salons to employ trainees who have not taken a course and gained a qualification. Detailed entry requirements for the principal qualifying bodies are:

NVQs/SVQs: no specific entry requirements.

City and Guilds: no set requirements but colleges may require three GCSEs/S grades (A-C/1-3), including biology.

BTEC national diploma: four GCSEs/S grades (A-C/1-3), including biology.

BTEC higher national diploma: one A level/two H grades and supporting GCSEs/S grades, including English and a science subject.

Confederation of International Beauty and Cosmetology (CIBTAC): three GCSEs/S grades (A-C/1-3) or equivalent, including English and preferably human biology, or another science subject.

International Health and Beauty Council (IHBC): no specific entry requirements.

Entry is also possible through training schemes for young people, which involves work experience in a beauty salon and off-the-job training. Further details are available from careers offices, TECS/LECS. Most courses can be started at age 16 years.

TRAINING

The most usual method of training is a full-time course at a further education college, or at a private beauty school. Courses in further education colleges usually last one to two years. Courses in private training schools are shorter, more intensive and require the payment of fees.

Courses should cover all the essential treatments mentioned above (facials, make-up, eyebrow and eyelash tinting, manicure, pedicure and some body treatments), plus some or all of the following: anatomy and physiology of the head, face and neck, to include bones and muscles, nerve, blood supply and lymphatic system; the structure of the skin (including skin diseases and disorders; skin types and skin care); the structure of nails; cosmetic science; organic and inorganic chemistry; electricity – high frequency, galvanic and faradic currents; hygiene, health and safety; first aid; salon procedure; business skills; communication skills; and professional ethics.

There are a number of qualifications. The principal ones are:

NVQs/SVQs. The emphasis is on practical assessment and the demonstration of professional competence, rather than on written examinations. There is no prescribed number of hours of training required for NVQs/SVQs. NVQs/SVQs are offered through college and some independent centres.

The NVQs/SVQs currently available are as follows:

Level 1 in Beauty Therapy. Appropriate for trainees and other salon staff working as assistants.

Level 2 in Beauty Therapy. Covers the essential facial, nail and wax treatments, together with basic sales skills. Additional units cover ear piercing and the control, handling and display of stock.

Level 3 in Beauty Therapy. Goes into greater depth and covers more skills, including management and supervisory skills.

There are also two further NVQs/SVQs at Level 3 in Epilation and Aromatherapy Massage.

City and Guilds. Most courses offered in further education colleges last one to two years (full-time), although many colleges are now offering part-time courses lasting a minimum of two years. They include: Beauty Therapy Certificate (3040), Electrical Epilation Certificate (3050), Cosmetic Make-Up (3020), Manicure (3030), Salon Management (3060), Introductory Certificate in Salon Services (3570).

BTEC/SCOTVEC. The BTEC National Diploma in Beauty Therapy normally lasts two years full-time and is available at a number of colleges of further education. The advanced BTEC Higher National Diploma is available only at a few colleges. In Scotland, SCOTVEC national certificate modules are available in beauty care and associated subjects.

Confederation of International Beauty Therapy and Cosmetology (CIBTAC). CIBTAC is the examining body of the British Association of Beauty Therapists and Cosmetologists (BABTEC). CIBTAC qualifications include a Beautician Diploma, a Body Therapy Diploma, an Electrical Epilation Diploma, Esthiticienne Diplomas, an Assistant Beautician Certificate, an Anatomy and Physiology Certificate (plus one with Massage) and an Aromatherapy Certificate.

Students are normally awarded a CIBTAC Diploma after a minimum of seven months training.

International Health and Beauty Council (IHBC). A number of courses and qualifications are available through IHBC including the International Beauty Therapy Diploma. Other courses and qualifications include remedial camouflage, electrology, sauna treatments, theatrical and media make-up, body massage and nail technology. The courses are modular, which makes it easier to study part-time over a period of time.

LATE ENTRY

There are good opportunities for late entrants, as maturity is a desirable quality for beauty work. Most mature entrants take part-time courses in FE colleges or private schools.

OPPORTUNITIES

Newly trained beauticians or beauty therapists usually start by working in a high street salon. There is no shortage of trained therapists and there is usually considerable competition for jobs. Jobs are advertised in the beauty press, eg *Health and Beauty Salon; International Therapist* in the local press, and through specialist recruitment agencies and Jobcentres.

There are also opportunities to work on cruise ships, in hotels, at health farms, fitness centres and spas. Many beauty therapists are self-employed and work either by visiting clients in their homes, or through fitness centres. Opportunities for make-up artists exist in photographic studios, theatres, films and on television, although entry to the work is highly competitive and mostly freelance. There are also opportunities to work abroad, for those who have a foreign language.

PAY AND CONDITIONS

There are no nationally agreed rates of pay – it varies from employer to employer. Salaries start at around £130 a week, rising to around £200 a week.

Most therapists can expect to earn more through commission. Perks may include free treatments, discounts on products, or free use of facilities at health farms and on cruise ships, where accommodation may also be included. Working hours are normally 9 to 5, although some salons stay open until about 8pm on some days. Beauty therapists normally work on Saturdays and receive one day off in lieu during the week.

PROSPECTS

Opportunities for promotion to managing a salon within about five years of qualifying are good. Many beauty therapists eventually open their own salons or become self-employed. Others move into teaching (or training); into professional make-up work (sometimes working in photographic studios, theatres, films or television); or into image consultancy work.

RELATED OCCUPATIONS

Hairdresser, make-up artist, massage therapist, image consultant, health and fitness instructor.

FURTHER INFORMATION AND READING

Please see article 2. BEAUTY CONSULTANT

2. BEAUTY CONSULTANT (IK)

THE WORK

Beauty consultants sell cosmetics and advise customers on choosing and using cosmetic products. These include skin creams and lotions, make-up and cosmetics. They may also include perfumes and hair care products as well.

The work is essentially that of a sales person: the job is to sell products. Beauty consultants must also be able to diagnose a customer's skin condition and advise on the appropriate type of product. In most cases, beauty consultants are employed by a particular cosmetics company (Revlon, Clarins, Clinique, Elizabeth Arden, Estie Lauder, Lanctme and Max Factor are some of the best known) rather than by the store, although in smaller shops and high street chemists, some beauty consultants may be employed directly by the shop to sell a range of products. Consultants advise customers on the best combination of products to suit a range of different skin types and faces. They are also responsible for product displays, and may be involved in ordering stock. Some beauty consultants may be involved in doing demonstration make-overs. Experienced consultants may find opportunities organizing special sales campaigns and promotions, demonstrating the products, training staff and in area management.

Consultants normally wear the uniform of the cosmetic company they are representing and are expected to use the company's products.

WORK ENVIRONMENT

Beauty consultants work behind counters in department stores or shops. Most of the working day is spent standing behind a sales counter. Occasionally, a consultant may be involved in demonstrating products or giving a customer a make-over. A small amount of time may be spent in the stock-room.

SKILLS AND INTERESTS

Beauty consultants are essentially salespeople. They must be confident and used to dealing with the public. An outgoing personality, a friendly manner, a clear voice and a certain amount of persistence are important. Beauty consultants are also required to maintain a high standard of personal appearance. They must be well groomed and appropriately made up, using the company's products. Good health is important: firstly, because it affects physical appearance, and secondly, because the work can be strenuous and tiring.

Consultants must be familiar with the products they are selling and be able to advise customers on the best range of products for their particular skin type.

Beauty consultants usually work as members of a small team and need to be able to co-operate and get on well with colleagues.

Numeracy is required for the cash-handling aspect of the work.

ENTRY REQUIREMENTS

There are no set entry qualifications other than a good general education. Applicants are assessed on their general physical appearance, presentation skills, interest and knowledge of cosmetics, and sales experience.

Most cosmetics companies prefer applicants to be over 18 and usually prefer consultants in their twenties, thirties, and forties.

TRAINING

The individual cosmetic companies normally offer short training courses for their consultants. This training covers product knowledge, the structure of the skin, skin care, make-up techniques, dealing with the public, stock-taking and sales techniques. Some cosmetic companies have their own examinations and award diplomas.

Currently NVQs/SVQs are being developed.

LATE ENTRY

Many employers prefer to employ older people, because of their experience.

OPPORTUNITIES

Beauty consultants generally work in department stores, where they are usually employed by one particular cosmetics company to sell their products, or in large high street chemists. Most of the opportunities are in towns and cities. There are also opportunities in the duty-free shops at airports, on cruise ships or ferries, in hotels and occasionally in health farms. Although many beauty consultants are employed by individual cosmetic companies to sell only their branded products, there is a trend towards stores employing staff to sell a number of different products. There is considerable competition for jobs in the large stores. Opportunities exist for temporary employment during busy times such as Christmas. A number of agencies supply the beauty houses with temporary staff at these times and give two to three-day courses on the products of different cosmetic companies.

PAY AND CONDITIONS

Starting salaries are usually between £5,000 and £7,500 plus commission, rising to about £9,000. Rates of pay are higher in most of the London stores. Most consultants are paid commission on everything they sell and are expected to reach sales targets. They normally work the same hours as any other retail sales staff and are expected to work on Saturdays. Temporary and part-time work is possible. Staff are usually required to wear a special uniform. Discounts on products and allowances for make-up are normally available.

PROSPECTS

There are prospects of promotion from junior consultant to senior consultant and then to supervisor and regional manager. Experienced beauty consultants may also have the opportunity to give make-up demonstrations, or move into training. There are also some senior posts in organizing special sales campaigns and promotions.

RELATED OCCUPATIONS

Make-up artist, beauty therapist, image consultant, retail manager, sales assistant, sales representative.

FURTHER INFORMATION

Health and Beauty Therapy Training Board, PO Box 21, Bognor Regis, West Sussex PO21 2PF

Vocational Training Charitable Trust/Vocational Awards International*, 46 Aldwick Road, Bognor Regis, West Sussex PO21 2PN, 01243 842064

Confederation of International Beauty Therapy and Cosmetology (CIBTAC)*, Parabola House, Parabola Road, Cheltenham, Gloucestershire GL50 3AH, 01242 570284 (please send sae)

Federation of Recruitment and Employment Services, 10 Belgrave Square, London SW1X 8PH (for advice on agencies which find temporary work for beauty consultants)

FURTHER READING

Leaflets/booklets available from the addresses marked*.

Working in Beauty, Fitness and Hairdressing – COIC
Getting Jobs in Beauty – Cassell
Careers in Hairdressing and Beauty Therapy – Kogan Page

In the careers library classified under IK; OFM.

HAIRDRESSER CLCI:IL

BACKGROUND INFORMATION

In recent years, hairdressing has become increasingly linked with fashion. As fashions in clothes change, so do hair fashions. The development of new hairdressing techniques and treatments now allows a greater range of styles to be created than ever before.

Hairdressers play an important part in helping both males and females to make the most of their appearance. Many males now demand treatments that were once associated just with females – tinting, perming and styling. Most salons no longer specialize in men's or women's hairdressing, but offer a service to both sexes.

THE WORK

Hairdressers cut and style hair. They begin by giving client consultations, in which they discuss what clients require and may make recommendations on style or hair treatment. They may diagnose any basic problems clients may have with their hair or scalp, and suggest how improvements can be made.

Stylists (trained hairdressers) shampoo, condition and rinse hair, cut it wet or dry and may perm, colour, tint or bleach hair. They then style clients' hair, either by setting, blow-drying, or using other techniques, and may apply hairspray or gel. They may recommend hair-care products stocked by the salon and sell them to clients. Some hairdressers also fit wigs, which is a specialized area of work, requiring careful and painstaking handiwork.

Some tasks may be undertaken by a junior or apprentice – tasks such as washing and rinsing clients' hair and applying conditioner. Juniors may also help stylists by handing them rollers, rods, end papers, scissors, combs, and so on.

Stylists use a variety of equipment, including scissors, clippers, combs, razors, pins, curlers, tongs, straightening irons, hot brushes, heated rollers, highlighting materials and dryers. They use shampoos and conditioners, lotions for perming, colouring, bleaching, blow-drying and setting and products such as mousse, gel, polish, wax and sprays. Some of the chemicals used are powerful and hairdressers wear thin protective gloves while working with them.

An important part of hairdressing is customer contact. Hairdressers talk to clients to build up a good relationship. Some of their discussions with clients concern hairdressing, for example, styles and hair products, such as shampoos and conditioners, but much is social. Hairdressers gauge whether clients want to chat or whether they prefer to relax quietly.

Hairdressers may be responsible for other tasks – reception, answering the telephone, making appointments, stock control, sorting towels and gowns, keeping the salon well supplied with clean linen, sweeping up, cleaning basins, helping clients with their coats and bags and making tea and coffee for staff and clients. These tasks are normally done by an apprentice or junior in a salon.

Some hairdressers specialize in ladies' hairdressing. Others specialize in barbering (men's hairdressing), which can include all the treatments offered in ladies' hairdressing, but also beard and moustache trimming. Most hairdressers, however, cut and style both men's and women's hair.

Some hairdressers specialize in Afro-Caribbean styling.

WORK ENVIRONMENT

Hairdressers work indoors. Most of them work in salons, although some work in private homes. Salons are usually clean and light, but can become warm and humid in summer.

Hairdressers spend all their time standing and bending.

Most hairdressers work in local salons. Some work on a mobile basis and travel locally to clients' homes. A driving licence is necessary for mobile work. A few hairdressers work on cruise ships and are away from home for much of the time.

SKILLS AND INTERESTS

Hairdressers should have good hand skills for cutting and styling hair. An interest in art and fashion is useful, to be able to appreciate different styles and keep up to date with changing styles. An interest in science is desirable, to understand the use of chemical products in hairdressing.

Hairdressers need a friendly manner and should be capable of getting on well with people of all kinds. They must be good listeners and be able to talk easily to clients.

Hairdressers need patience and concentration for their work. A careful approach is required, particularly when working with scissors, razors and chemical products.

Fitness and stamina are important, as hairdressers stand all day. They ought to be free from skin complaints, such as eczema, as the chemical products used tend to aggravate these conditions.

Hairdressers should be clean and well-groomed, with a general appearance that gives their clients confidence.

Hair-styles change with fashion. Hairdressers must keep up to date with new styles and hairdressing products and be willing to put them into practice.

ENTRY REQUIREMENTS

There are no minimum qualifications for entry to hairdressing, but GCSEs/S grades in English, science, maths and art are useful.

Although no education qualifications are necessary to work towards NVQs/SVQs, some colleges offering full-time courses leading to NVQs/SVQs may ask for specific subjects and/or grades at GCSE/S grade.

BTEC National Diploma in Design Fashion Styling for Hair and Make-up requires either: four GCSEs/S grades (A-C/1-3); or Intermediate GNVQ Art and Design/GSVQ Level II Design. Candidates also need a portfolio of art and design work that includes several life and fashion images.

BTEC Higher National Diploma in Design Fashion Styling for Hair and Make-up requires either: one A level/two H grades, normally including art, and four GCSEs/S grades (A-C/1-3); or a relevant BTEC national diploma; or Advanced GNVQ Art and Design/GSVQ Level III Design. Candidates also need a portfolio of art and design work that includes several life and fashion images.

Entry may be possible for young people through Modern Apprenticeships leading to at least an NVQ/SVQ Level 3. Contact your local careers office, TEC/LEC for details.

Experience of salon work with a Saturday or holiday job can be an advantage.

TRAINING

The traditionally recognized qualifications in hairdressing are NVQs/SVQs.

NVQ/SVQ in Hairdressing at Level 1 is concerned with reception, stock control, health and safety, personal presentation, working with others and the first steps of hairdressing.

NVQ/SVQ in Hairdressing at Level 2 includes: working as part of a team, reception, client consultation, conditioning hair and scalp, shampooing, cutting, blow-drying, setting, perming and neutralizing and setting and colouring. Afro-Caribbean hairdressing is available as part of Level 2, along with barbering, and are available as optional units.

NVQ/SVQ in Hairdressing at Level 3 involves higher technical skills, such as perming, colouring, cutting and long hair work, and also includes training, supervisory skills, improving systems and procedures and organizing promotional activities for the salon.

There are several routes into hairdressing, most of which involve working towards NVQ/SVQ qualifications:

Training schemes for young people. The majority of 16 and 17-year-olds entering hairdressing do so via training schemes. Trainees combine on-the-job training at a salon with day release to college or a training centre. They work towards NVQ/SVQ Hairdressing Level 2, which normally takes around two years.

Modern Apprenticeships in hairdressing are available for young people. Apprenticeships may take up to three years and combine training in a salon with day release to college to work towards at least an NVQ/SVQ in Hairdressing at Level 3. Contact your local careers office, TEC/LEC or the Hairdressing Training Board for details.

Full-time college courses. Many local colleges throughout the UK offer full-time courses that lead to NVQs/SVQs in Hairdressing at Levels 2 or 3. Some offer qualifications such as the National Diploma of Hairdressing, which is awarded by the Guild of Hairdressers.

Courses usually last for two years and combine theory and practice. Practical work may include working with members of the public in a training salon at the college, and regular work experience within salons.

The London College of Fashion offers a BTEC National Diploma and a Higher National Diploma in Design Fashion Styling for Hair and Make-up (both two years full-time). These courses are designed to prepare students for work as a make-up and hair artist in the fashion-related fields of beauty, editorial, catwalk and advertising.

Apprenticeships. Some salons offer three-year apprenticeships. Apprentices assist qualified hairdressers and are trained by them. They may gain additional experience with customers on 'model evenings' and usually attend a local college or training centre to work towards an NVQ/SVQ in Hairdressing at Level 2.

Private hairdressing schools. There are many privately-run hairdressing schools that offer full-time courses, where students pay their own tuition and examination fees. The courses are usually shorter and more intensive than courses offered by local colleges or training centres.

Students at some private hairdressing schools work towards NVQs/SVQs, while some work towards other hairdressing qualifications. Students are advised to check how far other qualifications are recognized by the hairdressing industry, before deciding on a course at a private hairdressing school. Check with local careers offices.

After training, hairdressers are expected to work for at least one year as an improver, before being considered experienced. Those with an NVQ/SVQ in Hairdressing at Level 2 may apply to the Hairdressing Council to become state-registered hairdressers.

LATE ENTRY

There is no strict upper age limit for entry to hairdressing, but most entrants are school-leavers. Adults who enter hairdressing often do so after a full-time course.

There may be specific training opportunities, directed at adults, in some areas for this type of work. Candidates may have to satisfy certain conditions to be eligible. Contact your local Jobcentre, careers office or TEC/LEC for details.

OPPORTUNITIES

There are approximately 170,000 hairdressers, most of whom work in the 36,000 salons throughout the UK. Most salons are unisex, with a minority for males or females only. The number of hairdressers decreased during the recession in the early 1990s, but has begun to stabilize.

Salons range from one-person businesses to large, national chains of salons. Most hairdressers work in high street salons, while others work in department store salons, beauty salons, health farms, hotels and clubs, the Armed Forces and in hospitals. There are a few opportunities for hairdressers to work on cruise ships, in film and television work and with fashion photographers.

Self-employment is possible in a number of ways. Some hairdressers rent a chair from a salon owner and work with their own customers. Others offer hairdressing at their own homes, while some operate on a mobile basis, travelling to customers' homes. Many hairdressers open their own salon. It is also possible for hairdressers to open their own salon by entering a franchise arrangement with a regional or national hairdressing company.

Work abroad is possible, particularly at European holiday resorts that are popular with English-speaking tourists.

PAY AND CONDITIONS

The suggested wage scales in hairdressing are:

Trainee – £36.50 a week plus £3.25 per unit of NVQ/SVQ Level 2 passed.

Trainee with NVQ/SVQ Level 1 – £40.50 a week plus £3.25 per unit of NVQ/SVQ Level 2 passed.

Stylist with NVQ/SVQ Level 2 or three years salon experience – £79.50 a week plus £3.90 per unit of NVQ/SVQ Level 3 passed.

Senior stylist with NVQ/SVQ Level 3 or Level 2 plus two years salon experience, or five years salon experience – £142 a week.

These exclude commission and are suggested wage scales. Some salons pay more than these, while others pay less.

Hairdressers usually work a 39-hour week over five days, including Saturdays. They may work one late evening a week.

Part-time work is common.

PROSPECTS

In most small salons there is no scope for promotion. In large salons it may be possible to specialize, perhaps as a perming technician or colour technician. Salons that are part of a large group can offer promotion to salon manager and further management positions within the organization.

Hairdressers with an NVQ/SVQ in Hairdressing at Level 3 may train for management by working towards an NVQ/

SVQ in Management at Level 4. An NVQ/SVQ in Hairdressing at Level 4 is being developed and will be concerned with management, rather than additional hairdressing skills.

There are opportunities for experienced hairdressers to teach hairdressing in a local college, or at a private hairdressing school. Colleges usually require applicants to have a further education teaching qualification. Relevant qualifications outside Scotland include: the Certificate in Education, which is available (one-year full-time) at Bolton Institute of Higher Education and the Universities of Huddersfield, Greenwich and Wolverhampton; City and Guilds Further and Adult Education Teacher's Certificate, which is offered part-time at many colleges in England, Wales and Northern Ireland.

In Scotland, hairdressers with SVQ Level 2 or 3 may prepare for management, or for teaching hairdressing at college, by studying for the SCOTVEC Higher National Certificate in Hairdressing and Salon Organization. Courses are offered at a number of Scottish colleges, full-time for one year or on a day release basis for one to three years.

A few hairdressers become technical consultants for hair product companies and teach hairdressers the most effective ways of using hairdressing products.

RELATED OCCUPATIONS

Beautician/beauty therapist, beauty consultant, receptionist, fashion model, trichologist, retail assistant, retail manager.

FURTHER INFORMATION

Hairdressing Training Board*, 3 Chequer Road, Doncaster DN1 2AA, 01302 342837 (please include sae)

FURTHER READING

Leaflets/booklets available from the address marked*.

Job Outlines – Hairdressing – COIC
Working in Beauty, Fitness and Hairdressing – COIC
Careers in Hairdressing and Beauty Therapy – Kogan Page

In the careers library classified under IL.

FUNERAL DIRECTOR/EMBALMER
CLCI:IP

BACKGROUND INFORMATION

Funerals, which are ceremonies organized for the disposal of the bodies of the deceased, take the form of burials or cremations. In Great Britain there are strict regulations governing the procedures to be followed from the time a death occurs to the actual burial or cremation. Funeral directors or undertakers are responsible for preparing the deceased for burial or cremation and for arranging and supervising funerals. This involves a variety of duties. In large organizations, the tasks may be divided between employees – different workers may be responsible for driving, pall bearing, doing the paperwork, etc. The majority of funeral directors, however, are small family firms, with one person having responsibility for the broad range of tasks. Extra staff may be hired, for example, as bearers or drivers, when required.

Many funeral directors also carry out embalming, which is concerned with preserving bodies until they are buried or cremated. Embalming, however, is a separate profession and may be carried out by fully qualified embalmers who are not concerned with the other aspects of undertaking.

THE WORK

Funeral Director

Funeral directors are usually contracted by the relatives or friends of a deceased person to arrange a funeral. Having received notification of a death, the funeral director arranges to collect the remains, and establishes basic information about the deceased, such as the name and age and date of death.

Arrangements are made for further visits to the clients so that detailed preparations can be made for the funeral. Funeral directors offer advice and make all the practical arrangements for families. This includes organizing transport, flowers, catering, accommodation and obituary notices. Having decided upon a burial or cremation, funeral directors negotiate times and dates with the officials involved – clergy, cemetery staff, crematorium officials, and so on, on their clients' behalf. Funeral directors may deal with all the financial arrangements and transactions. In addition, they ensure that all the legal requirements are satisfied. They assist their clients in obtaining the necessary paperwork, such as the death certificate, and clients may also need advice about claiming death grants, and other things.

The body must be prepared for burial or cremation. This may include embalming, and general preparations such as washing/setting hair, shaving men, and applying cosmetics discreetly to faces. Pads are inserted under the eyelids and the mouth is sutured to stop the jaw opening.

The prepared body is placed into a coffin which will have been fitted with a lining and handles chosen by the clients. On the day of the funeral, funeral directors are responsible for ensuring that everything runs smoothly and according to the agreed routine and timetable. They usually ride in the hearse and precede the cortege to the ceremony. All legal aspects, such as handing over certificates to the crematorium officials, are also dealt with.

Embalming

Embalming is linked to funeral directing and is carried out by a professional embalmer. The process is concerned with the disinfection and preservation of bodies until burial/cremation. Embalming is not a legal requirement in this country, but it is increasingly carried out for reasons of hygiene. The main objectives of modern embalming are to: prevent deterioration prior to the funeral; remove obvious and distressing signs of death; restore as normal an appearance as possible; and ensure that there is no health risk to those who come into contact with the deceased.

The treatment of deceased people, to arrest or retard the process of decay, involves washing the body with germicidal soap, and injecting the body with sterilizing fluid. The process may be more complicated when the embalmer is dealing with severely injured persons, and after post-mortem investigations have taken place complete embalmment may be necessary. It may be necessary to restore normal appearance to parts of the body, particularly visible aspects such as faces, which have become misshapen or disfigured.

Embalmers use materials such as wax and plaster of Paris for this purpose, and apply cosmetics to provide colour.

WORK ENVIRONMENT

The premises of a funeral director are often fairly large and comprise warm, pleasant, comfortable reception rooms, offices, store rooms, and an embalming area. Although based inside and working in fairly comfortable conditions for much of the time, undertakers are required to work outside in all weathers when attending funerals. The work also involves quite a lot of travelling, which usually entails driving – to collect the remains, visit clients, attend funerals, etc. Funeral directing and embalming work can be heavy, as it entails lifting and carrying.

Embalmers work in a clinically clean environment, often part of the funeral director's premises. The temperature of the work area is usually slightly lower than normal room temperature. They may spend long periods standing in one position with few opportunities to sit whilst working. Those who do not combine the work with funeral directing have little contact with the public. The vast majority of embalmers are required to drive and travel a fair amount during the day, for example to provide services for different funeral directors, or carry out undertaking duties.

SKILLS AND INTERESTS

Funeral directors must have good communication skills and be able to deal with people of all ages and from a variety of social backgrounds. They should be well spoken, tactful and understanding. They have to be able to cope with people in a very unhappy and distressed condition. Genuine sympathy and sensitivity are necessary, but funeral directors must not allow themselves to become too deeply and emotionally involved. Smart and conventional dress is required, and individuals must be prepared to conduct themselves in a serious and dignified manner.

Administrative and organizational ability is required for carrying out the office work and to co-ordinate funeral arrangements. It is essential that funerals proceed without problems. Attention to detail, therefore, is vital, so that nothing is forgotten or mistimed. Management skills are also necessary, in order to negotiate with representatives of other organizations, organize and control staff, make financial arrangements, etc. Familiarity with religious rituals is useful; however, it is not essential, in general, that individuals are religious or are of any particular religious persuasion. It is essential that individuals are not squeamish, do not mind handling corpses and are able to endure unpleasant sights and smells. They should be able to adopt a professional, mature and responsible attitude to the duties involved. Embalmers are required to have an interest in science, particularly anatomy and chemistry. Manual dexterity is also necessary for handling surgical instruments and tools. Cleanliness and neatness are essential.

ENTRY REQUIREMENTS

No formal educational qualifications are required for entry into funeral directing or embalming work. Some employers, however, prefer new recruits to have GCSEs/S grades (A-C/1-3), including English.

Candidates may find the study of subjects such as English, maths, chemistry, biology and religious studies useful. A background of business and secretarial studies may also be advantageous for carrying out the administrative and office-keeping tasks.

Funeral directors and embalmers are often required to drive, so a full driving licence is desirable and often essential.

TRAINING

Undertaking

There may be opportunities for those entering jobs as drivers or pall bearers to learn all aspects of funeral directing work and to become funeral directors. Individuals interested in becoming funeral directors should check with employers as to the possibility and availability of training. In some companies, employees start and remain in the same jobs.

Training is on-the-job and new entrants usually begin in operative jobs, such as driving, cleaning the vehicles and carrying out routine maintenance. Other routine duties include cleaning out the embalming room and collecting the deceased from homes and hospitals. Supervision is by the funeral director or an experienced worker. Trainees may move on to finishing coffins – fitting handles, linings, plaques, and so on – and placing bodies into them. They will gradually be introduced to tasks of increased responsibility, such as bearing at funerals, driving the hearse and assisting with the office work.

Having gained experience of all the different aspects of funeral directing, individuals may firstly assist the funeral director and then arrange and conduct funerals alone. Those who express an interest may be trained in embalming.

The British Institute of Funeral Directors runs, through its qualified instructors, part-time training courses leading to the *Diploma of Funeral Directing* – the recognized professional qualification. Students must already be in employment with a firm of undertakers. Candidates must pass a preliminary examination set by the National Association of Funeral Directors or hold other acceptable qualifications, such as two GCSEs/S grades (A-C/1-3), in English and maths. Exemption is also given to those who hold the Certificate of the British Institute of Embalmers, or the Registered General Nurse qualification, or the Certificate and Diploma in Mortuary Hygiene and Technology. Training is usually over one year and is mainly on the job with part-time tuition from an approved tutor

during weekends and evenings, at a training centre or by correspondence course. Students must successfully complete theoretical and practical examinations, and candidates may then be considered for membership of the Institute.

Embalming

Many funeral directors train as professional embalmers, although individuals may train solely in embalming. Trainees are normally in full-time employment, although this is not essential. The British Institute of Embalmers is the professional body and members are normally required to pass theoretical and practical examinations set by the National Examinations Board of Embalmers.

Contact the Institute for a list of schools and accredited tutors.

Training is by the modular system of education, comprising a foundation module, followed by five further modules in preparation for the final theory and practical examinations. Candidates must pass the foundation module examination before they are allowed to commence the course. There are no educational requirements to join a study course for the foundation module.

Candidates are required to sit an end-of-module test under exam conditions, and obtain a minimum pass mark of 60 per cent in each of the five modules before they are permitted to sit the theory examination. Marks gained from the five end-of-modules tests account for up to 60 per cent of the total marks awarded for the final theory examination requirement.

The majority of courses are run on a part-time basis for those in work, although a small number are full-time. Practical training is mainly on the job, with part-time tuition from a registered tutor during weekends or evenings, or via a correspondence course. Home study will be required if candidates are to reach the standard required to pass the examinations.

Successful candidates may apply to be considered for membership of the Institute.

LATE ENTRY

The opportunities for mature candidates to enter funeral directing or embalming work are favourable, as compared to those for school-leavers. Many employers look for candidates with a full driving licence and some driving experience. Skills and interests are very important, and a mature attitude to the work is essential. Entry is usually into operative posts, for example as drivers or pall bearers. There may be opportunities to train in undertaking or embalming, depending on the employer. Training for adult entrants is as described in TRAINING.

OPPORTUNITIES

Funeral directors and embalmers may be employed by large or small firms throughout the country. Many funeral directors are self-employed and run their own businesses. This type of business is often kept as a small family concern and consequently may be difficult to get into.

Individuals may run other types of business, such as building or cabinet making, in conjunction with funeral directing. This is particularly the case in the smaller towns and villages. There is, however, no specific link between undertaking and carpentry/joinery, as most coffins are now bought in from specialist manufacturers. Larger organizations (such as the Co-operative Society) specialize in providing funeral directing services, and employ staff to carry out funeral directing. Embalmers may work for the larger organizations or become self-employed – serving local funeral directors within an area, as required. Many individuals will provide both funeral directing and embalming services.

Work is available for funeral directors and embalmers throughout the UK. Some entrants to the work find themselves unsuitable and the work distasteful, but many find it a satisfactory, steady job and there is a low turnover of staff. Funeral directing is generally difficult to get into unless the business is in the family. Recruitment by the larger organizations is at a fairly low level. There are few opportunities for school-leavers and openings are mainly for drivers and/or bearers. There may then, however, be a chance to learn the other aspects of the work.

Individuals may set up in business on their own, providing they can raise the capital – a substantial amount may be required. In addition, it will be necessary to have learned the trade with an established funeral director. There may be slightly better opportunities to enter embalming work and, depending on demand in local areas, embalmers may become self-employed.

Vacancies for qualified embalmers are advertised in the publication *The Embalmer* (British Institute of Embalmers).

PAY AND CONDITIONS

It is difficult to give figures. Earnings depend on duties, and may be supplemented by a series of bonuses, for example for attending funerals, working unsocial hours and being on-call during unsocial hours. Generally, funeral directors earn slightly more than bearers/drivers, and may receive additional payments for embalming.

Salaries for funeral directors and embalmers working on a self-employed basis vary according to the amount of work they are able to obtain. Earnings are generally favourable, compared to the wages of employees of larger companies.

Funeral directors may have very irregular hours and are required to be on-call 24 hours a day for seven days a week. Most of the administration and organizing is carried out during office hours but they must be prepared to turn out at any hour when notified of deaths. Visits to relatives often take place in the evenings. The demand for services may also be irregular and may provide work on a part-time basis only. Those concerned solely with embalming may be able to work more normal office hours – Monday to Friday, for 37 hours a week. However, demand for their services is also variable.

PROSPECTS

Promotion prospects are generally very limited for funeral directors and embalmers. Those working for large organizations as employees may have opportunity to train in embalming, and there may be a formal career structure that provides opportunities of progression into management. Similar opportunities may be available for embalmers. Those funeral directors and embalmers working as employees for large or small businesses may aim to become self-employed owners of their own businesses, or partners of existing firms.

RELATED OCCUPATIONS

Hospital porter, grave digger, crematorium technician, mortuary attendant, pathology technician, car/van driver.

FURTHER INFORMATION

British Institute of Embalmers*, 21c Station Road, Knowle, Solihull B93 0HL, 01564 778991

British Institute of Funeral Directors*, 140 Leamington Road, Coventry, CV3 6JY (please include sae)

National Association of Funeral Directors*, 618 Warwick Road, Solihull, West Midlands B91 1AA, 0121 711 1343

FURTHER READING

Leaflets/booklets are available from the addresses marked*.

In the careers library classified under IP.

1. GENERAL PRACTITIONER CLCI:JAB
2. HOSPITAL DOCTOR CLCI:JAB

1. GENERAL PRACTITIONER (JAB)

THE WORK

GPs (general practitioners), or family doctors, play an important part in the life of a community. Their job is to listen to patients, perform examinations if necessary and, using their extensive knowledge of medicine, provide a diagnosis of the illness. The illness may not be apparent at first, or one set of symptoms may be masking the real problem. GPs advise patients on how to manage the illness, disability or problem, and prescribe appropriate medicines. They may also perform minor surgery. When appropriate, GPs will refer patients to a hospital specialist, or for X-ray examinations, or other tests. GPs may also refer patients to a social worker, psychologist, psychiatrist, or speech therapist, if appropriate.

After surgery, doctors have telephone calls to make to specialists or colleagues, as well as referral letters to write to hospitals. Notes on patients must also be completed, and GPs must keep fully up to date with changes in medical practice, law, ethics, drugs, and so on. There is a great deal of paperwork; GPs are called upon to certify a patient's state of health for social security, insurance or employment purposes, and to sign death certificates.

Preventing illness is an increasingly important aspect of the work of GPs; they are involved in immunizations, developmental checks on babies and young children, and health education during consultations.

GPs have the chance to get to know their patients and their families, as they often treat them over a period of many years. A relationship of trust is built up, which puts the GP in a position of great responsibility. GPs usually work as partners in group practices, or at health centres provided by the local health authority. Reception and secretarial services are often shared. There is an increasing trend towards large practices; nurses, health visitors, midwives, and physiotherapists may also be employed, ensuring a full service to patients.

WORK ENVIRONMENT

Although doctors in a practice are part of a team, much of their working day is spent on a one-to-one basis with patients. The average consultation lasts seven minutes, with the result that the work is extremely busy. Surgeries are normally pleasant environments. Home visits in rural areas may involve driving long distances. Modern, purpose-built health centres now provide professional accommodation for an increasing number of doctors.

SKILLS AND INTERESTS

GPs must be good listeners. Patients often find it difficult to explain what is wrong with them, and the GP needs to ask the right questions, and often look beyond the presenting symptoms.

GPs need to be responsible and trustworthy, with the ability to remain calm in a crisis. Practical ability and a steady hand are necessary for examining patients. GPs need the ability to absorb large amounts of information, normally of a scientific or technical nature. Good written skills are required for letters, reports, etc.

ENTRY REQUIREMENTS

A qualified doctor in the UK must hold a degree in medicine awarded by a university medical school and recognized by the General Medical Council. The first degree lasts five years for candidates who have taken science subjects at A level or H grade, or six years for candidates with non-science subjects, who study a pre-medical year. The pre-medical year is offered in some medical schools only. Candidates holding non-science A levels/H grades should offer excellent grades in sciences and maths at GCSE, or equivalent. English language at GCSE/S grade (A-C/1-3) is also required. GCSE/S grade and A level/H grade requirements vary between medical schools.

The competition for places at medical school is intense, and in most years less than half the applicants are successful in gaining a place. For the five-year course, candidates should have chemistry or physical science A level, and two others from physics, biology and maths. (See below for Scottish requirements.) Students not offering biology may find parts of the course particularly difficult. Occasionally, the third A level may be offered in an arts subject, usually at a very high grade. The grades requested at A level vary from three grade As to three grade Cs. However, most candidates for medicine obtain excellent grades at A level, mainly As and Bs at one sitting. One A level (not chemistry) may often be replaced by two AS levels; consult admissions tutors for acceptable combinations.

Most medical schools in Scotland require candidates to obtain five H grades at grades A and B. Chemistry and physics are normally required. The Scottish Certificate of Sixth Year Studies should also be passed. English and another language may be requested at S grade (1-3).

Academic ability is not the only prerequisite for a career in medicine. Commitment, perseverance, determination, initiative, originality, concern for others, and the ability to communicate are essential. High grades at A level/H grade are normally asked for because the course is long and intellectually demanding.

TRAINING

The total training period for doctors varies. All medical students spend five or six years as undergraduates and obtain a bachelor of medicine and surgery – MB BS, MB ChB, or a diploma from a non-university licensing body. There is some variation between medical schools, according to the way in which the degree is taught, but the following is a general description of medical training. It is important to research courses carefully; consult books listed in FURTHER READING in article 2. HOSPITAL DOCTOR.

The **one-year pre-medical course – 1st MB –** is offered by some medical schools and provides a preliminary course in chemistry, physics and biology, lasting 30 weeks. It is aimed at students who have done arts or mixed subjects at A level or H grade, not for those who have performed poorly in sciences.

The **two-year pre-clinical course – 2nd MB –** involves a study of the basic medical sciences, including anatomy (the structure of the human body), physiology, biochemistry, psychology, medical sociology, pathology and pharmacology. This part of a doctor's training involves memorizing and understanding a tremendous amount of knowledge. Some courses offer more contact with patients than others in the pre-clinical stage. At the end of the pre-clinical stage, some students transfer to other medical schools to continue their training.

The **one-year intercalated degree course** gives medical students the opportunity to take a degree in a science subject, usually related to medicine, before progressing on to the next part of a doctor's training. It is a built-in feature of some courses, whilst at other medical schools the opportunity is only offered to the most successful students.

For some students the **three-year clinical course** provides the first real contact with patients. The clinical course aims to help students develop practical skills and acquire knowledge, whilst taking responsibility for their own decisions. In some schools the clinical training starts with a nursing attachment, and continues with training on the ward. Student doctors are attached to a 'firm', comprising a small group of consultants, and senior and junior doctors, who are responsible for a number of patients. Student doctors assist in theatre, help deliver babies, and take blood. Clinical training involves working hospital hours, and taking a share of night duties. The training takes place on ward rounds, in out-patient clinics, and during seminars. Various specialities are taught via the firms, including pathology, haematology, obstetrics, paediatrics, and psychiatry. There may be an attachment to the accident and emergency unit, as well as placements in general practice and community medicine. Throughout the three years, students attend lectures on medical practice.

The qualifying examination for a doctor is known as the final MB, part of which is taken between six and twelve months before the end of the clinical course. Even though doctors hold a bachelor of medicine and surgery degree, they only have provisional registration until they have completed a year as a pre-registration house officer. House officers work long hours, with many nights spent on-call. This part of the training includes six months' supervised work in medicine and six months in surgery, after which registration with the General Medical Council is possible.

NB: Many medical schools are in the process of restructuring their courses, with the emphasis changing to the integration of the teaching of basic science and clinical medicine.

All doctors have to undertake one year's training in a hospital after their medicine degree (lasting five or six years), before they can be fully registered by the General Medical Council.

Postgraduate training

About half of all medical students eventually become GPs, for which the training lasts three years. Twelve months is spent as a trainee general practitioner, as well as two periods of six months working in a relevant speciality, such as paediatrics, geriatrics, psychiatry, or accident and emergency. A further year is spent in a hospital post. It is then possible to take the examination for membership of the Royal College of General Practitioners (MRCGP), although this is not compulsory. The total training period for a doctor who becomes a GP therefore lasts nine or ten years.

LATE ENTRY

Medical schools have different policies regarding entry for mature students. Thirty years is generally considered to be the upper age to start training, although many schools are reluctant to take people beyond the age of 25. Entrance requirements are not normally relaxed. Some candidates enter medical training after taking a degree in another subject, in which case they may have to finance themselves for all or part of the course. Even if the first degree was taken in a relevant subject, the length of training will not normally be shortened, although exemptions from certain courses may be given. An upper-second-class degree is the minimum entry requirement for graduates, and some schools will only consider candidates with relevant degrees. This route is an extremely difficult one.

OPPORTUNITIES

There are about 34,000 GPs in the UK. They are contracted by the NHS and receive fees and allowances for the work they do.

A very small number work in the Armed Forces. Doctors wishing to work abroad may find opportunities in the EU; there are very few openings in Australia, Canada, New Zealand and the USA. Voluntary organisations provide jobs in poorer countries, although remuneration is small.

PAY AND CONDITIONS

GPs partners should be available to their patients for not less than 26, 19 or 13 hours a week (depending on their contract) for consultations and home visits (this includes travelling time to the home visits). In practice, most GPs work a 50-hour week, including administration, reading, etc. Two-and-a-half hours are normally spent in the surgery, seeing patients each morning and afternoon, or early evening. Visits are usually offered during the afternoons. A Saturday morning surgery is often required. All GPs are expected to be 'on-call' for emergencies, but the frequency depends on the number of partners in the practice, and whether a deputising service is used.

General practice offers a higher income at an earlier stage than a career in hospitals. The average income of a GP is about £44,000, but this can vary, depending on the area and the number of services offered by the GP. Terms and conditions of service are negotiated with the National Health Service, although GPs are self-employed, being independent contractors to the NHS. Some GPs may also hold their own budgets to purchase hospital treatment, drugs, etc. A minority of GPs have a small number of private patients.

The money GPs receive has to pay the salaries of nurses, receptionists and other staff, as well as overheads for premises, rates, and rents. Some partners buy a share in the premises, although they never 'buy in' to the goodwill of the partnership.

PROSPECTS

A minority of GPs combine their work as a general practitioner with part-time work in a hospital, or as a journalist writing medical articles for magazines or newspapers. Other GPs might work as a medical adviser to a pharmaceutical company, occupational health service, or the Benefits Agency, or work as a police surgeon or part-time prison medical officer.

RELATED OCCUPATIONS

Dentist, optometrist/ophthalmic optician, psychologist, social worker, pharmacist.

FURTHER INFORMATION AND READING

Please see article 2. HOSPITAL DOCTOR.

2. HOSPITAL DOCTOR (JAB)

THE WORK

Hospital doctors work in various specialities, and the nature of the work they do depends on their grade. The junior grades of hospital medical staff are training posts, and are known as house officer, senior house officer, and specialist registrar. At the top of the hospital ladder is the consultant, who has the ultimate responsibility for patient welfare.

The first training grade is **pre-registration house officer,** which all doctors must undertake for one year before they can be fully registered with the General Medical Council. House officers examine patients as they arrive, take notes, and organize the initial investigations and treatment. They prescribe drugs for minor symptoms, and ensure that any intravenous infusions are working. They undertake most work under direct supervision.

Senior house officers gain increasing responsibility for patient care and develop the necessary wide range of general and relevant specialist skills.

Specialist Registrars supervise the work of house officers and usually examine and treat patients who have the diseases in which they have specialized whilst undergoing structured higher specialist training.

Consultants are the career grade of hospital doctor. They are considered fully trained and capable of acting independently. Consultants are personally responsible for the treatments they prescribe, and supervise the work and training of all doctors in training grades.

There are over 50 specialities in hospital medicine, which can be divided into four main types:

Medicine. There are various specialities in medicine, although many doctors are experienced in a variety of areas; general medical emergencies may demand a varied knowledge. Doctors examine patients, diagnose their condition and decide upon a suitable treatment. Specialities within medicine include paediatrics, cardiology, dermatology, geriatrics, neurology and tropical medicine. Doctors work in teams comprising a number of specialists, and they supervise and co-operate with nurses, hospital technicians and ward staff.

Surgery. Surgeons are concerned with patients who need operations, and they are responsible for each patient before, during, and after the operation. Many surgeons are general surgeons, but most have a special area of expertise. Neurosurgeons diagnose disorders and injuries of the brain and nervous system, performing lengthy operations. Orthopaedic surgeons diagnose and treat injuries and diseases affecting the bones, tendons, joints and ligaments. Plastic surgery involves the delicate surgical repair of deformities, either those present since birth, or those caused by injuries or burns in later life. Surgeons liaise closely with physicians and other specialists before performing operations.

Pathology. Pathologists investigate the causes and effects of disease. They work in laboratories, supervising the work of other laboratory staff, and often have little contact with patients. Histopathologists diagnose disease from changes in tissue structure, whilst the chemical pathologist looks at the biochemical nature of disease. Other specialities within pathology include blood transfusion and medical microbiology.

Psychiatry. Psychiatrists work with people suffering mental illness, and with those with mental disabilities. They often work within a team of professionals, including social workers, psychologists, and occupational therapists. Psychotherapy is a speciality within psychiatry, although not all psychotherapists are qualified doctors.

Specialities include: **anaesthetists** who provide pain relief or anaesthesia during surgical operations, childbirth, and diagnostic procedures; **obstetrics,** the care of pregnant women; **gynaecology,** the specialty dealing with diseases confined to women; **radiologists,** involved with taking X-rays and the resulting diagnosis; and **oncologists,** who treat cancer patients with radiation, and are closely involved with their patients' progress within the medical team.

WORK ENVIRONMENT

Hospital doctors work as part of a team with other doctors, health professionals such as nurses, radiographers, and physiotherapists, and administrative staff. They deal with patients and their families on a day-to-day basis. Hospital doctors work in a number of hospital departments, for example in accident and emergency, in maternity, in wards and in operating theatres. Pathologists are based in laboratories.

SKILLS AND INTERESTS

Please see article 1. GENERAL PRACTITIONER. In addition, surgeons need a very high level of manual dexterity and practical ability.

ENTRY REQUIREMENTS

Please see article 1. GENERAL PRACTITIONER.

TRAINING

Pre-registration training. This is as for GENERAL PRACTITIONER; please see previous article.

Postgraduate training. Once the pre-registration period has been completed, doctors may choose a speciality, either general practice, hospital medicine, public health medicine, or one of the less usual areas, such as occupational medicine, research, or working for the Armed Forces. Most specialist training posts begin after pre-registration training and a year or two's experience as a senior house officer, which gives doctors a chance to consider the area of medicine in which they may wish to specialize. Doctors will normally spend about five years as a specialist registrar applying for consultant posts. During training, various examinations must be passed, including those set by the appropriate Royal College, for example the Royal College of Obstetricians and Gynaecologists. Training for consultants takes at least seven years after registration by the General Medical Council. In the past, the ladder to consultant posts has taken much longer, with some not gaining a post as a consultant. Each trainee will be given a national training number which will ensure the right number of doctors are being trained.

LATE ENTRY

Please see article 1. GENERAL PRACTITIONER.

OPPORTUNITIES

There are some 43,700 hospital doctors in the NHS. Opportunities for hospital doctors vary considerably according to the chosen speciality. Surgery, general medicine, and paediatrics have traditionally been very competitive, whereas promotion in fields such as anaesthetics and geriatric medicine may be a little easier to obtain. Hospital doctors may have to move to different parts of the country several times during their career, as jobs can arise anywhere.

Some consultants working in the NHS also see private patients. The NHS is going through a number of changes, which may affect opportunities for doctors.

Doctors in the Army may have the opportunity of working in hospitals overseas, in places such as Hong Kong, Cyprus, and Gibraltar.

PAY AND CONDITIONS

Salaries for hospital doctors within the NHS are as follows: house officer – £14,880 to £16,800; senior house officer – £18,560 to £23,560; specialist registrar – £20,745 to £30,260; consultant – around £42,170 to £54,430. Additional payments are made for extra hours for doctors in training. Consultants may receive additional discretionary points and staff in London receive London weighting allowances.

The hours for hospital doctors are long and irregular, but the hours of all junior doctors must not exceed 72 a week.

Hospital doctors work two types of shift system, full and partial, in addition to the on-call rota system. The maximum number of hours per week must not exceed 72.

Terms and conditions of service may differ for consultants working in NHS trust hospitals, although doctors in the training grades work on a national model contract.

PROSPECTS

There are four grades of hospital doctor: pre-registration house officer, senior house officer, specialist registrar, and consultant. There is keen competition for promotion, and hospital doctors have to take a series of examinations in their chosen speciality if they want to progress. After becoming a senior house officer, many doctors go on to train as general practitioners.

Doctors, in the past, may have had to wait many years for a suitable post. However, there have been changes to the structure of training which will shorten the training period and ensure a more structured approach.

RELATED OCCUPATIONS

Please see article 1. GENERAL PRACTITIONER.

FURTHER INFORMATION

British Medical Association (BMA)*, BMA House, Tavistock Square, London WC1H 9JP, (please include A5 sae)

General Medical Council, 178-202 Great Portland Street, London W1N 6JE, 0171 580 7642

FURTHER READING

Leaflets/booklets are available from the addresses marked*.

Careers in Medicine, Dentistry, and Mental Health – Kogan Page Learning Medicine – British Medical Association
Medical Careers – A General Guide – British Medical Association
Thinking of a Career in Medicine? – Peter Richards – BMJ Publishing Group

In the careers library classified under JAB.

1. HOSPITAL NURSE CLCI:JAD
2. MIDWIFE CLCI:JAD
3. DISTRICT NURSE CLCI:JAD
4. HEALTH VISITOR CLCI:JAD
5. OCCUPATIONAL HEALTH NURSE
   CLCI:JAD
6. HEALTH CARE ASSISTANT/NURSING
   AUXILIARY CLCI:JAD

BACKGROUND INFORMATION

This section covers the work of those concerned with health care both in hospitals and in the community. Nurses are members of the primary health care team, which includes doctors, dentists, dental auxiliaries, etc. They work with and are supported by dietitians, psychologists, social workers, therapists, and so on, who provide other forms of treatment and services.

Those interested in nursing should read all the articles in the section, as qualified nurses with additional training can move into midwifery, health visiting, district nursing and occupational health nursing.

1. HOSPITAL NURSE (JAD)

THE WORK

Hospital nurses are responsible for the care of patients in hospital. They plan, assess and evaluate care for each patient, aiming to meet the needs – physical, emotional and social – of the whole person (holistic care). Nurses carry out the plan of care, adapting it as the patient responds.

They familiarize themselves with the patient's medical history and circumstances, keep careful records of treatment and response, and carry out doctors' instructions. They take into account both the psychological and the physical needs of the patient, and the needs of their relatives.

Nurses work as part of a ward team and participate in all aspects of care. There are four major branches for registered nurses: adult/general (RGN); children's (RSCN); mental health (RMN); and mental handicap (RNMH).

There are many different types of wards in which **adult/general nurses** may work: medical, surgical, orthopaedic, intensive care and geriatric, for example, all of which involve different activities. Nurses can take post-clinical courses so that they are able to deal confidently with particular aspects of specialist areas of nursing care.

At the practical level, nursing care in hospital wards consists of: taking temperature, blood pressure and respiration rates; giving injections; administering medications; cleaning and dressing wounds; applying lotions; draining wounds and ulcers; bandaging and splinting; administering blood transfusions and drips; as well as the more routine tasks, like making beds. They are involved in any actions that contribute to the direct comfort and ease of their patients.

In other situations, nurses may work in theatre, preparing the appropriate instruments for use by the surgeons. In intensive care, in theatre and in other wards, they use highly technological equipment, such as life-support systems, applying the use of renal equipment for kidney malfunction, etc.

Children's nurses carry out similar duties to adult/general nurses, but apply their specialist knowledge of the particular needs and problems of children, from birth to adolescence. The work involves a more flexible approach to routines, and anticipation of the needs of children, who are not always able to communicate as easily as adults.

Mental health nurses aim to provide care appropriate to the individual, so that they may achieve the highest possible level of independence.

Nursing mentally ill people involves providing practical care, as in general nursing. Much more time may be spent in counselling and exploring ways of helping patients overcome or come to terms with their illness.

Mental handicap nursing involves helping and encouraging patients to develop to their full potential, and providing support to people with learning difficulties and their families. Nurses help adults and children with mental handicaps to gain everyday skills and so increase confidence. The aim is to enable people to achieve as much independence and quality of life as possible.

There are very many sources of satisfaction and success in nursing, but nurses also have to cope with failures of treatment and death. The work may be at times messy and distressing, although experienced nurses generally come to terms with this. Occasionally, nurses have to comfort grieving relatives.

WORK ENVIRONMENT

Types of hospital vary widely from large general hospitals with numbers of specialized departments and wards, out-patients and accident and emergency departments, to much smaller specialist units treating patients with particular health problems, eg orthopaedic and geriatric units. There are also psychiatric hospitals, some of which are 'secure' in that they are custodial, as well as therapeutic, units. Most hospitals are modern, light, airy, and very clean. Some of the older buildings, however, are dark and comparatively dismal. Most hospital nurses are based on one particular ward at a time but may quite regularly move around – escorting patients to X-ray or theatre, for example.

SKILLS AND INTERESTS

Nursing is very demanding work and calls for a great deal of personal commitment. An interest in, and an ability to get on well with, a wide variety of people is essential. Nurses need both physical and mental stamina. They must be alert, observant, show initiative and be able to act decisively. Tact, patience and sensitivity are called for, as are maturity and a sense of humour. Both in their nursing activities and as part of a team, they should be able to get on with and work with others effectively. Communication skills are very important for dealing with patients, their relatives and members of staff.

Increasingly complex technology and sophisticated systems, along with in-depth psychological care, make greater demands today on the intellectual capacity of nurses. An interest in science is useful. Common sense and a down-to-earth approach are highly valued.

ENTRY REQUIREMENTS

Applicants for (RN) pre-registration nurse education training may take either a diploma or degree course.

Minimum entry requirements for a diploma course are five GCSEs/S grades (A-C/1-3) or equivalent. Those without these qualifications may be able to sit an entrance test (DC test). Schools or colleges often ask for higher than minimum qualifications, including A levels or H grades, and may require specific subjects, such as English and/or science.

Entry into degree courses leading to some of the 'Registered' designations is with a minimum of two or three A levels/three H grades plus two or three GCSEs/S grades (A-C/1-3). Science subjects are usually required, as is maths and English, at least at GCSE/S grade (A-C/1-3).

Graduates can train for the general part of the Register by taking either the three-year RN course or a shortened postgraduate RN course. Relevant degrees are required for most of the shortened courses, usually in a physical, biological or behavioural science.

Pre-nursing – some colleges of further education offer full-time and/or part-time courses.

The United Kingdom Central Council (UKCC) has agreed that the minimum age of entry to nurse training is 17½ years. The minimum age of application to nurse training through the English National Board Nurses' Central Clearing House, is 16½ years.

Individual schools and colleges may have other stipulations, particularly concerning standards of health and height.

TRAINING

Diploma courses last three-years. The course is made up of an 18-month common foundation programme, which provides a general introduction to nursing, and an 18-month branch programme in one of the four branches – Adult, Child, Mental Health or Mental Handicap.

The common foundation programme covers core skills and subjects, including the theory and practice of nursing; communications; social, life and behavioural sciences; ethnic and rural issues; organization structure and processes; and social care provision. The programme includes placements in the community and hospital wards or departments.

Branch programmes prepare students for nursing in one of the four branches, and include theoretical study and practical experience.

Degrees in nursing

Courses lead to a degree, either in nursing plus registration, or to a degree in the social or natural sciences as well as registration. The degree in nursing takes about four years to complete, whilst the degree combining nursing and another subject can take from four-and-a-half to five years, although it leads to two qualifications. Some degree courses offer opportunities for specialization, for example, in psychiatric nursing, and some lead to health visitor qualifications (England only).

Postgraduate qualification

Those with relevant degrees, which normally means a degree including behavioural or natural sciences (depending on individual nursing schools/colleges) may take a shortened course lasting around two to two-and-a-half years, and leading to registration in general nursing. Graduates in non-related subjects may be accepted onto a three-year postgraduate course. Those with a degree in a non-relevant subject and A level/H grade in physics, chemistry or biology may be accepted onto shortened courses. Competition for postgraduate courses is intense.

Further training

There is an increasingly wide range of further training possibilities for nurses after registration. Courses are available in a wide range of clinical specialisms, such as geriatric, coronary care and orthopaedic, for first and second-level nurses. Other training courses are available for qualified nurses to prepare them for specialized work, such as district nursing and midwifery. Some courses are only open to nurses on certain parts of the register – for example, health visiting is only open to registered general nurses.

There are also some part-time, day and block release degrees offered for qualified general nurses.

LATE ENTRY

Nursing is an area where mature entry is possible. There is no statutory upper age limit for entry to nurse training and schools of nursing may use discretion in accepting older applicants. This is particularly the case in mental health nursing. Some schools may set an upper age limit of 45 years.

Mature applicants may be offered the opportunity of taking the DC educational test if they do not hold the academic entry qualifications of a minimum five GCSEs/S grades (A-C/1-3), or equivalent. Some schools/colleges offer this method of entry to mature candidates only.

OPPORTUNITIES

The NHS is by far the largest employer of hospital nurses, although there are opportunities for work in non-NHS hospitals, self-employment and agency nursing work and private nursing.

The number of hospital nurses in the NHS is around 400,000. Private hospitals and nursing homes employ more than 7,000 nurses.

The Armed Forces also provide nursing opportunities with the Queen Alexandra's Royal Army Nursing Corps (QARANC), the Queen Alexandra's Royal Navy Nursing Service (QARNNS) and the Princess Mary's Royal Air Force Nursing Service. QARANC and QARNNS offer training for registration.

Qualified female nurses are employed in women's prisons, young offender institutions and selected men's prisons.

British nursing qualifications are acceptable in many countries abroad, including those in Europe, the Middle East and Australasia.

Advertisements for posts in the NHS, private hospitals and nursing homes, and for positions overseas appear in *Nursing Times; Midwifery; Health Visitor.* Vacancies for qualified nurses also appear from time to time in local newspapers.

PAY AND CONDITIONS

Salaries vary according to skills, responsibilities and experience. Staff nurse basic salaries range from £11,645 to £13,720. Sisters/charge nurses earn basic salaries of £14,330 to £19,190.

Nurses in psychiatric, geriatric and other chronic-illness departments receive extra allowances. The NHS also provides free uniforms and subsidized meals, and pays inner and outer London weighting allowances.

Terms and conditions of service may differ for nurses working in NHS trust hospitals. Nurses in private hospitals and nursing homes receive similar, and sometimes higher, wages.

In the National Health Service, the agreed working hours are 75 over a two-week period. Hospital nursing, of course, takes place around the clock throughout the year, and the work can therefore involve shift, weekend and bank holiday duties. Nurses working on the wards have a three-shift system, but arrangements can vary between different hospitals and areas. Part-time work is available for qualified staff.

Nurses in nursing education and management positions usually work around normal office hours, and those in out-patient units work straight shifts that do not involve overnight cover.

Night duty is required during training; after qualification it depends on circumstances. Some nurses work permanent nights.

PROSPECTS

Promotion for registered nurses is usually to charge nurse/ sister – in charge of the ward or clinic. There are opportunities for general nurses to specialize in other branches of nursing, such as district or occupational health nursing, or midwifery or health visiting. There may also be opportunities for registered nurses to move into health service management, nurse education, or one of the statutory nursing bodies developing training or giving careers advice. There are opportunities for general nurses to specialize in clinical nursing, or to undertake further training for midwifery or community nursing jobs.

Qualified and experienced nurses can move into fields such as social and counselling work, particularly if they also have good academic qualifications.

RELATED OCCUPATIONS, FURTHER INFORMATION AND READING

Please see article 6. HEALTH CARE ASSISTANT/ NURSING AUXILIARY.

2. MIDWIFE (JAD)

THE WORK

Midwifery care involves making antenatal examinations and monitoring the health of the mother and development of the foetus by taking blood pressure, as well as giving other physical checks.

Midwives supervise and conduct deliveries, sometimes administering drugs and other aids. After the birth, they continue to monitor the health of the mother and baby, weighing and examining the baby, and administering medicines when necessary.

There are some minor differences between hospital-based and community-based midwifery practice.

In hospital, midwives are involved in pre-natal and post-natal care and with parent-craft education. The expectant woman may need to be admitted to an antenatal ward for rest and observation before the baby is due, but in the majority of cases the mother goes into hospital when she begins labour, and the midwife looks after her during labour and conducts the delivery of the baby. Midwives are then concerned with the post-natal care of the mother and child.

In the community, the work also includes total antenatal care. The work is similar to that of the hospital midwife, except that the antenatal care is given in health care centres and GPs' surgeries, where the midwife regularly examines the expectant woman, assesses her condition and that of the developing baby, and advises the mother throughout pregnancy.

The help midwives give is active, but also advisory and caring. If a baby dies, the midwife must give support and comfort. In carrying out all their duties, midwives take into account the psychological and emotional needs of mothers and their families and the economic and environmental factors that affect them.

WORK ENVIRONMENT

Hospital-based midwives work in the maternity units of general hospitals, or in maternity hospitals. Community midwives make home visits and work in hospitals, antenatal clinics, community health centres and GPs' surgeries.

In private practice they may work in nursing homes or private hospitals.

Community midwives can do quite a lot of travelling, particularly in rural areas. Conditions can vary considerably, and sometimes can be much less airy and less sterile than in hospitals.

SKILLS AND INTERESTS

As described in article 1. HOSPITAL NURSE, but in addition it is particularly important for community midwives to work responsibly and effectively alone. Working in other people's homes can require a different and more independent approach from that used in hospitals.

Stamina, good physical health and robustness are required, as midwifery can be physically demanding.

Increasingly complex technology and sophisticated systems, along with in-depth psychological care, make greater demands today on the intellectual capacity of nurses. An interest in science is useful. Common sense and a down-to-earth approach are, however, still much valued.

A driving licence is useful, especially where the midwife practises in the community.

ENTRY REQUIREMENTS

There are two methods of training as a midwife.

Direct entry: minimum educational requirements for direct entry into training for registration as a midwife are five GCSEs/S grades (A-C/1-3), including English and a science subject, or approved educational equivalents. This is very much the minimum requirement; places are limited and competition for entry is intense. Most nursing/midwifery schools ask for one A level/two H grades.

Post-basic training: some trainee midwives are already registered general nurses. RGNs (part 1 of the register) may apply for 18-month courses (minimum). No additional qualifications are laid down, though schools may expect GCSEs/S grades (A-C/1-3).

In Scotland, applicants must be registered general nurses before they can begin training. For information about training for general nursing registration please see article 1. HOSPITAL NURSE.

Student midwives beginning direct-entry training in England and Wales must be at least 17 years old. In Scotland, because training cannot start until after nursing registration, training is usually from 20 years onwards (the maximum age is 50). Among other requirements for trainee midwives is that they enjoy good health (a medical is usual).

TRAINING

Direct entry. Applicants who are not registered general nurses (RGNs) are required to take the full course of midwifery training. All colleges of nursing and midwifery offer a three-year pre-registration midwifery course. There are waiting lists. Contact the English National Board for Nursing, Midwifery and Health Visiting for details.

Post-basic training. Some midwives begin training in this specialism after completing training as general nurses. Midwifery training lasts a minimum of 18 months.

Training courses take place in schools/colleges of midwifery, and include theoretical and clinical instruction and practical experience in the care of pregnant women, mothers and babies. The courses cover all aspects of midwifery and the complications that may occur, neonatal paediatrics, the use of analgesics, obstetrics, the care of newly born infants, the principles and practice of health education, and the social and psychological aspects of child bearing.

The successful completion of training, at either entry stage, leads to registration by the United Kingdom Central Council for Nursing, Midwifery and Health Visiting. This is a statutory requirement to practise as a midwife. Midwives have to notify their intention to practise annually.

LATE ENTRY

By far the majority of midwives begin their training after initial general nursing registration, and midwifery is very much an occupation for adult entry. There is potential for qualified nurse returners to specialize in midwifery. There are refresher courses for qualified midwives who return to work after a career break. The upper limit for entry is 50 years.

OPPORTUNITIES

Around 28,000 midwives work in Great Britain, including those employed by the National Health Service and private nursing homes and clinics, and other miscellaneous organizations. This occupation is equally open to men and women, although, so far, few men have trained.

The major employer of midwives is the National Health Service. There can be opportunities in private hospitals and clinics and for part-time and agency work. As United Kingdom midwifery qualifications are accepted in the EU and Commonwealth countries there are possibilities for work abroad. There can be opportunities, too, for voluntary or paid work in the developing world – this is particularly true for midwifery teachers. The Armed Forces also have opportunities for midwives to train and practise. Midwives may also be self-employed and practise independently.

Vacancies for qualified midwives are held by Jobcentres, and some private employment agencies deal with this type of work, while others actually specialize in this field. Advertisements for the agencies and for NHS posts appear in *Nursing Times* and *Midwife, Health Visitor* and *Community Nurse.*

PAY AND CONDITIONS

Salaries for NHS midwives start from £11,645. Midwifery sisters/charge nurses earn between £14,330 and £19,190. Salaries in the private sector vary.

Community midwives receive car mileage and telephone allowances. Free uniforms, subsidized meals and pension schemes are also available within the NHS. The NHS pays London weighting allowances.

Hospital-based midwives work shift systems, which are broadly the same as those worked by general nursing staff in hospitals.

Midwives who work solely in the antenatal clinics of NHS hospitals usually work normal office hours.

Midwifery staff in the NHS community nursing service normally work days only on an office-hours basis, although they have periods when they are 'on-call.'

Terms and conditions of service may differ for midwives working in NHS trust hospitals.

PROSPECTS

Post-basic courses enable midwives to specialize in various clinical areas, such as special care baby units and labour ward intensive nursing care. There are also courses for advanced midwifery diplomas (and in Scotland, the Midwife Clinical Teaching Certificate) which precede courses for midwifery teaching positions. There are other opportunities and also appropriate courses for those who wish to pursue a management career in the National Health Service.

There are openings for qualified midwives in other fields, such as health visiting.

RELATED OCCUPATIONS, FURTHER INFORMATION AND READING

Please see article 6. HEALTH CARE ASSISTANT/ NURSING AUXILIARY.

3. DISTRICT NURSE (JAD)

THE WORK

District nurses provide skilled nursing care for patients in the community – either in their own homes or in residential care homes. They care for those released from hospital after acute illness, the chronically ill before and after hospitalization, the dying and the bereaved. Their patients can be any age, but usually include a large number of elderly people.

In their practical nursing care they give injections, apply dressings, drain wounds, and wash and clean their patients. They are concerned with both the physical and psychological well-being of their patients and teach care skills to their families, which can include, for example, showing them how to give injections. At the same time, they give support to patients and encourage as much independence as possible. They may visit some patients several times a day to give supervision support and medication, or other treatment. This is particularly the case when patients are terminally ill.

District nurses liaise with other agencies within the community, such as social workers, occupational therapists, and voluntary agencies, as well as with hospital colleagues and other members of the community health team.

They work in a district team that includes GPs, health visitors and community midwives. Methods and programmes of treatment of individual patients are discussed and drawn up, and a careful record kept of decisions, action and progress. In some areas, particularly thinly-populated rural areas, one person takes on the triple responsibilities of district nurse, midwife and health visitor (see relevant articles). In urban areas duties may include giving advice and treatment in a community health centre, or GP or group surgery.

As a result of changes in the treatment of psychiatric illnesses, a growing number of district and community nurses are now providing health care and advice to patients discharged from psychiatric hospitals to live in the community.

WORK ENVIRONMENT

District nurses make home visits and work in residential care homes, GPs' surgeries, community health clinics and hospital day centres. Those in rural areas may have to travel considerable distances.

SKILLS AND INTERESTS

These are similar to the skills and interests for a HOSPITAL NURSE (see article). In addition, it is important that they are good listeners, can give advice tactfully and are tolerant. A mature attitude is important, as well as the ability to work responsibly and independently. As with community midwives and health visitors, working within patients' own homes can call for a different approach from hospital nursing and sensitivity to varied situations.

Stamina is very important as the work is usually very demanding. District nurses are sometimes the main contact for people who are socially isolated, frightened, in pain, or dying.

A driving licence is necessary in most cases.

ENTRY REQUIREMENTS

To enter training in district and community nursing, candidates must be qualified as a general nurse (see article 1. HOSPITAL NURSE). For the District Nursing Certificate, individuals must have a minimum of five GCSEs/S grades (A-C/1-3), or meet the college selection standards and **in addition** be already qualified as a registered general nurse and have additional nursing experience. A pass in an entrance test is also required by some colleges.

TRAINING

Training lasts for at least 38 weeks and includes a period of supervised clinical practice. Courses are held at higher education institutions. Subjects include psychology, physiology, sociology and epidemiology. Skills in communication are taught, as well as counselling and teaching.

LATE ENTRY

Most entrants are in their mid to late-twenties, and many others take up training after a career break or after working abroad, though they may in these cases have to take an entrance test set by the individual college. A period of hospital-based nursing may also be required before secondment for training.

There is no official upper age limit.

OPPORTUNITIES

District nurses are employed in the UK only in the NHS, but there are also opportunities for work overseas, particularly in the developing countries.

PAY AND CONDITIONS

Salaries range from £16,940 to £19,600, depending on duties.

Telephone and car mileage allowances are paid and there is a London weighting allowance.

Hours of duty vary depending on the area. In some areas shifts are worked; in others a rota system for being on-call during nights is used, coupled with day work between 9am and 6pm. Some unsocial hours can be expected. Opportunities exist for part-time work, particularly for evening and night duties.

PROSPECTS

As qualified registered nurses (in addition to their specialist qualifications) district and community nurses have the same promotion and other prospects as hospital nurses (see article 1. HOSPITAL NURSE). In addition, with further training, they can become practical work tutors (continuing with their own case load) or district and community nurse tutors.

RELATED OCCUPATIONS, FURTHER INFORMATION AND READING

Please see article 6. HEALTH CARE ASSISTANT/ NURSING AUXILIARY.

4. HEALTH VISITOR (JAD)

THE WORK

Health visitors promote health and help prevent illness by teaching people to attain a relevant standard of health and to stay healthy. They also help chronically ill and disabled people to learn to live with their disabilities.

The work involves giving advice on health matters, teaching people about diet, hygiene, exercise, the hazards of smoking, drugs abuse, infection control, etc. They check and monitor people's health, particularly young children and elderly people. They identify problems – mental, physical and social – by working with, and talking to, individuals and families, and they alert doctors/social workers where necessary. They may run clinics for mothers and babies and give talks to groups in schools and health centres. They visit all new babies at home to monitor the baby's health and offer the parents support and advice about feeding, safety, normal child development, etc. In rural areas, those qualified may combine the role of midwife, district nurse and health visitor.

Health visitors are responsible for organizing their own work within the framework of their health authority's policies and work much more independently than other nurses.

WORK ENVIRONMENT

Health visitors are usually attached to work with a group of GPs, or alternatively work in a defined geographical area. They may be based at clinics, health centres or GP group practices.

The work involves visiting people in their own homes, health and community centres, schools, playgroups, day centres, and special schools and centres for the disabled, GPs' surgeries and old people's homes. In some rural areas mobile health clinics are used.

SKILLS AND INTERESTS

As described in article 1. HOSPITAL NURSE.

In addition, health visitors need the ability to communicate effectively with a wide range of people and should have tact and understanding. They need to be able to write clear reports, liaise with other members of the primary health care team and other agencies, and teach and counsel patients. When dealing with people from a variety of social backgrounds, health visitors must have both an understanding of social pressures and sympathy with people.

The capability to observe, evaluate and anticipate potential health problems in individuals, families and groups is essential.

Health visitors must be able to work independently, as they spend much of the time working alone, and should have the stamina to be out and about a good deal.

A driving licence is useful and/or required.

ENTRY REQUIREMENTS

To become a health visitor, it is necessary to first qualify for registration; most are registered general nurses (RGNs) and have had some experience of nursing (see article 1. HOSPITAL NURSE). Some health authorities also require nurses to have had some experience in obstetrics or midwifery.

Postgraduate courses are available for RGNs who also hold a relevant degree.

Some degree courses lead to both nursing and health visiting qualifications. Entry is with a minimum of five GCSEs/S grades (A-C/1-3) with two A levels/three H grades, or equivalent. However, candidates should check prospectuses, as requirements are often higher and specific subjects may be asked for.

TRAINING

These are the main training routes for registration as a qualified health visitor:

Post-registration courses for experienced nurses

Post-registration courses for general nurses (RGNs) who have midwifery/maternity care/obstetrics nursing qualifications and experience, extend over 51 or 52 weeks. There are a few part-time courses lasting two years. They are held at institutions of higher education.

Modified post-registration courses for graduates in relevant disciplines

Modified post-registration courses for graduates with relevant degrees – which usually means nursing studies, natural or social sciences – are available for people who have the professional pre-entry requirements.

Degree courses with health visiting option

Registered general nurses with the approved obstetric qualification may take a degree course in relevant studies that includes an option leading to health visitor registration. Such courses are available at Southampton University, University of East London and Coventry University.

Integrated degree courses

Nursing degrees are available at a number of institutions of higher education. Courses last for around four years and combine practical nursing with theoretical instruction usually in science or social sciences. Courses most often lead to a registered general nursing (RGN) qualification and some provide options for candidates to qualify as a registered health visitor (RHV). These include courses available at Southampton, Manchester, Liverpool and King's College, London.

The content of the training for the health visiting certificate in these courses covers the study of human growth (psychological, physiological and social), social policy and administration, and social aspects of health and disease. The skills taught include those of observation, developing relationships with, and teaching, both individuals and groups, and planning and organization. The courses include practical field work experience and involve a period of supervised practice with a small case-load.

Registration

On qualification, in order to practise, health visitors must be registered with the United Kingdom Central Council for Nursing, Midwifery and Health Visiting, which operates through four national boards (in England, Northern Ireland, Scotland and Wales). The boards are responsible for the training, examination and professional certification of health visitors.

LATE ENTRY

The majority of health visitors enter the profession having gained general nurse registration and midwifery/obstetric nursing qualifications and experience. Adult entry is therefore an important feature of the work.

OPPORTUNITIES

In Great Britain there are around 11,500 health visitors and about 1,100 people enter health visitor training each year. The work is nation-wide and covers rural, urban and inner-city communities.

Vacancies for qualified health visitors are held by Jobcentres. Advertisements appear in *Nursing Times*, *Nursing Standard*, *Midwife*, *Health Visitor* and *Community Nurse*.

PAY AND CONDITIONS

Salaries for health visitors are between £16,940 and £19,600. The NHS also pays London weighting allowances.

Health visitors usually work office hours, Monday to Friday. However, hours are dictated by the nature of the work and can involve evening work (giving talks or lectures on health-care matters) and occasional weekend work.

There are sometimes opportunities for part-time working and job share.

PROSPECTS

There are further education courses in specialist aspects of health visiting, and health visitors with a minimum of two years' full-time experience can take a field-work teacher course and go on to help train student health visitors. With further training as a teacher it is possible to move into health visitor lecturing in the further/higher education sector. There are also appropriate courses for those who wish to pursue a management career within the NHS.

RELATED OCCUPATIONS, FURTHER INFORMATION AND READING

Please see article 6. HEALTH CARE ASSISTANT/ NURSING AUXILIARY.

5. OCCUPATIONAL HEALTH NURSE (JAD)

THE WORK

There are three main aspects of occupational health (OH) nursing.

The first is concerned with identifying potential health hazards in the workplace. This means being aware of possibly dangerous materials, substances, plant and machinery, and can involve environmental surveillance and biological monitoring.

The second is the promotion and maintenance of health and the prevention of ill-health. OH nurses have an educational role, both in promoting the personal health of individual employees, and health and hygiene related to work.

The third aspect is the organization of emergency treatment of people who are injured at work, and the treatment of minor illnesses and injuries people may suffer while at their workplace. OH nurses may have to give initial care to people who have suffered heart attacks, experienced injury involving broken bones, burns, and so on, and may also have to administer prescription-only medicines provided by a doctor.

Added to these core functions can be rehabilitation work with employees who have been ill, counselling, and referral work.

OH nurses may make assessment of previously ill or injured employees and make recommendations as to their suitability for the same or different work. They also maintain confidential records.

In providing a nursing service, OH nurses have an administrative role and may have responsibilities for organizing the service in the workplace, liaising with management, formulating nursing policy, providing advice to management on nursing salaries and conditions of service, preparing and working within budgets, and appointing nursing personnel.

WORK ENVIRONMENT

The majority of OH nursing posts are in industry, where the working environments vary depending on the type of industry concerned. In all these various areas, nurses have to be familiar with the whole plant and will have to spend some time on the shop floor. The majority of openings are in the manufacturing industry, but there are many jobs in universities, hospitals, large department stores, food shops, etc.

In some posts, the nurse needs to be mobile between the different premises of the organization; a driving licence is useful for this type of work.

SKILLS AND INTERESTS

As described for HOSPITAL NURSE, but, in addition, OH nurses require business-like efficiency because of the administrative aspects of their work.

ENTRY REQUIREMENTS

Occupational health work is open to registered and enrolled nurses – they need to be qualified **and** on the register of the UKCC. Please see article 1. HOSPITAL NURSE for details of the entry qualifications required for training as a registered nurse.

Training as an RGN takes three years and nurses need a further two years' experience before studying for the Occupational Health Nursing Certificate/Diploma.

TRAINING

It is not a statutory requirement for nurses to have specialist occupational health nursing training for an occupational health nurse job. However, it is the policy of the RCN Society of Occupational Health Nursing that all nurses should be trained for the work. The number of courses provided to train OH nurses varies across the country.

The Occupational Health Nursing Certificate/Diploma courses are held at institutions of higher education in England, Scotland and Wales and last for one year full-time, or three years part-time. Students can also study through distance learning. Students on the part-time or distance learning course should be employed in appropriate occupational health nursing work.

Subjects include: legislation relating to health and safety, social security and industrial relations; committee procedure; interviewing techniques; the duties of the nurse and ethical responsibilities; principles and methods of treatment of common clinical conditions; how to survey the workplace; and other principles of monitoring the environment. Accident cause and prevention is also studied, based on factors such as psychological stress and fatigue, machine guarding and ergonomics.

An important part of the course is the study of the concept of total health needs and levels of care, with emphasis on health supervision, screening tests, conditions and diseases caused by exposure to the work environment, etc. Record keeping, elementary statistics for application to epidemiology, teaching and health education programmes are also covered.

A list of colleges offering courses may be obtained from the Royal College of Nursing.

LATE ENTRY

People who move into occupational health nursing are already qualified nurses, so adult entry is the norm.

Although many nurses have a range of hospital experience before moving into occupational health nursing, it is possible to study for OH nursing qualifications following first qualification. It is desirable, however, to have at least two years' post-registration experience. There is no official upper age limit for training, but colleges may apply their own age limits on entrants to courses.

OPPORTUNITIES

There are about 5,000 nurses employed in occupational health services in Great Britain. Something like 300 people enter training each year.

PAY AND CONDITIONS

Salaries start at £13,000 to £27,000. Senior occupational nurses can earn in excess of £27,000.

The NHS provides uniforms and subsidized meals, and pays travelling and London weighting allowances.

Working patterns vary. In a large plant involved in continuous-process production, there may be a team of nurses (and doctors) who work shifts to provide total cover. In other organizations, the pattern may be normal office hours. There are opportunities for part-time work.

PROSPECTS

In large occupational health departments, there can be opportunities to move into nursing management positions.

There can be prospects in the development and administration of occupational health services in some NHS districts/areas.

RELATED OCCUPATIONS, FURTHER INFORMATION AND READING

Please see article 6. HEALTH CARE ASSISTANT/ NURSING AUXILIARY.

6. HEALTH CARE ASSISTANT/NURSING AUXILIARY (JAD)

BACKGROUND INFORMATION

Since the launch of Project 2000, health care assistants have been introduced in the NHS. New schemes of training mean that health care assistants perform some of the tasks that used to be carried out by student nurses. They undertake many of the activities previously performed by nursing auxiliaries, but can now achieve NVQs/SVQs that recognize their competence in the workplace. This allows them to progress to more complex duties and undertake some supervision.

THE WORK

Health care assistants/nursing auxiliaries work in hospitals, homes and in the community. They support professionally trained staff – nurses, midwives, health visitors, occupational therapists, physiotherapists, speech therapists and chiropodists – in caring for patients. They are sometimes called ward assistants. In psychiatric hospitals, they are usually known as nursing assistants. They often work as part of a nursing or care team made up, for example, of a sister or staff nurse, registered nurse, student nurse, health care assistant and nursing auxiliary.

Duties vary according to the level of training and local policy. All tasks are performed under the supervision of a qualified professional and, on **wards** , may involve:

Treatment – take and chart patient's temperature and pulse; take urine and sputum samples; perform urine tests; weigh patients; put on simple dressings; take patients to theatre and for X-rays; help with treatments – set up trolleys, explain procedure to patients, assist professionals during treatments, and clear up afterwards. Health care assistants/nursing auxiliaries do not give drugs or injections.

Nutrition –- help patients feed themselves; feed incapacitated patients; encourage children to eat; make snacks and hot drinks.

Hygiene and cleanliness – give out and empty bed-pans; help patients use the toilet; change incontinence pads/ sanitary towels/nappies; give bed-baths; help patients wash themselves; accompany patients to bathroom or shower; bathe children and babies.

Mobility – help patients dress and undress; support patients who are unsteady on their feet; help patients carry out therapists' instructions.

Comfort and emotional support – turn bed-bound patients to prevent pressure sores developing; change soiled linen and clothing; provide extra blankets, pillows, etc; help patients with radio headphones, position of television, contents of locker, etc; talk or read to patients; comfort anxious or frightened patients; play with children; help patients make the most of recreational facilities.

Death of patients – help with last offices; help with related paperwork and administration.

General duties – health care assistants/nursing auxiliaries also have duties such as escorting patients to other departments, making beds and tidying the ward, checking and sorting stock such as linen, and helping with the department's paperwork.

In **psychiatric hospitals**, many activities centre on helping patients build confidence and independence, perhaps in preparation for their return home, or a move into the community after a long stay in hospital. Nursing assistants may help patients learn/relearn basic skills such as dressing themselves or – when professional supervision is not required – may accompany them on trips, to libraries, theatres or restaurants, for example, which will help them adjust to life in the community.

In **hospital clinics and out-patient departments**, duties may include taking clients from one area to another; weighing and measuring; helping with treatments; taking and testing urine samples; and ensuring medical staff have correct files.

Community health care assistants/nursing auxiliaries visit clients in their homes. They provide nursing support, such as giving baths, renewing simple dressings, and so on; or provide social care to clients who might otherwise have to stay in hospital.

Health care assistants/nursing auxiliaries usually wear protective clothing. Uniforms are not worn in a psychiatric setting.

WORK ENVIRONMENT

Health care assistants/nursing auxiliaries work in wards and clinics in general, specialist and psychiatric hospitals, and in clients' homes. They also work in homes for the elderly and for those with enduring mental illness.

They are active for much of the day and may have to do a lot of heavy lifting, for which they are trained. On some wards, they deal regularly with blood, vomit, excreta, etc.

SKILLS AND INTERESTS

Health care assistants/nursing auxiliaries need to be practical and well-organized. They must be able to work well under supervision and as part of a team, and to follow instructions clearly. They must be reliable, hardworking and able to remain calm in an emergency. The work is often stressful, because suffering, and perhaps death, are involved, so resilience is needed to cope.

They must be fit and healthy. Stamina is needed; health care assistants/nursing auxiliaries work on their feet most of the time and need the strength to do whatever lifting is required. They have to be prepared to do unpleasant jobs. Health care assistants/nursing auxiliaries work in an environment where hygiene and safety are particularly important.

Health care assistants/nursing auxiliaries care for patients from many different backgrounds. They need to be sympathetic and tactful, and discreet with confidential information. They must be firm when necessary, but always treat patients as human beings and with respect, however dependent they may have become. They need a pleasant and courteous manner and a good sense of humour.

Illness, anxiety or senility can make patients awkward or angry, and health care assistants must respond with understanding and patience.

ENTRY REQUIREMENTS

No formal academic qualifications are needed, but candidates must be literate and numerate. Some authorities require some GCSEs/S grades or equivalent. Applicants need to be at least 17 to 18 years old.

Candidates have to complete a medical questionnaire and may have to undergo a medical examination.

There are a number of courses relevant to work as a health care assistant/nursing auxiliary.

SCOTVEC national certificate – requires a good general education. Check with individual colleges, as they may have their own entry requirements.

BTEC First Certificate/Diploma in Care – requires a good general education.

BTEC National Certificate/Diploma in Caring Services (Social Care) – needs either: four GCSEs/S grades (A-C/1-3); or a BTEC first award; or an Intermediate GNVQ/GSVQ Level II.

NVQ in Care/SVQ in Health and Social Care – needs no particular exam passes.

Intermediate GNVQ in Health and Social Care – does not need particular entry requirements but educational institutions may specify their own requirements.

Advanced GNVQ in Health and Social Care – usually requires either: Intermediate GNVQ; or four GCSEs/S grades (A-C/1-3); or a BTEC/SCOTVEC national award.

GSVQs in Care Levels II and III – have no formal entry requirements. Colleges may admit students they feel can benefit from the courses. In the case of Level III, this includes students who have passed Level II.

TRAINING

Pre-entry

SCOTVEC national certificate – a number of colleges offer one-year or two-year courses that lead to national certificate modules in care.

BTEC First Diploma in Care – just a few colleges now offer this one-year course.

BTEC National Diploma in Caring Services (Social Care) – many colleges offer this two-year course.

NVQ in Care/SVQ in Health and Social Care – a number of colleges offer care courses that provide students with a basis of knowledge and work experience to prepare them for relevant NVQs/SVQs at Level 2. Some also offer training to Level 3.

GNVQ in Health and Social Care/GSVQ in Care – some schools and many colleges now offer GNVQ in Health and Social Care at Intermediate level (one year) and Advanced level (two years). A number offer GSVQ in Care Level II (one year) and Level III (two years).

On entry

Local employers take different approaches to training. Applicants seeking vocational qualifications should ensure training allows for assessment towards NVQs/SVQs.

Health care assistants may register for assessment for NVQs/SVQs in Care. These may be available at Levels 1, 2 and 3. There is no set time limit for NVQ/SVQ assessments to be completed.

Training may be on the job, or a combination of on-the-job training and time spent in a school of nursing or local college. Basic skills, such as bed-making and lifting, are taught; lectures are given on such subjects as first aid, infection control, and health and safety.

The City and Guilds (C&G) course 3560 Practical Caring Skills (Levels 1 and 2) is a two-year programme of on and off-the-job training.

Details of local training opportunities are available from NHS/private hospital personnel departments, FE colleges and Jobcentres. Also see local newspapers.

LATE ENTRY

There is no upper age limit and no formal qualifications are needed. Because of the demand of the work, mature entrants may be particularly well-suited to it, provided they meet the physical and emotional requirements.

Adults can gain recognition of their skills and experience by working towards NVQs/SVQs. There is open access to NVQs/SVQs – no academic qualifications are required, and there are no age limits. NVQs/SVQs are based on competence, and it does not matter how that competence has been gained – through experience, company training programmes, college courses or open learning. Past experience can be put forward as evidence of competence, via Accreditation of Prior Learning (APL).

OPPORTUNITIES

Most health care assistants/nursing auxiliaries work for the NHS, in general and psychiatric hospitals, hospitals for those with enduring mental illness, and in the community. There are also opportunities in specialist NHS hospitals.

Openings also arise in private hospitals and clinics and private homes for the elderly, or the physically or mentally impaired.

Opportunities are related to local recruitment policies and vary from area to area. It may be necessary to move to find a job.

Openings are advertised at Jobcentres and in local papers. Details of vacancies are also available from hospital personnel departments.

PAY AND CONDITIONS

Nursing auxiliaries employed by the NHS are paid on Whitley Council incremental scales. Scale A employees earn £7,325 to £8,960; Scale B employees (working in the community with less direct supervision) receive £8,625 to £9,790.

In England and Wales, local agreements are made for health care assistants. Their pay tends to be a little higher and may be linked to undertaking assessment for NVQs/SVQs. In Scotland, health care assistants are paid the same as nursing auxiliaries.

Allowances may be paid to nursing auxiliaries for shifts worked at night and on Saturday or Sunday. These may not be payable within the new local pay and conditions.

Full-time NHS health care assistants/nursing auxiliaries work 37½ hours a week. There are often three shifts: first, back and night. Many hospitals have flexible working hours and there are many opportunities for part-time work.

Terms and conditions of service may differ for health care assistants/nursing auxiliaries working in NHS trust hospitals. Privately employed workers are paid on Whitley Council scales, or on the hospital/home/clinic's own scale.

PROSPECTS

There are opportunities for those nursing auxiliaries prepared to take extra responsibility, to move from supervised work in hospitals to less directly supervised work in the community.

RELATED OCCUPATIONS

Care assistant, home help, special needs teaching auxiliary, ward clerk, hospital porter, operating department assistant, nurse, social worker, occupational therapist, dietitian, physiotherapist.

FURTHER INFORMATION

British Red Cross*, Central Headquarters, 9 Grosvenor Crescent, London SW1X 7EJ, 0171 235 5454

British Red Cross in Scotland, Scottish Central Council Branch, Alexandra House, 204 Bath Street, Glasgow G2 4HL, 0141 332 9591

Care Sector Consortium Secretariat*, Occupational Standards Council For Health and Social Care, 3 Devonshire Street, London W1N 2BA, 0171 436 8712

Careers Section*, ENB for Nursing, Midwifery and Health Visiting, PO Box 2EN, London W1A 2EN

National Board for Nursing, Midwifery and Health Visiting for Northern Ireland, Centre House, 79 Chichester Street, Belfast B1 4JE, 01232 238152

Nurses and Midwives Central Clearing House, ENB, PO Box 9017, London W1A 0XA, 0171 391 6279

Royal College of Midwives*, 15 Mansfield Street, London W1M 0BE, 0171 872 5100

Royal College of Nursing*, Library, 20 Cavendish Square, London W1M 0AB, 0171 409 3333

Society of Occupational Health Nursing*, 20 Cavendish Square, London W1M 0AB, 0171 409 3333

St John Ambulance*, 1 Grosvenor Crescent, London SW1X 7EF, 0171 235 5231

Welsh National Board for Nursing*, Midwifery and Health Visiting, Floor 13, Pearl Assurance House, Greyfriars Road, Cardiff CF1 3AG, 01222 395535

FURTHER READING

Leaflets/booklets are available from the addresses marked*.

Job Outlines – Hospitals – COIC
Working in Work with Children – COIC

In the careers library classified under JAD.

1. DENTIST CLCI:JAF
2. DENTAL NURSE CLCI:JAF
3. DENTAL HYGIENIST CLCI:JAF
4. DENTAL TECHNICIAN CLCI:JAF

BACKGROUND INFORMATION

Dentistry is the branch of medical science concerned with the diagnosis and treatment of diseases and disorders of the teeth, gums and surrounding tissue.

Dentists, dental nurses, dental technicians and dental hygienists are employed in private or NHS general practice, in the community dental service or in hospitals. They also work in the Armed Forces and in the health centres of large organizations.

1. DENTIST (JAF)

THE WORK

There are several different branches of dentistry, and the work varies in each area.

General practice

Dentists in general practice are responsible for the dental health of their patients, using a variety of preventive and restorative measures.

They start their work with patients by taking a medical history and examining their teeth and mouth. They often have to reassure patients that the treatment will be conducted as painlessly and quickly as possible. X-rays may be taken to reveal any areas of decay undetected by examination.

The dentist may administer a local anaesthetic to reduce any discomfort experienced by the patient. Dentists restore teeth by filling them with silver-coloured amalgam and white composite materials. They restore gaps in the mouth by fitting bridges and dentures, which are made by a dental technician. Badly decayed teeth may be removed, although they are often saved nowadays by root fillings.

Dentists are helped by a dental nurse, who assists in (four-handed) dentistry, passing instruments and other materials to the dentist as required. Dentists also scale, polish, and clean teeth, unless a dental hygienist is employed to perform those tasks. Dentists also apply fissure sealants, formed from an acrylic-like substance that bonds to the surface of the tooth, helping to prevent decay.

Prevention of dental decay and disease is becoming increasingly important, with many dentists employing hygienists to help them in this role. With the advent of fluoride toothpaste and fluoridated water in some parts of the UK, dental decay is becoming far less common. 'Dentists must encourage their patients to return for further treatment where necessary, and to attend regular check-ups.

Dentists in general practice may work single-handed, or as part of a group of several professionals. A dentist in general practice may concentrate on orthodontics, which involves straightening teeth using braces, and is used mainly with children who have overcrowded mouths. Other dentists may have a special interest in restorative work for damaged or missing teeth, which includes crowning teeth and fitting bridges. Others may be specially trained and qualified in anaesthesia, although anaesthetics at the local dental surgery are much less common than in the past.

Hospital work

Hospitals offer dentists the opportunity to carry out treatments that may not be possible within general practice. Dentists may work in a specialized dental hospital, or in the dental department of a general hospital. Much of the work is concerned with out-patients, with only a minority staying in hospital for any length of time.

In a dental hospital, patients are often treated by student dentists, closely supervised by senior members of staff. Patients may be referred to a dental hospital for complex bridgework, or periodontal surgery, where the dentist performs surgical procedures to the gums. The dentist may remodel a patient's gums by trimming diseased tissue and applying stitches.

The hierarchy for dentists in hospital is similar to that for doctors, starting at the house officer grade, and progressing through registrar and senior registrar to the rank of consultant. All grades other than consultant are considered to be training grades. Hospital dentists seeking promotion normally take a series of higher qualifications. Dentists wishing to make a career in hospital work normally specialize in one of the following areas:

Orthodontics. Dentists in general practice work on straightening teeth by the use of mechanical appliances, but more complex cases are frequently referred to a hospital. The dentist in general practice may ask the hospital orthodontist for specialist advice, although the actual treatment may be performed in the general practice.

Oral and maxillo-facial surgery. Oral and maxillo-facial surgeons treat people who have been born with facial defects, such as a cleft palate, as well as those who have been damaged by accidents and cancers of the jaw and face. This is highly skilled and demanding work, requiring co-operation with other members of the medical team, including ear, nose and throat specialists. Many oral and maxillo-facial surgeons are qualified in medicine, as well as dentistry.

Community dental service

Community dentists work in clinics, providing a service to young children, expectant mothers, and people with special needs, such as those with physical or mental disabilities. State school children are required by law to receive dental checks, and community dentists visit schools to ensure these take place. The community dental service is also involved in surveys and research into dental disease and health education.

Industrial dentistry

Some large companies employ dentists to provide dental services for their employees. The work is similar to that performed in general practice.

Armed Forces

The Armed Forces offer some cadetships, similar to sponsorships, during training. After training, dentists can serve for a short commission of five years, or may sign up as a regular officer.

University teaching

Highly qualified and experienced dentists may be able to teach undergraduate and postgraduate students within a dental school or hospital. They also publish the results of any research they are engaged in.

WORK ENVIRONMENT

Dentists in general practice work in a surgery, which may be in their own house or elsewhere. Dentists may work in a company dental surgery, or in community health clinics and schools, which can involve some travelling. Within a hospital, the dentist may work in a surgery, in a clinic, and in the operating theatre. The working conditions are clean, hygienic, and well lit.

SKILLS AND INTERESTS

Dentists need an interest in their patients as people. Many patients are anxious and worried about dental treatment. A friendly manner helps to put patients at their ease, whilst a sense of humour helps both the dentist and the patient. Good verbal communication skills are important in order to relate well, both to patients and other members of the dental team. Manual dexterity and an interest in science are also essential. Dentists must be hard-working and, in general practice, possess good business sense, because they have to manage the financial and administrative side of the practice. Dentists are increasingly required to market their services in an attractive and imaginative way.

ENTRY REQUIREMENTS

Before dentists can practise, they must be registered by the General Dental Council. To qualify for registration, most students take the Bachelor of Dental Surgery (BDS), and a few take one of the diplomas of the Royal College of Surgeons, who award the Licentiate in Dental Surgery (LDS) following satisfactory completion of an approved course in a UK dental school.

Dental schools normally ask for three good A levels for the BDS – chemistry and two from biology, maths, and physics. Occasionally an arts subject may be offered as the third A level – requirements vary between dental schools. Students are normally asked to obtain grades between BBB and BCC at A level. Two AS levels can sometimes be substituted for one A level. Between five and six H grades are normally requested, to include chemistry and other science subjects, at grades between A and B. Candidates normally need a GCSE/S grade (A-C/1-3) in English language, and many schools ask for physics, maths and biology at this level also. Some dental schools offer candidates with non-science A levels/H grades the opportunity of taking a pre-dental year, which is really a conversion course to science A levels/H grades. Competition for all courses is intense, with admissions staff looking for evidence of a candidate's suitability for dentistry as well as academic strength. All prospective candidates should visit a dentist for work shadowing, to find out whether they might be suited to dentistry.

TRAINING

Training for the BDS degree lasts five years. A further preliminary year is involved if non-science A levels are held.

Pre-dental course

This course is only available at some of the dental schools, and covers the study of physics, chemistry, and biology for candidates without A levels/H grades in these subjects. Candidates already holding sciences at A level/H grade are exempt.

Five-year dental course

The first part of the course introduces student dentists to the study of anatomy (the study of parts of the body), dental anatomy, physiology (the study of body function), biochemistry and histology (which is the microscopic study of parts of the body). These subjects are taught via lectures, practicals, tutorials, and clinical demonstrations, and are normally examined during the first two years of the course.

As the course progresses, students learn how to examine, diagnose and care for patients. Practical skills are learnt, initially in the laboratory, and, later in the course, students work with patients under supervision. Courses also include theoretical and practical teaching in general medicine – to enhance the student's knowledge and all-round experience – as well as visits to general dental practices, community dental services, and so on.

A wide variety of subjects are studied, which include: preventive dentistry; children's dentistry and orthodontics; anaesthetics; oral surgery; periodontics, which is the study of gum disease; radiology; drugs or pharmacology; oral pathology, or the study of diseases of the mouth; community dentistry; restorative dentistry including crown and bridge work; the construction of dentures and associated laboratory work, known as dental prosthetics; dental materials science. After the final examination has been passed, the dentist can apply for admission to the Dentists Register to begin practising.

It is sometimes possible for suitable students to take an *intercalated degree*, after the first two or three years of the dental course, and obtain a Bachelor of Science (BSc) qualification. This entails an extra one to two years of study. In addition, it is usual to take an *elective*, which gives the opportunity to gain work experience in the UK or abroad.

Postgraduate training

New graduates can join a practice on a one-year vocational training scheme, under the supervision of trained and experienced dentists. This will supplement their existing knowledge of general practice, with lectures and demonstrations attended outside the surgery. Vocational training is mandatory for those wishing to work in NHS general dental practice.

Various postgraduate courses are provided by the university dental schools and the Royal Surgical Colleges (contact the Royal College of Surgeons of England, the Royal College of Surgeons of Edinburgh or the Royal College of Physicians and Surgeons of Glasgow for further details). Community dental officers spend two years on a special training course, which emphasizes health education and the prevention of oral and dental disease. It is possible to take the Diploma in Dental Public Health of the Royal College of Surgeons, after which community dentists may apply for promotion to more senior posts.

LATE ENTRY

It is possible to enter dental school training up to the age of 30 years, although individual schools have different policies regarding the admission of mature students. It is unlikely that dental schools will relax entry requirements for mature students.

OPPORTUNITIES

There are approximately 27,000 dentists in the UK, with about 800 new graduates each year. Over half of all dentists work in general dental practice. Only about five per cent work in hospitals, with a similar percentage working in the Community Dental Service. Many dentists spend a short spell working in a hospital to improve their all-round experience. It may be possible to work in Australia, New Zealand and South Africa, with the necessary work permits, and in countries of the European Union without restrictions. In America, British dental qualifications are not fully recognized, and State Board examinations must be sat, which are similar to dental school final examinations. Voluntary organizations employ dentists to work in developing countries.

PAY AND CONDITIONS

Most dentists in general practice are governed by NHS regulations. The NHS fees are calculated according to an average net income, which is around £38,379. However, the amount that each dentist earns depends upon the amount and type of work they do, as each piece of work attracts a fee laid down by the NHS. Fees for private work vary considerably between dentists, who may earn much more than the recommended average, depending on the number of private patients they have and the way in which they manage their NHS practice. They may also earn less than the recommended average, particularly if their surgery is not fully booked on most days. Dentists in general practice have to meet all their own overheads for premises and so on, and usually have to buy into the 'goodwill' of the practice if they wish to become partners. This can be very expensive.

For children's routine dental treatment, dentists receive a fixed monthly fee, which varies according to the age of the child. For adults, they receive a small per capita payment, but 90 per cent of the dentists' fees for treating adults come from set fees for different items of treatment.

Salaries for dental officers in the Community Dental Service range from £20,660 to around £30,080. Senior dental officers earn from around £30,080 to £40,445. Assistant district and district dental officers earn salaries which vary according to the population of the area. These salaries range from around £33,105 to £48,290. In the hospital service, a house officer starts at about £14,740, while consultants can earn up to £53,900.

Dentists in general practice can arrange their own working hours to fit in with the needs of their patients. Most dentists in general practice start work between 8.30 and 9am and finish between 5.30 and 6pm, and may work some evenings and Saturday mornings on a rota basis. Dentists in NHS general practice have to provide emergency cover. The community dental service offers more regular hours, 9am to 5pm, Monday to Friday. Some hospital dentists can expect to work more irregular hours, with those in oral and maxillo-facial surgery, where emergencies are most likely to occur, working at night and during weekends on occasions. They will also be expected to be on-call during some of their free time.

Dentistry, particularly in general practice, provides opportunities for part-time work. Dentistry, as a whole, is one vocation to which women are turning in increasing numbers.

PROSPECTS

The use of fluoride toothpaste and fluoridated water has greatly reduced the need for fillings. This means that the type of treatment performed by dentists is changing, and many are more involved in preventive work. Competition for places at some dental schools is now severe, because fewer dentists are being trained, although this means that there will be less people applying for jobs after qualifying. Within the hospital service, there are often more people applying for senior posts than there are vacancies, and dentists may have to move to another area of the country for a suitable job.

RELATED OCCUPATIONS

Doctor, pharmacist, medical laboratory scientist, dental therapist, dental hygienist.

FURTHER INFORMATION

The British Dental Association, 64 Wimpole Street, London W1M 8AL, 0171 935 0875

Faculty of General Dental Practitioners (UK), The Royal College of Surgeons of England, 35/43 Lincoln's Inn Fields, London WC2A 3PN, 0171 405 3474 ext 3534

National Advice *Centre for Postgraduate Education, Faculty of Dental Surgery, Royal College of Surgeons of England, 35 Lincoln's Inn Fields, London WC2A 3PN, 0171 405 3474.

FURTHER READING

Leaflets/booklets are available from the address marked*.

Job Outlines – Dentistry and Dental Auxiliary Occupations – COIC

Careers in Medicine, Dentistry, and Mental Health – Kogan Page

In the careers library classified under JAF.

2. DENTAL NURSE (JAF)

THE WORK

Dental nurses perform an important job in the dental team by providing support to dentists, hygienists, and therapists. Their work can combine administrative and clerical duties with practical work in the surgery, thus ensuring the patients receive a good service.

Dental nurses prepare the dental surgery before patients arrive, making sure all the equipment is ready, and clear up the surgery at the end of a day's work. They may also make sure the waiting area is a clean and welcoming place. Sterilizing dental equipment is an important part of the dental nurse's job, and is something that continues throughout the day. Dental nurses play an important part in helping to make patients feel comfortable and relaxed, by being friendly and interested in them.

During a check-up, the dental nurse may amend a patient's records, noting down details dictated by the dentist on a specially designed chart. Dental nurses work quickly, mixing fillings and materials for impressions, and pass these to the dentist as required, along with any necessary instruments. They sometimes hold suction instruments to remove saliva from a patient's mouth. All the work is done under the direction of the dentist, and can vary according to the preferences of individual dentists. Dental nurses also process and mount X-ray films.

Patients may undergo treatment with general anaesthesia in dental surgeries and dental hospitals. Appropriately qualified dental nurses look after patients while they are unconscious and help care for them during recovery. This involves checks on their pulse and breathing rates, appearance, and colour. Patients are carefully monitored at all times by the dental team, with the dental nurse assisting the dentist as a nurse would a surgeon.

In a smaller practice the dental nurse may act as a receptionist – answering the phone, greeting patients and making appointments, as well as dealing with all the NHS paperwork needed for the proper payments to be received. Dental nurses often organize and file record cards, as well as maintaining supplies of stationery and materials. Reminder cards may be sent out to inform patients of the need to make regular appointments. Dental nurses keep patient records up to date, noting information on the state of their teeth and a history of the work that has been done. In larger practices and hospitals, a receptionist may be employed.

Dental nurses wear a uniform or white coat and, when assisting the dentist, a protective mask and rubber gloves should always be worn during clinical procedures.

WORK ENVIRONMENT

Dental nurses work in dental surgeries, or in company surgeries, community health clinics, or dental or general hospitals. They may work alone with the dentist in a very small practice, or may be part of a much larger team. They work with people from a variety of different backgrounds, and in community health centres their work is mainly with children. The environment is always clean and well lit, and many dentists make their surgeries even more attractive places, with music playing to help patients feel relaxed. Most of the work is done standing up, which can be physically tiring.

SKILLS AND INTERESTS

Dental nurses need a warm, friendly, willing personality and a liking for people. They need to be understanding and sympathetic, since many people are very anxious about visits to the dentist. They need to be able to communicate clearly, both verbally and in writing. A sense of humour is an asset, along with the ability to remain calm under pressure.

An interest in health, oral hygiene, and biology is important. Dental nurses should be fit and healthy since the work can involve standing for long periods. They should be clean and neat with healthy-looking teeth. Practical ability, or manual dexterity, is important in order to handle instruments and prepare fillings.

Dental nurses need to be well-organized and methodical to cope with the administrative aspects of the work.

ENTRY REQUIREMENTS

Many dentists in general practice are willing to train dental nurses who do not have any experience and may not have any academic qualifications. A good general education is normally requested, and GCSE/S grade qualifications, perhaps in English and biology, would be an asset. There are no formal entry requirements for the National Certificate of Dental Nurses' examination.

Entry requirements for the full-time course for dental nurses vary according to the dental hospital or school attended. Between two and four GCSEs/S grades (A-C/1-3) are normally requested at present, preferably including English language and biology or human biology, although personal qualities and a suitability for the work are also important. The minimum age for entry varies between dental schools, but is usually 16 or 17 years. Applicants should be physically fit.

TRAINING

Many dental nurses train on the job within a general dental practice, where they receive instruction from the dentist. It is advisable for young people training in this way to study for the National Certificate for Dental Nurses, available on a part-time evening basis at colleges of further education. Candidates are awarded the Certificate after they have successfully completed 24 months' practical experience in a dental surgery and passed the final examination.

An alternative method of training is to take a full-time, national certificate, one or two-year course for dental nurses at a dental school or hospital, for which a salary at the appropriate rate is paid. The course combines practical work with theory, and includes lectures, small group seminars, and individual tuition. A wide variety of relevant topics are studied, including: anatomy and physiology; the use of dental instruments and materials; prevention of cross-infection and sterilization; the use and storage of drugs; anaesthesia and sedation; elementary orthodontics; oral surgery; the care of patients; the causes of decay and gum disease; the maintenance of dental records and charting; the preparation of fillings; general principles of dental radiography; dental health; law and health safety. The final examination consists of a written paper, an oral examination, and practical tests.

LATE ENTRY

There is no upper age limit for the full-time and part-time national certificate courses for dental nurses (as described in TRAINING). Some dental schools expect mature candidates to possess the normal academic entry requirements, whilst others may offer an entrance test to applicants over the age of 23 years who do not hold formal qualifications. The test examines written communication skills and ability in English. Evidence of practical ability will be assessed at interview, along with a suitable personality for the work. Mature students generally do well on the course, and find that their maturity and experience is valued by their future employers. As an alternative to the full-time college course, mature students may find employers willing to train them on-the-job, providing they are prepared to accept the low salaries generally offered during training.

OPPORTUNITIES

There are about 25,000 dental nurses in the UK. Job prospects are good in most areas of the country, with a shortage of experienced staff in some areas, such as the South East of England. Dental nurses work in several areas: in general practice, both private and NHS, or a combination of the two; in dental hospitals and the dental departments of some general hospitals; in community dental services; in the Royal Navy, Army and RAF; and in private industry and commerce.

Opportunities for working abroad are limited, although possibilities exist, particularly in the Middle East.

Jobs may be advertised in the careers office, or Jobcentre, as well as in local newspapers.

PAY AND CONDITIONS

The British Dental Association and the British Association of Dental Nurses have jointly agreed guidelines for minimum salaries for general dental practice. The recommended minimum for 38 hours a week is approximately £100.28 rising to £198.78. In addition, a bonus of £24.00 a week is payable to dental nurses on the Voluntary National Register.

However, these are guidelines only, not statutory rates, and many employers do not pay salaries in accordance with the guidelines.

In hospital or community service, salaries are agreed by the Whitley Council. The minimum for a trainee aged 18 years is around £6,370. When qualified, a dental nurse can expect to earn between £8,290 and £10,400. Senior dental nurses earn between £10,800 and £13,650.

Dental nurses in general practice rarely work a 9 to 5 day. They may start at 8 or 8.30am and finish at 5.30pm, or later. Many dentists work one or more late nights, and some Saturday mornings, when the dental nurse will also be expected to work, although in a large practice these duties may be shared on a rota basis. During busy periods they may work through lunch hours. The hours are more regular in a community health centre, perhaps 8.30am to 4.30pm, or 9am to 5pm. Hospital work may involve working unsocial hours. Part-time work is sometimes possible.

PROSPECTS

There is no set pattern of promotion for dental nurses within general practice. However, in larger practices there may be scope for more senior dental nurses to train new recruits, or to move into practice management and administration, after management and financial training.

In dental hospitals and in community dental services, career progression is more obvious. After one or two years' training within a hospital, student dental nurses become qualified dental nurses. After three years' experience they can then become senior dental nurses, with responsibility perhaps for a specialized department within the hospital. Dental nurses can also progress by taking various other qualifications, such as specialist certificates in oral health education, dental radiography and conscious sedation, which may enhance promotion prospects.

Within hospitals there is also the possibility of moving into teaching, after taking the Further and Adult Education Adult Teacher's Certificate. Most dental hospitals have posts for a principal of a school for dental nurses.

Many dental nurses undertake further training to become dental hygienists, which is possible after two years' experience. There is also a combined course in dental hygiene and dental therapy at the Dental Auxiliary School of the London Hospital Medical College, for which experienced dental nurses may apply.

RELATED OCCUPATIONS

Dental hygienist, dental therapist, dental technician, nurse, nursing auxiliary/health care assistant, receptionist, medical secretary.

FURTHER INFORMATION

British Association of Dental Nurses, 110 London Street, Fleetwood, Lancashire FY7 6EU, 01253 778631 (please include sae)

National Examining Board For Dental Nurses, 110 London Street, Fleetwood, Lancashire FY7 6EU, 01253 778417

FURTHER READING

Job Outlines – Dentistry and Dental Auxiliary Occupations – COIC

In the careers library classified under JAF.

3. DENTAL HYGIENIST (JAF)

THE WORK

Dental hygienists are involved in preventing tooth decay and gum disease, enabling people to keep their own teeth in a healthy condition for as long as possible. They work under the direction of dentists, who devise and prescribe treatment plans.

Dental hygienists scale, clean, and polish teeth, remove stains, and apply fluorides and fissure sealants to reduce decay and deterioration, using a variety of special instruments. Hygienists perform post-operative hygiene work on the mouth after gum surgery, and in hospitals they look after patients' mouths before and after oral surgery of any kind. In a small minority of cases they are assisted by a dental nurse. They do not do fillings or remove teeth.

Preventive dentistry is an important part of dental hygienists' work. They advise adults and children on the proper care of teeth and gums. Detailed instruction is given on the correct use of toothbrushes and how to remove plaque, along with advice on diet. Hygienists may talk to groups of children or adults in schools, clinics, and community centres, as well as giving advice to individual patients. One of the most satisfying aspects of the work is when patients follow the advice of their dental hygienist and thus improve the condition of their teeth, mouth, and gums. Hygienists often see the direct results of their work.

WORK ENVIRONMENT

Dental hygienists work in dental surgeries, as well as visiting clinics and community centres. They may travel to two or three places in the course of a week, although about half of dental hygienists are employed in one place. Hygienists work with people of all ages. Their work environment is clean and well lit. Hygienists wear protective clothing, such as a white coat, a mask and gloves to reduce the risk of infection.

SKILLS AND INTERESTS

Dental hygienists need good communication skills to explain to patients, both individually and in groups, about the importance of caring for the mouth and teeth. The hygienist must gain the confidence and co-operation of patients. Dental hygienists also need to establish a good working relationship with the dentist. They need good eyesight and concentration, along with practical ability. Hygienists need an ability and interest in science, whilst a sense of humour helps to put anxious patients at their ease. Dental hygienists should also be well-presented, clean, and tidy.

ENTRY REQUIREMENTS

Entry requirements for dental hygiene vary from school to school. Applicants need a minimum of two years' experience as a dental nurse plus a recognized Certificate in Dental Nursing. Five GSCEs/S grades (A-C/1-3) are normally required, including English language and either biology or human biology; some schools also ask for two A levels. A suitable personality for dental hygiene work is also necessary. Applicants should normally be at least 20 years old. Student dental hygienists are not paid a salary, but can apply for bursaries from the Department of Health.

TRAINING

Full-time courses in dental hygiene, leading to the examination for the Diploma in Dental Hygiene, last two years and are offered at most dental schools throughout the UK.

During the first part of the training, students supplement their theoretical training with practical experience on 'phantom heads'. The syllabus is very broad, and includes the following subjects: general histology, which is the study of the cells and tissues of the body; dental histology; general anatomy and physiology – the study of the body and its functions; first aid; diet and nutrition; microbiology and sterilization; oral pathology – the study of diseases of the mouth, especially tooth and gum disease; dental radiography; the study of tooth form; preventive dentistry; dental health education; and operative techniques such as scaling, polishing, and applying fissure sealants.

Tests are normally given weekly during the course, and the final examinations comprise written papers, a practical test, and an oral examination. Once the Diploma in Dental Hygiene has been obtained, dental hygienists may become enrolled dental hygienists by having their name entered in the roll of dental hygienists kept by the General Dental Council. Dental hygienists may not practise in the United Kingdom unless they are enrolled.

Some hygienists take the Certificate in Oral Health Education awarded by the University of Nottingham. Other refresher courses are available as well. It is also possible to take a joint course in dental hygiene and dental therapy, at the Dental Auxiliary School of the London Hospital Medical College, which lasts for two years.

LATE ENTRY

The majority of applicants for dental hygiene training are about 21 years old, although there is no upper age limit. Dental hygiene is a relatively new profession, with most staff having qualified since 1970. Most dental hygienists are currently under 40 years of age. Dental schools do not normally relax entry requirements for mature candidates.

OPPORTUNITIES

Preventive dentistry is increasingly important in the UK, with dental hygienists playing a vital role. Demand for dental hygienists varies in different parts of the UK, particularly in Scotland and Wales; it can therefore be difficult to find work readily. At present there are about 3,000 dental hygienists in the UK.

Dental hygienists may find work in the following areas:

General dental practice: about 85 per cent of hygienists spend at least part of their working week in general practice.

Community dental services include working with pregnant women, and disabled and elderly people, as well as children.

Hospital services: hygienists may work in a specialized department of a dental hospital, or in the dental department of a general hospital.

Teaching and research employs a few hygienists.

Armed Forces: dental hygienists are normally trained by the branch they have joined. Occasionally the Army has spare places on its courses; civilians may take up the places, although they have to pay their own course fees.

Occupational dental practice: hygienists occasionally work in the dental surgery of a company. Toothpaste manufacturers sometimes employ dental hygienists to take part in exhibitions, displays, and so on.

Outside general practice the majority of dental hygienists are employed in hospital or community service. There are some opportunities overseas, for example in continental Europe and the Middle East.

PAY AND CONDITIONS

Salaries vary according to whether hygienists work in general practice, in hospitals or in the community service.

In general practice, they are paid by the dentist; salaries are not agreed by the NHS. It is up to individual hygienists to negotiate their salaries with their employers. The British Dental Hygienists' Association (BDHA) recommended rate starts at £11,674 and rises to £16,495. Salaries are reviewed annually.

Dental services have become increasingly flexible. It may be possible to work an adjusted working day, or there may be the opportunity to work part-time.

Most hygienists in general practice work surgery hours, which may start between 8.30 and 9am, and finish between 5.30 and 9pm. They may be required to work late on one or more evenings, and sometimes on Saturday mornings. Dental hygienists who work in hospitals may have to be on-call at night. Those in the community dental service work more regular 9-to-5 hours.

PROSPECTS

There is no clear career path for dental hygienists within general dental practice. Within a dental school or hospital there is the possibility of becoming a tutor once a Further and Adult Education Adult Teacher's Certificate has been obtained. Prospects are improved if dental hygienists take further qualifications, such as the Certificate in Oral Health Education of the University of Nottingham. This could possibly lead to posts in dental health education within the community dental service. Candidates with joint qualifications in dental hygiene and dental therapy will find they are sought after by employers.

RELATED OCCUPATIONS

Dental nurse, dental therapist, nurse, health visitor, teacher.

FURTHER INFORMATION

The British Dental Hygienists' Association*, 13 The Ridge, Yatton, Avon BS19 4DQ, 01934 876389 (please include sae)

Assistant Director, Army Dental Service*, AMD 6, Keogh Barracks, Ash Vale, Aldershot, Hampshire GU12 5RQ, 01252 340321

British Association of Dental Nurses (BADN), 110 London Street, Fleetwood, Lancashire FY7 6EU, 01253 778631

FURTHER READING

Leaflets/booklets are available from the addresses marked*.

Job Outlines – Dentistry and Dental Auxiliary Occupations – COIC

In the careers library classified under JAF.

4. DENTAL TECHNICIAN (JAF)

THE WORK

Dental technicians make dental appliances from prescriptions given to them by dental surgeons. Using a variety of traditional and more modern materials, technicians use several techniques in their work that demand a high level of skill. These include plaster casting, wax carving, metal casting, moulding plastic, bending wire, sand-blasting, grinding and polishing, involving the use of specially designed equipment. Dental technicians work in the following areas:

Prosthodontics. Dental technicians make dentures, which can be removed from the mouth, in plastic and cast metal alloys. Either complete or partial dentures may be made, according to the needs of the patient. Technicians have to understand exactly what the dentist requires in order to make a comfortable and visually pleasing denture. They must also ensure that a partial denture does not harm the health of any remaining natural teeth.

Various materials are used for making dentures, including plaster, wax, acrylic, cobalt chrome, stainless steel and precious metals.

Crowns and bridges. Dental technicians help dentists in their restorative work by making crowns and bridges, which are permanently fitted into the mouth. Crowns or caps are made in acrylic, porcelain or metal, and are cemented to the prepared roots of remaining natural teeth. Bridges are made in a similar way, but fit into gaps in the dentition. Plaster, wax, acrylic, porcelain, metal alloys and precious metals are used to make crowns and bridges.

Orthodontic appliances. Orthodontists and dental surgeons in general practice rely upon dental technicians to make orthodontic appliances (braces – special clasps and springs) that help to straighten a patient's teeth. Plaster of Paris, stainless steel wire and tape, and acrylic resins are all used to make orthodontic appliances.

Maxillo-facial surgery. Dental technicians working mainly in hospitals help dental and oral surgeons in their work with patients who have suffered facial or jaw injury or illness, or who have been born with an abnormal or deformed face. They make artificial parts of the face, known as prostheses. These are skilfully modelled in plastic, and fitted to the patient's face. The prostheses help to improve patients' appearance, as well as enabling them to eat and speak. Dental technicians play a crucial part in the recovery of these patients, and have a vital role in the dental team. Technicians also make splints for patients with broken jaw bones so that the oral surgeon can perform urgent operations.

In addition to practical work, dental technicians are sometimes involved in administrative and clerical tasks, particularly if they are self-employed.

WORK ENVIRONMENT

Whatever branch of dental technology they are employed in, dental technicians work in laboratories. They may work alone (particularly if they are self-employed), with one or two other people, or as part of a larger team. Dental technicians do not usually have contact with patients. The work is mainly performed whilst sitting down.

SKILLS AND INTERESTS

Dental technicians are involved in highly skilled craft-work, and therefore need to be practical and good with their hands, preferably with an interest and ability in art. A good eye for detail, along with well-developed colour perception, is also required. Dental technicians need good concentration to cope with the often painstaking work. An interest and ability in science is also important, as they will be expected to follow and interpret detailed scientific instructions.

ENTRY REQUIREMENTS

Good eyesight (aided or unaided) is essential, along with good colour vision for some aspects of the work. The initial qualification the dental technician should aim for is the BTEC/SCOTVEC National Diploma/Certificate in Science (Dental Technology).

Candidates should possess either a BTEC/SCOTVEC First Certificate/Diploma in Science or Engineering; or four GCSEs/S grades (A-C/1-3), to include maths and a science, or Intermediate GNVQ/GSVQ Level II in Science.

For dental technician trainees in hospitals entrance requirements may vary. Some ask for four GCSEs/S grades (A-C/1-3), in English, maths, physics and biology, or Intermediate GNVQ/GSVQ Level II in science.

Occasionally, other qualifications or experience may be acceptable as alternatives, particularly for mature entrants over the age of 21 years or by Accreditation of Prior Experience and Learning.

Entry requirements for commercial laboratories vary, with many laboratories requesting four GCSEs/S grades (A-C/1-3) to enable candidates to study for the BTEC/SCOTVEC National Diploma/Certificate in Science (Dental Technology). It is now possible to take a BTEC First Certificate in Science with an option in dental technology, which leads on to the BTEC National Diploma. Entry requirements for the BTEC First Certificate are GCSEs grade E in a science, English and maths, although specific requirements may vary between colleges. Candidates may be accepted for apprenticeships with fewer qualifications if employers consider they have the ability to succeed as a dental technician with education and training.

TRAINING

There are three main ways of training to become a dental technician, all of which combine practical experience with theory work:

Paid training in a commercial dental laboratory or in a dental laboratory associated with a dental practice. Students train for five years, and normally attend college for one day and one evening a week to study for the BTEC/SCOTVEC National Diploma in Science (Dental Technology). The first two years of the training may be organized as part of a training scheme for young people. Most dental technicians in Scotland (outside hospitals) train via this method, which includes day release. The SCOTVEC National Diploma in Science (Dental Technology) is normally studied on a day release or block release basis for four years.

The following subjects form part of the courses for the BTEC/SCOTVEC National Diploma/Certificate in Science (Dental Technology): dental anatomy, dental materials; basic laboratory techniques; complete denture prosthetics; dental materials technology; orthodontics; partial prosthetics and conservation, porcelain and metal bridges.

Students normally spend four days a week in the laboratory, and start by learning the more straightforward tasks, such as making 'trays' for impressions, and wax 'bite blocks'. They may then make repairs to dentures, before moving on to making dentures, crowns and bridges, and eventually more advanced work.

Full-time college course. The full-time courses for the

BTEC National Diploma in Science (Dental Technology) last for three years, and include practical experience in a commercial or hospital dental laboratory as part of the training. Grants for full-time courses at this level are discretionary. The subjects covered are as above.

Higher training. After taking the BTEC/SCOTVEC National Diploma/Certificate in Science (Dental Technology), it is possible to take a BTEC/SCOTVEC higher national diploma or certificate, on a two-year day release basis, covering more advanced aspects of dental technology. Degree courses are also becoming available, following successful completion of the BTEC/SCOTVEC National Diploma/Certificate in Science (Dental Technology).

It is also possible to take advanced City and Guilds 7390 courses in dental ceramics, crown and bridge work, orthodontics, and maxillo-facial work. These are usually taken on a part-time evening basis.

Paid training within a hospital. Eight hospitals in the United Kingdom recruit student dental technicians for a training programme, which lasts up to four years, and includes block release for the BTEC National Diploma in Science (Dental Technology). Hospital trainees receive a salary whilst training.

LATE ENTRY

Some hospitals are reluctant to accept trainee dental technicians over the age of 30 years. Employers are often unwilling to train adults for a five-year apprenticeship, mainly because the wages of trainees are fairly low.

There may be specific training opportunities directed at adults available in some areas for this type of work. Candidates may have to satisfy certain conditions to be eligible. Contact your local Jobcentre, careers office or TEC/LEC for details.

Colleges may be prepared to relax entry requirements for mature students; contact individual colleges for more information. The Accreditation of Prior Experience and Learning may provide exemption of units/modules of the programme of study.

OPPORTUNITIES

Dental technicians work in the following four main areas, where they may perform specialist or general work:

Commercial dental laboratories – dental technicians provide a variety of services to dentists, mainly to those working in general practice. The dentist may be based at some distance from the laboratory, and the technician must interpret the dentist's prescription accurately. Commercial laboratories often undertake highly specialized work. Qualified and experienced dental technicians may be able to set up their own laboratory and become self-employed.

General practice – dental technicians may be employed on a dentists premises to provide work for the dentists, usually of a fairly general nature.

Community dental service – dental technicians provide the necessary appliances for the work of community dentists – those working for the school dental service and in clinics. Much of the work involves supplying orthodontic braces.

Hospital work – involves maxillo-facial work as well as the more general work of a dental technician.

In total there are about 6,000 dental technicians working in the UK.

There are prospects for dental technicians to work abroad.

PAY AND CONDITIONS

NHS salaries are payable in hospitals. Student dental technicians earn from about £6,371 to £8,627. Trained dental technicians are paid on a salary scale of £10,821 to £13,693. Senior grade technicians earn from £14,242 and chief technicians from £17,326. Senior chief technicians earn from £21,079 to £24,660.

The National Joint Council negotiates minimum pay and conditions for qualified dental technicians following an agreed consolidating period working in commercial dental laboratories. The minimum rate is about £182.00 for a 39-hour week, or £197.38 if certain qualifications are held, such as the BTEC National Diploma in Science (Dental Technology). An extra £7 a week is payable to people registered with the Dental Technician Education and Training Advisory Board (DTETAB). Trainee dental technicians earn a percentage of the full rate, which ranges from 45 per cent in the first year, to 75 per cent in the fifth and final year of training. Dental technicians, particularly if self-employed, can earn higher salaries.

Within the NHS, dental technicians normally work approximately 37 hours, from 8.30am to 5pm, Monday to Friday. In commercial laboratories a 39-hour week is worked, although there may be the opportunity to work paid overtime. Technicians employed in maxillo-facial work may work irregular hours with occasional on-call duties. There is the opportunity to work part-time.

PROSPECTS

Within the NHS there is a clear promotional ladder. After three years' training and a consolidation year a student becomes a qualified dental technician. Promotion to senior grade technician may be possible after two years in a basic grade post. Further prospects are to become a chief dental technician in charge of either a laboratory or a section of a larger laboratory. The senior chief dental technician may be in charge of a large laboratory or group of laboratories, and it is unlikely that anyone would reach this level until the latter part of their career. There are often many more applicants than vacant posts at the higher levels, and candidates are expected to have gained higher qualifications during their career.

Prospects within commercial dental laboratories are good, and experienced dental technicians may move on to become quality controllers, or section or laboratory managers. It may also be possible to move into dental research, or dental supply company employment.

RELATED OCCUPATIONS

Laboratory technician, orthotist/prosthetist, medical physics technician, physiological measurements technician, dental nurse.

FURTHER INFORMATION

Dental Technician Education and Training Advisory Board (DTETAB)*, Partners In Practice, 5 Oxford Court, St James Road, Brackley, Northamptonshire NN13 7XY, 01280 702600

Dental Laboratories Association Ltd, Chapel House, Noel Street, Nottingham NG7 6AS

FURTHER READING

Leaflets/booklets are available from the addresses marked*.

Job Outlines – Dentistry and Dental Auxiliary Occupations – COIC

In the careers library classified under JAF.

1. PHARMACIST CLCI:JAG
2. PHARMACY TECHNICIAN CLCI:JAG

BACKGROUND INFORMATION

Pharmacy is a scientific profession concerned with the development of drugs, their preparation, dispensing and eventual use. There are three main areas of work available to qualified pharmacists: community (or retail) pharmacy; hospital pharmacy; and industrial pharmacy.

Pharmacists wishing to practise must be registered with the Royal Pharmaceutical Society of Great Britain, which has approximately 40,000 members.

1. PHARMACIST (JAG)

THE WORK

Community pharmacist

Community or retail pharmacy is the largest branch of the profession and involves a qualified pharmacist working in a retail environment.

The main duties of a community pharmacist are to prepare and dispense drugs on prescription to the general public, although there is now a general trend towards pre-packaged and prepared medicines. Prescriptions, dosages and labels must be checked for legality and accuracy.

A pharmacist gives advice to customers on how to use prescribed drugs and ensure that customers realize when prescriptions should not be taken in conjunction with alcohol or with other medication. They also provide information on the sale of over-the-counter medicines and general health care issues. If a patient's condition is serious, then a pharmacist may need to refer them to a doctor or dentist.

The community pharmacist is in frequent contact with the public. However, they also oversee stock control, stock rotation and ordering. Records must be maintained, such as the Poisons Register, and use is increasingly made of computer technology. Pharmacists normally undertake the supervision and training of assistants and technicians. It is unlawful for a pharmacy to operate without the presence of a qualified pharmacist.

A community pharmacist is also likely to be a business manager and must run a chemist shop efficiently and profitably. Most sell a wide range of products, including toiletries, cosmetics and photographic materials. The work therefore includes financial management, merchandising and responsibility for staff and premises.

Hospital pharmacist

Hospital pharmacists prepare and dispense medicines and drugs. They are involved in stock control, ordering, labelling and financial management. Computer technology assists the pharmacist with administration.

In many hospitals, the pharmacist meets patients during ward rounds to discuss the supply and form of appropriate medicines, in addition to consulting with doctors, nurses and other hospital staff.

Newly qualified staff join the NHS at basic grade A under the supervision of more experienced staff. After this transitional period, pharmacists may choose to specialize, for example, in radiopharmacy (preparing radioactive substances for administration to patients, in collaboration with radiologists).

Senior pharmacists may also supervise the training of pre-registration trainees and junior pharmacists.

Industrial pharmacist

Industrial pharmacists are concerned with researching and developing pharmaceutical products. There are many different areas in which an industrial pharmacist can specialize. One field is clinical trials, where drugs are tested for safety and effectiveness with the co-operation of volunteers and patients. Another branch is production, where medicines and drugs are manufactured, packed, stored or delivered. Other areas are research and development, marketing and quality assurance.

WORK ENVIRONMENT

Community pharmacists employed in large chemist shops work as part of a team of pharmacists, technicians and sales staff. In smaller community outlets, the pharmacist works with only one or two other staff.

Hospital pharmacists work in health centres or hospital laboratories or dispensaries. They work as part of a team including biochemists, technicians and other hospital staff. In addition to providing in-patients and out-patients with medicines, they may visit patients on the wards.

Industrial pharmacists are normally based in a laboratory.

Pharmacists operate in clean and sometimes sterile conditions. Protective clothing may be necessary.

SKILLS AND INTERESTS

All pharmacists must have an interest in science and medicine, and the ability to study a scientific subject to degree level. The ability to work carefully and accurately is essential. Pharmacists should be able to work methodically and think logically when carrying out laboratory tasks and ordering supplies. It is important that a pharmacist is able to co-operate with others as part of a team. Pharmacists dealing with the public or patients must have a caring and sympathetic manner, a friendly personality and excellent communication skills.

Pharmacists with staff responsibility must have effective management skills and the ability to supervise and delegate work to junior staff. Pharmacists may also have to provide training for other staff.

Those working in the retail sector require merchandising, selling and financial management skills in order to run a successful business.

ENTRY REQUIREMENTS

Pharmacists must have a degree in Pharmacy from an approved school of pharmacy.

Minimum entry requirements to degree courses are two A levels/three H grades plus five GCSEs/S grades (A-C/1-3). Most candidates, however, hold three A levels or four/five H grades with high grades in scientific subjects. A level/H grade chemistry is essential for entry to all pharmacy degree courses. For full details of entry requirements, candidates should consult the Royal Pharmaceutical Society and the appropriate university prospectuses.

Postgraduate courses

Many of those working in research posts as pharmacists have studied for postgraduate qualifications. Candidates normally require a first or second-class degree in pharmacy, or a related discipline, to be considered for entry to a higher degree programme.

TRAINING

Registration as a pharmacist leading to membership of the Royal Pharmaceutical Society of Great Britain is essential, to practise in retail, hospital and in some forms of industrial pharmacy. Registration is available only to those who have: obtained a degree in Pharmacy from an approved school of pharmacy, satisfactorily completed a one-year period of pre-registration training in a pharmacy, and passed the Society's registration examination. Both the pharmacy and the tutor appointed to supervise the graduate must be approved by the Royal Pharmaceutical Society for training purposes.

Degree courses

Degree courses are available at the universities of Aberdeen (The Robert Gordon University), Aston, Bath, Belfast (The Queen's University), Bradford, Brighton, Leicester (De Montfort), Liverpool (John Moores University), London (King's College and The School of Pharmacy), Manchester, Nottingham, Portsmouth, Strathclyde, Sunderland and Wales (Cardiff).

Courses last four years. However, there is a five-year sandwich course at the University of Bradford, which incorporates two six-month blocks of professional training. This enables the student to graduate and register simultaneously. In Scotland, degree courses last for four years, with the first year spent studying the basic sciences – chemistry, physics and a biological subject.

Both hospitals and community pharmacies welcome graduates wishing to complete their pre-registration year, and provide valuable practical experience.

The National Pharmaceutical Association provides part-time and distance learning courses for pharmacists in areas such as business management and drugs.

Postgraduate courses are offered by the following universities: Aberdeen (Robert Gordon University), Aston, Bath, Belfast (The Queen's University), Bradford, Brighton, Derby, Keele, Leicester (De Montfort University), Liverpool (John Moores University), London (King's College and the School of Pharmacy), Manchester, Nottingham, Portsmouth, Strathclyde, Sunderland and Wales (Cardiff).

LATE ENTRY

There are no upper age limits for training or entry to work. All applicants follow the training route described in TRAINING. Occasionally, educational establishments may encourage older applicants by reducing the entry requirements to courses, although candidates must be able to demonstrate that they are capable of academic study at this level. Details are available from individual institutions. The recruitment policy of particular employers determines employment prospects.

OPPORTUNITIES

There are numerous opportunities for qualified pharmacists. However, the majority enter community pharmacy.

The size of a chemist/pharmacy varies, and a community pharmacist may be the owner of a small chemist's shop or may work for one of the high street chains. There are excellent opportunities for promotion within the larger companies.

Hospital pharmacists can work within the National Health Service, in private hospitals and in health centres. In hospitals, qualified pharmacists enter at a basic grade and diversify or specialize after they have gained some experience. For those who want temporary work, locums are employed in both hospital and community pharmacies.

The pharmaceutical industry has grown considerably in recent years and there are an increasing number of varied posts available to qualified pharmacists. Pharmacists are usually employed in clinical trials, production and quality assurance, or research and development. There are also opportunities available in chemical plants producing such items as fertilizers. Pharmacists may also find work in establishments that specialize in agricultural and veterinary products, animal medicines and drugs.

Opportunities for advancement in the pharmaceutical industry are considerable. Higher management positions are available to pharmacists from all branches of industry.

Information about vacancies is available from the *New Scientist, Pharmaceutical Journal,* and the local and national press.

PAY AND CONDITIONS

A pre-registration pharmacist working in the NHS can expect a starting salary of £8,181. On qualifying, Grade A pharmacists can expect to earn £12,836. A senior pharmacist working at a regional level could earn up to £38,400. Terms and conditions of service may differ for pharmacists working in NHS trust hospitals.

There is a wide range of salaries for community pharmacists. A pre-registration pharmacist working in a high street chemist could expect a salary of approximately £7,500. Employed pharmacists usually receive salaries between £18,000 and £28,000. Many of the large high street chains also offer staff discounts, pensions schemes and private health insurance. The income of those who are self-employed varies considerably.

Industrial pharmacists start at around £17,000 rising to £57,500 in a senior management position.

Community pharmacists usually work shop hours – 9am to 5.30pm or 6pm for five or six days a week. The use of a rota system is common in all pharmacies. Some stores are open for late evening dispensing until 10pm and, in major cities, some are open all night. Hospital pharmacists are likely to work on a shift system. Industrial pharmacists normally work regular hours from Monday to Friday.

PROSPECTS

Newly qualified pharmacists enter employment at a basic level, but some high street chemists have in-house training schemes, which enable employees to move to a managerial level quickly. Promotion prospects are excellent in larger chemist shops and may lead to regional management. Some pharmacists may wish to run their own establishments, although this requires capital.

Pharmacists working in a hospital pharmacy may be able to specialize in a particular area such as database management or geriatric care. Career progression can also lead to district or regional management within a health authority.

Industrial pharmacists may move into specialist managerial positions in personnel, or marketing and sales, within the pharmaceutical industry.

RELATED OCCUPATIONS

Dentist, doctor, pharmacologist, biochemist, chemist.

FURTHER INFORMATION AND READING

Please see article 2. PHARMACY TECHNICIAN.

2. PHARMACY TECHNICIAN (JAG)

THE WORK

Community (retail) pharmacy technicians assist qualified pharmacists with their work in retail outlets. They help pharmacists with labelling and dispensing drugs and issuing pre-packaged prescriptions. Prescriptions received must be checked for legality, accuracy, and the absence of errors or forgery. Technicians may need to make simple dilutions or count the prescribed number of tablets. It is important that technicians are familiar with the range of different drugs and brand names for similar products and arrangements for emergency supply of drugs.

An important task of the technician is record keeping. Individual records of patient's prescriptions are usually stored on a computer. A community pharmacy technician also helps the pharmacist in a range of other duties such as stock checking and ordering.

Technicians may have to sell over-the-counter medicines and other items stocked by the chemist, such as cosmetics, toiletries, baby food and photographic supplies. Customers may seek advice and information on the use of medicines or general health issues, and the pharmacy technician must know when to refer the customer to the pharmacist or other health care professional.

Hospital pharmacy technicians assist the hospital pharmacist or senior pharmacy technician. The majority of work involves dispensing drugs and medicines under close supervision by hospital staff. Hospital technicians also manufacture individual medicines. They ensure that each hospital department and ward has sufficient supplies and the correct dosages for patients. Technicians also check stock levels and ensure that the correct orders are made to the pharmaceutical companies. These orders are often made with the use of a computer.

Senior technicians can specialize, for example, in analytical control for checking the quality of hospital medicines, or in the preparation of radioactive materials.

Industrial pharmacy technicians work as chemical or laboratory technicians and assist the pharmacists who have specialized in a certain field, such as research and development, clinical trials or production. The work may involve setting up scientific tests of medicines to ensure their safety and effectiveness before they go to the production and manufacturing stage. They maintain accurate records of results.

WORK ENVIRONMENT

Please see article 1. PHARMACIST.

SKILLS AND INTERESTS

Technicians should have an interest in medicine, science and technical subjects. They need a basic understanding of the contents and use of common medicines. They should be accurate and meticulous when carrying out practical work. An understanding is required of the basic physiology of the body, together with the action and uses of drugs. As much of the work is routine, a high level of concentration is required, and they must be methodical and logical. It is important that a pharmacy technician is able to operate with other colleagues and work as part of a team.

Technicians employed in the retail sector should be friendly, patient and sympathetic when they deal with patients who may be worried about their condition, or seeking advice about their medication. They may also require sales ability, as a wide variety of products are sold in community pharmacies.

ENTRY REQUIREMENTS

Entry as a trainee technician is from 16 years. Applicants should have studied science subjects at GCSE/S grade level. The following qualifications are available to pharmacy technicians:

BTEC National Certificate in Science (Pharmaceutical): four GCSEs/S grades (A-C/1-3) are normally required.

SCOTVEC Certificate in Science (Pharmaceutical): candidates require three GCSEs/S grades (A-C/1-3), including chemistry and preferably two other science subjects.

BTEC Higher National Certificate in Science (Pharmaceutical): minimum entry requirements are four GCSEs (A-C) and one A level *or* four S grades (1-3) and two H grades.

National Pharmaceutical Association Correspondence Course for Dispensing Technicians: no formal qualifications are required, but entrants must have completed one year's full-time work in a retail pharmacy and be at least 17 years old.

TRAINING

On-the-job training is often given and can be supplemented by part-time study for one of the recognized qualifications to develop existing skills. Many hospitals run training sessions for technicians on a regular basis. The courses listed below are widely available.

BTEC National Certificate in Sciences (Pharmaceutical): the main subjects covered are human physiology, pharmaceutical microbiology, pharmaceutics and pharmacy law, actions and uses of drugs, pharmacology and therapeutics. Courses are two or three years part-time with study on a day release basis. A correspondence course is also available. This course is essential for those who wish to work in a hospital pharmacy.

SCOTVEC Certificate in Sciences (Pharmaceutical): this certificate is similar to the BTEC award. The two-year part-time day release course includes lectures and practical training.

National Pharmaceutical Association Correspondence Course for Dispensing Technicians: this two-year distance learning course covers pharmacy law and ethics, human physiology, microbiology, dispensing practice and procedure, and actions and uses of drugs. There is a one week compulsory summer school between the first and second year.

NVQs/SVQs are due to be introduced in late 1996.

LATE ENTRY

Opportunities for late entry and training depend on individual employers.

OPPORTUNITIES

There is a steady demand for pharmacy technicians. Many work for the high street chains. Self-employed community pharmacists may employ one or two pharmacy technicians as assistants in their practice.

Hospital pharmacy technicians can work within the National Health Service, in private hospitals and in health centres. There is a continuous demand for all levels of hospital technicians.

PAY AND CONDITIONS

Community pharmacy technicians at 21 years can expect a starting salary of £6,668 for a 39-hour week. Technicians in the retail sector follow usual shop hours – 9.30am to 5.30pm or 6pm, five or six days a week on a rota system. Part-time work and Saturday jobs are offered by some chemists.

The average salary of a pharmacy technician working in a hospital is approximately £8,600 rising to £13,500. With two or three years' experience, this salary could rise to £15,500. Most hospital pharmacists operate shift and rota systems. In some hospitals part-time work may be available.

The salaries of industrial pharmacy technicians vary, depending on which field they are working in, but the hours worked would be similar to office hours.

PROSPECTS

Pharmacy technicians are unable to pursue a career as a pharmacist without successfully completing the relevant degree course and the compulsory pre-registration training period (see article 1. PHARMACIST).

Technicians in a large community pharmacy may be able to work in management or specialize in marketing or sales. Technicians employed in hospitals must complete a training programme and have appropriate experience to be considered for promotion to a higher grade of senior technician. (In NHS hospitals there are five grades of technicians.) In some hospitals there are chances for technicians to specialize in areas such as quality control – analysing the medicines that are dispensed – and

radiopharmacy – acquiring expertise in the handling of radioactive materials.

There are numerous fields of specialization available in the pharmaceutical industry, such as research and production.

RELATED OCCUPATIONS

Laboratory technician, medical laboratory technician, physiological measurement technician, medical physics technician, pharmacist.

FURTHER INFORMATION

The Association of The British Pharmaceutical Industry, 12 Whitehall, London SW1A 2DY, 0171 930 3477

The National Pharmaceutical Association of Great Britain*, Mallinson House, 38-42 St Peter's Street, St Albans, Hertfordshire AL1 3NP, (please enclose sae)

The Royal Pharmaceutical Society of Great Britain*, Education Division, 1 Lambeth High Street, London SE1 7JN, 0171 735 9141 (please include sae)

The Society of Apothecaries*, Apothecaries Hall, Blackfriars Lane, London EC4V 6EJ, 0171 236 1189

FURTHER READING

Leaflets/booklets are available from the addresses marked*.

Job Outlines – Pharmacy – COIC
Working in Chemistry – COIC
Working in Hospitals – COIC
Careers in Medicine, Dentistry and Mental Health – Kogan Page

In the careers library classified under JAG.

1. OPTOMETRIST/OPHTHALMIC OPTICIAN CLCI:JAL
2. DISPENSING OPTICIAN CLCI:JAL
3. ORTHOPTIST CLCI:JAL

BACKGROUND INFORMATION

Optometrists (also known as ophthalmic opticians) examine eyes and prescribe and dispense optical aids. Dispensing opticians supply optical aids but are not qualified to examine eyes. Working under medical direction, orthoptists investigate and treat vision defects and abnormal eye movements such as squints. Optometrists and dispensing opticians must register with the General Optical Council. Regulations on spectacle sales have been relaxed, but it is still illegal for unregistered vendors to examine eyes, supply contact lenses, or supply spectacles to children and those who are registered blind or partially sighted.

1. OPTOMETRIST/OPHTHALMIC OPTICIAN (JAL)

THE WORK

Optometrists, when examining a patient, determine the reason for the visit, the symptoms and history of the patient, their present state of health and any current or past medication. They also establish whether the patient is a driver, their sports, hobbies, etc.

Optometrists have a series of tests available for examining the eyes: objective – that do not need the patient's input, such as retinoscopy (which determines the optical status of the eyes); and subjective – where the patient answers questions about how they see test objects. By combining the results of the various tests, the optometrist prescribes lenses to correct any optical errors.

They may also carry out other tests, such as colour vision tests, tonometry (to measure the pressure in the eyes), or visual field plots (to ensure the eyes are not suffering from glaucoma, neurological, or other pathology, effecting the visual field).

Optometrists examine the inside of the eye with an ophthalmoscope to see if there are indications of disease or injury. A slit-lamp biomicroscope is used to reveal scratches and scars on the surface of the eye, to help with the prescription of contact lenses, and for internal examination, using supplementary lenses.

When optometrists detect early signs of eye abnormalities, such as glaucoma or detached retina, or of general conditions, such as hypertension or diabetes, they refer the patient to their GP for further investigation, and possible referral to a hospital eye department.

Prescriptions for spectacles consist of mathematical instructions on the lens powers, such as the cylindrical (astigmatic) power and axis, needed. Optometrists are qualified to fit and supply spectacles, but this may also be done by dispensing opticians (please see article 2. DISPENSING OPTICIAN). The lenses they supply must give clear and comfortable binocular vision at the distance needed for the patient's work or recreation. Frames must hold the lenses securely in the right position, be comfortable, and suit the patient, and must take account of any protective requirements of sport and some occupations.

When contact lenses are appropriate, optometrists choose from a range of hard, soft and gas-permeable lenses, tell the patient how to insert, remove, and care for the lenses, and ensure the patient returns for regular check-ups.

Optometrists provide magnifiers, electronic devices and other aids for people whose vision is so poor that spectacles or contact lenses are of little use.

Optometrists also give advice on eye care; some give orthoptic treatment (see article 3. ORTHOPTIST) and advise people such as pilots, VDU operators and others who have particular vision needs connected with their occupations.

In private practice, optometrists fit contact lenses, spectacles and eye products. They also have administrative and managerial duties.

Hospital optometrists do the tests described above and help eye surgeons in the diagnosis and post-operative treatment of complex eye conditions. They can specialize in certain types of vision disorder.

WORK ENVIRONMENT

Optometrists in private practice work in owned or rented premises, often with a shop front, or in rooms. They work in clean and comfortably furnished examination rooms. They sometimes leave their premises for home visits.

Optometrists also work in eye hospitals and hospital eye departments, where they may have research facilities, as well as examination rooms, and in university departments, where they teach and conduct research.

SKILLS AND INTERESTS

Optometrists require scientific and mathematical aptitude. Patience and precision are essential, as well as the manual dexterity to use delicate instruments and fit contact lenses.

Optometrists must have the enthusiasm and flexibility to respond to the rapid advances in their field, but also be willing to do repetitive, sometimes mundane tasks.

They must like people and deal with them confidently and sympathetically. An interest in style and fashion is an asset.

All optometrists need to be self-motivated and well-organized, but in private practice they also require organizational and administrative skills.

ENTRY REQUIREMENTS

Practising optometrists must be registered with the General Optical Council. They need a degree in Optometry (Ophthalmic Optics), a year's clinical experience under supervision and to have passed the Professional Qualifying Examination of the College of Optometrists. Requirements for entry to a degree course vary and often depend on the candidate's performance at an interview.

Usual entry requirements in England and Wales: three A levels including maths and science, plus five GCSEs (A-C), including English, maths and physics. Average entry grades vary, usually between 20 and 22 A level points. Equivalent entry qualifications may also be considered.

Entry requirements in Scotland: four or five H grades or three H grades and two S grades (1-3). H grades must include two from maths, physics, chemistry and biology. Maths and English are required at H grade or S grade (1-3). BTEC/SCOTVEC and other qualifications are considered, when equivalent to normal entry requirements.

Prospective applicants are advised to make several half-day visits to an optometrist to see what the work entails. Only 50 per cent, or fewer, applicants are accepted onto courses each year.

TRAINING

Candidates must undertake a three-year BSc Degree in Optometry (Ophthalmic Optics) at one of six universities in England, Wales, or Northern Ireland (Aston, Bradford, City (London), Wales at Cardiff, Ulster and UMIST) or equivalent four-year BSc course at Glasgow Caledonian University. Subjects studied include: anatomy and physiology, optics, optometry, pharmacology, recognition of ocular abnormality, and dispensing practice. A satisfactory degree usually exempts trainees from Part I of the professional qualifying exam run by the College of Optometrists.

The degree is followed by a pre-registration year of training and experience supervised by a registered optometrist. This includes attendance at hospital out-patient departments, or is worked in full at a hospital. A small salary is paid. Part 2 of the qualifying exam (practical and oral) is taken towards the end of the year. Successful candidates are eligible for registration with the General Optical Council and elected to membership of the College of Optometrists (MCOptom).

Optometrists' basic training qualifies them to fit and supply contact lenses, but advanced training is available in this growing field, as well as in orthoptics, children's sight problems, vision in industry, low vision and other topics.

LATE ENTRY

Optometry attracts a number of late entrants. There is no upper age limit and requirements are relaxed for mature students entering university or college, providing they have equivalent qualifications or experience.

Some dispensing opticians retrain to be optometrists but, though entry requirements may be relaxed, they still have to obtain an Optometry degree and work the pre-registration year.

OPPORTUNITIES

There are 7,500 registered optometrists in the UK, of whom the great majority work in general practice. About 55 per cent work for small independent firms or run their own business, alone or in partnership.

Opportunities exist in the high street multiples, in independent firms run by optometrists and dispensing opticians, and in hospitals.

PAY AND CONDITIONS

Trainee optometrists in their pre-registration year are paid £7,600. Newly registered optometrists in private practice earn £15,000 to £25,000, their earnings rising, as they become more experienced, to £30,000 or more.

Hospital Eye Service salaries are graded and extra responsibility payments are made within the grades. Salaries range from £11,823 for newly registered optometrists to £39,877 (or exceptionally, £48,517). London allowances are paid. Terms and conditions of service may differ for optometrists working in NHS trust hospitals.

Most optometrists work a 35-hour week, though in private practice hours vary according to local demand. Optometrists working on Saturday take time off in lieu during the week. Some large practices work rotas in which days-off vary. In the Hospital Eye Service optometrists work a 35-hour week, Monday to Friday.

Part-time opportunities are readily available.

PROSPECTS

Career structures vary from firm to firm. Small companies may only employ an assistant optometrist, while the multiples have assistants and branch managers, regional directors, and head office personnel. Advanced qualifications increase prospects of promotion (see TRAINING).

Optometrists hoping to start their own business or enter a partnership usually work as an assistant for two or three years first, to gain experience of patient and practice management. The chances of becoming self-employed are better than in many professions. The Association of Optometrists gives advice on the financial assistance available to optometrists setting up their own practice. The newly self-employed often take part-time or locum work elsewhere for two or three days a week until their own practice is established.

Opportunities are available in teaching and research in universities or colleges, or consultancy or research work in the optical industry.

RELATED OCCUPATIONS

Dispensing optician, ophthalmologist, hospital doctor, orthoptist, speech and language therapist.

FURTHER INFORMATION AND READING

Please see article 3. ORTHOPTIST.

2. DISPENSING OPTICIAN (JAL)

THE WORK

Dispensing opticians work mainly in private practice. They dispense, fit and supply spectacles and other optical aids.

Dispensing opticians interpret prescriptions from optometrists and ophthalmic medical practitioners; these give details of the power and angle of lenses needed. They advise patients on lens type – spherical or aspherical, clear or tinted, single vision or bifocal, etc – and on spectacle frame, weight, colour and style. They fit sample frames – several sizes are available in each style – and specify lens measurements accordingly. Frames must be chosen that position the lenses correctly in front of the eyes, and opticians may need to take exact measurements to establish, for example, the distance between the pupils, the height of the segment in bifocals, etc. Helping patients choose frames is time-consuming, as they must suit the face and general appearance, as well as holding the lenses securely in the right position.

Dispensing opticians order the spectacles from prescription houses. When the finished spectacles are returned, opticians make sure that they meet specifications and fit the patient correctly and comfortably.

Dispensing opticians may see the same patient a number of times if their spectacles need to be adjusted or repaired, if their vision requirements change, or if their sight deteriorates.

Demand for contact lenses is growing, and many dispensing opticians take the additional training that qualifies them to fit and supply contact lenses. Others specialize in areas such as aids for the partially-sighted.

Selling is an important part of a dispensing optician's work.

Management skills are essential for those wishing to run a branch or start their own business.

WORK ENVIRONMENT

Dispensing opticians usually work in high street shop premises. Reception and sales areas are clean and comfortable, designed to welcome the public. Many practices have separate fitting rooms.

SKILLS AND INTERESTS

The work of dispensing opticians is intricate and requires exceptional accuracy and precision. As well as interpreting scientific and mathematical information, dispensing opticians must be able to handle ophthalmic instruments and fit spectacles, and probably contact lenses. They come into contact with a variety of people, and their communication skills are as important as their technical ability. They should like people and deal with them confidently and sympathetically. A pleasant manner, tidy appearance, patience and a sense of humour are essential. An understanding of fashion and design is a great asset.

Dispensing opticians in private practice need good sales ability. Management skills and drive are vital when they are holding a responsible post or running their own business.

ENTRY REQUIREMENTS

Dispensing opticians have to be registered with the General Optical Council. They must complete a three-year training and pass the Association of British Dispensing Opticians examinations before being eligible for registration and fellowship of the association (FBDO).

Minimum requirements for entry to diploma courses in ophthalmic dispensing at 16 years or over are: five GCSEs (A-C), including English literature or English language, maths or physics, and another science subject, *or* five S grades (1-3). Subjects must include English and maths; preference is given to applicants offering science subjects as well. Equivalent qualifications will be considered.

TRAINING

There are three methods of training to be a dispensing optician:

1. A two-year full-time course in ophthalmic dispensing at Bradford and Ilkley Community College, City and Islington College, or Glasgow Caledonian University. Subjects studied include maths, anatomy and physiology, visual optics, ophthalmic lenses and frames, spectacle making, dispensing, and social ophthalmics. Courses feature practical sessions in laboratories and workshops as well as lectures. This is followed by a pre-registration year of salaried work supervised by a registered optometrist or dispensing optician.

2. A three-year day release course in ophthalmic dispensing at Bradford and Ilkley Community College, City and Islington College, or Anglia Polytechnic University. Students have to be employed throughout as trainee dispensers supervised by a registered optometrist or dispensing optician. Courses include practical work as well as lectures, and cover subjects such as anatomy and physiology, anatomy of the eye, visual optics, ophthalmic lenses and frames, dispensing, customer care, product knowledge and selling skills.

3. A three-year distance learning course in ophthalmic dispensing run by the Association of British Dispensing Opticians. Students have to be employed throughout as trainee dispensers supervised by a registered optometrist or dispensing optician. The course provides only the theoretical knowledge needed for the association's examinations. Practical examination experience is gained in the practice.

Anglia Polytechnic University offers a BSc (Hons) Optical Management. This three-year full-time degree gives qualifications in ophthalmic dispensing and retail management.

Advanced part-time courses for qualified dispensing opticians are available in contact lens dispensing, low vision, and spectacle lens design. Short, full-time refresher courses are also available.

Some firms sponsor full-time students, who are expected to work for them during vacations and probably in their pre-registration year. Details from the Federation of Ophthalmic and Dispensing Opticians.

LATE ENTRY

Entry requirements may be relaxed for applicants with at least ten years optical experience, though they require a GCSE/S grade (A-C/1-3) (or equivalent) in maths or physics. There is no upper age limit. A number of people train late to be dispensing opticians, particularly those with previous optical experience, eg optical technicians or receptionists for dispensing opticians.

OPPORTUNITIES

There are more than 3,400 registered dispensing opticians in the United Kingdom. Of these, 65 per cent are employed in private practice, 30 per cent are self-employed or in partnership, and the rest work in hospitals, in prescription houses, as college lecturers, etc.

Opportunities arise for dispensing opticians to work for independent optometrists and dispensing opticians, and in the multiple practices – the largest of which has 700 branches. The job market has become more competitive in recent years but prospects remain good, particularly for dispensing opticians willing to relocate and undertake managerial responsibility. Increasing numbers are starting their own businesses.

Registration with the General Optical Council is recognized in many countries abroad. Positions are advertised in the *Optician*.

PAY AND CONDITIONS

Trainees in full-time employment can earn about £6,000. Incremental payments are made as trainees complete key stages of their training. On registration, dispensing opticians employed in private practice earn £10,000 to £15,000, rising to £25,000 or more as experience and responsibility increase. The earnings of self-employed dispensing opticians may be substantially higher.

Dispensing opticians work a five-day, 35-hour week. Many work half or all day Saturday, which is often the busiest time of the week, and take time off in lieu. It is possible for dispensing opticians to work part-time and as locums.

PROSPECTS

Each company has its own career structure, but many trainees reach the position of assistant manager by the time they are qualified. In multiple stores, dispensing opticians' promotion may be to managerial positions in larger branches or a move into regional or head office management. Promotion depends on ability to deal courteously and efficiently with customers and on willingness to take responsibility.

Advanced training increases promotional prospects, and geographical mobility is essential at all career stages.

Outside private practice, dispensing opticians work in hospital eye departments, in prescription houses, where they provide technical support for other opticians, in lens and frame manufacture, as college teachers, or as sales consultants for ophthalmic instrument manufacturers, lens suppliers, and frame-makers and importers.

RELATED OCCUPATIONS

Optical technician, ophthalmic instrument technician, optometrist/ophthalmic optician, orthoptist, retail manager.

FURTHER INFORMATION AND READING

Please see article 3. ORTHOPTIST.

3. ORTHOPTIST (JAL)

THE WORK

Orthoptists diagnose and treat disorders of vision and eye movement, including squint, reduced vision and double vision.

Most orthoptists work in hospitals, assessing patients referred by general practitioners and local consultants. Many of their patients are children under eight, although increasing numbers of adults are being referred, including elderly patients with impaired binocular vision.

Orthoptists carry out a range of tests, then decide on appropriate treatment and monitor its progress at subsequent appointments. They aim to re-educate the eyes by exercises to improve eye co-ordination, and this may include giving patients eye patches to wear. Sometimes they refer patients back to a consultant to discuss and recommend the next stage of treatment, which may be optical, pharmacological, or surgical. They may also find that brain scans or other special X-rays are needed.

Orthoptists work with equipment ranging from prisms (to measure a squint) to computerized visual field analysers. They also use charts and cards and – in assessing the vision of very young children – toys and games.

When surgery is needed for squint, orthoptists do the pre- and post-operative assessments and monitoring. They are also involved in the diagnosis and monitoring of glaucoma and the treatment of double vision caused by strokes, accidents and some illnesses, such as thyroid disorders. They often help neurologists, neurosurgeons and doctors diagnose complex disorders of eye movement. Orthoptists also assess the visual abilities of physically and mentally impaired children. Their diagnosis, observations and treatment have to be noted in the patient's records and written up in reports for consultants and GPs.

Some orthoptists are involved in screening pre-school and school children for vision defects.

WORK ENVIRONMENT

Orthoptists work in eye hospitals and in eye departments and clinics in general hospitals and children's hospitals. They spend time on the wards as well as in clinics, and may work at several different locations.

Most orthoptists work as a member of a team including dispensing opticians, nurses, optometrists and doctors, headed by an ophthalmic surgeon. They may have their own examination room or share one with another orthoptist.

Orthoptists in the community work in health centres and schools, and sometimes from specially equipped mobile units.

SKILLS AND INTERESTS

Orthoptists have to be enquiring and observant, able to work to high standards of accuracy and interpret the information supplied by their tests and examinations. They need the manual dexterity and technical competence to use ophthalmic instruments and computerized equipment.

They must also be able to communicate well with children and adults from widely differing backgrounds. Orthoptists see some patients over a long period of time and have to gain their confidence and put them and anxious relatives at ease. As well as patience, a pleasant manner and a sense of humour, they need the imagination to attract a young child's attention or to improvise when a patient is unable to respond to conventional methods of testing. They must retain their enthusiasm and persevere when a patient's progress is slower than expected. Their work with physically and mentally impaired children may be particularly demanding, but also very rewarding.

Orthoptists need to be self-motivated and well-organized, working confidently and professionally in a team or on their own. Management skills are necessary for career advancement.

ENTRY REQUIREMENTS

Orthoptists working in the National Health Service have to be registered with the Council for Professions Supplementary to Medicine. Entrants to the profession are now required to obtain an Orthoptics Degree. Three-year degree courses are run at Sheffield, Liverpool and Glasgow Caledonian universities.

Entry requirements for Liverpool University: three A levels (grade C), including at least one science subject, preferably biology, or equivalent; plus five GCSEs (A-C), including English language and maths, or equivalent.

Entry requirements for Sheffield University: three A levels (grades B-C), including at least one science subject, preferably biology (but excluding general studies), or equivalent; plus five GCSEs (A-C), including English language and maths, or equivalent.

Entry requirements for Glasgow Caledonian University: three/four H grades (grades B-C), including English and at least one science subject, or at least three equivalent A levels; plus S grades (1-3) in at least two more subjects, including maths if not offered as a H grade, or equivalent.

Prospective candidates are advised to spend time in an orthoptic clinic before applying. Some hospitals run careers days for schools, which feature orthoptics.

Potential applicants are advised to check course entry requirements and that the courses they are interested in have been approved by the Orthoptists Board for Professions Supplementary to Medicine.

TRAINING

The three-year degree courses combine theory and practice and lead to a degree in Orthoptics. Course content includes:

general study of anatomy and physiology, cell biology, child development, behavioural sciences, and genetics; detailed study of the eyeball, ocular muscles, brain and central nervous system; ophthalmology and diseases affecting the eye.

Students gain practical experience on day and block placements in hospitals, child development centres and assessment centres for the physically and mentally impaired. Training also covers refraction techniques and methods of diagnosing and monitoring glaucoma.

A Certificate in Advanced Study in Education (Orthoptics) is available for those wishing to teach in a clinical setting.

LATE ENTRY

There is no upper age limit, though applicants over 35 years may find it hard to obtain a place on a training course. Professional qualifications and work experience are considered in the absence of standard entry qualifications.

OPPORTUNITIES

There are about 1,000 orthoptists working in the United Kingdom, most of them employed by the National Health Service.

Opportunities arise for orthoptists to work in hospitals (NHS, NHS trust and private practice), in the community and in universities. It may be necessary to move location in order to find a suitable position.

A list of vacancies – including a few overseas – is circulated with the British Orthoptic Society monthly newsletter.

PAY AND CONDITIONS

National Health Service salaries range from £12,635 for a basic grade orthoptist to more than £27,190 for the highest grade head orthoptist. A senior orthoptist in charge of a unit or department earns a minimum of £17,355. Annual increments are paid within each of the eight grades. Allowances are paid to orthoptists working in inner and outer London.

Orthoptists work a 36½-hour week, usually Monday to Friday.

NHS trust hospitals may set their own scales of pay and terms of employment.

Part-time jobs are available in the NHS and in private practice, and some orthoptists work in both sectors. Locum work is also available.

PROSPECTS

The National Health Service has a well-defined career structure which recognizes special skills and responsibilities. It is possible for a basic-grade orthoptist working in a team to progress to senior orthoptist in charge of a department and then move on to clinical or district management.

Promotion depends on willingness to take increased responsibility, and to move from one region to another.

Some orthoptists work in private practice and a few are employed as researchers, teachers or lecturers. Opportunities may be available in management positions in other areas of health care.

RELATED OCCUPATIONS

Physiotherapist, speech and language therapist, optometrist/ophthalmic optician, medical technical officer.

FURTHER INFORMATION

Association of Optometrists*, Bridge House, 233-234 Blackfriars Road, London SE1 8NW, 0171 261 9661

The Association of British Dispensing Opticians*, 6 Hurlingham Business Park, Sulivan Road, London SW6 3DU, 0171 736 0088

College of Optometrists*, 10 Knaresborough Place, London SW5 0TG, 0171 373 7765

British Orthoptic Society*, Tavistock House North, Tavistock Square, London WC1H 9HX, 0171 387 7992

The Federation of Ophthalmic and Dispensing Opticians*, 113 Eastbourne Mews, Paddington, London W2 6LQ, 0171 258 0240

General Optical Council*, 41 Harley Street, London W1N 2DJ, 0171 580 3898

FURTHER READING

Leaflets/booklets are available from the addresses marked*.

Working in Hospitals – COIC

In the careers library classified under JAL.

1. **PHYSIOTHERAPIST CLCI:JAN**
2. **RADIOGRAPHER CLCI:JAP**
3. **OCCUPATIONAL THERAPIST CLCI:JAR**
4. **SPEECH AND LANGUAGE THERAPIST CLCI:JAS**
5. **CHIROPODIST/PODIATRIST CLCI:JAT**
6. **DIETITIAN CLCI:JAV**

1. PHYSIOTHERAPIST (JAN)

BACKGROUND INFORMATION

Most physiotherapists work for the National Health Service. They are important members of the health care team, working in close co-operation with doctors, nurses, social workers, other therapists and specialists.

Physiotherapy is concerned with the rehabilitation of people who are suffering from injury, disability or other conditions. Increasingly, physiotherapists undertake preventive work, health education and research.

THE WORK

Physiotherapists aim to return or develop patients to as near normal function of body and limbs as possible, so that the patient can resume an active life with maximum independence. When treating patients with progressive diseases, they aim to make the best of the functions that remain at each stage.

Techniques of physiotherapeutic treatments are mainly based on movement and manipulation. Other treatments may include electrotherapy, ultrasound and heat treatments.

Some patients are treated in groups, but most of the work is with individuals. Those who are too ill to be moved are treated in bed. The emphasis is on encouraging patients to exercise, rather than on prescribing passive treatments. However, some patients may not be able to move at all, for example paraplegics, and it is necessary to move their limbs for them. Physiotherapists encounter a wide range of disabilities. These include the result of certain diseases (such as arthritis, multiple sclerosis and cystic fibrosis), post-operative conditions, and disabilities resulting from injury or that have been present since birth.

At some stage in their careers physiotherapists usually deal with patients who have suffered strokes. They must encourage them to reach their full potential and cope with permanent disabilities.

The work can be very strenuous – moving limbs, helping patients to move and providing support. It is important that physiotherapists are able to lift without strain.

Physiotherapists must monitor and evaluate the progress of each patient at each session. This involves making records and carefully documenting progress. Where treatments are not as successful as they could be, the physiotherapist may refer back to the doctor to discuss alternatives.

Physiotherapists work with people of all ages, from babies to the elderly.

After gaining experience of general physiotherapy, usually in a hospital, it is possible to specialize in: developing a major skill, such as manipulation; treating specific conditions, such as intensive care or respiratory disorders; or treating a particular group, such as children or the elderly. An increasingly important area of work is with mentally disabled and mentally ill people – physiotherapy can help to improve quality of life and assist rehabilitation.

Patients in all types of hospital departments require physiotherapy. In maternity wards physiotherapists may advise expectant mothers on relaxation and exercise and help them regain muscle strength after childbirth. Most physiotherapists begin work in hospitals but the trend is towards community-based health care – patients are treated in their own homes, at local health centres, at schools and in nursing homes.

WORK ENVIRONMENT

The majority of physiotherapists work in the National Health Service; physiotherapists work on hospital wards with patients, or in specially equipped gymnasia and treatment units.

There are some opportunities for physiotherapists to work on a full or part-time basis, in different kinds of sports clubs, including gymnasium work in health clubs, work for GP's, professional football clubs, etc. There are also jobs to be found on-site in industrial concerns, where therapists treat employees and give health education information.

SKILLS AND INTERESTS

Skills in teaching and counselling are needed; physiotherapists must teach the patient exercises, explain the treatment plan and gain their co-operation. It may be necessary to persuade patients to persevere and reassure those who lack self-confidence or are in pain. Progress can be slow and disappointing, but the physiotherapist must be prepared to provide encouragement and build up determination. A tactful and sympathetic personality, patience, and tolerance are essential qualities.

Physiotherapists should be able to work well with their hands and have the ability to give manipulative treatments. Lifting and supporting patients can be physically strenuous and individuals should have the stamina and physique required to carry out these duties. Physical fitness and good health are essential. An interest in physical education, as well as in science (particularly biology), is an advantage.

ENTRY REQUIREMENTS

The usual academic qualifications for a degree in Physiotherapy are three A levels (grade C or above) plus five GCSEs (A-C) or five H grades plus five S grades (1-3) to include English, maths and two science subjects. Alternative qualifications are also considered. Course requirements often specify additional or specific qualifications – contact relevant institutions for details.

Applicants have to pass a medical before being admitted into training. The minimum age for entry into training is normally 18 years, but those achieving satisfactory qualifications early may be accepted at 17 years. It is also useful to be able to swim.

It is recommended that those considering training in physiotherapy should arrange to visit a physiotherapy department to observe the work, before applying.

TRAINING

Candidates training in physiotherapy take an approved degree course that is acceptable for membership of the Chartered Society of Physiotherapy and for state registration.

All those working in the National Health Service must be state registered. Members of the Society are entitled to call themselves 'chartered' physiotherapists and use the letters

MCSP after their names. First degree courses are for three or four years of full-time study and are available at a number of institutions. (Contact the Chartered Society of Physiotherapy for details.) A two-year accelerated postgraduate degree is available at Glasgow for good honours graduates from a biological or sports science background.

Courses are run at: Aberdeen; Birmingham; Bradford; Bristol; Cardiff; Coventry; Eastbourne; Edinburgh; Glasgow; Hatfield; Keele; Leeds; Liverpool; London; Manchester; Middlesborough; Newcastle-upon-Tyne; Norwich; Nottingham; Salford; Sheffield; Southampton; Ulster; Wakefield.

Courses combine theoretical and practical training and cover a wide range of subjects including anatomy, physiology, physics, behavioural science, pathology, and the theory and practice of therapeutic movement and manipulation.

LATE ENTRY

Applications from adult students are welcome. Schools may waive some of the academic entry requirements for applicants aged 21 years and over who can show some evidence of recent successful academic study, for example A levels/H grades, Open University or access courses.

Separate guidelines for mature applicants are available from the Chartered Society of Physiotherapy.

OPPORTUNITIES

There are over 25,000 practising members of the Chartered Society of Physiotherapy. About 15,000 are employed by the National Health Service – they may be either hospital or community-based. About 2,000-3,000 physiotherapists are self-employed, running private practices. Employment has been rising for a number of years, but entry to training is very competitive, with three to four applicants for each place.

Vacancies for qualified physiotherapists appear in *Physiotherapy Frontline* (a publication of the Chartered Society of Physiotherapy), which is published and circulated twice monthly to members of the Society.

PAY AND CONDITIONS

National Health Service pay scales range from £14,803 for the newly qualified, to a maximum of £26,831 for a physiotherapy service manager. Employees are covered by pension arrangements and may have uniform allowances or other benefits. Terms and conditions of employment may differ for physiotherapists working in NHS trust hospitals.

Salaries in employment outside the NHS are negotiated individually, but are generally related to NHS scales. The Chartered Society of Physiotherapy has a recommended scale for physiotherapists working in industry and private practice.

Working hours in the sport and leisure sector can involve weekend working (mainly Saturday) and evening work (to cover evening football matches, for example). Otherwise, daytime working is usual and there are opportunities for part-time work.

Full-time posts usually follow the five-day week pattern, although there may be demands to work early mornings and evenings, and for on-call duties.

PROSPECTS

There are opportunities for physiotherapists working in the NHS to progress to senior and superintendent physiotherapist grades. Promotion routes extend into senior management positions. Training continues throughout their careers and physiotherapists may attend postgraduate courses. Some choose to become clinical specialists, rather than moving into management, and career paths are available for those taking this route. Research is a small but growing area and provides opportunities for experienced physiotherapists.

There are also opportunities to teach physiotherapy, once experience has been gained clinically in the profession. Prospective teachers are normally expected to have gained a higher degree.

RELATED OCCUPATIONS

Osteopath, chiropractor, radiographer, occupational therapist, speech therapist, teacher, nurse, prosthetist/orthotist.

FURTHER INFORMATION

The Chartered Society of Physiotherapy*, 14 Bedford Row, London WC1R 4ED

Institute of Sports Medicine, Burlington House, Piccadilly, London W1V 0LQ

FURTHER READING

Leaflets/booklets are available from the addresses marked*.

Job Outlines – Physiotherapy – COIC
Job Outlines – Working with Children – COIC
Working in Hospitals – COIC

In the careers library classified under JAN.

2. RADIOGRAPHER (JAP)

BACKGROUND INFORMATION

Radiography is a health care profession with two distinct branches of education and training: diagnostic and therapeutic. Both types of radiographer need considerable technological, anatomical, physiological and pathological knowledge to carry out their work.

THE WORK

Diagnostic radiographers are specialists who use ionizing radiation and other imaging techniques such as ultrasound, radioactive isotopes and magnetic resonance imaging. This helps doctors in the diagnosis of a wide range of diseases or injuries, or to monitor processes within the body. This could mean, for example, taking an X-ray of a suspected broken limb or an ultrasound scan to ensure all is well in pregnancy.

While most diagnostic radiographers carry out a range of procedures in their daily work, there are also opportunities to specialize in areas such as computerized tomography (CT) scanning, ultrasound, radionuclide imaging, and magnetic resonance imaging. Special post-qualifying courses are available in these areas.

Therapeutic radiographers administer radiation to patients, as prescribed by a doctor, to treat diseases such as cancer. Therapeutic radiographers often work with the same patients over a period of time and build relationships with them; diagnostic radiographers more often only see patients once. The therapeutic radiographer administers the radiotherapy treatment, keeps detailed records, and ensures that the patient's needs are looked after through liaison with other professionals in the team. Patient care is a vital part of therapeutic radiography.

WORK ENVIRONMENT

Most radiographers work in a hospital. The imaging or radiotherapy department is usually in a central position convenient to all referring departments and wards.

Diagnostic radiographers carry out most of their work in the hospital imaging department, but where necessary they work in wards and operating theatres using mobile units. Large modern hospitals have a series of X-ray rooms, each specially equipped for different procedures. Diagnostic radiographers often work alone on a specific procedure although they are part of a departmental team.

Therapeutic radiographers work almost exclusively in a radiotherapy department. Their work involves working closely with other colleagues, such as clinicians, physicists, nurses, and social workers.

SKILLS AND INTERESTS

Both diagnostic and therapeutic radiographers need the skill to deal with patients of all types and ages, some of whom will need reassuring about the radiographic procedures. They also need to be able to work with complex high-technology equipment. The work of all radiographers involves knowledge of the anatomy. Safe use of radiation and knowledge of the equipment and techniques are vital. A radiographer needs the ability to give great care and attention to detail, combined with the flexibility to treat each patient as an individual case.

The many new developments in radiographic techniques and treatments mean that radiographers are constantly learning new skills and the work is normally very varied.

ENTRY REQUIREMENTS

The minimum academic qualifications for a degree in Radiography are five GCSEs/S grades (A-C/1-3) and two/three other subjects at A level or four at H grade. English, maths or physics and another science are required. Alternative qualifications are also considered, such as Advanced GNVQs/GSVQs Level III. Individual education centres may require higher grades or specific subject requirements.

TRAINING

All radiography qualifying courses are at degree level and most are three-year honours degrees (except in Northern Ireland, where the course is a four-year honours degree). Students are normally based in a university and in clinical departments for an equal amount of time.

LATE ENTRY

There is no upper age limit for training but entrants require good health to undertake the physical requirements of the job. There is a special entry scheme for adults aged 21 years and over who do not hold the normal minimum entry requirements.

OPPORTUNITIES

The NHS employs 90 per cent of all radiographers, with other opportunities in private clinics and industry. There are about 17,500 state registered radiographers in the UK. The ratio of diagnostic to therapeutic radiographers is ten to one.

Radiographers who can speak an appropriate foreign language can often obtain jobs overseas. There are a small number of diagnostic radiographers in the Armed Forces.

The NHS has a formal career structure for radiographers. Promotion is by interview and based on merit. Once qualified, a radiographer can progress to senior radiographer. Radiographers in charge of departments are graded as superintendents. There are two grades of senior radiographer and four grades of superintendent radiographer. The grades are related to the level of skill or expertise, as well as the number of staff for whom a superintendent is responsible. The most senior posts are managerial posts.

There are courses designed to enhance promotion prospects. A number of postgraduate courses are available in areas such as medical ultrasound and radionuclide imaging. Radiographers who wish to go into teaching need teaching qualifications.

PAY AND CONDITIONS

Salaries for newly qualified staff in the NHS start at about £12,390 and rise to about £14,320. Staff working in the London area receive an additional London allowance. Senior radiographers grade II earn from £14,320 to £17,015 and Senior I from £17,015 to £19,490. Superintendent scales range from £17,015 at grade IV to £25,750 at grade I. NHS trust hospitals may set their own scales of pay and terms of employment.

Posts in private clinics do not normally offer higher salaries. Posts in industry might offer a higher salary but are normally only available to experienced radiographers. The Armed Forces pay radiographers a higher basic salary, linked to service grades, but do not provide for emergency payments.

Radiographers employed in the NHS normally work a five-day, 35-hour week. Diagnostic radiographers are normally required to participate in an on-call scheme, to provide cover for emergencies at night, weekends and during public holidays.

There are growing opportunities for both part-time work and for job sharing up to the most senior levels.

Annual leave starts at five weeks a year and increases by three days after ten years.

PROSPECTS

The NHS has a formal career structure for radiographers. Promotion is by interview and based on merit. There are courses designed to enhance promotion prospects. A large number of postgraduate courses are available in areas such as medical ultrasound, radionuclide imaging, clinical magnetic resonance and other specialities. There are also opportunities in university education and research.

RELATED OCCUPATIONS

Medical photographer, radiologist, medical physics technician, physiological measurements technician, nurse, medical laboratory technician.

FURTHER INFORMATION

The College of Radiographers*, 2 Carriage Row, 183 Eversholt Street, London NW1 1BU, 0171 391 4500

FURTHER READING

Leaflets/booklets are available from the address marked*.
Working in Hospitals – COIC
In the careers library classified under JAP.

3. OCCUPATIONAL THERAPIST (JAR)

BACKGROUND INFORMATION

Occupational therapists (OTs) treat patients with temporary or permanent physical or mental disability or mental illness. 'Activity' therapy might be a more accurate description of the treatment, which is designed to rehabilitate patients physically, psychologically and socially, and to help them become as self-reliant as possible. Much of the work is hospital-based but, increasingly, many OTs work for local authority social services departments, in the community and in patients' homes.

THE WORK

Occupational therapists (OTs) assist people to build up confidence and independence after injury, illness or disability, and adjust to everyday living. They assess and treat clients of all ages, through tests, interviews and practical tasks. OTs design treatments to increase clients' self-reliance, teach skills in self-care and offer activities suited to the person's lifestyle and interests. They enable clients who have problems to cope with work, leisure and everyday tasks. Occupational therapists help people with mental health problems gain confidence and a sense of purpose through group work, which improves memory and social skills, and workshop activities, which could lead to employment. They help elderly people look after themselves in their own homes or maintain full, meaningful lives in residential accommodation.

OTs give individual treatments and facilitate group work/ group treatments. Those who make home visits work with patients and their families, teaching them how to deal with and adjust to disability. Counselling both the client and the family is a major part of the job. Prevention of illness and promoting a healthy lifestyle are also inherent in the counselling process, as are planning and preparation for coping with increasing stages of illness (if the client has a deteriorating condition).

WORK ENVIRONMENT

Occupational therapists work as part of the health care team in hospitals and the community, in clinics, schools, day centres and patients' homes.

Some posts, involving local travel, require a driving licence.

SKILLS AND INTERESTS

In addition to their medical knowledge and practical skills, OTs must have good judgement – to make accurate assessments and plan courses of treatment – and have keen powers of observation. Their work brings them into contact with a wide range of people – health care workers and clients – so they need a sympathetic and understanding personality, good communication skills and the ability to encourage and teach both individuals and groups. They need energy and stamina.

ENTRY REQUIREMENTS

The minimum age to start training is 18 years.
The minimum academic qualifications for the degree in Occupational Therapy are two A levels plus five GCSEs (A-C) or three H grades plus five S grades (1-3). The passes should include English and a science subject. Alternative qualifications are also considered.

The requirements of individual schools vary and applicants are advised to consult prospectuses. A candidate's personal qualities are very important and are assessed at interview.

TRAINING

Occupational therapists must be state registered for employment in the NHS or in local authorities. This is attained by taking a degree in Occupational Therapy. Courses are three or four years full-time and are run by schools of occupational therapy based in universities. Students learn anatomy, physiology, psychology, psychiatry, the pathology of conditions that can be treated by OT, and practical skills and techniques. One third of the course is practical placement in a variety of clinical settings.

In England and Wales, graduates in relevant disciplines – preferably scientific – can, in some cases, take a shortened two-year course.

Occupational therapy helpers, who have qualified via further education courses, NVQs/SVQs, or have one year's supervised experience, may undertake a four-year in-service course leading to a degree which gives professional qualification and state registration (England and Wales).

LATE ENTRY

The minimum age for entry to training is 18 years. There is no maximum age limit. Adults are welcome to apply for training, and normal academic requirements may be relaxed to some extent for applicants with suitable experience. Applicants should be able to provide evidence of a broad general education, including science. Evidence of a recent study is usually expected, for example of A levels/H grades, Open University or access courses.

OPPORTUNITIES

The NHS is the largest employer of OTs. Experienced OTs can find work in local authority social services departments, in prisons and with voluntary organizations. Job opportunities are good; the demand for qualified OTs exceeds supply. An increasing number are self-employed in private practice.

PAY AND CONDITIONS

NHS salaries start at £12,145, rising to £14,040 in the basic grades. The next grade is Senior Grade II with a salary of £14,040 to £16,680, followed by Senior Grade I at £16,680 to £19,110. The most senior posts have salaries around £29,000, depending on opportunities and range of responsibilities.

NHS occupational therapists work a five-day, 36-hour week. Occasionally they have on-call, weekend and holiday duties. Conditions similar to these are usual with other employers of OTs. Part-time work and job share opportunities are available. Pay and conditions of service may vary in NHS trust hospitals.

PROSPECTS

There are a number of NHS management grades leading up to occupational therapy managers or professional managers responsible for OT services within a health district or trust. OTs with additional qualifications can move into teaching or research. The career path for OTs in local authority social services departments is less well defined. Most posts are held by OTs who have had NHS experience.

RELATED OCCUPATIONS

Music therapist, drama therapist, art therapist, speech and language therapist, physiotherapist, nurse, counsellor.

FURTHER INFORMATION

The College of Occupational Therapists*, Education Department, 6/8 Marshalsea Road, Southwark, London SE1 1HL, 0171 357 6480 (please include sae)

FURTHER READING

Leaflets/booklets are available from the address marked*.

Job Outlines – Occupational Therapy – COIC
Working in Social Work – COIC

In the careers library classified under JAR.

4. SPEECH AND LANGUAGE THERAPIST (JAS)

BACKGROUND INFORMATION

Speech and language therapists treat speech, language fluency and voice defects. The profession is closely linked to medicine, education and psychology. Speech and language therapists are responsible for the assessment, diagnosis and treatment of patients. Speech and language therapy should not be confused with elocution, which improves poor speech that is otherwise normal.

THE WORK

Patients may be referred to speech and language therapists by GPs, hospital consultants or teachers. Therapists deal with all types of communication problems, but mainly treat disorders of fluency, articulation, voice and language, that may be caused by congenital deformities (for example, a cleft palate, deafness, mental or physical disability) or may be acquired (for example, through illness and disease, psychological or neurological problems).

To assess patients' problems and devise remedial programmes, speech therapists spend a lot of time observing and getting to know the patients and gaining their confidence. When the cause of a problem is not obvious, the speech therapist has to use a combination of skills and personal qualities and relies upon medical and scientific knowledge (for example phonetics, psychology, anatomy, physiology, neurology and acoustics), acquired during training.

Much of the work is concerned with children, for instance those who are slow to talk, have stammers, or have hearing difficulties. Many of the children have learning difficulties or are physically disabled. A lot of work with adults involves the rehabilitation of people after accidents or illnesses. Someone who has had cancer of the larynx for example, must be taught to speak using the oesophagus or a speaking valve. A patient whose brain has been damaged by an accident or a stroke may have to re-learn how to speak or use a communication aid.

Speech and language therapists spend much of their time with individuals on a one-to-one basis, but they also organize group sessions for either adults or children.

They attend case conferences and liaise with other specialists, such as doctors, teachers, social workers and psychologists. They write reports and keep records, some of which are for the use of other professionals. Speech and language therapists counsel relatives to help them cope with the problems created by a patient's disability, so that they can assist with the treatment.

WORK ENVIRONMENT

Most speech and language therapists work for the NHS. Some work in one location, but many divide their time between clinics, hospitals, schools and patients' homes; their jobs therefore involve a lot of travelling. Those in rural areas may have to travel long distances.

SKILLS AND INTERESTS

An interest in and an aptitude for science are essential. Speech and language therapists must be effective communicators with clear, accurate speech, a sensitive ear and a good command of written English. Speech and language therapy is demanding and responsible and calls for understanding, patience and the ability to get on well with people and win their confidence.

The work can be very rewarding in terms of results; however, some patients recover very slowly and some do not recover at all. Speech and language therapists need a positive, encouraging approach, particularly where the treatment is long and difficult. They work on their own, arranging their schedules and deciding treatments, so they need initiative and good organizing skills.

ENTRY REQUIREMENTS

Entry to the profession is all graduate. The minimum educational requirements for a relevant degree course are: two A levels plus five GCSEs (A-C), or three H grades plus five S grades (1-3), including English or equivalent. Many colleges require an A level/H grade in a science – contact the Royal College of Speech and Language Therapists for details. Competition for student places is strong, and successful applicants normally have more than the minimum qualifications.

TRAINING

A speech and language therapist must be issued with a certificate-to-practise from the Royal College of Speech and Language Therapists, in order to practise in the NHS. There are two methods of achieving this:

1. By completing a recognized three or four-year honours degree course usually including an honours project; *or*

2. Candidates holding a degree (usually in a related subject, such as linguistics or psychology) can qualify by successfully completing a two-year postgraduate course. These are available at City University and University College London, Reading, Sheffield and Newcastle universities and all lead to a masters degree.

The courses combine theory and clinical practice; the theoretical work has a strong scientific bias. Subjects include psychology; phonetics and linguistics; anatomy and physiology, language pathology and therapeutics; acoustics; audiology; disorders of ear, nose and throat; education; neurology; orthodontics; plastic surgery; psychiatry; research methodology; and statistics and sociology.

Practical work includes visits to clinics, schools and hospitals and observing, assisting and working under the supervision of a qualified speech and language therapist. Students also have to prepare case studies.

Successful completion of a course makes students eligible for membership and registration by the Royal College of Speech and Language Therapists. They may then seek employment as qualified speech and language therapists. After qualifying there is a period of, normally, one year of supervised practice before members of the Royal College of Speech and Language Therapists enter the professional body's practice register.

LATE ENTRY

There are no age restrictions on entry to the profession, and mature students are accepted onto degree and postgraduate courses. Some colleges relax entry requirements and take relevant experience into account.

It is possible to take a career break and return to the profession. Refresher courses are available; it is essential to keep up with current knowledge and practices.

OPPORTUNITIES

Most speech and language therapists are employed by the NHS, usually based in clinics and responsible for a geographical area. There are some static posts in specialist hospital departments (for example ear, nose and throat clinics), or in special schools for mentally and physically disabled children. Some voluntary and charitable organizations offer employment, for example with disabled children or the hearing-impaired. Some therapists work in independent practice.

It may be possible to get health authority approval to work in private practice, but it would not normally be possible to make a living working solely in private practice.

PAY AND CONDITIONS

Salary scales for speech and language therapists range from £12,296 to £31,983.

Speech and language therapists in the NHS usually work 9am to 5pm, Monday to Friday. There are part-time posts available.

Terms and conditions of employment may differ for speech and language therapists working in NHS trust hospitals.

PROSPECTS

There is a promotion ladder that depends on ability and experience. Further qualifications are an advantage. There are good prospects for advancement in clinical and management fields. Experienced speech and language therapists can move into teaching or research.

RELATED OCCUPATIONS

Social worker, drama therapist, clinical psychologist, teacher, music therapist.

FURTHER INFORMATION

The Royal College of Speech and Language Therapists*, 7 Bath Place, Rivington Street, London EC2A 3DR, 0171 613 3855 (sae required)

FURTHER READING

Leaflets/booklets are available from the address marked*.
Job Outlines – Speech and Language Therapy – COIC
Job Outlines – Working with Children – COIC
Working in Hospitals – COIC
In the careers library classified under JAS.

5. CHIROPODIST/PODIATRIST (JAT)

BACKGROUND INFORMATION

Chiropodists, also known as podiatrists, diagnose and treat ailments, diseases and deformities of the foot and advise patients how to avoid a recurrence of some foot problems.

Patients can see a chiropodist without having to be referred by their GP, so chiropodists must be able to distinguish between conditions local to the foot and the symptoms of a general disease, for example a circulatory disease or metabolic disorder, which requires medical or surgical attention.

State registration is required of all chiropodists working in the NHS. To become state registered, candidates need to have successfully completed a degree course approved by the Council for Professions Supplementary to Medicine. It is possible to train at private schools of chiropody; however, these schools do not offer state registration.

THE WORK

Much of a chiropodist's time is spent dealing with superficial conditions such as corns, callosities, warts, bursae, blisters, abrasions, disorders of the toenails, bacterial and fungal infections of the skin, and other conditions brought about by systemic disease, for example chilblains, ulcers, cysts and ganglia. They also treat structural and functional disorders, which may be congenital, or abnormalities caused during the period while the foot is growing. The chiropodist can cure many conditions if treatment starts early, but for many elderly patients treatment is palliative.

Chiropodists use heat and cold treatments, hydrotherapy (exercising the foot in warm water), ultrasound and wax baths. They give massage, and treatment may include the use of active and passive exercises, drugs, analgesics, and fungicides or antiseptics. They make dressings and appliances to ease pressure or redistribute weight. Occasionally they perform skin or nail operations under local anaesthetic. Some also undertake minor surgery, for example involving bones of the toe. Chiropodists have an educative and advisory role; they give foot-care talks in schools and health centres, and counsel on footwear and hosiery.

WORK ENVIRONMENT

NHS chiropodists work in a variety of environments. They see patients in clinics, hospitals, health centres, mobile surgeries, schools, residential homes and they make house calls. They spend part of their day travelling and often work in rooms not ideally suited to their requirements. They keep in contact with doctors, nurses, other chiropodists and specialized professions. Private practitioners see patients by appointment in a rented surgery, or in their own homes, and they make house calls. Chiropodists employed in industrial and commercial organizations usually work in the organization's clinic or sick bay.

SKILLS AND INTERESTS

Chiropodists need patience and understanding, as many of the patients they treat are in pain or discomfort. The work calls for dexterity and good eyesight. Sharp observation and attention to detail are needed.

Chiropodists should be well-organized, able to work to an appointments system and deal with administrative work in an orderly way. They need the initiative to work on their own and to take responsibility for their own judgements. They should also be able to work as members of a health-care team.

ENTRY REQUIREMENTS

The minimum age of entry is 18 years.

State registration is required of all chiropodists working in the NHS.

To apply for state registration, candidates need to have successfully undertaken a degree course in chiropody, podiatry or podiatric medicine, approved by the Council for Professions Supplementary to Medicine.

Minimum entry requirements are five GCSEs/S grades with two A levels/three H grades. Subjects should include English and preferably two sciences. Some schools require higher qualifications and may prefer A level/H grade science. Alternative qualifications are also considered.

TRAINING

The degree course lasts for three years, full-time. Some centres plan to offer the course on a part-time basis. Courses combine theoretical and practical training.

Universities adopt their own course structure but, typically, in the first year, students follow an introductory life skills course; they study theoretical chiropody under supervision, and begin practical work, which occupies at least half the total training time. There is a written examination and a practical examination, during which students are assessed in diagnosis, operating skills, therapeutic procedures and chiropodial appliances.

In the second year, they study anatomy and physiology, particularly in relation to the foot. Written and oral examinations cover anatomy, physiology and chiropody; there is a practical examination.

In the third year, students study the principles of medicine and surgery, with emphasis on their application to foot disorders, and pedology (the detailed study of the foot in health and disease), aetiology (the science of the cause of disease), pathology, diagnosis of foot abnormalities, and theory and practice of therapeutics. There are written and oral examinations and two sessions of practical chiropody. Students have to present appliances they have made, with supporting case notes.

On successful completion of the degree course, candidates are eligible for state registration.

LATE ENTRY

Most chiropody training schools accept mature students and may waive their entry requirements if students have relevant experience.

OPPORTUNITIES

The Society of Chiropodists and Podiatrists has about 6,500 members. Most work for the NHS.

Most chiropodists take a first post within the NHS but move on to private practice, supplementing their income with NHS session work. There are a few full-time and part-time posts with industrial or commercial firms. The Armed Forces employ civilian chiropodists. Vacancy information can be obtained from the newsletters of the Society of Chiropodists and Podiatrists.

PAY AND CONDITIONS

Salaries for full-time NHS chiropodists range from £12,145 to £16,680 for senior grade II chiropodists, and £16,680 to £19,110 for those at senior grade I. A small number of senior posts have salaries up to about £27,920. There are London weighting allowances. NHS sessional rates vary according to the chiropodist's grade and the number of sessions worked. Terms and conditions of service may differ for chiropodists working in NHS trust hospitals. Private practitioners can earn considerably more than those in the NHS.

Most NHS chiropodists work a five-day, 37½-hour week, as the main groups of patients (children, elderly people, expectant mothers, hospital in-patients) are available during normal working hours. Chiropodists in private practice must expect to work long and irregular hours, since most of their patients are not available during the day. Many private practitioners supplement their income by doing a number of sessions for the NHS; they receive a fixed sum for a three-hour clinic. There are many opportunities for part-time work.

PROSPECTS

There is a formal promotion structure in the NHS, and in the higher grades work is both clinical and administrative; however, there are very few senior posts. There are very limited prospects for advancement in private practice. There is a formal promotion structure for chiropody teachers, but very few posts.

RELATED OCCUPATIONS

Nurse, orthotist/prosthetist, occupational therapist, physiotherapist, health visitor.

FURTHER INFORMATION

Society of Chiropodists and Podiatrists*, 53 Welbeck Street, London W1M 7HE, 0171 486 3381

Private (non-state registered) courses:

British Chiropody and Podiatry Association, New Hall, Bath Road, Maidenhead, Berkshire SL6 4LA, 01628 32440

Institute of Chiropodists*, 27 Wright Street, Southport, Merseyside PR9 0TL, 01704 546141 (please include sae)

FURTHER READING

Leaflets/booklets are available from the addresses marked*.

Job Outlines – Chiropody – COIC
Working in Nursing – COIC
Working in Social Work – COIC

In the careers library classified under JAT.

6. DIETITIAN (JAV)

THE WORK

Dietitians work in a wide range of settings, practically applying the science of nutrition to the diets of all groups of the population, from those who are sick through to preventing illness in the healthy person. Poor diet and ill health are closely linked to many present-day medical conditions, and dietitians play an important role in nutrition education, offering independent, consistent advice to health professionals, the public and many other agencies. In many ways, by encouraging people to look at the food they eat, one can help prevent disease and the dietitian has an important role to play in this aspect of health promotion. Dietitians also work with people who have illnesses or conditions that require major modification of their food intake. These 'special diets' can often be prescribed for life and it is important that people understand the implications of their diet from a person qualified to undertake this task.

The work is very diverse and varies according to which area of the profession the dietitian is employed in. The work of a dietitian must not be confused with that of a nutritionist. The latter name may be used by a dietitian practising outside the Health Service. However, a nutritionist is unlikely to call themselves a dietitian, as they must be state registered to operate in this capacity.

The main areas for employment for dietitians are as follows:

Within the National Health Service

Hospitals. In consultation with doctors, dietitians advise on therapeutic diets for patients, liaise with the catering department about their preparation, and ensure that all members of the care team – people such as the nurses and speech and language therapist – are aware of the implications of the diet. Dietitians are responsible for ensuring that the patient receives the appropriate therapeutic diet whilst in hospital, as well as advising them on the correct procedures to follow the diet at home. The dietitian's expertise is required in many areas of patient feeding. In some instances, this may be by tube feeding directly into the patient's stomach, looking at food consistency for those unable to chew, or by especially calculated diets for those on a kidney machine.

Within hospitals, the dietitian will be closely involved with general aspects of nutrition, for example, ensuring hospital menus provide healthy choices for patients and staff, education of medical staff about nutrition, as well promoting the important role food plays within a healthy lifestyle.

Many hospitals will have out-patient clinics. Patients may be referred to a dietitian by their GP or a consultant for a variety of reasons. They may be suffering from diabetes, intestinal disorders, allergies, weight problems (underweight or overweight) or heart disease. The dietitian helps and advises the patient in planning a suitable diet, bearing in mind their financial situation and any religious or cultural factors influencing diet. They may see up to 30 patients a day in this setting, although it is more usual for this to be a session of half that number of referrals.

Research. Within hospitals, dietitians may undertake varying areas of research that are diet or food-related. Such research involves working closely with other professionals, such as biochemists and statisticians. Dietitians may carefully analyse all the nutrients in a patient's diet, and measure its effect on the patient's health. They are involved with ensuring accurate diet histories are obtained and interpreting the results.

Community dietetics. Increasingly, the demand for dietetic expertise is required outside the hospital environment, within community settings. The service may be provided from a hospital nutrition and dietetic department, but more often today it is based within a community service. Dietitians working within the community are working with all groups of the population. However, they diversify into several different areas: the majority are either employed to undertake clinical out-patient work within general practice, being based in a health centre and providing training and support to all the members of the primary health care team, or they work solely in the area of nutrition education. As the demand for dietitians is high, they have to work as members of a multidisciplinary team, educating other health professionals, such as teachers, health visitors, social workers, home care workers. They will also be involved in the preparation of information packs and leaflets, covering many aspects of food, but especially healthy eating. These may be used by schools, residential homes for the elderly, community hospitals, etc.

Outside the National Health Service

The expertise of the dietitian outside the Health Service is highly valued and much sought after, such that the opportunities for employment are various and diverse. Dietitians may be employed in industry, by food manufacturers, public relations companies, trade associations. Many also work in a freelance capacity, working in the media, as consultants to outside bodies, in specialist areas such as sports nutrition and in private practice. Job opportunities also exist within higher education, teaching nutrition across a variety of courses, as well as training future dietitians.

WORK ENVIRONMENT

Dietitians may work in a variety of environments, depending on their specialism. The work may be performed within a hospital or health centre, and may involve travelling from place to place in the course of a day. Dietitians involved in research or working for a food manufacturer may be based in a laboratory. This usually involves less contact with people than work in a hospital or the community, where dietitians meet many people from a wide variety of backgrounds. The working conditions are generally good. Dietitians work as part of a team, and may work alongside other professionals such as nutritionists, biochemists, doctors, nursing and other staff allied to medicine, as well as care staff in the community.

SKILLS AND INTERESTS

Dietitians need an interest and ability in science, particularly chemistry, along with a practical approach to the work. An interest in diet and food is also important. Good verbal communication skills are very important in order to talk to people, both individually and in groups. Written communication skills are also important, as dietitians are often involved in writing leaflets and other material used in health education. Dietitians should enjoy working with people, and may need persuasive skills for those patients reluctant to change life-long patterns of eating. An understanding, non-judgemental approach is essential. Dietitians hoping to become managers need determination, resilience, and leadership qualities.

ENTRY REQUIREMENTS

Entry to the profession is all graduate. The entry requirements for a degree in Dietetics are five GCSEs/S grades (A-C/1-3), with two/three A levels (which may have to include chemistry and usually one other science subject, often specified as biology) or three/four H grades (including chemistry and one other science). Two AS levels may be offered as an alternative to one A level (not chemistry). A GCSE/S grade (A-C/1-3) in English is normally required if not passed at A level/H grade. Various institutions have other GCSE/S grade requirements, some specifying maths as essential. It is important to consult individual prospectuses, since the requirements vary between institutions, with some asking for Bs and Cs at A level/H grade. Alternative qualifications may also be considered; write to institutions for further information.

TRAINING

A dietitian must be registered by the Dietitians' Board of the Council for Professions Supplementary to Medicine in order to become state registered and practise in the NHS. Those who hold an approved degree or postgraduate diploma are eligible for registration. Two-year postgraduate diplomas are available to graduates holding degrees in other relevant subjects such as biochemistry or physiology.

Degree courses in dietetics, that include state registration, last four years in total. Sometimes the courses are integrated four-year BSc degrees; in other cases there is a three-year BSc degree followed by a postgraduate diploma lasting one to two years. Optional subjects vary between institutions; full details are given in prospectuses.

Subjects studied normally include human nutrition and dietetics, food and catering studies, sociology and psychology, biochemistry, physiology (the study of the structure and function of the human body), microbiology and medicine. Practical work forms an important part of all courses, with a period of practical training in a hospital undertaken by all students aiming for state registration. Management studies, quantitative methods, and interviewing and communication skills feature in most courses.

LATE ENTRY

Many institutions are prepared to consider mature applicants (over the age of 21 to 23 years) who do not have the traditional entry requirements. An approved access course in science may provide an appropriate bridge for the mature student, and colleges may consider mature students holding BTEC/SCOTVEC qualifications. Recent study of some sort is normally required, so that the college can assess whether the student has the necessary academic potential to complete a science degree. Relevant work experience, in a scientific, social, or health-related context, is useful in a profession where maturity is an asset.

OPPORTUNITIES

A significant number of dietitians work within the NHS, and a few are employed in private hospitals. There is also a widening area of opportunities for dietitians in many other fields, although these jobs often go to dietitians with experience, probably gained within the NHS.

Openings exist within food and pharmaceutical manufacturers and large caterers, as well as with promotional bodies such as the Meat and Livestock Commission. The Ministry of Agriculture, Fisheries and Food employs dietitians, who look at the nutritional quality of the food supply. Research is carried out by various bodies

employing dietitians, including the Medical Research Council.

An increasing number of dietitians work on a freelance basis, in an advisory or research capacity, and in this case are usually self-employed. If dietitians wish to work abroad, their skills and experience are valued in Third World countries, where they may work for an international relief agency or the Food and Agriculture Organization of the United Nations. British dietetic qualifications are not automatically recognized in the USA. In Australia or Canada, dietitians wishing to practise there may have to take examinations set in those countries. Opportunities are available in Europe for those who can offer the necessary language skills.

Dietetics is a small but rapidly expanding profession, expected to be the second of all professions to show significant growth within the NHS. Recently qualified staff should not experience difficulty in finding a first job, provided that they are prepared to be geographically mobile. Due to reorganization within the National Health Service there is significant demand for dietitians to work in the field of nutrition education within the community environment. Monthly lists of vacancies are published by the British Dietetic Association and circulated to members, but non-members can buy copies from the Association.

PAY AND CONDITIONS

Basic grade dietitians in the NHS start on an annual salary of around £12,490 and progress through four incremental points to £13,900. Senior dietitians grade 2 earn from £13,900 to £16,520, and seniors at grade 1 earn from around £16,520 to £18,920. At the top of the NHS ladder, dietitians can currently earn a maximum of almost £27,650. Dietitians also receive additional payments for on-call duties and training allowances.

NHS dietitians normally work a five-day 36½-hour week. Talks and lectures may involve occasional evening work, and dietitians working in the hospital environment may sometimes work on Saturdays. Dietitians whose work includes on-call duties sometimes work evenings and weekends. More flexible patterns of working are increasingly becoming established, with many opportunities for part-time and job share working.

NHS trust hospitals are increasingly setting their own scales on pay although at present they vary little from the above.

PROSPECTS

There is a formal career path for NHS dietitians, and a basic grade dietitian can expect a first promotion after about two years. Experienced dietitians (Senior II, Senior I, and Chief grades) either have clinical expertise, for example, in renal work, paediatrics, or community work, or they manage teams of dietitians. The dietetic manager or head of service is the top-grade post, and can hold responsibility for the whole dietetic service across a wide area. This is, however, now becoming less common, with the advent of trusts. A dietetic manager is normally responsible for staff only working within his/her unit or trust rather than across several trusts (provider units). A dietitian can also enter full-time teaching or lecturing, or move into health service management.

Whilst working within the profession, dietitians may take

various post-registration training courses, for example in paediatrics or care of elderly people. Dietitians wishing to teach may take the City and Guilds Teaching Certificate or a Health Education Diploma.

RELATED OCCUPATIONS

Health visitor, home economist, food scientist/technologist, health education officer, nurse, pharmacist.

FURTHER INFORMATION

The British Dietetic Association, 7th Floor Elizabeth House, 22 Suffolk Street, Queensway, Birmingham B1 1LS, 0121 643 5483

FURTHER READING

Job Outlines – Dietetics – COIC
In the careers library classified under JAV.

MEDICAL TECHNICAL OFFICER
CLCI:JOB

BACKGROUND INFORMATION

As medical technology is growing, so hospitals are using an increasingly wide range of complex equipment to diagnose and treat illness and then monitor the results of the treatment. The technologists and technicians who are responsible for operating and/or maintaining this equipment usually specialize in a particular area of work, with responsibility for a particular type of equipment.

Medical technical officers specialize either in **medical physics** or **physiological measurement**. **Medical technologists** (previously known as medical physics technicians) specializing in radiation protection, lasers, clinical instrumentation or engineering may have little or no patient contact; those specializing in radiotherapy, ultrasound, renal dialysis or nuclear medicine have a high rate of patient contact, dealing with them in a clinical situation and even, in the case of patients being treated by home dialysis, at the patient's home. They are involved in the research and development of new techniques and apparatus, the monitoring of its performance, the maintenance and service of the specialized equipment, together with some aspects of its operation. They work closely with scientists within the medical physics department and with medical staff.

Physiological measurement technicians (sometimes known as physiological measurement technologists), usually specializing in audiology, cardiology, neurophysiology or respiratory physiology, work closely with patients – measuring the capacity of various parts of the body to function – to help medical staff diagnose and treat diseases.

THE WORK

Medical technologists

Radiotherapy is one of the main treatments of cancer. A beam of radiation is directed at the tumour while the other areas of the body are protected. Medical technologists construct devices to hold the patient in the correct position during treatment and make masks and shields to ensure that areas of the patient are protected from radiation – vitally important in directing radiation beams at the affected area and away from the rest of the body. The tumour is thus treated in the safest and most effective way. Some technologists are involved in treatment planning, making sure that the doses of radiation given to the patient are accurate. The equipment used in planning and administering treatment to the patient in the radiotherapy department is maintained by medical technologists who work within the engineering specialities.

Radiation protection is a separate speciality, in which medical technologists are responsible for ensuring the safety of staff and patients. They carry out frequent tests and measurements to monitor the exposure levels of staff in radiotherapy and of patients and staff in nuclear medicine and diagnostic radiology, making sure that radiation doses are kept to a minimum and that staff follow safe working practices.

Ultrasound uses sound waves to monitor functions and identify abnormalities within the body. It is best known for its use with pregnant women, showing an image of the unborn baby on the screen to check the progress of development, but it is also used to study tissue structure, blood flow and other physiological functions. Medical

technologists working in this speciality offer routine technical support and back-up to the medical staff, sometimes becoming involved in research and development projects.

Nuclear medicine involves small amounts of radioactive material being introduced into the patient. The medical technologist may be responsible for preparing and purifying radioactive materials safely and for administering them to the patient. The patient is then positioned by the technician in front of a gamma scanner or radioactivity camera to measure the concentration and distribution of the radioactive material inside the patient's body, testing the uptake of a specific organ. The distribution and uptake of the radioactive material gives a good indication of organ function. It is also the technologist's job to safely and accurately dispose of these small tracer samples of radioactive material.

Engineering for medical technologists may involve electronic or mechanical specialization. Medical technologists are involved in the development, construction and maintenance of the specialized equipment that is used by clinicians within the medical physics department and throughout the hospital. Their work ranges from regular calibration, fault diagnosis, servicing and safety checks to designing and building particular pieces of apparatus. Bioengineering involves the development of artificial replacements for parts of the body that no longer work – such a hip or knee joints – or adaptations to help people with disabilities.

Clinical instrumentation demands considerable knowledge of electronics, using basic engineering skills to construct or adapt equipment or instruments. Some medical technologists may choose to specialize and work mainly in departments using X-ray equipment, lasers or ultrasonic equipment.

Renal dialysis involves an artificial kidney machine pumping a patient's blood, containing waste products, through miles of ultra-thin tubing so that only the waste products diffuse to the waste fluid. Medical technologists must continually check the pumps and electronic circuitry for accurate functioning and make sure that the dialysis fluid is of the correct composition. When repair is necessary, the technologist removes the apparatus to the workshop to correct faults. If equipment fails at a patient's home, the technologist visits, diagnoses the fault, replaces or repairs the part, and instructs the patient or family on how to operate the equipment and avoid the fault in future.

Lasers are increasingly used in ophthalmology, surgery and gynaecology to burn away tiny quantities of diseased tissue or repair torn tissue in otherwise inaccessible organs. The accuracy of the machinery must be very high and it is the responsibility of the medical technologist to check, maintain and calibrate it.

Physiological measurement technicians

Audiology involves the measurement and evaluation of people's hearing capacity. If a child or adult is suspected of having a hearing problem, the audiology technician's subsequent measurements will enable the medical staff to diagnose and prescribe the appropriate treatment. Audiology technicians also test balance and auditory-evoked potentials (electrical responses in the brain to test sounds). Another aspect of the work is to test and fit hearing aids and teach people how to benefit most from them; rehabilitation and counselling are an important part of the job. Technicians make minor adjustments to hearing aids and take impressions of the ear so that they can prepare specially moulded ear inserts.

Cardiology technicians work with patients who either have, or are suspected of having, heart disease. They measure the electrical activity of the heart, recording its electrical changes by fitting disposable electrodes onto the patient's limbs and linking them with wires to the ECG (electrocardiograph) machine to pick up the heartbeat. The machine reads the impulses and prints out a graph chart. Any irregularities are shown up and the doctor can decide on the correct course of action. Twenty-four-hour 'ambulatory' readings may be taken if a problem does not show up instantly, using a portable monitor and an audio tape. People with intermittent heart problems may be given a cardio-memo machine, which records the problem when it occurs. The patient then rings the technician and transmits the recording down the telephone line, for interpretation. In addition, cardiology technicians may give a 'stress test', where the patient walks on a 'conveyor belt' whilst linked up to monitors. The technician watches the trace of the heart and takes the blood pressure at regular intervals. Ultrasound may also be used to aid diagnosis. Having seen the results of the tests, the medical staff identify the problem and its severity, and decide on a course of action. Cardiology technicians monitor patients who have electronic pacemakers to regulate their heartbeat, making sure that they are working efficiently. They also may be called upon to monitor the condition of a patient's heart during surgery, or in the intensive therapy unit.

Neurophysiology involves the measurement and recording of the electrical activity of the brain and central nervous system. The physiological measurement technician monitors the measurements by using electrodes placed on the outside of the patient's head to transmit information to an EEG (electroencephalograph) machine. The results are recorded and printed out onto paper. An abnormal pattern may indicate disease. The EEG technician may also record evoked potentials, that are produced by the brain in response to specific stimuli.

Respiratory physiology refers to the functioning of a patient's breathing system. The respiratory physiology technician takes measurements that reflect the function and efficiency of the patient's breathing system. Patients are normally referred to the department with breathing problems, chest pain or abnormality on a chest X-ray. The tests vary in complexity. Usually, patients breathe into a mouthpiece attached to the equipment used by the technician to measure and record the volume of the lungs and how well they transfer gas; alternative tests could combine exercise studies and circulatory measurements in more complicated procedures. Respiratory technicians also analyse respiratory gas and do blood gas analysis. Computer technology is being used increasingly for test calculations.

WORK ENVIRONMENT

Technologists and technicians work within different hospital departments, according to their speciality. Radiation technologists, for instance, may work closely with medical physicists in laboratories, or spend much of their time in the hospital basement; those specializing in clinical instrumentation may work in clinical departments around the hospital, but are usually based in a workshop that contains the necessary sophisticated tools and instruments; engineering technologists may work in any department where there is electronic equipment; cardiology and respiratory technicians work in clinical departments, out-patient clinics or on wards; neurophysiology technicians in some hospitals may work on clinical departments, wards, intensive therapy units or operating theatres; audiology technicians spend much of their time with patients in out-patient clinics.

SKILLS AND INTERESTS

Technologists working in medical physics need to be responsible and meticulous since the medical staff rely on them to ensure that the equipment gives the most accurate results.

Manual dexterity is required to set up, operate and maintain complex equipment. Accuracy is needed in reading the equipment.

Technologists and technicians need to communicate effectively with patients and staff. They carry out tests on patients who may be anxious and unwell; it is important to be sympathetic and reassuring whilst ensuring that the tests are carried out fully and accurately. They need to be calm and competent, so that patients may have complete confidence in them.

ENTRY REQUIREMENTS

There are no formal entry requirements but employers usually require a minimum of either: four GCSEs/S grades (A-C/1-3) in English, maths and two science subjects or a double science award; or a relevant BTEC first award, eg science; or appropriate SCOTVEC national certificate modules; or a relevant Intermediate GNVQ/GSVQ Level II, eg science. These are the minimum requirements for entry to the BTEC National Certificate in Medical Physics and Physiological Measurement. Some employers may accept lower qualifications and arrange for entrants to take suitable courses to bring them to this standard.

Some entrants in engineering or clinical instrumentation have either: BTEC National Certificate/Diploma or SCOTVEC National Certificate in Electronics or Electrical/Electronic Engineering; or Intermediate GNVQ/GSVQ Level II in Engineering; or A levels/H grades. Some enter on completing a higher national award or degree in science or engineering. Physiological measurement technicians are usually age 18 or over on entry, because of the amount of direct contact with patients.

Entry may be possible for young people through Modern Apprenticeships leading to at least an NVQ/SVQ Level 3. Contact your local careers office, TEC/LEC for details.

TRAINING

Trainee technologists and technicians undertake a programme of in-service training related to their particular specialism. They also gain an insight into other specialisms. Training is mainly in the practical skills of the specialism but also includes lectures from senior technologists and technicians, scientists and medical staff.

Trainees specialising in physiological measurement, radiotherapy, radiation protection, ultrasound or nuclear medicine usually attend a college of further education part-time, on day release or block release, to work towards the BTEC National Certificate in Medical Physics and Physiological Measurement or the SCOTVEC Certificate in Medical Science. Areas studied include: physics, maths, medical physics and physiological measurement techniques, medical instrumentation, human physiology, core sciences, using computers and common skills.

Most trainee neurophysiology technicians also sit Part 1 of

the professional examination organized by the Electroencephalography and Clinical Neurophysiology Educational Board. There is also a two-year full-time course available to trainee neurophysiology technicians.

Trainee audiology technicians sit examinations set by the British Association of Audiology Technicians. A few hospitals run full-time courses for audiology technicians, rather than sending them to a college of further education.

Trainee cardiology technicians also sit either the associate membership examination organized by the Society of Cardiological Technicians, or the national training assessment examination, Part 1.

Respiratory technicians can take the in-service training examination set by the Association of Respiratory Technicians and Physiologists.

Entrants with relevant BTEC/SCOTVEC higher national awards, or degrees, complete a period of in-service training, rather than study for the BTEC national diploma or SCOTVEC certificate.

There are a few opportunities each year in England for supernumerary trainees, who are employed by a regional health authority rather than a hospital. They spend time in different departments over two years while attending the BTEC course, after which they decide on their specialism. Shortpost-qualification courses are available.

NVQs/SVQs in Health Care – Physiological Measurement are available at Level 3 in audiology, neurophysiology and respiratory physiology.

Modern Apprenticeships are designed for some young people entering work as audiology technicians, neurophysiology technicians and respiratory physiology technicians. Apprentices work towards the appropriate NVQ at Level 3 and the BTEC National Certificate in Medical Physics and Physiological Measurement. Apprenticeships are not for a set length of time but are likely to last for between two-and-a-half and three years. Contact your local careers office or TEC for details.

LATE ENTRY

Many technologists and technicians are recruited straight from school or college, although an increasing number enter as graduates. Physiological measurement technicians are not usually recruited under age 18. There is no upper age limit for entry to the profession.

OPPORTUNITIES

The majority of medical technologists and physiological measurement technicians work for the NHS. Most work with large and expensive equipment, found only in the bigger district or teaching hospitals; audiology technicians may work in any size of hospital or in community clinics. A few technologists and technicians are employed by the

Armed Forces, particularly the RAF. Vacancies are advertised in local newspapers, trade journals and scientific publications such as *New Scientist.*

PAY AND CONDITIONS

There are fixed pay scales for NHS employees, negotiated annually. There is one trainee grade and five other Medical Technical Officer (MTO) grades. All MTO posts are allocated to specific pay scales within a pay spine. Trainees' pay starts at £6,562 rising to £8,019. The salaries of qualified MTOs (grades MTO 1-5) range from £8,886 to £28,592.

NHS trust hospitals may set their own scales of pay and terms of employment.

Most technologists and technicians work a five-day, 37-hour week. This may include some weekend or on-call duties. There can be some overtime work in emergencies.

There are opportunities for part-time work, especially for audiology technicians who see patients by appointment.

PROSPECTS

To apply for promotion to senior MTO, applicants must have had at least three years' experience at basic grade. The next step is to chief MTO, a job that brings responsibility for planning, administration and training. Top of the scale is the senior chief or principal – managing a department.

RELATED OCCUPATIONS

Radiographer, medical laboratory assistant, laboratory technician, prosthetist/orthotist, pharmacy technician.

FURTHER INFORMATION

Association of Medical Technologists, Medical Physics Department, Royal Hospital, Wolverhampton WV2 1BT

British Society of Audiology*, (Audiology Technicians Group), 80 Brighton Road, Reading, Berkshire RG6 1PS (please include 29p sae), 01734 660622

Cardiothoracic Measurement Department, Derbyshire Royal Infirmary, London Road, Derby DE1 2QY, 01332 47141 ext 2252

Health Service Careers, PO Box 204, London SE5 7ES

Scottish Office Home and Health Dept, Police Division, Room 364A, St Andrew's House, Edinburgh EH1 3DG, 0131 244 2156

FURTHER READING

Leaflets/booklets are available from the address marked*.
Working in Hospitals – COIC
Working in Physics – COIC

In the careers library classified under JOB.

AMBULANCE PERSON CLCI:JOC

BACKGROUND INFORMATION

Ambulance services are often associated with emergency 999 calls to road accidents and major disasters, or to people suffering sudden illness or injury. However, this forms only a small, though very important, part of ambulance service work. The majority of calls are to non-urgent cases, such as elderly patients, who need ambulance transport to and from hospital and daycare centres.

There are 67 ambulance services in the UK; there is no national ambulance service, so there are some differences between individual services, particularly in recruitment and training patterns. The following sections describe common features; further information on local requirements can be obtained from local chief executives/ambulance officers.

THE WORK

All ambulance personnel spend most of their time working with people – patients, hospital staff, members of other services or agencies. Features common to the work of all personnel are: lifting and carrying patients; answering queries from patients, medical staff, etc; checking/replenishing stocks of first aid equipment and other supplies; basic vehicle checks (oil, water, tyre pressure); filling up with petrol; ambulance cleaning; completing log sheets.

Ambulance personnel sometimes work in pairs, one driving the ambulance, the other attending to patients' needs.

In most services, operational ambulance personnel are divided into three main grades: care assistants, technicians and paramedics. There are considerable differences in the levels of skill and range of tasks carried out by each grade.

Ambulance care assistants, sometimes known as dedicated day transport personnel, are mainly concerned with transporting infirm, disabled, mentally ill, elderly patients, or patients unable to get to and from hospital out-patient clinics, day centres, etc. They help patients into the ambulance and make sure they are secure and comfortable – fastening safety straps and seat belts, wrapping blankets around patients where necessary. Care assistants often enter the patient's home – particularly when the patient is elderly – to help the patient to the ambulance. While in the patient's home, care assistants may carry out simple safety checks, such as making sure the gas is turned off, or that the doors are locked. Assistants sometimes help with patient care in hospital units – carrying out nursing auxiliary duties – as well as undertaking ambulance work.

Ambulance technicians are involved in the full range of accident and emergency duties. They respond to 999 calls for assistance at road traffic accidents and other emergencies and incidents. They are also called on by GPs who require ambulance transport for urgent cases, and their services are needed for the admission, transfer and discharge of patients requiring skilled treatment – such as the administration of oxygen – whilst travelling by ambulance.

Technicians need to be able to make decisions about the treatment and movement of patients; this involves making provisional diagnoses. They give emergency treatment, such as splinting broken bones or using various types of life-saving equipment; these include ventilators, which introduce air into the lungs, or semi-automatic defibrillators, used to restore a co-ordinated rhythm to the heart.

Ambulance paramedics are technicians who have taken significant additional training, and are qualified to use the more advanced forms of life support equipment. They may, for example, administer intravenous infusion (setting up a drip to introduce substances into the patient's bloodstream) and endotrachial intubation (introducing a tube into the throat to create an airway). They are also qualified in coronary care, and may administer drugs in certain situations.

Both technicians and paramedics complete patient report forms, for the use of medical staff; these describe signs, symptoms and any actions that have been taken.

Control room assistants work in ambulance stations or central control units, answering emergency and urgent calls from GPs and the public, and maintaining radio contact with ambulance crews. They operate switchboards, receive and pass on messages, and use other communications equipment, such as computer terminals, fax machines and telex. Assistants may also be involved in planning ambulance crew journeys.

WORK ENVIRONMENT

Ambulance crew spend the majority of their time in vehicles, on the move. They start the working day at the ambulance station, and may return there in mid-shift for a meal break. Throughout the shift they are in radio contact with their control room. Technicians and paramedics work nights, and this may involve being outside in the dark, in all weather conditions – for example, at the scene of an accident. Physically, ambulance work is strenuous, involving heavy lifting, carrying and bending.

Ambulance personnel wear uniforms, and protective clothing for emergency work and where appropriate.

SKILLS AND INTERESTS

Ambulance personnel should enjoy working with people from a variety of backgrounds. A friendly personality is important, together with the ability to deal tactfully and compassionately with sick and injured people. Understanding and patience are essential.

A clear voice and good spoken communication skills are necessary for communicating with patients, hospital staff, representatives of other emergency services and organizations such as social services. Written communication skills are also required, particularly at technician and paramedic level, for completing patient report forms and for formal study on training courses.

A responsible attitude, reliability and punctuality are essential. A smart appearance is required, to inspire the public's trust and confidence.

It is important to be able to remain calm in crises and to be able to cope with distressing sights and situations. It is also necessary to take decisions about the treatment and movement of patients and to be responsible for the results of those decisions.

Ambulance personnel need to be physically fit, and capable of lifting and moving patients. Their weight and body size should be proportionate to their height.

Control room assistants need to be able to communicate clearly, both orally and in writing. Good eyesight and hearing are important. Keyboard skills are an advantage and may be required in some services.

ENTRY REQUIREMENTS

For ambulance crew, the minimum age is usually BETWEEN 18-21 years, although in some areas there are cadet schemes for 16 and 17-year-olds.

Applicants for entry as ambulance care assistants, aged 18 or over, need a full, clean, current driving licence. Experience of working with the elderly or disabled, or in a caring capacity, may be required. The selection process involves an interview and series of tests. Before the interview, applicants are sent a booklet on medical care, which they are expected to study; the assessment process includes questions on this material. Candidates are also tested on basic maths, English, manual dexterity, driving and knowledge of the Highway Code. They must pass a medical examination, including a test of normal colour vision.

In some ambulance services, direct entry as a technician is possible. The selection process is the same as for care assistants, but some employers require four GCSEs/S grades (A-C/1-3), preferably including English, maths and a science subject.

Academic entry requirements for cadet schemes vary, as they are set by individual ambulance services. Four GCSEs/S grades (A-C/1-3), preferably including English, maths and a science subject, are advantageous.

It is possible to enter as a control room assistant at a minimum age of 16-18 years, and to transfer to ambulance duties after reaching the age of 18-21 years. Applicants should have good communication skills and VDU experience – they may have to pass a test of keyboard skills.

TRAINING

Ambulance care assistants start by taking an in-house course, usually lasting for between two and four weeks. The course covers: basic health and safety at work; first aid; the role of the ambulance service in the community; ambulance driving; working with patients (including techniques for lifting and carrying); and sometimes experience in a hospital.

Ambulance technicians have normally completed the care assistant training course and gained experience in that position. Technician training starts with an eight-week residential course at a regional ambulance training school. Six weeks of the course are spent on the study of patient care, anatomy, physiology, diagnosis, treatment, casualty management, basic midwifery and related subjects. For the remaining two weeks, trainees receive instruction in advanced driving techniques.

The residential course is followed by twelve months' experience in the full range of accident and emergency work, with continuous assessment and exams at the end of the twelve-month period. Those who successfully complete the course and assessments, gain the National Ambulance Proficiency Certificate awarded by the National Health Service Training Directorate.

Paramedics. Those who have completed a minimum of twelve months' post-qualifying experience in the full range of ambulance duties, as ambulance technicians, are eligible to be selected for paramedic training. The selection process involves an interview with clinical staff and ambulance officers, and a written and practical examination in ambulance aid.

Those who are selected for paramedic training take a four-week intensive course at a nationally accredited training centre. The course covers advanced anatomy and physiology, with particular reference to the nervous, cardiovascular and respiratory systems, and training in the use of advanced life-saving equipment. The course is divided into modules of one week and three weeks, each followed by examinations of theory and practical procedure. After the course, there are four weeks of hospital training, supervised by clinical and medical consultants, which includes experience in different hospital departments. Successful completion of the course modules and hospital training, plus assessment by the Chairman of the local Ambulance Paramedic Advisory Council, leads to the Certificate for Ambulance Paramedic Skills, awarded by the National Health Service Training Directorate.

Cadet schemes are run by some ambulance services. The schemes usually last two years and include on and off-the-job training. Typically, they include driving instruction, outward bound courses, community projects, co-operative work with the police and fire service cadets, experience in hospitals and different departments within the ambulance service, and a trip abroad to observe how another country's ambulance service operates. Trainees may also study at a regional training centre for the licentiate grade examinations of the Ambulance Service Institute.

Some cadet schemes are linked to a five-year programme, enabling a person who enters as a 16-year-old cadet to become a fully qualified ambulance paramedic by the age of 21 years.

Ambulance Service Institute qualifications are not essential for ambulance personnel, but they are advantageous, particularly for staff who intend to train as paramedics, and for promotion to supervisory and management grades. Serving personnel (other than cadets) usually study for the examinations via distance learning courses. The Institute awards qualifications at four levels: licentiate, associate, graduate, and fellow.

Updating courses: ambulance personnel take further courses, to learn new skills and keep up with technical developments, at regular intervals throughout their careers.

Control room assistants receive on-the-job training in the use of switchboards, radio communications and other control room equipment.

LATE ENTRY

Ambulance work is often a second job, and employers recruit applicants who are over the minimum entry age of 18 years. Previous experience in nursing or with the elderly is an advantage, although recruits to ambulance services come from a wide range of backgrounds. The age range is about 18 to 55 years. However, because of the length of training, it is likely to be more difficult for people over the age of about 35 to 40 years to be selected for training as technicians and paramedics.

OPPORTUNITIES

The National Health Service employs about 15,000 operational ambulance personnel; the total number of people employed by ambulance services, including officers, is about 18,000.

The UK's ambulance services are usually run by district health authorities or NHS trusts.

Apart from the NHS, there are opportunities to train in ambulance work in HM Forces. Other employers include private ambulance services, catering for private hospitals, and large industrial firms that sometimes run small on-site ambulance services. Private sector employers usually engage staff with NHS training and experience.

Overall, employment in ambulance services is stable. The availability of vacancies varies in different parts of the country, with greater demand for staff in London and South East England. In rural districts and areas of high unemployment, there is likely to be considerable competition for vacancies. If an application to the local ambulance service is unsuccessful, it may be worth applying to an ambulance service in another area.

There are occasional opportunities to work overseas, for instance with Voluntary Service Overseas (VSO).

PAY AND CONDITIONS

Salaries vary between different services. Most entrants of 18 years or over start as ambulance care assistants, earning a salary of around £11,000 (pro-rata for part-timers). Ambulance technicians and paramedics earn around £14,000. London staff receive an additional London allowance.

Additional hours over and above the normal working week are paid, but at the basic rate.

Ambulance personnel work a 39 or 40-hour week. Ambulance care assistants usually work days, Monday to Friday; starting and finishing times vary. Many care assistants work part-time. Ambulance technicians and paramedics work a rotating shift pattern, including nights and weekends. In remote areas, additional stand-by and on-call duties may be required.

Control room assistants also work a 39 or 40-hour week. Some work days; others work rotating shifts.

Rates of pay and conditions of service may vary in NHS trusts.

PROSPECTS

All ambulance staff are eligible for promotion if they have the potential and meet the required criteria. Supervisory work involves responsibility for a group of staff. There are further opportunities to progress to management grades – specializing in operations, control room communications, training or administration.

The majority of senior management have risen through the ranks.

In some services, control room assistants can be promoted through various grades and reach management level without gaining operational ambulance experience. Other services require control room assistants to gain experience as care assistants/technicians before they can be considered for more senior posts.

RELATED OCCUPATIONS

Nurse, health care assistant/nursing auxiliary, care assistant, fire-fighter/officer, coastguard officer, police constable, hospital porter.

FURTHER INFORMATION

Contact the local chief executive/ambulance officer for further information; the address can be found in the telephone directory.

London Ambulance Service*, Personnel Department, 220 Waterloo Road, London SE1 8SD,

FURTHER READING

Leaflets/booklets are available from the address marked*.

In the careers library classified under JOC.

ALTERNATIVE/COMPLEMENTARY MEDICINE: JOD

1. ACUPUNCTURIST CLCI:JOD
2. AROMATHERAPIST CLCI:JOD
3. CHIROPRACTOR CLCI:JOD
4. HERBALIST CLCI:JOD
5. HOMOEOPATH CLCI:JOD
6. NATUROPATH CLCI:JOD
7. OSTEOPATH CLCI:JOD
8. REFLEXOLOGIST CLCI:JOD

BACKGROUND INFORMATION

Many of the therapies profiled in this article see themselves as complementary to conventional medicine, rather than as an alternative to it. They are complementary to each other as well, since different therapies may be seen as more appropriate for different patients, as well as conditions. They are sometimes called natural therapies, as their aim is to work with natural processes.

Complementary medicine can be described as holistic, which means it takes the whole person into account, examining their physical, mental, emotional and spiritual state. The patient's physical, social and personal environment is also taken into consideration. Holistic practitioners may encourage patients to take responsibility for changing elements in their life which may be contributing to their affliction – such as their posture or the amount of exercise they take. Often patients present chronic conditions.

On completion of training, practitioners become eligible for membership of a professional association with its own register, code of ethics and disciplinary procedures. Current changes mean both osteopaths and chiropractors are soon likely to have national registers regulated by law, the others remain voluntary.

GPs may refer patients for complementary treatment, especially from fund-holding practices, as long as they remain in charge of the patient. Most therapies are available privately, although homoeopathy has been available on the NHS since 1948. Interest in complementary medicine has increased in recent years.

THE WORK

1. Acupuncturist

Acupuncturists aim to regulate their patients' body functions and promote the restoration of health using methods from a system of medicine which originated in China thousands of years ago. As well as therapeutic acupuncture, some acupuncturists offer acupuncture anaesthesia, and ear acupuncture, a system to help people overcome addictions.

The main method used is insertion of very fine stainless steel needles into particular points beneath the skin. Sometimes the acupuncturist may treat these points by moxibustion – warming them with a burning aromatic herb (moxa or dried mugwort) – or by massaging them. The underlying theory is that the body has a network of channels (or meridians) along which vital energy (chi) flows. The acupuncturist aims to reduce or increase the flow as required by the stimulation that the inserted needles, or other methods, provide.

Acupuncturists take full case histories from their patients, including their food preferences and emotional reactions to various situations, to get a whole picture before they start a diagnosis. Then they take a series of pulse measurements on the patient's wrist and may examine their tongue. A recent technological introduction to the art is electro-acupuncture, where a machine examines the points on the patient's body, although many acupuncturists prefer to do their examinations by hand.

2. Aromatherapist

Aromatherapists treat a variety of conditions using essential oils extracted or distilled from flowers, trees, herbs, spices and fruit. Practitioners often massage their clients with these oils (blended with carrier vegetable oils), although they can be used in baths or inhaled.

The aromatherapist takes a detailed personal and medical history of the client, often covering areas such as diet, exercise, environmental factors, allergy and emotional problems. From this, the essential oils to be used in treatment are selected and administered in the way the aromatherapist thinks is most appropriate. Different oils are used, depending on the complaint, for instance to alleviate skin disorders, relieve stress or aid blood circulation.

3. Chiropractor

Chiropractors specialize in mechanical disorders of joints, especially of the spine. They use a wide range of manipulative techniques to improve movement and relieve pain and muscle spasm. In addition, they may offer advice about exercise, lifestyle and work. The history of chiropractic has roots in ancient Hindu and Chinese manuscripts.

Chiropractors take a detailed medical history of their patients, followed by a physical examination, which may include X-rays, blood samples and neurological examinations. They examine the patient's spine and joints with their hands, observing mobility and any changes in tissue. Treatment comprises of a wide range of adjusting and supporting techniques, taking the form of twists and pulls, with the practitioner and patient in different positions.

4. Herbalist

Herbalists use plant remedies to treat disease. Western pharmaceutical drugs use only the 'active' part of a plant, either concentrated or synthesized, while herbal drugs use extracts of the whole plant to achieve a more balanced effect. Herbal remedies include infusions (made like tea), tablets, liquids and lotions.

Herbalists take detailed medical histories, offer advice about diet and lifestyle, and prescribe herbal remedies for the specific complaint. While qualified herbalists treat a wide range of complaints, they also refer patients to a doctor or another therapist, where appropriate.

Herbal medicine is known as phytotherapy in Europe. Practitioners may specialize in the western tradition, using plants from all over the world, or in the Chinese tradition, using mainly Chinese herbs.

5. Homoeopath

Homoeopaths use a system of medicine, based on a Law of Similars, to treat disease with substances which produce similar symptoms in healthy people. The idea is to use very minute quantities of substances to stimulate the body's own natural healing powers. Homoeopathy aims to treat the underlying cause of a disease, rather than just its symptoms.

Homoeopaths take a wide range of detailed personal and medical information from their patients. They then prescribe remedies, normally in the form of a pill, suited to the individual patient and their illness. Remedies are usually derived from vegetable substances, but both animal and mineral substances are used as well. These substances are increasingly diluted and vigorously shaken in water and alcohol.

6. Naturopath

Naturopaths work on the basis that the body naturally knows how to heal itself, but that most people are out of touch with the knowledge, pointing to animals' instinctive tendency to fast or eat foods with healing properties when they are sick. In the naturopath's view, disease may be caused by congenital or developmental factors, or the patient's environment or diet, as well as by infection or trauma. Naturopaths use standard medical examination procedures to diagnose conditions and assess the patient's potential for health and vital reserves.

The naturopath's main work is to promote the body's own self-healing systems. This work often involves giving advice about nutrition, exercise and rest. Hydrotherapy may also be used, where patients are given special baths or hot and cold shower sprays. Herbs, or hot or cold packs, to be applied to problem areas may be prescribed. In some cases, the naturopath may provide psychological counselling. Where appropriate, if disease is outside the scope of naturopathy, patients are referred to conventional medicine. Naturopaths sometimes practise osteopathy as well.

7. Osteopath

Osteopaths manipulate patients' spines and joints to ensure they are properly aligned and move easily. They also use deep massage to ensure muscles and ligaments do not restrict joint movement. They are concerned with restoring and maintaining the balance of the human system. The work is quite physically demanding, although manipulative skills are required rather than particular strength.

Osteopaths take detailed medical histories before examining how the patient walks, stands and sits. They use their hands to examine muscles, ligaments and vertebrae and, in some cases, may use X-rays or other orthodox tests. If the problem cannot be helped by osteopathic treatment, the osteopath may refer the patient to a doctor or another type of therapist.

8. Reflexologist

Reflexologists work on the basis that every part of the body is connected by energy pathways, which end in reflex areas on the feet. By working systematically on the reflex areas on the feet, reflexologists apply controlled pressure to treat or improve the health of the corresponding body areas.

Reflexologists treat patients' bare feet, feeling for any tiny lumps under the surface of the skin, or imbalances in the feet. By working on these points, they aim to release tension and blockages, restore the body's energy flow, and improve circulation and elimination.

WORK ENVIRONMENT

Practitioners work mostly indoors, and often have a couch (or similar) for patients to lie on. Some practitioners work from a room in their home, others in very large buildings (such as the Royal London Homoeopathic Hospital or the British School of Osteopathy), or smaller rented rooms and in clinics or health centres. Some practitioners visit patients in their own homes, using a transportable table/couch. Practitioners may work outdoors at sports events, for example. Some chiropractors treat animals, especially horses.

SKILLS AND INTERESTS

It is essential for practitioners in complementary medicine to be ethical, and to be able to establish a good rapport with a wide range of patients. Good communication skills are vital, as are sympathy and understanding when treating patients who may be in some pain. Clear, logical problem-solving skills, and detached observation, help with case assessments.

A willingness to pursue their own personal development is required, since some self-knowledge and stability is necessary to help other people. A genuine desire to help people is essential, along with a certain amount of sensitivity, especially in therapies which involve touching the patient. For most complementary medicines, a lot of stamina is needed to cope with the physical and emotional demands of healing. For some, such as chiropractic and osteopathy, manipulative skills are needed as well.

ENTRY REQUIREMENTS

For some courses, especially for homoeopathic doctors and acupuncturists, training in orthodox medicine is required (as a medical doctor, nurse or paramedic).

1. Acupuncturist

In order to gain membership of the British Acupuncture Association and register, it is necessary to train at the British College of Acupuncture, or satisfy its board of examiners that at least equivalent training has been passed. Entry requirements for the British College of Acupuncture training is a degree and qualification in another branch of medicine – such as orthodox, naturopathy or osteopathy. Other colleges variously stipulate a minimum of two science A levels/H grades, or equivalent, a degree, or training in Chinese medicine. Some colleges state that they consider all serious applicants individually, whatever their qualifications.

2. Aromatherapist

To become a full member of the many associations under the umbrella of the Aromatherapy Organizations Council (AOC), candidates must attend courses approved by the relevant association and pass their exams. Entry requirements for training establishments offering approved courses vary. Some take entrants with no qualifications or previous experience in massage therapy. Others specify qualifications in chemistry, anatomy and physiology, or basic massage skills.

3. Chiropractor

Anyone practising as a chiropractor will be required by law to be registered with the General Chiropractic Council (GCC), once it is in place. To gain membership of the general register of chiropractors, it will be necessary to attend a recognized college. There are two colleges in Oxfordshire and one in Bournemouth which offer degree or HND level courses, all currently going through registration with the GCC. Entry requirements for these colleges are usually two or three A levels/three or four H grades, or equivalent, although mature applicants are considered on an individual basis. A background or qualification in chemistry and/or biology is required.

4. Herbalist

The register of the National Institute of Medical Herbalists only accepts graduates of the School of Phytotherapy in Hailsham, East Sussex, and of the BSc in Herbal Medicine at Middlesex University. Usual entry requirements for these courses are two A levels or equivalent, with at least one science subject. Candidates for the full-time course at the School of Phytotherapy must be at least 19 years old. Mature students may be assessed on an individual basis, and may need to demonstrate evidence of study skills and knowledge of science. There is a wide range of other courses available, some with no entry requirements, some seeking GCSEs/S grades, A levels/H grades, or equivalent. Chemistry and biology are useful.

5. Homoeopath

There are two different entry levels to homoeopathy. People listed by the British Homoeopathic Association have completed postgraduate courses run for medically qualified doctors, vets and pharmacists. These courses are governed by the Faculty of Homoeopathy, a body authorized by an Act of Parliament to train doctors in homoeopathy.

Alternatively, to be eligible to join the register of the Society of Homoeopaths, applicants must hold a qualification from a college recognized by the Society, followed by at least one year's clinical supervision. College entry requirements vary from no minimum academic qualifications to two A levels/three H grades, or equivalent. Most entrants are adults. A science background is useful.

6. Naturopath

To join the General Council and Register of Naturopaths, held by the British Naturopathic Association, applicants must have a Diploma in Naturopathy. This is usually gained as part of a BSc degree in Osteopathy and Naturopathy or as a postgraduate modular course in Naturopathic Medicine for qualified primary health care practitioners.

Entry requirements for the BSc course run by the British College of Naturopathy and Osteopathy are two A levels/H grades, or equivalent, in chemistry and biological science, although mature applicants are often considered on an individual basis. The postgraduate course run by the British Naturopathic and Osteopathic Association requires candidates to be fully trained in another primary health care discipline, such as osteopathy, chiropractic, medical herbalism and medical practice.

7. Osteopath

Practising osteopaths are required by law to become a member of the General Osteopathic Council. Membership requires osteopaths to have studied at one of its approved osteopathic schools. Entry requirements are generally two science A levels/H grades, or equivalent, (biological science and chemistry preferred) although mature candidates are considered on an individual basis.

8. Reflexologist

To join the register of qualified reflexologists run by the Association of Reflexologists, an independent representative organization, it is necessary to have studied at one of their accredited schools or colleges. To become a full member, a year's professional experience is also required.

Most colleges do not state any specific academic entry requirements, although a general ability in biology is useful. Personal qualities, such as sensitivity, caring for others and good listening skills, are considered more important than academic qualifications.

TRAINING

1. Acupuncturist

Courses vary between colleges, but typically last three or four years, either part or full-time. The British College of

Acupuncture's offers a Licentiate after two years' postgraduate study and a Bachelor degree which takes four years to complete.

Training covers methods of traditional Chinese acupuncture, laws of acupuncture and its philosophy, methods of diagnosis, therapeutic needling and moxibustion. Other subjects include anatomy, physiology and physical diagnosis. The basics of western medicine may be taught to those without a background in it.

2. Aromatherapist

The duration and depth of courses vary considerably, with introductory and refresher courses of only a few days or weeks to professional diploma courses lasting several months or years, depending on the level of previous experience and knowledge. Courses are usually part-time. They may be accredited by any of the dozen associations of the Aromatherapy Organizations Council (AOC).

The AOC stipulates a minimum standard for diploma training as 180 class hours. These break down into 80 hours of aromatherapy and essential oils, 60 hours of massage and 40 hours of anatomy and physiology.

The profession has begun research into the development of nationally recognized awards, such as NVQs/SVQs.

3. Chiropractor

At all of the three British schools, training lasts four or five years, whether full or part-time. Study includes subjects such as chiropractic palpation and adjustment techniques, along with standard medical subjects such as anatomy, neurology and pharmacology. The length and depth of the courses allows a considerable medical grounding. As well as theoretical and practical training, more senior students acquire clinical practice, examining and treating patients under close supervision.

4. Herbalist

Professional-level courses last three or four years, and can be studied full or part-time, or by distance learning. Academic subjects include pharmacy and herbal materia medica, as well as pathology and diagnostics. Students aiming for registration with the National Institute of Medical Herbalists also undergo clinical training, such as physical examination and diagnostic testing. Clinical experience of taking case histories and examining patients is conducted under close supervision of qualified practitioners.

5. Homoeopath

Courses usually run part-time over three or four years, although it is possible to study full-time. Although some study can be done by distance learning, it is not considered sufficient on its own to qualify at a professional level. Subjects include the principles, philosophy and practice of homoeopathy, anatomy, physiology, pathology, taking case histories and medical science.

The profession is working towards national recognition, either through NVQs/SVQs or university accreditation.

6. Naturopath

The two main courses are the four-year full-time course which is combined with the BSc degree in Osteopathic Medicine, and the postgraduate diploma course, which is modular and is typically completed over a two to three-year period. Subjects include the philosophy, history and development of naturopathy, as well as the principles and practice of therapeutic fasting, clinical nutrition and hydrotherapy. More detailed specific medical studies (such as infections, gastro-intestinal and neurological conditions) and psychological counselling are included. Clinical training is also available.

7. Osteopath

Most courses are four years full-time, although a part-time option for the first three years (five years in total) is available at the British School of Osteopathy. Courses lead to a BSc degree, except for the postgraduate course for doctors at the London College of Osteopathic Medicine, which leads to a fellowship of the college. This course is part-time for 13 months.

Students study anatomy, physiology, pathological processes, biomechanics and clinical methods. They learn about interpreting clinical tests and study relevant areas of psychology and sociology. They also get a wide range of clinical experience under close supervision.

8. Reflexologist

Professional-level courses at accredited schools and colleges are usually part-time, spread over at least nine months. Courses recognized by the Association of Reflexologists provide a minimum of 60 hours contact teaching time on subjects such as integral biology, anatomy and physiology, along with reflexology techniques. Most courses involve considerable amounts of home study and practical work.

The profession has begun research into the development of nationally recognized awards, such as NVQs/SVQs.

LATE ENTRY

Many entrants to complementary medicine are mature, often with previous qualifications in another branch of medicine. Some colleges actively welcome mature applicants, and state that they will be considered on an individual basis.

OPPORTUNITIES

Interest in complementary medicine has increased in the last few years, with demand exceeding supply in most areas, so that opportunities are generally good. Many areas lack complementary medicine practitioners, so there is often room for new practices to start. These opportunities are most apparent in cities and large towns, where there is a large population to provide potential patients.

Many practitioners are self-employed in private practice, although some work in multidisciplinary complementary health centres. It is sometimes possible for newly-qualified practitioners to start work as assistants to other practitioners before setting up their own private practice. This is often the case with osteopaths and chiropractors. Some practitioners work within or alongside the National Health Service, either in hospitals or GP practices.

PAY AND CONDITIONS

Many practitioners are self-employed, so income varies considerably. Most charge a session or hourly rate, which is usually in the range of £15 to £40 an hour. However, as the number and flow of patients can fluctuate, some practitioners supplement their income by practising more than one therapy, or by teaching and related work. The income of self-employed practitioners must also cover costs, such as rent of the therapy room and any administrative staff, such as receptionists. A number of practitioners work part-time.

PROSPECTS

Apart from private practice, where future prospects depend on building up the business alone or with partners, there is a variety of related careers to which practitioners can progress. Many practitioners opt to include teaching in their workload, or move into research. Another option is to move into journalism or publishing in the health care field.

Opportunities may sometimes exist in related manufacturing. This is particularly the case for medical herbalists.

Practitioners in one discipline may add others to their skill base and so build their career. For instance, a reflexologist may practise aromatherapy as well, or vice versa. Opportunities also exist to move into or add related disciplines, such as counselling.

RELATED OCCUPATIONS

Doctor, nurse, counsellor, midwife, occupational therapist, psychotherapist, physiotherapist, paramedic.

FURTHER INFORMATION

Institute for Complementary Medicine (ICM)*, PO Box 194, London SE16 1QZ, 0171 237 5165

Council for Complementary and Alternative Medicine (CCAM)*, 206-208 Latimer Road London W10 6RE, 0181 968 3862 (10am-5pm, Mon-Thu)

British Complementary Medicine Association (BCMA)*, 39 Prestbury Road, Cheltenham, Gloucester GL52 2PT, 01242 226770

British Acupuncture Association and Register*, 34 Alderney Street, London SW1V 4EU, 0171 834 1012

Aromatherapy Organizations Council*, 3 Latymer Close, Braybrooke, Market Harborough, Leicester LE16 8LN, 01858 434242

Anglo-European College of Chiropractic*, Parkwood Road, Bournemouth, Dorset BH5 2DF, 01202 436200

British Herbal Medicine Association*, Sun House, Church Street, Stroud GL5 1JL, 01453 751389

Society of Homoeopaths*, 2 Artizan Road, Northampton NN1 4HU, 01604 21400 (please include sae)

British Homoeopathic Association*, 27(a) Devonshire Street, London W1N 1RJ, 0171 935 2163

General Council and Register of Naturopaths*, Goswell House, 2 Goswell Road, Street, Somerset BA16 0JG, 01458 840072 (please include sae)

Osteopathic Information Service*, 56 London Street, Reading RG1 4SQ, 01734 512051 (please include sae)

Association of Reflexologists*, 27 Old Gloucester Street, London WC1N 3XX, 01273 479020

FURTHER READING

Leaflets/booklets are available from addresses marked*. Some are priced and some require an sae.

Working in Medicine – COIC
Job Outlines – Alternative Medicine – COIC
Working in Complementary and Alternative Medicine – A Career Guide – Kogan Page
A-Z of Alternative Medicine – Abercorn Hill Associates
In the careers library classified under JOD.

PROSTHETIST/ORTHOTIST CLCI:JOL

BACKGROUND INFORMATION

Prosthetists/orthotists are professionals who work with doctors and therapists as members of rehabilitation teams to provide care for disabled people. Prosthetists design and fit artificial limbs (prostheses) as replacements for limbs lost through amputation. These have to be functional, with working joints, and yet look natural. They are made from lightweight materials and have electronic and pneumatic mechanisms incorporated into the design so that, when fitted, they look and move like the limb they replace. Orthotists design and fit orthoses such as callipers, braces, neck collars and spine supports, which provide support to the patient's limbs or spine to relieve pain or prevent physical deformities from becoming worse. These may be worn permanently by the patient, or temporarily until natural healing restores the normal function of their body.

THE WORK

Prosthetists/orthotists work from a surgeon's prescription. They measure, make tracings and take plaster casts of the part to which the prosthesis/orthosis is to be fitted. They design the prosthesis/orthosis, producing drawings by hand or computer, or otherwise provide specifications for the technicians who will make the device. (Prosthetists and orthotists working at small centres may also be involved in making the prostheses.) Prostheses are all made to measure and, in designing them, the prosthetist needs to take the patient's life-style into consideration.

Once the prosthesis or orthosis is made, the prosthetist/orthotist fits it on to the patient, making sure that it fits well and is comfortable. In the case of prostheses, these may need further adjustments to give the patient a walking pattern which looks as natural as possible. They show the patient and their family how the prosthesis or orthosis works, how to put it on and take it off and, in some cases, they may have to help the patient to come to terms with wearing it. They later monitor the effectiveness of the appliance and carry out checks, adjustments and repairs as necessary.

WORK ENVIRONMENT

Prosthetists can work for the NHS, or manufacturing and service companies, and usually work in disablement service centres or artificial limb and appliance centres, which are normally in the grounds of a hospital. Orthotists may work for the NHS and be based in hospitals, or work for manufacturing and service companies, in which case they will spend some of their time driving to clinics to see their patients.

Prosthetists/orthotists spend much of their time seeing patients in clinic rooms – large spacious rooms where they measure patients and see how well they move with their prosthesis/orthosis. They also spend time in the centre's office and workshop.

SKILLS AND INTERESTS

Prosthetists/orthotists need both technical and practical skills to measure, design, fit and adapt prostheses and orthoses. They also need to be innovative, as all prostheses and many orthoses are designed for each individual patient. An awareness of computer technology is necessary, as it is becoming increasingly important in this work.

Prosthetists/orthotists need an interest in people, in how the body works, in mechanics, and a desire to help people with disabilities.

Good communication skills are vital in working with patients and other members of the team. They should be sensitive to the needs of the patients, tactful and understanding. The work may involve giving some patients physical assistance and so prosthetists/orthotists should be fit and healthy.

ENTRY REQUIREMENTS

Entry into this career requires an BSc (Hons) degree in Prosthetics and Orthotics. At present there are two such courses:

School of Prosthetics and Orthotics – University of Salford. The entry requirements for this course are: a combination of A and AS level passes, or equivalent qualifications, that gives a total of around 14 points (grades B and C). If maths is not offered at A level, other evidence of mathematical ability is required. Subjects should include maths *or* a choice of combined science, integrated science, physics coupled with biology. Alternatively, BTEC/SCOTVEC national diploma with distinctions in at least four relevant subjects, normally including maths or physics and human biology; or an Advanced GNVQ/GSVQ Level III in science, plus compulsory and optional additional units (for details of specific units required – contact the university).

The National Centre for Training and Education in Prosthetics and Orthotics–University of Strathclyde. The entry requirements for this course are: four H grades including maths at grade B, physics at grade B and preferably biology or chemistry, or three A levels including maths at grade C, physics at grade C and preferably biology or chemistry. Equivalent qualifications are considered on an individual basis.

TRAINING

Training for this career takes four years. The courses at the University of Strathclyde and the University of Salford qualify students in both prosthetics and orthotics. At the end of the course, students can decide in which discipline they wish to specialize.

University of Salford. This course comprises three interlinked elements: academic studies, practical training in the fabrication and forming of prosthetic and orthotic devices, and clinical experience in the assessment and fitting of patients. These three aspects of the course are developed together in the first three years. The fourth year is spent working in clinical practice in the Health Service or with an orthotic or prosthetic manufacturing company under contract to the NHS. The core subjects for this course are: life sciences and maths refresher (studied during weeks two to four of the course), electronic and engineering design and materials sciences, maths, computing, mechanics and biomechanics, clinical studies, prosthetic and orthotic science, health professional studies and research methods.

Students learn about the human body and the conditions that affect it, the biomechanics of normal and abnormal function, and the application of force to the body. They must also understand the properties of the materials from which devices can be made. In the practical side of the course students learn to design, fabricate and fit all types of prosthetic and orthotic devices. They work with volunteer patients to gain experience in prescription, measurement and fitting techniques. During these three years they spend short periods in NHS clinics. The final year is devoted to two blocks of six months clinical experience in each discipline, where students will gain practical experience in a clinical working environment. There is also an optional language training programme which runs throughout the first three years and includes a period of residence abroad in the summer holidays following the second year of their course.

University of Strathclyde. This is a four-year honours degree course combining academic studies, practical and clinical training, and clinical experience. Core subjects include life sciences, mechanics and biomechanics, prosthetics and orthotics science, maths and statistics, total design and graphical communication, electrotechnology, computer science, and materials technology. During the first three years students learn to fit and construct all types of prosthetic and orthotic devices using volunteer patients. The fourth year is spent in approved clinical centres applying the theory and skills they have learnt to real patients in the clinical situation. They work as part of the clinic team, spending six months in prosthetics and six months in orthotics.

LATE ENTRY

Applications from mature entrants are welcome for both courses. Each applicant is considered on their individual merit, and normal entry qualifications may not be needed. Applicants for the Salford course with no maths background are advised to first enrol on an access course in sciences.

OPPORTUNITIES

In England and Wales most prosthetists work for private manufacturing and servicing companies or private clinics. There are only limited job opportunities for prosthetists within the NHS. Orthotists can work for the NHS or for manufacturing and servicing companies.

In Scotland prosthetists/orthotists work for NHS, private clinics or private manufacturing and servicing companies.

At present there are about 200 prosthetists and 500 orthotists in Britain and it is possible that demand for them will increase.

The two courses only take about 28 students each year and so there is considerable competition for places. Opportunities for prosthetists/orthotists to work abroad are excellent. At present, graduates from Strathclyde are working in Canada and the USA, Australia, China and South East Asia, India, Africa and the Middle East and in the European Union. They can work for overseas health organizations and manufacturing and servicing companies, British companies with branches abroad, and voluntary organizations such as the Red Cross. It is expected that graduates from the new course at Salford will enjoy similar opportunities.

PAY AND CONDITIONS

Salaries for qualified prosthetists/orthotists range from approximately £12,000 to £28,000. Orthotists working for private companies usually have a company car provided. Most prosthetists/orthotists work a five-day, 40-hour week. Hours are normally from 8.30 to 5pm, Monday to Friday.

PROSPECTS

Although students, on graduating, choose to specialize in either orthotics or prosthetics, they are not restricted by their choice and can later change specialization if they wish. Promotion prospects are very limited in this career. There is no formal career ladder in either the NHS or with private companies. Some may become managers of teams of prosthetists/orthotists and technicians. There are also a few who move into education to train student prosthetist/orthotists or who move into sales posts with manufacturing companies.

RELATED OCCUPATIONS

Medical physics technician, dental technician, occupational therapist, biomedical engineer.

FURTHER INFORMATION

School of Prosthetics and Orthotics*, University of Salford, Blatchford Building, Statham Street, Salford M6 6PU

National Centre for Training and Education in Prosthetics and Orthotics*, University of Strathclyde, Curran Building, 131 St James Road, Glasgow G4 0LS

FURTHER READING

Leaflets/booklets are available from the addresses marked*.

In the careers library classified under JOL.

1. HOSPITAL PORTER CLCI:JOZ
**2. OPERATING DEPARTMENT
   PRACTITIONER CLCI:JOZ**

1. HOSPITAL PORTER (JOZ)

BACKGROUND INFORMATION

Porters move patients, equipment and other items around the hospital. During a typical day they have short social contacts with many people, including patients, nurses, technicians and other ancillary workers. Portering suits people who enjoy contact with the public and are physically active, as the work can be strenuous.

THE WORK

The organization of porters varies in different hospitals, but generally there will be a 'pool' of porters who serve all wards and departments, responding to requests from the nursing staff. There will also be other porters attached to particular departments or rostered to carry out specific duties, such as refuse disposal.

Porters in the 'pool' receive instructions from their supervisor – often by radio. A typical task would be to go to a ward, help a nurse to lift a patient from bed to a wheelchair and wheel the patient down to the X-ray department.

Sometimes porters move patients in their beds, when they are too ill to be transferred to wheelchairs. They also use trolleys or stretchers.

Other tasks may include moving furniture and heavy medical equipment, taking blood samples and specimens from wards to laboratories, delivering meal trolleys to wards, cleaning, and reception/telephonist duties.

One aspect of porter's work which may be distressing is the removal of dead bodies from wards and other departments. The body is prepared for movement by the nursing staff, then a porter takes it by trolley to the mortuary and helps to transfer the body to a storage container.

Porters who are not part of the 'pool' are attached to a particular department, such as accident and emergency, the operating department or pharmacy, or specialize in one specific type of duty.

Those who work in the operating department wear sterile clothing, and take patients who are under sedation from the wards to the theatre, and from the recovery room back to the wards. They are accompanied by a nurse.

Some porters are responsible for removing dirty laundry and refuse (including clinical waste, like used hypodermics and bloodstained dressings) from the wards, and for refuse disposal. Others work in the mail room, sorting and delivering post around the hospital.

Porters may be responsible for checking gas cylinders used on wards (usually oxygen cylinders, used by patients with breathing difficulties) and replacing them with new cylinders as necessary.

In some hospitals, porters are responsible for security – investigating suspicious circumstances and dealing with disturbances or intruders – but in other hospitals, this work is undertaken by separate security staff.

Porters may also be responsible for enforcing parking regulations in the hospital grounds.

Porter/drivers are employed in some hospitals, particularly those with split or spread-out sites. They drive minibuses to take patients from wards to clinics, and delivery vehicles to transport specimens, post and other items.

WORK ENVIRONMENT

Most of the time is spent indoors, walking from one part of the hospital to another. There may be some outdoor work, such as car parking duties. In hospitals with split sites, it is necessary to go out of doors when moving from one part of the building to another.

Portering is very active and physically demanding, involving a lot of walking, lifting, carrying and bending.

Porters wear uniforms – a heavy-duty jumper, dark trousers and shirt. They wear protective clothing for specific duties, such as rubbish disposal.

SKILLS AND INTERESTS

Porters need stamina and a good standard of physical fitness.

An outgoing disposition and friendly, cheerful personality are important – they meet a wide variety of people during the course of a working day.

They must be reliable, mature, and not easily upset by sickness and distress. As with all hospital work, it is essential to respect patient confidentiality.

At times, porters deal with people who are under severe stress, and the work may be pressured, for instance when there is a major road accident or other emergency.

They should be flexible, and prepared to carry out a variety of tasks.

ENTRY REQUIREMENTS

There are no specific educational entry requirements, although literacy is essential.

Most entrants are adults, rather than school-leavers, although there is no set minimum entry age.

Selection is by interview and medical examination, which includes a test of physical fitness.

A driving licence is required for porter/driver posts.

It is sometimes possible to work as a volunteer in a hospital, assisting porters; this experience is a useful background for those applying for paid jobs.

TRAINING

Porters may start by taking a short induction course covering general information about the hospital, health and safety, and lifting techniques.

Further training is carried out on the job, with guidance from experienced staff. New porters work under supervision for the first few weeks. They often rotate through the various duties until they have gained experience of all the different types of work.

LATE ENTRY

Most entrants are adults. Maturity is an advantage, and employers may prefer applicants who are over 30 years of age.

Experience in any kind of work that involves contact with the public is useful.

OPPORTUNITIES

Porters work in hospitals of all kinds, both in the public and private sectors. They may be directly employed by the hospital, or they may be employed by private contractors that provide ancillary services for hospitals.

A typical provincial hospital, with around 600 beds, would employ about 30 porters, plus supervisors and a head porter.

Many hospitals are cutting back on the numbers of porters they employ. There is keen competition for any vacancies that arise.

The majority of porters are men, but there is no barrier to the employment of women, provided they meet physical fitness requirements.

PAY AND CONDITIONS

Pay rates may be set locally, but generally porters are paid on the Whitley Council scale. This sets basic pay at between £134.92 and £140.40 a week, with additional payments for shift and weekend work, London allowances and bonuses. Hospital porters work a 39-hour week. They have to be prepared to work shifts, including nights and weekends. Some day jobs (8am to 5pm) are available. It is possible to work overtime.

Part-time work may be available.

PROSPECTS

Experienced porters may be promoted to supervisory posts and from there to head porter or porter-manager. However, opportunities for promotion are limited by the relatively small number of porters employed by each hospital.

It is possible to move into related areas such as health care assistant/nursing auxiliary.

RELATED OCCUPATIONS

Ambulance person, health care assistant/nursing auxiliary, sterile services assistant, hotel porter, security guard/officer, operating department practitioner, caretaker.

FURTHER INFORMATION

Further information about training and vacancies may be available from local careers offices and/or Jobcentres. Vacancies may be advertised in local newspapers. Local telephone directories may provide a suitable list of local employers.

FURTHER READING

Working in Hospitals – COIC

In the careers library classified under JOZ.

2. OPERATING DEPARTMENT PRACTITIONER (JOZ)

BACKGROUND INFORMATION

Operating department practitioners (ODPs) are part of a team that cares for patients during anaesthetic procedures and surgical operations. They provide essential support services for surgeons and anaesthetists, as part of the theatre team.

The term 'operating department practitioner' is relatively new. Until the mid-1970s, unqualified staff assisted in operating theatres. Then, in 1976, courses leading to a City and Guilds (C&G) qualification were introduced. Those

who achieved the C&G award were known as 'operating department assistants', and most non-medical, non-nursing staff currently working in operating departments still use this title.

Recently, with the introduction of NVQs, a new qualification and a new job title have been adopted, which reflect current practice in operating departments.

THE WORK

There are various different types of work:

'Scrubbed' ODPs are members of the operating team, working alongside surgeons and nurses. Like the rest of the team, they 'scrub up' – scrubbing their hands and arms up to the elbows, and putting on surgical masks, caps, sterile gowns and gloves.

Their duties involve handing instruments and dressings to the surgeon during the operation, anticipating the needs of the surgeon and providing the right instruments quickly, without being prompted. They also have to check instrument trays before the operation and keep account of all swabs and dressings used during the operation. Afterwards, they make a final check, the purpose of which is to make sure that no stray swabs, dressings or instruments are accidentally left inside the patient's body. They sign a register to confirm that they have carried out the necessary checks.

Other terms used instead of 'scrubbed ODP' are 'instrument person' and 'scrubbed assistant'.

Circulating duties involve supplying the surgical team with items such as dressings, drugs, swabs and equipment, and providing general assistance as required. ODPs on circulating duties do not wear sterile gowns, and can therefore fetch any additional items required during surgery.

Their duties also include overall care for patients, lifting them from beds or trolleys onto the operating table and positioning them correctly before surgery. They also check patients' identity before treatment, and make sure that all necessary records are available for medical staff.

Assistance to anaesthetists involves preparing the area to be used for administering anaesthetic, checking machinery and equipment for faults, and making sure that appropriate drugs are available. ODPs assisting anaesthetists have some responsibility for drugs, making sure they are stored correctly and that their use is recorded according to hospital policy.

ODPs help anaesthetists during the administration of general or local anaesthetic, handling equipment and instruments. In the operating theatre they help to monitor the patient's vital signs (such as blood pressure, heart rate and temperature) throughout the proceedings, acting as the anaesthetist's 'second pair of eyes'. They also assist the anaesthetist by fetching additional items such as drugs, intravenous fluids or blood. After operations, ODPs help monitor patients as they recover from the anaesthetic/surgical procedure.

ODPs are trained to carry out all the roles described above, and they rotate between the different duties. They work as a team and, during a typical working day with numerous operations, they swap roles – particularly between circulating and scrubbed duties. Those who are rostered to assist anaesthetists usually spend the whole day in that specialism.

WORK ENVIRONMENT

Most ODPs work in operating departments, which consist of operating theatres, anaesthetic areas and recovery rooms.

An increasing number of ODPs work in accident and emergency departments, intensive care units or as part of cardiac arrest teams. They are employed in these departments mainly for their skills in working with anaesthetists.

ODPs spend most of the time standing.

SKILLS AND INTERESTS

Communication skills and the ability to work with others, as a team member, are essential. A caring, sympathetic attitude is needed for dealing with patients – who may be conscious, and worried about their operations – when they are arriving at or leaving the operating department. Strict confidentiality about patients' treatment is essential.

ODPs need manual dexterity for handling equipment. They should be able to anticipate the needs of surgeons and anaesthetists. A careful, methodical and conscientious attitude is required.

Good health and fitness are important as the job involves a considerable amount of physical work – lifting patients and moving equipment. It is not suitable for people with back problems.

Working in an operating department can be distressing – for instance, some patients die on the operating table. ODPs need to be mature enough to cope with such situations.

ENTRY REQUIREMENTS

There are no set academic entry requirements, but a good general education is needed and numeracy and literacy are essential. Centres running ODP training usually set selection tests covering basic English, maths and reasoning. Candidates are selected by interview. They have to pass a medical examination. Normal colour vision is required, as it is necessary to be able to recognize colour-coded items.

Entry may be possible for young people through Modern Apprenticeships leading to at least an NVQ/SVQ Level 3. Contact your local careers office, TEC/LEC for details.

The minimum age for entry is usually 18 years. Younger people may gain experience in other types of hospital work – for instance, as health care assistants – and transfer to ODP work later on.

Courses leading to the GNVQ in Health and Social Care at Intermediate level or the GSVQ in Care at Level II are an appropriate background for those seeking to enter this type of work.

TRAINING

Student ODPs are hospital-based, attending ODP training centres for the theoretical part of their training. There are 27 ODP training centres, based at large hospitals or colleges/institutes of health studies around the country. A list of centres is available from the British Association of Operating Department Assistants or Theatre Personnel Nation-wide.

Students are normally trained over two years. Their education and training programme begins with a short induction course at the ODP centre and hospital. They then spend about eight weeks working in operating departments before returning to the ODP centre for a further one- or two-week theory course. A similar pattern of training continues throughout the two years, although the intervals between theory courses gradually become longer. Altogether, about 18-20 weeks are spent on theoretical training, and just over 80 weeks on practical training in hospitals.

The practical training includes experience in a variety of hospital departments – including surgical wards, intensive care units and accident and emergency departments – as well as in operating departments. The theoretical training covers subjects such as anatomy and physiology, basic chemistry and physics, pharmacology, microbiology, sterilization and disinfection, and infection control.

At the end of the two years students are expected to achieve an NVQ/SVQ in Health Care at Level 3: Operating Department Practice, awarded by City and Guilds in England and Wales and SCOTVEC in Scotland. The qualification is made up of seven units: health and safety in the workplace; controlling cross-infection; preparing the environment/workplace; preparing patients for clinical/operative procedures; providing assistance in clinical/operative procedures; providing immediate post-operative care; and providing initial emergency care. Continuous assessment of students is carried out in the workplace; theoretical knowledge is assessed via tests, exams and written case studies.

LATE ENTRY

Entrants are normally over 18 years, and the most usual age to enter this type of work is the mid-twenties.

There is keen competition for training places and it is an advantage to have hospital experience, particularly in a job with a reasonable amount of patient contact, such as health care assistant or nursing auxiliary. Experience in residential care is also useful.

Relevant qualifications may give exemption from part of the ODP training course, via Accreditation of Prior Learning (APL).

There is no fixed upper age limit, but entry after the age of about 45 is likely to be difficult.

OPPORTUNITIES

ODPs are employed by most hospitals with a sizeable operating department, both in the public and private sectors.

Because the ODP qualification is new, there are only around 300 to 400 people who have so far gained this award. About 2,500 to 3,000, nationally, hold the operating department practitioner qualification.

There are some opportunities to work abroad. Employment agencies recruit holders of the ODA/ODP qualification to work in hospitals in the Middle East. There are also opportunities in the Netherlands for qualified staff with at least two years' experience.

Temporary work is available in the UK through employment agencies.

PAY AND CONDITIONS

Pay varies according to local policy, but is usually on the Medical Technical Officers' scale. Students are normally paid about £7,390 to £7,640. Salaries for qualified ODPs range from about £10,100 to £17,500 (Senior ODP).

Operating departments are open 24 hours a day, 365 days a year, and the staff work shifts, including nights and Bank Holidays. They may have on-call and standby duties.

During training, students normally start by working days,

8am to 5pm. They transfer to shift work once they have gained some experience.

After qualifying, it may be possible to work part-time, depending on the employer's policy. Job share may be available.

PROSPECTS

Promotion is initially to Senior ODP – this involves responsibility for theatre suites, ordering, service contracts, staff management and supervision of students in training.

From Senior ODP it is possible to move into higher managerial positions. Some practitioners move into full-time education posts in health care – they may be able to take courses leading to NVQs/SVQs in Training and Development at Levels 3 and 4.

RELATED OCCUPATIONS

Nursing auxiliary/health care assistant, ambulance person, care assistant, hospital nurse, medical technical officer, hospital porter.

FURTHER INFORMATION

British Association of Operating Department Assistants*, 70a Crayford High Street, Dartford, Kent DA1 4EF, 01322 555755.

Theatre Personnel Nationwide* (formerly known as The National Association of Professional and Technical Theatre Personnel), 14 Roath Court Place, Roath, Cardiff, South Glamorgan CF2 3SJ, 01222 463695 (please include sae)

Health Service Careers*, PO Box 204, London SE5 7ES

FURTHER READING

Leaflets/booklets are available from the addresses marked*.

Job Outlines – Hospital Support Staff – COIC
Working in Hospitals – COIC

In the careers library classified under JOZ.

1. FIELD SOCIAL WORKER CLCI:KEB
2. RESIDENTIAL SOCIAL WORKER
CLCI:KEB
3. CARE ASSISTANT CLCI:KEB

BACKGROUND INFORMATION

The majority of social workers are employed by local authority social services departments in England and Wales, social work departments in Scotland, and area and local education departments. These are statutory agencies, responsible by law for the welfare of certain groups in their area, including children and young people, families under stress, people with disabilities, elderly people and people who are emotionally or physically chronically sick. In Scotland, the social work departments are also responsible for criminal justice services.

There are also a growing number of independent and voluntary social work agencies that fill gaps in statutory provision or provide specialist services. Many of these employ full-time professional staff. Increasingly, private agencies are offering services for aged and infirm people; many such agencies employ professional care staff.

The range of work carried out by individual social workers is varied, but it is possible to concentrate on certain areas such as field social work, residential social work and, in Scotland and Northern Ireland, probation work.

1. FIELD SOCIAL WORKER (KEB)

THE WORK

Field social workers work in the community, visiting individuals and families, where necessary taking some remedial action or organizing practical assistance. They generally work as part of an area team (which may include welfare assistants, an occupational therapist, a home help organizer and clerical staff) based in the district they serve, and supervised by senior social workers who are directed by an area team leader.

Increasingly, social services departments are organized in specialist sections, either for adults, or for children and families. Many departments have introduced a 'purchaser/ provider' split, where some social workers are employed as care managers, making assessments and putting together packages of care, while others provide a service direct to users. In all cases, however, the emphasis is on carers and service users working in partnership with each other.

A field social worker has a 'case-load' of clients who may include children at risk, young people in trouble with the law, families with financial or emotional problems, people coping with physical or mental disabilities or illness, and fostering and adoption work.

Social workers have to assess their clients' needs and determine short-term or long-term courses of action. Some situations can be quickly resolved with practical aid, such as a home help or financial provision, but others require careful planning over a period of time.

Some problems may be lessened by practical help, but actually stem from the attitude of clients themselves. Social workers need to build a relationship of trust with such clients and help them to accept what cannot be changed and direct them towards improvements in their lives that can be achieved.

Much of the social worker's time is spent in routine organization and planning, in arranging for services to be made available to clients, or in consultation with other professional people or agencies on their behalf. A social worker may take action to help clients help themselves, such as by setting up self-help or mutual support groups.

Legislation has given social work agencies the authority and responsibility to intervene in the lives of clients where the situation requires it. This may mean the social worker having to make the decision to take a child into care, or to commit to hospital an emotionally disturbed person.

Some social workers are employed by local authorities in England and Wales (social work departments in Scotland) to provide social work services to hospitals and health centres. They are sometimes known as 'medical' or 'psychiatric' social workers. Working alongside doctors, therapists, psychiatrists and nursing staff, they assess a patient's needs and take steps to reduce the social, environmental or emotional problems that have contributed to the patient's condition.

Social workers provide short-term help, such as arranging for the care of children while a parent is in hospital or arranging for patient after care by organizing, for example, visits from home helps. Social workers also help people with permanent disability to come to terms with their condition, and may provide support for terminally ill people and for bereaved families, by counselling and group therapy sessions.

In addition to direct work with clients, a social worker spends time writing casework reports, attending team meetings and case conferences, or liaising with other statutory, voluntary and private agencies. They work in close co-operation with doctors and medical staff, court officials, police and school staff. Part of every week is spent 'on duty', dealing with callers to the office or health centre, telephone enquiries and emergencies.

WORK ENVIRONMENT

Community-based social workers spend most of their time outside the office, visiting clients in their homes or in day or residential centres. They may have to travel outside their own area, to visit clients in special or custodial care.

Social workers may have to attend juvenile court to present a social inquiry report.

Working in rural areas normally requires the use of a car.

They must be prepared to meet with unpleasant or difficult situations in their work, from entering infested houses to coping with violent clients, utilising help from agencies such as environmental health services or the police. They must also be prepared for situations where resources are not available to meet the needs of users and carers.

Social workers may also work in hospitals, out-patient clinics, health centres and in doctors' surgeries.

SKILLS AND INTERESTS

Social workers need maturity and the ability to build good working relationships with people of all ages and from a wide variety of backgrounds. The work is varied and sometimes stressful; social workers need to combine a practical, calm approach with adaptability. They need excellent communication skills and an interest in people's problems.

Social workers need to be good listeners, and capable of conveying complex information in simple terms.

They must be able to co-operate with other professionals and work well as members of a team. They also need to have sound judgement and be able to work on their own initiative.

Social workers who work as care managers need to be able to control budgets and to be computer literate.

ENTRY REQUIREMENTS

The professional qualification for all social workers is the Diploma in Social Work (DipSW). Minimum entry requirements depend on age of entry to training for the DipSW.

For applicants under 21 years the minimum requirements for entry to DipSW programmes (courses) are either: two A levels/three H grades and three GCSEs (A-C)/two S grades (1-3) in other subjects; or NVQ/SVQ Level 3; or a BTEC/SCOTVEC national award; or the CACHE Diploma in Nursery Nursing (NNEB); or Advanced GNVQ/GSVQ III; or equivalent qualifications.

Most students under 21 years are only accepted on programmes that combine a degree course with preparation for the DipSW. Degree course entry is with a minimum of either: five GCSEs(A-C)/S grades (1-3) with two A levels/three H grades; or an appropriate BTEC/SCOTVEC national award; or an appropriate Advanced GNVQ/GSVQ Level III; or equivalent. A minimum age of 19 is required for entry to some degree courses that include the DipSW.

Applicants for DipSW programmes who are age 21 and over, may not need formal educational qualifications but must show that they can study at a higher education level. It is helpful if they can offer one of the entry qualifications described above.

Some courses combine a postgraduate social science qualification with the DipSW – entry is usually with at least a second class honours degree.

Certain types of criminal conviction may prevent people from entering social work. The provisions of the Rehabilitation of Offenders Act do not apply to social service employers, who may require applicants for posts to declare any convictions and may seek information from police records.

All applicants to DipSW programmes are normally expected to have had sufficient experience in paid or voluntary work to demonstrate an understanding of the nature and demands of social work as a career. Paid experience may be gained by working as unqualified staff for statutory or voluntary agencies, or as a residential care assistant, social work assistant or probation ancillary.

Valuable voluntary experience may be gained with local authority social services departments, agencies such as the Salvation Army or the Royal National Institute for the Blind, or through volunteer bureaux, which are in many towns and cities in the UK. Few successful applicants to DipSW courses, though, have voluntary experience only.

TRAINING

The Diploma in Social Work (DipSW) is the professional qualification for all social workers in all sectors and settings throughout the UK.

DipSW programmes are offered at many centres throughout the UK. They are designed to train entrants for all types of social work, but some courses offer the opportunity to concentrate on a particular client group. Programme structures vary to meet the needs of the wide variety of people entering social work at different stages in their lives, with different educational backgrounds.

Programmes may be college-based (two years) with lengthy periods of supervised practical experience, or be employment-based (two or three years) where students are in paid social work employment.

Programmes are also available part-time and, in Scotland, by distance learning.

DipSW programmes consist of academic study and a minimum of 130 days supervised practice. Areas of study include: knowledge and understanding of human growth and behaviour and of a range of human needs; the process of observation and assessment and transcultural factors. Various aspects of practice are covered, including aims, methods and theories, the settings in which practice is carried out and the administrative and legal systems which provide its framework. Clients' rights and ethical issues are also covered.

The award of the DipSW is based on the candidate being assessed against core competences and relevant knowledge and values.

Contact the Central Council for Education and Training in Social Work (CCETSW) for **Handbook 9.3, How to Qualify for Social Work**, which contains information on all DipSW programmes.

LATE ENTRY

Adult entry is usual, with maturity and experience of life and work being valued. There is no upper age limit for entry to DipSW programmes.

To gain acceptance onto a DipSW programme, adults must show that they can cope with the study involved. This can be done by successfully completing an approved higher education access course. Access courses are offered at local colleges and are usually one year full-time or one to two years part-time with daytime and/or evening attendance. It is also possible to prepare for entry to social work training by successful completion of the Open University's (OU) Foundation Module. CCETSW issues guidance notes on Access courses and OU courses for prospective DipSW students.

There are extended DipSW programmes designed for candidates with family commitments. Details of programmes are available from CCETSW.

OPPORTUNITIES

There are over 26,000 field workers employed by local authorities in England and Wales. Although field workers are employed throughout the UK, work may be easier to find in inner cities. There is usually competition for fieldwork positions and preference may be given to social workers with field rather than residential experience.

The statutory agencies are the largest employers of field social workers (local authority social services departments in England and Wales, local authority social work departments in Scotland). Social workers in educational welfare offices are usually employed by local education authorities, but in England and Wales no separate education social service exists, as in Scotland. The Department of Social Security employs some experienced social workers as inspectors and advisers. Health service social workers are employed, particularly where there are large hospitals. There are also opportunities to work in special units, such as alcohol, drug or solvent abuse clinics.

Those experienced in clinical psychiatric work are also employed by local education authorities to work in child guidance clinics.

There are increasing employment opportunities in the Armed Forces. The Ministry of Defence employs social workers in military hospitals. The Navy Personal and Family Service provides a social work service for the Navy, and the Soldiers', Sailors' and Airmen's Families Association (SSAFA) mainly looks after Army and Air Force families.

Independent social work agencies are increasingly employing professional social workers, to work in the community and for casework. They offer opportunities to specialize and to work in small flexible units.

There are openings for social workers to teach on training courses in universities and colleges and as training officers or practice placement teachers in social work agencies.

Vacancies for qualified field workers are advertised in *Community Care, Public Service, Local Government Appointments, The Voice, The Independent* and *The Guardian*.

PAY AND CONDITIONS

There are nationally agreed salary scales for field and medical social workers in local authority social services departments, but each employer sets its own starting points and length of scale. Salaries also depend on qualifications, experience, and the responsibilities of the post. Additional allowances are paid in areas where physical, social or economic circumstances cause recruitment problems, give rise to stress, or otherwise make it a particularly demanding place in which to work. Typically, though, a newly qualified social worker may start on £14,028 and may be on a scale up to £19,260. Care managers/senior practitioners may typically be on a scale from £19,260 to £20,748. At the top of the scale, directors of social services are paid considerably more. Scottish local authorities pay field social workers on a scale range from £15,438 to £19,617.

The pay scales of some large independent agencies are comparable to those offered by the statutory agencies, but salaries reflect the resources of the agencies concerned.

Social work is not a nine-to-five job; service users may have to be visited outside normal working hours, and problems can arise at any time. Most agencies and local authorities provide a 24-hour, seven-days-a-week emergency service. Team members may be on a rota for standby duty covering nights and weekends, for which they will receive extra pay or time off in lieu. Part-time work may be available.

Social workers in medical settings often work normal office hours, but may be required to go on a rota for standby duty.

PROSPECTS

Within the statutory agencies there is a well-defined career structure. There are opportunities for promotion from the basic grade of social worker to senior social worker in an area team and eventually to team leader. At that level it is possible to move into managerial or advisory posts, or to continue working with service users in an agency that provides special opportunities for experienced social workers with particular skills.

RELATED OCCUPATIONS

School teacher, further/tertiary education lecturer, probation officer, youth and community worker, residential social worker.

FURTHER INFORMATION AND READING

Please see article 3. CARE ASSISTANT.

2. RESIDENTIAL SOCIAL WORKER (KEB)

THE WORK

Residential social workers provide care in long-stay or short-stay residential centres, and in day-care units – which offer the advantages of residential care without actually removing people from their homes. The social workers themselves are not necessarily resident in the setting in which they practise. They are concerned with groups of people who have one factor in common, such as their age or disability, but are otherwise individual and unique in their various needs.

Children and young people: residential care is available for those needing permanent or, more often, temporary care. When possible, children are placed in foster homes, so those remaining in care usually have special needs or behavioural problems, or have been committed by the courts. Most children in children's homes are adolescents.

Social workers may work in family units caring for small mixed-age groups, or in homes providing special facilities. There are special boarding schools for disabled children and those with social and behavioural difficulties.

Adults: disabled people of any age, unless they require special treatment or therapy facilities, are usually cared for within the community, in family-sized units that provide the required support and help. More than half the residential homes in this country, and many of the day-care centres, are for elderly people.

There are hostels providing support for adults needing rehabilitation or an adjustment period before returning home. Also, there are hostels for ex-psychiatric patients, single parents, parents who need support with parenting, or young homeless adults, and rehabilitation units, providing temporary accommodation for families and for people with temporary disabilities.

All residential social workers are, to some extent, involved in the everyday routine of looking after their clients, including sharing meals, arranging for medical care if necessary, and ensuring that children go to school and adults to work, as relevant.

The work involves more than the residents' physical well-being, because their emotional, social, spiritual and recreational needs must also be provided for. A primary aim is to offer the benefits of living in a community, while allowing individuals independence and privacy. Where possible, residents are encouraged to achieve the independence and self-confidence required to return to their own homes.

Social workers attempt to build up relationships with their clients, and aim to promote favourable conditions for their clients' development, to improve their quality of life.

It may be necessary to identify psychological, emotional or social causes of problems, gain the individual's confidence and try to find realistic and achievable goals. Social workers have to be sympathetic to pressures on individuals in care. Clients may have behavioural and other problems. Skilled care is required in many cases, as clients are not always co-operative or responsive.

Residential social workers are trained in methods that can be applied in a variety of circumstances.

Group work: involves helping the residents by group discussion of mutual problems and, by providing an appropriate environment, employment and contact with the community.

Casework: social workers work with residents individually, establishing a relationship of trust. Casework can be valuable in assessing individual needs, establishing attainable targets and helping the client to accept situations that cannot be changed.

In addition to direct work with clients, a residential social worker spends time writing reports, attending team meetings and case conferences, and liaising with other professionals, such as teachers, hospital staff or court officials.

WORK ENVIRONMENT

The size and character of residential homes depends on the services they offer. Some are large, modern, purpose-built buildings with special facilities, while others are converted houses. A large number are small, family-sized units in ordinary urban houses with the minimum adaptation. Social workers may be required to live-in, usually in self-contained accommodation. Non-resident staff may be expected to sleep-in on a rota basis.

SKILLS AND INTERESTS

Residential social work calls for commitment; the work can be very demanding, both physically and mentally, and calls for emotional resilience and physical stamina. Tolerance and patience are required, and it helps to be a good listener. Residential social workers must be mature and capable of assessing their clients' needs. They should provide appropriate care for clients, yet also be able to establish effective control and show firmness where necessary.

Social workers should be able to develop relationships with clients, gain their trust, build up confidence, and develop a warm, supportive, environment for the benefit of the residents. It is important, however, to treat clients as individuals, respecting their need for privacy and independence.

Residential social workers also need administrative and managerial skills. Residential social workers work as part of a team, which includes care assistants, kitchen staff, domestics and other ancillary staff.

ENTRY REQUIREMENTS

The professional qualification for all social workers is the Diploma in Social Work (DipSW) – please see article 1. FIELD SOCIAL WORKER. The majority of residential workers, however, are not professionally qualified social workers. Depending on the nature of the work, heads and deputies may have qualifications in nursing, teaching or occupational therapy.

Entry may be possible for young people through Modern Apprenticeships leading to at least an NVQ/SVQ Level 3. Contact your local careers office, TEC/LEC for details.

TRAINING

Please see article 1. FIELD SOCIAL WORKER for details of social work training.

All Diploma in Social Work (DipSW) programmes provide training on residential care. Eight programmes, however, are part of the Residential Child Care Initiative and are particularly appropriate for senior residential child care staff. Further details can be obtained from CCETSW.

Care staff can work towards NVQs/SVQs in Care at Levels 2, 3 and 4 that are designed for people in a wide range of settings, including residential and nursing homes and day centres.

LATE ENTRY

Adult entry is usual, with maturity and experience of life and work being valued. There is no upper age limit for entry to DipSW programmes – please see article 1. FIELD SOCIAL WORKER.

It can be possible for interested adults to test whether they would be suitable for residential care work. This they may do by gaining temporary employment in a residential home or a day centre, possibly through an employment agency.

OPPORTUNITIES

There are around half a million people in residential care throughout the country. Emphasis on community care has led to an increase in the number of day centres for particular groups, such as elderly or disabled people.

Although many of those working in the residential sector are not qualified as social workers, a qualified social worker would probably find this type of work the easiest to enter.

There are good opportunities to obtain pre-qualification experience in residential work.

Local authority social services departments in England and Wales (local authority social work departments in Scotland) are large employers of residential social workers in residential and day-care centres. Voluntary organizations and private agencies also employ social workers in residential and day-care settings. Voluntary organizations may have strong religious or social convictions.

Vacancies may be advertised in *Community Care, Health and Social Services Journal, Public Service, Local Government Appointments* and *Care Weekly.*

PAY AND CONDITIONS

Salaries for staff in local authority residential homes for children or adults reflect the size of the home and level of responsibility required. Senior care workers may typically earn £13,197 to £14,472. Team leaders and unit managers may typically be on a scale from £15,438 to £22,053.

Some residential posts provide accommodation for staff. Others may include allowances for irregular hours or extra payments for overnight duties.

Pay scales of large, independent agencies are comparable to those of local authorities, but salaries reflect the resources of the agency concerned.

Residents need care around the clock and social workers must be prepared to work unsocial hours. Few are required to live-in. Most posts specify a number of hours to be worked in a week, including evenings and weekends, which are arranged in shifts or blocks of time-on and time-off.

Social workers may be required to sleep-in on a rota basis.

PROSPECTS

Advancement for qualified workers can be fairly rapid. The size of the units, and residential work itself, is so varied that there is no standard pattern of promotion. An experienced social worker may become an assistant or deputy to the officer-in-charge of a home, and then manager of a unit.

Formal structures exist within local authority departments; promotion to more senior grades may involve moving to different residential centres.

Opportunities exist at management level as group manager of a number of homes within an area. There is mobility between residential and other fields of social work, although relevant experience, in addition to residential work, may be required.

RELATED OCCUPATIONS

Nursery nurse, nurse, youth and community worker, playleader, field social worker, care assistant.

FURTHER INFORMATION AND READING

Please see article 3. CARE ASSISTANT.

3. CARE ASSISTANT (KEB)

THE WORK

Care assistants are involved in providing services for groups of people with differing needs. A wide range of care services includes provision for groups (including children and young people), people with disabilities, adults, families, and elderly people.

The work is about helping to improve the quality of life, or to ensure the best possible quality of life, for individuals/ groups.

Children and young people: residential care is provided for children and young people with special needs, such as those with physical or mental disabilities (whose parents or guardians are unable to look after them), or behavioural problems. Some children have been committed by the courts.

Care assistants are responsible for carrying out many of the practical tasks in residential centres for children and young people with special needs. They help with the physical care of the children, assisting with toileting, bathing, dressing and undressing. Care assistants are also increasingly involved in stimulating and encouraging children to learn and become responsible.

While children attend school, care assistants are often required to help other staff with domestic tasks such as washing up, clearing away, making beds, washing, ironing and mending clothes. After school and at weekends, care assistants encourage and supervise play or help children with interests. They may accompany children on outings and help with activities, such as swimming or horse-riding.

There may also be opportunities for care assistants to work with children in the community, perhaps in schools or nurseries, working with young children aged three to five. Duties include settling the children down when they arrive, preparing materials (such as paint, water, card and crayons) for play activities, playing with the children and clearing away afterwards. Care assistants may also prepare meals and help to feed the children, then assist them to wash and toilet.

People with disabilities: duties vary as individuals have different needs and abilities. The care assistant aims to help individuals to be as independent and live as normal a life as possible. In residential centres, care assistants help with practical tasks – washing, dressing, etc. People with disabilities may need help with walking or getting in and out of wheelchairs, and much of the work may involve helping individuals to do everyday things, such as handling cutlery, using telephones and shopping.

Similar duties are involved in work at day centres and training centres that provide support for people who are able to live in their own homes. Care assistants develop friendly relations with individuals and help them with practical activities. They may also assist with training classes, under the direction of an instructor, that may be concerned with social skills, for example, arts and crafts, physical education, or reading and writing.

Elderly people: care assistants may look after elderly people in residential homes, in day centres or in their own homes. They help in practical ways, such as carrying out household tasks and shopping, and they also befriend old people, helping to reduce feelings of isolation. Assistants organize activities and encourage independent living. At day centres, assistants help with meals and encourage interests – joining in with activities, as well as listening and talking to attenders.

Many residential homes are for elderly people – a small number cater for those with particular problems, such as blindness or mental infirmity. Duties vary according to individuals' needs: some may require help washing and dressing, or assistants may read and talk to residents.

Work with other groups: care assistants may work in homes/ hostels provided for other groups who may need temporary shelter in half-way houses, such as homeless people and single parents, or for people such as ex-prisoners or ex-drug abusers, needing support until they are able to adjust to life in the community.

WORK ENVIRONMENT

Residential homes vary in relation to the different services they offer – some are large, modern, purpose-built buildings designed with special facilities to meet the needs of the clients, others are set in converted country houses. A large number are small family-sized units occupying ordinary urban houses with the minimum adaptation.

Care assistants may be required to live-in, in which case they will probably be offered self-contained accommodation. The work becomes more of a way of life for live-in workers. Non-resident staff may be expected to sleep-in on a rota basis.

Care assistants who make visits to people in the community may travel quite a lot within the local areas, and a driving licence may be required.

SKILLS AND INTERESTS

Care assistants need to have a genuine interest in people. A mature attitude is essential. Reliable, responsible individuals are required for this type of work.

Care assistants must be able to communicate with people of all ages and from a variety of backgrounds. Talking to people and forming relationships of trust and friendship are important aspects of the work. It helps to be a good listener.

Patience and tolerance are essential. Caring for people – some of whom will be difficult at times, as a result of their problems or disabilities – can be physically and mentally demanding. Care assistants have to be prepared to become involved with people, which calls for emotional resilience and stamina. Practical duties, such as lifting and helping people walk, require individuals to be physically fit.

Sometimes the work is with sick and dying people. Care assistants must also undertake jobs that may be unpleasant and messy.

Care assistants must work well as members of a team in co-operation with other assistants, medical staff, domestics, kitchen assistants, etc.

ENTRY REQUIREMENTS

There are no minimum academic qualifications needed for entry into work as a care assistant. Most employers prefer applicants to be age 18 or over.

Training courses for young people – no minimum entry requirements.

Modern Apprenticeships in Care – entry may be possible for young people through Modern Apprenticeships leading to at least an NVQ/SVQ Level 3. Contact your local careers office, TEC/LEC for details.

There are a number of courses relevant to work as a care assistant:

SCOTVEC national certificate – requires a good general education. Check with individual colleges, as they may have their own entry requirements.

BTEC First Certificate/Diploma in Care – requires a good general education.

BTEC National Certificate/Diploma in Caring Services (Social Care) – needs either: four GCSEs/S grades (A-C/1-3); or a BTEC first award; or an Intermediate GNVQ/GSVQ Level II.

NVQ in Care/SVQ in Health and Social Care – needs no particular exam passes.

Intermediate GNVQ in Health and Social Care – does not need particular entry requirements but educational institutions may specify their own requirements.

Advanced GNVQ in Health and Social Care – usually requires either: Intermediate GNVQ; or four GCSEs/S grades (A-C/1-3); or a BTEC/SCOTVEC national award.

GSVQs in Care Levels II and III - have no formal entry requirements. Colleges may admit students they feel can benefit from the courses. In the case of Level III, this includes students who have passed Level II.

TRAINING

Pre-entry

There are a number of full-time courses that prepare students for a range of caring work. Courses can also be used as an entry qualification to a higher level course. All courses include some practical experience.

SCOTVEC national certificate – a number of colleges offer one-year or two-year courses that lead to national certificate modules in care.

BTEC First Diploma in Care – just a few colleges now offer this one-year course.

BTEC National Diploma in Caring Services (Social Care) – many colleges offer this two-year course.

NVQ in Care/SVQ in Health and Social Care – a number of colleges offer care courses that provide students with a basis of knowledge and work experience to prepare them for relevant NVQs/SVQs at Level 2. Some also offer training to Level 3.

GNVQ in Health and Social Care/GSVQ in Care – some schools and many colleges now offer GNVQ in Health and Social Care at Intermediate level (one year) and Advanced level (two years). A number offer GSVQ in Care Level II (one year) and Level III (two years).

On entry

Training schemes for young people – these schemes train young people in work with elderly people, disabled people and/orchildren. Trainees work towards relevant NVQs/SVQs at Level 2 or 3. Contact your local careers office, TEC/LEC for details.

Modern Apprenticeships in Care – apprenticeships are designed for care workers in different settings, for example, in residential nursing homes or day centres for elderly people or people with physical or learning disabilities. Apprentices work towards an NVQ/SVQ in Care at Level 3. Some may first achieve a Level 2. In addition they undertake training in communication, application of number, information technology, working with others, improving their own learning and performance and problem solving. Apprenticeships are not for a set length of time but are unlikely to last for less than three years. Contact your local careers office, TEC/LEC for details.

All care workers are trained by their employers. They may also be encouraged to attend local college on a day release or evening-basis to study courses such as: SCOTVEC national certificate care modules (varying length of time); or BTEC First Certificate in Care (one year); or BTEC National Certificate in Caring Services (Social Care) (two years).

Increasingly care assistants are being encouraged to work towards NVQs/SVQs in Care at Levels 2 and 3 that are designed for people in a wide range of settings, including residential and nursing homes, day centres, health care support services and community care projects.

LATE ENTRY

Maturity and experience are valued in care work and adult entry is encouraged. Most employers set a minimum age of entry at 18 years but there is no set upper age limit.

The City and Guilds Community Care Practice award (3250) has been designed particularly for adults employed in social care work. No qualifications are required for entry and many colleges offer the course on a day release basis.

Adult entrants may be encouraged to work towards NVQs/SVQs in Care.

OPPORTUNITIES

A large number of care workers are employed throughout the UK. The emphasis on community care has led to an expansion in community services, including day centres, that provide support for groups such as elderly people and those with mental or physical disabilities. The demand for care services is likely to continue to increase, especially as the number and proportion of old people in the population grows.

The statutory agencies are large employers of care workers. These include local authority social services departments in England and Wales, and local authority social work departments in Scotland. Voluntary organizations also employ care workers in residential and day settings. Some of these agencies, such as the Royal National Institute for the Blind, have been established for. many years, while others have developed more recently. In the voluntary sector, some of the organizations have strong religious or social convictions. Residential homes, especially those providing for elderly people, may be owned privately.

Vacancies may be advertised in *Community Care, Public Service, Care Weekly* and *Local Government Appointments*.

PAY AND CONDITIONS

Pay varies according to employer, location, type of work, and experience. Salary agreements differ considerably between local authorities. For day centre work (Monday to Friday, regular hours) care assistants may typically earn between £9,300 and £10,386. Those working in residential settings may typically earn £9,906 to £10,578. Posts with more responsibility, such as a senior care worker, may be on a scale that reaches in excess of £14,000.

Wages paid by private and voluntary agencies also vary, although rates are generally similar to those offered by local authorities.

Care assistants working in day centres and in the community may work regular hours from Monday to Friday, although occasional weekend work may be included, for instance, for outings. Staff working in residential homes often work shifts, on a rota basis, to cover 24 hours for seven days a week. Some assistants live-in, while others are non-residential; both residential and non-residential staff share night duties, on a rota basis.

Part-time work is possible.

PROSPECTS

There is no standard pattern for promotion for care assistants. Most assistants gain qualifications before they progress to supervisory level posts.

It is not possible to achieve professional social worker status through promotion without taking the qualifying Diploma (DipSW); see article 1. FIELD SOCIAL WORKER. Increasingly, employers are recruiting only social workers who are qualified. For entry to DipSW programmes, work experience as a care assistant is highly valued.

RELATED OCCUPATIONS

Nursery nurse, nurse, residential social worker, youth and community worker, play leader, nanny/home help, health care assistant/nursing auxiliary.

FURTHER INFORMATION

Central Council for Education and Training in Social Work*, *England:* CCETSW Information Service, Derbyshire House, St Chad's Street, London WC1H 8AD, 0171 278 2455 *Scotland:* 5th Floor, 78-80 George Street, Edinburgh EH2 3BU, 0131 220 0093 *Wales:* 2nd Floor, West Wing, Southgate House, Wood Street, Cardiff CF1 1EW, 01222 226257

Community Service Volunteers (The National Volunteer Agency), 237 Pentonville Road, London N1 9NJ, 0171 278 6601

London Voluntary Service Council, 356 Holloway Road, London N7 6TA, 0171 700 8107

National Association for Voluntary Hostels*, Fulham Palace, Bishops Avenue, London SW6 6EA, 0171 731 4205

National Council for Voluntary Organizations, Regents Wharf, 8 All Saints Street, London N1 9RL, 0171 713 6161

Scottish Council for Voluntary Organizations, 18-19 Claremont Crescent, Edinburgh EH7 4QD, 0131 556 3882

Social Work Admissions System (SWAS), Fulton House, Jessop Avenue, Cheltenham, Gloucestershire GL50 3SH, 01242 225977

Wales Council for Voluntary Action, Llys Ifor, Crescent Road, Caerphilly, Mid-Glamorgan CF8 1XL, 01222 869224

FURTHER READING

Leaflets/booklets are available from the addresses marked*.

Job Outlines – Social Work – COIC
Working in Social Work – COIC
Working in Work with Children – COIC
Careers in Social Work – Kogan Page
Careers Working with Children – Kogan Page

In the careers library classified under KEB.

PROBATION OFFICER CLCI:KEB

BACKGROUND INFORMATION

Probation officers are primarily 'officers of the court' dealing with offenders of all ages as part of the criminal justice system. They may also provide help to the courts in safeguarding the welfare of children in family proceedings.

The Home Office is responsible for the organization of the Probation Service in England and Wales. Probation officers are employed by local probation committees in 54 areas, rather than by local authorities. Typically they are based in an office located near the magistrates court to which they are attached.

In Scotland there is a separate statutory framework, whereby local authority social work departments have responsibility for providing criminal justice services. Social workers are employed in local authority social work departments responsible to the Regional and Islands Authorities. Those interested in probation work may work in these areas, but within a department that has a wider range of responsibilities.

THE WORK

Probation work is mainly concerned with the supervision of offenders in the community, although probation officers undertake an increasingly wide range of duties.

The aim of the work is broadly to work with offenders so that they lead law-abiding lives, in a way that minimizes risk to the public. Probation officers work in partnership with other bodies and services in using the most constructive methods of dealing with offenders and defendants.

Court work: in most cases the first main task for the probation officer is to prepare a pre-sentence report for the court. The purpose of the report is to advise the court about the offence that has been committed, the relevant circumstances of the offender and the report writer's opinion of the most suitable sentence that the court might decide to impose (for example, a community service order). In order to complete their reports the officers interview the offender at length and make inquiries into their personal affairs. Offenders are not always willing to co-operate and may resent the officer's attempts to help.

Probation orders: when the court makes this type of order the offender is placed under a probation officer's supervision; this may be from six months up to three years. The offender is allowed to remain at home, subject to certain conditions, including good behaviour. Supervision entails working with the individual, often on a one-to-one basis. Probation officers try to gain offenders' confidence, help them to recognize their problems, and attempt to find realistic and achievable goals. Officers try to identify any psychological, emotional or social causes of the offender's behaviour. They also help the offender sort out any personal, social or work problems, mobilizing and making effective use of the resources and services available.

Probation officers observe offenders in their home situations, assess their needs, strengths and weaknesses, and develop plans with offenders and their families to achieve the desired ends. There are no set formulas leading to solutions; each offender is an individual and much depends on the probation officer's approach and personal qualities.

Community sentence work: there are a range of community sentences available to the courts for offenders whose offences are not so serious to merit a term of imprisonment but serious enough to justify a community sentence. The main community sentences for adults aged 16 and over are the *probation order*, the *community service order* and the *combination order*. For young offenders between the ages of 10 and 17, the courts may impose a supervision order lasting for up to three years. This is similar to the probation order, but designed to take account of the needs of a young person.

If a probation order is made, the offender is placed under a probation officer's supervision for a period between six months and three years. The probation officer is responsible to the court for the planning, co-ordination and delivery of the supervision programme.

The community service order requires the person to perform unpaid work for between 40 and 240 hours, for example, gardening, building adventure playgrounds and decorating elderly people's homes. The hours set by the court should be completed within one year of the order, but it remains in force until the hours are completed. Probation officers organize and monitor community service, ensuring that placements provide positive, demanding and socially useful work.

If the court imposes a community sentence, the supervising probation officer is responsible for: ensuring that the offender obeys the terms of the order; securing the rehabilitation of the offender by tackling offending behaviour and helping the offender to lead a law-abiding life in the future; protecting the public from harm by the offender and preventing the offender from committing further offences; dealing with any unacceptable failure of the offender to comply with the sentence – this will result in enforcement action, including the possibility of a return to court, where the offender can be re-sentenced for the original offence.

Work with prisoners: some probation officers are seconded to prisons to assist in the rehabilitation of offenders and to help prepare for their release. They help offenders and their families to cope with custodial sentences and provide information about home leave or parole decisions. Some probation officers are employed as wardens of probation and bail hostels and a small number work in day centres.

Probation officers also provide newly released prisoners with an 'after-care' service, for example, by helping them to find accommodation and work, or directing them towards those statutory or voluntary bodies that can provide special help. On release, prisoners serving more than twelve months are supervised on licence by the probation service.

Family court welfare work: the probation service assists in family court welfare work, where its main aim is to help the courts in their task of serving the needs of children whose parents are involved in separation or divorce proceedings. The main duties of probation officers are to try to identify areas of agreement between the parties, carry out necessary enquiries and prepare a welfare report to assist the court to make decisions in the best interests of the children.

In addition to direct work with offenders, the probation officer spends time writing casework reports, and attending case conferences and meetings with other members of the service. Probation teams meet regularly to discuss problems and there may be case conferences. In addition to having contact with the law enforcement agencies (police and the courts), probation officers develop links with representatives of other statutory bodies and private/voluntary/charitable agencies that provide resources or services. Part of every week is spent on-duty, dealing with callers to the office, telephone enquiries and emergencies.

WORK ENVIRONMENT

Probation officers are usually based in an office and work in small teams under the management of a senior probation officer. They usually spend less than half of their time in the office and are required to visit clients and their families at home. In addition, there will usually be at least one day a week attending court sessions. A considerable amount of travelling, therefore, may be entailed.

SKILLS AND INTERESTS

The work is demanding and calls for a flexible approach. Probation officers must be capable of making objective appraisals and exercising clear judgement. They must be sympathetic to the personal pressures that may cause individuals to commit offences, but also able to establish effective control where necessary. It is important that probation officers are able to develop relationships with offenders, gain their trust and build up confidence. However, this may often prove difficult and the officer must be prepared to cope with hostile attitudes and resentment.

There will inevitably be disappointments when dealing with some individual cases. The officer should be able to cope with the stress and heavy responsibility of some aspects of the work. However, there will also be job satisfaction, for example, in providing help, getting offenders to accept their problems and constructively working towards a situation where they do not re-offend.

Probation officers rely on their powers of persuasion when dealing with unco-operative offenders and with the courts. They must be effective communicators – both in speech and in writing.

They must be able to work in close co-operation with other professionals, as well as with a case-load of up to 50 offenders of different ages and from a variety of backgrounds.

ENTRY REQUIREMENTS

England and Wales

Until recently, entry to probation work as a qualified probation officer in England and Wales was through a course of professional training leading to the Diploma in Social Work (DipSW). That is no longer the case. A new scheme is to be introduced which will allow probation committees to recruit trainees direct, following a regional selection procedure. Applicants will have to pass a range of tests, exercises and interviews, to be selected for training. Probation committees will be encouraged to draw on a wide range of backgrounds, skills and disciplines in order to provide a well-balanced workforce.

It is intended that the new arrangements will be in place in time for the first trainees recruited in this way to begin training in Spring 1997.

Scotland

Entry to criminal justice work as a qualified social worker in Scotland continues to be through a course of professional training leading to the Diploma in Social Work (DipSW) awarded by the Central Council for Education and Training in Social Work (CCETSW) – see ENTRY REQUIREMENTS – FIELD SOCIAL WORKER (KEB).

TRAINING

England and Wales

Details of the new training arrangements due to start in Spring 1997 have not yet been finalized. Training, however, will be mainly work-based and on a modular basis. Individual entrants' qualifications and previous experience will be taken into account in planning their training.

It is expected that training will lead to Qualified Probation Officer Status (QPOS) and to an appropriate-level NVQ. Contact The Home Office Probation Training Unit for further details.

Scotland

In Scotland the DipSW remains the qualification for social workers involved in criminal justice work. See TRAINING – FIELD SOCIAL WORKER (KEB) for full details of training leading to the DipSW.

LATE ENTRY

Maturity and experience of life are advantages in probation work and adult entry is encouraged.

In England and Wales, it is likely that entrants into probation work under the new training arrangements will be experienced adults.

As far as Scotland is concerned, please see FIELD SOCIAL WORKER (KEB) for information on late entry to DipSW training.

OPPORTUNITIES

In England and Wales the Probation Service is co-ordinated by the Home Office; probation officers are employed by local probation committees comprising magistrates and co-opted members. In Scotland, no separate probation service exists and the functions are carried out by local authority social work departments, within which it may be possible to specialize in criminal justice work. There may be opportunities for trained probation officers to find employment with some of the voluntary organizations working in the field. Independent agencies are increasingly employing professionally trained workers.

In Scotland, some students are employed as trainees by local authorities, seconded onto courses, then resume employment after completing the professional training course. Such secondments, though, are limited in number.

The number of social work posts is limited, according to available resources.

Job opportunities vary around the country and it may be necessary to move to another geographical location.

Posts are advertised in *Community Care* and in the national press.

PAY AND CONDITIONS

Qualified probation officers with the Probation Service in England and Wales receive at least £15,672 on appointment and are on a pay scale to £21,132. Senior probation officers are on a pay scale from £20,106 to £24,054. Probation officers working in certain areas may be entitled to additional allowances, as are those based at penal establishments.

Social workers in Scotland working in criminal justice work are paid on a scale from £15,438 to £19,617.

The working week is approximately 37 to 40 hours, Monday to Friday, but the exact hours worked are dictated by the demands of the job. Probation officers may have to be available outside normal working hours to visit offenders under supervision, to enable working offenders to report in, and to deal with emergencies – for example, attending the police station. There may be a rota for stand-by duty covering nights, weekends and bank holidays. Time off in lieu should be available for extra hours worked. Additional payments are made for working 'unsocial hours'.

PROSPECTS

Promotion is quite difficult to achieve in the probation service. It is possible to advance to senior, advisory or managerial posts. However, there are few opportunities to practise practical probation work at levels above senior probation officer. Most of the work will be of an administrative nature. Other avenues are to teaching posts as tutors, training officers or student supervisors, in educational establishments or with voluntary organizations.

RELATED OCCUPATIONS

Field social worker, residential social worker, counsellor, prison governor, teacher, youth and community worker.

FURTHER INFORMATION

Central Council for Education and Training in Social Work*, **England:** CCETSW Information Service, Derbyshire House, St Chad's Street, London WC1H 8AD, 0171 278 2455 **Scotland:** 5th Floor, 78-80 George Street, Edinburgh EH2 3BU, 0131 220 0093 **Wales:** 2nd Floor, West Wing, Southgate House, Wood Street, Cardiff CF1 1EW, 01222 226257

The Home Office, Probation Training Unit, Room 414, Queen Anne's Gate, London SW1H 9AT, 0171 273 3178

For addresses of voluntary organizations and opportunities for voluntary work, please see the SOCIAL WORK articles.

FURTHER READING

Leaflets/booklets are available from the addresses marked*.

Job Outlines – Social Work – COIC
Job Outlines – Working with Children – COIC
Careers in Social Work – Kogan Page

In the careers library classified under KEB.

NURSERY NURSE CLCI:KEB

BACKGROUND INFORMATION

Nursery nurses work with children, from new-born babies to seven-year-olds (eight in Scotland), in a variety of settings including nursery, infant or primary schools, day nurseries and hospitals, in both the private and voluntary sectors. They are also often employed in private households to care for children in their own home environment.

There have been enormous changes in the role of the nursery nurse over the last ten years, with an increasing emphasis on the pre-school education of young children, which requires teaching as well as the more traditional caring skills. The growing number of working mothers has meant that more children of pre-school age are being cared for in nursery provision and the demand for qualified nursery nurses remains high.

Nursery nurses work with a wide range of children, including those with disabilities and special needs, and often liaise with other professionals such as social workers, teachers and medical staff.

THE WORK

Nursery nurses are involved in planning, initiating and supervising work and play activities for individuals or groups of children, including story sessions, reading, cooking, computer activities and music sessions.

Promoting the physical, social, emotional and educational development of a child is an essential part of the work. This is done by encouraging children to make meaningful choices, have consideration for others, engage in exploration and develop self-esteem and confidence, through a programme of learning and play activities. A nursery nurse often has to take sole responsibility for children in outdoor areas where a variety of activities are available. Observing, monitoring and assessing individual children at play is also an important aspect of the job, as is reporting on areas of concern to parents, guardians, teachers or hospital staff. The work also involves carrying out domestic duties such as tidying up, preparing meals and washing soiled clothes. Caring for sick children and administering first aid when necessary as well as washing, feeding, dressing and toileting the very young are all part of the nursery nurse's work.

With the increasing emphasis on pre-school education, the maintenance of accurate records has become an important aspect of the job, as has the encouragement of, and assistance with, early reading and number work.

Nursery nurses often work as part of a multidisciplinary team providing care and education.

WORK ENVIRONMENT

Nursery nurses work in a variety of settings from private homes to large day nurseries. Working conditions can often be noisy, untidy and messy. Supervision of children can be indoors or outdoors and sometimes involves taking children on outings to local parks or places of interest. The workplace itself may be modern, light and airy or can be an older property with more outdated facilities.

SKILLS AND INTERESTS

It is essential that nursery nurses have a genuine interest in children and a desire to be involved in their social and educational development. Physical fitness and stamina are essential, as bending and being active are a major aspect of the job. Nursery nurses must be alert, in order to look out for any potential dangers. A responsible attitude is needed at all times. Children are not always predictable and their demands can be stressful, so patience and the ability to remain calm in crisis situations is crucial. Creative ability and imagination are important, in order to produce stimulating activities for children. A nursery nurse must be able to work as part of a team as well as being able to work alone. Planning, organization and presentation skills are necessary in order to provide an interesting programme of work and play. A cheerful disposition, along with a sense of humour are also invaluable. An awareness of the social, emotional and educational needs of a child and sensitivity to children are essential. Good communication skills are important when liaising with other professionals, as well as parents and guardians.

ENTRY REQUIREMENTS

In England, Wales and Northern Ireland the recognized qualifications are the Certificate in Child Care and Education (CCE), the Diploma in Nursery Nursing (NNEB), and the Advanced Diploma in Child Care and Education (ADCE) – all awarded by the Council for Awards in Children's' Care and Education (CACHE). The BTEC National Diploma in Caring Services (Nursery Nursing) is also a nationally recognized qualification. For those already involved in the care of children, NVQs/SVQs in Child Care and Education are available at Levels 2 and 3.

The Scottish Nursery Nurses Board (SNNB) in Scotland issues certificates of Registration to Nursery Nurses. The training consists of a two-year programme of SCOTVEC modules that provide both theoretical and practical areas of study. Potential applicants must be 16 years or over.

There are no specific academic requirements, but most institutions prefer two or three GCSEs/S grades (A-C/1-3) in English and other subjects such as sociology, music, human biology, psychology and art. The ability to play a musical instrument is useful, as is previous experience of care work either on a paid or voluntary basis. Most colleges of further education accept students at 16 years, although the private colleges have a minimum entry age of 18 years.

Entry may be possible for young people through Modern Apprenticeships leading to at least an NVQ/SVQ Level 3. Contact your local careers office, TEC/LEC for details.

TRAINING

The CACHE Diploma in Nursery Nursing (NNEB) and the SCOTVEC National Certificate in Caring Services (Nursery Nursing) consist of both theoretical and practical training on a continuous assessment basis.

The CACHE Diploma in Nursery Nursing (NNEB) is a two-year full-time course, but is also available part-time, which may take up to five years maximum. Forty per cent of course time is spent working in practical placements with children and families. The age groups covered are birth to one, one to four, and four to seven years – in a variety of settings. Amongst the areas of study are: work with young children, equality of opportunity, physical care and development hygiene, first aid, emotional and social development, and nutrition. Students are expected to demonstrate their competence in a variety of situations and show their ability to work in a professional and responsible manner.

The Certificate in Child Care and Education (CCE) is a

one-year full-time award. It is a module-based course, the two main areas being knowledge and understanding, and practical skills and competency. There are no academic entry requirements for the CCE other than a minimum age of 16 years. Students who successfully complete the CCE can progress onto the CACHE Diploma in Nursery Nursing (NNEB).

The Advanced Diploma in Child Care and Education (ADCE) consists of six modules that can be completed within a two to five-year period and is aimed at experienced professional child care and education workers. It may also be run as a one-year full-time course. Under the Credit Accumulation Transfer Scheme (CATS), the Open University awards credit points on completion of the ADCE to candidates who wish to progress to higher education.

The BTEC National Diploma in Caring Services is also available at many further education establishments; courses usually last two years full-time.

In Scotland, the SCOTVEC National Certificate courses consist of a combination of theoretical and practical work. The programme of SCOTVEC modules leads to a national certificate, as well as a higher national certificate.

NVQs/SVQs in Child Care and Education at Levels 2 and 3 are available nationally. At Level 2 the units covered are: work with babies, work in support of others, work in pre-school groups and work in community-run pre-school groups. Level 3 covers group care and education, family day-care, pre-school provision, family support and special needs.

Specific training opportunities for young people, including Modern Apprenticeships, may be available – contact your local careers office, TEC/LEC for details.

LATE ENTRY

There is no upper age limit for entry to nursery nurse training and adult students are welcome. Those with previous experience and skills may be able to go through the APEL route in order to gain recognized qualifications.

OPPORTUNITIES

Demand for qualified nursery nurses in both the private and public sector is high, and vacancies are available not only in the UK but often abroad. The majority of nursery nurses work in local authority nursery schools or classes, day nurseries and companies offering workplace creche or nursery provision.

Vacancies are normally advertised in the local press or in national publications such as *The Lady, The Times Educational Supplement* and *Nursery World*. Local authorities also provide details on all vacancies within various departments. There are several agencies who specialize in finding work for nannies both in the UK and overseas.

PAY AND CONDITIONS

Pay and conditions for nursery nurses vary depending on the type of employer and can range from £6,693 to £11,700 for those working in the public sector. Those in senior positions can earn from £11,000 to £28,800 depending on the size of the nursery and the number of children being cared for. Nursery nurses employed in private homes as nannies can receive an average wage of £80 to £90 a week, although this can vary depending on the location of the job and the number of children needing care. Private nannies who are required to live-in have accommodation provided and this is usually reflected in the salary.

Most nursery nurses work between 32 and 40 hours a week involving early starts and late finishes. Some workplace and day nurseries can be open from 7am until 8pm, and staff normally work on a shift basis. Staff employed in schools usually work school hours and have school holidays.

In residential nurseries it is essential that adequate supervision and cover is available all year round, 24 hours a day (including weekends and public holidays), so staff need to work to a strict shift system.

For nannies working in the private sector, the hours tend to be longer and time off is not always available on the same day or at weekends. Due to the fact that they 'live in', nannies are sometimes required to attend to, and care for, children during the night.

It is possible to obtain part-time work as a nursery nurse. Job share opportunities are available and encouraged.

PROSPECTS

Promotion prospects for nursery nurses are limited, particularly in the public sector. Eventually, it is possible to become an officer-in-charge, which involves managing budgets, administration duties and arranging and organizing supervision of children.

A qualified nursery nurse may open their own nursery, crhche or childminding provision but this would also require some business expertise.

RELATED OCCUPATIONS

Nurse, care assistant, childminder, teacher, social worker, youth and community worker, playgroup leader.

FURTHER INFORMATION

Council for Awards in Children's Care and Education (CACHE), 8 Chequer Street, St Albans, Hertfordshire AL1 3XZ, 01727 847636 (sae please)

Professional Association of Nursery Nurses (PANN), 2 St James' Court, Friar Gate, Derby DE1 1BT, 01332 343029

Scottish Nursery Nurses Board, 6 Kilnford Crescent, Dundonald, Kilmarnock, Ayrshire KA2 9DW (sae please).

FURTHER READING

Job Outlines – Nursery Work – COIC
Working in – Work with Children – COIC
Careers Working With Children and Young People – Kogan Page

In the careers library classified under KEB.

CAREERS ADVISER CLCI:KED

BACKGROUND INFORMATION

The Careers Service is undergoing significant change as a result of legislation in 1993. For many years, it has been run exclusively by local education authorities but, from 1994, the management responsibility has transferred to organizations that have successfully tendered to run local careers services.

Local careers services provide information, guidance and practical help to school or FE college students (and those who have recently left) to enable them to take up suitable education, training and employment.

The Careers Service is not responsible for work with students in universities and colleges of higher education; most of these institutions employ their own careers staff.

THE WORK

Careers advisers, sometimes known as careers officers, help their clients make informed, realistic decisions about their future education, training and employment, and to put these decisions into practice. Most careers officers' work is very varied, although some careers services have careers officers specializing in work with particular client groups, such as members of ethnic minorities, special needs, sixth-form and college.

Careers advisers spend much of their time in schools, often working in a team with other careers advisers and careers service support staff. They inform and advise young people at times when they make decisions that have career implications. Activities include interviewing young people, sometimes with their parents, and talking to and initiating discussions with groups. Careers advisers work closely with school staff to advise on schools' careers education and to arrange interviews and group work. They meet tutors in schools and may conduct training for teachers to advise them of developments in employment and training.

An increasing amount of careers advisers' time is spent in helping young people to draw up action plans, and in advising those seeking to enter work-based training on how best to use their **Youth Credits.** Youth Credits is a system of funding training, which enables young people to approach employers or training providers of their choice.

Careers advisers are responsible for providing support and advice to young people seeking work-based training, both when trying to enter, and once in, such training. That responsibility remains, whether young people are in Modern Apprenticeships or other forms of supported training. They also liaise with training providers.

Some careers advisers work in local sixth-form colleges, tertiary colleges and colleges of further education, with similar activities to those in schools.

Careers advisers keep in touch with unemployed young people. They advise them of job and training vacancies, arrange interviews for vacancies notified to the careers service, help them with applications and interview techniques and advise them of any financial help that may be available.

Careers advisers make frequent contact with employers for several reasons: learning about jobs and training; keeping up-to-date with the local labour market; seeking vacancies for clients; arranging work experience placements; setting up education-business projects; advising employers of developments in education and training and on recruitment of young employees; establishing what an employer needs from the careers service and marketing its services.

Careers advisers produce information for their clients on a range of subjects, such as local opportunities, career ideas and higher education. It may be in the form of booklets, leaflets or information from computer databases.

In addition, many careers services have some advisers who spend time working with adult clients.

All careers advisers are responsible for administrative tasks, including: making notes after each interview; writing reports; liaising with staff in educational establishments, social services, youth service, etc; attending meetings and committees; making frequent telephone calls. Some supervise clerical support staff.

WORK ENVIRONMENT

Careers advisers are based in offices that are open to the public, but spend much of their time in schools, colleges and on employers' and training providers' premises. Most of their work is in clean, light surroundings.

The work usually involves travelling in the local area and many jobs require that careers advisers hold a driving licence and own a car.

SKILLS AND INTERESTS

Careers advisers must be able to get on well with a wide range of people and be capable of establishing good working relations with them.

They have contact with all kinds of young people and their parents, teachers, headteachers, college and university lecturers, employers, training providers, social workers, etc.

Careers advisers should be interested in young people and understand and care about them without being judgmental. They need the ability to gain young people's confidence and motivate them. An interest in educational matters is important. Careers advisers must keep abreast of developments in education and interpret them to young people, parents, employers and training providers.

Careers advisers should understand and be interested in industry and commerce, if they are to advise clients realistically. This should include a thorough understanding of training matters, including new developments and qualifications.

An interest in information gathering is desirable, as information plays a central part in careers work. Careers advisers have to research information and communicate it clearly to clients.

Good communication skills are essential. Careers advisers need to be able to express themselves clearly and simply, both in speech and in writing. They also need the ability to speak effectively to groups of people, such as young people, parents or teachers.

Careers advisers are responsible for arranging much of their own work, which needs good organizing and time-management skills. They are, though, part of a team and must operate well as team members.

It is increasingly important that careers advisers can work with computers. Many of them use portable computers to produce clients' career action plans and summaries of advice given to clients. Computer-assisted guidance systems programs are also increasingly used in careers offices, schools and colleges.

Senior staff need to be capable of managing staff and careers service resources.

ENTRY REQUIREMENTS

The nationally recognized professional qualification for careers officers is the Diploma in Careers Guidance (DCG). Applicants to DCG courses normally need one of the following:

– a degree, for which the minimum entry requirement is normally two A levels/three H grades and five GCSEs/S grades (A-C/1-3), or equivalent;

– an approved diploma or certificate in social science or social studies;

– an approved diploma in municipal or public administration, political science or management studies;

– qualified teacher status;

– a certificate in municipal administration, higher national diploma, or certificate or other approved qualification of comparable standard;

– diploma in higher education.

In practice, most younger entrants have a degree.

Two courses can lead to a degree and Part 1 of the DCG:

1. A degree in Human Organizations at the University of Northumbria, Newcastle – needs three A levels/four H grades plus five GCSEs/S grades (A-C/1-3) or equivalent.

2. A degree in Occupational Psychology – requires three A levels/four H grades and five GCSEs/S grades (A-C/1-3) including mathematics or equivalent.

TRAINING

Most careers advisers achieve their DCG qualification through a one-year full-time course (Part 1) followed by one-year on-the-job training as a probationary careers adviser while employed by a careers service (Part 2). An increasing number, though, are being employed by a careers service and attending college part-time, in which case Part 1 and Part 2 run concurrently.

One-year full-time courses only are offered at: University of Northumbria at Newcastle, University of Paisley, University of Strathclyde, University of Reading, University of Glamorgan, Nottingham Trent University and South Bank University.

The following institutions offer both one-year full-time courses and two-year part-time courses: University of Central England (Birmingham), University of the West of England (Bristol), University of East London, University of Huddersfield, The College of Guidance Studies (Swanley), Manchester Metropolitan University and Napier University (Edinburgh).

Part 1 training is intensive and includes both theoretical study and practical training. Areas covered include: careers guidance and careers education; the careers service; the education system; employment and unemployment; training; equal opportunities. Skills training is given in interviewing and working with groups. Courses include visits to employers, educational establishments and training organizations, with practical placements at careers offices.

Part 2 of the DCG takes place in post as a probationary careers adviser. The year is closely supervised and activities assessed.

An open learning course is offered at The College of Guidance Studies. This involves working through open learning packages, attending several five-day residential blocks at the college, monthly regional tutorial meetings and two weeks placement at a careers office. Most students take two years to complete Part 1 of the DCG on this basis and may also complete Part 2 at the same time.

The University of Northumbria at Newcastle offers a three-year full-time Human Organizations degree that can lead to completion of Part 1 of the DCG during the third year.

A recently introduced alternative method of qualifying is via NVQs in Guidance available at Levels 3 and 4 awarded by the Local Government Management Training Board, the Institute of Careers Guidance, City and Guilds, the Open University Validation Service and SCOTVEC.

A new form of training is being piloted which involves on and off-the-job elements integrated into a complementary programme. These courses will lead to an NVQ/SVQ in Guidance at Levels 3 and 4.

LATE ENTRY

There is no upper age limit for entry. Mature applicants are particularly welcome for the experience they can bring to the work, particularly if that experience is relevant, for example, work in industry or commerce, teaching, social work or youth work. The normal entry requirement for entry to DCG courses may be waived for applicants of 25 years and over who have five years' good employment experience. Course tutors need to be satisfied that such applicants can cope with the academic demands of the course and they may have to demonstrate this by passing an entry test.

Adult entrants to DCG training with relevant qualifications or experience may be able to gain exemptions from some aspects of Part 1 through Accreditation of Prior Learning (APL).

Some careers service support staff, often known as **employment assistants** or **careers assistants**, become careers officers by attending a full-time DCG course or by being supported by their employer to study part-time for the DCG. The NVQs being developed for employment assistants (Level 3) and careers advisers (Level 4) should make it easier for mature entrants to progress in the careers service.

OPPORTUNITIES

Careers advisers work in careers offices in towns and cities throughout the UK. There are approximately 470 main careers offices and a slightly greater number of branch and sub-offices.

Until recently, the vast majority of careers advisers worked for local education authorities but, since 1994, it has been open for other organizations to tender to run a local careers service. In the future careers advisers will work for careers services run by a variety of organizations. Some colleges of further education and sixth-form colleges employ their own advisers.

The number of careers officers increased considerably during the late 1980s and there are currently over 4,500.

On completing DCG Part 1 courses, careers advisers may need to move to another location to find a post. Vacancies have tended to be more plentiful in South East England than elsewhere. Vacancies are advertised in *PORTICO* (the Institute of Careers Guidance's fortnightly vacancy bulletin), in the *Times Educational Supplement* and in the *Guardian* education edition on Tuesdays.

PAY AND CONDITIONS

Most careers advisers currently begin on a salary scale of approximately £13,000 rising to £18,000. Senior careers advisers can earn £18,000 upwards. Chief executives may earn £40,000 plus.

Most careers advisers work a 37-hour week, Monday to Friday. Most work is in normal office hours, but some evening work is usual to attend parents' evenings and careers conventions and to allow late evening opening of careers offices.

The new careers services are encouraging flexibility over working hours. In future, part-time work, job sharing and working on a supply basis (on-call to fill temporary vacancies) are likely to become common for qualified careers advisers.

PROSPECTS

Most careers advisers begin in a general post with a wide range of duties. After gaining experience they may specialize in work with, for example, special needs clients, the unemployed, sixth-form and further education students, careers information, industrial liaison, ethnic minority clients, and so on.

Promotion to senior careers adviser may involve either management of one of these specialist areas, supervising a team of careers advisers, or running a small branch office. Further promotion involves additional management responsibilities and, for instance, it is possible to progress to operations manager and chief executive.

Some graduate careers advisers seek employment careers advisers work in higher education institutions.

It is possible for careers advisers to study part-time for a masters degree in guidance.

RELATED OCCUPATIONS

Personnel officer, counsellor, teacher, social worker, youth and community worker, training manager, university careers adviser, employment agency consultant/ interviewer.

FURTHER INFORMATION

The Institute of Careers Guidance*, 27a Lower High Street, Stourbridge, West Midlands DY8 1TA, 01384 376464

Local Government Opportunities (LGO), Local Government Management Board*, 76-86 Turnmill Street, London

FURTHER READING

Leaflets/booklets are available from the addresses marked*.

Job Outlines – Careers Work – COIC
Guidance, Counselling and Advisory Work – AGCAS

In the careers library classified under KED.

EMPLOYMENT AGENCY CONSULTANT/ INTERVIEWER CLCI:KED

BACKGROUND INFORMATION

Employment agencies act as intermediaries between employers and job-seekers. They earn fees from employers by matching suitable applicants with permanent and temporary vacancies.

There are several types of employment agency.

General staff agencies deal mainly with office workers, but may place other categories of staff, such as drivers or factory workers, in employment. The large national chains – Brook Street, Reed and Alfred Marks, for instance – are general staff agencies. There are also smaller local chains and independent agencies, with just one office. The majority of employment agencies fall into this category.

Specialist agencies specialize in particular categories of staff, such as accountants or computer personnel.

Medical and nursing agencies supply nurses and other medical staff to National Health Service and private hospitals.

Executive selection agencies concentrate on permanent recruitment of managers and executives.

Executive search agencies (also known as 'head hunters') are concerned with filling senior posts, and usually make the first approach to potential candidates.

The employment agency business tends to expand rapidly in times of general economic prosperity, and to contract when the economy slows down.

THE WORK

The terms 'interviewer' and 'consultant' generally have the same meaning, although the terms 'consultant' or 'recruitment consultant' are more widely used within the industry.

The work includes the following aspects:

Contacting employers, by telephone, correspondence and in person. A lot of time is spent 'selling' job-seekers to employers. For example, if a skilled candidate is available, a consultant may telephone a number of potential employers to see if they have a suitable vacancy. Employers also telephone the agency when they are in need of extra staff, and it is the consultant's job to take details of their requirements and draw up job specifications. Consultants may circulate lists of candidates to potential employers. 'Prospecting' – finding new clients for the agency – is also important. It involves telephoning and/or making personal visits to local employers, with the aim of selling the agency's services.

Interviewing job-seekers and trying to match their experience, qualifications and personality with suitable vacancies. It may be necessary to advise or counsel job-hunters – for instance, to persuade them to take further training or to make realistic decisions about the types of work for which they are qualified. Consultants also test candidates' skills.

Organization and administration. Consultants advise on interview preparation, arrange interviews and ensure that candidates know the time, date and venue. Afterwards consultants make follow-up telephone calls, to find out whether the interviews were successful. They also keep records of applicants, introductions and placements – either on record cards or computers. Administration also includes drafting press advertisements and placing them in newspapers and magazines.

Many employment agencies deal with both temporary and permanent placements, but, within an agency, consultants tend to specialize in working with either permanent or temporary staff.

The pattern of work varies with different employers, but a typical consultant would probably spend about half the time dealing with client firms (essentially sales work) and the other half selecting and interviewing candidates and carrying out back-up administration.

WORK ENVIRONMENT

The majority of employment agencies are to be found in town or city centres. Some occupy shop premises, using the shop window to display job vacancy cards; others are situated in offices, usually above street level.

Most agency branches are small – typically employing no more than four or five staff.

The work is largely desk-based, but there may be some travel, to visit clients. A driving licence is useful for this aspect of the work.

SKILLS AND INTERESTS

The work involves a great deal of contact with people, and it is important to be able to gain the confidence of others and to put people at ease. Communication skills – especially a good telephone manner – are essential. Selling is an important part of the work, demanding persuasiveness and persistence. A smart, well-groomed appearance is required to inspire the confidence of clients and job-seekers.

Interviewers/consultants need to be able to cope with pressure, remaining calm and polite at all times. They deal with varying demands and conditions, requiring adaptability and a flexible approach. Good organizational skills are needed to schedule telephone calls, interviews and appointments, keep track of job-seekers and vacancies, and maintain accurate records.

ENTRY REQUIREMENTS

There are no specific entry requirements – a suitable personality is more important than academic qualifications. It is possible to enter this type of work with no exam passes, although it may be an advantage to offer some qualifications, such as GCSEs/S grades.

Most employers – and particularly executive recruitment and executive search agencies – welcome applications from graduates. Any subject is acceptable.

Employment agency consultant/interviewer is typically a second job, entered at the age of around 21 to 25 years (although there are no fixed minimum or maximum age limits). Previous experience in sales, personnel or office work is useful; other backgrounds may be acceptable. Initial appointment will generally be as a trainee consultant. Another entry route involves starting work as an administrator or secretary in an employment agency; promotion may then lead to consultant status.

TRAINING

The large general staff agencies run induction training programmes, lasting up to twelve weeks, which include on-the-job training and courses in the companies' own training centres. Smaller agencies often send staff on external courses run by the Institute of Employment Consultants (IEC).

The IEC offers courses at two levels:

The Foundation Vocational Award in Employment Agency Practice is a distance learning course and examination for recent entrants to employment agency work. The course lasts six months and covers: background to employment agencies; essential legislation and procedures; the agency and the client; and the agency and the applicant. The IEC organizes study and revision seminars, at which students have the opportunity to meet and discuss difficulties. (It is possible to take the Foundation Vocational Award before starting work with an agency.)

The Certificate in Recruitment Practice is a national qualification, offered in conjunction with the Associated Examining Board. Part-time evening courses lasting one year are offered by a number of colleges of further education; a list of colleges is available from the IEC. Distance learning courses are also available. The courses cover recruitment practice, interviewing (including a practical test of interviewing skills) and relevant legislation. The standard required is similar to A level. Consultants usually take the Certificate in Recruitment Practice after gaining some experience in an employment agency or other personnel-related fields.

IEC qualifications are not always required for employment, but they are an advantage. The IEC encourages employers to recruit qualified consultants, and recommends that people looking for employment as consultants check that potential employers recognize the value of qualifications and training.

Some consultants take the Institute of Personnel Management examinations, although this is less common than the IEC qualification route.

LATE ENTRY

Late entry is usual – the majority of entrants are in their twenties. There are no maximum age limits.

OPPORTUNITIES

There are over 16,000 employment agencies in Great Britain. About 70 per cent of these are general staff agencies. There is a greater concentration of agencies in London and South East England than in other parts of the country, although opportunities are available nation-wide.

Vacancies are advertised in local and national newspapers, and in the specialist magazines, *The Interviewer, Selection,* and *Recruitment International.* It is also possible to find work by making direct approaches to agencies. Sometimes applicants who have registered with an agency, seeking other types of work, are offered trainee consultant posts.

PAY AND CONDITIONS

Salaries are a combination of a basic payment and commission. Consultants in London are generally the highest paid, with a typical starting salary of £13,000 to £17,000. Outside London, starting salaries are likely to be between £8,000 and £12,000. With two to three years' experience, consultants – in London and elsewhere – can earn £30,000. However, earnings depend to a great extent on results.

Working hours are usually 8.30am to 6pm, Monday to Friday. Some evening work may be necessary. Specialist agencies – such as those dealing with nurses or industrial workers – may open early in the morning, or 24 hours a day (on shifts).

A company car is sometimes provided. Private medical insurance may be offered to senior staff.

PROSPECTS

Entrants usually start as trainee consultants, and can expect to become consultants/interviewers within a few months of joining an agency. Thereafter, prospects depend on the size of the agency – there may not be much scope for promotion in smaller local firms, although it is possible in most agencies to reach branch management level. Large firms have a more clearly defined promotion structure, with opportunities for promotion to divisional management and beyond.

There may be occasional opportunities for experienced consultants to work abroad, with the European divisions of major agencies.

Self-employment – running one's own employment agency – is common, but it is important to gain experience of the industry first.

Experienced consultants also move into related work, such as sales or personnel.

RELATED OCCUPATIONS

Sales representative/manager, sales negotiator (estate agency), telephone salesperson, careers adviser, personnel officer.

FURTHER INFORMATION

Federation of Recruitment and Employment Services Ltd, 36-38 Mortimer Street, London W1N 7RB, 0171 323 4300

Institute of Employment Consultants*, 6 Guildford Road, Woking, Surrey GU22 7PX, 01483 766442

FURTHER READING

Leaflets/booklets are available from the address marked*.

In the careers library classified under KED.

YOUTH AND COMMUNITY WORKER (ENGLAND AND WALES)/COMMUNITY EDUCATION WORKER (SCOTLAND) CLCI:KEG

BACKGROUND INFORMATION

Youth and community work involves a broad spectrum of activities, concerned with education in its widest sense, with encouraging active participation in community affairs, and with the promotion of equal opportunities, irrespective of age, gender, class, race or disability. A key theme in current practice is 'empowerment' – the idea that it is possible for individuals or groups of individuals to make significant changes to their lives and the life of their community, with appropriate support from professionals.

THE WORK

There is a wide range of jobs under the general heading of 'youth and community work'.

Youth work is the most easily defined area, and is concerned with the education and development, both social and emotional, of young people aged between eleven and 26 years, particularly those aged 13 to 19 years

Over 50 per cent of youth workers are club or centre-based. Youth workers in clubs or centres organize activities such as sports, art projects, drama, discothhques. Centres may provide an informal setting for young people to meet (a coffee bar, for instance), where youth workers provide guidance in an unstructured way. They may also be involved in more formal group discussions and individual counselling, and may focus on particular groups such as the young unemployed, or young people with special needs.

A great deal of face-to-face youth work is carried out by part-time and voluntary workers (who outnumber full-time staff). Full-timers are often responsible for centre management, and divide their time between administrative duties, supervising part-time and voluntary youth workers, and direct work with young people. They may also liaise with and support part-time and voluntary workers running youth clubs in village halls, churches, mosques and other places of worship.

Some youth workers are 'detached' – not based in a centre, but concerned with meeting young people on their own ground: in the street, arcades, pubs and cafes, and working with them on the central issues of their lives.

There are also some youth workers based at schools, who may divide their time between youth work, teaching or pastoral duties, and others who are neighbourhood or district-based, working, for example, on housing estates. Some youth services employ outreach workers, whose aim is to encourage young people to make use of youth provision.

Community workers work with a variety of people who share common concerns or problems, helping them to identify their problems and move towards a solution. They are concerned with giving people from all walks of life the opportunity and confidence to take part in social, community and political activities. They may, for instance: work with tenants' groups, working to improve facilities on housing estates; encourage parents to establish playgroups and toddlers groups; help to set up credit unions; or work with homeless people.

In Scotland, community education services are concerned with adult education, as well as youth and community development. Training covers generic skills, but once employed, some staff specialize in working with young people, community work or adult education. Community education workers in local authorities often continue to have a mixture of responsibilities, whilst those in voluntary organizations tend to specialize.

WORK ENVIRONMENT

Youth workers may be based in clubs, centres, schools, or premises owned and managed by voluntary organizations. Some youth workers, along with community workers, are based at community education centres, community schools, neighbourhood or district offices. In Scotland community education workers may be based in community centres, or have responsibility for a specific geographic area. Most jobs involve some travel; in rural areas, this can be quite substantial. A driving licence is useful.

SKILLS AND INTERESTS

Youth and community work and community education demands the ability to relate to, and communicate with, a wide variety of people. Empathy and good communication skills (especially the ability to listen) are essential. It is important to be sensitive and emotionally mature, with the capacity to earn the trust of others, and to be able to offer information, advice and guidance in a way that is acceptable and useful. Resilience and toughness may be needed to cope with conflict and deprivation. To get projects off the ground, initiative and enthusiasm are required. Planning and administrative skills are also necessary.

Many posts require a commitment to work unsocial hours.

Wide interests are useful, and for some posts it is an advantage to have specialist skills or interests such as sports or arts.

ENTRY REQUIREMENTS

In England and Wales, the minimum entry qualifications for initial training courses are usually five GCSEs (A-C) (if candidates are under 25); this requirement is generally waived for mature and experienced applicants.

In Scotland, standard entry requirements for the BA in Community Education courses are three H grades and one S grade (passes to include English at H Grade and a mathematical subject). Mature applicants with experience of paid or voluntary work in community education are accepted without these qualifications, provided they can demonstrate their ability to meet the academic demands of the course. Applicants who have completed Access courses or other non-traditional modes of study are also accepted, with appropriate experience.

A number of entrants have degrees in unrelated disciplines. Entry to degree courses is with a minimum of two A levels/three H grades and five GCSEs/S grades (A-C/1-3) or equivalent. These entrants qualify by taking postgraduate courses in youth and community work that are open to graduates in any subject (although some institutions prefer a 'relevant' discipline, such as social sciences). Applicants for training courses are usually required to have some experience of working with people, preferably in a youth or community work setting. Such experience can be gained by working as a volunteer or paid part-timer in a youth centre. Local training courses, run by local authorities or voluntary agencies, may be available; these may lead to some level of youth and community work qualification, and are a useful foundation for those who want to proceed to qualifying training at a later stage. Further information about part-time and voluntary opportunities is available from youth officers in local authorities and voluntary and independent bodies.

The majority of qualifying courses in youth and community work are for mature students (21 years and over); school-leavers are generally advised to gain experience before studying for a full professional qualification.

All prospective youth workers must be prepared to disclose any criminal record they may have, even if it would normally be considered 'spent'. However, a criminal record does not necessarily disqualify an individual from working with young people; factors such as the nature of the offence, and how long ago it took place, are taken into account

TRAINING

There are a number of different routes to becoming a qualified youth and community worker, and there are now different levels of qualification, local and national, part-time and full-time:

England and Wales

1. Two-year full-time initial training courses, leading to a professional qualification in youth and community work (in many cases the qualification is a diploma in higher education, which may be followed by an optional third year of study for a degree). Courses are available at a number of colleges.

2. Three-year part-time initial training courses, leading to a professional qualification as above.

3. One-year full-time postgraduate courses.

4. Two-year part-time postgraduate courses.

5. Degree courses, lasting three to four years (a diploma in higher education may be awarded after the first two years).

6. A three-year part-time distance learning course run by the YMCA National College, for unqualified full-time and part-time workers in the Youth and Community Service.

7. A limited number of apprenticeship/accreditation schemes, usually for local people without qualifications, but with considerable experience in youth and community work.

8. A teaching qualification gained before 31 December 1988 is, in theory, an acceptable alternative to a youth and community qualification. However, employers may not regard teaching qualifications and experience (particularly with infants or juniors) as relevant for work with adolescents, and in these cases it may be necessary to take a one-year postgraduate course. Those who qualified as teachers after 1988 have to take a further qualification in youth and community work.

9. The National Youth Agency may recommend that the JNC grant individual recognition to candidates with a social sciences diploma or degree completed in 1981 or earlier, or, in certain cases, other qualifications.

10. Part-time qualifications, which may be a 'stepping stone' to further qualification, are run by local authorities, voluntary and independent bodies, and are regionally accredited.

Scotland

Northern College of Education, Jordanhill Campus (Glasgow) and Moray House Institute (Edinburgh) run a three-year BA in Community Education. They also offer one-year postgraduate certificate/diploma courses in Community Education (for applicants with degrees or equivalent qualifications, for example, in social work).

LATE ENTRY

Late entry is positively encouraged, as maturity is important. It is also advisable to have gained some experience in youth and community work before starting a professional training course.

OPPORTUNITIES

The number of full-time posts for youth and community workers is relatively limited. The total for full-time youth workers employed by local authorities in England and Wales has been estimated at around 5,000, plus around 700 officers and advisers. There are also an unknown number of community workers employed by other local authority departments, such as leisure and recreation, social services and housing.

Additionally, youth and community workers are employed by voluntary organizations such as the YMCA (Young Men's Christian Association), the National Association of Boys' Clubs, and small neighbourhood-based community groups.

In Scotland, it has been estimated that there are about 1,300 to 1,400 full-time posts in community education with many other community education workers holding posts in voluntary sector organizations and other local authority services such as social work and economic development.

PAY AND CONDITIONS

Qualified full-time youth and community workers in local authority employment are paid on a scale that ranges from £11,769 (starting point of level 1) to £22,604 (top of level 3).

Hours vary, but most staff are contracted to work a set number of hours (35 to 37 a week) that may include specified evening and weekend sessions. In practice, the actual time worked may considerably exceed the contracted hours.

PROSPECTS

In local authority youth work and community education services in Scotland, a clear promotion structure exists. Usually a youth worker will start as an assistant, then move on to running a youth centre, then into a senior role, with responsibility for youth work in a particular neighbourhood. Thereafter, there are opportunities for promotion to management grades – area youth officer, county youth officer. It is also possible to become a lecturer or trainer.

There is less of a formal promotion structure in voluntary sector youth work and in community work.

RELATED OCCUPATIONS

Field social worker, residential social worker, careers adviser, probation officer, volunteer organizer, school teacher, play worker, leisure centre manager.

FURTHER INFORMATION

National Youth Agency*, 17-23 Albion Street, Leicester LE1 6GD, 0116 2471200

Scottish Community Education Council, Roseberry House,

9 Haymarket Terrace, Edinburgh EH12 5EZ, 0131 313 2488

Wales Youth Agency, Leslie Court, Lon-y-Llyn, Caerphilly, Mid-Glamorgan CF8 1BQ, 01222 880088

The Community Youth Work Association (CYDA), 122 Rochdale Road, Oldham OL1 1NT, 01457 834943

National Council for Voluntary Youth Services, 11 St Bride Street, London, EC4A 4AS, 0171 353 6909

FURTHER READING

Leaflets/booklets are available from the address marked*.

Working in Work with Children – COIC

Service to the Community – AGCAS Careers Information Booklet

NYA Guide to Becoming a Youth Worker – National Youth Agency.

In the careers library classified under KEG.

PSYCHOLOGIST CLCI:KEL

BACKGROUND INFORMATION

While psychology is a relatively young science, it has made an impact on most people's lives. Psychologists observe and interpret normal and abnormal human behaviour. The knowledge and understanding gained is applied in a wide range of situations.

This article covers the five main professional specialisms: **clinical psychology, educational psychology, occupational psychology, criminological and legal psychology** and **counselling psychology.**

The British Psychological Society (BPS) has set up a register of chartered psychologists. It is open to appropriately trained psychologists who are members of BPS. The BPS also approves first degree courses and professional training courses in psychology.

THE WORK

Clinical psychologists are concerned with their patients' mental health. They work in teams with psychiatrists, nurses and other professionals in hospital and community clinics, or even the patient's own home. Although there are no absolute boundaries between the work of psychologists and psychiatrists – one major difference is that psychologists do not prescribe medication.

Their clients are all kinds of people, such as the elderly, children and mentally or physically disabled people. They interview and assess their patients, using psychometric testing where necessary. Once a problem has been identified it is discussed with others in the team, and a treatment programme is drawn up and carried out.

Therapy is designed to suit each individual's needs. It helps to improve the quality of patients' lives by teaching them to avoid or control their problems.

Psychologists train nursing and other staff in strategies for coping with problems like disruptive and violent patients, or bereavement. They write reports, attend meetings and case conferences, and carry out research.

Educational psychologists deal with the needs and problems of children from birth to the age of 19 years. They liaise with teachers, social workers and other professionals in schools, hospitals, child guidance clinics and social service departments.

They deal with all types of children, from the unhappy or disruptive to those who have special needs or who are gifted children. They choose the most suitable course of action from a range including counselling, learning programmes or family therapy. They help parents and teachers when necessary, training them in skills like behaviour management.

Educational psychologists also look at wider issues, for example, the organization and management of a school or home, identifying strengths and weaknesses and solving problems. They provide in-service training for staff dealing with young people. The work includes meetings, case conferences, report writing and research.

Occupational psychologists specialize in the world of work. They advise companies on improving training, job satisfaction and productivity. They study and assess the functions of organizations or groups, preparing and presenting reports, as well as advising on performance, ergonomics (the interaction of people with their workplace, equipment and efficiency), health and safety and other factors. Their skills are used to help individuals' needs as well, handling such behavioural problems as low self-esteem or workplace bullying.

They may specialize in one topic, such as industrial relations, vocational guidance and counselling, or selection and recruitment.

Criminological and legal psychologists work in prisons, youth custody centres, special hospitals and secure units. They work with staff and inmates and provide a range of rehabilitative programmes, including social skills training, stress management and anger control. An important part of the work is assessing prisoners, and some psychologists prepare reports for mental health review tribunals. They provide individual and group therapy. They are involved in the day-to-day running of these institutions and provide support and training for prison staff.

All are involved in research to some extent. They examine criminal behaviour and evaluate their therapies. Senior staff help with policy making and planning. They advise other professionals in this field including prison staff, the police and probation officers. Some specialize in court work, assessing clients, preparing reports and giving 'expert' evidence.

Many of the techniques that psychologists use are common to all the specialisms. Computers, video recording and other specialized equipment are widely used in experimental work. Psychological investigation uses a variety of methods. These range from laboratory-controlled scientific testing to informal situations where people are assessed in a relaxed environment.

Counselling psychologists are concerned with helping people cope with stress, resolve their problems and make decisions for themselves. They may work with other health care professionals, or in an organizational setting, and deal with issues such as redundancy, organizational stress, management, etc.

Their clients may be young people, adults, families and couples, or other professionals seeking a consultancy service such as counsellors or medical staff.

WORK ENVIRONMENT

This varies depending on the specialism. Psychologists may work in laboratories, offices, clinics, schools and colleges, prisons, and in commercial or industrial settings. Some visit clients or patients in their own homes.

SKILLS AND INTERESTS

Psychologists need to be interested in people, their abilities, interests and temperaments. They should be keen to help others without getting too personally involved – working with clients and patients can be emotionally draining. As problem solving can be such a major aspect of the work, they should be able to think logically and creatively and to examine issues from every aspect.

The work needs above-average written and spoken communication skills, as psychologists spend much of their time listening and talking to clients, colleagues and patients, and writing reports and other material. Patients' and clients' confidentiality should be respected. There is an obvious ethical aspect to the work and psychologists need a mature attitude and sound judgement in deciding on the best interests of their clients. It is important to be tolerant and to refrain from judging others.

Team work is an important aspect of the work and psychologists must be able to get on with other people.

Psychology, like other sciences, uses statistics to evaluate the outcomes. This requires psychologists to be numerate, able to analyse and interpret figures, and use computers.

They should be accurate and methodical workers who are able to organize their own workload and meet their objectives.

ENTRY REQUIREMENTS

A psychology degree from a course recognized by the BPS is necessary for anyone wishing to work in most psychology posts. The minimum entry requirements for a degree course are five GCSEs/S grades (A-C/1-3) with two A levels/three H grades. Many courses expect a GCSE/S grade (A-C/1-3) in maths.

When choosing a degree it is helpful if applicants consider their future career choices, because some first degree courses are more relevant than others. The BPS awards 'Graduate Basis for Registration' to those applicants who have completed approved courses.

Competition for specialized training places and first appointments is very intense. It is essential that applicants obtain good honours degrees (minimum 2:2, more usually a first or 2:1) if they are to find a training place.

TRAINING

Clinical psychology training is mostly hospital-based, although some academic teaching may take place in a higher education institution. Graduates are usually employed as trainee clinical psychologists and complete either a three-year MSc or MPhil degree course. They are supervised by senior staff and gain experience in working with all client groups.

Those wishing to train as educational psychologists need to complete a Postgraduate Certificate in Education (PGCE) and two years' teaching experience (not required in Scotland) before undertaking a one to two-year MSc or MEd course in educational psychology, followed by about one year's supervised training as above.

Psychology graduates, especially those who have a first degree in occupational psychology, often go straight into occupational psychology. They work in areas relating to the best use of people and equipment. They must be supervised by a qualified chartered occupational psychologist and undertake a postgraduate qualification in occupational psychology.

Many graduates who are interested in criminological and legal work join the Prison Psychological Service on graduation, and follow a three-year programme of in-service training. Those working in prisons and other institutions that are not secure/special units need no extra professional qualifications, though many study further for a master's degree in criminology, criminological psychology or similar.

Those working in special hospitals or regional secure units often have to be qualified in clinical psychology.

LATE ENTRY

There is no upper age limit. Those without a degree need to complete a BPS-approved degree course to be eligible for further training. If applicants lack the usual educational requirements they should contact the institution of their choice to enquire if a mature entry scheme is available. Graduates with a non-relevant degree should contact the BPS and enquire about 'conversion' courses.

OPPORTUNITIES

Psychologists work in the public services and the private sector. Part-time and job share vacancies are sometimes available.

Clinical psychologists form the largest professional group. The NHS has about 2,200 posts in the United Kingdom and this number is increasing annually. There are generally regular vacancies at the basic grade. Local authorities employ psychologists mainly in education or social services departments, working in child guidance, assessment centres and community homes. The Civil Service employs psychologists in many departments, including the Home Office Prison Service, Department for Education and Employment and Ministry of Defence.

Those involved in research and teaching are often attached to institutes of higher, further and tertiary education.

Psychologists in the private sector are often found in human resources management, private practice, market research or freelance consultancy. Opportunities are increasing because psychology has such a wide range of applications, relating, as it does, so closely to people in their daily lives.

PAY AND CONDITIONS

Salaries vary depending on specialism, seniority and levels of responsibility. Psychologists working for the National Health Service, local education authorities and the Prison Service have national pay scales. The earnings of freelance psychologists and those in industry and commerce can reach the highest of the salaries mentioned below.

Trainee clinical psychologists start at £11,823. Senior clinical psychologists rise to £49,238. The starting salary for a qualified educational psychologist is around £20,460, which rises to about £37,689 for a principal educational psychologist. These salaries are slightly lower in Scotland. Occupational psychologists' earnings are more variable. In the public sector, they start at around £12,000 rising to about £26,000, but in the private sector they can rise as high as £40,000.

Those working in prisons have a pay scale linked to Civil Service pay and conditions, unless they are employed in a clinical capacity, when their pay is similar to NHS scales.

Working hours depend on their duties. Many work normal office hours, 8.30am to 5pm Monday to Friday. Some research projects and clinical appointments may require attendance out of office hours.

PROSPECTS

Promotion prospects are good for chartered psychologists. Membership of the Register is essential for most vacancies as it denotes a recognized standard of professional attainment and training.

The NHS, Prison Service, Civil Service and local education authorities all have clearly defined career paths for suitably qualified psychologists. The prospects in the private sector are as attractive. People seeking promotion may have to move to another area to take up a suitable vacancy.

RELATED OCCUPATIONS

Psychiatrist, ergonomist, psychotherapist, counsellor, field social worker, teacher.

FURTHER INFORMATION

The British Psychological Society (BPS)*, St Andrews House, 48 Princess Road East, Leicester LE1 7DR, 0116 254 9568 (please include sae)

The BPS has sections for all areas of specific interest, divisions for major professional groups and national branches in Scotland, Wales and Northern Ireland.

FURTHER READING

Leaflets/booklets are available from the address marked*.

Which Psychology Degree ? – A Gale – BPS
Compendium of Postgraduate Studies in Psychology in the UK and Ireland – BPS
How about Psychology ? – L Higgins – BPS
Career Choices in Psychology – L Higgins – BPS

In the careers library classified under KEL.

VOLUNTEER MANAGER CLCI:KEM

BACKGROUND INFORMATION

Voluntary work is unpaid activity which benefits the community. It is carried out in a wide range of settings, and includes activities such as working in charity or hospital shops, befriending the lonely, driving, decorating an elderly person's flat, counselling, fund-raising, delivering meals on wheels, countryside conservation and office administration.

As the scope and complexity of voluntary work has grown, it has become increasingly common for organizations in the voluntary sector to employ paid managers to recruit, train and manage volunteers.

Many different job titles are used in this area, for example, voluntary help organizer, volunteer development officer, voluntary services manager and volunteer bureau manager.

THE WORK

The work is concerned with relating to a very wide range of people; volunteer managers come into contact with a much broader cross-section of the community than is usual in most other jobs, even in related areas such as the social services and health care.

Prospective volunteers may come from any section of the community – from unemployed teenagers to retired executives. They are interviewed by the volunteer manager, who needs to be skilled at drawing people out and discovering their interests, skills and experience, as well as the degree of commitment they are able to make to voluntary work. Managers then try to match volunteers with work that they will find interesting and satisfying from the point of view of their own personal development – and where they will be able to make a useful contribution to whatever project is chosen.

Volunteer managers try to encourage the public to come forward and offer their services, by publicizing the need for volunteers in their organization. This may involve arranging advertising and public speaking.

Liaison with others is an important part of the job – it is necessary to obtain advice, consent, support and sometimes finance for projects. In the NHS, volunteer managers liaise with medical staff and management. In social services departments, they liaise with social workers and other staff, such as home-helps. In voluntary organizations, liaison can be with a wide range of other organizations, both statutory and voluntary.

The work may involve organizing training sessions for volunteers and providing ongoing support for them in their voluntary work (for example, checking that they are satisfied with the type of work they are doing and dealing with any difficulties that may arise). Managers also promote good practice in the recruitment and use of volunteers by local organizations within the voluntary sector.

Managers may manage/supervise volunteers, or advise and liaise with other organizations/individuals concerned with the day-to-day management of volunteers. Some recruit volunteers for a range of different tasks, whereas others are concerned with organizing volunteers in one specific field.

The work usually involves administration: keeping records/accounts, writing letters, reports, guidelines for volunteers and other documents, applying for grants, organizing fund-raising, attending committee meetings. Managers may be responsible for budgets and keeping accounts, and for supervising paid staff, such as secretaries, as well as volunteers.

WORK ENVIRONMENT

The work is office-based but is likely to involve travel to meetings with representatives of other organizations, to meet volunteers at their placements, etc.

SKILLS AND INTERESTS

The ability to relate to individuals from a very wide range of backgrounds is essential; this involves adaptability, tolerance, patience, open-mindedness and a sense of humour.

Excellent spoken communication skills are required for interviewing, managing and training volunteers, giving talks, etc. Volunteer managers also need to be able to express themselves clearly in writing. Self-confidence and a positive, outgoing attitude are required for liaising with people from other organizations.

The post of volunteer manager, even when the work takes place in a large institution, such as a hospital, can be somewhat lonely: manager's concerns are different from those of other professional staff, and at the same time they do not share the perspective of the volunteers with whom they work.

As many posts require the ability to lead and motivate others enthusiasm is important. Managers need initiative to start up and develop new projects.

The work requires adaptability and commitment – it is not a nine-to-five job – and it is important to be flexible about attending meetings and other events in the evening or at weekends.

Volunteer managers who keep accounts should be numerate.

ENTRY REQUIREMENTS

There are no specific entry requirements in terms of academic qualifications or previous experience, although a degree and/or professional qualification may be an asset.

Entrants are usually, but not always, older individuals with experience and training in other fields. Experience in any or all of the following is useful: volunteering; organizing people (perhaps in the NHS or in teaching); committee work. It is particularly helpful to have had experience in a field that includes voluntary workers. A full, clean, current driving licence and use of a car are an advantage and may be essential for some jobs.

TRAINING

Training varies according to the organization and area but usually involves learning on the job, possibly under supervision. There may be opportunities to take short courses, typically lasting between one and five days.

Some organizations, eg those in health care and social services, provide short training courses for all their staff. Volunteer managers may attend such courses on areas including counselling and health and safety.

Most training specific to the role of volunteer manager, however, is external. There are a number of organizations running training events of various kinds. They include the following:

The Volunteer Centre arranges a large number of training courses around the country. These normally last one or two days and cover topics such as training volunteers, recruitment and selection, and interviewing skills. Their training brochure also includes details of volunteer management courses run by other agencies.

VOLUNTARY HELP MANAGEMENT WORK: KEM

The National Association of Volunteer Bureaux (NAVB) provides one-day training courses throughout the UK for managers who have been in post for at least twelve weeks. NAVB also holds training seminars at its annual three-day conference for volunteer bureau managers.

The National Association of Voluntary Service Managers offers a number of short training events (usually lasting one day) for volunteer managers working in the field of health care.

National Association of Councils for Voluntary Service runs a wide range of short training courses throughout England, some of which are designed for volunteer managers.

Directory of Social Change offers a number of short training courses specifically for volunteer managers. Most take place in London but some are in other English cities.

Volunteer Development Scotland has a core training programme for volunteer managers, covering the recruitment, training, selection and support of volunteers. It also offers courses for newly appointed managers and for those with experience.

Wales Council for Voluntary Action runs short courses for volunteer managers at different centres throughout Wales. They include: managing for the first time, training skills and managing staff development.

Northern Ireland Volunteer Development Agency (NIVDA) organizes a number of training courses, lasting between a half day and three days, on such as recruitment and selection of volunteers, effective management of volunteers and training volunteers.

Regional networks of voluntary organizations may run their own training events. An NVQ for volunteer managers is being developed.

LATE ENTRY

All entrants are adults and there are no maximum age limits. Most have experience and training in other fields.

OPPORTUNITIES

The main employers are:

– Voluntary organizations such as MIND, Age Concern, or local Victim Support Schemes. Some staff in voluntary organizations combine the role of volunteer manager with other responsibilities.

– Hospitals, hospices, community health and social services departments, which employ about 400 volunteer managers.

– Local Volunteer Bureaux, which function like employment agencies, matching prospective volunteers with voluntary sector organizations needing their services. There are about 300 such bureaux in England, Wales and Northern Ireland, and about 34 in Scotland. Most are charities or part of charitable organizations. Bureaux respond to local needs, and the range of tasks they carry out varies from one part of the country to another.

Entry is competitive, and because many voluntary sector organizations are affected by constraints on local authority spending, there is little or no expansion of this work at present.

PAY AND CONDITIONS

Rates of pay vary widely. Some organizations recommend rates of pay, for example a minimum of £12,000 to £15,000 for basic manager duties, with more for increased and managerial responsibilities (and higher rates for working in London). However, not all volunteer managers are paid these rates. Many jobs are part-time (salaries may be pro-rata).

Full-time volunteer managers work a basic 35 to 37 hours a week, Monday to Friday; extra evening/weekend work may be required. Organizations in the voluntary sector rarely pay for any overtime work, but instead allow time off in lieu.

PROSPECTS

Promotion prospects are limited, but this type of work can be a good background for related careers, such as social work, and for other posts within the voluntary sector, at managerial level, for instance.

RELATED OCCUPATIONS

Field social worker, youth and community worker, employment agency consultant/interviewer, charity fund-raiser, personnel manager, health service manager, volunteer.

FURTHER INFORMATION

Directory of Social Change, 24 Stephenson Way, London NW1 2DP, 0171 209 4949

National Association of Councils for Voluntary Service, 3rd Floor Arundel Court, 177 Arundel Street, Sheffield S1 2NU, 0114278 6636

National Association of Voluntary Service Managers, Teresa Cullen (Hon. Secretary), University Hospital, Nottingham NG7 2UH, 0115 924 9924 ext 42836

National Association of Volunteer Bureaux, New Oxford House, 16 Waterloo Street, Birmingham B2 5UG, 0121 633 4555

Northern Ireland Development Agency, Annsgate House, 70-74 Ann Street, Belfast BT1 4EH, 01232 236100

The Volunteer Centre, Carriage Row, 183 Eversholt Street, London NW1 1BU, 0171 388 9888

Volunteer Development Scotland, 80 Murray Place, Stirling FK8 2BX, 01786 479593

Wales Council for Voluntary Action, Crescent Road, Caerphilly, Mid Glamorgan CF83 1XL, 01222 869224

FURTHER READING

Directory of Volunteering and Employment Opportunities -Directory of Social Change
How to Work for a Charity – Directory of Social Change
Voluntary Agencies Directory – Bedford Square Press
Graduate Guide: Working for Charities and Pressure Groups – University of Sussex Career Development Unit

In the careers library classified under KEM.

1. BARRISTER/ADVOCATE CLCI:LAB
2. SOLICITOR CLCI:LAC
3. BARRISTERS' CLERK CLCI:LAZ
4. LEGAL EXECUTIVE CLCI:LAD
5. SHORTHAND WRITER CLCI:LAG
6. COURT USHER/COURT OFFICER/
MACER CLCI:LAG

BACKGROUND INFORMATION

In the United Kingdom there is one legal system for England and Wales and a different one in Scotland. Each is based on its own set of legal principles.

Both systems consist of two separate, complementary branches – barristers and solicitors (England and Wales); advocates and solicitors (Scotland). They are trained in different ways to qualify for the specialist service they provide.

Solicitors are normally the first point of contact for any person wanting legal advice. They may be general legal experts or may specialize in a particular area of law. In many cases they deal with the matter personally; in others a barrister/advocate is briefed.

Barristers/advocates are consultants offering specialist legal advice or representing clients in court or before tribunals. They are not approached directly by clients but through a solicitor or, in some cases, through another professional who has the right to brief them, for example, accountants, architects and surveyors. They have almost exclusive rights to appear in the higher courts. Some barristers practise general common law, although the majority specialize in certain areas. The majority of advocates do not specialize, although a larger number build up expertise in particular areas through doing a considerable amount of work in them.

Other legal careers featured in this chapter are peculiar to one or other of the two legal systems. Court officer/macer, for example, is a Scottish profession; legal executive, an English and Welsh one.

1. BARRISTER/ADVOCATE (LAB)

THE WORK

Practising barristers/advocates are always consulted by a member of another profession – in most cases by a solicitor. They may not work directly for a member of the public. They do not at first meet the client, but are briefed by the solicitor or other professional intermediary who wishes them to give specialist advice to their clients or to represent them in court.

Barristers/advocates are often consulted on points of law on which they give their opinion – after conducting research into similar cases and analysing them.

Solicitors often ask for an opinion on the likelihood of a case succeeding should it come to court. Based on their knowledge of past decisions and of the courts, barristers/advocates advise. If, in their opinion, the claim or defence is not likely to succeed, matters may be taken no further.

If a case comes to court, barristers/advocates concentrate on the conducting of the case, while the preparatory work of collecting evidence is carried out by the solicitor. One of the barrister's/advocate's skills lies in presentation in the courtroom, but in order to do this they have to spend a lot of time in preparation. Their preparatory work consists of becoming thoroughly acquainted with the facts of the case, reading statements and law reports, understanding any relevant technical or scientific terminology, and consulting clients, as and when necessary, in the presence of a solicitor.

In court they present the facts of the case to the judge and jury, cross-examine witnesses who are giving evidence, and finally sum up the reasons why the court should decide in their clients' favour.

Court appearances are not always easy to plan, since it is difficult to predict how long a particular case will last. When delayed by one case, a barrister/advocate may not be able to appear as planned in another. This may mean finding someone else – where possible, a colleague, to take on the work.

The division of time between court appearances, advising and drafting written opinions, depends on clients, solicitors and the chosen area of specialism. Chancery work (trusts, property, estates, taxation and company law) involves much more advisory work, preparing detailed and complex opinions and drafting agreements. Common law (criminal, family, contract law, torts) may involve a lot of time spent on court cases, but, even here, civil cases are less likely to lead to proceedings and demand less time in court than on advisory work. (Ninety per cent of civil cases are, in fact, abandoned, or a compromise is reached.) Barristers specializing in criminal work spend a high proportion of their time in court.

Although the majority of barristers/advocates are in private practice and work for clients, about 25 per cent of barristers and a smaller proportion of advocates work at the **Employed Bar** – in industry, commerce and central and local government, where they work in specialist legal departments, advising only their own employers.

Barristers in commerce and industry may be generalist legal advisers, or may specialize in areas such as company law or taxation. The greater part of their work is likely to be concerned with drafting, advising on and negotiating contracts, but they may also advise on aspects of employment law, patents, health and safety law, and acquisitions and mergers.

Those working in central government departments provide an advisory service to civil servants and ministers. Others work for the Crown Prosecution Service, which conducts prosecutions on behalf of the police. Barristers review charges and evidence to decide whether a case should proceed to court. They may conduct the prosecution in magistrates' courts, but they brief practising barristers in cases going to the Crown Court.

More and more barristers are using computers in their work, for research, report writing and record keeping.

WORK ENVIRONMENT

Most of the barristers in private practice work in chambers – their base. Some sets of chambers are specialist, home to groups of barristers who have chosen the same branch of legal work.

In London, chambers were once all in the same area, near the Inns of Court and the High and Central Criminal Courts. Many still are, but some barristers are seeking a wider variety of accommodation just outside the Inns. Outside London, chambers tend to be near the court buildings.

Some barristers work from home or from rented offices. This accommodation is still technically chambers, but they are known as sole practitioners.

Barristers in practice may base themselves in London and travel anywhere in the country to attend court, or may practise almost exclusively on one of six circuits, or administrative areas, in England and Wales: Northern; North Eastern; Midland and Oxford; West; South East; Wales and Chester. Even within one circuit, they spend a lot of time travelling.

Most advocates work from the Advocates' Library in Parliament House, Edinburgh, which provides the facilities they need to practise and which is open 24 hours a day, 365 days a year. If they are based elsewhere, they must still arrange to collect papers delivered to them by solicitors at the Library.

Employed barristers/advocates work in their company's or employing authority's premises.

SKILLS AND INTERESTS

Barristers/advocates need intellectual ability. The work calls for the ability to assimilate facts quickly, analyze, distinguish the relevant from the irrelevant, weigh the evidence and apply the law to the current situation.

They need fluency, clear speech and excellent presentation skills. In court they must be able to persuade, convince, argue, explain obscure points of law for the jury, and interrogate or cross-examine defendants and witnesses to establish the facts for both judge and jury.

They must be self-confident and able to inspire confidence in others. They must not allow their own or others' prejudices to affect the work they do for a client, but consider every problem dispassionately. Barristers/advocates working in criminal law accept that everyone is entitled to representation, whatever their financial means and whatever crime they are alleged to have committed. Even if their clients are unpopular with the media and general public, they are obliged to defend them to the best of their ability.

They must have complete integrity of character and need mental and physical stamina in order to cope with long hours, travelling and stress.

ENTRY REQUIREMENTS

England and Wales

Entrants must have:

- a law degree of at least 2:2 honours standard that has included study of the seven foundations of legal knowledge: obligations I, obligations II, criminal law, equity and the law of trusts, the law of the European Union, property law and public law. Entry requirements for law degrees vary but are usually a minimum of five GCSEs/S grades (A-C/1-3) with three A levels/five H grades at high grades, or equivalent *or*

– a non-law degree at the same standard, plus completion of the one-year Common Professional Examination (CPE) course. Please see article 2. SOLICITOR. It is important to note, however, that not all CPE courses satisfy the Bar's requirements. Suitability must be checked with the General Council of the Bar.

Scotland

Candidates, known as **Intrants,** must:

– have a law degree from a Scottish university; *or*

– have a non-law degree; *or*

– possess the qualifications that would permit taking a law degree, that is, H grades (normally five at A or B grades).

TRAINING

England and Wales

Currently, to become a barrister a person must:

- complete the academic stage of training by one of the routes above; *and*

- join one of the four Inns of Court and eat three dinners there during each eight terms. (A system of 'double dining' has been introduced for students who find it difficult to get to London frequently, and students may join an Inn and complete dining terms while still undergraduates); *and*

- complete a one-year full-time vocational course. For the academic year 1996-7 the Bar Vocational Course (BVC) is only offered at the Inns of Court School of Law. Thereafter, the BVC will be offered at a number of institutions around the country. Presently, students are called to the Bar after successful completion of the BVC. However the Bar Council has agreed that call should be deferred until after successful completion of the first six months of pupillage.

Two-thirds of the vocational course is devoted to skills training. Students practise the techniques of interviewing clients, take part in mock trials, learn how to draft documents, develop writing, numeracy, communication and presentation skills. They also study legal research, problem solving and opinion writing.

Following completion of the BVC, barristers intending to practise must complete a period of pupillage. Pupillage consists of two six-month periods spent under the guidance of an experienced barrister. During the first six months, the non-practising pupillage, pupil barristers must work in chambers (that may be outside London), gaining experience in drafting, opinion writing, preparing cases, attending court and attending external short courses and conferences. Their activities must be recorded against an approved check-list. They are then given a Provisional Practising Certificate, may appear in court and accept work in their own right. The Final Certificate is issued after the second six-month period.

The second pupillage may be spent outside chambers, in the Government's Legal Service, in industry, the Crown Prosecution Service or even in another EU country or at the European Commission.

Pupillage must also incorporate a certain amount of continuing professional development. Compulsory elements involve attendance at a course entitled 'Advice to Counsel' and further advocacy training that each Inn administers for its own members. Optional courses are available in Accounts, and European and Human Rights Law.

On qualifying, a practising barrister must obtain a tenancy in a set of chambers and work from there for at least three years, or with someone who has had five years' experience.

Barristers choosing to work in commerce and industry usually complete a pupillage even though it is not a requirement. Otherwise, they are unable to represent their employers in court.

Scotland

Intrants first follow a one-year full-time postgraduate course at a Scottish university leading to the Diploma in Legal Practice.

They then serve a period of salaried training of 12 to 21 months in a solicitor's office, during which time they may experience all work undertaken by solicitors, not merely that concerned with litigation.

The final stage consists of a nine-month period of pupillage, known as *devilling,* spent with a member of the Scottish Bar approved by the Dean of the Faculty. This is a full-time pupillage, with devils forbidden to undertake any form of paid work which would interfere with their training.

During this time they must pass the Faculty of Advocates' examinations. There are no formal lecture courses or tuition for these. Since the majority are graduates in Scots Law, they are exempted from almost all of the examinations except those in Evidence, Procedure, Pleading and Practice. After successfully completing the devilling period and passing the examinations, they are called to the Bar. Only then do they decide whether or not to practise.

LATE ENTRY

England and Wales

There is no upper age limit. Adults may follow the normal entry routes described above.

Individuals over 25 years of age who do not intend to take a degree should first contact The General Council of the Bar to establish whether any qualifications they do hold would entitle them to enter training. The Council has discretion to rule on previous qualifications and experience.

The decision by a mature entrant to become a practising barrister demands careful thought, given the financial implications of funding CPE and vocational course (see below) and the uncertain income during the early years of practice.

Solicitors wishing to become barristers should apply to the Joint Regulations Committee.

Scotland

Adults may follow the normal entry route. Certain exemptions are, however, granted to:

– Scottish solicitors and English/Welsh barristers who have practised for a minimum of three years (they are automatically exempted from taking the Diploma in Legal Practice); *or*

– students who do not wish to become practising advocates; they may receive partial exemption from training in solicitors' offices and/or devilling.

Solicitors may apply to become advocates at any time.

OPPORTUNITIES

There are about 8,500 independent barristers practising at the Bar, of whom 22 per cent are women. Two-thirds are based in London; the remainder in large towns and cities on the circuits. Those with a strong concentration of barristers include Birmingham, Bristol, Cardiff, Chester, Leeds, Liverpool, Manchester and Newcastle. A Northern Chancery Bar has been formed, reflecting the increasing amount of this work done outside London.

Barristers/advocates in independent practice are self-employed. They have to build a reputation for themselves so that solicitors will return to them with cases. There is, however, no longer any prohibition on barristers advertising. They can now market their services.

It is thought that over 2,000 barristers work at the **Employed Bar** and approximately 500 work in central government departments. There are other opportunities in the Crown Prosecution Service. A fairly small number work for local authorities.

There are opportunities to specialize in European or international law, and some to work or travel overseas. Some barristers, for example, have chambers in both Brussels and London. Others work at international and EC institutions. Some barristers have links in Commonwealth countries, or North America, and may travel to represent clients in courts there.

There are increasing opportunities to work on behalf of overseas clients with interests in the UK. These clients may brief barristers direct, without using a solicitor or intermediary, where the work does not involve court proceedings. Barristers wishing to be approached for such work usually make this known to the International Practice Committee of the Bar, which provides guidance to clients on the selection of barristers.

There are about 530 advocates, 300 of whom are in practice. Most are based in Edinburgh. Those who choose not to enter practice work in industry, commerce, government service, etc.

PAY AND CONDITIONS

Training

Non-law graduates find the same situation as regards funding full-time courses as do solicitors. Please see article 2. SOLICITOR.

During pupillage, most pupil barristers receive a minimum award of £3,000 per half-year. This is a figure agreed between the Bar and all chambers. Pupillages served in commerce, industry and public service are salaried. Both the Crown Prosecution and Government Legal Services offer a limited number of sponsorships, under which pupil barristers serving the first six months of non-practising pupillage receive a salary before serving the second six months with them. They, in addition, occasionally sponsor students through the CPE and vocational course.

Intrants serving their period in a solicitor's office receive a salary on a scale laid down by the Law Society of Scotland. They receive no fees or salary during the nine months' pupillage. Some scholarships are available but the majority of intrants must finance themselves.

On qualification

Practising barristers/advocates are all self-employed individuals. (They are not allowed to form partnerships or associations in independent practice.) Earnings therefore vary considerably, depending on success and workload.

It can take three to five years to build up a practice.

Fees may not come in until sometime after a case, and in the meantime overheads have to be met. Barristers share the expenses of running chambers, paying a share of the cost of premises and the salaries of barristers' clerks and other staff. Advocates pay a sum, graduated according to earnings and seniority, to the Faculty, for use of the premises, and a percentage of fees received to a service company, which provides administrative and secretarial services. The latter are not payable until fees are received.

Employed barristers/advocates receive a salary. Salaries in industry and commerce vary. In the Crown Prosecution Service they range from £20,579 to £55,836.

Hours of work vary considerably, but are usually long and often involve unsocial hours and time spent in travelling.

PROSPECTS

Prospects for barristers/advocates employed in government service depend on their gaining promotion to higher grades. The same applies to those working in local government. They sometimes move out of legal work into administration and take up senior management posts with local authorities.

At the independent Bar there are obviously no guarantees of earnings, security or prospects. Newly qualified barristers/advocates spend the early years in building up a practice, getting themselves known while working in the lower courts and in industrial or rent tribunals. Work is allocated to them by the barristers'/advocates' clerks. (The group of advocates assigned to the same clerk at the Library is known as a *stable*, while barristers share a clerk in chambers.)

Barristers/advocates usually know by the end of three years whether or not they are going to succeed.

After ten to 15 years' experience they may apply to 'take silk' (become a Queen's Counsel), which is necessary if they wish eventually to become a High Court or Court of Sessions judge. Barristers may also become Circuit judges, Crown and County Court recorders (part-time judges) and stipendiary magistrates, while advocates may become sheriffs. Both may be appointed to tribunals.

Some become (salaried) justice's clerks in magistrates courts. Others move to salaried posts outside the profession.

RELATED OCCUPATIONS

Solicitor, justice's clerk.

FURTHER INFORMATION

The Faculty of Advocates*, The Clerk of Faculty, Advocates Library, Parliament House, Edinburgh EH1 1RF, 0131 226 5071

The General Council of the Bar of England and Wales*, Education and Training Departments, 2/3 Cursitor Street, London EC4A 1NE, 0171 440 4000

The Students' Officers at: Gray's Inn Treasury Office, 8 South Square, Gray's Inn, London WC1R 5EU, 0171 405 8164

Students Department, Treasurers' Office, Inner Temple, London WC2A 3TL, 0171 797 8250

The Honourable Society of the Middle Temple, The Treasury, Middle Temple, London EC4Y 9AT, 0171 353 4355

The Bar Association for Local Government and The Public Service*, c/o Milton Keynes Borough Council, Civic Offices, 1 Saxon Gate East, Milton Keynes MK9 3HG, 01908 682205

The Bar Association for Commerce, Finance and Industry*, 60 Temple Chambers, Temple Avenue, London EC4Y 0HP, 0171 583 4937

GLS Recruitment Team, Queen Anne's Chambers, 28 Broadway, London SW1H 9JS, 0171 210 3304

The Crown Prosecution Service*, Personnel Branch 2, 50 Ludgate Hill, London EC4M 3EX, 0171 273 8000

FURTHER READING

Leaflets/booklets are available from the addresses marked*.

Job Outlines – Law – England and Wales – COIC
Job Outlines – Law – Scotland – COIC
Legal Profession – AGCAS

In the careers library classified under LAB.

2. SOLICITOR (LAC)

THE WORK

Solicitors give legal advice to clients and act for them, when necessary, in legal matters. Clients may be individuals, organizations, businesses or government departments. The cases undertaken by solicitors depend on the area of work they have chosen, and on their employer. A small firm, or a solicitor working as a sole practitioner, may deal with business affairs, commercial property matters, residential conveyancing, family law, crime, injuries and probate. Medium-sized and large firms tend to specialize, or have specialized departments dealing with, for example, international law, litigation, insurance, probate, or company and commercial law.

The main areas of work are as follows:

Business and commercial law: contract law, tax and VAT legislation, employment law, patents, export law, acquisition and sale of companies. Small firms usually consult solicitors as the need arises; large ones have their own legal departments staffed by solicitors and possibly barristers.

Probate: wills, estates and property. Solicitors advise clients on how to draw up wills and ensure that their wishes are carried out when they die. They may act as trustees of estates left in wills and deal with the affairs of people who die without making a will.

Conveyancing: involves the buying and selling of both business and domestic property. Solicitors ensure that the vendor has the right to sell the property, obtain all necessary information which may affect the new owners – known as conducting searches (for instance, in a domestic purchase, on the existence of rights of way or the likelihood of future planning development) and draw up the contract. In commercial property transactions, they may work closely with the client's source of finance, such as a merchant bank; in domestic ones, help the client carry out transactions with banks or building societies.

Litigation: clients involved in any kind of dispute with another person might consult a solicitor, who advises on whether the matter could be settled by correspondence or the threat of action, or whether legal action will be necessary. In the latter case, solicitors may represent clients in magistrates' and county courts. In more serious cases heard in the higher courts, they brief barristers. Litigation covers civil law cases like unfair dismissal, debt, landlord-and-tenant disputes, breach of contract, divorce and custody of children. Examples of criminal cases include theft, motoring offences and personal injury.

Some solicitors choose to specialize in criminal law, defending clients against prosecution.

Others are employed in industry and commerce, where they deal solely with their employer's legal affairs. This work is likely to include drafting, advising on and negotiating contracts, and advising on aspects of employment law, patents, and health and safety law, and on the legislative implications of decisions made, often at board level.

Some work for local authorities, where their clients are the council's staff and the elected members or councillors. They advise on current legislation as it affects local authorities, on matters ranging from child care to planning enquiries, education provision, libraries and social services. They also represent the authority in court when necessary.

Those working for central government advise civil servants

and ministers about the legislation relevant to their own department and also oversee the implementation of appropriate legislation. The work varies according to that of their employing departments (for example Transport, Education and Employment, Health).

Solicitors employed by the Crown Prosecution Service (CPS) advise the police about prosecutions. If a case goes to prosecution following their recommendation, a CPS solicitor conducts the case in the magistrate's court.

Wherever they work, solicitors spend a lot of time interviewing clients. They ascertain the facts, form an opinion, and give advice, using their own legal knowledge and consulting books and legal references when necessary. There is a lot of paperwork in the form of letters and contracts.

WORK ENVIRONMENT

Solicitors are based in offices, but some travel may be involved to visit clients at their premises or homes. Solicitors working for big commercial firms may travel overseas. Those involved in litigation may spend a large proportion of their time in court. Some may have to visit clients held at police stations or in prison.

Offices vary in size from large city centre practices with hundreds of employees to smaller ones with less than ten. A small number practise alone, working with just one secretary or clerk. Solicitors employed in government services or by local authorities may work in a legal department housed in a large central government building or county hall.

SKILLS AND INTERESTS

Solicitors need a high level of academic ability. They must be able to assimilate and analyse large amounts of information and must pay great attention to detail. They must also be prepared to read widely and undertake post-qualification training by attending courses, in order to keep abreast with the Law, which is constantly changing.

Communication skills, both written and verbal, are important. Solicitors must be able to write clearly and succinctly. If appearing in court, they need excellent presentation skills and the ability to argue a case successfully. When dealing with clients they need the ability to explain the legal position clearly and simply to people who may find the concepts difficult to understand. Some clients are distressed and solicitors have to be tactful and sympathetic when interviewing them. They must also be discreet.

Numeracy is important in some branches of the work, when dealing with property purchase or divorce settlements, for example.

Solicitors working in large departments are sometimes expected to work as members of a team. Others, particularly on the private client side, work mainly alone. Solicitors running practices need business skills and the ability to manage staff. Those working on their own need self-discipline and motivation.

All solicitors must be able to work under pressure, to deadlines, and cope with large amounts of work.

ENTRY REQUIREMENTS

England and Wales

Trainee solicitors must:

– have a qualifying law degree, which may be in law or certain other subjects, provided that it includes the seven *Foundations of Legal Knowledge:* Obligations I, an outline of the law of restitution; Obligations II , torts; Foundations of Criminal Law; Foundations of Equity and the Law of Trusts; Foundations of the Law of European Union; Foundations of Property Law and Foundations of Public Law. (A list of approved degrees may be obtained from the Law Society.) A level/H grade subjects are not stipulated, other than that they must be academic ones, and high grades – usually A and B passes – are required; *or*

– have a non-law degree plus completion of the Common Professional Examination (CPE), a one-year full-time course that covers the Foundations of Legal Knowledge. The CPE is offered at the five branches of the College of Law and at a number of universities. It may also be studied two years part-time or through distance learning. (Some institutions offer a Diploma in Law course for graduates, which is accepted by the Law Society as an alternative to the CPE; *or*

– be a Fellow of the Institute of Legal Executives (please see article 4. LEGAL EXECUTIVE), be over 25 years old and have worked for five years in a solicitor's office.

These are the only accepted entry qualifications. The non-graduate entry route has been discontinued (other than for qualified legal executives, as above).

Scotland

Entrants must:

– hold a law degree from one of the five Scottish universities offering the study of law; *or*

– have completed three years' pre-Diploma training and have passed the examinations of the Law Society of Scotland (for which no formal tuition is provided).

Applicants intending to qualify by the latter (much less common and extremely difficult) route must have five H grade passes including English at B or above and either maths or a science subject or a foreign language. The total H grade passes must be at least eight points on a scale where A=3, B=2 and C=1. Applicants possessing a degree in any discipline, a Higher National Diploma in Legal Studies from an approved college, plus H grade English at B or above, automatically qualify to attempt this route to qualification.

The entry qualifications may be relaxed for applicants over the age of 23 years with experience of legal work.

TRAINING

England and Wales

Training is in three stages:

– gaining a thorough grounding in the main principles of law, through any of the methods outlined above; *and*

– completion of a two-year period of training with solicitors approved to offer training by the Law Society (the solicitors' professional body), known as a training contract (qualified legal executives are normally exempted from this stage); *and*

– successful completion of the Law Society's Legal Practice Course (LPC).

Law and non-law (CPE) graduates take the LPC *before* entering their two-year training contract. Qualified legal executives have the choice of attending the course or preparing for the exams as external candidates.

The Legal Practice Course is intended to teach both the legal knowledge necessary to practise as a solicitor and some of the essential skills – such as legal research and problem solving, interviewing skills, legal drafting, negotiation and advocacy (pleading).

The training contract combines on-the-job training with attendance at some external courses. With their employers – firms, local authorities or the Crown Prosecution Service – trainee solicitors gain practical experience in a minimum of three different areas of law from a list laid down by the Law Society (although many employers offer the chance to work in more than the minimum). Trainees are attached to qualified solicitors, at first observing, soon assisting and undertaking some of the work under supervision. Possible areas of experience vary according to the type of work done by the employer. Some might offer only commercial work, others might not offer crime or matrimonial law.

All LPC students have to undertake a Professional Skills course, covering a range of subjects and taking 20 days in total.

Scotland

All entrants must complete the following:

– a one-year full-time course at one of five universities, leading to a Diploma in Legal Practice. The course teaches the practical skills and knowledge required by solicitors; *and*

– two years under a training contract with a practising solicitor in Scotland. After the first year they may apply for a qualified Practising Certificate from the Law Society of Scotland that permits them to appear in court for their employer's clients. At the end of two years they are entitled to hold the full Practising Certificate.

The training contract may be served with solicitors in private practice, industry and commerce or with some public sector departments, for example regional and district councils or the Department of the Solicitor to the Secretary of State for Scotland.

Six months of the training contract may be spent in England or another EU country, with the employer's consent.

LATE ENTRY

There are no upper age limits. Mature entrants follow any of the training routes available to school-leavers. Some institutions may relax their degree course entry requirements, but all expect evidence of recent academic study – through part-time or evening classes for example.

In England and Wales the legal executive route is the most usual method of entry for mature entrants.

OPPORTUNITIES

There are about 60,000 qualified solicitors in practice in England and Wales: 7,600 in Scotland. The majority work in private practice, where they may choose from a range of employers and specialisms or be self-employed.

In England and Wales approximately 3,000 are employed in industry and commerce. A further 3,000 work for local authorities.

In Scotland approximately 6,000 work in private practice.

Others work in the Civil Service (central government departments), in the Magistrates' Court Service or in the Crown Prosecution Service/Procurator Fiscal Service, both of which have increasing numbers of openings.

Smaller numbers work for law centres, charities, Citizens' Advice Bureaux and in HM Forces and industry and commerce.

There are opportunities to travel or to work overseas by: working for an international practice that has branch offices in several countries; working for international and EU institutions like the United Nations or the European Commission; working for a firm engaging in public international law, which may require solicitors to attend the World Court, European Court of Human Rights or European Courts of Justice on behalf of clients.

It is possible to work in some Commonwealth countries that have legal systems based on English Common Law, but it is often necessary to attend a familiarization course in order to obtain a licence to practise.

The EU is committed to mutual recognition of professional qualifications. Solicitors wishing to be admitted in any of the EU member states may do so after passing a *transfer test*. It is therefore becoming easier for solicitors qualified in one member state to practise in another.

PAY AND CONDITIONS

Training

Non-law graduates usually have to fund themselves through the CPE course as local education authorities rarely give grants for this – and some do not give grants for the compulsory course in Legal Practice. Many trainees obtain bank loans. Some graduates opt for the longer training route of first becoming a legal executive, as most trainee legal executives study part-time whilst working full-time in a legal environment.

Some large commercial law firms offer sponsorships, under which they pay students' tuition fees and give them a further sum to cover living expenses. Students are then expected to complete the training contract with the firm.

During the training contract, trainee solicitors are paid a salary. The figure varies, but for trainees in England and Wales the Law Society stipulates a minimum of £12,150 in Central London and £10,850 elsewhere.

The Law Society of Scotland recommends trainee salaries of £8,840 and £11,960 for first and second-year trainees, respectively. These levels are, however, not mandatory.

On qualification

Once fully qualified, solicitors may earn from £15,000 in a small town practice, to £29,000 in the City of London. Within a few years of qualifying, salaries can vary enormously.

Solicitors normally work standard office hours, plus as much (unpaid) overtime as is necessary to complete the work. Many spend most of the day with clients and have to complete their research and paperwork at home, or in the office, during the evening and at weekends.

Some have to visit clients after working hours or may be called to police stations at any time.

Solicitors working in law centres see a lot of clients in the evenings.

PROSPECTS

Solicitors in private practice begin as salaried assistant solicitors. Later, they may become salaried partners (salaried associates in Scotland) or equity partners, investing a sum in the practice and taking a share of the profits. Many become partners in their early thirties.

They may become self-employed, or principals/sole practitioners, but, in England and Wales, they are not allowed to establish their own practices until they have practised for three years. No similar time restriction exists in Scotland, but they must attend a course on practice management within one year of becoming a principal.

Solicitors in commerce and industry may become heads of legal departments, or often become company secretaries. In local government they may progress in the legal department or may move into general local government administration. Many chief executives of councils are former solicitors.

In the Civil Service, solicitors may move to bigger or different departments to gain promotion. Some become parliamentary counsels, responsible for drafting legislation.

RELATED OCCUPATIONS

Barrister, justice's clerk, procurator fiscal, legal executive.

FURTHER INFORMATION

The Law Society, Legal Education Information Services, Ipsley Court, Berrington Close, Redditch, Worcestershire B98 0TD, 017124 21222 ext 3088

The Crown Prosecution Service, Personnel Branch 2*, 50 Ludgate Hill, London EC4M 3EX, 0171 273 8000

GLS Recruitment Team, Queen Anne's Chambers, 28 Broadway, London SW1H 9JS, 0171 210 3304

The Deputy Secretary (Legal Education)*, The Law Society of Scotland, 26 Drumsheugh Gardens, Edinburgh EH3 7YR, 0131 226 7411

FURTHER READING

Leaflets/booklets are available from the addresses marked*.

Job Outlines – Law – England and Wales – COIC
Job Outlines – Law – Scotland – COIC

In the careers library classified under LAC.

3. BARRISTERS' CLERK (LAZ)

THE WORK

Barristers' clerks work for groups of barristers, who all practise independently in a set of chambers.

The word 'clerk', although a historic term, can be misleading and some chambers now call their senior clerks 'practice managers' or 'chambers' directors'.

Barristers' clerks are responsible for the running of chambers as a business, developing its practice, managing the flow of work, liaising with solicitors and day-to-day administration. Most chambers have a team of clerks who, between them, normally carry out the following duties.

Junior clerks

Court work – accompany a barrister to court, carry documents, papers and robes. In cases being heard some distance from chambers they make travel and accommodation arrangements.

Messenger work – deliver documents by hand.

Administrative work in chambers – prepare the accounts, send out bills (sometimes done by clerical staff), keep the chambers reference library tidy and file reports.

Experienced clerks

Arrange the barristers' schedules: keep a master diary with the names of each barrister, the cases they are working on, the names of clients and instructing solicitors, information relevant to cases and barristers' daily engagements.

Run the chambers' petty cash system.

Senior clerks

The senior clerk (also known as clerk of chambers) is the office manager, responsible for the work, recruitment and training of junior barristers' clerks, and other clerical staff where employed – typists, receptionists and, sometimes, VDU operators.

Their most important role, however, is liaison with solicitors. It is through this that work comes into chambers and clerks must work to establish good relationships with solicitors. A solicitor wishing to brief a barrister first approaches the senior clerk who, through familiarity with previous similar cases and knowledge of the specialisms of the barristers in the set, can recommend particular barristers for the case. They can be extremely influential on the career development of young barristers.

Although it is in their interests to keep work for their own chambers, in some instances they will recommend the solicitor to consult another set, where barristers specialize in the matter in question.

They are also responsible for negotiating their barristers' fees, based on length and difficulty of the case, and the seniority of the barrister.

In Scotland, advocates' clerks fulfil the same duties.

WORK ENVIRONMENT

Barristers' clerks work in small teams in chambers, usually three or four clerks working for 15 to 20 barristers. Some of the London chambers can be very small and cramped. Others, and the majority of provincial chambers, are in more modern premises.

Junior clerks spend much of their time on messenger duties, or accompanying barristers to court. As they become more senior the work is more office-based. Even contact with solicitors is done largely by telephone.

Seventy per cent of barristers' clerks are based in London, with the remainder working in chambers near the courts in other cities in England and Wales.

Advocates' clerks all work at Parliament House in Edinburgh.

SKILLS AND INTERESTS

Barristers' clerks must be completely reliable and able to work under pressure to meet deadlines. They should be able to move from one job to another as the situation demands, putting one task to one side in order to deal with something more urgent. They must pay great attention to detail and make sure that all arrangements work smoothly. If they make mistakes in diary details or bookings for court appearances, the chambers could lose future business from solicitors.

They need a good command of written and spoken English and a good telephone manner.

Loyalty to chambers and discretion are expected. Clerks must be careful to respect client confidentiality, especially if barristers in their set are appearing for opposing sides in the same case.

Senior clerks need to be skilled financial negotiators, especially over the telephone; they must be tactful and at times persuasive. They are essentially the chambers' public relations officers and have to build good working relationships with solicitors. In order to do this they sometimes offer advice on the level of fees or market rate for a particular case without necessarily expecting to get the brief for one of their own barristers.

Although their job is to get business for their chambers, it is within their discretion to refuse a case; if they feel none of their barristers is an expert on a particular problem, they will do so, rather than risk an unsatisfactory outcome.

They need to know their barristers well, since they essentially act as agents. Clerks are particularly careful when selecting cases for young barristers, ensuring that they are not given work as yet outside their experience.

ENTRY REQUIREMENTS

The majority of new entrants start after completing GCSEs/S grades or A levels/H grades. Minimum entry requirements are four GCSEs/S grades (A-C/1-3) or equivalent, including English and maths.

Some junior clerks are expected to be able to type.

TRAINING

All training is carried out in chambers. Junior clerks are assigned to routine jobs of filing, delivering messages, carrying books and papers for barristers going to court and possibly typing out the accounts. They learn the more advanced duties by observing the work of senior clerks and assisting them.

Junior clerks may be given day release to attend a BTEC National Certificate course in Business, Finance and Chambers Management, which contains specialist modules devised in association with the Institute of Barristers' Clerks.

On obtaining employment in chambers, students may become members of the Institute of Barristers' Clerks.

There is no formal training or qualification for advocates' clerks. They begin as deputy clerks and are trained on the job by senior clerks.

LATE ENTRY

Most barristers' clerks start as school-leavers or graduates. Some chambers recruit adults with previous managerial or administrative experience.

OPPORTUNITIES

This is a particularly small profession. There are no more than 950 barristers' clerks in England and Wales. In Scotland, there are ten advocates' clerks and ten deputy advocates' clerks. Over half the jobs for barristers' clerks are in London, in chambers near the Inns of Court. The remainder are found in chambers in towns on the circuits. Please see article 1. BARRISTER.

The number of clerks' posts depends on the number of barristers in a set. Some barristers work in groups as small as six, and employ one clerk. The recent tendency is towards sets of approximately 20 barristers. A set of this size is likely to employ a senior clerk, three clerks and reception and typing staff.

Finding a first position is difficult. Although the more senior positions are frequently advertised in the national press, the majority of trainee vacancies are filled by word of mouth or through a scheme run by the Institute of Barristers' Clerks, under which people interested in working in London are notified of junior vacancies as they arise.

Vacancies for trainee advocates' clerks are advertised in the press. There is very little turnover, and so entry opportunities are severely limited.

PAY AND CONDITIONS

Junior clerks are paid a fixed salary. Figures vary, but £6,300 to £7,500 would be an average starting salary in London.

Senior clerks are paid in one of several ways. A small number receive a salary. The majority receive a percentage of the gross fee paid to each barrister. Traditionally, these were set at either five, seven-and-a-half or ten per cent, but no new ten per cent contracts are now negotiated. Five per cent is the average. A third practice is for the clerk to receive a fixed salary plus one or two per cent of fees, and this is becoming more usual, especially for new positions.

Earnings potential therefore varies and depends on the income of the set. A senior clerk in chambers where two or three barristers are earning £150,000 and the remaining twelve £80,000 could easily earn more than individual barristers.

Advocates clerks are all employed by the organization Faculty Services Ltd, which provides support services to **stables** of advocates. They are employed on a salary scale from £15,000 to £28,000.

The work involves long hours, including evenings and weekends.

PROSPECTS

Barristers' clerks begin as junior clerks, may obtain promotion to second clerk, then to a senior clerk. It is sometimes necessary to move to different chambers to achieve this.

Once in a senior clerk's position, it is usual to remain with that chambers. Most barristers' clerks do not move again.

There is no possibility of transferring to legal work as a barrister, other than by following the full training route.

RELATED OCCUPATIONS

Legal executive, office manager, administrator.

FURTHER INFORMATION

The Administrator of the Institute of Barristers' Clerks*, 4a Essex Court, Temple, London EC4A 9AJ

FURTHER READING

Leaflets/booklets are available from the address marked*.

Job Outlines – Law – England and Wales – COIC
Job Outlines – Law – Scotland – COIC
Careers in the Law – Kogan Page

In the careers library classified under LAZ.

4. LEGAL EXECUTIVE (LAD)

THE WORK

Legal executives work (in England and Wales) with solicitors in private practices, local authority and commercial companies' legal departments and in the Civil Service.

The work falls under three main headings:

Work with clients. Legal executives interview clients, advise them and do much of the preparatory work before cases come to court, wills are administered or transactions like sale and purchase of property are carried out. They may attend court to assist solicitors or barristers with the presentation of a case.

They are also able to exercise a right to audience before a judge sitting in Chambers and so undertake the same role as barristers and solicitors.

Administration. They do much of the practical and technical work in a solicitor's office or legal department. They may, for example, draw up wills, check titles to deeds, issue writs, take out summonses, collect information needed for affidavits and draft documents.

Management. In some law firms, legal executives are practice managers. They assign work to junior staff, supervise the work of clerks and secretaries, and do all the accounts.

Most legal executives specialize in one area of the law:

Probate

If specializing in this, they help to ensure that the property of people who have died is disposed of in the way they had wished. They calculate inheritance tax, work out the sum each beneficiary will receive and explain the terms of the will to relatives. They may work closely with appointed executors who are not relatives, including accountants or bank managers.

Conveyancing

Conveyancing involves helping the client through all the stages of house purchase, reading and checking documents, telephoning the seller's or purchaser's solicitors, estate agents and building societies and conducting searches. Please see article 2. SOLICITOR.

Litigation

Working in litigation involves working for clients who are in a dispute, interviewing them to find out the details and noting the information down. They may write letters on the client's behalf or prepare material for a court case.

There is no direct equivalent to a legal executive in Scotland. Some solicitors employ staff known as legal, or unqualified, assistants who may carry out some of the duties described above.

WORK ENVIRONMENT

Please see article 2. SOLICITOR.

Legal executives work mainly at a desk. Those specializing in litigation may go to court regularly.

SKILLS AND INTERESTS

Much of the routine work – of form filling, document drafting and doing calculations – requires concentration and precise attention to detail.

Legal executives must be able to write clear English, often first consulting documents that are written in complicated legal language. They must understand the legal terms and concepts.

They need to be able to relate well to clients of all backgrounds – some of whom are very distressed – be sympathetic when interviewing them, and be capable of explaining matters clearly. When dealing with court officials or representatives of banks, accountancy firms or other legal firms, they may have to be persistent, but at the same time polite and persuasive.

In probate and conveyancing work, numeracy is essential. Legal executives are expected to meet deadlines and work under pressure. They work on many different cases at the same time and may be responsible for the work of junior staff. They need to be good organizers, able to plan their time and priorities.

ENTRY REQUIREMENTS

The normal minimum entry requirements are four GCSEs/S grades (A-C/1-3) or equivalent. These must be in academic subjects and include English. Technical and craft subjects are not accepted.

In practice, many entrants have A levels, GNVQ Advanced *or* a BTEC national level qualification or equivalent.

An alternative entry qualification is the Vocational Legal Studies qualification, which may be taken by home study or by attending a college of further education. There is no entry requirement for this course.

TRAINING

In order to become a Fellow of The Institute of Legal Executives (that is, fully qualified) it is necessary to be aged at least 25, have passed membership examinations and worked for five years in **qualifying employment,** ie under the supervision of a solicitor in a practice, public authority, industry or commerce. Two of these years must be served after passing the examinations.

Most legal executives study for the exams on a part-time basis while in approved employment. Colleges throughout England and Wales run courses leading to the exams. The Institute has set up a home study programme for students who cannot or do not wish to attend a college.

Membership exams are in two stages. Part I, set at A level standard, consists of papers in law, legal practice and procedures. Part II, equivalent to a degree standard, contains one paper on legal procedure and three from specialist areas of law – land law, criminal law, conveyancing, contract law, etc. Students may choose papers appropriate to their specialism in their own offices.

It is possible to take a one-year full-time course at certain colleges leading to the Part I exams, then gain suitable employment to train for the necessary five years. A small number of people choose this route.

The average time taken to pass all the exams is four years, although some trainees complete them in three. At this stage they may become Members of the Institute.

Practical training, carried out at employers' premises, consists of assisting legal executives and solicitors with their work, observing, learning and then progressing to doing some casework under supervision, gradually assuming more responsibility.

It is common for trainee legal executives to work as 'outdoor clerks' for a period. This involves delivering documents, such as taking briefs to barristers, taking documents to court for entry by court officials and paying any fees required and attending court cases to take notes for senior colleagues. Some trainees start as secretaries in solicitors' offices and are given the opportunity to progress to legal work.

Scotland

There is no single route to qualify for similar work in Scotland. Some employers prefer to train their own staff. Others send staff to attend a Paralegal course at Strathclyde University; this involves attendance for two hours on 20 Saturday mornings.

Entry requirements are at the discretion of employers. Some expect four S grades (1-3), while others prefer entrants to hold a SCOTVEC Higher National Diploma in Legal Studies.

LATE ENTRY

About 60 per cent of legal executives are over 20 years of age. Some have worked as legal secretaries.

The Institute of Legal Executives is prepared to waive the entry requirements for mature students over 25 years with suitable references. Each application is considered individually.

OPPORTUNITIES

There are 22,500 members of The Institute of Legal Executives in England and Wales (5,200 of them Fellows). The majority work for solicitors, but they may also work for any of the organizations that employ solicitors. Most opportunities are with medium and large-sized law practices, in industry, commerce and with local authorities.

Registration with the Institute is not compulsory for employment, but only Fellows of the Institute may be described as legal executives.

Opportunities to work overseas are limited. There may be openings in countries which have a legal system based on English Common Law and in the EU with English firms that have offices in member countries.

PAY AND CONDITIONS

Salaries vary throughout the country and according to employer. There is no recommended minimum salary for trainees as there is for trainee solicitors, but most newly appointed trainee legal executives can expect to earn between £8,000 and £12,000. Fully qualified Fellows can earn between £20,000 and £24,000, and experienced Fellows of ILEX £25,000 plus; some receive salaries of £40,000 upwards.

Not all employers give help with course or examination fees, although over 70 per cent do make some contribution. (The total training costs, including fees and books is approximately £2,100 over the four years.)

Most legal executives work normal office hours over a five-day week, but, when necessary, may be expected to work overtime.

PROSPECTS

In large organizations, legal executives have prospects of promotion to head a department of legal executives. In a small number of law firms they may become the practice's manager. Promotion prospects are limited in small firms.

Legal executives may also qualify as solicitors and this is now the principal route for a non-graduate wishing to become a solicitor. Fellows of The Institute of Legal Executives may choose whether to attend a one-year Legal Practice course or to take a two-year part-time course whilst remaining in employment. They do not have to undertake the two-year training contract under articles. Please see article 2. SOLICITOR. They do, however, have to complete their training by undertaking a Professional Skills course.

RELATED OCCUPATIONS

Barrister, justice's clerk, procurator fiscal, barristers' clerk.

FURTHER INFORMATION

The Institute of Legal Executives*, Kempston Manor, Kempston, Bedford MK42 7AB, 01234 841000

The Institute of Legal Executives, Ilex Tutorial Services Ltd, Kempston Manor, Kempston, Bedford MK42 7AB, 01234 841010 (for details of home study courses)

FURTHER READING

Leaflets/booklets are available from the address marked*.

Job Outlines – Law – England and Wales – COIC
Job Outlines – Law – Scotland – COIC

In the careers library classified under LAD.

5. SHORTHAND WRITER (LAG)

THE WORK

Shorthand writers, who are also known as court reporters, shorthand reporters and verbatim reporters, attend court hearings and take records of the hearings in shorthand, either by hand or by the use of stenotype machines. Their work varies, depending on whether they work in England and Wales or in Scotland.

England and Wales

Shorthand writers attend most criminal cases, which are held in Crown Courts throughout the country. Today, most civil cases held in the High Court and all County Courts are recorded officially on audio tape, and shorthand writers are not used, although some are engaged privately in the High Court. Shorthand writers also attend private cases such as arbitration, public inquiries, industrial tribunals, trade union and political conferences, annual general meetings and disciplinary hearings. They are also employed in the House of Commons and House of Lords.

In most Crown Court cases, only one shorthand writer is present. They have to be in court before proceedings start and are present throughout the day's proceedings. They use computer-aided transcription (CAT) systems – which are rather like a small typewriter, but with a different keyboard, which enables whole words and phrases to be typed at one stroke. CATs writers can achieve very high shorthand speeds – over 200 wpm (words per minute).

The machines produce a paper tape, which looks rather like a till roll and enables the shorthand writer to read back what has been said when required. The machine also produces the shorthand on a computer disk and, if a transcript is needed of the days hearing, the shorthand writer can transfer the text to a computer, which transcribes it. The shorthand writer can then add any words not transcribed by the computer, correct any mistakes and edit the text.

Sometimes lawyers ask for a transcript of the proceedings to be completed before the next day – this means that the shorthand writer has to transcribe their work during the evening.

Some parts of the case, such as the witnesses statements, are transcribed verbatim, whereas other parts may be edited to make them grammatically correct. For instance, many judges do not like the use of colloquialisms – and shorthand writers make the necessary changes. The court reporter has to use common sense and experience to decide what should be changed or included. For example, some judges like their jokes included in the transcript. In private cases and very complex court cases, lawyers may want a daily copy of the proceedings and this requires the shorthand writers to use a real-time system. To do this, they sometimes work in teams of three. The CAT system is linked to a computer, which immediately transcribes the notes into English, and these can be seen by those participating in the proceedings. In the team, one shorthand writer types using the stenotype machine and one 'scopes', which means that they read what comes up on the screen and correct any unusual words that have not been translated by the writer's dictionary. A third member of the team proof-reads, checking for punctuation and grammar.

Shorthand writers also record and transcribe witness statements prior to the court hearing.

Scotland

At present, shorthand writers work in the Sheriff Courts (on civil cases), the High Court, Senior Criminal Court and the Court of Session, there is little private work in Scotland. In all other courts, tapes are used. In Scotland, although a few shorthand writers use CAT systems, most still write by pen. Writers again make a record of the proceedings, with the exception of the lawyer's summing up. If daily transcripts are needed, writers work in teams. After each period of reporting they then leave the court and dictate what they have written onto audio tape – this is then typed up by an audio typist.

WORK ENVIRONMENT

Shorthand writers spend much of their time working in courts. In private hearings such as arbitration, public inquiries, and so on, they travel to wherever the hearing is held – this could be in a conference room or a court. The work involves sitting for long periods of time. They usually have to do considerable travelling, carrying their CAT machine and computer, so the ability to drive is helpful. Some of their transcription work may be carried out in their homes.

SKILLS AND INTERESTS

Shorthand writers must be very responsible and work accurately. They need to be able to concentrate for long periods of time. Sharp hearing is important. It is vital that they have an excellent command of English – both written and spoken – and have a very good knowledge of grammar, to transform what might be ungrammatical speech into a grammatical record.

Punctuality is vital, as court cases cannot start until they are present. They have to be flexible in their approach to working hours, being prepared to work in the evenings with virtually no notice. They should be able to work on their own in what can be quite a lonely job. They also have to be able to work in teams when providing a real-time service. In operating stenotype machines, manual dexterity is needed.

Shorthand writers need to present a smart appearance. They need to be confident – if at any point in the proceedings they cannot hear what is being said, or if a witness is talking too quickly, they have to be able to ask for the proceedings to be stopped and for the witness or lawyer to repeat what they said. They also need a clear speaking voice to read back parts of the script when required.

ENTRY REQUIREMENTS

England and Wales

Employers usually require new applicants to have had training and gained qualifications in the use of stenotyping machines and to have reached a minimum speed of 140 wpm. Training for this is offered in a number of colleges – for addresses contact the British Institute of Verbatim Reporters, or the Association of Professional Shorthand Writers. Entry onto these courses usually requires three or four GCSEs (grades A-C) including English. Many students have A levels or degrees.

Scotland

There are no formal entry requirements, although most firms ask for some S grades (1-3) including English. Applicants must also have shorthand speeds of at least 120 wpm.

All would-be shorthand writers need excellent skills in both spelling and grammar. A familiarity with medical and technical terminology is also a distinct advantage.

TRAINING

England and Wales

Most shorthand writers start by undergoing a course in machine shorthand, either full-time at a college or by distance learning. Addresses of colleges running these courses are available from the British Institute of Verbatim Reporters and the Association of Professional Shorthand Writers.

When trainees are taken on by a firm they usually start by working in one of the courts which is taped, to gain experience of court proceedings, giving them practise at reporting and increasing their speeds. The trainee acts as a logger, keeping a detailed record of the times when each person starts and stops speaking. They also take records of the proceedings in shorthand. In addition, some firms also run evening training sessions, where trainees can practise transcribing.

This period of training usually lasts between three and twelve months. During this time, trainees also start to produce their own dictionary. All shorthand writers have their own way of writing things, so each writer has their own dictionary of how the computer should transcribe their shorthand. They start this dictionary when they first start training, and add to it as they progress in the work.

Once trainees achieve speeds of 160 wpm they can apply to become associates of one of the professional bodies. This involves taking a practical test in court, which consists of taking an hour's proceedings in shorthand and then transcribing it without the aid of tapes. They then become provisionally accredited shorthand writers and can work on their own in court.

After a further three years' experience, they can apply for membership of their professional body. This entails producing a transcript of another hour's court proceedings. Members can apply to become fellows two years later, at which time they have to undergo two tests in different types of court – for instance, one test in a civil court and one in a crown court.

Scotland

New shorthand writers in Scotland are trained by the firms they work for – there are no courses. Usually they start learning on straightforward cases, such as custody or divorce. They work with an experienced shorthand writer and both take notes of proceedings. This enables the trainee to practise and increase their speed, as well as become familiar with court procedures. During this time they are given regular tests to see if they are making progress. After about three months they are usually able to undertake a straightforward civil case on their own.

LATE ENTRY

There is no maximum age for entry into this career, and many firms prefer more mature entrants. See ENTRY REQUIREMENTS and TRAINING.

OPPORTUNITIES

Most are employed by firms of shorthand writers, who are contracted to provide reports of court proceedings. The British Institute of Verbatim Reporters (previously the Institute of Shorthand Writers) and the Association of Professional Shorthand Writers provide lists of the member firms who may employee trainees.

In England and Wales, firms hold appointments to the High Court, the Central Criminal Court and other courts, and outside London to the Crown Court centres which are in all the larger towns. They do not hold appointments to the County and Magistrates Courts and the district courts. Firms also undertake work for public inquiries, trade union and political conferences, industrial tribunals, board meetings and disciplinary hearings. Firms use their own employees and freelances.

In Scotland, they work for one of the three firms of shorthand writers, or are freelance. There is a move in Scotland towards taping cases, rather than using shorthand writers. This means that, over the next couple of years, opportunities for shorthand writers may decrease considerably. There is a shortage of suitably qualified shorthand writers in England and Wales. In addition to full-time work there are opportunities for part-time work and self-employment.

PAY AND CONDITIONS

England and Wales

Shorthand writers are paid a standard fee for each day's attendance at court with a separate fee for any transcripts they produce. The usual daily rate is about £45 to £70, unless they work privately, in which case they are likely to work in a team of three and can earn up to £200 a day.

Scotland

Shorthand writers earn about £12,500 if they are fully employed. Some are employed, but on piece rates, and are usually paid about the same as freelances – equivalent to a salary of between £9,500 and £16,000.

Shorthand writers may work irregular hours. Courts usually sit from 10am until 4pm, but if a court case continues into the evening, the shorthand writer is required to stay until the end. In situations where a transcript is needed for the next day the shorthand writer has to complete the work in the evening.

PROSPECTS

There is no promotional ladder for this career. However, there are opportunities for experienced shorthand writers to work freelance. They can also work for Hansard, producing reports of the day's proceedings in the House of Commons and House of Lords. There are also opportunities for caption writing for the deaf, and in television.

RELATED OCCUPATIONS

Shorthand typist, secretary, journalist, copy editor, legal executive, barrister's clerk.

FURTHER INFORMATION

British Institute of Verbatim Reporters, 61 Carey Street, London WC2A 2SG (please include sae)

Association of Professional Shorthand Writers, Edial Farm, Burnt Wood, Near Walsall, West Midlands ST17 9FS

Verbatim Reporters, 1 Atholl Place, Edinburgh EH3 8HP

FURTHER READING

Working in Law – COIC.

In the careers library classified under LAG.

6. COURT USHER/COURT OFFICER/ MACER (LAG)

BACKGROUND INFORMATION

In England and Wales, court ushers work in Crown Courts, the Court of Appeal and Magistrates Courts, all of which deal with both civil and criminal cases. They also work in County Courts and High Courts, which deal with civil cases only.

In Scotland, those working in Sheriff courts are known as court officers, those in the Court of Session (the Supreme Civil Court) and in the High Court of Justiciary (the Supreme Criminal Court) are known as macers.

THE WORK

England and Wales

The work of a court usher varies depending on the type of court they work in. For most ushers, the main part of their work is in ensuring that everything required for a hearing is in the right place at the right time. Before the start of a hearing, they gather all the necessary papers, ready for the court clerk or clerk of the court. They prepare the courtroom for the day's hearings, for instance, putting out glasses and drinking water. They also have a responsibility for safety, for example, making sure that fire exits are clear.

They check that witnesses, lawyers and defendants have arrived for the case and inform the court clerk of the situation.

In Crown Courts they also receive the judge on arrival and have their wig and gown ready.

At the start of the hearing, when the magistrate or judge enters the court, it is the usher who tells everyone to stand. During the case, they call the defendants and witnesses into the court and administer the oath – giving them the Bible (or other scripture, depending on the defendant's or the witness's religion) and hold up a card printed with the oath for the witness or defendant to read. They fetch anything required by the clerk and pass any evidence to the judge or jury. If the clerk wishes to communicate with one of the lawyers, then the usher passes the message. They also make sure that people waiting outside the court do not make too much noise.

In Crown Courts, which deal with more serious criminal

cases, there may be a small team of ushers. As these cases have a jury, one of the ushers acts as jury bailiff. This involves making sure that the jury are sent reminders before the case, so that they know which court they are in and what time to arrive. They welcome the jurors on their arrival at court and escort them to the jury waiting room. When the jury are assembled, they explain the procedures to them, for example how they will be sworn in. For most jurors this will be their first time in court and they may be nervous, so the usher needs to calm their fears and put them at ease. The usher escorts the jury into and out of the court and, during the hearing, passes the jury any evidence such as photographs or documents that they have to look at.

At the end of the hearing, while the jury deliberates its verdict, the usher remains outside the jury room and acts as the communications link between the jury and the court clerk. If the jury does not reach a verdict at the time and has to stay overnight, the usher organizes hotel accommodation for them, takes them to the hotel and stays there with them.

In County Courts with a number of district judges, the majority of hearings are held in chambers, not in public courts. In these situations, the usher acts as a receptionist, taking a note of people as they arrive and escorting them to the correct room for their hearing.

At the end of a session in any court, the usher clears the court or chambers and secures the rooms. They collect any papers and return them to the clerk; they also gather any lost property, record it and store it in a safe place.

Scotland

In Scotland, court ushers, known as either court officers or macers, are civil servants. In the Sheriff Courts they are known as court officers and their main job is to attend the sheriffs. In the Supreme Courts, they are macers and, here, they attend the judges. They also carry out similar jobs to the court ushers in England and Wales and may also deal with a range of other tasks, such as collecting and delivering the mail, and even operating a switchboard.

WORK ENVIRONMENT

Court ushers spend part of their time in the courtroom itself. They also usually have an office, often in the court buildings, from which they carry out their administrative work. Ushers in Magistrates Courts may have to travel between a number of different courts. In County Court chambers they work on the reception desk. If they are acting as jury bailiff they may occasionally have to spend a night away from home.

SKILLS AND INTERESTS

Ushers need a considerable amount of confidence and an authoritative manner. They need to be well organized and methodical, as they are responsible for making sure everything needed for a case, from the appropriate people to the relevant papers, is there. They need excellent communication skills as they deal with a wide range of people, from offenders to judges. Defendants are often frightened and witnesses may be nervous, so ushers need to be understanding and have the skills to calm them down and put them at their ease. They have a wide range of problems to cope with, from abusive defendants and people complaining about having to wait for their case to be heard, to lawyers who are not ready when their case starts. Dealing with these takes a considerable amount of patience and good interpersonal skills. Ushers work in a team with the clerk of the court/court clerk and sometimes with other ushers.

ENTRY REQUIREMENTS

There are no entry requirements for this work. The minimum age is 21 (16 years in Scotland) but most courts prefer to recruit more mature people. Courts often prefer ushers who have a background in the police or Armed Forces. In the more rural areas of Scotland, there can be considerable travelling and ushers may need to be able to drive. This is also the case with ushers whose work covers a number of Magistrates Courts in a rural area.

TRAINING

Training takes about a year. Some courts in England and Wales run short courses for ushers covering such areas as: security issues, dealing with difficult people, working with jurors and ethnic awareness. However, most training is given on the job, with ushers learning the operations of their particular court from experienced ushers.

LATE ENTRY

Many courts tend to employ more mature entrants. There is no upper age limit. Entry requirements are as described above.

OPPORTUNITIES

England and Wales – in the Crown Courts, County Courts, the Court of Appeal and the High Court, ushers work for the Court Service (part of the civil service). In Magistrates Courts they work for the Magistrates Court Committee. There are some 700 magistrates courts, 400 county courts and 100 high courts in England and Wales, which employ about 1,000 ushers between them. Courts are found in all cities and most major towns.

In Scotland, all court officers and macers are civil servants. Court officers work in Sheriff Courts, of which there are 49 – divided between the six Sheriffdoms of Grampian, Highlands and Islands, Tayside, Central and Fife, Lothian and Borders, Glasgow and Strathkelvin, North Strathclyde and South Strathclyde. There are 110 court officers at present. Twenty-two macers work in one of the two Courts of Session in Glasgow or Edinburgh and they also work in the High Court of Justiciary. Court ushers, court officers and macers can be employed full-time, part-time or work on a casual basis. Entry into the work is fairly competitive.

PAY AND CONDITIONS

In magistrates courts, some ushers are paid by the hour at about £4.30 an hour, plus their travelling expenses; others may be salaried. Ushers in England and Wales and macers in Scotland are usually paid between £8,602 and £10,227. A chief usher could earn up to £10,000. Ushers usually work Monday to Friday, starting about 8.30am in the morning and finishing about 5pm. However, occasionally they may have late sittings and be required to stay in the evening.

PROSPECTS

Within large magistrates courts, it is possible for an usher to be promoted to a supervisory role with responsibility for a number of other ushers; prospects, however, are limited. In other courts, ushers gain promotion to supervising usher or administrative officer (civil service) and could be promoted to more senior grades, such as court clerk. In Scotland, court officers/macers can be promoted to supervisory levels, running a team of officers or macers. They can also be promoted to the grade of support manager, where they would be in charge of officers, macers, messengers and other support staff. At present, there are only two people in these posts.

RELATED OCCUPATIONS

Court clerk, TV floor manager, receptionist.

FURTHER INFORMATION

England and Wales

Contact local Crown Courts or Magistrates Courts.

Scotland

The Scottish Court Service, Hayweight House, 23 Lauriston Street, Edinburgh EH3 9DQ, 0131 229 9200

FURTHER READING

Working in Law – COIC

In the careers library classified under LAG.

1. POLICE CONSTABLE CLCI:MAB
2. TRAFFIC WARDEN CLCI:MAB

1. POLICE CONSTABLE (MAB)

BACKGROUND INFORMATION

The Police Service in England and Wales is made up of 43 police forces and 8 in Scotland, all run under the command of a chief officer. The chief officer is responsible for the direction and control of the force and its day to day management. The primary responsibility for policing and for the police force lies with the police authority which has a duty to secure the maintenance of an efficient police force for its area.

The work of the police may be summarized as being to enforce the law, keep the peace and protect the community.

THE WORK

The work of a constable has been described as 'maintaining law and order, protecting people and property, preventing and detecting crime, providing reassurance and help, and coping with society's emergencies.

After training, all entrants begin work as uniformed constables. The largest proportion of constables are involved in work 'on the beat'. They are the first point of contact between police and public and act as a visible deterrent to the criminal.

Their work is extremely varied and includes dealing with accidents, disturbances and traffic problems, handling complaints, apprehending and interviewing suspects, investigating crimes, obtaining statements from witnesses, checking the security of premises, and answering questions from the public. They deal with large public events like sports meetings, shows and demonstrations.

Some constables work in car patrols, while others work in the police station, either on the front desk dealing with the public, or in the communications room in two-way contact with their colleagues out of the station. Some time is spent in court giving evidence.

A number of constables specialize some time after completing their two-year probationary period. The specialisms include:

The traffic department, which deals with traffic accidents and offences, promotes road safety and the smooth running of traffic.

Criminal Investigation Department (CID), which is concerned mainly with the investigation of more serious crimes and with crime prevention. It also includes specialist areas like the Fraud Squad and the Special Branch.

Dog handling, where dogs are used to catch and arrest criminals or find hidden drugs or explosives. Dog handlers are responsible for their own dogs, which live and train with them.

Mounted police, who are concerned with the use of horses for crowd control and countryside searches, etc.

River police, who patrol rivers and coastal waters. Their responsibilities include preventing theft and smuggling, life-saving and the recovery of bodies.

Underwater search units, which have teams of divers who have to search rivers, lakes, canals and deep ponds for missing people, stolen property and dumped weapons, etc.

WORK ENVIRONMENT

Police constables may spend much of their time outdoors in all weathers. They may be on foot or in a car. When indoors, they may be in a police station, a court of law, or in private or business premises.

Many constables drive regularly in their work.

SKILLS AND INTERESTS

Police constables should be tolerant and show courtesy to the public. They need physical courage and fitness to deal with incidents and disturbances. Mental resilience is needed to cope with difficult tasks such as informing people of the death of a relative.

Initiative is important, as constables often find themselves in charge of situations like road accidents.

Communication is a central part of a constable's work. Good written skills are necessary to record details of incidents and arrests – records that may later be used in court. Good spoken skills are needed to deal with the public in appropriate ways, for example, when giving advice, sympathy or a reprimand. Clear speech and confidence are required when giving evidence in court.

Police work is based on a team approach, so the ability to work as part of a team, as well as being able to work alone, is vital. A police force is a disciplined unit where a willingness and ability to accept discipline is necessary.

ENTRY REQUIREMENTS

1. The minimum age on entry is 18½ years, but forces prefer candidates who demonstrate maturity of outlook and some forces specify higher minimum ages. In England and Wales there is no specified upper age limit. In Scotland the upper age limit is forty years.

2. Entrants must be: British citizens; Commonwealth citizens whose stay in the UK is not subject to restrictions; *or* citizens of the Irish Republic.

3. All applicants must sit a standard entry test regardless of their educational qualifications. In England and Wales the test includes English language, maths, information checking, reasoning and observation. A slightly different test is used in Scotland, involving English language, maths and information checking.

4. There are no minimum or maximum height requirements.

5. Applicants must be in good health, of good physique and must pass a full medical examination.

6. Eyesight standards vary between forces, but all require good eyesight. Most forces accept officers with spectacles or contact lenses (although unaided vision must be of a reasonable standard). In Scotland, each Chief Constable has the discretion to decide, on advice from the force medical officer, the eyesight standard required for recruits to his force.

7. Applicants to the accelerated promotion scheme for graduates must have either a degree or be in the final year of a degree course. Any degree subject is acceptable.

TRAINING

All police officers do basic training and have a two-year probation. Initial training comprises a two-year modular system alternating work based training with college courses. Initial training in the Metropolitan Police is a little different and takes slightly longer.

Training usually involves three to four weeks at the force's local training centre, then a period at a police station. This is followed by a ten-week residential course at a national police training centre.

The course is followed by five weeks' practical experience at a police station under the supervision of a tutor constable, then, after assessment, constables begin to work on their own.

In Scotland, probationer constables attend the Scottish Police College at Tulliallan Castle for ten weeks after local induction. They return to the college for a further eight weeks after about 14 months' work and training with local forces.

During the first two years of a constable's career, training continues with various post-foundation courses, and attachments to specialized departments, like CID, traffic and the dog section.

LATE ENTRY

There is no specified upper age limit for entry to the police forces in England and Wales. Some forces may consider applicants in their forties.

In Scotland, chief constables may consider applicants from the Armed Forces or the merchant navy a year or two above the normal upper age limit of forty years.

OPPORTUNITIES

Only three forces recruit cadets – Durham, Staffordshire and West Midlands. All recruit only from their local area. There are few vacancies and entry is very competitive. In Scotland, four forces recruit cadets – Central, Fife, Grampian and Tayside. In England and Wales, some forces operate volunteer schemes for those in the 15-18 age group.

Approximately 6,000 police officers are recruited annually throughout England and Wales, and about 600 in Scotland, with fierce competition for places.

There is no annual quota of places open through the accelerated promotion scheme for graduates. The selection procedure is particularly rigorous, but there are places for all who meet the standards. Many other graduates join the police as standard entrants.

In addition to the regular police forces, there are other separate police organizations: for example, the British Transport Police – responsible for railways, docks and harbours, stations, etc; and the UK Atomic Energy Authority Constabulary – responsible for security of nuclear establishments.

PAY AND CONDITIONS

Constables begin on £14,412 during initial training and then move to either £15,648 or £16,710, depending on age skill or experience. They are on a pay scale that reaches £22,809 after 14 years' service. London officers receive additional allowances. Salaries on promotion depend on rank and length of service: for example, sergeants earn between £22,014 and £25,674, superintendents between £38,724 and £46,362.

Constables and sergeants work an eight-hour day on a shift system with two days rest a week. Overtime, or work on a rest day, is paid at an increased rate, or compensatory time off is taken for officers in the ranks of constable or sergeant.

PROSPECTS

After their initial two years, constables may specialize in branches such as the CID, traffic, dog section, mounted branch, community relations, crime prevention.

Promotion is on merit and is initially to sergeant, which may be achieved within about five years by passing a promotion examination in police subjects and being recommended by senior officers.

RELATED OCCUPATIONS

Security officer, prison officer, fire-fighter, private detective, Armed Forces serviceman/woman, traffic warden.

FURTHER INFORMATION

British Transport Police*, Force Headquarters, PO Box 260, 15 Tavistock Place, London WC1H 9SJ

Police Graduate Liaison Office*, Room 553, Home Office, Queen Anne's Gate, London SW1H 9AT, 0171 273 3353

Police Recruitment Department*, Police, Personnel and training Unit, Room 514, Home Office, 50 Queen Anne's Gate, London SW1H 9AT, 0171 273 3797

Scottish Office Home Department*, Police Division, Room 364A, St Andrew's House, Edinburgh EH1 3DG, 0131 244 2156

UK Atomic Energy Authority Constabulary*, Building E6, AEA Technology, Abingdon, Oxfordshire OX14 3DB, 01235 463757

FURTHER READING

Leaflets/booklets are available from the addresses marked*.

Working in Police and Security – COIC
Careers in the Police Force – Kogan Page

In the careers library classified under MAB.

2. TRAFFIC WARDEN (MAB)

BACKGROUND INFORMATION

The 1991 Road Traffic Act decriminalized parking offences and led to the introduction of a new, related job known as parking attendant, which has been introduced in some areas. The role of parking attendants is to enforce on-street parking restrictions, together with supervising car parks and ensuring that vehicle owners have paid to use them. Some of their duties are broadly similar to those of a traffic warden, described as follows, although they do not share their responsibility for keeping traffic moving freely.

Parking attendants are employed by local authorities or by private companies contracted to them, whereas traffic wardens are employed by the police force.

THE WORK

The traffic warden's main duty is to keep vehicles moving freely through cities and towns which are increasingly under heavy pressure from the volume of traffic. They monitor schemes which have been introduced to prevent traffic problems, including: waiting restrictions, parking meters and one-way street systems, plus controlled parking zones and restrictions on loading and unloading of goods (identified by yellow lines). They also report parking offences and issue fixed penalty notices, commonly known as tickets, to offenders. In addition, they are frequently asked for information and directions by members of the public.

At the beginning of a shift, traffic wardens report to their office and receive instructions from a senior traffic warden, who allocates them to specific areas. Wardens are not necessarily always assigned to the same part of a town every day. They are given notice of any special events which may be occurring, such as weddings, funerals, parades or festivals that are likely to cause delays to traffic flow or increase parking problems.

When out on duty, they patrol the streets, acting as a visual deterrent to illegal parking and looking out for vehicles that are wrongly parked and may cause an obstruction, or that may be parked at meters whose time has overrun. When necessary, they issue fixed penalty notices and may have to arrange for a vehicle to be clamped or to be removed by the police to a parking 'pound'. They make checks to ensure that parking meters and car park ticket machines are in working order.

While on patrol, they also watch for vehicles displaying out-of-date motor vehicle licences (tax discs) or no disc at all. They also assist the police by keeping a look out for vehicles which have been reported stolen.

Their other duties include advising drivers on where they may park and answering questions from pedestrians who may be unfamiliar with the town and need directions.

Sometimes they do point duty – directing traffic by means of hand signals. This may happen when traffic lights have failed or when traffic has to be re-routed through a town centre due to an event being held. They may also patrol school crossings.

A further duty may be at police car pounds, where they receive vehicles being brought in and register the details.

At the end of a shift, traffic wardens return to the office to hand in duplicate copies of any tickets they have issued and to report incidents, like road accidents, that are causing delays – necessary information for wardens on the next shift.

Occasionally they have to appear in court to give evidence against offenders.

Parking attendants do the above duties with the exceptions of: point duty, school crossing patrol and attendance at police pounds.

Traffic wardens wear a distinctive uniform. They have protective clothing for wet weather. Parking attendants wear the uniform of their own employers. These vary in design, the only requirement on employers being that parking attendants' uniforms must be clearly distinguishable from those worn by traffic wardens or police officers and must state clearly the name of the employing local authority.

WORK ENVIRONMENT

Traffic wardens and parking attendants work outdoors in all weather conditions. They are on their feet for most of the day and may walk as far as five miles during one shift. They are based at offices in police stations and may share canteen and social facilities there with police officers.

SKILLS AND INTERESTS

Both traffic wardens and parking attendants must be fit and active.

They work alone for much of the time and must be capable of working without close supervision. They should be observant and honest.

They must be assertive, yet polite and tactful, when dealing with people. Motorists are often aggressive and hostile. They must be able to cope with this and not be easily upset. Self-confidence is important. They need good communication skills, as they are constantly in contact with the public. Traffic wardens also work in close co-operation with the police.

ENTRY REQUIREMENTS

Exact requirements vary from area to area.

No formal educational qualifications are required. Applicants should, however, have a good standard of education and are sometimes expected to pass a written entrance test in maths and English.

Many areas have a minimum age requirement of 18 years; in others it is 20 or even 25 years.

Applicants should be in good health and are usually required to take a medical examination. Good eyesight is necessary. Glasses are permitted. Some employers stipulate a minimum height. Others insist that applicants are British subjects and/or reside in the area.

Experience of previous employment in a job which involves dealing with the public is an advantage.

TRAINING

Traffic wardens and parking attendants receive much of their training on the job, from experienced colleagues, and in the case of wardens, sometimes from a police officer with responsibility for supervising traffic wardens. They usually spend several weeks working with an experienced colleague before going out alone.

Since they are often recruited as specific vacancies arise, there is not usually a sufficiently large number of entrants joining at the same time to warrant the provision of a full-time instruction course.

However, in many areas a special introductory course may be arranged for a large intake and, in London, all traffic wardens attend a training course at the Metropolitan Police Training Centre in Hendon.

Trainees learn traffic regulations and how to complete and issue tickets for parking offences. They may also learn methods of note-taking and of writing short reports. The training of traffic wardens also covers the techniques of giving evidence in court. In some areas they also take a short first aid course so that they may deal with emergencies that occur on the street.

LATE ENTRY

This type of work is very suitable for older entrants, as it requires maturity and evidence of ability to deal with people. Because of this, there is a minimum age limit in most areas. There may, however, be a maximum entry age limit of 55 to 59 years.

OPPORTUNITIES

Approximately 4,000 traffic wardens and parking attendants are employed in the UK. Opportunities vary from area to area and the largest number of openings is in cities and large towns.

Traffic wardens are civilians who work in local police districts under the general control of the police force.

Parking attendants are employed by local government district authorities, that is by town or city councils. The London boroughs have contracted-out the work to private companies, who directly employ the staff.

The number of opportunities for parking attendants is increasing, as more local authorities take over the responsibility for enforcing parking regulations from the police force. The number of openings for traffic wardens is consequently decreasing.

Vacancies may be held by local Jobcentres or be advertised in the local press. Alternatively, contact local police headquarters (traffic wardens) or council headquarters (parking attendants) directly to enquire about current opportunities. In London, enquiries about traffic warden vacancies should be made to the Metropolitan Police Recruitment Branch.

PAY AND CONDITIONS

Pay scales vary in different areas. A trainee might begin on a salary of approximately £9,600 rising to approximately £10,150 in annual increments. In London, the starting salary is £10,265 with no annual increments. Performance related pay is now in force. A London weighting allowance is paid and there are opportunities for paid overtime.

Uniform and protective clothing allowances are paid. Some employers also provide a shoe allowance.

Duties are carried out during the times when traffic regulations are in force. Hours of work could be between 6.30am and 8pm. It is normal to work a 42-hour week on a shift system spread over seven days.

PROSPECTS

Traffic wardens and parking attendants may gain promotion to senior grades. Career prospects vary in different areas and may be extremely limited in areas where few are employed.

Progression is based on ability. Staff employed in the more senior grades become increasingly involved in the administrative, supervisory and training aspects of the work.

RELATED OCCUPATIONS

Police constable, security officer, HM Forces personnel, store detective.

FURTHER INFORMATION

From local police constabularies/district councils. Addresses in the telephone directory.

Metropolitan Police Recruitment Branch, 26-27 Aybrook Street, London W1M 3JL, 0171 321 9569/70

FURTHER READING

Working In Police and Security – COIC

In the careers library classified under MAB.

1. PRISON GOVERNOR CLCI:MAD
2. PRISON OFFICER CLCI:MAD

BACKGROUND INFORMATION

Her Majesty's Prison Service serves the public by keeping in custody those committed by the courts. It also has a responsibility to treat prisoners with humanity and to help them lead law-abiding lives in custody and after release.

The Prison Service in England and Wales is a Home Office Agency, whilst the Scottish Prison Service is an Executive Agency of the Scottish Office. Staff are public employees. Both prison services are going through a period of considerable change, with many of the functions previously undertaken centrally by the Home Office or Scottish Office now devolving to individual prisons. In England and Wales, this includes recruitment of prison officers. Some prisons in England have been 'contracted out' to the private sector and are run by private companies, who employ their own staff.

Some prisoners in the care of the prison service are on remand, still waiting for trial or for sentencing by the courts, following their conviction. Others have been sentenced for varying lengths of time and are dealt with according to their category. Category A prisoners are the most dangerous and are dispersed between top security prisons, whilst Category D can be trusted not to attempt escape and may be housed in open prisons. Categories B and C fall between these extremes. Other types of prison establishment include remand centres and young offender institutions, which provide training for young people under 21 years of age. Local prisons keep a cross section of prisoners, and security varies from one part of the prison to another.

The situation in Scotland is slightly different, with local closed prisons, specialized closed prisons, open prisons and young offender institutions.

1. PRISON GOVERNOR (MAD)

THE WORK

Governors are the managers in the prison service. They are responsible for the control and security of prison establishments, managing both staff and resources. The work varies considerably with the size and type of establishment and the grade and level of experience of the governor.

A senior governor is in overall charge and is assisted by a team of governor-grade staff who have responsibility for particular functions or areas of the prison.

Governors organize the work of prison officers and carry out staff training. They supervise security, oversee the maintenance of prisoners' records, deal with parole requests, and have responsibility for discipline procedures. They may also chair admission, release and parole boards.

Governors have frequent contact with prisoners, either in a one-to-one situation, or as part of regular 'walkabouts' to check what is happening in the prison. They are responsible for organizing and supervising prisoners' development and progress. They counsel and advise prisoners and liaise with other professionals including doctors, chaplains, probation officers and psychiatrists. They also arrange prisoners' educational, leisure and work activities. Much of the inmates' work is carried out on a commercial basis for organizations outside the prison, and governors oversee contracts.

As governors progress through the grades, they take on more responsibility and may eventually be in charge of a prison. Before this, however, there may be times when they are the most senior member of staff on duty and are responsible for the prison for short periods. Governors also have the opportunity of working at headquarters, perhaps as part of a team looking after several prisons in an area, or offering strategic support to individual prisons when a major disturbance occurs. They may also work at a prison service college, training other staff.

'Contracted out' prisons have a different structure and may not use the term 'governor'. However, similar functions are undertaken by their management teams.

WORK ENVIRONMENT

Governors usually work in prisons, although some are based at headquarters, or in a prison service college or field training unit.

Prisons vary from very modern buildings to old and overcrowded centres, although a great deal of refurbishment is going on in some of the older establishments. The environment will also vary, depending on the amount of security in the prison.

Governors often work in offices within the prison, but their jobs take them to all parts of the establishment. They also spend time in meetings, conferences and courses outside the prison.

SKILLS AND INTERESTS

Governors need management skills to organize the prison and its resources. They must be able to lead and motivate both staff and prisoners. Good communication skills (both written and verbal) are essential. The ability to make decisions, sometimes in response to an urgent situation, is needed. Decisions must be well thought out and clear.

Governors need maturity and patience to help the prisoners, and must be interested in their welfare. They should be able to understand and sympathize with inmates, without condoning their behaviour.

The ability to enforce discipline without being authoritarian is essential. Difficult situations may arise and must be dealt with. The work can be stressful and demanding and requires a flexible approach.

ENTRY REQUIREMENTS

In England and Wales, entry to governor grade is by promotion to governor 5 (the first governor grade) from principal officer (the highest prison officer grade), or by open competition – the accelerated promotion scheme (APS). The APS is open to serving prison officers and to graduates from outside the prison service. All applicants must pass an examination to progress to a three-day extended interview.

Scotland. Entry to governor grade is by promotion from prison officer (as above), or by direct entry. Direct entrants must have considerable management experience.

Applicants must be at least 20 years old. All entrants must be physically fit with good eyesight (glasses and contact lenses may be acceptable). They must pass a medical examination. Nationality, residency and conviction rules apply – please see article 2. PRISON OFFICER. Minimum height regulations of 1.7m (5 feet 7 inches) for males and 1.6m (5 feet 3 inches) for females apply in Scotland.

Entry requirements and methods are under review. 'Contracted out' prisons operate their own systems.

TRAINING

England and Wales. Entrants to the APS spend a week at the Prison Service College, followed by two weeks' observation in a prison near their home. A nine-week residential course at either Wakefield or Newbold Revel Prison Service College (near Rugby) follows. This deals with the practical skills of prison work, including cell searching and controlling violent inmates. It also covers assertiveness skills and issues such as race relations and suicide prevention. This is the course undertaken by newly appointed prison officers, as all APS entrants begin by spending nine months as a basic grade prison officer. During this time they sit the senior officer examination and, if successful, take the principal officer board. (APS entrants who were serving prison officers continue from the grade they had reached.) Before taking up a twelve-month posting at principal officer rank they undergo two months' training, and have a further two months' training before their next placement as governor 5. The APS ends when candidates have spent two years at governor 5 level and have passed their governor 4 Board.

Scotland. Direct governor entrants undergo a twelve-month 'Governor 5 On Appointment Programme'. This is competency-based, and a probationary year runs at the same time. Trainees are based in prisons and work as governor 5 whilst training.

LATE ENTRY

The upper age limit for entry to the prison service is 49½ years in England and Wales, and 42 years (46 for those in HM Forces) in Scotland. Mature entrants must undertake the same pattern and length of training before being appointed to governor grades.

Most entrants to the APS in England and Wales are young graduates, but older candidates will be considered, particularly if they have appropriate experience, such as HM Forces or police work. In Scotland, relevant management experience is essential for direct entry to a governor post.

'Contracted out' prisons may have different age limits.

OPPORTUNITIES

Over 40,000 people are employed in prisons in Britain, including over 1,000 governors in England and Wales and about 150 in Scotland. The number of staff in the prison service has increased by around a third in recent years.

Governors are employed by the Prison Service (England and Wales), the Scottish Office or by private companies operating 'contracted out' prisons. There are over 130 prison establishments, including headquarters, colleges and training units in England and Wales, with more planned. Scotland has 21 prisons, plus a headquarters and a prison service college. Prisons are located all over the country in both urban and rural locations. Male and female prisoners are usually housed separately, but a long-established tradition of 'opposite sex posting' means male governors can work with female prisoners and female governors with male prisoners. Governors must be prepared to move, as they can be posted to any prison establishment within the Prison Service (England and Wales) or within the Scottish Office. Those working for private companies are employed at a particular prison.

Entry is very competitive, whether through APS, by direct promotion from principal officer grade, or by direct entry. The APS does not run every year, but is advertised in the national press in October of the year it is to run. Opportunities for direct governor entrants in Scotland are advertised in the national and Scottish press and on television (STV).

PAY AND CONDITIONS

Except for direct entrants in Scotland, governors start their careers on prison officer grades. Please see article 2. PRISON OFFICER.

Governor salary scales range from basic pay for governor 5 of £26,978 to £47,629 for governor 1. A London supplement is also payable. Governors wear civilian clothes.

Governors work the hours needed to complete the job, and busy working days may extend beyond eight hours. There are no additional payments for extra hours. The nature of the job involves some evening duties and working weekends, but night hours are less common. There are opportunities to work part-time.

'Contracted out' prisons have their own salary and working patterns, and managers may be required to wear uniform.

PROSPECTS

The first governor grade is governor 5 and the most senior (which might mean running a large prison) is governor 1. Someone at governor 3 grade (governor 4 in Scotland) may be in charge of a smaller prison.

Promotion to higher grades is on merit through promotion board and the length of time taken varies between candidates. For example, someone entering the service on the APS could reach governor 4 in five years, whereas the non-accelerated route would take considerably longer.

Experienced governors can work at headquarters on the administrative side, for example, as area managers or operational directors with responsibility for several prisons. They may also work at prison service colleges or training units running courses for other staff.

Grades and promotion routes are under review in both England/Wales and Scotland. 'Contracted out' prisons have their own structures.

RELATED OCCUPATIONS

Police constable, probation officer, HM Forces – commissioned officer, social worker, Civil Service executive officer, Civil Service administration trainee, prison officer.

FURTHER INFORMATION AND READING

Please see article 2. PRISON OFFICER.

2. PRISON OFFICER (MAD)

THE WORK

Prison officers' work varies with the type of prison and its level of security as well as with the category and age of the prisoners.

They have security duties that ensure prisoners remain in custody. These involve supervising prisoners in all areas, including work areas and cells, and in all activities such as eating, recreation and exercise. They also patrol buildings and grounds and carry out cell searches. They have to deal with disruptive behaviour and ensure the safety of inmates and staff.

Officers are involved in tasks such as receiving new prisoners, issuing clothing, completing reports and other paperwork, and passing on prisoners' requests to senior staff.

An important part of the work is rehabilitating prisoners. This involves helping them with their problems and preparing them for life outside the prison. Prison officers advise and counsel prisoners and ensure they have access to professional help when needed. They are also responsible for prisoners' training.

Entrants with specific skills can carry out specialist work after prison officer training. They remain prison officers with discipline duties, but may become catering officers, health care officers, PE instructors, works officers (building trades), etc. They practise their skill and teach it to prisoners who work with them in workshops, on farms, in prison hospitals or kitchens, on building sites or in maintenance programmes and in trade training schemes. Inmates can take appropriate vocational qualifications.

Higher grade prison officers have additional responsibilities, such as supervising other officers or looking after an area or wing of the prison.

'Contracted out' prisons have a different structure and may not use the term 'prison officer', but staff carry out similar work.

WORK ENVIRONMENT

Prison officers usually work in prison establishments as part of a team. Some are based at headquarters or in a prison service college or field training unit.

Prisons vary from very modern buildings to old and overcrowded centres, although a great deal of refurbishment is going on in some of the older establishments. The environment will also vary depending on the amount of security in the prison.

Except for certain trades, the majority of a prison officer's work will take place indoors, although patrolling and supervisory duties may mean spending time outside. Escort duty and some trades mean spending time away from the prison.

SKILLS AND INTERESTS

Prison officers must like working with people, gaining their trust and helping with their problems. They need patience, understanding and tact, but must also be firm and be able to exercise authority. They must be able to deal with a variety of people, from those who are abusive and potentially violent, to those lacking in self-confidence and personal skills. Difficult situations may arise and prison officers must be able to use their leadership skills to cope. Prison officers should be able to understand and sympathize with inmates without condoning their behaviour.

They must be able to work as part of a team and liaise with others concerned with the welfare of the prisoners. Good communication skills are very important. The work can be stressful and requires a flexible approach. Self-control, resilience and a sense of humour are all essential.

ENTRY REQUIREMENTS

No formal qualifications are required, but applicants have to pass an aptitude test before being interviewed. There is also a full medical examination.

Applicants must:

– be aged 20 (in England and Wales there is an upper age limit of 49½ years);

– be a British citizen, a British protected person, a Commonwealth citizen with indefinite leave to remain in the UK, or an EU national;

– have been resident in the UK for at least three years at the time of application;

– be physically fit and in good health;

– have a minimum standard of vision (glasses and contact lenses are not necessarily a bar);

– be fully mobile (although basic grade officers are recruited locally by prisons in England and Wales, postings for senior and principal officers are controlled centrally. In Scotland, officers themselves apply for postings or promotions in other establishments but, under some circumstances, postings may still be controlled centrally);

– declare any convictions (including Armed Forces) on the application form. An offence is not an automatic bar, as each case is considered on its own merits.

'Contracted out' prisons have their own entry requirements.

TRAINING

England and Wales. New prison officers spend one week on pre-training experience at the prison that appointed them before undertaking a nine-week residential course at one of the two Prison Service Colleges (Wakefield or Newbold Revel, near Rugby). This course covers a wide range of skills necessary for the care and control of prisoners, including cell and body searching, radio procedures, court and escort duties, supervision, physical restraint and self-defence. It also includes a strong element of physical training. After the course there is a one-week induction at the prison before prison officer duties start. New prison officers have a twelve-month probationary period.

Scotland. Newly appointed officers undergo a training year that is also a probationary period. After a week spent in a prison, officers take a two-week course in the Prison Service College at Falkirk to learn the skills and procedures required in the job (see England and Wales above). Two more weeks' training in the prison follow, after which officers become operational. During the rest of the training year a further two weeks are spent in college and the remainder in the prison.

NVQs/SVQs in Custodial Care are available at Level 2.

'Contracted out' prisons provide their own training for staff.

LATE ENTRY

The upper age limit for entry to the prison service is 49½ in England and Wales. All entrants must meet the requirements listed above and follow the same pattern of training.

Relevant experience such as HM Forces or police work is useful.

'Contracted out' prisons may have different age limits.

OPPORTUNITIES

Over 40,000 people are employed in the prison service in Britain and, of these, more than 27,000 are prison officers. The number of staff in the prison service has increased by approximately one third in recent years.

Prison officers are employed by the Prison Service (England and Wales), the Scottish Office, or by private companies operating 'contracted out' prisons. There are over 130 prison establishments, plus headquarters, colleges and field training units, in England and Wales, with more planned. Scotland has 22 establishments, a headquarters and a college. Prisons are located all over the country and, in England and Wales, each is responsible for recruiting prison officers locally. Vacancies are advertised in Jobcentres. In Scotland, recruitment is still carried out centrally, although no recruitment is taking place at present. The recruitment system in Scotland is under review.

Prison officers must be prepared to move, as they can be posted to any prison establishment within the Prison Service (England and Wales) or within the Scottish Prison Service. They can also transfer between the two. Those working for private companies are employed at a particular prison. Male and female prisoners are usually housed separately but 'opposite sex postings' mean that female officers can work in male prisons, and male officers in female prisons.

PAY AND CONDITIONS

The starting salary for a basic grade prison officer (England and Wales) is £14,430, rising to £20,037 after 15 years. The basic pay for a senior officer is £21,275 and that for a principal officer is £22,056. Shift allowances and London supplements are also payable. Specialist officers, such as trade instructors and hospital officers receive an additional £936 a year. Officers are provided with a free uniform.

New recruits in Scotland have a starting salary of £12,500 and with satisfactory or better performance may progress to £16,000.

Officers work a 39-hour week in shift patterns that vary between establishments. Night, evening and weekend working are likely to form part of the shift pattern. There are opportunities to work part-time.

'Contracted out' prisons have their own salary and working patterns.

PROSPECTS

Prison officers can progress to senior officer grade (after a minimum of four years in England and Wales) by examination. After this, promotion to principal officer grade is by merit, and officers go before a promotion board. Principal officers are eligible for promotion to governor grades (please see article 1. PRISON GOVERNOR).

Prison officers in England and Wales can also apply to join the accelerated promotion scheme (APS) (please see article 1. PRISON GOVERNOR), although this does not run every year.

Experienced officers who wish to specialize can take additional training courses. For example, those without nursing qualifications, who wish to work as hospital officers, can take an intensive course that includes NHS hospital placements as well as classroom and practical instruction.

Grades and promotion routes are under review in both England/Wales and Scotland. 'Contracted out' prisons have their own structures.

RELATED OCCUPATIONS

Police constable, prison instructor, HM Forces serviceman/woman, probation officer, social worker, youth and community worker, prison governor, security officer.

FURTHER INFORMATION

England and Wales – individual establishments: see Yellow Pages for addresses/telephone numbers.

England and Wales – Accelerated Promotion Scheme: The APS Section, Directorate of Personnel, Prison Service HQ*, Room 418, Cleland House, Page Street, London SW1P 4LN, 0171 217 6437/6055 (please include sae)

Scottish Prison Service*, Central Recruitment Board, Room 131, Calton House, 5 Redheughs Rigg, Edinburgh EH12 9HW, 0131 244 8591/2

FURTHER READING

Leaflets/booklets are available from the addresses marked*.

Job Outlines – Prison Service – COIC

In the careers library classified under MAD.

FIREFIGHTER/FIRE OFFICER CLCI:MAF

BACKGROUND INFORMATION

The Fire Service exists to save and rescue people and property from all types of accident and disaster. In fact only one in five calls on average, is for help at a fire.

Fire-fighters respond to fire calls, road traffic accidents, floods, bomb incidents, spillages of dangerous substances, rail and air crashes and also rescue people and animals who are trapped inside buildings, lifts and other confined spaces. They often work closely at the site of a disaster with members of the other emergency services, including the ambulance and police services.

The Fire Service also has a role in promoting fire safety (including safety when using fireworks) and is responsible for enforcing standards of fire safety in public and commercial premises.

There is no national fire service. Instead, there are 63 local fire authorities, each under the command of a chief fire officer (firemaster in Scotland). There are 55 separate fire brigades in England and Wales, provided by county councils, metropolitan authorities and in London by the London Fire and Civil Defence Authority. Each fire brigade divides its geographical area of responsibility into Divisions. In addition to an overall Brigade Headquarters it has Divisional Headquarters in the charge of a Divisional Commander, responsible for several fire stations.

There are two types of firefighter, whole-time and part-time, or 'retained'. The Home Office (for England and Wales) and the Scottish Office lay down guidelines based on the risk of fire occurring in each area and how severe the damage might be to the people. These help determine whether a fire station is staffed by whole-time or retained fire-fighters. Retained fire-fighters are usually found in rural areas and small towns. They are paid an annual fee or retainer plus fees for attending drill nights and training sessions in addition to a fee for each call they attend. They must live or work within four minutes of the fire station.

In some of the remoter parts of Scotland there are units of volunteer fire-fighters who serve their local communities.

THE WORK

Fire-fighters work in teams and respond to an emergency call or 'shout' as it happens. They may be required to attend an incident in which they have to use cutting and lifting gear to free people who are trapped under masonry or in vehicles and may have to give first aid before the ambulance crew arrive. They may be called to a fire which produces toxic fumes and heavy smoke, which necessitates the use of special breathing apparatus. Whatever the situation, their responsibility is to save life and property with minimum damage and to clear and check the safety of the site.

Fire-fighters work in crews of five or six allocated to one appliance (fire engine). When a shout comes a controller assesses how many appliances will be required and, from information on high risk buildings and hazardous materials that is kept on the control room computer, decides whether specialist equipment will be required. A sub-officer or station officer is briefed before leaving the station, then takes charge of the operation and leads the crew(s). With a major incident, a more senior officer attends and co-ordinates the work.

Fire-fighters' appliances are fully equipped with ladders, water hoses, foam equipment, bolt cutters, air cutting saws, sledge hammers, slate rippers, breathing apparatus and sometimes thermal imaging cameras to help them to locate people in smoke-filled rooms. They wear helmets and protective equipment and, for attendance at chemical spills, they have additional protective suits. They may carry personal radio sets with them to enable them to stay in contact with each other and with the fire station.

When the crews arrive at an incident the officer in charge must assess the situation as quickly as possible, noting, for instance, whether a fire involves any hazardous substances or modern materials such as foam-filled furniture, which generates heavy smoke. The fire officer decides on the method of containing the fire or dealing with other incidents and directs the crew who work in close co-operation with each other. Team work is vitally important. Every member of a crew is responsible for the lives of colleagues and of people involved in the situation. They have to deal with unforeseen circumstances as they arise and think quickly.

After dealing with an incident, fire-fighters clean up the site then return to the station, where the officer in charge has to write a full report of the incident.

Between shouts, whole-time fire-fighters are based at their station, where they have a variety of duties. They inspect, clean and maintain their appliance and its equipment, do drills and physical training, and study and learn new techniques. If they have the time, they may study for promotion exams. The night shift, or watch, are able to rest if they are not called out. Each station has sleeping quarters.

Other duties carried out by fire-fighters, and particularly by fire officers, include: providing specialist advice to institutions, such as hospitals and residential establishments, and to local authorities, which are responsible for licensing places of entertainment; inspecting premises and issuing fire certificates; talking about fire safety in schools and to local organizations.

Fire officers have a dual role. In addition to leading teams of fire-fighters at incidents they have managerial duties. The most senior officers spend a large part of their time on administrative and training duties and in giving talks on fire prevention and safety.

WORK ENVIRONMENT

Most full-time fire-fighters work in urban areas, whereas retained fire-fighters cover rural ones.

Fire-fighters work in dangerous and often very unpleasant conditions: heat, cold, at heights, in enclosed spaces, in smoke-filled buildings, and in all kinds of weather conditions. They are exposed to danger from collapsing buildings or vehicles, explosion and fumes.

The work is hard physically and can be very uncomfortable,, since fire-fighters have to wear heavy protective clothing and breathing apparatus and carry heavy and awkward equipment.

Crews normally stay in the same watches, which is important for building up team spirit.

Fire-fighters spend much of their time at the station, where they carry out routine duties, study or do physical training. Sometimes they leave the station to carry out practice drills and to give talks and lectures.

SKILLS AND INTERESTS

Fire-fighters require stamina and a high level of physical fitness. They need quick reactions and the ability to stay calm in hazardous situations. Their work requires courage and determination. They must be able to accept discipline and enjoy working as a member of a close-knit team. At the same time they are expected to use their initiative and respond to changing circumstances when at an incident.

They must be prepared to accept restrictions on their personal appearance. Most brigades insist that hair should not show below the helmet. Male firefighters are not generally permitted to have beards or sideburns which could impinge on the breathing apparatus face mask.

They need to be practical and able to work with a range of tools and equipment.

Communication skills are important. Verbal skills and a reassuring manner are required when dealing with members of the public who are injured or in a state of shock. They must be able to deal firmly but politely with bystanders who may be hampering rescue work at an incident.

Written communication skill is essential when writing incident reports. These will often be used by accident investigators and insurance companies as a basis for their work.

ENTRY REQUIREMENTS

There is no minimum educational entry standard. A good general education is required and some brigades may ask for GCSEs/S grades (A-C/1-3) or equivalent in English, mathematics and science.

All recruits begin as fire-fighters. There is no separate officer or fast stream entry, although many entrants have A levels or degrees and they are expected to pass promotion exams more quickly. Some fire brigades advertise specifically for graduates (in any subject) with leadership potential.

In some areas, applicants have to take an educational entry test which includes English, numeracy, mechanical comprehension and spatial awareness.

They must be between the ages of 18 and 30 and must be between 1.68m (5 feet 6 inches) and 1.93m (6 feet 4 inches).

Each brigade has a range of fitness entry tests that include lung function and aerobic capacity, muscle strength, hand grip and lifting. Applicants must be in good health and must pass a medical examination. They must have good vision in each eye without the aid of glasses or contact lenses and must not be colour blind.

Brigades also set a series of initiative and physical tests – often over a two-day period.

Entry may be possible for young people through Modern Apprenticeships leading to at least an NVQ/SVQ Level 3. Contact your local careers office, TEC/LEC for details.

TRAINING

New recruits in England and Wales follow a full-time training course of 12 to 16 weeks. This is held at their own or a nearby fire authority's residential training centre (some authorities do not maintain their own centres but send their recruits to do their initial training at one run by another authority). In Scotland, 16-week recruit training courses are provided at the Scottish Fire Service Training School, which is maintained by the Scottish Office.

Induction training is rigorous, with military-style discipline and much time spent on drill. It is divided between theory and practical work covering basic rescue techniques: use of fire-fighting and breathing equipment; entering smoke-

filled rooms; foam and fire extinguishers; ladders, hoses, knots, hydraulic and other equipment; fire safety; and first aid.

Recruits next move to their fire station, where they spend up to two years as probationary fire-fighters, learning from experienced fire-fighters. There is continuous assessment during this period.

Training continues throughout a firefighter's career. Refresher courses are held in fire safety, use of breathing apparatus and appliance driving. Lectures and courses are held on new techniques. Fire Service training centres often have buildings which can be filled with smoke and whose layout – floors, walls, staircases – can be changed so that both recruits and experienced fire-fighters can practise rescues continually in realistic conditions – while carrying heavy breathing packs.

Fire-fighters are encouraged to gain specialist qualifications, such as an LGV licence, necessary for driving a fire appliance, or in fire safety, and to study for statutory promotion exams. Most brigades encourage fire-fighters who wish to do so to take additional professional qualifications, such as membership of the Institution of Fire Engineers, or a degree in Fire Engineering or qualifications in public administration or management studies.

Officers attend short courses on technical fire-fighting and management skills at the Fire Service College in Gloucestershire.

Retained fire-fighters do basic training over a series of weekends and attend weekly drill nights throughout their service. They may occasionally have to attend some short courses held during the day.

LATE ENTRY

In some areas the maximum age of entry is 30 for full-time fire-fighters; 45 for retained fire-fighters.

OPPORTUNITIES

There are about 40,000 whole-time fire-fighters in England and Wales and approximately 17,000 retained fire-fighters. In Scotland there are 7,000 whole-time and retained fire-fighters.

The majority of fire-fighters work for local fire brigades. Competition for entry is fierce and there are always far more applicants to the full-time Fire Service than there are vacancies. Many brigades have periods when they do no recruitment at all. There is almost always a shortage of retained fire-fighters.

There are opportunities to work for a small number of other employers, like the British Airports Authority, which maintains fire brigades at airports, and for the Defence Fire Service of the Ministry of Defence.

PAY AND CONDITIONS

A firefighter earns £12,984 on entry, rising to £16,497 over five years. Leading fire-fighters earn from £17,667 to £18,396. Sub-officers and officers earn higher salaries. A station officer, for example, earns £21,012 to £22,659 and a senior divisional officer £29,946 to £32,304. Assistant chief officers and chief officers/firemasters are not paid on fixed scales. Their salaries vary with different fire authorities.

Retained fire-fighters are paid £1,440 to £1,575 a year plus attendance and turn-out fees.

Fire-fighters work a 42-hour week, which is divided into day and night shifts. They have an average of at least two days off each week. Many stations operate a system under which fire-fighters work two day shifts from 8am to 6pm followed by two night shifts from 6pm to 8am. The four shifts are then followed by four days' leave. When necessary, paid overtime is worked.

PROSPECTS

All recruits start in the same grade and promotion is on merit. Progression through the ranks is as follows: leading firefighter, sub-officer, station officer, assistant divisional officer, divisional officer grades 1-3, senior divisional officer, assistant chief fire officer/firemaster, chief fire officer/firemaster.

A firefighter who has passed the promotion exams could rise to the rank of station officer after five years' experience. This, however, would be exceptional. It normally takes longer than the minimum possible period to gain each promotion.

Up to the rank of station officer, promotions are made internally. After this grade, vacancies which arise are advertised throughout the Service, so that anyone with appropriate experience and qualifications may apply.

It is usually necessary to move to different areas for promotion and most senior officers have worked in several brigades.

RELATED OCCUPATIONS

Police constable, security officer, HM Forces serviceman/woman, ambulanceman/woman.

FURTHER INFORMATION

Contact the personnel or recruitment departments of local fire services; addresses are in the local telephone directory.

FURTHER READING

Job Outlines – Emergency Services – COIC
Working in the Emergency Services – COIC
In the careers library classified under MAF.

SECURITY WORK: MAG

SECURITY OFFICER CLCI:MAG

BACKGROUND INFORMATION

Security is often required by both private and public organizations whose premises and property may be at risk of theft, malicious damage, or accidents such as fire and flood. Many organizations have their own security staff, while others make use of services provided by specialist security companies.

Services offered by contract security companies include: transporting cash and valuables in secured vehicles; guarding premises; planning and installing security systems; protection against industrial espionage; protecting retail premises; and protecting people.

THE WORK

The prime function of security officers (sometimes known as security guards) is loss prevention (one of the major causes of this is fire). They protect property, goods, money and people for commercial, industrial and public organizations. Their work can range from patrolling industrial premises to guarding ships and their cargoes, providing security for important meetings or conferences, being guards at sporting events or providing protection for important people.

There are three main types of security officers: static security officers; mobile security officers; and security drivers/cash-in-transit security officers.

Static security officers – are based in one place, which could be an office block, a factory, warehouse, building site, etc. Part of their work may involve working in the reception area, where they receive visitors to the company, get them to sign the visitor's book, issue them with a pass and direct them to where they are going. Security officers are usually responsible for personnel and visitors in case of an emergency such as fire, so they need to know where a visitor will be. Their work may include checking delivery vehicles in and out of premises; in factories and other large premises, guards may be on the gate checking all who enter and leave.

If an emergency does arise, security officers are usually responsible for ensuring that everyone can leave the building easily – so they control all doors and gates and ensure that fire exits are kept clear. They also ensure all personnel are out of the building and accounted for, and that no one re-enters until the emergency is over.

At night, security officers use closed circuit television to watch the premises. They also patrol the premises regularly, checking doors and windows, making sure that no one has broken in, and looking for fire and flood hazards.

Security officers may be issued with two-way radios, so that, if they come across intruders, they can radio for assistance.

Mobile security officers – do similar work to the static guards but are not based in one place. Mobile security officers patrol and visit a number of sites. Part of their job may be visiting premises as the staff are leaving at the end of the day.

Throughout the night and at weekends they carry out patrols of the outside of buildings, checking windows, gates and doors. They also patrol the inside of the building, checking to see that there are no water leaks or fire hazards. They also need to be on the alert to deal with intruders, if found.

A security company may act as a key holder for a number of

premises, so that if an alarm goes off, mobile guards are sent to premises to find out what has happened. They open the premises for police or fire brigade, assist them while they are there and then make sure the building is secure when they have left. It is important that mobile security officers vary their routine for visiting premises. Some mobile security officers also use dogs.

Cash-in-transit operatives – collect valuables such as cash, precious metals or jewellery and transport them in safety to their destination. The operatives wear protective clothing and they are in constant radio contact with their base station. Drivers may also be used as couriers: delivering packages, documents, computer data and almost any other important item.

WORK ENVIRONMENT

This varies depending on the job. Static security officers could be based in offices, building sites, industrial premises, retail premises, etc. They may work alone, although some companies may have a number of static security officers on duty at one time. Mobile security officers often work alone and spend a considerable amount of their time driving from one set of premises to another. Both static and mobile security officers' work involves patrolling the inside and outside of buildings and this can mean being outside in the dark in all weathers. Cash-in-transit operatives spend much of their time in security vehicles.

SKILLS AND INTERESTS

All security officers need the qualities of honesty, common sense and reliability. It is vital for this work to be able to think quickly and clearly in an emergency, and confidence is essential, as security officers are expected to approach and challenge suspicious persons in the course of their duty. They must have a firm, polite and helpful manner, and be fit and in good health. Mobile and static security officers need to be able to work alone and on their own initiative, while cash-in-transit operatives must be able to work in a team.

ENTRY REQUIREMENTS

Most newcomers into this work are recruited as static or mobile security officers or cash-in-transit operatives. There are no specific entry requirements; personal qualities and good health are considered more important than educational qualifications. Applicants will have to provide a checkable record of employment, self-employment or unemployment, and may have to pass a medical examination. For some jobs, a current clean driving licence is required.

Entry may be possible for young people through Modern Apprenticeships leading to at least an NVQ/SVQ Level 3. Contact your local careers office, TEC/LEC for details.

TRAINING

Training varies depending on the organization for which the security officer works. Most organizations run their own training, and their staff are often encouraged to take City and Guilds or other relevant qualifications. Security staff can also gain NVQs at Level 2 in Security, Safety and Loss Prevention, which provide specialisms in Security Officer, Retail Security Officer, Door Supervisor, Dog Handler, Aviation Security Officer and CCTV Operative. An NVQ is also available at Level 2 in Transporting Property under Guard (CIT). Training for this work may be both on and off-the-job. It usually starts with an induction course that covers such subjects as: the legal powers of security officers; physical security – how to check doors, windows, etc; dealing with customers; car searching, etc. Some organizations also run a range of further courses, for instance in first aid. Some companies send their staff on courses run by the Security Industry Training Organization (SITO) or the International Professional Security Association (IPSA).

SITO offers a range of courses, including distance learning packages and courses at regional training centres in such subjects as professional guards parts 1 and 2, which leads to SITO/City and Guilds 7274 and 7278, retail security, cash-in-transit and aviation security.

IPSA courses range from induction courses through career foundation and supervisory courses to management courses and seminars. On-the-job training is done under the supervision of an experienced security officer.

Those wanting promotion to more senior supervisory and management jobs may find that, for these jobs, some employers may look for the professional qualifications of the International Institute of Security (IISec) or SITO's National Examining Board for Supervisory Management (NEBS) qualifications; however, this is not essential. There are no academic requirements to take these courses. Study for IISec is usually by correspondence course, available through the IPSA, and takes 28 weeks. Study for SITO qualifications is through distance learning and residential courses.

LATE ENTRY

Most security organizations want more mature applicants and the usual age for recruitment into this work is between 21 and 45 years. There are good opportunities for ex-servicemen and women, police, prison officers and fire-fighters. There are no formal academic requirements for this work – see ENTRY REQUIREMENTS for details.

OPPORTUNITIES

This area of work is expanding by about 15 per cent each year and employs about 200,000 people. Employers include industrial and commercial organizations, retail stores, property companies, central government, local government, and contract security firms. Amongst the specialist security companies, there are a few large companies and many smaller ones. With large international security companies, there may be chances to work abroad.

PAY AND CONDITIONS

In contract security companies, security officers tend to earn between £180 and £220 a week. Shift allowances may be paid and overtime is common. Security officers working for in-house security teams may earn slightly more – often between about £200 and £300 a week (or possibly even more). Hours vary – most security officers work shifts. Some officers work permanently at night. Cash-in-transit operatives and some static security officers may work mainly during the day. The normal hours worked by security officers in the contract side of the industry is 60 a week. The in-house security officers tend to work a maximum of 40 hours.

PROSPECTS

Opportunities for promotion are usually better in large companies. Security officers can be promoted to supervisory posts, for instance, supervising a number of static security officers, visiting them to make sure that all is going smoothly and being on hand in case they have any problems they cannot deal with. There are also opportunities for promotion from supervisory posts to management.

RELATED OCCUPATIONS

Police constable, prison officer, store detective, safety officer.

FURTHER INFORMATION

The Security Industry Training Organization, Security House, Barbourne Road, Worcester WR1 1RS, 01905 20004

The International Professional Security Association, IPSA House, 3 Dendy Road, Paignton, Devon TQ4 5DB

The International Institute of Security, 3 Dendy Road, Paignton, Devon TQ4 5DB

FURTHER READING

Working in Police and Security – COIC
In the careers library classified under MAG.

COASTGUARD: MAZ

COASTGUARD OFFICER CLCI:MAZ/YAL

BACKGROUND INFORMATION

Her Majesty's Coastguard is responsible for the co-ordination of all civil maritime rescue operations around the coastline of the UK and for 1,000 miles into the North Atlantic. The Coastguard Agency is a civilian, uniformed service and an executive agency of the Department of Transport.

HM coastguard is organized in six Maritime Search and Rescue Regions (SRRs), each of which contains a number of districts. SRRs are the responsibility of regional controllers operating from Maritime Rescue Co-ordination Centres (MRCCs), and each district is controlled by a district controller working from a Maritime Rescue Sub-centre (MRSC).

Within each district, there are companies of auxiliary coastguard, who are volunteers but are under the management of coastguard sector officers.

Regular coastguards are civil servants and this article is concerned with their role and duties.

THE WORK

Coastguards in rescue centres keep a 24-hour radio watch on the international UVF distress frequencies and also deal with telephone, telex and facsimile messages through specially designed consoles.

Search and rescue

Coastguards co-ordinate all civil marine search-and-rescue operations and are responsible for radio monitoring, calling and co-ordinating emergency services, and leading and training rescue teams.

Radio monitoring: coastguards keep a close watch over the radio frequencies used by ships in distress.

Rescue co-ordination : on receipt of a distress message at the MRSC/MRCC, the coastguard decides on the action to be taken, requests assistance from the appropriate authorities and co-ordinates operations.

Coastguards may call on RNLI offshore and inshore lifeboats, fixed-wing aircraft and helicopters allocated by the Ministry of Defence, civil helicopters under contract, and coastguard equipment and teams. They may also request assistance from vessels in the vicinity of a ship in distress. They keep in constant radio contact with rescue services and pass on accurate information, ensuring that messages, signals, and so on, are dealt with promptly and that information is disseminated correctly.

Coastguards also alert and liaise with other interested bodies such as the police, fire brigades and harbour authorities.

Rescue team work: coastguards train and supervise auxiliary coastguards, and lead rescue teams of auxiliaries in cases of cliff rescue.

Channel Navigation Information Service (CNIS)

The HM Coastguard MRCC at Dover operates CNIS on behalf of the Department of Transport. They broadcast information for navigators regularly on VHF, and monitor vessels not complying with collision regulations. Unusually large ships and those carrying bulk liquid and gas cargoes must report to the coastguard and receive instruction on passing through the strait. CNIS is in constant contact with its French equivalent.

Reporting pollution

The coastguard is often first to hear about pollution incidents at sea because of its communication coverage. It is responsible for reporting incidents to the Department of Transport's Marine Pollution Control Unit (MPCU).

Miscellaneous duties

Coastguards provide shipping and casualty information to the Marine Accidents Investigation Branch and Lloyd's of London. They also give safety at sea education and assistance to other government departments – such as Customs and Excise, and the Ministry of Defence – and report infringement of Merchant Shipping Acts.

Certain coastguard stations maintain a daily log of weather conditions, and may provide local meteorological offices with weather reports. Readings are collected of wind direction and speed, rainfall, pressure, humidity and hours of sunshine. This may involve taking straightforward readings from meteorological instruments, and some computation.

Coastguards also: deal with press enquiries; may be asked to give talks or lectures to local clubs/other bodies on coastguard matters; give navigational information; answer general enquiries; and recommend safety equipment for use in small vessels.

WORK ENVIRONMENT

Most coastguards work solely in rescue centres, but a number work at sector offices where some patrol work at sea can be involved, using small boats in surf and moderate sea conditions. Coastguards work as part of a team in rescue centres.

For the majority of coastguards, most of the work is light and indoors, but for sector officers it may involve going out in all weathers. Rescue work can entail climbing, heavy lifting, pulling and carrying, and can demand a great deal of physical effort at times.

SKILLS AND INTERESTS

Coastguards must be self-reliant, and able to work well alone or in a team. They should be calm and reliable and able to maintain concentration throughout the shift. It is important that they can assess situations quickly, have good judgement and are able to make decisions. Coastguards must be prepared to take the lead and instruct auxiliary coastguards in the event of an emergency.

Coastguards spend much of their time communicating by telephone and radio; they should therefore be competent at handling communications equipment, and have good hearing and a good clear speaking voice. Physical fitness is important in order to carry out the strenuous activities that can be involved in rescue work.

ENTRY REQUIREMENTS

Applicants should:

1. have at least six years' practical maritime experience *or* three years' practical search-and-rescue experience;

2. hold at least three GCSEs/S grades (A-C/1-3), or equivalent, including English and maths;

3. be between 27 and 45 years of age;

4. hold a full current UK driving licence;

5. have good sight and hearing and pass a medical examination;

6. be prepared to work anywhere in the UK; and

7. be a British subject or member of the Commonwealth.

TRAINING

Coastguards are employed as probationers for the first year of service. Most of the training is given on the job, with a seven-week training course at Coastguard Training Centre, Highcliffe, Dorset, after first appointment, and a further short course after nine months' service. After satisfactory completion of the probationary period and passing the proficiency examinations, a probationer becomes a watch officer. A second attempt to pass the test is permitted, but failure at this stage is usually followed by service being terminated.

Candidates must achieve satisfactory theoretical and practical knowledge of a variety of subjects. These include: the organization of HM Coastguard; search-and-rescue principles and procedure; navigation and chart work.

LATE ENTRY

Entry to work as a coastguard is open to adults up to the age of 45 years. All applicants must have six years' previous maritime experience or three years' practical search-and-rescue experience. See ENTRY REQUIREMENTS for further details.

OPPORTUNITIES

HM Coastguard is organized by the Coastguard Agency, an executive agency of the Department of Transport. There are around 500 regular coastguard officers, located around the British coastline. Coastguards must be prepared to work anywhere in the UK; it is possible to apply for transfer but applicants must usually have served at least three years at one station before a transfer will be considered. Some stations are in remote areas.

PAY AND CONDITIONS

Coastguard officers (probationer) are paid a scale of £9,524 plus £2,381 allowance. Coastguard officers (watch officer) start on a salary of £10,544 rising to £13,460 depending on performance, plus additional coastguard allowance of 25% of salary. Additional allowances may be payable to officers stationed in the Scottish Islands. Uniforms are provided.

Coastguard watch officers work on average a 42-hour week in 12-hour shifts.

PROSPECTS

A formal promotion structure exists, leading to the higher posts of station officer and district officer.

Promotion is dependent on success in qualifying examinations. District officers may go on to achieve inspector grade through promotion via a selection board. Opportunities to progress are limited by the small number of higher-grade posts.

RELATED OCCUPATIONS

Air traffic controller, Merchant Navy officer, Royal Navy officer/rating, RAF officer/airman/airwoman, police constable, firefighter/fire officer, lifeboatman/woman.

FURTHER INFORMATION

The Coastguard Agency, Room 1/18, Spring Place, 105 Commercial Road, Southampton SO15 1EG, 01703 329100

FURTHER READING

In the careers library classified under MAZ; YAL.

1. PRIVATE PRACTICE ACCOUNTANT CLCI:NAB
2. INDUSTRY AND COMMERCE ACCOUNTANT CLCI:NAB
3. PUBLIC SERVICE ACCOUNTANT CLCI:NAB
4. ACCOUNTING TECHNICIAN CLCI:NAB

BACKGROUND INFORMATION

Accountants are concerned with the management of the financial affairs of individuals and organizations. They control funds, analyse financial and statistical information, check accounts, provide financial advice, and audit company accounts. Although they work in a numerate environment, the emphasis of their work is on the interpretation and effective communication of financial information. All accountants share common accountancy skills, but, broadly, they work in either financial accounting, or cost and management accounting. In some organizations the two accounting functions overlap.

Financial accounting deals largely with recording, analysing and reporting financial transactions through the maintenance of accounting records. Accountants extract information from these to draw up an annual profit and loss account and balance sheet (which show a company's results), for a wide range of interested parties within and without the organization: shareholders, investors, employees, creditors and suppliers, and government departments. All registered public and private companies are required by law to have their accounts audited by a qualified chartered or certified accountant.

Cost and management accounting deals with the production and analysis of periodic reports which show the current status of a company, and 'one-off' reports which measure performance, for example, actual cost against a predetermined budget, or product cost and profitability. This information is used by managers within an organization to help them to make informed decisions on the running of the business, to arrive at a price for a product or service, or to plan whether (and when) to make a significant capital expenditure.

All accountants routinely use calculators and computers in their daily work.

Around 100,000 accountants in the UK work in the three main areas of accountancy: private (public) practice, industry and commerce, and public service.

1. PRIVATE PRACTICE ACCOUNTANT (NAB)

THE WORK

In private practice (also known as public practice) the range of work varies depending on the size of the firm and its location. In a small practice, accountants deal mainly with individuals and small firms, which involves a high level of personal client contact. Medium and large firms offer more opportunities to specialize:

Financial services – maintaining accounting records, making returns, analysing and explaining financial results, advising on loans and providing tax advice.

Audit – checking the accounts of a registered public or private company and certifying them as a 'true and fair' account of the company's financial state in accordance with the Companies Act. Evaluating and commenting on the control and management of internal accounting systems.

Insolvency – administrating the financial affairs of an individual or company when serious financial difficulties arise; restructuring it to help it survive, selling the business as a going concern, or selling off its assets to repay creditors.

Management consultancy – advising on a wide range of issues, from computer systems to personnel; from corporate strategy to marketing and investments. Acting as executor of a will or trustee.

Taxation – assisting with tax compliance – corporate or personal, minimising clients' tax bills (as far as is legitimate), negotiating tax assessments with government departments on behalf of a client, advising on the tax consequences of specific deals.

Corporate finance – dealing at the highest levels; identifying suitable companies to acquire, evaluating their worth and then negotiating the purchase on behalf of a client.

Information technology – advising clients on selection, installation, management, application, and evaluation of systems.

WORK ENVIRONMENT

Most work is office-based. Accountants in private practice divide their time between the practising office, the clients' premises, or, for meetings, other places of business such as banks or building society offices.

Accountants may work away from home.

SKILLS AND INTERESTS

Accountants must enjoy working in a numerate environment, and have a good working knowledge of accounting information technology. They should have an inquiring, analytical mind and be able to work logically, consistently and accurately even when under pressure. They need to be self-motivated individuals with the ability to manage their time effectively.

They need a wide knowledge of economics, business law and the general economic environment in which they operate. They need to keep themselves up to date with regularly changing financial rules and regulations and have the ability to recognize quickly the implications of such changes on their clients affairs.

Accountants in private practice deal with people from a wide variety of backgrounds and at all levels so they need strong interpersonal skills. They should be confident individuals with the ability to put people at their ease and inspire confidence.

They should have excellent written and spoken communication skills and be able to discuss and explain financial issues with both fellow professionals and those with little or no financial background.

ENTRY REQUIREMENTS

Qualifications for accountants working in private practice are offered by the Institutes of Chartered Accountants (England and Wales, Scotland, Ireland), or by the Chartered Association of Certified Accountants (ACCA). About 90% of the intake to the Institutes of Chartered Accountants, and 40% of the intake to ACCA, are graduates.

Entry requirements to the Institutes are: five GCSEs/S

grades (A-C/1-3) with English language and maths, and two A levels/three H grades, or equivalent; The Association of Accounting Technicians (AAT) Technicians qualification; or a BTEC higher national diploma; or relevant NVQ/SVQ Level 4 qualification.

TRAINING

All accountancy training is recognized as being extremely rigorous and demanding.

Traditional route – the most common route to qualification as a chartered accountant is to undertake a three-year (for graduates), or four-year (for non-graduates), training contract whilst in employment with an authorized firm of chartered accountants. Graduates with non-relevant degrees must first complete a Foundation Stage examination (graduate conversion course). Higher national diploma holders take the same examination. AAT holders are treated differently from other non-graduates – check with ICAEW.

Prospective Student route – allows students to take ICAEW Foundation and Intermediate examinations outside a training contract, though candidates must obtain a training contract in order to take the Final examination.

The Training Outside Public Practice scheme (TOPP) is also available with approved organizations in industry and commerce, and the public sector.

Tuition for ICAEW exams is provided by accredited tuition bodies and combines block study at external tutorial organizations, and private study packs (see below for ICAS training).

For the ICAEW qualification, students take two sets of professional exams consisting of five and four papers, respectively. Graduates take the exams in their second and third year; foundation course students in their second and fourth.

Students must take and pass the Intermediate exams within four years of registration as a student, and take and pass the Final exam in six years (five years and seven years, respectively, for those on four-year training contracts). Students are not normally allowed more than two attempts to pass exams.

For the Institute of Chartered Accountants of Scotland (ICAS), there are three parts to the exams for non-relevant graduates: the Professional Examination, Test of Professional Competence Part I and Test of Professional Competence Part II. Graduates with approved accounting degrees are exempt from the Professional Examination. Students prepare for examinations by attending block release courses in either Glasgow, Edinburgh, Aberdeen or London. Students must keep a log book of their practical work experience for approval by the Institute.

The Institute of Chartered Accountants in Ireland (ICAI) membership examination is in four parts; Professional One, Two, Three and Final Admitting Examination. Exemption from Professional One is granted to all graduates and to members of the Institute of Accounting Technicians in Ireland (IATI) who have passed their technician examinations with credit. Further exemptions are available to graduates with relevant degrees (further details from the Institute). Study is by block release, linked by regular lectures, study weekends and/or home study material. During training, students must keep a record of their work experience, which has to be approved by the Institute. Before admission to membership, all students are required

to have successfully completed a programme in IT – 'Personal Computing for Accountants'.

For details of training with ACCA, please see article 2. INDUSTRY AND COMMERCE ACCOUNTANT.

LATE ENTRY

Most candidates enter through one of the routes mentioned in TRAINING. Mature candidates may find it more difficult to obtain a training vacancy; however, opportunities do exist and a significant number of the Institutes' student intake is aged over 25.

Entry requirements may be relaxed for those with relevant financial or accounting experience – these applications are judged on individual merit.

OPPORTUNITIES

Opportunities exist in all areas of the UK, in EU countries and elsewhere abroad.

Employers range from the small one-person firm, to the medium-sized practice with two or three partners employing several accountants and accountancy staff, to 'the big six' practices that employ hundreds of accountancy personnel nationally and internationally. Medium and large firms offer the best opportunities to specialize.

ICAEW publish a comprehensive annual guide to training vacancies.

Vacancies are advertised in the local and national press and journals such as: *Accountancy Age*, *Accountancy*, *Accountant*, *Local Government Chronicle*, *Management Accounting* and *PASS* magazine.

PAY AND CONDITIONS

Salaries for accountants vary greatly. The size of a practice and its location affects salaries at all levels – lower in Northern Ireland, Wales and Scotland, and higher in London, for example.

Starting salaries for trainees in public practice are about £6,000 to £8,000; graduates might expect £10,000 to £15,000. Newly qualified accountants salaries range from £15,000 to £25,000 (higher in London). Thereafter salary levels vary according to seniority and merit.

Usual working hours are 9am to 5pm, Monday to Friday with occasional late/weekend work required in busy periods.

Part-time work, flexible hours and job share may be possible after qualification. Some practices may offer part-time training contracts.

PROSPECTS

In private practice an accountant can become a partner in a firm, though this can take up to ten years to achieve. It is not unusual for accountants to move between firms in order to gain promotion or experience in a specialized field. Those who intend to set up in practice independently require a Practising Certificate. This is awarded by the qualifying body to those with a minimum of two years' practical experience with an approved firm.

RELATED OCCUPATIONS

Please see article 3. PUBLIC SERVICE ACCOUNTANT.

FURTHER INFORMATION AND READING

Please see article 4. ACCOUNTING TECHNICIAN

ACCOUNTANCY: NAB

2. INDUSTRY AND COMMERCE ACCOUNTANT (NAB)

THE WORK

Accountants working in industry and commerce work for a single business concern in financial accounting, internal audit and management accounting.

Financial accountants are responsible for the day-to-day financial operations of a business. They control company funds both within and outside of the business, and liaise with government departments on behalf of the company.

They ensure that all transactions are properly recorded in the company's (usually computerized) ledgers. They maintain accounting systems and ensure controls are in place to maximize the efficient operation of the accounting function.

They analyse company accounts and extract relevant information to compile financial reports and statements for managers, such as cash-flow forecasts. A major task is to keep account of funds coming in and funds going out of the company, including stocks and fixed assets.

Internal audit accountants are involved with checking the efficiency and effectiveness of current systems, ranging from finance procedures, stock control systems, staff working hours, and information systems. Most internal auditors develop expertise in information technology as the information they record is computerized. Their role often covers examining the effectiveness of an operational system and making a recommendation to install new software as packages become obsolete.

Management accountants operate as integral members of the management team. They are concerned with identifying, interpreting and presenting financial and statistical management information. They prepare periodic reports which provide a 'snapshot' of the company's trading position. They advise on borrowings, carry out in-depth studies to evaluate elements of the company's activity in the context of the wider commercial environment, and investigate and forecast the likely outcome of business decisions. In this way, management accountants contribute to formulating company policy, budgeting resources, planning business strategy and managing change, often reporting to senior management.

WORK ENVIRONMENT

Accountants in industry and commerce spend the majority of their time in offices at one location. Depending on the size of company for which they work, they may be required to travel locally, nationally or even internationally, to other company locations, or to other business environments for meetings with fellow business professionals.

SKILLS AND INTERESTS

Accountants working in industry and commerce should enjoy working in a fast-moving, sometimes pressured environment. They should be numerate, possess good analytical and reporting skills and be capable of logical thought.

They should have a thorough appreciation of the aims of the company for which they work, understand how their company's business fits in to the wider commercial environment, and have a thorough knowledge of relevant legislation.

Accountants in industry and commerce should be resourceful individuals, with the ability to evaluate alternative courses of action and suggest solutions to sometimes complex business problems.

They need to be confident communicators, quick-thinking, with a flair for presenting ideas and information clearly, both in speech and in writing, to both fellow professionals and those with little or no accounting background.

ENTRY REQUIREMENTS

Qualifications are available via the Chartered Association of Certified Accountants (ACCA), or the Chartered Institute of Management Accountants (CIMA).

Usual minimum entry qualifications to ACCA and CIMA are three GCSEs/S grades (A-C/1-3) with English language and maths, and two A levels/three H grades or equivalent, such as the Advanced GNVQ/GSVQ Level III in Business.

TRAINING

ACCA – study can be full-time, or part-time whilst in employment, by day release, evening classes, distance learning, correspondence, at home using manuals, or any combination of these.

To qualify, ACCA students must complete a series of professional examinations and complete a minimum of three years relevant training, which can be done before, during, or after studying for the exams. The examinations comprise three stages of 14 papers: Foundation Stage (four papers), Certificate (four papers) and Professional (six papers). Students have a maximum of ten years from the time of registration to complete the examinations, but students usually achieve the qualifications in one to four years.

Those with the AAT final examination, BTEC Higher National Certificate/Diploma in Business and Finance, or SCOTVEC Higher National Certificate in Accountancy, or NVQ/SVQ in Accounting at Level 4, are exempt from the Foundation Stage. Non-relevant graduates from recognized institutions obtain exemptions from papers 2 and 4; graduates with more relevant qualifications may be awarded further exemptions in the Professional Stage.

CIMA – study can be full-time, or part-time whilst in employment, by day release, evening classes, by distance learning, or any combination of these. Achieving the CIMA qualification means passing exams at four separate stages, (each stage consists of four papers) and completing three years' practical experience.

Most students gain practical experience in a training post with an employer whilst studying for exams. Practical experience can be gained in any of the three accounting sectors or combination of sectors during or after qualification, and is documented in three areas; basic accounting, management accounting, and financial management.

Those with the AAT Technician stage, BTEC Higher National Certificate/Diploma in Business and Finance, SCOTVEC Higher National Certificate/Diploma in Accountancy, or graduates with a relevant degree (and non-relevant degree holders who have successfully completed a graduate conversion course) may all claim exemption from certain papers in stages one to three. Exemptions granted depend on options and levels taken. For full details of exempting qualifications contact CIMA. There are no exemptions from the stage four examination.

Students take about three years to qualify and can continue their studies overseas if necessary.

LATE ENTRY

There are no age restrictions.

ACCA – mature students (21 and over) who lack the minimum qualifications can apply via the Mature Students Entry Route (MSER). Registration as an external student allows four consecutive attempts to pass papers one and three. Those who successfully complete these papers are transferred to the main student register and go on to take the remaining examinations in the Foundation Stage. Employer-confirmed experience gained prior to registration, by MSER candidates, can count towards ACCA's three-year experience requirement.

CIMA – mature students (25 years or over) who lack the minimum qualifications, but who have employer-confirmed, substantial experience of accountancy, may be considered for student membership.

OPPORTUNITIES

More than half of all qualified accountants work in industry and commerce. Though competition can be stiff, there is a vast range of employment options. Accountants in industry and commerce may be employed in every conceivable type of business – from small, local firms to giant multinationals.

Opportunities occur throughout the UK, EU countries and elsewhere overseas.

Both ACCA and CIMA produce vacancy lists, available free of charge.

Vacancies are advertised in the local and national press and journals such as: *Accountancy Age, Accountancy, Certified Accountant, Accountant, Local Government Chronicle* and *Management Accounting.*

PAY AND CONDITIONS

Salaries for accountants in industry and commerce vary greatly. Factors which affect levels of pay are size, type of business and location, with salary levels generally higher in London than other areas of the UK. Salaries for trainees begin at about £5,000 to £7,000; graduates might expect £10,000 to £15,000.

Newly qualified accountants salaries range from £14,000 to £23,000 (higher in London). Thereafter, salary levels vary according to seniority and merit.

Usual working hours are 9am to 5pm, Monday to Friday. Occasional late/weekend work may be required in busy periods, especially at year-end.

PROSPECTS

The large number and different types and size of businesses offer a variety of career prospects.

Some accountants fulfil appointments as finance director, business analyst, or production accountant, whilst others work outside accounting, specializing in marketing or computer services. Others choose to make their careers in the wider field of general management, rising to managing director or chief executive status. It is also possible to work independently as a consultant.

Opportunities for part-time work and job sharing are far fewer in industry and commerce than in, for example, public practice. It is not unusual for accountants to change employers or move to other areas of the country in order to achieve advancement.

RELATED OCCUPATIONS

Please see article 3. PUBLIC SERVICE ACCOUNTANT.

FURTHER INFORMATION AND READING

Please see article 4. ACCOUNTING TECHNICIAN

3. PUBLIC SERVICE ACCOUNTANT (NAB)

THE WORK

Accountants working in public service organizations are concerned with all aspects of the financial management and effective accountability of funds in the provision of public services.

In common with their colleagues in industry and commerce, public service accountants deal with financial accounting and management accounting. However, the element of public accountability lends an extra (and often high-profile) dimension to both aspects of their work.

In local government, accountants have a public stewardship role: they maintain financial records and prepare accounts for audit and public scrutiny. They act as financial advisers to the council on borrowing, budgeting and (increasingly) on commercial decisions. They concern themselves with protecting public funds and ensure that the public and the organization they work for receive value for money.

Accountants in the National Health Service (NHS) fulfil a similar role to their colleagues in local government. They exercise local control over budgets, deal with purchaser/provider accounting systems in the Service's internal market, and offer financial advice to senior managers, which they use to plan and implement change.

The national audit bodies (The Audit Commission, The Accounts Commission, The National Audit Office, and the Northern Ireland Audit Office) employ accountants as technical advisors – they advise on accounting and auditing and lead value-for-money studies in their specialist area of public service; and as field auditors – carrying out studies, visiting public service providers, schools, hospitals and local authorities.

These bodies have a statutory duty to verify local government accounts and ensure budgets are spent lawfully. In addition, they offer advice to local authorities on the effective provision of public services. A major function of the national audit bodies is to audit and certify the accounts of local authorities, government departments and the NHS.

The National Audit Office provides Parliament with impartial information and advice, and advances ideas for the effective and efficient use of public funds.

Where they work for a private company that supplies a public service, accountants have a duty to shareholders and investors to ensure the most efficient use of the company's financial resources.

WORK ENVIRONMENT

In central and local government, public service accountants are usually office-based in one location. Those who work for the statutory auditing bodies may be required to travel to other locations in the UK. In private companies, the work is office-based, with local travel to other business environments for meetings with fellow business professionals.

SKILLS AND INTERESTS

Accountants working in public service should be numerate, questioning, creative-thinkers and possess good analytical skills. Changes in the public services market means that accountants should enjoy working in a dynamic, sometimes volatile, and often pressured environment.

They need to have a thorough understanding of the concept of providing public services, whilst remaining open-minded to change. They should possess a thorough knowledge of relevant legislation, and keep themselves up to date with procedural changes.

Accountants in public service need to be resourceful, confident communicators with excellent spoken and report-writing skills. They should be diplomatic, with the ability to rationalize conflicting arguments.

ENTRY REQUIREMENTS

Usual minimum entry qualifications to the Chartered Institute of Public Finance and Accountancy are: five GCSEs/S grades (A-C/1-3) with English language and maths, and two A levels/three H grades; or Advanced GNVQ/GSVQ Level III; or NVQ/SVQ Level 3; or BTEC/SCOTVEC national certificate. Alternatively: the AAT Technician stage, BTEC/SCOTVEC higher national certificate/diploma, or degree.

Many accountants in the public sector hold other accountancy qualifications, particularly ACCA. Please refer to relevant article for entry and training details.

TRAINING

Candidates enrol in CIPFA's Education and Training Scheme. Study is part-time whilst in employment and combines distance learning, supported by a link tutor, and optional day/block release, evening classes and residential weekends at higher education institutions.

The CIPFA syllabus comprises four stages: Foundation, P1, P2 and P3. There are four papers in each of the Foundation, P1, and P2 stages. P3 stage is the Final Test of Professional Competence, comprising a case study examination and a project thesis.

Students with CIPFA must obtain employment in a public service organization in a post undertaking accountancy, financial management or audit work, and complete 400 days validated workplace experience during training. Most qualify within three years, though students have a maximum of six years from registration in which to qualify.

Relevant degree holders are exempt from the Foundation stage and certain papers in P1 and P2 exams. Non-relevant degree holders may claim exemption from certain papers in Foundation Stage, P1 and P2. Those with AAT Technician level and holders of the SCOTVEC Higher National Certificate/Diploma in Accounting are exempt from the foundation stage. For full details of exemptions contact CIPFA.

There are no exemptions from either element of the P3 examination.

LATE ENTRY

There are no age restrictions.

Most trainees follow the training route set out in TRAINING. CIPFA will consider applications from those who lack the minimum formal entry qualifications and from those over 21 with three years' employer-confirmed work experience.

Those over 25 years who lack formal qualifications, but have at least five years' relevant experience may apply for membership under CIPFA's Senior Entrant Scheme.

OPPORTUNITIES

Opportunities exist in all areas of the UK.

The public services represent about 45 per cent of the UK economy. Public service accountants work for a very wide range of employers in the public sector, including: central and local government, the National Health Service (largest employer in Europe) and the national audit bodies – The Audit Commission, The Accounts Commission, The National Audit Office, and the Northern Ireland Audit Office.

Other public service providers include the utility industries: water, gas and electricity. Educational institutions, housing associations and charitable organizations all employ public service accountants.

In the private sector, an increasing number of organizations, including the major accountancy firms, are keen to recruit financial managers who understand the public sector.

CIPFA has about 12,000 members and more than 3,000 students, and produces a regular vacancy listing service for potential CIPFA students.

Vacancies are advertised in the local and national press and journals such as *Health Service, Public Finance, Local Government Chronicle, Management Accounting* and *Accountancy Age.*

PAY AND CONDITIONS

Salaries vary depending on the area of the country, with higher rates in London. Salaries in public finance begin at around £9,000, rising to about £14,500 on qualification (more in London). Thereafter, salary levels vary depending on type of employer, seniority, and promotion. At the top of the salary scale, directors of finance can earn between £40,000 and £80,000.

PROSPECTS

For accountants qualified in public service it is relatively easy to move between employers in the different sectors, and to any area of the country, to gain experience in a specialized field, or to move up the promotional ladder. Promotion structures and job titles vary according to the employer and employment sector. Those who rise to the most senior appointments, such as chief executive status, usually have a finance background.

In the national audit bodies, career progression follows a set structure.

RELATED OCCUPATIONS

Actuary, bank manager, economist, stockbroker, building society manager, local government service manager, health service manager, investment analyst, operational researcher, statistician, insurance loss adjuster.

FURTHER INFORMATION AND READING

Please see article 4. ACCOUNTING TECHNICIAN

4. ACCOUNTING TECHNICIAN (NAB)

THE WORK

Accounting technicians are highly skilled support staff, many of whom work in support of, and under the supervision of, professionally qualified accountants. However, in recent years they have assumed many of the duties which qualified accountants traditionally carried out. Consequently, qualified, experienced technicians occupy positions of senior responsibility as company accountants or finance directors with sole responsibility for the accounting function of their firm, or as managers, section supervisors or specialists. They are widely employed in public finance, industry and commerce and private practice.

Technicians share common accountancy skills in financial accounting and management accounting, though the emphasis of their work differs according to the sector in which they are employed.

They deal with financial accounting – recording sales and purchase transactions, carrying out internal audits of the accounts system, and managing credit control systems – ensuring clients make prompt payment and do not exceed set levels of credit. They deal with payroll – calculating staff wages and salaries; stock control – accounting for stock levels and the movement of stock; invoicing and payments – ensuring invoices and statements are correct, sent out on time and payments made to creditors.

They work as a member of an audit team – checking elements of a company's accounting system to decide whether the accounts are being properly maintained. They also advise clients on book-keeping methods, and gather information that will assist the professional accountant to advise clients on such matters as tax planning, trusteeship, insolvency, receivership and executorship.

They deal with management accounting; collating and analysing financial and statistical information, and report this in written form to business managers. They produce periodic reports, review elements of a company's business, and advise on the suitability and operation of computerized accounting systems.

All accounting technicians routinely use computers and calculators in their work.

WORK ENVIRONMENT

The work is desk-based, usually in comfortable offices. Local travel may involve visiting clients and working on their premises. Accounting technicians work alone or in a team.

SKILLS AND INTERESTS

Accuracy and attention to detail are essential qualities of the accounting technician. They need to be able to work quickly and methodically and be able to analyse financial information and interpret the results for other professionals and lay-persons. They should have good written and spoken communication skills and a good working knowledge of computer operation. They also need a wide knowledge of accountancy practice and business law and need to keep up to date with changes in financial practice. As well as being good team workers, they should be capable of working on their own initiative and be able to take responsibility.

ENTRY REQUIREMENTS

Though no formal educational qualifications are required for registration with the Association of Accounting Technicians (AAT), entrants do need a reasonable standard of literacy and numeracy.

Entry may be possible for young people through Modern Apprenticeships leading to at least an NVQ/SVQ Level 3. Contact your local careers office, TEC/LEC for details.

TRAINING

Candidates enrol in the AAT Education and Training Scheme and work toward the awards of NVQs/SVQs in Accounting at Levels 2, 3, and 4; Foundation, Intermediate and Technician stage.

The education and training scheme is offered at institutes of further and higher education and private training organizations throughout the UK. Provision may be full-time or part-time via evening classes, day release, or by distance learning. Some employers offer trainees the opportunity to achieve the AAT qualification through in-house training schemes. Most students are employed in accounting whilst they complete the scheme. Those in full-time employment, on average, spend about a year on each stage to qualify in three years, but there is no time limit and students can complete each stage at their own pace.

To achieve full membership of the AAT and use the designatory letters MAAT, students must complete all stages of the scheme and have at least one year's approved work experience in accounting, gained during or after qualification. Those with one A level/H grade in accounting, plus one other H grade, or two A levels in academic subjects, or who hold a BTEC/SCOTVEC national certificate in business and finance and gain accreditation at Intermediate and Technician stage, are eligible to apply for membership. Those who hold a UK degree in accounting and gain accreditation at the Technician stage are eligible to apply for full membership. All membership applicants must gain accreditation at the Technician stage.

LATE ENTRY

There are no age restrictions. Adult entrants can join the education and training scheme as described in Training.

OPPORTUNITIES

Opportunities for qualified personnel are increasing and are available throughout the UK. A wide range of employers include central and local government, health and public service industries, manufacturing industry, and commercial concerns such as banks, building societies and insurance companies. Some opportunities may also occur in EU countries and elsewhere abroad. The Association of Accounting Technicians has around 90,000 members and students world-wide. For further information on various employers in the main categories of accountancy, see previous articles.

Vacancies are advertised in a variety of publications: local and national press and in journals such as: *Accountancy Age, Accountancy, Accountant, Certified Accountant, Local Government Chronicle, Management Accounting* and *Accounting Technician.*

PAY AND CONDITIONS

Salary levels vary widely according to the type of business and area of the country; technicians in the London area can expect to earn more than in other areas of the country. Generally, salaries for trainee technicians begin at about £6,500. Fully qualified technicians can expect £10,000 to £18,000. Salaries thereafter vary according to level of responsibility, seniority and merit. Self-employed members of the AAT can attract levels of income in excess of average salary levels.

Usual working hours are 9am to 5pm, Monday to Friday, though this can vary according to the demands of the job. A number of employers offer flexible working hours. There is good scope for part-time work, and home-based work is also possible.

PROSPECTS

A wide range of employment options, at various levels of responsibility, are available to qualified accounting technicians. Though most specialize in one of the three areas of accountancy, it is possible to change from one branch to another, and it is common to move between employers in order to specialize or gain promotion.

Promotion structures vary according to the organization for which they work, but qualified and experienced accounting technicians often hold appointments in the ranks of senior management, whilst others choose self-employment.

Qualified accounting technicians can go on to study for the examinations of the professional accountancy bodies and can usually claim exemptions from foundation-level examinations. Over 1,500 AAT finalists a year register with ACCA.

RELATED OCCUPATIONS

Taxation technician, accounts clerk, finance clerk, bank officer, insurance clerk, insurance broker, building society clerk, accountant.

FURTHER INFORMATION

The Association of Accounting Technicians*, Student Services, 154 Clerkenwell Road, London EC1R 5AD, 0171 837 8600

The Association of Taxation Technicians*, 12 Upper Belgrave Street, London SW1X 8BB, 0171 235 2544

The Chartered Association of Certified Accountants*, Student Services Department, 29 Lincoln's Inn Fields, London WC2A 3EE, 0171 396 5800; *Scottish Branch**, 1 Woodside Place, Glasgow G3 7QF, 0131 409 4099; *Irish Branch**, 9 Leeson Park, Dublin 6, Eire, 00353 1 496 3412
The Chartered Institute of Management Accountants*, Press and Publicity Department, 63 Portland Place, London W1N 4AB, 0171 637 2311

The Chartered Institute of Public Finance Accountancy*, Recruitment Liaison Officer, 3 Robert Street, London WC2N 6BH, 0171 895 8823

The Institute of Chartered Accountants in England and Wales*, Student Recruitment, PO Box 433, Moorgate Place, London EC2P 2BJ, 0171 920 8677

The Institute of Chartered Accountants in Ireland*, Student Recruitment, Chartered Accountants' House, 87-89 Pembroke Road, Dublin 4, Eire 00353 1 668 0400, and 11 Donegal Square South, Belfast, BT1 5JE Northern Ireland, 01232 321600
The Institute of Chartered Accountants of Scotland*, Student Recruitment, 27 Queen Street, Edinburgh EH2 1LA, 0131 225 5673

The Institute of Financial Accountants*, and The International Association of Bookkeepers, Burford House, 44 London Road, Sevenoaks, Kent TN13 1AS, 01732 458080

FURTHER READING

Leaflets/booklets available from the addresses marked*.

Job Outlines – Accountancy – COIC
Working in Accountancy – COIC
Careers in Accountancy – Kogan Page

In the careers library classified under NAB

1. BANK MANAGER CLCI:NAD
2. BANK OFFICER CLCI:NAD

BACKGROUND INFORMATION

Banks traditionally looked after customers' money, paid interest to them on the money deposited in their accounts and lent them money, charging interest for this service.

Nowadays their role has broadened. They also provide foreign exchange facilities and financial services, which include investment and insurance advice, mortgages, personal and business loans. They also act as executors and trustees. For each of these services they charge a fee or commission.

Many services are also offered by other financial services institutions such as insurance companies and building societies. This means that banks are in a very competitive environment and their employees must be prepared to sell their services.

There are four main types of bank:

Clearing or retail banks look after the accounts of personal and business customers. The best known names are the 'big five', Barclays, Lloyds, Midland, National Westminster and TSB, together with the Abbey National, Clydesdale, Coutts, the Co-operative Bank, the Bank of Scotland and the Royal Bank of Scotland.

The Bank of England is banker to the Government, providing advice to the Treasury, raising finance for the Government and issuing bank notes. It also acts as banker to all the other banks. All clearing banks have accounts there. Its other role is to supervise all the banks that operate in the UK. It does not operate personal or business accounts.

Investment or merchant banks provide banking services to companies (corporate clients), to governments and to a small number of very wealthy individuals. In addition to the investment banks themselves there are investment banking divisions in many retail banks.

International banks have overseas branches or own banks in other countries. Most of the overseas banks in Britain are based in London, with some in other major cities. British banks have branches in different countries. In general, branches of international banks offer the services provided by both retail and investment banks. The tendency is to recruit mainly local staff except at management level.

Managers are often seconded to work abroad for periods of varying lengths.

1. BANK MANAGER (NAD)

THE WORK

The management team in a branch of a retail bank is responsible for providing quality customer service, running the branch, managing and motivating staff and for marketing the bank's services and products. Branches are set targets by their regional head offices and are expected to achieve these by selling the bank's services. The number of staff known by the title *manager* varies according to the size of the branch. In a small branch there may be only one manager, while in larger ones there are more: an administration manager, who deals with the day-to-day running of the branch and staff training and assessment; a lending account manager, who supervises the work of the lending team and makes sure that all loans are repaid; and, in overall charge, the branch manager.

The branch manager has overall responsibility for staff training and for encouraging all staff to reach sales targets. They also deal with any complaints.

All managers have to know their area well, the type of customers they have and what their needs are. They must be familiar with all the bank's services and 'products' – the word used to describe savings schemes, insurance policies, etc. A good deal of their time is taken up in interviewing customers: to advise them or to decide whether to agree their requests for loans or overdrafts. Individual managers who deal with requests for loans usually have a maximum sum which they may agree to lend. Above this limit they must refer to a senior manager or, where large sums are concerned, to the bank's regional office.

Managers spend a proportion of their time visiting customers, or potential customers, to promote the bank's products and generate new business.

Managers do not all work in branches. In the regional and head offices, the term may describe a level of seniority in specialist functions like marketing, personnel and training. Other managers specialize in investment, taxation, corporate finance (particularly in investment banks) or trust work, which involves administering the estate of a person who has died and left money and property to be invested on behalf of another person named in their will. They may advise branch managers, or have clients referred to them for detailed advice. Some managerial-level staff work as inspectors, visiting and assessing the work of branches.

In the Bank of England, employees who would be described as managers in other banks are 'senior banking officers', who hold managerial responsibility or who work in high-level economic research.

WORK ENVIRONMENT

Branch managers have their own offices. Other managers often work in an open plan office, but may take customers to interview rooms to discuss confidential matters.

Many managers spend up to half their time out of the branch visiting business customers at their premises, where they can assess how the business is being run. They are usually expected to be active members of local business and community organizations and to attend evening meetings.

Specialist managers are usually based in regional or head offices. Many head offices are in London.

SKILLS AND INTERESTS

All managers need general management skills. They need to be able to lead and motivate their staff, to arrange for them to attend appropriate training courses and to recommend suitable staff for promotion. They conduct annual appraisals of the staff who work directly for them.

They need good communication skills, both verbal and written for dealing with their own staff and with customers. They need to be able to form accurate judgements, negotiate and take decisions.

Numeracy is important. They must be willing to work in what is increasingly a sales-orientated environment.

Managers must also be honest and demonstrate integrity in their dealings with customers and staff.

They also need technical knowledge, that is they must have a thorough understanding of banking procedures, services and products.

ENTRY REQUIREMENTS

Most managers spend a period working as bank officers. It is possible to enter in a junior grade and gain promotion to management level. For entry qualifications to this level please see article 2. BANK OFFICER.

The largest number of managers, however, enter as A level (or equivalent) or graduate trainees on programmes that are designed to give them experience of most of the jobs done by bank officers (please see article 2. BANK OFFICER) and help them to reach managerial level in a shortened period of time, provided that their work is suitable.

Investment banks normally recruit entrants with degrees for their management training programmes.

All banks accept any degree subject, although banking, business studies, law and economics are particularly relevant.

Great stress is laid on the personal qualities and skills outlined above.

Some graduates with relevant degrees enter as specialist managers.

TRAINING

Most retail banks run two kinds of accelerated management training programmes: one for applicants with A levels/H grades or Advanced GNVQs/GSVQs Level III; the other for graduates. Training is a combination of on-the-job training, attendance on courses at the banks' training centres and study for Chartered Institute of Bankers' (CIB) qualifications. Practical experience is normally gained by working briefly in most of the bank officer grades. This is normally done in several different branches. Trainees must be willing to be mobile. The length of scheme varies with the different banks. Graduates, however, are normally expected to pass the Institute's examinations within three years. Some programmes include all aspects of a bank's work – domestic, corporate and foreign, while some have separate programmes for those who wish to work in UK banking.

University sponsorships are offered by Barclays, Midland, NatWest, TSB and the Yorkshire Banks.

To become a manager, it is usually necessary to have passed the examinations leading to associateship of the Chartered Institute of Bankers (CIB) or the Chartered Institute of Bankers in Scotland. From September 1996, associateship of the Chartered Institute of Bankers (England and Wales) will be linked to a BSc (Hons) Financial Services degree. The examinations consist of compulsory papers in: law relating to banking services; the monetary and financial system; accountancy and management in banking; plus a further four papers chosen from a range of options such as: administration of trusts; investment; trade finance; branch banking, law and practice; taxation and regulation, market practice and treasury management.

In England and Wales, candidates must follow an approved course of study based on tuition material provided by the Institute and reviewed by the University of Manchester. Courses are offered through a network of academic centres in England and Wales. Courses may include, lectures, groupwork, tutorials, distance learning and revision seminars. Candidates have a maximum of six years to complete the associateship/BSc (Hons) Financial Services. The Chartered Institute of Bankers in Scotland offers training via distance learning and also has a higher-level members' course which is taken on block release over 16 weeks at a university.

Staff who join as bank officers may also study for CIB qualifications via the Banking Certificate as they work their way up through the bank. Please see article 2. BANK OFFICER.

The Bank of England's specialist economists must all have at least a postgraduate degree in economics, but the Bank sponsors a small number of graduates in non-relevant degrees through a two-year postgraduate course in economics. All job-related training is done within the Bank. School leavers with A levels join as senior clerical entrants. They attend courses at the Bank's own training centre and may be given day release to obtain CIB qualifications or a Higher National Certificate in Business Studies. They may apply to join the Accelerated Training Programme for non-graduate entrants at any stage of their careers.

Investment banks run their own training programmes which are much shorter than those in other banks. They have their own training departments and also make use of external training centres. They do not normally require staff to take CIB examinations, although support is given to these and other relevant professional qualifications.

LATE ENTRY

There is no maximum age limit for entry to banking. Applicants over 30 years old, however, are unlikely to be recruited direct to management training programmes.

OPPORTUNITIES

The retail banks' total intake of graduate trainees is about 700 graduate management trainees each year. This has declined from over 1,000 a few years ago. Most are recruited for national schemes, on which they are expected to work anywhere in the UK, but some banks have separate regional programmes for graduates who wish to restrict their careers to working in one geographical area. Figures for A level entry vary and are difficult to calculate since recruitment is done at regional or branch level.

They may work in any one of 12,500 branches.

Investment banks recruit in much smaller numbers – about 100 to 150 graduate trainees annually.

PAY AND CONDITIONS

Managers' salaries depend on the size of the branch and their level of responsibility. Newly appointed managers could expect to earn approximately £24,000, while a very senior manager could earn over £70,000. They may also receive performance-related bonuses if branch targets are met. Additional allowances are paid to managers working in the London area.

Managers also receive benefits in the form of company cars, reduced rate mortgages and other loans, pension and insurance schemes.

Hours of work are officially 9am to 5pm Monday to Friday with some Saturdays worked on a rota basis. Some banks now open on Sundays. Most managers work far in excess of these hours and may have to attend early morning or evening meetings to suit customers' convenience. They have around 30 days annual holiday entitlement.

PROSPECTS

Promotion is strictly on merit and managers have regular appraisals. The first appointment as a manager is either to branch manager of a small branch with no more than ten staff, to manager of a department within a larger branch, or to a specialist head or regional office position. They may eventually be responsible for over 200 staff, or head a specialist department.

Career development depends on ability and on the degree of mobility of a manager – that is the amount of relocation he/she is willing to undertake. The best prospects are for those who are willing to move frequently and work wherever the bank has a need for their skills.

A career in investment banking or in the Bank of England is spent mainly in London with openings in some other cities.

RELATED OCCUPATIONS

Building society manager, accountant, retail manager, insurance underwriter, insurance broker, financial services consultant, bank officer.

FURTHER INFORMATION AND READING

Please see article 2. BANK OFFICER

2. BANK OFFICER (NAD)

THE WORK

The term bank officer is used to describe bank employees below management grade (formerly known as bank clerks). In retail banks, bank officers do a variety of different jobs which are graded according to difficulty. Some banks still use the terms grade 1 officer to grade 5 office;: others now use the job title alone.

Some bank officers work in a branch office on the administration of customers' accounts, while others work in the banking hall, where they have direct contact with customers. In a small branch, one person may combine several duties; in larger ones jobs are specialized.

Bank officers have different roles with different levels of seniority. As they gain experience, they may be promoted to higher grades. They may spend considerable time in each job before moving on.

Grade 1 or processing officers feed information on customers' accounts into computer terminals, answer telephone enquiries and process the cheques paid into the branch each day.

Processing the cheques and credits paid into customers' accounts is done by passing the cheque through an encoding machine which enters the amount written on each cheque and the account details written at the foot. The computer sorts the cheque and credits customers with the correct withdrawals and deposits. Processing officers have to check, at the end of each day, that the total amount shown on the computer balances with the cheques paid in.

Grade 2 officers usually meet customers and, in some banks, these officers are known as customer service officers. They may work on the counter as cashiers, paying money in and out of accounts, or as personal banking advisers, opening and closing accounts and dealing with enquiries. They are expected to suggest use of the bank's financial services and products to customers. Another job is that of standing order officer, arranging for regular payments to be made from customers' accounts for items such as mortgages or bills.

Grade 3, 4 and 5 officers do more complicated work. This varies in different banks. Some work in a branch's foreign section, where they issue foreign currency and travellers' cheques and help customers with business overseas to settle their invoices and arrange insurance. Others arrange for customers to purchase or sell stocks and shares or advise on insurance policies. At this stage, officers are often supervisors, responsible for the work and training of junior staff in the processing office, or in one section of the branch.

They also do more technical banking duties. They may work as loans officers with authority to lend customers sums up to a certain amount. They undertake more complicated investment and advisory work and, at grade 4 or 5 level, often work as assistants to one of the managers. Managers' assistants write letters to customers, analyse balance sheets, prepare reports for managers, frequently interview customers and agree loans and overdrafts. They work closely with the management team and, at this level, are gaining management experience.

WORK ENVIRONMENT

Bank officers are based in branches, which may have from ten, to over 200 members of staff. In some banks, processing officers work together in the branch 'machine room'. Other banks have removed all processing functions to regional processing centres, which are staffed by processing and customer service staff.

Bank officers at grade 2 and above work in the part of the branch which is open to customers. In larger branches this is known as the banking hall. Cashiers and some officers who handle enquiries work behind counters. In some branches, cashiers sit behind security glass. Some banks however, have introduced counter areas with no protective glass. Staff are given certain protective devices and procedures that they can follow in an emergency – for example, panic buttons.

Bank officers who advise customers often have their own desks in the open plan banking hall. They are normally able to move to private interviewing rooms if they sense that a customer does not wish to discuss business in an open area.

SKILLS AND INTERESTS

Bank officers must enjoy providing a service to customers. They must be accurate and pay great attention to detail, even when they are under pressure because several customers are waiting for attention, or a particular customer is in a hurry.

They must be honest and work in what is increasingly a sales-orientated environment.

They must be tactful in their dealing with customers and must respect confidentiality.

Bank officers must also have sufficient knowledge of the bank's products to be able to advise customers on them. Those working in the higher grades also need further technical knowledge and understanding of banking procedures and services.

ENTRY REQUIREMENTS

Although there are no minimum entry requirements to retail banks in England and Wales, some banks require a minimum of two to four GCSEs/S grades (A-C/1-3), normally including English and maths. Some training programmes for young people are also run. However, many banks recruit at well above the minimum, often preferring holders of A levels/H grades or Advanced GNVQs/GSVQs Level III.

The Bank of England recruits junior clerical staff with GCSE/S grades (A-C/1-3), including maths and English, and senior clerical staff with the aforementioned, plus at least two A levels/H grades, or equivalent qualifications.

Entry may be possible for young people through Modern Apprenticeships, leading to at least an NVQ/SVQ Level 3. Contact your local careers office, TEC/LEC for details.

TRAINING

Bank officers learn their work on the job from more experienced bank officers and supervisors. They may also attend short courses at banks' residential training centres.

If they wish, they may study for the examinations of the Chartered Institute of Bankers (CIB). These are not compulsory but are almost essential for promotion. The first stage is the Certificate in Financial Services Practice, followed by the Banking Certificate/degree foundation. Candidates are allowed a maximum of four years to complete the Banking Certificate. Subjects studied include: the business of banking; business calculations; and business communications, plus an optional subject from a wide range, including: banking operations; customer services; introduction to accounting, and the legal environment.

The Scottish Certificate in Financial Services takes up to two years.

See BANK MANAGER for further training details.

Banking NVQs and SVQs are available at Levels 2, 3 and 4.

LATE ENTRY

It is now easier than it used to be to enter banking as an adult, particularly for work in a regional processing centre. Retail banks now recruit many more older applicants, although promotion prospects are likely to be limited, due to the length of time required to work through the grades and take examinations.

The majority of entrants are still aged 18 to 25 years.

OPPORTUNITIES

There are approximately 12,500 branches of retail banks where bank officers may work, but the number is falling as banks close more branches.

Openings for new entrants to grade 1 work are at ten per cent of the levels in the late eighties, due to new technology and the introduction of automatic cash machines. For some years, recruitment to many branches has been very low. Retail banks are beginning to recruit again at this level, but in small numbers.

There are opportunities for job sharing and part-time employment. The number of jobs open in investment banks to applicants with GCSEs/S grades (A-C/1-3) has also declined.

Some retail banks now offer short-term contracts of two to three years. Banking can no longer be seen as a career for life.

PAY AND CONDITIONS

Bank officers are paid on salary scales from £5,900 (£6,750 for an A level entrant) to approximately £15,000, depending on their seniority. They also receive benefits in the form of cheap loans, mortgages and profit sharing schemes after working in the bank for a qualifying period of time.

Hours are usually 9am to 5pm, Monday to Friday, but may vary. If the computer records and till balances do not match at the end of the day, some bank officers have to stay on to find the mistake. At busy times some overtime may be required.

Most banks are open on Saturdays and some have limited Sunday opening times. Bank officers are expected to work on these days and are paid extra for doing so. Sufficient volunteers may be found: otherwise weekend work is done on a rota basis. Career break schemes, flexible hours and job sharing are very common.

PROSPECTS

Bank officers may progress through the grades to reach higher positions. Promotion prospects vary, however, according to the movement of staff in the higher grades and the number of staff who may leave. Bank officers may be qualified and ready for promotion only to find that they have to wait a considerable time for a vacancy in the next grade to arise.

All promotion comes on merit and on consideration of officers' annual appraisals. Bank officers can increase their prospects by taking professional examinations and by being willing to move to different branches for promotion.

Bank officers hoping to reach senior supervisory grades normally take the CIB certificate examinations, while those who hope to become managers study for the associateship. Please see article 1. BANK MANAGER.

There is a shortened route to associate level for bank officers who have one A level/Advanced GNVQ plus GCSE (A-C) in English. They may take a shorter 'fast track' pre-associateship route instead of the Banking Certificate. There is no standard time scale for this route but candidates are allowed a maximum of three attempts at the examination.

RELATED OCCUPATIONS

Building society customer service assistant, accounting technician, post office counter clerk, bank manager.

FURTHER INFORMATION

The Banking Information Service*, 10 Lombard Street, London EC3V 9AS, 0171 398 0066

The Chartered Institute of Bankers*, Emmanuel House, Burgate Lane, Canterbury, Kent CT1 2XJ, 01227 762600

The Chartered Institute of Bankers in Scotland*, 19 Rutland Square, Edinburgh EH1 2DE, 0131 229 9869

London Investment Banking Association*, 6 Frederick's Place, London EC2R 8BT

The Bank of England*, Schools Liaison Officer, Threadneedle Street, London EC2R 8AH

FURTHER READING

Leaflets/booklets are available from the addresses marked*.

Working in the Money Business – COIC
Careers in Banking and Finance – Kogan Page

In the careers library under NAD.

1. BUILDING SOCIETY BRANCH MANAGER CLCI:NAF
2. BUILDING SOCIETY CLERK CLCI:NAF

BACKGROUND INFORMATION

When they were first founded, building societies had two purposes: they looked after money for savers, paid them interest, and lent money, in the form of mortgages, to the same customers when they became borrowers who wished to purchase houses. Societies earned money from the interest rates charged on mortgages.

These remained their two functions for over 200 years until, in 1987, an Act of Parliament allowed building societies to introduce a wider range of financial services. Some building societies have chosen not to offer all the permitted services and the administration of savings accounts and mortgage lending remain the major activities of most societies.

They may, however, now run current accounts for their customers; provide travellers' cheques; advise on and arrange investment services, pensions and insurance schemes; and run services linked to property purchase, such as conveyancing and surveying.

They have become more like banks and are now in direct competition with them for some customers. In order to adjust to the new environment, both managers and clerks have had to learn to promote financial services and gain new customers, rather than simply manage savings accounts.

1. BUILDING SOCIETY BRANCH MANAGER (NAF)

THE WORK

Branch managers are responsible for the work of their staff and for the profitability of the branch. They make sure that staff are trained to deal promptly and politely with customers and know how to do every aspect of their work correctly. They are usually responsible for recruiting staff, supervising their training and compiling annual progress reports. In a small branch, the manager may train staff personally in operating procedures and product knowledge. In larger branches, where managers have senior staff who can deputize for them, they may delegate some of this work to the assistant manager or senior cashier.

Managers often interview customers personally, usually those who request very large loans, those with repayment problems – particularly if their property may have to be repossessed – and those who ask for more complex financial advice. They sometimes have to make difficult decisions which their customers may find unpleasant – such as refusing mortgage applications or deciding whether to honour cheques written by customers who are overdrawn. Sometimes they try to help customers, who are in financial difficulty, to plan their expenditure in order to avoid problems happening again. They also have to deal with any complaints.

Building society branches are set annual targets by their regional or head offices. They are expected to produce a given amount of profit by persuading new customers to open accounts and existing customers to save more or to use some of the financial services. Sometimes, individual employees within a branch are given personal targets. It is important that the manager ensures that all the staff are aware of the targets and are trained to achieve them.

Branch managers also spend a good deal of time out of the office. Some of this time is spent in visiting potential customers and encouraging them to use the branch. They also spend a lot of time building up links with professionals who are in a position to recommend clients to use the branch, such as estate agents, solicitors and surveyors.

They are also expected to make the society well known in the local community by supporting charities and sponsoring activities. They are usually expected to join local business organizations.

WORK ENVIRONMENT

Building society managers work in branches, which may have fewer than ten, to over 60 staff. Branches are normally situated in town centres for ease of access by customers. Managers are office-based and usually have their own private office even in the smallest branches. They spend 25 per cent, or more, of their time out of the office making visits.

SKILLS AND INTERESTS

Branch managers need to have the management and leadership qualities common to all managers. They must be able to organize the work of their team, and know when and how to delegate and assess the potential of individual employees for development and promotion.

They must also be able to motivate the staff to take an interest in the society's products and to help to achieve the branch targets. They have to acquire knowledge of their society's products as they come on to the market, need enthusiasm for generating new business and must be happy working in a selling environment.

They need to be tactful when dealing with some customers who are in financial difficulties and who may not be able to keep up their mortgage repayments.

They need good communication skills, both verbal and written, for dealing with their own staff and with customers. They need to be able to form accurate judgements and take decisions.

Numeracy is important. Managers must also be honest and trustworthy.

ENTRY REQUIREMENTS

Building society managers may begin work as clerks and become managers through promotion. Please see article 2. BUILDING SOCIETY CLERK for details of entry requirements and training.

The larger building societies run management training programmes, for which they expect entrants to have A levels, H grades or Advanced GNVQs/GSVQs Level III. Some societies recruit holders of BTEC/SCOTVEC higher national awards and graduates. Diplomas and degrees in any subject are acceptable, although business studies, economics or financial services are particularly relevant.

TRAINING

Managers must have experience of working as clerks and cashiers in order to understand the duties of all their staff. Direct entrants to management training schemes follow a planned training programme. This gives them experience of working for a period in all the different jobs. Training usually takes place in more than one branch and also includes attachments to regional and head offices. In addition, managers may attend short courses in sales techniques, interviewing skills and people management.

To become a manager, it is usually necessary to have passed the examinations leading to associateship of the Chartered Institute of Bankers (CIB) or the Chartered Institute of Bankers in Scotland. From September 1996, associateship of the Chartered Institute of Bankers (England and Wales) will be linked to a BSc (Honours) Financial Services degree. The examinations consist of compulsory papers in: law relating to banking services; the monetary and financial system; accountancy and management in banking; plus a further four papers chosen from a range of options such as: administration of trusts; investment; trade finance; branch banking, law and practice; taxation and regulation, market practice and treasury management. Building society employees take the optional subjects relevant to their work.

In England and Wales, candidates must follow an approved course of study based on tuition material provided by the Institute and reviewed by the University of Manchester. Courses are offered through a network of academic centres in England and Wales. Courses may include, lectures, groupwork, tutorials, distance learning and revision seminars. Candidates have a maximum of six years to complete the associateship/BSc (Hons) Financial Services.

The Chartered Institute of Bankers in Scotland offers training via distance learning and also has a higher-level members' course which is taken on block release over 16 weeks at a university.

Staff who join building societies as clerks may also study for Chartered Institute of Bankers' qualifications. Please see article 2. BUILDING SOCIETY CLERK.

LATE ENTRY

There are no upper age limits. Mature applicants may, however, find it an advantage to have had previous experience in some kind of financial or sales work. There are no special entry schemes for adults. Some societies however, may recruit graduates in their mid-twenties to accelerated management training programmes.

OPPORTUNITIES

There are about 80 building societies in Britain with building society branches in every high street – a total of approximately 5,000. Some societies have merged recently and more are expected to do so, with the result that the number of branches reduces each year as surplus offices are closed.

There are limited opportunities for work overseas, since building societies are an almost uniquely British institution. There may be possibilities of working abroad in related careers.

PAY AND CONDITIONS

Managers' salaries depend on the location of the Society and size of the branch. They are between £12,000 and £48,000. They may also receive profit-related bonuses if they reach their targets. They usually receive benefits in the form of subsidized mortgages, cheap loans, company cars, medical insurance and London allowance, if appropriate.

Hours are usually 9am to 5pm, Monday to Saturday, but many managers work much longer hours. They may have to work on one Saturday in two, or it could be one in four, depending on the availability of other management and senior staff.

They may have to attend early morning or evening meetings with clients.

PROSPECTS

There are prospects of promotion to manage larger branches and to become area and regional managers. A different promotion route is to move into a head office position in a specialist post such as training, personnel, marketing or product development. An ambitious manager must be willing to move for promotion. A head office position does not normally, however, mean a move to London, since very few building societies have their head offices there.

It has become more common than it once was for managers to move between building societies in order to gain experience and promotion.

Since the various sectors of the financial services industry now have much in common, it is also possible to move from building society work into insurance work, banking or estate agency.

RELATED OCCUPATIONS

Bank manager, insurance broker, retail manager, accountant, estate agent, financial consultant, building society clerk.

FURTHER INFORMATION AND READING

Please see article 2. BUILDING SOCIETY CLERK

2. BUILDING SOCIETY CLERK (NAF)

THE WORK

Building society clerks have a variety of duties. The combination of duties varies from society to society and also according to the size of the branch. Usually, when they first join a society, they begin by doing general office duties such as opening and distributing post, filing and answering telephone enquiries, together with specialist tasks, like making sure that automatic cash dispensers are stocked with money and checking mortgage application forms have been filled in correctly.

In small branches, building society clerks may share these duties and work in turn on the counter. In many branches, counter work is done by experienced clerks who may be known as cashiers or, more often, as customer service assistants.

Cashiers/customer service assistants deal with queries from customers regarding their accounts, assist new customers to complete the paperwork necessary to open an account and process information from the application forms into a computer, issue travellers' cheques and, if working on the counter, balance the till at the end of each day.

Cashiers/customer service assistants normally have computer terminals at the counter with a personal password known only to them. They also have their own key to the cash drawer beneath the counter. When they come on duty they log in the password and collect an amount of money from the safe to put in their drawer. Whenever they leave the counter they log off the computer and lock the cash drawer. Every evening they count the cash they have and enter the total figure into the computer which keeps a running record of transactions. If the two totals do not balance, cashiers/customer service assistants have to find the mistake, which may involve getting a computer print-out of all the day's transactions and checking through them.

Cashiers/customer service assistants working at the counter

are expected to use opportunities to sell their society's services (known as products). If, for example, a customer mentions that they are about to go on holiday, the cashier might offer to supply travellers' cheques. When they are issuing travellers' cheques, they might ask whether the customer has already arranged travel insurance, and if not, suggest the society's policy.

They also answer enquiries as far as they are able and give basic information on the society's services before making an appointment for the customer to see a customer service assistant or manager who can advise them further. They might explain the society's terms for arranging mortgages and make an appointment for the customer with a mortgage adviser. In the case of investment queries, they refer the customer to a manager who is qualified to give investment advice.

Sometimes they have to explain to people what they must do in order to close an account and obtain the money in it. If a customer has died, the cashier/customer service assistant has to explain to the relatives what legal steps have to be taken and may help them fill in forms.

More experienced cashiers/customer service assistants may also arrange for some of the services associated with house purchase, such as property valuations and surveys, to be carried out for customers. Senior cashiers/customer service assistants may be responsible for a small team of staff and for running the branch in the manager's absence.

In some larger branches, cashiers/customer service assistants who have received further training are given some of the responsibilities of a manager. They interview customers in private to give advice on investments and other financial services. They may also have the authority to decide whether a customer may be given a mortgage and the amount that will be loaned.

WORK ENVIRONMENT

Building society cashiers/customer service assistants work in branches which may have fewer than ten, to over 60 staff. Branches are normally situated in town centres for ease of access by customers.

The premises are normally comfortable and light.

In most branches cashiers/customer service assistants who work at the counter sit behind security glass. Some societies, however, have introduced counter areas with no protective glass. Staff are given certain protective devices and procedures that they can follow in an emergency – for example, panic buttons.

If they are dealing with a customer who wishes to talk in private they are able to move to a private interview room.

SKILLS AND INTERESTS

Building society cashiers/customer service assistants should enjoy working with the public and must enjoy providing a service. They must be willing to work in a selling environment, promote the society's products, and help the branch to meet its targets. They should enjoy getting to know customers who visit the branch regularly. They must be tactful in their dealings with customers and must respect confidentiality.

Numeracy is important, as are accuracy and attention to detail. They must be able to work accurately, even when under pressure because customers are waiting in a queue or are in a hurry. Honesty is essential.

ENTRY REQUIREMENTS

In some building societies there are no minimum academic entry requirements. Personal qualities are seen as more important. However, the majority of societies expect four GCSEs/S grades (A-C/1-3) including English and maths, or equivalent qualifications, such as Intermediate GNVQs/GSVQs Level II.

TRAINING

Training is given on the job by managers and senior staff. When they first begin to work at the counter, cashiers/customer service assistants first observe an experienced colleague then begin to do the work themselves with the colleague in the background to give them any assistance they need.

They may attend short courses organized by their society's regional training departments.

Regular training to keep all members of staff up to date and informed of new developments is also carried out in branches by the manager, assistant manager or senior cashier/customer service assistant. Staff may meet together on a regular basis to learn about the society's new products.

NVQs/SVQs Levels 2, 3 and 4 are available, and the opportunity to gain these is increasingly offered by building societies. Level 2 is predominately aimed at cashier staff; Level 3 for supervisors.

Building society cashiers/customer service assistants may also study if they wish, for the examinations of the Chartered Institute of Bankers. Please see BANK OFFICER (NAD).

LATE ENTRY

There are no upper age limits. Mature applicants may, however, find it an advantage to have had previous experience in some kind of financial or sales-related work.

OPPORTUNITIES

Please see article 1. BUILDING SOCIETY BRANCH MANAGER. However, cashiers/customer service assistants are unlikely to look for work outside their immediate home area and, although there are building society branches in every high street, openings depend on the size of the branch.

Computerized systems and the introduction of automatic cash dispensers have caused a general decline in openings. There are usually very good opportunities for part-time work and job sharing.

PAY AND CONDITIONS

Salaries vary in the different building societies and also according to age, experience and responsibility. Starting salaries are usually around £8,000 rising to £13,000 for experienced/senior cashiers/customer service assistants.

Societies often give benefits to their staff in the form of subsidized mortgages and health insurance.

Hours of work are normally from 9am to 5pm, Monday to Friday and from 9am to 3pm or 5pm on Saturdays. Staff are often asked to work one or two Saturdays in each month and have compensatory time off during the week. They are normally paid extra for Saturday working. Sometimes they have to work late – if the day has been busy and the cash takes longer to balance or if there have been some till mistakes.

BUILDING SOCIETY WORK: NAF

PROSPECTS

There are prospects of promotion to senior cashier/customer service assistant, or to move into branch management. Staff who hope to become managers find it advisable to study for the associateship level of the Chartered Institute of Bankers. Please see article 1. BUILDING SOCIETY MANAGER and BANK MANAGER (NAD).

A special route is available for cashiers/customer service assistants who have one A level plus GCSE (A-C) English. They may take a shorter 'fast track' pre-associateship route.

RELATED OCCUPATIONS

Bank officer, insurance clerk, insurance broker, accounting technician, building society branch manager.

FURTHER INFORMATION

The Building Societies Association*, 3 Savile Row, London W1X 1AF, 0171 437 0655

The Chartered Institute of Bankers*, Emmanuel House, Burgate Lane, Canterbury, Kent CT1 2XJ, 01227 762600 (for information on examinations)

FURTHER READING

Leaflets/booklets are available from the addresses marked*.

Working in the Money Business – COIC

In the careers library under NAF.

1. **INSURANCE UNDERWRITER CLCI:NAG**
2. **INSURANCE BROKER CLCI:NAG**
3. **INSURANCE SALESMAN/WOMAN CLCI:NAG**
4. **INSURANCE CLAIMS OFFICIAL CLCI:NAG**
5. **INSURANCE CLERK CLCI:NAG**
6. **INSURANCE SURVEYOR CLCI:NAG**
7. **INSURANCE LOSS ADJUSTER CLCI:NAG**

BACKGROUND INFORMATION

Insurance exists to provide people with security. Many activities – travelling, running businesses, owning vehicles and property – carry a risk of accident or loss. Insurance cannot remove the risk, but it can compensate for the damage by providing the financial means to replace the damaged goods. It works on the principle that a large number of people pay sums of money or insurance premiums into a common fund, but a smaller number will need to draw money out when the risk happens that has been insured against. The funds are invested in order to ensure there is sufficient money to pay claims and, in some years, to make a profit.

When people want to insure something, they buy a policy that states the risk covered and the terms on which it is done. Normally they start by getting advice from an insurance broker – who acts as go-between between customers and a number of insurance companies – or from an insurance company's salesperson.

When they have been advised on the best policy for their needs, they complete a proposal form, which is sent to the company. There, an underwriter calculates the degree of risk and decides the amount of premium that the customer must pay. An insurance surveyor may be asked to conduct an evaluation in order to assist the underwriter. When a claim is made, it is handled by the claims official who is responsible for authorizing payment to the policy holder. In the case of some claims, an independent loss adjuster is called in to make investigations.

There are seven main classes of insurance: aviation, marine, property, motor, liability, life, and pensions. The last two are more properly known as assurance. Insurance is the term normally used for risks that may or may not happen, such as theft or illness; assurance is the term used for certainties such as death and retirement.

Insurance is a major industry that employs over 300,000 people in the UK. There are three main areas in which the majority of insurance employees work: in insurance companies, in insurance broking, and in Lloyd's of London.

Insurance and assurance companies may be composite companies that offer a range of insurance cover, such as motor, life and property, or they may specialize in just one type. They vary in size from small privately-owned companies to multinational organizations. Lloyd's of London is an insurance market consisting of syndicates or groups of members, each with an underwriter who accepts risks on behalf of the syndicate. Lloyd's syndicates often specialize in covering large-scale risks, like oil rigs or spacecraft, or in unusual ones like a wine-taster's palate.

1. INSURANCE UNDERWRITER (NAG)

THE WORK

Underwriters are the experts who decide whether to accept an insurance risk and, if so, how much to charge for a policy and whether to impose any special conditions.

When they receive a proposal form they study it carefully, assessing all the information contained in it. If the answers to questions are straightforward and the sum that might have to be paid out if a claim is made is not very large, they issue the policy immediately, following company guidelines and imposing a standard premium.

If they have reason to suspect that the person requesting the policy might present a high risk, they may either refuse to accept the risk, impose special conditions, or ask for an increased payment. If, for example, a person asking for household insurance has had a burglary in the past, they might refuse to issue a policy until the premises have been made more secure, with locks fitted to doors and windows. They would ask a higher premium for car insurance from a young person who has recently learned to drive, or from a motorist with a history of accidents, than from a person with years of accident-free driving. In some cases, they might first ask for advice from other experts. They could ask a doctor for an opinion on a person's medical history and the likelihood of certain illnesses occurring, or ask the person to have a medical examination. They might ask an insurance surveyor to visit the person and assess the value of a building or a valuable antique.

In some cases, they are able to call on specialist information already provided. The company's actuaries will have drawn up life expectancy tables that are used when calculating life assurance premiums. Previous experience will have shown them the likelihood of burglaries taking place or cars being stolen in particular areas, and so on.

When they have all the necessary information, they decide whether to issue the policy and, if so, provide the person with a quotation. This must be high enough to cover any likely costs and low enough to be competitive, since the person has probably asked several insurance companies for quotations.

In the case of a very large risk, underwriters have to decide whether they are prepared to accept the whole risk or whether they need to share it with other insurers. This is particularly true at Lloyd's, where underwriters may accept only a tiny percentage of one risk.

Many underwriters specialize in one type of insurance.

WORK ENVIRONMENT

Insurance underwriters are based in offices, where they work in teams with other underwriters and with clerks. They may travel to attend meetings and to visit clients and brokers at their premises. If they work for companies that undertake risks in other countries, they may travel abroad and be away from home for short periods.

SKILLS AND INTERESTS

Underwriters must be capable of acquiring a thorough knowledge of the class or classes of insurance they are dealing with. This often means keeping up with developments in technology and changes in the law. They need to be able to absorb information and should be numerate.

They are responsible for deciding what evidence they need

and must learn to know when they can make the decision alone and when they need to consult experts. They must always pay attention to detail.

They need good written and verbal communication skills. They have to gather information from brokers or potential clients, be able to negotiate with brokers, and often to explain their reasons for issuing a policy on certain terms.

They must be able to word the terms of a policy so that it is absolutely clear what the company has undertaken to cover, whether any special conditions have been imposed, and whether there are any exceptions. They must be discreet, as they are dealing with confidential and often sensitive information about clients.

They make much use of computers in their work.

ENTRY REQUIREMENTS

Most insurance companies recruit entrants who have the minimum qualifications required to become a student member of the Chartered Insurance Institute (CII). These are:

– two A levels/three H grades, plus two GCSEs (A-C) or S grades (1-3), including English; *or*

– three A levels/four H grades; *or*

– an Advanced GNVQ/GSVQ Level III award; *or*

– a pass in the CII Certificate of Insurance Practice; *or*

– a pass in the Advanced Financial Planning Certificate (held by qualified investment planners and financial advisers); *or*

– to be aged 25 or over.

Although it is not essential to register as a student member and take the CII examinations, most companies promote only those employees who have taken them.

Many new entrants are graduates. Any degree is accepted. There are, however, some degrees in business studies or financial services that offer insurance options, and a small number in insurance itself.

Entrants who do not have A levels/H grades, or equivalent qualifications, can start as insurance clerks and study for more qualifications before being promoted to trainee underwriter. Please see article 5. INSURANCE CLERK.

TRAINING

Training varies from company to company and depends on the trainee's background and previous experience. Most, however, start with an induction course, introducing them to the insurance business and to their company's methods.

They next work under the supervision of experienced underwriters, at first doing some of the administrative and clerical work before learning how to issue standard policies. As they become more competent they are assigned a number of proposal forms and are allowed to issue policies up to a given figure. They then begin to specialize and to learn about more complex risks.

Some companies run training schemes for graduates and school or college-leavers with A level and equivalent qualifications, on which they spend periods in several departments, including underwriting, before deciding on a specialization.

They attend short courses as necessary to learn about their particular subjects. The CII has its own college in Sevenoaks, Kent, where many such courses are held.

Underwriters are normally expected to study for the Associateship examinations of the CII, which usually takes three to four years. They may be given time off work to attend a college, or may be expected to study through evening classes or by correspondence course. Most employers give study leave before examinations. The examinations consist of ten subjects, three of which are compulsory (risk and insurance, contract law and insurance, and the business environment). The remaining seven are chosen according to the trainee's area of specialization.

From April 1997, in addition to the compulsory core subjects, a pass in either principles and practice of management in insurance, **or**, accounting and finance for managers in insurance, **or**, as above, but with special reference to Lloyd's, will be a compulsory requirement for the award of the Associateship examinations of the CII

Degree courses in insurance are available at Bangor, Buckingham, Central England (Birmingham), City (London), London Guildhall and Nottingham universities.

LATE ENTRY

There are no official maximum age limits for entry to this career. People over 30 years of age may find it difficult, however, unless they have relevant experience of working with people and in a business environment.

OPPORTUNITIES

There are over 450 insurance companies in Britain. Insurance underwriters may work for both specialist and composite companies and for Lloyd's. Although the latter does not have a tradition of taking graduate entrants, openings are increasing.

Underwriters who have language skills may have the opportunity to work abroad, either for a short time for the overseas office of a British company, or for an overseas company.

PAY AND CONDITIONS

Trainees with A levels/H grades could expect a starting salary of around £7,000 to £9,000. Graduates could expect to start at about £11,000 to £14,000.

Salaries for experienced underwriters depend on performance and responsibility, but an underwriter with five years' experience could expect a salary of between £16,000 and £25,000.

Most insurance companies provide benefits such as pension schemes, mortgage subsidies, medical insurance and life assurance.

Hours are usually 35 to 37 a week, Monday to Friday, but work outside these hours may be necessary.

PROSPECTS

Underwriters usually gain promotion to more responsible posts dealing with more unusual risks and greater sums of money. Others gain promotion and a higher salary by specializing in a particular field such as fire, life or marine insurance. They may also move into management, taking charge of an underwriting team. There are also opportunities to move into other branches of insurance, such as loss adjusting, claims or broking.

RELATED OCCUPATIONS, FURTHER INFORMATION AND READING

Please see article 7. LOSS ADJUSTER.

2. INSURANCE BROKER (NAG)

THE WORK

Insurance brokers are independent intermediaries between clients who have something they wish to insure and insurers who provide cover. Clients range from individuals wishing to insure a sole item, such as a car or a holiday, to large companies wishing to insure very large risks like business premises and stock.

When they first meet a customer, brokers ask the questions necessary to establish exactly what cover is required and, if necessary, advise clients to buy more than they had themselves estimated would be sufficient. From their knowledge and experience, they are normally able to advise the customer what sort of price they will have to pay for the policy and, in many cases, can provide quotations there and then from different companies who charge standard prices. In more complicated cases they need to negotiate with several underwriters to find the type of cover required at a suitable price. This may involve writing a detailed report on the risk to be insured, including having a survey conducted and photographs taken. When they have obtained a number of satisfactory quotations from insurers, they return to the client and advise on which one to accept.

Lloyd's brokers often deal with the more complicated risks, which require negotiation and drawing up tailor-made policies. Lloyd's of London is not a company, but an insurance market. It is a society of members who have all invested money in Lloyd's on the basis of unlimited personal liability, and professional underwriters accept risks on their behalf. These members are grouped into syndicates, each of which employs an underwriter to handle each type of insurance the syndicate handles. A Lloyd's broker acting on behalf of a client approaches several different Lloyd's underwriters with a document or 'slip' containing full details of the risk to be insured. (These are often very large items such as oil rigs or aircraft.) As a syndicate very rarely accepts the entire risk, the broker approaches several and arranges for them to accept a proportion of the risk – which may in some cases be as little as one per cent. When the broker has negotiated an acceptable rate with each underwriter, they draw up the policy, indicating what share of the total risk each syndicate has accepted. This is then produced as a formal policy document incorporating all the signatures.

Some brokers specialize in certain types of insurance, such as fire or property. They have a completely free choice as to which insurance provider to approach and are expected to find the most appropriate one for their client on the basis of their professional knowledge. Although all brokers' earnings come in the form of commission from the insurer with whom they successfully place business, they are legally obliged to put the interests of the client first.

Some brokers may place business with insurance companies and with Lloyd's; others with one or the other only. A limited number of 'accredited' brokers are permitted to transact business at Lloyd's.

In addition to negotiating cover, brokers also assist clients who have to make a claim by advising them on how to proceed: in simple cases by letter and phone; where the situation is more complex they see the client personally.

They also have to keep records, and maintain contact with existing clients to ensure that their needs have not changed and that the level of cover is adequate. They may be involved in marketing their services and acquiring new business.

Some specialize, and are either placing or claims brokers.

WORK ENVIRONMENT

Brokers are based in offices which may be small high street premises with a small number of staff, or much bigger premises – mainly in large cities. Depending on the nature of their business they may spend a good deal of time out of the office, visiting clients or insurance underwriters. Lloyd's brokers are usually out of the office for two or three days each week. If a broker works for a firm that negotiates policies for clients with overseas interests, they travel abroad as part of their job.

SKILLS AND INTERESTS

Communication skills are most important for an insurance broker. They must be able to establish relationships with both clients and underwriters and win their confidence. They need the ability to persuade and negotiate. Many employers regard personality as more important than academic qualifications.

Brokers must also be scrupulous and entirely honest. While trying to obtain the best deal for their clients, they must never attempt to mislead an underwriter, since all underwriting transactions are conducted on the basis of utmost good faith.

They need a comprehensive and detailed knowledge of the insurance market and of risks. They must be able to acquire and assimilate information. They need to be able to write clear and precise reports and must pay great attention to detail when drawing up a policy.

If arranging cover in a hurry, they need the ability to think quickly.

Numeracy is important. If brokers are dealing with overseas business, an interest in other countries' financial services and the ability to learn languages are useful.

Brokers must be persistent and calm when things go wrong, particularly when a client takes their custom elsewhere after a great deal of time and effort on the broker's part.

They must be willing to take responsibility for their own decisions and to manage their time without being under constant supervision.

ENTRY REQUIREMENTS

Insurance brokers have varying academic backgrounds. It is possible to enter with no formal qualifications (provided, of course, that they are numerate and literate), work as a technical clerk, dealing, for example, with simple renewals of policies or claims, and work one's way up to becoming a broker.

Many broking firms prefer however, to take people with A level, H grade or Advanced GNVQ/GSVQ Level III qualifications. Some recruit graduates and holders of higher national diplomas.

If the firm expects its trainees to study for CII examinations, they must hold appropriate entry qualifications. Please see article 1. INSURANCE UNDERWRITER.

Some small high-street brokers prefer to recruit people with previous experience of insurance work such as underwriting.

TRAINING

The length and type of training varies from firm to firm. The larger ones, especially those that take graduate entrants, offer more structured training programmes, which move trainees around different departments to gain experience. In all cases though, brokers learn by first doing the simpler jobs – dealing with more straightforward requests for cover – then observe senior colleagues at work and do part of the work required to write a policy under supervision. As they become more competent, they take on larger amounts of responsibility until they are judged ready to work alone.

Many firms send trainees on short courses on the insurance industry and broking skills, or run their own courses in-house. Most expect their trainees to take CII examinations. Please see article 1. INSURANCE UNDERWRITER.

Trainees with firms of Lloyd's brokers must sit the Lloyd's Introductory test within 15 months of joining.

The British Insurance and Investment Brokers' Association runs a national YT scheme that requires entrants to have a minimum of two GCSEs (A-C) in English and maths, or equivalent qualifications. Trainees are able to obtain NVQ/SVQ Insurance Intermediaries at Level 2, which is linked to CII studies.

NVQs/SVQs in Insurance (Intermediaries) are available at Levels 2, 3 and 4. (Further information may be obtained from the Insurance Industry Training Council.)

LATE ENTRY

There is no upper age limit for this work, although many firms recruit school and college-leavers. Previous background in insurance or other financial work, such as banking, may be helpful for adults hoping to become brokers.

Entry requirements and training are the same for all entrants.

OPPORTUNITIES

There are approximately 4,000 broking firms in Britain. Some have several thousand employees and offices in several countries; others employ only half a dozen people.

Some of the firms specialize in different types of insurance, for example, motor or aviation insurance, or insurance cover for financial institutions. Others provide a more general service. Brokers, therefore, may have the opportunity to specialize themselves if they wish, either by working for a specialist firm, or by becoming the specialist in a particular aspect within their firm.

They may also choose to become a specialist type of broker, concentrating on either negotiating or claims work.

In the international firms, or in British firms with overseas clients, there are opportunities to travel or work abroad. Self-employment and job sharing are possible.

Vacancies can be found by registering with insurance recruitment agencies or by making speculative applications.

PAY AND CONDITIONS

Trainees with A levels/H grades, or equivalent, could expect to earn between £7,000 and £9,000, depending on location. Graduates would start on £11,000 to £14,000. Pay for experienced brokers depends on their type of work, ability and responsibility, but a broker with five years' experience could expect a salary of between £16,000 and £25,000. Brokers working in London earn higher salaries.

Working hours are normally 35 to 37 hours a week, Monday to Friday, but work outside these hours is often required,

particularly when closing a contract for work, arranging cover for a client at very short notice or when dealing with overseas clients on different time zones.

Most firms provide a range of benefits including life assurance, medical insurance, subsidized loans and pension schemes.

PROSPECTS

Brokers may be given senior positions within their firms according to their ability. In large firms they could be put in charge of a team of brokers, become heads of departments and eventually partners. Alternatively, they could opt for self-employment and become owners or partners in their own businesses.

To gain senior posts in large firms it is usually necessary to have passed CII examinations at associateship level.

RELATED OCCUPATIONS, FURTHER INFORMATION AND READING

Please see article 7. LOSS ADJUSTER.

3. INSURANCE SALESMAN/WOMAN (NAG)

THE WORK

Sales people are very important to any insurance company. They are responsible for bringing in new business. They do this by selling insurance to the general public, insurance brokers and to insurance agents.

There are three main types of salesman/woman who are employed by insurance companies. All of them establish contact with new customers, maintain contact with established ones and advise them on the kinds of policies best suited to their needs.

Agency inspectors (life inspectors with life assurance companies) are a link between an insurance company and its agents, who may be insurance experts themselves – ie brokers – or one of a range of other people who arrange insurance for customers on behalf of the company. These include estate agents, car sales staff, building society managers and solicitors in a specified geographical area. They visit them to establish new contracts, and to make the agents aware of new products. They do not sell direct to members of the public. Agency inspectors are responsible for appointing agents, training them, maintaining contact with them, keeping them abreast of new products and dealing with any enquiries they may have. Some may also deal with surveys and handle small claims.

Direct selling representatives deal directly with the public, mainly in the field of life assurance and various financial packages, such as unit trusts and financial planning advice. They have to establish contact with potential clients, find out what their needs are, gain their confidence, then suggest suitable policies and plans, and persuade them to buy. It is a selling job, similar to that of other sales representatives.

Home service agents do very similar work but with a different emphasis. They sell mainly life, fire and accident policies to clients who prefer to be visited in their own homes. They explain policies, help clients to fill in forms and give them general financial advice if asked to do so. After selling the policy, the salesman/woman visits clients regularly to collect the premiums, which may be paid once a year, once a month or in weekly instalments.

A fourth category of salesman/woman is the **financial**

adviser. They may sell the products of one company only – as 'tied' advisers' – or they may be independent advisers making recommendations from the policies of different companies. They may sell life assurance policies, other types of insurance or pension plans. Their clients may come to them directly or be referred by solicitors or accountants.

WORK ENVIRONMENT

Insurance salesmen/women are generally based in offices, although some may work from home. They spend most of their time visiting clients at their business premises or at their homes. Although most of them work in sales teams, in the charge of a sales manager and attending team meetings, they spend most of their time working alone.

SKILLS AND INTERESTS

Most employers see personal qualities as far more important than academic qualifications. Insurance salesmen/women must have outgoing friendly personalities and be able to win people's trust and confidence. They must be able to establish relationships with all types of people.

They must be willing to listen to clients' needs and be able to work out which is the best product for them. Home service agents, in particular, must be able to explain the benefits of different policies simply and clearly. Persuasive skills are important.

They have to keep accurate records of clients and payments made, so must be numerate and able to pay attention to detail.

All salesmen/women need a good grasp of the policies available and must be able to assimilate information about new ones. Financial advisers need an especially wide-ranging knowledge of the products from different companies.

ENTRY REQUIREMENTS

Most companies like their trainee salesmen/women to have four GCSEs/S grades (A-C/1-3) or equivalent qualifications. However, because of the importance of personality, applicants, particularly older ones, without these qualifications may be accepted.

Some companies recruit people at the age of 18 years direct from school or college, but the majority do not. For most entrants it is a second career (see LATE ENTRY). School-leavers are usually best advised to gain experience first, either in sales work or in clerical work, with an insurance company, before applying.

A driving licence is almost essential, although this depends to some extent on where the salesman/woman works.

TRAINING

Training in general insurance (household, motor, etc) is mainly given on the job, learning from experienced sales people and attending short courses on product knowledge and selling skills.

Most inspectors study for the CII examinations. Agents and representatives may do so. Please see article 1. INSURANCE UNDERWRITER.

Anyone who sells financial services or advises on investment must be qualified. The Financial Planning Certificate (for which there are no formal entry requirements) and Advanced Financial Planning Certificate are available through a company's accredited in-house training scheme, or through the Chartered Insurance Institute. Compulsory subjects are: life assurance, investment, pensions, taxation and trusts. Options include: personal general insurance, mortgages, personal investment planning, corporate investment planning, business management and marketing.

LATE ENTRY

Late entry is usual in that most insurance salesmen/women have previous relevant experience and are rarely recruited under the age of 20. Most direct selling representatives and home service agents are at least 25. Many move from other careers in their thirties and forties. They normally have experience in another sales field, or in clerical work in an insurance company.

Agency inspectors are normally recruited from insurance company staff who hold the CII qualifications.

OPPORTUNITIES

There are over 450 insurance companies in Britain. There are opportunities to work for composite companies – that cover all kinds of insurance – or ones that specialize in one type, for example, life assurance companies. There are no opportunities for self-employment as direct selling representatives or home service agents, but tied agents or independent financial advisers may be self-employed or run their own businesses and employ other staff.

There are openings throughout Britain, since customers must be visited at their own premises.

PAY AND CONDITIONS

Salaries vary considerably in this work, as they are mainly based on commission.

Agency inspectors receive salaries, but may receive some commission in addition.

Direct selling representatives are paid by results, with almost all their salary coming from commission. The work is difficult but earnings can be high. Conversely, if they are not successful, earnings are very low. A small number of companies pay no salary at all. The majority pay a fixed salary of £6,000 to £12,500, with commission paid on top.

Home service agents are usually paid partly through salary and partly through commission.

Financial advisers are paid in one of two ways: through commission on the services they sell, or on a fee basis, charging clients for the time they spend on advising them and arranging services.

Hours also vary according to the type of work. Agency inspectors normally work a 37-hour week, Monday to Friday. Direct selling representatives, home service agents and financial advisers choose their own hours to some extent, depending on the level of earnings they wish to achieve. Home service agents usually do most of their work during the evenings or at weekends and have free time during weekday mornings and afternoons.

PROSPECTS

Home service agents and direct selling representatives can progress to managing an area sales team or to district manager, managing a number of teams. Agency inspectors can become area or regional managers in charge of a number of agents or may move to senior 'indoor' positions within their companies.

RELATED OCCUPATIONS, FURTHER INFORMATION AND READING

Please see article 7. LOSS ADJUSTER.

4. INSURANCE CLAIMS OFFICIAL (NAG)

THE WORK

Claims officials are responsible for checking claims made by policyholders who have suffered some loss or damage, assessing whether they are fair and deciding whether or not to pay the sum involved.

There are two types of claims official: indoor staff (claims settlers) and outdoor staff (claims inspectors). Claims settlers usually deal with phone calls, claims forms and letters from policyholders. Claims inspectors investigate claims by visiting clients, and sometimes their solicitors, in person.

Their work begins when a policyholder reports a loss or damage and asks to make a claim. In a straightforward situation, such as lost or damaged property, the claims official checks that the client is still insured with the company and has paid the premium, and issues a form on which the client will provide relevant details. If there seems to be no problem and the sum claimed is not excessive, they arrange for payment, send a cheque to the claimant and ask them to sign a receipt. If larger sums are involved, or further investigations are needed, they may ask the client to obtain several different estimates for repairing the damage – from builders or vehicle repairers, for example – before authorizing the policyholder to proceed with the work.

If the claim involves a motoring accident, they may have to get reports from the police and any witnesses and again ask the claimant to obtain estimates for repair work.

Alternatively they may pass the matter over to a claims inspector.

The claims inspector visits the claimant, makes a report, interviews witnesses and police officers as necessary or makes an assessment of the cost of putting the damage right. They then report back to the claims settler. When the claim has been authorized, it is the claims inspector who may have to go back to see the client and agree a sum to be paid.

If the claim is large, or complex investigations are required, or fraud might be suspected (or simply as a matter of routine in some companies), a loss adjuster is called in instead of a claims inspector. Please see article 7. LOSS ADJUSTER.

WORK ENVIRONMENT

Most indoor claims officials are entirely office-based. Many insurance companies have smart, modern offices with pleasant working environments and good facilities. Many staff work in large open-plan offices. They have contact with a wide variety of people by phone and letter.

Outdoor claims inspectors spend much of their time visiting claimants at their homes or business premises. They meet the company's clients face to face.

Claims staff work in teams of settlers, inspectors and clerks, although the inspectors spend most of their time working alone with clients and return to the office periodically to attend meetings and deliver reports.

SKILLS AND INTERESTS

The reputation of an insurance company depends on the speed with which claims are met, and the manner of its staff.

Good verbal communication skills are important, as is the ability to deal with a wide variety of people. They need a sympathetic manner when dealing in person or on the telephone with people who are in distressing situations and are upset or angry, yet they must be sure to obtain all the relevant information from them. In the case of a policyholder who is phoning to report a car accident, they often have to reassure them, ascertain whether anyone has been injured and whether the police have been informed, before they can proceed any further. They also need to be tactful if they have to explain that a claim is not valid and cannot be met.

Inspectors must be able to work with solicitors, police officers and, sometimes, forensic experts.

Claims officials need a thorough knowledge of the policies their company issues. A knowledge of typical repair costs is also useful.

Integrity and fairness are very important qualities. Policyholders expect to have their claims met in full, or a reasonable compromise to be agreed.

They should be able to work well when under pressure, because speed in settling claims is vital to the company's reputation, yet the amount of work in hand at any one time can never be planned. It all depends on the number of claims that are made each day.

ENTRY REQUIREMENTS

The usual minimum requirements are four GCSEs/S grades (A-C/1-3), or equivalents such as Intermediate GNVQ/ GSVQ Level II qualifications.

Many companies, however, recruit trainees who have the qualifications necessary to commence study for the CII examinations. Please see article 1. INSURANCE UNDERWRITER.

Graduate entrants are also recruited by many companies. Claims inspectors usually need a current driving licence.

TRAINING

Training varies from company to company and depends on the trainee's background and previous experience. Most, however, start with an induction course introducing them to the insurance business and to their company's methods.

They next work under the supervision of experienced claims officials, at first doing some of the more routine clerical work, before being allowed to deal with some straightforward claims under supervision.

For details of short courses, professional examinations and relevant pre-entry university degrees, please see article 1. INSURANCE UNDERWRITER.

Some companies run training schemes for graduates and school or college-leavers with A level and equivalent qualifications, on which they spend periods in several departments, including claims work, before deciding on a specialization.

LATE ENTRY

There are no official maximum age limits for entry to this career. People over 30 years of age may find it difficult, however, unless they have relevant experience of working with people and in a business environment.

OPPORTUNITIES

There are over 450 insurance companies in Britain. Insurance claims officials may work for both specialist and composite companies and for Lloyd's.

It is usual to begin in indoor work as an assistant claims settler.

Experienced claims officials may have the opportunity to work abroad, either for a short time for the overseas office of a British company, or for an overseas company.

PAY AND CONDITIONS

Trainees with A levels/H grades could expect a starting salary of around £7,000 to £8,000. Graduates could expect to start at about £10,500 to £13,000.

Salaries for experienced claims officials depend on performance and responsibility, but a claims official with five years' experience could expect a salary in excess of £14,000. Most insurance companies provide benefits such as pension schemes, mortgage subsidies, medical insurance and life assurance.

Hours for indoor staff are usually 35 to 37 a week, Monday to Friday, although work outside these hours may be required. Inspectors must expect to work some evenings.

PROSPECTS

Indoor claims staff may be promoted to manage a section, followed by a department within the company. Some decide to move to outdoor inspection work. It is also possible to move into other jobs within insurance companies or into broking or loss adjusting.

RELATED OCCUPATIONS, FURTHER INFORMATION AND READING

Please see article 7. LOSS ADJUSTER.

5. INSURANCE CLERK (NAG)

THE WORK

Insurance clerks, sometimes known as insurance technicians, are indoor staff who assist senior colleagues by providing clerical support. They work in all insurance departments, but particularly in claims processing, underwriting and broking.

Their duties include: opening and sorting post, delivering letters to the appropriate professionals, updating customer records, dealing with customer queries by phone, producing policy documents, preparing cover and debit notes, making financial calculations, and general office duties such as filing and photocopying.

Some insurance offices, particularly those of small high-street brokers, are open to the public. Clerks working in such offices may have a lot of personal contact with customers over the counter. In other offices – insurance companies' head or regional offices – most of their direct customer contact work is done by phone.

There are four main types of insurance clerk:

Brokers' clerks' particular responsibilities include checking clients' completed proposal forms (requests for insurance) for mistakes or omissions and sending them on to insurance companies once they are satisfied that they are correctly completed, contacting clients by phone and over the counter. They may advise clients on suitable policies for uncomplicated risks.

Claims clerks deal with the claims forms and correspondence that come addressed to the claims officials in their departments. When a claim is received, they check the records to make sure that the person is covered for the claim and that the policy is up to date. They check that forms have been fully completed. They deal with clients and brokers, in person, over the counter and by phone.

Processing clerks work in underwriting departments. They transfer information from clients' proposal forms onto computer. When policy documents have been issued, they post them to new clients and they send regular, usually annual, reminders to pay the premiums due. They keep customers' records up to date and add any changes notified to the company. They may collect some statistical information for underwriters.

Underwriting clerks deal mainly with giving insurance quotations for straightforward policies. When a proposal form comes in, they check it, then use reference books to calculate the amount of premium to be paid. They notify the broker or client of this by phone or letter and wait to see whether the quotation has been accepted. They often work in specialist sections for underwriters who deal, for instance, in motor or personal property insurance, in order to gain knowledge in one field.

WORK ENVIRONMENT

Clerks are office-based. They work in teams with other clerks, underwriters, brokers or claims officials, depending on their specialism. Some offices, particularly those of high street brokers and agents, may be very small, with only one or two staff working there. Insurance companies' premises are usually large, with large numbers of staff working in open-plan offices.

SKILLS AND INTERESTS

Insurance clerks need excellent communication skills. In many cases, they are the only representative of their company who deals directly with a client. They need good verbal skills to talk to clients in a helpful manner on the phone or in person. Claims clerks also need to be sensitive as they often communicate with clients who are distressed, have had an accident, lost something valuable or may have suffered a bereavement.

All clerks must be methodical and pay attention to accuracy and detail when dealing with paperwork and clients records.

Their command of written English must be good, since they usually draft their own letters. Numeracy is also important, as many insurance clerks deal with figures.

They should be willing to acquire keyboard skills and to learn to use VDUs and computers.

ENTRY REQUIREMENTS

Although it is possible to enter this work with no formal qualifications, the majority of employers expect their clerks to have four GCSEs/S grades (A-C/1-3), including English and maths, or equivalent qualifications (such as an Intermediate GNVQ/GSVQ Level II in Business).

TRAINING

Training varies from company to company. In large ones, where several new clerks may join on the same day, the clerks' training begins with an induction course, introducing them to the insurance business and to their company's methods. They next move to their own departments and learn their work on the job from their immediate supervisor. In smaller companies, there will be no induction course, but an office manager will explain the company's methods to a new trainee.

They will be given training in-house and may attend short courses on, for example, telephone technique, at an external training centre or in the company's own training department. Most clerks are encouraged to study for CII examinations and it is essential to do so if they are aiming at eventual promotion. Insurance clerks with no formal academic qualifications may take the Certificate of Proficiency (COP). This requires between approximately 75 and 100 hours of study time through a correspondence course run by the Institute. Examinations are held four times a year and trainees may sit them when they feel ready to do so. The Institute however, recommends that the study should be spread over several months. There are two papers that may be taken at the same time, consisting of a core element subject (insurance, the market and legal principles), plus a choice of either general (non-life) or life.

Trainees who have four GCSEs/S grades (A-C/1-3) or equivalent, *or* hold the Certificate of Proficiency, *or* hold the Financial Planning Certificate, *or* are aged 21 or over, may take the Certificate of Insurance Practice (CIP). This consists of five examination papers/subjects at three levels – foundation, branch and specialist. You can choose subjects which are relevant to your job or which particularly interest you. The length of time taken to qualify varies, but the CII estimates that 104 hours of study are required for each subject over a period of six months. The examinations are held twice a year and it is possible to pass all five papers in two examination sessions. Holders of COP are excused one paper.

Most trainees study by correspondence course. In some areas part-time courses are run by colleges of further education. Possession of the CIP qualifies insurance clerks for membership of the Society of Technicians in Insurance and they are exempted from three subjects in the CII Associateship examinations, should they wish to study further.

The CII is currently working to link its professional qualifications with NVQs, so that successful completion of the COP examinations will give holders an NVQ at Level 2. Employees who pass the core subjects of CIP will receive an NVQ Level 3 and those who pass the relevant specialist papers, a Level 4.

LATE ENTRY

There are no official maximum age limits for entry to this career. People over 30 years of age may find it difficult, however, unless they have relevant experience of working with people and in a business environment.

OPPORTUNITIES

There are over 450 insurance companies in Britain. Insurance clerks may work for both specialist and composite companies, for firms of brokers and for Lloyd's of London.

PAY AND CONDITIONS

Salaries vary from company to company and depend on qualifications and previous experience, but a clerk with five years' experience could expect a salary of between £8,500 and £12,500.

Most insurance companies provide benefits such as pension schemes, mortgage subsidies, medical insurance and life assurance.

Hours are usually 35 to 37 a week, Monday to Friday.

PROSPECTS

There are opportunities for promotion to supervisory positions, managing a small team of perhaps four clerks, then moving on to take charge of larger teams or groups of teams in a department. Insurance clerks who take the qualifying examinations may go on to train as underwriters, claims officials, sales people or brokers.

RELATED OCCUPATIONS

Clerk, receptionist, civil service administrative assistant/ officer, insurance claims official, insurance salesman/ woman.

FURTHER INFORMATION AND READING

Please see article 7. LOSS ADJUSTER.

6. INSURANCE SURVEYOR (NAG)

THE WORK

Underwriters often require more detailed information than can be contained on a proposal form, before they can decide on the terms on which to issue a policy covering premises such as warehouses, shops and factories. In such cases they ask an insurance surveyor to prepare a report for them.

Insurance surveyors often specialize in different types of insurance: fire and flood; accidents and liability; engineering; or theft.

Fire and flood surveyors visit the premises to be insured and establish what materials have been used in their construction. They examine the fire protection arrangements and the condition of heating and ventilating systems. They normally draw an outline plan showing the main features. Following a detailed inspection, they write a report, noting any factor that might affect the insurance. If, in the course of the survey, they have discovered safety hazards such as faulty wiring for example, or unsafe storage of flammable liquids, they advise the owner on how to put these right.

In a **liability and accident survey**, they find out what business or manufacturing processes are carried out there and what safety measures are in place to protect employees and visitors. They inspect the condition of premises and machinery, examine safety systems and try to establish whether all safety regulations are observed.

Burglary and theft surveys involve them in noting what kind of goods are stored at the premises and investigating security arrangements and access to the building.

Engineering surveyors usually specialize in examining electrical or mechanical plant and equipment and reporting on its condition and safety.

WORK ENVIRONMENT

Insurance surveyors' place of work is their own office and wherever the survey is to be conducted. They divide their time almost equally between visiting sites and writing reports in the office. Sites can be office blocks, factories, shops and building sites. Some may be dirty and noisy. Part of the survey can require them to work at heights, for example, climbing on to a roof.

Insurance surveyors work largely alone, although they are in constant contact with clients and they do have periodic meetings in their offices with underwriters and other surveyors.

SKILLS AND INTERESTS

Insurance surveyors have to be observant and thorough and pay close attention to detail. They need an investigative and enquiring mind in order to be able to find out everything necessary concerning the risk they are evaluating. They need the ability to absorb the technical knowledge needed to inspect buildings and equipment.

They must be able to write clear reports in language that can be understood by non-technical colleagues and by clients. They also need to be able to work with a wide range of people and be able to explain matters clearly to them.

ENTRY REQUIREMENTS

Entry requirements vary from company to company. Most insurance companies, however, recruit new entrants who have the minimum qualifications required to become student members of the Chartered Insurance Institute. Please see article 1. INSURANCE UNDERWRITER.

An increasing number of graduates become insurance inspectors. Any degree is acceptable, although ones in scientific or technical subjects may be preferred. Engineering surveyors are normally qualified engineers.

People who are already working in insurance companies and have gained relevant experience may also become insurance surveyors, particularly if they have taken the CII examinations.

A current driving licence is a usual requirement.

TRAINING

Insurance surveyors need a knowledge of general insurance work, especially underwriting. With the exception of a few engineering and science graduates who are recruited directly into surveying work, it is therefore usual for surveyors to have spent some time working in other departments in an insurance company. Some may intend to become surveyors when they join; others decide to change career after working in a different job like underwriting or claims settling.

Some companies run training schemes for graduates and school or college-leavers with A level and equivalent qualifications, on which they spend periods in several departments before deciding on a specialization.

For information on training courses and professional examinations please see article 1. INSURANCE UNDERWRITER.

LATE ENTRY

Few people begin training for insurance surveying before their early twenties. They are, however, expected to have gained experience in other branches of insurance work. It is rare to begin training without such experience after the age of 30.

Exceptions are made for engineers with appropriate backgrounds and experience, who may be recruited at any age.

OPPORTUNITIES

Insurance surveyors are employed by the largest insurance companies. They may also work for insurance brokers and for companies in industry and commerce as risk managers, advising on ways of reducing or minimizing hazards and recommending the type of insurance cover to be obtained.

PAY AND CONDITIONS

Fully trained insurance surveyors with five years' experience could expect a salary of between £16,000 and £25,000.

Most insurance companies provide benefits such as pension schemes, mortgage subsidies, medical insurance and life assurance.

Hours of work are usually 35 to 37 a week, Monday to Friday, but work outside these hours may be necessary.

PROSPECTS

There are prospects of promotion to senior surveying positions in charge of other staff. Some insurance surveyors move into underwriting, specializing in fire, accident and liability or theft insurance. Others may become risk managers.

RELATED OCCUPATIONS, FURTHER INFORMATION AND READING

Please see article 7. LOSS ADJUSTER.

7. INSURANCE LOSS ADJUSTER (NAG)

THE WORK

Loss adjusters are independent insurance claims specialists who work on behalf of insurance companies. Their job is to ascertain the insurance company's liability for a loss within the terms and conditions of the insurance policy. This entails visiting the insured person (policyholder), establishing the exact nature of the loss or damage, making sure that any conditions attached to the policy were followed and enquiring about the probable amount of the claim.

They then advise the policyholder how to claim, suggest a figure that is acceptable to both claimant and insurance company, negotiating this where necessary, and write a report for the insurance company, in which they suggest a suitable amount of payment.

Once, they were appointed mainly by companies who suspected a policyholder might be making a fraudulent claim, or where a large sum of money was involved. Nowadays, insurance companies employ loss adjusters in a wider range of situations: where a claim exceeds a set figure; where there are complications; when they are particularly busy and their own claims staff are not able to do the work; and sometimes as a matter of course, preferring them to do all the initial visiting to policyholders.

When investigating a claim, loss adjusters first survey and physically assess the damage. This could involve climbing on the roof in the case of storm damage, asking to see photographs or valuation certificates relating to stolen items, or obtaining a fire brigade report on the circumstances of a fire.

They also help arrange for damage to be put right – by contacting reputable builders and arranging for repairs to be carried out, or in the case of a burglary, contacting the police and private investigators and possibly arranging for advertisements to be published offering a reward for information.

If they do suspect fraud, they investigate further, sifting through wreckage to look for evidence, checking a company's accounts or calling in independent consultants like forensic experts.

Before they leave a policyholder's premises, they normally explain what recommendation they are going to make to the insurers. They also explain if they are going to recommend that certain steps should be taken before the company issues a new policy. (Following a burglary for instance, they might require the householder to fit new locks on doors and windows or replace a flimsy door.)

They may have to explain to a person that their property is not fully insured and therefore not all of the loss is covered. In such situations, they will suggest that insurance cover is immediately increased. They also advise a policyholder if he or she has under-claimed.

WORK ENVIRONMENT

Loss adjusters are based in offices but usually spend at least two-thirds of their time visiting claimants in their homes or at their business premises. Some of the work can be dirty or involve climbing heights.

They may travel overseas, if they are working for a company that has insured foreign property.

It is essential to be able to drive and hold a clean driving licence.

Loss adjusters' work often brings them into contact with other specialists: lawyers, accountants, engineers, police, fire and rescue service officers, and forensic scientists.

SKILLS AND INTERESTS

Loss adjusters must be able to maintain complete impartiality. Although they are appointed by insurance companies, they are acting for both the company and the insured person and must be fair to both parties.

Good communication skills are essential. Loss adjusters must be good at dealing tactfully and sensitively with people who are distressed. They need written communication skills in order to write clear and accurate reports.

They also need to be firm when necessary, confident of their judgement, and not easily swayed if put under pressure.

They need to be physically fit and able to work in all kinds of places that have suffered damage, including rooftops and burnt-out buildings.

They need a wide-ranging knowledge, in order to deal with a variety of claims, and the ability to assimilate technical knowledge if dealing with particular kinds of claim – such as fire.

They should be flexible and able to put aside work they are currently engaged on when a new and more urgent claim comes up that must be dealt with immediately.

Good powers of observation are necessary.

ENTRY REQUIREMENTS

It is necessary to have two years' experience in practice as a loss adjuster and a relevant professional qualification, before beginning to study for the examinations of the Chartered Institute of Loss Adjusters.

A small number of entrants join firms of loss adjusters straight from school with A levels, H grades or Advanced GNVQ/GSVQ Level III awards, or from a higher education institution with a degree or higher national diploma. They usually study first for the Chartered Insurance Institute examinations. The minimum entry requirement for the CII examinations are two A levels or H grades plus two GCSEs/S grades (A-C/1-3), or an Advanced GNVQ/GSVQ Level III award.

Most entrants, however, have previous experience as accountants, engineers, surveyors, insurance claims officials or lawyers, and already hold the qualifications appropriate to their own profession.

TRAINING

Loss adjusters train on the job, learning from experienced and qualified colleagues. Study for the examinations of the Chartered Institute of Loss Adjusters (CILA) is undertaken part-time. The examination subjects include: principles and practice of insurance in relation to loss adjusting; accident and liability claims and commercial claims; and a number of optional subjects such as building, or theft. Students may not sit any of the exams until they have had at least two years' experience in a firm of loss adjusters.

Study for the exams is usually undertaken through private study, although the Institute and some of the larger firms provide assistance through seminars and tutorials.

Entrants with professional qualifications normally pass the CILA exams in three to four years.

LATE ENTRY

Most people joining this profession are late entrants, in the sense that they have already gained training and experience in a relevant career. However, there is no upper age limit for anyone prepared to take all the necessary examinations.

OPPORTUNITIES

Loss adjusters work for specialist firms that range in size from the small ones with only one or two loss adjusters, to those with up to 200. Firms are situated throughout the country.

There are opportunities to work abroad for a foreign firm, or the overseas branch of a British firm. There are also possibilities for self-employment and to open one's own firm.

Some loss adjusters specialize in a branch of insurance, such as motor or aviation. Those specializing in marine work are known as average adjusters.

PAY AND CONDITIONS

Hours of work can be long. Although they may officially work from 9am to 5pm, Monday to Friday, loss adjusters have to be prepared to work unsocial hours when visiting clients. They may be called out at weekends in emergencies. When they have been involved in visits all day, but still have to complete reports so that other claimants can be reimbursed, they must be prepared to work late or to take work home.

Salaries vary with previous qualifications and experience. A loss adjuster with five years' experience could expect a salary of approximately £18,000.

PROSPECTS

In a large firm the promotion route would be from loss adjuster to branch manager, then to area manager or to a head office position. In smaller firms, promotion would be to partner or director.

There are possibilities of moving into insurance work, especially claims assessing or surveying.

RELATED OCCUPATIONS

Actuary, bank manager, building society manager, financial consultant, insurance claims official, insurance salesman/woman, insurance underwriter, investment analyst, market maker, pensions manager, stockbroker.

FURTHER INFORMATION

The Chartered Insurance Institute*, Careers Information Officer, 20 Aldermanbury, London EC2V 7HY, 0171 417 4424

British Insurance and Investment Brokers Association, BIIBA House, 14 Bevis Marks, London EC3A 7NT, 0171 623 9043

The Chartered Institute of Loss Adjusters*, Manfield House, 376 Strand, London WC2R 0LR, 0171 240 1496

The Insurance Industry Training Council, Churchill Court, 90 Kippington Road, Sevenoaks, Kent TN13 2LL, 01732 450888

FURTHER READING

Leaflets/booklets are available from the addresses marked*.

Job Outlines – Insurance – COIC

Insurance – Ivanhoe Career Guide

In the careers library classified under NAG.

ACTUARY CLCI:NAJ

BACKGROUND INFORMATION

Actuaries form a small but influential professional group. Most of them are concerned with life assurance, pension schemes and other forms of insurance, but all are concerned with long-term financial planning. They design the policy, fix the premiums and repayment values, and decide how to invest the policyholders' money in order to keep the company viable.

THE WORK

Actuaries apply the mathematical theories of probability, compound interest, and statistical techniques to matters with long-term implications, such as life assurance or pension schemes. From their evaluations of past performance, they construct mathematical models for future developments. These valuations and predictions are used to draw up individual schemes for their clients, and to determine long-term policy for their own companies. Increasing use is made of computers, but an understanding of mathematical theories and statistical techniques is essential.

Insurance: almost 50 per cent of actuaries in Britain work in insurance companies. They carry out an annual valuation – the financial stock-taking required by law. They are concerned with developing new financial products, calculating premium costs and surrender values and investing the vast sums that are received in premiums. The larger insurance companies invest over two million pounds every working day.

Life assurance: the 'appointed actuary' of the company has a statutory responsibility for certifying that millions of pounds of policyholders' money is safe. The actuary to a pension fund similarly has a responsibility to make sure that the finances are sound and that there is money available to pay the benefits that have been promised to present and future pensioners.

Consultants deal with a variety of clients, but most of their work is concerned with advising commercial companies and businesses on pension arrangements for their staff. They advise smaller insurance companies who do not have their own in-house staff, give specialist advice on such matters as take-overs or mergers, and where necessary the level of damages to be awarded.

Government service: the Government Actuary Department is responsible for devising public service pension schemes, inspecting life assurance companies for the Department of Trade and Industry, and advising the DSS on benefit rates.

Stock Exchange actuaries give investment advice based on analyses of the market. Their clients are usually insurance companies or pension funds seeking to invest money from premiums. They need specialist advice because they are subject to particular legal liabilities.

A few actuaries work in education, industry and commerce. The jobs range from university teaching to administering the pension funds of multinational companies.

WORK ENVIRONMENT

Actuaries are usually office-based, but those in consulting practice spend a lot of time visiting clients.

SKILLS AND INTERESTS

Actuaries need a flair for maths and an aptitude for analysing facts and figures. The ability to express facts and ideas clearly and simply in speech and writing is essential. They need to be able to explain details to non-specialists and make reports. They also need an intellectual interest in problem solving and in the practical analysis of business problems.

Concentration and attention to detail are essential. Actuaries must be able to amass large quantities of facts, to organize this knowledge, and apply it methodically and accurately.

ENTRY REQUIREMENTS

To qualify as an actuary, candidates must register as a student member of the Institute of Actuaries (England and Wales) or the Faculty of Actuaries (Scotland).

For the Institute of Actuaries, minimum entry requirements for student membership are five GCSEs (A-C), including English; plus two A levels, one of which should be maths at grade B or further maths at grade C, and the other must be at grade C.

For the Faculty of Actuaries, minimum requirements are three H grades, including maths at grade A, and English.

Over 90 per cent of entrants are graduates.

There are several degree courses in actuarial science in the UK. Graduates are accepted from a wide variety of disciplines, providing that they can either meet the A level/H grade requirements, or their degree covers the required mathematical studies.

TRAINING

Training time varies, but an average estimate is from three to five years, combining part-time study and supervised work experience. Tuition for the examinations is mainly through correspondence courses run by the Faculty's or Institute's Education Service. Most employers allow time off for study, but much of it has to be fitted in at evenings and weekends. Tutorials are arranged in London and other major centres. Regular discussion groups are held in Edinburgh and Glasgow.

There are nine joint Institute and Faculty examinations divided into two groups. The earlier four examinations cover mathematical, statistical and financial techniques. The later four examinations test the application of these principles and techniques to institutional investment, life assurance, general insurance and pension funds. In addition, there is a fellowship examination which aims to list the candidate's deeper understanding of the four later subjects. It is also necessary to have at least three years' relevant experience of actuarial work to qualify as a fellow of the Institute.

In Scotland, the Faculty examinations are the same, but there is no prescribed period of practical experience.

Actuarial science degrees, and some maths degrees, give exemption from parts of the Institute or Faculty examinations.

LATE ENTRY

The Institute of Actuaries prefers training to begin within four years of achieving A levels or a degree. Exceptions can be considered, depending on previous experience and proven aptitude.

OPPORTUNITIES

The Institute of Actuaries has over 4,000 members. The Faculty of Actuaries has over 900 members. Approximately 50 per cent work in insurance or life assurance companies, 40 per cent in firms of consultants, two per cent on the Stock Exchange and a few in industry, commerce, government service and education.

Members of the Institute and the Faculty are employed all over the world, especially in Australia, Canada, the USA, New Zealand, South Africa and the West Indies.

PAY AND CONDITIONS

Salaries start at around £13,600 to about £16,500 for a trainee in London, rising to over £25,000 on qualification. A chief executive can earn £100,000, or more, a year, depending on location.

Actuaries work normal office hours. Trainees have to set aside several hours of their own time every week for studying.

PROSPECTS

Actuarial training can prove an effective foundation for any type of management. It involves analysing facts and figures, perceiving trends and planning ahead. Actuaries are widely respected in business and financial circles, since they play a significant role in many matters. Many actuaries achieve senior management positions.

RELATED OCCUPATIONS

Insurance broker, insurance underwriter, accountant, economist, investment analyst, stockbroker, market maker, statistician.

FURTHER INFORMATION

The Faculty of Actuaries (FOA)*, 40-44 Thistle Street, Edinburgh EH2 1EN, 0131 220 4555

The Institute of Actuaries*, Napier House, 4 Worcester Street, Oxford OX1 2AW, 01865 794144

FURTHER READING

Leaflets/booklets are available from the addresses marked*.

In the careers library classified under NAJ.

1. **MARKET MAKER CLCI:NAL**
2. **STOCKBROKER CLCI:NAL**
3. **INVESTMENT ANALYST/FUND MANAGER:NAL**

BACKGROUND INFORMATION

Stockbrokers, market makers (previously known as stock jobbers) and investment analysts are all concerned with the buying and selling of stocks and shares (otherwise known as securities). Bonds are mostly issued by government, as a way of borrowing money to provide public services. They carry a fixed level of interest. Shares, meanwhile, are issued by companies as a way of raising money to help them carry on their business. They pay variable interest from year to year depending on the performance of the company.

Individuals and institutions, such as pension funds, buy and sell securities in the Stock Market as a form of investment. They hope their shares will produce a good rate of return and will, therefore, be worth more when they sell them than when they bought them, after allowing for the effects of inflation. Pension funds use their investments to provide for their members' pensions, while insurance companies use the money to pay the claims they receive.

Stockbrokers act as investors' agents and advisors in the buying and selling of securities. The job of the market makers, meanwhile, is to buy and sell securities on their own account, or for institutional clients, and to make markets in securities by quoting buying and selling prices. Both stockbrokers and market makers are members of the Stock Exchange. Some firms act as stockbrokers and market makers.

Investment analysts, by contrast, are employed by stockbrokers (the 'sell side') or institutional investors (the 'buy side') to undertake research into companies, industries, markets or individual securities.

1. MARKET MAKER (NAL)

THE WORK

Market makers trade in securities as 'principals'. In other words, they buy and sell securities on their own account with the aim of making a profit on each transaction, ie by selling securities at a higher price than they bought them for. They may also buy and sell securities for institutional investors, but they do not give investment advice.

The system is based on competition between market makers to ensure the best prices. Throughout the day market makers are obliged to quote continuous firm buying (bid) and selling (offer) prices for the securities in which they are registered, whether or not there are any orders for those securities on that day.

Market makers can choose to register to trade in one or more of four main securities: UK equities (shares), international equities, the gilt-edged market (loans issued on behalf of the government to fund its spending), or fixed-interest securities. Some securities are traded infrequently and cannot support competition between market makers. In many of these cases, a sole market maker quotes prices; for other securities the prices are simply decided on the basis of Stock Exchange member firms' orders.

Market makers decide what prices to quote by studying the supply and demand for securities. For instance, rival take-over bids mean that a company's shares may be in demand, so current shareholders can sell their holdings at a high price. On the other hand, disappointing profits may mean that demand for a particular company's shares falls, so that they can be bought for a low price.

Market makers gather this and similar information by reading the financial press and consulting investment analysts. It is important for them to be immediately aware of any changes in the securities markets. This means that they make heavy use of computerized information services, which can be updated continuously to take account of events that affect the markets.

WORK ENVIRONMENT

Market makers no longer work in the hectic atmosphere of the Stock Exchange trading floor. They work from their firm's dealing rooms, which are large modern work spaces surrounded by banks of VDUs and telephones. The atmosphere can be busy and noisy.

SKILLS AND INTERESTS

Market makers need be constantly alert, quick thinking, and interested in and sensitive to emerging trends in the stock market. They must also have the confidence to trust their own judgement in what are often stressful situations.

In order to make good judgements, it is necessary to have the capacity to pick out relevant information and think rapidly in order to make instant decisions on what prices to quote to customers. As their income depends on the quality of their decision-making, they need to be able to cope with high levels of risk. They need the maturity and responsibility to work unsupervised and on their own initiative. Clarity of thought and an ability with figures is important for calculating prices and profits.

ENTRY REQUIREMENTS

Although there are no formal entry requirements, in practice the majority of firms now have a policy of recruiting only graduates. Whilst any degree is acceptable, it is often considered that a background in economics or a demonstrable interest in the securities industry and the financial and business world is essential. Previous work experience or familiarity with the City is valuable. A good knowledge of the financial press is also important.

TRAINING

New recruits are trained in-house by working in a firm's different departments and watching established colleagues at work. Some large financial houses that offer a variety of services, including market making, train new recruits by introducing them to all branches of the firm before they decide to which section they would be best suited. This type of training programme can last for 18 months.

Before they can trade on the Stock Exchange, however, market makers must be registered with the Securities and Futures Authority (SFA). This requires them to pass an examination which consists of a multiple-choice paper with about 150 questions, and takes three hours. Preparation for the examinations can be by home study, evening classes or intensive day courses (lasting five to seven days plus 40 hours private study) provided by commercial training organizations. Employers usually offer candidates financial support or study time to prepare for these exams.

Some employers may also expect market makers to take the Securities Institute examinations, leading to the Institute's Diploma. This consists of a choice of three out of ten papers. Usually, one paper is taken at a sitting, and sittings take place twice a year. Preparation for these examinations may be via day courses provided by commercial training organizations (lasting seven to eight days plus 80 hours private study), evening classes or home study. Candidates are usually allowed a certain amount of time off to prepare for these exams. It is expected to take 18 months to three years to study for and pass them.

LATE ENTRY

This may be possible for people who have passed the SFA registered persons examinations. In most cases, late entrants are expected to have had some other relevant experience and to be able to bring the necessary personal qualities (see ENTRY REQUIREMENTS). It is also possible that individuals with experience in the Armed Forces may be welcomed, especially because they are trained in and are accustomed to making quick decisions under pressure. It is essential, nonetheless, to be well-informed about and committed to the financial world.

OPPORTUNITIES

This is a relatively small field. In total, there are just 29 firms which are registered as market makers in UK equities, 50 as market makers in international equities, 20 as market makers in gilts and ten as fixed interest market makers. One firm may register to trade in more than one type of security. Market-making firms are now usually part of larger organizations, made up of banks, stockbrokers and investment advisers. Although these all recruit from time to time, openings for market makers as such are few and competition is fierce. There are opportunities for work overseas, especially in the Far East.

PAY AND CONDITIONS

Pay may be very high (often well over £100,000 a year at the top) but can vary significantly from year to year, depending on a firm's trading results. There is a strong emphasis on youth and it is sometimes suggested that, because of 'burn-out' (exhaustion), market makers reach their peak in their thirties and early forties, before moving on to other forms of employment. The working day is from 7am to 7pm, Monday to Friday, but it may be necessary to work longer hours.

PROSPECTS

Prospects are limited, as most firms do not have a well-defined promotional ladder. It may be possible to move into work in other branches of the employing organization.

RELATED OCCUPATIONS

Actuary, commodities broker/merchant, futures trader, insurance underwriter, investment analyst, stockbroker.

FURTHER INFORMATION AND READING

Please see the article 2. STOCKBROKER

2. STOCKBROKER (NAL)

THE WORK

Stockbrokers buy and sell securities as agents on behalf of individual clients, or as principals with institutional investors. They also advise clients on their investments. Some stockbrokers specialize in private client work and others in institutional work. The clients vary in their approach. Some decide themselves what to buy and sell, and choose brokers who specialize in dealing only, while others decide what to buy and sell after discussions with their stockbroker and choose firms who specialize in advisory work. A third group give their stockbrokers discretion to buy and sell on their behalf as they think fit and choose firms who specialize in discretionary work. The ultimate responsibility for the transaction remains, however, with the client. The better the advice given by the stockbroker, the more clients they attract. Stockbrokers earn their income from commissions on the transactions they carry out.

Trading in securities no longer takes place in the hectic atmosphere of the Stock Exchange floor. The introduction of new technology has meant that stockbrokers now work from their firms' dealing rooms, using computer screens and telephones. Trading prices for UK securities are displayed on computer screens via SEAQ (Stock Exchange Automated Quotations system), while foreign securities appear through SEAQ International – brokers buy and sell at these prices over the telephone. They have a legal obligation to buy at the lowest price available in the market at the time of the deal. Once a transaction has taken place, the Stock Exchange uses a computerized settlement system to transfer the shares between buyer and seller.

Stockbrokers also spend time assessing their clients' portfolios (securities holdings). They advise on a wide range of investment products, including unit trusts and options (the right to buy or sell securities at a fixed rate within a specified period). They make their judgements on what to buy and sell by reading the financial press, consulting computerized information systems and talking to investment analysts, or reading their reports.

Privately owned UK and overseas companies may also seek advice from stockbrokers on going public, ie on raising money by selling their shares to the public and trading them on the Stock Exchange. Companies whose shares are already being traded may also approach stockbrokers for advice on the nature and timing of new securities issues. Some stockbrokers specialize in new issue work.

WORK ENVIRONMENT

Most stockbrokers work from their firms' dealing rooms, which are large modern workspaces surrounded by banks of VDUs and telephones. The atmosphere can be busy and noisy.

SKILLS AND INTERESTS

Stockbrokers need to be confident with figures and clear-headed, so as to reach decisions quickly on what to buy and sell. They should respond well to working under pressure and be able to cope with high stress levels, as their income level, promotion and job security depend on their performance. They need good communication skills for attracting clients, advising them and explaining the reasons for their advice.

They must be people of honesty and integrity, as they are dealing with large sums of other people's money. The maturity and responsibility to organize their own time and work without supervision are also necessary.

ENTRY REQUIREMENTS

There are no formal minimum entry requirements, but, in practice, firms recruit graduates with good degrees (minimum 2:1), preferably in economics. Recruits without an economics degree should be able to demonstrate interest in their chosen field: for example, they may have done vacation work with a stockbroking firm.

TRAINING

Before stockbrokers conduct investment business, they must be registered with the Securities and Futures Authority. This requires them to satisfy the SFA's 'fit and proper' criteria (further details from the SFA, see FURTHER INFORMATION), and pass a registered persons examination. There is a choice of papers, but stockbrokers normally take the Securities Representative paper. This is a three-hour multiple-choice paper consisting of about 150 questions. There are various ways of studying for it, including home study, evening classes and attendance at intensive training courses provided by commercial training companies. The latter last from five to seven days plus 40 hours private study.

Many employers also require stockbrokers to take the Securities Institute examinations leading to the Institute's Diploma, though this may not apply to British branches of foreign securities houses. Candidates take a choice of three out of ten papers, usually one paper at a sitting. Sittings take place twice a year. Preparation for these examinations may be through day courses (lasting about seven or eight days plus about 80 hours private study) provided by commercial training organizations, evening classes or home study. Candidates are normally allowed some time off to prepare for the examinations. It is expected to take 18 months to three years to study for and pass the examinations.

Training also takes place 'in house'. Many new recruits follow formal training programmes for a year or 18 months, during which they work in all sections of the firm and are assigned projects to complete. They are then given the job of assistant account or fund manager. Employers offering a variety of financial services, including stockbroking, may take on graduate recruits and train them in all branches of the firm before they decide what type of work they are best suited to.

LATE ENTRY

Mature entrants who have passed the SFA Registered Persons examinations may be considered.

OPPORTUNITIES

There about 400 member firms of the Stock Exchange. Many of these are part of larger organizations that offer other services including banking, market making and investment advice.

Competition for vacancies is fierce. Some large firms recruit about 15 to 20 graduates a year, other smaller firms recruit just one. Others recruit only when a vacancy arises. A number of stockbroking firms attend university recruitment fairs.

Most stockbroking firms are located in London, though a number are to be found in Liverpool, Birmingham, Manchester, Bristol, Bournemouth, Leeds, Edinburgh and other large towns. There are also opportunities for overseas work, mainly in the Far East.

PAY AND CONDITIONS

Starting salaries range from around £17,000 to £23,000. An average salary is around £75,000, while a top broker can earn well over £100,000.

The working day is from about 7am to 7pm, Mondays to Fridays, though stockbrokers must be prepared to work longer hours if necessary.

PROSPECTS

In most stockbroking firms, there is no well-defined promotional ladder. In private client work, assistant account managers who perform satisfactorily can expect to progress to account manager after about five years. Institutional brokers who perform well should progress from assistant fund manager to fund manager. Thereafter, in both types of work, promotion depends on their record and has to be earned. The better advice managers give and the more clients they bring in, the more likely they are to proceed to senior manager or director.

RELATED OCCUPATIONS

Commodities broker/merchant, futures trader, market maker, insurance broker, investment analyst, statistician.

FURTHER INFORMATION

Please see article 3. INVESTMENT ANALYST

The Securities Institute*, Centurion House, 2-4 Monument Street, London EC3R 8AJ

FURTHER READING

Leaflets/booklets are available from addresses marked*.

In the careers library classified under NAL.

3. INVESTMENT ANALYST/FUND MANAGER (NAL)

THE WORK

The work and training of an investment analyst and a fund manager is so similar in content that, often, fund managers carry out their own analysis, so the following information is relevant to both titles. Investment analysis and fund management also includes the work of portfolio managers and investment managers.

Investment analysts attempt to predict the long and short-term future performance of securities and decide what will be a good buy for investors, who may be their clients (for stockbroker analysts) or their employers (for institutional analysts). Investment analysts do not analyse only UK securities. They study foreign securities and other investment media, such as commodities, futures and options. They also look at economies and markets in general, to help them get the full picture of the prospects for a particular company or sector. Investment analysts working for stockbrokers tend to specialize in a particular field, such as utilities (gas, water and electricity) or building materials, building up long-term relationships in their specialist sectors.

Investment analysts study financial and other data, such as past performance of particular securities, published government statistics, company annual reports, government regulations, and legislation which could affect companies in their sector. They also gather information by speaking to contacts via the telephone and by meeting representatives of, and visiting, the companies they analyse. They use this information to produce models and forecasts for internal use, written reports for clients (often accompanied by a presentation) or reports on proposed changes within an investment portfolio. These reports often have to be produced at short notice.

Stockbrokers' investment analysts have regular meetings with clients. Their expertise is important in attracting potential clients. They can become involved in assisting their firm to advise companies in their sector on raising money through issuing shares. In large firms they work as part of a team, all contributing to produce one report, but in small firms, one investment analyst may do all the research necessary to produce a report.

Institutional investment analysts work closely with fund managers (the people who manage an institution's portfolio of investments) and help them decide what to buy and sell; in fact, the distinction between the two is often blurred. They also make presentations to representatives of the funds they manage. These representatives may be fellow employees, in the case of life assurance companies or self-managed pension funds, or they may be clients, for instance, trustees of pension funds or charities who have appointed an external fund manager to look after their investments.

WORK ENVIRONMENT

Investment analysts are based in offices; however, they spend a lot of time out of the office, conducting research and meeting people. They may have to travel long distances to meetings or spend time away from home or even abroad.

SKILLS AND INTERESTS

Investment analysts need to have outgoing personalities and be able to sell their skills and knowledge to clients and relate to people at all levels. They need the maturity and responsibility to organize their own or their employer's time and work without supervision. At the same time, a capacity for team work is essential. As they often receive unexpected last-minute requests for detailed information, flexibility, emotional resilience and the ability to work under pressure are vital. Tact and resourcefulness are also useful when gathering information, perhaps from companies that are being studied as investment prospects. A high level of commitment to the job is required.

Investment analysts need to be able to extract relevant information from a mass of detail, in order to prepare useful reports on a company as an investment prospect. Numerical fluency, or the readiness to improve it, is important for understanding statistical and financial information. Accountancy skills are useful too. Fluency in written and spoken communication is needed for writing readable reports and making presentations to clients. They need to have, or be prepared to acquire, computer skills.

ENTRY REQUIREMENTS

There are no formal minimum entry requirements, but it is increasingly difficult to get a job or be accepted as a trainee investment analyst without a degree or professional qualification. Many applicants will have both. The most useful degrees or qualifications for prospective entrants are in economics, statistics or accounting, but this does not rule out candidates from other disciplines. For instance, languages may be useful when applying to a firm specializing in overseas work. Relevant industrial experience may also be useful.

TRAINING

Training varies according to the size of the employing organization, but most training takes place on the job. Trainees usually start off as part of a team, with a senior analyst assigned to supervise them. They are given regular tasks, such as updating internal forecasts, and larger projects – designed to teach them how to approach analysis, such as collecting published data on a company or sector and writing a report on it. They can expect to contribute to the decision-making process within six to twelve months of joining.

At the same time, they study for a test set by the regulatory authority, such as the Investment Management Certificate, usually followed by a professional qualification: associate membership of the Institute of Investment Management and Research. This is gained by passing the Institute's examination. Exam subjects include: economics and applied statistical analysis; interpretation of accounts and corporate finance; portfolio management; and investment regulation and practice. Depending on the size of the employing organization, trainees are usually given financial support and time off work to study for these exams. Study for the exams takes three years and can be by block or day release, evening classes or correspondence courses.

Some stockbroker analysts study for the Securities and Futures Authority registered persons examinations as an alternative. Passing one or more of these examinations allows employees of SFA member firms to manage investments and give investment advice. The Securities Representative examination, for example, consists of 150 multiple-choice questions and lasts about three hours. Investment analysts may study for alternative qualifications offered by other professional financial services institutions, such as the Chartered Institute of Banking.

LATE ENTRY

Maturity and experience are useful attributes. The majority of new entrants are over 25 years.

OPPORTUNITIES

Investment analysts usually work for stockbrokers or financial institutions, ie pension funds, life assurance companies, unit and investment trusts and banks, including merchant banks and the Bank of England, and large companies who manage their own investments. There are opportunities for work abroad, particularly in the Far East. The employer's size can vary from a small firm with a handful of professionals, to an integrated financial conglomerate with hundreds of investment professionals.

Overall numbers within the profession (around 5,000) are stable and competition for vacancies is fierce. Vacancies occur fairly often, as investment analysts tend to move around within the profession. Jobs are concentrated in the South East of England, Birmingham, Liverpool, Manchester and Edinburgh, and it is necessary to be mobile to secure work.

PAY AND CONDITIONS

Annual salaries are within a range of £20,000 to £22,000 for new entrants to over £50,000 for experienced analysts. Analysts work long and irregular hours to get the job done, as stock markets around the world operate on different time zones. They often come into work very early, before the London Stock Market opens.

PROSPECTS

Career analysts tend to work for stockbrokers, while institutional analysts who do well can expect to progress to assistant fund manager and then to fund manager. It is also possible to become self-employed as a partner in a consultancy or stockbroking firm, though partners in a firm of stockbrokers must pass the Securities and Futures Authority exams.

RELATED OCCUPATIONS

Accountant, actuary, economist, statistician, stockbroker, fund manager.

FURTHER INFORMATION

The Institute of Investment Management and Research*, 211-213 High Street, Bromley, Kent BR1 1NY, 0181 464 0811

Publicity and Promotions Department*, The London Stock Exchange, London EC1 1HP, 0171 797 3628

The Securities and Futures Authority Ltd*, Cottons Centre, Cottons Lane, London SE1 2QB, 0171 378 9000

FURTHER READING

Leaflets/booklets are available from the addresses marked*.

Working in the Money Business – COIC

In the careers library classified under NAL.

1. MARKETING MANAGER CLCI:OB
2. MARKET RESEARCH EXECUTIVE CLCI:OB
3. MARKET RESEARCH INTERVIEWER CLCI:OB

BACKGROUND INFORMATION

The purpose of marketing is to provide customers with the goods and services they want, when and where they want them, at a price that suits both the customers and the company.

Marketing involves making sure that the company offers what the customer wants to buy, and that the customer buys it. This entails a marketing campaign in which all departments, from design to distribution, work together with the client's wishes in mind.

The main sectors in marketing are:

– fast-moving consumer goods, such as food, drink, toiletries;

– consumer durables, such as furniture, cookers, washing machines;

– industrial products, sold within industry, such as machine tools, engine components, laboratory equipment, raw materials;

– services, including financial, computing, travel, leisure;

– public sector, for example, charities, theatres, schools and colleges.

This division applies to both the home and export market.

1. MARKETING MANAGER (OB)

THE WORK

The main stages in marketing – the 'marketing mix' – are market research, product development, pricing, sales, distribution and promotion. Marketing managers are responsible for planning and co-ordinating each of these stages.

Market research provides managers with information about customer preferences and competitors' activity. They attend meetings with their research executives or a market research agency, deciding what information they need and how to gather it. They use the findings of the research in planning the marketing strategy.

Product development involves the marketing manager advising the design and production departments of the customers' requirements, agreeing what changes need to be made to existing products and discussing the introduction of new ones. They attend meetings, give presentations and write reports based on market research findings.

Pricing means working out prices that are realistic in terms of both production, costs, sales targets, and an acceptable profit level. Managers co-ordinate production and promotion with sales and distribution.

Sales and distribution – the marketing manager makes sure that the demand can be met. They analyse the sales figures to find out how effective the promotion campaign has been and to help in planning future production. In some companies, sales and marketing management are combined, and the marketing manager takes personal accountability for sales.

Promotion campaigns involve working and liaising with design consultancies, advertising, direct marketing and self promotion agencies and PR consultancies if not done in-house, also liaising with advertising agencies to discuss the advertising campaign and choice of media.

Export marketing is usually separate from the home marketing department. It often combines responsibility for marketing and sales. Managers have to adapt the marketing mix to local demand and can face problems of communication, cultural differences or consumer legislation. Some managers appoint local agents to handle market research, sales, distribution and promotion. Others become personally involved in assessing the market, setting up promotion campaigns and negotiating with customers. While overseas they often work by themselves, arranging transport and storage, dealing with documentation, customs, local taxes and legal problems. Some spend most of their time overseas; others handle much of the administration from the UK. In multinational companies, the marketing manager works in liaison with overseas branches.

WORK ENVIRONMENT

Marketing managers are office-based but spend much of their time in discussion with other departmental managers and in travelling to visit customers and agencies. Travel overseas may be required.

SKILLS AND INTERESTS

Marketing managers should be good communicators, able to talk and write clearly and persuasively to people at all levels both inside and outside the company. It is important to
be a good listener, able to understand other people's points of view without losing sight of the original objective.

Qualities of leadership are very important: the ability to organize and motivate others, set targets, encourage co-operation and accept responsibility. They should also be willing to adapt plans to the needs of the market-place and to work within the management team.

Numeracy is a basic requirement; marketing managers use figures much of the time, in analysing sales and research data, in planning and in pricing. They must be aware of the need for profit.

In initiating and carrying through a project, imagination should be combined with enthusiasm, attention to detail and sound judgement.

ENTRY REQUIREMENTS

The minimum qualifications for a trainee post in marketing are four GCSEs/S grades (A-C/1-3) including English and maths, and one A level/two H grades or BTEC/SCOTVEC National Certificate/Diploma in Business Studies. Entrants are usually over 18 years.

These qualifications enable a trainee to study for higher national certificates/diplomas or the Certificate in Marketing, to be followed by the Postgraduate Diploma in Marketing of The Chartered Institute of Marketing (CIM). Minimum qualifications for the professional examinations of the Institute of Export are four GCSEs/S grades (A-C/1-3) including English, and one A level or equivalent.

Many employers require a degree or higher national diploma. The degree may be in any subject, but a business-related course that includes marketing may be most directly relevant. Some employers prefer a language qualification or, for industrial marketing, a scientific or technical subject.

Minimum entry qualifications for a degree course are two A levels/three H grades with five GCSEs/S grades (A-C/1-3) or equivalent qualifications.

BTEC/SCOTVEC Higher National Diploma in Business Studies with marketing specialisms is widely available. Minimum entry requirements are a BTEC/SCOTVEC national award *or* one A level/two H grades with five GCSEs/S grades (A-C/1-3) or equivalent. Subject requirements should be checked with each institution but nearly always include English and maths at GCSE/S grade.

An increasing number of graduates (any discipline) take a full-time postgraduate course in marketing, a Diploma in Management Studies, or a Diploma in Export Marketing.

For export marketing, it is often important to acquire a knowledge of the language of the company's customers.

A driving licence is often required.

TRAINING

A number of full-time courses are available that include marketing studies. Marketing may be combined with languages, computing, economics or other subjects and it forms part of most business and management science courses.

Whether or not the new entrant has an academic qualification in marketing, some measure of training at work is provided. Much of it is informal, through working alongside experienced marketing assistants and managers. Employers arrange short in-company or external courses on topics such as public speaking or computer techniques, and may encourage part-time study for a professional qualification, usually the Postgraduate Diploma in Marketing of The Chartered Institute of Marketing.

An increasing number of marketing trainees study for the CIM qualification usually via part-time courses or distance learning. The syllabus covers the economic and legal aspects of marketing, accounting, statistics, business organization and marketing practice. Alternatively, many short courses/seminars are also available on all aspects of marketing.

The Institute of Export conducts professional examinations in two parts leading to graduate membership of the Institute (MIEx (Grad)). Courses may be studied by part-time or distance learning. Part 1 (Advanced Certificate in Overseas Trade) includes principles of marketing, principles of law, international trade and payments, and physical distribution. Part 2 (Diploma in Export Management) covers international marketing, export markets, selection, research, statistics, and principles of management in export.

NVQs/SVQs in Marketing Products and Services are available at Levels 3 and 4.

LATE ENTRY

Most recruits to marketing begin in their early twenties and expect to become marketing managers at 25 to 35 years. Older candidates usually have experience in a related field such as sales, market research or advertising.

Most institutions of higher education welcome applications from adult students. Candidates who lack the normal entry qualifications are considered according to individual circumstances.

OPPORTUNITIES

Most industrial and commercial organizations have their own in-house marketing departments, responsible for the marketing process as a whole. Marketing services agencies also offer opportunities for marketing managers. Some agencies specialize, for example, in communications, or other areas such as advertising or market research. Others offer a broad range of marketing support services.

Opportunities exist in the consumer sector, particularly fast-moving consumer goods, for marketing trainees with both manufacturers and retail chains. In industrial marketing, where the products are often complex, expensive and adapted to the requirements of individual customers, the sales and marketing functions may be combined, so that the marketing manager deals directly with the customers. Opportunities also exist in the relatively new and growing service and public sectors.

Opportunities in marketing vary with the state of the economy. Competition for jobs at any level is intense. Vacancies are advertised in the national press, *Marketing, Marketing Weekly* and *Campaign.*

PAY AND CONDITIONS

Salaries for trainees in marketing start at around £10,400 and rise with success in the job. A salary of £35,000 or more is not uncommon for an experienced manager.

Most marketing managers work normal office hours of 37 to 40 hours a week but these are often extended to meet deadlines and attend meetings.

PROSPECTS

It is usual for a new entrant to marketing to make several changes, between jobs and between employers, in order to gain experience. Promotion depends on success in the job. It generally implies taking responsibility for the marketing of an increasing number or range of products. Marketing managers may become marketing directors or go into general management. Some set up their own consultancy.

RELATED OCCUPATIONS

Advertising agency account/media executive, market research executive, sales manager, public relations officer, store manager, sales representative.

FURTHER INFORMATION

The Chartered Institute of Marketing*, Moor Hall, Cookham, Maidenhead, Berkshire SL6 9QH, 01628 427500

The Institute of Export*, Export House, 64 Clifton Street, London EC2A 4HB, 0171 247 9812

FURTHER READING

Leaflets/booklets are available from the addresses marked*.

Working in Marketing – COIC
Marketing and Sales – AGCAS
How to Get on in Marketing – A Career Development Guide (Second Edition) – Kogan Page

In the careers library classified under OB.

2. MARKET RESEARCH EXECUTIVE (OB)

BACKGROUND INFORMATION

The purpose of market research is to find out what customers want and why, so that the suppliers of goods and services may meet that need. There are three main types of market research: consumer, industrial, and social.

Consumer research is concerned with goods and services sold to the public. Companies that provide these ask questions such as: how do customers react to new prices or packaging? How satisfied are they with the after-sales service? Could this town accommodate another hypermarket? A market research agency usually conducts the research on behalf of the company.

Industrial or 'business to business' research is concerned with goods and services bought for use within industry, such as machine tools or raw materials. It often calls for technical knowledge and is carried out either by a specialist research agency or by the firm's own market research executives. They deal with matters such as the market for electronic components, trends in textile manufacture, potential coal exports.

Social and political research is used by central and local government to investigate people's views on political or economic issues. They use the findings to help plan their policy on, for example, health or housing provision.

THE WORK

Consumer research executives working for an agency, identify exactly what the client wants to find out, then prepare a proposal outlining the research programme and detailing the costs. They 'sell' this to the client in a written and oral presentation. Once the deal has been negotiated and secured, agency executives control progress. They decide what sample of the population to target and what quantitative or qualitative research methods to use. These could include face-to-face or telephone interviews, postal questionnaires and group discussions. Executives usually train a team of field interviewers to help with face-to-face surveys – interviewing passers-by – while they themselves conduct in-depth discussions and write the questionnaires. They monitor sales and stock records from stores. They also use published information from sources such as government statistics and company reports. Using computers to analyse the data, executives collate and interpret the findings of the research. Finally they deliver a written or verbal presentation to the client.

Many firms supplying the consumer market employ their own market research executives. Their job is seldom to carry out the research themselves but to commission an agency to do it. This means agreeing objectives, terms and methods of enquiry with the agency, and interpreting the results to management.

Industrial research executives gain much of their information from personal or telephone interviews with users of the product in question. Interviews tend to be more detailed than in the consumer sector, and to be based less on a questionnaire than on a discussion about how the product is bought or used in that particular firm. Desk research can also be particularly helpful.

Social researchers work in many different settings on a wide range of subjects. These include unemployment, racial harassment, women's health care, drug dependency. Methods vary with subject and sample, but include questionnaires, interviews, and door-to-door enquiry, followed by statistical analysis using computers.

In large agencies and research institutes, the work may be divided into quantitative and qualitative research. Quantitative researchers spend more time on computing and statistical analysis. Qualitative work calls upon interests in psychology and behaviour, and involves writing questionnaires, conducting in-depth interviews and interpreting the results.

WORK ENVIRONMENT

Market research is mainly office-based, either in agencies or within the firms that supply goods or services. However, executives may travel extensively to meet their clients, at home and, increasingly, abroad. Most agencies are found in large cities.

SKILLS AND INTERESTS

For quantitative research a numerate and analytical mind is essential. Market research executives dealing with numbers and statistics have to analyse the data clearly and objectively. A grounding in statistics and computing is often required. Industrial research executives may need particular scientific or technical knowledge. Qualitative researchers require an interest in psychology and behavioural science.

Executives need the ability to appreciate the client's requirements and to frame a questionnaire that elicits the appropriate information. They should be able to express themselves clearly in speech and writing, for compiling and presenting reports.

Market research executives should like working with a wide variety of people. The work can involve discussions with consumers, managers, technical staff and others; executives should feel at ease in meeting and talking to everybody. Agency executives also require sales ability to some extent, as part of their job is to win commissions.

Market research executives should be good administrators. A thorough, logical approach, and willingness to take responsibility, are important. Pressure can be considerable – working to deadlines, sometimes handling several projects at once.

ENTRY REQUIREMENTS

No formal academic requirements are specified but almost all market research executives hold a degree or higher national diploma. Any degree subject is acceptable, though the most relevant include business studies, social sciences, maths, statistics and economics. A science or engineering degree may be appropriate for industrial market research. Languages can be an advantage for international work.

The minimum entry requirements for a degree course are: two A levels and five GCSEs (A-C); three H grades and five S grades (1-3); or equivalent. Minimum requirements for higher national diploma are: BTEC/SCOTVEC national certificate/diploma; one A level/two H grades and three GCSEs/S grades (A-C/1-3), preferably including English and maths; or equivalent. Applicants should check course requirements for each institution.

Students in further and higher education may take the Market Research Society's Foundation and Certificate examination as part of their degree, higher national diploma or A level studies. These professional examinations can also be taken independently if no arrangement exists within the under graduate or postgraduate course. Details of these schemes are available from The Market Research Centre.

TRAINING

Postgraduate courses in marketing, market research or social research are available at several institutes of higher education. A degree course lasts three or four years, a higher national diploma course lasts two to three years. Many degree and higher national diploma courses in business subjects offer options in marketing or market research.

Much training is carried out within the company and may be supplemented by short courses and seminars run by the Market Research Society (MRS). Practising researchers who hold the Market Research Society's Certificate may progress to the Diploma.

NVQs/SVQs in Marketing Research are available at Levels 3 and 4.

LATE ENTRY

Most research assistants or trainee market research executives begin in their early twenties. It may be possible to go into market research after experience in other marketing fields – such as advertising or sales – or with a background in statistics, economics or maths. Some find an opening as research assistants after experience in field or telephone interviewing.

Many universities and colleges welcome applications from older candidates who lack the usual formal academic entry requirements. Each application is considered on its merit.

Candidates over 21 years who lack the usual academic qualifications may register for the MRS Certificate and Diploma examinations provided they are working full-time in market research or marketing at an appropriate level.

OPPORTUNITIES

The Market Research Society has about 6,500 members, of whom half work in agencies. There are about 300 market research agencies, mostly in London. They range from one or two-person businesses to firms of several hundred. Most agencies handle consumer research, a few specialize in industrial topics or social and political research.

Opportunities in social research arise with local and central government, in higher education, with independent agencies and with institutes such as Social and Community Planning Research. There are occasional openings in employer or trade associations. The Social Survey Division of the Office of Population Censuses and Surveys handles much of the research for central government.

Other executives work in industry. Most large industrial and commercial organizations have their own research departments. Advertising agencies employ market researchers, mainly to study the effectiveness of the advertising.

There are about 250 vacancies a year in market research for new graduates. Many start as research assistants, helping with desk research and administration and briefing field workers. Some graduates start as general marketing trainees, with research as one of the options. Vacancies appear in the national press, industrial trade press, *Marketing* and *Marketing Week*.

The MRS publish directories of market research organizations.

PAY AND CONDITIONS

Starting salaries range from £10,000 to £15,000. These rise to £26,000 plus, for senior executives; well over that for managers.

Most executives work normal office hours but may be required to work extra as deadlines approach.

PROSPECTS

Early responsibility and rapid promotion are possible within market research for those with ability and ambition. In consumer research, it is usual to change jobs fairly frequently, and to move between industry and agencies to gain experience.

Market research trainees can expect to take early responsibility for their own clients and their own projects, then to manage a research department or team. Specialization is possible, for example in attitude research or overseas work. Agency executives may become directors, or set up in business themselves. Some market research executives move into advertising or other marketing functions.

Industrial market researchers may gain promotion within their department, or move into other marketing or managerial posts.

In social research institutes, central and local government and higher education, a career structure, dependent on experience, leads to senior grades. However, many posts are on a short-term contract basis.

RELATED OCCUPATIONS

Advertising executive, public relations officer, marketing manager, statistician, psychologist, sales representative, purchasing officer.

FURTHER INFORMATION

Please see article 3. MARKET RESEARCH INTERVIEWER.

3. MARKET RESEARCH INTERVIEWER (OB)

THE WORK

Market research interviewers collect facts and opinions by interviewing the public and members of organizations in person or by telephone. The main areas of work are consumer, executive or specialist research. Interviews may be with individuals or groups and range from brief objective questions-and-answers to lengthy in-depth discussions. Most interviews are one-to-one, but some interviewers hold group or panel sessions. These involve, for example, asking members of the public to keep a diary of the brands they are using.

To make sure that they obtain the information they want, interviewers normally follow a guide and in many cases a very detailed questionnaire, specifying not only what is to be asked but how. They note down answers as they proceed – by ticking boxes and/or writing, word for word, what each person says. They may use tape or video recorders in group situations. Telephone interviewers may key the responses directly into a computer.

Consumer research can take place on the pavement, inside shops, in local halls or in people's homes. A vast range of topics is covered, from shopping habits and food preferences to political opinions and local transport policy. On the high street, interviewers approach members of the public who, in their opinion, belong in certain selected categories. In most cases, interviewer and respondent together complete a brief questionnaire, which may cover any social, political or consumer subject. In hall tests, respondents are invited into a local meeting place to sample a new product or comment on a display. For home visits, interviewers may be supplied with addresses or may choose their own. They may conduct the interview there and then, or they may leave a questionnaire for the householder to fill in, returning at a later date to collect it or assist with it. They may leave samples on home placement, for example, new brands of washing powder or disposable nappy, and call back to discuss them later. Some interviews may be conducted by telephone from home or office, often during the evening.

Executive interviews are usually long detailed discussions, by telephone or in person. They are arranged by appointment with people in positions of responsibility, such as senior executives, purchasing officers or company secretaries. They may investigate industrial or commercial subjects such as the import of raw materials, choice of machine tools or use of desktop computers in the office.

Specialist interviews are similarly detailed. The interviewer might, for example, question doctors, pharmacists and physiotherapists on the supply of certain medicines or orthopaedic equipment, or visit farmers to compare fertilizers or feedstuff. In-depth interviews demand careful preparation as the interviewer should be sufficiently well-informed to discuss the subject with experts.

WORK ENVIRONMENT

Many market research interviews take place in town or city streets amid noise, bustle and any sort of weather. Others are held in shopping malls, stores, places of work or in private homes. Interviewers usually work in or near their home area. Telephone interviewers usually work from their own homes but sometimes from an office.

SKILLS AND INTERESTS

Market research interviewers should enjoy meeting people and should not be shy to approach them. They should find it easy to talk confidently to anyone, explain what they are doing and ask direct unambiguous questions. They should also be good listeners, careful and observant in noting responses. Legible handwriting and the ability to write clear, concise reports are required.

Gaining people's confidence and winning their co-operation demands tact and patience. Most people are pleased to respond to a courteous, friendly approach, but some object. It can be especially difficult to gain interviews with busy executives. Completing a full quota of interviews can take a great deal of perseverance and self-discipline. A thorough, methodical manner of working is required. Interviewers need to be reliable and work without direct supervision.

Good health and stamina are essential for most field work, as it often takes place outdoors in all weathers and can involve a great deal of walking and standing.

ENTRY REQUIREMENTS

No particular academic qualifications are required. Personal qualities and enthusiasm are more important. These are tested during training and the first experiences of field work, which commonly deter a number of new entrants.

Applicants should have their own telephone, so that they can be contacted when work is available. They should be able to work at short notice and to devote sufficient time each day to complete the job within the allocated period. Except in inner cities, a driving licence and a car are nearly always essential.

TRAINING

Market research agencies organize their own training. Typically this consists of a two or three-day intensive course covering the principles and practice of market research interviewing. Trainees are taught to recognize socio-economic categories. They learn how to select and approach respondents, what to ask and how, how to complete the returns and write reports. Where appropriate they also learn the skills of telephone interviewing. A supervisor accompanies them on field-work training, and again at twice-yearly intervals. A percentage of their field work is back-checked by telephone.

The Market Research Society's Foundation and Certificate examinations provide a qualification for those new to the industry. Contact the Market Research Society for details. NVQ/SVQ in Marketing Research (Interviewing) is available at Level 2.

LATE ENTRY

Market research interviewers are recruited at any age over 18. There is no maximum age limit. Some agencies may express a preference for older applicants with some experience of dealing with the public.

The availability of part-time work also makes it particularly suitable for adults with domestic commitments.

OPPORTUNITIES

Most interviewers are employed by market research agencies. A smaller number work for research institutes, government departments or opinion pollsters. There are about 300 agencies, mostly based in the London area but using field interviewers throughout the country. The larger agencies undertake all types of market and social research. Consumer research is the main area of employment for interviewers, but a few agencies specialize in industrial or business-to-business research. Social research is carried out either by independent research institutes, the Social Survey Division of the Office of Population Censuses and Surveys, other government departments, or by the social research units of large market research agencies. Some interviewers are self-employed and may work for more than one agency.

Demand for market research interviewers varies with the state of the economy. In recent years many small independent agencies have closed, or amalgamated with larger firms. Vacancies are advertised in the local press. Jobcentres and careers offices may be able to help with the addresses of potential employers.

PAY AND CONDITIONS

The work is part-time and irregular. Agencies contact interviewers already on their pay-roll, or advertise for trainees, as required. Interviewers are allocated work to be completed within a set period. To some extent they can arrange their hours to suit themselves and their family commitments. However, some jobs, such as those involving home visits, have to be done in the evening and at weekends. Field interviewers are normally expected to work about six hours a day. Interviewers may be paid on an hourly or daily rate, but most are paid by the job. The average basic rate for a six-hour day is about £26 a day plus mileage allowance. Bonuses may be added.

PROSPECTS

Experienced field interviewers may develop preferences and build up skill in certain types of work, such as social surveys, home placement or group interviewing. Some branch into industrial research, which involves learning to interview executives or specialists in depth.

In large agencies there are prospects of promotion to senior interviewer, supervisor and area field-work manager. Occasionally an opportunity to become a research assistant may arise.

RELATED OCCUPATIONS

Telephone salesperson, sales representative, employment agency consultant/interviewer, store demonstrator, market research executive.

FURTHER INFORMATION

The Market Research Centre*, Leicester Business School, The Gateway, Leicester LE1 9BH, 0116 257 7222

The Market Research Society*, 15 Northburgh Street, London EC14 0AH, 0171 490 4911

FURTHER READING

Leaflets/booklets are available from the address marked*.

Market Research and Social Research – AGCAS

In the careers library classified under OB.

1. ACCOUNT EXECUTIVE CLCI:OD
2. ACCOUNT PLANNER CLCI:OD
3. MEDIA EXECUTIVE CLCI:OD
4. COPYWRITER CLCI:OD

BACKGROUND INFORMATION

Advertising is concerned with promoting goods, services and ideas. Advertisements appear in newspapers and magazines, on posters, commercial radio and television, in cinemas and in the form of direct mail and circulars.

Advertising is big business, with thousands of millions of pounds spent on advertising in Britain each year. It is an industry that has to keep aware of changes in the business environment, such as the development of advertising on satellite and cable television and on Teletext.

The advertising industry can be seen as having three parts:
– the organizations that buy advertising;
– the owners of the media who sell advertising, such as newspapers, magazines, commercial radio and television;
– the link between the two, which is usually an advertising agency.

This article deals with four of the main specialist jobs in advertising agencies – account executive, account planner, media executive and copywriter.

THE WORK

1. Account executive

Account executives, also known as account handlers, act as the link between the advertising agencies that employ them and the clients that wish to advertise. In effect, they represent the client to the agency and the agency to the client.

Account executives receive a brief (instructions) from the client. They find out from the client information about the company, its business methods, products or services and who it wishes to attract with its advertising (the target group).

They work with account planners to devise a marketing strategy and advertising campaign (an advertising programme usually consisting of a series of advertisements) within a given budget. When the client approves the campaign, account executives brief the creative team of copywriter and art director, whose job is to develop ideas for the campaign. They also brief the media planner and buyer, who are responsible for recommending the most effective form of advertising and buying the advertising space or time.

Account executives monitor the progress of the creative and media teams, leading to them giving a presentation of the creative work to the client and advising the client of the media plan (which media are to be used, when and the costs involved). The client may ask for modifications and the account executives negotiate these changes with the agency's creative and media teams.

When the client finally accepts the agency's proposals, account executives arrange for the advertisements to be produced and make sure that deadlines are kept.

Once an advertising campaign has begun, account executives monitor its progress in consultation with the client's marketing staff. If results are not up to expectations they may negotiate with the client to modify the campaign, eg switching from one form of advertising to another.

Account executives work under the supervision of account directors. Typically they handle three or four accounts at the same time. Approximately 80 per cent of their time is spent in discussion with clients, agency colleagues and suppliers. The other 20 per cent is taken up with writing reports, briefs and business correspondence.

2. Account planner

Account planners use their knowledge of consumer attitudes and reactions to make sure that advertising campaigns are targeted effectively. They do this by acting as the consumer's representative at each stage in the development of an advertisement.

At the presentation, agencies try to secure a client's business (the account); account planners contribute their specialist knowledge of consumers.

If the agency is awarded the account they study the brief (instructions) given by the client and decide what research they must do. They need to know who buys the product or service to be advertised, why they buy it and what distinguishes it from competitors' products or services. They also need to understand consumers' attitudes towards their clients and their competitors, their products or services and their advertising.

There may be existing research information available in the form of published market reports, surveys on usage and attitudes, and advertising research. It may, however, be necessary to arrange for fresh market research. Account planners may commission another organization to carry out this research or they may conduct it themselves. This may involve discussions with consumers likely to buy the particular product or service.

Account planners analyse and interpret the research information and decide on a strategy for the advertising campaign based on a thorough understanding of the target audience – the consumers at whom the advertising is aimed. They seek the client's approval for the strategy, then brief the creative team of copywriter and art director. In particular, they seek to describe very clearly the nature of the target audience.

Account planners liaise with the creative team while they are coming up with ideas and join them in presenting ideas to the client for approval, interpreting the appeal of the proposals to the target group.

When a campaign has been approved account planners may arrange for it to be pre-tested to check that the intended message is getting across and the brand name remembered.

While a campaign is in progress account planners research its effectiveness by getting consumer reaction to the campaign. They try to gauge consumer awareness of the campaign and the image of the product or service, and they monitor sales figures. If account planners do not think that a campaign is going as well as expected they may suggest alterations.

Account planners work on several different campaigns at the same time. Much of their time is spent in discussion with account executives and creative staff in the advertising agency, the agency's clients and with consumers.

3. Media executive

Media executives recommend the media that should be used for a client's advertising and buy the advertising space and time. Their aim is to place the advertisements where they will be seen or heard by the maximum possible number of the target audience at the lowest possible price.

In small agencies the planning and buying work may be combined and dealt with by a media executive. Large agencies usually have separate planners and buyers, each of whom may further specialize in 'time' (radio, television and cinema advertisements) and 'space' (newspapers, magazines and posters).

Media planners may work alongside the account executive in preliminary discussions with a client. Alternatively they may be briefed by the account executive or account planner on the product or service to be advertised, the advertising strategy, the target audience and the available budget.

When considering the advertising media to use planners have to take into account information about the different media. They consider circulation and readership figures for newspapers and magazines, viewing figures for different commercial television stations, listening figures for commercial radio stations and figures for cinema audiences. They also consider the costs for each form of advertising. Some information is readily available, such as readership figures from NRS (National Readership Survey) and viewing figures from BARB (Broadcasters' Audience Research Board). Sometimes planners ask their agency's research department to conduct some necessary survey or research.

Planners finally decide on a detailed media plan showing which media are to be used, when, and the costs involved in each. When the client has agreed the plan, planners brief the media buyer.

Media planners spend much of their time in discussion with clients and agency colleagues. They use computers to help in analysing the information they must consider before arriving at the media plan.

Media buyers are instructed by media planners on which media are to be used for an advertising campaign, the budget available and the approximate number of the target audience the agency and the client hopes to reach.

Buyers negotiate with media owners for the advertising space in newspapers, magazines, posters or time on television, radio or in cinemas. They aim to get the best possible deal for the client, which can include being aware of any available discounts.

Much of media buyers' time is spent on the telephone. They keep detailed records of all their transactions and check that they are staying within their budget.

In large agencies media buyers may specialize in one particular medium, such as television.

4. Copywriter

Copywriters work in agency creative departments, providing the words (copy) that are read or heard in advertisements. This can range from slogans, jingles and headlines to more detailed text for catalogues, brochures, leaflets, trade papers and journals. They may also be involved in writing scripts for film, radio and television advertisements. Some copywriters specialize in a particular form of advertising.

Copywriters usually work in partnership with one particular art director who is responsible for the visual part of the campaign.

Copywriters and art directors receive their brief (instructions) from the account executive and/or account planner, with detailed information about the advertiser, the product or service to be advertised and who it wishes to attract with its advertising (the target group). They may want further information, including research material, and may visit the client to learn more about the product or service.

The essential skill of copywriters lies in understanding the product and the target group and in linking them persuasively. Copywriters and art directors together look for an idea that will catch the attention of the target group and put across the selling point of the product. They may produce many ideas, both pictures and headlines, most of which they will discard. In this ideas stage copywriters and art directors discuss visual and textual ideas with each other.

Copywriters and art directors show their more successful ideas to the creative director who may suggest modifications. Neater drawings are then produced and presented to the client, who may also ask for changes. Once the client accepts the concept the layout is modified and the copywriters write the 'body copy' (smaller print containing more detailed information).

Copywriters must always keep in mind the need for their writing to meet legal requirements and be within the Codes of Advertising Practice. They are involved in constant revision and rewriting of their work, either to seek improvement or following a request for modification.

After the client has approved the design and copy, the work is handed on to the production team for typesetting and the production of photographs and drawings (in the case of printed advertisements), or recording or filming (for radio or television commercials). Copywriters and art directors may attend recording and filming (shoots) to make sure that the creative aspects meet their requirements.

Copywriters work under the supervision of a creative director and usually work on several briefs at any one time. Although coming up with ideas and writing copy is central to their work, copywriters spend much of their time in talking to people – agency colleagues, clients and others.

WORK ENVIRONMENT

Account executives, account planners, media executives and copywriters work indoors in office surroundings that are usually comfortable and well furnished.

All spend some time travelling to meetings with clients. Account executives, in particular, may spend up to a day a week travelling to and attending meetings with clients and suppliers outside the agency. Copywriters may travel to studios or locations when advertisements are being recorded or filmed.

All spend much of their time sitting.

SKILLS AND INTERESTS

Advertising is, above all else, a commercial activity. However attracted staff feel towards the creative aspects of advertising they need both an interest in and a commitment to advertising as a business.

Communication skills and the ability to get on well with people are essential in all these jobs, as much of the working day for account executives, account planners, media executives and copywriters is spent in discussion with clients, agency colleagues and others.

Writing skills are important for producing briefs and reports.

Advertising is based on team work, so the ability to work well in a team is essential.

Having to meet deadlines is a feature of advertising work, as is the need to cope with several different jobs at the same time. Ability to work under pressure is therefore important, as is willingness to work long, irregular hours.

Account executive

As the link between clients and the agency, account executives have to balance clients' wishes with the agency's recommendations. This needs self-confidence, diplomacy, persuasiveness and good negotiating skills.

Account executives should be able to present ideas and strategies clearly and accurately, both in speech and in writing.

They must be systematic and well organized, as they have to co-ordinate different activities in several accounts at the same time.

Good staff management skills and the ability to lead a team and work within it are important. They must be able to motivate staff to give of their best, although they are under pressure themselves.

Account planner

An interest in human nature is essential. If account planners are to represent consumers to their colleagues and clients they must be able to understand people, what motivates them, how their attitudes are formed and why they behave as they do.

Account planners must keep constantly aware of changes in society that affect consumer attitudes, such as the state of the economy, the role of women in society, changing leisure patterns and changing eating habits. They need to be alive to trends and fashions and take them into account.

Account planners should be numerate and imaginative in order to translate research data into advertising action.

Media executive

Media planners must be able to express themselves well in speech and in writing in order to negotiate with clients and to brief agency colleagues. A persuasive manner is necessary to gain acceptance of recommendations.

Planners need computer aptitude and numerical and statistical ability for analysing data.

Media buyers should have a confident telephone manner, as much of their time is spent on telephone work. They should have good negotiating skills if they are to get the best possible deals for their clients.

Numerical ability and computer aptitude are important, as buyers have to analyse statistics, calculate expenditure and keep within their budget. They have to be well organized, attentive to detail and capable of careful record keeping.

Copywriter

Copywriters need the ability to write well. They must be able to express themselves in writing in a clear, concise and persuasive way. They need to have imagination and a good command of different writing styles. It is important that they are capable of the painstaking rewriting and polishing necessary to produce quality work.

It is not enough for copywriters to be interested only in the creative side of their work. They must also have a strong interest in the commercial aspects of advertising if they are to understand the products and services they are advertising and the readers, viewers or listeners they are targeting.

Visual understanding is important. Although they are responsible for the written and spoken parts of advertisements, copywriters should be able to contribute ideas about the visual aspects.

Copywriters must be able to accept criticism and be prepared to modify their work if requested by their creative director or the client.

ENTRY REQUIREMENTS

There are no minimum educational requirements but entry to advertising is fiercely competitive and most entrants have at least A levels/H grades. Many agencies only recruit graduates.

Degree courses in communication studies, media studies and business are useful and there are some higher national certificate/diploma and degree courses that specialize in advertising. While these courses are good preparation for a career in advertising they do not guarantee acceptance into the industry. Most employers do not ask for degrees in any particular subject and select the applicants they think are most suitable.

BTEC Higher National Diplomas require either: four or five GCSEs/S grades (A-C/1-3) and one A level/two H grades; or a BTEC/SCOTVEC national award; or Advanced GNVQ/GSVQ Level III. Some colleges offer a BTEC HND in Design with an advertising option. They usually require a Foundation art course or Advanced GNVQ/GSVQ Level III in Art and Design.

Aberdeen College's SCOTVEC Higher National Certificate in Advertising, Marketing and Public Relations requires either two H grades, including English, or a SCOTVEC national certificate with appropriate modules.

Central College of Commerce, Glasgow offers a SCOTVEC Higher National Diploma in Advertising and Public Relations that requires either two S grades and two H grades, including English or a language-based subject, or a SCOTVEC national certificate with appropriate modules, including communication 4.

Degree courses require a minimum of either: two A levels/three H grades plus five GCSEs/S grades; or Advanced GNVQ/GSVQ Level III; or BTEC/SCOTVEC national award. Specific grade and subject requirements vary from course to course.

West Herts College has three relevant courses: the Diploma in Advertising requires five GCSEs/S grades (A-C/1-3) and two A levels/three H grades; or a BTEC/SCOTVEC national award; or Advanced GNVQ/GSVQ Level III. The Postgraduate Diploma in Advertising requires a higher national diploma or degree in any subject. Applicants for the Postgraduate Diploma in Copywriting/Art Direction wishing to specialize in copywriting should be at least 18 and have two A levels/three H grades.

West Thames College's Higher National Diploma in Graphic Design and Advertising prefers a good grade in A level English or equivalent for entry to its copywriting option. Ability in art and design is not essential but basic visual understanding is.

The Communication Advertising and Marketing (CAM) Education Foundation's Certificate in Communication Studies requires either: a degree; or BTEC/SCOTVEC national award in business studies; or two A levels/H grades and three GCSEs/S grades (A-C/1-3); or five GCSEs/S grades (A-C/1-3) and at least one year's relevant UK employment; or at least five years' relevant work experience; or the London Chamber of Commerce and Industry Third Level Group Diploma in Advertising, Marketing and Public Relations. Some qualifications give full exemption from the Certificate examinations, such as the University of Ulster's degree in Communications, Advertising and Marketing, and West Herts College's Diploma and Postgraduate Diploma in Advertising. Other courses allow partial exemption.

For the CAM Diploma in Advertising, entrants must have the CAM Certificate or have exemption from it.

TRAINING

Pre-entry

There are several courses that specialize in advertising:

- BTEC Higher National Diploma in Marketing and Advertising is offered by the London College of Printing and Distributive Trades (two years full-time). It is concerned with the business aspects of advertising.

- SCOTVEC Higher National Certificate in Advertising, Marketing and Public Relations is offered by Aberdeen College (one year full-time), while SCOTVEC Higher National Diploma in Advertising and Public Relations is offered by Central College of Commerce, Glasgow (two years full-time). These courses introduce students to advertising techniques and practices.

- Degree courses are offered by Bournemouth University (Advertising Management), Lancaster University (Advertising and Marketing) and London College of Printing and Distributive Trades (Marketing and Advertising). These courses are all full-time for three years. Ulster University offers a four-year full-time course in Communications, Advertising and Marketing. All courses are good preparation for work as an account executive, account planner or media executive.

- A number of universities and colleges offer Higher National Diploma and Degree courses in Graphic Design that offer an advertising option that includes either copywriting or the business aspects of advertising. These courses are designed primarily for those with art and design ability.

- West Herts College's Diploma in Advertising and Postgraduate Diploma in Advertising (both one year full-time) include: advertising and sales promotion, media, advertising administration, marketing, market research, psychology, print processes and production, copywriting, design and typography.

- West Herts College's Postgraduate Diploma in Copywriting/Art Direction (one year full-time) trains students in the working practices of advertising agencies. They learn the copywriting skills relevant to a broad range of media. During the course copywriters have the opportunity to form creative partnerships with those training for art direction.

- West Thames College's Higher National Diploma in Graphic Design and Advertising (two years full-time) has a copywriting specialism that includes studying advertising, scriptwriting, copywriting, television and radio. Copywriters team up with art directors during the course to form creative partnerships.

On entry

Training received by new staff varies between agencies. In some agencies entrants begin work straight away and learn from experienced staff. Other agencies have a more formal programme of training that includes lectures, periods of time spent in different departments within the agency and visits to media owners.

In addition the Institute of Practitioners in Advertising (IPA) runs a number of courses for staff employed by an IPA member agency.

Account planners may attend short courses on specific skills run by the Market Research Society and the Account Planning Group.

Media executives may attend a series of introductory lectures by the Media Circle followed by an intermediate level course. They may also attend a four-day Media Business Course organized by The Advertising Association.

Copywriters may attend Advertising Creative Circle seminars and workshops.

Account executives who deal with overseas clients and have at least three years' experience may study for The International Advertising Association's diploma by attending a six-month evening course at Martran College, London.

Some agencies encourage their staff to study for the qualifications of The Communication Advertising and Marketing (CAM) Education Foundation:

- CAM Certificate in Communication Studies: students must pass examinations in: marketing, advertising, public relations, media, sales promotion and direct marketing, and research and behavioural studies.

- CAM Diploma in Advertising: students must pass an examination in management and strategy and two examinations from a choice of three advertising papers – consumer, business-to-business and international.

Both the Certificate and the Diploma can be studied full-time but are usually studied part-time on a day release, evening, weekend or distance-learning basis. Thirty-four colleges throughout the UK offer tuition for the Certificate and 13 for the Diploma. The length of time needed to complete the courses varies, but is typically around two years for the Certificate and one year for the Diploma.

There are a range of NVQs/SVQs that those in advertising may work towards. They include Marketing Communications at Level 2 and Advertising, Marketing Products and Services, Marketing Research, Direct Marketing and Sales Promotion, at Levels 3 and 4.

LATE ENTRY

There are no upper age limits for entry but advertising is largely a young person's profession. Fifty per cent of agency staff are under 30, 80 per cent under 40. Mature applicants find entry very difficult unless they have previous relevant experience, such as in marketing or communications work. Some agency staff such as secretaries, media assistants, production assistants and administrative assistants may manage to progress to become account executives.

Account planners have often had previous experience in advertising, research being a common background.

Late entry to media planning and buying is more likely with experience of selling advertising for a media firm or in marketing.

Mature applicants may be considered for the courses described in TRAINING without the usual minimum entry requirements.

OPPORTUNITIES

There are approximately 800 recognized advertising agencies in the UK. Most agencies are small and employ fewer than 50 staff, although two agencies employ over 500. Most of the larger agencies are subsidiaries of American companies and are situated in London.

The Institute of Practitioners in Advertising has 220 member agencies, which employ a total of 11,800 staff. They include most of the larger agencies and account for over 80 per cent of those employed in advertising in the UK. Approximately three-quarters of that 11,800 work in London.

Large agencies are often 'full service agencies' that offer a complete range of advertising services to clients. Many small and medium-sized firms specialize in one area of work and buy in expertise in other areas when required.

The number employed in advertising decreased considerably during the late 1980s and early 1990s but has begun to stabilize. There is always intense competition for all posts. Those seeking to enter advertising should approach agencies direct, rather than seek job advertisements. It can help if applicants have had some voluntary or vacation work experience in an agency.

It is not usual for those in advertising to work abroad, although there may be some opportunities for those who work for multinational agencies.

PAY AND CONDITIONS

Rates of pay vary according to the size of agency and the geographical area, with salaries usually higher in London. The starting salary for a graduate entrant may be between £10,000 and £14,000.

Account executives and account planners earn an average of £16,000, while media executives earn between £20,000 and £26,000. Senior posts for account executives, account planners and media executives can command over £27,000. Copywriters usually earn between £20,000 and £40,000, while successful copywriters working for a top agency may earn over £50,000.

Advertising staff tend to work long, irregular hours, Monday to Friday, although pressure of work can often lead to weekend work.

PROSPECTS

Large agencies have a promotion structure that may allow account executives and account planners to become account supervisors or account directors, media executives to become media directors, while copywriters may become senior copywriters or creative directors. Moving to another agency is common, either for a salary increase or for promotion, although most agencies regularly promote staff internally.

Experienced account executives may set up small advertising agencies of their own, possibly offering a specialist service and buying in expertise as required.

Media executives may transfer to media specialists – organizations that specialize in buying and, sometimes, media planning and research.

Copywriters may become freelance.

RELATED OCCUPATIONS

Market research executive, buyer, public relations officer, graphic designer, illustrator, marketing manager.

FURTHER INFORMATION

Account Planning Group*, 16 Creighton Avenue, London N10 1NU

The Advertising Association*, Abford House, 15 Wilton Road, London SW1V 1NJ, 071 828 4831 (2pm – 4pm, Tue – Thu)

The CAM Foundation*, Abford House, 15 Wilton Road, London SW1V 1NJ, 071 828 7506

Institute of Practitioners in Advertising*, 44 Belgrave Square, London SW1X 8QS

FURTHER READING

Leaflets/booklets are available from the addresses marked*.

Job Outlines – Advertising – COIC
Working in Marketing – COIC
Careers in Marketing, Advertising and Public Relations – Kogan Page
Advertising, Public Relations and Market Research – AGCAS
Getting Into Advertising – The Advertising Association

In the careers library classified under OD.

1. **STORE MANAGER CLCI:OE**
2. **STORE ASSISTANT CLCI:OE**
3. **STORE DEMONSTRATOR CLCI:OE**
4. **SUPERMARKET WORKER CLCI:OE**
5. **TYRE/EXHAUST FITTER CLCI:OFM/RAE**
6. **FORECOURT ATTENDANT CLCI:OFM**
7. **RETAIL BUTCHER CLCI:OFM**
8. **FLORIST CLCI:OFM**
9. **DISPLAY PERSON CLCI:OFM/ET**
10. **SHOE REPAIRER CLCI:OFZ**

BACKGROUND INFORMATION

Retailing is the final stage in getting goods and products to the final user, the consumer. Although it includes mail order operations, its main aspect is the wide variety of shops and stores from which we do our shopping. The retail industry has a workforce of over two million. Some 45 per cent of these work part-time.

Its range covers anything from a market stall to a big chain of supermarkets. The main categories are: small individual or independent shops, often specializing – such as a fashion boutique, a greengrocer or a newsagent; department or variety stores which sell a range of different products, though often with a separate department specializing in each product type (a carpet department, a hardware department, etc); and multiple retailers which operate chains of stores, though these stores may be small or large, specialist or variety, self-service or traditional.

They may be run by an owner/manager whose staff may be mainly members of the family, by a co-operative of friends, or by a limited company whose head office is in the same building, in a town miles away, or, in the case of a multinational, in another country.

The range of specialisms includes chemists, DIY and hardware, books, antiques, builders merchants, cars, clothing and footwear, florists, furniture, jewellery, toys, sports equipment, stationery and office equipment, as well consumer durables like cookers and refrigerators.

The industry is still undergoing change. Supermarkets, hypermarkets and out-of-town shopping centres have already had a major impact on the types, style and location of stores. Electronic tills connected direct to central computers keep a running record of goods sold and initiate re-ordering processes, as well as simplifying analysis of changing consumer demand and staff performance. Giant warehouse-style operations and shopping from home by phone and computer may affect stores in the future. Also, experiments with eliminating cash and having customers in self-service stores tally up their own bills with portable bar-code readers could affect staffing levels.

1. STORE MANAGER (OE)

THE WORK

Store managers are sometimes called retail sales managers or, increasingly, customer services managers, and there are other titles denoting level on a promotion ladder. The manager of an independent store or of a branch of a specialist multiple may, in a department store, be the department manager, sometimes called controller. In fact they may manage more staff and have a bigger sales turnover.

The work of a store manager is similar to that of the store assistant – please see article 2. STORE ASSISTANT – except in self-service stores. Store managers may work as a senior salesperson, selling to customers, dealing with complaints, and leading by example. They deal with problems that junior staff cannot handle, give special attention to regular customers, and listen to their suggestions. They supervise and direct the assistants to ensure that shelves and counters are fully stocked and neat, and that everything is clean, tidy and safe. As managers, they also have to encourage and motivate the assistants in order to meet sales targets devised by themselves or imposed by head office. They draw up rotas for staff, deal with holiday arrangements, interview and recruit new staff, arrange and conduct training, discipline and sometimes dismiss staff who cannot achieve the required standard.

The manager may have responsibility for stockroom staff or for receiving deliveries themselves. They may initiate special offers, promotions of specific items or ranges, and decide or recommend price changes. They may see sales representatives from suppliers, place orders, complain about quality or late delivery, and handle or oversee the accounts. They also deal with paperwork – instructions from head office and forms to complete. They have a responsibility for the security and safety of premises and stock as well as for staff and customers.

Generally, the manager of an independent store is likely to have much more freedom to use their own initiative than a manager within a multiple, who has to work within standardized procedures.

In many stores, there are supervisors and assistant or deputy managers who may handle some of these responsibilities. In some large stores, duties are divided so that a trading or commercial manager looks after stock levels, display areas and their staffing and running, a customer service manager looks after the checkout area and the cash received, and a systems manager oversees the operation of the computerized aspects of the work. In a large department store, there may also be a personnel manager who handles hiring and training, an accounts manager, a marketing manager, a purchasing manager, etc. In a major multiple, these would be roles occupied by senior managers at a regional or head office.

WORK ENVIRONMENT

The offices of managers are often small and cramped and may be windowless, because space devoted to selling goods is more profitable. Except when managing specialist departments such as personnel, store managers are expected to spend as much time as possible supervising in the sales areas and as little as possible on paperwork, telephoning, etc.

The work involves a lot of standing and walking. Sales areas of stores are usually open, light and attractive. All areas of large stores are likely to be lit mainly by artificial light and be air-conditioned.

SKILLS AND INTERESTS

This is a labour-intensive industry, so skills in leading and managing people are essential. This includes the ability to communicate clearly, and to lead and encourage, often by example. Good communication skills, tact and politeness are also important in dealing with customers, when handling their suggestions and criticism. Store managers have to be able to think quickly and take decisions to cope with emergencies and solve often complex problems. They must be able to work within the procedures laid down by the company to ensure efficiency, safety and accuracy. Self-confidence and self-motivation are essential. Attention to detail, ability to plan and set priorities, and analytical skills are all important, as is a constant commercial awareness of the possible impact on takings and profits of any course of action. Managers should know the role of their staff and be able to take over in the event of absence or sickness. Managers are expected to be smartly dressed in the style required by the company. It is often necessary to move to different parts of the country during training and during employment with multiples.

ENTRY REQUIREMENTS

Direct entry to management training schemes operated by medium-sized and large companies is usually between 18 and 23 years. Some of these schemes are open to graduates (degrees in any subject), others accept people with BTEC/SCOTVEC National Certificate/Diploma or Higher National Certificate/Diploma in Business Studies, Distribution or Retailing, and some ask for GNVQ/GSVQ or two A levels/three H grades in any subject. In addition, many companies expect GCSEs/S grades (A-C/1-3) in English and maths. Specialist qualifications may be useful for work in specific sectors such as food marketing or food science for the grocery sector, or a functional department such as accounts.

Entry may be possible for young people through Modern Apprenticeships leading to at least an NVQ/SVQ Level 3. Contact your local careers office, TEC/LEC for details.

Sound health and physical fitness is a requirement and some employers give applicants a medical examination. Employers look for a pleasant personality, neat appearance and evidence of an interest in retailing.

However, many people reach store management after entering as a store assistant and subsequently being placed on a management training course or by working their way up via supervisory positions, sometimes gaining relevant qualifications whilst in employment (see LATE ENTRY). Entry to junior clerical and accounts posts may also offer the possibility of promotion within function departments.

TRAINING

Most management training schemes involve a period as a sales assistant in a selling department followed by attachments in a junior capacity to departments such as buying, marketing, personnel. Training involves gaining experience in positions of greater responsibility in various sales departments or at stores in different parts of the country. Between these assignments are periods that are spent in the company's training department or, for higher level entrants, at a management training college following a specialist course or, for lower level entrants, at an FE college studying for a BTEC/SCOTVEC qualification. Some graduate entry schemes involve study for a postgraduate qualification.

The structure of schemes varies from company to company as does duration. Graduate entry schemes are from three months to 18 months, lower level entry schemes two years.

Training is to NVQ/SVQ Level 3 or 4 in Retail Operations. Modern Apprenticeships also lead to NVQs/SVQs in Retail Operations plus units of Advanced GNVQs/GSVQs in Distribution at Level III and other broad-based skills. For these some training may be off the job in a training centre or FE college. Modern Apprenticeships are expected to average three years.

LATE ENTRY

Though graduate trainee schemes normally recruit people in their early twenties, some of them are officially open to individuals up to 35 years. Other companies accept applicants of any age to management and trainee vacancies if they have supervisory or management experience elsewhere.

Sales and supervisory staff in stores who show ability and potential may be encouraged and assisted to take management courses with a view to promotion. Most companies have a policy of promoting from within. Individuals working as store assistants may increase their chances of promotion to management by taking distance learning courses and exams with bodies such as the Institute of Sales and Marketing Management (ISMM) or the British Shops and Stores Association (BSSA). Other organizations cater for specialist and functional areas.

Anyone may become a manager at any age by raising the necessary finance to buy or rent premises, purchase stock to sell and open their own store.

OPPORTUNITIES

Despite a decline in the total numbers employed in retailing in recent years, the number of managers has declined much less than lower levels of staff. The need for effective management has led to a growing tendency for large concerns to seek management recruits with higher qualifications at higher national certificate/diploma or degree level. Openings still exist for those with lower qualifications. However, competition for places on management training schemes is intense, especially with the major publicly recognized companies.

Stores of all kinds exist in towns and cities throughout Britain but, for major multiple chains, management recruitment is often at national level through company headquarters.

PAY AND CONDITIONS

Salaries differ widely at different points on the promotion ladder. A graduate trainee may start at around £12,000. Managers may earn from £8,000 in a small store or branch to £50,000 plus for a managing director, general manager or chief executive in a large concern. Team and individual bonuses may increase these figures significantly. The range of other benefits also tends to increase with promotion and may include concessions on purchases, subsidized meals, assistance with loans and mortgages, free health insurance, and company cars.

Managers generally tend to start work before other staff and finish afterwards. This leads to long hours, although generally over five days, alternating with other managers to cover Saturdays (and Sundays in some cases). Above junior levels, overtime is not paid for the extra hours.

PROSPECTS

Compared to many industries, retailing offers the possibility of reaching a responsible managerial position very early, often in one's twenties. Department stores and retail chains have established promotion ladders and often have a policy of promoting from within. This may lead from assistant or deputy departmental manager, to departmental manager, to deputy store manager, and store manager, or possibly sideways into a functional department within a big store in a managerial role in one of the functions of personnel, marketing, buying, systems, etc. In a multiple, the ladder may go on to area or district manager, regional manager and national manager, or sideways to management of one of the functions at any of these levels.

In independent stores, the promotion ladder is limited but may give a greater degree of responsibility over a wider range of activities. Experience even at relatively junior management levels is valuable in applying to other retail concerns or if one decides to set up one's own store or take over an existing business. Taking a retail franchise is a step some managers take.

There are chances to work abroad either in the overseas outlets of British chains or by applying directly, once experienced, to overseas companies in Europe, the USA and other countries.

RELATED OCCUPATIONS

Sales manager, buyer, marketing manager, personnel manager, store supervisor, store assistant, warehouse manager, distribution manager, restaurant manager.

FURTHER INFORMATION AND READING

Please see article 4. SUPERMARKET WORKER.

2. STORE ASSISTANT (OE)

THE WORK

Store assistants are also called general assistants, customer care assistants, or sales assistants. The move to self-service in many stores has narrowed the job in these shops to the tasks of making sure shelves and counters are fully stocked and attractively displayed, taking the customer's payment and wrapping or bagging the purchases. (Please see article 4. SUPERMARKET WORKER.) However in many stores, especially department stores and smaller specialist shops and boutiques, the complex and varied task of selling is still important. In larger stores, the trend towards multiskilling means that various duties are rotated among staff, giving greater work variety.

Every customer is different and has different needs, and reasons for coming into the store. Some know exactly what they want, ask for it and buy it, but many are not sure and, if not dealt with correctly, may go somewhere else to buy. The store assistant must assess when and how to ask if the customer wants help, win their confidence with the appropriate amount of questioning about their requirements, and give information and advice about suitable products which might best suit their needs. To do this, assistants draw on their interpersonal skills and also on their product knowledge. Outlining possible payment methods, especially easy-payment ones, may also be important in gaining a sale.

Finally they have to edge the customer into making the decision to buy and 'close the deal'. If the customer is merely assessing possibilities to buy the store assistant offers efficient and friendly service, so that they may return next time they need that type of product or goods. Many stores depend on their regular and repeat customers for survival. Assistants also handle returns and complaints.

Actual tasks vary with the type of product sold. In a men's outfitter, these could include measuring a customer for a suit. In an electronics store, it may be vital to be able to demonstrate how a computer or hi-fi unit works, and to ensure the customer has any accessories they need. In food areas, cutting and weighing the quantities requested may be part of the service.

In smaller independent stores, the work may include tasks such as arranging window and in-store displays, lettering sales and special offer cards, and helping to receive deliveries from suppliers into the stockroom.

WORK ENVIRONMENT

Please see article 1. STORE MANAGER.

Store assistants are normally expected to wear a uniform provided by the employer or to be smartly dressed. They are on their feet most of the time, except for assistants regularly on till duty at checkouts who sit most of the time in a confined area. Most big stores are located in city centres or on the outskirts of urban areas.

SKILLS AND INTERESTS

It takes physical and mental stamina to stand and walk around a store or department for long hours each day. Considerable self-reliance, patience and resilience are needed during quiet periods with few customers and the hectic rush of busy times. They should enjoy working with people and must be able to remain polite even when they are tired, under pressure or dealing with a complaining customer. A lively mind and good memory are valuable in learning about a product range and answering queries or offering advice. They must be able to work in a team yet accept responsibility for their own tasks.

ENTRY REQUIREMENTS

No minimum qualifications are required, though there may be basic tests of reading, writing and ability with numbers. Many employers look for some GCSEs/S grades (A-C/1-3). They also expect physical fitness, normal eyesight (with or without glasses) and hearing. Many companies offer training schemes for young people as an entry route at 16 to 17 years, but entry is possible at later ages.

Entry may be possible for young people through Modern Apprenticeships leading to at least an NVQ/SVQ Level 3. Contact your local careers office, TEC/LEC for details.

Candidates have to be able to speak clearly and present themselves well. An interest in the store and its product range is useful. This means an interest in sports may help in obtaining work in a sportswear and equipment shop, or hi-fi and photography in an electronics or camera store.

TRAINING

In independent stores, a new recruit is likely to be trained on the job by working alongside experienced staff in a succession of duties and departments. At a later point, they may be sent on short courses in sales techniques at training centres or in product knowledge with manufacturers.

In large department stores and multiples, where several assistants may be recruited at the same time, initial training is more likely to be away from the shop floor in a training room or department. It includes company structure and policy, the product range, operation of tills and the various methods of taking payment (cheque, credit card, debit card, etc). Short videos and role-play sessions may be used to teach techniques for handling customers wanting to buy or to complain. Further training may follow after a probationary period.

Specific training opportunities for young people, including Modern Apprenticeships, may be available – contact your local careers office, TEC/LEC for details.

Training programmes may include part-time study at

college for a relevant qualification or NVQs/SVQs in Retail Operations at Levels 1 and 2.

LATE ENTRY

Though there are no age limits, in practice many store assistants are recruited after leaving school or college. However, increasingly employers are recruiting older staff. Some supermarkets and chains now deliberately seek staff over 50 for some positions, though those with some experience of jobs involving contact with the public are likely to be preferred. People returning to work after family commitments are generally welcomed.

OPPORTUNITIES

Numbers employed in retailing have fallen significantly in recent years and many stores have closed, especially in rural areas and smaller communities, with supermarkets taking over from small local shops. However, there are still opportunities in most urban areas. Part-time and temporary work is available in many stores.

Vacancies may be advertised in stores themselves, in local newspapers and in Jobcentres. Even where vacancies are not advertised, direct application to the personnel manager at large stores or at the head office of retail chains should obtain information on recruitment policy and availability of jobs.

PAY AND CONDITIONS

Different sizes and types of employer pay at different rates. Hourly rates average between £2.50 and £3.50, increasing with experience and seniority and sometimes for special skills or knowledge. This may be supplemented by some employers by individual or group commission or bonuses. Seasonal work may be paid at a lower rate.

The basic working week is usually 35 to 39 hours spread over five days. However, most stores open Saturdays (though some close on Mondays), many open late on at least one or two evenings, and an increasing number open on Sundays for a few hours. This may mean working rotas or shifts and overtime, with overtime pay or time off in lieu as compensation. In small local and family shops hours may be very long.

PROSPECTS

Although, with independent stores, promotion possibilities are limited, retail chains, department stores and supermarkets offer opportunities for their own staff who show ability and keenness, for promotion to senior store assistant and supervisor. They may also consider such people for further training, for transfer to a specialist department or for a place on a management training scheme. Many managers in retailing have started as store assistants. Some assistants study in their spare time for appropriate qualifications to improve their chances of promotion. The NVQ/SVQ system of validating growing experience may form a way of proving readiness for promotion. For those with fluency in another language, there may be the possibility of work for a branch of a British multiple store in a European country.

RELATED OCCUPATIONS

Counter service assistant, supermarket worker, receptionist, store demonstrator, forecourt attendant, store supervisor, store manager, ticket agency clerk, travel agency clerk.

FURTHER INFORMATION AND READING

Please see article 4. SUPERMARKET WORKER.

3. STORE DEMONSTRATOR (OZ)

THE WORK

Demonstrators show potential customers in a store or at an exhibition or roadshow how to use an appliance or gadget, explain the advantages of a product, offer free samples or tastings of food or drink, and hand out leaflets or recipe cards, stickers, badges or cut-price coupons. Their purpose is to promote interest in a new product or increase sales of an established product.

Freelance demonstrators are normally hired by a manufacturer or supplier or, sometimes, by a large store, to promote a product. This could be a washing machine or a washing powder, an item or range of food, drink or confectionery such as French cheeses, household goods, a DIY tool, or a kitchen gadget such as a new fruit and potato peeler.

The demonstrator receives a training session or written brief about the item, so that they can talk knowledgeably about it and answer questions. They may use wording provided or have to prepare their own speech. They set up a table or specially made unit in the relevant department of the store or at the manufacturer's or supplier's exhibition stand. They unpack and put out examples of the product and any accessories needed such as glasses for a wine-tasting, portions of cheese, a small grill for cooking sausage samples, lengths of carpet for demonstrating a carpet cleaner, etc. For some items, a small room, area or theatre with seating may be provided and demonstrations advertised for set times. They may offer samples or a demonstration to individuals passing, by or draw a small audience around them before starting their routine.

The demonstrator may be responsible for ensuring point-of-sale material about the product is displayed on the shelves where it is sold, and for taking some record of sales before and during the promotion period. Promotions often coincide with a TV or poster advertising campaign. In some instances, a competition may be involved, or an element of consumer research requiring forms to be completed and returned to their employer.

At the end of the promotion they pack up and leave the area clean and tidy. They may be engaged for one or a few days, a week or for the duration of an exhibition. They may travel with a roadshow, or visit stores or pubs in different towns or areas on successive days.

WORK ENVIRONMENT

Demonstrators work in all kinds of stores, shopping centres (indoors and outside), pubs and hotels, exhibitions, motorway service stations, etc. They may need their own transport and spend time travelling between locations. In some cases, overnight stays may be involved.

Work situations are usually pleasant but may be crowded. Demonstrators stand for long periods. They may have to wear a uniform or costume and an apron or tabard and hat are supplied when handling foodstuffs. Otherwise they wear their own clothes but are expected to maintain a smart appearance.

SKILLS AND INTERESTS

Demonstrators should be sociable, self-confident and able to converse easily with strangers of a variety of ages and backgrounds. They need to remain cheerful and friendly, however unsympathetic the response of their audience may be. A clear voice that projects well is important.

Manual dexterity may be needed and the ability to learn quickly both how to use a new product and the information about it. Demonstrators have to appear to believe fully in the value of the items, whatever their personal preferences.

Although demonstrators may work with a wide variety of goods, individual promotions may be repetitive. Resilience and a sense of humour are essential, as well as the energy and physical stamina to stand in one place for long periods.

Owning a car and a clean driving licence may be important.

ENTRY REQUIREMENTS

A clear speaking voice and attractive appearance are essential requirements. No exam qualifications are needed but knowledge of the retail industry, and experience or qualifications in home economics, technology, cookery, bar work and DIY activities can help obtain certain types of demonstrating engagements.

Demonstrators are normally hired through marketing services companies, employment agencies, model agencies or performers' agencies. To register with such companies and agencies, individuals may need to show good photographs of themselves, both portrait and full length in smart clothes, together with a cv giving relevant experience such as performance/modelling, public speaking, teaching, work as a store assistant, party plan or catalogue selling. Most demonstrators are aged 20 years and over but some individuals are younger.

A Food Hygiene Certificate may be needed for demonstration involving food.

TRAINING

There are no training courses for this occupation. Some marketing or merchandising agencies which keep a register of approved demonstrators run short training programmes for new candidates which cover persuasion techniques, how to handle questions and complaints, safety, hygiene and food handling, and aspects of appearance and body language.

Those engaged to demonstrate more technical products may attend briefing sessions given by the manufacturer or supplier to learn their features. Some types of presentation may require briefings/rehearsals in ways of moving and speaking in a special costume, slogans and catchphrases.

Courses which provide certificates in elocution, public speaking, acting, modelling, selling, cookery and homecrafts may be useful.

One-day courses leading to a certificate in food hygiene are available at many FE colleges and training centres.

LATE ENTRY

Many agencies only accept applications from people over 20 years. Some product demonstrations may call for a specific age-range of demonstrator.

OPPORTUNITIES

Most store demonstrators work on a freelance basis. To obtain a reasonable amount of work, it is sensible to register with several agencies. Once registered with a few agencies, work should be possible but this may average no more than a day or two a week even for the most popular demonstrators. Few people make a full living as demonstrators and there is always considerable competition for the available work. A few stores employ their own demonstrators, usually at specific times of the year such as Christmas. Obtaining the first engagement is the most difficult, but, after a few successful engagements, obtaining work usually becomes easier.

Generally, there is more demonstration work in London and the big cities, though even here it varies considerably by region.

PAY AND CONDITIONS

Freelance demonstrating is paid at a daily rate of £30 to £60 a day. Rates are higher in London and major cities. Travel, subsistence and incidental expenses may be paid. Engagements are normally only for one or a few days but may last for several weeks. They are usually on days when stores are busiest, ie Thursday, Friday, Saturday, and may extend into evening opening hours. Most work often takes place over periods such as Christmas, Easter, bank holidays or local anniversaries or festivals. A day's hiring is normally eight hours, excluding travel time, but may be longer. Tea and meal breaks may be allowed.

PROSPECTS

As this is a freelance occupation, promotion prospects are limited. Some demonstrators are engaged regularly or full-time by marketing, merchandising or advertising companies as field supervisors or booking agents to supervise and/or book demonstrators. This may open up channels into other aspects of marketing, merchandising or promotions.

It may also be possible to move into party plan selling where similar skills are required.

RELATED OCCUPATIONS

Store assistant, market research interviewer, telephone salesperson, merchandiser, receptionist, beauty consultant, catalogue sales agent, party plan sales agent.

FURTHER INFORMATION AND READING

Please see article 4. SUPERMARKET WORKER.

4. SUPERMARKET WORKER (OE)

BACKGROUND INFORMATION

Supermarkets differ from most other types of store since they are self-service. As the customer selects products from shelves themselves, the sales function performed by store assistants in other stores is eliminated. Most supermarkets are based on grocery products, but the same principles are applied in some cases, to clothing, DIY products, and other areas. This field includes medium and large supermarkets, superstores, hypermarkets, and cash and carry operations.

THE WORK

The main operations are: receiving products from delivery trucks into the warehouse or stockroom attached to the shop floor; placing the products onto the shelves as needed and possibly attaching prices to them; and taking payment from the customer. These may be seen as separate jobs or stages in a training and promotion process. These duties may be rotated among staff providing variety of work known as multiskilling. In smaller neighbourhood supermarkets, the same workers may perform all these tasks at different times during the day or week.

Checkout operator

The checkout operator sits at an electronic till and feeds into the till the prices of goods chosen by the customer. This is increasingly done by passing each item over a device that reads the bar-code on it and automatically registers this in the till. In other cases, the operator presses numerical keys to enter the price or may use a light-pen to read a code. They may weigh some products such as fruit on a weighing scale by the till. When the till provides a total, the operator takes payment in cash, by cheque or by credit or debit card, and gives a till receipt and any change required. They provide plastic bags and may help the customer to pack. They change paper till rolls when necessary, and make sure there is enough change, credit card forms, and plastic bags. The operator rings a bell or buzzer to summon a supervisor to help with problems, and bags up notes and cheques for periodic collection. They enter their personal details and start and finish time in the till, so that their performance can be analysed later. General cleanliness and tidiness of the till area is their responsibility.

They may also have to deal with customers changing their mind or not having enough money to pay for the full load, broken or split packaging, unreadable or missing price labels and other problems.

Shelf fillers

Working under instruction from a supervisor, shelf fillers take quantities of products from the warehouse or stockroom on a wheeled trolley into the store. They place these onto the appropriate shelves, display stands or refrigerator cabinets, making sure that the older items remain at the front. If the packages are not already priced by bar-code or otherwise, they use a gun to attach small sticky labels with the price to each item. They generally clean and tidy shelf and display areas, clear any breakages or spillages, and answer questions from customers or call a supervisor for any they cannot answer. They may also have the duty of moving empty baskets and trolleys from the checkout area to where customers enter. Major shelf refilling work may be done by part-time staff after closing time.

Warehouse/stockroom staff

They receive and check in deliveries from suppliers or the company's main warehouse and move them by lift truck or hand truck onto the correct racks and shelves in the warehouse/stockroom. They may unpack some products from larger containers. They may take quantities off the racks and load them onto hand trolleys for the shelf fillers.

Supervisors

Most large supermarkets have a number of supervisors on duty at any time. They direct the shelf fillers and are available to answer queries from customers and staff and to deal with problems as they arise. They may also collect money from tills, bring extra change and other supplies to operators, move staff to different duties to deal with customer demand, and tell staff when to go for mealbreaks. Some supervisors act as managers of specialist areas.

Specialist workers

Some supermarkets contain within them specialist areas which operate like small shops with products which do require individual attention to make, prepare or serve.

Principal among these are: butcher areas, where meat is cut or minced, weighed and packed into suitable portions; bakery areas, where bread and pastries may be baked and packed; and delicatessen counters, where cooked meats, cheeses and salads are sliced, weighed and portioned often to individual order. These workers need appropriate skills and knowledge of hygiene rules.

WORK ENVIRONMENT

The store area of supermarkets is usually a big open space with rows of shelving and cabinets divided by wide gangways. Despite this functional layout, they are usually decorated in light colours, have good even lighting and are warm. Specialist areas may be like their small shop equivalents: meat and fish areas may be cooled with refrigerated areas, bakeries may be hot because of ovens, sometimes in view of the customers. Warehouses/stockrooms are big open spaces with tall racks. They also have refrigerated coldstores for meat, fish and frozen foods, and chilled areas for other perishables. Checkout operators work in a very restricted space. Some aspects of warehouse and shelf-filling work may be dirty and messy.

Supermarket workers are usually required to wear distinctive uniforms supplied by the employer. This often includes a hat, especially in areas of high hygiene requirements. Plastic gloves are worn for handling unwrapped foods.

SKILLS AND INTERESTS

A pleasant, polite personality and patience are important in dealing with customers and coping with their problems and complaints. Supermarket workers must be willing to work under close supervision. The ability to work fast and accurately is called for, especially on checkouts, where performance is measured from till records via the computer. The lifting, bending and stretching involved in shelf filling and warehouse work demands physical fitness.

Workers must be honest and trustworthy.

ENTRY REQUIREMENTS

There are no minimum academic requirements, though there may be basic tests of reading, writing and ability with numbers. Some employers look for a few GCSE/S grades (A-C/1-3). They also expect physical fitness, normal eyesight (with or without glasses) and hearing. Many companies offer training schemes as an entry route at 16 to 17 years, but entry is possible at later ages.

Previous experience in retailing in a part-time capacity or in work involving contact with the public helps in obtaining full-time employment. Staff for specialist areas may be recruited from those with experience and training in these fields in independent butchers, bakers, etc.

TRAINING

Supermarkets in large chains give a short induction training in a training room. This covers company policy on employment, welfare, holidays, health and safety, and food and hygiene. Some tuition is given in store and warehouse/stockroom layout, range of products and stock control systems, use of any tools such as trolleys and sticker guns, and safe lifting techniques. Unless recruited specifically for checkout duties, instruction in use of the till may follow at a later stage. This is complex and is normally given away from the shop floor though linked into the computer by a training simulation programme. Tuition in cheque and credit card handling procedures is also given. A period of working under supervision of experienced workers follows. Trainees may handle duties like bagging up customers' purchases during busy periods and checking missing prices or replacing damaged packets. Warehouse/stockroom workers may be sent on a short course in lift truck operation after an initial period of work. Workers in specialist areas may receive training in the specific craft involved.

In independent supermarkets, training on the job is the common practice, with the new recruits receiving instruction from an experienced worker in the simpler activities and performing these before moving to instruction and practice in the more complex and responsible areas.

Specific training opportunities for young people, including Modern Apprenticeships, may be available – contact your local careers office, TEC/LEC for details.

Training to NVQ/SVQ in Retail Operations at Levels 1 and 2 is available.

LATE ENTRY

Though there are no age limits, in practice many store assistants are recruited after leaving school or college (or before that for part-time work). However, increasingly employers are recruiting older applicants. Some supermarkets now deliberately seek staff over 50 for some positions, though those with some experience of jobs involving contact with the public are likely to be preferred. Those with experience in specialist shops such as butchers may be recruited directly as supervisors of specialist areas.

OPPORTUNITIES

There are supermarkets in most towns and cities, though superstores and hypermarkets are much fewer and generally on large sites away from towns. Despite the decline in the retail industry in recent years and the impact of electronic till systems on staffing levels, the number of self-service stores continues to grow. Recruitment is more or less continuous, due to promotion and people leaving for study or other types of work, and is usually handled at local store level.

PAY AND CONDITIONS

Different employers pay at different rates. Hourly rates average between £2.50 and £3.50 an hour, increasing with experience and for skills in a specialist area. Some employers pay group bonuses to staff for meeting sales targets for the store.

The basic working week is usually 39 hours spread over five or five-and-a-half days. Saturday working may be obligatory. Many supermarkets open late on at least two evenings, and an increasing number open on Sundays for a few hours. This may mean working rotas or shifts and overtime, with overtime pay or time off in lieu as compensation. In neighbourhood supermarkets, hours may be very long.

Supermarkets in large chains usually offer a subsidized canteen and staff concessions on purchases in the store.

PROSPECTS

Many supermarket chains have a policy of promoting from within, at least to supervisor level. Workers who show ability and enthusiasm may be offered supervisory training.

Some go on from this to management training to become supermarket managers or even move into senior management. Such promotion may involve having to move to other parts of the country.

The possibility of promotion in independent supermarkets is more limited, but experience in them could form a good basis for applying for posts with larger concerns. Some workers study in their own time for relevant qualifications, which make them eligible for supervisory or managerial posts or for management training schemes.

RELATED OCCUPATIONS

Store assistant, counter service assistant, store demonstrator, forecourt attendant, supermarket manager, ticket office clerk, box office clerk, warehouse worker.

FURTHER INFORMATION

British Shops and Stores Association (BSSA)*, Middleton House, 2 Main Road, Middleton Cheney, Oxfordshire OX17 2TN, 01295 712277

National Retail Training Council (NRTC)*, Bedford House, 69-79 Fulham High Street, London SW6 3JQ, 0171 371 5021

Distributive Industries Training Trust (DITT)*, 5 Bridge Street, Bishop's Stortford, Hertfordshire CM23 2JU, 01279 506125

Scottish Distributive Industries Training Council, The Alpha Centre, University of Stirling, Stirling FK9 4NF, 01786 51661

Institute of Grocery Distribution*, Careers Information Service, Grange Lane, Letchmore Heath, Watford, Hertfordshire WD2 8DQ, 01923 857141

Consortium of Retail Training Companies (CORTCO), Bedford House, 69-79 Fulham High Street, London SW6 3JW, 0171 371 5185

London College of Printing and Distributive Trades*, 30 Leicester Square, London WC2H 7LE, 0171 839 1547

FURTHER READING

Leaflets/booklets are available from addresses marked*.

Job Outlines – Shop Work – COIC
Working in Retail Industry – COIC
Retailing and Buying – AGCAS
Careers in Retailing – Kogan Page
Running Your Own Shop – Kogan Page
Marketing, Retailing and Sales Casebook – Hobsons
A Guide to Careers: Retailing and Wholesaling – DITT

In the careers library classified under OE.

5. TYRE/EXHAUST FITTER (OFM/RAE)

BACKGROUND INFORMATION

Tyre and exhaust fitters work alongside mechanics in garages and commercial and public service vehicle workshops, and in specialist tyre and exhaust centres.

In garages, it is usually up to the tyre/exhaust fitters to decide on whether tyres are so damaged or worn as to require repair or replacement, although customers may initially have been informed by a mechanic carrying out a repair or MOT test. In the larger tyre and exhaust fitting centres, instructions and work assignments usually come from supervisors.

THE WORK

Tyre/exhaust fitters check and fit tyres and exhausts to vehicles. Some may only carry out tyre fitting, although many fit both tyres and exhausts. They may work on cars or light vehicles or large goods/public service vehicles.

Tyre fitting

Cars and light vehicles. It is usual to replace a damaged tyre rather than attempt a repair, as modern car tyres are mostly tubeless. The first step is to remove the wheel from the vehicle; in most tyre and exhaust centres, large garages and workshops this is done very quickly, by raising the vehicle on a hydraulic jack or ramp and using semi-automatic machines to remove the wheels from the axles. In small garages, however, the work is often still done by hand – the hub-cap/wheel trim is removed, the wheel nuts are loosened with a box spanner or power tool, the axle is raised with a jack until the wheel clears the ground, the wheel nuts are removed and the wheel is taken off. The valve is then removed, and the tyre is deflated and separated from the wheel. Again, this may either be done on an automatic machine that breaks the seal between tyre and wheel, or by hand on a wheel stand, breaking the seal on each side using a hand tool and levering the tyre free. The above steps are reversed when fitting the replacement tyre.

The wheel must then be 'balanced' on a balancing machine to ensure even wear in road use and avoid steering vibration. A machine is run to rotate the wheel, and an indicator is read to determine the size and position of lead weights that are attached to the wheel rim. The machine is then re-run to check that the wheel is in balance. In some garages, fitters may also adjust the brake shoes and brakes of a vehicle for maximum efficiency and safety.

Fitters may also advise customers on whether tyres need switching round to even out wear patterns, on which treads are best to use according to their driving needs, and on legal requirements for tread depth and tyre type.

Large goods/public service/passenger vehicles. In large-vehicle garages and workshops, fitters undertake regular inspections of the tyres looking for stones, nails and so on, embedded in the tyre, and any serious cuts or cracks. The stones/nails are removed, the tyre pressure is checked and the fitter decides if the tyres need repositioning because of wear, or need repair or replacement. To remove tyres from commercial vehicles up to twelve tons, procedures are as for light vehicles, but the removal of tyres for vehicles over twelve tons is more complicated. The size of the wheels makes them awkward to handle, and special equipment is needed to remove and replace them. Once the tyre is removed it is inspected on the inside for any defects and it is then repaired or replaced. Special care is again taken when assembling and re-inflating the tyres; large vehicle tyres must be inflated within a protective steel cage. In some workshops and depots, the wheels are removed and replaced by mechanics, though any check and repair work is carried out by the tyrefitters.

Field duties. Some fitters work on agricultural and construction plant vehicles on-site. This mainly involves using a water pump to pump water into tyres to act as ballast for large vehicles.

Exhaust fitting

This requires a wider range of tools than tyre fitting, and is carried out on both cars and light vehicles and large goods and public service vehicles. The vehicle is lifted up on a ramp, the manifold is unbolted and the straps holding the exhaust onto the vehicle are undone. The faulty parts are then replaced and the exhaust refitted to the vehicle.

WORK ENVIRONMENT

Fitters work in awkward places, sometimes in cramped conditions, for example, lying down under a car. Some workshops can accommodate several large lorries at a time, whilst others are much smaller. All are equipped with work benches, power tools, ramps and pits. Strong artificial lights may be used, and the work is oily and greasy.

SKILLS AND INTERESTS

This is heavy and dirty work, especially if done by hand, so candidates should be physically fit, able to stand all day and do heavy lifting and carrying. Fitters may also work in cramped conditions, when working under a car.

As team work is involved it requires a person that can get on well with work-mates. Fitters dealing with the public need to be polite and be able to explain things clearly and give customers advice. They may have to handle cash and credit card transactions, so require numerical ability.

ENTRY REQUIREMENTS

No educational qualifications are required. Some employers require their fitters to be able to drive or be willing to learn. Evidence of practical ability (for example, qualifications in school subjects such as technology) and/or an interest in motor vehicles may be an advantage. For entry to C&G 3981 Exhaust Fitting, there are no minimum academic requirements.

TRAINING

Training is on the job, working alongside an experienced fitter. Some companies also have their own internal training programmes. Trainees learn the exact procedure to adopt depending on the type of tyre involved, which tools and equipment to use, which tyre types are best for various makes and size of motor vehicles, and which combinations of tyres are best for certain types of motoring. They must also know the standard rate of pressures for tyres of various makes of vehicles. It can take as little as six weeks to train a fitter to a reasonable standard in one of the specialist fitting centres, but to become a fully trained fitter, able to work on all sorts of vehicles and use all types of equipment, can take up to two years. NVQs/SVQs in Vehicle Maintenance: Service Replacement are available at Levels 1 and 2. Fitters can also study for City and Guilds qualifications such as C&G 3981 Exhaust Fitting. This is usually obtained through day release at a local college.

LATE ENTRY

No upper age limit is set, but the heavy physical nature of the job demands a very high standard of physical fitness, which limits opportunities for those over 40 years.

OPPORTUNITIES

The major employers of fitters are the specialist tyre and exhaust centres. Their purpose is to provide a quick tyre/exhaust replacement service for car owners. Garages vary from one or two-person businesses to big main dealers specializing in a certain make of vehicle. The smaller businesses do not generally employ tyre/exhaust fitters. Transport firms employ tyre fitters in their workshops to carry out regular inspections, repairs and maintenance work on commercial/passenger vehicles.

PAY AND CONDITIONS

The average rate of pay for a tyre or exhaust mechanic or fitter is about £146 for a 39-hour week, Monday to Friday. Most fitters do some overtime in the evenings and at weekends, boosting average earnings to £165 plus, a week.

Fitters employed by transport companies do most of the work at night when most of the firm's vehicles are off the road; such fitters will usually work shifts. Many tyre and exhaust fitting centres offer a Monday to Sunday service, with late evening opening. Staff work a duty rota with days off in lieu.

PROSPECTS

Experienced fitters working for specialist tyre and exhaust fitting centres or large garages or workshops can progress to supervisory positions. In the smaller establishments, however, there may be no opportunity to progress without moving to a larger firm.

RELATED OCCUPATIONS

Auto-electrician, motor vehicle body repairer, AA/RAC patrolman/woman, motor vehicle technician/mechanic, motor partsman/woman.

FURTHER INFORMATION AND READING

Please see article 6. FORECOURT ATTENDANT.

6. FORECOURT ATTENDANT (OFM)

BACKGROUND INFORMATION

Forecourt attendants work for petrol filling stations. Some filling stations offer an attended service where the forecourt attendant (also known as a petrol pump attendant) puts petrol or diesel into the customer's car. Most, however, are self-service; the forecourt attendant acts primarily as a cashier, performing similar duties to those of a cash till operator at any other retail outlet.

THE WORK

Attended service

The attendant asks how much petrol/diesel the customer wants. Various types of petrol are available, such as unleaded and four star, which can be measured in gallons, litres or money value, for example £5 worth. The attendant establishes what type of petrol the customer wants, and removes the car's petrol filler cap. The nozzle of the petrol pump is then put into the tank, checking that all the pump dials have returned to zero, before putting in the required amount of petrol. The attendant then replaces the filler cap and returns the petrol pump nozzle to its housing, before taking the customer's money and issuing change.

Some customers may require additional services such as filling up with oil or water, checking battery and brake fluid levels, checking and adjusting tyre pressures, or washing windows and lights.

Self-service stations

Forecourt attendants spend most of their time in an office as a cashier.

Customers come to the forecourt and help themselves to air, petrol and water before coming into the office/shop to pay for their purchases. The attendant operates a 'console' machine which has a series of lights and buttons relating to each petrol pump on the forecourt. When a pump is in use a button lights up. When the nozzle is replaced the 'pay' sign lights up and the console displays the amount of petrol sold and the price. The attendant can then re-set the pump dials to zero in preparation for the next customer. If a customer leaves the forecourt without paying for their petrol, the attendant must note their registration number and telephone the police immediately.

Most other functions are common to both self-service and attended petrol stations. Many customers pay cash for their petrol; the amount must be entered on a cash register and change given. Modern cash registers display how much change should be given but in other stations the attendant will need to calculate this. The attendant must also know how to deal with cheques and debit/credit card sales. Regular customers at the garage may hold an account whereby they just sign a receipt for their petrol and a bill is sent to them – usually on a monthly basis.

Many stations have a shop where they sell a range of foods, sweets, drinks and cigarettes, and car accessories such as dusters, polishes and sponges. Some also stock a small supply of replacement parts, for example thermostats, windscreen wiper blades, bulbs and fuses. The attendant may need to advise the customer on what type they need for their car.

At the end of each working day, or in 24-hour stations at the end of each shift, the attendant balances the cash in the till with the purchases recorded by the till. They also read a meter on each petrol pump and compare the readings with those taken at the start of a shift. The pump readings should correlate with the recorded sales on the cash register. Cashiers must be very security conscious and most companies enforce a maximum amount which should be held in the cash register at any one time. Anything over this amount should be transferred to the safe and a record kept of all such transfers.

In addition to sales work, attendants perform a number of other tasks concerned with the day-to-day running of the station such as dealing with petrol deliveries; re-ordering supplies for the shop; keeping the forecourt area safe, clean and tidy (including cleaning toilets); and giving directions to motorists.

WORK ENVIRONMENT

At self-service stations, attendants spend most of the shift indoors in the office/shop, only going outside occasionally to take readings from pumps, deal with petrol deliveries, etc.

At petrol filling stations with attended service, attendants work outdoors for most of the time in all types of weather conditions. The smell of petrol fumes can be quite strong. Forecourt attendants work largely alone with minimum supervision.

SKILLS AND INTERESTS

Attendants must be able to get on well with people and should have a pleasant, polite and helpful manner. For large parts of the day they will have control over the station and must therefore be able to work with minimal supervision. It is important to work well under pressure without becoming flustered and making mistakes. Forecourt staff handle large sums of money, so must be trustworthy and security conscious.

An interest in cars and some mechanical ability is an advantage.

ENTRY REQUIREMENTS

No minimum educational qualifications are required. Some employers set an arithmetic test at the interview. Local by-laws set minimum ages for people able to sell petrol; this is usually 18 years, but can vary from area to area.

TRAINING

Training takes place on the job under the supervision of an experienced attendant or other qualified individual. Trainees learn how to use the petrol pumps in an attended station, how to use the console in a self-service station and how to operate the cash register. They are also shown the various routine maintenance tasks, such as how to change the till rolls, how to balance cash a the end of the shift and how to cancel a sale that has been entered incorrectly. Where relevant they will also be trained on how to handle deliveries of fuel to the site. All training emphasizes the importance of health and safety awareness.

Forecourt attendants need to be familiar with company procedures for dealing with cheques, credit/debit cards and customer accounts. NVQs/SVQs are being developed in Petrol Retailing.

LATE ENTRY

This work is ideally suited to adults. Many employers favour older applicants due to the responsibility of working alone in the station and handling large sums of cash.

OPPORTUNITIES

Forecourt attendants are employed by all types of filling station. Many stations operate under franchise from the oil companies. Some stations are attached to garages offering car sales and/or servicing and repairs. Others are linked to supermarkets. Filling stations are found throughout the country with higher concentrations in urban areas. Staff turnover is quite high, so jobs occur quite regularly in most areas.

PAY AND CONDITIONS

The average rate for forecourt staff is £131 for a 39-hour week. Earnings can be improved by additional payments for overtime and unsocial hours including nights, weekends and bank holidays.

Filling stations are usually open for long hours, and some are open 24 hours a day, so shift work is often available. Many stations are open from about 8am to 10pm; they usually operate a two-shift system whereas 24-hour stations usually have a three-shift system. Saturday, Sunday and bank holiday working is normal, with compensatory time off in the week.

There are many opportunities for part-time work, often covering just the evening period or weekends and bank holidays.

PROSPECTS

Prospects of progression into managerial positions is severely limited for those without qualifications.

Attendants who particularly enjoy handling cash and helping other people may find that jobs in other areas of retailing are open to them. Those whose particular interest is in cars may find it possible to progress into car sales work or tyre/exhaust fitting.

RELATED OCCUPATIONS

Store assistant, supermarket worker, tyre/exhaust fitter, counter service assistant, filling station manager.

FURTHER INFORMATION

The Motor Industry Training Standards Council, 201 Great Portland Street, London, W1N 6AB, 0171 436 6373

Retail Motor Industry Federation Ltd*, 201 Great Portland Street, London W1N 6AB, 0171 580 9122

The Scottish Motor Trade Association*, 3 Palmerston Place, Edinburgh EH12 5AF, 0131 225 3643

FURTHER READING

Leaflets/booklets are available from the addresses marked*.

In the careers library classified under OFM.

7. RETAIL BUTCHER (OFM)

BACKGROUND INFORMATION

The meat retailing sector is the major employer in the meat industry. Some 70,000 people work in independent retailers and 8,000 in the meat operations of supermarkets and multiple stores. This article is concerned particularly with the independent retailers.

Retail butchers' shops increasingly offer a range of foods – including cheeses and delicatessen – as well as meat. Customers are demanding higher quality and a wider choice of goods, particularly products such as stir-fry or kebabs.

THE WORK

The main activity is selling meat and related products. Retail butchers need a thorough knowledge of the products they are selling, so that they can advise customers and answer enquiries about preparation, cooking, nutrition, etc.

In some shops, one or more staff work in a back room, cutting, boning and trimming meat to prepare it for sale, whilst staff at the front of the shop concentrate on serving customers. Both in the back room and in the store itself, staff must maintain a high standard of safety and hygiene.

Meat arrives at butchers' shops as carcasses, bone-in primal cuts and boneless pre-packed primal cuts, from which butchers prepare joints, chops, mince and meat products.

Buying and ordering supplies is an important part of the work; butchers need to take into account the quantities they have in stock and the anticipated demand – for instance, customers usually buy more joints in colder months, whereas in the summer, when barbecues are popular, there is a greater demand for chops, chicken joints, burgers and steaks.

Some retail butchers visit meat markets to purchase supplies. Others receive deliveries from wholesalers. When a delivery arrives, it is important to check the contents against the order form. Stock is transferred from the supplier's van either manually, or with trolleys, hoists, lifts, etc. The meat is examined, any unsuitable products are rejected, and supplies are then transferred to the coldstore. Operating the coldstore involves following the correct procedures governing temperature indicators and controls. (There are legal requirements governing temperature and hygiene in meat retailing.)

Another important aspect of the work is setting up attractive, eye-catching displays in the store, using both the shop window and internal display cabinets. Sometimes there are practical promotions to arrange (for example, encouraging customers to buy more lamb), with posters and leaflets advising customers on preparation and cooking.

Accurate handling and processing of payments is essential, as in all retail operations. Butchers need to operate the till and understand payment procedures. They weigh many purchases, using either electronic or manual scales, and wrap products hygienically. They may use an automatic ticketing system.

Some retail butchers run their own delivery services.

Butchers working in supermarkets are mainly backroom staff, engaged in cutting, boning and packaging. There is less contact with customers than in independent retailers' shops. However, there is a trend to develop in-store serve-over butchery counters within supermarkets.

WORK ENVIRONMENT

Butchers' shops are generally well-ventilated and well-lit. The selling area is maintained at a controlled, cool temperature. Staff also enter chill rooms and cold stores, mostly for brief periods.

Much of the working day is spent standing. Unloading and storing stock involves lifting and carrying, although mechanical aids may be used.

Some jobs involve driving vans to markets, wholesalers and customers' premises – for these posts, a full driving licence is required.

SKILLS AND INTERESTS

It is important to enjoy meeting customers and advising them on choice of products, cooking and preparation. An outgoing personality is essential for success as a retail butcher. Good spoken communication skills, with the ability to listen as well as to give information, are required. Butchers work as a team and need to be able to get on well with colleagues.

An interest in cooking and a taste for good food is a distinct advantage. Some visual flair is useful for producing attractive window/counter displays.

Butchers need manual dexterity and good hand-to-eye co-ordination for cutting and preparing meat.

Personal cleanliness and strict attention to hygiene are essential.

Numeracy is required for cash handling.

ENTRY REQUIREMENTS

No specific educational qualifications are required, although The Meat Training Council recommends entrants have GCSEs/S grades (A-D/1-4) in English, maths and a science subject. Some larger firms may set aptitude tests. A Saturday job or work experience placement in a butcher's shop is a useful background for applicants.

Completion of a training scheme for young people (as an unemployed trainee) and attainment of NVQ Meat Processing (Retailing) at Level 2 is an advantage for those seeking employment with retail butchers.

TRAINING

For school-leavers, the most common route is via training schemes for young people. Training both on and off the job normally lasts two years and can lead to an NVQ in Meat Processing (Retailing) at Level 2. Contact your local careers office, TEC/LEC for details.

Opportunities may be available to train via Modern Apprenticeships leading to at least an NVQ Level 3 in Supervisory Management (Meat Processing).

To attain the NVQ in Meat Processing (Retailing) at Level 2, trainees have to reach set standards in a specified number of units. These include hygiene and cleaning procedures, use of tools and equipment for cutting and boning, displaying and selling meat and meat products, and health, safety and security procedures. Optional additional units may be taken by those wishing to gain a wider level of competence. Units are awarded on the basis of continuous assessment at training centres and in the workplace. Holders of NVQ Level 2 are eligible to become affiliates of the Worshipful Company of Butchers, Guild of Freemen.

In Scotland, the Scottish Federation of Meat Traders' Associations runs an on-the-job training scheme for independent retailers, based on the assessment of competencies in the workplace. It leads to awards at two levels, accredited as SVQs. Level 1 is an introductory award, particularly for those who enter retail butchers as trainees; Level 2 is a more detailed assessment of craft training and is a recognized qualification for entry into more advanced courses. The length of training is flexible, but generally a trainee would take three to four years to reach Level 2.

The Meat Training Council offers further qualifications leading to associateship and graduate membership. These are aimed at those seeking advancement in the industry. They include modules in: abattoir; catering butchery; manufacturing plant; poultry industry; retailing; supermarket butchery; and wholesale distribution. Each module is accompanied by practical training and experience, and there is a written and practical examination.

Over 50 educational establishments offer courses leading to the Meat Training Council qualifications; most also offer NVQs/SVQs. Courses are generally part-time, over two years, but one-year full-time courses are available at some centres.

Opportunities for specialist study and work experience abroad are available through the Worshipful Company of Butchers Guild. Participants can gain experience in the continental meat trade and study specialist subjects such as *charcuterie*.

LATE ENTRY

Traditionally, employers have preferred to recruit school-leavers. However, as the number of 16-year-olds is declining, there may be better opportunities for adults, particularly those with experience in other retail sectors, to enter this type of work.

Related NVQs or SVQs are useful; it may be possible for adults with experience, who lack formal qualifications, to gain NVQs/SVQs via Accreditation of Prior Learning (APL). Further information is available from the Meat Training Council.

There may be specific training opportunities directed at adults available in some areas for this type of work. Candidates may have to satisfy certain conditions to be eligible. Contact your local Jobcentre, careers office or TEC/LEC for details.

OPPORTUNITIES

In the independent retail sector there are opportunities for employment with firms that run a single shop, or a chain of shops. Traditionally, many independent retailers have been family businesses, handed down from generation to generation, but this is now becoming less common. However, there are opportunities for others – without family connections but with training and experience as retail butchers – to start their own businesses.

In some areas (mainly in large cities) there are halal and kosher butchers catering for the specialist needs of local communities.

PAY AND CONDITIONS

Wage rates and hours of work are a matter of negotiation between employer and employee. Rates of pay vary considerably in different areas of the country. In general terms, for a 40-hour week, 18-year-olds earn between £83 and £130 a week; general assistants, aged 20 or over, £127 to £156 a week; skilled butchers £152 to £204 a week; shop managers £189 to £250 a week. Paid overtime may be available.

Most butchers work Saturdays, with a day off during the week. Part-time work may be available.

PROSPECTS

There are opportunities, particularly in supermarkets and major chains, for rapid progress. Many people reach managerial positions in their twenties.

It is possible, after further training, to become a meat inspector. The Royal Society of Health (RSH) qualification for meat inspectors may be taken after the associateship of the Meat Training Council, via a one-year part-time course, or as part of a one-year full-time course leading to the graduate membership and the RSH. Inspectors, who are employed by local authorities, check quality and standards in abattoirs and meat plants.

RELATED OCCUPATIONS

Meat process worker, meat inspector, store assistant, store manager, self-employed franchisee, food scientist/technologist.

FURTHER INFORMATION

Meat Training Council*, PO Box 141, Winterhill House, Snowdon Drive, Milton Keynes MK6 1YY, 01908 231062

The Worshipful Company of Butchers Guild, Butchers' Hall, Bartholomew Close, London EC1A 7EB, 0171 236 1060

The Scottish Federation of Meat Traders' Associations, 8/10 Needless Road, Perth PH2 0JW, 01738 637785

FURTHER READING

Leaflets/booklets are available from the address marked*.

Careers information, including a booklet and related video, from The Meat Training Council.

Working In Retailing – COIC
In the careers library classified under OFM.

8. FLORIST (OFM)

BACKGROUND INFORMATION

Although most floristry shops are small, the floristry industry is a significant part of the retail trade, with sales each year in the UK exceeding one billion pounds.

Florists use their creative skills to make up floral designs and sell flowers and plants.

THE WORK

Florists create and make bouquets, wreaths and floral tributes to order and sell them to the public. They also sell cut flowers, pot plants and sometimes dried and artificial flowers and vases.

Florists buy fresh flowers, taking into account customers' orders and likely sales to passing trade. They may visit a wholesale market or buy from a wholesaler who delivers to florists. Some florists also buy direct from local nurseries, while some telex or telephone orders to overseas growers, particularly in Holland.

They also buy other items they need for making up bouquets and wreaths and for sale in the shop, such as special wire, ribbon, cellophane, oasis (water absorbent foam), silk, dried and other artificial flowers, cards, tools and fertilizers. This can involve visiting a wholesale market or warehouse or having the goods delivered.

Florists use flowers to make up bouquets and wreaths, often for special occasions, such as weddings, anniversaries, birthdays, funerals and gift presentations. Many designs are traditional but customers may have their own ideas or may leave the design to the florist. They use a knife or scissors to make the design with fresh flowers and materials such as wire, tape, oasis, sprays of leaves and evergreen, baskets and cellophane.

Care of the flowers is important. This involves removing damaged branches, cutting the stems and putting them into deep water containing flower nutrient, watering pot plants and checking them for pests and treating them if necessary. They keep the premises clean and tidy.

Florists display flowers, plants and accessories and price goods for sale. They serve customers, both in person and by telephone, advise them on their choice and on how to care for their flowers or plants. They may arrange for orders to be delivered and process orders by the flower relay services like Interflora, Teleflorist and Flowergram. They handle cash, give change and process credit card orders.

Florists who are managers or who run their own shops must keep accounts and other business records.

Some florists arrange flowers away from their shops in other premises such as hotels, offices, public buildings, private homes and at exhibitions. They may also supply and care for the house plants in these premises, which is known as 'interior landscaping'.

Florists usually wear protective overalls and comfortable shoes.

WORK ENVIRONMENT

Florists work indoors, mainly in shops open to the public. While the selling areas are bright and cheerful, many shops also have cold rooms that are designed to provide the right environment for flower care. They are cool and shaded.

Florists spend much of their time standing, either when working at a bench or in dealing with customers. Work can be dirty, wet, heavy and strenuous.

Work can involve travelling to wholesalers, nurseries or customers' premises.

SKILLS AND INTERESTS

Florists should be creative and have artistic ability. A sense of colour, shape and design is important, both when discussing customers' requirements and when making up bouquets and wreaths.

Good hand skills are required, together with nimble fingers for wiring flowers. They need to work carefully and gently when making up designs, as flowers are easily damaged.

Florists should be able to work well as part of a team and get on well with other staff, as well as with customers. They need good communication skills to advise customers, understand their instructions and sell to them. Clear speech is necessary, particularly in dealing with telephone orders. They need to be particularly sympathetic and tactful when dealing with customers who may be upset, such as when ordering designs for a funeral.

Figurework ability is necessary for estimating the cost of orders, handling cash and giving change. Those who manage or run a business also need this ability for keeping financial records.

Florists must be able to work under pressure when completing orders by an agreed time and at busy times of the year, such as Mothers' Day, Easter, Valentine's Day and Christmas.

ENTRY REQUIREMENTS

There are no minimum requirements for entry to floristry, although some employers prefer some GCSEs/S grades (A-C/1-3). English, mathematics, art and craft subjects are particularly useful. It is important that entrants can write clearly and spell well. Good health and stamina are required.

It is possible to enter floristry direct, or following a full-time course. Many direct-entry school-leavers begin on training schemes for young people – contact local careers offices for details.

BTEC First Diploma in Floristry. No particular entry qualifications are required, although some GCSEs/S grades are useful.

BTEC National Diploma in Floristry. Usually requires either: four GCSEs/S grades (A-C/1-3); or a relevant BTEC first award; or Intermediate GNVQ/GSVQ Level II.

BTEC Higher National Diploma in Floristry. Usually requires either: one A level/two H grades and some GCSEs/S grades (A-C/1-3); or a relevant BTEC/SCOTVEC national award; or Advanced GNVQ/GSVQ Level III.

NVQs/SVQs in Floristry. Require no set entry qualifications.

National Certificate in Professional Floristry. Usually requires NVQ/SVQ Level 2 in Floristry.

The Intermediate Certificate of the Society of Floristry (ICSF). Requires evidence of at least three years' practical experience in floristry plus attendance at a one-day seminar run by the Society. Seminars are held at various locations throughout the UK.

The National Diploma of the Society of Floristry (NDSF). Requires entrants to hold the ICSF.

TRAINING

Pre-entry

There are a number of full-time courses that can be taken to prepare for entry into floristry.

BTEC First Diploma in Floristry. Courses are offered at a few English colleges and last for one year. They are designed as an introduction to floristry.

BTEC National Diploma in Floristry. Courses are offered at several colleges in England and Wales and last for two years full-time or three years on a sandwich basis. They aim to provide thorough training in the principles and practice of floristry.

BTEC Higher National Diploma (HND) in Floristry. Two and three-year courses are offered at some colleges. Higher National Diploma courses prepare students for managerial work or self-employment.

NVQ Floristry Levels 1 and 2. Many colleges offer one-year courses preparing students for NVQ Levels 1 and 2.

SVQ Floristry Levels 1 and 2. Banff and Buchan College of Further Education offers a two-year course preparing students for SVQ Levels 1 and 2.

National Certificate in Professional Floristry. A number of colleges offer one-year courses that allow students to develop existing floristry skills to a higher level. Successful completion of the course helps students to prepare for ICSF and NDSF qualifications, but is not essential for this purpose.

Advanced and Intermediate GNVQ/GSVQ Level II and III courses that include floristry are being developed.

On entry

Entrants are trained by an experienced florist. On starting work they learn shop procedures, the care of flowers and plants, flower and plant names, the principles of colour and design, techniques of making bouquets, wreaths and other displays, selling skills, cash handling, estimating costs and customer relations.

Those on training schemes and others wanting to gain qualifications work for NVQ/SVQ qualifications in floristry, often through part-time attendance at a local college.

NVQ/SVQ in Floristry at Levels 1 and 2 are designed for a wide range of floristry activities including: producing designs; conditioning and caring for fresh materials; product presentation; providing a service to customers; selling; handling stock; display. Topics covered include: customer care; health and safety; plant care; flower arrangements; merchandising; wedding floristry; gift wrapping; communications; funeral designs; tied assemblies.

NVQ/SVQ in Floristry at Level 3: includes assessing and evaluating designs and displays; work planning; floristry designs; receipt, storage and condition of stock; receipt of payments; security; health and safety; customer care; complaints and returns; information; staff training; working relationships. It also has an optional unit on assessing performance.

NVQ/SVQ in Floristry at Level 4: is being developed.

Florists can also attend short courses on specific topics that are run by colleges and flower relay services.

Experienced florists can gain the **Intermediate Certificate of the Society of Floristry (ICSF)** by passing examinations on the theory and practice of floristry. Holders of the ICSF can take further theory and practice examinations to gain the **National Diploma of the Society of Floristry (NDSF)**.

The NDSF is intended for professional florists with full practical experience and a thorough knowledge of the flower industry. It is the highest award in the UK and has international recognition. Some colleges offer courses to prepare for the ICSF and NDSF.

LATE ENTRY

There is no upper age limit for entry to floristry.

Mature applicants may be considered for the courses described in TRAINING without the usual minimum entry requirements.

There may be specific training opportunities directed at adults available in some areas for this type of work. Candidates may have to satisfy certain conditions to be eligible. Contact your local Jobcentre, careers office or TEC/LEC for details.

OPPORTUNITIES

Most florists work in small specialist shops that are in every town and city throughout the UK. Some work in floristry shops based in large hotels or shops that are departments within larger stores or garden centres. Shops tend to be small and often employ fewer than ten staff.

The number of florists decreased during the recession in the early 1990s but has since stabilized.

Vacancies may be advertised in Jobcentres, local newspapers and trade magazines such as *The Florist Trade Magazine* and *Complete Florist.*

There is an increasing trend for those leaving higher-level full-time courses to seek financial backing to open their own shop, possibly having first gained experience as an employee.

There are opportunities for experienced florists to work abroad.

PAY AND CONDITIONS

There are no set pay scales for florists. Their earnings tend to be similar to those in retail work generally and can range from approximately £65 to £200 a week, depending on the size and location of the shop.

Florists usually work normal shop hours for 40 hours a week including Saturdays. Early starts are often necessary to complete large orders for such as weddings or funerals or if visiting a wholesaler to buy stock. Sunday work may be necessary on occasion.

There are opportunities for part-time work.

PROSPECTS

It may be possible to become a buyer in a large floristry shop, or be promoted to supervisor or manager. Experienced florists with business skills may choose to set up their own business.

There are openings for some florists to teach floristry full-time or part-time and opportunities for part-time work demonstrating floristry and judging competitions.

Florists may use their experience to transfer to supervisory or management work in the retail trade outside floristry.

RELATED OCCUPATIONS

Window dresser, horticultural worker, garden centre worker, interior landscaper, gardener, store assistant, store manager.

FURTHER INFORMATION

Floristry Training Council*, Roebuck House, Hampstead Norreys Road, Hermitage, Thatcham, Berkshire RG18 9RZ, 01635 200465 (please enclose an sae)

The Secretary, Society of Floristry, 70a Reigate Road, Epsom, Surrey KT17 3DT, 01372 463688 (please include sae)

FURTHER READING

Leaflets/booklets are available from the address marked*.

Job Outlines – Floristry – COIC

In the careers library classified under OFM.

9. DISPLAY PERSON (OFM/ET)

BACKGROUND INFORMATION

The primary purpose of display design is to sell goods. It is usually intended to interest customers in merchandise, to encourage them into the shop and to focus the customers' attention on goods that the company's marketing plans are currently concentrating on selling. In-store and exhibition displays should make it easy for sales people to demonstrate and sell the products and make it easy for customers to find and examine the goods they want.

A good display can inform and advise, introduce new merchandise and products, help to establish new fashions, educate public tastes in furnishing fashion, promote the company's corporate image and keep customers in contact with price changes.

THE WORK

This varies considerably depending on where they work. In some cases, display personnel can use all their creativity with other employers, for example cosmetic manufacturers, or high street chains, the style of display may be dictated by the employer.

The work of a display person often starts months before the display is needed. In department stores for example, plans are made in January for the displays for the following Christmas. Designers, together with store directors, shop managers or manufacturers, plan future displays bearing in mind the image they want to create and the message they want to communicate, and what their competitors might be doing.

Many displays are based upon a theme or event, for example Christmas, Easter, spring, summer holidays, back to school, or autumn. In some cases they may be based on a show or film in the area, a national celebration or a topical occasion. The choice of merchandise for display depends on a number of factors – time of year, fashion, the location of the shop, the corporate identity of the manufacturer or shop and whether there is a national or local promotion for the goods at the time.

Once plans have been decided, design personnel draw designs for windows, shop interiors, show cases, exhibition stands, etc. In doing this they consider the areas to have displays, the size and shape of the areas and where they are positioned. For instance, in a store some windows facing a main street may be more important than those down a side street which may not be seen by so many people.

Display personnel design the displays to be pleasing to look at and to show the merchandise off to its best advantage. They consider such things as the shapes and colour of the merchandise and the balance and grouping of props. They decide what they want the customer to focus on in the display, how they will draw their eye to that area and the impression they want the display to create.

Lighting is a vital part of displays as, depending on the atmosphere required, the display may be softly lit, dim, bright or have coloured lighting. Lighting is also used to focus the customers' attention on particular parts of the display.

The next stage is planning what they need to create the impression they want, and how the props used in the display are to be made. In some cases the display team make their own display props, in other cases they contract the work out or may hire items. They plan the time needed, the materials, and the resources for the display.

In making props for the display they require a range of skills including painting, carpentry and plastering and use a variety of tools from sewing needles and pins to hand drills and saws. A window displaying ski clothing, for instance, may require them to paint panels with snow scenes on them to go at the back of the window. They would also have to create artificial snow for the floor of the window. For a display based on an Egyptian theme they might make models of pyramids and the Sphinx.

Before the display is ready to assemble, display personnel dismantle the previous display and return the merchandise to the relevant departments and clean the window areas. Assembling the new display may involve placing panels at the back of the window, laying the flooring, arranging the merchandise, dressing mannequins, etc.

Although the description above details the work of display personnel in a store the principles are similar in all types of display and exhibition design.

WORK ENVIRONMENT

Display personnel usually work indoors – in studios where they make the props being used to create the displays, in shop windows, on shop floors, and on exhibition stands. Some work in theme parks, advertising, TV or film studios, in museums or art galleries, airports, seaports or on board ship.

The work can involve climbing ladders, lifting carrying and bending. Display people working for manufacturers, high street chains or for a group of shops may have to travel and a driving licence could be an advantage. Occasionally they may be required to stay away from home overnight.

SKILLS AND INTERESTS

Display people need a considerable amount of creativity and artistic flair, with a good eye for colour, balance and composition. They also need imagination, ingenuity and the ability to improvise and adapt available materials. They need good hand skills and the ability to work with a wide range of materials – wood, paper, polystyrene, fabric, etc.

They work in teams and so need good interpersonal skills. They also meet customers and should be able to communicate well with them. Display staff also need to be reasonably fit as this can be physically hard work.

ENTRY REQUIREMENTS

It is possible to start straight from school with no academic qualifications and train on the job, together with day release to college. However, the majority of display people start with a full-time college course.

Entry requirements vary depending on the course applied for.

British Display Society (BDS)

The Technicians Certificate and BDS General Certificate Grade I do not require any academic qualifications. In order to apply for the BDS General Certificate Grade II it is necessary to have passed Grade I.

The BDS National Diploma Advanced Level course in Retail Display requires three GCSEs/S grades (A-C/1-3), including art and English.

The BDS National Diploma Advanced Level course in Exhibition Design requires three GCSEs/S grades (A-C/1-3), including art, English and a technical subject, plus a one-year foundation course such as the BDS General Certificate Grade I.

BTEC

The BTEC National Diploma in Design (Display) requires four GCSEs/S grades (A-C/1-3), including art or a related subject, or Intermediate GNVQ in Art and Design/GSVQ in Design Level II. Applicants should take a portfolio of their work along to the interview.

SCOTVEC

The GSVQ Level III in Design requires GSVQ Level II in Design, or five S grades (1-3).

Higher National Diplomas/Certificates require two H grades, or GSVQ Level III in Design. Applicants should take a portfolio of their work along to the interview.

TRAINING

Training may be full-time at colleges or part-time working as a display assistant and attending college on a day release basis. There are three major bodies offering qualifications in display – the British Display Society, BTEC and SCOTVEC. Courses may be full- or part-time.

British Display Society (BDS)

BDS General Certificate grade I – a one-year full-time course. Entry at 16 years.

BDS General Certificate grade II – one-year full-time course entry. Entry at 17 years.

BDS National Diploma Advanced Level in Retail Display – a two-year full-time course. Entry at 16 years.

BDS National Diploma Advanced level in Exhibition Design – a full-time two-year course.

BDS Technician Certificate – a three-year, day release course with three levels – Preliminary, Intermediate and Final stages. Students who successfully complete the BDS National Diploma Advanced Level courses, the BDS General Certificate course grade II or the final part of the Technicians Certificate can use the letters Cert BDS after their name on becoming members of the Society.

Students at colleges recognized by the BDS offering BTEC national diplomas or SCOTVEC GSVQ Level III in Design, are eligible on qualification to apply for Cert BDS membership.

BTEC

The National Diploma in Design (Display) is a two-year full-time course and is offered at a number of colleges throughout the country. However, at present there is only one college offering the BTEC National Certificate in Design (Display) and one college offering a National Diploma in Design (Exhibition).

SCOTVEC

In Scotland the equivalent college course is the GSVQ Level III in Design which has options in display design and exhibition design. This is a two-year full-time or three-year part-time course. SCOTVEC Higher National Diplomas and Certificates are also available in Design. Titles of these courses vary but include Retail Display, Exhibition Design, Visual Merchandising and Marketing Design. SCOTVEC courses may be full- or part-time and some parts may be available through distance learning.

There is also a considerable amount of on-the-job training in this work which can lead to NVQs/SVQs in Interior or Exhibition Design at Levels 2, 3 and 4.

New display personnel usually start as juniors and learn from more experienced staff.

LATE ENTRY

There is no upper age limit for the work. Entry and training for mature entrants is as described above. However, applicants for college courses with relevant experience and a very good portfolio may be accepted without the usual academic entry qualifications.

OPPORTUNITIES

Display personnel are employed by many different types of employers. They work for shops, this includes large department stores, high street chains and small groups of shops. They can also work for manufacturers doing displays for them in shops, exhibitions or pubs.

There are opportunities for work in advertising, in films and TV and in airports or seaports designing and dressing show cases. They can also work on board cruise liners.

It is also possible to work on a freelance basis and display personnel can work anywhere in the world. There are also opportunities to move into other types of design work such as interior design or theatre set design.

The chances of finding employment for those leaving college with recognized display qualifications is good.

PAY AND CONDITIONS

This depends on the type of work but on the whole most staff work flexi-hours, usually about 40 a week. Display staff work on Saturdays and Sundays and sometimes may have to work during evenings. Occasionally they may have to work on bank holidays.

Salaries vary tremendously depending on where the display person works and for whom. An assistant or new assistant may be paid in the region of £10,000 to £12,000.

PROSPECTS

Promotion prospects vary depending on where display people work but usually the prospects are good. For instance, in a large department store they start as a junior, progressing to display assistant and then to senior in charge of windows. They could then progress to assistant manager and then to display manager. Although it is not absolutely necessary to do the more advanced courses in order to gain promotion they can be a considerable advantage.

There are also opportunities for those with the necessary experience and qualifications to become lecturers in colleges offering display design courses.

RELATED OCCUPATIONS

Store manager, merchandiser, model maker, TV and theatre set designer, graphic designer, interior designer, store assistant.

FURTHER INFORMATION

British Display Society Ltd*, 70a Crayford High Street, Dartford, Kent DA1 4EF

FURTHER READING

Leaflets/booklets are available from the address marked*.

Working in the Retail Industry – COIC

In the careers library classified under OFM/ET.

10. SHOE REPAIRER CLCI:OFZ

BACKGROUND INFORMATION

There are different kinds of shoe repairer. Most are skilled craftspeople based in shops who take in repairs to be collected a few hours or days later. An increasing number of shoe repairers work in heel bars and provide a more limited range of services but do so quickly, often while customers wait. A small number of shoe repairers work in factories that make shoes. They deal with shoes returned to the factory for repair, usually shoes that have cost at least £90 a pair.

THE WORK

Shoe repairers mend shoes and boots. This can involve replacing soles or heels, re-stitching, replacing faulty fasteners (eg zips), dyeing, staining and polishing.

Shoe repairers begin by examining the damaged or worn footwear to decide whether repair is possible. They use their knowledge of how the shoes were manufactured and how different materials respond to wear and tear to decide on the most appropriate materials for the repair. They advise the customer of the recommended repair, the cost involved and when the footwear will be ready for collection.

Shoe repairers use pincers to remove the worn sole or heel. They then attach the replacement sole or heel. This may be done by using adhesive (glue) and a compressed-air staple gun, brad (nail) gun or hammer and nails. Leather soles are stitched to the shoe by using a stitching machine. When they have fitted the replacement sole or heel shoe repairers use a knife to trim away the excess material. They may then use an electrically operated trimmer to produce an exact fit to the shape of the shoe.

Shoe repairers use a brush to stain the edges of leather soles and heels to match the colour of the shoe. They use an electrically operated machine to polish footwear when repairs have been completed. The shoes are then wrapped, labelled with the customer's name, address, code number and price, and stored ready for collection.

Most shoe repairers are responsible for keeping their own machines and equipment in good working order. They sharpen cutting tools frequently and regularly service the electrically operated machinery.

Shoe repairers working in shops and heel bars usually offer a repair service for leather goods, such as stitching leather belts, jackets, handbags and suitcases, which often involves using sewing machines. They also sell a range of products, such as polishes, dyes, laces, insoles and keyrings.

An important part of retail shoe repairers' work is key cutting. They use a range of small electrically powered machines to cut a variety of commercial, domestic and vehicle keys. Some also use machinery to engrave items such as keyrings, nameplates and trophies.

Retail shoe repairers collect money from customers and deal with cash, cheques and credit cards.

Shoe repairers need to work quickly when trying to meet a promised deadline for repair. All shoe repairers wear protective clothing.

WORK ENVIRONMENT

Shoe repairers work indoors. Most work in small shops, either alone or with one or two others. A small number of shoe repairers work in workshops in shoe manufacturing companies.

The work can be dirty, with fumes from strong adhesives and smells from leather and rubber. It can be very noisy when operating machinery.

Most work is done sitting or standing at a workbench or machines.

SKILLS AND INTERESTS

Repairing shoes is practical work, so shoe repairers should have good hand skills, be nimble fingered and enjoy working with machines. They must be able to work neatly and accurately for repairs to be of acceptable quality to customers.

Shoe repairers should be safety conscious as some hand tools and machinery they use are potentially dangerous.

Product knowledge is important to decide on the most suitable method of repair. Initiative is required to complete each job alone.

Those working in shops must be able to get on well with customers. They need good communication skills to listen to customers' requirements and to explain the repairs they recommend. They should also be capable of working in a team with others in the shop.

Shoe repairers should be able to cope with pressure when working to meet promised deadlines and when their work is interrupted to serve customers. Lunch-times and Saturdays can be particularly busy. They must have the ability to estimate the cost of work and cope with handling money and giving change.

Good eyesight is needed to cope with small, neat stitching. Normal colour vision is required for matching dyes.

ENTRY REQUIREMENTS

There are no minimum entry qualifications required for shoe repairers, although some employers prefer applicants who have GCSEs/S grades (A-E/1-5) in English, maths and practical subjects, such as CDT or technology.

Some national organizations require applicants to pass an aptitude test that includes English, arithmetic and practical skills.

TRAINING

Most 16 and 17-year-olds entering shoe repairing do so via training organized by the Shoe Repair Industry Training Organization Ltd (SRITO). Contact your local careers offices, TECs/LECs for details.

Training in shoe repairs is usually on the job, with the trainee learning from an experienced repairer. National companies have their own training schemes that can include trainees attending their national training centres.

Trainees who enter through training organized by SRITO work towards an NVQ/SVQ in Footwear Repair at Level 2, as can other trainees. This includes: dealing with customers, advising on repairs, selecting materials, preparation work, attaching/benching, using adhesives, scouring, trimming, finishing, health and safety, maintenance, security and good housekeeping. SRITO has an open learning package that reflects the NVQ/SVQ and which is followed by entrants and available to others.

Some trainees use the open learning package produced by Accrington and Rossendale College, although not designed specifically to prepare trainees for an NVQ/SVQ in Footwear Repair at Level 2. It consists of twelve modules – footwear construction, footwear materials, repairing heels, repair of stuck-on footwear, repair of welted footwear, repair of moulded footwear and Doc Martens, finishing, maintaining shoe repair machinery, operating sole stitching machines, upper repairs, customer relations, shoe repair costings and key cutting.

LATE ENTRY

There is no upper age limit for entry to shoe repair and the majority of entrants are adults rather than school or college leavers.

The six-week intensive shoe repair course offered by Accrington and Rossendale College is designed particularly for mature applicants.

There may be specific training opportunities directed at adults available in some areas for this type of work. Candidates may have to satisfy certain conditions to be eligible. Contact your local Jobcentre, careers office or TEC/LEC for details.

OPPORTUNITIES

There are between 7,000 to 8,000 shoe repairers in the UK. Nearly all of them work in the estimated 6,000 shoe repair outlets. An increasing percentage of shoe repair outlets are part of national companies or part of larger shops, such as department stores or shoe retailers. About 70 per cent of outlets, though, are small, independent businesses, each typically having one to three workers.

The number of shoe repairers employed by factories is less than 50.

Vacancies may be advertised in *Shoe and Leather News*.

The shoe repair industry is influenced by footwear fashion. Fashions can either produce a lot of work for shoe repairers (eg court shoes with high heels that need frequent repair) or little work (eg trainers, which are not usually repaired).

The recent influx of cheap imported shoes has not helped shoe repairers, as people are reluctant to spend money on repairing very cheap shoes, preferring to buy a new replacement pair.

On the positive side, key cutting has become an increasingly important part of most shoe repairers work. The recent increase in interest in security has led to a strong demand for additional and replacement keys, and key cutting now accounts for up to 40 per cent of business for some shoe repairers.

PAY AND CONDITIONS

There are no standard rates of pay for shoe repairers. The earnings of shoe repairers with their own business depend on the shop's takings. Employed shoe repairers may earn between £4 to £7 an hour, with national companies commonly offering a bonus scheme.

Shoe repairers usually work a 40-hour week. This includes Saturdays, except for those in factories. Part-time work is possible.

PROSPECTS

Shoe repairers working for small, independent businesses have little or no chance of promotion. Instead, many choose to set up in business on their own.

National organizations have a structure that allows promotion to assistant manager and store manager.

RELATED OCCUPATIONS

Saddler, leather craftworker, footwear manufacturing worker, sewing machinist, upholsterer, store assistant, textile operative, store manager.

FURTHER INFORMATION

Footwear Open Tech Unit, Accrington and Rossendale College*, Haslingden Road, Rawtenstall, Lancashire BB4 6RA, 01706 211181

Shoe Repair Industry Training Organization Ltd*, 27 Coleshill Street, Sutton Coldfield, West Midlands B72 1SD, 0121 355 2033

Society of Master Shoe Repairers*, 21 Station Road, Desborough, Northamptonshire NN14 2SA, 01536 760374

FURTHER READING

Leaflets/booklets are available from the addresses marked*.

In the careers library classified under OFZ.

PUBLIC RELATIONS OFFICER CLCI:OG

BACKGROUND INFORMATION

Public relations (PR) is concerned with presenting a favourable understanding of an organization to various audiences or publics, such as consumers, businesses, the financial community and employees.

The Institute of Public Relations (IPR) describes PR as having 'the responsibility of managing an organization's reputation, credibility and corporate image: shaping, protecting and promoting it'.

Many kinds of organization use PR – commercial and industrial, central and local government, hospitals, charities, religious bodies, educational institutions, trade unions, trade and professional associations, lobbyists and arts organizations. They use PR to present their organization in the best possible light, so that their policies, products or services are regarded favourably.

PR is a two-way activity. PR staff seek to influence others on behalf of an organization but also to gather and feed back outside opinions of the organization.

PR operates in two distinct settings. **In-house PR** departments are concerned solely with their employing organization, while **PR consultancies** provide a service to a number of clients. Some organizations have an in-house PR department but also use an external consultancy.

THE WORK

Public relations officers plan, organize and conduct activities that bring favourable attention to an organization's image, policies, products or services. This involves a number of functions, including:

Programme planning. Public relations officers analyse PR problems in consultation with clients or management. They agree on aims and objectives and plan activities to meet them within an agreed budget.

Writing and editing. A major function of PR work is writing and editing press releases, reports, articles, newsletters, annual reports, leaflets, brochures, speeches and film and video scripts.

Production. Public relations officers co-ordinate the production of radio tapes, company newsletters, leaflets, brochures, videos and films.

Liaison with the media. Public relations officers make sure that the message they want to put across is published or broadcast. They make and maintain good relationships with newspaper, magazine, radio and television staff to help make that more likely.

Public speaking. The work involves talking to individuals and groups through interviews, meetings, presentations and conferences.

Special events. Public relations officers plan events and participate in them. Press launches, news conferences, exhibitions, open days, trade fairs and corporate hospitality, at sports events, for example, are an important part of PR activity.

Research and evaluation. Surveys, interviews and opinion polls are used to gauge how a PR activity may be received. After an activity, public relations officers may use similar methods to judge its effectiveness.

In-house PR is often more specialist than work in consultancies. This is reflected in some job titles used, such as press officer, publicity officer, information officer, publications officer.

PR consultancy work is usually conducted in a team with an account director, two or three account executives and a secretary. Teams may specialize in different types of account – corporate, financial, consumer, business-to-business, public affairs or employee communications.

WORK ENVIRONMENT

Public relations officers are based in offices but their work involves travelling for a variety of purposes – to meet clients, to attend press conferences, exhibitions, trade fairs, radio and television studios and design studios.

SKILLS AND INTERESTS

Public relations officers must be able to get on well with many different people, including journalists, managers and employees of an organization, and members of the public.

They should be able to express themselves clearly in speech and in writing. Oral skills are needed for press briefings, meetings, conferences and presentations. Written ability is required for preparing news releases, leaflets, reports, articles, etc.

PR work demands good organizational skills to cope with a number of different activities that staff work on at any one time and to arrange events, such as news conferences, open days and exhibitions.

Numeracy is important as PR work must be costed and kept within budget.

Public relations officers must be able to analyse problems before deciding on action. Initiative and enterprise are needed to devise activities that provide solutions.

It is important to be able to work well in a team. Self-motivation and the ability to work under pressure are necessary.

ENTRY REQUIREMENTS

Although no specific qualifications are required, in practice most entrants have a degree. Any degree subject is acceptable. The minimum requirements for entry to degree courses are five GCSEs/S grades (A-C/1-3), plus two A levels/three H grades.

There are some BTEC Higher National Certificate/Diploma courses in Business Studies with a PR specialism. They require either one A level/two H grades with four GCSEs/S grades (A-C/1-3), or a BTEC/SCOTVEC national award.

Postgraduate courses in PR require a degree for entry.

Some entrants to PR have taken the Communication Advertising and Marketing (CAM) Foundation's Certificate in Communication Studies. Candidates applying for Certificate registration must be age 18 or over with a minimum of: *either* two A levels/three H grades and three GCSEs/S grades (A-C/1-3); *or* a BTEC/SCOTVEC national award in business studies; *or* five GCSEs/S grades (A-C/1-3) and one year's relevant work experience; *or* at least three years' relevant experience.

Most entrants to PR have had previous experience of other work, such as journalism, marketing, advertising, engineering, science or law.

TRAINING

Pre-entry

There are a number of relevant full-time courses, although none guarantees entry to PR.

Degrees in PR are run at the University of Bournemouth, the University of Exeter, the University of Central Lancashire, the College of St Mark and St John, Plymouth and at Leeds Metropolitan University and Napier University.

Some degree and BTEC/SCOTVEC higher national diploma courses in business studies, communication or media studies include PR.

Relevant postgraduate courses are offered at the University of Stirling, Manchester Metropolitan University, and West Herts College.

A few entrants have studied full-time for the CAM Certificate in Communication Studies which gives a broad introduction to the communication industry. Tuition is offered at a number of colleges, course length varying from centre to centre.

On entry

The Institute of Public Relations (IPR) lists three PR consultancies with in-house graduate training programmes. They involve experience in various departments of the consultancy, internal training sessions, attending talks and visiting media organizations.

Training for most entrants to PR is given in-house. They may also attend workshops, seminars, courses and conferences organized by IPR and by the Public Relations Consultants Association (PRCA).

Public relations officers are encouraged to study for the CAM Certificate in Communication Studies and the CAM Diploma in Public Relations. The diploma is concerned specifically with management and PR. Courses are available at 28 centres, full-time, part-time or by distance learning. Course length varies from centre to centre.

NVQs/SVQs in Public Relations are available at Levels 3 and 4.

LATE ENTRY

Most entrants to PR have had experience of other work. Journalism, marketing and advertising are particularly useful. Other experience, such as engineering, financial management or law, can be useful in relevant areas of PR work.

Entry beyond the age of 35 becomes increasingly difficult.

Adults may be able to enter higher education courses described in TRAINING without the usual entry qualifications.

OPPORTUNITIES

There are approximately 11,000 professional PR practitioners in the UK, although it is estimated that there are over 28,000 with substantial PR experience. Approximately 70 per cent work outside London.

In-house PR staff are employed by a wide range of organizations. The largest single employer is the Government Information Service with over 1,300 employees. Other employers include local authorities, commercial companies, professional bodies, trade associations, charities, cultural organizations and television companies.

There are approximately 2,000 consultancies, which employ about one-third of all PR staff. Consultancies vary from those run by one or two individuals to large national firms employing over 100 staff.

Entry to PR work is extremely competitive. Vacancies are advertised in *Campaign, PR Week* and *Public Relations Consultancy* and in the national press, but those seeking entry are advised to contact potential employers direct. It may be necessary to begin in PR as an information assistant or publicity assistant with an in-house department, with the aim of later becoming a public relations officer.

PAY AND CONDITIONS

There are no set salary scales in PR. Starting salaries can be around £10,000. Experienced public relations officers earn between £15,000 and £22,000. Senior managers in PR earn over £30,000.

Public relations officers usually work a five-day week, with pressure of work sometimes leading to evening and weekend work. An average working week may be approximately 45 hours.

PROSPECTS

Both in-house departments and consultancies have promotion possibilities but both are very competitive.

In-house public relations officers may seek promotion to management posts, such as communications manager or media relations manager.

Consultancy staff may progress from junior account executive to account executive, senior account executive or account manager, associate or account director.

Movement from company to company for advancement is a common feature of PR careers. Some public relations officers move to the related fields of advertising or marketing, while others set up consultancies on their own or in partnership.

There are some opportunities for experienced public relations officers to work abroad for international companies and consultancies.

RELATED OCCUPATIONS

Market research executive, advertising account executive, advertising copywriter, marketing manager.

FURTHER INFORMATION

CAM Foundation*, Abford House, 15 Wilton Road, London SW1V 1NJ, 0171 828 7506

The Institute of Public Relations*, The Old Trading House, 15 Northburgh Street, London EC1V 0PR (please include sae)

Public Relations Consultants Association*, Willow House, Willow Place, Victoria, London SW1P 1JH, 0171 233 6026

Scottish Public Relations Consultants Association, Scottish Council for Development and Industry, 23 Chester Street, Edinburgh EH3 7ET, 0131 225 7911

FURTHER READING

Leaflets/booklets are available from the addresses marked*.

Job Outlines – Public Relations – COIC
Working in Journalism – COIC
Working in Marketing – COIC
Careers in Marketing, Public Relations and Advertising – Kogan Page

In the careers library classified under OG.

SALES REPRESENTATIVE/MANAGER
CLCI:OM

BACKGROUND INFORMATION

Every product and service needs to reach prospective customers – whether that product or service is food, clothes, hi-fi equipment, roads, aircraft, stationery, insurance or cleaning services.

The jobs of all the people who design and manufacture goods or provide services depend on the work of the sales people. For instance, however good a new novel is, it will not sell unless the sales team do their job well and get the book into the bookshops.

Sales representatives may be involved in selling their products to shops or retail outlets or may sell direct to the customer who may be an individual buying double glazing or a developing country buying major engineering works or road-building programmes.

THE WORK

Sales representative

The work of sales representatives – who may also be known as sales executives, sales consultants, agents or technical representatives – varies considerably from company to company. Most sales representatives are responsible for a particular area (usually called territory) of this country or abroad. In some companies, especially new companies or ones that have a new product and no existing customers, representatives may have to decide on the potential market for the product and then build up their list of customers. Other representatives have already established customers on whom to make regular calls.

Some sales people working in consumer sales sell their company's products to retailers, whereas others in technical or specialized sales sell products such as parts and components or items such as road systems or aircraft to other industries.

Selling to retail outlets. The products sold by representatives working in this field depends on the company they work for. They could be selling shoes, sports equipment, jewellery, cleaning materials, food, stationery, electrical goods, etc.

Representatives work in partnership with shop owners, managers and buyers. They find out what their customer wants then advise on appropriate products. They supply information about the product and any other information the customer needs to know. They visit their retail outlets on a regular basis to show the buyers or managers new products, or invite buyers to a showroom to show them the products.

When buyers have decided what they want to buy, representatives help them build an order, which may be done on computer. As stock is sold the company notifies the representative who arranges to replace it.

Sales representatives also help shop owners and managers to sell the products. This may include advising about display and providing the shop's sales staff with product information.

Services may be sold in a similar way. For instance, insurance sales people work closely with brokers to keep them up to date on their company's products and services.

Technical sales. Technical sales representatives usually sell to technical experts, such as aeronautical or civil engineers or architects, and need technical knowledge about their products. One sale may take months of negotiating and when the sale is completed the sales representative may oversee the installation of the product – the building of a road system, for example – so projects may take years to complete. Other technical sales, such as medical or pharmaceutical products, are sold to doctors and hospitals in the same way as consumer product sales people sell to retail outlets.

All representatives have considerable paperwork to complete, they keep records and accounts of all their sales that may be on paper or computer. They handle most complaints from their customers.

Sales manager

A large part of sales managers' work is to manage their teams of representatives. They recruit representatives, which involves arranging for job vacancy advertisements, interviewing and appointing staff. They are usually responsible for organizing training courses for their staff in such areas as product knowledge, company procedures, communication skills and sales techniques. In some cases they may carry out some of the training themselves. Sales managers have regular meetings with their teams to motivate and manage them, carrying out assessments, appraisals and counselling.

They organize their sales force, allocating the territories to be covered by each representative, and they set sales targets. They compile accounts and analyse sales results (often using computers), monitor the progress of all their team, and use sales figures to plan and budget for future sales campaigns. Sales managers also organize regular sales conferences where the company's new products are explained to the representatives. In some companies sales managers may deal with a number of customers themselves.

Another large area of their work is in dealing with problems or complaints that customers have. Some problems are dealt with by representatives but major problems such as the customer having large batches of faulty stock usually require the sales manager to resolve the situation.

Sales managers can also be involved with market research carried out on a product before it is ever manufactured. They attend meetings with other managers and advise on whether a product is likely to meet a market need (however good a product is, it is not worth making unless it is going to sell). Sales managers may also be able to advise other managers on what products the buyers want.

WORK ENVIRONMENT

Representatives usually spend a considerable amount of their time driving to visit customers who may be within a relatively small geographical area like Avon or a much larger area such as the North of England. They may use their homes as a work base, only visiting their companies very occasionally. Others may spend a day or two a week in their offices.

Some representatives spend much time abroad selling anything from chocolates to aircraft, catering equipment, to road systems. Representatives may have to spend days or even weeks staying in hotels away from their home.

Sales managers spend considerable time in the field advising sales representatives and visiting major customers. They also spend time in their office. They travel to attend trade fairs and exhibitions.

SKILLS AND INTERESTS

Representatives should be friendly, outgoing, self-assured and able to get on with all types of people. They need excellent interpersonal skills to build good relationships with customers and to negotiate sales with them. They must be able to work on their own, and be very self-motivated. Determination and perseverance is also needed. Representatives should have good numerical skills to deal with orders and costings, and the ability to absorb large amounts of information about products and customers needs.

Sales managers need many of the same skills as representatives with the addition of administrative abilities, and management skills to motivate their teams.

ENTRY REQUIREMENTS

There are no set entry requirements for this work other than a clean driving licence. However, more and more companies are recruiting graduates. Technical and scientific products usually need representatives with relevant qualifications and experience. For instance, engineering sales representatives are invariably engineering graduates.

Some companies recruit trainees, usually graduates, with no experience; others recruit people with relevant experience. This can usually be gained in the following way: working in a sales office carrying out clerical jobs such as maintaining sales records and dealing with customers by phone and letter; starting in a particular profession or speciality such as engineering and moving into technical sales; working in the retail industry, gaining experience of sales work.

The Management Marketing and Sales Association (MAMSA) offers training and qualifications for sales staff. To study for the Diploma in Salesmanship requires: five GCSEs/S grades (A-C/1-3), including English and a mathematical subject; or to have reached a minimum age of 20 years with two years' approved and certified employment; or by assessment of the college/institute lecturer. Sales representatives can also study for City and Guilds/Institute of Sales and Marketing Management (ISMM) examinations in Operational Salesmanship – candidates are usually required to have GCSEs/S grades (A-C/1-3) in English and maths.

Most sales managers have previous experience as sales representatives. Some companies recruit graduates as direct-entry trainees.

TRAINING

Sales representative

Most training is given on the job with representatives learning from experienced members of the team. Companies often run courses in the practical skills of selling such as: how to take an order, negotiating, presentation skills, and finance. Representatives can study for the Diploma in Salesmanship from MAMSA which covers communication, salesmanship, organization and business, and market distribution; or City and Guilds/ISMM 6701 Operational Salesmanship which covers salesmanship, organization for selling, communication, advanced salesmanship, and marketing practice.

Sales manager

Training is also usually given on the job. MAMSA offer an advanced Diploma in Sales Management which covers: communication control, advertising and marketing research, personnel control, time control, cost control, legal control, and statistical control. ISMM/City and Guilds offer an examination in Sales Management.

A number of NVQs/SVQs are available, including: Selling at Levels 2 and 3; Sales Supervision at Level 3; and Field Sales Management at Level 4.

LATE ENTRY

There is no maximum age limit for entry into this career, indeed adult candidates are often preferred. However, applicants should be healthy, with considerable stamina because of the travelling and long hours required. Many people move into sales work from other careers.

OPPORTUNITIES

Most sizeable manufacturing companies and companies offering commercial services such as insurance companies provide opportunities throughout the country and have their own sales representatives and sales managers. Employment is also possible overseas. There are opportunities for self-employment as freelance sales agents, who may sell products for a number of different companies.

PAY AND CONDITIONS

Pay varies enormously from one company to another. Some representatives work on a salary; some have a salary plus commission; others may just work on a commission-only basis. Many companies have bonus schemes as well. Starting salaries for representatives commence at £6,500, and top representatives' earnings are very high. Most companies provide a company car and expense allowance to cover meals and hotel expenses. Working hours are not regular and there may be some evening work.

Sales managers – again pay varies a great deal. Managers can earn between £18,000 and £47,000; some firms pay a bonus if the company does well. Managers usually have a company car and an expense account.

PROSPECTS

The promotion route for representatives is usually to become field sales managers, running a team of representatives. Many move on to become sales managers and from there into general management, and then possibly become directors of a company.

RELATED OCCUPATIONS

Insurance salesperson, marketing executive, buyer/purchasing officer, sales assistant.

FURTHER INFORMATION

The Institute of Sales and Marketing Management (ISMM), National Westminster House, 31 Upper George Street, Luton, Bedfordshire LU1 2RD, 01582 411130

Managing and Marketing Sales Association (MAMSA), New House, School Lane, Warmingham, Sandbach, Cheshire CW11 0GD

FURTHER READING

Job Outlines – Buying and Purchasing – COIC
Working in Marketing – COIC

In the careers library classified under OM.

BUYER/PURCHASING OFFICER CLCI:OP

BACKGROUND INFORMATION

Every organization needs to purchase supplies, whether they be for its own internal use (office stationery), for the manufacturing process (raw materials, components) or for re-sale (goods purchased by retail, wholesale and mail order businesses). As well as goods, many organizations purchase services such as cleaning, transport and consultancy.

Purchasing can make a direct contribution to the effectiveness and profitability of an organization, by cutting costs, by ensuring that sources of supply are reliable, and by reducing the amount of capital tied up in stock. Greater management awareness of the importance of these factors has improved the status of purchasing departments in recent years.

Various different terms are used to describe the purchasing function and the people who carry it out. Retailers generally refer to 'buyers'. Buyers are also found in industry, as are 'purchasing' or 'supplies' officers. In the public sector, the terms most commonly used are 'procurement' and 'supplies'.

THE WORK

Buyers/purchasing officers aim to obtain goods and services 'of the right quality, in the right quantity, from the right source, delivered to the right place at the right time, at the right price'. These aims may be difficult to reconcile – for instance, a company that can supply goods of the 'right' quality may not have the capacity to deliver them at the 'right' time. Buyers and purchasing officers have to achieve a balance between often-conflicting objectives, with the aim of making the best possible arrangement that circumstances allow.

There are a number of stages in the purchasing process:

– define requirements, in consultation with other departments such as design and production;

– obtain quotations from potential suppliers;

– negotiate with suppliers, in response to their queries – both technical and commercial;

– choose supplier(s) and commit to purchase, in the form of a contract. The buyer needs to be confident that the product will meet specifications and that the supplier can deliver by the due date. Price is an important, but not overriding factor; buyers aim to achieve a fair price, rather than the lowest possible figure;

– monitor the progress of the contract;

– accept delivery and check that the product or service is of an acceptable standard; and

– pay, processing suppliers' invoices, taking advantage of any discounts for prompt payment, and checking that suppliers are paid on time.

Purchasing is often seen in the wider context of the management of materials, storage and stock control. Buyers may have additional responsibilities in these areas, such as making sure that supplies arrive 'just in time' for use, but not too soon (because it is wasteful for an organization to hold unnecessary stock).

In retailing, the fundamental aspects of purchasing are similar to those in other organizations; however, retail buyers need a keen awareness of consumer tastes and preferences, with the ability to pick out merchandise that will sell successfully in the shops. This can be particularly difficult in areas such as fashion buying, where it is important to predict future trends and consumer buying patterns.

Retail buyers, and purchasing officers in other sectors, often specialize in buying a particular category of merchandise.

The work usually involves a great deal of contact with people, including members of other departments within the organization and suppliers' representatives. Buyers and purchasing officers are likely to spend a lot of time on the telephone and in meetings.

Handling, sifting and evaluating information is another important aspect of the work. This involves tasks such as reading catalogues, consulting trade directories, and using computers for recording and analysing supplier performance, or monitoring stock levels.

WORK ENVIRONMENT

The work is office-based, but there may be trips out of the office to visit suppliers. These journeys may involve staying away from home for short periods.

It is usual to work as a member of a team, except in the case of small firms, where there may only be one buyer or purchasing officer.

SKILLS AND INTERESTS

Purchasing is very responsible work, demanding sound judgement, decisiveness, maturity and the ability to cope with pressure and crises. Buyers and purchasing officers need a firm, tough, business-like approach. Absolute integrity is essential; there are greater temptations (for instance, to accept gifts from suppliers) than in many other jobs.

Excellent communications skills – oral and written – are required for liaising with other departments and negotiating with suppliers.

Buyers/purchasing officers need to be well-organized and methodical, with an eye for detail (to read the small print in contracts, for instance). The ability to assimilate information is also important. Numeracy is required to interpret market data, to make commercial decisions and negotiate effectively.

Buyers need initiative to seek out new sources of supply.

A driving licence is useful; it is usually required for posts involving travel.

ENTRY REQUIREMENTS

Entry qualifications vary with different employers. No specific academic entry requirements are laid down but, increasingly, employers are looking to recruit candidates with A levels, H grades, BTEC/SCOTVEC national or higher national awards, or degrees.

A degree in any subject is acceptable. Business studies or closely related subjects are usually regarded as the most relevant disciplines, and graduates in these may be granted exemption from all or part of the foundation stage of the Chartered Institute of Purchasing and Supply (CIPS) examinations. Technical and scientific disciplines are useful, where relevant to the employers' business. Foreign languages are an asset in international companies, or for jobs involving contact with overseas suppliers.

Holders of BTEC/SCOTVEC Higher National Certificates

or Diplomas in Business Studies may also be granted full or part-exemption from the CIPS foundation stage. Entry to BTEC/SCOTVEC higher national certificate/diploma courses is with one/two A levels or three H grades, or a BTEC/SCOTVEC national certificate diploma.

The minimum entry qualifications for student registration with CIPS are: two A levels or three H grades and three additional GCSEs/S grades (A-C/1-3); an Advanced GNVQ/GSVQ Level III; a BTEC/SCOTVEC national certificate/diploma; a relevant NVQ/SVQ at Level 3, or an equivalent qualification. Exact details are available from the CIPS.

About 60 per cent of CIPS students have degrees or BTEC/ SCOTVEC higher national awards.

Applicants without the necessary qualifications listed above may register for the CIPS Supervisory Qualifications (First and Second Certificates in Purchasing and Stores). These provide the opportunity to start working towards a professional qualification.

In retailing, it is possible for people with sales experience, but no formal qualifications, to become buyers. Increasingly, however, employers are recruiting A level or H grade school-leavers and graduates – either providing general management training or direct entry to buying departments.

TRAINING

Many employers run their own training schemes. Graduates or A level entrants may start on a general-management training scheme and then specialize in purchasing, or they may enter a purchasing or buying department directly, typically as trainee buyers or purchasing clerks. They may take part-time courses for CIPS qualifications; these are becoming increasingly necessary for career progression.

The majority of CIPS students qualify via part-time day/ evening courses, with employers paying tuition and examination fees. However, block release, full-time and correspondence or distance learning courses are also available. Over 120 educational establishments offer courses for the CIPS examinations.

The examinations are in two stages.

1. The Foundation Stage covers introduction to purchasing and supply chain management, management principles and practice economics, quantitative studies, and business accounting.

2. The Professional Stage includes four compulsory papers in purchasing and supply chain management: strategy; tactics and operations; legal aspects; and a case study. This stage also includes specialist option papers and electives.

Courses for BTEC/SCOTVEC Higher National Certificate or Diploma in Business Studies, with purchasing options, are available at a number of colleges. Both full- and part-time courses may be taken, usually over a period of two to three years.

The CIPS Supervisory Qualifications (First and Second Certificates in Purchasing and Stores) are aimed at young people with fewer academic qualifications, who are typically employed in purchasing at a clerical level, or in stores and warehouses. They may, after obtaining the qualifications, proceed to courses for the CIPS qualifications, as described above, although this is a lengthy training route. First and Second Certificates in Purchasing and Stores are offered by many of the colleges running CIPS courses. The majority of courses are part-time; it takes one year to complete each certificate.

NVQs/SVQs in Purchasing at Levels 2, 3 and 4, and completion of Levels 3 and 4 offers a route to membership of the CIPS, subject to the completion of a project and a case study examination.

LATE ENTRY

There are good opportunities for adult entry. Most CIPS students are aged 23 or over. Academic entry requirements for CIPS examinations are waived for candidates aged 23 or over, providing they are working in a business or commercial environment. Study for the CIPS Supervisory Qualifications is open access.

OPPORTUNITIES

Purchasing/buying departments vary enormously in size and scope. In a small organization, one person may be responsible for all purchasing. In a large organization there may be a centralized purchasing department with a number of purchasing officers or buyers, each specializing in buying a particular category of goods or services. Alternatively, purchasing may be decentralized, so that it serves the needs of the individual branches of the organization more closely. Sometimes purchasing is partly centralized, with certain supplies being purchased centrally, others at local level.

Buyers and purchasing officers are employed by organizations of all kinds – including manufacturing and service industries, retailing and mail order firms, wholesalers, the Civil Service, the National Health Service, local authorities, public service industries, and HM Forces.

The Chartered Institute of Purchasing and Supply (CIPS) has around 21,000 members, but this figure does not represent the total number of people employed in purchasing.

Recruitment is competitive; employers are looking for well-qualified candidates. Those who are prepared to be mobile are at an advantage.

There are some opportunities to work abroad, particularly with multinational firms. There is also the possibility, in organizations of many kinds, of making short overseas buying trips.

PAY AND CONDITIONS

Starting salaries for trainee buyers are dependent upon industry and location and range from £10,000 to £15,000. Three to four years after qualifying via the Chartered Institute of Purchasing and Supply, a typical salary would be in the range £12,500 to £22,000 with an average of £16,000. Managerial posts offer salaries from around £20,000 to £45,000 plus a company car and health insurance.

Holiday entitlement varies with different employers, but is likely to be around 20 to 35 days a year.

Purchasing staff normally work office hours, sometimes with extra hours in the evenings or at weekends.

PROSPECTS

There are good promotion prospects in larger organizations with sizeable purchasing departments. People who enter as trainee buyers or purchasing clerks can become assistant buyers within two to three years; thereafter, progress is very much dependent on ability, as well as formal qualifications. It is quite possible to become a purchasing manager by the age of 28 to 30 years.

Some buyers/purchasing officers move into other, related areas of work, usually within their own organizations. Computing, distribution, logistics, stores and materials control, marketing or sales are the most likely areas for a career move.

Small firms offer more limited prospects, and people employed by small companies should be prepared to move in order to progress.

RELATED OCCUPATIONS

Distribution manager, warehouse manager, marketing manager, market research executive, store manager, sales representative.

FURTHER INFORMATION

Chartered Institute of Purchasing and Supply*, Easton House, Easton on the Hill, Stamford, Lincolnshire PE9 3NZ, 01780 56777

FURTHER READING

Leaflets/booklets are available from the address marked*.

Job Outlines – Buying and Purchasing – COIC
Retailing, Retail Buying and Purchasing – AGCAS

In the careers library classified under OP.

FASHION MODEL CLCI:OT

BACKGROUND INFORMATION

Fashion modelling has a very glamorous image. Top models are constantly in the news, shown in exotic locations or on the catwalks in designer shows. For a select few, fashion modelling can be glamorous and well paid. For the majority, however, it is a tough, competitive, insecure and short-lived career.

The main areas of modelling are catwalk and photographic work. There is much overlap between the two and many models do both.

THE WORK

Fashion models display clothes and/or accessories to potential customers to the best effect, either live at a fashion show or in photographs.

Live modelling

'House' models work for wholesale or retail fashion houses displaying garments to private buyers, professional fashion buyers and fashion journalists from newspapers, magazines and television.

They work closely with designers who create clothes on a live model. The model must stand still for long periods of time while the designer drapes and pins the fabric and makes adjustments to the garment.

House models display the finished garments. This involves walking and turning with natural, flowing movements and bringing details of the garments to the attention of spectators. They must allow spectators to have a close view of the garments and may answer their questions about available fabrics, colours and sizes.

House models are expected to undertake other duties when not modelling, such as greeting clients, answering telephones and helping visitors.

Freelance show models work in fashion shows at a variety of venues, displaying clothes produced by fashion houses. High fashion models demonstrate *haute couture* (exclusive fashion) and *pret-a-porter* (ready-to-wear) collections, while general show models display all types of clothes as required. These models are often also photographic models.

The major international fashion shows take place in the spring and autumn. They are generally more flamboyant than showroom work, designed to give an overall impression of the clothes. Shows are often fast-paced and choreographed. Models rehearse the schedule of clothes and display the garments by performing movements to music, sometimes to simple dance routines. During the show there is very little time allowed for models to change outfits and the atmosphere can be hectic.

Designers also take stands at fashion exhibitions held in major cities. Models stand and walk about for much of the day, although exhibitions usually include at least one large show each day.

Models may also do some promotional non-fashion work, for example, at motor shows, product launches and exhibitions.

Photographic modelling

Photographic models work in a studio or on location. A small number of top models obtain work with high fashion and women's magazines but most opportunities are with mail order catalogues and advertisements that appear in magazines, newspapers, advertising brochures and on posters.

Mail order catalogues are produced twice a year and models are used to display clothes in a simple and straightforward way. They are also used to display other catalogue products, such as furniture.

Some models have exceptionally good features, for example, teeth, hands, eyes or hair, and can specialize in modelling particular products that emphasize these features. Some experienced models appear on television and cinema advertisements.

In photographic work models have to follow the photographer's directions on pose, movement and facial expression. They may have to hold a particular pose for a long time. The work involves sitting, standing, moving and posing, while looking natural and relaxed. Photographic sessions can be lengthy, with periods of inactivity while the photographer adjusts the set and lighting.

All models spend time caring for their complexion, hair and figure. When not modelling, freelance models spend much of their time seeking work by attending auditions, and visiting fashion editors and designers.

WORK ENVIRONMENT

Fashion models work mainly indoors in showrooms, studios, stores, hotels or exhibition centres. Dressing rooms and studios can be hot, cramped and overcrowded. Working conditions can be uncomfortably hot or cold. When on location, models may work outside in all weathers.

Models are likely to spend all day on their feet, either standing or walking to display clothes.

Modelling involves travelling to auditions and jobs. Some jobs result in long and short stays away from home.

SKILLS AND INTERESTS

Fashion models should have an interest in fashion and an awareness of new trends in clothing, make-up and hairstyling.

Models must be well groomed at all times. They must look after themselves if they are to keep a good complexion and not put on weight.

Good physical co-ordination is required for the natural, flowing movements of live modelling and for interpreting directions during photographic work. An interest in dance and drama is helpful for this.

Personality is very important in modelling – models work closely with others, including designers, photographers and agents. This requires a pleasant manner and the ability to get on well with people.

Models need to develop a professional approach and be punctual and well prepared for each job. Patience is vital – models may spend long periods waiting around. They must keep smiling and look interested even when they are tired or bored. Self-confidence is important, and models must be able to accept criticism and rejection.

ENTRY REQUIREMENTS

There are no minimum educational qualifications required for fashion modelling, although a good general education is desirable. Appearance and personality are more important than qualifications.

Models should have a slim figure, be well proportioned with

good even physical features. A clear and healthy complexion is required, as are good hands, skin, teeth and hair. Photographic models, in particular, should have a good facial bone structure and be photogenic.

Modelling is physically demanding and tiring, so models need to be fit, healthy and energetic to cope with live shows or lengthy photographic sessions.

Females. The Association of Model Agents recommends that females should be approximately 86-61-86cm (34-24-34 inches) and at least 1.72m (5 feet 8 inches) tall, although most top models are taller. Some females begin modelling part-time before they are 16 years of age.

Males should be at least 1.83m (6 feet) tall. Many male models are taller. The Association of Model Agents recommends that males should also have at least a 97-102 cm (38-40 inch) chest, 76-81cm (30-32 inch) waist and 84cm (33 inch) inside leg measurement. Males usually begin modelling between 17 to 35 years.

The London College of Fashion's College Certificate in Modelling and Grooming prefers students to have three GCSEs/S grades (A-C/1-3). Females must be at least 1.72m (5 feet 8 inches) tall and should maintain size 10-12 (81-61-86/86-66-91cm; 32-24-34/34-26-36 inches). Males should be at least 1.83m (6 feet) tall. Selection is by interview and audition and entry is very competitive.

Commercial modelling schools have no educational entry requirements for their courses. Reputable schools only accept applicants they feel have a chance of succeeding as a model.

Those seeking to enter modelling need at least two photographs, one full face, the other full length, to forward to modelling agencies (with a prepaid envelope for their return).

Whether or not a model has completed a training course, entry to modelling is usually by acceptance onto the books of a reputable modelling agency. Less often, entry is by gaining employment in a showroom.

TRAINING

It is possible to take a training course before trying to enter modelling. Such training is not essential and certainly cannot guarantee success in finding work as a model.

The London College of Fashion's College Certificate in Modelling and Grooming is the only non-commercial modelling course. It is a one-year full-time course and allows students to build confidence and gain experience in modelling in college and often on outside assignments. It also gives students a general introduction to fashion. The course includes hair and make-up, styling, movement and choreography, dance, exercise and health care. Students may build up a basic portfolio during the course.

A number of commercial modelling schools offer training courses. They vary from courses that last for a few evenings to those that are full-time for several weeks. Courses provide the basic techniques of fashion and photographic modelling and may also cover grooming, hygiene, diet, exercise, skin care and make-up, deportment and fashion clothing and accessories. Commercial modelling courses tend to be very expensive.

When models are accepted onto an agent's books they are advised about dress, appearance and hair styles. Agents may recommend hairdressers and cosmetic experts. Experienced models teach new recruits basic walks, turns, stands and poses.

LATE ENTRY

There is no strict upper age limit for entry to modelling. Most female models, though, begin in their teens, while most males start between the ages of 17 and 25 years. Entry beyond those ages is unusual and extremely difficult.

OPPORTUNITIES

Most fashion models work freelance and find work through model agencies, some of which specialize in either show or photographic work. Model agencies are regulated by the Employment Agencies Act, 1973, which does not allow them to charge a model for joining an agency.

It is important that models seek representation with reputable agencies, such as those belonging to the Association of Model Agents (AMA). Reputable agencies only accept models they feel may be successful in finding modelling work.

Entry to modelling is highly competitive. Even after acceptance onto an agency's books it may be very difficult to obtain work.

There are few openings for permanent positions as a house model with wholesale and retail fashion businesses.

Most modelling work is for females, although there has been an increasing demand for male models over the past few years. Male models are employed more in photographic work than in live modelling.

Most work for fashion models is in London and it can be very difficult to make a reasonable living from modelling outside London. The AMA, for example, has 19 member agencies in London and just two outside (in Dublin and Glasgow).

Modelling careers tend to be short. Some live models may continue modelling into their thirties but photographic models usually finish before they are 30. There are some opportunities for experienced, older models to promote products aimed at a more mature market.

PAY AND CONDITIONS

Most models are self-employed and earn only when they work. Earnings can therefore vary tremendously. They obtain work through modelling agencies which negotiate fees for each job. The agencies deduct a percentage of the modelling fees as commission, typically 20 to 25 per cent.

It is unusual for most new models to find regular work and earnings can be low – often below £4,000 a year – unless and until they establish a reputation for their work. Few people ever make a living from modelling. Successful models, however, can earn £200 to £400 a day for photographic work. Catalogue work earnings vary according to a model's popularity, but may be up to £250 a day, although the work is seasonal. Advertising can pay up to £100 an hour. Editorial work pays less than these rates – from £35 a day – but it is very useful for getting models seen and in building up their careers.

Freelance models often have to pay their own expenses, such as travel to auditions and jobs and maintaining a wardrobe.

There are no set working hours for freelance models, although a working day can be as long as ten hours.

Models employed full-time by fashion houses work more regular hours, with overtime usual at show times. These models receive a set wage.

There is little opportunity for part-time work.

PROSPECTS

Modelling has no career structure. Successful employed models may seek to increase their income by becoming freelance. Freelance models progress by being offered more prestigious and highly paid jobs.

When their modelling career is finished models may seek to use their experience in a number of ways. They may teach in a modelling school. Some run or manage a modelling agency. It may be possible to enter fashion journalism, fashion consultancy, public relations in a fashion house or store, retailing or sales work.

RELATED OCCUPATIONS

Beauty therapist/beautician, beauty consultant, make-up artist, actor, dancer, fashion designer.

FURTHER INFORMATION

The Association of Model Agents*, The Clockhouse, St Catherine's Mews, Milner Street, London SW3 2PX, 071 584 6466 (enclose sae), Model Information Line 0891 517 644

London College of Fashion*, 20 John Princes Street, London W1M 0BJ, 0171 514 7400

FURTHER READING

Leaflets/booklets are available from addresses marked*.

Job Outlines – COIC
Working in Fashion – COIC
Careers in Fashion – Kogan Page

In the careers library classified under OT.

1. **SCIENTIST/TECHNICIAN CLCI:QOB-QOM**
2. **FOOD SCIENTIST/TECHNOLOGIST/TECHNICIAN CLCI:QON**
3. **MATERIALS SCIENTIST/TECHNOLOGIST/METALLURGIST CLCI:QOS**

1. SCIENTIST/TECHNICIAN (QOB-QOM)

BACKGROUND INFORMATION

Scientists are involved in the systematic study of the nature and behaviour of the material and physical world, based on observation, experiment and measurement. The scientific subjects taught at school – biology, chemistry, maths and physics – form the basis for an enormous range of scientific careers. It is possible to qualify and work in these familiar subject areas or to choose a more specialized field, such as biochemistry, metallurgy, food science, forensic science, environmental monitoring or a related subject like computer science or engineering.

Employment opportunities range from laboratory-based posts in areas such as research and development or quality control to work in technical marketing, production management or science teaching. Professional scientists and technicians work for both public and private sector organizations, in this country and overseas.

Most professional scientists and technicians qualify in one of the following disciplines, although much scientific study and many fields of scientific work combine two or more of these.

Biological science is concerned with the study of living organisms and includes many different specialisms. Zoology is concerned with animals, botany with plants. Microbiology involves the study of micro-organisms, while biochemistry and pharmacology are concerned with chemical compounds and reactions in living organisms. All of these areas of biology are important in the pharmaceutical and food industries and in medicine. Biotechnology, where the scientific theory of biological processes is applied to technological development, is an expanding area. It involves the production of man-made molecules, such as hormones and enzymes, and is closely linked to genetic engineering.

Chemistry is concerned with the composition, reactions and properties of substances. Laboratory-based chemical research leads to the development of new products, such as drugs for combating disease, foodstuffs, dyes and paints, fertilizers, detergents, synthetic fibres for textiles, plastics and cosmetics. Analytical chemistry is vital in areas such as environmental protection and medicine and is important in ensuring the quality of production in the chemical, pharmaceutical and food and drink industries. It also plays an essential part in public health protection and in such work as forensic science.

Physics is based on the properties of matter and energy, and the relationship between them. Through physics we can understand how and why things behave as they do. It includes topics such as heat, light, magnetism, electricity, electronics, sound, atomic physics, laser optics, cosmology, astrophysics, quantum physics, plasma physics, opto-electronics and low temperature physics. The work of physicists often involves both experimental investigations and theoretical analysis, and forms the basis for solving a wide range of scientific and engineering problems.

Mathematics forms the basis for increasingly important fields such as computing, systems analysis, statistics and operational research. Mathematical operations and processes are therefore involved in the solution of many scientific problems in industry and commerce. Mathematics is also very important in physics and engineering fields.

Professional scientists and technicians are also active in more specialized areas:

Food science concentrates on developing processes of cooking, preserving and storing food, and on quality control procedures. Food scientists and technologists are employed by industrial and manufacturing companies as well as government bodies such as the Ministry of Agriculture, Fisheries and Food. Please see article 2. FOOD SCIENTIST/TECHNOLOGIST.

Medical laboratory sciences cover a wide range of related fields including pharmacology, biochemistry, microbiology, cytology, immunology, cellular pathology and haematology. Medical laboratory scientists and technicians work in the National Health Service and private hospitals, government departments, higher education institutions, manufacturing industry and the Armed Forces.

Materials science involves the study of a wide range of natural and man-made materials including glass, ceramics and polymers, while **metallurgy** is concerned with metals and alloys. Metallurgists and materials scientists/technicians are therefore involved in the development of new materials and in the selection of appropriate materials for new products. Metallurgists are also employed in the mining industry. Please see article 3. MATERIALS SCIENTIST/TECHNOLOGIST/METALLURGIST.

Environmental science has become increasingly popular as awareness of green issues increases. Environmental scientists work in such diverse areas as geology, hydrogeology, geophysics, meteorology, ecology and astrophysics, to improve and maintain our environment.

Other areas in which professional scientists and technicians are active include: agriculture, horticulture, natural resources, biomedicine, health care and education.

THE WORK

Scientists often work as part of a multidisciplinary team in a laboratory experimenting, monitoring and analysing the results. They are required to write up the results of tests and experiments, perhaps using a computer for analysis of data. Information technology skills are increasingly important.

There is also a growing emphasis on being able to communicate scientific information in an understandable way to non-specialist audiences, for example, to marketing staff and customers.

Many scientists have a management role, including responsibility for staff, premises and work scheduling. They may also have financial responsibilities in areas such as purchasing, planning and managing a department budget. Scientists must pay close attention to health and safety requirements.

It is essential for scientists to devote time to keeping up to date with new developments in their area of specialization, for example, through reading scientific journals, membership of a professional body, or attending conferences.

Technicians play an important role as part of the scientific team. The work varies enormously from one environment to another – from analysing blood samples in a hospital to operating physical testing equipment in a research centre, from assisting with the development of a new polymer to preparing equipment for use by students at a college. The work frequently involves taking measurements, so accuracy is vital. A working knowledge of computers is often necessary as complex calculations are common. Technicians also have to keep equipment – such as measuring devices – clean and in good working order. Senior technicians require good financial and management skills.

The main areas of work are:

Research, design and development (R&D) covers a wide spectrum of activity from basic, original research through applied research to the development of new products to meet a particular market need. Research requires innovative ideas, together with the ability to develop creative and practical solutions. Universities often undertake pure research, and some projects may have no immediate practical application. Others, such as those undertaken by commercial organizations, are designed to develop saleable new products or to improve existing ones. Scientists and engineers often work together on exciting and challenging projects to design and develop new products.

Analysis involves a wide variety of tests using highly sophisticated equipment, as well as complex manual procedures. The work of analysts ranges from quality assurance to aid manufacturing production, to testing samples of water, food, drugs or chemicals. In medical laboratories, the majority of the routine tests are carried out by technical staff (medical laboratory scientific officers), while scientists are involved in specialized analyses and the development of new techniques.

Production is usually a commercial enterprise and involves the manufacturing of products. Scientists and technicians work as part of a production team to ensure that the manufacturing process is carried out efficiently, safely and practically. The end product must also be tested for quality and effectiveness.

Management services covers a broad range of activities which include: marketing and sales, technical support, operational research and data processing. Marketing and sales is a vital area for many businesses, such as chemical and pharmaceutical companies, as international competition is fierce. An excellent understanding of the customer, the product and its competitors is vital.

Technical support staff provide a back-up for the marketing and sales team, offering technical advice and information. If there is a problem with a product, they have to resolve it.

Education. There is a great demand for science teachers in schools and colleges, particularly teachers of the physical sciences. Please see TEACHING articles (FAB). Many science graduates find work within institutions of higher education as lecturers or choose to carry out research and gain further qualifications. Others train to teach young people at schools, tertiary colleges and colleges of further education. Teachers and lecturers need to be able to communicate effectively, and to demonstrate their enthusiasm for science.

WORK ENVIRONMENT

Many scientists/technicians are laboratory-based, but scientists/technicians also work in offices, on production lines, building sites, mines and weather centres.

Scientists work with team members of every discipline, supervising technicians and other support staff, as well as working alone. Many scientists travel to other laboratories or libraries, attend meetings, seminars and conferences, both in this country and overseas. Some scientists take part in video conferences and may communicate via the Internet.

SKILLS AND INTERESTS

Both scientists and technicians need to have a keen interest in science. It is important to have a clear logical mind and a practical approach to problem solving. Accuracy and attention to detail are vital. Technicians should be methodical, as they often carry out routine tests and applications. Research activities require persistence.

Imaginative and creative abilities are required to find solutions to problems. Good communication skills, both spoken and written, are important. Scientists/technicians need to be able to explain clearly scientific and technical concepts to the non-specialist. It is also important to work well with others as a team member.

ENTRY REQUIREMENTS

Graduate entry

A recognized science degree is necessary. Minimum entry requirements for degree courses are either: two A levels/three H grades and GCSEs/S grades (A-C/1-3) in three other subjects – specific subjects may be required, eg maths, English and relevant sciences; or a relevant BTEC/SCOTVEC national award; or a relevant Advanced GNVQ/GSVQ Level III.

Applicants with non-science A levels may be accepted onto a foundation year preceding the first year of a degree course in some institutions. Many professional bodies offer recognized qualifications equivalent to a first degree, which also allow membership at different grades.

Technician level entry

The minimum requirements for technician entry are either: four GCSEs/S grades (A-C/1-3); or a relevant BTEC first award; or appropriate SCOTVEC national certificate modules; or Intermediate GNVQ/GSVQ Level II.

BTEC/SCOTVEC higher national diploma/certificate courses require a minimum of either: one A level/H grade and three GCSEs/S grades (A-C/1-3); or a relevant BTEC/SCOTVEC national award; or a relevant Advanced GNVQ/GSVQ Level III.

BTEC national diploma and certificate courses usually require either: four GCSEs/S grades (A-C/1-3); or a BTEC first award; or Intermediate GNVQ/GSVQ Level II.

SCOTVEC national certificate courses have no set entry requirements. Applicants should check with individual colleges, who may set their own requirements as they wish, to be satisfied that students are able to benefit from the courses.

Advanced GNVQs/GSVQs Level III usually require either four GCSEs/S grades (A-C/1-3), or Intermediate GNVQ/GSVQ Level II.

The Institute of Science Technology's (IST) Ordinary Diploma and Certificate have a preferred minimum entry requirement of four GCSEs/S grades (A-C/1-3), preferably including a science subject, or equivalent. Candidates for the IST's Higher Diploma should have A levels/H grades or equivalent. There are no formal entry requirements for the IST/City and Guilds Core Vocational Qualification (CVQ).

Modern Apprenticeships have been introduced for young

people in some areas of chemical work, including process operations and laboratory operations. There are no set entry requirements and selection is based on entry tests and evidence of relevant academic success. Contact your local careers office, TEC/LEC for details.

TRAINING

A number of professional and industrial organizations offer sponsorship to science students. Bursaries are available from a number of organizations and salaries are normally paid while students are on industrial placement at the company/organization.

Graduate training

A wide range of degree courses in scientific subjects is offered by many universities and colleges of higher education. Courses are either three or four years in duration. Four-year sandwich courses allow a period of time for placement with an employer, where students can get 'hands-on' experience. Courses include: biological and medicinal chemistry, pharmacology, immunology, agricultural science, laboratory science and administration, food technology, textile science, and environmental science, as well as the more familiar basic sciences.

Many graduates with a science degree follow this with a postgraduate course. A good degree (first or upper second class) is normally needed to progress to a research degree. There are specialized options from which to choose for both taught courses and research degrees.

Technician training

Technicians may take a full-time course before joining an employer. They may study for either: a higher national diploma with a view to entry as a higher level technician (two years full-time or three years sandwich); or a BTEC national diploma (two years); or a SCOTVEC national certificate (one year); or an Advanced GNVQ/GSVQ Level III.

Those seeking to work in animal science can take the Institute of Science Technology's (IST) Ordinary Diploma (one year full-time) in Animal Science at Blackpool and The Fylde College, West Cheshire College or Swindon College.

Alternatively technicians may enter work and study part-time on a day release or evening class basis for either: BTEC higher national certificate (two years); or SCOTVEC higher national certificate (one year); or BTEC national certificate (two years); or SCOTVEC national certificate (one year). Those working in animal science can study for the IST's Ordinary Certificate in Animal Science by attending one of the colleges listed above, part-time for two years.

IST's Higher Diploma is intended for employed technicians. It is not a taught course but is designed to recognize technicians' understanding and competence. It is offered in the following subjects: analytical chemical laboratory techniques, biochemical laboratory techniques, electron microscopy laboratory techniques, physiology and pharmacology laboratory techniques and microbiological laboratory techniques. It consists of two written papers and a practical project overseen by the candidate's employer.

The IST, in conjunction with City and Guilds, has introduced the Core Vocational Qualification (CVQ), a work-based qualification for laboratory technicians. Preliminary, Intermediate and Advanced levels are being planned.

Those on Modern Apprenticeships work towards a relevant NVQ/SVQ at Level 3, eg Process Operations or Laboratory Operations. They also undertake training in team work, communication, application of number, problem solving, information technology and self-development. There is no set length of time for Modern Apprenticeships, but training is likely to take at least three years.

In-service training is provided by most public and private sector organizations for both scientists and technicians, through external short courses, in-house programmes or distance learning. This training may cover advanced technical skills or business management areas. Many employers also encourage staff to participate in the career development opportunities offered by professional bodies.

There are a number of NVQs/SVQs available in science areas up to level 4.

LATE ENTRY

There are no upper age limits for entry to scientific work, but adult entrants must have science qualifications. However, as scientific knowledge develops so rapidly, opportunities may be limited. Refresher courses are run by some colleges for scientists wishing to return to work after a career break.

Access courses for adults, who wish to study for a degree but do not have the necessary qualifications, are offered at many local colleges. Courses are usually one year full-time or one/two years part-time with daytime and/or evening attendance.

Mature applicants may be accepted onto a foundation year preceding the first year of a science degree or higher national diploma course in some institutions.

OPPORTUNITIES

Within specialized scientific fields, there is a massive range of jobs available to qualified scientists and technicians. For example scientists can choose a laboratory-based career or work in sales and marketing. Starting a career in one sector of industry does not mean staying there, and scientists are able to move around as their career develops.

The main areas of employment are within industry. Scientists and technicians are employed in a wide range of private sector organizations, such as pharmaceutical companies, food manufacturers and research consultancies.

Public sector organizations are also major employers of scientists, including education establishments, government departments and the National Health Service.

Jobs are advertised in magazines and newspapers such as: *The New Scientist, The Institute of Biomedical Science Gazette, Laboratory News, Chemistry in Britain, Chemistry and Industry, Process Engineering, Energy World, Physics World, Food Manufacture, Food Processing, Farmers' Weekly, The Guardian, The Daily Telegraph, The Independent, The Sunday Times, Times Educational Supplement, Times Higher Educational Supplement.*

PAY AND CONDITIONS

Laboratory technicians may earn between £8,500 and £13,300, assistant scientists £12,000 to £18,000 and senior scientists £17,000 to £26,500.

Figures for scientists/technicians employed in industry depend on qualifications, experience, ability and employer location. Large manufacturing and industrial companies offer highly competitive salaries.

Many scientists/technicians work normal office hours, 9am to 5pm, Monday to Friday. Laboratories in hospitals, however, operate 24 hours a day, and staff work to a rota. Weekend and evening work may also be necessary for scientists and technicians employed in industry, who are often required to meet tight deadlines.

Temporary and part-time work and job sharing are sometimes available.

PROSPECTS

Promotion and prospects vary within private and public sectors. Medical laboratory science officers follow a grading scale within the National Health Service as do scientists/technicians who are part of the Scientific Civil Service. Within private organizations promotion can be fast and scientists are likely to be given managerial responsibilities, including the possibility of director-level posts.

Some scientists may have to move around the UK to obtain promotion. Employment opportunities exist not only in the UK but elsewhere in the world, particularly Europe and North America.

Scientists can use their knowledge to enter careers in other areas such as production, scientific publishing and information technology.

RELATED OCCUPATIONS

Engineer, telecoms engineer, pharmacist, pharmacy technician, technical brewer, geologist, oceanographer, meteorologist.

FURTHER INFORMATION

The Association of Clinical Biochemists, Burlington House, Piccadilly, London W1V 0BN, 0171 437 8656

The Biochemical Society*, 59 Portland Place, London W1N 3AJ, 0171 580 5530

Bio-Industry Association, 14-15 Belgrave Square, London SW1X 8PS, 0171 245 9911

British Pharmacological Society, 16 Angel Gate, City Road, London EC1V 2PT, 0171 417 0113

Food and Drink Industry Training Organization, Training and Careers Executive, 6 Catherine Street, London WC2B 5JJ, 0171 836 2460

The Institute of Biology*, 20-22 Queensberry Place, London SW7 2DZ, 0171 581 8333 (sae required)

Institute of Biomedical Science*, 12 Coldbath Square, London EC1R 5HL, 0171 636 8192

The Institute of Food Science and Technology*, 5 Cambridge Court, 210 Shepherd's Bush Road, London W6 7NL, 0171 603 6316

The Institute of Materials*, 1 Carlton House Terrace, London SW1Y 5DB, 0171 839 4071

The Institute of Physics*, 76 Portland Place, London W1N 4AA, 0171 470 4800

Institute of Science Technology, Mansell House, 22 Bore Street, Lichfield, Staffs WS13 6LP, 01543 251346

Institution of Mining and Metallurgy, 44 Portland Place, London W1N 4BR, 0171 580 3802

The Royal Society of Chemistry*, Burlington House, Piccadilly, London W1V 0BN, 0171 437 8656

FURTHER READING

Leaflets/booklets are available from the addresses marked*.

Job Outlines – Food Science and Technology – COIC
Job Outlines – Laboratories – COIC
Job Outlines – Management Services – COIC
Working in Food and Drink – COIC
Working in Chemistry – COIC
Student Helpbook Series – Careers With a Science Degree – CRAC/Hobsons

In the careers library classified under QOB/QOD/QOF/QOM.

2. FOOD SCIENTIST/TECHNOLOGIST/TECHNICIAN (QON)

THE WORK

Food scientists examine the chemical, biological and nutritional aspects of food from raw materials through to the finished product while food technologists use their expertise to turn raw materials into finished products, but the two overlap and most food scientists/technologists use a combination of both subjects in their work.

They work in four main fields.

Applied research

Food scientists/technologists work on projects to solve problems that occur in the development or processing of new food products as well as on the safety of food and its processing.

They work as part of a small team on their own, on both long and short-term projects, normally on several at the same time. They design experiments, use the latest equipment, much of which is computer controlled, and prepare reports on their findings. Examples of projects include: testing a starch in a range of mayonnaise, ice creams and low-fat spreads to establish whether it could be an effective substitute for fat; evaluating the effect of microwave cooking on raw ingredients; or investigating the safety of irradiation as a method of preserving food.

Technicians assist the scientists and technologists by operating equipment under guidance. They help to collate results and statistics and may be in charge of one section of the laboratory, and responsible for ordering supplies and controlling stock.

Research of this nature is carried out in institutions of higher education, government-funded and independent research establishments and large food companies. Trouble shooting and problem solving are also carried out in small to medium-sized companies, or consultancies to the food industry.

Product/process development

This can mean development of new products, making changes to existing ones or improving the manufacturing process.

In most food manufacturing companies this type of work goes on all the time. Food scientists/technologists make up small batch samples and test them on panels of tasters, often drawn from the general public. They note suggestions and comments and prepare full-scale trial runs on processing equipment. Problems often occur at this stage, in transferring small samples to factory processes. If the product is not of the required quality or safety standard they analyse the ingredients at each stage of manufacture. Problems can occur at any stage, including packaging.

Product development involves food scientists/technologists in liaison with other departments in the company, such as sales and marketing. They often have to work within a strict budget and to tight deadlines.

Quality control

This involves analysing raw materials, monitoring stages of production and checking storage and distribution conditions. Food scientists/technologists conduct tests on taste, texture, nutritional value, colour, and ensure that products conform to government regulations regarding additives and safety. They are also responsible for the overall appearance of a finished product, ensuring for instance that all the biscuits in a batch look the same after baking.

They use varying techniques including sophisticated gas chromatography for compositional analysis of oils and fats and near-infra-red reflectance spectroscopy to determine the moisture, fat and protein content of foods.

Much routine testing is done by machines, some of which may be operated by technicians. Quality control technicians carry out the bulk of the testing and monitoring work, take samples from the conveyor belt, analyse them and keep records at each production stage. Statistical evaluation is important.

Production management

Food scientists/technologists have to make sure that production is as efficient as possible. When there is a drop in quality or a time delay, they try to find out which stage of production is causing the problem. Many of the problems are technical, for example, to do with faulty equipment, but this specialism also requires them to manage people and resources. They are often involved in recruitment and training, and may take part in negotiating industrial relations.

Other work

Some food scientists/technologists work for government departments, investigating food safety, collecting and interpreting information and acting as advisers. In the Ministry of Agriculture, Fisheries and Food (MAFF) Scottish Link they also deal with problems of pesticides and food contamination. Others specialize in packing technology or process equipment engineering.

Other opportunities exist in retailing, consultancy, technical sales, technical journalism, trading standards, education and, increasingly, in environmental health.

WORK ENVIRONMENT

Food scientists/technologists involved in research and development work mainly in laboratories or pilot plants. Those specializing in food manufacturing spend much of their time on the factory floor: those with management responsibilities may be based in an office.

Food scientists/technologists who work for food manufacturers may spend time away from their own research laboratories visiting other factories in the group where different products are made, and visiting firms that supply ingredients. Those working for retailers spend a lot of time visiting the companies that manufacture their products.

SKILLS AND INTERESTS

Food scientists/technologists need a strong interest and ability in science combined with an enquiring mind. They should be accurate and methodical and enjoy applying an analytical approach to problem solving. It helps to be

innovative and creative, particularly in the area of product development.

Self-motivation is important as much work has to be completed to deadlines. Since the job often requires them to work on several different projects simultaneously they should also be flexible and able to allocate time to different priorities. Personal hygiene is also a priority for anyone involved with food handling, due to the responsibility for people's safety.

Many jobs also require management skills, the ability to communicate with all different types of people and to write clear reports.

ENTRY REQUIREMENTS

Food scientists/technologists. Most qualify by taking a full-time or sandwich degree or higher national diploma in food science and/or technology.

Degrees in Food Science/Technology usually require a minimum of either: two A levels, preferably including chemistry, with the other either biology, physics or maths, plus three GCSEs (A-C) in other subjects; or three H grades, preferably including maths, chemistry and physics, plus two S grades (1-3) in other subjects; or a relevant BTEC/SCOTVEC national award (eg science or food technology); or a relevant Advanced GNVQ/GSVQ Level III (eg science).

BTEC higher national diploma and certificate courses usually require either: one science A level, preferably chemistry, plus GCSEs (A-C) in maths and English; or a relevant BTEC/SCOTVEC national award (eg science or food technology); or a relevant Advanced GNVQ/GSVQ Level III (eg science).

SCOTVEC higher national diploma and certificate courses usually require either: two H grades, including a science, plus three S grades (1-3); or a relevant BTEC/SCOTVEC national award (eg science or food technology); or a relevant Advanced GNVQ/GSVQ Level III (eg science). Those with a higher national diploma may be eligible for third-year entry to a degree course.

Different institutions prefer different combinations of subjects and it is advisable to check entry requirements.

Applicants with non-science A levels may be accepted onto a foundation year preceding the first year of a food science/technology degree or higher national diploma in some institutions.

It is also possible to enter most areas of employment with a qualification in a closely related subject, such as chemical engineering, microbiology, biology or analytical and applied chemistry. Some graduates in these areas take a postgraduate course in food science or food technology, entry to which is with a first degree.

Technician entry. The usual entry qualifications are either: a minimum of four GCSEs/S grades (A-C/1-3), often including English, maths and a science subject; or a relevant BTEC first award (eg science); or appropriate SCOTVEC national certificate modules; or a relevant Intermediate GNVQ/GSVQ Level II (eg science).

BTEC national diploma and certificate courses usually require either: four GCSEs/S grades (A-C/1-3); or a BTEC first award; or Intermediate GNVQ/GSVQ Level II.

SCOTVEC national certificate courses usually require a minimum of four S grades (1-3), including chemistry, or equivalent.

Advanced GNVQ courses usually requires either: four

GCSEs/S grades (A-C/1-3) preferably including science; or a BTEC first award; or Intermediate GNVQ/GSVQ Level II.

Defective colour vision or skin allergies may be a problem in this career.

TRAINING

Food scientist/technologist. A number of universities and colleges offer degree courses in food science/studies/technology. Titles vary as does course content. Most cover the basic disciplines of food processing, biochemistry, microbiology, physics, mathematics and statistics, nutrition, quality control, management studies and basic engineering. Each course also offers additional options and specialisms. Courses usually last three or four years full-time or four years on a sandwich basis, where some time is spent on placement with an employer. All honours degree courses in Scotland last for four years.

Graduates in other science subjects may either take a postgraduate course in food science or food technology or find employment with an employer who arranges any necessary training for them.

A number of colleges offer higher national diploma courses relevant to food science and technology. Courses usually last two years full-time or three years on a sandwich basis. For some students these courses can lead to eventual transfer to a degree course.

The Institute of Food Science and Technology (UK) – the food scientists' and technologists' professional body – awards its own Postgraduate Diploma in Food Control. Graduates working full-time in the food and allied industries may join the programme. The Diploma combines academic study with work-based experience and requires the successful completion of three of six modules. Final assessment is by case study and oral examination.

Technicians may take a full-time course before joining an employer. They may study for either: a higher national diploma with a view to entry as a higher level technician; or a BTEC national diploma (two years); or a SCOTVEC national certificate (one year); or an Advanced GNVQ in Science with food technology specialism that is offered at Grimsby College (two years).

Alternatively they may enter work and study part-time on a day release or evening class basis for either: BTEC higher national certificate (two years); or SCOTVEC higher national certificate (one year); or BTEC national certificate (two years); or SCOTVEC national certificate (one year).

Many BTEC/SCOTVEC courses, particularly those that are part-time, have specialisms geared to the needs of the local industry, for example, baking or meat, while others have options in business or management studies.

NVQs/SVQs relating to food science and technology are currently being developed.

LATE ENTRY

Late entry is not difficult for mature graduates in food science and related subjects due to the national shortage of food scientists/technologists.

Access courses for adults who wish to study for a degree or higher national diploma course but do not have the necessary qualifications are offered at many local colleges. They are usually one year full-time or one or two years part-time with daytime and/or evening attendance.

Late entry technicians may have difficulty in finding posts if not able to move to another location.

OPPORTUNITIES

There are about 4,000 food scientists/technologists working in the UK. About one-third in research and development and another third in production and quality control.

The majority of opportunities are with: the food processing and manufacturing industry – with manufacturers of products or ingredients, packaging and equipment manufacturers; in research laboratories and in government departments (especially the Ministry of Agriculture, Fisheries and Food); and with retailers. Supermarket chains are now major employers. They have teams of food technologists who are concerned with new product development, food control and product distribution. The latter requires knowledge of refrigeration and packaging techniques, and shelf-life of individual products.

Food scientists/technologists may work as public analysts in laboratories, move into the catering industry or become specialist environmental health officers with local authorities. It is possible to work for consultancy organizations.

There are also opportunities in education. Food scientists/technologists may work in universities and colleges that teach food science and technology as specific subjects but also may teach courses concerned with agriculture, catering, dietetics, nutrition and food management and marketing.

There are some opportunities to work for international organizations like the United Nations and to work overseas on short-term projects in developing countries.

Jobs are available throughout the UK, although most of the research establishments are in the South East of England (with the exception of the MAFF research station in Norwich and the Campden Food and Drink Research Association in Gloucestershire).

Recruitment is fairly regular and as there is a shortage of well-qualified food scientists and especially technologists, there is a good choice of openings. There is competition, however, for entry to the food research associations which may only need a small number of new entrants each year.

PAY AND CONDITIONS

Earnings vary according to employer, specialism, qualifications and location. A new graduate may expect from £10,000 to £15,000.

Hours of work depend on the type of work being done. Food scientists/technologists working in research and development may work a standard five-day 37-hour week, Monday to Friday. Those involved with food manufacturing processes may have to work the usual hours of the factory which can include some shift, evening or weekend working.

PROSPECTS

Promotion prospects for food scientists/technologists depend on where they work. In central or local government there is a structured career path with prospects of promotion to a higher grade, ultimately running a research laboratory, selecting research topics and managing staff.

Some similar positions exist in the private sector, but senior positions in industry generally depend on business and management skills or may mean a move away from bench laboratory work into more general management.

Those who want promotion in a particular field may have to move between companies or between employment sectors.

Self-employment in consultancy work is possible. A small

number become journalists, technical writers and information scientists.

RELATED OCCUPATIONS

Analytical chemist, dietitian, nutritionist.

FURTHER INFORMATION

The Institute of Food Science and Technology (UK)*, 5 Cambridge Court, 210 Shepherd's Bush Road, London W6 7NJ, 0171 603 6316 (please send 9x6 inch sae)

Food and Drink Industry Training Organization, Training and Careers Executive, 6 Catherine Street, London WC2 5JJ, 0171 836 2460

FURTHER READING

Leaflets/booklets are available from the address marked*.

Job Outlines – Food Science and Technology – COIC
Where to Study for a Career in Food Science and Technology – Institute of Food Science and Technology
An A-Z of Careers in Food Science and Technology – Institute of Food Science and Technology

In the careers library classified under QON/SAB.

3. MATERIALS SCIENTIST/ TECHNOLOGIST/METALLURGIST (QOS)

BACKGROUND INFORMATION

All kinds of products used in daily life are made from materials. Some, like wood and stone, are used in their natural state, as is gold in some manufacturing processes. (Fine gold wires are used in microelectronics.) Most materials, however, are made by applying physical and chemical processes to natural raw materials and their compounds to make **polymers** like plastics (which are derived from oil, coal, natural gas and salt) and rubbers; **metals** (eg steel, stainless steel); and **ceramics** including glass.

Materials science/metallurgy has been responsible for the development of products as different as bathroom fittings, computer disks, house guttering, contact lenses, double glazing, cling film, car bodies and replacement hip joints.

Materials scientists/technologists and metallurgists are concerned with the behaviour of metals and materials in their natural state and improving our knowledge of what they can be made to do or how they can be exploited, finding answers to questions such as: 'Why does steel rust? Why is glass brittle?'. The results of research are applied to the manufacture and production of the alloys, compounds, etc.

There is much overlap between the disciplines of materials science/metallurgy; so much so that they are often studied together, although there are specialist courses.

Some people use the name of the material in which they specialize in their job titles, calling themselves ceramics, glass, plastics technologists or paper scientists instead of using the more general term. There is no standard materials scientist.

Strictly speaking however, metallurgists study metals alone; polymer scientists, polymers; while people who study *all* materials, ie, metals, polymers and ceramics, are called materials scientists. Similarly, the job titles scientist, engineer and technologist are used interchangeably.

THE WORK

Materials scientists/technologists and metallurgists use the three basic subjects, of physics, chemistry and maths, in their work. Since the area of materials is so vast, however, specialization is common.

Materials scientists apply the principles of chemistry and physics to structures, uses and production of all kinds of materials, but may specialize in working on one or two only, depending on the research and manufacture undertaken by their employers.

Materials technologists and engineers are concerned with: selecting the most appropriate material for a particular product whether it is a cutting tool, component for electronic devices or artificial limb; design; and the fabrication of materials into products.

Metallurgists normally specialize in one of the two sciences.

Chemical metallurgists are concerned with the extraction and purification of metals from their ores, the reclamation of metals from scrap, corrosion prevention and the development of new, lighter alloys.

Physical metallurgists specialize in the structure and physical properties of metals and alloys, and in particular, how they behave when subjected to stress and overload.

Process metallurgists work in a third area; they are concerned with the actual manufacturing process. They are the experts on the best way to produce the required product, deciding whether to use forging, welding, bonding, or other techniques, and how to alter a metal's properties by controlled heat treatment.

Materials scientists/technologists and metallurgists work in three main areas.

Research and development

This is carried out in laboratories in educational establishments, government research institutes or on manufacturers' premises.

Government and university-funded projects are usually concerned with finding solutions to problems over a long period. Industry supports research for results in the short term, designed to improve, invent or modify its own products, often with a very short time-scale.

Scientists work at a laboratory bench – the term used is actually 'bench research'. They work in a team with colleagues, some of them specialists in other scientific disciplines. They have junior staff to supervise and, depending on their seniority, may be responsible for managing the project's budget and staying within the agreed sum made available for research.

Research is undertaken into new ways of using existing materials and also into improving methods used in processing. Development involves developing new ideas from existing products. Of the two, research tends to be more chemistry-based, while development uses mathematical and engineering knowledge.

Research and development staff make use of traditional laboratory tools – microscopes, testing equipment, sophisticated analytical machinery, much of it controlled by computer. They make considerable use of computers when analysing data and results of experiments. All staff, but particularly the project director, have to keep accurate written records of the project's progress. The senior scientists and director have to write the final report.

Scientists working in universities and government establishments are able to publish their findings in the form of research papers. Those in industry are often prohibited from doing so because of the need for commercial secrecy.

Technicians assist the scientists and technologists by setting up experiments and operating equipment under guidance. They also help to collate results and statistics and may be in charge of one section of the laboratory, and responsible for ordering supplies and controlling stock.

Quality control

All products have to be tested at stages during manufacture to ensure they meet the purpose for which they were designed, are safe, with all components reaching the same standard. In addition to standards imposed by individual manufacturers, British Safety Standards (laid down by government) must be met. Quality control is also responsible for ensuring that goods are being produced as economically as possible.

Materials scientists/technologists take samples for analysis; this is done either in the laboratory or on the factory floor, depending on the size of the parts being tested. Testing may be done by chemical, physical or mechanical methods – a process known as destructive testing, since the product is deliberately broken down or changed, for example, by abrasion – or electrically. Testing done by the latter method, using X-rays for example, leaves the component in its original state, and is known as non-destructive testing.

Routine testing is done by machine. Samples that need to be tested by hand or bench equipment are usually the responsibility of technicians who carry out the bulk of the testing and monitoring work, taking samples from the conveyor belt, analysing them and keeping records at each production stage.

Production

Some materials scientists/technologists and metallurgists become production managers or manufacturing engineers.

Production managers and manufacturing engineers use managerial rather than scientific skills, although in this career a technical background and understanding of the processes involved is important.

They are responsible for the manufacture of products or components on time and in line with the agreed budget. Their work includes planning every stage of production to ensure that equipment is being used to full capacity and that parts and supplies arrive on schedule in order to keep the production process in operation.

Anyone working in research, quality control or production, but particularly the latter, may have to wear protective clothing. This depends on the materials being worked with. Some substances are dangerous and there are strict government health and safety regulations regarding the control of substances hazardous to health (COSHH regulations). In other cases, protective clothing is used to protect the product. Processing of silicon, for example, is done in clean rooms with all the staff wearing full head-to-toe anti-contamination suits, gloves and face masks to protect the silicon from dust.

Other opportunities exist in technical sales and marketing, technical journalism, information work, consultancy, teaching and lecturing.

WORK ENVIRONMENT

The workplace of materials scientists/technologists and metallurgists depends on their specialism. They might work in laboratories, in scrupulously clean production plants wearing special suits or in very noisy and possibly dangerous conditions. A metallurgist or metallurgical technician may use portable testing equipment outdoors. Others have to spend time on noisy factory floors or visit industrial plants operating furnaces at very high temperatures to assess the possibility of using specially designed materials in them.

Most materials scientists/technologists and metallurgists also spend time in offices, writing reports or attending meetings.

SKILLS AND INTERESTS

Materials scientists/technologists and metallurgists must be interested in maths, physics and chemistry. Scientific ability, curiosity and an interest in the application of science is essential. They should enjoy accurate and methodical work. They must be capable of clear, logical thought, and be able to work with patience and accuracy, even when conducting the same test or experiment repeatedly.

As research and development work is normally carried out by teams, they must be able to work well as a team member. Tact and diplomacy are required, and the ability to relate to all levels of staff.

Good communication skills, both written and spoken, are important. Many jobs also require the ability to write clear, concise reports.

ENTRY REQUIREMENTS

The usual qualification to become a materials scientist, materials technologist or metallurgist is a degree in such as metallurgy, materials science, polymer chemistry or ceramics. Some entrants may also have degrees in physics, chemistry or engineering.

Minimum entry requirements for degree courses are either: two A levels from physics, chemistry and maths plus GCSEs (A-C) in three other subjects; or three H grades (in maths, physics and chemistry) plus five S grades (1-3); or a BTEC/SCOTVEC national award in science or an applied science, such as polymer technology; or a relevant Advanced GNVQ/GSVQ Level III, eg science.

Applicants with non-science A levels may be accepted onto a foundation year preceding the first year of a relevant degree course in some institutions.

For a career in an academic research establishment, a higher degree is usually required. Entry to a higher degree is with a first degree.

The minimum qualifications for technician entry are usually either: four GCSEs/S grades (A-C/1-3) or a BTEC first award in science; or appropriate SCOTVEC national certificate modules; or Intermediate GNVQ/GSVQ Level II.

BTEC Higher National Diploma/Certificate in Materials Science/Metallurgy requires either: study of two A levels from physics, chemistry or maths, with one being passed; or a relevant BTEC/SCOTVEC national award; or a relevant Advanced GNVQ/GSVQ Level III. In Scotland those with H grades normally complete the last year of a SCOTVEC certificate before starting the higher certificate/diploma, but direct entry is possible with the Certificate of Sixth-form Studies.

BTEC national diploma and certificate courses usually require either: four GCSEs/S grades (A-C/1-3); or a BTEC first award; or Intermediate GNVQ/GSVQ Level II.

SCOTVEC national certificate courses have no set entry requirements. Applicants should check with individual colleges, who may set their own requirements, as they wish to be satisfied that students are able to benefit from the courses.

Advanced GNVQ Science usually requires either four GCSEs/S grades (A-C/1-3), or Intermediate GNVQ/GSVQ Level II.

Modern Apprenticeships have been developed in polymer processing for some young people. There are no set entry requirements, but employers need to be sure that entrants can benefit from training and are capable of achieving NVQ/SVQ Level 3 qualifications.

Defective colour vision or any skin or respiratory problems could present difficulties in this career.

TRAINING

A number of universities and colleges of higher education offer degree courses in materials science/technology/engineering or metallurgy. Course titles vary, as does the emphasis of each course. It is important, therefore, to check carefully before choosing a course. Lists of recommended degree courses can be obtained from the Institute of Materials and from the Plastics and Rubber Advisory Service. Please see FURTHER INFORMATION.

Degree courses last three years full-time or four years on a sandwich basis, where students spend a period of time on placement with an employer. Some courses concentrate on a particular group of materials, while others are initially more general but allow specialization later in the course.

Technicians may take a full-time course before joining an employer. They may study for either: a higher national diploma (two years full-time or three years sandwich) with a view to entry as a higher level technician; or a BTEC national diploma (two years); or a SCOTVEC national certificate (one year); or an Advanced GNVQ/GSVQ Level III science (two years).

Alternatively they may enter work and study part-time on a day release or evening class basis for either: BTEC higher national certificate (two years); or SCOTVEC higher national certificate (one year); or BTEC national certificate (two years); or SCOTVEC national certificate (one year). Those in polymer processing may work towards an NVQ/SVQ at Level 3 in Polymer Processing Product Development or in Polymer Processing Technology.

Those on Modern Apprenticeships in polymer processing work towards one of the Level 3 NVQs/SVQs. There is no set length of time for Modern Apprenticeship training but it is likely to be at least three years. Contact your local careers office, TEC or LEC for details.

Training is provided by employers for both materials scientists and technicians. They may work towards membership of The Institute of Materials and the status of Chartered Engineer, Incorporated Engineer or Engineering Technician.

LATE ENTRY

There is no set upper age limit for entry to this work but depends on the attitude of individual employers.

Mature applicants may be accepted onto a foundation year preceding the first year of a degree or higher national diploma course in some institutions.

Access courses for adults who wish to study for a degree but who do not have the necessary qualifications are offered at many local colleges. They are usually one year full-time or one to two years part-time with daytime and/or evening attendance.

OPPORTUNITIES

Materials scientists/technologists and metallurgists work in three main areas: in government research establishments, in academic research institutions of higher education, and in industry.

The largest employing government department is the Ministry of Defence, but materials scientists/technologists and metallurgists also work in the Health and Safety Executive. These establishments are found in various geographical locations.

The largest employer of materials scientists/technologists and metallurgists, however, is private industry. Much of the heavy manufacturing industry offering suitable employment is concentrated in the North and Midlands of England.

Major employers include: British Steel, British Nuclear Fuels, the Atomic Energy Authority, the gas and electricity companies, the major chemical companies, the aircraft and car industries, the firms making components for these industries, and companies manufacturing plastics, polymers, paper goods, rubber, etc.

It is possible to be self-employed as a consultant, working on a contract basis on projects for companies.

Britain is the base for several foreign companies that employ materials scientists/technologists and metallurgists. In addition, some companies based in mainland Europe recruit British graduates. Anyone who has combined technical study with learning a language, therefore, has opportunities to work abroad.

PAY AND CONDITIONS

The hours are usually 9am to 5pm or 8.30am to 4.30pm (often the case in industry) Monday to Friday, with some employers offering flexitime. Scientists working to deadlines or travelling to visit clients at different sites may work extra hours when necessary.

Work in quality control and production management usually involves shift work. Patterns vary with different employers.

Salaries vary widely between companies. A newly qualified graduate might expect to earn at least £13,500 a year. The average salary for an experienced materials scientist is £35,654.

Technicians also receive differing rates of pay with different employers. An average salary range might be £9,000 to £11,800 while training, rising to £17,000 with seniority. Incorporated engineers earn an average of £25,725.

PROSPECTS

It used to be common for research and development scientists to reach a certain salary level, then to move out of bench work and into general management. To reduce the risk of losing good staff in this way, some companies have introduced better career grades and higher salaries for research work. Such companies usually provide training in communication skills, report writing and management skills before promoting staff to become senior scientists or project directors.

Materials scientists/technologists and metallurgists who do wish to move from the research side have a wide choice. There are good prospects of progression in production management. Others move into different jobs, becoming raw materials buyers, sales or marketing managers. Others leave industry altogether and work as information officers, technical writers or even journalists on specialist magazines.

RELATED OCCUPATIONS

Medical laboratory scientist, engineer, textile technologist, scientist, medical technical officer.

FURTHER INFORMATION

The British Polymer Training Association, Coppice House, Halesfield 7, Telford, Shropshire TF7 4NA, 01952 587020

Institute of Materials*, 1 Carlton House Terrace, London SW1Y 5DB, 0171 839 4071

Plastics and Rubber Advisory Service*, 6 Bath Place, Rivington Street, London EC2A 3JE, 0171 457 5000

FURTHER READING

Leaflets/booklets are available from the addresses marked*.

Working in Chemistry – COIC
Working in Physics – COIC
Scientific Research and Development – AGCAS
Processing Technology – AGCAS

In the careers library classified under QOS.

STATISTICIAN CLCI:QOG

BACKGROUND INFORMATION

Statistics is the science of collecting, classifying, presenting, analysing and interpreting numerical information.

This is a relatively new career area, which has expanded greatly since the 1950s, when industry and commerce recognized the value of employing specialist statisticians rather than relying solely on scientists or managers to analyse their own numerical data. Computers also have had a major impact – extending the range and scope of the work.

Statisticians are employed in many different fields: government service; industry; finance; teaching; research and development; market research; medicine; agriculture and forestry; environmental health; commerce. In addition they are involved in a wide variety of different tasks. Examples of a few of these include: economics and resource forecasting; management services; quality control and production problems; health and safety research (such as the risks of work-related diseases); medical research (the relationship between disease and smoking, the spread of epidemics, effects of new drugs, etc); road safety (eg optimum speed limits); ecology (extinction rates of plants and animals); planning (future needs of housing, schools, roads, etc); and insurance (probabilities of death or accident).

THE WORK

Statistical analysis

Figures can be used to indicate current situations, currency reserves and census figures, for instance. Taken alone such figures are of little interest, but after analysis the information can be used by decision makers. Statisticians compare the latest figures with previous ones; they can then produce information about changes, such as percentage increases in users of a product or rises/falls in population. Decision makers may use the information when determining policies, such as where to market products.

Efficiency evaluation

Statistics can be used to assess the efficiency of policies, new products, equipment, etc. In industry this could mean using figures to assess whether production plant is being used efficiently and economically. Another example is where a policy of increasing salaries may have been intended to boost the number of recruits entering a particular profession; statisticians could review the effectiveness of the policy through analysing the recruitment figures, taking into account other variable factors.

Forecasting

Statistical techniques are used to forecast the results of policies, future requirements, marketing campaigns, performance of products or industrial processes, etc. Information may be obtained by interviewing random samples of the population and analysing replies to a range of carefully worded questions, or by observing a range of measurements which predict trends or changes in processes, etc.

Quality assurance

Statistical techniques are used to ensure that all types of products/services are of an acceptable and consistent standard. Statisticians may help to define the precise specifications and standards that must be achieved, as well as advising on methods of collecting data, evaluating quality control tests and reports, and devising new tests.

Activities involved in statistical work

Statisticians work in a variety of fields and may specialize in particular applications. However, the work involves a number of common tasks.

It is first important to consider whether statistical methods can be applied to the problem and, if so, how this should be done. Clear and accurate definitions are essential to ensure that those collecting the information gather exactly what is required so that findings may have a wide application. Statisticians also need to establish valid, reliable and efficient research designs, in both experimental and survey studies.

Statisticians must have knowledge of the mathematical theories and principles of probability. Statisticians analyse the information and must indicate the reliability with which any conclusions can be drawn.

Computers are widely used in statistics; they can be programmed to act as working models and determine the effects of changing variables. When analysing a mass of information, statisticians take account of the variables that might affect the results.

Interpreting figures is a major element of a statistician's work. Presenting the results of an investigation is part of the work, but decision makers often need to know the reasons behind the results, the likely effects and implications. After analysing information, the statistician must present it in a meaningful way. This can involve making written and oral reports, explaining details in a way that is understandable to non-specialists. They may use diagrams, graphs and tables to show results and the relationships between factors.

WORK ENVIRONMENT

Many statisticians are office-based and can expect to work in fairly comfortable surroundings. They often work in teams with other professionals such as scientists, market researchers, management services personnel, engineers and managers.

Work on some investigations may involve travelling to different locations, and sometimes may include trips abroad. Scientific work may include surveys and experiments away from the office.

SKILLS AND INTERESTS

Statisticians need a high level of numeracy and a thorough understanding of the maths of statistics. Statisticians should be methodical, logical and show a high level of reasoning, as well as having problem-solving skills. Statisticians must be able to handle large amounts of information easily and must work accurately with attention to detail. Interests and skills in computers are essential.

The work offers opportunities for initiative and creativity in problem solving; however, it is also necessary for statisticians to carry out work that is routine.

Communication skills are also important for statisticians who need to work alongside specialists in other disciplines and use their skills of persuasion to influence managers. They should be able to weigh up the evidence and communicate their results. It will often be necessary to explain complicated aspects of the work to non-experts in a clear and straightforward manner.

ENTRY REQUIREMENTS

Most entrants to statistician jobs have qualifications at higher national diploma, degree level or above, or The Royal Statistical Society examinations. Entrants to BTEC/SCOTVEC higher national certificate or diploma courses generally require an appropriate BTEC/SCOTVEC national award or one A level plus three to four GCSEs (A-C), *or* two H grades plus two or three S grades (1-3) (including study of a mathematical subject to A level/H grade).

Degree courses

Candidates for degree courses need a minimum of two A levels plus five GCSEs (A-C), *or* three H grades plus five S grades (1-3). Mathematical subjects are often required at A level/H grade, and three A levels/four H grades, with high grades, may be necessary. Other useful subjects include computing, sciences and economics. Contact universities for details of specific requirements.

Postgraduate courses

Suitably qualified graduates may undertake research degrees leading to PhD, DPhil or MPhil qualifications. Those with degrees in related subjects – such as engineering sciences, psychology and social sciences – may attend postgraduate diploma or MSc courses in statistics.

The Royal Statistical Society examinations

Examinations are run at several levels for candidates with different qualifications. Entry to the Ordinary Certificate is with good GCSEs/S grades or equivalent, or with relevant work experience. The Higher Certificate follows on from the Ordinary Certificate and may be accepted for degree course entry or entry to the Graduate Diploma, which is widely recognized as a degree equivalent.

The Civil Service, which is one of the largest employers of statisticians, sets entry requirements:

Trainee statistician–a first-class or second-class honours degree or higher degree plus A level/H grade maths or equivalent. Candidates who do not have a degree in maths, statistics, or a combination of the two, must have good knowledge of one of these subjects and demonstrate ability to undertake a postgraduate course in statistics.

NB: For year 1996, there will be no recruitment of trainees.

Assistant statistician – candidates must have a first or second-class honours degree that includes study of statistics or computing science (minimum 25 per cent).

Exceptions may be made for candidates with relevant experience who have passed certain Royal Statistical Society exams.

Senior assistant statistician – candidates must hold the qualifications as for assistant statistician posts and relevant experience in industry, research or the public sector.

TRAINING

Most statisticians have undertaken a full-time or sandwich training course leading to a relevant qualification.

BTEC/SCOTVEC higher national diplomas/certificates

Several institutions of higher education offer full-time courses leading to BTEC/SCOTVEC higher national awards. Appropriate subjects include, for example, maths, statistics and computing, statistics and physics, and applicable maths. A number of sandwich courses are available; these include placements to give work experience.

Degree courses

Full-time or sandwich degree courses are available at higher education institutions throughout the UK. Statistics can be taken as a single subject or combined with other subjects such as maths, operational research, or computer science. Combined courses are considered useful for future employment prospects.

It is important that candidates check the syllabuses of courses, as there may not be a strong enough statistical content to qualify the graduate as a specialist statistician. Most specialist courses include study of maths, statistics and computing.

Postgraduate courses

Those with a good degree in statistics may go on to take higher qualifications such as PhD, DPhil or MSc. Study may last for up to three years for research degrees. Students may specialize in particular applications or fields, such as medical or agricultural statistics.

Candidates who have taken degree courses with less of an emphasis on statistics may take one or two-year postgraduate courses leading to a Diploma or MSc in Statistics.

The Royal Statistical Society examinations

It is possible for candidates to achieve a standard equivalent to that of a good honours degree in statistics through taking the examinations. Courses are available at some institutions of higher education in the UK, mainly on part-time day release or evening class basis, for those in work. A small number of full-time courses are available and it is possible to study through correspondence courses. Contact The Royal Statistical Society for further details.

Ordinary Certificate in Statistics. The aim of this qualification is to provide a grounding in the principles and practice of statistics. The emphasis is on practical data collection, presentation, and interpretation. It is intended as a qualification, for example, for clerical assistants in statistics, or as a basis for the more advanced exams. Exemptions to the exam are granted to those with two A levels/three H grades, including one in statistics, maths and statistics or pure maths.

Higher Certificate in Statistics. For this exam students are expected to have knowledge to the level of the Ordinary Certificate. It consists of three three-hour written papers on theoretical and applied statistics. It is intended for those in relevant work, for example at assistant level, and for those wishing to progress to graduate level work in statistics.

Graduate Diploma in Statistics. This exam follows on from the Higher Certificate and is regarded as equivalent to a good honours degree in statistics. The diploma consists of five three-hour written papers: two on theoretical statistics; two on applied statistics; and one from a choice of biometry and medical statistics, industrial statistics and operational research, economic statistics and econometrics. Statistical computing features in all parts of this examination.

In the Civil Service, training takes place mainly on the job, with recruits working alongside experienced staff. It may also include formal courses, including classroom training, to cover specialist elements of the work, such as computing. The training period will vary according to the type of job, organization and experience of the individual. New statisticians often work on a number of projects with experienced statisticians, until they have sufficient experience to work alone.

Membership of professional organizations

The Royal Statistical Society is the professional body representing statisticians. Candidates need to have passed the Society's exams or approved equivalent qualifications, and have practical experience to become Grad Stat and C Stat. Anyone with an interest in statistics may also join as a (non-professional) fellow. It publishes several journals and arranges regular meetings on a variety of topics. Contact The Royal Statistical Society for details.

LATE ENTRY

Entry to this type of work is normally via the routes described.

Adult candidates may achieve promotion from clerical posts in statistical work. They often take The Royal Statistical Society qualifications on a part-time basis. Adults may also gain entry to relevant degree and/or postgraduate diploma courses. Many higher education institutions waive their entry requirements for adult students. However, applicants are normally able to show that they are academically capable of the level of work and, often, also have relevant experience in business, industry or commerce.

Appropriate Open University degrees can be acceptable.

OPPORTUNITIES

Computers have had an enormous impact on the profession. They have taken over many of the complicated and time-consuming calculations. The statistician's expertise is still necessary and it is unlikely that they will be replaced by new technology. The practice of statistics requires skills of judgement which cannot be automated. This is a fairly small profession, however, with around 2,000 professionally qualified members of The Royal Statistical Society and a further 4,000 (non-professional) fellows.

Statisticians work in many sectors of the economy. In industry and commerce, employers include those involved in manufacturing, market research and finance.

Opportunities also exist within local government, for example, in planning. The Civil Service is a large employer. The main employing departments include the Inland Revenue, the Cabinet Office (Central Statistical Office), Department for Education and Employment, Employment Service, Department of Energy, Department of Trade and Industry, Department of Transport, Home Office, Ministry of Agriculture, Fisheries and Food, Ministry of Defence, Office of Population Censuses and Surveys, Scottish Office, Treasury and Welsh Office.

In addition, statisticians may also be employed by higher education and by research institutions. There are opportunities for statisticians to work abroad, either with overseas employers or representing British companies on overseas projects.

Statisticians may also work on a self-employed basis, often as members of management consultancy teams.

Advertisements may be carried in the national press, and also in the monthly newsletter of The Royal Statistical Society, *RSS News,* which goes to all members of the Society.

PAY AND CONDITIONS

Salaries vary according to employer, location and experience. Assistant statisticians are expected to progress rapidly, on merit, to statistician (grade 7) with a salary of £26,000 to £40,000. Assistant statisticians normally start at £13,396 and rise to £24,589. In addition some posts may attract a recruitment and retention allowance of up to £1,776 which is awarded at the discretion of each department. Starting salaries outside the Civil Service are likely to be comparable. Average salaries for people with experience are £16,000 to £25,000, with those in senior posts able to earn in the region of £35,000.

Most statisticians work standard office hours, 9am to 5pm, Monday to Friday. Some organizations offer opportunities for working flexible hours – where starting and finishing times can vary to suit an individual's preference or needs.

When working on particular projects, it may be necessary to work extra hours so that deadlines can be met.

PROSPECTS

Many statistician groups are small and there may, therefore, be limited opportunities for internal promotion. However, statisticians are not restricted to one area of application and there may be promotion opportunities by moving between companies into areas making increasing use of statistics, such as the pharmaceutical industry, environmental sciences and market research. Prospects may exist for progression to senior statistician, then to project leader and department head. There are opportunities for statisticians, usually with experience, to work for consultancies – either specialist or general management consultancies. There may also be opportunities for statisticians to progress into general management; statistics can provide a useful background for senior management positions.

RELATED OCCUPATIONS

Operational researcher, actuary, computer systems programmer, computer hardware designer (electronics), economist, professional scientist.

FURTHER INFORMATION

The Royal Statistical Society*, 12 Errol Street, London EC1Y 8LX, 0171 638 8998

Government Statistical Service, SGMU, Room 1802, Central Statistical Offices, Millbank Tower, Millbank, London SW1P 4QQ, 0171 217 4367/4369

Office of Public Service and Science (OPSS)*, Cabinet Office, Fastream and European Staffing Division, Room 127/2, Horse Guards Road, London SW1P 3AL, 0171 270 5697

FURTHER READING

Leaflets/booklets are available from the addresses marked*.

In the careers library classified under QOG.

ECONOMIST CLCI:QOK

BACKGROUND INFORMATION

Economics is a small profession – comparable in size with actuarial or archive work. Competition for entry is fierce, and only the most able economics graduates become professional economists.

However, there are many other careers for which an economics degree is a useful background, including other financial professions such as accountancy, banking or insurance, general business careers such as marketing, market research or management services, economic journalism and lecturing/teaching.

THE WORK

Economists perform an advisory role in government and business, providing information on which policy decisions can be based. They analyse and research economic problems, and produce forecasts of future developments.

The work of professional economists varies considerably according to the sector in which they are employed, but there are certain tasks which are common to all jobs.

1. All economists are experts in finding information from sources such as databases, libraries, newspapers and government departments. They manipulate data drawn from these sources, using mathematical and logical tools to find answers to questions such as:
– What have the recent economic trends been?
– What are the driving forces behind these trends?
– What forecasts can be made for the future?

2. The problems economists deal with may be macro-economic – concerned with large economic units such as nation-states; or micro-economic – concerned with the financial characteristics of firms, industries, individual households, and so on, and the way individual elements in an economy (such as consumers, or commodities) behave. A typical macro-economic task might be to forecast the GDP (gross domestic product) of the USA in the coming year, or to assemble the arguments for and against a change in interest rates, whilst the kind of question dealt with at micro-economic level could be concerned with predicting the demand for furniture in South East England over the next quarter, or analysing the costs and benefits of regulating or taxing some form of pollution.

3. Personal computers are essential tools for professional economists, who use them to access information, make calculations, run economic models and word process reports and other documents.

4. There is a public relations aspect to the work of most professional economists. They may be required to speak at seminars, conferences and other public gatherings, or to present their views via the media. They go out and meet representatives of other organizations, and may deal with their employers' clients.

In specific sectors, the emphasis of economists' work is as follows:

Government Economic Service (GES)

Economists in the Government Economic Service advise ministers and senior officials on a broad range of economic issues. Work on macro-economic problems, especially in the Treasury, involves forecasting, policy development and analysis of trends in incomes, output, prices, balance of payments, etc.

They advise on micro-economic issues in the Treasury and in all the major departments – including, for example, Health, Social Security, Agriculture, Transport, Environment, Education and Employment, Industry and Overseas Development – and in some other government bodies.

Some economists specialize in particular policy areas, but it is usual for them to change jobs every few years, either within or between departments.

Bank of England

Economists employed by the Bank of England specialize in areas such as monetary economics, financial economics, international economics or econometrics.

Other banks and financial institutions

Economists investigate and analyse national and international trends affecting financial markets. They may specialize, for instance in particular sectors of the economy such as housing, or in producing reports on foreign countries.

Commerce and industry

Economists are concerned with the effect of economic trends and changes in the economy on their own industry or organization. They produce forecasts which managers can use as a basis for forward planning.

Only the largest 'blue chip' companies employ their own economists – and then only in very small numbers.

Consultancies

Many management and specialist consultancies employ economists to help produce reports for governments, local authorities, commercial enterprises and other customers, on a wide range of issues from macro-economic forecasting to capital project appraisal.

WORK ENVIRONMENT

Economists are mainly desk-based. They spend much of the time working alone, but are usually part of a small team.

Some jobs involve travel, for instance to meet clients. Travel is likely to be mainly within the UK, except when the economist is working for an overseas client, or attending the occasional international conference.

SKILLS AND INTERESTS

Economists need to be good at working with figures. They should enjoy looking at a page of numbers and working out what they mean. Mathematical and information technology skills are essential.

Economists need to be able to explain their ideas simply, in plain English, to non-specialists. They should be able to express themselves clearly, both in writing and in speech.

Once they have drawn conclusions from a set of figures, economists should be prepared to stand by their judgements and argue a case. They should not be swayed easily by the views of others.

Economists need to be decisive, logical, quick-thinking and able to cope with pressure – they may, for example, be given only a few minutes to come up with a reasoned reaction to a set of statistics.

It is important to be able to get on well with a variety of people, both inside and outside the employing organization.

ENTRY REQUIREMENTS

The minimum entry requirement is normally a good first degree in Economics (first or upper second class).

Entry to first degree courses is with a minimum of five GCSE/S grades (A-C/1-3) with two A levels/three H grades, or equivalent. Maths at A level or H grade is often required for entry to courses, and is increasingly regarded as essential for those who intend to become professional economists.

Many entrants have postgraduate qualifications – masters' degrees or doctorates.

TRAINING

Government Economic Service

Economics graduates join the GES as Assistant Economists. Their training is largely given on the job but is supplemented by a structured programme of courses. In addition to academic ability in economics, they are expected to develop administrative and managerial skills.

There are also opportunities for economists to join the GES via the European Fastream, which helps candidates to prepare for the recruitment competitions of the European Community institutions. If successful, they leave the GES for employment with one of the Community institutions; if not, they have the option of staying in the GES.

Bank of England

The Bank runs a graduate training programme, covering all the Bank's operational and policy areas. There are also two postgraduate sponsorship schemes:

Postgraduate studentships – undergraduates studying economics can apply for sponsorship on one-year masters' degree courses.

Postgraduate cadetships – graduates in other subjects are sponsored on a one-year diploma course followed by a one-year masters' in economics.

In other organizations training is largely given on the job. Some employers encourage staff to study for higher degrees via part-time or evening study.

Many economists join the professional bodies – the Royal Economic Society and the Society of Business Economists – but these bodies do not confer specific qualifications.

LATE ENTRY

Adults may qualify by taking first degrees and postgraduate qualifications in economics. Entry is so competitive, however, that in most cases they are not likely to find employment as professional economists unless they have closely related experience.

There is no upper age limit on entry to the GES, apart from the European Fastream, but most successful applicants have graduated in the past ten years.

OPPORTUNITIES

With 510 staff in the Government Economic Service, government departments are the main employers of economists in the UK. Each year there are up to 40 vacancies for assistant economists, plus up to ten in the European Fastream, and a few for the Cadet Economist Scheme. Most posts are in London, but there are some opportunities in Birmingham, Sheffield, Leeds, Edinburgh, Glasgow and Cardiff.

The Bank of England is another major employer of economists. Most begin their careers in the Monetary Analysis Division, which employs around 90 economists, but there are some opportunities in other divisions. As their careers develop, economists are able to choose between remaining as specialists or becoming all-round central bankers.

Other banks and financial institutions such as building societies, insurance companies and securities houses also have some openings for economists.

There are some opportunities in local government, particularly in larger urban authorities which may employ economists as economic development officers.

Some large industrial and commercial firms employ economists, but in very small numbers. There are also a few opportunities with other large organizations such as health authorities and utilities. In some cases a specialist qualification such as health or transport economics may be required.

Opportunities for teaching and research are available in universities and colleges. Independent economic intelligence units also offer a few posts.

An increasing number of organizations prefer to use the services of economic consultants, rather than to employ their own economic teams. There is therefore a growing number of opportunities with firms of consultants.

Overseas work with international organizations such as the European Community institutions, the World Bank or the Organization for Economic Co-operation and Development (OECD) is possible, although the number of posts is small and competition intense.

PAY AND CONDITIONS

Starting salaries for assistant economists in the Government Economic Service are in the range of £13,396 to £18,154. In other sectors starting salaries may be higher – up to about £20,000 in financial institutions. In the Bank of England, the minimum graduate entry salary is about £18,000; those with relevant further degrees and/or experience may be offered a higher starting figure.

For experienced economists, the salary range is very wide, with the most successful commanding six-figure salaries. In general, however, salaries are likely to be in the £30,000 to £50,000 bracket. There may also be fringe benefits such as a company car, assisted loan for house purchase, medical insurance, non-contributory pension, profit shares and an annual bonus.

Economists work a five-day week, but are likely to work long hours – in the financial sector, for example, twelve-hour days are common.

PROSPECTS

Promotion prospects are generally rather limited, because economists are employed in such small numbers by most organizations.

In the GES, however, there is a promotion structure and staff can expect to be promoted through the grade of assistant economist to economic adviser (Civil Service grade 7). Economists at that level, if they stay in the Civil Service, fairly often transfer into administration. There are, however, some prospects of promotion, as an economist, to grade 5, and to a very few more senior posts.

Experienced economists may become self-employed, setting up their own consultancies. Alternatively, they may move into more specialist areas of economics – for example, experience in the GES or Bank of England can be a useful background for work in one of the international organizations. It is also possible to move into related careers such as financial or investment management.

RELATED OCCUPATIONS

Statistician, mathematician, accountant, investment analyst, bank manager, actuary, financial consultant/ adviser.

FURTHER INFORMATION

Society of Business Economists*, 11 Bay Tree Walk, Watford, Herts WD1 3RX, 01923 237287

Government Economic Service*, Economist Group Management Unit, HM Treasury, Room 46/2, Parliament Street, London SW1P 3AG, 0171 270 5622/5073

Bank of England (Personnel Division)*, 1-2 Bank Buildings, Princes Street, London EC2R 8EU

FURTHER READING

Leaflets/booklets are available from the addresses marked*.

Job Outlines – Economics – COIC
Management Services and Economic and Statistical Work – AGCAS Careers Information Booklet

In the careers library classified under QOK.

1. GEOLOGIST CLCI:QOL
2. METEOROLOGIST CLCI:QOL
3. OCEANOGRAPHER CLCI:QOL

1. GEOLOGIST (QOL)

BACKGROUND INFORMATION

Geology is the science of the Earth's history, composition and structure. It has applications in mining, civil engineering and the exploitation of natural resources such as oil, gas, minerals and underground water.

Geology covers a range of specialisms including: petrology – the composition, character and origin of rocks; mineralogy – the composition, occurrence and origin of minerals; palaeontology – the study of fossil remains; stratigraphy – the interrelationship of layered rocks; structural geology – study of the stresses and strains in the Earth's crust; and geomorphology – the origin and development of land forms.

Two closely related subjects are geophysics and geochemistry. Geophysics is the scientific study of the physical properties, structure, composition and dynamic changes which affect the Earth and its atmosphere. Geophysics uses the principles of physics to measure and analyse the Earth's seismic activity (earthquakes and related phenomena), electromagnetism, gravity and radiant energy. Geochemistry is the study of the chemical composition of the Earth – it provides information about, for example, the evolution of the oceans and the atmosphere, the ages of rocks and fossil remains, the occurrence of elements and the effects of pollutants in the earth, oceans and atmosphere.

The term 'geoscience' is sometimes used to cover all the geological disciplines, particularly since geologists, geophysicists and geochemists are increasingly required to engage in multidisciplinary studies.

THE WORK

Geologists identify and survey areas where valuable natural resources may be present. They take samples in the field, test and evaluate them, and use the results as a basis for maps, reports and computer models.

The main areas of work are:

Exploration for natural resources such as oil, gas, coal, ground water and raw materials for industry

Geologists identify areas where resources are likely to be found, both onshore and offshore. In the oil industry, for example, geologists carry out seismic surveys, generating seismic waves and recording reflections from sub-surface layers. They evaluate the data collected, and, if the results are favourable, drilling and further geophysical and geochemical testing are carried out to confirm the presence of oil. Geologists then assess whether oil is present in sufficient quantities to justify commercial development. Comparable activities, with a heavy emphasis on geochemistry, sustain the minerals industry.

Hydrogeologists are responsible for identifying, measuring and analysing sources of water. They evaluate the quality and quantity and assess the possible threats posed by pollution. In the case of reservoirs, geologists advise on siting, accessibility and suitability of construction materials.

Engineering and environmental geology

Geologists are involved in carrying out investigations before the foundations and earthworks for large civil engineering projects – such as roads, dams or tunnels – are constructed. They assess the condition of bedrock and sub-soil, and evaluate risks such as slippage or earthquake. Once projects are under way, they monitor progress. They may also advise on the suitability of materials used in construction, such as sand, gravel and limestone.

Environmental geology can involve dealing with questions such as disposal of waste of all types – from household rubbish to nuclear waste – or evaluating the environmental impact of construction projects.

Geological surveying

Geologists collect geological information, both on land and at sea, which is used as a basis for maps and databases.

The subject is so important to national economies that most countries have geological surveys or equivalent bodies. The British Geological Survey, founded in 1835, surveys and maps the British land-mass and offshore areas. It provides a national geoscience information service, and has extensive international experience.

Education and research

Many geologists are concerned with teaching and academic research in universities, or with teaching Earth sciences and related subjects in schools and colleges.

There are also geologists working as museum curators.

WORK ENVIRONMENT

The work often involves travel, sometimes to areas with extreme climates and arduous conditions. However, an increasing proportion of the work is laboratory and office-based, mainly as a result of the greater emphasis now placed on the use of information technology.

SKILLS AND INTERESTS

A scientific approach is essential. Geologists need to be observant, objective and analytical, and capable of thorough, methodical work. They need investigative and enquiring minds, with the ability to think logically and clearly, to deal with numerical data, statistics, maps, and so on, and to interpret them with clarity and precision. Most jobs involve the use of information technology.

Geologists should be flexible, prepared to adapt to new theories, techniques and practices. It is important to keep abreast of new developments and current research.

Good communication skills – spoken and written – are required. It may be necessary to explain complex information clearly to non-specialists.

Geologists should be able to work alone (when carrying out field work, for example) and as members of a team. They need to be practical and resourceful and willing to act on their own initiative. A sense of responsibility is important. Some jobs require the ability to supervise the work of technicians.

Manual dexterity is needed for using surveying instruments. Many jobs require good health and normal colour vision.

ENTRY REQUIREMENTS

Entry is usually with a first degree in one of the geological sciences, although some enter the profession after taking a first degree in a subject such as maths, physics or chemistry, followed by a postgraduate degree in one of the geosciences.

Minimum entry requirements for degree courses are five

GCSEs/S grades (A-C/1-3) and two A levels/three H grades, or equivalent, in scientific subjects – but for some geoscience courses, more than the minimum requirements may be needed. Preferred subjects include physics, chemistry, biology, geology, mathematical subjects. A level/H grade geography is accepted for entry to some courses.

Minimum entry requirements for the British Geological Survey, at scientific officer level, are a good degree or higher national certificate/diploma in a scientific, engineering or mathematical subject.

TRAINING

Many universities and other institutions of higher education offer first degree courses, lasting three or four years, in the geological sciences. Subject choices include geology, geophysics, geochemistry and applied courses – for instance, engineering geology, petroleum geology or exploration geology. Almost all courses include practical experience of field work.

Geologists often go on to take higher degrees in specialist or applied geoscientific subjects. One-year taught masters' degree courses provide the specialist vocational training, required by some employers. For research posts or teaching in universities, a PhD is usually required.

For those wishing to teach, postgraduate teacher training courses are available at nearly 100 educational institutions. Specialist courses in teaching Earth sciences are offered at Bath and Keele Universities.

Employers usually provide induction training and an initial period of supervised work. Some sponsor staff on postgraduate courses. Further in-service training may be provided as necessary. Large organizations such as the British Geological Survey run extensive internal training programmes for staff at all stages of their careers.

LATE ENTRY

Most geology departments welcome applications from mature students, and may accept older applicants with non-standard qualifications, depending on their background and experience. Science Access courses are a useful background. Check detailed requirements with individual institutions.

For mature applicants intending to teach, experience in industry, and of working with young people (for example, in a voluntary setting), are useful.

OPPORTUNITIES

There are about 6,000 geologists and other geoscientists employed in the UK. The largest single employer is the British Geological Survey, which is part of the Natural Environment Research Council (NERC). The NERC, which is the leading UK agency for research and surveying of the natural environment, also offers some opportunities for geologists in its other research institutes and units.

Other major employers of geologists are oil and gas companies, mining and quarrying firms, and companies which provide these industries with technical services.

Some geologists are employed by the water industry, civil engineering companies and environmental agencies. Others work as teachers in schools, colleges and universities.

In the long-term, there is likely to be a steady increase in demand for geologists. Growth areas include hydrogeology, pollution control and other work related to environmental problems.

It is possible to enter employment directly after taking a first degree. Initial employment, for instance in junior posts in seismic exploration, provides entry to the profession and can lead on to more responsible technical or managerial work.

Evidence of commitment to the subject – for instance, through junior membership of the Geological Society, or relevant vacation work – is helpful for those seeking employment.

Mobility is necessary for those who want to take full advantage of job opportunities. Many geologists – particularly those working in the oil industry, mining or civil engineering – spend part of their careers working abroad.

PAY AND CONDITIONS

Short-term contracts are common, both in industry and academic research.

Many jobs involve office hours, Monday to Friday, but in areas such as oil exploration, civil engineering or mining, shift work may be necessary.

In the British Geological Survey, salaries are similar to those of the scale for the science group in the Civil Service. This starts at £11,584 for a scientific officer, rising to a top rate of £30,455 for a senior scientific officer, and supplemented by a range of allowances.

Rates of pay are likely to be higher in industry, particularly for those with postgraduate qualifications. There may be special allowances for those working overseas.

PROSPECTS

Promotion prospects vary in different organizations. There may be opportunities to progress to senior scientific or managerial posts. Experienced geologists may become self-employed consultants.

RELATED OCCUPATIONS

Meteorologist, oceanographer, engineer: chartered civil/structural, surveyor: land/hydrographic, surveyor: mineral/mining, scientist, laboratory technician.

FURTHER INFORMATION

Geological Society*, Burlington House, Piccadilly, London W1V 0JU, 0171 434 9944

British Geological Survey*, London Information Office, Natural History Museum, Earth Galleries, Exhibition Road, London SW7 2DE, 0171 589 4090

British Geological Survey*, Keyworth, Nottingham NG12 5GG, 0115 936 3100

Natural Environment Research Council*, Polaris House, North Star Avenue, Swindon SN2 1EU, 01798 341 1500

FURTHER READING

Leaflets/booklets are available from the addresses marked*.

Job Outlines – Geology, Mining and Quarrying – COIC
Exploration, Extraction and Protection of Natural Resources – AGCAS Careers Information Booklet
Degree Course Guide – Geological and Environmental Sciences – Hobsons
Periodicals: British Geologist, New Scientist
In the careers library classified under QOL.

2. METEOROLOGIST (QOL)

BACKGROUND INFORMATION

Meteorologists monitor and interpret changes in the Earth's atmosphere and analyse and predict their effects. All aspects of the atmosphere are relevant, from the Earth's surface to the beginning of 'outer space'.

The science of meteorology is developing rapidly, leading to a greater understanding of the natural environment and climate. It is now possible, thanks to the development of Earth satellites and extremely powerful computers, to study the weather over the entire globe in a way that could not be done in the past.

The work of meteorologists varies from regular collection and forecasting of weather information for airlines, the media, farmers, shipping, industry, government departments and other organizations, to research into the long-term effects of climate change such as global warming.

THE WORK

Operational – meteorologists collect and interpret information continuously from sources such as weather stations, satellites, observation vessels, and civil and military aircraft. The information has to be co-ordinated and processed via computer systems and the resulting charts and computer models analysed. General and specific forecasts and maps are prepared.

Research – the research conducted by meteorologists is very varied. Many researchers try to improve the scope and range of forecasting. Their studies can extend to the oceans and polar regions and a long-term view of climatic change.

Applied – meteorologists also give specific advice on many practical matters, such as crop spraying, the effects of atmospheric pollution (eg acid rain, car exhausts), or the siting of bridges, oil rigs and power stations.

A large proportion of meteorologists work for the government's Meteorological (Met) Office. Met Office staff are best known for presenting weather forecasts on TV and radio, but this is only a small part of their work. Other major activities include providing meteorological services to government departments, civil and military aviation, local government and industry. For example, electricity, water and gas companies rely on information from the Met Office to predict demand; and local authorities use frost warnings to save money, by salting the roads only when necessary.

Met Office headquarters in Bracknell houses one of the most powerful computer complexes in the UK, used for forecasting and research. Over 100,000 messages from weather observation stations are received every day at the Met Office's telecommunications centre; they are fed into computers which generate global forecasts. The Met Office also operates a national network of local weather centres, many of which provide specialist services – such as shipping forecasts.

The Met Office undertakes an extensive research programme in meteorology and geophysics. Its Hadley Centre for Climatic Prediction and Research makes it possible for meteorologists to study large-scale changes in the world's climate, caused by the 'greenhouse effect'.

WORK ENVIRONMENT

Work environments vary from comfortable offices to remote weather stations at airfields, defence bases, and so on. Some posts involve spending time out of doors, collecting weather information.

SKILLS AND INTERESTS

Meteorologists need a methodical and practical approach to collecting information, analysing data and solving problems. Meticulous accuracy, patience, attention to detail and good powers of observation are essential.

Good communication skills – written and spoken – are needed for answering enquiries, interacting with colleagues and advising clients. Meteorologists should be able to work with others as members of a team. Some posts require supervisory and management skills.

Meteorologists should be responsive to new ideas and technological developments. A flexible approach, together with a willingness to acquire new skills, are important.

ENTRY REQUIREMENTS

Entry at meteorologist level is with a degree or higher national certificate/diploma. Minimum entry requirements for degree courses are two A levels/three H grades and five GCSEs/S grades (A-C/1-3) or equivalent. Many institutions' requirements are above the minimum – for example, some require three A levels, with good grades. For higher national certificate/diploma courses, entry is normally with one A level/two H grades and four GCSEs/S grades (A-C/1-3), or equivalent. The most useful A level/H grade subjects are maths and physics.

Relevant first-degree subjects include meteorology (as a single subject or as part of a combined degree), mathematics, physics or computing. Other subjects which may be acceptable include astrophysics, electronics and physical chemistry. Environmental science may be accepted if applicants have a good grounding in maths and physics.

Meteorological Office

To enter the Met Office at scientific officer grade, applicants need one of: a degree in Mathematics, Physics or Meteorology (or a combination of these), Computing Sciences or Electronics; *or* a BTEC/SCOTVEC Higher National Certificate/Diploma in Mathematics, Computing or Applied Physics; or an equivalent qualification. The Met Office also gives consideration to applicants who have a degree in a relevant subject such as Physical Chemistry, Oceanography, Environmental Science or Geography, together with proven ability (usually A level or equivalent) in maths and physics, or if they have a relevant higher degree, for example in computing, together with a less relevant first degree.

Applicants must meet Civil Service residency requirements.

TRAINING

The main centre for the study of meteorology at first degree level is the University of Reading. Reading offers a single subject degree in Meteorology, combined first- degree courses in Meteorology with Mathematics or Physics, and an interdisciplinary course in Environmental Science of the Earth and Atmosphere.

Other universities offering a substantial amount of meteorology as an option within more general degree courses include: East Anglia – Environmental Sciences; Edinburgh – Physics; Lancaster – Environmental Science or Geophysical Science; Plymouth – Ocean Science; Southampton – Geophysical Sciences.

The following postgraduate courses are appropriate: Birmingham – MSc Applied Climatology and Meteorology; Dundee – MSc Remote Sensing, Image Processing and Applications; East Anglia – MSc Atmospheric Sciences; Edinburgh – MSc Remote Sensing and Image Processing Technology; London, Imperial College – MSc Remote Sensing; Reading – MSc Applied and Agricultural Meteorology, MSc in Weather, Climate and Modelling.

The Meteorological Office College provides practical training at graduate and non-graduate level, both for Met Office staff and for sponsored students from other organizations.

The Royal Meteorological Society organizes meetings in London and at its Local Centres. It also has a professional qualification, Chartered Meteorologist.

LATE ENTRY

Adults may be accepted on relevant degree or higher national certificate/diploma courses – many educational institutions encourage adult applicants, and may relax entry requirements to courses. Enquiries should be made to the university or institution concerned.

The Met Office does not set age limits for entry (apart from normal retirement age). Adult applicants are welcome, provided they have appropriate scientific background. Previous experience in any kind of scientific work, and IT skills, are useful.

OPPORTUNITIES

The main employer is the Meteorological Office, which is an agency within the Ministry of Defence, and employs over 2,000 staff. About half of them work at Met Office headquarters in Bracknell, Berks. Others work at around 100 smaller offices at locations throughout the UK, or overseas – mainly in Germany, Cyprus, Gibraltar and the South Atlantic. Met Office staff must be willing to move to another location.

Other employers include research councils such as the National Environment Research Council or the Agricultural and Food Research Council, universities and other educational institutions, government departments and industry – particularly oil, gas, electricity and water. Small numbers of meteorologists are employed by instrument manufacturers and geophysical contractors. An increasing number of consultancies offer forecasting services, and consultancy work offers opportunities for self-employment for experienced meteorologists.

The Overseas Development Agency and United Nations technical aid programmes, as well as the Met Office, offer opportunities for overseas employment.

PAY AND CONDITIONS

Current Met Office salary scales for graduates start on a salary band starting at £12,750 rising to £15,300.

These scales are supplemented by additional allowances, for shift work, for example. Many posts in meteorology involve shifts, because information about the weather is collected on a round-the-clock basis.

In the Met Office the basic working week is 42 hours, including meal breaks.

It may be possible to work part-time.

PROSPECTS

There are opportunities within the Met Office to transfer from one type of work into other areas – for instance, from

forecasting to research or computing. Staff are encouraged to study for further qualifications which may be useful when they are considered for promotion.

Other organizations employ only small numbers of meteorologists, so promotion prospects are likely to be limited.

RELATED OCCUPATIONS

Scientist, geologist, oceanographer, hydrographic surveyor, ecologist, physicist, laboratory technician.

FURTHER INFORMATION

Royal Meteorological Society*, 104 Oxford Road, Reading, Berkshire RG1 7LJ, 01734 568500

Meteorological Office*, Personnel Department, London Road, Bracknell, Berks RG12 2SZ, 01344 856032/3

FURTHER READING

Leaflets/booklets are available from the addresses marked*.

Job Outlines – Physics – COIC

Exploration, Extraction and Protection of Natural Resources – AGCAS Careers Information Booklet

Periodicals: New Scientist

In the careers library classified under QOL.

3. OCEANOGRAPHER (QOL)

BACKGROUND INFORMATION

Oceanography, the study of the seas, is a multidisciplinary field, drawing on biology, chemistry, physics, geology and geophysics, supported by mathematics, computer sciences and engineering. It encompasses the study of the shoreline, estuaries, coastal waters, shelf seas and deep oceans – including their history, present state and likely future development.

THE WORK

Two major issues that currently preoccupy oceanographers are:

– pollution of the seas, through their use as a dumping-ground for waste;

– climate change, and how this is affected by, and affects, the oceans.

Both these questions need to be approached from a multidisciplinary point of view. For instance, to study the effects of pollution on organisms requires, in addition to a knowledge of biology, an understanding of the chemistry of the ocean environment, together with a knowledge of physics and geology, to understand how the pollutant is carried from its source by currents and turbulence and how pollutant particles find their way to the seabed and become part of its geographical structure. Similarly, the study of climate change involves not only physics, which is closely connected with meteorological forecasting, but also marine biology, chemistry and geology.

Nevertheless, within oceanography there is some degree of specialization:

Oceanographers whose interests are primarily biological are concerned with organisms living under the sea or on the shoreline. There are practical applications to biological research in fisheries research and in other branches of oceanography – for example, the development of medicines based on aquatic plant life.

Chemists are concerned with the ocean as a chemical system, and with understanding how chemicals are distributed within the ocean and are eventually transferred into the rocks and seabed. Chemical oceanography has applications in the study of pollution – and it is linked closely to physics, because the distribution of material in the water is largely determined by the laws of physics.

Geologists working in oceanography are concerned with the formation of sediments – this has practical applications, varying from the study of the effects of offshore dredging on beaches to the effects on the environment of offshore extraction of natural gas. On a much larger scale, they are concerned with plate tectonics – large-scale movements of the Earth's crust – much of which is occurring beneath the oceans.

Physicists study the movements of waves, tides, ocean currents, turbulence and the temperature and salinity of the ocean. Currently an international programme is under way to study currents on a global scale – including the polar regions, which provide evidence of climate change.

Much of the work of an oceanographer involves gathering data, for instance, from moored or drifting instruments deep below the sea surface, and recording the results. Techniques such as acoustics or satellite remote sensing are also used to collect information.

At some stage in their careers, all oceanographers carry out field work, going to sea on research vessels for periods lasting from around two weeks up to about two or three months. They may go down to the seabed, using diving equipment or submersible vehicles.

Onshore, oceanographers may be engaged in delicate laboratory work, using sophisticated analytical equipment. They use computers, for example, to produce forecasting models. They also write and present reports, attend meetings and conferences.

Many oceanographers are purely concerned with research, but others work in a more commercial environment. In this context, they may, for example, carry out surveys and advise on the siting of sewer outlets, or the environmental consequences of extracting gravel from the seabed.

WORK ENVIRONMENT

Much of the work is laboratory or office-based. In some cases – depending on the area of specialization – oceanographers may spend up to about three months a year at sea, on research vessels.

There is an international dimension to oceanography, which may involve attendance at conferences in Europe and elsewhere, as well as seagoing research on foreign vessels.

SKILLS AND INTERESTS

Oceanography, like other scientific disciplines, demands an enquiring mind, good powers of observation, meticulous accuracy and close attention to detail.

Research work in oceanography is often carried out on an individual basis, but there are many situations in which it is important to interact well with others and work as a member of a team.

Good communications skills – oral and written – are essential. Mathematical ability and information technology skills are also important.

For carrying out research at sea, a reasonable standard of physical fitness is required – but disability is not necessarily a barrier to employment in this field.

ENTRY REQUIREMENTS

Entry is usually with a degree in oceanography, or a related subject, such as marine science or meteorology. Alternatively, graduates in chemistry, physics, mathematics, biology and other scientific/technological disciplines may be able to enter employment related to oceanography, and/or to train via specialist postgraduate courses.

Entry to first degree courses is with a minimum of five GCSEs/S grades (A-C/1-3) with two A levels/three H grades, or equivalent. For most courses, maths at GCSE/S grade (A-C/1-3) is essential; technological subjects and one or more foreign languages are useful. At A level/H grade intending oceanographers need at least two sciences; maths or statistics are the most useful third subjects.

TRAINING

There are three universities offering broad-based first degrees in oceanography, covering the four main disciplines: physics, chemistry, biology and geology.

Bangor (University of Wales) offers single honours courses in ocean science, geological oceanography, marine biology and marine chemistry. Joint honours courses in marine biology with oceanography, applied zoology, biochemistry or zoology, and in physical oceanography with mathematics, or oceanography with soil science, are available.

Southampton University offers a degree in marine sciences and combined degrees in oceanography with acoustics, biology, marine biology, marine environmental chemistry, geology, mathematics, physics or physical geography.

University of Plymouth offers a single honours degree in ocean science. It is also possible to combine ocean science with a range of other subjects.

In addition, a number of other universities offer more specialized first-degree courses in relevant areas – for example, marine biology, applied marine biology.

At postgraduate level, it is usual to specialize in the study of marine aspects of one of the four main disciplines. Postgraduate facilities are therefore available at a wider range of universities.

Specialist on-the-job training may be provided by employers.

LATE ENTRY

Adults may apply for first-degree or postgraduate courses on the same basis as school-leavers or graduates. Universities may be prepared to waive or lower standard entry requirements in the case of mature applicants – check with individual institutions.

OPPORTUNITIES

The Natural Environment Research Council (NERC) is the main employer of oceanographers. The council, which was established in 1965, is responsible for planning, encouraging and carrying out scientific research to explain the natural processes of the environment. It runs two institutions concerned with oceanography:

– the Southampton Oceanography Centre (which brings

together the former Institute of Oceanographic Sciences' Deacon Laboratory and the James Rennell Centre, the NERC's Research Vessel Services and the University of Southampton's departments of geology and oceanography);

– the Centre for Coastal and Marine Science, which comprises the Plymouth Marine Laboratory, the Proudman Oceanographic Laboratory in Birkenhead, and the Dunstaffnage Marine Laboratory in Oban.

Other employers include the National Rivers Authority, water companies, university departments, pharmaceutical companies and the Royal Navy. Some government departments – mainly the Department of the Environment, the Ministry of Agriculture, Fisheries and Food, and the Ministry of Defence – employ oceanographers. There are opportunities abroad, particularly in Europe.

Consultancies providing advice on environmental matters offer a growing number of opportunities for employment. These bodies may, for instance, advise on matters relating to construction of offshore structures. Advisory and consultancy work is likely to increase in the next few years as more legislation concerned with environmental matters is introduced. It is expected that there will be opportunities in fields such as marine environmental law – for those with legal training coupled with relevant scientific knowledge.

It is also expected that, in future, interest in predicting changes in climate will lead to greater emphasis on the observation and study of the oceans. The creation of a 'Wet' Office – similar to the Met Office – has been proposed, and another possible development is the setting up of a Global Ocean Observing System (GOOS) to aid in climate prediction.

PAY AND CONDITIONS

The pay scale for scientists employed by the NERC is similar to the scale for the science group in the Civil Service. This starts at £11,138 for a scientific officer, rising to a top rate of £27,998 for a senior scientific officer and supplemented by a range of allowances.

In universities, lecturers are paid between £14,756 and £25,735; senior lecturers £27,108 to £30,533.

Short-term contracts lasting between one and four years are common.

Oceanographers are likely to work normal office hours when engaged in onshore work, but they may work round-the-clock when engaged in research at sea.

PROSPECTS

The growing prevalence of short-term contracts means that it can be difficult to predict long-term career paths. A series of sideways moves – from university into the NERC and back, or between contracts and fellowships, for example – are possible.

RELATED OCCUPATIONS

Geologist, chemist, biologist, physicist, meteorologist, hydrographic surveyor, laboratory technician.

FURTHER INFORMATION

Southampton Oceanography Centre, Empress Dock, Southampton SO14 3ZH, 01703 596435

Natural Environment Research Council*, Polaris House, North Star Avenue, Swindon, Wiltshire SN2 1EU, 01793 411500

Society for Underwater Technology*, 76 Mark Lane, London EC3R 7JN, 0171 481 0750

FURTHER READING

Leaflets/booklets are available from the addresses marked*.

Exploration, Extraction and Protection of Natural Resources – AGCAS Careers Information Booklet

Periodicals: New Scientist, Nature

In the careers library classified under QOL.

FORENSIC SCIENTIST CLCI:QOT

BACKGROUND INFORMATION

Forensic scientists examine materials associated with crimes to provide information or evidence which may be used in the legal process.

Forensic scientists are independent of police authorities although most of their work is undertaken for the police.

Forensic evidence has become increasingly important in crime investigation as techniques have advanced. Research is constantly being undertaken to make forensic techniques faster, more specific and more precise and the information and evidence provided more useful.

The importance of forensic science cannot be overstated. In many crime investigations it can provide the only hard evidence to indicate the guilt or innocence of an individual.

THE WORK

The work carried out in forensic science laboratories is usually dealt with in three main sections:

Chemistry. The main concern is with crimes against property such as burglary and arson. The work includes examination of glass, paint, chemicals, shoe-prints and tool marks. Forensic scientists also deal with fire investigation and vehicle accident reconstruction.

Biology. This involves offences against people, such as murder, assault and rape. The work includes blood grouping, blood pattern analysis, DNA profiling, and the examination of damage to clothing and of weapons, hairs, fibres, paper and other such materials.

Drugs and toxicology. Forensic scientists examine materials for restricted drugs and other toxic substances and look into cases of suspicious death, such as overdose or poison.

Laboratories have wide-ranging facilities, including, in some cases, for examining vehicle engines, defective parts and tyres, and for the analysis of blood and urine samples in drink-driving cases. Some work is undertaken in specialist departments, for example, at Huntingdon for the examination of firearms, and at Birmingham for the examination of forged documents.

The work of forensic scientists depends on their grade and specialism. Scientists examine exhibits arising from a wide variety of crimes, make comprehensive notes, handle small samples, analyse a range of materials and work with appropriate instruments. Techniques used include gas and high-pressure liquid chromatography, infra-red spectroscopy, specialized microscopy, microspectrophotometry, electrophoresis and DNA analysis techniques.

On completion of tests, scientists present the results of their examinations in the form of written statements for production in court. The more experienced scientists may be required to produce reports for court and give verbal evidence in court.

Senior scientists also allocate work to other staff and support their work. Assistant forensic scientists in England and Wales and technicians sand trainees in Scotland are involved in examining and analysing a range of materials under the supervision of qualified scientists.

WORK ENVIRONMENT

Most forensic science work is laboratory-based. Some time is spent travelling to and attending scenes of crime, which can be indoors or outdoors in any conditions or weather. Good personal mobility may be required at scenes of crime, with bending and crouching necessary. The more experienced scientists attend court to give evidence.

SKILLS AND INTERESTS

Forensic scientists need an interest and ability in science. Mathematical ability is required as test results may be in numerical form. Their work demands a logical, methodical, problem-solving approach. Painstaking attention to detail, accuracy and sound judgement are essential.

Good written ability is necessary. Forensic scientists compile detailed reports on all examinations, with conclusions they have drawn from the scientific evidence. The reports must be clearly written and capable of being understood by whomever hears them in court.

Forensic scientists should be articulate and self-confident, as they may have to give evidence in court and be cross-examined.

It is important that forensic scientists are not squeamish, as scenes of crime can be unpleasant and distressing.

Forensic scientists must be able to work in a team. Although scientists tend to specialize in one area of forensics, they often need to work closely with scientists from different sections during a major police inquiry, as well as with police officers and lawyers.

ENTRY REQUIREMENTS

England and Wales

The minimum entry requirements are those for entry as an assistant forensic scientist.

Assistant forensic scientist. Entry is with a minimum of either four GCSEs/S grades (A-C/1-3) including English and either maths or a science, or Intermediate GNVQ/GSVQ II. In practice, most entrants have A level/H grade in chemistry and two from physics, maths and biology. BTEC/SCOTVEC higher national diploma in a science is accepted, entry to which requires a minimum of either: one relevant A level/H grade and three GCSEs/S grades (A-C/1-3); or Advanced GNVQ/GSVQ III science; or a relevant BTEC/SCOTVEC national award.

Forensic scientist. Entry requires either: a degree in science or maths; or degree-standard membership of a professional institution; or a BTEC/SCOTVEC higher national diploma/certificate in science or maths.

In practice, most entrants have a degree in science, such as chemistry, physics or biology, or in an appropriate technology, such as metallurgy. Entry to degree courses is with either: two or three A levels/three or four H grades, usually including sciences and sometimes maths, and three GCSEs/two S grades (A-C/1-3) including maths and usually English; or a relevant Advanced GNVQ/GSVQ III; or a relevant BTEC/SCOTVEC national award.

Applicants with non-science A levels may be accepted onto a foundation year preceding the first year of a degree course in some institutions.

The University of Strathclyde's degree in Forensic and Analytical Chemistry requires either: three A levels including chemistry and maths and preferably either physics, biology or a modern European language; or four H grades including chemistry, maths and physics and preferably either English or a modern European language; or Advanced GNVQ/GSVQ III science with evidence of sufficient chemistry and maths and some physics; or BTEC/

SCOTVEC national award, again with evidence of sufficient chemistry and maths and some physics.

The University of Bradford's degree in Chemistry with Pharmaceutical and Forensic Science requires either: three A levels including chemistry and at least one other science and a minimum of grade B in GCSE maths; or four H grades including chemistry and at least two other science or maths subjects; or Advanced GNVQ/GSVQ III science plus A level/H grade chemistry; or a BTEC/SCOTVEC national award with sufficient chemistry content.

NB: The Universities of Strathclyde and Bradford require considerably above minimum grades for entry to these degree courses. Consult the university prospectuses for detailed entry requirements. Postgraduate courses in forensic science require a relevant degree for entry.

Senior forensic scientist. Entry is with a first or second-class honours degree in a relevant subject, such as science or technology, and a number of years' relevant postgraduate experience.

Scotland

The minimum entry requirements are those for entry as a technician. Few are recruited at this level, however, the majority entering as basic grade forensic scientists.

Technician Entry is with a relevant SCOTVEC national award.

Basic grade forensic scientist. Entry is with at least a first or second-class honours degree in chemistry, biology or another relevant subject.

Good colour vision is essential. There are nationality rules that restrict entry to British, Commonwealth, EU and Irish Republic citizens and British protected persons.

TRAINING

Pre-entry

The University of Strathclyde offers a degree in Forensic and Analytical Chemistry (three or four years for A level entrants, four or five years for H grade entrants), which includes an industrial placement of five or twelve months' duration.

The University of Bradford offers a three-year degree in Chemistry with Pharmaceutical and Forensic Science. The course combines pharmaceutical chemistry, forensic archaeology and electronic image analysis with a foundation of chemistry.

Neither of these courses is exclusively concerned with forensic science and graduates can seek openings in other fields open to chemistry graduates.

Strathclyde also offers postgraduate courses in forensic science – a diploma (nine months full-time) and an MSc (one or two years full-time). Kings College, London, offers an MSc course (one year full-time).

Although extremely useful, none of the above courses guarantees employment in forensic science.

On entry

Most forensic science training is in-house. It is laboratory-based and provided by experienced staff at the establishment concerned. Forensic Science Service staff may attend induction training at the training unit at Chepstow. All forensic science staff may attend specialist courses at Chepstow, dealing with subjetcs such as examining techniques, blood grouping and note taking.

Where appropriate, assistant forensic scientists and technicians are encouraged to continue their education up to degree level by day release.

NVQ/SVQ in Investigating Scenes of Incident at Level 3 and NVQ/SVQ in Recovery of Evidential Material (Laboratory Based) at Level 3 are being introduced. NVQs/SVQs at Levels 4 and 5 are being developed.

LATE ENTRY

Mature entrants must have the qualifications described in ENTRY REQUIREMENTS and recent relevant experience, such as scientific research.

Adults may be considered for relevant higher education courses without the usual entry requirements. They may also prepare for application to higher education by taking an access course. Access courses are offered at many colleges throughout the UK. They are usually one year full-time or one/two years part-time, with daytime and/or evening attendance.

OPPORTUNITIES

Most forensic scientists in England and Wales are employed by government or police laboratories. The largest single employer is the Forensic Science Service, an agency of the Home Office that employs approximately 500 scientists. That number has increased slightly in recent years, particularly at assistant forensic scientist level. The Service has six operational laboratories at Aldermaston, Birmingham, Chepstow, Chorley, Huntingdon and Wetherby, and a Central Research and Support Establishment at Birmingham, where forensic techniques and equipment are developed.

The Metropolitan Police Service Forensic Science Laboratory employs over 200 scientists.

Forensic scientists in Scotland are employed by the police in four laboratories – Strathclyde (Glasgow), Lothian and Borders (Edinburgh), Grampian (Aberdeen) and Tayside/Fife/Central (Dundee). The Scottish laboratories employ approximately 100 forensic scientists – an increase on past years.

There are also a number of private forensic science consultants in the UK and many official forensic laboratories abroad that may recruit British staff.

Vacancies are scarce. Any vacancies for assistant forensic scientists and technicians are advertised in the local press and at Jobcentres. Vacancies for other grades are advertised in the national press and in scientific journals such as *New Scientist.*

PAY AND CONDITIONS

The Forensic Science Service and Metropolitan Police forensic staff are on similar annual salary scales, with starting points depending on qualifications and experience.

The ranges are from £9,880 to £16,168 for assistant forensic scientists. Trainee forensic scientists begin on £9,800 but progress after one year's satisfactory service onto a scale from £12,396 to £20,057. Senior forensic scientists can earn up to £37,563. Those working in London receive an additional allowance.

Forensic scientists in England and Wales usually work a 41 or 42-hour week (inclusive of lunch breaks) over five days. They work an on-call rota outside those hours to deal with serious crimes.

In Scotland annual salaries range from £9,500 to £16,200 for technicians. Basic grade forensic scientists start at £14,000 rising to £23,000. Senior scientists earn between £24,000 and £26,000. Principal scientists' pay rises to £33,000.

Forensic scientists in Scotland work a 36-hour five-day week (excluding lunch breaks), with an on-call rota outside standard hours.

PROSPECTS

In England and Wales promotion is from assistant forensic scientist to forensic scientist, higher forensic scientist and senior forensic scientist. Further promotion in the Forensic Science Service is to grade 7 and beyond. With the Metropolitan Police further promotion is to principal scientific officer, senior principal scientific officer, assistant director and director. Promotion boards interview candidates recommended by their line managers as suitable for promotion. Transfer from one regional laboratory to another for promotion is common.

In Scotland, technicians who obtain a relevant degree may apply for a vacancy as a basic grade forensic scientist. Thereafter, promotion is to senior chemist or biologist, head of chemistry or biology (in Strathclyde only), deputy principal scientist and principal scientist. Transfer between laboratories for advancement is possible when vacancies arise.

RELATED OCCUPATIONS

Chemist, biologist, medical laboratory technician, biochemist, microbiologist, pharmacologist, laboratory technician.

FURTHER INFORMATION

The Forensic Science Service*, Priory House, Gooch Street North, Birmingham B5 6QQ, 0121 607 6800

The Forensic Science Society*, Clarke House, 18A Mount Parade, Harrogate, North Yorkshire HG1 1BX, 01423 506068

Forensic Science Laboratory, Grampian Police Office, Nelson Street, Aberdeen AB2 3EQ, 01224 639111

Lothian and Borders Police Forensic Science Laboratory, 11 Hewden Hall Road, Edinburgh EH16 6TF, 0131 666 1212

Metropolitan Police*, Forensic Science Laboratory, 109 Lambeth Road, London SE1 7LP, 0171 230 6181

The Police Forensic Science Laboratory, PO Box 59, West Bell Street, Dundee DD1 9JU, 01382 312291

Strathclyde Police Forensic Science Laboratory, Police Headquarters, Pitt Street, Glasgow G2 4JS, 0141 204 2626

FURTHER READING

Leaflets/booklets are available from the addresses marked*.

Job Outlines – Forensic Scientist – COIC
Working in Chemistry – COIC

In the careers library classified under QOT.

1. ENGINEER CLCI:RAB
2. ENGINEERING CRAFTSMAN/WOMAN CLCI:RAB
3. ENGINEERING OPERATIVE CLCI:RAB

BACKGROUND INFORMATION

Engineering is one of the largest and most diverse careers – with engineers working on products as varied as oil rigs, aeroplanes, bridges, telecommunication systems and artificial limbs as well as on processes such as food processing, water purification and oil refining. There is a wide range of specializations within the industry such as mechanical, electrical and civil engineering, and within these specializations a variety of different functions such as design, research and development and production.

Branches of engineering

Aeronautical engineering covers the design and building of civil and military aircraft and their engines and space systems. It also includes the design and manufacture of electronic and electrical equipment and advanced navigation systems in aircraft.

Agricultural engineering is concerned with the design, production and maintenance of agricultural and forestry machinery and buildings, and environmental engineering such as irrigation systems.

Automobile engineering is concerned with the development, production and maintenance of cars, vans, lorries, buses, plant machinery and their components.

Biomedical engineering is a combination of electronic, electrical and mechanical engineering and physics. It involves designing and producing a wide range of medical devices, instruments and equipment such as surgical lasers, kidney dialysis machines, biosensors, aids for disabled people, body scanners and body replacement parts such as artificial joints.

Building services engineering is a combination of mechanical, electrical and structural engineering and deals with the design and manufacture of heating, air-conditioning, acoustics and refrigeration systems to fit in with the overall construction and use of a building.

Chemical, or processing engineering involves plant design, installation, testing, operation and maintenance in the production of food and drink, chemicals, dyes, petrol, pharmaceuticals, fertilizers, plastics, etc.

Civil and structural engineering involves the design, planning, construction and maintenance of structures such as roads, bridges, railways, airports, harbours, dams, canals and tunnels. It also includes structures and systems for services such as electricity, water treatment and distribution, sewerage and sewage treatment.

Electrical engineering is concerned with the applications of electricity for heavy-current applications such as power generation and power supply. Electrical engineers are involved in the production and distribution of electricity to homes, factories, schools, and so on, and the manufacture of equipment and transmission systems to provide power. Their work is concerned with the design, manufacture, installation and maintenance of electrical equipment on trains, aircraft, ships and road vehicles.

Electronic engineering is concerned with the use of electricity for light-current applications like communications and control systems. Electronic engineers design, manufacture, operate and monitor computers, telecommunications, control systems such as satellite tracking devices.

Manufacturing engineering – manufacturing engineers are responsible for all aspects of engineering manufacture of products ranging from satellites to paper-clips. Their work includes the planning, managing and maintenance of these processes.

Marine engineering is a specialized branch of mechanical and electrical engineering and involves the design, construction, maintenance and operation of machinery used at sea and on offshore platforms.

Materials engineering deals with the process for making materials such as plastics, rubber, wood, stone, concrete, metal and the operations used to convert them into saleable items.

Mechanical engineering is the largest area of engineering and is concerned with the design, development, manufacture, operation and maintenance of machinery of all kinds from a dentist's drill to a giant crane.

Mining engineering deals with the extraction of coal, ore and metals from the ground. Mining engineers plan the extraction and supervise the control of operations. They provide pumping and ventilation systems for mines and make them safe from gas, dust and flooding.

Naval architecture/shipbuilding deals with the design, construction, maintenance and repair of all craft that float or hover above the water including ships, tankers, submarines, oil rigs and hydrofoils.

Nuclear engineering is concerned with the production and use of nuclear fuel and its safe reprocessing. It covers a wide range of disciplines including mechanical, chemical, electrical, electronic and materials engineering.

1. ENGINEER (RAB)

THE WORK

This article covers the work of three levels of engineer: chartered engineers, incorporated engineers and engineering technicians. The main difference in the work of these people is in the level of responsibility they have.

Chartered engineers work on design, development, manufacture and sale of products. They are often team leaders, managing incorporated engineers and engineering technicians.

Incorporated engineers are often responsible for a number of engineering technicians. Their work may be similar to that of chartered engineers.

Engineering technicians include draughtsmen/women using CAD, estimators, quality assurance technicians, inspectors, planners and laboratory technicians. They are usually part of a team headed by an incorporated or chartered engineer.

In addition to specializing in one of the branches of engineering, engineers usually also specialize in one of the main engineering functions, which are:

Design

Design engineers produce designs for new products, plant and engineering processes. These designs may be for completely new products or modifications to existing ones. They usually work to a brief – for instance, designers working for a car manufacturer may be asked to come up with a design for a car that is more modern in design, smaller, and more economical than an existing model.

Design engineers work in teams with other engineers such as manufacturing engineers and between them they consider many factors as it is important that the product they design is safe, efficient, economical and fit for its purpose. These factors may include: **strength** – will the product stand up to stresses and strains; **safety** – is it safe to operate; **cost** – the cost of production and the cost to the customer; **shape** – this is important with some products such as cars and planes which have to be streamlined to reduce wind resistance. Appearance is also important in some products so that they appeal to the buyer, and the product has to be designed with the user in mind, for example, making sure that car controls are within easy reach for the driver. Design engineers also decide on the materials to be used in the product. They may use computer models to test their designs and when they are satisfied they produce, often on computer, details of specifications and outline designs.

The specifications and outline designs are then passed on to incorporated engineers and engineering technicians who support chartered engineers in design work, usually working as design or detail draughtsmen/women.

Design draughtsmen/women are incorporated engineers. They examine design specifications from which they calculate the dimensions and weights of components using a calculator or computer. They also work out the most effective and economical means of manufacturing the article, see if it is possible to incorporate standard parts and materials, and check the safety of the design. These processes involve maintaining liaison with production managers and senior shop-floor workers. The next stage is to produce a general arrangement drawing to scale, showing the position, size, shape and inter-relations of components. Design draughtsmen/women normally use computer-aided design (CAD) to produce initial 'scheme' drawings. Drawings can include a lot of detail but must be clear to the user. Design draughtsmen/women prepare the working material and specifications from which detail draughtsmen/women work, and then supervise their work.

Detail draughtsmen/women are engineering technicians. They take the scheme drawings and, under the supervision of the design draughtsman/woman, redraw them often using computer-aided design (CAD) to produce very accurate and detailed drawings for use by craftspeople. They may use a different scale or projection, or break down the general arrangement drawing into a series of drawings for production. It is impossible to give a full picture of a three-dimensional object from a simple two-dimensional drawing; production workers need this additional information. So detail draughtsmen/women draw individual components, parts and sections of a variety of mechanical, electrical, electronic, civil and other engineering items. Design draughtsmen/women may incorporate some measurements into their general arrangement drawings, and detail draughtsmen/women add the rest. They use mathematical calculations, for example, using formulae to work out the diameter of gear wheels from other given measurements. They may also incorporate production guidance into the drawings, for example where holes should be drilled. Detail drawings have to be standardized: details and symbols must be uniform throughout and information must always be listed in the same order.

Detail draughtsmen/women need to be familiar with the work on the shop floor in order to appreciate what craftworkers can and cannot do on a particular machine. Those who work for the gas, electricity and telephone services spend a lot of time updating maps showing the location of cables and pipes: the safety of workers depends on maps being clear and accurate.

Detail draughtsmen/women often have to do routine office work, such as making lists of components and alterations, keeping drawing records and manual filing systems.

Research and development

Engineers working in research and development (R&D) find solutions to engineering problems. Chartered engineers work in teams with incorporated engineers and engineering technicians. They work with design engineers on the development of new products and modifications to existing ones, and test designs.

They work closely with manufacturing engineers who look for ways to reduce costs and make manufacturing more efficient.

Finding solutions to problems (trouble shooting) found in manufacturing is a large part of their work. They carry out tests to find the causes of problems, analyse the results, and then look for a solution.

Manufacturing

Manufacturing is both a branch and a function of engineering. The work of manufacturing engineers involves planning, managing and maintaining manufacturing processes within a manufacturing industry. This could be the manufacture of a single item or mass manufacture. They design new manufacturing systems and plan the layout of manufacturing lines. They look for ways to improve existing manufacturing processes, to make them cheaper and more efficient, while maintaining the quality of the product and the safety of the work environment. This may involve assessing the machinery used in manufacture and modifying it where necessary, introducing computers into the manufacturing process, or working with designers to alter the product in order to improve manufacturing.

Their day-to-day work includes making sure that the materials used in manufacturing are available at the right time and that the manufacturing work is on schedule. There is a large element of staff management in their work, and they also deal with industrial relations, sorting out problems on the shop floor.

Within manufacturing engineering some engineers specialize in planning, where they decide on the steps that have to be taken to make a particular product and work out the time that the process will take, the people that will be needed and the cost of the operation. As with the other two functions of engineering, chartered engineers are supported by incorporated engineers and engineering technicians.

Sales and marketing

In this function, engineers find customers and visit them to explain about, and sell, their company's products. They find out what the customer needs in the way of new products or modifications to existing ones and pass this information on to their company to develop and manufacture. (Please see article SALES REPRESENTATIVE/MANAGER.)

WORK ENVIRONMENT

Engineers' work environment depends on their specialization and function. For instance, many civil engineers may spend considerable time out of doors on construction sites, whereas automobile design engineers are more likely to spend most of their time in their company.

Design engineers usually work in design offices but may also visit the factory floor. They may also travel to other parts of the country to meet customers or to see the site where the product is to be used. **Research and development engineers** work in laboratories, development workshops and on factory floors. They may travel to other parts of the country to attend conferences and exhibitions to look for new ideas that can be used in production. **Manufacturing engineers** usually work both in offices and on the factory floor. **Sales and marketing engineers** spend most of their time away from the office visiting clients. Depending on their company, they may spend time abroad.

SKILLS AND INTERESTS

Engineers need an interest in, and aptitude for, maths, science and technology. They apply scientific principles to solve practical problems. They should be able to think in an orderly, methodical way and have good judgement and sound reasoning skills. They need analytical skills to analyse and interpret data. They should have a logical, inventive and enquiring mind to be able to sort out problems and look for more efficient ways of working. They work to deadlines and therefore need to be able to work under pressure. Communications skills are very necessary in liaising with other engineers and with customers, to produce written reports and to make presentations to convince others of their ideas. It is important to work well as a team member; they often supervise staff, and need management and leadership skills. Particular skills may be needed depending on the branch and function of engineering, such as technical drawing, formulating test techniques and persuasive sales techniques.

ENTRY REQUIREMENTS

There are three levels of registration with The Engineering Council:

Chartered engineer

To be eligible to register with The Engineering Council as a chartered engineer requires: a relevant accredited Honours Degree in Engineering, plus successful completion of two years' industrial training, a further two or three years' relevant experience with professional responsibility, and corporate membership of a chartered engineering body. There is a final test of competence called a professional review. The minimum age to register is 25 years.

Degree course entry requirements are five GCSEs/S grades (A-C/1-3) with two, usually three, A levels/three to four H grades usually including maths and a science subject or equivalent.

At some universities offering engineering courses, students without maths and science A levels/H grades may first do a conversion course. These may be a year longer than usual engineering courses and give students the necessary maths and science teaching.

European Engineer (Eur Ing) – engineers with an accredited degree in engineering plus a further period of training and professional experience making a total of seven years from the beginning of their higher education are eligible for the title of European Engineer. All chartered engineers are eligible for the title of Eur Ing.

Incorporated engineer

To be eligible to register with The Engineering Council as an incorporated engineer requires: a BTEC/SCOTVEC Higher National Certificate/Diploma or ordinary Degree in Engineering accredited for incorporated engineer status plus a minimum of two years' relevant industrial training and a further two to three years' experience with appropriate responsibility. The minimum age to register is 23 years.

BTEC/SCOTVEC Higher National Diploma/Certificate in Engineering course entry requirements are: five GCSEs/S grades (A-C/1-3) including English, maths and science (or an engineering subject) plus one A level/two H grades (usually including maths or physics) or BTEC/SCOTVEC National Certificate/Diploma in Engineering Studies.

Engineering technician

To be able to register as an engineering technician with the Engineering Council requires: a BTEC/SCOTVEC National Certificate/Diploma in Engineering Studies plus a minimum of two years' suitable industrial training and a further two years' experience. Minimum age to register is 21 years.

BTEC/SCOTVEC national certificate/diploma entry requirements are: four GCSEs/S grades (A-C/1-3) including maths, English and a science or engineering subject.

TRAINING

Chartered engineer

Degree courses may be general, such as engineering science – which is a mixture of mechanical, civil and electrical subjects – or specialized in one branch such as mechanical, marine or manufacturing engineering.

Courses may be three-year full-time, or four-year sandwich courses that include periods of practical training in industry. There are also integrated courses that involve a year in industry before the course begins and a ten-week industrial placement each year.

MEng courses are for particularly able students who may transfer on to these courses after the first or second year of their degree course, and take four years to complete.

Professional training usually lasts two years and includes induction training to introduce graduates to the company's organization, products, customers and safety policies and on-the- job experience in several departments including design, manufacturing and computer applications.

Incorporated engineer

It is possible to follow an educational programme full-time through a BTEC/SCOTVEC higher national diploma course. These are two-year full-time or three-year sandwich courses. Alternatively, it is possible to train with a company, studying part-time for a BTEC/SCOTVEC higher national certificate.

Industrial training is broad and similar to that of the chartered engineer, and leads to an NVQ/SVQ Level 4 qualification.

Engineering technician

Apprenticeships last two to three years, and training includes time in the company's training centre covering craft skills such as welding combined with part-time study for BTEC/SCOTVEC national certificates. This leads to NVQ/SVQ Level 3 qualification.

Full-time training – BTEC/SCOTVEC national diplomas at colleges of further education.

Sponsorship – a number of companies run sponsorship schemes combining a degree or BTEC/SCOTVEC course with on-the-job training in the company. Students gain practical experience alongside their studies and are paid a bursary/salary during the sponsored period.

LATE ENTRY

There are no maximum age limits for engineering, and adults should be able to enter this career. However, entry depends on the individual company's requirements and the applicant's previous experience.

Many institutions of higher education have special entry procedures for mature candidates. Access courses are available for adults who wish to study for a degree but do not have the required entry qualifications.

Many institutions have a mature candidate route to enable people over the age of 35, with considerable design experience but without the required educational qualifications, to become chartered or incorporated engineers. There are also other similar routes for engineering technicians. It is also possible to qualify via the Open University or the Engineering Council's own examinations.

OPPORTUNITIES

At present there are about 300,000 engineers and technicians registered with the Engineering Council, although the actual number is far higher. In future there is likely to be an increasing need for engineers.

The range of opportunities for engineers depends to a great extent on their specialization. However, there are opportunities for most types of engineers in the following areas.

Manufacturing industry – opportunities exist both in industries that manufacture engineering products such as cars, trains or cookers as well as industries that produce non- engineering products such as food, textiles or pharmaceuticals.

Process industries – these include chemicals, plastics, rubber and paper industries.

Public service industries – which includes electricity generation and distribution, water and sewage treatment, coal mining, railways.

Local government – where engineers are employed in departments such as building services, engineering and transport departments.

National government – engineers are employed by a range of departments including the Ministry of Defence, Department of Trade and Industry, Department of the Environment and the Patent Office. Engineers are also employed in the Armed Forces and by engineering contractors. There are opportunities for engineers to work in research organizations and as lecturers in institutions of higher education.

PAY AND CONDITIONS

Salaries vary from company to company but qualified and established engineers may be in the ranges: chartered engineer, £13,000 to £30,000+; incorporated engineer, £12,000 to £22,000; engineering technician, £10,200 to £20,931 (senior technician).

Hours are usually 37½ a week, Monday to Friday, but may be variable to suit the needs of the job. Overtime may be required and some engineers may have to work shifts or carry out stand-by duties.

PROSPECTS

Promotion prospects within engineering depend on the company, but usually there is a formal structure. Technicians may be sponsored for higher national certificate/diploma or degree courses enabling them to become incorporated or chartered engineers. Incorporated engineers may be sponsored onto degree courses enabling them to become chartered engineers. All engineers can move up the promotional ladder gaining more responsibility and may eventually move into general management.

Engineers can become self-employed as consultant design engineers. There are increasing opportunities for engineers to work abroad and it is now possible to register in Europe (see ENTRY REQUIREMENTS).

RELATED OCCUPATIONS

Scientist/technician, materials scientist, micro-electronics designer/engineer, surveying technician, architectural technician, engineering craftsman/woman.

FURTHER INFORMATION

The Association of Cost Engineers*, Lea House, 5 Middlewich Road, Sandbach, Cheshire CW11 9XL, 01270 764798

British Computer Society, PO Box 1454, Station Road, Swindon SN1 1TG, 01793 480269

British Institute of Non-Destructive Testing*, 1 Spencer Parade, Northampton NN1 5AA, 01604 30124

Chartered Institution of Building Services Engineers*, Delta House, 222 Balham High Road, London SW12 9BS, 0181 675 5211

Chartered Institution of Water and Environmental Management, 15 John Street, London WC1N 2EB, 0171 831 3110

Engineering Training Authority (EnTra)*, Engineering Careers Information Service, Vector House, 41 Clarendon Road, Watford, Hertfordshire WD1 1HS, 0800 282167

Engineering Council*, 10 Maltravers Street, London WC2R 3ER, 0171 240 7891

Institute of Acoustics, Agriculture House, 5 Holywell Hill, St Albans, Herts AL1 1EU, 01727 848195

The Institute of Materials, Shelton House, Stoke Road, Stoke-on-Trent ST4 2DR, 01782 202116

Institute of Energy*, 18 Devonshire Street, London W1N 2AU, 0171 580 7124 (for careers enquiries)

Institute of Engineers and Technicians, 100 Grove Vale, East Dulwich, London SE22 8DR, 0181 693 1255

Institute of Highway Incorporated Engineers, 20 Queensberry Place, London SW7 2DR, 0171 823 9093

The Institute of Healthcare Engineering and Estate Management*, 2 Abingdon House, Cumberland Business Centre, Northumberland Road, Portsmouth PO5 1DS, 01705 823186

Institute of Marine Engineers*, The Memorial Building, 76 Mark Lane, London EC3R 7JN, 0171 481 8493

Institute of Measurement and Control*, 87 Gower Street, London WC1E 6AA, 0171 387 4949

The Institute of Materials, 1 Carlton House Terrace, London SW1Y 5DB, 0171 839 4071

Institute of Physics and Engineering in Medicine and Biology, 4 Campleshon Road, York YO2 5PE, 01904 610821

Institute of Plumbing*, 64 Station Lane, Hornchurch, Essex RM12 6NB, 01708 472791

Institute of Quality Assurance*, National Quality Information Centre, 10 Grosvenor Gardens, London SW1W 0DQ, 0171 730 9986

Institute of Road Transport Engineers, 22 Greencoat Place, London SW1P 1PR (please include sae)

Institution of Chemical Engineers*, Davis Building, 165-189 Railway Terrace, Rugby CV21 3HQ, 01788 578214

Institution of Civil Engineers*, 1 Great George Street, Westminster, London SW1P 3AA, 0171 222 7722

The Institution of Electronics and Electrical Incorporated Engineers (IEEIE)*, Savoy Hill House, Savoy Hill, London WC2R 0BS, 0171 836 3357

Institution of Electrical Engineers*, Schools Education and Liaison Service, Michael Faraday House, Six Hills Way, Stevenage, Herts SG1 2AY, 01438 313311

Institution of Engineering Designers*, Courtleigh, Westbury Leigh, Westbury, Wiltshire BA13 3TA, 01373 822801 (please include sae)

Institution of Engineers and Shipbuilders in Scotland, 1 Atlantic Quay, Broomielaw, Glasgow G2 8JE, 0141 248 3721

Institution of Gas Engineers*, 21 Portland Place, London W1N 3AF, 0171 636 6603

The Institution of Incorporated Executive Engineers, Wix Hill House, West Horsley, Surrey KT24 6DZ, 01483 222383

Institution of Lighting Engineers*, Lennox House, 9 Lawford Road, Rugby CV21 2DZ, 01788 576492

Institution of Mechanical Engineers, Schools Liaison Service*, Northgate Avenue, Bury St Edmunds, Suffolk IP32 6BN, 01284 763277

Institution of Mechanical Incorporated Engineers, 3 Birdcage Walk, Westminster, London SW1H 9JN, 0171 799 1808 (please include sae)

Institution of Mining Electrical and Mining Mechanical Engineers, Danum House, 6(a) South Parade, Doncaster DN1 2DY, 01302 360104

Institution of Mining and Metallurgy*, 44 Portland Place, London W1N 4BR, 0171 580 3802

Institution of Nuclear Engineers, Allan House, 1 Penerley Road, London SE6 2LQ, 0181 698 1500

Institution of Plant Engineers*, 77 Great Peter Street, Westminster, London SW1P 2EZ, 0171 233 2855

Institution of Railway Signal Engineers, 'The Cutting', 1 Badlake Close, Dawlish, Devon EX7 9JA, 01626 888096

Institution of Structural Engineers*, 11 Upper Belgrave Street, London SW1X 8BH, 0171 235 4535

The Institution of Water Officers, Heriot House, 12 Summerhill Terrace, Newcastle-upon-Tyne NE4 6EB, 0191 230 5150

Local Government Management Board*, 4th Floor, Arndale House, Luton LU1 2TS, 01582 451166

The Minerals Engineering Society, 2 Ryton Close, Blyth, Worksop, Nottinghamshire S81 8DN, 01909 591787

Royal Aeronautical Society*, 4 Hamilton Place, London W1V 0BQ, 0171 499 3515

Royal Institution of Naval Architects*, 10 Upper Belgrave Street, London SW1X 8BQ, 0171 235 4622

Scottish Engineering, 105 West George Street, Glasgow G2 1QL, 0141 221 3181

The Welding Institute*, Abington Hall, Abington, Cambridge CB1 6AL, 01223 891162

Women's Engineering Society*, Imperial College, Dept of Civil Engineering, Imperial College Road, London SW7 2BU, 0171 594 6025

FURTHER READING

Leaflets/booklets are available from the addresses marked*.

Job Outlines – Engineering Technicians and Incorporated Engineers – COIC
Working in Engineering – COIC
The European Engineering Yearbook – Cambridge Market Intelligence
Engineering Graduate Handbook – Westlake Publishing
Awards, Courses, Visits – The Engineering Council*
Careers in Chemical Engineering – IChemE*
Engineering Careers in Scotland – EnTra*

In the careers library classified under RAB.

2. ENGINEERING CRAFTSMAN/WOMAN (RAB)

THE WORK

Engineering craftsmen/women work from engineering drawings and turn the designs of chartered engineers and technicians into a range of engineering parts. They use both hand and computer-controlled machines to shape, cut, drill or grind metal very precisely to shape and may specialize in one or more skills.

Turners use lathes that rotate a workpiece. Metal is removed by using a cutting tool to produce round bars or cylinders, or to cut holes, screw-threads and grooves.

Millers use milling machines to produce flat surfaces, or cut special shapes, curves, slots, grooves and spirals by means of a cylindrical cutter or disc.

Borers use their machines to enlarge or modify large holes in metal components and perform certain milling operations.

Grinders use machines to produce very flat and smooth surfaces on flat or curved areas, usually finishing operations begun by turners and millers.

Planers and shapers cut or plane to produce a flat surface or special shape.

Drillers use drilling machines to produce holes up to 50mm in diameter. It is rare to specialize as a driller.

Engineering craftsmen/women order any materials required. They decide the order in which the machine carries out certain tasks and set up and operate the machine.

Most craftsmen/women make small batches of two to 2,000 items. They may also set up production machines for semi-skilled operators. When machinists make complete items they may have to fit machine parts together using more than one type of machine tool. Some craftsmen/women manufacture replacement parts or work in a team producing the prototype for a new model.

Toolroom machinists must be able to use all of the machine tools described above, and hand tools. They build specialist machine tools or the patterns, discs and cutters used to guide machine tools.

Some craftsmen/women machinists may be required to supervise semi-skilled and unskilled machine operators.

Personal safety is an element in the work. It is necessary to wear overalls, safety shoes, safety glasses and, sometimes, barrier creams (against dirt and infection).

WORK ENVIRONMENT

They work mainly indoors. Conditions can vary from a small production unit or workshop to a large factory which can be noisy.

SKILLS AND INTERESTS

This is a job that requires practical ability and physical fitness. Craftsmen/women must be able to read engineering drawings and visualize in three-dimensions what the end product will look like. They need to be very precise in their work as it has to be accurate to within one thousandth to ten thousandths of an inch. A steady hand and good concentration is required. They should be careful and pay attention to safety. Numeracy is needed for taking measurements and making calculations.

They need to be able to understand and give spoken and written instructions in their work. Craftsmen/women may work on their own, with other craftspeople or part of a team with other skilled workers and technicians.

ENTRY REQUIREMENTS

Entrants are usually 16 or 17 years old. Entry requirements are usually GCSEs/S grades (A-G/1-7) in maths, physics (or other scientific subject) and English. Other useful subjects are design and technology. Some employers use aptitude tests.

TRAINING

Training is through Modern Apprenticeships and often starts with one year off-the-job training in engineering workshop skills. This is followed by up to three years on-the-job training working alongside experienced craftsmen/women. There may be day/block release study at college for a City and Guilds (C&G), BTEC/SCOTVEC qualifications. Assessment is to NVQ/SVQ Level 3 or above.

LATE ENTRY

It has previously been unusual for adults to enter this career, and most new entrants have been school-leavers aged 16 to 17 years. However, most companies are now accepting adults, especially those with relevant experience in related areas of work, such as mechanical engineering crafts.

OPPORTUNITIES

Craftsmen/women are employed in manufacturing industries such as car, aircraft, ship, hospital equipment and office furniture manufacturers. These range in size from those employing a few craft machinists to large multinational companies. There are also opportunities in the Armed Forces.

About 500,000 craftworkers are employed throughout the engineering industry.

Opportunities for self-employment are very limited. There are good opportunities for working abroad either for British or overseas companies.

PAY AND CONDITIONS

Wages depend on the type of industry, location, experience, and responsibility of position held. Wages are around £170 a week for people aged 20 years and over, though they may be higher depending on the employer and local agreements. Shift allowances and bonus payments are common.

Hours are usually between 37 and 39 a week. Shift work may be necessary.

PROSPECTS

Craftsmen/women with good examination passes from training can transfer to a BTEC/SCOTVEC National Diploma/Certificate in Engineering and study for engineering technician level qualifications. There are links to technician level studies in most craft subjects. Many engineering craftsmen/women can be promoted to supervisory or inspector posts.

RELATED OCCUPATIONS

Please see article 3. ENGINEERING OPERATIVE.

FURTHER INFORMATION AND READING

Please see article 3. ENGINEERING OPERATIVE.

3. ENGINEERING OPERATIVE (RAB)

THE WORK

Engineering operatives carry out routine but key jobs in the production of items manufactured in the engineering industry.

Assembly workers put together part or whole products. It can involve carrying out simple routine tasks or more complicated assembling, following detailed instructions. Assemblers use tools such as screwdrivers, soldering irons, spot welders or hand riveters. Some workers (for example, those on a television assembly line) sit all day at a work bench; others (for example, those assembling cars) have to stand and move about the item they are working on. An item may take several minutes or a whole day to assemble depending on its size and complexity. Operators are usually given regular breaks to rest their eyes, if they are working on very small components.

Machine operators control automatic and semi-automatic machine tools, such as capstan lathes, borers, drilling machines, grinders, etc. Sometimes this is just a matter of switching on the machine and keeping it fed, or switching off the machine if anything goes wrong. Some jobs require operators to be able to set up and run their machines; they need to align cutting or shaping tools, set the speed of work and follow instructions and diagrams to manufacture items. This sort of work is almost as skilled as a craft-level machinist, but operators usually specialize in one type of production. Most machine operators do large batch work (200 to 1,000 items a day).

Finishers usually give a special treatment. This can be putting on a final protective coating (for example, chrome plating or paint spraying) or preparing the article for the next stage in the manufacturing process (for example, heat treatment or vapour blasting). Dangerous substances (such as acids) can be used in finishing processes and operators must do their work carefully and methodically. They need skill to set up the work and ensure that it is done correctly.

Viewers and checkers are part of the quality control process that is carried out at all stages of production. It can involve visual inspection with or without the use of optical aids; physical measurement using micrometers; or ensuring that a component works properly, for example, by using electrical equipment to check circuit boards. Operators carry out routine checks; craft workers or technicians carry out more complex technical tests.

Some jobs require protective clothing – aprons, goggles, boots, etc.

WORK ENVIRONMENT

Machine operators spend a great deal of their time standing or sitting at their machines and the work can be tiring when heavy materials are involved.

Generally the work environment depends upon the type of product being manufactured. They work mainly in workshops and factories that can be noisy.

SKILLS AND INTERESTS

Operators require concentration to carry out repetitive tasks. They also have to follow instructions – both written and spoken. It is important that they work carefully and pay attention to safety rules. Finishers may work with dangerous chemicals.

Engineering machine operators need stamina as they spend long periods of time standing and watching machines, some need strength to lift and move parts around. Some operatives have to be very accurate as they work to very precise measurements. An eye for detail may be needed for assembling or checking work. Operatives need to be able to work well on their own but also co-operate as part of a team.

Those who work with machine tools need some understanding of mechanical processes.

ENTRY REQUIREMENTS

There are no educational requirements for entry. Physical fitness, however, is important for some jobs and operatives may have to pass a medical. Although it is possible to enter work at 16 years, most operatives are over 18 years.

Some employers require applicants to pass a manual dexterity test and, for certain electrical assembly work, a colour vision test.

TRAINING

Training varies according to the type and complexity of the job. Usually entrants start with induction training: an introduction to the firm; its structure and policy; company practices; health and safety; amenities; trade unions, etc. It may take place in the firm's training centre or may be a brief introductory talk and tour.

Skills training may take place at a work bench under the supervision of an experienced operator or supervisor, or in a training centre. Skill and proficiency training can take a few hours or two to three weeks. Some employers give operators day or block release to study for City and Guilds (C&G) examinations. These offer an introduction to the tools and machinery used in engineering firms and sometimes include broader courses to improve operators' general education. Firms may train experienced and skilled operators to set and operate specialist machine tools. Such

training can take several months but does not have the scope or depth of craft level training.

A number of NVQs/SVQs in engineering are available at Levels 1 and 2.

LATE ENTRY

There are no age limits for this work. Adults with experience of production work may have an advantage over school-leavers in finding work. Adults should be physically fit.

OPPORTUNITIES

Engineering operatives work in manufacturing industries such as car, aircraft, ship, ventilation and office furniture manufacturers. These range in size from those employing a few operatives to large multinational companies employing hundreds of operatives. There is a declining demand for operatives, with the introduction of robotics, although opportunities may vary in different parts of the country. In certain regions there is a concentration of heavy engineering (eg shipbuilding or steel manufacture) or light engineering (eg domestic appliance or electrical goods manufacture).

PAY AND CONDITIONS

Wages vary according to industry, employer and location of job being done and the experience and age of the worker. Wages are approximately £125 to £250 a week for people aged 20 and over. Wages may be higher depending on employer and local agreements. Shift allowances and bonus payments are common within the industry.

Hours are generally 37 to 39 a week. However, firms generally follow a production schedule and may require shift work (including evenings and weekends) and overtime work. Some firms may also operate production machinery during the night, requiring night shifts to be worked.

PROSPECTS

Where opportunities exist, the more skilled and experienced operators may be put on to more complex and responsible tasks, such as machine setting or quality control, or promoted to supervisory posts.

RELATED OCCUPATIONS

Production worker, assembler, packer, building operative, foundry worker, welder, carpenter/joiner.

FURTHER INFORMATION

Engineering Training Authority (EnTra)*, Engineering Careers Information Service, Vector House, 41 Clarendon Road, Watford, Hertfordshire WD1 1HS, 0800 282167

FURTHER READING

Leaflets/booklets are available from the address marked*.

In the careers library classified under RAB.

1. MOTOR MECHANIC/VEHICLE TECHNICIAN CLCI:RAE
2. AUTO-ELECTRICIAN CLCI:RAE
3. VEHICLE BODY REPAIRER CLCI:RON

BACKGROUND INFORMATION

The number of motor vehicles on Britain's roads continues to increase. These include commercial trucks and vans, buses and taxis, as well as private cars and motorcycles. They all require regular routine servicing to ensure they keep operating efficiently and reduce the risk of breakdown. They also need repair after breakdowns and accidents. Specialists in these three occupations deal with different aspects of that work. They work not only for the garages, sometimes attached to showrooms but also in the garages and depots of companies and organizations which operate fleets of vehicles, ranging from ambulances and dustcarts to police cars and lorries.

THE WORK

1. Motor mechanic/vehicle technician

This divides into two main jobs: light vehicle or car mechanics, who deal with cars and small vans; and heavy or commercial vehicle mechanics, who handle large vans, trucks, buses and other large vehicles; motorcycle mechanics are another smaller category. Many employers now use the title vehicle technician rather than motor mechanic.

Their responsibility is for all the mechanical aspects of vehicles, primarily the engine but also all other working parts. For cars, this may be either petrol or diesel. For large vehicles, it is usually diesel, but includes pneumatically and hydraulically operated elements. Where a garage has no vehicle body repairers, some of their tasks may fall to mechanics.

For a periodic service, the mechanic conducts the routine checks laid down in the service manual, replaces any faulty or worn components, renews the oil and tops up other fluids, and checks and adjusts brakes, windscreen wipers, etc.

Repair normally entails diagnosing the cause of a fault and the removal of damaged or faulty units (engine, transmission, gearbox, etc) from the vehicle. They are then stripped down on a bench or the workshop floor, damaged or worn parts are repaired or replaced, the unit put back together and tested, and then returned to the vehicle. In car repair, faulty units are often replaced by new ones and the old ones scrapped. Heavy vehicles may also have major overhauls when all major parts are stripped down, cleaned and re-assembled. Some heavy vehicle mechanics specialize in one aspect such as gearboxes.

In some garages, servicing and repair requirements are assessed by more experienced mechanics or technicians, who also do the more complex work, while the more routine and simple tasks are performed by trainees, apprentices, assistants and less experienced mechanics.

Mechanics may road test a vehicle after repair. They may on occasion drive a breakdown truck to breakdown or accident sites to fix or retrieve vehicles. They may also be involved in MOT testing, in tuning engines or, in vehicle showrooms, in pre-delivery inspections.

They use a wide range of hand tools and power tools (with heavy vehicles this may include machine tools). They refer to service manuals and technical drawings. Multiskilling

means they may handle some basic electrical and electronic tasks as well when necessary.

Motorcycle mechanics form a separate sector. They specialize in servicing and repair of motorcycles only. As employers are usually small, these mechanics also handle electrical, electronic and body aspects. New motorcycles are delivered in kits of parts and assembled by mechanics at sales outlets.

2. Auto-electrician

They service and repair the many electrical items in a vehicle and the complex wiring harness which connects them. They also look after the electronic aspects including computers controlling different systems, and the dashboard display.

Routines of service and repair are similar to that carried out by motor mechanics, though auto-electricians are aided by ammeters, voltmeters and complex electronic test devices in their fault-finding. Complete units which may be removed for testing, repair and adjustment include starter motors and alternators. Routine servicing includes legally required testing of batteries and lights and may involve topping up batteries, changing bulbs, and re-aligning headlamp beams, though, in some sectors, these simple tasks may be handled by trainees or garage assistants. Electronic repairs may be effected by replacing a complete element such as a printed circuit board or microchip. Auto-electricians may also be involved in pre-delivery inspections and MOT tests.

They use a variety of hand and power tools, and test appliances and refer to manuals and circuit diagrams. Installation and servicing of accessories such as security alarms, radio/cassette players and car phones are often their responsibility, as are ticket/cash systems on buses, catering and video equipment on coaches and tachographs in heavy vehicles.

Though the same job title applies for all road vehicles, auto-electricians are normally trained on and specialize in one type of vehicle and sometimes one make, depending on their employer. As a result of multiskilling, they may handle basic mechanical tasks such as removing non-electrical items to reach electrical/electronic ones.

3. Vehicle body repairer

Repair of damage caused to the bodywork and windows, and in some cases the chassis, is carried out by vehicle body repairers. This ranges from scratches, dents and rust damage to the crumpling of whole panels in accidents. Repairs may involve hammering out dents or filling them with plastic compounds, by cutting and shaping sheet metal (or sometimes fibreglass) and welding it into place, or by fitting new or replacement panels, doors, windscreens, bumpers, etc.

They may also prepare areas for painting by cleaning with solvents, sanding, and priming, then mix paint to the correct colour match and spray on the appropriate number of coats and finally polish. They remove fittings such as door handles before painting and re-fit them after, and mask off windows and non-removable fittings. In larger garages, spray painting is done by a specialist craftsperson.

Body repairers may work on the restoration of classic vehicles and the customising of cars, where special transfers, colour schemes and painting designs may be involved. Company slogans and logos may be screen-printed or applied by transfer.

The only sector where the job includes routine servicing is with buses and coaches. Here vehicle body repairers regularly check and adjust door handles and locks, window mechanisms and windscreen wipers, though these tasks are often delegated to trainees or garage assistants. In other sectors, this work is carried out by a mechanic.

WORK ENVIRONMENT

Though some garages are small and dark, handling only one or two vehicles at a time, most are large, light, airy spaces with concrete floors. They have pits or ramps over or onto which vehicles can be driven to give workers access below. They can be cold in winter and hot in summer. Garages for buses/coaches and big trucks have to be big. There may be separate smaller workshops, or specific areas where specialist work is carried out.

For some activities such as paint-spraying or welding, body repairers may work in enclosed or screened booths to restrict spread of spray or fumes. They wear gloves, face-masks and eye-shields or goggles for these types of work and for sanding or grinding.

Overalls or boiler suits are worn for all garage work. Mechanics are exposed to oil, grease and dirt, but these also affect auto-electricians and vehicle body repairers. Motor mechanics and auto-electricians have to lean into engine and dashboard spaces or reach up from underneath vehicles from standing, kneeling or lying positions.

Some mechanics may work outdoors in all weathers when carrying out breakdown repairs on roads.

SKILLS AND INTERESTS

Good hand skills are essential when handling tools, test equipment, wires and components, some of which may be small. Workers should be fit and agile to stretch and reach into engine spaces, to bend and sometimes to lift heavy items. This is particularly the case for heavy vehicle mechanics and body repairers handling chassis repairs. Tracing the reason for a fault calls for diagnostic skills, though, for some aspects, electronic diagnostic devices may be used.

Mechanics and auto-electricians need patience and a logical mind to conduct a servicing procedure step by step and to take an item apart and put it together again in the correct order. Good hearing and colour vision are needed. The ability to work on one's own as well as in a team and to follow instruction from a foreman/woman are required. They need to be able to follow manuals and read instrument/computer displays. Discussing faults with drivers or owners of vehicles calls for good communication skills, as does the writing of reports or completing of forms. Changing vehicle designs and technologies requires a willingness to keep up to date with details of new models. Safety consciousness is vital. A driving licence may be needed for recovery duties.

ENTRY REQUIREMENTS

Entry is usually at 16 years to a three/four-year Modern Apprenticeship, or to a two-year training scheme for young people which may lead to a full apprenticeship. The minimum entry requirement is a reasonable ability in maths and English to ensure entrants can cope with the college elements to training. However, some employers look for exam passes and a few require GCSEs/S grades (A-C/1-3) in maths, physics and English. Engineering or craft subjects also help, as does an interest in cars and how they work and model-making. GNVQs/GSVQs in engineering may be acceptable. There may be an aptitude test to check manual dexterity and other abilities.

An alternative is to take a relevant full-time FE course at a college leading to a GNVQ, City and Guilds (C&G) or BTEC/SCOTVEC qualification, such as repair and servicing of road vehicles or motor vehicle engineering, before applying to employers for work and further training. This may be especially relevant to work at technician level. Colleges normally require four GCSE/S grades (A-C/1-3) for entry to BTEC/SCOTVEC courses. No set exam passes are required for C&G courses.

TRAINING

Training is to NVQ/SVQ Level 2 or 3 after a two-year training scheme for young people and at least Level 3 after a three/four-year Modern Apprenticeship. This is a modular system which involves skills and competence assessment and collection of evidence of tasks successfully completed. Training is largely given on the job in the garage working alongside skilled personnel. It also includes day or block release at college, or at other training organizations, working towards NVQs/SVQs.

Entrants with a GNVQ, C&G or BTEC/SCOTVEC qualification may have a period of further training with an employer when NVQ/SVQ assessments are completed for full craft or technician status.

Relevant NVQ/SVQs are:

Motor mechanic: Maintaining Passenger Carrying Vehicles (PCVs) – Mechanical at Levels 2 and 3, or Vehicle Mechanical and Electronic Systems Unit Replacement at Level 2 and Vehicle Mechanical and Electronic Systems Maintenance and Repair (for Light or Heavy Vehicles or Motorcycles) at Level 3.

Auto-electrician: Maintaining PCVs – Electrical at Levels 2 and 3 or Electrical Engineering Maintenance at Level 3.

Vehicle body repairer: maintaining PCVs – Body Trades at Levels 2 and 3 or Vehicle Body Fitting at Level 2 and Vehicle Body Repair at Level 3. Vehicle Re-finishing at Level 3 covers painting.

LATE ENTRY

Adult entry is relatively rare. Mature entrants may come, within the industry, from garage assistant jobs (mainly found in bus and coach sector) or from related occupations in other industries such as plant mechanic or engineering maintenance fitter. Some enter direct from vehicle maintenance in the Armed Forces. With the increase in electronics aspects, some individuals with electrical/electronics qualifications and experience gained in other industries may transfer to the work, especially at technician level. Garage assistants may be able to progress by gaining NVQs/SVQs.

Training opportunities specifically for adults may exist in some areas. Contact your local TEC/LEC, Jobcentre or careers office.

OPPORTUNITIES

While the number of road vehicles is expected to continue to increase, some factors have tended to reduce employment prospects in recent years. Many companies have cut back on the size of their fleets. Vehicle manufacturers have improved their technology and methods, so that vehicles are more reliable and less likely to develop faults. Modular construction, especially of electronic elements, makes it easier to replace components rather than repair them. There has also been a tendency by big concerns to sub-contract their vehicle maintenance to independent garages. Privatization of bus services has created more employers but reduced the number of formal apprenticeship systems. On the other hand, the increasing presence of electrical/electronics elements (computers, in-car entertainment, car phones) has increased the importance of auto-electricians. However, multiskilling and replaceable components, has led to the elimination of this job and its merging into vehicle technician.

The main categories of employer are independent garages, which service and repair private cars and the vehicles of small firms, and the vehicle maintenance departments of large concerns, which take care of their fleets of vehicles. The latter, and larger garages, may offer a more established training system and some form of promotion ladder. The range of these is very wide and includes: local authorities, public services (electricity, gas, water, telephone, post companies and so on), police forces, haulage and delivery companies, removals firms, bus and coach concerns, large manufacturers and retail chains, taxi and vehicle hire companies, security firms and many more. They are situated all over Britain, though most employers are in urban areas. Generally, there are more opportunities for motor mechanics and vehicle body repairers than for auto-electricians, and four times as many openings for trainee light vehicle mechanics than for heavy vehicle mechanics. Specialist body building and repair companies also employ body repairers

PAY AND CONDITIONS

Basic rates of pay for these occupations are within the band £2.85 to £4.10 an hour. Bonuses and overtime/shift allowances normally increase take home pay to well above this level. Employed trainees and apprentices are paid in the region of £1.80 an hour at 16 years, increasing with age and achievement. Some employers provide overalls and laundry service. Bus and coach companies often give travel concessions to employees and their families.

Normal working is 8am to 5pm, Monday to Friday. Some garages work evening or weekend overtime. In some sectors, such as bus and haulage, shift work including night work on a rota system is common to ensure vehicles are on the road during daytime hours. In some instances, repair/servicing work is done only at night. Some garages operate an on-call system outside normal working hours to deal with breakdowns of their vehicles.

PROSPECTS

Increasing sophistication of vehicle engineering means that technician level expertise is in demand and additional training to gain this offers one promotion route. Another is to foreman/woman and manager. As one in seven garage employees is a supervisor or manager and many of these come from the shop floor, such promotion prospects are good. Work on service reception or providing repair estimates may be another possibility.

Some experienced motor mechanics obtain employment as patrolmen/women with motoring organizations such as the AA and RAC. Other individuals start up a small garage business on their own or with colleagues. A small number move on to teach their skills in colleges or training centres. Some become assessors with motor insurance companies.

There may be possibilities of work abroad either in the overseas depots of multinationals or with native companies, especially within the EU or in developing countries.

RELATED OCCUPATIONS

Plant fitter/mechanic, engineering maintenance fitter, service engineer – office equipment, service engineer – domestic appliances, sheet metal worker/fabricator, AA/RAC patrolman/woman, tyre/exhaust fitter.

FURTHER INFORMATION

Automotive Management and Development Ltd (AMD)*, Regency House, 43 High Street, Rickmansworth, Hertfordshire WD3 1ET, 01923 896607

CENTREX*, Apprentice and Youth Training Department, Training and Conference Centre, High Ercall, Telford, Shropshire TF6 6RB, 01952 770441

Institute of the Motor Industry*, Fanshaws, Brickenden, Hertford SG31 8PQ, 01992 511521

REMIT*, 201 Great Portland Street, London W1N 6AB, 0171 580 9122

Retail Motor Industry Training*, 2nd Floor, Chestnut House, 32 North Street, Rugby CV21 2AH, 01788 576465

RTITB Services Ltd (same address as CENTREX, Telford)

Scottish Motor Trade Association, 3 Palmerston Place, Edinburgh EH12 5AF, 0131 225 3643

Vehicle Builders and Repairers Association, Belmont House, Finkle Lane, Gildersome, Leeds LS27 7TW, 0113 253 8333

FURTHER READING

Leaflets/booklets are available from the addresses marked*.

Job Outlines – Garages and Vehicle Repair – COIC
Working in – Work with Motor Vehicles – COIC
Jobs in Garages – Kogan Page
Apprenticeships within Youth Training – CENTREX

In the careers library classified under RAE/RON.

ELECTRICIAN CLCI:RAK

BACKGROUND INFORMATION

Although the skills and knowledge of the craft electrician apply to all electricians, their actual jobs vary considerably depending on the industry in which they are trained and employed.

Installation electricians install the wiring in new buildings and conversions of old buildings. The wiring includes that needed for equipment and machinery as well as for light, heat and power points.

Maintenance electricians maintain the basic circuitry, and service the machines used in manufacturing processes.

Production electricians install the wiring and electrical components in more complex electrical and electronic appliances and products.

Electricians in the electricity supply industry install and maintain transformer stations and **in electricity power stations** maintain the electrical aspects.

Service electricians repair faults in domestic appliances and office and factory machines. Please see article DOMESTIC APPLIANCE SERVICE ENGINEER/BUSINESS MACHINE SERVICE ENGINEER (ROK).

Auto-electricians service the electrical wiring and components in cars, trucks and buses. Please see article AUTO-ELECTRICIAN (RAE).

Safety

Electricity is dangerous; electricians rarely work where the system is live. Installation electricians' work is often done before the electricity supply is connected. The work of production electricians only receives current when the test technicians take over. A first rule for electricians, whether in homes or in factories, is to isolate the circuit before starting work.

However, some faults can only be located with the current flowing, for example, electronic circuits. Specially insulated tools and test instruments are used for these.

Where high voltages are involved, as in electricity generation and distribution, a strict 'permit to work' system is enforced. Electrical engineers certify that equipment being serviced is isolated from power.

THE WORK

Installation electricians install the wiring in houses. They decide from the architect's or contractor's drawing where to run the wiring (carcassing). The 'first fix' is to put in the boxes that will hold power points and to put protective strips over the cables. The 'second fix' is to strip the insulation off the ends of the wires and connect the fitments – light fittings, wall sockets, fuse box, immersion heater, central heating controller, etc. The system is earthed and tested to make sure all circuits are correctly installed, before calling in the regional electricity company for a connection to the supply.

Working on an office block or factory will involve a similar pattern. Cables may be laid in metal trunking in the floor and in metal pipes, called conduit. Cables for lifts or machinery may be bigger to carry higher currents.

On a conversion of an old building, the work starts with stripping out the old wiring and installation system.

Much of the work can be non-electrical – lifting floorboards, bending and cutting conduit or trunking, fixing cables, boxes or other equipment to walls, drilling holes for cables or screws, etc.

Production electricians' work may involve interpreting drawings provided by the drawing office or production engineers. The electrician decides the best way to make the connections, probably working at a bench or in a workshop.

Maintenance and service electricians' work involves travelling to where the faulty equipment or wiring is located. They use visual indications, past experience and instruments to check the faults.

WORK ENVIRONMENT

Installation electricians normally work in private houses, shops, offices or on building and construction sites. They can be exposed to cold, damp, dirt and dust. Electricians may also wire the lights on airfields, signals on railways and instruments in oil refineries and chemical plants. Some of the work can be in very exposed locations. Long journeys to and from work or staying away from home may be necessary.

Maintenance electricians in factories work indoors, but servicing machine tools, for example, may be oily and greasy.

Production electricians may work in the same workshop all the time, connecting up the wiring inside a complex product with a range of variations, or they could, for example, be in a shipyard, wiring out a cross-channel ferry.

SKILLS AND INTERESTS

Good hand skills are needed to deal with often quite intricate connections and to handle a range of tools skilfully and quickly. The work is active and can involve standing for long periods, bending, stretching, pulling, kneeling and lifting heavy equipment. Electricians should be able to work at heights and in confined spaces and in the heat or cold, damp and dust of building sites.

Electricians often work on customers' premises so they need to be tidy and clean and respectful of other people's property.

An ability in maths and physics is needed to follow technical drawings and calculate formulae. Electricians have to be able to work without supervision and to make decisions either on their own or in a small team. They must be meticulous and careful when working on installations/ equipment that carry high voltages. Patience is needed to locate and diagnose faults.

ENTRY REQUIREMENTS

Entry is mainly at 16 or 17 years by applying for an apprenticeship with an electrical contractor, an engineering company or an electricity supply company. Vacancies may also be advertised in local newspapers.

Training opportunities for young people may be available, including Modern Apprenticeships, leading to at least NVQ/SVQ Level 3. Contact your local careers office, TEC/ LEC for details.

Though not essential, GCSEs/S grades in English, maths, science or a practical subject are desirable. Craft and technology subjects can be useful. Applicants take aptitude and selection tests followed by an interview.

They also need to be physically fit with normal colour vision.

TRAINING

Training of **installation electricians** in England and Wales is usually supervised by JT Limited which is owned jointly by the Electrical Contractors Association (ECA) and the Amalgamated Engineering and Electrical Union (AEEU). In Scotland, training is supervised by SECTT (Scottish Electrical Charitable Training Trust) on behalf of the Scottish Joint Industry Board (SJIB).

The training programme in England usually leads initially to NVQ Level 2 in Installing Electrical Systems and Equipment. This requires apprentices to attend college on a day/block release course and take City and Guilds (Part 1) and the Achievement Measurement (AM) 1 practical test. Following success in Part 1 and AM 1 apprentices continue to attend college to undertake City and Guilds (Part 2). Apprentices also gain on-site experience which is recorded by them in a Field Evidence Record Book. When it is considered that apprentices are nearing full competence they undertake the industry's final practical test, Achievement Measurement (AM) 2.

Success in all units of NVQ/SVQ Level 3 in Installing and Commissioning Electrical Systems and Equipment leads to NVQ/SVQ Level 3 and recognition as a qualified electrician.

Apprentice training in other industries follows a similar pattern to these. The Electricity Training Association co-ordinates training in the electricity supply industry throughout Britain.

LATE ENTRY

It may be possible for adults to do a Joint Industry Board (JIB)-approved course through government sponsored training for adults. The JIB gives recognition, through employers. No formal route exists for engineering but some employers will take on adults and train them, increasingly so in view of the shortage of school-leavers. The electricity supply industry does recruit adult entrants for craft training.

OPPORTUNITIES

There are approximately 35,000 electricians in the electrical contracting industry, 112,000 in engineering, and 42,000 in electricity generation and supply.

The wide range of employers includes specialist electrical contractors, building contractors, manufacturers of electrical appliances and products with a significant electrical and electronic content, local authorities, hospitals, colleges, retailers and rental companies of domestic appliances, and power generating and supply concerns.

PAY AND CONDITIONS

Wages vary according to employer and experience. In many large firms, the basic wages are £237 (£240 in London) a week. Pay rates determined by the Joint Industry Board for the Electrical Contracting Industry are around £222 a week for an electrician, and £240.75 (£256 in London) a week for

an approved electrician, for a 37½-hour week. Hours depend on the company; shift work may be involved.

Overtime and holiday arrangements vary between industries and firms. Overtime is common; maintenance electricians, for instance, often do their work when everyone else has gone home, which means work at night, at weekends and during holidays.

PROSPECTS

After at least two years' experience, installation electricians may become eligible for re-grading to approved electrician. In all areas, promotion to senior hand, chargehand or forehand is available with the possibility of moving on to managerial positions.

Further training can lead to transfer into non-craft and supervisory grades, working on estimating, designing or planning electrical installations, or specializing in electronics. Some people go on to take degrees in electrical engineering, sometimes with the financial support of their employer.

It is possible to work freelance or start a small business.

RELATED OCCUPATIONS

Auto-electrician, domestic appliance service engineer, business machine service engineer, telephone technician, electrical/electronic assembler, telecoms technician.

FURTHER INFORMATION

Amalgamated Engineering and Electrical Union (AEEU), EETPU Section*, Hayes Court, West Common Road, Bromley, Kent BR2 7AU, 0181 462 7755

Electricity Training Association (ETA), 30 Millbank, London SW1P 4RD, 0171 344 5700 (electricity supply industry in England, Wales, Scotland and Northern Ireland)

Engineering Training Authority (EnTra)*, Engineering Careers Information Service, 41 Clarendon Road, Watford WD1 1HS, 01923 238441, 0800 282167 (freephone)

JT Limited*, South Block, Central Court, Knoll Rise, Orpington, Kent BR6 0JA, 01689 891676

Scottish Electrical Charitable Training Trust (SECTT)*, Bush House, Bush Estate, Penicuik, Midlothian EH26 0SB, 0131 445 5659 (electrical contracting industry in Scotland)

FURTHER READING

Leaflets/booklets are available from the addresses marked*.

Working in Construction – COIC
Working in Engineering – COIC

In the careers library classified under RAK.

TELECOMS TECHNICIAN CLCI:RAL

BACKGROUND INFORMATION

At one time, telecommunications essentially meant telephones and it was a British Telecom monopoly plus private systems within large organizations. Since privatization and deregulation, the industry has changed, extending the range of possible employers to some 5,000 organizations and increasing the technical knowledge demanded of technicians. The technology is now a complex mix of telephone cable (metal or fibre-optic), radio and computers, with some technicians being specialists, others multiskilled.

Public telephone services are provided by BT and Mercury with a separate company for Hull, although another major company is likely to appear using the British Rail (now Railtrack) communications network and energy companies are expected to enter this field as well. Major manufacturing and commercial companies have internal telecommunication systems spanning office and manufacturing complexes, regions and countries. These have been expanded to computer networking as well as voice and fax communication. Some use telecoms systems to transmit signals automatically from unstaffed plant and to adjust switches and valves remotely from a control room a considerable distance away. All of these use microwave radio links as well as cable (whether metal or fibre-optic), and, in some cases, satellite uplinks.

Major concerns which have their own telecommunications systems include: Railtrack, London Transport, British Gas, Powergen and other electricity companies, big oil and chemicals companies, water utilities, etc.

In addition, there are now two cellular phone networks (which work on a basis of interlinking radio areas or cells) and a number of private mobile radio network operators. Cable TV companies offer local telephone connections as well as TV programmes, and satellite companies have a role to play in international communications.

Other technical developments include digital telephone exchanges and digitized signals, fibre-optic cable, car phones and pagers. The interface with computers often calls for some knowledge of computer hardware and software. The incorporation of live and recorded moving pictures into computer and phone systems will change things further.

The titles telecoms technician and telecoms engineer are used to cover a wide range of jobs and include craft, technician and incorporated engineer qualifications.

THE WORK

There are a whole range of jobs and the work varies accordingly. Many telecoms technicians work on the installation and maintenance of communication systems at customers' premises. These could be switchboards (PBXs), telephones, telex and fax machines, and the internal cabling for phones and for computer networks. Installation of a whole system in a new office block, or in an old office being modernized, could take weeks or even months, laying cables in ducts below flooring, then connecting up equipment and testing it, using complex test equipment.

A maintenance technician might travel in a van from customer to customer, responding to calls following faults, discovering the cause of the fault and then correcting it. If based at the exchange (sometimes called a switch or switching centre or distribution node), they might install extra capacity, test lines where a fault has been reported, connect new or additional circuits for subscribers, and locate and repair faults within the exchange responding to flashing codes on a screen indicating the area of a fault.

Based at a satellite earth station, they could work either on operations and maintenance, ensuring the satellite dish is lined up correctly with the satellite and correcting faults, or on connecting circuits through the satellite to a telecoms system in another country.

With a cellular network, they could be based at the switching centre, as described above, or work as a radio base station (RBS) engineer, travelling by van to each base station in their area, either on routine testing of circuits or responding to faults reported by the engineers at the exchange.

With a user company, the work may be designing a system or preparing a detailed brief of what is required as well as installation and fault-finding. This may involve detailed talks with other departments in the company, and then liaising with suppliers and contractors who provide the appropriate equipment and software, cabling or radio links.

With an equipment manufacturer, technicians may be involved in the design, construction, inspection, testing, installation or technical sales of switchboard or exchange equipment, fax, telex and answering machines, mobile phones and radios, etc.

WORK ENVIRONMENT

Workplaces vary. A technician could be based permanently at a telephone exchange. Here they would divide their time between the control room/area and the switchroom. Or they might travel in a van between sites (homes, offices, etc) of customers, or to radio base stations. This may involve carrying heavy test equipment from van to site.

Some technicians work outdoors laying and connecting cables in the street or in uncompleted buildings on construction sites. Other telecoms technicians work in factories or design offices or development laboratories.

Many technicians work on their own. They communicate with base by radio or mobile telephone, apart from occasional visits to pick up spare parts, etc. Whether they wear overalls, a uniform or smart clothes depends on the type of work and the degree of contact with customers.

SKILLS AND INTERESTS

Dexterity is a prime requirement for using a wide range of hand tools and meters and making connections of tiny wires and electronic components. Engineering calculations and the use of meters require some mathematical skills. Deductive ability and a methodical approach are needed in analysing a fault and tracing its cause. Technicians often have to work alone and take responsibility for their own work, but also have to perform quickly under pressure when customers, or their employer, want facilities back in operation as quickly as possible.

They need good communication skills to discuss requirements and the symptoms of faults with customers or users. An interest in technology and a willingness to read magazines to keep abreast of new developments is valuable. Wires and electronic components are colour-coded so normal colour vision is required. Physical fitness may be important for lifting, carrying, bending and stretching. A clean driving licence is a requirement for some posts.

ENTRY REQUIREMENTS

BT have three levels of entry. Both craft and technician IIB entry require no prior qualifications only the passing of aptitude tests, though for technician IIB experience of relevant subjects at school or in previous work is required. Technical and commercial trainee entry, requires four GCSEs/S grades (A-C/1-3), for the BTEC/SCOTVEC national certificate/diploma course. It is likely that, with the introduction of Modern Apprenticeships and NVQ/SVQs, BT and other telecoms employers will recruit trainees via Modern Apprenticeships.

Modern Apprenticeship: The minimum requirement is a good general education but many successful applicants have three or four GCSEs/S grades (A-C/1-3), including maths, English and a science subject (physics is preferred). Technology and engineering subjects may be useful. Intermediate GNVQs/GSVQs Level II may be an alternative. Application is direct to employers. Entrants who perform well may be moved on to a higher level of training/study/qualification.

Incorporated engineer level: entry to a traineeship is with a relevant BTEC/SCOTVEC higher national diploma/certificate in, for example, electronic engineering or telecommunications. For higher national certificate/diploma level study, one A level/two H grades or BTEC/SCOTVEC national certificate/diploma or Advanced GNVQ/GSVQ Level III in Manufacturing or Telecommunications is required.

TRAINING

Modern Apprenticeship: an extended period of off-the-job workshop training, as well as tuition in theory at college, followed by work alongside experienced technicians under supervision. Assessment is to at least NVQ/SVQ Level 3.

Incorporated engineering: training is likely to be similar to Modern Apprenticeship above. Assessment to NVQ/SVQ Level 4.

Professional engineering: for engineering technicians, this gives the letters EngTech after their name. Those with national certificate/diploma qualifications and three years' engineering experience, including two years' training, may obtain this by registering with The Engineering Council direct or through the Institution of Electronics and Electrical Incorporated Engineers (IEEIE). Incorporated engineers gain the letters IEng, by the same process, after achieving higher national certificate/diploma standard qualifications plus five years' practical experience including two years' training.

LATE ENTRY

Adult entry is fairly common. BT has traditionally accepted mature entrants up to age 58 for technician IIB entry and up to age 41 for technical and commercial trainees. Newer, rapidly growing companies, needing capable technicians quickly, have recruited to a large extent from experienced or qualified people. Individuals from comparable posts in the Armed Forces, on radio/radar, for example, have been welcomed, as have those from electronic engineering with craft and technician skills/qualifications.

The NVQ/SVQ system makes possible the assessment of competences, however gained, which is valuable when applying to new employers. Training periods are usually shortened for recruits with relevant experience. Full-time and part-time college courses are open to mature applicants for whom formal educational requirements may be lowered or waived.

OPPORTUNITIES

Downsizing of major companies, especially privatized ones, has led to a reduction in staff numbers and severe restrictions on recruitment of apprentices and trainees. BT (traditionally the biggest employer) is now taking only 24 apprentices each year nationwide and Mercury is not currently recruiting.

However, some cellular companies are still expanding and cable is a growth area with 100 companies employing over 9,000 technical staff. This is expected to double over the next five years and companies are recruiting young people as trainees. The demands of computer networking, checkout tills linked directly to computers for stock re-ordering and sales analysis, travel agencies making bookings directly with tour operators' computers, bank accounts debited electronically, and so on, means that large companies increasingly find they need telecoms technicians as well as computer experts on their staff.

The major employers, especially public and cellular telephone systems, function throughout the UK, though their offices are likely to be in major towns and cities. The big industrial and commercial companies, such as gas, electricity and water utilities, and transport such as Railtrack, which maintain their own internal communications systems are also usually found in towns and cities.

Telecommunications equipment manufacturers employ technicians in the more complex assembly roles, in test and inspection, in design and development, and in installation and service areas. Suppliers of imported equipment and specialist service companies have technicians for installation and service work.

An increasing number of technicians now work freelance, subcontracting their skills to large companies and developing business skills to obtain customers. Others set up small businesses supplying telephone or communications equipment to domestic or commercial customers or offering a maintenance service.

Some move into inspection or regulatory work in manufacturing or with supervisory bodies or government departments.

Installation work can take technicians to other countries. Opportunities arise for employment in Europe, USA, the Middle East, etc.

PAY AND CONDITIONS

Salaries are generally supplemented with payments for overtime and shift working and some companies also pay bonuses. However, salaries and conditions such as holiday entitlement can vary significantly.

In most areas, the basic working week is 37 to 38 hours, many technicians work evenings/weekends as part of their normal working hours.

PROSPECTS

Job titles and promotion routes vary depending upon the employer. With BT, it would be to technical officer, and possibly assistant manager and manager of a service or a facility, such as a telephone exchange.

On the customer service side with Mercury, it would be assistant customer engineer, customer engineer, senior then principal customer engineer, customer department manager. In a telephone exchange for Mercury or a cellular network, it could be assistant network engineer, network engineer, assistant network manager, network manager. With Thomson, the tour operators, promotion is from telecoms technician to telecoms analyst, telecoms project manager, to telecoms manager.

In some cases, in order to gain promotion it may be necessary to take further courses, to gain BTEC/SCOTVEC higher national certificate/diploma qualifications or a relevant degree.

RELATED OCCUPATIONS

Maintenance fitter (instrument/electronics), broadcasting engineer, computer service engineer, aircraft maintenance engineer (avionics), contract electrician, production fitter (electronics), railway signal/telecoms technician, incorporated engineer/technician (electronics).

FURTHER INFORMATION

Telecommunications Industry Association (TIA)*, 20 Drakes Mews, Crown Hill, Milton Keynes MK8 0ER

Telecommunications Vocational Standards Council (TVSC), Blackfriars House, 399 South Row, Central Milton Keynes MK9 2PG, 01908 240120

Institution of Electronics and Electrical Incorporated Engineers (IEEIE)*, Savoy Hill House, Savoy Hill, London WC2R 0BS, 0171 836 3357

Scottish Engineering*, 105 West George Street, Glasgow G2 1QL, 0141 221 3181

Cable Television Association, 5th Floor, Artillery House, Artillery Row, London SW1P 1RT, 0990 111777

Federation of Communication Services (FCS)*, Keswick House, 207 Anerley Road, London SE20 8ER, 0181 778 5656

Fibreoptic Industry Association, 10-15 The Arcade Chambers, High Street, Eltham, London SE9 1BG, 0181 859 6617

Mobile Radio Training Trust, PO Box 10, Twyford, Reading RG10 8AZ, 01734 223 828

Confederation of Aerial Industries, Fulton House Business Centre, Fulton Road, Wembley Park, Middlesex HA9 0TF, 0181 902 8998

FURTHER READING

Leaflets/booklets available from the addresses marked*.

Job Outlines – Radio and Telecommunications – COIC
Working in Telecommunications – COIC
Working in Electronics – COIC
Your Choice for Life – A Career in Electronic, Electrical and Mechanical Engineering – IEEIE Periodicals

Periodicals: Communications Monthly, Electronics Weekly

In the careers library classified under RAL.

OIL AND GAS PRODUCTION AND DRILLING: ROB

1. ROUSTABOUT CLCI:ROB
2. ROUGHNECK CLCI:ROB
3. DERRICKMAN CLCI:ROB
4. DRILLER/ASSISTANT DRILLER
   CLCI:ROB
5. TOOLPUSHER CLCI:ROB
6. PRODUCTION STAFF CLCI:ROB

BACKGROUND INFORMATION

Oil is one of our most valuable commodities. We need it to run cars, ships, aircraft and railways; to provide power, heat and light, and to lubricate machinery. From oil we also get chemicals and other products used in industry, agriculture and our homes. The UK offshore oil and gas industry only started 30 years ago and is still a relatively new employment field.

From offshore oil platforms two operations take place – drilling and production. In addition to drilling on oil platforms, drilling is also done from a number of other marine drilling units. There are mobile drilling rigs, which can be moved from place to place then installed. When the water is shallow, different types of rigs which are mounted on floating barges or platforms and supported on the seabed by legs, are used. In deeper water semi-submersible drilling rigs are used.

The first process is exploratory drilling to establish whether there is an oil field suitable for commercial production. When this is confirmed the temporary rigs are replaced by a permanent fixed oil platform, which is attached to the sea bed. This platform houses facilities for both drilling and production as well as living quarters, storage areas for all the equipment and supplies, a helicopter pad and engine room for generating power for the platform.

Drilling – is normally done using a rotary drill which revolves at the end of a string of drill-pipe rather like a giant power drill. The drilling string is suspended from the derrick – steel framework which may be up to 140 feet high. At the top of the derrick is a crown block from which the drill string and casing is raised and lowered. During drilling, mud is circulated around the drill to make the process easier.

Drilling is done from both offshore and onshore drilling rigs. Onshore rigs are mobile and can be dismantled and moved from one site to another.

Production – once the well is drilled and completed, production starts. The drill is replaced by lighter-weight tubing through which hydrocarbons – a mixture of oil and gas can flow to the well head. These then have to be separated so the oil is free of dissolved gas and ready for pipeline or tanker transport. Salt water is often produced with the oil and also has to be separated. The gas must be purified and free of any liquids. If the hydrocarbons cannot reach the surface unaided then other methods such as pumping or injecting gas or water may be required.

This article concentrates on the work of drilling and production teams; however there are many other jobs on an oil platform – engineers, geologists, safety officers, divers, caterers and medical orderlies.

THE WORK

Drilling

Offshore drilling crews consist of a toolpusher, drillers, derrickmen, roughnecks and roustabouts. Onshore drilling crews are often smaller and usually have a toolpusher, driller, derrickman and roughnecks. They rarely employ roustabouts.

1. Roustabout

This is the basic manual labouring job on a drilling platform or rig. Roustabouts work in both oil drilling and production. They keep work areas clean, remove rust from structures and paint them. They offload supplies from boats and store them in storage areas and move supplies from storage areas to where they are going to be used. Some more experienced roustabouts lead a small team.

2. Roughneck

This is the next level up from roustabout. Working under the direction of the driller, they do the manual work associated with the drilling operation. They run the drill pipe into the hole and pull it back out. They make up the appropriate length of drill string by joining lengths of drill pipe together. As drill bits become worn the roughnecks pull the drill string out of the hole, disconnect the lengths of pipe and put a new drilling bit in, then reconnect the drill string. This operation may be necessary every few hours depending on how much drilling is being done. In doing their work roughnecks use hoisting tackle, ropes and air winches.

In addition to working on the drill string they clean the de-sanding and de-silting equipment through which the mud passes. They also maintain drilling equipment. Roughnecks also carry out some of the duties of the roustabout.

3. Derrickman

Derrickmen work on platforms up the derrick. Under the direction of the driller, they handle the sections of drill pipe, latching and unlatching the lifting equipment used to support the pipe when it is being pulled out of or run into the hole. Derrickmen also have responsibility for the proper working of the mud pumps, the condition of the drilling mud system and the supervision of the roughnecks. They supervise the mud pumping operators.

4. Driller/assistant driller

Drillers control the drilling equipment and are in charge of the drilling crews. They control operations on the drill floor and operate the machinery which raises and lowers the drill string and bit. Under the advice of the drilling supervisor they maintain the speed of rotation of the drill string and the weight on the bit. In addition they keep records of the drilling and its progress. Assistant drillers do the same job as drillers but under the supervision of the driller.

5. Toolpusher

The toolpusher is the rig superintendent in overall control. They oversee the entire drilling operation. They ensure that everything runs smoothly and that all the necessary equipment and materials are available. They are also responsible for the crews, shifts, rotas and safety. The toolpusher is the link with the oil company's representative who makes regular visits and inspections.

Production

6. Production Staff

The production team is involved in the management of the hydrocarbons (oil and gas) from the reservoir to the initial customer. They deal with production from the wells and the processes through which the hydrocarbons go. The team comprises a production supervisor, control room operators, foremen/women operators, lead operators and operators.

Roustabouts also work in production. Operators work in one of three areas: utilities, oil production and gas compression.

New operators start working in utilities – controlling the systems providing such things as sanitation and electricity. With experience they move to oil production and then gas compression – the most complex of the operations.

Operators in oil production keep a constant watch on the instrumentation, making sure all the valves and instruments work properly. If there are problems they correct them – often by operating valves manually. In gas compression they look for abnormalities in flow rates and pressure and condition of gas.

Their work varies depending on their level of experience. Less experienced operators carry out manual tasks such as opening and shutting valves, offloading tankers, and warehouse work. Skilled operators work in the control room, taking and analysing samples for quality, operating computers, and managing equipment used to measure and control the substances being refined. They are responsible for making sure that equipment is working properly and safely. If the flow rate of a substance slows down they are responsible for finding out the reason and having the fault repaired.

From operator (gas compression) they can be promoted to lead operator (utilities), then lead operator (oil production) and on to lead operator (gas compression). In this job they are chargehands supervising a team of operators. Their next promotion is to foreman/woman operator, running the plant and instructing the operators. The next level is control room operator – these people control the whole operation. They monitor everything that is happening in all three areas. If, for instance, the gas is not up to the correct standard they recycle it. They also manage the crews.

The most senior job in production is that of production supervisor. They have a more strategic role involved in forward planning, as well as having overall responsibility for the production operation and safety. They also handle any major problems that arise. A major part of their work is controlling the production of oil. There are limits to the amount of oil that can be produced at any one time. These limits are determined by OPEC and by the oil buying market. So, under the direction of the oil company, the production supervisor controls the production rate. This is done by shutting down a well or reducing the rate of flow. The production supervisor decides on the most appropriate method and then instructs the crew.

WORK ENVIRONMENT

Crews working offshore may be on oil platforms or rigs and are away from home for two weeks at a time. Those involved in offshore drilling are often exposed to dirty, wet and noisy conditions. Production operators, however, work mainly in control rooms. Derrickmen work at heights. Drilling jobs involve a great deal of bending and lifting.

On the platform there are leisure facilities such as games rooms, films, videos and libraries. Smoking on the platforms is restricted to certain areas and no alcohol is allowed.

Roustabouts and production operators sleep in two-berth cabins, but only one sleeps there at a time, as the other one will be working. Food and accommodation are provided free.

SKILLS AND INTERESTS

It is very important that crew members are able to cope with periods spent away from home. They should be able to live with and get on with other people and to work as a team. They are transported to the platform by helicopter, so punctuality is necessary. Work on oil platforms can be hazardous so employees must be responsible, reliable and safety conscious. Those involved in drilling must be willing to work outside in all weathers.

ENTRY REQUIREMENTS

There are no minimum academic entry requirements to start as a roustabout, although applicants must be physically fit. They also have to be able to work at heights and have no speech defects. There is a tendency nowadays for companies to prefer operators to be multiskilled, for instance, as operator/mechanics or operator/electricians, and employers look for relevant training and experience. Those who wish to become operators but have no transferable skills can start as roustabouts. For some jobs defective colour vision is a bar. All applicants undergo a medical which may include tests for substance abuse. The minimum age for this work is 18 years although many companies prefer applicants who are between 25 and 35 years.

Graduate entry – there are schemes for graduates with relevant degrees in science to enter and progress quickly in production or drilling to production supervisor or toolpusher.

TRAINING

All offshore employees must first undertake an offshore survival course which covers safety, survival and firefighting. Some companies sponsor new employees for this course. The cost of this course is between £450 and £550. For a list of centres running this course contact the Institute of Petroleum.

Other training is given on the job under the supervision of chargehands, combined with relevant short courses which crew members may do during their shore leave. This can lead to NVQs/SVQs in Process Operations: Hydrocarbons at Levels 1, 2 and 3 and Offshore Drilling Operations at Levels 1, 2 and 3.

LATE ENTRY

It is unusual for applicants to be accepted after 35 years, unless they have transferable skills such as engineering or mechanic work or they have a background in the Armed Forces.

OPPORTUNITIES

The UK offshore industry is mainly based off the east coast of England and Scotland, in Morecambe bay and Liverpool bay and west of the Shetlands. There are three types of offshore companies – operating companies (usually major oil companies) hold the exploration and production licences and operate the production platforms, drilling companies are contracted to undertake the drilling work. There are also service companies providing assistance to both operating and drilling companies, such as caterers, cementing companies, and so on. Operators usually work for the operating companies and drilling teams for drilling contractors.

There is considerable competition for jobs, so the more

skills and relevant work experience applicants have the better. Experience in offshore installation construction yards or an onshore drilling company is useful. For experienced personnel there are opportunities to work anywhere in the world.

PAY AND CONDITIONS

Roustabouts and production operators earn up to about £17,000 with increases on promotion. Offshore crews work on the rig for two weeks followed by two weeks' shore leave. The crews work in shifts of twelve hours on and twelve hours off. Onshore crews also work night shifts but they usually work a week of days followed by a week of nights.

PROSPECTS

Drilling

Most people start as a roustabout. Promotion is gained on experience and ability. Promotion to roughneck usually takes from one to three years. From there to derrickman another two to three years and a further four to six years to reach assistant driller. To reach driller takes about five to eight years and then eight to ten years to become a toolpusher.

Production

Production operator (utilities) is the first rung on the ladder for those who have relevant experience. Those without relevant experience start as roustabouts. From utilities the next steps are to production operator (oil) and then production operator (gas). This is followed by promotion to chargehand (utilities), chargehand (oil) and chargehand (gas). Then it is possible to move to control room operator and then to production supervisor.

There are accelerated training schemes in both drilling and oil/gas production for graduates who can reach senior jobs more quickly. There are a range of courses in both these areas, which can enhance promotion prospects – information on these is available from individual training schools (for addresses contact the Institute of Petroleum).

RELATED OCCUPATIONS

Chemical plant process operator, construction operative, crane driver, motor mechanic, dock labourer.

FURTHER INFORMATION

The Institute of Petroleum*, 61 New Cavendish Street, London W1M 8AR, 0171 467 7100

OPITO*, Inchbraoch House, South Quay, Ferryden, Montrose, Angus DD10 9SL, 01674 662500

For information about firefighting and survival courses only, contact OPITO.

FURTHER READING

Leaflets/booklets are available from the addresses marked*.

In the careers library classified under ROB.

1. MAINTENANCE FITTER CLCI:RAB
2. BUSINESS MACHINE SERVICE ENGINEER CLCI:ROK
3. DOMESTIC APPLIANCE/GAS SERVICE ENGINEER CLCI:ROK

BACKGROUND INFORMATION

Our society depends upon the continued and efficient running of its machines and appliances, whether these are machines used in manufacturing processes in industry, business machines in offices or domestic appliances in our homes. Yet, due to overwork, misuse or the simple wear and tear of normal operation, these machines are liable to break down.

The answer to this is called maintenance or servicing. This may be routine inspection and maintenance where, at set intervals, the equipment is checked, cleaned, lubricated, the parts most liable to wear replaced, and the machine adjusted to work as well as possible. This gives longer life and trouble-free performance. Or it may follow a breakdown, after which the cause of the failure has to be found and corrected, possibly including repair or replacement of a faulty part.

In many cases, the people responsible for maintenance also deal with the installation and commissioning of machinery, though for more complex equipment this may be a separate occupation, often at technician or incorporated engineer level.

Some trends have lessened the amount of servicing required such as greater built-in reliability and modular construction which allows major components to be replaced and either discarded or taken to a workshop for repair. With computer/microchip control, some machines now have in-built diagnostic ability and signal the cause of common faults which may then be corrected by the user, or which simplifies the task of the engineer, indicating where the fault lies and what is required to repair it.

Engineers who go into customers' premises are often called field engineers as opposed to workshop engineers who remain in the repair workshop.

In industry

In manufacturing and process industries, maintenance has traditionally been split between different engineering disciplines, with fitters skilled in mechanical, electrical or electronic/instrument aspects, partly because each field is so complex. Although there has been a measure of multiskilling, which avoids having to call out someone with one of the other skills when the fault is predominantly in one area, this split still broadly applies. It has broken down most in areas of strong automation and robotization, though these tend to require technician level knowledge and skills.

In offices

Increasingly, business machines of all kinds are leased or rented from an agent or dealer rather than bought from a manufacturer. Part of the deal may be a service contract under which the agent or dealer takes responsibility for maintenance. If the equipment is purchased, there is a period under guarantee during which the manufacturer or dealer is responsible for maintenance. After that, they may offer a service contract or the user company may contract with a service company.

Some of these providers have regional and local workshops with their own maintenance staff. Others use a network of small independent service companies subcontracted to them. Some organizations such as large educational establishments employ a small number of maintenance staff to deal with most problems.

In homes

The increased reliability of appliances, which has reduced the number of breakdowns, has led to a reduction in the need for domestic appliance servicing in recent years. This is especially true of electronic devices where the microchip has greatly reduced the number of components that can go wrong. In addition the much lower cost of small appliances, such as electric irons and hair dryers, means that it is often cheaper for the user to buy a new one than to pay for repair.

In gas appliance servicing, the major change is the downsizing of British Gas following privatization and the increase of competition. This has drastically curtailed the main entry and training route for gas service jobs.

1. MAINTENANCE FITTER (RAB)

THE WORK

Maintenance fitters ensure that machinery and equipment used in making or processing products keeps working and that, when it breaks down, it is put back into order as quickly as possible. Another group of maintenance fitters may perform similar tasks for the plant services, ensuring that supplies of electricity, water steam, compressed air, and so on, continue and that lighting, heating, lifts, conveyor belts, security and sprinkler systems and communications networks function as required.

Following instructions from a work docket or call-out sheet, or working to a routine maintenance schedule, fitters leave the workshop to repair/service machines. A mechanical fitter involved in servicing isolates the machine from power, replaces parts which have worn, or can be expected to wear out shortly, and lubricate and adjust machines as necessary. Their field includes pneumatic and hydraulic aspects.

An electrical fitter checks the electrical components, they may replace items such as brushes, check that contacts are free from dirt and oil, replace and repair the electric motor or overhaul the old motor in the workshop.

The electronics or instrument fitter examines the instrument and control aspects which have increased with computerization and the microchip. This may involve mechanical aspects such as the delicate moving of arms that draw pens across revolving graph sheets to record changes in temperature or pressure. Increasingly machines have a built in electronic monitoring system so that a printout indicates the fault or the area of a fault. For these, it may be necessary to keep the power flowing to be able to check faults which may call for additional safety precautions such as insulation mats and insulated tools.

Periodically equipment needs a major service or complete overhaul, involving dismantling, and repair or replacement of any damaged parts, re-assembly and testing. A large factory may do this during the shutdown of the annual summer holiday.

Maintenance fitters are also involved in the installation of new machines, instrumentation and facilities, possibly working alongside suppliers or contractors from whom the new machines or services have been bought.

Maintenance fitters may repair parts in the workshop – machining, welding, etc. In some firms they may be employed solely in the workshop as specialist maintenance fitters.

Fitters work on their own or with a semi-skilled mate to assist with heavy lifting, handing them tools, etc. They use a wide range of hand and power tools, measuring and testing devices, and may refer to technical manuals and drawings.

WORK ENVIRONMENT

Fitters are based in a workshop which may be within the manufacturing area or away from it. This is equipped with workbenches, specialist machine and power tools, and test equipment for checking and repair. These workshops are usually well-lit and warm.

From this base, fitters go out into manufacturing areas where environments vary. Engineering machinery may be dirty and greasy. Shipyards and coal-fired power stations may be dirty and dusty. Some chemicals plant is in the open air. So work areas may be cold in winter, and involve long walks. In contrast the surroundings of a highly automated food processing plant are clean, warm and comfortable.

SKILLS AND INTERESTS

Good powers of observation are necessary to be able to deduce the reason for a failure from the symptoms reported by the machine operator. This may involve good hearing, good eyesight for anything out of the ordinary, and even smell and touch. The work involves checking meticulously all the possible faults.

Fitters need good communication skills to question the operator and to understand their instructions and the manual. They also have to complete forms reporting on their tasks. With production held up until they can restore the machine or conveyor belt, they have to be able to work quickly and accurately under pressure.

Nimble fingers, dexterity with hand and machine tools, understanding of engineering principles, and ability to follow technical descriptions and diagrams are all involved.

ENTRY REQUIREMENTS

Normal entry in future will be through a Modern Apprenticeship at craft level. GCSEs/S grades in maths, physics and English are required, although many successful applicants have three/four GCSEs/S grades (A-C/1-3). Engineering and technology subjects help, as does an interest in mechanics/electrics/electronics illustrated by hobbies such as model making. GNVQ/GSVQs in engineering may be accepted.

An alternative route may be to take a course at an FE college leading to a City and Guilds (C&G) or BTEC/SCOTVEC national certificate/diploma qualification such as mechanical and manufacturing engineering or electrical and electronic craft studies, and then apply to an employer. For BTEC/SCOTVEC national certificate/diploma, entry is usually with four GCSEs/S grades (A-C/1-3).

TRAINING

Modern Apprenticeships are structured on an established pattern. They initially involve one-year off-the-job training in a company training centre or a group or industry training centre, primarily in general engineering craft skills with day or block release at a college. This is followed by on-the-job training, working alongside experienced fitters, in relevant modules (at least two) accompanied by assessments towards NVQ/SVQ in Engineering Maintenance at Level 3 and college study towards a C&G craft or BTEC/SCOTVEC qualification. In engineering, this leads to the

EnTra Modern Apprenticeship Certificate as well as an NVQ/SVQ in Engineering Maintenance at Level 3.

Modern Apprenticeships are skill-based not time-based, but usually take three to four years.

LATE ENTRY

The NVQ/SVQ system may make it possible for engineering operators, assemblers or craftsperson's mates to acquire and be accredited with the relevant skills and knowledge and so be accepted as qualified fitters.

Some employers may train people with an appropriate C&G or national certificate/diploma qualification gained in further education; or retrain in maintenance skills those with similar experience, for example, a production fitter.

OPPORTUNITIES

There is a continuing demand for maintenance fitters. However, the decline in manufacturing industry generally has reduced the number of openings and the recruitment of apprentices. Also the application of computer control and the introduction of integrated manufacturing systems has tended to mean more reliable machinery with less need for servicing/repair. When servicing/repair is needed, technician level skills are required.

Employers include:

– large concerns in engineering, manufacturing, process and extraction industries;

– manufacturers of industrial machinery and equipment who employ fitters as field engineers to install, test, service and repair on customers' premises;

– service industries and commercial concerns including hospitals, local authorities, universities, chains of stores and restaurants, insurance companies, and so on, who may retain or call in maintenance staff to service heating and ventilation systems, communication systems, lifts, lighting, computers/tills, conveyor belts, catering equipment, and so on;

– the Armed Forces.

However, not all of these recruit and train apprentices.

Opportunities to work abroad may come through working on overseas contracts for UK or multinational companies or by employment by foreign companies in other EU countries, the USA, Eastern Europe, Middle East, etc.

PAY AND CONDITIONS

Average earnings for a qualified fitter are about £340 a week, including overtime and bonuses. The basic week is 37 to 39 hours. Shift work may be involved, especially in process industries such as chemicals and power generation. In others, overtime in evenings or weekends allows servicing or repairs to be done when machines are not in use. In some cases, fitters may have to be prepared to be called out by phone in off-duty hours to deal with a breakdown. In large companies that close down for annual holidays, fitters may work through on major overhauls or installations, taking their own holidays at another time.

Protective clothing, such as overalls, boots, helmets and earmuffs, are normally provided by employers. Apprentices are expected to build up their own toolkit of hand tools and basic measuring devices during training while the employer makes available power and machine tools, electrical or electronic test equipment, etc.

PROSPECTS

The promotion route is to senior fitter, chargehand, foreman/woman and possibly to workshop manager or maintenance department manager, though these higher level posts are more likely to be held by incorporated or chartered engineers in large companies. Some fitters go on to train further to engineering technician or incorporated engineer level by studying for BTEC/SCOTVEC national certificate/diploma or higher national certificate/diploma qualifications or through the NVQ/SVQ system. It is also possible to qualify for Engineering Council examinations leading to professional engineer status by open learning through a National Extension College course.

The detailed knowledge of machines gained during maintenance work makes possible specialization in installation work or transfer to inspection and testing or to sales and marketing posts for those with the appropriate abilities.

RELATED OCCUPATIONS

Production fitter, motor vehicle mechanic, business machine service engineer, domestic appliance service engineer, gas service engineer, incorporated engineer/ technician (mechanical), aircraft maintenance engineer, auto-electrician, computer service technician, construction plant mechanic, plumber, telecoms technician.

FURTHER INFORMATION

Engineering Careers Information Service (ECIS)*, Engineering Training Authority (EnTra), Vector House, 41 Clarendon Road, Watford, Hertfordshire WD1 1HS, freephone 0800 282167

Scottish Engineering*, 105 West George Street, Glasgow G2 1QL, 0141 221 3181

FURTHER READING

Leaflets/booklets are available from the addresses marked*.

Job Outlines – Craftworkers and Operatives in Engineering – COIC

Working in Engineering – COIC

Engineering Explained – ECIS

Training and Working in Engineering – ECIS

In the careers library classified under ROK.

2. BUSINESS MACHINE SERVICE ENGINEER (ROK)

THE WORK

Business machines on which modern offices depend include: word processors, personal computers, printers, photocopiers, facsimile (fax) and telex machines, paper-handling machines such as folders, collators, trimmers and shredders, and others.

The work of business machine service engineers falls into three major activities: installation, servicing and repair. Installing a business machine includes setting it up in the position requested by the user, making appropriate connections to electricity supply, ensuring that it is loaded with materials such as paper and ink, testing its operation and making adjustments. The engineer may also be responsible for ensuring that the stationery the client wishes to use is suitable for the machine and for instructing a staff member in its operation and also providing a user's manual where appropriate.

Under a routine servicing contract, an engineer calls at agreed intervals of six to twelve months. They look for worn parts and replace them, clean and lubricate working parts and make adjustments as necessary. They generally make sure it is working to the maximum efficiency possible.

Repair is sometimes necessary following a breakdown or a serious failure of the machine. A call-out is made to bring the service engineer. Experience may tell them immediately the most likely cause of the symptoms reported by the user, enabling a part to be replaced or an adjustment made. Otherwise meters and electronic test devices may be required to locate the fault, possibly referring to technical manuals. If necessary, they may dismantle the machine or part of it to locate or clear a problem. Nowadays it is more common to replace a faulty unit or even the whole machine and remove the broken-down one for repair by the workshop engineers. Their work may include renovation and updating of older models for resale or rehire as second-hand.

Engineers handle mechanical, electrical and electronic aspects, using appropriate tools and instruments and taking steps to ensure safety and cleanliness. They fill in standard forms with time taken and spare parts used, for invoicing and other purposes, or enter the information directly onto a computer terminal. They may have to obtain a user's signature and advise them on any misuse of the machine which has caused a fault to develop.

Workshop engineers have the facilities, tools and test equipment for complete analysis, dismantling and re-assembly of appliances, including the complete renovation or updating of older appliances for resale or rehire as second-hand models. Some smaller items of business equipment may be brought in by customers for repair to the retail outlet attached to a workshop, with larger appliances only arriving when brought in by field engineers. In some companies, field engineers spend some time, eg one day a week, in the workshop on workshop repairs. Only a small number of specialists stay in the workshop.

WORK ENVIRONMENT

Field engineers travel between a series of user-clients by car or van, collecting details of calls periodically from base or receiving them by radio, mobile 'phone or pager. They carry tools and spare parts with them. They work in users' premises which are normally warm and clean. Engineers may have to bend, kneel or lie down, sometimes in cramped situations, to get access to the parts of machines they are servicing. The insides of machines may be dirty and greasy but engineers have to leave offices clean and tidy and work quietly. They wear neat overalls or uniform, or, in many cases, a suit and tie.

Workshop engineers, who do not normally meet users, work in overalls in a workshop with test equipment and more sophisticated tools.

SKILLS AND INTERESTS

Service engineers need to be self-assured and able to work on their own without supervision, even to the extent of planning their own work routine and programme of calls to keep travel time to a minimum. Normal colour vision is essential for identifying the colour-coded wires and components. They use detective and problem-solving ability in diagnosing and tracing the cause of faults, which often calls for a logical, methodical approach. Users want the machine back in use as quickly as possible, so engineers have to be able to work quickly but accurately under pressure. As they are acting as the representative of the manufacturer or service company that employs them, a neat appearance, a tactful manner and a tidy way of working are needed. Good communication skills are also important in speaking with the user's staff to find out the symptoms of the fault or to explain how to use the machine and deal with any complaints about delays, repeated faults, etc.

Physically, they should be fit and agile, and have nimble fingers. There could be lifting and bending involved and reaching into awkward spaces. The form-filling, record-keeping and technical calculations aspects call for an ability with numbers. They must know and observe safety regulations, on their own behalf and on that of users.

ENTRY REQUIREMENTS

Few people enter direct from school. Employers usually look for people who have already gained a City and Guilds (C&G) or BTEC/SCOTVEC qualification such as electrical and electronic craft studies, electronics servicing or electronics. Advanced GNVQ/GSVQ Level III in Engineering may also prove acceptable in the future. Employers also recruit individuals who have worked in a job in another industry where the training and experience are appropriate, such as in another maintenance area or as an assembler or fitter on electrical or electronic products. NVQs/SVQs in Engineering at Levels 2 and 3, may also be accepted.

Normal colour vision and a clean driving licence may be other important requirements.

Entry requirements to FE courses vary. Three GCSES/S grades, at any level, may be adequate for C&G courses. For BTEC national awards, it is four GCSEs (A-C); for SCOTVEC national courses, requirements vary from college to college. Entry to BTEC/SCOTVEC higher national courses is with four GCSEs/S grades (A-C/1-3) and one A level/two H grades, or equivalent, such as Advanced GNVQ/GSVQ Level III. Details of entry to Advanced GNVQ/GSVQ Level III courses should be obtained from colleges or schools.

Some employers offer training with part-time or day release to study at college for C&G or BTEC/SCOTVEC qualifications.

NB: It is possible that Modern Apprenticeships may make a difference to this entry pattern at some stage but apprenticeships are not normally an entry route at present.

TRAINING

College courses include workshop skills as well as engineering theory. After recruitment by an employer, practical training specific to servicing business machines is normally in the employer's own workshops and by going on calls with an experienced engineer, watching how they work and assisting them, before handling tasks under their supervision. Trainees may be sent on short courses provided by manufacturers or suppliers of particular machines. Training covers maintenance routines, fault-finding, use of tools, safety, etc.

Assessment for NVQ/SVQ in Servicing Office and IT Equipment and Systems Levels 2 and 3 may form part of the further education and training process.

During employment, knowledge of new models or new machines is provided by short courses given by the manufacturers.

LATE ENTRY

As the industry does little training itself, many enter after work in other industries on electrical/electronic maintenance or work as a production fitter or assembler on light machinery. A craft or technician level qualification or NVQs/SVQs gained in these areas are particularly useful.

For those without work experience or qualifications, it is possible to take the full-time college courses mentioned above. For applicants over 21 years, formal educational requirements may be reduced or waived.

OPPORTUNITIES

The increase in the range and sophistication of office machines has led to a growth in the need for skilled service engineers. However, improvements in reliability, and the ability of some machines to signal the cause of a fault so that the user can correct it, have reduced the frequency of call-outs.

The workshops of employing companies are situated in urban areas throughout the UK. Service engineers work for office machine manufacturers or suppliers/importers and for agents or dealers who rent or sell office machines, all of which may provide servicing under guarantee or contract. Specialist service companies are another, and growing, area of employment, due largely to the spread of equipment rental or leasing, though many of these are small firms. Employment is also possible with some local authorities, large educational establishments, office complexes, and so on, as an in-house service engineer, though this entails knowledge of a wide range of equipment.

PAY AND CONDITIONS

Pay varies within different parts of the country, and with factors such as complexity and novelty of the machines involved and the engineer's experience and qualifications. Average earnings for a service engineer are around £373 a week, including overtime and bonuses.

Working hours relate to those of user-clients, ie normal office hours Monday to Friday. Engineers may have to start earlier to be at a client's premises by 9am and have to work into the evening to complete work on the last call or do a service outside normal working hours when the machine can be spared. Some employers operate on a 24-hour emergency call-out basis for which stand-by bonuses and call-out payments are made.

A van or car is normally provided to ensure speedy response and to transport tools and spare parts.

PROSPECTS

In larger companies, the promotion route is to senior engineer, supervisor and manager, with consequent responsibility for a number of engineers and user-clients in a town, area or region. Though this is generally a craft-level job, where machines are especially complex or computerized, the possibility of training to technician level or higher may be offered or required. The detailed knowledge of a product line and its capabilities gained from this work may make possible transfer to technical sales and marketing posts.

Companies with overseas branches or customers may provide the opportunity to work abroad on a regular or occasional basis. Going independent as a freelance service engineer or by setting up a small business is a possibility for experienced engineers.

RELATED OCCUPATIONS

Domestic appliance engineer, photocopier service fitter, TV/video repairer, computer service technician, telecoms technician, auto-electrician, incorporated engineer/technician (electrical/electronic), assembler: electrical/electronic.

FURTHER INFORMATION

Federation of the Electronics Industry (FEI), Russell Square House, 10-12 Russell Square, London WC1B 5EE, 0171 331 2000

Electronic Office Systems Maintenance Lead Body, c/o Electronics Examination Board, Savoy Hill House, Savoy Hill, London WC2R 0BS, 0171 836 3357

Amalgamated Engineering and Electrical Union (AEEU), Hayes Court, West Common Road, Bromley, Kent BR2 7AU, 0181 462 7755

FURTHER READING

Working in Electronics – COIC

In the careers library classified under ROK.

3. DOMESTIC APPLIANCE/GAS SERVICE ENGINEER (ROK)

THE WORK

Appliances on which we depend in our homes include cookers, washing machines, tumble dryers, TV sets and video recorders, microwave ovens, vacuum cleaners, heaters and central heating installations.

When a new or second-hand appliance is bought or rented, a domestic appliance or gas service engineer installs it in the home. They connect to electricity, water or gas supply as necessary, laying new cables or pipes if needed. Testing and adjustment follows and instructing the owner in correct use, safety, etc.

Engineers also visit homes under routine service agreements to service, for example, a central heating system or a cooker once a year. This involves inspection, cleaning, replacing worn parts, adjusting and testing.

However most visits are call-outs when an appliance has broken down or is performing badly. The engineer has to detect the cause of the fault, tracing it with meters or other test devices or relying on past experience, to correct the fault. This may be replacing a basic component, or involve dismantling a part of the appliance. Increasingly, serious faults are dealt with by removing the whole appliance or a faulty sub-unit to the workshop for repair, replacing it with a working appliance or sub-unit.

Engineers question the owner to find out the symptoms of the fault and how it came about, suggest ways to prevent it happening again, provide estimates of cost for work to be done, make out invoices or receipts, and take payment by cash or cheque if the work is not covered by a guarantee or service agreement. Gas engineers, especially, may have to inform the owner if an appliance is unsafe, fixing a tag prohibiting its continued use.

Engineers handle electrical, electronic and mechanical/plumbing aspects – even gas appliances often have electrical and electronic aspects. They make use of a wide range of hand and power tools and test devices, equipment for bending and cutting pipe, etc. Some tasks call for reference to technical manuals. Links with base are maintained by mobile 'phone or radio. Spare parts are kept in the van and replenished on occasional visits to the workshop. Domestic appliance service engineers may be trained in one manufacturer's range or be capable with several types of appliance. Gas service engineers are normally trained in the range of gas domestic appliances, unless working for one manufacturer.

Field service engineers may also be involved in installing appliances in new houses and in installing and servicing appliances in non-domestic premises, such as cookers in company or school canteens or in restaurants, tumble dryers in launderettes, heating in offices, etc.

Workshop engineers have the facilities, tools and test equipment for complete analysis, dismantling and re-assembly of appliances, including the complete renovation or updating of older appliances for resale or rehire as second-hand models. With smaller local shops, members of the public may bring portable appliances to them for service, with larger appliances only arriving when brought in by field engineers. In some companies, field engineers spend some time, perhaps one day a week, in the workshop on workshop repairs, and only a small number of specialists stay in the workshop.

In British Gas, special teams in each area deal with reports of gas leaks as a top priority.

WORK ENVIRONMENT

Field service and gas engineers travel between customers in a car or van, and communicate with base by radio or 'phone. Actual work is done mainly in people's homes, so conditions vary. Usually, they are warm and clean, but they may be cluttered. Engineers must work carefully and neatly.

Bending, kneeling and physical effort may be involved. With electrical and gas appliances safety is of prime importance, including explaining safety factors to customers.

Workshop engineers normally remain in the workshop, where they have use of more sophisticated tools and test equipment.

SKILLS AND INTERESTS

Tact, friendliness and the ability to converse easily are essential in getting customers to explain symptoms, to deal with complaints about the breakdown or delays and to explain what has gone wrong and advise on future use of the appliance. Engineers need analytical skills to diagnose and trace faults and a methodical approach. They need to build up, from training and experience, a thorough knowledge of the appliances and what can go wrong with them.

They must have a concern for safety, be fit and agile with manual dexterity. Those dealing with electronic devices need normal colour vision. They should be self-motivated, working alone without supervision at speed to achieve the number of calls required in a day. Representing their employer, they must be neat in their appearance, usually in a uniform suit or overall. Technical calculations, estimating what to charge the customer, and record-keeping all call for mathematical ability. Field engineers also require a clean driving licence, though some large employers may assist with training for this during an apprenticeship.

ENTRY REQUIREMENTS

Domestic appliance service engineer

For craft level and a City and Guilds (C&G) qualification, a general education including maths, physics (or other science) and English may be acceptable. Those employers who train to BTEC/SCOTVEC national level may ask for three to four GCSEs/S grades (A-C/1-3). Most entrants have some GCSEs/S grades (A-E/1-5) or equivalent such as an Intermediate GNVQ/GSVQ Level III in Engineering.

Another route is to acquire training through the further education system by taking a full-time college course for a C&G or BTEC/SCOTVEC qualification before applying to an employer.

Gas service engineer

Responsibility for recruitment within British Gas has been devolved to the regional gas companies and their policies have not yet been announced. No apprentice recruitment is taking place at present. Previously entry at 16 to 17 years to British Gas apprenticeships required five GCSEs/S grades (A-C/1-3) including maths, science, and English.

Most gas installation and service companies do not offer apprenticeships. They require previous experience, such as with British Gas, or a C&G qualification acquired on a full-time college course, such as gas studies craft, or one in plumbing or in heating and ventilating fitting.

All gas installation/service companies must be registered with the Council of Registered Gas Installers (CORGI).

TRAINING

Domestic appliance service engineer

Apprenticeships may include a period of off-the-job training in a training centre and on-the-job training in a workshop followed by working alongside an experienced field engineer, observing, assisting and performing increasingly complex tasks under supervision. Day or block release may be included to study at college in theoretical and practical aspects of a C&G or BTEC/SCOTVEC qualification. Short courses on specific appliances and models provided by appliance manufacturers may form part of or supplement this training. NVQs/SVQs in Domestic Service Engineering at Level 3 are available.

Gas service engineer

Training policy within British Gas companies is not yet settled. Previously apprentice training was similar to that described above but incorporating study for C&G Gas Service Engineering. Both apprenticeship training and college courses are likely to incorporate assessment for NVQs/SVQs in Mechanical Engineering Services, Gas Services Installation and Maintenance Domestic at Level 2, and Gas Services Installation and Maintenance at Level 3.

Additional training provided by employers to people with plumbing and heating and ventilating equipment (H&V) fitting qualifications is likely to be CITB/ACOP (Construction Industry Training Board/Approved Code of Practice) short courses covering aspects of gas appliance and central heating installation and gas safety.

LATE ENTRY

Many individuals enter these occupations after training and experience in other fields, including gaining craft or technician qualifications. This might be in electrical and electronic maintenance, or work as an assembler or production fitter in light engineering. For gas work, it might be as a plumber or heating and ventilating fitter/welder.

Mature entry is possible to college courses mentioned above. Formal entry requirements may be reduced or waived for applicants over 21 years.

OPPORTUNITIES

Domestic appliance service engineers are employed by electricity supply companies, stores and chains selling or renting appliances, local electrical shops, manufacturers of appliances, and specialist service companies. However, the electricity companies and the large chains are the most likely to recruit apprentices. Others prefer to recruit people with training in and/or experience of maintenance and give additional training in specific appliances.

Gas service engineers are employed by regions of British Gas and by independent gas installers, gas appliance stores, department stores retailing gas appliances, and central heating companies. They all have to be members of CORGI (Council of Registered Gas Installers), which maintains the necessary safety standards. However, British Gas is reducing its workforce and not currently recruiting apprentices. Other employers tend to recruit people who have already acquired basic maintenance training and possibly experience and then provide the training in gas service work.

Employers or their workshops are situated throughout the UK, mainly in urban areas. The growth in the range of appliances and the steady consumer demand mean there is a continuing need for service engineers. However, the increased reliability of appliances and the practice of removing and replacing faulty units such as printed circuit boards has cut down on the number of calls and the amount of work per call, allowing fewer engineers to handle the total work. Disposability of small appliances has reduced the amount of repair work, though renovation of large second-hand appliances continues.

PAY AND CONDITIONS

Salaries vary around the country and with different employers. Average earnings in some fields are about £280 a week. Overtime, call-out, shift and bonus payments may operate. A nominal working week is 38 hours, but an actual average of 40 to 45 hours is more common, including early starts to collect instructions and spares from base and reach the first call at an early hour, as well as continuing into the evening to complete calls at the only time when the customer can be at home. Most companies operate a five-day week, but some offer Saturday service. A few, like British Gas, have a 24-hour emergency service, staffed on a shift basis.

Overalls or uniform are often provided, as is a car or van.

PROSPECTS

Some maintenance teams are small, offering little chance of promotion. In larger companies, the promotion route goes from engineer to senior engineer, then supervisor and service manager. With the increasing computerization of products, some engineers go on to train for technician-level qualifications. The detailed knowledge gained of appliances allows some to transfer to sales and marketing posts or, if employed by a manufacturer, to inspection and test jobs in the factory.

Some gas engineers receive additional training to install and service large-scale industrial heating equipment and gas-fired manufacturing plant for industrial and commercial customers. Gas-fired power stations may present other opportunities. Some experienced engineers opt to start their own small service business or open electrical shops, or they may become freelances, contracting to large concerns or to specialist service companies.

RELATED OCCUPATIONS

TV/Video repairer, business machine service engineer, plumber, incorporated engineer/technician (electrical/electronic).

FURTHER INFORMATION

Electrical and Electronics Servicing Lead Body, c/o Electronics Examination Board, Savoy Hill House, Savoy Hill, London WC2R 0BS, 0171 836 3357

Amalgamated Engineering and Electrical Union (AEEU), Hayes Court, West Common Road, Bromley, Kent BR2 7AU, 0181 462 7755

Personnel departments of regional headquarters offices of British Gas plc. Consult local telephone directories for addresses.

FURTHER READING

Working in Engineering – COIC
Working in Electronics – COIC
British Gas – Flame

In the careers library classified under RAN/ROK.

FABRICATION ENGINEERING: RON

1. SHEET METAL WORKER/PLATER/ FABRICATOR CLCI: RON
2. WELDER CLCI: RON

BACKGROUND INFORMATION

These are major occupations involved in making or constructing engineering products or processing plant by shaping and joining metal parts, which is often called fabrication. In the main, these parts are tubes, pipes, cylinders, boxes, flat or shaped plates or sheets of metal. Usually this concerns fixed metal constructions; mechanical fitters are responsible for assembling and adjusting aspects of metal machines with moving parts. Machine operators or foundry workers may have been involved in the creation of some of the metal parts.

The products made cover a massive range from laboratory sinks to oil rigs and refineries, ships, and aeroplanes. Industries involved include domestic appliance and industrial machinery manufacture, aerospace, engineering construction, shipbuilding and civil engineering. However, there is a major difference between the manufacture of light engineering products and heavy engineering ones.

In light engineering areas, the metal involved is in sheets up to 3mm thick and often thinner (and, therefore, light and easily shaped). This is what sheet metal workers work with.

Heavy engineering and construction use metal plate which is thicker, and often much thicker, than 3mm. This is handled by platers or fabricators (a job title increasingly used in shipbuilding). Welders work in both sectors using the same basic skills, but the quality demanded of the weld and the level of weld inspection and testing are often much higher in heavy engineering.

1. SHEET METAL WORKER/PLATER/ FABRICATOR (RON)

THE WORK

Sheet metal workers: use thin metal sheets that can be bent and formed into different shapes by beating it with hammers. Skill is needed to create a smooth, regular curve or bowl shape without dents, and without the metal becoming significantly thinner and weaker at any point. Sheet metal workers use small presses, roller machines and hammers for the simpler bends and curves and they cut it with snips, with hand or machine saws, and with guillotines.

They use a technique called pattern-development, which involves mathematical calculations, when marking out (drawing) the shapes on flat metal, so that stretching and contraction of the metal is allowed for. The joining of shaped pieces is done by riveting or welding. Often the welding work is done by a specialist welder, though the sheet metal worker may set up the workpiece for the welder.

Platers/fabricators: the techniques for handling heavy metal plate are quite different. Cranes and hoists are needed to move the metal plate around, with platers possibly doing the guidance and slinging (fixing the chains securely). Straight cuts may be done by powerful guillotine machines. More complex shapes are cut out by computer-controlled burning machines which are programmed by technicians and operated by platers or by caulker-burners using hand-operated flame burners.

The marking on the plate of lines for cutting and of codes for assembly is done by marker-offs, who are senior platers,

working to drawings prepared by technicians. Shaping is done by massive machines called rollers and presses capable of creating curves and bends. A complex shape like a bowplate may take a series of partial bends at slightly different angles. Some platers (usually in a team of two) specialize in the operation of these machines.

Other platers specialize in assembly – setting up the cut pieces of metal in the positions specified by the drawings. They use metal wedges and blocks and clamps to hold it in place until it can be tack-welded (small temporary pieces of weld). They use power grinders or hand files to prepare cut edges for a craft welder to do the finished weld and, after the weld is done, they may grind down surplus weld metal to leave a smooth surface. They may build sub-assemblies in a big workshop, or work outside putting sub-assemblies and units together to create the finished ship, chemical plant, etc.

They may work closely with others, not only welders and crane drivers, but, in shipbuilding, for example, caulker-burners, who prepare edges and who cut with hand burners, and shipwrights who are especially concerned with the shape of the hull. On repair work, damaged plates may have to be cut away and replaced or patched.

WORK ENVIRONMENT

Sheet metal workers work alone or in small teams. Their workshops are usually relatively small. Work items normally fit onto a bench with devices for holding them.

Platers work in huge workshops or on construction sites outdoors in all weather conditions. They may work in a team with other craftspeople.

They both use earmuffs to protect against noise and wear boilersuits, gloves, helmets and safety boots. Goggles or visors are needed when close to welding activity.

SKILLS AND INTERESTS

Both need physical fitness for lifting, bending and using a range of hand and machine tools. Good hand and eye co-ordination is called for, especially from sheet metal workers. They should be meticulous and logical in planning how to tackle each task.

Sheet metal workers: need good eyesight to spot a blemish or dent, however small, and a subtle sense of touch to feel any too small to see. An ability with numbers is vital in handling the formulae and calculations involved in working out the size of the flat shape from which the three-dimensional one can be made. They have to be able to imagine the three-dimensional shape they will be making from looking at two-dimensional technical drawings. Powers of concentration are important to see a job through accurately.

Platers: should be able to visualize the finished assembly and have an eye for the right line or curve. Good colour vision may be important in differentiating colours used in codes marked on the plate to show which edge butts against which, various kinds of metal and so on. As well as hand and power tools, they use spirit levels, water levels, laser devices, and so on, to ensure accuracy of positioning. In much plating work, a head for heights is important, as is willingness to live away from home and to work in all weather conditions.

ENTRY REQUIREMENTS

Engineering – the minimum requirement for entry to a Modern Apprenticeship at 16 to 17 years is a good general education, but most successful applicants have three/four GCSEs/S grades (A-C/1-3), including maths, English and a science subject (physics is preferred). Technology and engineering subjects may help. GNVQs/GSVQs may be an alternative.

Shipbuilding/repair – for Modern Apprenticeship entry, there are no minimum requirements but preference is given to those with GCSEs/S grades (A-C/1-3) in maths or a science or a related GNVQ/GSVQ.

Engineering construction – the National Apprenticeship Scheme for Engineering Construction (NASEC) caters for craft level occupations. For NASEC apprenticeships, entrants are expected to gain GCSEs/S grades (A-C/1-3) in maths, English and a science. Those with, in addition, engineering drawing, metalwork or other practical subjects have an advantage.

Hobbies that show a keen interest in technology always help. The selection process may include aptitude tests (to show manual dexterity, co-ordination, and so on) and interviews.

An alternative route may be to do A levels/H grades, or undertake a course at an FE college leading to a City and Guilds (C&G), BTEC/SCOTVEC, or Advanced GNVQ/GSVQ Level III qualification, covering subjects such as sheet metal working and fabrication skills or mechanical and manufacturing engineering, and then apply to an employer.

TRAINING

Engineering – training often starts with one year of off-the-job training in engineering workshop skills. This is followed by up to three years' on-the-job training, working alongside experienced sheet metal workers or platers. There may be day or block release throughout for study at college for a C&G or BTEC/SCOTVEC qualification, such as sheet metal working and fabrication skills or fabrication and welding competences. They also take assessments for an NVQ/SVQ in Engineering Materials Processing at Level 3 and receive an EnTra or M&ETA Modern Apprenticeship Certificate.

Shipbuilding/repair – skill training may be to NVQs/SVQs Levels 1, 2 or 3. It can include off-the-job and on-the-job training for an NVQ/SVQ in Engineering Foundation at Level 2. It may include day or block release as above. A Modern Apprenticeship Certificate is awarded to trainees achieving NVQ/SVQ in Engineering Assembly (Fabrication) at Level 3 and other required standards.

Engineering construction – NASEC apprentices do two years' off-the-job training at a training centre in Stockton-on-Tees in North East England. Apprentice platers start with general workshop skills, then do basic training in fabrication and welding skills and go on to specialized plating training. The college element is a C&G course. On-the-job training on actual engineering construction sites follows for 12 to 18 months. They are assessed for an NVQ/SVQ in Engineering Construction at Level 3, and receive a Modern Apprenticeship Certificate.

LATE ENTRY

College courses are open to mature applicants but adult entry to these occupations is rare except for individuals from related skill areas, for instance, a vehicle body repairer. People in other heavy engineering trades may be able to re-train as platers or extend their training into this field. Semi-skilled platers' assistants or mates may be able to add to their basic plating skills and confirm their competence using the NVQ/SVQ system.

OPPORTUNITIES

The decline in manufacturing industry in the UK, and especially of shipbuilding, aerospace and defence work, has reduced the number of jobs and the amount of apprentice recruitment. Computer-controlled manufacturing systems and robotization have also had an impact in some areas, as has machine pressing of sheet metal and the use of plastics for housing some appliances.

Heavy engineering companies and the bases of engineering construction companies, which employ platers, tend to be in Scotland and the North of England. Shipbuilding/repair is now found in cities on a very few major rivers only. The Midlands, South Wales and London and the South East probably offer most sheet metal work opportunities. Large engineering companies may have a sheet metal work department, but there are also smaller companies that specialize in sheet metal work for other manufacturers or direct to end-users.

Employers are usually companies making or constructing one-off or small batches of products where machine-pressing would be uneconomic. For sheet metal workers, these products could be aircraft, railway carriages, lorry cabs or coaches, laboratory sinks and other equipment, housings for packaging or other manufacturing or agricultural machinery, ventilation ducting, etc. For platers, they would be ships, tanks, oil refineries, chemicals plant, power stations, large storage vessels, oil rigs, etc.

PAY AND CONDITIONS

Average earnings, including overtime and bonuses, are in the region of £230 a week for sheet metal workers, and £308 for platers. However, this depends on the industry, the scale of the company, experience and responsibilities, as, to some extent, do conditions such as holiday entitlement. The basic week is 37 to 38 hours, but there may be overtime or shift working in some areas. Protective clothing, steel-capped boots, or helmets are usually provided by the employer.

PROSPECTS

Promotion is to marker-off (marking out the lines for cutting or shaping on metal plate or sheet from engineering drawings), foreman/woman, and manager. Some platers and sheet metal workers become inspectors, checking the work done by others, usually after specialist training. Others move into training. Some study for technician or incorporated engineer qualifications on part-time or full-time BTEC/SCOTVEC courses, and move into design, planning, production control, estimating or similar fields.

In engineering construction and civil engineering, there may be possibilities of freelance work, contracting as an individual or as a small team to a construction company for the duration of specific projects. Some individuals start their own metal-working business, either alone or with colleagues.

There is the possibility of work on construction projects in other countries, either for UK companies or for foreign ones.

Multiskilling may ultimately create a new trade that merges plating, welding and other metal-handling/construction skills into a new occupation.

FABRICATION ENGINEERING: RON

RELATED OCCUPATIONS

Motor vehicle body repairer, pipefitter, heating and ventilating fitter/welder, steel erector, mechanical fitter, shipbuilding caulker/burner, plumber, welder.

FURTHER INFORMATION

Engineering Careers Information Service (ECIS)*, Engineering Training Authority (EnTra), Vector House, 41 Clarendon Road, Watford, Hertfordshire WD1 1HS, freephone 0800 282167

Marine and Engineering Training Association (M&ETA)*, Rycote Place, 30-38 Cambridge Street, Aylesbury, Buckinghamshire HP20 1RS, 01296 434943

NASEC Administration*, Engineering Construction Industry Training Board (ECITB), Blue Court, Church Lane, Kings Langley, Hertfordshire WD4 8JP, 01923 260000

Institute of Sheet Metal Engineering, Exeter House, 48 Holloway Head, Birmingham B1 1NQ, 0121 622 2860

Scottish Engineering*, 105 West George Street, Glasgow G2 1QL, 0141 221 3181

FURTHER READING

Leaflets/booklets are available from the addresses marked*.

Job Outlines – Craftworkers and Operatives in Engineering – COIC
Working in Engineering – COIC
Engineering Explained – ECIS
Training and Working in Engineering – ECIS
Modern Apprenticeships in the Engineering Construction Industry – ECITB NASEC – ECITB
Leaving School at 16+ – ECITB
Fact Sheet 11, Welding as a Career – TWI
Providing a Wealth of Opportunity – M&ETA
National Standards and Qualifications for Engineering – M&ETA

In the careers library classified under RON.

2. WELDER (RON)

THE WORK

Welding uses intense heat to join together pieces of metal with a joint. The heat may melt the edges of two pieces of thin metal butted up together so that they merge, or, for thicker metal, it may melt 'weld metal' from a rod or electrode to fill a V-shape gap between the pieces of metal or to join pieces at right angles. The pieces to be welded are often be set up by other craftspeople, such as a plater or sheet metal worker.

The five principal fusion welding methods are: oxy-acetylene (OA); manual metal arc (MMA); metal inert gas (MIG); metal active gas (MAG), and tungsten inert gas (TIG). Not all welders are expert in all of these, as different processes suit the work of different industries or companies, and relate to which metals and thicknesses are involved.

Their work instructions or welding procedure specification gives the welder technical information to support the engineering drawings showing what is required. Depending on size, the items are welded at the welder's workplace or where the weld is needed. They connect equipment to power and to gas cylinders with cables and pipes. They plan the weld, deciding how to do it most effectively. In some cases, they make sure the metal surfaces are clean, though often this preparation is done by another craftsperson.

With the equipment correctly adjusted to suit the job to be done, the welder switches on and strikes an arc, which is the hot bright zone between the metal and the electrode tip. In OA and TIG welding, a filler rod has to be held in the other hand to supply the extra metal to fill the gap. In MAA, MIG and MAG, the electrode becomes molten and is used to fill the gap, so the welder has to maintain a constant distance between the electrode tip and the work to ensure the arc does not go out.

Welds can be downhand or overhead – looking down or up at them. They may be on a curve, an angle, in any direction.

Welds in critical products are subject to strict inspection to check their quality, using measuring instruments and non-destructive testing methods such as X-ray, ultrasonic and dye testing, so welds are expected to be of a standard that will not fail these tests.

Automatic and robotic welding equipment is more usually set up and operated by welding technicians than by craft welders. Spot-welding may be of sheet metal panels, a robot operation as in car manufacture or is carried out by semi-skilled operators.

WORK ENVIRONMENT

Factory workshops may be large or small, with the noise of machine and hand tools. The welder may work in a small booth created by heavy curtains to protect other workers from glare. Other work situations might be in the hollow sections in the bottom of a ship's hull or, exposed to the weather, welding sections of a pipeline or chemical plant.

A head shield with protective filter glass, or tinted goggles, give essential protection for the welder's eyes from the glare. Overalls, apron and gloves give protection against sparks and molten metal. Where fumes could be a problem there is an extractor above their work and, in some situations, breathing apparatus is used. In noisy work situations, they wear earmuffs. On construction sites, hard helmets have to be worn.

Except for welders based permanently in a factory workshop, they are likely to travel to different locations for long or short periods, which could be a long way from home, living in site accommodation or lodgings.

Though they may work closely with a sheet metal worker or plater, they essentially work on their own.

SKILLS AND INTERESTS

Obtaining a good weld calls for the ability to concentrate intensely, with acute co-ordination of the hand and eye. Strength and a steady hands are needed to be able to work holding a torch.
Other attributes are good eyesight to see into the welding glare through tinted goggles or mask, and good hearing to spot changing sounds of the welding arc. Welders need fitness and strength to carry heavy equipment, climb ladders and crawl into cramped spaces.

They need mental and physical stamina to keep up the level of concentration all day and withstand the loneliness of much of the work. They must take full responsibility for their work, adhere to safety regulations and technical instructions, and may liaise closely with platers, sheet metal workers and other craftspeople.

ENTRY REQUIREMENTS

Engineering – the minimum requirement for entry to a Modern Apprenticeship at 16 to 17 years is a good general education but most successful applicants have three/four GCSEs/S grades (A-C/1-3), including maths, English and a science subject (physics is preferred). Technology and engineering subjects may help. GNVQs/GSVQs may be an alternative.

Shipbuilding/repair – for Modern Apprenticeship entry, there are no minimum requirements but preference is given to those with GCSEs/S grades (A-C/1-3) in maths or a science or a related GNVQ/GSVQ.

Engineering construction – the National Apprenticeship Scheme for Engineering Construction (NASEC) caters for craft level occupations. For NASEC apprenticeships, entrants are expected to gain GCSEs/S grades (A-C/1-3) in maths, English and a science. Those with, in addition, engineering drawing, metalwork or other practical subjects have an advantage.

Hobbies that show a keen interest in technology always help. The selection process may include aptitude tests (to show manual dexterity, co-ordination, and so on) and interviews.

An alternative route may be to do A levels or to undertake a City and Guilds (C&G) 229 or CENTRA/EMFEC 165 course, or equivalent, at an FE college, and then apply to an employer. However, it is not clear yet how this system may operate for this particular occupation.

TRAINING

Engineering – training often starts with one year of off-the-job training in engineering workshop skills. This is followed by up to three years' on-the-job training working alongside experienced welders. There may be day or block release throughout for study at college for a C&G or BTEC/SCOTVEC qualification. The resulting qualification is an NVQ/SVQ in Joining Materials by Welding at Level 3 plus an EnTra or M&ETA Modern Apprenticeship Certificate.

Shipbuilding/repair – skill training may be to NVQ/SVQ Levels 1, 2 or 3. It can include off-the-job and on-the-job training for an NVQ/SVQ in Engineering Foundation at Level 2. It may include day or block release as above. A Modern Apprenticeship Certificate in Welding is awarded by M&ETA to trainees achieving NVQ/SVQ in Joining Materials by Welding at Level 3 and other standards.

Engineering construction – NASEC apprentices do two years' off-the-job training in one of three training centres (Grangemouth in Scotland, Stockton-on-Tees in North East England and Tipton in the West Midlands). They start with general workshop skills, then would-be welders do basic training in fabrication and welding skills and go on to specialized welding skills. The college element is a C&G course. On-the-job training on actual engineering construction sites follows for 12 to 18 months. The resulting award is NVQ/SVQ in Engineering Construction at Level 3 and a Modern Apprenticeship Certificate.

To find employment, a skilled welder must be able to pass a Welder Approval Test which demonstrates their skill on that type of welding work. These tests conform to national, European and international standards. The main one is European Standard EN287. This may mean frequent retesting, as with Ministry of Defence work, which is retested every six months.

LATE ENTRY

Adult entry is not common without previous experience in a related area. With multiskilling, basic welding has become a small part of other jobs, such as plater, which may offer the possibility of additional training to become a welder. The Welding Institute (TWI) and other organizations run training courses of two to ten weeks leading to a recognized Welder Approval Certificate. Contact your local Jobcentre, TEC/LEC for details.

OPPORTUNITIES

Skilled welders are important in heavy engineering, where products like vessels and pipework for chemical plants or boilers and turbines for power stations are made, or in similar industries, such as shipbuilding/repair and engineering construction, which handles the building of chemical plants and power stations. In this area the decline in manufacturing, construction and shipbuilding generally and cuts in arms manufacture mean fewer welders are needed. In light engineering, they work with thinner metal sheet alongside sheet metal workers who prepare the metal for welding. There is reduced demand in this area due to the increase in plastics and the shaping of metal sheet by giant presses with panels joined by robotic welding processes. Welders also work in building engineering services (heating and ventilating) and civil engineering.

In all areas, multiskilling has passed some basic welding tasks such as tack-welding to hold a piece of metal plate in position, to other trades such as platers or shipwrights. In time, there may be some merging of these crafts, as has already happened in heating and ventilating where the title fitter/welder applies. However, at its most skilled levels, welding is a distinct and important skill.

PAY AND CONDITIONS

Different skill classifications, ie certification for different types and qualities of welding, demand different levels of pay. An average would be around £296 a week, including overtime and bonuses. In some areas, piecework rates may apply. The basic working week is 38 hours. There may be shifts or overtime.

PROSPECTS

In companies with a team of welders, promotion may be possible to foreman/woman and supervisor and possibly to fabrication shop manager over welders and other craftspeople. With additional training and qualifications, some welders move on to technician or higher level work and into inspection and non-destructive testing. Further training is also needed to obtain European qualifications such as European Welding Practitioner, Specialist and Technologist.

In construction and engineering construction industries, some welders operate on a freelance basis, contracting their skills for the duration of a job such as the laying of a gas or oil pipeline. In some instances, welders work abroad on overseas construction projects.

RELATED OCCUPATIONS

Heating and ventilation fitter/welder, vehicle body repairer, sheet metal worker/plater, shipbuilding caulker/burner, gas distribution worker, plumber, blacksmith.

FURTHER INFORMATION

Engineering Careers Information Service (ECIS)*, Engineering Training Authority (EnTra), Vector House, 41 Clarendon Road, Watford, Hertfordshire WD1 1HS, freephone 0800 282167

The Welding Institute (TWI)*, Abington Hall, Abington, Cambridge CB1 6AL, 01223 891162

Marine and Engineering Training Association (M&ETA)*, Rycote Place, 30-38 Cambridge Street, Aylesbury, Buckinghamshire HP20 1RS, 01296 434943

NASEC Administration*, Engineering Construction Industry Training Board (ECITB), Blue Court, Church Lane, Kings Langley, Hertfordshire WD4 8JP, 01923 260000

Scottish Engineering, 105 West George Street, Glasgow G2 1QL, 0141 221 3181

FURTHER READING

Leaflets/booklets are available from the addresses marked*.

Job Outlines – Craftworkers and Operatives in Engineering – COIC
Working in Engineering – COIC
Engineering Explained – ECIS
Training and Working in Engineering – ECIS
Modern Apprenticeships in the Engineering Construction Industry – ECITB NASEC – ECITB
Leaving School at 16+ – ECITB
Fact Sheet 11, Welding as a Career – TWI
Providing a Wealth of Opportunity – M&ETA
National Standards and Qualifications for Engineering – M&ETA

In the careers library classified under RON.

1. **PRODUCTION MANAGER CLCI:SAB**
2. **QUALITY CONTROLLER/TESTER CLCI:SAB**
3. **PRODUCTION WORKER CLCI:SAB**
4. **ASSEMBLER (LIGHT INDUSTRY) CLCI:SAB**
5. **PACKER CLCI:SAB**

BACKGROUND INFORMATION

Almost all products in everyday use – domestic items, food and drink, electrical goods and furniture – are provided by manufacturing industry, which also supplies different industries with components such as bricks, tubing, integrated circuits and optical fibres. Manufacturing is divided into sectors: biotechnology; ceramics, glass and minerals; chemical industry; defence industries; electrical, electronic and information technology; energy; food and drink manufacturing; mechanical engineering; metal manufacturing; packaging; paper making; plastics processing; printing; shipbuilding; textile, clothing and related industries; timber and furniture; and the vehicle industry.

Production is central to manufacturing; methods of production vary from industry to industry and according to type of product. The major aspects of production are described below.

Production/processing takes a number of forms. Though in some industries, traditional techniques are still used, increasingly the emphasis is on introducing new technology to automate production. Production workers are required mainly to monitor the working of the machinery/equipment, operate controls, maintain a supply of raw materials, etc.

Assembling – components are brought together to produce partly assembled or finished products. Workers may assemble on a line, bench or floor and may be involved with assembling light or heavy goods.

Packaging may be the final stage on a production line or a separate procedure. It may be automated, or carried out by skilled or unskilled workers.

Quality control – all the way through production, the quality must be monitored, and tests carried out to ensure the specifications are being met. The types of checks made by quality controllers and/or checkers/testers vary in sophistication, though there is an increasing trend to give production workers greater responsibility for checking the quality of their own work.

Production management is an essential element of efficient manufacturing, necessary to ensure forward planning, scheduling, co-ordination and organization.

Manufacturing engineering is concerned with planning, managing and maintaining manufacturing production/processing. Manufacturing engineers plan and set up the production line, so that goods are manufactured making the most efficient use of resources.

Research and development engineering is concerned with practical problem solving on current and new products, taking into account the often continuous and rapid product changes that are necessary to keep up with and beat competitors in world markets. Research and development departments work closely with design and production teams.

Design engineering involves consulting other experts and drawing up the specifications of the plans and processes to be used in manufacturing a product. Normally the work is done within tight financial and time restraints.

These articles are concerned with the work of production managers, quality control inspectors, production workers, assembly workers and packers who are employed in almost all manufacturing industries. For information about engineering, see ENGINEER (RAB).

1. PRODUCTION MANAGER (SAB)

THE WORK

A production manager's role is to oversee the activities associated with production. Functions include ensuring that production targets are met, planning and controlling resources, product quality, labour relations and discipline, avoiding disruptions to the continuous operation of the production line, and future planning. Their main concern is to make the best use of available resources to achieve given objectives. Customers are given a delivery date and estimate of costs when ordering manufacturing products. It is the responsibility of the production department to ensure that orders are completed by the agreed date and conform to requirements.

The production manager has overall responsibility; however, tasks may be carried out by members of the production team.

The numbers and titles of jobs vary within different production management departments. The production supervisor may be called the shift supervisor and may be responsible to a production controller and/or planner at middle management level. Controllers and planners may have a number of staff under their control, for example progress chasers/clerks or production clerks or planning technicians, and can be responsible to senior planners and/or the production manager.

In general, as managers become more senior, they spend less time on the factory floor and become increasingly involved in future planning, attending management meetings, co-ordinating, etc.

The major production functions include:

Planning and control

On receiving an order, the planner must devise a production programme to be agreed by the manager and/or production director. The type of programme required depends on the method of production:

continuous/flow production – the programme may remain unchanged for long periods of time;

batch production involves limited numbers (batches) of each of a range of different products, or of the same product with variations of style, colour, aroma, etc, being produced in succession. The production programme may be based on sales estimates and previous experience, or on orders from customers, and is likely to be adjusted quite regularly;

non-standard item/job production – every order is of a different specification, involving frequent machine changes and for which it is very difficult to draw up a regular programme. Where the item being produced is big and complex, eg a turbine for a power station or an aircraft, the production schedule may stretch over many months and involve input from a large number of departments or factories and even countries.

The production programme states the output figures for each quantity and type of product for each period – day, week, month, etc. It is necessary to calculate the number of machines and time required to produce the operations, taking into account constraints such as time required for servicing equipment.

The allocation of resources – people, equipment and time – to production operations is known as loading. The aim is to achieve optimum loading – parity between supply and demand – which may be difficult since there are often conflicting requirements.

Production control involves making sure that production is maintained and refining the master programme – scheduling and re-scheduling work to ensure that the targets are met, taking day-to-day problems into account.

Data is received from all production departments giving details of the current position. Many problems arise, such as machine failure, staff shortages or increasing rates of machine rejections or scrap. Adjustments must be made to daily schedules according to the established priorities.

Planning and control involves liaison with many other people including senior managers and production workers, managers of design, estimating, sales and purchasing departments, and outside suppliers. The collection and analysis of data entails a great deal of figure work, which in larger companies is computerized. Various techniques may be employed for planning, analysing, scheduling and controlling, including critical path analysis.

Production supervision

This is mainly concerned with supervising the production workers involved.

Much of the work takes place on the shop floor, and involves touring production areas. Supervisors observe work and ensure that the production schedule and targets are adhered to. They anticipate problems, take action to forestall them, or deal with them if they do arise. They are required to take frequent decisions. Decisions are mostly of a short-term and immediate nature, but must be made independently as higher management is often unavailable, for example during night shifts.

Day-to-day duties vary considerably. Supervisors receive production reports and check that production is proceeding to schedule. They take a co-ordinating role – liaising with planners, controllers and departmental managers, co-operating with colleagues (for example, in quality control and dispatch), and organizing and motivating production workers. It is essential that they establish good working relationships.

Supervisors take responsibility for handling problems of absenteeism, maintaining good labour relations and attending to health and safety. They need to consider the workloads on individual operatives and sort out group problems, directing the workforce towards achieving the overall production goals.

Other activities may include taking corrective action to reduce sudden increases in rejects, ensuring that operatives adhere to specified procedures, making sure that machine fault analysis is correct, anticipating future problems, etc.

Production management and supervision may include: preparing and submitting budgets; cost control; responsibility for productivity and efficiency, for planned maintenance and equipment replacement, and for employee training programmes; negotiating with employees and trade union representatives on industrial relations matters; health and safety; as well as problem-solving on a day-to-day basis.

WORK ENVIRONMENT

This depends on the type of manufacturing unit and, to some extent, on the type of production. Modern factories are often light, airy and clean, but there are exceptions in some industries and workshops, eg foundries.

The more senior members of the production management team tend to be office-based. Offices may be clean and fairly comfortable, large and open-plan, or small and cramped. Middle and junior managers may have offices close to the shop floor and spend a proportion of their time in the manufacturing facility. Supervisors may have office space within the manufacturing area but spend most of their time on the shop floor, touring the production areas, dealing with problems, etc.

SKILLS AND INTERESTS

Personal qualities are very important in production management. Managers in junior grades are primarily concerned with dealing with people. They should have good skills in persuading and influencing and must develop good working relationships with production workers, colleagues and senior managers. It is necessary to be approachable as well as being a good leader.

Good communication skills, both spoken and written, are essential at all levels. Production managers are required to present arguments, write reports and keep records. For planning and controlling work, individuals need to be numerate, and should be able to master basic analytical and planning techniques. Production managers need also to understand the processes involved. The emphasis on technical knowledge varies according to the industry and products being manufactured. A knowledge of marketing and finance is also helpful.

Problem-solving skills are required to find the cause of the problem, initiate corrective action and carry out follow-up procedures. Managers need good investigative skills and should be able to set priorities.

Individuals must be self-reliant and capable of making decisions quickly. Many problems can arise and it is important to be able to work under pressure while remaining calm and in control.

Supervisors may spend much of their time on their feet on the shop floor, and require energy and stamina to endure work that can be physically as well as mentally demanding.

ENTRY REQUIREMENTS

There are no minimum qualifications for production management. However, for direct entry to a management trainee scheme, which may result in a post in production management, candidates are normally educated to degree level or equivalent. Direct entry to a post as assistant or trainee production manager may be possible with a degree in a relevant subject and/or a management qualification. Other production managers are recruited after experience in other posts in manufacturing industry such as production supervision, quality control, production planning and control, sometimes by internal promotion.

Entry to degree courses is with a minimum of five GCSEs/S grades (A-C/1-3) with two A levels/three H grades or equivalent, such as Advanced GNVQs/GSVQs Level III in Manufacturing. Exact requirements vary and applicants should check prospectuses.

Any degree may be acceptable although the subject may affect the type of industry the graduate enters. The high-technology sectors often require entrants with degrees predominantly in technical subjects, such as technology, science, or maths. Degrees in specific engineering disciplines may be needed for some jobs. Other industries prefer a qualification specifically in management.

In some industries there may be openings for some candidates with BTEC/SCOTVEC higher national awards.

Industrial experience, such as that gained on a sandwich course or in an industrial placement, can be an advantage.

TRAINING

It is possible for an individual to work up to production supervisor level through the ranks – for example, from production worker to chargehand to production supervisor. Some entrants move into production from other functions such as work study, quality control, purchasing or works engineering.

Direct entrants to production departments may start their training by following an induction course, lasting anything from a few weeks to several months. Specific job-related training follows; this normally entails working alongside experienced staff. Trainees may start on the factory floor in a manufacturing/production supervisor role, or in a related department, such as production planning or control, to get an overview.

Classroom training in specialist functions may be provided, particularly if there are specialist elements in the work, such as complex production processes or computer applications. Trainees may take courses in management or technical subjects at further/higher education establishments on a part-time or full-time basis.

Some companies recruit management trainees into broad-based schemes that do not involve a commitment to production – trainees spend time in different functions, for example, sales, personnel and finance departments as well as production. Trainees gain wide experience and may then specialize in one function as a route to senior management.

There are a number of qualifications relevant to production management. They include:

National Examining Board for Supervisory Management (NEBSM) courses which relate to supervisors and first-line managers. These may be formal courses, open learning, or through NVQs/SVQs at Levels 3 and 4;

the Institute of Management's Certificate in Supervisory Management, Certificate in Management, and Diploma in Management. These relate to NVQs/SVQs at Levels 3, 4 and 5 respectively. A postgraduate diploma is also offered for senior managers;

the Certificate in Management Studies (CMS) awarded by BTEC/SCOTVEC for people in junior management posts;

the Certificate in Management (CM) and Diploma in Management Studies (DMS) which are postgraduate or post-experience courses offered by colleges and universities. In some cases, the CM is the first year of a two-year linked course; in others the DMS is a two-year stand-alone course.

Master of Business Administration (MBA) courses at colleges, universities and private sector business schools, usually for individuals already in, or aiming at, senior manager posts.

NVQ/SVQ in Supervisory Management (Level 3), First-line Management (Level 4) and Middle Management (Level 5) to standards set by the Management Charter Initiative (MCI) and awarded by organisations such as BTEC, SCOTVEC, IM, NEBSM, Henley Management College and the Institute of Supervisory Management. This can be by workplace assessment or courses at colleges, universities and private sector organizations.

NVQ/SVQ at Level 4 relevant to specific manufacturing industries, eg engineering manufacture and production planning in engineering.

Though some of these qualifications can be gained on a full-time course before a first management job, many are intended for those with management experience and already in post, so they can be taken on a part-time, open or distance learning basis.

These qualifications do not specialize in production management but choice of topics, modules or units allows a degree of specialization.

Several years' experience in relevant functions such as production planning and control or production supervision are often required for production manager posts.

LATE ENTRY

Production management is a career highly suitable for adult entrants, though increasingly it is necessary to acquire one of the qualifications listed in TRAINING to be considered eligible.

Experience of production work at any level can be an advantage. There are no upper age limits specified, although individual companies may set their own. It may be more difficult to be accepted for posts at production level if aged over 40 and considering production work for the first time.

There may be specific training opportunities directed at adults available in some areas for this type of work. Candidates may have to satisfy certain conditions to be eligible. Contact your local Jobcentre, careers office or TEC/LEC for details.

OPPORTUNITIES

Production managers are employed by manufacturing companies. Prospects vary according to sector, individual factory location, and a variety of local and economic factors. The nature of manufacturing industry is changing, for example, with the decline of the traditional heavy industries and the increasing introduction of automation. This may have implications for production managers. In future, recruits with technical knowledge who are able to understand the more complex production technology may be favoured by employers. In addition, as production lines are increasingly automated, fewer workers (including production supervisors) may be required on the shop floor. However, the need to maintain competitiveness and the pressure to meet production targets will ensure a continuing demand.

Experienced individuals employed by large companies with overseas subsidiaries or connections, may have opportunities to work overseas. This will depend on company policy; it may be necessary to speak a foreign language.

PAY AND CONDITIONS

Salaries vary according to the company, its location, the responsibility of the job and experience of the manager.

Production supervisors receive in the region of £11,500 to £17,800. Extra payments are made for overtime and shift work. Production controllers and planners receive between £12,900 and £20,700, and production managers from around £17,000 to £30,000. Senior production managers working for large companies can earn in excess of £40,000.

Official working hours are usually from Monday to Friday, 37 to 40 hours a week. However, the demands of production often mean that flexibility and overtime are required, making the actual hours very irregular. In senior positions, this overtime may be without additional pay.

Supervisors and junior managers are required to work the same hours as production and process workers. This can often involve shift work, including nights and weekends. In addition, they deal with immediate problems, and some supervisors in continuous production industries are effectively on-call day and night for seven days a week. Overtime is often required.

PROSPECTS

Career development depends on the organization and the manager's individual performance. Production managers may advance into general management. Some people move into different functions at a senior level to gain wide experience before moving into general management. There is a formal promotion hierarchy in most organizations. Individuals may also move to different employers to improve their position.

RELATED OCCUPATIONS

Work study/organization and methods officer, transport manager, general manager, engineer, marketing manager, quality controller, warehouse manager, distribution manager.

FURTHER INFORMATION

Institute of Operations Management, University of Warwick Science Park, Sir William Lyons Road, Coventry CV4 7EZ, 01203 692266

The Institute of Management*, Management House, Cottingham Road, Corby, Northamptonshire NN17 1TT, 01536 204222

The Institute of Manufacturing, 58 Clarendon Avenue, Royal Leamington Spa, Warwickshire CV32 4SA, 01926 855498

National Examining Board for Supervisory Management, 1 Giltspur Street, London EC1A 9DD, 0171 294 2468

FURTHER READING

Leaflets/booklets are available from the address marked*.

Production and Plant Management – AGCAS

In the careers library, classified under SAB.

2. QUALITY CONTROLLER/TESTER (SAB)

THE WORK

Quality controllers, or testers, ensure that everything from raw materials entering a factory to finished goods leaving the factory are tested and meet the specified requirements.

Inspection and testing involves a wide range of duties, determined to some extent by the product. In the food and drink industry, for example, inspectors may test for consistency, flavour, colour and nutritional value. Pharmaceutical products may be tested for composition, purity and safety. In textiles, yarns may be tested for strength, colour/dye, grease and water content. Packages must also contain correct quantities and be in perfect condition.

Methods of inspection include visual inspection, which involves checking the product by viewing with or without aids, such as microscopes or magnifying glasses. Products are also checked for physical characteristics, such as weight or size. Functional tests may be required to ensure that products perform adequately. Electronic measuring instruments are often used and are being introduced to take over some of the more routine tasks. Complicated scientific testing can involve using a wide range of instruments and scientific equipment. Accuracy and precision is vital to ensure meaningful results.

Analysing and interpreting the results of tests is a major part of the work. Quality controllers, or testers, may use a variety of distribution charts and statistical and arithmetical techniques to translate their results and determine whether specifications eg British Standards, etc – have been met. The analyses are also used to determine whether the production processes are drifting even if the product is within specification. This can involve calculating percentages, averages, means and modes, determining whether results fall within normal distribution ranges, and identifying deviations.

Some tests may be very straightforward and take only a few minutes to complete; others are complicated, and it can take hours or days to obtain the results. Quality controllers, or testers, make notes of the tests for each product as they work, and write up detailed reports on completion.

Quality controllers, or testers, advise shop-floor staff who are increasingly responsible for the quality of their output.

WORK ENVIRONMENT

The work environment depends on the type of factory, and product being manufactured. In most cases the quality control department is located in a room, similar to a laboratory or workshop, away from the shop floor.

For some tests a dust-free and scrupulously clean environment is essential for accurate results. Materials and products may also be dangerous and must be handled safely and carefully. It may be necessary to wear protective clothing and head coverings.

For sample collecting and liaising with workers, quality controllers, or testers, spend time on the shop floor. The temperature in factories is often controlled but in some places it may be very hot or cold. In addition, the shop floor may be noisy, dusty, dirty, etc – depending on the type of manufacture.

SKILLS AND INTERESTS

Carrying out test and inspection work requires practical skills and manual dexterity. The work is often precise and requires careful attention to detail and a thorough approach. Inspectors should have an interest in science subjects. They must be prepared to carry out routine tasks, time and time again, while maintaining concentration and accurately following specified procedures.

Some quality control is based on statistical sampling and arithmetical methods; controllers or testers therefore should be numerate and be comfortable working with figures.

Quality controllers, or testers, must be able to deal with people and therefore need a mature outlook. They need to gain the co-operation of shop-floor workers and encourage operators to produce work of a satisfactory quality.

ENTRY REQUIREMENTS

There are no minimum academic qualifications required to become a quality control inspector.

Many individuals gain shop-floor experience as production workers and then move into quality control. School-leavers without qualifications may enter quality control departments as assistants and progress to inspector posts; however, it is more likely that employers will ask for qualifications – typically a minimum of four GCSEs/S grades (A-C/1-3), including maths, English and science subjects.

Some employers may train inspectors/testers via a Modern Apprenticeship or technician training scheme and may ask for some GCSEs/S grades or A levels/H grades. Employers in high technology industries may require BTEC/ SCOTVEC NC/D or HNC/D or, in some cases, relevant degrees, eg in electronic engineering, materials science, or chemistry.

The City and Guilds (C&G) does not ask for formal qualifications for entry to the 7430 Certificate in Quality Assurance.

TRAINING

Training varies according to the type of industry and methods of production. It takes place mainly on the job, with instruction from experienced staff and/or senior instructors. The length of training varies but it may take up to four years. Classroom training may be organized to give instruction, for example, in specific techniques, complicated production methods or computer applications.

Many trainees are required to study for qualifications on a part-time basis through day release and/or evening classes. The main qualification for inspectors is the C&G 7430 Quality Assurance. Courses are normally run at educational establishments and the C&G examinations are usually taken after one or two years' study.

The certificate is in two parts, which may be taken separately. Candidates who pass both parts are then exempt from the first of the Institute of Quality Assurance's (IQA) series of associate membership examinations – contact the IQA for further details.

Training may include further specialist courses in aspects of quality control/quality assurance, and courses specifically geared towards quality control inspectors working in particular industries, such as engineering or food processing.

Other relevant qualifications include BTEC/SCOTVEC higher national certificate/diploma courses with quality control/quality assurance elements. Such courses tend to have a manufacturing bias.

A small number of first degree courses in technology include quality control/assurance elements. Several MSc courses are also available.

NVQs/SVQs for quality controllers at Levels 2 and 3 are being introduced by different manufacturing industries under titles relevant to those industries. In engineering, for instance, Control of Quality is one possibility within the Providing Technical Services NVQ/SVQ. Other NVQ/ SVQs up to Level 4 for different manufacturing industries have quality assurance units and/or testing elements. In engineering, Engineering Manufacture (Testing) Level 4 would be appropriate for some posts.

LATE ENTRY

There are opportunities for mature entrants in quality control. This is particularly true for those already working in production with a company; those who show the necessary aptitude may be offered opportunities to move into quality control. Background experience will be taken into account.

Dealing with people in ways which may be critical of their work demands individuals with maturity, who can rely on experience and personal qualities. Mature applicants may, therefore, be preferred by employers for inspector posts.

There may be specific training opportunities directed at adults available in some areas for this type of work. Candidates may have to satisfy certain conditions to be eligible. Contact your local Jobcentre, careers office or TEC/LEC for details.

OPPORTUNITIES

Quality controllers, or testers, are employed by manufacturing companies of all types. Firms employing quality controllers, or testers, vary in size and type from the highly automated to basic factories with large or small workforces. High technology sectors, with complicated production and processing techniques, may tend to employ those with higher-level and scientific or technological qualifications.

The Institute of Quality Assurance issues a monthly magazine *Quality News* which usually contains advertisements for quality control assurance vacancies.

PAY AND CONDITIONS

Salaries vary according to employer, location, responsibility and experience. Quality control inspectors have starting salaries of around £9,000 to £12,000, depending on age, experience and qualifications. This can rise to over £14,000 for experienced and senior staff. Overtime rates are usually payable and there may be shift allowances.

Regular working hours – of 37 to 40 hours a week – are available in manufacturing industry. Some companies run shift systems and may require quality control departments to be staffed 24 hours a day. Shift systems can involve day and night shifts and include work at weekends. Working to production schedules may mean that overtime is available or required.

There are some opportunities for part-time working.

PROSPECTS

Quality controllers, or testers, may progress to senior technician/team leader posts and to quality control management positions. Several years' experience is necessary and inspectors often study for advanced qualifications.

Other avenues for quality controllers, with sufficient experience and expertise, may be into supervisory or management posts in production or research and development.

RELATED OCCUPATIONS

Engineer/technician, work study/O&M officer, production manager, laboratory technician, safety officer, production worker.

FURTHER INFORMATION

Institute of Quality Assurance*, PO Box 712, 61 Southwark Street, London SE1 1SB, 0171 401 7227

Engineering Training Authority, Careers Information Service (ECIS)*, Vector House, 41 Clarendon Road, Watford, Hertfordshire WD1 1HS, 01923 238441, freephone 0800 282167

FURTHER READING

Leaflets/booklets are available from the address marked*.

In the careers library classified under SAB.

3. PRODUCTION WORKER (SAB)

THE WORK

Operatives carry out key, though often routine, jobs in order to produce the variety of items manufactured in industry. As many as 60 people may work on a production line, requiring workers to co-operate as members of a team. Other workers work as individuals either sitting or standing at a bench or table. There are wide individual variations between jobs at this level. However, they may be grouped into the following areas of work.

Machine minding and operating is concerned with the monitoring and/or operating of the automatic and semi-automatic machinery involved in producing manufactured products. The level of skill required and the types of tasks performed vary.

With automated processes, certain levels – temperature, pressure, rates of flow or speed of lines – need to be maintained. Deviations from specified conditions must be recognized immediately. The appropriate action by operatives may involve calling in the maintenance or engineering staff, or operatives may be required to make adjustments – opening and closing valves or altering levers, switches, etc. Operatives, such as those working in the food or chemical industries, may follow menu-type directions that require the weighing and measuring of different materials or ingredients for adding to the main mixture at specified times.

Those working with machines are required to be aware of, and adhere to, safety regulations. This may involve, for example, wearing protective clothing or ensuring that machine guards are properly fitted.

Finishing work is concerned with adding the finishing touches to the manufactured product – often metals, plastics or textiles – usually involving special treatments, such as adding protective coatings, smoothing down rough edges, and heat or special cleaning processes.

As dangerous substances may be used, such as acids or other corrosive/explosive chemicals, a careful and systematic approach is necessary in this sort of work. Skill is required in setting up the work and ensuring that the part has been adequately treated, cleaned, protected, etc.

In addition, workers may label finished items with their name or number and batch identification tag. Items must go for inspection on completion, and those that are not passed will be returned to be done again.

Other duties: operatives may have other duties combined with production. Much of the work is now on automated production lines, for example, those where machines fill, cap, label and pack items including pharmaceuticals, food products, paint or chemicals. On semi-automated lines, operatives may undertake a variety of duties, along with other workers, possibly on a rota, and may be concerned with assembling and packing (please see articles 4. ASSEMBLER (LIGHT INDUSTRY) and 5. PACKER).

Some workers may be responsible for checking products for faults or testing products as they come off the production line, checking aerosol cans for leaks or weighing samples to ensure they are of the correct weight, for example (please see article 2. QUALITY CONTROLLER/TESTER).

WORK ENVIRONMENT

The work may be light or heavy. For some types of work, a dust-free and scrupulously clean environment is essential – pharmaceuticals or food in particular – and workers may wear special clothing, such as head coverings, gloves and slippers.

Those working in a dusty environment may wear face masks, for example, when dealing with flour or refractories. Other types of protective clothing, including goggles, aprons and boots, may be required when dealing with dangerous substances or heavy materials. In some factories workers may be subject to hot or cold conditions and unpleasant smells or fumes.

The work can be tiring and entail remaining in one position, either sitting or standing, throughout the day.

It is important that production workers are able to work well as members of a team, particularly when working on production lines with others.

SKILLS AND INTERESTS

Workers require stamina to cope with long periods of sitting or standing, and those handling heavy materials or products require a degree of physical strength. The work can be repetitive, and operatives have to work consistently and may have to work quickly.

Workers should be able to get on with people of all ages and co-operate, if required, as members of a team.

Operating and monitoring machines requires attention to detail, concentration and a sense of responsibility. Good timekeeping and reliability are important personal qualities.

ENTRY REQUIREMENTS

No educational qualifications are required to enter work as a production operative. Proof of proficiency in practical subjects can be advantageous.

Some employers set an aptitude test for applicants, particularly where the work requires good manual dexterity and/or following detailed instructions. Tests are used to determine the individual's practical ability and suitability for the type of work. Good eyesight and accurate colour vision may be essential in some areas, eg electronics. For some posts, physical fitness and stamina may be important, though mechanical aids are usually available for heavy lifting and moving.

TRAINING

This varies according to the employer and type of product manufactured. The training may be in two parts.

Induction training is an introduction to the company – its structure and policy, company practices and products. Subjects usually include: conditions of employment; layout of the factory – medical facilities, restaurant/canteen, recreation areas, and so on; staff welfare; and health and safety matters. Induction training may be held in the firm's training centre, or may be a brief introductory talk and tour round the factory.

Skills training is largely given on the job, and normally involves supervision from an experienced worker, chargehand or supervisor. For routine work, new recruits may receive instruction for a few hours or two to twelve weeks, depending on the job. It may take some time for individuals to learn all the aspects of the work and to develop speed, if required.

For semi-skilled and or more specialist jobs, there may be short classroom training courses held on the premises and supervision for longer periods.

In some industries, employers send operatives to study on a part-time basis at technical colleges. Training may be through day or block release and can lead to relevant qualifications, including NVQ/SVQs, awarded by City and Guilds or other bodies. Subjects may include operating equipment and machinery, instrumentation and production and process techniques, and safety or emergency procedures.

NVQs/SVQs are available at Levels 1 and 2 in a number of manufacturing industries, with each industry setting its own standards and requirements. For instance, in the engineering industry, relevant titles might be Engineering Machining, Engineering Material Processing, Engineering Assembly or Engineering Finishing. Level 3 may be available for those who move into supervisory or more technically skilled positions.

Specific training opportunities for young people may be available, including Skillseekers in Scotland. Contact your local careers office, TEC/LEC for details.

LATE ENTRY

Manufacturing is an area of work providing many opportunities for adult entrants. Acceptability will vary according to the policy of the individual employer. Most companies consider adult applicants on an equal basis to school-leavers. Personal qualities are most important, especially reliability. There are also opportunities for part-time working at times that fit in with personal and family commitments – these vacancies are often more attractive to the adult entrant or returner.

There may be specific training opportunities directed at adults available in some areas for this type of work. Candidates may have to satisfy certain conditions to be eligible. Contact your local Jobcentre, careers office or TEC/LEC for details.

OPPORTUNITIES

Production workers are employed throughout the country by manufacturing companies of all types. The Engineering Training Authority covers almost half of those employed in manufacturing. Production or process workers are required in all sectors including ceramics, glass and mineral products, chemical industry, electrical, electronic and information technology, energy production, food and drink manufacturing, mechanical engineering, metal manufacturing industry, packaging, paper making, plastics processing, textile, clothing and related industries, timber and furniture, and the vehicle sector.

Employment in manufacturing is changing with the introduction of new technology, and the number of semi-skilled and unskilled jobs is falling. Future opportunities are likely to be for production workers who monitor machines that carry out a variety of tasks.

PAY AND CONDITIONS

Rates of pay vary according to employer, location, the type of job, experience and age. Wages may also vary if a piecework rate is paid, that is, a rate of pay set by the rate of production.

Production workers, after training and with sufficient experience to have built up speed, earn around £180 to £250 a week.

Additional payments may be made for shift work and as productivity bonuses. Extra pay for overtime may also significantly increase wages.

Regular working hours, of 37 to 40 hours a week, are available in manufacturing industry. Some companies have shift systems that include work in the evenings, and at nights and weekends. Meeting the requirements of production schedules may mean that overtime is available or required. There are good opportunities for part-time working. Some firms operate production machinery during the night, and may require permanent night shift workers.

PROSPECTS

Promotion prospects are fairly limited for most production workers.

There may be opportunities, for those with speed and aptitude, to move on to more specialist and complex work; some may become skilled craft workers and undertake formal training programmes.

Some individuals may progress to supervisory grades such as inspector, chargehand or supervisor. Another alternative may be to move into quality control work.

There may be opportunities for some production workers to move into related areas such as transport, distribution, storage, warehouse or clerical work.

RELATED OCCUPATIONS

Packer, bottler, brewery worker, chemical plant process operator, quality control inspector, assembler, sewing machinist, engineering machine operator, textile operative, ceramic/pottery maker, lift truck operator.

FURTHER INFORMATION

Engineering Training Authority, Careers Information Service (ECIS)*, Vector House, 41 Clarendon Road, Watford, Hertfordshire WD1 1HS, 01923 238441, freephone 0800 282167.

FURTHER READING

Leaflets/booklets are available from the address marked*.

In the careers library, classified under SAB.

4. ASSEMBLER (LIGHT INDUSTRY) (SAB)

THE WORK

Assemblers are involved in fitting together components, made by others, to produce finished products or sub-assemblies – used as components of other products. Assemblers are responsible for carrying out one or more stages of the making-up procedure. Some assemblers construct complete products; most assemble part of an article, such as integrated circuits or mechanical components, for hearing aids, washing machines or vacuum cleaners, for example. Goods may be completed within the factory, or sub-assemblies may go to other factories, companies or industries for fitting into finished products.

On an assembly line, each assembler may carry out a different task – adding bits to an item as it moves on a conveyor – to result in a finished product or complex component.

The parts required to carry out the assembly, such as clips, screws, pins, washers, wires and transistors, are usually at hand in trays or bins.

Partly assembled items may be taken from a conveyor belt, or a batch brought to the assembler. Each assembler fits components to the items and then replaces them on the conveyor belt or trolley ready for the next person.

The assembler normally remains in one place, and is brought new supplies by warehouse/stores staff as required. Items are often kept in order on the assembler's bench and there is usually a specified routine for fixing parts together. This is so that the operations may be carried out quickly and efficiently.

The work can involve a series of simple, repetitive tasks. It may be necessary to follow sets of detailed instructions and diagrams.

The work may be held in a jig or frame, which allows the assembler to fix pieces more easily and rotate the part. Simple tools may be used, such as screwdrivers, pliers or tweezers, and some assemblers use soldering irons to link wires between pins on circuit boards, etc. Where components are very small, regular breaks are given to allow rest and avoid eye strain. Some assemblers use simple machinery, eg crimping machines for soldering tags on to wires, drills or grinding equipment – operated by foot pedals, switches or hand levers.

WORK ENVIRONMENT

This varies according to the type of manufacturing unit and to some extent to the type of product being assembled. Modern factories are often light, airy and clean. For some types of work, a dust-free, scrupulously clean environment is essential – in electronics, for example, conditions resemble those of a science laboratory. Workers may have to wear overalls and head coverings.

The work can be tiring and may require assemblers to remain in one position, either sitting or standing, all day. Using a soldering iron for lengthy periods may mean that the worker is subject to hot conditions with unpleasant fumes.

SKILLS AND INTERESTS

For light assembling, individuals should have patience and good manual dexterity.

It is important to have good eyesight and, for some operations, such as wiring, good colour vision is essential. The work demands accuracy, neatness and well-developed powers of concentration. Assemblers should be quick and methodical, and capable of following instructions or diagrams.

Particularly on production lines, it is important that assemblers are able to work as members of a team.

ENTRY REQUIREMENTS

No educational qualifications are required to enter assembly work. GCSEs/S grades or equivalent qualifications in English and maths are useful. Proof of proficiency in a practical subject can be advantageous.

Some employers set an aptitude test for candidates, particularly when the work is the assembly of very small components, demanding a high level of accuracy. Tests are used to determine an individual's manual dexterity and suitability for the type of work. Good eyesight may be essential, and accurate colour vision is vital for jobs in electrical and electronic assembly, because of the colour-coding of components.

TRAINING

Training is given on the job, or there may be a short training course, lasting up to a month, for the more complex assembly work. This can entail classroom instruction where trainees learn to identify different components and follow instructions and diagrams accurately. Special techniques – such as wiring, soldering and inspection – will be taught.

NVQs/SVQs are available at Levels 1 and 2 in a number of manufacturing industries, with each industry setting its own standards and requirements. For instance, within engineering, Cable and Wiring Loom Manufacture, or Electronic Product Assembly, or Engineering Assembly, or another title, might be appropriate to a specific job. Level 3 may be available for those who move into supervisory or more technically skilled positions.

Specific training opportunities for young people may be available, including Skillseekers in Scotland. Contact your local careers office, TEC/LEC for details.

LATE ENTRY

Manufacturing is an area of work providing many opportunities for adult entrants. Personal qualities are most important to employers, especially reliability. There are also opportunities for part-time working at times, which can fit in with personal and family commitments. These vacancies are often more attractive to the adult entrant or returner.

There may be specific training opportunities directed at adults available in some areas for this type of work. Candidates may have to satisfy certain conditions to be eligible. Contact your local Jobcentre, careers office or TEC/LEC for details.

OPPORTUNITIES

Assembly is traditionally very labour-intensive work. However, with increasing automation the divisions between different stages of work and types of jobs – production, assembly and packing, for example – are breaking down. It seems probable that future jobs will be mainly concerned with machine monitoring and maintenance, or at technician and professional level.

Much of the work for assemblers is in the electrical, electronic and information technology sectors. Assemblers may be concerned with assembling components for: domestic appliances such as refrigerators, washing machines, vacuum cleaners and dishwashers; TV, video and audio equipment; air conditioners; office equipment; aerial, aeronautical, scientific and medical equipment and instruments, etc. Many components are assembled for use by different companies and for industries in different sectors, such as electronics for the defence industry.

Assembly work of components and/or complete items is also required in the metal manufacturing, paper-making, plastics processing and timber and furniture sectors. Individuals should also refer to ENGINEERING OPERATIVE (RAB) for details of heavy assembly work and SEWING MACHINIST (SAH) for textile and clothing assembly.

PAY AND CONDITIONS

Assemblers, after training and with sufficient experience to have built up speed, earn around £180 to £227 a week. Additional payments may be made for shift work and as productivity bonuses. Extra pay for overtime may also significantly increase wages.

Regular working hours, of 37 to 40 hours a week, are available, although some companies have shift systems. There are good opportunities for part-time working.

PROSPECTS

Promotion prospects are fairly limited for most light assemblers. Some individuals may progress to supervisory grades such as inspector, chargehand or supervisor. Another alternative may be to move into quality control work (please see article 2. QUALITY CONTROLLER/ TESTER).

RELATED OCCUPATIONS

Engineering operative, production worker, quality control inspector, packer, electronic bench tester, sewing machinist, domestic appliance repairer, electrician, telephone technician.

FURTHER INFORMATION AND READING

Please see article 3. PRODUCTION WORKER.

5. PACKER (SAB)

THE WORK

Modern packaging has a variety of functions: as well as containing the product, the package may help to preserve perishable goods, make transportation easier, prevent damage, advertise, and provide directions/instructions. A package can form a constituent part of a product – as with aerosol cans, matchboxes, etc.

Goods of all types are packed in the factory ready for sale. A variety of materials are used for packaging including paper, board, cellulose film, thermoplastics, glass, tin plate, aluminium foil, textiles, laminates and wood.

Products may be in liquid (eg beverages, chemicals and pharmaceuticals), powder or solid form, and are packed into packages including bottles, jars, cartons, tubes, boxes, bags, cans, crates, drums and sacks.

Packing may be divided into two main types:

Routine packing. The tasks involved in packing vary according to type of product. Bottles/jars, for example, may be packed into cartons of a dozen or more. The packer makes up cartons from flat sheets and inserts dividers to protect the bottles. Using both hands, the packer picks up a number of bottles at once, for slotting into the boxes. Other items may be packed into bags, sacks or drums, or put into trays for shrink-wrapping – this involves loading batches into a machine that shrinks plastic-film wrapping by heat.

Different methods of sealing packages – tape, staples, glue, etc – are used and can entail operating various types of equipment, tools and machinery, such as staple guns or banding machines.

Packing may be a full-time job or combined with other work. Much of the packaging in factories is now automated and many of those working on production lines are concerned with machine operating (see article 3. PRODUCTION WORKER). Operators monitor equipment carrying out filling, capping, labelling, and so on, and make adjustments to the speed of operations and the quantities being packed into individual containers. They ensure that the machines are supplied with raw materials, component parts, boxes, labels, etc.

In routine packing, a continuous flow or batches of a product are all packed in the same way. It may take anything from a few hours to several weeks to complete a batch.

Specialist packing. Different-sized, awkwardly shaped and particularly heavy or fragile articles need special attention. A great deal of skill is required to pack delicate items, such as scientific instruments, ceramics and glassware.

Packers normally work alone or in small teams of three or four people.

Additional duties. All types of packing work often entail carrying out other relevant duties, including labelling. Products may be labelled automatically on production lines, although it may still be necessary to mark packs with information such as the batch number, date and destination. In addition, some packers are responsible for checking items for faults and testing products as they come off the production line, by weighing samples, for example.

WORK ENVIRONMENT

Working conditions vary. Certain products need to be packed in sterile conditions. The workplace may in some cases be dusty or hot. Packing may involve long periods of sitting or standing.

Protective clothing – such as overalls or head coverings – may be worn.

SKILLS AND INTERESTS

Packers should enjoy practical tasks and take pride in producing neat and tidy work. They should be able to work quickly and carefully. Specialist packers should be patient and able to decide how to pack items securely. Those who label packages need clear handwriting.

Good timekeeping and reliability are important.

ENTRY REQUIREMENTS

No educational qualifications are required. Proof of proficiency in practical subjects can be an advantage.

Ability to read and write is important for reading labels and filling in forms. Some employers set aptitude tests for manual dexterity, etc. Physical fitness and stamina may be important in some industries.

TRAINING

Training is largely given on the job. Large companies may run short induction courses for new staff, covering conditions of employment, company policies, health and safety, etc.

Skills are gained through experience, with entrants learning from experienced workers or supervisors.

NVQs/SVQs are available at Levels 1 and 2 in a number of manufacturing industries, with each industry setting its own standards and requirements. The pharmaceuticals industry has a specific title, Packaging Operations (Pharmaceuticals), while, in other industries, packing units of a more general NVQ/SVQ might be relevant. Level 3 may be available for those who move into supervisory positions.

Packer in the removals industry is a specialist occupation due to the skills required for packing delicate and valuable items. Short courses for removals staff, which include packing for export, are run by CENTREX.

Specific training opportunities for young people may be available, including Skillseekers in Scotland. Contact your local careers office, TEC/LEC for details.

LATE ENTRY

Packing is an area of work providing many opportunities for adult entrants. Personal qualities are most important to employers, especially reliability. There are also opportunities for part-time working at times which can fit in with personal and family commitments. These vacancies are often more attractive to the adult entrant or returner.

There may be specific training opportunities directed at adults available in some areas for this type of work. Candidates may have to satisfy certain conditions to be eligible. Contact your local Jobcentre, careers office or TEC/LEC for details.

OPPORTUNITIES

Packers are employed throughout the UK by manufacturing companies of all types. They are also employed to pack manufactured goods by export firms, shipping and forwarding agents, mail order companies and warehouse/storage services. Similar work is available with large stores and other retail outlets, removal firms and specialist exporters dealing with antiques, fine arts, etc.

In manufacturing, the introduction of new technology is reducing the demand for routine packing, and opportunities are decreasing. Demand for specialist packers is more stable.

PAY AND CONDITIONS

Packers usually work a 37 to 40-hour week. Some work shifts. Overtime may be available. There are opportunities for part-time work.

Rates of pay vary according to employer, location, the type of job, experience and age. Wages may also vary if a piecework rate is paid, that is, a rate of pay set by the rate of production.

Packers, after training and with sufficient experience to have built up speed, earn around £150 to £250 a week.

Additional payments may be made for shift work and as productivity bonuses. Extra pay for overtime may also significantly increase wages.

PROSPECTS

Promotion prospects are limited. It may be possible to progress from routine to specialist packing, but this may involve moving to another company. Some packers progress to supervisory grades such as chargehand or supervisor.

RELATED OCCUPATIONS

Production worker, checker, quality control inspector, assembler, engineering machine operator, warehouseman/ woman, removal man/woman, fork lift truck operator, post-room worker, laundry/dry cleaning worker.

FURTHER INFORMATION

CENTREX Training and Conference Centre*, High Ercall, Telford, Shropshire TF6 6RB, 01952 777777

FURTHER READING

Leaflets/booklets are available from the address marked*.

In the careers library, classified under SAB.

BAKER CLCI:SAC

BACKGROUND INFORMATION

The large white sliced loaf is still the most popular type of bread in Britain, but other types of bread such as wholemeal, French sticks, pitta bread, malt loaves, and organic bread have grown in popularity. Bread sales declined for a number of years but are now static; however, 'morning goods' – products such as rolls, croissants, crumpets, muffins and pastries – are being bought in increasing quantities. Public interest in a more varied range of bakery products means there is scope for the small, specialist concern, as well as for the large-scale bread producer.

Bread and morning goods are made by three main types of bakery:

Plant bakeries are mainly large firms, with a factory-like environment. They use modern technology to bake on an automated production line. Their main product is bread, but some have separate departments making cakes and pastries.

Traditional craft bakeries bake bread for sale in their own shops and also supply local outlets such as hotels, pubs and sandwich bars. Craft bakeries vary in size – some may consist of a single shop and bakery, others own a network of shops in a local area. As well as bread and morning goods, many craft bakeries produce cakes, pies and pastries, and offer sandwiches and snack meals.

In-store bakeries are found in supermarkets and other large stores. The growth of these outlets has been helped by technical developments that enable retailers to purchase pre-mixes, part-baked or unbaked frozen dough. These can be stored until needed, then processed and baked on site – enabling stores to sell freshly baked bread throughout the day.

About 80 per cent of Britain's bread is produced by plant bakeries, about 8 per cent is made by craft bakeries, and the rest by in-store bakeries.

THE WORK

The main difference between the work in craft, plant and in-store bakeries is the degree of mechanization involved. In plant and in-store bakeries, most operations are mechanized and routine, whereas in craft bakeries, some proportion of the work may be carried out by hand, or with hand-operated machinery, and is usually non-routine.

The main operations in all types of bakery are: weighing and measuring ingredients; mixing doughs and other mixtures; portioning and shaping mixtures (for loaves, rolls, etc); conditioning and baking mixtures; cooling, slicing, wrapping and labelling where required; and delivery to customers.

In plant bakeries, baking is a continuous operation, with dough and loaves moving automatically through the various stages of production on a conveyor belt. The baker's work involves operating machinery and ensuring that each stage of the process progresses smoothly. Bakers may move between different tasks during the course of each working week, so there may be some variety in the work, though the number of production lines is usually limited.

In-store bakeries operate on the same lines as plant bakeries, but not usually with a continuous production line, as batches are smaller. There is more manual work – such as lifting and carrying trays of bread from one stage of production to the next.

Craft bakers use fewer machines and may carry out some processes – such as moulding dough and check-weighing finished loaves – by hand. They need to develop the skills necessary to adjust recipes, taking into account the variability of ingredients (such as the quality of flour used). There is more variety of tasks and products in craft baking, as batches are smaller and it may be necessary for a small team to produce a wide range of different products. Craft bakers may also make and decorate cakes, as well as other jobs such as driving delivery vans, ordering supplies, or cleaning the bakery.

WORK ENVIRONMENT

Plant bakeries are a factory environment. In-store bakeries are large rooms, attached to a supermarket or store. Craft bakeries are usually attached to a baker's shop.

Conditions are often noisy – with tins clattering against racks, and the sound of machinery. There may also be dust from flour, although this problem has been virtually eliminated in the larger, automated bakeries and is controlled in others. Conditions for people working near ovens are hot, but not all jobs involve working in a hot environment; putting cream on cakes, for instance, is a task that must be done in a cool room.

There are legal requirements covering health, safety and hygiene, which all bakeries must meet.

Bakers work as members of a team: the number of people working together varies considerably, from two or three in a small craft bakery to 200-300 in a large plant bakery.

Protective clothing and equipment, consisting of hats and overalls and, for some tasks, safety shoes, gloves and ear-defenders, is normally provided by employers.

SKILLS AND INTERESTS

As the work involves food handling, a high standard of personal hygiene is essential. It is important to be conscious of safety procedures when operating machinery and using hot ovens.

Bakers need to be able to work quickly. Good timing is crucial in baking, and it is important, particularly in craft bakeries where there may be several different types of bread being baked at once, to be well organized – remembering to take each batch out at the right time.

Good health and physical fitness are important; bakers are on their feet all day, and the work can be tiring. In smaller bakeries (craft and in-store), staff may need to lift sacks of flour, tins of loaves, etc; some strength is required.

Manual dexterity and some artistic ability are required for hand moulding of dough (to make bread plaits, for example) and decorative work. Some jobs require numeracy, for measuring ingredients, ordering supplies, working out costings and calculating cooking times.

Bakery work may be unsuitable for people who suffer from dust allergies, asthma and certain skin complaints.

ENTRY REQUIREMENTS

In the majority of cases, there are no formal educational entry requirements; however, GCSEs/S grades in English, maths, science or home economics are useful.

Entry requirements for the BTEC national diploma or SCOTVEC national certificate modules are four GCSEs/S grades (A-C/1-3) including English, maths and a science subject, or equivalent qualifications.

TRAINING

There are a number of different training routes:

On-the-job training. Many entrants begin as trainees and receive on-the-job training from employers. In some cases this may be supported by flexible and video learning material produced by the National and Scottish Associations of Master Bakers. Training may also include day release study at a local college.

Skillseekers. In Scotland only, Skillseekers opportunities are available for young people in all LEC areas, with entry usually at 16-18 years but also possible, in some areas, up to 25 years. This is a structured form of youth training, mainly on the job, which may lead to an SVQ in Craft Baking at Level 2. It can also lead to a Modern Apprenticeship and SVQ Level 3. For placements, contact the Scottish Association of Master Bakers (see FURTHER INFORMATION).

Modern Apprenticeships. Available for young people mainly in craft bakeries. Training is on the job, plus college studies, and normally takes about three years. The Apprenticeship leads to NVQ/SVQ in Craft Baking at Level 2 and NVQ/SVQ in either Craft Baking (Technical Operations) or Supervisory Management at Level 3. Additional qualifications may be acquired such as GNVQ/GSVQ units or BTEC Baking Technology modules/SCOTVEC Craft Baking units.

NVQs/SVQs. Available in Craft Baking at Level 2 and at Level 3 in Supervisory Management and Craft Baking (Technical Operations). Employees of any age can be assessed for these, as they are based on competences acquired.

For plant bakers, the relevant NVQs/SVQs are in Food and Drink Manufacturing Operations at Levels 1 and 2. Level 3 in Supervisory Management and Technical Operations will soon be available.

BTEC National Diploma in Science (Baking Technology) is a two-year full-time course, which may be taken before applying to employers, available at a number of colleges, including Thomas Danby College, Leeds, and the University of the South Bank, London. BTEC qualifications are particularly useful for intending supervisors and managers. In addition to the national diploma, first diploma/certificate, national certificate and higher national diploma/certificate courses are available.

SCOTVEC Scottish National Certificate in Craft Baking is a one-year full-time course, which needs no formal entry qualifications. A SCOTVEC Higher National Certificate in Bakery and Confectionery Production is also available, for which entry requirements may be the SNC, SVQ Level 2, or appropriate work experience within a bakery. The HNC is particularly useful for people aiming to work at technician or supervisory levels.

Basic hygiene training is compulsory for all food handlers and health and safety qualifications are recommended for all bakers.

LATE ENTRY

There are no age restrictions on entry, but employers have, traditionally, tended to favour school-leavers. However, shift working in the plant baking industry means that employees usually have to be at least 18 years.

There may be specific training opportunities directed at adults available in some areas for this type of work. Candidates may have to satisfy certain conditions to be eligible. Contact your local Jobcentre, careers office or TEC/LEC for details.

OPPORTUNITIES

There are estimated to be about 125,000 people employed in the British baking industry of which about 50 to 60,000 work as bakers. There are opportunities throughout the country. Overall, employment in the industry has been decreasing for a number of years, as baking processes have become increasingly automated. The decrease in employment has been mainly in the plant baking sector, which currently employs about 25,000 people in about 70 bakeries. The majority of employees in the plant baking industry are adults.

In-store bakeries are increasing their share of the bread market, and most large supermarkets now have their own in-store bakery. There is a growing number of jobs in this sector.

The National Association of Master Bakers, which represents craft bakeries in England and Wales, has some 1,600 member firms. Some of these are very small, with just one shop and a bakery attached; others are chains, supplying five or six shops or, in a few cases, a much larger number of outlets. In Scotland, some 350 craft bakeries – also varying considerably in size – are represented by the Scottish Association of Master Bakers.

PAY AND CONDITIONS

In craft and plant bakeries, there are negotiated agreements between employers and trades unions, although not all employers are party to these agreements. Negotiated rates range from £153 a week for a skilled bakery worker depending on starting time or £191 for very early starts and night shifts. Apprentices are paid a percentage of the agreed rate, such as 70 per cent at 17 years and under. Some employers pay more than the negotiated minimum.

Standard working hours are 39 a week, over five days. Very early starts (4am or earlier) are less often required than in the past, and starting times of 6 to 7am are now more common. Plant bakeries operate 24 hours a day; staff work shifts, on a rota system. Shift and overtime working for full-time workers is usually compulsory.

In craft and in-store bakeries, Saturday work (to produce bread for sale the same day) is fairly common. This may attract overtime rates of pay, or may be part of a standard Tuesday to Saturday week.

In plant bakeries, employees covered by negotiated agreements receive 25 days paid holiday after completing one year's service. In craft bakeries, the agreements allow for 20 days paid holiday a year, plus one extra day holiday over the Christmas and New Year period. After five years' service, staff are entitled to an extra two days' holiday. Holiday entitlement for in-store bakery staff depends on the policy of individual employers.

There are limited opportunities for part-time employment. Some specialist types of work – such as cake decoration – are quite often done on a part-time basis.

PROSPECTS

Plant bakeries offer a full range of career opportunities. It is possible for young people entering plant baking at any level to reach production management, provided they gain an understanding of production techniques and have managerial capabilities.

In-store and craft bakeries, which are generally fairly small, offer prospects for promotion – to supervisor level, for example. Prospects are better for those who are prepared to be mobile, moving to different areas to take up more responsible posts.

Self-employment – setting up and running a small bakery – is possible for those with several years' experience of the work. The National Association of Master Bakers offers guidance on self-employment and runs a finance company that provides loans to people wishing to purchase a bakery business.

Some bakers transfer into related areas of work, for instance, with flour-milling companies and baking equipment manufacturers. These firms employ test bakers, who experiment with different baking methods and ingredients, and they also employ bakers as technical advisers, trainers or sales representatives.

There are also opportunities to teach bakery skills at colleges of further education.

RELATED OCCUPATIONS

Chef, cook, kitchen assistant, production operative (food manufacturing), retail assistant (bakery).

FURTHER INFORMATION

The Federation of Bakers*, 20 Bedford Square, London WC1B 3HF, 0171 580 4252

The National Association of Master Bakers (NAMB)*, 21 Baldock Street, Ware, Herts SG12 9DH, 01920 468061

The Scottish Association of Master Bakers (SAMB)*, Atholl House, 4 Torphichen Street, Edinburgh EH3 8JQ, 0131 229 1401

The Craft Bakery Training Organisation (Scotland)* – as for SAMB

FURTHER READING

Leaflets/booklets are available from the addresses marked*.

Working in Food and Drink – COIC

In the careers library classified under SAC.

MEAT PROCESS WORKER CLCI:SAC

BACKGROUND INFORMATION

The most visible part of the meat and poultry industry is the high street butcher, but independent retailers (who are covered in a separate article: RETAIL BUTCHER: OFM) only form one part of the meat chain. There are also those who work in abattoirs, process plants, wholesalers, manufacturers, supermarkets and those who work as meat inspectors and catering butchers. Increasingly, these activities overlap – for instance, slaughtering, processing and manufacturing may be combined on one site. Factories combining these operations are known as meat plants.

THE WORK

Meat process workers usually specialize in one of the following:

Abattoirs. Animals are humanely slaughtered in abattoirs, which may be part of meat plants or may be separate. Livestock arrive at the meat plant or abattoir in lorries. Some workers are responsible for unloading the animals and receiving them into pre-slaughter pens (known as 'lairage'), where they are kept for a short time. The animals are then moved from the lairage to the stunning pen. Slaughtermen/women stun the animals, to render them insensitive to pain, then kill them quickly. The carcasses are hoisted onto a conveyor belt where they are bled. Further on, the hides are removed. After skinning, carcasses are 'dressed', which involves trimming, cleaning and the removal of the edible offals.

The carcasses are now ready for cutting into sides and quarters (known as 'primary cutting'). In some abattoirs they are then prepared for dispatch as whole carcasses, to be further cut up (or processed) at wholesalers or retail butchers. In the larger meat plants, further cutting and boning continues, both mechanically and by hand, to prepare joints and cuts. In poultry plants, slaughter and processing is largely an automated process.

All work in an abattoir is subject to strict public health controls, monitored by the Meat Hygiene Service.

Meat wholesalers. Some staff of meat wholesalers buy livestock from markets; others cut and prepare carcasses that have been supplied by the abattoir; others sell to retailers and other customers, including meat manufacturers, from depots and meat markets, including overseas customers.

Catering butchers. Companies vary in the type of work they do. Some workers take deliveries from abattoirs and meat plants, process and distribute them to restaurants, caterers or public institutions. Some carry out primary cutting, leaving the final preparation to the caterer. Others are involved in producing cuts, joints, oven-ready dishes and other products to the caterer's strict specifications. There is particular emphasis in catering butchery on portion size, weight, cost and packing.

Meat manufacturing. In larger meat and poultry plants, some of the meat passes through to the manufacturing stage, but meat manufacturing is also carried out in specific factories, large and small, which may not be related to abattoirs. Workers produce sausages, pies, pâtés, ready-made dishes, frozen foods and other meat products, and cure bacon and ham. Much of the work is broken down into simple, repetitive tasks, carried out on a continuous production line, in factory conditions. In smaller companies, more traditional craft skills are required, with staff carrying out a wide range of processing operations.

In all sectors of the meat processing industry, there is an emphasis on cleanliness, hygiene and food safety. In smaller factories the cleaning and maintenance may be carried out by the process workers, but in larger factories this will be a specialist function.

WORK ENVIRONMENT

Abattoirs and meat plants are cool and airy. The environment is designed to protect the health and safety of workers and to ensure the food safety of products, with hygienic practices observed at all stages. All workers wear protective and hygienic clothing, including head coverings.

Many workers (though not all) experience very cold conditions during brief periods spent in chill rooms and refrigerated areas, used for storage. Special clothing is provided for this.

In abattoirs and meat and poultry processing plants conditions can be noisy, and it may be necessary to wear ear defenders. Smells can be unpleasant, particularly in abattoirs.

Much of the work involves standing.

SKILLS AND INTERESTS

All staff working with meat must pay strict attention to food safety and hygiene. Personal cleanliness is essential.

Most jobs demand the ability to work with others as a member of a team.

Workers who are directly involved in slaughtering need a straightforward, unsentimental approach to killing animals for food. In the abattoir and in other stages of the meat-processing chain, it may be necessary for some workers to handle carcasses, and for these manual lifting and carrying jobs some strength is required.

Manual dexterity is required for jobs that involve cutting and boning meat.

On the production line, it is important to be able to carry out repetitive tasks consistently and quickly.

ENTRY REQUIREMENTS

There are no formal educational entry requirements. However, for those aiming to reach supervisory or technical level, it is an advantage to have some GCSEs/S grades or GNVQs/GSVQs.

The job of slaughterman/woman is restricted by law to people aged 18 or over.

Every slaughterman/woman involved in killing must, under European Union legislation, be licensed by the Local Authority. Licences must be renewed annually.

TRAINING

Some companies offer opportunities for young people via a Modern Apprenticeship leading to NVQ/SVQ Level 3 in Technical Operations or in Supervisory Management (Meat Processing). For school-leavers in England and Wales, some larger employers have their own recruitment and training schemes. In Scotland, Skillseekers may be available, funded by youth credits. In both cases, on and off-the-job training normally lasts up to two years and can lead to NVQ/SVQ Level 2. Skillseekers can lead on to SVQ Level 3 and a Modern Apprenticeship. Others may be recruited to on-the-job training only, though NVQ/SVQ

Levels 1 and 2 may be available when sufficient experience and competence has been gained.

To attain NVQ/SVQ Level 2, candidates have to reach specified standards in three core units covering hygiene, health and safety, and communications.

Additional units, appropriate to the competencies required for the trainee's sector of the industry, are also taken. On successful completion of training, the title of the NVQ/SVQ Level 2 is one of: Meat and Poultry Plant Operations; Meat and Poultry Butchery Operations; Meat and Poultry Processing and Manufacturing Operations; or Selling and Distributing Meat, Poultry and Related Products. Units are awarded on the basis of continuous assessment at colleges, training centres and in the workplace.

The Meat Training Council offers further qualifications leading to associateship and graduate membership. These are aimed at those seeking advancement in the industry. They include modules in: abattoir; catering butchery; manufacturing plant; poultry industry; and wholesale distribution. These qualifications are examination-based.

Nearly 60 educational establishments offer courses leading to Meat Training Council qualifications, including NVQs/SVQs. Courses are generally part-time, over two years, but one-year full-time courses are available at some colleges.

The Royal Society of Health (RSH) qualification for meat inspectors may be taken after the associateship of the Meat Training Council, via a one-year part-time course, or as part of a one-year full-time course leading to the associateship and RSH.

LATE ENTRY

Adult entry is very common, particularly in the manufacturing sector of meat plants. Most employers welcome applications from mature people. There are good opportunities in manufacturing for women returners, and part-time jobs are plentiful. Experience on a production line is useful, but not essential.

Related NVQs/SVQs are useful; it may be possible for adults with experience, who lack formal qualifications, to gain an NVQ/SVQ via Accreditation of Prior Learning (APL).

There may be specific training opportunities directed at adults available in some areas for this type of work. Candidates may have to satisfy certain conditions to be eligible. Contact your local Jobcentre, careers office or TEC/LEC for details.

OPPORTUNITIES

It is estimated that about 60,000 people are employed in meat manufacturing. A further 15,000 work in abattoirs, and about 4,000 in catering butchers and wholesalers.

The overall trend is towards consolidation into larger units, combining all or most of the stages in the meat chain from slaughter to shrink-wrapping for supermarkets. At the same time, however, there has been an increase in the number of small firms that concentrate on specialist products, such as pâtés.

The number of abattoirs not linked to meat plants has been decreasing for some time, and further closures are expected, as more stringent European Union legislation governing meat hygiene comes into force.

PAY AND CONDITIONS

Minimum wage rates for adults are between £125 and £145 a week, depending on the individual's level of skill and the area of the country. However, bonus and other incentives boost take-home pay significantly for most people.

Full-time staff work a 40-hour week, usually Monday to Friday. Some employers may operate a shift system. There are many part-time jobs in meat manufacturing.

PROSPECTS

There are prospects of promotion to supervisory and management posts, and into quality control, product development and other related specialisms.

After further training it is possible to become a meat inspector; inspectors are employed by the Meat Hygiene Service to check quality and standards in abattoirs and meat plants.

NVQs/SVQs in Supervisory Management (Meat Processing) at Level 3 and in Management (Meat Processing) at Level 4 and/or Meat Training Council qualifications may be advisable for the more responsible posts.

RELATED OCCUPATIONS

Retail butcher, meat inspector, production worker, quality control inspector, packer, warehouse worker.

FURTHER INFORMATION

Meat Training Council*, PO Box 141, Winterhill House, Snowdon Drive, Milton Keynes MK6 1YY, 01908 231062

Worshipful Company of Butchers, Butchers' Hall, Bartholomew Close, London EC1A 7EB, 0171 606 4106

Scottish Federation of Meat Traders' Associations, 8-10 Needless Road, Perth PH2 0JW, 01738 637472

FURTHER READING

Leaflets/booklets are available from the address marked*.

In the careers library, classified under SAC.

TECHNICAL BREWER CLCI:SAC

BACKGROUND INFORMATION

British brewing companies produce about 30 million pints of beer every day. There are over 1,200 brands of beer on the market, each with its own special flavour and characteristics. Almost half of all beer produced is now lager; the more traditional bitters, mild, pale ale and stout make up the remainder.

There are about 60 substantial brewing companies in the UK, operating around 100 breweries. There are also regional brewing companies and small companies. The small breweries offer few opportunities for employment. The majority of openings for technical brewers are with the large firms.

THE WORK

Brewing is a biochemical process in which malt, barley and other cereals or cereal products, water, hops and yeast are combined to produce beer. Variations occur in the properties of these ingredients; it is the brewer's responsibility to ensure that beer of a consistent quality, which suits public taste, is produced.

Technical brewers (also called technical or process managers) manage the complex process of beer production, which in most breweries is highly automated. They are responsible for resources – raw materials, plant and equipment – and for managing the work of operators and technicians. They monitor the production process, testing samples (for instance, to check specific gravity, which determines the strength of a beer). Where necessary, technical brewers make adjustments to processes in order to maintain product consistency.

Technical brewers' responsibilities vary according to the size of the company. In a large firm, they are likely to specialize in managing one stage of the brewing process, such as production of wort (malt liquor), fermentation, packaging or quality control. In a small company, a technical brewer may be responsible for several or all aspects of beer production.

In both large and small organizations, technical brewers need a knowledge of the chemistry, biochemistry and biology of the raw materials and their conversion into the finished product. To understand the plant and equipment used in brewing, they also need some knowledge of mechanical, chemical and electrical engineering. The work is likely to involve the use of computers for large-scale operations such as process control; technical brewers may also use personal computers for tasks such as technical calculations.

WORK ENVIRONMENT

Technical brewers spend much of their time in production areas, where conditions can be noisy, hot, wet and sometimes dusty. The work involves a lot of walking and standing; it may involve climbing up and down ladders (fitted to fermentation vessels, for instance). Only a small part of the working day is likely to be spent in the office.

Managing people is an important aspect of the work and there is continual contact with staff at all levels in the organization.

Technical brewers wear protective clothing – laboratory coats, rubber gloves, rubber boots or stout shoes. In noisy parts of the production area they may wear ear defenders; in dusty areas, face masks.

SKILLS AND INTERESTS

Technical brewers need leadership qualities, including initiative, the ability to manage people, and the capacity to develop general business management skills. They have to be able to interact well with other people and to communicate easily.

An interest in science and its practical application is important. Some aptitude for mechanical engineering is required, to understand the operation of plant and machinery.

Numeracy and computer literacy are essential.

Brewers need to be fit and active. Normal colour vision is required to read colour-coded control panels. Good hearing is important, for safety reasons.

ENTRY REQUIREMENTS

Most entrants are now graduates. They enter through one of two routes.

1. A degree in a pure or applied scientifically based discipline such as chemistry, biochemistry, food science/technology, microbiology or chemical engineering.

2. A BSc (Honours) in Brewing and Distilling at Heriot-Watt University. Entry to the course is usually with three A levels/four H grades including chemistry, biology and maths or physics. Maths must be offered at GCSE/S grade (A-C/1-3) if not at A level/H grade.

Entrants are usually expected to sit and pass the Institute of Brewing (IOB) Associate Membership Examination (AME), which covers the underlying scientific and engineering knowledge required. The BSc (Hons) in Brewing and Distilling at Heriot-Watt University gives associate membership and exemption from the exam.

TRAINING

The large companies run graduate technical management training programmes, consisting of intensive on and off-the-job training, together with practical experience, over a period of between one and four years.

Trainee technical managers study for the AME of the IOB. The examination syllabus covers scientific and engineering topics. Candidates may attend intensive modular courses, run by the IOB, covering engineering, malting, wort production, fermentation, and post-fermentation treatments. They are also expected to carry out a substantial amount of private study in their own time.

The practical aspects of technical brewing training are covered by the Brewers' Guild Certificate of Brewing Competence (CBC). This scheme has been introduced to replace the former pupillage system, and to ensure that entrants to the industry obtain practical experience in all aspects of brewing production, in addition to their academic training. The minimum time to complete the syllabus is twelve months, but a considerably longer period may be required. Assessment, in the form of an oral examination in a brewery, is carried out by an experienced senior brewer.

Alternative entry and training routes include the following.

1. Entry to laboratory-based research and development or quality control in a brewing company, with a relevant degree. After several years it may be possible to transfer to technical management.

2. Candidates with relevant degrees and experience in other industries are sometimes recruited as 'direct replacements',

taking up operational appointments without going through the normal management training scheme route.

3. A level/H grade entry, with day release or evening study for higher national certificate qualifications. This route is now rare. People who enter via these routes will be expected to study for the AME of the IOB, as above.

Advanced qualifications

Brewers may take the Diploma Master Brewer Examination (DME) of the IOB. A pass in or exemption from the AME is a prerequisite for those taking the DME.

An MSc and a postgraduate diploma in brewing are available at Heriot-Watt University. Employers may sponsor recruits with non-brewing degrees on these.

LATE ENTRY

The majority of entrants are recruited directly from institutions of higher education. There are no special provisions for mature entrants, although they may be accepted on relevant degree courses. It is now rare for people to enter technical brewing by promotion from operative and supervisory jobs in the industry.

OPPORTUNITIES

The majority of opportunities are with the large brewing companies, which recruit via the university 'milk round'; smaller companies tend to advertise when they need to fill a specific technical vacancy.

As a result of automation, employment in the production side of brewing has been declining over the years. The number of vacancies for technical brewers is very limited.

Related areas of work in brewing companies, where entry may be easier, include laboratory-based research, development and quality control, brewing engineering, sales, marketing, personnel and distribution.

With large brewing companies, which often have overseas divisions, there may be opportunities to work abroad. Foreign languages may be required.

A list of brewing companies and their addresses is included in the Brewers' and Licensed Retailers' Association (BLRA) information pack, *Technical Management in the Brewing Industry.*

PAY AND CONDITIONS

The large brewing companies have graduate recruitment schemes, and generally offer starting salaries of up to £15,000.

Technical brewers who have completed company training

schemes are likely, in their first operational appointments, to earn up to £17,000. Earnings vary according to the size of the brewery, and geographical area. Salaries for experienced brewers can be substantially higher.

Large breweries operate a two or three-shift system, and technical brewers are expected to work shifts and weekends. Small breweries may only brew one batch a day, and so do not operate shifts. However, hours of work in a small brewery are likely to be variable and irregular, and on-call duties may be required.

Working away from home for short or long periods of time may be necessary. This is particularly likely during training, when it is important to gain experience in a wide range of operations, but it may happen at any time in a brewer's career – for instance, if the company is setting up a new plant in another area of the country.

PROSPECTS

The IOB Diploma, which may be taken by technical brewers with at least four years' production experience, is recognized as the standard of technical excellence by employers. In major companies, it is unlikely that individuals will advance in their careers without this qualification.

For those with the IOB Diploma, appropriate personal qualities and management skills, promotion to a significant managerial appointment is possible by the early 30s; and director level can be reached before the age of 40.

RELATED OCCUPATIONS

Scientist/technician, food scientist/technologist, microbiologist.

FURTHER INFORMATION

Brewers and Licensed Retailers Association*, 42 Portman Square, London W1H 0BB, 0171 486 4831

Brewers' Guild*, 8 Ely Place, Holborn, London EC1 6SD, 0171 405 4565

The Institute of Brewing, 33 Clarges Street, London W1Y 8EE, 0171 499 8144

FURTHER READING

Leaflets/booklets are available from the addresses marked*.

Working in Food and Drink – COIC

In the careers library classified under SAC.

GLASSMAKER CRAFTSMAN/WOMAN
CLCI:SAD

BACKGROUND INFORMATION

Glass is a transparent, hard, brittle substance used for a wide range of purposes in modern industrial societies. It is formed from certain liquids that have the property of cooling below their freezing point without crystallizing. They become liquids of increasingly high viscosity (stiffness) until they are, to all intents and purposes, solid.

The main ingredient of most glasses is silica (sand). This is combined with lime and soda in varying proportions to make the soda lime glass used for many purposes, including windows, light bulbs, bottles and inexpensive tableware. Glass can also be given special qualities by adding other ingredients. Flint glass, used widely for cut-crystal glassware, is made from silica, potassium carbonate, potassium nitrate and red lead. Coloured glasses are produced by adding metallic oxides.

Glass is made by heating the ingredients (together with cullet (scrap glass) of the same type being made) to a very high temperature in a furnace. At these temperatures glass behaves like a normal liquid, but as it cools it becomes malleable. It can then be fabricated into the shape required by one of three main methods: mouth blowing; pressing; and pouring, rolling or drawing. Although all these operations were originally performed by hand, automatic processes have been developed for large-scale production and by far the majority of glass products today are made in this way.

Automated production lines employ relatively small numbers of staff. Many are professionally trained engineers and technologists, but there are also jobs for production workers who tend the machinery and intervene when problems arise. These occupations are discussed in articles elsewhere in this book. The most common items still hand-made by traditional methods are lead crystal glassware, other decorative glassware and tableware, and special scientific glass articles.

The glass industry today can be divided into four main sectors. These are: **the container sector,** which produces bottles, jars, light bulbs, vacuum flask interiors, and so on; **the flat glass sector,** which manufactures flat glass for window and vehicle glazing and mirrors; **the fibre sector,** which produces glass fibre products such as glass wool and optical fibres for use in communications systems; and **the tableware and scientific products sector.**

The article below deals with the work of craftsmen/women who produce hand-made tableware and scientific products, as well as art and sculptural glass.

THE WORK

Glassblowers orm glass roughly into the shape of the finished article by blowing down a tube, spinning the tube and swinging it backwards and forwards. They then either pass the pipe on to the chairman/servitor to complete the article, or blow it into a mould to shape it further.

Chairmen/servitors (sometimes called **finishers**) receive the partly shaped object still attached to the blow pipe or rod and form it into shape using shaping tongs, a palette knife, wooden blocks and other implements. They usually sit in a chair with long, horizontal, metal-plated arms and roll the blow pipe backwards and forwards to help them shape the glass.

Glass benders bend glass by placing sheet glass or smaller pieces of glass over moulds and putting them in a furnace or kiln. When heated the glass becomes pliable and falls into or over the shape of the mould. Products made this way include curved shop windows, roof-lights and glass domes. Glass benders place the glass and moulds in the kiln and remove them when the glass has bent. They also check the kiln temperature and adjust this if necessary.

Scientific glassblowers (sometimes called **bench glassblowers**) make scientific and industrial glassware by heating glass tubes in a bench burner until they are pliable. They can then make bends and bulbs in them by bending by hand and by blowing into the tubes. Blowing is also used to even out constrictions or sagging in the glass caused by bending.

Glass lathe workers use lathes for large pieces of glassware that cannot be handled on a bench. They join separate pieces of glass together, such as the neck and bulb of a scientific flask, and, like benchworkers, make straight joins and 'T' joins. They also shape glass on the lathe as it rotates heated by burners. Lathe workers use thermally protective gloves where necessary.

Designers develop new designs and products in glassware, taking into account the production methods and costs involved. Some combine this with working as glass decorators.

Glass decorators apply decorative designs and finishes to glassware. They use a variety of techniques, including mitre wheel cutting, engraving, sand blasting and stencilling, acid etching and polishing. Decorators work to traditional designs or to new ones created by designers or, in some cases, themselves. Some decorative work involves freehand drawing. This is highly skilled.

Designer craftsmen/women combine the work of designer, glass-blower, chairman/servitor and decorator to produce glass articles from start to finish. They make mainly decorative glassware in small craft workshops or studios. Some craftsmen/women specialize in stained glass work, restoring old stained glass windows and screens, or creating new products. Recent advances in technology mean that it is now possible for craftsmen/women to build and operate their own small glass-making furnaces.

WORK ENVIRONMENT

Conditions in a glass factory can be hot, particularly in the summer months and when workers have to go near the furnaces and kilns. For the most part, however, working conditions are warm though not uncomfortable. Glass factories can also be noisy and dusty.

Glassblowers and glass benders have to be on their feet for much of the day, whereas chairmen/servitors, scientific glassblowers and lathe workers tend to do most of their work sitting down. Designers, decorators and designer craftsmen/women also do much of their work seated.

Chairmen/servitors and glassblowers usually work in teams, with workers passing articles from one to another for further shaping. Glass benders, scientific glass blowers and lathe workers work largely alone, though they may occasionally join with others on large jobs.

SKILLS AND INTERESTS

Chairmen/servitors and glassblowers need to be good with their hands and in the use of tools and equipment to control the distribution and shaping of the hot glass. Some physical strength and stamina are needed to manipulate the weight of the rod and metal. Scientific glassblowers need to have nimble fingers and a steady hand. The main requirements of a glass bender are patience and care.

All glass workers need a good eye for shape and size, and to be able to work quickly and accurately. They need to be able to work with others as part of a team.

Self-employed craftsmen/women need to have or develop a range of business skills, including marketing, book-keeping, pricing and estimating, negotiating and time management.

Glass decorators and designer craftsmen/women may, depending on the nature of their work, require good colour vision.

ENTRY REQUIREMENTS

For jobs as glassblowers, scientific glassblowers, lathe workers, benders and chairmen/servitors, most employers do not require any specific educational qualifications, although exam passes in science and craft subjects are an advantage.

The main way to become a designer or a craftsman/woman is to take a course in design with an option in glass. These are mostly degree level courses, for which the minimum requirement is five GCSEs/S grades (A-C/1-3) and two A levels/three H grades, or an equivalent qualification, such as the BTEC National Diploma in Design or Advanced GNVQ/GSVQ in Art and Design. Applicants are also usually expected to show practical evidence of their ability and commitment to art and design by submitting a portfolio of work.

A non-degree full-time course is available at Dudley College of Technology. No specific academic qualifications are required for this course, but enthusiasm and commitment, as well as satisfactory references, are needed.

In Scotland the requirements for degree-level design courses are five GCSEs/S grades (A-C/1-3) including English, and three H grades or two A levels. Art and English at A level or H grade are normally expected, but not mandatory.

TRAINING

Glassblowers and chairmen/servitors learn mainly by working alongside experienced workers, by being shown and by carrying out the operations themselves. The same applies to glass benders, though in a few cases a trainee bender may attend college on day release to study for the City and Guilds award in Glass Technology.

For scientific glassblowers and lathe workers, some companies have training schools where trainees learn how to manipulate glass, how to form bends and constrictions, and how to join pieces of tubing together. Similarly, lathe workers learn by starting on simple jobs and gradually develop skills and expertise. In many firms trainees learn both scientific glassblowing and lathe work.

Some London-based firms send trainees to college on day release to study for the qualifications of the British Society of Scientific Glassblowers (BSSG) or City and Guilds. Braintree College of Further Education and Hounslow Borough College run courses for the BSSG awards. All these courses can be taken full-time, and Hounslow Borough College also runs an evening course.

Designers are usually graduates from courses where they learn all aspects of glass making and decorating. Glass decorators are often trained on the job, and may also be sent on part-time college courses.

Youth training in the glass industry is managed by Glass Training Limited (GTL). Schemes are run by a number of firms, each of which adapts the programme according to the type of glassware it produces. Trainees are first given an all-round introduction to the glass industry followed by specialist training suited to their abilities and needs.

All trainees study an open learning course called Glass Manufacture which was set up by Glass Training Limited in conjunction with Dudley College of Technology. This course is also available to other employees. Students who successfully complete the course receive a Dudley College/Glass Training Limited certificate. They may also sit for the City and Guilds 0690 examinations (sections 1 and 2) in Glass Manufacture.

Another open learning course is the BTEC National Certificate in Engineering Process Technology (Glass), run via Wakefield College and St Helens College. The section of the course relating to glass is mainly provided by the Glass Manufacture open learning course materials.

Entry through Modern Apprenticeships, leading to NVQ/SVQ Levels 3 and 4 may also be available in your area. Contact your local careers office, TEC/LEC for details.

Designer craftsmen/women usually take a full-time training course such as the BA Honours Degree in Three-dimensional Design. Centres offering such courses with options in glass include the University of Sunderland, Edinburgh College of Art, West Surrey College of Art and Design, and Stourbridge College of Technology and Art. Many other design courses include glass as an option, though not always to the same extent as those mentioned.

A non-degree course in glass techniques and technology is run by Dudley College of Technology at its International Glass Centre in Brierley Hill. This is a full-time 36-week course starting in September and lasting till June. It is primarily aimed at students who wish to work in a glass studio, or set up their own businesses. The course is, however, accredited by the West Midlands Access Federation, which means that students can gain credits towards higher education entrance requirements. Students spend about a third of their time on glass making, a third on the technology of glass (including furnace building and design) and a third on glass decoration. Dudley College also organizes short courses on demand.

NVQs/SVQs in Glass Processing and Scientific Glass Product Fabrication are available at Levels 1 and 2. NVQs/SVQs in Glass Batch Processing Operations, Glass Melting Operations, Glass Forming Operations, Glass and Glazing Production (Replacement Fabrications), and Production Support Operations – Glass (Cold End Operations) are also available at Level 2.

LATE ENTRY

Many of the colleges running the courses mentioned in TRAINING are prepared to waive their normal entry requirements for mature candidates.

The course at Dudley College is particularly popular among adults changing career.

OPPORTUNITIES

Opportunities for craft glass workers are limited. Only a very small number are being recruited at present. Manufacturers of glass articles of this kind are situated in all parts of the country, but with a particularly strong concentration in London, the West Midlands and the North East of England, and Perthshire in Scotland.

Self-employment as a designer craftsman/woman is possible by setting up a workshop or studio. As well as excellent craft skills, a range of business skills are needed for success.

PAY AND CONDITIONS

The average earnings of the glass craft workers covered in this article are around £249 a week. Chairmen/servitors and scientific glassblowers usually earn more than other craft workers as their work is the most skilled. Some workers such as glass decorators are paid at piece-rates, so their earnings can vary.

Most craft glassmakers work a 39-hour week, Monday to Friday, usually starting at 8am. Overtime may sometimes be required. Some companies operate a shift system. Craft crystal workers often work 6am to 2pm.

PROSPECTS

Glassblowers can go on to become chairmen/servitors, but for the most part, craft glass workers are limited to reaching positions as supervisors or foremen/women. There is no promotion ladder for self-employed designer craftsmen/women. For them a rising income depends on hard work, business acumen, skill, and – to some extent – luck.

RELATED OCCUPATIONS

Glazier, three-dimensional designer, carpenter/joiner, ceramic glazer/painter/decorator, carpenter/joiner, materials scientist/technologist, glass technologist, production worker.

FURTHER INFORMATION

Glass Training Limited*, BGMC Building, Northumberland Road, Sheffield S10 2UA, 0114 266 1494

British Society of Scientific Glassblowers, 21 Grebe Avenue, Eccleston Park, St Helens, Merseyside WA10 3QL

Dudley College of Technology*, International Glass Centre, Moor Street, Brierley Hill, West Midlands DY5 3EP, 01384 455433 (ext 4267)

Glass and Glazing Federation*, 44-48 Borough High Street, London SE1 1XP

Guild of Glass Engravers*, 19 Wildwood Road, London NW11 6UL

Rural Development Commission*, 141 Castle Street, Salisbury, Wiltshire SP1 3TP, 01722 336255

Made in Scotland Ltd, Station Road, Beauly, Inverness-shire IV4 7EH, 01463 782578

Scottish Glass Society*, 32 Farington Street, Dundee DD2 1PF, 01382 669864

University and Colleges Admissions Service, UCAS*, Fulton House, Jessop Avenue, Cheltenham, Glos GL50 3SH, 01242 227788

FURTHER READING

Leaflets/booklets are available from the addresses marked*.

Working in Glass – COIC

In the careers library classified under SAD.

1. LEATHER TECHNOLOGIST CLCI:SAF
2. LEATHER CRAFT WORKER CLCI:SAF

BACKGROUND INFORMATION

Leather is made in a tannery from animal skins and hides. In Britain the main animals used are cows, pigs, sheep and goats. The raw hides and skins are cured or preserved immediately to prevent decay.

After pre-treatment to remove unwanted components such as flesh, hair and salt, the hides and skins are ready for tanning. Tanning agents cement together the protein fibres in the skin, giving leather its unique, flexible, hard-wearing qualities.

A variety of tanning substances may be used. The most common are chromium salts, though for environmental reasons traditional tanning methods using vegetable extracts are enjoying a revival. Other tanning substances include aluminium and zirconium salts, oil (used mainly for chamois leather) and synthetics.

Tannages are often used in combination, consecutively or simultaneously, to produce leather with just the right qualities for the application intended. Vegetable-tanned leather, for example, is retanned with chrome to produce semi-chrome shoe uppers and suede and glove leather.

After tanning, and retanning if required, the leather is then dressed and finished, through processes such as shaving, dyeing, rolling, fat-liquoring, softening, lubricating and surface coating. It is then ready to be crafted into any of the wide range of domestic and industrial leather products.

Domestic leather products include: boot and shoe soles, heels, inner soles and uppers; saddles, bridles and harnesses; horse collars; travelling bags, suitcases and briefcases; straps; book bindings; handbags, purses and wallets; gloves; upholstery; belts, jackets and other garments; razor strops; and footballs, cricket balls and other sporting goods. Industrial products include: aprons; buffing wheels; textile carders and combers; washers; hydraulic packings; lithographic equipment; and machinery belting.

The leathercraft industry in the UK is made up mainly of small firms with an average of 25 to 30 employees, though there are a few larger firms that make luggage. The major geographical centres are Walsall, where saddles and harnesses and small items such as purses and wallets are produced, and London, where handbags are made. Leathercraft businesses do, however, exist in all parts of the UK.

1. LEATHER TECHNOLOGIST (SAF)

THE WORK

Leather technologists apply scientific and technical principles in the process of leather manufacture. They aim to ensure that the leather's aesthetic appeal is maintained without compromising physical attributes such as durability. Technologists must be familiar with: all the processes and operations that are needed to prepare skins for tanning; the tanning process itself; and the many subsequent operations that determine the thickness, softness, texture, colour and water resistance of the leather.

Leather technologists must continually balance the practical requirements of day-to-day production (including the need for the tannery to make a profit) with the strict disciplines of the pure sciences.

Technologists have to understand the nature of the materials used in leather production and the ways in which they react. They control these reactions by methods such as varying the time a reaction is allowed to proceed and altering the mix and concentration of chemicals used. They test and analyse the finished products in laboratories, using chemicals, dyestuffs and small-scale apparatus, to ensure that the leather produced has all the required qualities.

Technologists do some office work, writing reports on research projects and on management topics such as plant production and performance. This may involve statistical analysis, which is likely to require the use of computers.

Depending on the size and the nature of the company, technologists may supervise operatives and technicians, and may in turn be responsible to senior managers or to a board of directors. The UK leather industry is becoming increasingly automated, and technologists are responsible for designing production layouts and for engineering aspects of processing. They have to ensure that plant performs efficiently, by minimizing costs incurred on items such as energy, labour, time and raw materials.

Finally, leather technologists are responsible for the monitoring and control of effluent, as well as ensuring the health and safety of the workforce.

WORK ENVIRONMENT

Most leather technologists work indoors in tanneries. Much of the work is practical, dealing with hides and chemicals and controlling and monitoring large-scale machinery. Some office work is also involved.

Although modern tanneries are usually clean, light and airy, some noxious substances are used, and protective clothing has to be worn at least some of the time.

The leather industry obtains its supplies and sells its products all over the world. Hence the job of the technologist may well involve travel, both within the UK and overseas.

SKILLS AND INTERESTS

Technologists must be flexible and adaptable, always seeking to solve problems in new and different ways. An aptitude for science, particularly chemistry, is essential, and practical ability is required for working with large-scale machinery.

An aptitude for staff management is important for supervising operatives and technicians. Good communication skills are needed when giving verbal and written reports to senior staff. The work is occasionally physical so technologists should be reasonably fit, but they are not required to do any heavy lifting.

Colour-blindness may be a disadvantage, and an allergy to chemicals or hides would cause major difficulties.

ENTRY REQUIREMENTS

Entry is possible at several levels. For courses leading to the City and Guilds (C&G) Operatives Certificate (4560) and the C&G Craft Certificate (4570), no formal qualifications are required, but candidates would normally already be employed in the leather industry.

For the BTEC Certificate of Achievement in Leather Technology, GCSEs/S grades (A-C/1-3) in maths, chemistry, a second science and a subject showing use of English are the minimum requirements. City and Guilds qualifications provide an alternative entry route.

Students with some science qualifications (GCSE or

equivalent) and relevant industrial experience (normally of at least two years' duration) can be admitted to the Nene Certificate course.

Applicants for the BSc Honours Degree in Leather Technology at Nene College normally require a minimum of five GCSEs/S grades (A-C/1-3) including maths, physics and chemistry, with two A levels/three H grades including at least one from maths, physics and chemistry. The BTEC Certificate of Achievement in Leather Technology also gives entry to the BSc course. Alternative qualifications with a similar physical science content are also considered.

TRAINING

The following courses are available at the British School of Leather Technology (BSLT) at Nene College, Northampton, which is the only establishment in the UK offering formal training for leather technologists. The school's purpose-built Leathersellers Centre has a well-equipped modern tannery as well as testing and research laboratories.

For those joining the industry direct from school, on-the-job training is supplemented by courses leading to City and Guilds Operatives and Craft Certificates. The Operatives Certificate (4560) gives an introductory overview of leather manufacture, while the Craft Certificate (4570) is a more advanced and comprehensive course which covers the operations of leather processing in more detail, with reference to the underlying science, mathematics and management principles. These courses are normally studied via open learning. Students on open learning courses work at their own pace, assisted by a mentor at their workplace and a tutor based at BSLT.

The one-year full-time BTEC Certificate of Achievement in Leather Technology is designed as a preliminary course to the BSc honours degree, and successful students would normally progress to the degree course in the next session. The subjects covered are: maths, physics and chemistry; the principles and practice of leather production; laboratory techniques; chemical engineering; tannery engineering; quality assurance; the use of computers; health and safety; and environmental issues (clean technology).

The major course offered by the British School of Leather Technology is the BSc Honours Degree in Leather Technology. The major themes of the course developed through the three years are: leather science and technology; evaluation and testing; chemistry and engineering; and the management of production. A final-year project brings together these themes in a practical investigatory study.

A one-year taught MSc in Leather Technology is available for graduates working in the leather producing and allied industries. Higher degrees (MPhil and PhD) are also available by research. It is possible for a student with no initial qualifications to progress from the C&G Operative's Certificate via BTEC qualifications and a BSc degree to a PhD.

All courses at Nene College are flexible, and it is possible for students to have different entry and exit points according to their needs and experience. It is also possible for students to take a break from their studies and return later to complete their education.

LATE ENTRY

Adult entry at technologist level is normally restricted to applicants who have followed one of the formal training courses described above.

Graduates in related subjects such as chemistry may be recruited into the industry. They are often sponsored to take a course such as the one-year MSc in Leather Technology. Students who already have at least one year of previous tannery experience (and, normally, have reached the age of 20) can take the one-year full-time Nene Certificate in Leather Studies. This course combines the study of practical leather-making with leather science, management and other relevant subjects.

OPPORTUNITIES

Most technologists work in tanneries. Centres of production have been traditionally sited near rivers. The main production areas today are in the East Midlands, the West Country, Lancashire, Yorkshire and the Scottish lowlands.

Leather manufacturing in the UK has contracted in recent years due to factors such as increased foreign competition and the replacement of leather in some applications by synthetic products such as plastics. However, a number of companies with high quality products and modern manufacturing methods are trading successfully, and appear to have good prospects for the future.

A number of companies in the UK employ leather technologists, though the job may not always be given that title. Job descriptions vary between companies, particularly with regard to areas of responsibility and the amount of supervisory work involved. Generally, smaller companies offer greater variety of work, a shorter management hierarchy and, therefore, more responsibility. In larger companies, the technologist can expect a more clearly demarcated job and a more clearly defined position on the management ladder.

Most leather technologists are directly involved in leather tanning and processing. Technologists also work in the footwear industry, in companies specializing in the import or export of leather, and in companies supplying chemicals and equipment to tanneries. There are many opportunities to work overseas. Teaching posts are occasionally available, as are research and commercial posts with BLC The Leather Technology Centre, the technical centre for leather world-wide.

PAY AND CONDITIONS

Newly qualified leather technologists earn between £10,500 and £20,000, with about 20+ days paid holiday, plus public holidays. Many firms have private pension schemes.

Leather technologists usually work the same hours as the factory. As leather production is a continuous process they may be required to work outside these hours, especially if problems arise.

PROSPECTS

A technologist may progress to production manager or technical manager. It is also possible to become a works chemist, or to work on the commercial side of the business in buying, sales or marketing. Formal qualifications in leather science and technology are increasingly a necessity for promotion to senior positions.

RELATED OCCUPATIONS

Scientist, technician, materials scientist, engineer, textile technician, production manager, leather craft worker.

FURTHER INFORMATION AND READING
Please see article 2. LEATHER CRAFT WORKER.

2. LEATHER CRAFT WORKER (SAF)

THE WORK

The range of leather goods manufactured is wide and varied. Many products are now made using modern machinery and production methods, but many jobs in the industry still involve the application of craft skills. In recent times there has been a revival of interest in articles made by traditional methods, and this has created a whole range of opportunities for enterprising craft workers.

Leather craft workers use many different hand tools. They include measuring and cutting tools; punches for making holes in leather for stitching and for fasteners and buckles; stitching tools, which include needles, awls and lacing pliers; roughing, grooving and edging tools; and a variety of tools for special jobs such as snap setters and screw creasers. Machine tools used include sewing and stitching machines, power drills and press cutters.

Most leather craft products are created from patterns similar to those used in making garments. Patterns are produced on paper, which is often divided into small squares to assist in drawing and copying. Experienced craft workers may design and make their own patterns, or they may use or adapt existing ones. The pattern is laid over the leather to be used and taped into place. The leather is then cut to the desired shape using scissors or a knife.

Before hand-stitching thicker leathers, it is usually necessary to punch holes in the material with a rotary or drive punch or a pricking iron. It is usually possible to sew lighter materials, such as soft suede, with needle and thread without the need to pre-punch holes. Many materials may also be machine sewn or stitched.

When larger holes are required for drawstrings or laces they may have to be reinforced with eyelets or grommets. Materials may also be joined together or reinforced with rivets or snaps. Special tools are required to perform these operations.

Craft workers may make their own thread by rolling strands of hemp together and waxing them, or they may purchase waxed thread ready-made. For some purposes they use leather lacing, which is leather cut into very thin strips. This is known as thonging.

For stitching the worker commonly uses a harness needle and waxed thread. A simple running stitch may be employed, but for strength and decorative effects more elaborate alternatives such as saddle-stitch or whipstitch may be preferred.

Craft workers may perform a number of other operations. These include: cementing, where two pieces of leather are glued together, usually with rubber cement; staining, which is done after cutting but before stitching to produce decorative effects on part or all of the finished product; edge finishing, where the cut edges of the leather are trimmed and polished, and possibly stained or waxed; and the addition of buckles, straps or handles, which may be sewn on or fixed by rivets.

Finally, a variety of techniques may be used to decorate the finished product. These include drawing, painting, staining, appliqui and hot and cold tooling, including the use of decorative stamps and dies.

Saddlery

Saddlers make and repair saddles, bridles and harnesses. The work involves intricate cutting and stitching. The leather used is thick and strong, and is usually stitched with hand-made thread.

A rural saddler often spends more time on repairs than on making new saddles or bridles. Rural saddlers tend to deal mainly in harnesses and horse clothing, while urban saddlers concentrate on new production.

WORK ENVIRONMENT

Most leather craft workers are self-employed or work for small firms. Many work on their own, but some, for example handbag makers, may work together as a team, each carrying out one particular task or operation.

Work is steady rather than pressured. Although saddlers are physically active, much of a craft worker's time may be spent seated in a workshop. The smells of leather and the chemicals used to polish and preserve it are always present.

Some self-employed craft workers travel regularly to craft fairs, displays and exhibitions to assist in marketing their work. These events are usually held in the summer months.

SKILLS AND INTERESTS

Practical ability is needed; most of the work is done by hand. Leather craft workers need to pay close attention to detail and have a patient approach to their work; concentration is required for close detailed work. Self-motivation and the ability to work alone are also required.

Creative flair is an advantage, particularly if the job involves designing leather goods. An eye for colour is needed for matching leather pieces.

Self-employed people need to have, or to develop, a range of business skills, including marketing, book-keeping, pricing and estimating, negotiating and time management.

ENTRY REQUIREMENTS

The national centre for training in leathercraft is Cordwainers College in London. Applicants for the college's full-time diploma courses must be at least 16 years and have either four GCSEs/S grades (A-C/1-3), or an equivalent qualification, such as a BTEC First Diploma or an Intermediate GNVQ/GSVQ Level II. Applicants for the BTEC Higher National Diploma in Saddlery Technology must be at least 18 years and have four GCSEs/S grades (A-C/1-3) and one A level/two H grades, or equivalent.

Applicants are invited to attend the college for an interview. All interviewees have to show a portfolio demonstrating their aptitude for this type of work. In certain circumstances the college may waive the entry requirements stated above. For part-time day and evening classes at Cordwainers College there are no special entry qualifications.

A range of part and full-time courses in leathercraft is also available at Walsall College. For most courses, no specific educational qualifications are required.

TRAINING

Most leather craft workers in employment are trained on the job by their firms, although the Rural Development Commission provides short courses for those already employed in this industry. Cordwainers College offers full-time training courses in leather crafts, as follows.

The two-year Leather in Three Dimensions course

provides practical training in the use of leather, ranging from high fashion to traditional hand-crafted items and experimental art forms. The third term of the first year provides a chance to sample the two options from which a specialist subject for the final year of study is chosen.

OPTION 1: Leather Arts and Fine Craftsmanship, concentrates on the uses of leather for hand-sewn, high quality bespoke items and on leather as an art form medium.

OPTION 2: Fashion Bags and Travel Accessories, concentrates on machine-made fashion bags and small personal accessories.

The whole of the second year consists of project work in the chosen specialist option. The course leads to a College Diploma in Leather Arts and Fine Craftsmanship or Fashion Bags and Travel Accessories, depending on the chosen specialist option. During the course students sit for City and Guilds Certificate exams in Leather Goods Manufacture at Stages I and II.

The two-year Diploma in Saddlery Studies aims to introduce students to the work of a saddler, and includes both traditional rural saddlery and modern factory-based production methods. Subjects covered include bridle, harness and saddle making, tack repairs and lorinery (the production of bits and other metal fittings for horses' tack). Students take the City and Guilds Certificate exams in Saddlery at Stages I, II and III and the two Loriners' Certificate examinations.

The two-year Higher National Diploma in Saddlery Technology is an advanced course covering not only saddlery (including bridle and harness making) but also horse studies. In the second year students choose between two options: (1) The Saddle, and (2) Harness and Bridle. The course is designed to equip students for a career in saddlery or in management in an equestrian-related company.

Students who have attained a high enough standard in any of the above courses, and who are supported by their course leaders, may enter for relevant skill tests and submit work for assessment by the Guild of Master Craftsmen and/or the Society of Designer Craftsmen.

All courses include a good grounding in business matters, to assist the many students who go on to become self-employed.

Cordwainers College also offers a range of courses in footwear technology and footwear/accessories which include the design and production of a variety of leather goods and accessories.

A range of part-time and full-time courses in leathercraft is also available at Walsall College, including a two-year full-time course in saddle and bridle manufacture, and part-time courses in book-binding and leather carving and tooling. City and Guilds qualifications and/or NVQs may be available.

NVQs/SVQs in Leathergoods Manufacture are available at Levels 1 and 2. Level 1 is an introductory qualification, while Level 2 covers a range of skills including sewing, machining, hand-stitching, pattern-cutting and so on. A Saddlery NVQ is available at Level 2, and covers cutting and preparing saddlery components and stitching them by hand. It also includes establishing and maintaining effective working relationships and contributing to the continuity of workflow and overall profitability of the production process.

LATE ENTRY

There are no upper age limits for leather craft workers. Cordwainers College actively encourages mature students and adult returners to apply for places on their courses. Previous experience may be accepted in lieu of formal academic qualifications under Accreditation of Prior Learning.

OPPORTUNITIES

In recent years the leather industry has contracted and the number of jobs and student places has fallen. Employment opportunities for leather craft workers are concentrated in London and the West Midlands, though self-employed people may work anywhere they can produce and sell their goods.

There is a small but steady demand for skilled saddlers and bridlers. Opportunities exist across the UK, both in urban and rural areas. Competition for training places and apprenticeships in saddlery has increased in recent years, and applicants need to be prepared to move to another part of the country to secure work.

The majority of leather craft workers are either self-employed, working from home or small workshops, or work for small firms producing leather goods.

PAY AND CONDITIONS

There are no set rates of pay in the British leathergoods industry. Payment is often negotiated between workers and employers. The starting wage for newly trained craft workers ranges from £100 to £200 a week. Saddlers are generally much better paid than other leather craft workers and may earn between £15,000 and £20,000 a year.

Self-employed people initially have to work long hours to establish a business, but if they can meet deadlines, they can be flexible in their working hours. For some products, demand may vary according to the time of year, and this means workers may be busier at certain times than others.

As with pay, holidays and hours of work vary greatly within the industry and are subject to negotiation. It is unusual for workers to contribute to a company pension scheme.

PROSPECTS

Those employed as craft workers may, with experience and further training, move on to positions as supervisors and managers. They may also move into design, buying, sales and marketing or administrative posts.

There is no promotion ladder for the self-employed. A rising income depends on hard work, business acumen, skill, and – to some extent – on luck.

RELATED OCCUPATIONS

Tailor/dressmaker, cutter, shoe repairer, fashion/clothing/footwear designer, bookbinder, upholsterer, sewing machinist, leather technologist.

FURTHER INFORMATION

BLC The Leather Technology Centre*, Leather Trade House, Kings Park Road, Moulton Park, Northampton NN3 1JD, 01604 494131

The British Leather Manufacturers' Research Association (BLMRA), Leather Trade House, Kings Park Road, Moulton Park, Northampton NN3 1JD, 01604 494131

The British School of Leather Technology*, Nene College, Moulton Park, Northampton NN2 7AL, 01604 735500

Cordwainers College*, 182 Mare Street, London E8 3RE, 0181 985 0273

Industrial Leathers Federation (address as for BLC)

Leather Industry Suppliers Associates (address as for BLC)

Leather Institute (address as for BLC)

Leather Producers' Association (address as for BLC)

National Union of the Knitwear, Footwear and Apparel Trades, 55 New Walk, Leicester LE1 7EB, 0116 255 6703

Rural Development Commission*, 141 Castle Street, Salisbury, Wiltshire SP1 3TP, 01722 336255

The Society of Dyers and Colourists*, Perkin House, PO Box 244, 82 Grattan Road, Bradford BD1 2JB, 01274 725138

Society of Leather Technologists and Chemists Ltd, 1 Edges Court, Moulton, Northampton NN3 7UJ, 01604 647318

Society of Master Saddlers*, Kettles Farm, Mickfield, Stowmarket, Suffolk IP14 6BY, 01449 711642

FURTHER READING

Relevant books are available from the Nene College bookshop.

In the careers library, classified under SAF.

1. TEXTILE TECHNICIAN CLCI:SAG
2. TEXTILE DYEING TECHNICIAN
CLCI:SAV/SAG
3. TEXTILE OPERATIVE CLCI:SAG

BACKGROUND INFORMATION

Technology has transformed the textile industry in recent years. Intricate and time-consuming jobs, such as splicing yarn or threading the loom, have been largely automated. In many modern textile mills, computers govern the pattern of warp and weft in weaving, the degree of twist and tension in spinning, and can translate a design on the drawing board into an electronic pattern-card controlling the looms or knitting machines.

The result of such changes is ever-increasing productivity from a decreasing workforce. Even so, textile manufacture remains one of the largest industries in Britain. It employs 160,000 people in firms that range from small businesses specializing in a single process, such as spinning or weaving, to big conglomerates dealing with every stage from raw fibre to finished garment.

The raw materials of the textile industry are natural fibres (such as cotton, wool, angora, silk or jute), man-made ones (such as nylon or viscose) and combinations (such as cotton/polyester). Textile mills turn these materials first into yarn, then into fabric. The products include lace, rope and carpets as well as woven and knitted cloth for fashions, furnishing or industrial uses.

The four main stages of textile production are: yarn preparation; yarn production; weaving or knitting; and dyeing and finishing. New bales of wool or cotton are first sorted and cleaned. Carding machines spread out and straighten the fibres to form a sliver, or soft rope. Man-made fibres may be added at this stage. The sliver is further drawn out, combed and twisted until it is fine and strong enough to be spun into yarn.

Weaving and knitting are the basic processes of cloth production. Cloth comes off the looms or knitting machines in continuous lengths. Some circular knitting machines produce garment shapes such as stockings in linked chains.

Bleaching, dyeing, printing and finishing impart colour, pattern and qualities such as water-resistance, fire-resistance or lustre to the cloth.

1. TEXTILE TECHNICIAN (SAG)

THE WORK

Textile technicians work in most sections of a mill – in production, in design and in dyeing, printing and finishing.

Technicians are responsible for the machinery. They make sure all the mechanical and electrical parts work efficiently, installing the equipment, stripping it down and servicing it regularly. Before each production run they set up the machines for the operatives. When something goes wrong, the technician finds and repairs the fault. Technicians learn to operate the computers that control the machines and some learn basic electronic engineering skills as well, to help them diagnose problems in the electronic components.

Each technician usually looks after the machinery for one particular process, such as spinning or weaving. Weaving technicians, or supervisory technicians, are in charge of the looms, which are large, complex and expensive. Warp (lengthwise) threads are raised and lowered in step as the weft (crosswise) yarn flashes to and fro between them. In the most modern looms, tension, pattern and speed are automatically controlled. With older machines the supervisory technician adjusts and checks the settings. Jacquard looms, which weave the design into the cloth (as opposed to having it printed) are governed by pattern cards. These control a 'harness' of wires, which raise and lower individual warp threads. In some firms a computer translates the design on the drawing board into an electronic pattern card. In others, technicians code the design onto paper pattern and fix up the intricate mesh of wires which forms the harness.

In addition to machine maintenance and adjustment, supervisory technicians are responsible for making sure that the work of their section goes on safely and efficiently. This involves showing the machine operators what to do, explaining safety procedures and making sure the area is kept tidy. They fill in timesheets and write reports.

WORK ENVIRONMENT

Conditions in textile mills vary widely, but modern factories are spacious and bright. In some sections the noise level may be high, and ear protectors are worn. Some of the processes make the atmosphere warm and humid. Dust is no longer a problem as it is virtually eliminated by dust extractors.

Much of the work involves standing, stretching and walking about.

SKILLS AND INTERESTS

Technicians should enjoy solving mechanical problems. Practical ability is essential. Setting up and adjusting machinery calls for accuracy in measurement and calculations. They should be interested in the rapidly changing technology of the textile industry.

Technicians should be able to work alone, but also to fit in well with others, for example, discussing problems with designers, managers or operatives. They need to express themselves clearly in speech and writing, to give instructions, keep records or write reports.

Technicians need good eyesight, with or without glasses, and, for most jobs, good colour vision.

ENTRY REQUIREMENTS

Candidates for technician training at 16 or 17 years usually require GCSEs/S grades (A-C/1-3) in maths, English and science, with an additional subject at grade D/4 or above, or a qualification of similar standard such as Intermediate GNVQ/GSVQ Level III in relevant subjects such as manufacturing or science. They are also required to show some practical/mechanical ability and for most jobs they need good colour vision. Other qualifications may be considered at the employers' discretion. People over 18 may also apply for technician training. Entry standards are similar, but most employers are willing to consider a fairly wide range of qualifications and experience provided the candidate is keen and able. Employers may set their own selection tests.

It is also possible to enter technician training after full-time study on the following courses:

BTEC National Diploma in Textiles. Entry requirements are three or four GCSEs/S grades (A-C/1-3).

BTEC National Certificate in Science (Textile Coloration). Entry requirements are three or four GCSEs/S grades (A-C/1-3). For SCOTVEC national certificate modules in textiles, no formal entry requirements are stated.

BTEC/SCOTVEC Higher Diploma in Textiles. Entry requirements are either: BTEC/SCOTVEC national certificate/diploma; or Advanced GNVQ/GSVQ Level III; or four GCSEs/S grades (A-C/1-3) including maths, English and science, plus one A-level/two H grades.

TRAINING

Opportunities are available via a Modern Apprenticeship. This lasts about three years. Apprentice and employer sign a training agreement, underwritten by the local TEC, to follow a training plan which combines work-based modules with off-the-job training at a college or training centre. This leads to nationally recognized qualifications and underpins the practical knowledge gained at work.

All apprentices work towards NVQ/SVQ Level 3 or above. During their training they may also take appropriate City and Guilds and/or BTEC/SCOTVEC national certificates in textiles. Apprentices who are already part-qualified on entry – for example, they may have begun a college course – are expected to cover the same training and achieve NVQ/SVQ Level 3 in a shorter time. The training programme for each entrant is modified to take into account existing qualifications and experience. There are similar arrangements for older entrants.

In the wool industry, apprenticeships are integrated into the Career Structure Scheme of the Confederation of British Wool Textiles. This is a training programme for technicians and supervisory technicians of any age. Trainees under 21 years follow the terms and conditions of a modern apprenticeship. The scheme combines structured experience on the job, under continuous monitoring, with part-time study for appropriate qualifications. These include NVQs/SVQs up to at least Level 3. In year two, trainees also take C&G exams or BTEC/SCOTVEC national certificate. In the third year, they may begin studying for BTEC/SCOTVEC Higher National Certificate in Textiles and/or supervisory studies leading to NVQ/SVQ Level 4 or NEBSM (National Examining Board for Supervisory Management) qualifications.

LATE ENTRY

Most candidates for technician training are aged 16-24 years. However, adults over this age are welcome to apply. They are selected by test and interview. Training takes account of previous qualifications and experience. People of any age can take NVQs/SVQs. Existing qualifications may afford exemption from part or all of the units at any level (Accreditation of Prior Learning).

OPPORTUNITIES

West Yorkshire, Lancashire, the Midlands and the borders of Scotland are the main areas of textile manufacture, with smaller centres all over the country. Many craft and operative jobs have disappeared. However, there is great demand for people with technical interests and abilities who want to learn about the new and developing technology of textile production.

The journal *Textile Month* carries job vacancies.

PAY AND CONDITIONS

Rates of pay differ from place to place, and are usually enhanced by shift allowances, overtime, etc. A 16 or 17-year-old trainee starts at about £80 to £90 a week. Salaries for fully trained and experienced technicians range from about £10,000 to £16,500 (£190 to £320 a week).

PROSPECTS

Promotion to senior technical positions can lead on to more specialized scientific and technical work in quality control or research and development.

Technicians who are following the Career Structure Scheme of the Confederation of British Wool Textiles, and experienced technicians who like to teach or take responsibility for others, may go on to supervisory grades. From there they may go into professional management, technical sales or business management. Study to at least BTEC/SCOTVEC higher national certificate level is required. It is possible to continue studying part-time for a BSc honours degree in textile technology.

These professional qualifications open up a wide range of opportunities in textile research, marketing and management both in the UK and abroad.

RELATED OCCUPATIONS

Textile operative, textile technologist, textile designer, textile dyeing technician, engineering technician, scientist/technician.

FURTHER INFORMATION

The Confederation of British Wool Textiles Ltd*, Merrydale House, Roydsdale Way, Bradford BD4 6SB, 01274 652207

The Cotton and Allied Textiles Industry Training Organization*, Reedham House, 31 King Street West, Manchester M3 2PF, 0161 832 9291

FURTHER READING

Leaflets/booklets are available from the addresses marked*.

Job Outlines – Textile Manufacture – COIC

In the careers library classified under SAG.

2. TEXTILE DYEING TECHNICIAN (SAV/SAG)

THE WORK

Dyeing technicians are responsible for dyeing materials to the shade the customer wants. Dyeing involves a series of chemical processes, and each type of material requires different treatment. Technicians decide which dyes and which machine processes to use. They work out the dye recipes for each shade of dye and calculate the machine settings that govern temperature, heating rate and timing. In some dyehouses this information is specified on a computer database.

Recipes are tested in laboratories before being applied in quantity. On the factory floor, dyeing technicians supervise operatives, who mix the dyes and feed the materials through the machines. They make sure the machinery is running smoothly, check the dyeing process at each stage, and take samples for testing.

Quality control is an important part of the job. Dyeing technicians are responsible for testing the treated materials for colour fastness, colour match, finishes, and so on, using a variety of physical and chemical tests. Computers are often used in colour matching.

Technicians keep records of orders, materials, recipes and processes. They may be involved in choosing and buying the dyestuffs. Assistants or trainees may work under their direction in the laboratory.

Most dyeing technicians specialize in dyeing, but their training includes printing, finishing and the preparation processes of bleaching and cleaning. They may be involved in these, for example by choosing pigments for printing or by making sure that the chemicals used are compatible with the dyestuffs.

WORK ENVIRONMENT

Bleaching, dyeing, printing and finishing may take place either in a general textile mill or in specialist bleach and dye works. In a textile mill, the dyehouse is usually set apart from the main shop floor. Conditions vary from place to place. Modern dyehouses are warm but spacious and airy, so the fumes and steam from the dyeing processes are well dispersed. Dyeing technicians spend a good deal of their time in laboratories or in the dyer's office partitioned off from the shop floor.

SKILLS AND INTERESTS

Dyeing technicians should be interested in science, particularly chemistry and physics, and should enjoy practical laboratory work. Mathematical ability and an interest in working with computers are desirable. Good colour vision is essential. A thorough, methodical approach is called for, checking and testing at every stage in the dyeing process.

Dyeing technicians should be prepared to take responsibility for planning and organizing their own and other people's work, for making decisions and supervising staff.

ENTRY REQUIREMENTS
Please see article 1: TEXTILE TECHNICIAN. Good colour vision is essential for work in dyeing.

TRAINING

Coloration and Finishing is one of the programmes available under a Modern Apprenticeship in the textile industry. Apprentices gain practical experience of all processes in dyeing and finishing. This is combined with off-the-job study and leads to NVQ/SVQ Level 3. They may also take a BTEC/SCOTVEC national certificate in textile coloration in the second year. Students are encouraged to begin studying for Higher National Certificate in Science (Textile Coloration) during the third year of the Apprenticeship, and to continue with this during subsequent training. Some also take courses in supervisory studies, leading to NVQ/SVQ Level 4 and/or NEBSM qualifications. The higher national certificate includes advanced study of dyeing, printing and finishing, together with applied science, textile and fibre technology, machine technology, computing and management studies. This can lead on to part-time courses for associateship of the Society of Dyers and Colourists, the professional qualification granting the title chartered colourist. Applicants who fall outside the age limits for apprenticeships follow a similar training plan. The programme can be modified to take account of existing qualifications and experience.

LATE ENTRY

There is no upper age limit. Adults for whom a full NVQ/ SVQ or BTEC/SCOTVEC course would be inappropriate may take single units from the programme, or short college courses complementing intensive training at work. Mature applicants with alternative qualifications or experience may be considered for full-time courses at the discretion of the college.

OPPORTUNITIES

West Yorkshire, Lancashire, the Midlands and the Scottish Borders are the main areas of textile production, with smaller centres elsewhere. Dyeing technicians work either in textile mills or in specialist dye works.

PAY AND CONDITIONS

Technicians are usually salaried, paid monthly on rates agreed by local negotiation. Salaries vary widely, from about £10,000 to about £17,000.

Hours vary from factory to factory. Some run a 24-hour three-shift system; others work 35 to 40 hours, daytime only.

PROSPECTS

Promotion to senior posts can lead to work in research and development, technical or general management, or technical sales. Associates of the Society of Dyers and Colourists find a wide range of career prospects in management, marketing, research and development, both in Britain and abroad. Some transfer from the textile industry to other areas of colour science and technology, such as the manufacture of dyes and pigments or the coloration of paper, plastics, leather, etc. Demand for dyeing technicians from the trainee level upwards is high and increasing.

RELATED OCCUPATIONS

Textile technician, printing technician, scientist/technician, leather technologist, paint technologist, materials scientist/ technologist.

FURTHER INFORMATION

Confederation of British Wool Textiles Limited*, Merrydale House, Roydsdale Way, Bradford BD4 6SB, 01274 652207

Cotton and Allied Textile Industry Training Organization*, Reedham House, 31 King Street West, Manchester M3 2PF, 0161 832 9291

Society of Dyers and Colourists*, Perkin House, PO Box 244, 82 Grattan Road, Bradford, West Yorkshire BD1 2JB, 01274 725138

FURTHER READING

Leaflets/booklets are available from the addresses marked*.

In the careers library classified under SAG/SAV.

3. TEXTILE OPERATIVE (SAG)

THE WORK

Textile operatives work in every section of a textile mill. Some work in the warehouse on loading, unloading, packing and dispatch. Others run the machines that turn raw fibre into yarn or yarn into fabric. Their jobs include scouring, carding, combing, spinning, weaving, knitting, bleaching and dyehouse work.

Operatives engaged in any of these processes start the machine and watch the passage of the material through it. They look out for faults that could indicate breakages or mechanical failure and report these to a technician. On some spinning or weaving machines broken threads have to be repaired by the operative, who finds the broken ends and joins them together. On modern machines the yarn is automatically mended. Weavers check cloth as it comes off the loom and mark any flaws for the attention of the mender. Badly damaged sections are removed. Operatives are always moving along the rows of machinery watching for problems. They may also replace empty bobbins and take off the cones of spun yarn or the completed lengths of cloth. A knitting operative may control a bank of high-precision machines; a weaver attends to several looms.

Operatives in the dyehouse load the grey (untreated) cloth onto rollers and start the machine that feeds it through vats of dye and fixative, through the drying chambers or over the stenter to stretch it to shape. They make sure it runs smoothly and evenly, and watch for any problems which need the attention of a technician. In between batches they clean the dye off the rollers.

Operatives are responsible for keeping their work area as tidy as possible. As with any machine work, they need to pay attention to safety procedures in handling the machines or moving between them.

WORK ENVIRONMENT

Conditions in textile mills vary widely, but modern factories are spacious and bright. In some sections, the noise level may be high and ear protectors are worn.

Some processes, such as scouring, make the atmosphere warm and humid. Dust is no longer a problem as it is virtually eliminated by dust extractors.

Operatives spend much of the day on their feet. Lifting, bending and stretching are unavoidable.

SKILLS AND INTERESTS

Textile operatives should enjoy practical work using machines. Many operative jobs require nimble fingers and good eyesight (with or without glasses) and, in some cases, good colour vision. They need to remain alert and observant, and be able to concentrate while carrying out routine tasks. They should be reliable and conscientious workers.

ENTRY REQUIREMENTS

There are no particular academic requirements. Some employers test eyesight and colour vision before entry.

TRAINING

Training is mainly on the job but may include part-time attendance at a training centre or college. Trainees take NVQs/SVQs at Levels 1 and 2. They follow one of 13 routes, depending on which job they do. Each route consists of several units covering skills used at each stage of the production process. For example, a weaver learns beaming, card cutting, spool-setting, warping and weaving. Fibre preparation units include blending, carding and combing.

Dyehouse operatives learn colour mixing, line systems, spray systems and vessel systems. Some companies train operatives in more than one job. Some jobs, such as operating a bank of knitting machines, are multiskilled in themselves.

LATE ENTRY

There are no upper age limits. Older people, job changers and returners may enter the work. Special training and re-training courses may be arranged for them by the company.

OPPORTUNITIES

West Yorkshire, Lancashire, the Midlands and the Scottish Borders are the main areas of textile manufacture, but there are smaller centres elsewhere.

Many older mills have been closed and many workers have been made redundant in recent years. However, there is now a shortage of people skilled in using modern equipment, and new entrants at all levels are in demand.

PAY AND CONDITIONS

Wage rates are fixed by negotiation with local unions and differ from place to place. A 16-year-old trainee might expect to start at about £90 to £95 a week. Basic wages for those aged 18 years or over range from £127 to £163. This would be the basic minimum, invariably boosted by overtime, shift allowance, bonus schemes, etc.

Hours vary. Some factories work round the clock in three eight-hour shifts. Others work a 37 to 40 hour week. Overtime and part-time work are often available.

PROSPECTS

Promotion is initially to supervisor or instructor, then section management, sales or administration. It is usually an advantage for people seeking promotion to gain BTEC/SCOTVEC qualifications. These can lead eventually to positions in management.

RELATED OCCUPATIONS

Production worker, textile technician, textile dyeing technician, machine printer, warehouse worker, sewing machinist.

FURTHER INFORMATION

Confederation of British Wool Textiles Ltd*, Merrydale House, Roydsdale Way, Bradford BD4 6SB, 01274 652207

Cotton and Allied Textile Industry Training Organization*, Reedham House, 31 King Street West, Manchester M3 2PF, 0161 832 9291

FURTHER READING

Leaflets/booklets are available from the addresses marked*.

Job Outlines – Textile Manufacture – COIC

In the careers library, classified under SAG.

CLOTHING: SAH

1. TAILOR/DRESSMAKER CLCI:SAH
2. PATTERN CUTTER/GRADER CLCI:SAH
3. SPREADER/CUTTER CLCI:SAH
4. SEWING MACHINIST CLCI:SAH
5. CLOTHING PRESSER CLCI:SAH

BACKGROUND INFORMATION

Clothing is one of the United Kingdom's largest manufacturing industries, with over 175,000 employees. Companies usually specialize in making certain types of garments, for example rainwear or sportswear, in a range of styles and fabrics.

Wholesale manufacturing is the largest sector, producing off-the-peg clothes for high street stores and mail order, and special clothing for specific companies. Most modern factories are highly automated and often use computers to help control the work and systems. Some people, however, still prefer to buy individually made clothes. Their needs are catered for by haute couture houses, tailors and dressmakers. Haute couture houses make designer garments, available from high-class fashion houses at very high prices. Only one or two copies of each garment are made, almost entirely by hand. Individual clothes are made-to-order for customers by bespoke tailors and dressmakers.

In every case, the production cycle begins with design followed by the creation of a pattern, fabric cutting, sewing, pressing and checking for quality before despatch. With the increase of working in teams, checking for quality is now more often done by workers at each stage in the production process rather than by specialist garment examiners or quality controllers.

Intense competition from abroad and new technology are affecting the whole industry, demanding increased professionalism from management and a more highly skilled and adaptable workforce.

1. TAILOR/DRESSMAKER (SAH)

THE WORK

Bespoke tailors make made-to-measure suits and heavy outer clothes; dressmakers make dresses and other light clothing. Tailoring and dressmaking involve very similar techniques.

In a small firm the tailor/dressmaker is responsible for the garment from commissioning to collection; in a larger firm some of the tasks may be shared with others.

Tailors/dressmakers firstly take the customer's measurements and advise on fabric and style. When the fabric is selected they quote a price for the work, taking into account the time involved and the cost and quantity of the material. If the quote is accepted, the measurements are converted into a cardboard or paper pattern, which the tailor/dressmaker cuts round on the cloth, also cutting linings, canvas interlinings and tapes as required. The cardboard pattern can be stored and used again for the same customer. Occasionally, the pattern may be drawn straight on the cloth. Cutting is delicate work, demanding a high level of accuracy; allowances have to be made for fitting ease and possible alterations in the future. Wastage must be kept to a minimum.

After cutting, the tailor/dressmaker carefully sews the garment together. Various stitches are used, to hold the garment firm or to produce special effects such as making a collar lie neatly. A sewing machine may be used on long seams, but hand sewing is used wherever it produces a better finish.

The tailor/dressmaker presses each part of the garment as it is completed using an iron known as a goose. The customer may be fitted with the garment on two or three occasions, and it is altered where necessary. Bodies are not symmetrical; left and right sides can differ markedly. A skilful tailor or dressmaker can disguise shoulders that are different heights, or a slightly curved spine.

Tailors/dressmakers must keep up with changing fashions and must be aware of new techniques and materials. Each customer has different needs and the garments have differing wear and tear; a sports jacket may be worn daily, for example, while an evening dress or kilt may be used once a year.

It is possible to specialize in particular garments. Dressmakers may concentrate on children's clothes or wedding dresses, while tailors may specialize, for instance in military uniforms.

WORK ENVIRONMENT

Many firms are based in town-centre premises comprising a small shop with workroom attached. Some clothing factories have small tailoring and dressmaking sections, while many people work in workrooms in their homes. Accommodation is generally well-lit and clean.

SKILLS AND INTERESTS

Tailors and dressmakers need an aptitude for, and interest in, sewing, and the ability to concentrate on fine work for long periods. They should enjoy seeing a task through from the beginning to end, and have an interest in fashion and design. Good eyesight and good colour vision are essential. Numerical ability is useful for doing calculations and measurements, and good communication skills are required to deal effectively with clients and colleagues.

Self-employed tailors and dressmakers require good business skills. They need to monitor buying and spending, pricing their work realistically.

ENTRY REQUIREMENTS

Modern Apprenticeships are available, though some employers may still offer a traditional apprenticeship. No formal educational qualifications are stipulated, but some firms prefer candidates with GCSEs/S grades (A-C/1-3) in maths and English.

Personal aptitudes are more important than academic achievement.

TRAINING

A Modern Apprenticeship is not time-based, relating instead to the time it takes the individual trainee to acquire competences, but it is expected to take two to three years as against the four to five years of a traditional apprenticeship. Modern Apprenticeships lead to an NVQ/SVQ in Handcraft Tailoring at Level 3. On-the-job instruction by experienced tailors/dressmakers and work experience is combined with day/block release or evening study at local colleges for underpinning knowledge. With traditional apprenticeships, this study would be for City and Guilds 4600 craft certificates.

The City and Guilds 4600 certificates are available through full-time study at a few centres around the country. Some people take these courses as a pre-entry qualification before applying to an employer.

LATE ENTRY

Some colleges are making increasing provision for mature students. It is also possible to apply direct to employers who may either train or re-train applicants, as required. The NVQ/SVQ system may allow individuals with experience in the industry to be trained and assessed for Level 3 qualifications.

OPPORTUNITIES

There will always be a demand for made-to-measure garments from people who do not conform to standard sizes or who value hand-crafted, well-fitting clothes. Most large bespoke tailoring houses are in London, but openings also occur with shops and factories throughout the country. Dressmakers work for fashion retailers or clothing manufacturers nationwide. Opportunities for self-employment are particularly good, both for dressmakers and for tailors. Many firms employ outworkers, who visit the firm to collect bundles of work and are paid as pieceworkers.

Several employment agencies in the West End of London specialize in tailoring and dressmaking vacancies. Vacancies may also be found in *Drapers Record* – a weekly publication.

PAY AND CONDITIONS

Workers over 18 years earn about £110 a week or over. Experienced tailors and dressmakers are paid according to their skill, experience and responsibility. Many are self-employed, with earnings linked directly to business prosperity.

Waged tailors and dressmakers work a standard 39-hour, five-day week. Those employed in retail outlets may work Saturdays. Extra hours are common, bringing in overtime payments or enhancing piecework productivity. Self-employed tailors and dressmakers can arrange hours to suit themselves and their customers, and can put in a lot of hours if demand warrants it.

PROSPECTS

Tailors and dressmakers may progress to become supervisors in charge of a workroom, or may enter self-employment with their own small shop. Some tailors/dressmakers specialize in cutting and move into larger-scale production, while others develop the selling side and spend more time dealing with customers. There is a wide range of courses to prepare staff for management positions; details can be obtained from the CAPITB. There are a few opportunities for teaching in colleges of further education.

RELATED OCCUPATIONS, FURTHER INFORMATION AND READING

Please see article 5. CLOTHING PRESSER.

2. PATTERN CUTTER/GRADER (SAH)

THE WORK

Pattern cutters make the patterns that enable a designer's sketch to be made into a garment. Pattern graders work from a basic size pattern and create the patterns needed for a range of garment sizes. Jobs vary from company to company. In small companies the designer may also be responsible for pattern cutting and grading. In larger companies there are specialist pattern cutters and/or graders.

There are two ways of making patterns; the method used depends on the style of garment concerned.

Flat pattern cutting. The pattern cutter works from the designer's sketches or working drawings and makes a pattern for each part of a garment by creating a block (a cardboard pattern piece). Some pattern cutters create their own blocks, while some companies have their own basic blocks and the pattern cutter adapts the shape of these for the new garment. Increasingly, computers are used to help in designing garments and creating patterns.

Modelling onto a dummy. Working from the designer's drawings the pattern cutter drapes and pins fabric onto a dummy and fits it in accordance with the drawings. The fabric is then cut and the resultant pattern shape or toile is pinned to paper which is cut out to form the pattern shape.

With both processes, the pattern cutter produces patterns as near as possible to the designer's sketches, while taking into account the type of fabric to be used and the demands of the manufacturing process. When the pattern has been completed, it goes to a sample machinist who produces a sample garment. When the designer and pattern cutter inspect the sample garment they may decide on slight alterations before the final patterns are made.

Pattern grading has become increasingly computerized. The pattern grader pastes a standard size 12 pattern onto a computerized digitizing table and assigns rule numbers. There are different rules for different garments. The grader feeds the rule numbers into the computer with a cursor pen and the computer automatically grades the pattern into different sizes and plots the patterns full-size onto paper. Some companies do not use computers for pattern grading, working instead from size charts and using conventional drafting skills to draw up the patterns.

WORK ENVIRONMENT

Pattern cutters' and pattern graders' work environment can vary considerably from employer to employer. Some work in a factory, sharing their work space with others involved in garment manufacture. Others work with clothing designers in studios. Work can involve long periods sitting or standing, with some bending.

SKILLS AND INTERESTS

Pattern cutters/graders should be interested in fashion if they are to appreciate what their designers are aiming for.

Numerical ability is essential for measurement and calculation. It is useful if pattern cutters and graders have some technical drawing skill, both for understanding drawings and for adapting existing blocks. Aptitude for working with computers is very helpful. Accuracy and a meticulous approach are important as patterns must be exact. An eye for proportion and shape are necessary, as is good manual dexterity.

Their work demands patience but pattern cutters and graders often work to deadlines. They must be able to work under this pressure while maintaining accuracy and quality of work.

Pattern cutters and graders should be able to work as part

of a team. Good communication skills are needed, as they must liaise with designers and sample machinists.

ENTRY REQUIREMENTS

Most entrants come into these jobs after pre-entry training, usually full-time, on a course leading to one of the qualifications listed below. These include pattern cutting and grading within general clothing manufacture skills and knowledge. However, by selection of units, the SCOTVEC courses mentioned below can be tailored specifically towards pattern cutting and grading. Increasingly, employers look for design expertise as well.

City and Guilds (C&G) 4600 Clothing Craft Certificate. No specific qualifications are required for entry but applicants should have practical ability and numerical skills.

London College of Fashion Foundation Course in Clothing. No specific qualifications are required.

London College of Fashion Certificate in Clothing Production. Applicants must be at least 21 and have a minimum of four GCSEs/S grades (A-C/1-3), including English.

BTEC National Diploma in Clothing. Requires either four GCSEs/S grades (A-C/1-3), or a relevant BTEC first award.

SCOTVEC National Certificates in Fashion Technology; Clothing Technology; and Clothing Studies. No particular qualifications are required, but an interest in this type of work is essential.

BTEC Higher National Diploma in Clothing. Requires one A level/two H grades and four GCSEs/S grades (A-C/1-3), or, more usually a BTEC National Diploma in Clothing.

SCOTVEC Higher National Diploma in Fashion Technology; Clothing Technology. Applicants should have evidence of having achieved national certificate modules in garment making.

Degree in Clothing Studies. Entry is with either two A levels/three H grades and three GCSEs/S grades (A-C/1-3) including English, maths and a science subject, or a relevant BTEC national diploma.

Some fashion design courses include pattern making and grading skills. Entry requirements range from having a good portfolio of drawings and designs, to those required for entry to degree courses.

A Modern Apprenticeship in Product Development leading to at least an NVQ/SVQ Level 3 may be an alternative route into this work. Most employers would look for GCSEs/S grades (A-C/1-3) in maths, English and art as entry qualification.

TRAINING

Pre-entry

C&G 4600 Clothing Craft Certificate (two years full-time) is offered at a number of centres in England.

London College of Fashion Foundation Course in Clothing (one year full-time) prepares students for entry to a national diploma course in, for example, clothing or fashion. It includes the possibility of taking C&G 4600 Clothing Craft Certificate.

London College of Fashion Certificate in Clothing Production (one year full-time) concentrates on the design, cutting and making of sample garments.

BTEC National Diploma in Clothing (two years full-time) is offered at eight centres in England.

SCOTVEC National Certificates in Fashion Technology;

Clothing Technology (one year full-time) are offered at Cardonald College, while the SCOTVEC National Certificate in Clothing Studies (one year full-time) is run by Motherwell College.

BTEC Higher National Diploma in Clothing (two years full-time) is run at Handsworth College, Birmingham, Leeds College of Art and Design, Kent Institute of Art and Design, City of Liverpool Community College, and Manchester Metropolitan University.

SCOTVEC Higher National Diplomas in Fashion Technology; Clothing Technology (two years full-time) are run at Cardonald College.

Degrees in Clothing Studies are offered at London College of Fashion and Heriot-Watt University (four years sandwich), Manchester Metropolitan University, and Nottingham Trent University (both three years full-time).

On entry

Pattern cutters and graders receive further training from experienced staff. There are a number of courses they may attend on a day release or evening basis to develop their skills. Courses are of varying length and include C&G 4600 pattern cutting stages 1, 2 and 3 and courses leading to individual college's certificates or diplomas. In Scotland, SCOTVEC national certificate modules in clothing are offered by Cardonald College, Motherwell College, and North Glasgow College.

After entry, pattern cutter/graders may be assessed on relevant units of NVQ/SVQ in Product Development at Level 3.

LATE ENTRY

There is no upper age limit for entry to pattern cutting and grading. Adults may find that they can be accepted for courses described in ENTRY REQUIREMENTS without the usual academic entry requirements. Some people move into these jobs from work in the industry as machinists or spreaders/cutters and are given additional training. They may be assessed on units of NVQ/SVQ in Product Development at Level 3.

Access courses may be available in some areas to prepare adults for entry to higher national diploma and degree courses in clothing studies.

OPPORTUNITIES

Pattern cutters and pattern graders may work for individual designers, for large manufacturers, for specialist pattern cutting and/or pattern grading firms, or they may work on a freelance basis. Pattern graders have first had experience of pattern cutting. Most employers require both pattern-making and grading skills.

The clothing manufacturing industry is large, with garment manufacturers in many towns and cities. The industry has, however, decreased in size over the past few years and computerization has speeded up much pattern cutting and grading. In spite of this, there is a shortage of skilled pattern cutters and graders. Vacancies are advertised in periodicals, including *Drapers' Record, Fashion Weekly* and *Manufacturing Clothier.*

PAY AND CONDITIONS

There are no set salary scales for pattern cutters and pattern graders, with individual employers paying their own rate. Some pay annual salaries, while others pay on a piecework basis. Earnings vary tremendously and range from £6,000 to £20,000.

Working hours are usually between 37 and 39 a week, Monday to Friday. Many firms in the clothing industry finish early on Friday afternoons. Part-time work is possible. Overtime may be worked.

PROSPECTS

Pattern cutters and pattern graders may seek to improve their situation by moving from one employer to another. They may become head pattern cutters and head pattern graders, either within their employing organization or by moving to another employer. Although difficult to achieve, a few become clothing designers, particularly if their original training specialized in design.

The clothing industry is important world-wide and there are openings for trained pattern cutters and pattern graders overseas.

There are opportunities for pattern cutters and graders to become self-employed and work on a freelance basis.

RELATED OCCUPATIONS, FURTHER INFORMATION AND READING

Please see article 5. CLOTHING PRESSER.

3. SPREADER/CUTTER (SAH)

THE WORK

The spreader or cutter checks the cloth for flaws – it must be smooth and free of wrinkles, and any patterns or other features must match up when it is sewn together. This laying-up process can be done manually by two people, or by machine. The next step is to put a lay-plan on the cloth, sometimes using tailors' chalk or spray paint. The lay-plan is worked out by a technician, sometimes using a computer. The fabric is then ready for cutting, either by hand, machine or dies.

Hand cutting is done using shears, an electric knife, or a vertical band knife. Cutters must ensure that the bottom pieces of the lay remain in unison with the top ones to avoid distortions in shape, and must try to minimize fabric wastage.

Die-cutting is done by machine. A press, whose blades have been set according to the lay-plan, is lowered on to the fabric, cutting the pattern shape right through the lay. This process is very accurate but uses more fabric than does cutting by hand. It is often used when large numbers of identical garments are being made, or for cutting linings and trimmings where the fabric is less expensive. New computer-controlled die-cutting machines are gradually being introduced, capable of cutting up to 250 inches per minute, depending on the depth of the lay.

Laser cutting. With this, computer images are used to operate the laser cutter with great accuracy.

After cutting, the cloth is made into bundles containing everything necessary to make up a given number of a particular garment.

WORK ENVIRONMENT

Cutting rooms are generally clean and well-lit. There may be some dust in the air, and it can be noisy at times. Cutters must be safety-conscious, as the cutting edges are very sharp; chain mail gloves are worn as protection for band knife cutting.

Cutters spend much of the day standing.

SKILLS AND INTERESTS

Cutters need to be physically fit, able to bend over tables and lift heavy bales of cloth. Good eyesight and perfect colour vision are important, and it is useful to be able to visualize the finished garment so as to minimize marking-up errors. Some numerical ability is required.

The work demands a methodical and meticulous approach; mistakes can rarely be rectified, so accuracy is very important. Cutters should be able to cope with pressure, be decisive and able to rely on their own judgement – cutting an expensive pile of cloth is a big responsibility. Cutters work directly with the designers and sometimes technicians, trainees and other assistants, so ability to work well in a team is important. An interest in fashion is useful cutters must keep up with new styles, ideas and techniques.

ENTRY REQUIREMENTS

No educational qualifications are necessary, but a good standard of secondary education is expected. Some GCSE/S grade qualifications are an advantage; maths is particularly useful.

TRAINING

Training is largely given on the job. Some employers offer the HEADstart training programme with Kingscourt training organization (details from local careers offices or from Kingscourt). This leads to an NVQ/SVQ in Manufacturing Products from Textiles at Level 2.

Trainees experience a variety of work before specializing in pressing.

Trainees learn about: different types of fabric and all the flaws which may be found; how to interpret written and spoken instructions; correlation of pattern parts with the garment sample; using the laying-in instructions on a pattern; cutting procedures and routine maintenance of cutting tools; spreading fabrics by hand and machine; lay planning; pattern grading; marker making; and advanced computerized cutting-room methods.

LATE ENTRY

As the industry comes out of recession and with the challenge of new technology, employers are increasingly willing to take on adults with experience in other industries or returners. Training is mainly on the job, and usually shorter than for youth entrants. Adults can also be assessed for NVQ/SVQ and previous experience may be taken into account.

OPPORTUNITIES

Garment manufacturers are found in towns throughout the country, producing a great variety of clothes from sober suits to high fashion. Firms vary greatly in size and in the techniques and manufacturing equipment used. Some employment is part-time.

PAY AND CONDITIONS

Please see article 4. SEWING MACHINIST.

Experienced cutters are paid according to their skill and the level of responsibility in their job.

PROSPECTS

There is no fixed promotion pattern. It is also possible to move into haute couture, wholesale couture or sales work, or become a tailor or dressmaker.

RELATED OCCUPATIONS, FURTHER INFORMATION AND READING

Please see article 5. CLOTHING PRESSER.

4. SEWING MACHINIST (SAH)

THE WORK

Machinists guide fabric through a sewing machine. Different machines do different jobs: lockstitch for plain seams; overlocking for neatening and stretching a seam with extra thread; button-holing; lace attaching; etc.

Traditionally, machinists were trained to use one particular machine. By sewing one type of seam over and over again, they could build up their speed and skill. Now, however, it is increasingly common for machinists to work together in teams to produce a whole garment – individuals carry out several operations, and this makes the work more interesting.

Sample machinists make up a few examples of every new style, to show to potential buyers.

WORK ENVIRONMENT

Clothing firms range in size from small businesses with half a dozen people in a workshop, to large factories where there may be up to 500 machinists. However, factories tend to be split into small units working with individual unit supervisors.

People with chest complaints may have to wear face masks as dust and fluff are sometimes a problem. Most, though not all machinists, work sitting down. The work is often done by artificial light.

SKILLS AND INTERESTS

Machinists need good eyesight, manual dexterity, a liking for fine, close work and the ability to concentrate on a repetitive job for hours at a time.

It is important to be able to work quickly, neatly and accurately. Nimble fingers are required for tasks like changing needles and cleaning machines, as well as for guiding fabric through the machine.

An interest in fashion and design is useful for visualizing the appearance of the completed garment. An eye for colour is useful for matching pieces together.

Machinists need to be able to get on with colleagues and work as part of a team.

ENTRY REQUIREMENTS

No formal entry qualifications are required. Most companies give applicants a practical aptitude test, plus a medical which includes an eyesight test.

A qualification awarded by Qualifications for Industry, 'Introductory Industrial Stitching', can be taken by pupils at school or students in further education. It accredits the basic skills needed for entry to the industry.

TRAINING

Training is largely given on the job. Some employers offer the HEADstart training programme with Kingscourt training organization (details from local careers offices or from Kingscourt). This leads to an NVQ/SVQ in Manufacturing Products from Textiles at Level 2.

Trainees experience a variety of work before specializing in machining. During the scheme, trainees have approximately 20 weeks' off-the-job training, usually on the employer's premises.

Most companies have a training section, where new machinists spend the first few weeks learning to operate a machine. While training, they receive a basic weekly wage. It takes about three weeks to become skilled enough to go out onto the factory floor. Re-training goes on constantly, as new products are introduced. Keen workers with aptitude can train to operate several different machines, so increasing their choice of jobs.

LATE ENTRY

As the industry comes out of recession and with the challenge of new technology, employers are increasingly willing to take on adults with experience in other industries or returners.

Adult entrants follow the training described above. Employers normally offer a few weeks' training or re-training to those who have experience working with other companies or machines, or who have taken the City and Guilds Certificate, so that machinists become familiar with the firm's machines and procedures.

Adults can also be assessed for NVQ/SVQ and previous experience may be taken into account.

There may be specific training opportunities directed at adults available in some areas for this type of work. Candidates may have to satisfy certain conditions to be eligible. Contact your local Jobcentre, careers office or TEC/LEC for details.

OPPORTUNITIES

There are plenty of vacancies for skilled or trainee machinists in all areas. The biggest employer is the clothing industry but machinists also work in other parts of the textile industry, for example making household goods such as bed-linen or curtains, or special-purpose items like sails and tents. They work in the furniture industry on upholstery, and even in the motor car industry making seat covers.

Many machinists work as outworkers.

PAY AND CONDITIONS

An experienced person's minimum rate is £2.78 an hour. Many machinists get bonuses or sew for piece-rates. The more practised and skilled they become, the more they can earn.

A 39-hour week is normal. Some factories work shifts and there are often opportunities for part-time work.

PROSPECTS

Experienced machinists can become supervisors in charge of a unit of up to 30 workers. Supervisors are responsible for keeping the unit supplied with work, for monitoring output and doing an initial check on the work as it comes in. Alternatively, machinists could turn to garment examining, packing or sample-room machining. Experienced machinists could also become instructors or go into quality control. Instructors are responsible for training new machinists, and for re-training existing workers in new methods, or when a style is changed.

RELATED OCCUPATIONS, FURTHER INFORMATION AND READING

Please see article 5. CLOTHING PRESSER.

5. CLOTHING PRESSER (SAH)

THE WORK

Pressers use steam, pressure and temperature to press clothes. Pressing of separate pieces of garments may be done during production before they are made up, known as underpressing. Pressing also takes place at the end of production, when the garments are given a final pressing before they are put on sale.

Different machines and methods of pressing are used depending on the type of garment and the fabric concerned. Pressers have to follow set procedures for all pressing work, whatever the machinery used.

A common type of pressing involves a hand iron and ironing table/board. The hand iron is fed with steam from a central boiler, and the board has a vacuum on it. The presser places the iron onto the garment and steam is drawn through the cloth, which presses and dries the garment, while preventing the board from becoming wet. The irons have to be set for temperature and steam control according to the fabric concerned and may be fitted with a Teflon shoe to protect the garment.

Some pressers use a steam dolly, which looks like a tailor's dummy. The presser puts a garment such as a skirt or shirt on the press and steam is blown from inside the shape to get rid of creases.

Garments such as trousers are pressed on a flat press, where the presser lowers a large press onto the whole garment, which has been laid on a flat surface.

Some pressing is automatic with sophisticated machinery, often computer controlled. With tunnel presses and carousel presses, pressers carefully hang garments onto shaped supports, which are then fed into the machine and then are steam-pressed automatically.

Pressers working manually have to work quickly, while those on automatic machines have to work to the speed of the machine.

In small factories, pressing may be just part of a job, with some time spent on machine sewing. In larger factories it is usual for people to specialize in pressing – some use one machine; others use different pressing processes.

WORK ENVIRONMENT

Clothing pressers work in factories. Conditions in clothing factories vary. Some are light and spacious, with extractor systems to keep the working temperature reasonable and prevent an uncomfortable build-up of steam; others can be cramped and hot.

Pressing involves standing all day, with some bending.

SKILLS AND INTERESTS

Clothing pressers should be interested in practical work. Some pressing operations, such as hand ironing, require manual dexterity.

There are set procedures to follow in pressing different types of garment to produce the best finish in the quickest time. Pressers need to be methodical and able to follow those set procedures. Pressing is done to shape a garment or to remove creases. Speed of work is important. Pressers should be able to work quickly while maintaining good quality work.

Pressers should be able to concentrate and work consistently at what tends to be repetitive work. An eye for detail is required.

Pressers should be flexible and prepared to operate different types of machinery depending on the type of garment that is being produced and the fabric concerned. They need also to be willing to learn the operation of new pressing machines which may be introduced.

Some pressing work is energetic. It is important for pressers to like active work and to have the stamina to cope with it.

ENTRY REQUIREMENTS

No formal academic qualifications are required for entry to pressing, although an aptitude for practical subjects is helpful. Employers are concerned with personal qualities, seeking reliable, conscientious workers who can follow instructions.

Some employers give applicants a practical test. Some arrange for a medical examination to make sure that applicants are fit for the work.

TRAINING

Training is largely on the job. This may lead to an NVQ/SVQ in Manufacturing Products from Textiles at Level 1. Trainees experience a variety of work before specializing in pressing.

On starting work all pressers are trained by an instructor. They may begin by practising on training garments, then on reject garments, before progressing to full-quality garments. It can take several weeks to become efficient on one type of pressing operation, but years to gain full proficiency and experience on a range of pressing operations.

As new pressing machines are introduced into the factory, pressers are trained in their use by an instructor.

LATE ENTRY

There is no upper age limit for entry to pressing. As the industry comes out of recession and with the challenge of new technology, employers are increasingly willing to take on adults with experience in other industries or returners. Training is mainly on the job and usually shorter than for youth entrants. Adults can also be assessed for NVQ/SVQ and previous experience may be taken into account.

There may be specific training opportunities directed at adults available in some areas for this type of work. Candidates may have to satisfy certain conditions to be eligible. Contact your local Jobcentre, careers office or TEC/LEC for details.

OPPORTUNITIES

There are more than 4,000 clothing factories throughout the UK making all kinds of clothing – skirts, dresses, sweaters, jeans, sports wear, men's and boys' clothes, overalls, uniforms, etc. Most of them employ pressers. The clothing industry has been decreasing in size over the past few years, however, with a consequent reduction in the number of pressers employed.

Opportunities may be available via training schemes for young people. Contact your local careers office, TEC/LEC for details.

Vacancies for pressers may be advertised in *Drapers Record*, *Manufacturing Clothier*, or local newspapers. Those seeking work as a presser should contact local clothing manufacturers to ask about vacancies.

PAY AND CONDITIONS

There are no national pay scales for pressers. Most pressers are paid on a piecework basis. Trained pressers may receive between £120 and £240 a week. Working hours vary between 37½ and 39 a week, Monday to Friday. Many firms finish early on a Friday afternoon. Some part-time work is available. Overtime is common.

PROSPECTS

Pressers may be promoted to supervisor and be responsible for a number of pressers – allocating their work, monitoring output, and checking the quality of work.

It may be possible to become an instructor, responsible for training new staff and re-training existing staff on new presses that are introduced into the factory.

Promotion to supervisor or instructor is usually internal. Most companies prefer to promote internally rather than bring in supervisors from outside the firm.

The clothing industry is world-wide. Pressers who move abroad may find pressing work in any one of a number of countries.

RELATED OCCUPATIONS

Clothing alteration hand, textile operative, packer, theatre costume maker, window dresser.

FURTHER INFORMATION

CAPITB Trust*, 80 Richardshaw Lane, Pudsey, Leeds LS28 6BN, 0113 239 3355
Qualifications for Industry (address as for CAPITB).

FURTHER READING

Leaflets/booklets are available from the address marked*.
Working in Fashion – COIC
In the careers library classified under SAH.

1. CABINET MAKER CLCI:SAJ
2. UPHOLSTERER CLCI:SAJ
3. FRENCH POLISHER CLCI:SAJ

BACKGROUND INFORMATION

Making fine furniture by hand and restoring furniture requires three main skills: cabinet making, upholstery and French polishing. Many of these craftspeople work on their own or with one or two other craftspeople, but their skills are also needed by furniture manufacturers.

1. CABINET MAKER (SAJ)

THE WORK

Cabinet makers are craftsmen/women who make fine furniture mainly by hand. In addition to making cabinets, which are pieces of furniture containing shelves, drawers or cupboards used for storage or display, they may also make other items such as chairs and tables. Cabinet makers usually specialize in traditional designs; others produce furniture, sometimes one-off pieces, to their own designs and are often called designer/makers. Cabinet makers may also restore damaged furniture.

The first stage in their work is to make a drawing of the piece to be made, the joints to be used, and so on. They calculate the timber required to make it, then select and buy the wood. Usually they work with hardwoods such as oak, tropical hardwoods, walnut or American cherry. They rarely work with softwoods such as pine.

When they have selected the appropriate timber, they cut it using circular, hand and band saws, and plane to get a smooth finish. This is a very important process as the timber has to be cut and planed in such a way as to get exactly the grain effect the cabinet maker wants. The pattern of grain on the fronts of drawers for instance, may be cut so that the grain pattern on each one is identical. Decorative veneers, if used, are normally applied to panels before they are cut to size. They are bought in sheets and cut to give the right grain effect in the right place.

The cabinet maker then assembles the piece of furniture. Any decorative effects such as mouldings or inlays are added, and the whole piece is then carefully sanded. The latter is a lengthy operation, some of which is done by machine and some by hand. Sometimes the cabinet maker will then pass the piece on to a French polisher to provide the final finish; others may do this themselves.

WORK ENVIRONMENT

Most cabinet makers work in workshops that are light and airy, though conditions in some smaller workshops can be cramped. There may be dust from sanding but most workshops have dust extractors, and masks are also worn. The workshop may be noisy when using machinery, and ear defenders are worn. Some cabinet makers may have to travel to timber yards to buy wood and deliver their goods. Occasionally they may have to work at the customer's premises, in the case of making and fitting kitchen units, for example. The work involves considerable standing and walking as well as bending and carrying.

SKILLS AND INTERESTS

This work requires excellent hand skills and hand-eye co-ordination. Cabinet makers need a great deal of patience and perseverance – to carry out very detailed accurate work. They also need a certain amount of artistic ability – an eye for what looks good and a sense of proportion. Numeracy is important in calculations, measuring and estimating costs.

Self-employed cabinet makers need good business skills, self-discipline and self-motivation. They also require good interpersonal skills to deal with customers.

ENTRY REQUIREMENTS

No minimum educational qualifications are required, however, the courses leading to relevant qualifications may have specific entry requirements. There are a number of appropriate courses for cabinet making:

City and Guilds 5550 in Furniture Craft subjects and 5640 in Furniture Crafts (Special). There are no formal entry requirements for City and Guilds courses; however, some colleges may look for about three GCSEs in maths, English and a science subject.

BTEC/SCOTVEC National Diploma/Certificate in Design (Crafts). Entry requirements are four GCSEs/S grades (A-C/1-3), or an Intermediate GNVQ/GSVQ Level III.

BTEC/SCOTVEC Higher National Diploma/Certificate in Design (Furniture), Design (Restoration) or Furniture. Entry requirements are usually: five GCSEs/S grades (A-C/1-3), with two or three subjects studied to A level/H grade and one or two passed; or an Advanced GNVQ/GSVQ Level III; or a BTEC/SCOTVEC national diploma/ certificate.

Degree courses, national diplomas/certificates in subjects such as restoration and conservation, furniture design and craftsmanship, and furniture restoration and craftsmanship. Entry requirements for degree courses vary. Normal qualifications for some courses are: five GCSEs/S grades (A-C/1-3) including English, plus an art foundation course; Advanced GNVQ/GSVQ Level III; or BTEC/ SCOTVEC diploma in art and/or design. Other courses may require two A levels/three H grades or equivalent.

TRAINING

Training may be either full-time at college or by becoming a trainee with a cabinet maker learning on the job and attending college on day release. There are a number of colleges offering full-time courses.

Courses include City and Guilds 5550 in Furniture Crafts, a one-year full-time or three-year part-time course which covers: timber preparation and construction; metal and plastics preparation and construction; upholstery and bedding preparation and construction; finishing preparation and modern finishing; soft furnishing; carcass and wooden frame construction; and hand-made furniture construction. This can lead to City and Guilds 5640 Furniture Crafts: Cabinet Making (Special), a one-year full-time or three-year part-time course.

BTEC/SCOTVEC national diploma and higher national diploma courses vary. A typical BTEC national diploma is a two-year full-time course and is likely to cover the skills needed to design and make furniture, working with wood, metal and plastics. Courses also include material and workshop technology, information technology, business studies and design history.

A BTEC Higher National Diploma in Furniture Design is a two-year full-time course and is likely to cover both traditional and modern methods of making furniture, restoration of furniture and replica-making, as well as design and business management.

There is also a range of relevant BSc and BA courses for cabinet makers, eg the BA (Hons) Furniture Design and Craftsmanship course at Buckinghamshire College (a college of Brunel University). This covers designing and producing furniture, with instruction in creative design and practical skills, together with business training.

There are also private fee-paying courses in cabinet making lasting from a couple of days to two years.

NVQs/SVQs in Furniture Production are available at Levels 1 and 3, and in Assembled Furniture Production and Upholstered Furniture Production at Level 2. NVQs/SVQs are also available at Levels 2 and 3 in Woodmachining, and at Levels 1, 2 and 3 in Producing Hand-crafted Furniture.

A Modern Apprenticeship Programme is available in cabinet making leading to at least NVQ/SVQ Level 3. Further information is available from BFM Training Ltd, the furniture industry training organization.

LATE ENTRY

There are no maximum age limits for this work and some colleges run full and part-time courses especially for mature students.

The BA (Hons) Furniture Design and Craftsmanship course at Buckinghamshire College accepts many mature students (over 22) who do not have the normal minimum academic qualifications for a degree course but can demonstrate ability and commitment.

OPPORTUNITIES

Cabinet makers are found in many cities, towns and rural areas throughout Britain. They may be self-employed or work for companies of cabinet makers. A few may specialize in one type of furniture, but most design and make a range of different items.

PAY AND CONDITIONS

As some cabinet makers are self-employed, pay may vary considerably. Hours are also variable to suit the needs of the job. Self-employed cabinet makers may work more than 39 hours a week.

PROSPECTS

Cabinet makers can progress by moving from working for a company to owning and running their own company. Some move into teaching.

Cabinet makers starting their own business need capital. This may be borrowed from a bank. There may also be some grants available, for instance from the Rural Development Commission.

RELATED OCCUPATIONS

Furniture designer, boat builder, musical instrument manufacturer, patternmaker, upholsterer, French polisher, carpenter/joiner.

FURTHER INFORMATION

BFM Training Limited*, 30 Harcourt Street, London W1H 2AA, 0171 724 0851

Buckinghamshire College*, Queen Alexandra Road, High Wycombe, Buckinghamshire HP11 2JZ, 01494 522141

The Crafts Council*, 44A Pentonville Road, Islington, London N1 9BY, 0171 278 7700

Guild of Master Craftsmen*, 166 High Street, Lewes, East Sussex BN7 1XU, 01273 478449

Rural Development Commission, 141 Castle Street, Salisbury, Wiltshire SP1 3TP, 01722 336255

FURTHER READING

Leaflets/booklets are available from the addresses marked*.

Woodworkers' Career and Educational Source Book – Guild of Master Craftsmen

In the careers library, classified under SAJ.

2. UPHOLSTERER (SAJ)

THE WORK

Upholsterers build up a piece of furniture from a frame into a finished covered item; they cover chairs and sofas with fabric or leather. Much of their work is re-upholstering and covering furniture. Their first job is to discuss with the customer what they want. Once the customer has chosen the material to be used, upholsterers measure the furniture to work out how much material is needed, so they can quote a price.

In re-upholstering, they first remove all the previous upholstery using a staple remover and chisel. If it is an old piece of furniture they may have to tighten the frame by removing the old dried-out glue and regluing it. They then upholster the furniture following the way it was made originally. If it had springs, they start by stretching hessian and tacking it to the frame and they then attach webbing to the frame. Springs are then placed on the webbing and tied with twine to the frame and the hessian. More hessian is stretched over and attached to the frame, and padding of horsehair, soft cotton wadding or felt is added. This is often followed by calico, before covering with material.

To cover the chair or sofa the upholsterer carefully cuts out the material making sure patterns match and that little material is wasted. They then stretch the pieces of material over the part to be covered and tack it down. When it is covered they then add braid, piping, fringing or other trimmings. They also make cushions if required.

Backs of chairs and sofas are upholstered in a similar way but by weaving threads into the base layer of hessian and tucking stuffing such as horsehair under the threads. This is repeated and followed by adding a layer of felt or flock to stop the hair coming through. Finally the item is covered in the chosen material.

Most modern furniture uses latex, polyurethane or polyester foam rather than the traditional stuffing materials. In the mass production of furniture, much of the work is done by machine. Upholsterers working in factories are generally responsible for handling one particular operation rather than the entire job.

Many factories employ a few upholsterers to upholster and cover sample pieces of furniture (eg for trade shows and exhibitions). They may also make patterns for cutting the material, and work out templates for the production line.

WORK ENVIRONMENT

Most upholsterers work in workshops that are light and airy; there may be some dust when removing old upholstery. Some work in factories. Self-employed upholsterers may have to visit customers' houses to measure, collect and deliver furniture. They may occasionally do some upholstery on the customer's premises. The work involves considerable standing, bending and walking. There is also a lot of carrying of material, chairs and sofas.

SKILLS AND INTERESTS

This work requires a good range of hand skills from sewing to hammering. Considerable patience and perseverance is needed to carry out detailed work with accuracy. Upholsterers need to work carefully and neatly. A certain amount of artistic ability is helpful and an eye for colour and co-ordination is needed for matching fabrics, patterns and colours. Numeracy is important in calculations, measuring and estimating costs.

Self-employed upholsterers need good business skills, self-discipline and self-motivation. They also require good interpersonal skills to deal with customers.

ENTRY REQUIREMENTS

There are no formal educational requirements for this career although some employers may look for GCSEs in subjects such as technology, maths, English, and science, and courses leading to relevant qualifications may have specific entry requirements.

The main courses for upholstery are City and Guilds 5550 in Furniture Craft Subjects and 5642 in Upholstery. There are no formal entry qualifications for City and Guilds courses but some colleges may ask for three GCSEs in maths, English and a science subject.

TRAINING

Training may be full-time at college or part-time working as a trainee with skilled upholsterers, learning on the job and attending college on day release. Study is usually via a two-year part-time course for City and Guilds 5550 in Furniture Crafts or via a one-year full-time/three-year part-time course for City and Guilds 5624 in Upholstery. Furniture Crafts covers: timber preparation and construction; upholstery and bedding preparation and construction; metal and plastics preparation and construction; finishing preparation and modern finishing; soft furnishing; carcass and wooden frame construction; and hand-made furniture construction. There are also modules in upholstery that can be taken with this course.

City and Guilds 5640 Furniture Crafts: Upholstery (Special) includes: basic traditional techniques in upholstery; use of tools and equipment; upholstery construction materials; and upholstery and soft furnishing fabrics and trimmings. It also covers: soft furnishing; furniture history; frame making and repair; wood finishing and polishing; small business studies; and applications of information technology.

Further study can lead to City and Guilds 5550 Advanced Studies (Upholstery) which takes the studies to a deeper level and introduces workshop management.

For a list of colleges offering the courses contact the Guild of Master Craftsmen. All courses are listed in *The Woodworkers' Career and Educational Source Book*.

NVQs/SVQs in Upholstered Furniture Production are available at Level 2. A number of other NVQs/SVQs are available in the furniture industry at Levels 1 and 3. For full details, please see article 1. CABINET MAKER.

A Modern Apprenticeship Programme is available in upholstered furniture production leading to at least NVQ/SVQ Level 3. Further information is available from BFM Training Ltd, the furniture industry training organization.

LATE ENTRY

There are no maximum age limits for this work. Some colleges run full and part-time BTEC continuing education courses, designed for mature students, in relevant subjects such as furniture restoration, which includes upholstery.

OPPORTUNITIES

Upholsterers are found in many cities, towns and rural areas throughout Britain. Many work for or in association with furniture restorers or antique dealers. Others are self-employed, work for other upholsterers, or work for furniture manufacturers.

PAY AND CONDITIONS

As some upholsterers are self-employed, pay may vary considerably. Hours are also variable to suit the needs of the job. Self-employed upholsterers frequently work far more than 39 hours a week. Those employed by furniture manufacturers are likely to work a 39-hour week, Monday to Friday.

PROSPECTS

Upholsterers can gain more advanced qualifications by studying for City and Guilds 5553 – Advanced Studies (Upholstery). They may progress by moving from working for another upholsterer to owning and running their own company. In factories there may be possibilities of moving into supervisory or management posts. Some upholsterers move into teaching.

Upholsterers starting their own business need capital (though the cost of tools and equipment is much less than for cabinet making). This may be borrowed from the bank. There may also be grants available, for instance from the Rural Development Commission.

RELATED OCCUPATIONS

Tailor, dressmaker, French polisher, cabinet maker.

FURTHER INFORMATION

The Association of Master Upholsterers, Francis Vaughan House, 102 Commercial Street, Newport, Gwent NP9 1LU, 01633 215454

BFM Training Limited*, 30 Harcourt Street, London W1H 2AA, 0171 724 0851

The Guild of Master Craftsmen Ltd*, 166 High Street, Lewes, East Sussex BN7 1XU, 01273 478449

Rural Development Commission, 141 Castle Street, Salisbury, Wiltshire SP1 3TP, 01722 336255

The Guild of Traditional Upholsterers, 5 Station Road, West Runton, Near Cromer, Norfolk, NR27 9QD

FURTHER READING

Leaflets/booklets are available from the addresses marked*.

Woodworkers' Career and Educational Source Book – Guild of Master Craftsmen

In the careers library, classified under SAJ.

3. FRENCH POLISHER (SAJ)

THE WORK

French polishers work on the sheen and colour of a piece of wood to fill in the grain, give it a smooth finish and bring out the beauty of the timber. They work on pieces of furniture and occasionally other wooden items such as staircases, doors and panelling in old houses. They may work on new items or on the restoration of old ones.

Before polishing, French polishers have to prepare the piece of furniture. For restoration work they may carry out simple repairs, if necessary – more complex ones are usually sent to a cabinet maker or restorer. If the furniture has previously been painted, varnished or lacquered, they remove this with paint stripper, steel wool and possibly sandpaper. They fill in any holes in the wood and ensure that it has a smooth surface.

Once the wood is prepared they decide on the type of stain needed to produce the colour they want. This is mixed and then applied using a rubber (which is a piece of cloth with wadding inside it) or mop. French polish consists of shellac dissolved in meths – and this is applied to the wood using the rubber. The shellac is applied by rubbing it onto the wood, using an overlapping circular motion. This process is repeated many times until the correct finish is achieved.

Furniture may also be lacquered, varnished, painted, oiled or waxed, and many French polishers apply these finishes. They also reproduce and create other different types of finishes. These processes may be quicker than French polishing. For instance, in the case of a lacquer, the furniture may first be sprayed with a tinted lacquer, or stained and then sprayed with a clear lacquer.

French polishers are sometimes employed in factories which mass-produce furniture. As very little mass-produced furniture is French polished, their job is usually to work out how to achieve the finish the designer requires in the manufacturing process. If the factory does produce furniture French polished then machines may do some of the work, but French polishers polish parts, such as chair legs, that cannot be done by machine.

WORK ENVIRONMENT

Most French polishers work in workshops that are usually light and airy. There may be dust from sanding and masks are worn. There may also be some fumes from the lacquers and polishes, although most workshops are well-ventilated. Some types of finish require the use of protective clothing, masks and (when using polyurethane, for example) a respirator hood with air supply. French polishers may have to visit a customer and may occasionally work in customers' homes. Some work in factories which may be noisy. The work involves considerable standing, bending and lifting.

SKILLS AND INTERESTS

French polishers should enjoy working with natural materials and have an appreciation of (and a good eye for) colour. They require good hand skills to apply stains and polishes. The work needs a great deal of patience and perseverance as it can be slow and repetitive. The work can be physically demanding and French polishers should be agile and fit. An interest in antique furniture and the history of furniture production is useful. French polishers should have an appreciation of the pattern, texture, feel and design of wood.

Self-employed polishers need good business skills, self-discipline and self-motivation. They need good interpersonal skills to deal with customers. Numeracy is important for calculating quantities and estimating costs. A knowledge of science is useful in working with chemicals.

ENTRY REQUIREMENTS

There are no specific entry requirements for this career although some employers may look for GCSEs in subjects such as technology, maths, English and science. Courses leading to relevant qualifications may have specific entry requirements.

The main course for French polishing is City and Guilds 5550 in Furniture Craft Subjects. There are no formal entry qualifications for City and Guilds courses but some colleges ask for three GCSEs/S grades in maths, English and a science subject.

TRAINING

Training may be full-time at college or part-time working as a trainee with skilled French polishers, learning on the job and attending college on day release. Study is usually for City and Guilds 5550 in Furniture Craft Subjects, with specialist modules in finishing.

City and Guilds 5550 in Furniture Craft Subjects covers: timber preparation and construction; metal and plastics preparation and construction; upholstery and bedding preparation and construction; finishing preparation and modern finishing; soft furnishing; carcass and wooden frame construction; and hand-made furniture construction. All students follow a common course during part 1 (normally one year block or day release), and select from a range of specialist modules for part 2 (which normally takes two years). All courses are listed in the *Woodworkers' Career and Educational Source Book.*

There are also private fee-paying courses in French polishing, such as those run by the Midland School of French Polishing, in Nottingham.

A number of NVQs/SVQs in Furniture Production are available at Levels 2 and 3. For full details, please see article 1. CABINET MAKER.

A Modern Apprenticeship Programme is available in polishing and finishing leading to at least NVQ/SVQ Level 3. Further information is available from BFM Training Ltd, the furniture industry training organization.

LATE ENTRY

There are no maximum age limits for this work. Some colleges run BTEC continuing education courses, both full and part-time, in relevant subjects, such as furniture restoration, which includes French polishing.

OPPORTUNITIES

French polishers are found in many cities, towns and rural areas throughout Britain. Many work for or in association with furniture restorers or antique dealers. Others are self-employed, working for other French polishers or for furniture manufacturers.

PAY AND CONDITIONS

As many French polishers are self-employed, pay may vary considerably, although the minimum wage rate is £165 a week. Hours are also variable to suit the needs of the job. They may work in excess of 39 hours a week.

PROSPECTS

French polishers can progress from working for another French polisher to owning and running their own company. Those working for furniture manufacturers may have promotion routes into supervisory and management posts. Some move into teaching.

French polishers starting their own businesses need capital. This may be borrowed from a bank. There may also be some grants available, for instance, from the Rural Development Commission.

RELATED OCCUPATIONS

Boatbuilder, musical instrument manufacturer, museum conservation officer, cabinet maker, upholsterer, painter/decorator.

FURTHER INFORMATION

BFM Training Limited*, 30 Harcourt Street, London W1H 2AA, 0171 724 0851

The Guild of Master Craftsmen Ltd*, 166 High Street, Lewes, East Sussex BN7 1XU, 01273 478449

Rural Development Commission, 141 Castle Street, Salisbury, Wiltshire SP1 3TP, 01722 336255

FURTHER READING

Leaflets/booklets are available from the addresses marked*.

Woodworkers' Career and Educational Source Book – The Guild of Master Craftsmen

In the careers library, classified under SAJ.

THE FOUNDRY INDUSTRY: SAM

1. FOUNDRY WORKER CLCI:SAM
2. PATTERNMAKER CLCI:SAM
3. MOULDER/COREMAKER CLCI:SAM

BACKGROUND INFORMATION

The foundry industry makes metal castings, such as engine blocks, turbine blades for jet engines, surgical instruments, crankshafts and other car parts. They also make products such as church bells, taps, ornate metal garden furniture and gates. Castings are made in a wide variety of metals including iron, aluminium, brass, bronze, steel and even silver, gold and platinum. They can range in size from large ships' propellers to delicate pieces of jewellery. Foundries usually specialize in one type of metal although some deal with a range of materials.

In foundries, metal ingots and other raw materials, and, in some cases, scrap metal, are put into a furnace and melted down. The molten metal is then poured into moulds made of sand or metal, where it solidifies into the correct shape.

1. FOUNDRY WORKER (SAM)

THE WORK

Foundry workers carry out a wide range of tasks within a foundry ranging from jobs such as cleaning or lift truck driving, to more complex work such as that of furnace operators. Many of the foundry workers assist specialist craftspeople in the foundry. For instance, some assist moulders/coremakers by mixing the moulding sand to the correct specification, adding water and binders. The main types of workers are:

Furnace operators load the furnaces with the correct specification of metal which can include new and scrap metal. After melting the metal, a sample is taken to the laboratory for testing or, in more modern foundries, the furnace operators may carry out their own analysis with special equipment. Temperatures are also taken to ensure they are correct for casting. Operatives check that furnace linings are not worn out. They may have to re-line the furnace.

Casters use ladles to pour molten metal into the prepared moulds. They are also involved in lining the ladles with a heat-resistant material and checking that the temperature in the ladles is correct. However, in more modern foundries this process is automated.

Knock out operators remove castings from moulds when they are cool and break the sand after it has been used, in foundries where this process is not automated.

Fettlers and grinders cut off any unwanted pieces of metal from castings and grind off any rough edges, in foundries where this process is not automated.

Machine moulding operators operate machinery. In fully automated foundries, their main task is controlling the moulding machine which may make as many as 300 moulds in a day. In other foundries, they may work hand-operated moulding machines set up for the production of small batches of castings. If this is not automated, they place cores into the moulds, and close the mould prior to casting. When the castings have been produced in the moulds they knock the castings out and put them into a shot blaster to knock the sand off.

WORK ENVIRONMENT

Foundry workers work mainly indoors in the foundry itself, although some work outside in all weathers sorting out scrap metal. Work in the area of the furnaces can be hot. The work may be physically strenuous with some lifting and carrying, but European legislation and the introduction of mechanical aids have removed most strenuous tasks. Foundries may be dirty and dusty and there may be fumes from moulds and cores, although most modern foundries have fume and dust extractors. In some iron foundries, coal dust is used in the sand, which makes the environment very dirty, though many have introduced an alternative that is dust-free.

SKILLS AND INTERESTS

Traditionally, foundry workers have needed to be fit and strong for the physical work, which involved a lot of lifting, but, increasingly, automation and mechanical aids and the use of sophisticated equipment mean there is more mental activity involved. Hand skills are very important for some jobs – such as fettling, and controlling the moulding machine. Basic communication skills are needed to be able to understand instructions and communicate with other workers.

Foundry workers should be careful, thorough in their work and able to understand and follow safety regulations. Foundries can be potentially dangerous, with hot metal and metal splinters being some of the hazards. Adaptability is also needed so that workers can do more than one job in the foundry. They need to be able to work on their own, although under supervision, and to work as part of a team.

ENTRY REQUIREMENTS

There are no academic entry requirements for this work. Physical fitness, however, may be vital and workers usually have to pass a medical examination. Although it is possible to come into this work at 16 years, this is unusual; most workers are over 18 years.

TRAINING

Training varies according to the needs of the person and the complexity of the job. Usually all new foundry workers will go through induction training and a course in safety. The rest of their training is given on the job and can take from a couple of hours to a couple of months, depending on the work they are to do. Lift truck drivers, for instance, require a couple of weeks' training. Furnace operators may take five to six months to train. In some cases a worker will start with a job such as general labouring work at the furnace, gradually learning more complex work. Many workers are now being trained to carry out a wide range of different tasks.

NVQs/SVQs in Engineering Material Processing or High Pressure Aluminium Diecasting at Levels 1 and 2 are available.

LATE ENTRY

There is no upper age limit for this work and many employers accept or prefer adults, especially those with experience of production work. Some jobs require physical strength and fitness; workers may have to pass a medical examination.

There may be specific training opportunities directed at adults available in some areas for this type of work.

Candidates may have to satisfy certain conditions to be eligible. Contact your local Jobcentre, careers office or TEC/LEC for details.

OPPORTUNITIES

Foundry workers are employed in independent foundries, and in large engineering companies that have their own foundries. Most opportunities are in independent foundries. Foundries fall into two types – automated and jobbing foundries, with some foundries being both. Automated foundries make large quantities of identical castings and the work is done by machines, whereas jobbing foundries make small quantities of castings and much of the work is done by hand. Foundry workers work in both types of foundry.

There are about 700 foundries throughout England, Wales and Scotland, ranging from very large foundries to small ones with fewer than 25 staff. They are found in most industrial areas, particularly in the Midlands, but many foundries are also found in Lancashire, Yorkshire, the North East coast, the Clyde, South Wales and the South East of England.

PAY AND CONDITIONS

Basic pay for foundry workers is likely to be around £180 a week, or £150 in a small foundry, though, for skilled and experienced workers, it can be in excess of £250. Hours are usually 37 a week Monday to Friday. They may have to work shifts, weekends and overtime depending on the foundry. It is possible, although not common, for foundry workers to work abroad for overseas companies.

PROSPECTS

Promotion is usually to supervisor or foreman/woman where NVQ/SVQ in Supervisory Management at Level 3 is available. Foundry workers often progress further into management and even senior management, as local knowledge and experience are highly valued.

RELATED OCCUPATIONS

Patternmaker, moulder/coremaker, blacksmith, forklift truck driver, engineering operator, production worker.

FURTHER INFORMATION AND READING

Please see article 3. MOULDER/COREMAKER.

2. PATTERNMAKER (SAM)

THE WORK

Patternmakers make the models or patterns of the required casting shape from which the moulds are produced. Patterns can be of wood, metal, plastic, resin or polystyrene.

Patternmakers work from a technical drawing of the part required, they plan how to make the pattern and then produce a full-scale working drawing by hand or computer. They decide from which material the pattern should be made, and then decide on the type of wood or metal. For instance, some woods such as mahogany are very long lasting, while others are particularly good for cutting with a chisel. For complicated shapes they may first make a metal template to assist them. Next they make the pattern parts using machines and hand tools including saws, planers, and milling and grinding machines working to extremely fine tolerances. During this process they use precision instruments to measure the dimensions of the pattern to make sure they are accurate. They then assemble the patterns and finish them by hand. Finally the pattern may be painted or varnished.

Some patterns are made on computer numerically controlled machines (CNCs), which are operated by a machine operator, the job of the patternmaker being to program the machine.

WORK ENVIRONMENT

Patternmakers usually work in a workshop. Modern dust and fume extraction systems mean that these are not particularly dusty. However, working with wood can produce dust that may cause problems for people with chest complaints. They can be noisy on occasion.

SKILLS AND INTERESTS

Patternmakers need good hand skills and the ability to work with both machines and hand tools as well as a variety of different materials including wood and metal. They should be able to visualize in three dimensions to work out how to construct patterns. Mathematical ability is needed for calculations and a good understanding of engineering drawings is vital.

Communication skills are important as they liaise with others involved in the design and use of their patterns. They should be able to work as part of a team but also on their own if necessary. They should be safety conscious, thorough and methodical. They also need the self-motivation to see a job through from start to finish.

ENTRY REQUIREMENTS

Entry for young people is possible in England via a Modern Apprenticeship in Patternmaking and Foundry Work, or, in Scotland, Skillseeker training. Application may be made to an employer, or through a TEC/LEC, or, for Modern Apprenticeships, through one of the three colleges which are approved training providers: Coventry Technical College, Sandwell College and Chesterfield College.

Qualifications may vary but many companies look for GCSEs/S grades (D/4 or above) in maths and an engineering subject. GNVQ/GSVQ in Engineering could also be helpful.

TRAINING

Both Modern Apprenticeships and Skillseekers lead through an NVQ/SVQ in Engineering Material Processing: Foundry or Patternmaking at Level 2 to Level 3 in Patternmaking. This is based on the time taken to acquire competences and usually takes about three years. Apprentices may also study for C&G 2110 Part 3 in Patternmaking.

Training varies but usually consists of one year's broad-based off-the-job training in a college or company training school followed by modular training within the company and day or block release to college. Modules/units will be chosen to suit the requirements of the particular employer.

Practical training includes pattern construction and how to make patterns in different materials, such as wood, metal and plastic.

LATE ENTRY

Traditionally most new entrants into this career are school-leavers aged 16 to 17 years. However, nowadays some companies employ adults, especially those with relevant experience in related areas of work, such as mechanical engineering crafts, or construction crafts, such as woodmachining or joinery, and give them additional training.

Training for adults varies from employer to employer and usually depends on the qualifications and experience of the trainee. Training is likely to be shorter and more condensed than that of a school-leaver. Adults may also be assessed for NVQs/SVQs, and skills acquired in other industries can be taken into account.

There may be specific training opportunities directed at adults available in some areas for this type of work. Candidates may have to satisfy certain conditions to be eligible. Contact your local Jobcentre, careers office or TEC/LEC for details.

OPPORTUNITIES

Please see article 1. FOUNDRY WORKER.

In addition to patternshops attached to foundries, patternmakers also work for specialist pattern-making companies.

PAY AND CONDITIONS

Basic pay for trained patternmakers is about £203 to £241 a week, though overtime can bring this up to £250 to £300. Pay varies with the size of the foundry or patternshop. Hours are usually 37 a week, Monday to Friday. Patternmakers may have to work shifts, weekends and overtime, depending on the foundry.

PROSPECTS

Promotion for patternmakers is usually to supervisor or foreman/woman and from there they may move into management. It is also possible for patternmakers with good results in their C&G examinations to move on to technician training in a range of areas, such as: quality control, estimating, work study, production planning, or mechanical testing.

Employers may give some patternmaking apprentices the opportunity to attend university for degree courses in materials sciences.

Work abroad is possible, as British C&G qualifications are recognized world-wide. Patternmakers can become self-employed.

RELATED OCCUPATIONS

Carpenter/joiner, engineering craft machinist, foundry moulder/coremaker, wood machinist, engineering toolmaker.

FURTHER INFORMATION AND READING

Please see article 3. MOULDER/COREMAKER.

3. MOULDER/COREMAKER (SAM)

THE WORK

Moulder/coremakers make the moulds in which metal castings are made, by packing sand into a box, round a pattern usually made of wood or metal that is the same shape as the required casting. They start by deciding how the mould should be made choosing the correct size of box for the job as it has to hold enough sand to make the mould strong, yet not use too much sand as that would be too expensive. They then carefully position the pattern into the box. Before putting the sand into the box and packing it firmly round the pattern they check that the sand mix is right.

When the sand is hard they carefully remove the pattern. If the mould shape is damaged they repair it using hand tools. Often they apply a mould coating, which means mixing the coating to get the right consistency then applying it with a brush or hose pipe to give a better surface finish on the castings.

If the casting has hollow sections, they make a core – a mass of sand in the shape of the hollow – and place it carefully into the mould ensuring the correct space for the molten metal to pass between the core and the mould walls. Some very intricate castings may have a large number of cores. Finally the mould halves are closed ready for the molten metal to be poured in.

WORK ENVIRONMENT

Moulder/coremakers' work environment varies depending on the type of mould they are working on. They could be working with a moulding box at a workbench or, in the case of very large moulds, they work in specially designed moulding pits. The work is physically strenuous with some lifting and carrying. Their environment may be dirty, hot if near the furnaces, and there may be fumes, although most foundries have fume and dust extraction systems. In iron foundries, coal dust is used in the sand, which makes the environment very dirty.

SKILLS AND INTERESTS

Moulder/coremakers need good hand skills. Care and patience are needed as some of the work can be very delicate, such as smoothing the sand in the mould. It is important that they work accurately; measurements for moulds and cores may need to be accurate to 1mm. Care is also needed to follow safety procedures. They need the ability to visualize in three dimensions to work out how to make moulds. Physical fitness is important as the work involves some lifting and bending. Moulder/coremakers need good communication skills to follow instructions and communicate with other moulder/coremakers and foundry workers.

They also need an understanding of the casting process and how sands and metals react. They should be adaptable as they have to work on both simple moulds and complex moulds which have a number of cores. They need to be organized, able to think for themselves and be methodical, to plan and make moulds.

ENTRY REQUIREMENTS

In England, it is possible to enter via a Modern Apprenticeship or, in Scotland, Skillseeker training for young people. Application may be made to an employer, or through a TEC/LEC, or, for Modern Apprenticeships, to one of the three colleges involved: Coventry Technical College, Sandwell College and Chesterfield College.

For these, companies may look for GCSEs/S grades (D/4 or above) in maths and an engineering subject. GNVQ/GSVQ in Engineering could also be helpful.

However, moulder/coremakers may also be recruited directly as trainee moulder/coremakers within an in-company training scheme, or start as foundry workers and progress to become moulder/coremakers. For this, no formal educational qualifications may be required, as many employers consider practical ability to be more important than academic ability.

TRAINING

Both Modern Apprenticeships and Skillseekers lead to an NVQ/SVQ in Engineering Material Processing at Level 3. This is based on acquiring competences and usually takes about three years. Modules/units selected are relevant to the requirements and processes of specific employers. Apprentices may also study for C&G 2100 Part 3 in Foundry Craft Studies.

Training varies. In many foundries, trainees spend their first year in a training centre learning the basic skills of moulding and coremaking. During this time they may also spend one day a week at a college learning the theory. At the end of that year they start work in the foundry, beginning with straightforward jobs such as making a smaller mould from a plated pattern, gradually progressing to more and more complex work, such as moulds with many cores and complex joints. On more complicated jobs they often assist an experienced moulder/coremaker, to learn their skills.

LATE ENTRY

There is no maximum age limit for this work although some foundries may not recruit people over the age of 30 years. Previous experience, especially in relevant work such as other foundry or engineering work, may be an advantage in getting a job. Length of training may vary depending on the previous experience of the trainee. Adults may be assessed for NVQs/SVQs and previously acquired knowledge and skills can be taken into account.

There may be specific training opportunities directed at adults available in some areas for this type of work. Candidates may have to satisfy certain conditions to be eligible. Contact your local Jobcentre, careers office or TEC/LEC for details.

OPPORTUNITIES

Please see article 1. FOUNDRY WORKER.

Moulder/coremaker is a traditional craft. While opportunities for training in it still exist, computerization and automation, together with pressure for higher production rates, mean that there is a tendency for these positions to be replaced by multiskilled machine operators in some foundries. In some instances, this is within a team-working system that includes maintenance skills. This craft may be re-defined or a new one evolve to replace it.

PAY AND CONDITIONS

Pay for trained moulder/coremakers is likely to be around £220 a week. Hours are usually 37 a week, Monday to Friday. They may have to work shifts, weekends and overtime, depending on the foundry.

PROSPECTS

Promotion for moulder/coremakers is usually to supervisor or foreman/woman and from there they may move into management. It is also possible for moulder/coremakers with good results in their C&G examinations to move on to technician training, in a range of areas, such as: quality control, estimating, work study, production planning, or mechanical testing.

RELATED OCCUPATIONS

Patternmaker, foundry worker, engineering craft machinist, engineering operative, engineer.

FURTHER INFORMATION

British Metal Castings Council*, Bridge House, Smallbrook, Queensway, Birmingham B5 4JP, 0121 643 3377

Institute of British Foundrymen*, Bordesley Hall, The Holloway, Alvechurch, Birmingham B48 7QA, 01527 596100

Metcom*, Savoy Tower, 77 Renfrew Street, Glasgow G2 3BZ, 0141 332 0826

Engineering Training Authority (EnTra)*, Vector House, 41 Clarendon Road, Watford, Herts WD1 1LB, 0800 282167

EnTra Publications*, PO Box 75, Stockport, 0161 480 5285

FURTHER READING

Leaflets/booklets are available from the addresses marked*.

Job Outlines – The Cast Metals Industry – COIC

In the careers library, classified under SAM.

PLASTICS PROCESS OPERATIVE
CLCI:SAN

BACKGROUND INFORMATION

Plastics are used throughout the world – everything from household goods to the most advanced science and technology. The range of uses is endless because plastics are so versatile. There are roughly 24 main types, including polythene, polypropylene, melamine and glass reinforced plastic (GRP), which is very hard. Plastics have many properties – they are strong and light, soft and flexible; can be moulded; are heat-resistant and free from corrosion. They can be welded, pre-coloured, printed upon or be used to coat or laminate goods. Another type of plastic, known as thermosetting plastic is malleable when it is first heated and formed, but, when further heat is applied, it is 'cured', setting like pottery in a kiln, and remaining permanently shaped and heat-resistant.

THE WORK

Process operatives – also called machine operators – are responsible for product quality, feeding raw materials into machines and removing the finished product. They weigh and measure, then remove and trim the finished product checking its quality. Some process operatives also label and pack the finished goods.

Process operatives check that semi-automatic and non-automatic machinery involved in producing plastic products runs correctly. They check the machines' pressures and temperatures, and ensure the goods are being produced at the right speed. Machines are set by machine setters but operatives may need to make minor adjustments to machines, altering valves and switches to check the machines run smoothly. When there is a fault, operators may need to tell the chargehand or supervisor, or call in the maintenance team.

Process operatives need to work at a steady, quick pace. Some machines produce goods at a set rate, others can be altered to produce goods to different speeds so the operator can work at their own rate. Some operators may be responsible for more than one machine.

The operative may work on a range of different goods; one machine may make a variety of products. The operative may also move from machine to machine and learn how several different machines work.

WORK ENVIRONMENT

Process operatives work on the shop floor, in factories and workshops.

There may be fumes from the raw material but most shop floors are well-ventilated. In most factories, operators work in clean, well-lit surroundings.

SKILLS AND INTERESTS

Process operatives need to work quickly and steadily to handle the regular flow of goods being produced by the machine.

Operating machinery can be repetitive and requires concentration and careful attention. All operators need to be responsible and check that safety regulations are followed.

Technical knowledge is necessary for monitoring and correcting machines. A scientific understanding is useful, as plastics processing involves the effect of chemical reactions and heat treatments.

Operatives may need to make some straightforward calculations when measuring and mixing quantities of raw materials.

Working on the shop floor involves team work – the ability to co-operate with other workers and follow instructions is needed.

Workers should be physically active – long periods are spent standing or sitting, and some work may involve lifting heavy materials.

ENTRY REQUIREMENTS

For many operative jobs, no educational qualifications are required, but exam passes can be useful.

Applicants should be able to follow instructions and understand straightforward calculations as the work may involve weighing materials.

However, increasing complexity of machinery and processes means that qualifications are becoming more important. To meet this, a new entry route is a Modern Apprenticeship, leading to an NVQ/SVQ in Polymer Processing at Level 3. Entry requirements are GCSEs/S-grades (A-C/1-3), or being able to demonstrate the ability to cope with an NVQ/SVQ Level 3.

In Scotland, entry to Modern Apprenticeships is through Skillseekers.

TRAINING

Training for modern apprentices includes on the job skills training to acquire competences which are assessed and study for underpinning knowledge. Apprentices also study to obtain a BTEC/SCOTVEC Certificate in Polymer Technology and some BTEC/SCOTVEC Foundation units in Engineering.

Other entrants learn specific tasks mainly on the job, but a wide range of other courses are offered to meet the needs of the industry; these combine both study and practical work. Trainees may be sent on BPTA short courses, lasting three or four days, related to new technology and specific job duties. These include courses about plastic materials, the physical testing of plastics, the use of additives such as stabilizers and colourants during processing and their effect on production.

Other courses teach operators to recognize faults in finished goods and carry out tests for quality to British Standards Institute (BSI) standards.

LATE ENTRY

Opportunities are available for older entrants to work as a process operative. Most companies consider adults who meet their requirements; see ENTRY REQUIREMENTS and TRAINING. Adults can also be assessed towards NVQ/SVQ qualifications, and previous relevant experience in other industries may be taken into account.

OPPORTUNITIES

There are over 2,000 plastics processing companies employing 99,000 people, a large number being process operatives.

After falling for a number of years, there has been some increase lately in the number of people employed in plastics processing. Indeed, the plastics processing industry has been identified by the government as a growth sector both for output and for employment, so opportunities will increase for individuals willing to obtain the appropriate qualifications.

PAY AND CONDITIONS

Rates of pay vary and depend on the company and its location. An experienced operative can earn an average basic wage of around £260 a week. Extra may be paid for shift work and productivity bonuses. Opportunities may also exist for overtime work.

Some companies have shift working which includes evening, night and weekend work. Some firms may require permanent night-shift workers.

PROSPECTS

For those interested in, and with an aptitude for, working with machines, machine moulding or setting is a possible prospect.

The BPTA runs various courses to enable process operatives to increase their skills. Courses include practical knowledge about how to set up and close down machines and correct faults. Some operatives may progress to supervisory grades, such as chargehand, inspector or supervisor.

Other prospects may include moving into quality control work.

RELATED OCCUPATIONS

Production worker, chemical plant process operative, engineering operative, brewery worker, foundry worker.

FURTHER INFORMATION

The British Polymer Training Association (BPTA)*, Coppice House, Halesfield, Telford, Shropshire TF7 4NA, 01952 587020

Institute of Materials, 1 Carlton House Terrace, London W1Y 5DB, 0171 839 4071

FURTHER READING

Leaflets/booklets are available from the address marked*.

In the careers library, classified under SAN.

PAPER MANUFACTURING WORKER
CLCI:SAP

BACKGROUND INFORMATION

The paper manufacturing industry makes paper and board which are converted into a wide range of products from packing boxes and writing paper to kitchen work surfaces. In Britain we produce half our paper; the other half is imported. Over half the paper made in Britain is made from recycled wastepaper. Most of the rest is made from wood pulp, either imported or home-grown. A little is made from other vegetable fibres, such as cotton or grasses – bank notes are made of cotton, for example. Most paper is made by machines, but there are a few remaining paper mills where paper is hand made.

THE WORK

Pulpmen/women

Pulpmen/women operate the machinery that converts the raw material into fibres called pulp which is suitable for further processing. To do this, they use conveyors to load the raw materials into the pulpers, control the process time, add chemicals and adjust the temperature and pressure of machines. They then test the pulp to make sure it is suitable for papermaking. The mixture of treated raw materials eventually becomes the paper or board known as stock.

Beatermen/women

Beatermen/women operate the mechanical and chemical processes that refine the stock so that it is of the correct colour, fibre length and wetness to provide the characteristics of the paper or board required. For instance, they operate the control systems from a computer keyboard or by opening and closing valves that add the correct colourings at the right temperature and in the right amount, to produce paper of the required colour. In addition to operating the machinery, they monitor the processes, making sure that the machines are working correctly.

Machinemen/women

The stock then passes to the papermaking machine where the fibres are intermeshed to form a continuous sheet. Machinemen/women control the papermaking machine, usually by computer. They use a variety of data such as laboratory tests and readings from the computer to keep a constant check on the quality of the paper being produced. They also maintain the condition of the machines by ensuring that all moving parts are working correctly, sensors are operating and worn parts are replaced. Often this means liaising with engineers. They also supervise and train other members of the machine crew.

Dryermen/women

The water is then removed to leave a dry continuous sheet of paper, and sprayed with size to seal its surface. Dryermen/women or backtenders control the dryers to make sure that the paper dries uniformly, and monitor and control the size press. They use VDUs to monitor the processes and the condition of the paper, making sure the processes are working correctly.

Reelermen/women

They operate the reeler that converts the reels of paper at the end of the production into finished reels of the right size for the customer. They set and change the knives used to do this. They check any sub-standard reels for re-winding.

Coating machinemen/women

They control the coating machines, usually by computer, making sure the machines run at the right speed and apply a coating of the right quality. They make sure that the coating is mixed to the right consistency and add appropriate chemicals. They supervise the rest of the coating crew.

Inspection windermen/women

Sometimes paper gets damaged in the manufacturing process and the job of the inspection windermen/women is to cut out any marked or damaged paper from the reels and remake any bad joints. If the paper is to be coated it then goes through another process.

Cuttermen/women

These workers operate a sheet-cutting machine that cuts the paper into sheets. They set up the machine to cut the paper to the correct size and inspect the paper for faults. They also direct their crew.

Finally, the paper passes to a finishing area, called the *salle*, where packers and sorters take out any faulty sheets of paper.

Paper testers

At various stages during the manufacturing process paper testers, using a variety of types of measuring equipment, carry out tests to determine the paper's thickness, weight, smoothness, strength and moisture content.

Effluent operative/fibre recovery attendant

Paper making uses a lot of water, but at the end of the production process most of the water is recycled. Mills use millions of gallons each day. The effluent operative/fibre recovery attendant operates and maintains the water systems and operates the plant that recovers fibres for re-use. They make sure the correct volume of effluent is directed to the appropriate stage in the process. They do this by checking flow rates and by opening and closing gates or valves. Many modern effluent treatment plants have systems containing live microscopic organisms that devour the effluent, and the attendants have to ensure that the organism's environment is correctly maintained.

WORK ENVIRONMENT

Paper mills can be noisy and workers may have to wear ear defenders when working near machinery. However, nowadays most of the processes are controlled by computers and workers work within soundproof rooms. Paper testers work in laboratories. The work can involve a lot of standing and, as mills are usually very large, walking. There is some lifting, although most is done by machine.

SKILLS AND INTERESTS

Paper manufacturing workers need an interest in mechanical and computer-controlled equipment. Some ability in science, technology and maths is useful, to make calculations and to understand the manufacturing process.

They need to be very observant as much of the work is observing the various processes to check that the paper is being produced to the right quality.

Communication skills are required in order to give and understand instructions.

Paper manufacturing workers need to be able to work as part of a team.

ENTRY REQUIREMENTS

There are no minimum entry requirements for this work. Most employers look for a good general education and some may give candidates a maths test.

For Modern Apprenticeships, employers may require GCSEs/S grades (A-C/1-3) in maths, English and science, plus passes in two other subjects (D/4) , or equivalent awards such as GNVQs/GSVQs.

Physical fitness is important and candidates usually have to pass a medical.

TRAINING

Training varies from employer to employer. Most training is given on the job, with trainees starting with more straightforward jobs, such as testing, reeler's assistant, machine assistant, dryerman/woman's assistant.

Some employers encourage trainees to study for the City and Guilds 5120 in Paper and Board Making, either at college or in the mill's own training department. This covers the technology of paper and board manufacture plus related industrial studies, and students can study at a pace to suit themselves. In Scotland, Skillseekers may be available.

Some mills offer a Modern Apprenticeship. In Scotland, this is via Skillseekers. Apprentices spend their first weeks moving round the different sections of the paper mill and then start their on-the-job training, at the same time going to college on day release, or studying in the mill's training department. The training leads to an NVQ/SVQ in Paper and Board Making at Level 2 and in Controlling the Process of Making Paper and Board at Level 3.

In Scotland, SCOTVEC National Certificate in Paper Production can be taken by workers with appropriate qualifications and/or experience. S grade (1-3) is preferred.

LATE ENTRY

There are no age limits for entry into this work. However, it is important for all workers to be physically fit. Adult applicants with previous experience in relevant work, such as other manufacturing work, may be preferred.

OPPORTUNITIES

Paper mills are mainly found in the South East and South West England, Lancashire and Scotland, although there are few mills in other areas. As a great deal of water is used in the papermaking process, mills are normally found close to rivers, well away from towns.

The size of mills varies from quite small recycling firms to enormous sites covering acres of land.

There are currently 110 mills operating in the UK, employing over 33,000 people.

Opportunities for paper manufacturing workers are decreasing because of new technologies enabling greater output per employee.

PAY AND CONDITIONS

Paper manufacturing workers work a range of day and shift systems with the majority employed on seven-day shift-working systems. Weekly hours vary between 37 and 39 dependent upon the shift system.

Minimum pay ranges from £140 to £254 a week for adult employees. Actual rates paid by paper mills are higher than the minimum and are further supplemented through bonuses and overtime payments.

PROSPECTS

Promotion for paper manufacturing workers is usually, first, to shift supervisor – possibly in charge of a couple of machines and then to superintendent, where they might be in charge of the preparation area or the papermaking machines, or dealing with waste products from manufacturing and the warehouse.

RELATED OCCUPATIONS

Textile operative, chemical process worker, production worker.

FURTHER INFORMATION

Paper Education and Training Council (PETC)*, Papermakers House, Rivenhall Road, Westlea, Swindon SN5 7BD, 01793 886086

FURTHER READING

Leaflets/booklets are available from the address marked*.

In the careers library, classified under SAP.

1. KEYBOARD OPERATOR CLCI:SAR
2. MAKE-UP COMPOSITOR CLCI:SAR
3. CAMERA/SCANNER OPERATOR, PLANNER AND PLATEMAKER CLCI:SAR
4. MACHINE PRINTER CLCI:SAR
5. BOOKBINDER/PRINT FINISHER CLCI:SAR

BACKGROUND INFORMATION

These articles refer only to the general, commercial sector of the printing industry and not to national newspapers.

Printing is one of Britain's largest industries; over 6,000 firms all over the UK – ranging in size from fewer than five employees to more than 5,000 – employ in excess of a quarter of a million people. Printers tend to specialize in the kind of work they do, primarily because each end product requires slightly different printing presses and folding, binding and gluing processes. The main specializations are: general printing (anything from mail order coupons to catalogues); books; high-quality colour printing (for brochures, cards, line art reproduction); newspapers; security printing (for banknotes or bond issues); carton (for food and other packaging); magazines; labels; stationery; and print on metal (beer cans, metal badges).

A number of different processes are used in printing, depending on the end product: lithography; letterpress (now uncommon); gravure; and screen printing.

Seventy-five per cent of firms use two or four-colour lithography, but web-offset is increasingly used because it can do long runs quickly. The equipment involved is extremely costly, so consequently there has been considerable growth recently of firms, many of them trade printers, that specialize in just part of the printing process, rather than following a product through from beginning to end. This particularly applies to the origination processes (typesetting, layout and platemaking) and finishing (cutting, stapling, binding, etc).

Nowadays computer control of many of the production processes is commonplace. For example, many people in printing use visual display units (VDUs) as an integral part of their work. With computerized typesetting, whole pages of text can now be produced in seconds. Most of the old craft jobs, such as letterpress printing, have consequently become rare, and the work calls increasingly for people with technical skills.

Jobs and training are now grouped under four main stages of production: origination; printing; finishing; carton converting.

Origination is the first stage in any printing process and includes all the jobs involved in preparing the products for the actual printing process. A few firms employ their own design and graphic artists, but this work is usually undertaken by advertising agencies or by the customers with assistance from the keyboard operators or make-up compositors.

In many smaller firms, the jobs outlined below may all be done by one person or may be shared by several people, all trained and skilled in the various different stages.

1. KEYBOARD OPERATOR (SAR)

THE WORK

Most typesetting is done by keyboard operators who use a computer keyboard and visual display unit (VDU) to produce a designed text. Either the customer or a designer passes the text to the keyboard operator and they discuss design requirements such as typeface and layout. The operator types it on a keyboard similar to a QWERTY keyboard but with more controls and buttons.

Some machines allow the text to be moved around on the screen, increasing the design facility. The text is often reproduced on floppy disk and in print which, in some large companies, will be passed to a reader for checking. More usually though, operators do their own checking in consultation with the customer.

Operators often make their own decisions about whether the design is right or the text correct – this involves considerable responsibility for the operator since the end product is largely dependent on correct work at this stage.

WORK ENVIRONMENT

Keyboard operators work in clean, light, office conditions.

SKILLS AND INTERESTS

Keyboard operators must be good at English language, particularly spelling and must be conscientious, meticulous and accurate. They must be able to concentrate for long periods in front of a VDU. If operators are employed in general origination, doing a range of jobs where colour assessment is involved, it is essential that they have accurate colour vision.

ENTRY REQUIREMENTS, TRAINING AND LATE ENTRY

Please see article 5. BOOKBINDER/PRINT FINISHER.

OPPORTUNITIES

As more and more computers are used in the printing industry, keyboard operating is an expanding field and there is a current shortage of skilled people.

PAY AND CONDITIONS

The British Printing Industries Federation (BPIF) has recommended a minimum grade rate for skilled occupations of £197.07 a week. Apprentices under 20 years are paid £98.54 a week. Wages vary from firm to firm and many pay considerably more. In addition, extra payments up to £30.20 may be payable depending on the equipment used. There may also be opportunities to earn more with overtime.

Most operators work day shifts; some work double days (6am to 2pm and 2pm to 10pm); some operate treble shifts (continuous running), and a few work nights. Holidays are five weeks plus bank holidays, and the standard working week is 37½ hours, after which overtime is payable.

PROSPECTS, RELATED OCCUPATIONS, FURTHER INFORMATION AND READING

Please see article 5. BOOKBINDER/PRINT FINISHER.

2. MAKE-UP COMPOSITOR (SAR)

THE WORK

Make-up compositors make up the page to its final design, using the copy and illustrations passed to them by the keyboard operator or, sometimes, the customer. They may either use their discretion and make their own decisions about how best to design the layout, or they may be guided by a designer or the customer.

The make-up compositor usually cuts and trims the copy and illustrations to the required size so that they fit into the page design and then fixes them in place with adhesive, ready for subsequent photography.

WORK ENVIRONMENT

Layouts must be kept free of blemishes so make-up compositors work in clean, light, airy offices. They liaise with other staff involved in origination work and between offices and photographic processing rooms.

SKILLS AND INTERESTS

Design flair, spatial awareness and an eye for balance are very important. Make-up compositors must be able to make their own decisions about design, often under the pressure of deadlines. They need to apply meticulous attention to detail coupled with concentration and care, since their work has a vital effect on the finished product.

ENTRY REQUIREMENTS, TRAINING AND LATE ENTRY

Please see article 5. BOOKBINDER/PRINT FINISHER.

OPPORTUNITIES

There are opportunities with specialist origination houses and with local and provincial newspapers, magazines and free papers.

PAY AND CONDITIONS

Please see article 1. KEYBOARD OPERATOR.

PROSPECTS, RELATED OCCUPATIONS, FURTHER INFORMATION AND READING

Please see article 5. BOOKBINDER/PRINT FINISHER.

3. CAMERA/SCANNER OPERATOR, PLANNER AND PLATEMAKER (SAR)

THE WORK

Camera operators are given the colour transparencies, photographs, or artists' originals that are to be reproduced and printed, and set the controls on the equipment that photographs them to produce negative or positive images. These go to a planner who lays them according to the number of pages. A lithographic plate is then produced from which the final printed article eventually emerges.

Procedures vary, because of the range of equipment used. With less sophisticated units, operators have to calculate the correct exposure to ensure the best reproduction. Electronic scanners are increasingly used for colour processing; with more traditional cameras, operators have to produce films and plates for each of the one, two, three or four printing colours. Scanners also produce films for separate colours, but the colour separation itself is done automatically according to the operators' input.

Platemaking involves the exposure of the prepared plate with the negative or positive to ultraviolet light in a vacuum frame to obtain perfect contact.

Some methods mean that platemakers must process the plate to reveal the image. Any blemishes must be removed carefully with special fluids and the plate treated to protect it.

In small firms, camera operating, planning and platemaking may be processes performed by one person. Larger firms usually have separate operators for each job, and platemakers may also be involved in layout design.

WORK ENVIRONMENT

Conditions are clean and dry, although some processes involve handling chemicals and water. The job inevitably means working in subdued light for some of the time. Operators spend much of their time on their feet but in relatively quiet surroundings.

SKILLS AND INTERESTS

Camera operators, planners and platemakers must have good colour vision. They may have to carry out simple mathematical calculations, and they must be meticulous. They need to be able to work well with other people since strong team work is called for.

ENTRY REQUIREMENTS, TRAINING AND LATE ENTRY

Please see article 5. BOOKBINDER/PRINT FINISHER.

OPPORTUNITIES

Camera operators, planners and platemakers are employed in all sections of the printing industry. Because the equipment is extremely expensive, and large, there are few opportunities for self-employment, unlike other areas of origination.

Please see article 5. BOOKBINDER/PRINT FINISHER.

PAY AND CONDITIONS

Please see article 1. KEYBOARD OPERATOR.

PROSPECTS, RELATED OCCUPATIONS, FURTHER INFORMATION AND READING

Please see article 5. BOOKBINDER/PRINT FINISHER.

4. MACHINE PRINTER (SAR)

THE WORK

Machine printers set up (make ready) and operate the machines for the final printing of the product. They all use different techniques because the machinery differs according to the printing process involved, but the essential task is to transfer the image on to the paper, plastic or board.

In lithography, machine printers are given a separate plate for each colour to be printed and fix them in the correct position around rotary press cylinders. Having done that, they fill ink ducts, set the controls to ensure a regular flow of ink and dampening solution, and start the machine for a trial run. Any necessary adjustments are made before the machine is set for the required run. If there are any difficulties during the run it is the machine printer's job to stop the machine and correct any problems, such as blemishes.

For letterpress printing, the printer is given a *forme*, which is a metal frame holding composed pages of type and illustrations. The forme is then fixed in a type bed. On rotary machines, a 'stereo' is made to fix round the cylinder. The letterpress is run in a similar manner to a litho machine.

Machines now have control consoles – units at the end or side of the machine from where the machine printer controls the printing process. With the larger machines involved in gravure and other four-colour processes, the machine printer is in charge of a team of one or more printing machine assistants, not only because of the size of the machine but also because of the speed of the printing (sometimes as many as 13,000 sheets an hour), which makes the process difficult to control alone.

WORK ENVIRONMENT

Machine printers work in a factory environment, sometimes with very noisy machines, and they need to be prepared to handle ink and maintain machinery.

SKILLS AND INTERESTS

As well as a mechanical ability and manual dexterity, an appreciation of electronics is increasingly important. The work requires constant vigilance and concentration as well as careful attention to detail. The ability to work well as part of a team is important and printers must have leadership ability if they are in charge of a team of assistant machine minders. Good colour vision is essential.

ENTRY REQUIREMENTS, TRAINING AND LATE ENTRY

Please see article 5. BOOKBINDER/PRINT FINISHER.

OPPORTUNITIES

Machine printers work in all parts of the printing industry. There is a demand for skilled litho printers in this field.

PAY AND CONDITIONS

Please see article 1. KEYBOARD OPERATOR.

In addition, extra payments in excess of £80 a week are payable for the operation of large machines.

PROSPECTS, RELATED OCCUPATIONS, FURTHER INFORMATION AND READING

Please see article 5. BOOKBINDER/PRINT FINISHER.

5. BOOKBINDER/PRINT FINISHER (SAR)

THE WORK

Skilled work in the finishing department involves operating the machinery that performs one or more of the finishing processes, completing the product.

There are numerous other workers in this section of the industry who assist the skilled machine operators.

Machines include guillotines to cut paper or card, folders,

hole-punchers, stitchers, staplers, and collators. Die-makers produce formers to crease or cut cards for cartons.

After the work has been completed, the operators stack paper, card, booklets or book sections before setting up their machines and making them ready for the work. Some operators work on a number of different kinds of machine and others perform one particular function in the finishing process.

Some machines combine a number of processes, sometimes including cutting, collating pages, assembling, stitching and binding books on a single machine.

WORK ENVIRONMENT

Most bookbinding and finishing work is carried out in workshop conditions, sometimes resembling a warehouse, with partially and completely finished products stacked over wide areas. The work may be dusty and noisy because of the machinery. Some machines need more than one person to operate them and finishing processes can involve team work.

SKILLS AND INTERESTS

Good hand skills are needed as well as the ability to work with machinery. Some jobs involve team work, so it is important to work well with other people.

ENTRY REQUIREMENTS

There are no minimum academic requirements for entry, although employers may prefer GCSEs/S grades (A-C/1-3) in English, maths, a science or technology. However, the recruitment policies of individual firms vary enormously.

TRAINING

In England and Wales, new trainees may be recruited to training schemes. These may combine work experience with college study on a day or block release basis.

The main course is the City and Guilds in Graphic Communications, which normally takes two years to complete.

The course has various streams including machine printing, origination, reprography and screen printing.

In Scotland, trainees take the SCOTVEC National Certificate in Printing, by day or block release or on a full-time basis.

NVQs/SVQs are available in Machine Printing.

Bookbinding. There are various courses in bookbinding available.

It may be possible, occasionally, to find opportunities to train with a master bookbinder who specializes in hand binding and conservation and repair work.

LATE ENTRY

Theoretically there is no general bar to entry for adults of any age, although individual firms may have independent policies.

OPPORTUNITIES

There are opportunities for skilled workers in finishing departments in most sections of the industry. A number of independent finishing houses also do trade work for printing firms.

PAY AND CONDITIONS

Please see article 1. KEYBOARD OPERATOR.

PROSPECTS

Promotion prospects vary depending on the section of the industry and whether the person is single-skilled or has experience in a number of aspects of printing work. Appointment to supervisor or manager of a department is not uncommon; alternatively, an employee may move into administration where opportunities abound.

RELATED OCCUPATIONS

Word processor operator, computer operator, sub-/copy editor, layout artist, model maker, graphic designer, cameraman/woman, production worker.

FURTHER INFORMATION

British Printing Industries Federation (BPIF)*, 11 Bedford Row, London WC1R 4DX, 0171 242 6904

Institute of Printing (IOP)*, 8A Lonsdale Gardens, Tunbridge Wells, Kent TN1 1NU, 01892 38118

Scottish Print Employers Federation*, 48 Palmerston Place, Edinburgh EH12 5DE, 0131 220 4353

FURTHER READING

Leaflets/booklets are available from the addresses marked*.

Job Outlines – Publishing – COIC
Working in Publishing – COIC

In the careers library, classified under SAR.

CHEMICAL PLANT PROCESS OPERATOR
CLCI:SAV

BACKGROUND INFORMATION

The chemicals industry is Britain's fourth largest manufacturing industry and its highest-value exporter. It spends heavily on research and development – to keep at the forefront of science and technology – and on high-cost manufacturing plant. Its products include plastics, paints, medicines, fertilizers, adhesives, pesticides, herbicides, inks, dyes, polishes, and cosmetics.

The industry includes firms that refine feedstocks such as oil and natural gas to make base chemicals, firms that use these to create more sophisticated chemicals for industrial use, and firms that mix together chemicals to make finished products such as paints. Process plant is found mainly in the first two types of firm.

Chemicals manufacture is carried out either on a continuous process or by batch production. Continuous process plant runs 24 hours a day, seven days a week. A batch process may last for 24 hours or longer, and the same equipment may be used to make different chemicals. Usually one or more chemical reactions occur during these processes. Production in both cases can take place in massive vessels connected by large amounts of pipework.

THE WORK

Chemical plant process workers operate and look after the process plant that makes the chemicals. On continuous process plant, operators walk around the plant. They check what is happening by taking meter and instrument readings.

To start another stage of the process, or to speed up or slow down the process, they open or close valves by hand or automatically. They draw off small samples of the product to test that its quality meets the specification. They may do a simple chemical reaction test themselves by adding another substance or pass the sample to technicians in a laboratory.

However, in the main, they are looking to prevent a fault occurring in the process – a leaking pipe-joint, for example – that may need attention or maintenance. Usually they report faults to the relevant expert, to a maintenance fitter, for example, but increasingly process operators carry out the less complex and time-consuming maintenance tasks themselves.

They may also spend time in the control room, operating a computer-controlled process by taking readings from an electronic instrument panel. This is to check that everything is proceeding normally and to identify any sign that a process is going wrong and take corrective action. This is usually carried out by the plant controller, who is an experienced process operator.

Normally a team – of three to four workers a shift – looks after a large section of plant. The team might consist of, for example, a senior controller, a plant controller and one or two process operators.

On batch production, the process operator cleans out and prepares the equipment and pipework, measures out the ingredients and adds them into the reaction tanks in the correct sequence. They then switch on any heating, cooling or other operations, take readings as the process continues, make adjustments manually or by pressing control buttons, and take samples for testing. On completion of the process, they close down the plant and may run off the finished product into barrels, container lorries, railway trucks, etc. The work involves learning the different processes under supervision first and then working carefully to written instructions.

WORK ENVIRONMENT

The control room, which serves as base, is dry, clean and usually air-conditioned because of the electronic equipment. Increasingly chemical plants themselves are being updated to protect the environment and may also be modern and clean, though there remain some older, dirtier plants. There may be dust and fumes.

Workers wear protective overalls, helmets and boots. Some of the chemicals in some plants may be hazardous and involve the process operator wearing additional protective clothing including breathing apparatus, face masks and gloves.

The work may involve climbing stairs to considerable heights and walking long distances along catwalks around the tanks and pipework. It may also include long periods of sitting or standing. The plant may be covered or outdoors.

At night, lit by floodlights, parts of the plant may be dark and in shadow so that a torch is needed, for example, to examine pipework. Communication with the control room is by phones at key points, a mobile phone or a two-way radio.

SKILLS AND INTERESTS

Process operators need to have the patience to cope with regular routines, during which times little may happen, yet be able, if a problem or emergency arises, to react quickly, make the right decisions and take the correct actions.

An interest in science and technology is important.

They should be able to work in a team, yet be self-sufficient enough to cope with the responsibility of patrolling the plant on their own. Physical fitness is needed for climbing, walking, being out in all weathers and lifting or loading chemicals into containers.

Good eyesight and colour vision are required for reading meters, dials and instrument charts. An eye for detail and a good memory for what should be happening at each part of the plant and at each stage of the process is valuable.

ENTRY REQUIREMENTS

Employers seek people who are mature and responsible, so they tend to recruit people over 18 years (and in some cases over 23) who have held at least one other job since leaving school.

However, this is beginning to change with the introduction of Modern Apprenticeships. Specific training opportunities for young people, including Modern Apprenticeships, may be available – contact your local careers office, TEC/LEC for details.

In many companies, there are no formal educational requirements, though basic numeracy and literacy and a good general education is an asset. Applicants may be asked to take numeracy and general intelligence tests. Some companies ask for GCSEs/S grades (A-D/1-4) in maths and science subjects.

However, the increasing complexity of process control systems has resulted in some companies looking for technical qualifications for control staff roles. Relevant qualifications include City and Guilds and NVQs/SVQs (see TRAINING).

TRAINING

On-the-job training is provided. Some new process operators accompany an experienced worker, watching what they do and learning from them, then doing the tasks under their supervision. Normally this follows classroom induction training which includes health and safety information and precautions, and a basic understanding of the main chemical processes involved.

For more complex processes, there may be additional in-company courses. In some plants, there may be day release to study for a City and Guilds qualification in, for example, Instrumentation and Control, Materials Processing, Industrial Studies, and Scientific Calculation.

Increasingly, process operators are assessed in the workplace, carrying out their duties. These assessments of competence lead to NVQs/SVQs in Process Operations at Levels 1, 2 and 3.

LATE ENTRY

There is no maximum age limit, though company policies vary. Many firms prefer mature applicants, who have worked in other jobs or have experience in other process industries.

OPPORTUNITIES

There have always been relatively few openings for plant operators. In recent years, the number of posts has reduced even more due to factors such as recession, improvements in remote sensing, and computerization and electronic control of operations.

Employers range from big multinational chemical and oil companies to small firms producing specialist chemicals. The larger chemical process plants tend to be located near ports where feedstocks arrive by sea and where facilities for export are convenient. They may also be sited near natural sources of mineral feedstocks or in major industrial centres close to potential customers.

With the multinationals, there may be opportunities to work overseas, for example, in Europe, the Middle East, Far East and the Americas.

PAY AND CONDITIONS

Pay varies from company to company. However, process operators usually earn £15,000 to £20,000, plus overtime and productivity/bonus payments.

Basic hours are 38 a week. Plants operate 24 hours a day, seven days a week, so shift-working is common, involving night and weekend work. The shift pattern may change every week or two, so as to rotate everyone through the different duties. There are opportunities for overtime.

PROSPECTS

Promotion is from trainee plant operator (who works under instruction) to plant operator (who carries out normal routine operations) and then to plant controller (who runs the team from the control room). Beyond that are senior controller (who is responsible for that area of the plant) and shift supervisor (who is responsible for all areas of plant).

In smaller companies and on batch processes, there are fewer levels. Plant manager positions are normally held by graduate chemists or engineers.

There may be opportunities to take courses in craft maintenance and laboratory work to increase the range of practical skills or to take appropriate C&G/BTEC/SCOTVEC qualifications to transfer to craft or technician posts.

RELATED OCCUPATIONS

Plastics process operative, brewery worker, water/sewage treatment plant operator, electricity generation worker, engineer, meat process worker.

FURTHER INFORMATION

Chemical Industries Association (CIA), Kings Buildings, Smith Square, London SW1P 3JJ, 0181 834 3399

FURTHER READING

In the careers library, classified under SAV.

BLACKSMITH CLCI:SAW/RAB

BACKGROUND INFORMATION

Blacksmiths are concerned with shaping and constructing metalwork using both traditional and contemporary forge-work techniques. People often confuse the two trades of blacksmith and farrier: farriers shoe horses using blacksmithing skills to make the horseshoes. Only farriers are permitted by law to shoe horses. Some blacksmiths are farriers as well.

THE WORK

Blacksmiths work with a variety of metals. Mild steel is the main material, but wrought iron is increasingly used. Some also work with stainless steel, copper, brass and bronze. Other metals used are carbon tool steels, cast iron and alloys. First the metal is cut to the sizes laid down in drawings. Basic forge work is a series of different techniques involving heating, shaping, cooling, re-heating and re-shaping using a wide variety of tools. The blacksmith holds a piece of metal in an open coke, coal or gas fire – the forge or hearth – with a pair of tongs until it is hot and pliable. This is then transferred on to an anvil, where it is gradually shaped with blows from a variety of hammers or tools.

A variety of tools can be used for decoration and other techniques such as twisting, pinching and texturing. The design of traditional blacksmiths' hand tools has changed little over the centuries. Blacksmiths often make their own tools. Power tools are also now used such as power hammers, drills, air chisels and hydraulic presses. Engineering machinery such as centre lathes, millers and grinders may be used. Modern fabrication equipment, including plasma cutters, is used too. Sheet metal is often worked cold and shaped by cutting and manipulation.

Once the pieces of metal have been shaped they are fixed together by, for example, riveting, fire and arc welding, or soldering. A range of equipment such as MIG, TIG and oxy-acetylene torches is used in welding. Surface finishing ranges through gilding, zincing, galvanizing, to grit blasting. Decorative techniques similar to those used by jewellers, such as *repoussage* and *relevage*, are used for intricate work. A wide selection of paints and dangerous chemicals are also employed. Protective clothing – leather aprons, overalls, face masks, ear defenders, safety glasses, and shoes – are worn when required.

Blacksmiths make anything from gates for stately homes and canal locks, metal housing for industrial machinery and road barriers, to candlestick holders and decorative brackets. Most blacksmiths specialize in an area of work.

They work in agriculture, making, for example, farm trailers and sheep feeders, and mending agricultural machinery. Some steel farm buildings are made and erected by them.

The building trade uses blacksmiths to make and fix fire escapes, security grills and steel doors. Engineering companies may sub-contract to, or employ, blacksmiths with a knowledge of mechanical engineering for fabrication and welding of manufacturing equipment. Industry also uses blacksmiths for heavy forging, fabrication and tool production.

Some blacksmiths have conservation and restoration skills. They use their detailed knowledge of architectural history, maintenance, materials and finishes in the heritage industry, restoring and replacing ironwork in and around old buildings.

Other blacksmiths design, produce and market decorative work for indoor domestic and garden use, and for the tourist trade. Some make limited editions of art objects, both decorative and functional items, for sale in museums and galleries.

Architects employ blacksmiths to work on modern office buildings and shopping centres, producing and installing railings, staircases and decorative ironwork. Local councils employ them to design and make street furniture such as seats, lamps and litter bins.

WORK ENVIRONMENT

Forges vary in size from a large engineering workshop to a small brick shed. Most of the work is carried out under cover but installation can involve working outdoors. They work in extremes of temperature from the heat of the area around the forge to freezing site conditions. Some jobs involve visiting customers and fetching supplies.

Blacksmiths' forges are usually uncomfortable, noisy, dirty and smelly due to the nature of the work. Safety practices are strictly enforced due to fire hazard and use and storage of dangerous chemicals. Most of the work is done standing up and involves a lot of bending and lifting.

SKILLS AND INTERESTS

Fitness and stamina rather than strength are essential, as the craft is physically demanding. Power tools are now used for much of the heavier work. Good hand-to-eye co-ordination is important for working accurately. As the craft uses technical skills a logical approach is required. Artistic ability and design skills are needed by artistic blacksmiths. Much of the work is repetitive and progress can be slow. Persistence and strong powers of concentration are therefore important.

Blacksmiths tend to work alone, so they must be well-motivated and self-disciplined.

Many blacksmiths are self-employed. Running a business requires sound business and administration skills. An important element of the job is sales and marketing, which means being confident and sociable, and able to get on with people at all levels.

ENTRY REQUIREMENTS

There are no formal entry requirements for those seeking employment with a blacksmith or entry on to specialist smithing courses. Attendance on short courses, related qualifications and/or examples of metalwork are helpful.

Related areas include:

Engineering, including welding and sheetmetal work: useful subjects include maths, engineering, workshop theory and practice, craft (metal), design technology, and integrated science. These are also basic entry requirements for BTEC/SCOTVEC, NVQ/SVQ or City and Guilds qualifications.

Art and design: three-dimensional (3-D) design in metalwork – the usual entry requirements for higher national diploma courses are BTEC National Diploma/Certificate in General Art and Design; or three GCSEs/S grades (A-C/1-3) with one A level in a relevant subject; or five GCSEs/S grades (A-C/1-3) and successful completion of a foundation course in art and design. For degree courses, five GCSEs/S grades (A-C/1-3) are required, with two A levels/three H grades or equivalent.

TRAINING

On the job

Occasionally, job opportunities occur where specific skills such as welding, sheetmetal work, fabrication or 3-D metalwork design are sought. Other blacksmithing and forging techniques are taught on the job.

For those already working in blacksmithing in rural areas, the Rural Development Commission has a programme of courses designed to extend and develop skills and techniques. Contact the Rural Development Commission for further details.

The Worshipful Company of Blacksmiths is active in developing training. It promotes standards of excellence and professional practice through a system of awards made at all levels from apprentices upwards. Diploma holders are associates of the company and are entitled to use AWCB after their name. Medal holders are fellows (FWCB) and licentiates (LWCB).

Apprenticeships

Few blacksmiths are able to offer apprenticeships. Prospective apprentices have to find their own Masters. The Worshipful Company of Blacksmiths administers apprenticeships. Other apprenticeships are administered by the National Joint Apprenticeship Council (NJAC) through the National Association of Farriers, Blacksmiths and Agricultural Engineers (NAFBAE). Attendance at Herefordshire College on a block release basis is a NJAC requirement (see below).

Courses

Herefordshire College of Technology

1. College Diploma in Blacksmithing and Metalworking – one year full-time. The course covers the full range of blacksmithing including: the use of hand and machine tools; cutting and welding; farm machinery maintenance; metal fabrication; wrought iron design; materials; costing; art and design; and business skills.

2. College Diploma in Blacksmithing and Restoration Crafts – one year full-time. A specialized course for those wishing to pursue a career in restoration work. It covers blacksmithing and related areas including: heat treatment and corrosion control of metals; preservation, conservation and restoration techniques; drawing and design; and business skills. Students visit museums and heritage sites. A project portfolio is produced, and the course includes two weeks' practical experience.

3. College Certificate in Rural Smithing – four years, block release. This course is designed for those employed in small firms catering for the rural market. It covers smithing, gas and arc welding, bench fitting, machine shop practice and agricultural implement repair. Subsidiary subjects include electrical safety requirements, engineering science, reading drawings, workshop calculations, and business skills. Apprentices indentured with NJAC sit trade tests in smithing, welding and bench fitting, with implements repair option.

4. College Certificate in Industrial Smithing – four years, block release. This course is suitable for those working in small urban workshops handling work for industry, builders, local government, etc. Blacksmithing and fabrication craft work is combined with welding, sheetmetal work, bench fitting and lathework. Ornamental ironwork option. See College Certificate in Rural Smithing (above) for subsidiary subjects and details of NJAC tests.

5. BTEC National Diploma in Three Dimensional Design: Blacksmithing – two years, full-time. This course is offered jointly with Herefordshire College of Art and Design. It provides a basic understanding of drawing and design principles, coupled with practical workshop introductions into the structure and use of materials.

6. BTEC Higher National Diploma in Design Crafts: Blacksmithing – two years, full-time. This course is also offered jointly with Herefordshire College of Art and Design. It has been devised to prepare students to enter or establish a workshop in order to produce originally designed works directed towards high quality outlets. There is also provision for students to concentrate on restoration work, should that be where their strengths lie.

West Dean College runs a programme of residential courses lasting from two to five days in basic blacksmithing, wrought ironwork and decorative techniques.

Camberwell College of Arts – BA Hons Three-dimensional Design, Ceramics or Silversmithing/Metalwork. The course develops the creative use of materials and processes. Students produce individual pieces as well as learning about batch production. The metalwork option covers blacksmithing and architectural metalwork.

Art and design courses at higher national diploma and degree level, in three-dimensional design specializing in jewellery or metalwork, is another route into blacksmithing. Contact the British Artist Blacksmiths' Association.

Craft engineering/craft training schemes with engineering companies are run through a local network of group training associations (GTAs). Trainees work towards BTEC/SCOTVEC, NVQ/SVQ or City and Guilds qualifications in welding and fabrication. Usual age of entry is 16 or 17 years. Contact Engineering Careers Information Service.

Training schemes for young people.

Wye Valley Training, based at Herefordshire College of Technology, is the main training provider for blacksmithing. Placements are organized through the agency. The NJAC recognizes the first two years of training as the equivalent of the first two years of its four-year apprenticeship, subject to passing trade tests. For further information, contact Wye Valley Training or your local careers office, TEC/LEC.

The New Entrants' Training Scheme (NETS) in Forgework, run by the Rural Development Commission, provides training for young people aged 16-25 (though older applicants may be considered). Applicants must be employed in a rural area in England. Trainees receive twelve weeks' training over a two-year period. Successful trainees gain a range of qualifications, including two Worshipful Company of Blacksmiths' awards and City and Guilds awards or NVQs.

LATE ENTRY

There is no upper age limit and many take up blacksmithing as a second career. Entry requirements to art and design courses may be waived for adults.

There may be specific training opportunities directed at adults available in some areas for this type of work. Candidates may have to satisfy certain conditions to be eligible. Contact your local Jobcentre, careers office or TEC/LEC for details.

OPPORTUNITIES

Around 900 UK companies employ blacksmiths in mining, docks and engineering for maintenance, repair and production. Job opportunities are limited. There are few artist blacksmiths, but opportunities are increasing. Most are self-employed, working to commission for architects, interior designers and the public.

PAY AND CONDITIONS

Minimum rates of pay, hours of work and holidays laid down by the National Joint Wages Board (NJWB) of the Blacksmithing and Agricultural Engineering Trades are as follows. For apprentices: first year, £69.23 a week; second year, £78.84 a week; third year, £107.69 a week; fourth year, £136.54 a week. Qualified craftsmen/women earn £196.42 a week.

NJWB recommended hours of work are between 38 and 38½ hours a week, Monday to Saturday. Holidays are four working weeks a year, plus eight days statutory bank holidays.

NB: NJWB rates are not mandatory. Pay and hours are subject to individual negotiation between employer and employee.

PROSPECTS

In larger firms there are opportunities for promotion to supervisory posts.

RELATED OCCUPATIONS

Bladesmith, goldsmith/silversmith, farrier, agricultural mechanic, welder, sheetmetal worker, mechanical engineer, machine operator.

FURTHER INFORMATION

British Artist Blacksmiths' Association (BABA)*, Honorary Secretary, Carlton Husthwaite, Thirsk, North Yorkshire YO7 2BJ, 01845 501415 (please send first class stamp)

Engineering Careers Information Service, Vector House, 41 Clarendon Road, Watford, Hertfordshire WD1 1HS, 0800 282167 (freephone)

Herefordshire College of Technology, The Library, Folly Lane, Hereford HR1 1LS, 01432 352235 ext 216

National Organizer, National Association of Farriers, Blacksmiths and Agricultural Engineers (NAFBAE)*, The Forge, Avenue B, 10th Street, National Agricultural Centre, Stoneleigh, Kenilworth, Warwickshire CV8 2LG, 01203 696595

Rural Development Commission, 141 Castle Street, Salisbury, Wiltshire SP1 3TP, 01722 336255

Training Co-ordinator, Wye Valley Training, Herefordshire College of Technology, Folly Lane, Hereford HR1 1LS, 01432 276899

West Dean College, West Dean, Chichester, West Sussex PO18 0QZ, 01243 811301

Worshipful Company of Blacksmiths, 27 Cheyne Walk, Grange Road, London N21 1DB, 0181 364 1522

FURTHER READING

Leaflets/booklets are available from the addresses marked*.

In the careers library, classified under SAW/RAB.

1. ARCHITECT CLCI:UB
2. ARCHITECTURAL TECHNOLOGIST CLCI:UB

BACKGROUND INFORMATION

Architects are concerned with the design of new buildings and the alteration of existing buildings. New buildings may be single structures, such as houses, shops, schools, factories, warehouses, offices and hospitals, or may be complete housing estates, shopping precincts, industrial estates and office blocks.

Alterations to existing buildings may mean extending them, converting them to a different use or modernizing them.

Architects are not only concerned with design. They are often responsible for every stage of a building project, through to completion of the building work.

Traditionally, architectural technologists worked entirely under the supervision of architects. Many still do so, but the responsibilities of other technologists have expanded considerably and some technologists now work independently of architects.

1. ARCHITECT (UB)

THE WORK

Architects design new buildings and design alterations to existing buildings. They may also be responsible for complete projects from design to the completed structures.

Architects receive a brief (instructions) from a client, which details the work the client requires and the budget available. They discuss the brief and advise the client, taking into account the type of building required, the proposed site, legal and planning matters and costs involved.

Architects may undertake preliminary research by arranging for the site and its surroundings to be surveyed and by discussing the proposals to decide how they will affect people who will use the building.

The next stage involves architects in preparing a design at a drawing board or, increasingly, on a computer. The design must take into account how the building will be used, its appearance, the materials to be used, how all the services will work and the costs involved. Architects must make sure in their design that the building can be built and maintained safely. In preparing the design, architects combine their creativity with a high level of technical knowledge and social awareness.

Architects present the client with a visual idea of the proposed design, which may include a model of the project, and an estimate of the cost.

When a client has approved the design, architects produce 'working drawings', which are detailed drawings specifying exact dimensions, materials, fittings, services and costings. In some cases the working drawings are produced by an architectural technologist rather than an architect. During this stage architects may work closely with other professionals, including civil and structural engineers, mechanical and electrical engineers, surveyors, landscape architects and quantity surveyors. They may negotiate and agree contracts with those needed for the project.

In many projects architects are in overall charge until completion. In these cases architects make constant visits to sites to check progress, see that the work is of the necessary quality, issue instructions to contractors' agents, authorize payments to contractors, and generally take responsibility for solving any problems that may arise.

Some architects specialize in areas such as project management, building investigation, safety planning and energy advisory work.

WORK ENVIRONMENT

Most of architects' work is office-based, in clean, light surroundings. They may be outside their own offices for a good deal of time when visiting clients, planners, builders and others.

Architects responsible for a project until completion spend some time on site, which involves being outdoors in all weathers.

Much of the time indoors is spent sitting, while site work includes walking.

Travelling to meetings and sites can take up a considerable mount of architects' time. The work may involve being away from home for extended periods.

SKILLS AND INTERESTS

Architects need drawing ability as they design by drawing. They must be creative to be able to work through problems to achieve a finished structure that will satisfy both their clients and public opinion. Creativity must be matched by a practical approach to enable them to design buildings that are safe and suited to their purpose.

Ability in science is essential for solving design problems and understanding the properties of building materials. Mathematical ability is necessary for preparing costings and for dealing with financial matters. As computer-aided design (CAD) techniques are increasingly being used for design, architects need to be confident in using CAD instead of a traditional drawing board when appropriate.

Architects must have an awareness of social and environmental factors, as the people who use their buildings can be greatly affected by the design.

Good communication skills are important. Architects are constantly involved in meetings and discussions with clients and others involved in a project.

Architects should have good management skills to organize and lead several projects at the same time. Ability to negotiate and persuade is desirable.

Architects should be physically fit to cope with site inspections. There is, however, scope for people with disabilities to qualify and succeed as architects.

ENTRY REQUIREMENTS

The minimum entry qualifications are those required to enter a degree course accredited jointly by the Royal Institute of British Architects (RIBA) and the Architects Registration Council of the United Kingdom (ARCUK). Minimum requirements are:

– two A levels/three H grades with five GCSEs/two S grades (A-C/1-3) in other subjects. Both the A levels/H grades must be in academic subjects. They should include English, maths and either physics, chemistry or dual award science.

Some schools of architecture will accept either:

– Advanced GNVQ Construction and Built Environment/ GSVQ Construction Level III Construction, *or*

– BTEC National Certificate/Diploma in Building Studies, or SCOTVEC National Certificate in Building/Building Construction plus GCSE/S grade (A-C/1-3) in English.

Many schools of architecture require more than the minimum requirements. They may also specify certain subjects. Details of each school's requirements are listed in a booklet published by the RIBA–*Schools of Architecture with Courses Recognized by the RIBA.*

It is not essential to have an art qualification but applicants must be able to sketch and draw freehand. Most schools of architecture ask to see an applicant's portfolio of drawings and sketches.

TRAINING

To use the title architect it is necessary to register with ARCUK. Registration is permitted when applicants have gained exemption from Parts 1, 2 and 3 of the RIBA Examination in Architecture and spent at least two years working in an architect's office. Most achieve this by following a full-time course that is offered at 38 schools of architecture in the UK.

Training takes at least seven years. There are variations between schools but there are usually four stages in training:

1. Three or four years at a school of architecture to work for a degree in architecture and exemption from RIBA Part 1. (Those who do not wish to continue beyond this stage may seek to become architectural technologists or can use their degree to enter any one of a range of careers open to all graduates).

2. One year, usually spent working in an architect's office.

3. Two years further study at a school of architecture to obtain a diploma or higher degree and exemption from RIBA Part 2. This does not necessarily have to take place at the same school at which Part 1 was taken.

4. One year (at least) working in an architect's office before taking the RIBA Part 3 Professional Practice Examination. Successful completion of Part 3 allows registration with ARCUK and membership of the RIBA.

Some schools of architecture offer part-time training on a day release basis for students already working in an architect's office. The degree takes four or five years and the diploma course three years. A further year must be spent in an architect's office before taking the Professional Practice Examination.

A large part of the time at a school of architecture is spent on project work, where, individually or in groups, students design buildings. Subjects studied include design, building science and technology, construction and structure, history and theory of architecture, environmental science, urban studies, town planning, social studies, economics, communication, computer-aided design, and professional practice.

LATE ENTRY

There is no upper age limit for entry to architecture. Adult entrants normally follow the route described in TRAINING, which takes a minimum of seven years.

Alternatively, adults with at least six years continuous practical architecture experience who have the minimum qualifications needed for entry to an architecture degree may become external candidates. They may work towards the RIBA Examination in Architecture and Examination in Professional Practice and become qualified architects.

Those who have already gained RIBA Part 2 from attending a school of architecture need only three years' practical architecture experience to become an external candidate.

OPPORTUNITIES

There are approximately 19,800 architects in full-time employment in the UK. Sixty-nine per cent of them work in private practice, with practices varying in size from those with one or two staff to those with over 50. About half have five or fewer staff. The majority of those in private practice are self-employed. Seven per cent of architects work for private companies such as retail organizations, building and civil engineering firms, industrial firms, and commercial organizations such as banks and breweries.

Fifteen per cent of architects work for local authorities and nine per cent for central government.

Architects are employed throughout the UK, although almost half are located in London and South East England.

Architecture is closely linked with the building industry, which is subject to the state of the economy more than most industries. The number of unemployed architects rose from one per cent of those in the workforce in 1990 to seven per cent in 1994 and about a fifth of those in work were not working to full capacity. As a result, newly qualified architects have found it difficult to find a first job, although some continue in employment with the organization with which they worked towards Part 3 of the RIBA exams.

Work overseas is a possibility, either for UK-based private practices that win contracts abroad, or with government bodies such as the Overseas Development Administration.

Vacancies for architects are advertised in *Building Design, Architects' Journal, RIBA Journal, Architect, Building,* and *Planning.*

PAY AND CONDITIONS

In 1994 the average salary for an architect's assistant with Part 1 of the RIBA examination was £12,000. An architect's assistant with the Part 2 examination earned an average of £14,217, while a newly qualified architect aged 27 averaged £20,685 a year. A partner or director of 45 years with 14 years' experience earned an average salary of £36,814. There were slight regional variations with those in London earning above average in each case.

Architects have a basic working week of 9am to 5pm, Monday to Friday, but pressure of deadlines can mean that they must work some evenings and weekends.

Architects involved in site management have to deal with problems whenever they arise. They can be on-call 24 hours a day or have to be on site while building is being carried out.

Part-time work is common.

PROSPECTS

Architects may become partners in private practices. Many architects set up on their own.

In central and local government there is a promotion structure that enables architects to progress to chief architect.

Some architects achieve further qualifications and become planners, landscape architects or conservation specialists. Others move into teaching in schools of architecture. A few use their architectural experience to become writers, journalists or researchers.

RELATED OCCUPATIONS

Town planner, engineer, surveyor, landscape architect, construction manager, interior designer, architectural technologist.

FURTHER INFORMATION AND READING

Please see article 2. ARCHITECTURAL TECHNOLOGIST.

2. ARCHITECTURAL TECHNOLOGIST (UB)

BACKGROUND INFORMATION

In 1994 the British Institute of Architectural Technicians became the British Institute of Architectural Technologists (BIAT). This change reflected the increased responsibilities of architectural technicians over the past few years. Members of the BIAT are now known as architectural technologists. Others in the field may be known either as architectural technicians or architectural technologists. For the purposes of this article they are all called architectural technologists.

In the past, architectural technologists worked under the supervision of architects. Many still do so but increasingly they operate as professionals in their own right.

THE WORK

Architectural technologists are concerned with the technological aspects of building design and construction, from the initial client briefing to completion of the project.

There is considerable variation in the work of different architectural technologists, depending on the organization worked for and the experience and seniority of the technologist. Some experienced architectural technologists are responsible for managing the whole building process from start to finish; others may specialize in just one part of the process.

Duties may begin with discussions with a client to understand what the client requires and to advise what is possible.

Architectural technologists conduct preliminary investigations based on the client's brief. They gather, analyse and prepare all the technical information that is necessary before a design can be produced. This can involve surveying sites and buildings and collecting specialist advice and opinion from other professionals, such as structural and civil engineers.

The design itself may be the responsibility of an architect but in routine building or conversion work the design may be done by an architectural technologist. The technologist may prepare drawings or a model of the design and be involved in a presentation of the design to the client.

Whether or not the architectural technologists has been responsible for the design, it is usually the technologist who prepares detailed technical drawings specifying, for example, dimensions and materials to be used. These may be drawn at a drawing board but are increasingly produced by computer-aided design (CAD) techniques. In both design and detailed drawings architectural technologists use their technical knowledge and take into account the legislation and regulations that affect the project.

Architectural technologists may be responsible for inviting tenders for the building work, which can involve liaising with quantity surveyors to prepare the necessary information, and for negotiating contracts with building contractors.

When the building work takes place architectural technologists monitor schedules to check that the project is progressing on time, deal with any problems on site, make sure that the correct materials are used, and carry out regular inspections. They are also concerned with routine project administration tasks, such as the issue of instructions and certification of work satisfactorily completed.

Some architectural technologists manage the day-to-day running of an architect's office. Some operate within architects' offices as CAD systems managers.

WORK ENVIRONMENT

Much of architectural technologists' work is office-based in clean, light conditions, although they frequently may be out of their offices to attend meetings, collect data and visit sites.

Some of their time is spent on-site, involving being outdoors in all weathers and wearing boots and safety helmets.

Much of the time indoors is spent sitting, while site work includes walking.

Architectural technologists spend some of their time travelling between their office and meetings on-site and elsewhere. For most that involves driving. For some, the work can include spending extended periods away from home.

SKILLS AND INTERESTS

Architectural technologists should have an interest in design and be able to draw. The ability to visualize objects in three-dimensional (3D) form is helpful. An interest in architecture and the environment is desirable.

Aptitude with figures is required, both for technical and financial calculations. Scientific ability is necessary to understand building technology.

A methodical, accurate approach with an eye for detail is demanded to be able to produce detailed drawings. As computer-aided design (CAD) techniques are increasingly used for design, architectural technologists need to be confident in using CAD when appropriate.

The ability to get on well with people and operate effectively within a team is essential, as architectural technologists spend much of their time in discussions and consultations with clients, architects, contractors and others. They need good listening, spoken and written communication skills, together with a diplomatic but persuasive manner. These skills are also important as architectural technologists may have an important role in co-ordinating the professional consultants involved in a project.

Architectural technologists should be physically fit to cope with site inspections.

ENTRY REQUIREMENTS

There is no specified minimum qualification required for entry to work as an architectural technologist, although in practice most entrants have at least four GCSEs/S grades (A-C/1-3).

BTEC National Certificate/Diploma in Building Studies

requires four GCSEs/S grades (A-C/1-3). Useful subjects include English, maths, science, technology and art.

SCOTVEC National Certificate in Building/Construction Studies has no formal entry requirements. Colleges admit students they feel can benefit from the course.

Advanced GNVQ Construction and the Built Environment usually requires either four GCSEs/S grades (A-C/1-3) or Intermediate GNVQ Construction and the Built Environment.

GSVQ Level III Construction has no formal entry requirements. Colleges admit students they feel can benefit from the course, including students who have successfully completed GSVQ Level II Construction.

BTEC Higher National Certificate/Diploma in Building Studies usually requires either: two A levels to have been taken and one passed, plus four GCSEs (A-C); or a relevant Advanced GNVQ (for example, Construction and the Built Environment, or Science); or a relevant BTEC national certificate/diploma.

SCOTVEC Higher National Certificate/Diploma in Architectural Technology/Building usually requires either: two H grades and three S grades in separate subjects, with a preference for English, maths and science; or a relevant GSVQ Level III (for example, Construction or Science); or appropriate SCOTVEC national certificate modules.

Degree courses require either: two A levels/three H grades with three GCSEs/two S grades (A-C/1-3) in other subjects, with English, maths and science often being required; or a relevant Advanced GNVQ/GSVQ Level III (for example, Construction and the Built Environment, Construction, or Science); or a relevant BTEC/SCOTVEC national award. Candidates with a relevant higher national diploma may be accepted onto the second or third year of a degree course.

TRAINING

British Institute of Architectural Technologists (BIAT)

The BIAT is the professional body that represents architectural technologists and many employers expect entrants into architectural technology to work towards full membership of the BIAT. To become a member requires one of the following qualifications:

– a degree in architectural technology or a built environment subject with a technology base;

– an approved BTEC/SCOTVEC higher national certificate/diploma in building studies that includes a number of specified units;

– an alternative BIAT-approved higher level qualification, eg Royal Institute of British Architects (RIBA) Part 1 or Chartered Institute of Building (CIoB) Part 2.

Those who have followed a full-time course of study must have a further year of work experience. All applicants must complete a logbook for two years during practice and pass a professional interview.

The BIAT intends moving to degree entry for membership, probably by the late 1990s.

Pre-entry

There are a number of courses that prepare entrants for architectural technology.

BTEC National Diploma in Building Studies (two years full-time) is offered at many colleges throughout England, Wales and Northern Ireland.

SCOTVEC National Certificate in Building or Building Construction (one year full-time) is offered at almost 20 colleges in Scotland.

Advanced GNVQ Construction and the Built Environment (two years full-time) is offered at colleges throughout England, Wales and Northern Ireland.

GSVQ Construction Level III (normally two years full-time) is offered at colleges.

BTEC Higher National Diploma in Building Studies (two years full-time or three years on a sandwich basis) is offered at many colleges in England, Wales and Northern Ireland. Fifty-two of the courses include the units required by the BIAT for membership.

SCOTVEC Higher National Diploma in Architectural Technology/Building (two years full-time). Five colleges and universities in Scotland offer courses that include the units required for BIAT membership.

Degree courses in architectural technology (three or four years full-time, or four years on a sandwich basis) that are currently accepted by the BIAT as qualifying towards membership are offered at Huddersfield University, University of Luton, South Bank University, Glasgow College of Building and Printing in association with Glasgow Caledonian University, Napier University, and the University of Ulster.

On entry

Many architectural technologists enter work and attend college on a day release basis for a course appropriate to their entry qualifications.

BTEC National Certificate in Building Studies (two or three years). Courses are offered at many colleges throughout England, Wales and Northern Ireland.

SCOTVEC National Certificate in Building Construction (two years). Courses are offered at almost 20 colleges throughout Scotland.

BTEC Higher National Certificate in Building Studies (two years). Seventy-six colleges in England, Wales and Northern Ireland offer courses that include the units required for BIAT membership.

SCOTVEC Higher National Certificate in Building (two years). Twelve Scottish universities and colleges offer courses that include the units required for BIAT membership.

Subjects studied on national award courses may include all or some of the following: construction drawing, construction processes, the built environment, construction science, construction technology, construction materials, measurement, organization and procedures, site surveying and levelling, communication studies, building construction, design procedures, environmental science, structural mechanics and architectural detailing.

Higher national award courses include similar subjects plus: advanced building construction, building services and equipment, contractual procedures, computer-aided design (CAD), law and economics, and architecture administration and practice.

Degrees include similar subjects but may also include: history of building craft techniques, advanced technology, management theory, advanced CAD, interior architecture, and business studies.

GNVQ/GSVQ courses are designed to develop the general skills, knowledge and understanding that underpin a wide range of occupations relating to construction and the built environment. They are modular courses with units relevant to architectural technology.

LATE ENTRY

There is no upper age limit for entry. Mature applicants may be accepted for courses described in TRAINING without the usual minimum entry requirements, particularly if they have relevant experience, in construction, for example.

Those age 30 and over with at least ten years' relevant experience may become members of the BIAT through a special entry route called the profiling route.

OPPORTUNITIES

Architectural technologists work throughout the UK, mostly in private practice for firms headed by architects, architectural technologists or other professionals in the building industry. Others work for building contractors, property developers, housing associations, banks, building societies and commercial and manufacturing companies.

A number of architectural technologists work in the public sector for central government organizations such as the Property Services Agency, and for local authorities in the architects or planning departments.

An increasing number of architectural technologists are self-employed.

The number of architectural technologists has decreased in the past few years as a direct result of economic recession and there are now just under 20,000 in the UK, including approximately 6,000 who are members of BIAT.

Vacancies for architectural technologists are advertised in *Building Design, New Builder, Building, Architects Journal, Opportunities,* and *RIBA Journal.*

There are opportunities to work overseas, either for UK-based private practices that win contracts abroad or for government bodies.

PAY AND CONDITIONS

A survey in 1994 showed that junior architectural technologists at age 18 with BTEC/SCOTVEC national qualifications earned £8,174 to £12,100. Those age 24 with higher national qualifications and at least three years' experience earned £12,520 to £16,717, while 30-year-old architectural technologists with higher national qualifications and ten years' experience earned £15,688 to £20,333.

The earnings of architectural technologists who are partners or directors of a practice depend on the profitability of the practice.

The standard working week is 9am to 5pm Monday to Friday but pressure of deadlines can involve working in the evenings and at weekends. Architectural technologists in site management may have to be on site while work is going on, or possibly be on-call 24 hours a day.

Some architectural technologists work part-time.

PROSPECTS

Architectural technologists may be promoted to senior technical positions within their employing organization, which may include responsibility for supervising other staff.

Many architectural technologists with good experience in private practice set up on their own or go into partnership with other architectural technologists, architects or other building professionals.

It is possible to train to become an architect. Qualified architectural technologists interested in this should approach schools of architecture to check the acceptability of their existing qualifications for entry to an architecture degree.

Alternatively, architectural technologists with at least six years' practical experience who have the minimum qualifications needed for entry to an architecture degree may become external candidates. They may work towards the RIBA Examination in Architecture and Examination in Professional Practice and become qualified architects. Those who have already gained RIBA Part 1 from attending a school of architecture need only three years' practical experience to become an external candidate.

Some architectural technologists train for surveying by studying for the examinations of the Royal Institute of Chartered Surveyors.

RELATED OCCUPATIONS

Town planning technician, quantity surveying technician, design draughtsman/woman, civil engineering technician, construction manager, building surveyor, surveying technician, architect.

FURTHER INFORMATION

Architects Registration Council of the UK*, 73 Hallam Street, London W1N 6EE, 0171 580 5861

British Institute of Architectural Technologists*, 397 City Road, London EC1V 1NE, 0171 278 2206

Royal Incorporation of Architects in Scotland*, 15 Rutland Square, Edinburgh EH1 2BE, 0131 229 7545

Royal Institute of British Architects*, 66 Portland Place, London W1N 4AD, 0171 580 5533

FURTHER READING

Leaflets/booklets are available from the addresses marked*.

Job Outlines–Architecture–COIC

In the careers library classified under UB.

PROFESSIONAL BUILDER/TECHNICIAN CLCI:UD

BACKGROUND INFORMATION

The construction industry employs over one million people in the UK and accounts for around 10 per cent of gross national product. Forecasts of future demand for construction work indicate that 80 per cent of new projects over the next decade will be in building (as opposed to civil engineering). For this reason, and because the technical demands of building are becoming ever more complex, there is a growing need for qualified building professionals.

The following article describes four professional roles in building: estimator; buyer; planner; and construction manager. To understand the relationship between these and allied professions such as architects and quantity surveyors, a brief outline of the various stages in the management of a building project is necessary. These stages are as follows:

Design

The client defines a need – for instance, for a housing estate, factory or office block. The architect interprets the client's ideas into a design, and the architectural technologist produces working drawings. At the design stage, other professionals such as the consulting civil engineer, landscape architect and building services engineer may be involved. The drawings and specifications produced by this design team are then translated by the quantity surveyor into the **bill of quantities**; this document sets out in writing every operation that the building contractor will have to carry out in order to complete the contract, with lists of materials and methods of working. A number of firms of building contractors are then invited to submit tenders for the contract.

Tender stage

Once the contractor receives the design and the bill of quantities, the estimator can calculate the cost of labour, plant and materials. At this stage the planner starts work on planning a programme of operations, and the buyer obtains information on prices, availability and delivery dates. The construction manager advises on potential construction problems, and other professionals – such as the plant specialist, who is consulted on the use of machinery – are called in. At the end of this process, an estimate of the amount it will cost the contractor to complete the contract is reached, and a further amount is added for profit. This represents the tender price, which is submitted to the client.

Site preparation

If the tender is accepted by the client, then a considerable amount of preliminary work must be carried out before construction starts. The main role here is that of the planner, who works out the sequence of operations in detail, liaising with the buyer, construction manager, subcontractors, the design team and others.

Construction

Under the supervision of the construction manager, building work starts. Progress is continually monitored by the construction manager and planner, to ensure that work proceeds according to schedule.

THE WORK

Estimator

The estimator calculates the cost of labour, materials, subcontractors, plant and overheads. Estimating is closely linked to the process of tendering. A tender must reflect all the costs to the company, otherwise no profit will be made, but the price must be competitive or the contract will be won by another firm. It is therefore important to forecast costs as accurately as possible, working from architects' and engineers' drawings, the bill of quantities, and information on prices supplied by subcontractors and the company buyer.

The estimator is a member of the pre-tender team, liaising with the planner, buyer and technical staff to ensure that estimates are realistic, and that the tender submitted to the client will enable the contractor to make a profit.

Estimators are also concerned with comparing actual costs against estimates throughout the building process.

Buyer

The buyer sends out enquiries for quotations and once the most suitable quotation has been selected purchases materials, equipment and services required for the contract. The work involves negotiating the most competitive price and making sure that materials can be delivered on time.

Buyers usually invite potential suppliers to submit competitive tenders. They may screen suppliers, investigating their past track record to ensure that they have the ability to supply and deliver materials and/or labour to a set programme.

When tenders have been received, the buyer assesses each one from a commercial point of view, and to check its compliance with the required specifications.

The buyer then selects a particular firm from those that have submitted tenders, and proposes acceptance of a suitable contract to the management team.

The buyer's other responsibilities include checking that materials are to be delivered on time, and monitoring the quality of supplies. From time to time the buyer may be involved in commercial disputes over problems such as late delivery or poor quality.

In large firms some buyers specialize, for instance, in purchasing timber or steel.

Planner

The planner selects the most appropriate method and sequence for building operations. The aim is to schedule building work so that it can be completed within the shortest possible time.

The work involves planning and co-ordinating all the project's requirements for materials, equipment and labour. Planners make sure that everything is available at the right time, and they set target dates for completion of each stage of the construction process, for example, excavating, completing the structure, installation of services. They may be responsible for setting completion dates for whole projects.

Working from designs, plans and bills of quantities, planners construct a programme of the sequence of operations. The programme is usually diagrammatic, with some explanatory text, and is produced on computer. It involves complex calculations, for example, of quantities of materials required.

To plan the sequence of building operations, the planner needs to gather detailed information from the design team, buyer, estimator and others. Precise information on designs and specifications, and how they can be practically translated into bricks and mortar, are needed in order to set a target date for completion of each stage of the project. The planner also has to pass on information to the construction manager, subcontractors and other interested parties. The information gathering and disseminating role involves the planner in a lot of telephone liaison work.

Once construction has begun, planners usually need to modify the programme, taking into account any problems that have arisen, for instance delays caused by bad weather or late delivery of materials. If at all possible, they must try to re-schedule work so that the pre-arranged completion date can still be met. Monitoring the programme involves planners in site inspections.

In a small company planning may be combined with buying.

Construction manager

The construction manager usually oversees between four and six contracts and has overall responsibility for a building site, monitoring three main elements: quality, cost and speed. The construction manager co-ordinates operations, making sure they are carried out to the correct standard, and on schedule. A site manager or agent carries out the detailed work of overseeing the production process, in a similar way to the construction manager, but is usually only responsible for one site.

The majority of the work is at the construction stage, but at the tender and site preparation stages the construction manager liaises with the estimator, buyer, planner and other professionals. It is important that the planner and construction manager agree on the scheduling of operations, as it is the construction manager who actually puts the planner's programme into operation.

At the site preparation stage, the manager visits the site to check on matters such as access, environmental factors (trees, for example, may be left standing) and car parking. Services such as electricity and telephones have to be arranged, and site offices erected.

Once construction is under way, the manager leads and controls practical operations on site. On a large building project, this involves leading a team of professionals and co-ordinating the work of heads of section and supervisors. On a small site, there is more contact with the labour force, and the manager may act as a general foreman/woman. Much of the work involves trouble-shooting: sorting out problems such as labour disputes, non-arrival of plant or materials, and safety matters.

Another major aspect of the work is monitoring or taking overall responsibility for standards of materials and workmanship. On a small project, this can involve going out on site to check records of deliveries, completed work and measurements, then comparing these with plans and specifications; on a larger project, the manager supervises staff carrying out these tasks.

In the site office, records are kept, covering matters such as instructions received from the client and issued to subcontractors, hours worked, materials and plant used, health and safety, etc. The records are kept by clerical staff, but the construction manager is involved in the paperwork and is responsible for its organization tend maintenance. This may involve the use of computers.

Technician

Technicians provide support to professional staff and act as a link between management and the labour force on site.

In large and medium-sized companies, technicians usually specialize in one of the areas described above, carrying out the less complicated types of work. For example, in the buying area they may deal with purchasing for smaller contracts, working under the supervision of the company buyer.

In small companies, if technicians are employed, they may carry out aspects of all the areas described above.

WORK ENVIRONMENT

Estimators and buyers are generally office-based, working either at the company's head office or regional offices. They sometimes travel to visit sites.

Planners are usually site-based, but they sometimes work at regional or head offices.

Construction managers usually work in a site office – often a temporary structure, such as a Portacabin. They also spend a considerable proportion of the time outdoors, in all weathers, inspecting work on site. Inspection may involve climbing ladders and scaffolding. Travel is an important part of the construction manager's job and it may be necessary to work a long way from home, living in lodgings, whilst a contract is in progress. Construction managers also travel to meetings with clients, architects and other professionals.

Depending on the type of work involved, technicians may be site-based or office-based, or may combine both.

SKILLS AND INTERESTS

Professional builders and technicians need to be able to work well with other people as members of a team, and to liaise with other professionals. Good spoken and written communication skills are important.

A thorough knowledge of building techniques and materials is needed, and it is helpful to have site experience.

Numeracy is required for all professional and technician-level building work, and is particularly important for estimators and buyers, much of whose work involves interpreting figures and making calculations.

Self-motivation and the ability to plan and organize one's own workload are important. It is essential to be able to think logically.

Buyers need commercial awareness, with good negotiating skills, as well as an understanding of the technical aspects of building.

Estimators need to be able to work accurately, and assimilate details quickly.

A driving licence is useful and may be required.

ENTRY REQUIREMENTS

The most common entry route at professional level is via a relevant degree course. Minimum entry requirements are three GCSEs (A-C) or two S grades (1-3) and two A levels or three H grades. English and maths may be required at GCSE/S grade and some colleges require A level/H grade maths.

Entry to degree courses is also possible with a relevant BTEC/SCOTVEC national certificate or diploma, or with Advanced GNVQ/GSVQ Level III in a relevant subject, such as Construction and the Built Environment.

Technicians qualify via BTEC/SCOTVEC national or higher national awards. Normally, the minimum entry requirements for national level courses are four GCSEs/S grades (A-C/1-3), or Intermediate GNVQ/GSVQ Level II. However, less-qualified candidates may be admitted at the discretion of the college. Entry to higher national diploma/certificate courses is with: one A level/two H grades and supporting GCSEs/S grades (A-C/1-3); or a BTEC/SCOTVEC national award; or Advanced GNVQ/GSVQ Level III.

TRAINING

Degree level: degree courses in building, building management, building technology, construction, construction management and related subjects last three/four years; some are sandwich courses, including practical experience in the building industry. Employer sponsorship may be available for degree courses – contact the Construction Careers Service for further details. The degree is normally followed by three years' practical experience in construction, with continuing professional development (this may include further training courses, organized by employers). Membership of the Chartered Institute of Building (CIoB) can then be obtained after assessment at a professional interview.

Higher technician level: training is via a BTEC/SCOTVEC Higher National Certificate or Diploma in Building Studies (or equivalent). The higher national certificate is a part-time day release course, over two years, whilst the student is in employment. The higher national diploma is studied as a two-year full-time course, or three-year sandwich course.

Technician level: this involves entering employment and studying on day release for the BTEC/SCOTVEC national certificate (two to three years), or taking a full-time BTEC/SCOTVEC National Diploma course in Building Studies (or equivalent).

NVQs/SVQs in Building Site Supervision are available at Level 3 and Building Site Management at Level 4.

LATE ENTRY

There is no age limit on entry for candidates with previous experience in the construction industry (for instance at craft level), but it is difficult for adults with unrelated experience to enter this field.

The CIoB has a special entry route to corporate membership for mature candidates, normally non-graduates over 35 who hold higher national certificate or equivalent and are working in the industry at higher technician level or above.

Colleges may, at their discretion, accept adult candidates with relevant experience but who lack the usual academic entry qualifications.

There may be specific training opportunities directed at adults available in some areas for this type of work. Candidates may have to satisfy certain conditions to be eligible. Contact your local Jobcentre, careers office or TEC/LEC for details.

OPPORTUNITIES

Professional builders and technicians are employed by national and international firms of building contractors. Building contractors vary in size and scope, and it tends to be the medium-sized and larger firms, some of which combine building and civil engineering, that employ staff at professional and technician level. There are alsoopportunities with central and local government, and with other organizations that carry out or supervise their own construction projects – for instance, public utilities and major retailers.

Major international contractors offer opportunities to work abroad.

Self-employment is possible; a planner, for instance, can work on a self-employed basis for several small building companies.

Technicians also need to be prepared to be mobile.

PAY AND CONDITIONS

Salaries vary with individual employers, but typically are in the region of £10,000 to £12,000 for a graduate entrant. This could quickly rise to around £15,000, with additional benefits such as a company car. The most responsible posts command considerably higher salaries.

Technicians, once qualified to national certificate/diploma level, earn from around £9,000.

The standard working week is 37 to 40 hours, but actual hours worked may be irregular and include evenings and weekends.

PROSPECTS

Building graduates tend to start as planner, buyer, estimator or assistant to a construction manager, usually on the more straightforward building contracts. With experience it is possible to move on to larger and more complex projects, or into construction management. Further promotion could lead to the post of contracts manager, responsible for a number of different projects.

Some professional builders work in teaching or building research.

Higher-level technicians may qualify as chartered builders by gaining practical experience, part-time study for the membership exams of the Chartered Institute of Building and the professional interview.

Technicians may proceed via the higher national certificate/diploma route or study part-time for the associate grade of the Chartered Institute of Building, followed by further part-time study for the membership examinations and the professional interview, although the associate route is becoming less common.

RELATED OCCUPATIONS

Architect, building services engineer, building surveyor, civil engineer, clerk of works, quantity surveyor, town planner.

FURTHER INFORMATION

Careers in Construction, Construction Industry Training Board, Bircham Newton Training Centre, Bircham Newton, Kings Lynn, Norfolk PE31 6RH, 01553 776677 ext 2466

Chartered Institute of Building, Englemere, King's Ride, Ascot, Berkshire SL5 8BJ, 01344 23355

FURTHER READING

The Construction Industry Handbook of Professional and Management Careers – CITB Professional and Management Careers in Building – CITB

Periodicals: Building Construction News; New Builder

In the careers library classified under UD.

1. BRICKLAYER CLCI:UF
2. CARPENTER/JOINER CLCI:UF
3. FLOOR LAYER CLCI:UF
4. GLAZIER CLCI:UF
5. PAINTER AND DECORATOR CLCI:UF
6. PLASTERER CLCI:UF
7. PLUMBER CLCI:UF
8. ROOFER CLCI:UF
9. SCAFFOLDER CLCI:UF
10. WALL AND FLOOR TILER CLCI:UF

BACKGROUND INFORMATION

The construction industry, which employs about one in ten of the working population, is engaged in an enormous variety of projects ranging from roads and airports through to house extensions. The traditional focus of the industry has been on the building of houses, offices and factories, and on large-scale civil engineering projects such as bridges and motorways. Now, however, a considerable amount of work involves the restoration and refurbishment of existing buildings.

The industry is constantly tackling new and increasingly complicated projects, which require a well-trained, skilled workforce. Essential to any project are the traditional trade or craft skills described below, which offer many opportunities for interesting and challenging work. In construction no project is the same, so the work is varied and every day is different.

1. BRICKLAYER (UF)

THE WORK

Bricklayers build the interior and exterior walls of buildings, and other types of walling, for example, the linings of tunnels, archways, ornamental brickwork. The work may be on new buildings or on the extension, maintenance and restoration of old buildings.

Engineers usually set out the positions at which walls are to be constructed, although on smaller sites bricklayers themselves may be responsible for setting out. Working from these positions, bricklayers build the walls, starting with the corners of the building. They use spirit levels and bricklayers' lines to check vertical and horizontal alignment of walls. They use a trowel to spread mortar, a club hammer and bolster to cut bricks to size, and a brick hammer to trim the brick.

Labourers are usually employed to keep the bricklayers supplied with a steady stream of bricks and mortar. Several hundred bricks may need to be laid in one working day.

Depending on the size of the structure involved, it is usual for teams of bricklayers to be engaged in working on different sections of the site.

WORK ENVIRONMENT

Bricklayers must work on scaffolding when working at high levels. They work outside in most weather conditions. The work can be dirty and dusty.

Working as a bricklayer involves a lot of standing, kneeling, climbing ladders and constant physical motion. Sometimes quite heavy loads of tools, bricks and mortar have to be carried.

Building work inevitably involves travelling from site to site, working on a particular property or building project and then moving on when the job is completed. It may be necessary to work away from home for short and long periods.

SKILLS AND INTERESTS

Bricklaying is primarily a practical craft requiring good hand skills. It also requires a careful and methodical approach to the work and an ability to plan the job well in advance and set about the various tasks in the right order. Arithmetical ability is important as is the ability to understand drawings, plans and written or oral instructions easily.

The work can be physically demanding and it is important to have good health, agility and enough strength to lift and carry tools and equipment. A head for heights is also required.

Safety awareness is essential in all work in the construction industry. Basic safety equipment includes a safety helmet and protective footwear. Items such as gloves, goggles and ear defenders are provided as required.

Team work is a vital aspect of working in construction as each person relies on others to carry out their work to a high standard.

ENTRY REQUIREMENTS

No minimum educational qualifications are required for a trainee bricklayer. However, a good standard in maths, English and science at GCSE/S grade can help with the measurements, calculations and instructions in the job, and also with the theoretical part of the training.

Candidates for apprenticeships or training schemes may have to take a selection test. Contact your local careers service, TEC/LEC for details.

A driving licence is useful, especially for the self-employed.

TRAINING

Many young people now enter the building crafts/trades through specific government-assisted training schemes, and then extend the period of training through a nationally approved training agreement or a modern apprenticeship.

A modern apprenticeship is an agreement between a young person aged 16-20 and an employer or training provider, with the signed approval of the parents and the local TEC. Both apprentice and employer undertake to follow a training programme approved by the Construction Industry Training Board, leading to NVQ/SVQ Level 3 (minimum) in approximately three years. The apprentice receives a wage or training allowance.

Whether on a scheme or an apprenticeship, training combines site experience on the job, in-company training and day or block release to a local college. Some employers provide training for C&G qualifications as well as NVQs/SVQs Levels 1, 2 and 3.

Several of the building crafts follow this system of entry and training. They are: brick-laying, carpentry and joinery, painting and decorating, plastering, roofing.

LATE ENTRY

NVQs/SVQs can be taken at any age. Awards can take account of previous experience and qualifications (Accreditation of Prior Learning.) However, opportunities for adult entry are limited, except for those with compatible skills and experience. It can be difficult to find an employer willing to provide training. A building craft training scheme for adults is available in Scotland.

OPPORTUNITIES

The demand for construction workers varies according to a variety of local and economic factors. In recent years recruitment has been low in the building/construction industry. However, the CITB has offered opportunities for training and entry into many of the building trades, including bricklaying.

Bricklayers are often self-employed, working on a subcontract basis for building contractors. They may work as 'labour only' subcontractors, with all their materials provided by the building contractor.

Some are directly employed by building contractors, local authorities and other public organizations. Specialist bricklayers work in foundries and in mining.

PAY AND CONDITIONS

Pay rates are agreed nationally, and minimum rates for skilled workers start from £183.69 a week. Some employers pay above minimum rates, and bonus and overtime pay can increase wages considerably.

Allowances may also be paid for travelling time, travel expenses and cost of lodgings, though this will vary from employer to employer.

The standard working week is 39 hours, worked over five days, Monday to Friday. It is usual for starting and finishing times to vary in summer and winter to take advantage of available daylight. Construction and maintenance contracts usually have to meet deadlines and schedules, so evening and weekend overtime is common.

PROSPECTS

Progression may be made through craft supervisor up to the construction management team.

Qualifications like BTEC/SCOTVEC national and higher national certificates/diplomas are useful.

There may also be the opportunity, for the self-employed, to run one's own specialist firm.

RELATED OCCUPATIONS

Carpenter/joiner, plasterer, painter and decorator, scaffolder, roofer, stonemason, construction operative, building technician.

FURTHER INFORMATION AND READING

Please see article 9. SCAFFOLDER.

2. CARPENTER/JOINER (UF)

THE WORK

The main types of work or jobs carried out by carpenters and joiners are:

Formwork joiner. Formwork consists of moulds, made of timber (or other materials such as metal or plastic), used to support and shape wet concrete until it has set. This 'shuttering' is used on major structures such as multi-storey car parks, bridges and motorways, and buildings. The formwork carpenter cuts, shapes, drills and fits together timber or plywood to make the formwork according to required measurements, drawings or instructions.

First fixer. All first fixing work is concerned with the wooden parts used in the basic structure of a building and any wooden fittings fitted prior to having the walls plastered. This includes 'carcassing', which is concerned with fitting floor and roof joists and roof timbers, floorboards, staircases, partition walls, and door and window frames. The work involves setting up the wooden posts in the right position (many of them are now prefabricated) and fixing them in place. Modifications may have to be made and the posts must be checked for correct positioning and fit according to drawings and plans.

Second fixer. This includes putting in skirting boards and door surrounds, hanging doors, and fitting any kitchen cupboards, sink units, wardrobes, shelves, etc. Door handles and locks must also be fitted. Again, many parts will have been prefabricated and some items (for example, windowsills) are now made from PVC. However, a variety of materials must be handled, modifications must be made where necessary, and a high level of finish is required, particularly where quality materials are used.

Bench joiner. All of the prefabricated parts fitted by carpenters and joiners on site (like roof timbers, staircases, cupboards, etc) have been made by bench joiners in a joinery workshop. All carpenters and joiners are trained in bench and site work, though usually bench joiners remain in the workshop while others work on site. Timbers are marked and cut to the required lengths, planed and smoothed down and then put together to form the prefabricated part. Complicated formwork can also be done in workshops by joiners (though usually these workshops are on site).

Most wood fabrication work is done in joinery workshops sometimes miles from any building site.

Shopfitter. This is a specialist craft engaged in producing and fitting shop fronts and interiors. It is also concerned with hotels, restaurants, banks, offices and other prestigious buildings. It can involve both bench joinery work (producing items such as shop counters and special panelling) and fixing and installing these items on site.

Carpenters and joiners may specialize in one of the major skills, although those employed by small non-specialist firms that carry out a lot of maintenance/repair work and wood fabrication will probably need skills in most aspects of the work.

WORK ENVIRONMENT

Carpenters and joiners may spend a good deal of their time standing, kneeling or crouching to carry out the work. On site, agility is important in order to climb up ladders and onto scaffolding or to enter narrow and cramped spaces or to go out onto roofs and work at various heights.

It is necessary to carry heavy equipment such as ladders and tools; some of the prefabricated parts such as roof timbers need more than one person to move them. Team work is an important part of construction industry work; most carpenters and joiners will find themselves working with other skilled workers.

Bench joiners work in workshops; other carpenters/joiners work on site, both indoors and outside. Outdoor work can involve cold and wet conditions.

Working with timber creates wood dust, although in some workshops it may be minimized by extraction systems.

Site work and shopfitting involves travel; it may be necessary to spend short or long periods away from home.

SKILLS AND INTERESTS

Practical hand skills and good hand-to-eye co-ordination are essential. Carpenters and joiners need to work accurately, carefully and methodically. They should be able to plan and organize their work. It is important to be able to follow plans, diagrams and written instructions. Numeracy is required for measuring and calculating quantities of materials.

Physical fitness is important. Some strength is required to lift and carry timber and tools.

Safety awareness is essential in all work in the construction industry. Basic safety equipment includes a safety helmet and protective footwear. Items such as gloves, goggles and ear defenders are provided as required.

ENTRY REQUIREMENTS, TRAINING, LATE ENTRY

Please see article 1. BRICKLAYER.

OPPORTUNITIES

Carpenters and joiners work for construction companies of all sizes, for local authorities and other public organizations, and for demolition companies. Many are self-employed. Some work in specialist areas such as restoration of old buildings or furniture making.

Shopfitters usually work for specialist firms.

PAY AND CONDITIONS, PROSPECTS

Please see article 1. BRICKLAYER.

RELATED OCCUPATIONS

Plasterer, painter and decorator, glazier, tiler, cabinet maker, designer: three-dimensional (craft), wood machinist.

FURTHER INFORMATION AND READING

Please see article 9. SCAFFOLDER.

3. FLOOR LAYER (UF)

THE WORK

Floor layers work with three main types of floor covering:

– carpets, of all qualities, from Axminster and Wilton through to carpet tiles;

– vinyls, linoleum and rubber, including sheet material and tiles;

– hardwoods, which include hardwood strip – often used in sports halls – hardwood blocks, and mosaic panels, which are similar to parquet.

Floor layers usually follow plans, diagrams and written instructions.

In occupied buildings it may be necessary to move furniture and fittings before starting work.

The skills used in laying vinyls, linoleum and carpet are similar. With these materials, the first consideration is the condition of the sub-floor, which must be flat, because any undulations or damage will spoil the appearance of the floor covering.

Often, the floor layer prepares a flat surface by spreading a layer of levelling compound. Sometimes it is first necessary to remove an existing floor covering. This may be done mechanically, especially in large areas. It is also important to remove all traces of old adhesives.

With a level surface prepared, the next task is to measure the floor area and measure and cut the material. It is usually cut slightly over size before laying, because the room may not be exactly regular in shape.

Vinyls, linoleum and some types of carpet are stuck down with adhesive, which is evenly spread with a trowel or roller. Adhesives have to be handled carefully, and it may be necessary to wear a mask or even, in enclosed areas, to use breathing apparatus.

The flooring material is laid to protrude up the skirting board and is cut by hand, with a carpet knife, round the perimeter, to give a snug, neat fit.

Carpet, instead of being fixed with adhesive, may be laid on to a 'gripper' – a piece of wood with upwardly protruding nails. The gripper is fitted at the perimeter of the room, around the underlay. The carpet is then placed over the underlay and gripper. The edges, which protrude over the gripper, are neatly turned under.

Some types of flooring material, including carpet, are simply laid side to side and stuck down with adhesive. But with carpet, the edges may be sealed together with heated tape, or hand sewn. Vinyls are welded at all seams, after they have been stuck down. The simplest types of work involve laying carpet, lino or vinyl tiles. The main concern is maintaining the 'bond', ie laying the tiles straight.

Laying the more expensive types of carpet, particularly carpet with a repeating pattern, can be complicated. Large areas of high-quality carpet are often laid in buildings such as hotels or offices, and the work needs to be carefully planned so that offcuts from one room can be used elsewhere, with as little wastage as possible. The appearance of the fitted carpet is extremely important, and it may be necessary to stretch it to give a good fit, using special equipment. Sometimes a plain border is fitted around a patterned carpet, and doing this neatly is a highly skilled job.

Hardwood flooring involves different techniques. Hardwood strip is laid on battens, and secret-nailed (ie the nails are invisible). The battens provide a level surface; sometimes they are laid on rubber pads, to create a semi-sprung floor. Hardwood blocks and mosaic panels are laid on the sub-floor, which must first be prepared and levelled. Blocks are set out in a pattern, such as herringbone. The floor layer usually works from the centre of the room, moving out to the perimeter. The blocks are dipped into adhesive. Hardwood mosaic panels, on the other hand, are laid on to adhesive, which is spread by trowel on the sub-floor. Electric saws are used to cut hardwoods so that they fit neatly at the perimeter. The finished floor is then sanded with an electric sander.

Floor laying includes all the above types of work, but in practice floor layers tend to specialize in one or two areas: laying expensive carpet; laying lower-cost carpet, vinyl and linoleum; or hardwood flooring.

WORK ENVIRONMENT

The work environment can be a building of any type – including shops, offices, schools, hospitals, sports halls or private houses. It may be a building site or a building that is currently in use. Floor layers call at their employer's office or yard to collect materials, receive instructions, and so on, but most of their time is spent at customers' premises.

The work involves a considerable amount of travel, which may be in the local area or further afield. It may be necessary to spend the working week away from home, although it is usual to return at weekends. There may be opportunities to work abroad, on contract.

Some adhesives used in floor laying give off unpleasant and potentially dangerous fumes. However, there are strict safety procedures to minimize the risks, and modern adhesives are considerably safer than they were in the past.

SKILLS AND INTERESTS

Physical fitness is important – floor layers spend much of the working day on their hands and knees. They need to be able to lift and carry rolls and boxes of flooring material.

Practical hand skills are required for accurate fitting and cutting of materials.

A courteous and pleasant manner is required for dealing with clients, who may include private householders.

Work on building sites takes place at the final stages of the construction programme, and floor layers often face a situation where other trades, such as electricians or carpenters, are trying to finish their work at the same time as the floor is being laid. This situation requires tact and flexibility.

Floor layers also need to co-operate with others in their team – they normally work in pairs, but may work in groups on larger jobs.

Basic numeracy is required for measuring.

An appreciation of design is useful, particularly for laying and matching patterned carpet.

ENTRY REQUIREMENTS

There are no minimum academic entry qualifications, although a reasonable standard of maths, English and science subjects is desirable for career progress.

Applicants may be asked to take an aptitude test, administered by the Construction Industry Training Board.

Good colour vision is desirable.

Transport to jobs is often provided by the employer. However, a driving licence is almost essential (trainees may be accepted without).

TRAINING

The Contract Flooring Association, together with the Construction Industry Training Board, offers a three-year modern apprenticeship. After initial experience on the job, apprentices attend courses, on block release, at Erith Training Centre in Kent, Salford College, or Glasgow College of Further Education. In their third year they may attend manufacturers' short courses, covering specialist aspects. They are expected to attain NVQ/SVQ Level 2 in Floor Covering.

Alternatively, employers may train staff on the job, usually over two years. Again, this leads to NVQ/SVQ Level 2. Trainees are assessed at the end of their first and second years.

NVQs/SVQs Level 3 in Floor Covering should be available by 1997.

There are no college facilities for training in hardwood floor laying – all training is with employers.

Specific training opportunities for young people may be available – contact your local careers office, TEC/LEC for details.

LATE ENTRY

The majority of entrants are school-leavers, but some employers do recruit adult entrants.

A background in carpentry/joinery is very useful for laying hardwood floors.

There may be specific training opportunities directed at adults available in some areas for this type of work. Candidates may have to satisfy certain conditions to be eligible. Contact your local Jobcentre, careers office or TEC/LEC for details.

OPPORTUNITIES

The main employers are firms of flooring contractors, who provide services to the construction industry.

Flooring contractors are, by and large, small family businesses, typically employing about eight to ten people. There are, however, some larger firms with a hundred staff or more.

There are a few opportunities for employment with the manufacturers of flooring materials.

Retailers of carpets and other flooring materials generally use the services of self-employed flooring contractors, and rarely offer direct employment.

Self-employment is common, both in the domestic and contracting sides of the industry.

The market for flooring is dependent on the state of the construction industry, declining in times when the industry is stagnant, expanding when there is a construction boom.

There are no particular regional trends in employment – firms of flooring contractors are found throughout the country.

PAY AND CONDITIONS

The standard wage rate, laid down by the Building and Allied Trades Joint Industrial Council, is £183.69 a week. Additional payments are made for specialist skills and there are allowances for travel, lodgings and tools.

The standard working week is 39 hours. When laying flooring in premises such as shops, it may be necessary to work nights and/or weekends, so that there is no interruption to business.

Overtime may be available or required.

PROSPECTS

There are opportunities in flooring contracting firms for promotion to leading hand, supervisor and contracts manager. It is also possible to become self-employed.

RELATED OCCUPATIONS

Tiler: wall/floor, carpenter/joiner, ceiling fixer, painter and decorator, upholsterer, interior designer.

FURTHER INFORMATION

Careers in Construction, Construction Industry Training Board*, Bircham Newton Training Centre, Bircham Newton, King's Lynn, Norfolk PE31 6RH, 01553 776677

Contract Flooring Association, 4c St Mary's Place, The Lace Market, Nottingham NG1 1PH, 0115 941 1126

FURTHER READING

Leaflets/booklets are available from the addresses marked*.

In the careers library classified under UF.

4. GLAZIER (UF)

THE WORK

Slightly different techniques and installation methods are required depending on the type of glass/glazed unit being fitted.

Window fixing

Most house windows can be installed by a glazier and assistant/trainee or two glaziers working together. When working on new property under construction it may be necessary to refer to drawings/written instructions to ensure that the right type/size of glass is installed in the right location.

If a broken window is being replaced, then any remaining pieces of the glass must be removed. Large pieces may need to be scored through and broken in sections; pliers are used to remove awkward pieces. If the glass is held in position by wooden or metal beading this must also be removed. The old putty/mastic is then chipped away or cleared off. To fit a new pane into position it may be necessary to trim it to the correct size for an exact fit. This is done by holding the glass in position by hand and using a hand glass cutter.

High-wind/security/safety glass

This is used in shops and offices and in multi-storey buildings above the first two to three floors where wind force would break ordinary glass. The methods of fixing are otherwise much the same as described above, but it is usual to put in some sort of spacers, made of wood or plastic, or spring clips (for metal frames) to help absorb the weight of the glass. Sometimes as many as ten or even 20 glaziers are needed to help move and position the glass (with the aid of webbing straps). Fewer glaziers are needed if a wheeled lifting machine is used – this has a big suction pad to hold the glass plate safely while it is moved into position.

Pre-glazed/double glazed units/doors

While double glazed panes of glass are fitted as described above, with the help of wood/metal beading to hold it in position, a very different method is required for pre-glazed units. These usually come complete in a wooden, metal or PVC framework. Instead of only removing any existing glass, the entire frame must be removed before the new unit can be installed. Installation requires the unit to be screwed directly into the surrounding brickwork and sealed in with a waterproof mastic. Any pre-glazed doors have hinges and handles fitted by the glazier. Security glass used in banks/post offices and elsewhere also comes as a pre-glazed unit with its surrounding framework.

Roof glazing

Skylights and dormer windows are re-glazed in the same manner as house windows or doors. Skylight units are fitted by experienced roofers because of the amount of work required in making the roof good, but there are workshops/offices, and so on, that are built with glass roofing. Here the glass (normally in two-feet widths) is held in position between bar-strips acting as clamps. The glazier must first attach the bar-strips (up to twelve feet long) parallel to each other to the roof beams. This is done by drilling holes into the beams and bolting the strips to them. A pane of glass is then fitted between two bar-strips (into channels in the strips) and fixed in place. A further strip is then attached over the end of the fitted pane, the next pane slipped into position and so on. Finally the glazier fits lead/aluminium flashings to waterproof the glass roof.

Although glaziers may specialize in any of the above different types of glazing, it is also common for glaziers in the smaller glazing firms to be able to employ any of the above techniques and undertake any type of work.

WORK ENVIRONMENT

A feature of glazier work is having to work at heights. This can be done from a ladder, when fitting small, manageable panes of glass; tower scaffolding is also used. When working on multi-storey buildings where it is not possible to glaze from the inside then a suspended cradle is required.

A lot of the work can be carried out by one glazier, though a team of glaziers or a trainee acting as an assistant will be needed when working with large and heavy panes of glass.

The work can take place indoors or outside.

A lot of travel may be required.

SKILLS AND INTERESTS

Glazing requires considerable hand skills and material-handling ability.

It is not easy to cut glass in straight lines, neatly and without breaking it. Safety considerations also call for a careful, methodical approach. It is important to be able to measure accurately and interpret drawings and written instructions. Glaziers must be physically fit, able to carry quite heavy loads and climb easily up and down ladders and along scaffolding. They must not be afraid of working at heights. Neatness and tidiness in their work is also required when carrying out glazing work in people's homes or in offices and factories where people are working.

ENTRY REQUIREMENTS

Please see article 1. BRICKLAYER.

TRAINING

In most cases, young people enter the glazing industry through a Modern Apprenticeship or Youth Credits. An apprenticeship lasts at least three years and follows nationally agreed guidelines.

Apprentices work towards NVQ/SVQ in Glazing Installation, or Installing Architectural Glazing Systems, at Level 3. Some employers also provide training for C&G or BTEC/SCOTVEC qualifications.

LATE ENTRY

Please see article 1. BRICKLAYER.

OPPORTUNITIES

Although there is less new building work being carried out at present, existing structures are still in need of constant repair and maintenance. Glass, in particular, is fragile and tends to break and need replacement regularly. Windows in houses, shops, offices, and so on, cannot usually be left broken.

Glaziers are employed by any firm that sells, cuts and installs glass. These can be very small one or two-person businesses, requiring skilled glaziers capable of undertaking a wide variety of tasks. Then there are middle-sized firms employing several teams of three to four glaziers that will also undertake any type of glazing. There are also the larger glazing firms that employ hundreds of people – glass cutters/general glass operatives in the workshops and glaziers/glazing installers out on the road fixing glass. They may have glaziers specializing in different types of glazing, such as domestic, or pre-glazed units, or leaded and decorative glass. Other glazing firms may specialize totally in one aspect of glazing work, such as glass roofing contractors or commercial greenhouse glaziers.

Self-employment is always a possibility, but it is usually advisable to gain full training and qualification, followed by experience, before attempting self-employment.

PAY AND CONDITIONS

Please see article 1. BRICKLAYER.

PROSPECTS

If a firm is large enough to offer promotion prospects then there may be a chance to become a supervisor in charge of a team of glaziers and responsible for overseeing their work on site and elsewhere, or to become a surveyor of glass installations.

An alternative would be to specialize, for example, in double glazing, security glass, or decorative glazing, and obtain a specialist post within the firm or move to a specialist firm offering these sorts of services. Presentation and accuracy is most important.

RELATED OCCUPATIONS

Window fitter, carpenter and joiner, tiler: wall and floor, floor layer, painter and decorator, scaffolder, ceiling fixer, construction operative, building technician.

FURTHER INFORMATION AND READING

Please see article 9. SCAFFOLDER.

5. PAINTER AND DECORATOR (UF)

THE WORK

The sort of work carried out depends on the size of the employing firm and the type of work it does. Generally the smaller the firm the wider the range of work and duties performed, although firms tend to specialize in domestic or industrial work. Even within these fields there can be further specialization – shop and office decoration, civil engineering structures or ships, for example. All of this affects the type of skills an individual is expected to use and the types of tools used to carry out the work.

The work involves:

Preparation work: moving furniture, stripping wallpaper, ensuring the surface is smooth and clean, and so on, as necessary. This is not necessary on new buildings.

Painting. Before any paint can be applied to a surface, a primer or sealing coat is needed if the surface is absorbent, an undercoat is then added and then the required paint. Depending on the finish required and the scale of the job, paint may be applied by brush, roller or spraying equipment; each requires a different application technique.

Wall hanging. Wallpaper is still the most popular form of wall and ceiling covering. However there is a wide range of other types of wall hanging available, such as hessian, silk, wool, felt, suede and cane. The method of hanging therefore varies according to the covering used. Generally, each roll has to be measured, cut, pasted and hung using the correct type of paste for that type of covering, and making sure the material does not stretch during hanging. Sometimes a lining paper is required. Usually a plumb-line and spirit level are used to ensure correct vertical lines.

WORK ENVIRONMENT

The work takes place indoors and outdoors. It involves lifting, carrying, bending, climbing ladders and long periods of standing.

Some paint gives off fumes; it may be necessary to wear a mask and to use extraction equipment.

The work involves travelling to different sites, usually in the local area.

SKILLS AND INTERESTS

Painters and decorators need practical hand skills, with the ability to work accurately and neatly. An eye for detail is important; some appreciation of form and colour is an advantage. Good colour vision is desirable for mixing/matching paints.

Painting and decorating can be repetitive, but it is important to be self-motivated and to maintain a high standard of work at all times.

Often painters and decorators work in teams or pairs, but they may work alone. They need to be able to co-operate and work well with others.

A head for heights is required, as it is necessary to work from ladders or scaffolding.

ENTRY REQUIREMENTS, TRAINING, LATE ENTRY

Please see article 1. BRICKLAYER.

OPPORTUNITIES

Painters and decorators are employed by building contractors, specialist painting contractors, local and national bodies. Some painting and decorating firms concentrate on particular techniques, such as Artexing, marbling or graining, or on high quality work for prestigious clients, such as banks.

Many painters and decorators are self-employed; they may work as subcontractors and/or for private householders.

There is always a demand for painters and decorators, and the level of demand is fairly constant. However, the type of work depends on the state of the housing market and other local and national factors. During a housing boom, there is more contract work available, especially on new buildings; when houses are hard to sell, there is more demand from private householders who have decided to redecorate rather than move.

PAY AND CONDITIONS

Please see article 1. BRICKLAYER.

PROSPECTS

Promotion is usually to a supervisory position, organizing the work of others in the same specialist craft. Beyond this, a small number may progress to become general supervisors in charge of a number of different trades.

RELATED OCCUPATIONS

Carpenter/joiner, bricklayer, plasterer, electrician, scaffolder, glazier, floor/wall/ceiling tiler, interior designer, construction operative.

FURTHER INFORMATION AND READING

Please see article 9. SCAFFOLDER.

6. PLASTERER (UF)

THE WORK

There are two types of plastering – solid and fibrous.

Solid plastering simply means that the plaster used is not mixed with any hair or fibre to help hold it together. This is the usual type of work associated with plasterers and involves working mainly on the inside of buildings, plastering walls and ceilings, putting down solid flooring, and fitting cornices and mouldings. Plasterers may also give a protective covering to the external walls of the building.

Working on interior walls it is usual to fix angle beads (metal strips) to all exterior corners to achieve a straight and vertical edge (checked by spirit level and plumb line). A screed of rough plaster is then applied to the wall to form a box around the area to be covered. Once these horizontal and vertical bands are done the rest of the wall is covered up to the level of the screed. The plaster is then ruled off level and the surface scratched with a bevel (board with nails) to provide a key for the final fine coat of plaster. Some high quality jobs require three coats. The final coat is smoothed over with a water brush and trowel.

Floors are built up in the same way as walls, with plaster or cement screeds on top of which various floor coverings can be laid. Various qualities of floor plasters are available; some are tough enough for hard-wearing use, for indoor car parks, for example, and some plasterers specialize in this sort of work.

Exterior walls are also done in the same way as interior walls except that a board is nailed up to provide a level to work to and a sand and cement mix is normally used in the place of plaster. Various finishes may be required and it is possible to give the impression of stone work, by careful marking off, or a pebble dash finish, achieved by coating the wet cement and sand mix with small pebbles. Other coverings (for example, Hi-build) may need to be rollered on or applied by spray gun.

Maintenance and repair work requires the same skills and covers the same sort of work as outlined above. It also involves removing old plaster and bad patches before fresh plaster can be applied.

Fibrous plastering involves short lengths of fibre being used to hold the plaster mix together to produce a particular form or decorative pattern. It is the fibrous plasterer who is responsible for producing all sorts of decorative plaster work like cornices and ceiling roses found in most types of older houses, bars and restaurants, and the columns and architraves found in stately homes and public buildings. This sort of work was being replaced by the use of plastic mouldings until new fire regulations banned a lot of plastics from use in buildings.

Fibrous plasterers usually work in specialist firms that produce ornamental plaster work from moulds (synthetic rubber or resin). They may follow architect's or artist's drawings.

The fixing of the decorations in buildings can be done by solid plasterers; they are nailed or screwed into place. More complex and delicate work is usually carried out by fibrous plasterers working on site, although in some firms this is split into two jobs – with fibrous makers working all the time in the workshop and fibrous fixers working on site.

WORK ENVIRONMENT

Plasterers are less affected by the weather than other building trades, in that most of their work is done under cover. However, conditions for solid plastering can be cold and draughty.

Fibrous plasterers work in workshops, and may visit sites.

Plastering may involve working at moderate heights from ladders or scaffolding.

Travel may be necessary, including short/long periods away from home.

SKILLS AND INTERESTS

Plasterers need to be physically fit and active. The work involves continuous movement and demands good co-ordination. Plasterers spend a lot of time standing, bending and kneeling; strong wrists and arms are needed. The plaster, which is held on a board, can be quite heavy.

They should be able to work quickly but carefully to produce flat, smooth plasterwork. Good hand skills are needed for handling trowels and floats. Plasterers may work as part of a team; it is important to be able to co-operate with others.

Some artistic skills are needed for fibrous plastering and other decorative work.

ENTRY REQUIREMENTS, TRAINING, LATE ENTRY

Please see article 1. BRICKLAYER.

OPPORTUNITIES

Plasterers are employed by specialist plastering firms, building contractors, and by local authorities and other public organizations.

Many are self-employed.

PAY AND CONDITIONS

Please see article 1. BRICKLAYER.

PROSPECTS

Please see article 5. PAINTER AND DECORATOR.

RELATED OCCUPATIONS

Bricklayer, floor layer, painter and decorator, roofer, tiler: wall and floor, ceiling fixer, construction operative, building technician.

FURTHER INFORMATION AND READING

Please see article 9. SCAFFOLDER.

7. PLUMBER (UF)

BACKGROUND INFORMATION

Plumbing – more accurately termed 'plumbing and mechanical engineering services' – is concerned with the installation of most systems that make a building pleasant and hygienic to work in. These include water supplies, systems of soil and waste disposal, heating and ventilation pipes and appliances.

Plumbers are also responsible for a range of external work on buildings including sheet weathering, cladding, and rainwater discharge systems – pipes and gutters – in various materials.

The role and work of the plumber provides an important service for the community as a whole. Unlike some other building trades, the plumber is not dependent on new construction work and a good deal of time may be spent on maintenance and repair work on existing properties. A house owner is more likely to call for a plumber than for any other building trade worker. The same techniques and skills used in general plumbing work are also used in more specialized plumbing work in the chemical, ship and gas-fitting industries.

THE WORK

In plumbing work the provision of water supplies and facilities can be divided into two main areas.

Internal plumbing: hot and cold water supply; sanitation and waste disposal systems; oil, gas, and solid fuel appliances; and space/heating systems. In industrial buildings, offices, shops, hospitals and schools, plumbers will be responsible for a much wider range of piped services.

External plumbing: weatherproofing joints in roofs and walls against rainwater, and conveying it away in gutters and rainwater pipes. External works may also include the covering of roofs or external walls in sheet metals or non-metallic sheet material.

Each area involves the plumber in different operations, tools and materials. The type of skill and technique required also depends on whether the work is on new property, or maintenance and repair work on existing structures.

New work

In construction contracts involving housing and industrial estates, a lot of detailed planning will have been carried out by the professional design team. Plumbers must, therefore, be able to follow drawings and instructions on the various stages of work required, including details on the types, lengths and sizes of pipes and the kind of joints to be used. A lot of the plumbing can be assembled in the on-site workshop, leaving a minimum of assembly and jointing work to be done in the buildings. Smaller contracts involve the plumber in a lot more individual decision making.

The main tasks for a plumber are as follows:

1. Roof weathering: plumbers make and fit flashings or weatherings of copper, aluminium, zinc, lead or non-metallic sheet, to joints between roof tiling/slates, chimney stacks, dormer windows, etc. A range of techniques, such as bossing, welting and welding, are used to form details in the different materials.

2. Rainwater, soil and drainage pipes: rainwater pipes and gutters are fitted to a building to take rainwater discharged from roofs. Soil pipes and drains are fitted to take the discharge from sanitary fittings. These pipes may be in plastic material, which is easily fitted and jointed, but which nevertheless must be fitted properly to avoid problems due to the high expansion rate of plastics. They may otherwise be in cast iron, with the fixing and jointing methods being dependent upon the purpose and situation in which the pipe or gutter is fixed.

3. Hot and cold water supply, heating systems, gas supply, sanitation and waste disposal – these are fitted as other crafts complete the various stages of the building.

A variety of pipe materials are used for the different systems, and different installation techniques – cutting, jointing, bending, fixing – are used for the different materials and systems. Each system will also have various appliances – baths, toilets, washbasins, sinks, boilers, pumps, storage cylinders, storage cisterns, showers, and so on, which must be correctly fitted to ensure that they work properly.

Maintenance and repair work/jobbing

This is an important part of a plumber's work and many small firms specialize in this type of work. It covers all the types of work and skills required in the plumbing industry. In addition it can involve the plumber in a lot more planning and decision making than is usual in large-scale construction work. Plumbers must decide for themselves the types of material to use, the pipework layout, and how best to tackle the job. The plumber may also have to advise the property owners on the type of system required for their needs. The type of job to be done can range from very simple to complex: from replacing a worn-out washer to replacing out-of-date pipework and installing the new system.

The plumber will also be required to carry out routine servicing on central heating installations, and must be able to diagnose and rectify faults on plumbing systems.

Plumbing in other industries

Shipbuilding: marine plumbing – the same skills and abilities as plumbers in the building industry. As well as sanitation and water supply, however, refrigeration pipework is also fitted.

Chemical: plumber's skills and abilities are employed in the chemical industry. Due to dangerous corrosive chemicals used in the industry, lead and plastic pipes are used extensively in their plumbing systems.

Gas: this covers the provision of gas supplies to all types of buildings for central heating, cooking and refrigeration purposes.

It is also important that all plumbers ensure that systems and appliances are fitted safely, correctly, and in accordance with regulations.

WORK ENVIRONMENT

Plumbing involves working both indoors and outdoors (depending on the particular job to be done) and involves work in cold, wet and dirty conditions. Particularly severe wet and cold weather can halt external plumbing work, but even if working indoors it may be cold and draughty in properties and structures lacking any means of heating.

All plumbers often have to work in extremely cramped and uncomfortable positions fitting pipework to baths and wash-basins or crawling about under floorboards. It will also be necessary to be able to work at heights on roofs to fix flashings and gutters. This involves climbing and working from ladders and a variety of scaffolding.

It is usual for plumbers in building and jobbing work to work at a site or building until a particular task is complete and then move on to the next site or property. Usually firms will be operating locally, so requiring workers to travel no further than normal daily travelling distances.

Occasionally, and in particular with large contracting firms, it may be necessary to work away from home for a certain period of time (this can also involve working abroad). The only plumber not likely to travel to varying workplaces is the marine plumber based in a single shipyard.

SKILLS AND INTERESTS

Plumbing is a practical craft and it is important to have a mechanical aptitude and the ability to use a wide range of hand tools and equipment.

However, the plumber also requires a wide range of knowledge of plumbing systems and appliances which must be installed correctly, safely and in accordance with building regulations, water by-laws and codes of practice.

The ability to read drawings and plans, follow oral and written instructions, produce working drawings and carry out craft calculations is essential.

Since plumbers often come into contact with a company's customers, a polite and courteous manner is important. The work can be physically demanding and can involve working at heights and in confined spaces.

ENTRY REQUIREMENTS

There are no minimum stated qualifications for entry into the plumbing industry. However, most employers prefer candidates with GCSEs/S grades, particularly in technical subjects – maths, technology, etc.

Some companies have formal selection tests.

A driving licence is useful as most companies operate their own vans.

TRAINING

The industry operates a traditional four-year apprenticeship scheme. Under this scheme, apprentices either go straight into employment on leaving school, with payment of a wage by the employer, or go first into government-assisted training for young people. An increasing number of employers offer modern apprenticeships instead of the traditional type. Modern apprenticeships have no fixed term and provide training in waged-employment.

In all cases, once employment has commenced, the employer should apply to the appropriate apprentice registration body to take out a Training Service Agreement (or indenture) for the apprentice.

The apprentice registration bodies for the plumbing industry are: England and Wales – the Joint Industry Board (JIB) for Plumbing Mechanical Engineering Services in England and Wales; Scotland and Northern Ireland – Scottish and Northern Ireland Joint Industry Board for the Plumbing Industry.

The Training Service Agreement is a written agreement between the JIB, the employer and the apprentice (and the parent/guardian if the apprentice is under 18 years old) under which the employer agrees to pay the appropriate wages, employ the apprentice under the correct terms and conditions, and support the apprentice's training, usually at a college or training centre, for NVQs/SVQs in Mechanical Engineering Services (Plumbing) at Levels 2 and 3. Full details of the working rules and training regulations may be obtained from the appropriate JIB.

The Institute of Plumbing is concerned with promoting technical aspects of the plumbing industry and maintaining nationally accepted standards. Membership is available to any plumber holding technical qualifications and/or whose training and experience satisfies the Institute's Articles and Bylaws. The Institute publishes the annual directory listing over 5000 registered plumbers in business. Details of the Institute's other activities are obtainable from the Institute itself.

LATE ENTRY

Entrants are usually school-leavers, but mature applicants are welcome. Adults are normally required to complete the same qualifications as apprentices, over a time-span agreed with the employer, but existing qualifications may count towards their NVQ/SVQ awards (accreditation of prior learning).

Previous experience in related skills which can be transferred to plumbing (for example, certain types of engineering work) is particularly useful.

There may be specific training opportunities directed at adults available in some areas for this type of work. Candidates may have to satisfy certain conditions to be eligible. Contact your local Jobcentre, careers office or TEC/LEC for details.

OPPORTUNITIES

Plumbers work mainly with the following types of employer.

Plumbing contractors. The greater proportion of plumbers are employed by plumbing contractors or mechanical engineering services contractors. These companies range from the small one or two-person companies to national/international companies employing 100+ plumbers. Some of the larger companies employ other skilled trades people, such as gas fitters, electricians, and welders. Where a large building is being erected, the plumbing company will usually be subcontracted to the main building contractor.

Building contractors. Many building contractors, especially those involved in house building, employ their own plumbers.

Public sector bodies. Local authorities, health authorities and government departments all employ plumbers who are mainly employed on the maintenance of plumbing systems in buildings.

Ship, chemical and gas industries. These represent an important branch of the plumbing industry, employing between them thousands of skilled plumbers. Plumbers in the gas and chemical industries will be employed directly by firms operating in these fields or by contracting firms.

Self-employment is always a possibility for plumbers, as for other building trade skilled workers.

PAY AND CONDITIONS

Pay rates are agreed nationally and are normally reviewed every year.

Within the JIB National Agreement for England and Wales there are three grades of plumber; the rates are: £5.24 an hour for trained plumbers; £5.86 an hour for advanced plumbers; and £6.55 an hour for technical plumbers (for a basic week of 37½ hours). Similar rates apply in Scotland. Some employers operate bonus schemes, and, on jobs where it is necessary to meet a customer's deadline, overtime may be worked.

National rates are also agreed for travelling time, accommodation allowances, tool money, etc.

Plumbers with certain additional qualifications, such as the JIB Certificate of Competency in Welding, qualify for an increased hourly rate.

The standard working week is 37½ hours, worked over five days, Monday to Friday.

It is usual for starting and finishing times to vary in summer and winter to make the most of available daylight. Construction and maintenance contracts usually have to meet deadlines and schedules, so evening and weekend overtime is common. It may also be necessary to work unusual hours if business or industrial activities cannot be interrupted for maintenance work during normal working hours.

PROSPECTS

Under the JIB structure, companies operate a grading scheme, by which plumbers are able to progress from trained to advanced to technical plumber, as their qualifications and experience increase, and according to the size of company.

NVQs/SVQs at Levels 4 and 5, when available, will enhance promotion prospects.

RELATED OCCUPATIONS

Electrician, heating and ventilating fitter/welder, domestic appliance/gas service engineer, maintenance fitter (mechanical), building technician, construction operative.

FURTHER INFORMATION AND READING

Please see article 9. SCAFFOLDER.

8. ROOFER (UF)

THE WORK

Roof slater and tiler

Despite the fact that most modern houses now use roof tiles there is still a lot of work for specialist slaters, especially re-slating and repairing the roofs of old buildings. In any event slates and tiles are fixed to a roof in a similar way.

The technique used in fitting a new roof to an old house is much the same as when working on a completely new house. First of all, reinforced roofing felt is laid over the roof timbers and secured; this increases weatherproofing. Wooden battens are then attached horizontally across the roof to which the slates/tiles are to be nailed. As slate is a natural material it varies in size and thickness. A slater must, therefore, sort slates/tiles according to size before use, needing to vary the batten distance according to the length of the slates. Tiles, although of uniform manufacture, come in a variety of shapes and materials each requiring a different approach.

When fixing slates/tiles the slater/tiler begins at the lowest part and lays them in horizontal rows; the larger slates are laid at the bottom of the roof, smaller ones towards the top. If re-using old slates any flaking edges must be trimmed down. Many modern tiles are moulded to hook over the battens and are nailed down on alternate rows.

Where surfaces meet, such as gable ends, the slates/tiles have to be cut to size. Special capping tiles/slates are fitted along the ridge of a roof. These are bedded in place with cement.

Felt-roofer

On timber roofs a layer of felt is first of all nailed down. Further layers of felt and bitumen are laid on top of this by pouring hot bitumen onto the felt surface, and laying more felt over the bitumen. Modern techniques also include using torch-on materials, a blow lamp being used to melt the bitumen on the back of the felt as it is being laid. Some roofs are then finished off with paving tiles of fibre cement, or slabs, or granite chips.

Mastic asphalter

Mastic asphalt is used to seal and waterproof concrete roofs and other flat surfaces such as car parks, bridges and basements.

Normally the work is carried out by a gang including: the potman/woman who melts the asphalt; a labourer who carries buckets of hot asphalt and pours it out for the two spreaders. It is possible for two people to do the work, one as the potman/woman and bucket carrier and one as a spreader.

For hot roof surfaces the area to be covered must have been swept clean and felt laid down first. Wooden battens are used only to mark the area being worked on and two layers of asphalt are spread using a laying float. A layer of sand may be rubbed into the top surface to form a finish.

Roof sheeter/cladder

This work involves fixing profiled/corrugated iron sheets to roofs (sheeting) and to walls (cladding). The sheets can be made of fibre-cement, plastic, steel or aluminium. The sheets are normally 1m wide and vary in length. They can be difficult to handle in high winds and freezing weather.

This work is always carried out by a team. A worker on the ground hoists up the sheets by hand or rope and tackle while the others stay up on top to position and fix the large sheets. At least two people are needed to handle and fix the sheets.

WORK ENVIRONMENT

The roofer works at heights (often several storeys high) and climbs ladders and works from scaffolding. The work is dusty and dirty at times, especially when removing an old roof; it can also be quite cold.

Travelling to sites is necessary. Some roofers work away from home for long or short periods.

SKILLS AND INTERESTS

The roofing trades suit people who like to work with their hands. It is essential to have a head for heights and be able to climb ladders and scaffolding. The work is mainly outdoors and physically demanding; roofers need stamina, agility and strength.

They need to plan out each job in advance and set about various tasks in the right order. They must be able to understand drawings, plans and written or spoken instructions. Ability to work as part of a team and get on well with other members of the gang is essential.

ENTRY REQUIREMENTS, TRAINING, LATE ENTRY

Please see article 1. BRICKLAYER.

OPPORTUNITIES

The main employers are specialist roofing companies. Roofers may be directly employed by these companies or work as self-employed subcontractors.

PAY AND CONDITIONS

Please see article 1. BRICKLAYER.

PROSPECTS

Please see article 5. PAINTER AND DECORATOR.

RELATED OCCUPATIONS

Ceiling fixer, carpenter/joiner, scaffolder, glazier, floor/wall tiler, steeplejack, roadworker.

FURTHER INFORMATION AND READING

Please see article 9. SCAFFOLDER.

9. SCAFFOLDER (UF)

THE WORK

Access scaffolding

Putlog scaffolds or bricklayers' scaffolds are erected using scaffold tubes tapered and flattened at one end (putlogs) inserted into gaps left by the bricklayer at regular intervals between the courses of bricks. Upright tubes (standards) and horizontal tubes (ledgers) are attached with fittings using a special spanner to tighten the bolts.

Existing buildings do not have gaps in the brickwork, and the scaffold is tied to the building with 'positive ties' and 'reveal pins' which clamp the structure to window apertures, arches and other convenient openings. All the tools used by scaffolders are hand operated and simple to use, such as spirit levels, string lines and plumb-lines, pulleys and winches.

In erecting scaffolding, safety regulations will need to be strictly adhered to – for example, relating to the maximum distance between uprights, minimum width of working platforms, and minimum height of toe-boards and guard rails.

Different trades also have different requirements – bricklayers require a more solid platform for themselves and their stacks of bricks so the standards have to be closer together than for a painter or plumber cleaning gutter-work. Hoists and lifts may also need to be erected so that workers and materials can be taken quickly and easily to higher levels. Scaffolders also need to ensure the safety of any passers-by below and erect safety nets, covered walkways and street-level illumination.

Access scaffolding is not only needed around the exterior of buildings. A lot of repair, cleaning and restoration work is also carried out inside buildings, such as churches. For this a tower scaffold may be used. This consists of special horizontal and upright pieces that slot into each other. The whole tower can be mounted on castors for easy movement.

Falsework scaffolding

Falsework scaffolding uses similar techniques to those used in access scaffolding but for very different purposes. In this sort of scaffolding the scaffold provides a framework to support the wooden framework (formwork or shuttering erected by carpenters and formworkers) and reinforcement bars used in reinforced concrete structures such as large buildings, motorway bridges, etc. The scaffolding is removed once the liquid concrete has been poured into the formwork and has set. With some formwork the scaffolding is designed to just slot and bang together without using bolts.

WORK ENVIRONMENT

Erecting scaffolding involves a lot of work at heights (anything from one metre off the ground to several storeys high). It also involves a lot of movement, climbing up and down ladders, and balancing on narrow structures, while building up parts of the scaffold, and carrying heavy metal poles up to 6.3m long and heavy wooden boards.

Scaffolders work outside in all weather conditions.

The work involves travel to different sites and working away from home for short/long periods.

SKILLS AND INTERESTS

Scaffolders need to be physically fit and active, and a certain amount of strength is needed. The work involves a lot of bending, lifting and carrying. A head for heights is essential.

They need practical skills and the ability to work with hand tools.

Scaffolders must be extremely safety-conscious – those working on the scaffolding depend on this.

They should be able to work as part of a team, usually of three people.

ENTRY REQUIREMENTS

Please see article 1. BRICKLAYER.

TRAINING

Training follows the Scaffolders' Record Scheme. After gaining some work experience, and with their employer's agreement, new entrants apply for a trainee scaffolder's record card. They then attend a basic training course at a CITB-approved training centre. After a year's satisfactory experience, including some formal training, they may qualify for a basic scaffolder's record card. After 18 months' experience as a basic scaffolder they may take a further course leading to an advanced scaffolder's record card. Trainees take NVQs/SVQs up to Level 3 during their training. The type of work given to an individual by an employer and its complexity will depend on whether a basic or advanced card is held.

Alternatively, the employer may send the trainee on a one-year full-time course at the Civil Engineering College (CECOL) at Bircham Newton. Here they gain a trainee scaffolder's record card, then, after six to twelve months' experience, a basic record card.

LATE ENTRY

Adult entrants may gain experience as scaffolder's labourer in order to obtain a trainee scaffolder's record card. With training and support from the employer they may go on to gain a basic scaffolder's record card. A background in relevant practical work is essential.

OPPORTUNITIES

Scaffolders work on new buildings and those that are being repaired. These include houses, factories, office blocks, steel works, nuclear power stations, oil refineries, oil rigs and cathedrals. Scaffolders work for organizations such as oil and power companies, or for scaffolding firms, which can range in size from large multinational firms to small companies with fewer than ten staff. Some scaffolders are self-employed.

There is a steady need for new scaffolders. They work all

over the country in both urban and rural areas; there are also opportunities to work abroad.

PAY AND CONDITIONS

Please see article 1. BRICKLAYER.

PROSPECTS

Please see article 5. PAINTER AND DECORATOR.

RELATED OCCUPATIONS

Bricklayer, carpenter/joiner, roofer, steel erector, ceiling fixer, steeplejack, construction operative.

FURTHER INFORMATION

Careers in Construction, Construction Industry Training Board*, Bircham Newton Training Centre, Bircham Newton, King's Lynn, Norfolk PE31 6RH, 01553 776677

Glass and Glazing Federation*, 44-48 Borough High Street, London SE1 1XB, 0171 403 7177

Glass Training Ltd*, BGMC Building, Northumberland Road, Sheffield S10 2UA, 01142 661494

The Institute of Plumbing, 64 Station Lane, Hornchurch, Essex RM12 6NB, 01708 472791

Joint Industry Board for Plumbing and Mechanical Engineering Services in England and Wales, Brook House, Brook Street, St Neots, Huntingdon, Cambridgeshire PE19 2HW, 01480 476925

National Association of Plumbing, Heating and Mechanical Services Contractors*, Ensign Business Centre, Westwood Way, Coventry CV4 8JA, 01203 470626

National Association of Scaffolding Contractors, 18 Mansfield Street, London W1M 9FG, 0171 580 5588

FURTHER READING

Leaflets/booklets are available from the addresses marked*.

Job Outlines – Construction: The Building Trades – COIC

In the careers library classified under UF.

10. WALL AND FLOOR TILER (UF)

THE WORK

Tilers fix tiles made of ceramics, and sometimes of other materials such as stone, terracotta or marble. Tiles come in a variety of shapes, sizes, surface textures and colours, and may be laid in intricate decorative patterns.

Ceramic tiles are fixed on exterior and interior floors and walls, and on other surfaces, for instance in swimming pools, or on worktops. Tiling is used in kitchens and bathrooms in domestic premises, in commercial settings such as shopping centres, and in industry, for instance, in food preparation areas.

Tilers work from plans, diagrams and written instructions.

Before tiles are laid, most surfaces need to be prepared. This may involve removing existing floor or wall coverings, levelling floors by putting down a layer of sand and cement (known as screed), occasionally plastering walls or, for tile panels, fixing grounds (made of timber or other materials) to walls. Tiling is also used on partitioned walls, where special preparations have to be carried out.

Tilers measure the area where tiles are to be laid, using a ruler, square, plumb-line, spirit level, theodolite and/or laser level. They calculate the quantity of tiles needed for the area and work out how to keep cutting to a minimum (for the sake of cost and appearance).

They select a starting point, spread a layer of sand and cement mix or adhesive with a trowel or serrated float, and onto this they lay the tiles, leaving joints in between. They cut tiles to fit at sides, around pipes, columns, etc – wherever necessary. Cutting methods depend on the type of tile used; for household tiles a hand-operated tile cutter is used, whereas heavy industrial tiles are cut with a bench-mounted mechanical cutter.

The adhesive or sand/cement is allowed to dry and the joints between the tiles are then filled with grouting cement. Sometimes the work can involve making and matching of patterns, or creating a mural effect. It may also involve the use of large or small mosaic tiles.

On larger contracts tilers work as a team, but on smaller jobs they work in pairs or alone.

WORK ENVIRONMENT

About 90 per cent of the work takes place indoors. Locations vary tremendously and can include, for instance, shopping centres, underground stations, factories and building sites, as well as private houses. Most of the time is spent at customers' premises.

The work involves kneeling, bending and lifting. It is sometimes necessary to work at moderate heights, and in confined spaces. Adhesives, used for fixing tiles, may give off unpleasant and/or potentially dangerous fumes, but there are strict safety procedures governing their use. Protective clothing is worn as appropriate.

The work involves travel to different sites, both in the local area and further afield, and it may be necessary to work away from home for short or long periods.

SKILLS AND INTERESTS

Practical hand skills, with good hand-to-eye co-ordination, are required. Tilers need an awareness of shape and colour and an eye for the design aspects of their work. Accuracy is essential – tiles, once laid, may be in place for many years, and any faults are easily visible.

Physical fitness is important, as the work is quite strenuous. Safety awareness is essential and safety equipment or personal protective equipment – such as gloves and goggles – must be used as appropriate.

Basic numeracy is required for measuring and calculating areas and quantities. Tilers need to be able to follow quite complex plans, diagrams and instructions – both written or spoken. They need to be able to plan and organize their work carefully, thinking ahead to ensure tasks are carried out in the right order.

A polite, pleasant manner and good spoken communications skills are required, particularly for working in private houses, where the occupant may be present. It is important to be flexible, to enjoy meeting people and working in different settings.

ENTRY REQUIREMENTS

There are no minimum academic entry qualifications, although a reasonable standard of maths, English and science subjects is desirable for career progress. Entry is either direct to an apprenticeship or traineeship, or through a CITB training scheme. The CITB sets an aptitude test.

A driving licence is usually required, but young people can enter training before they have passed their driving test.

TRAINING

Training involves a three-year apprenticeship or traineeship. It follows guidelines set by the industry and is not a modern apprenticeship as such. Training on site is combined with block release attendance at a college or training centre. The periods on block release courses total 20 weeks over a period of two years.

Colleges and training centres running courses include: Glasgow College of Building; Salford College; Leeds College of Building; Birmingham College of Building; Lambeth College, London.

Apprentices and trainees take NVQs/SVQs Levels 1, 2 and 3, supplemented by additional specialist courses. Specific training opportunities for young people may be available at several of the above colleges/training centres or through other organizations. Contact your local careers office, TEC/LEC for details.

LATE ENTRY

Adult entry is possible, but unusual. Experience in any practical type of work involving hand skills is useful.

Adults normally follow the training routes described in TRAINING.

There may be specific training opportunities directed at adults available in some areas for this type of work. Candidates may have to satisfy certain conditions to be eligible. Contact your local Jobcentre, careers office or TEC/LEC for details.

OPPORTUNITIES

Employment is with specialist tiling companies, which are either concerned with tiling alone or, in a few cases, with tiling and an allied area, such as plastering. They are generally small firms: the smallest employ just one or two tilers; the largest firm belonging to the National Master Tile Fixers' Association employs around 80 tilers. Opportunities for employment depend on the state of the construction industry as a whole; in times of recession, it can be very difficult to find work or training places with tiling companies.

Tiling firms are found throughout the country, although most of them are based in towns or cities.

There may be occasional opportunities to work on contracts abroad.

Self-employment is common: many tilers work as self-employed subcontractors.

PAY AND CONDITIONS

The minimum weekly wage for trained craftspeople is £183.69 for a 39-hour week. Companies may pay in excess of this rate.

Certain projects involve night and/or weekend work.

Paid overtime may be available or required.

PROSPECTS

There are prospects for promotion to supervisory posts. It is possible to move from supervisory posts into contracts management.

Many tilers, once they have been trained and gained experience, become self-employed.

RELATED OCCUPATIONS

Floor layer, roof slater and tiler, plasterer, ceiling fixer, painter and decorator, building/civil engineering operative, professional builder.

FURTHER INFORMATION

National Master Tile Fixers' Association, 39 Upper Elmers End Road, Beckenham, Kent BR3 3QY, 0181 663 0946

Careers in Construction, Construction Industry Training Board*, Bircham Newton Training Centre, Bircham Newton, King's Lynn, Norfolk PE31 6RH, 01553 776677

FURTHER READING

Leaflets/booklets are available from the address marked*.

In the careers library classified under UF.

1. CONSTRUCTION OPERATIVE CLCI:UF
2. CONSTRUCTION PLANT OPERATOR CLCI:UV

BACKGROUND INFORMATION

Construction operatives are employed throughout the building and civil engineering industries. They are multiskilled and carry out a variety of general tasks that are as important to the overall success of a project as any of the craft trades.

In building, they are involved in the construction of houses, factories, offices, etc. In civil engineering, they work on roads, tunnels, bridges, docks, airports and roads.

Some construction operatives develop one particular area of work as a specialist occupation, particularly on the civil engineering side.

Contractors' plant, or machinery, is used in building and civil engineering to prepare the site for construction and to transport soil and materials.

Plant is particularly important in the first stage of construction, for trench digging and preparing foundations, and for roadworks. On a major civil engineering project, huge amounts of earth need to be moved and the machinery used is heavy and powerful. On smaller sites, plant that can be adapted to a variety of purposes is more suitable.

Throughout the construction process, materials need to be moved around the site, and different types of plant, including trucks and cranes, are used for this purpose.

1. CONSTRUCTION OPERATIVE (UF)

THE WORK

Building

Construction operatives play an important role in preparing the ground for building. Before holes and trenches are dug for the foundations and drains, they help to set out the areas to be excavated. This involves positioning wooden or metal stakes (profiles) at set reference points, and laying string lines between the stakes. They check line and level, so that excavation is done in the correct place.

Most excavation work is carried out mechanically, by plant operators using earth-moving equipment. However, operatives may dig shallow holes and trenches manually. They also trim and square trenches previously excavated by machine, and erect and dismantle timbering to shore up trenches. They lay drains – including pipes, manhole covers and inspection chambers – and cover them with earth, stone or rubble (backfilling).

Other tasks include:

– erecting hoardings, safety signs, barriers and temporary site huts;

– setting up and dismantling access equipment, including trestle scaffolding, ladders and small scaffolding towers;

– preparing materials for use on site, which involves mixing concrete, mortar and plaster;

– transporting, stacking and removing materials and components.

Construction operatives use, clean and maintain a variety of tools and equipment, including hand tools, power tools and small plant such as pumps and compressors. They may drive dump trucks.

All types of work may involve interpreting drawings, specifications, schedules, manufacturers' technical information and written or spoken instructions.

Some operatives specialize in assisting craft workers such as plasterers or bricklayers.

Civil engineering

In civil engineering, the work is similar to the tasks carried out in building, but also includes:

Formwork – this term is used to describe temporary moulds that support and shape liquid concrete until it hardens. Formwork is constructed from wood or metal or a combination of both, and can be made in a wide variety of shapes. Operatives assist with its erection and dismantling, taking care not to damage the finished concrete structure.

Steel fixing and bar bending – concrete structures that have to withstand heavy loads are reinforced with steel rods. The steel rods have to be bent to the required shape – a task known as bar bending. This may be carried out by specialist companies, but on smaller sites bar bending is often done by operatives. Operatives are also concerned with steel fixing – fitting the steel reinforcement in position. Some specialize in this type of work.

Concreting – operatives place liquid concrete, to make foundations, columns, beams, floors, etc. The concrete is placed in several layers, vibrated by mechanical vibrators to consolidate, and the top surface smoothed off.

Steel piling – involves the insertion of interlocking steel sheets into the ground. The sheets form a temporary retaining wall, allowing earth to be removed on one side. Operatives transport, place and remove the steel sheets.

Drain laying – in civil engineering, operatives lay large-diameter pipes, for main drainage systems, for example. The sections of pipe are lowered into trenches by crane, with teams of operatives guiding them into position. Operatives seal the sections of pipe together. The trench is then filled in by a plant operator, using earth-moving equipment.

Roadworks – civil engineering operatives carry out most road building, including concreting, kerb laying, paving and surfacing. Some operatives specialize in kerb laying or slab paving. Kerb laying involves laying kerb stones in straight lines or curves, to the correct alignment. They are held in place by a concrete backing (haunching), and joined end to end with dry butted joints. Slab paving involves laying a base of stone or hard-core (rubble) and then bedding the slab on a sand/cement mix. Paving slabs are sometimes laid in patterns, and may require cutting.

WORK ENVIRONMENT

Construction operatives work mainly outdoors, on site. Conditions may be cold, dirty, dusty and muddy. They wear protective clothing, including safety helmets, ear defenders, goggles and boots.

The work involves travelling to different sites, and may involve being away from home for short or long periods.

SKILLS AND INTERESTS

A practical approach and common sense are needed. Construction operatives need an understanding of the basic terminology used in building and civil engineering, together with a knowledge of the materials used, the basic structures and the order of events in the construction process.

A good standard of physical fitness, strength, stamina and agility are required to cope with lifting, climbing ladders and scaffolding, working outdoors in all weathers.

An aptitude for team work and the ability to get on well with others are important.

Working on a construction site can be hazardous; a responsible attitude to safety regulations is essential.

ENTRY REQUIREMENTS

No minimum educational qualifications are required. However, to cope with the theoretical side of the training, GCSEs/S grades in maths, English and science are desirable.

Entrants to training schemes for young people may have to take a selection test.

Those entering the Construction Industry Training Board (CITB) Civil Engineering Apprenticeship Training Scheme should be sponsored by an employer who is prepared to give the trainee on-site training experience. The CITB is usually able to assist applicants in finding a sponsor.

A driving licence is useful, especially for the self-employed.

TRAINING

The Construction Industry Training Board's Civil Engineering College at Bircham Newton, Norfolk runs two courses:

The Civil Engineering Apprenticeship Training Scheme (CEATS) includes 21 weeks' instruction in year one, covering: personal effectiveness and general studies; industrial relations; safety, security and site knowledge; hand and power tools; excavation work; concrete; paving; formwork; steel fixing; proprietary system scaffolding; drainage and pipe laying; timbering and support to excavations; kerb laying. The remainder of year one, and year two, consist of on-site training, except for those who choose the option of further training as plant operators, gas distribution operatives, scaffolders or formworkers.

At the end of two years (known as stage A), trainees qualify as general construction operatives. An optional third year (stage B), including off-the-job training in more advanced skills, leads to qualification as general construction craftsman/woman.

The course leads to NVQ/SVQ in General Construction Operations at Level 2. Additional units may be taken to acquire NVQ/SVQ Level 3. The CEATS course is also available at the CITB's training centres in Glasgow and Birmingham.

The Construction Course includes 43 weeks' instruction in year one, covering the following practical skills: use of hand tools, power tools and site and plant equipment; recognition and handling of construction materials; operating and routine maintenance of small plant; concreting; formwork erection; pipe laying and other drainage work; kerb laying; scaffolding; steel fixing and bar bending; timbering for trenches and shafts; levelling and setting out; road surfacing; sheet piling and oxy-acetylene cutting; project work; and an Outward Bound course. The second year consists of work experience.

The course leads to NVQs/SVQs in General Construction Operations at Levels 2 and 3. Similar courses are available at other centres.

Either course may be taken through a government-assisted training scheme, or as part of a Modern Apprenticeship or an approved training agreement. A training scheme can be extended into an apprenticeship. The total period of training lasts three to four years. The Construction Industry Training Board (CITB) acts as the primary managing agent for government-assisted training in the construction industry.

An alternative pattern of training is a modern apprenticeship or approved training agreement with part-time study by day or block release at a local college, leading to NVQs/SVQs in General Construction Operations at Levels 1, 2 and 3.

In other cases, all or most of the training may be given on the job. The trainee is placed with a skilled worker who demonstrates an operation, then asks the trainee to carry it out under supervision. It is usually necessary to repeat the operation a number of times before becoming proficient. Ideally, on-the-job training covers a wide variety of tasks, so the trainee obtains maximum benefit. Within the NVQ/SVQ framework, each skill represents a unit or element, which counts towards the eventual award. Trainees may collect a range of units at their own pace, depending on the tasks they do within the job. They may be taught and assessed at the workplace or by attending a college or training centre part-time.

LATE ENTRY

Some employers tend to favour older, more mature applicants for this type of work, particularly if they have related experience. On-the-job training may be provided. However, the CITB courses described under TRAINING are not open to adults.

OPPORTUNITIES

Construction operatives work on all types of building and civil engineering projects, from house building to motorways, bridges and tunnels.

The UK construction industry as a whole employs nearly one million people. The industry consists of a small number of relatively large companies and a very large number of smaller building and subcontracting firms, usually with fewer than ten employees.

Operatives are very often self-employed, working on a subcontract basis for building or civil engineering contractors. They may work as 'labour only' subcontractors, with all their materials and tools provided by the main contractor.

Over the past decade, most large contractors have made substantial cuts in their permanent workforce, and now rely to a much greater extent than in the past on smaller subcontracting firms and self-employed workers.

There are, however, still some opportunities for permanent employment with building and civil engineering contractors, with local authorities and other public organizations.

Demand for construction workers varies according to a variety of local and national economic factors. In times of recession there are fewer construction projects and reduced opportunities for employment. However, although the amount of work carried out by the industry varies, there is always demand for construction.

PAY AND CONDITIONS

In civil engineering, rates of pay for trainees start at around £55 a week. On completion of training the pay is around £154 a week. Employers may pay more.

Very similar rates apply in the building industry.

A 39-hour week is standard. Overtime is common, to meet

construction deadlines. It may be necessary to work unusual hours if business or industrial activities cannot be interrupted for maintenance work during normal working hours.

Some jobs are short-term or seasonal.

PROSPECTS

The CEATS scheme is designed for those who have the potential to become foremen/women, after they have gained relevant experience. Others who take the construction course or receive on-the-job training may also progress to foreman/woman level. Beyond that they can move into site management, particularly if they are prepared to study for relevant qualifications such as the Chartered Institute of Building exams.

RELATED OCCUPATIONS

Plant operator, scaffolder, fencer, steeplejack, bricklayer, roofer, demolition specialist.

FURTHER INFORMATION AND READING

Please see article 2. CONSTRUCTION PLANT OPERATOR.

2. CONSTRUCTION PLANT OPERATOR (UV)

THE WORK

Plant operators operate and control machinery, usually specializing in one particular type of machine. The main types of equipment used are:

Excavators: these machines are used to dig and transport soil, clear and level sites, break up hard surfaces, and load lorries. One of the most commonly used types is a rubber-wheeled machine with a front loading shovel and bucket and a rear digging arm (often known as a JCB). Relatively small, versatile and manoeuvrable, JCBs are widely used on both building and civil engineering sites. There are also larger but less versatile steel-tracked machines, which are used for heavy digging and levelling, and machines known as draglines, with a jib like a crane, which are used for deep or hard-to-reach excavations.

Compaction equipment: includes rollers for compacting materials or soil, mainly on roadworks or civil engineering projects, and smaller machines, known as whacker plates, used for compaction in smaller or restricted spaces.

Cranes: these are used to pick up equipment and materials and deposit them at different parts of the site. They include mobile cranes, which can be moved along normal roads and are fast, efficient and versatile. Rough terrain mobile cranes are also available. The other types of crane are the conventional crane, mounted on steel tracks, which is more complicated to transport and assemble, and the static tower crane, which is bolted to a concrete base.

Trucks: dumper trucks, with a capacity of up to five tons, and dump trucks, with a larger carrying capacity, are used to carry earth, sand and other materials. Rough terrain lift trucks are used to move materials such as bricks, scaffolding and timber. Crawler loaders are used for loading heavy materials, etc.

There are also various specialist machines used in road and motorway construction.

All plant has to be operated safely, and it is very important for operators to be aware of other workers close to the machine.

Plant operating frequently involves carrying out work to certain heights and depths – for instance, foundation digging. This must be done to the correct level. A banksman/woman on the ground works with the plant operator, checking the position and depth of the dig according to pre-fixed site guide rails and profiles. The banksman/woman also gives directions to the operator when visibility of any part of the operation is restricted, either by hand signals or by radio.

As well as operating plant, operators change buckets and other attachments – which can be heavy. Operators are also responsible for maintaining their machinery in good working order. They grease the machines and check the water, fuel, oil and hydraulic systems, as well as making daily safety checks.

WORK ENVIRONMENT

The work is outdoor, but much of the time is spent in the cab, which is enclosed and heated.

Conditions can be dusty and noisy (although ear defenders are worn if necessary). In winter, sites can be dirty and muddy; in summer, cabs can become very hot (although some are air-conditioned).

Some jobs (such as operating a tower crane) involve working at heights.

Travel to different sites is involved and it may be necessary to spend short/long periods working away from home.

SKILLS AND INTERESTS

Plant has the potential to be dangerous and operators need to be alert and aware of their surroundings, so as not to cause damage to other workers, equipment, etc. Adherence to safe working practices is essential.

Operators need to be able to concentrate for long periods.

Good hand-to-eye co-ordination is required for operating controls.

It is important to be physically fit, as the work involves some lifting and carrying, when changing buckets, for example. Agility is needed for climbing in and out of drivers' cabs. Good eyesight (with glasses if worn) and hearing are important for following directions and maintaining awareness of surroundings. Certain medical conditions – such as vertigo or fits – are a bar to this type of work.

Some knowledge of basic motor mechanics is required, and an understanding of construction processes and materials is desirable, although this can be gained through experience.

ENTRY REQUIREMENTS

Regulations require operators to be over 18 years, and because of the potentially hazardous nature of the work, some employers prefer older applicants. However, it is possible to start as a trainee at 16 years.

A full current driving licence is required.

No minimum educational qualifications are laid down. However, GCSEs/S grades in maths, English and science are desirable, particularly for those planning to take the CEATS course (please see TRAINING).

TRAINING

Training for plant operators is largely given on the job, supplemented by short courses (one week, for example) covering the operation of different categories of plant. Off-the-job induction courses are also available.

Under the **Certificate of Training Achievements (CTA) Scheme**, administered by the Construction Industry Training Board, construction plant operators have to demonstrate that they have attained an acceptable level of basic skills and safety awareness before they are awarded a certificate. These tests are specific to a particular category of machinery. After obtaining a CTA Operator Card for one type of machinery, additional types may be added by taking further tests. All operators are required to obtain a CTA Card.

The objective of the CTA Scheme is to ensure that all plant operators have attained an acceptable standard of basic skills and safety awareness.

Over 80 centres offer CTA testing. They include company training centres, CITB training centres and other CITB-accredited organizations.

School-leavers may train via the Construction Industry Training Board's CEATS scheme (please see article 1. CONSTRUCTION OPERATIVE). In their second year they take a 20-week course in plant operating, followed by 25 weeks' work experience.

NVQs/SVQs are available at Level 1 (Plant Occupations,) Level 2 (Plant Maintenance, Plant Operations, Earthmoving, Lifting) and Level 3 (Plant Maintenance, Plant Operations). Assessment is built into the CTA Scheme.

LATE ENTRY

Operators must be over 18 years and employers often prefer older applicants, especially if they have experience in the construction industry, for instance at operative level.

OPPORTUNITIES

Plant operators are employed by building and civil engineering contractors and other organizations, such as local authorities, that employ their own construction workforce.

There are more opportunities in civil engineering, because this involves a greater need for plant, both for earth moving and for transportation of materials.

There are also opportunities with specialist plant hire companies.

Self-employment is common, either as an owner-operator or labour-only subcontractor. Owner-operators have their own machines (for instance, a JCB); labour-only subcontractors use contractors' plant.

It is possible to work overseas – there are some specialist employment agencies that arrange contracts.

PAY AND CONDITIONS

The basic working week is 39 hours, Monday to Friday. However, it may be necessary to work overtime in the evenings and at weekends in order to meet deadlines. Minimum rates for trainees (under 19 years) start at £69 a week. Trainees over 19 start on pay of around £130 a week for 39 hours.

After training, employed operators earn around £160 for a 39-hour week; the self-employed (labour only) earn around £220 to £240 a week. However, pay depends on the level of skill – those who are able to operate more than one type of machine may earn more.

PROSPECTS

It may be possible for operators to move into general foreman/woman positions. Beyond that they can move into site management, particularly if they are prepared to study for relevant qualifications such as the Chartered Institute of Building exams.

Experienced operators can also become plant co-ordinators, selecting the machinery used for each contract and evaluating new plant.

RELATED OCCUPATIONS

Construction operative, plant mechanic, lift truck operator, LGV driver, scaffolder, roofer, plant co-ordinator.

FURTHER INFORMATION

Careers in Construction, Construction Industry Training Board*, Bircham Newton Training Centre, Bircham Newton, King's Lynn, Norfolk PE31 6RH, 01553 776677

FURTHER READING

Leaflets/booklets are available from the addresses marked*.

Job Outlines – Construction: the Building Trades – COIC
Working in Construction – COIC

In the careers library classified under UF/UV.

HOUSING OFFICER/MANAGER CLCI:UH/ CAG

BACKGROUND INFORMATION

Over the last decade, the number of people in Britain owning their own homes has increased considerably. Many people, however, still need or prefer to rent accommodation, from either local councils, housing associations (collectively known as the social housing movement) or the private rented sector.

Government legislation has changed the role of local authority housing departments, which are no longer direct providers of housing, but have a strategic role for ensuring that an area's housing needs are met – including ensuring the availability of land for building purposes. Increasingly, responsibility for providing new housing is moving to housing associations, which also own and manage properties, although local authorities still provide the majority of properties available for rent.

Council tenants are able to buy their homes. Those who remain as local authority tenants may choose their own landlords. Some groups are doing so, with the result that in some areas council estates are now managed by housing associations or housing action trusts. With the advent of compulsory competitive tendering for the housing management service, the role of the local authority in housing management is set for further change, with the possibility of private companies taking over the management function.

Various types of accommodation are owned and managed by local authority housing departments and housing associations. Apart from general needs accommodation, special needs accommodation is provided, suited to the needs of particular groups such as the elderly and people with physical disabilities.

Local authorities have, in addition, a statutory duty to house or provide temporary accommodation for certain groups of homeless people.

Some private sector landlords own large blocks of flats or other properties, which are run by professional managers.

Housing officers (sometimes called housing managers) may work for any of the above, but the work they do varies according to the type of employer.

THE WORK

Housing officers oversee the day-to-day running of rented properties on behalf of the owners, arranging for the signing of leases or tenancy agreements, organizing rent collection, arranging for any necessary maintenance work and repairs to be carried out, appointing and managing caretakers and wardens, and possibly interviewing prospective tenants.

They may allocate properties to waiting-list applicants and arrange transfers or mutual exchanges between tenants. They may also advise on welfare benefits and the statutory rights of private sector tenants.

Housing officers consult with tenants on all relevant matters. Some also attend meetings with tenant groups at which tenants can raise any problems and grievances and, sometimes, participate in decisions about the management of their homes.

As the local authority role is increasingly one of enabling other organizations to meet housing demand, housing officers working for local authorities may be called upon to assess the housing needs of particular localities and make recommendations for improvement.

Some housing officers may specialize in assisting homeless people. This includes making decisions concerning whether clients are homeless in the eyes of the law, giving people assistance in finding their own accommodation, arranging for emergency accommodation or rehousing.

The work involves contact with tenants and other people concerned with housing provision such as social workers. They may also liaise with people connected with house building and repair, such as builders and architects.

WORK ENVIRONMENT

Housing officers are based in offices but spend a lot of time visiting tenants, inspecting properties and attending meetings.

SKILLS AND INTERESTS

Housing officers must be committed to providing a service, which often includes improving people's living conditions. They must be sensitive to the needs of all clients. Good interpersonal skills with the ability to communicate clearly in speech and in writing are required.

Housing officers need to be able to work on their own and make decisions and explain the reasons for these. They must learn to deal with disappointed, angry and sometimes abusive clients.

Numerical skills are important. All housing managers are expected to work within pre-set budgets, to analyse statistics, the findings of reports and surveys and to assess priorities. Some technical understanding is required when examining structures and assessing the need for repair or improvement.

Housing officers need to be organized, with good administrative skills. Many are responsible for junior staff – housing assistants and clerical workers.

ENTRY REQUIREMENTS

Some posts require no qualifications but most employers expect or encourage staff to work towards membership of the Chartered Institute of Housing (CIH).

Minimum entry requirements for full corporate membership of the CIH are either: five GCSEs grade (A-C) plus two A levels; or five S grades (1-3) plus three H grades; or a BTEC/SCOTVEC national award in a relevant subject area, such as housing or public administration; or Advanced GNVQ/GSVQ Level III.

Many entrants have degrees or BTEC/SCOTVEC higher national awards. Minimum entry requirements for a degree course are usually either: two A levels/three H grades plus five GCSEs/S grades (A-C/1-3); or a BTEC/SCOTVEC national award; or Advanced GNVQ/GSVQ Level III; or equivalent.

Entry to BTEC/SCOTVEC higher national award courses is usually with a minimum of either: one A level/two H grades plus GCSEs and S grades; or a BTEC/SCOTVEC national award; or Advanced GNVQ/GSVQ III; or equivalent.

Entry to postgraduate courses is with a first degree.

Housing Modern Apprenticeships for young people have been introduced. There are no standard entry requirements but employers need to be sure that entrants can benefit from training and are capable of achieving an NVQ/SVQ in Housing at Level 3.

TRAINING

Training is carried out in the workplace. A trainee may work towards the professional qualifications of the Chartered Institute of Housing through a combination of work experience and part-time study or on a full-time course with placements in housing organizations.

There are several methods of obtaining the qualification.

– Graduates and those with a relevant BTEC/SCOTVEC higher level award (business studies, building studies, land administration, public administration or surveying) take a one-year Graduate Foundation Course and the Institute's Test of Professional Practice, followed by a two-year Professional Diploma course.

– Non-graduates take a two-year BTEC/SCOTVEC Higher National Certificate in Housing Studies followed by the two-year Professional Diploma course and the Institute's Test of Professional Practice. Those who have an NVQ/SVQ in Housing at Level 4 are granted exemption from the higher national certificate.

The Graduate Foundation, Professional Diploma and higher national certificate courses are all offered part-time at universities and colleges, and may also be studied through distance learning. UNISON offers the higher national certificate and Telford College (Edinburgh) the SCOTVEC higher national certificate as distance learning.

Alternative routes are available through:

– a four-year degree course that includes housing placements, eg degrees in housing management and development, housing policy and management and housing studies;

– a two-year full-time postgraduate Masters' Diploma in housing that includes housing placements;

– a three-year part-time postgraduate course recognized by the CIH.

All students must complete the Test of Professional Practice which consists of structured practical experience in the workplace. In addition, students are required to keep a logbook and complete case studies.

NVQs/SVQs in Housing are available at Levels 2, 3 and 4. They assess and certificate competent practice in housing.

Those on Modern Apprenticeships work towards an NVQ/SVQ in Housing at Levels 2 and 3. They also undertake training in communication, application of number, information technology and personal effectiveness. There is no set length of time for Modern Apprenticeship training but it is likely to be at least three years. On completion of the Apprenticeship it will be possible to progress to an NVQ/SVQ in Housing at Level 4. That allows entry to the Professional Diploma course to work towards membership of the CIH. Contact your local careers office, TEC/LEC for details of Modern Apprenticeships.

LATE ENTRY

There are no upper age limits. Maturity is considered an advantage, as is previous experience in a relevant job or in voluntary work. Many people enter housing as a second career.

Adults applying for courses may find that they are accepted without the normal entry requirements. They can prepare for applications to degree and higher national courses by undertaking an approved higher education access course. Access courses are offered at local colleges and are usually one year full-time, or one to two years part-time, with daytime and/or evening attendance.

OPPORTUNITIES

The Chartered Institute of Housing has about 12,500 members.

Most housing officers still work for local authorities, which at present own about 23 per cent of the country's housing stock. With the gradual transfer of responsibilities to housing associations, opportunities for employment with these are increasing. There are already over 2,000 associations, between them managing homes for over one million people.

Openings are also found with voluntary organizations, housing trusts, private landlords and property companies.

Employment is available throughout the UK. Most opportunities are found in large population centres.

Trainee positions are advertised in the local government bulletin *Opportunities*, in *Inside Housing*, the Institute of Housing's weekly magazine, in *Housing Associations Weekly*, the magazine of the National Federation of Housing Associations, and in the local and national press.

PAY AND CONDITIONS

Pay varies from employer to employer. Local authorities pay new entrants £7,000 to £10,000. Senior posts carry salaries of about £20,000. Salaries in excess of £50,000 are sometimes paid to Directors of Housing in large local authorities. Salaries in private organizations vary, but in the main are comparable with those paid in local government.

Housing managers normally work a 35 to 40-hour week, within normal office hours – 9am to 5pm, Monday to Friday. Some overtime may be necessary as may some evening work, particularly at more senior levels. Meetings may be held outside office hours.

Flexi-time systems are operated by many local authorities.

Part-time/job-share posts may be available.

PROSPECTS

There is a clear promotion path in local authorities, from housing officer to senior and principal officer level. It may be necessary to move to another location in order to reach the higher grades.

Some private sector employers have similar structures but many are individually organized to reflect the services they provide. It is often necessary to change employers in order to gain higher salaries and more responsibility.

In larger organizations and departments it is often possible to specialize in one aspect of the work such as research, housing advisory services, homelessness, welfare benefits, housing finance, development, or administering house purchase schemes and grants.

Many housing officers work for a variety of different organizations during a career.

RELATED OCCUPATIONS

Surveyor, community worker, estate manager, local government administrator, social worker, welfare rights officer.

FURTHER INFORMATION

Chartered Institute of Housing*, Octavia House, Westwood Business Park, Westwood Way, Coventry CV4 8JP, 01203 694433

Chartered Institute of Housing in Scotland*, 6 Palmerston Place, Edinburgh EH12 5AA, 0131 225 4544

Chartered Institute of Housing in Wales*, 4th Floor Dominions House North, Dominions Arcade, Queen Street, Cardiff CF1 4AR, 01222 397402

The National Federation of Housing Associations*, 175 Grays Inn Road, London WC1X 8UP, 0171 278 6571

Scottish Federation of Housing Associations*, 38 York Place, Edinburgh EH1 3HU, 0131 556 5777

Local Government Opportunities, Local Government Management Board*, Arndale House, Arndale Centre, Luton LU1 2TS, 01582 451166

FURTHER READING

Leaflets/booklets are available from the addresses marked*.

Working in Local Government – COIC

In the careers library classified under UH; CAG.

1. BUILDING SERVICES ENGINEER/ TECHNICIAN CLCI:UJ
2. HEATING AND VENTILATING FITTER/ WELDER CLCI:UJ

BACKGROUND INFORMATION

Building services are all those services that help a building to run: plumbing, lighting, heating, ventilating, air conditioning, power supply, lifts and escalators, refrigeration, cabling for computers, internal telephone systems, fire alarm and sprinkler systems, etc. These all relate to control of the working or living environment hence the alternative title environmental engineering. Environmental concerns have increasingly led to more efficient systems being fitted to minimize energy loss.

It is increasingly common for these services to be designed together and installed by the same contractor. In large buildings, the pipes, cables, ducting, and so on, needed for these services, are normally hidden from view above false ceilings or below floors, with boilers, pumps, refrigeration or air-conditioning plant in basement rooms and on the roof. The installation of these services can typically represent 20 to 35 per cent of the cost of a building. The buildings range from houses (central heating) to offices, factories, schools and hospitals.

In practice, the title engineer is used for all three grades working on the design, planning and management of this work, whether trained at chartered engineer, incorporated engineer or engineering technician level. A large design or contracting company may employ staff at all three levels, in which case the title technician may be used for the less-qualified staff. Smaller companies undertaking the less complex installations may have only engineering technicians. In some instances, heating and ventilating fitters/welders are also referred to as engineers.

1. BUILDING SERVICES ENGINEER/ TECHNICIAN (UJ)

THE WORK

Building services engineers and technicians perform a range of roles and tasks in the marketing, design, estimating, planning, installation, commissioning, upgrading and maintenance of building engineering services.

A **chartered engineer** is more likely to take the more senior and managerial roles such as direct negotiation with potential and actual clients, preparing the overall designs and specifications, overseeing the whole project as project engineer or the on-site installation work as site engineer, etc.

An **engineering technician** is more likely to work as a design draughtsman/woman, estimator, purchaser (of materials and equipment), inspector (of quality materials and workmanship), or as an installation technician. Installation technicians install the more complex and sophisticated equipment requiring a high level of engineering knowledge, or supervise craftspeople and sometimes semi-skilled workers in the more routine aspects of the work.

An **incorporated engineer** could carry out duties similar to those undertaken by a chartered engineer or engineering technician, though, in general, they fill more senior roles than the engineering technician.

While work must be done with skill and accuracy, building services technicians are frequently working to meet tight production schedules and deadlines. This may involve liaison with the client, the architect, civil and mechanical engineers, representatives of other contractors, craftspeople of a range of trades working on site and their supervisors, etc. At higher levels this may include site meetings regarding progress, co-ordination, any changes to plans, etc.

Design and draughting may be done on traditional drawing boards with a pen or on computer design terminals. Estimating, planning, scheduling and control may also involve computers. Installation, testing, quality control and maintenance may require a range of tools and instruments/ meters, depending on the activity. Use of the telephone, including portable ones, will be important for communications. Accurate record-keeping and regular reports may be required.

WORK ENVIRONMENT

For a design engineer, work may be mainly in a drawing office at a drawing board or computer design terminal. For a planner or purchaser, it may be primarily office-based with occasional visits to or from customers or suppliers, or to sites. Installation work is carried out on a construction site and, for a project engineer or site engineer, a major part of the time may be spent in a temporary office on site or outdoors on site.

Work on site at different stages in the construction or refurbishment of a building may mean areas open to the wind and cold, though normally under cover, and with no heating or only temporary industrial heating. On site, a protective helmet is worn and a coat or overalls to protect clothes against dust and dirt.

Some tasks could involve dirt, dust, grease and noise. Climbing ladders and working at heights may also be required. There may be considerable walking from area to area and the work may involve standing, crouching and kneeling.

There may be long distances to travel from home to reach the work site which may change every few months. This could involve spending long or short periods away from home.

SKILLS AND INTERESTS

Mathematical ability and an understanding of physical science and engineering principles are important. An ability in design and technical drawing, as well as an interest in computers and computer graphics, are useful in understanding and creating designs and drawings.

Communications skills are needed for liaising with clients, architects, colleagues, suppliers and staff of other contractors in person and by phone, as well as for writing reports.

The ability to work with technical accuracy under pressure and yet make sound decisions is vital, as is being able to work as a member of a team. Maintenance and commissioning require the application and analytical ability to locate a fault and trace the cause before deciding on a solution.

Good health and physical fitness are needed when working on site in all weathers.

Foreign languages are an asset for those wishing to work overseas.

ENTRY REQUIREMENTS

Chartered engineers require an accredited honours degree in Building Services Engineering or Environmental Engineering. Degrees in Mechanical or Electrical Engineering are also accepted but may be less highly regarded. Courses may be three-year full-time, or four-year sandwich, with work experience periods in the industry which may count towards training requirements. Sponsorship may be available. Entry to degree courses is with five GCSEs/S grades (A-C/1-3) with two to three A levels or three to four H grades, including maths and physics. GCSE/S grade English is also required. Other acceptable qualifications are BTEC/SCOTVEC national certificate/diploma or higher national certificate/diploma.

Incorporated engineer/engineering technician: normal entry is at age 16 to 18 as a student engineering technician apprentice or student incorporated engineer apprentice for a four to five-year apprenticeship. Entry requirement for this is one A level/H grade in maths or physics plus four GCSEs/S grades (for incorporated engineer) *or* four GCSEs/S grades (A-C/1-3) in maths, physics and English (for engineering technicians). Those with less than four passes at this standard can take BTEC/SCOTVEC first certificate to qualify. An alternative route is to take a BTEC/SCOTVEC national diploma (for engineering technician) or higher national diploma (for incorporated engineer) course full-time at a college; a shorter apprentice training may then be available. But few colleges offer such courses. A relevant ordinary degree also gives entry at incorporated engineer level.

TRAINING

Chartered engineer: a graduate engineer receives two years' training in employment. This includes induction training in the activities and practices of the employing company, and work under supervision in a number of departments including the final department, where the trainee will be given gradually increasing responsibility. After two further years' work experience, candidates can register with the Board for Engineers' Registration of the Engineering Council via the Chartered Institution of Building Services Engineers (CIBSE). This brings the title chartered engineer (CEng).

Incorporated engineer and engineering technician: training, in a large company, may involve some training in a training centre in more basic aspects, followed by work under supervision in different departments, involving increasing individual responsibility in later years of the apprenticeship. Performance in these will determine the job role they are finally placed in, if the company offers them a job on completion. Training will include practical skills as well as design, estimating and programming. Training includes day or block release to study both theoretical and practical aspects at college for a BTEC/SCOTVEC higher national certificate (incorporated engineers) or national certificate (engineering technicians).

Following completion of the apprenticeship and three years' work experience, incorporated engineer candidates may register with the Board for Engineers' Registration of the Engineering Council via the CIBSE. This brings the title Incorporated Engineer and initials IEng. Engineering technician candidates need a total of three years' training and experience before they can register. They gain the title engineering technician (EngTech).

LATE ENTRY

The CIBSE offers a mature candidate route for those over 35 with extended and increasing responsibility in the industry to achieve chartered engineer status.

Incorporated engineers with experience can take appropriate honours degrees to upgrade to chartered status, either full-time (possibly sponsored) or part-time on accredited courses or via Open University. Engineering technicians can also take higher national certificate plus a continuing education diploma (or higher national diploma) in their spare time or with help from employers. Experienced employees at craft or operator level may also find their experience helps them achieve higher technical or educational qualifications.

Many universities and colleges may waive the usual entry requirements for degree courses.

OPPORTUNITIES

Concerns that employ building services engineers and technicians include:

– building services departments of major building contractors;

– building services contractors, which may specialize in one area, such as heating and air conditioning or refrigeration or electrical;

– design consultancies or architectural practices which design building services installations;

– equipment manufacturers, such as lift manufacturers;

– users of large buildings, such as industrial and commercial concerns, big stores, hospitals, local authorities, or government departments, which may have building services engineers and technicians to maintain existing services, plan new ones and liaise with contractors/suppliers;

– specialist servicing and maintenance companies.

These are spread throughout the country, though the larger concerns with most employees are in cities and large towns.

For those prepared to travel, there are opportunities for employment in Europe and in other countries.

Membership of the CIBSE is 15,500, of whom 5,000 are chartered engineers.

PAY AND CONDITIONS

Pay at start of training is from £5,218 (first year) for student apprentices (technician levels). On completion of a technician apprenticeship, it is between £9,388 to £11,886. For graduate engineers, it is likely to be in the range of £13,047 to £16,026.

Those working on design, planning, estimating, purchasing, and so on, normally work 36½ hours a week, Monday to Friday, with overtime when project deadlines require it.

Those involved in installation or site management may have to work variable hours to suit the project. This can include weekends and evenings as overtime or with weekdays off in lieu. Servicing and maintenance, especially, may be done in evenings and weekends, and engineers may be on-call to attend to breakdowns.

PROSPECTS

Promotion is to team leader, project leader, project manager or section manager, and department manager. In the larger concerns, chartered engineers will normally fill these posts, but, in many cases, it is managerial skills that determine promotion rather than qualifications. Some move on to general management positions or to become directors of companies. Others start their own companies or become self-employed as consultants, especially in the design field.

Employers may send suitable candidates on short training courses to increase supervisory and management skills and/or familiarity with new technical developments and equipment. Engineering technicians and incorporated technicians may take additional courses part-time on their own initiative, or with the support of their employer to gain higher-level qualifications.

RELATED OCCUPATIONS

Chartered electrical engineer, chartered structural engineer, quantity surveyor, incorporated electrical engineer, architectural technologist, building technician, heating and ventilating fitter/welder.

FURTHER INFORMATION

Chartered Institution of Building Services Engineers (CIBSE)*, Delta House, 222 Balham High Road, London SW12 9BS, 0181 675 5211

Professional and Management Careers Service*, Construction Industry Training Board (CITB), Bircham Newton, King's Lynn, Norfolk PE31 6RH, 01553 776 677

HVCA Careers Service*, ESCA House, 34 Palace Court, London W2 4JG, 0171 229 2488

Institute of Domestic Heating and Environmental Engineers, 37a High Road, Benfleet, Essex SS7 5LH, 01268 754266.

FURTHER READING

Leaflets/booklets are available from the addresses marked*.

Working in Construction – COIC

In the careers library classified under UJ.

2. HEATING AND VENTILATING FITTER/ WELDER (UJ)

THE WORK

Heating and ventilating fitters/welders install the heating and ventilation equipment in all types of buildings. They install pipes, boilers, pumps, radiators, control valves and other equipment associated with heating and air-conditioning systems. The materials they work with include steel, copper, iron, plastic and stainless steel.

Fitting involves the installation of parts in the correct places with the right amount of space around them. Welding involves joining different metal parts by melting them with intense heat so that they flow together and become permanently joined as they cool.

The heating and ventilating fitter/welder works sometimes in existing buildings, but more often on building sites when a great deal of the construction work has been finished. Pipes can be fitted on the surface of walls or concealed above false ceilings or in ducts constructed in brick and concrete.

For large contractors, a chargehand or foreman/woman directs the work of the heating and ventilating fitter/welders. Otherwise, their first task is to check the plans that

detail where everything should go, what length and diameter of pipe is required, and where joins and bends are required. At the same time, they must check what tools they are going to need. A variety of tools are used for pipe fitting, including bending machines to bend pipes, stillsons (pipe-wrenches) that are used to tighten pipes into their fittings, pipe cutters to cut pipes to the required length, and an assortment of hand and power tools to fit valves, pumps and boilers. For welding, different types of gas and arc welding equipment are used. Fitting domestic heating systems may involve minor electrical wiring of boilers, control valves or thermostats.

Heating and ventilating fitters/welders perform a wide range of fitting work. They may start by fixing supports, which need to be stable and strong enough to support the weight of pipes and to withstand expansion stresses. They fit the pipes that link the boiler and other plant to the radiators and other heating units. They also install control valves and other parts to vary the system's output as the weather or time of day changes.

To join the pipework for the heating and ventilating systems, they may use one of a number of different welding techniques. These involve applying an electric arc or gas flame to heat and melt the parts to be joined (please see WELDER:RON) to make permanent, load-bearing, leak-tight joints in the pipes. While welding is more commonly used for joints in metal than plastic pipes, the practice of plastics welding is growing.

Protective clothing is essential, such as a hard hat, leather gauntlets and aprons, and masks or goggles for welding.

WORK ENVIRONMENT

Heating and ventilating fitters/welders frequently work on building sites, towards the end of the construction phase. The site may be dirty, dusty and unheated, and work may be required at heights or on ladders. They may also work in completed buildings that require a new or replacement system. In either case, they sometimes have to work in cramped conditions. They may have to travel some distance to particular building sites, and be prepared to work away from home.

SKILLS AND INTERESTS

Heating and ventilating fitters/welders must enjoy working with their hands and using tools. Good eye-to-hand co-ordination is necessary, and good colour vision is vital for any electrical work. Numerical ability is needed to ensure accurate measurements and fittings.

Fitters/welders need to be able to read plans and diagrams to see exactly where different parts need to be fitted. Working very accurately is essential, as the safety of many people, as well as the efficient working of the system, can depend on their work.

Heating and ventilating fitters/welders should enjoy solving practical problems. They need to be able to work on their own initiative as well as part of a team. If they are working in someone's home, they need to exercise tact and work cleanly and tidily.

ENTRY REQUIREMENTS

Formal qualifications are not essential, but an aptitude for maths, physics and science subjects as well as English is helpful for studies at college. All potential apprentices are required to sit a numerical paper and in some cases defective colour vision may restrict entry. Heating and ventilating fitters/welders must be physically fit.

Specific training opportunities for young people, including Modern Apprenticeships, may be available – contact your local careers office, TEC/LEC for details.

TRAINING

Training normally lasts four years, comprising on-the-job training and work experience with study leading to NVQs/SVQs. During this time, apprentices usually study at college on day release or block release.

Learning programmes designed to meet the requirements of NVQs/SVQs have been developed. Welding awards are under development but are not yet accredited.

The appropriate NVQs for heating and ventilation fitting are at Levels 2 and 3 in Mechanical Engineering Services – Heating and Ventilating (MES – H&V) and include:

– MES H&V Installation Industrial and Commercial Level 2 (Q1014150)

– MES H&V Installation Domestic Level 2 (Q1014149)

– MES H&V Installation Level 3 (Q1014151), Core and Option routes to either Domestic Installation or Industrial and Commercial Installation

– MES H&V Service and Maintenance (Maintenance of System Components) Level 2 (Q1014554)

– MES H&V Service and Maintenance (Rectification of Systems) Level 3 (Q1014555)

– MES H&V Ductwork Installation Level 3 (Q1014556)

– MES Ammonia Refrigeration Systems Level 3 (Q1018014)

The appropriate SVQs for heating and ventilation fitting are at Levels 2 and 3 in Mechanical Engineering Services (MES) and include:

– MES H&V Installation Industrial and Commercial Level 2 (SFO304202)

– MES H&V Installation Domestic Level 2 (SFO304203)

– MES H&V Service and Maintenance of System Components Level 2 (SFO304204)

– MES H&V Installation Level 3 (SG0304202)

– MES H&V Rectification of Systems Level 3 (SG0304203)

– MES H&V Ductwork Installation Level 3 (SG0304204)

Specific training courses for young people that include college attendance are often credited as part of craft training recognized by the Heating and Ventilating Contractors' Association (HVCA). For further details contact your local careers office, TEC/LEC or local office of Building Engineering Services Training Ltd (BEST).

LATE ENTRY

It is sometimes possible for adults to enter some training schemes, especially if they have relevant experience or skills. There may be specific training opportunities directed at adults available in some areas for this type of work. Candidates may have to satisfy certain conditions to be eligible. Contact your local Jobcentre, careers office or TEC/LEC for details.

OPPORTUNITIES

There are about 30,000 heating and ventilating fitter/welders employed at craft level in the UK.

Although the construction industry has suffered from the recession, new building work is still underway. In the South East of England, major new products include the opening of international terminals in London and Kent linked to the Channel Tunnel and the extension of the Jubilee underground line. Elsewhere, many companies and government departments are relocating to the North and West, with business parks and shopping centres opening to accommodate the moves.

Contact companies direct for information on apprenticeship opportunities, and look for advertisements in local and national newspapers. Your local careers office and the local office of BEST may also have details.

PAY AND CONDITIONS

Heating and ventilating fitters/welders earn on average about £208 a week. Pay, holidays and other benefits are agreed annually by the employers' association and the trade union.

Employees usually work 38 hours a week Monday to Friday and may be required to work shifts or overtime to meet client deadlines.

PROSPECTS

Heating and ventilating fitters/welders with organizational abilities may seek promotion to foreman/woman or supervisor. With appropriate further City and Guilds, BTEC/SCOTVEC or NVQ/SVQ qualifications, it is possible to progress to inspector or instructor. It is also possible to specialize in, for example, either service and maintenance of system components or domestic installation by following appropriate NVQs/SVQs.

For those who wish to progress to engineering technician or incorporated engineer, it is possible to become a building services technician (please see article 1. BUILDING SERVICES ENGINEER/TECHNICIAN). The usual route would be through following BTEC/SCOTVEC or NVQ/SVQ courses at higher levels.

RELATED OCCUPATIONS

Welder, sheet metal worker, plumber, engineering craftsman/woman, building services technician.

FURTHER INFORMATION

Heating and Ventilating Contractors' Association (HVCA)*, ESCA House, 34 Palace Court, London W2 4JG, 0171 229 2488

Building Engineering Services Training Ltd (BEST)*, 3 Mill Court, 51 Mill Street, Slough, Berkshire SL2 5DA, 01753 531188

Building Engineering Services Training Ltd*, Bush House, Bush Estate, Penicuik, Midlothian EH26 0SB, 0131 445 5580

City and Guilds (C&G)*, 1 Giltspur Street, London EC1A 9DD, 0171 294 2468

Institute of Domestic Heating and Environmental Engineers, 37a High Road, Benfleet, Essex 01268 754266

EnTra Careers*, Vector House, 41 Clarendon Road, Watford, Hertfordshire WD1 1HS, freephone 0800 282167

The Welding Institute*, Abington Hall, Abington, Cambridge CB1 6AL, 01223 891162

The Construction Industry Training Board*, Bircham Newton, King's Lynn, Norfolk PE31 6RH, 01553 776677

FURTHER READING

Leaflets/booklets are available from the addresses marked*.

Job Outlines – Craft Workers and Operatives in Engineering – COIC

Working in Engineering – COIC

Working in Construction – COIC

In the careers library classified under UJ.

LANDSCAPE ARCHITECT CLCI:UL

BACKGROUND INFORMATION

Landscape architects, also known as landscape designers, are concerned with the planning, design and construction of the whole outdoor environment.

Landscape architecture is often associated with planning fine gardens and parks but in fact most of the work is concerned with: the grounds and surroundings of public buildings and factories; open spaces on urban estates; playgrounds and recreational areas; or urban schemes in derelict inner cities. Some landscape architects work on water catchment areas and reservoirs, coastal regions and marinas, motorways, and mineral and quarry workings.

In any development that sets out to change the existing scenery – for example, the erection of a building, the excavation of a quarry or the creation of a park – landscape architects aim to create harmony between what is new and what already exists. They try to ensure that developments blend in, with minimal environmental damage.

In addition to landscape architects, other landscape professionals include landscape scientists and landscape managers. Information about these careers can be obtained from the Landscape Institute.

THE WORK

Landscape architects ideally become involved in the early stages of a development project, working alongside architects, planners and surveyors, in which case they can suggest alterations to plans that will help the new development to blend into the existing landscape.

They work to a brief (client's instructions). A project usually begins with an initial site visit to survey and record in detail the nature of the land and soil, the condition and life span of existing vegetation, together with any features such as buildings and roads.

Many different factors influence landscape architects in the drawing up of their plans. Their designs must be practical and make users feel at ease. Scientific considerations are also important; landscape architects must know what plants will flourish where – they must, therefore, have an extensive knowledge of horticulture, geology, soil science, and local ground and weather conditions. Technological considerations – for example, what methods and materials can and should be used to get particular effects and withstand various levels of use – must also be taken into account.

Having evaluated the project bearing all the above factors in mind, they produce drawings/diagrams of their proposals plus complementary written reports; together, these documents set out the possibilities of sites within the clients' guidelines. Negotiations then take place between landscape architects and clients to produce design schemes on which both are agreed. They then produce financial specifications and estimates for the work, which must include maintenance costs.

Having produced an acceptable plan, they put the project out to tender and select contractors who will carry out the digging, planting, etc. Landscape architects make regular site visits throughout the duration of the project, checking that the work is progressing according to contract and that the client is getting value for money. They also often negotiate the long-term maintenance contract.

WORK ENVIRONMENT

Landscape architects divide their time between office work and site visits. The office environment is normally warm, clean and comfortable, usually with good natural light for the drawing work. Site visits can, however, be cold and wet, and can also involve considerable amounts of travelling.

Those employed in the public sector may only be responsible for projects in a given area, but those in private practice may have to travel quite long distances.

SKILLS AND INTERESTS

Landscape architects must have a genuine interest in the creation and maintenance of an attractive physical environment. This requires an interest in both architecture and horticulture.

Design skills and technical drawing ability are important, since a lot of material is presented in the form of plans, sketches and detailed drawings.

Landscape architects work as part of a team alongside architects, planners, surveyors and engineers, and must therefore be able to communicate effectively, both verbally and in writing. The ability to negotiate – persuading clients to accept plans, and contractors to work to specifications – is also important, particularly for those working in private practice. Sound business sense is essential for those considering self-employment.

The work can be physically demanding, requiring site visits in all weather conditions.

ENTRY REQUIREMENTS

Entry is with a first degree or with a postgraduate qualification accredited by the Landscape Institute.

Entry to first degree courses is with a minimum of five GCSEs/S grades (A-C/1-3), including English and maths, plus two A levels or three H grades or equivalent. Useful A level/H grade subjects include biology, botany, design, environmental studies and geography. Check prospectuses for detailed entry requirements.

Entry to postgraduate courses is with a good first degree, usually in a related subject such as planning, geography, architecture, biology or horticulture. Some relevant practical experience is useful.

TRAINING

The recognized qualification for landscape architects is Associate of the Landscape Institute (ALI). To gain this qualification, it is first necessary to obtain graduate membership of the Landscape Institute by completing an accredited first degree or postgraduate course.

First degree courses are available at Cheltenham and Gloucester College of Higher Education, Edinburgh College of Art/Heriot-Watt University, Leeds Metropolitan University, The Manchester Metropolitan University, Sheffield University, and the University of Greenwich.

Postgraduate courses (two years full-time or three to five years part-time) are available at the universities of Edinburgh, Newcastle-upon-Tyne, Sheffield, Central England in Birmingham, and Greenwich.

A degree or postgraduate qualification is then followed by a period of practical experience, normally lasting two years, and the Landscape Institute's professional practice examination. This completes the requirements for associate of the Landscape Institute (ALI).

NVQs/SVQs in Amenity Horticulture/Constructing Landscapes are available at Levels 3 and 4.

LATE ENTRY

All professional landscape architects must follow one of the training routes outlined in TRAINING. Adult applicants are encouraged on all courses.

OPPORTUNITIES

Over 50 per cent of landscape architects work in private practices, which are usually small; most have fewer than ten professional staff.

There are also opportunities with local authorities, public bodies like the Forestry Commission, water authorities, and in the construction industry. Some landscape architects are employed as lecturers in higher education.

Landscape architecture is a small profession, with around 1,800 fully qualified practitioners, but it is growing fast. Most students completing courses in landscape architecture find employment in this field. There tend to be more vacancies in visually unattractive areas – such as inner cities – because in these places there is a greater need to improve the appearance of the outdoor environment.

There are opportunities to work abroad, particularly in other European countries and the Middle East.

Vacancies appear in the following journals: *Landscape Design, Landscape Design Extra, Building Design* and *Architects Journal.*

PAY AND CONDITIONS

Salaries are comparable to those earned by other similarly qualified professionals, such as architects. The starting salary for a degree-qualified entrant is around £9,000 to £15,000. Professionally qualified experienced landscape architects in private practice can expect to earn from £19,000 to £25,000 plus, depending on location and experience.

In the public sector, landscape architects normally work a 37-hour five-day week. Some employers operate a flexi-time scheme. Site visits can involve unforeseen difficulties and may occasionally lead to overtime. Extensive travelling can also lead to long working days.

Hours in private practice can be long and irregular. Meetings with clients must usually be held at their convenience and may involve occasional evening and weekend working. Overtime may be available or necessary in order to meet project deadlines.

PROSPECTS

Public sector employers, particularly local government, usually have well-defined promotion structures. Senior positions are difficult to achieve, however, because of the small numbers employed.

Experienced practitioners often move into private practice, where they can aim to become partners or set up their own practice. Some may also move into lecturing at higher education institutions.

RELATED OCCUPATIONS

Architect, town planner, design draughtsman/woman, civil engineer, horticultural manager, interior designer, forest officer, landscape manager, landscape scientist.

FURTHER INFORMATION

The Landscape Institute, 6/7 Barnard Mews, London SW11 1QU, 0171 738 9166

FURTHER READING

Job Outlines – the Landscape Profession – COIC
Architecture, Landscape Architecture and Town and Regional Planning – AGCAS

In the careers library classified under UL.

SURVEYOR CLCI:UM

BACKGROUND INFORMATION

Surveyors are involved in a wide range of roles related to the measurement, management and development of land, natural resources, buildings, other types of property and infrastructure, such as harbours, roads and railway lines. They work closely with other professionals, including architects, geologists and civil engineers, to provide expert services associated with land management and development.

Professional surveyors are supported by technical surveyors, who are less academically qualified but perform a vital role across the whole range of specializations.

There is a variety of different specialisms. The main areas identified by the Royal Institution of Chartered Surveyors are as follow:

Land surveyors measure, pinpoint, collect and manage information about the land's natural and man-made features. Such information enables them to determine where to site building projects.

Hydrographic surveyors are involved in all aspects of inshore and offshore marine surveying. The information they gather is used to manage the marine environment and its territorial limits, and to prepare charts.

Marine resource management surveyors are concerned with coastal engineering, land reclamation, mineral extraction, fisheries and ocean energy resources.

Minerals surveyors work with other professionals in the exploration of mineral deposits. They prepare planning applications, negotiate with local authorities and land owners, negotiate contracts and advise on the restoration of sites after the extraction has been completed.

Rural practice surveyors advise landowners, farmers and others with an interest in the countryside. They are responsible for the management of estates and farms, the planning and execution of development schemes for agriculture, forestry and recreation, and the valuation and sale of property and livestock.

Planning and development surveyors are involved in a wide range of both public and private sector building projects from their earliest planning stages through to completion. The job may involve raising finance from financial institutions and investors, overseeing the actual implementation of the project, controlling budgets and deadlines, and marketing the scheme to potential buyers.

Surveyors in general practice are concerned with valuation, investment, management and agency. It is possible to specialize in one of these elements of general practice work, or to specialize in a particular area, such as housing or fine art.

Building surveyors advise on the construction, maintenance, repair and refurbishment of all types of residential and commercial property. This includes surveying sites, drawing up plans and advising on design.

Quantity surveyors evaluate the costs of new developments, including housing, commercial property and infrastructure projects, such as bridges and airports. They also advise on alternative proposals, contract arrangements and construction conditions.

Professional surveyors are supported by technical surveyors. In many instances, the work undertaken by surveyors and technical surveyors is very similar. However, technical surveyors are less likely to be involved in project management.

THE WORK

Land surveyors are basically map makers. They compile information and measurements to determine the exact location and relative positions of both natural and man-made features. Their work involves the use of a range of equipment and instruments, from measuring tapes and theodolites to satellite positioning systems and laser alignment devices. Surveys are plotted at different scales for different purposes and are used by commerce and industry when planning new buildings and by central and local authorities in developing and managing road, bridges and other public sector projects. Some land surveyors specialize in the production of one type of survey. They work closely with other professionals, including civil engineers and cartographers, and are frequently required to provide technical analysis and advice.

Hydrographic surveyors produce surveys for use in nautical charts, and for the construction and maintenance of harbours, sea defences and inland waterways, such as canals. The work often involves establishing the position of rocks, sandbanks and other hazards, and locating navigation channels. The action of the sea means that nautical charts are subject to frequent revision.

Hydrographic surveyors are also involved in the positioning of oil and gas rigs, helping to lay underwater cables, defining marine boundaries and dredging harbours. They use equipment similar to land surveyors as well as instruments like echo sounders to measure water depth.

Marine resource management surveying is an expanding area of the profession. The work can include helping to extract minerals from the sea, reclaiming land, establishing and maintaining fisheries, and coastal engineering schemes.

Minerals surveyors work with other professionals, such as geologists, in the exploration of mineral deposits, from coal or gravel to gold and gemstones. The work involves surveying existing mine workings and valuing mines, quarries and mineral deposits. The valuation of mines and minerals require an understanding of the principles of rating valuation and taxation relating to the acquisition and sale of mineral assets.

When new developments or extensions to existing sites are proposed, the work includes preparing planning applications, anticipating any possible objections, negotiating with local authorities and land owners, and suggesting suitable amendments to overcome problems such as noise, dust or subsidence. They prepare contracts covering infrastructure, facilities, access rights, and infill and restoration of sites after extraction is completed.

The minerals surveyor is also likely to be involved in mine planning, including the design, development and surveying of quarries and underground mines, requiring a knowledge of earth sciences. They are responsible for ensuring the safety of mine workings and tips, and for minimizing the risk of subsidence and land movement, which could lead to claims for compensation. Once mineral extraction is completed, the quarry or mine workings must be left safe and may need to be sealed up, with the location of shafts fully recorded. Tips of mineral waste continue to be surveyed to ensure that they remain stable and arrangements may need to be made for tips to be landscaped to enhance the environment.

Rural practice surveyors are involved in a number of aspects of management and development in the countryside. They are often responsible for the management of estates, farms and forests, including financial and staff management. The supervision of agriculture and forestry activities is an important part of the job, including activities such as managing planting, ensuring the well-being of livestock, protecting crops and trees from damage and pests, harvesting and the marketing of estate or farm products. They may be employed to manage one estate or, alternatively, be responsible for a number of smaller properties.

Increasingly, this work involves the operation of leisure and recreation facilities, such as riding or golf, and perhaps the management and marketing of tourism accommodation. They may also be concerned with granting fishing or shooting licences.

Rural practice surveyors are also concerned with developments in the countryside, and advise on sales and purchases of rural holdings. Chartered surveyors in rural practice are employed to value land, property, livestock, agricultural produce and machinery, requiring a good knowledge of trends in the market. They may also organize and conduct auctions.

Planning and development surveyors in the private sector work on behalf of developers, advising them on the planning implications of their proposals. The work could include identification of suitable sites, analysing the viability of a project, preparing valuations, preparing planning applications, and negotiating with local authority planners to obtain planning permission. Developments normally have to conform to statutory requirements, such as county structure plans, and must be in line with complex legal and administrative requirements.

In the public sector, planning and development surveyors are involved in environmental planning at national, regional and local level. Working with other professionals, they help to plan where new developments, such as housing estates or shopping centres, are to be located and how competing demands for land use are to be reconciled, and priorities set. They balance the economic, social, financial and environmental benefits of different development proposals and recommend the most appropriate solution.

Planning and development surveyors are often required to prepare planning briefs, advise on legal aspects and to give evidence at public enquiries. Surveyors working in this area of the profession may also be concerned with financial arrangements and preparing tenders for building contracts.

Surveyors in general practice are involved in valuation, marketing and management of commercial and residential property, and investment management. Valuation is a key activity and surveyors are therefore experts in property markets, land and property values, valuation procedures, construction methods, property and planning law. Surveyors may act for vendors, purchasers, landlords or tenants, and visit different properties to value them.

Some surveyors specialize in the identification, valuation and auctioning of furniture, carpets, fine art, plant and machinery. This work can involve making detailed inventories, arranging for goods to be insured and safely transported to salerooms, producing a catalogue or arranging and conducting an auction.

Surveyors can also handle a property portfolio on behalf of pension funds, insurance companies, charities and other major investors, ensuring that they obtain the best possible return on their investment. Property management services are provided by surveyors in all sectors of the economy, including public sector organizations, property companies and charitable trusts.

Estate agency work involves the sale and acquisition of all types of property, from a family home to an office block or industrial estate. A prime role is negotiating between the vendor and the purchaser of a property. A survey is undertaken and a valuation agreed with the vendor. It is then necessary to market the property, which is likely to include preparing written information on the property, arranging for the display of 'For Sale' signs and, perhaps, organizing press advertisements. Prospective buyers are shown the property and the surveyors may be involved in negotiations with solicitors or organizations being asked for a mortgage on the property. An excellent knowledge of property law is required, together with an understanding of local market trends and sales skills. In some instances, estate agents may be responsible for organizing property auctions.

Building surveyors cover a very wide field of work, which frequently overlaps with other specialisms. Their work is mainly concerned with existing buildings of all types, sizes and uses. It includes undertaking detailed surveys of buildings, preparing accurate plans, advising clients on the suitability of the buildings for specific purposes, preparing schemes for conversion or repair, advising on relevant government legislation and the availability of grants.

If a client decides to go ahead with alterations to a building, the surveyor works with an architect to prepare constructional drawings, detailed specifications and obtain estimates for the work. Schemes may need to be submitted for planning approval. They also advise on the selection of contractors, then supervise the work to ensure that it is undertaken according to the specification. The work involves liaising with a number of different individuals and keeping them informed of progress.

Some building surveyors are employed by local authorities and specialize in building control, which includes administering building regulations, public health legislation and improvement grants. They check plans and ensure that work is undertaken to a satisfactory standard and that all health and safety requirements are met.

Quantity surveyors specialize in calculating what projects will cost. In private practice, they often work in conjunction with the architect, the client and others in undertaking feasibility studies to examine the kind of building required in relation to the money available for the project. Throughout the design stage of a building, the quantity surveyor continually appraises the cost of the work being undertaken using his or her knowledge of the quantities and prices of materials being used and the labour charges likely to be involved.

When the design is completed, a Bill of Quantities is prepared for selected contractors to use as a basis for preparing tenders and detailing what they would charge for the work. The quantity surveyor advises on which estimate should be accepted, monitors expenditure as the project progresses and arranges stage and final payments. It is important to keep an accurate check on the value of work in progress and to ensure that any variations are agreed by all relevant parties.

Quantity surveyors also work for contractors and civil engineers. This role involves providing cost and other financial advice, preparing estimates and invoices for work undertaken, establishing the quantities of materials that will be required for a project, agreeing the accounts submitted by subcontractors and preparing work schedules.

Central and local government also employ quantity surveyors, where the type of work is likely to be similar to that performed in private practice.

WORK ENVIRONMENT

Surveyors are frequently office-based, and most spend some time at a desk dealing with administration, writing reports, or preparing plans. However, the work is likely to include external meetings and site visits. Travel within the UK is an essential part of many posts and travel overseas is increasingly common. Employers may require surveyors to have a full driving licence.

Quantity surveyors and planning and development surveyors are likely to spend more time working at their desks than other branches of the profession. However, they are also involved in travelling to meetings and some site visits.

Land surveyors spend much of their time out of doors, in all weathers. Hydrographic and marine resource management surveyors often work from on board a ship and must be prepared for bad weather and rough seas. Hours of work are often determined by the availability of daylight, and are likely to include weekends. Both are likely to spend long periods away from home, sometimes in harsh or isolated conditions.

Minerals surveyors often work underground in mines and quarries where conditions are dirty and can be hazardous. Many posts are based overseas.

Rural practice surveyors, particularly those involved in estate management, are likely to spend some of their time outdoors regardless of the weather conditions.

SKILLS AND INTERESTS

Surveyors should be practical problem-solvers, able to obtain and analyse information, apply scientific and technological principles, and reach logical decisions within agreed deadlines and budgets. A methodical approach is required, together with an ability to pay attention to detail.

It is important for surveyors to understand fully the economic, social, legal, business and environmental background to a project. They therefore need to acquire technical, financial and legal expertise.

Surveyors and technical surveyors need to communicate effectively with a wide range of different people, face-to-face, on the telephone, and in writing. It is important to be able to present complex information, views and recommendations in a coherent and persuasive manner, sometimes to non-specialists. Surveyors are usually part of a team and therefore need to be able to work effectively with others. Chartered surveyors are often project managers, and leadership skills are therefore valued by employers.

Many posts require surveyors to possess a full driving licence.

ENTRY REQUIREMENTS

The entry requirements for professional bodies vary considerably. Those undertaking a relevant course or working in surveying are, however, usually eligible to join as student members.

BTEC/SCOTVEC National Certificate/Diploma in Surveying requires either: four GCSEs/S grades (A-C/1-3), with English, maths, science and geography being useful subjects; or a BTEC first certificate in a relevant subject, such as construction; or Intermediate GNVQ/GSVQ Level II in a relevant area such as Construction and the Built Environment/Construction; or an equivalent qualification.

BTEC/SCOTVEC Higher National Certificate/Diploma in Surveying requires either: at least one A level/two H grades and GCSEs/S grades (A-C/1-3), with physical science, maths, geography and economics the preferred subjects; or a relevant BTEC/SCOTVEC national award such as surveying or construction; or a relevant Advanced GNVQ/GSVQ III such as Construction and the Built Environment/Construction; or equivalent qualification.

Degree courses relevant to a career as a surveyor require a minimum of two A levels plus three other subjects at GCSE (A-C) or three H grades plus two other subjects at S grade (1-3). The GCSEs/S grades should include English and maths. A relevant BTEC/SCOTVEC national award, such as surveying or construction, may be accepted for degree entry, as may a relevant Advanced GNVQ/GSVQ III such as Construction and the Built Environment/Construction.

TRAINING

A number of organizations are involved in the training and professional development of surveyors:

Royal Institution of Chartered Surveyors

This is the principal body representing surveyors in the United Kingdom. To become a full member or a professional associate, it is necessary to satisfy the Royal Institution of Chartered Surveyors (RICS) in three areas: academic qualifications (a degree or equivalent), approved probationary training and experience, and professional assessment.

Relevant academic qualifications can be obtained via:

– a RICS-accredited full-time degree course in, for example, quantity surveying, land management, estate management, building or surveying, and normally lasting three years; or

– a RICS-accredited sandwich course that includes a year of practical work experience; or

– employment with a surveyor whilst studying for a RICS-accredited degree or diploma on a part-time basis by block release, day release or distance learning.

Graduates with a degree not directly related to surveying, such as geography or economics, can undertake a postgraduate conversion course. These can either be one year full-time, two years part-time or through distance learning.

As well as meeting academic requirements, it is necessary to complete an Assessment of Professional Competence (APC). This requires a minimum of two years of practical training. While working for a firm of chartered surveyors, a record of training and experience must be kept for submission to RICS. It is then necessary to demonstrate ability in an assessed practical assignment.

Architects' and Surveyors' Institute

This organization was formed by the amalgamation of the Faculty of Architects and Surveyors and the Construction Surveyors' Institute. Full membership is available to those who successfully complete the Stage 3 of the Institute's examination and have relevant practical experience. Exemption is given to those with a degree related to surveying. Licentiateship is available to those qualified to higher national certificate/diploma level. An alternative entry route is available to mature candidates with industry experience.

ISVA–The Professional Society for Valuers, Auctioneers and Estate Agents

ISVA is the principal society within the property profession involved with valuation services. There are several entry routes to become an associate of ISVA including: entry with a minimum of five GCSEs/S grades (A-C/1-3) including English language and maths; an NVQ/SVQ Level 2; Intermediate GNVQ/GSVQ Level II; or age 21 and over with relevant experience.

The ISVA Syllabus has six units, each consisting of a number of subject areas. Study can be part-time by day release at various universities and colleges throughout the UK or by distance learning. To achieve associate membership students must pass the six units (or be granted exemption from some or all of the units) and satisfy the Professional Assessment. That is undertaken over a two-year period of approved employment and comprises a journal and an assignment.

The Association of Building Engineers

The Association of Building Engineers (ABE) was formerly known as The Incorporated Association of Architects and Surveyors and is the professional body for those specializing in the technology of building.

Student membership of the ABE is open to those undertaking a full-time course of study leading to the award of an ABE accredited degree.

Associate membership (ABEng – senior technician grade) is awarded to those with an appropriate higher national award with two years relevant experience in a professional office.

Entry to professional membership is through an ABE accredited honours degree in a construction related subject. Members have an Evaluation of Professional Competence (EPC), success at which leads to becoming corporate members (MBEng). The EPC consists of two years' approved professional experience, a project and a professional interview.

The Institute of Revenues, Rating and Valuation

The Institute of Revenues, Rating and Valuation (IRRV) is a professional body for those involved in valuation, property taxation, and local authority revenues and benefits. Full professional membership is available to those who pass the Institute's professional examinations and to those qualified members of certain other professional bodies, including the RICS and the ISVA.

The Society of Surveying Technicians

The Society of Surveying Technicians (SST) works in partnership with the RICS to establish a nationally recognized organization for technical surveyors.

Surveying technicians/technician surveyors can start their training by working for an employer and following, part-time, a BTEC/SCOTVEC National Certificate in Surveying. Alternatively, it is possible to study full-time on a BTEC/SCOTVEC National Diploma in Surveying course. Associate membership requires successful completion of a Higher National Diploma/Certificate in Surveying. Full membership of SST also requires completion of the Joint Test of Competence, a searching practical test of the surveying technician's skill, which has been developed jointly by the Society and the RICS.

Those with two years' full membership of the Society of Surveying Technicians may be eligible to progress to corporate membership of the RICS.

Training for young people

For those aged 16 or 17 years, it is possible to enter the profession via training that includes a work placement as well as part-time study for a BTEC/SCOTVEC National Certificate in Surveying. Trainees specialize in either commercial and residential property surveying, building surveying or quantity surveying. Further information is available from the Chartered Surveyors Training Trust.

Continuing professional development

A growing range of post-qualification courses are available for surveyors who wish to specialize in a particular area, such as project management, property investment or building conversion. Surveyors may also participate in overseas technical study tours. It is also possible to upgrade knowledge and skills through distance learning programmes, such as those offered by the College of Estate Management.

Larger organizations offer in-house training to surveyors and surveying technicians/technician surveyors in areas related to technical as well as business and management skills. Even in smaller organizations, surveyors must continue to develop their professional skills, perhaps by attending external courses or seminars, to ensure that they keep abreast of new technical or legal requirements relating to their area of specialization.

NVQs/SVQs relating to surveying are currently being developed.

LATE ENTRY

Adults applying for degree or higher national courses may not need the normal entry requirements. They may prepare for application for such courses by successfully completing an approved higher education access course. Access courses are offered at local colleges and are usually one year full-time or one to two years part-time with daytime and/or evening attendance.

Professional bodies associated with surveying are also willing to accept mature candidates and most have special late-entry criteria for those with appropriate experience. It may be more difficult for those aged over 30 years to find a first post, though, unless they have relevant experience.

Refresher courses are available for those wishing to return to work as a surveyor after a career break.

OPPORTUNITIES

Demand is generally good for surveyors and surveying technicians, although it does vary with the state of the property market and the level of construction activity being undertaken. There are over 72,000 fully qualified members of the Royal Institution of Chartered Surveyors.

Opportunities occur most frequently in general practice and quantity surveying as these are the largest areas of specialization. In contrast, there are relatively few land, hydrographic, minerals, or planning and development surveyors.

In the private sector, surveyors and surveying technicians are employed by organizations of all types, from utility companies such as British Gas or Thames Water to firms of builders and civil engineers, auction houses to rural estates.

Government departments and executive agencies employ some surveyors, including the Valuation Office Agency, the Ministry of Defence and the Ministry of Agriculture, Fisheries and Food, and the Mapping and Charting Group. Local authorities are also large employers.

Vacancies are advertised in *Building, Property Week, Estates Gazette, Estates Times* and *New Builder*.

PAY AND CONDITIONS

Surveying salaries vary considerably depending on age, qualifications and experience. Demand for staff in particular specialisms also has a major impact on salary levels. Salaries are currently depressed owing to the recession in the UK economy, especially the construction industry, and low levels of house sales.

A school-leaver starting work and studying part-time might expect a salary anywhere between £5,000 to £10,000. For newly qualified chartered surveyors, salaries average £24,000 dependant on location.

Progression within the private sector is likely to be based on merit with salaries for experienced practitioners rising to £30,000 plus. Income for partners, for example in general practice, depends on the profits achieved by the business.

Local authorities and other public sector organizations have salary scales, although overall salaries are usually lower than in the private sector.

PROSPECTS

Prospects for surveyors and technical surveyors are generally good. Larger firms in the private sector and public sector organizations usually have a recognized career structure with promotion opportunities leading to managerial posts.

Promotion prospects can be more limited in smaller organizations and it may be necessary to move around to gain experience. However, these organizations can be very flexible and career progression can be rapid for the most able. It is often possible for experienced chartered surveyors to become partners in commercial organizations or even to start their own firm.

RELATED OCCUPATIONS

Estate agent, land agent, civil engineer, construction site manager, town planner, town planning technician, architect, housing manager, forestry manager, valuer/auctioneer.

FURTHER INFORMATION

Architects and Surveyors Institute*, 15 St Mary Street, Chippenham, Wiltshire SN15 3WD, 01249 444505

The College of Estate Management*, Whiteknights, Reading RG6 6AW, 01734 861101

Construction Industry Standing Conference, The Building Centre, 26 Store Street, London WC1E 7BT, 0171 323 5270

The Association of Building Engineers (ABE)*, Jubilee House, Billing Brook Road, Weston Favell, Northampton NN3 4NW, 01604 404121

ISVA, The Professional Society for Valuers and Auctioneers, 3 Cadogan Gate, London SW1X 0AS, 0171 235 2282

The Institute of Revenues, Rating and Valuation, 41 Doughty Street, London WC1N 2LF, 0171 831 3505

The Royal Institution of Chartered Surveyors*, Training Department, Surveyor Court, Westwood Way, Coventry CV4 8JE, 0171 222 7000

The Society of Surveying Technicians, Surveyor Court, Westwood Way, Coventry CV4 8JE, 0171 222 7000

FURTHER READING

Leaflets/booklets are available from the addresses marked*.

Job Outlines – Chartered Surveying – COIC

Working in Construction – COIC

In the careers library, classified under UM.

CIVIL ENGINEER CLCI:UN

BACKGROUND INFORMATION

Civil engineers are concerned with major construction projects – roads and railways, tunnels and bridges, docks and airports. Reservoirs, dams, water supply and sewerage systems are designed and built by civil engineers; so are power supply systems such as hydroelectric or nuclear power installations.

Structural engineers design large free-standing structures, such as dams, bridges, oil rigs, multi-storey car parks or office blocks. They are responsible for the foundations and structural framework of the building, making sure it is strong enough to withstand loads such as the weight of traffic or water, and forces such as heat, cold or earth tremors. They also carry out structural surveys of existing buildings and advise on repair.

Municipal engineering is the public service branch of civil engineering. It involves working for local government, other public authorities or utilities, on projects such as road building, traffic management, water supply or sewerage. Municipal engineers may undertake design, construction and maintenance themselves, or arrange contracts with consulting engineers or contractors.

Highway and traffic engineers are concerned with road building and traffic management. Traffic management entails assessing road use and planning one-way systems, cycle lanes, traffic lights, parking facilities, etc.

Water engineers specialize in water supply, sewerage systems and pollution control.

This article deals with opportunities in civil engineering and its specialisms.

THE WORK

Professional (chartered) engineers initiate, design and manage projects. Other members of the team, normally incorporated engineers or engineering technicians, translate overall plans and designs into drawings and instructions. At the design stage they produce calculations and make detailed drawings, often using computers. They may be involved in estimating costs, buying materials, planning the sequence of work and quantity surveying. During construction they help to set out the site, using surveying instruments to check lines and levels. They pass instructions to the supervisors and craft workers and make sure that any alterations in the plan are noted and acted upon.

Incorporated engineers are usually team leaders within the design office or on the construction site who take responsibility for sections of the work, solve day-to-day engineering problems and advise on choices of action.

Engineering technicians apply standard techniques in practical situations.

Civil and structural engineers are involved in all stages of a construction project. The two main areas of work are design and construction management.

Design is based on knowledge and structures of materials their properties and behaviour and the forces that can be applied to them. It demands an understanding of mechanics, statics and aerodynamics, of hydraulics (the movement and storage of water) and of geotechnics (the properties and behaviour of soil and rock). Civil and structural engineers use their knowledge to create the most efficient and economic design.

The design of a project involves collecting data about the site, planning in detail, producing design calculations and drawings, plans and specifications and estimating costs. The overall plan is turned into a series of working drawings by civil engineering draughting technicians. Computers are widely used in drawing.

Structural design for large buildings involves selecting materials, calculating stresses and making drawings. Structural engineers work in liaison with the architect, builder, building services engineer and quantity surveyor. Their aim is to balance strength and safety against economy and appearance.

Construction management. Civil engineers may work as project managers or site engineers. Project management entails detailed planning: working out the sequence of operations at each stage and organizing workers, equipment and materials. Managers make regular inspections on site, checking measurements, materials and workmanship. They are responsible for the work of site engineers, buyers, planners, quantity surveyors, supervisors and craftworkers.

Site engineers make sure that the design is carried out in detail on site. First they set out the site and establish the site infrastructure (making a compound for workshops and offices, laying on water and erecting fences). Next they supervise ground preparation – excavating topsoil, felling trees, laying foundations. Thirdly the main structure goes up. Site engineers mark out the positions for buildings, check measurements and levels, assess the quality of the materials and the standard of work. They give instructions to technicians and supervisors and sort out day-to-day problems, such as drainage, mechanical breakdown or the non-arrival of supplies, as they arise. They liaise with gas and electricity authorities over realigning pipes and cables, and consult with local people and pressure groups to explain what they are doing.

WORK ENVIRONMENT

Civil and structural engineers work both in offices and on site. Site work can involve working outdoors in all weathers and at heights on scaffolding or ladders.

Jobs at a senior level usually involve working on several projects, visiting sites, attending meetings and working in an office.

Engineers may work on sites away from home for varying periods of time.

SKILLS AND INTERESTS

Civil and structural engineers are both creative and practical; design and problem-solving call for creative thinking combined with a practical outlook and logical method of working.

It is necessary to be able to make neat, accurate plans and drawings and to use advanced maths to calculate stresses etc, although much of the routine work is done by computers.

Both design and management involve team work. On site, the engineer may be in charge of 100 or more people. Organizing and motivating the workforce demands qualities of leadership, and the ability to deal with problems in detail without losing sight of the overall plan.

Good communication with staff at all levels is essential. Civil and structural engineers need to give clear instructions and hold discussions with everyone on the project, from the client and architect to the site supervisor and plant operatives. They also have to write regular progress reports for the management team.

Dealing with all the problems that occur on a large project, from bad weather to land slippage, demands a great deal of perseverance and adaptability.

ENTRY REQUIREMENTS

Chartered engineer

To become a chartered engineer requires an honours degree or equivalent in civil engineering or engineering science, accredited by the Joint Board of Moderators on behalf of the Institution of Civil Engineers, The Institution of Structural Engineers, and the Chartered Institute of Building Surveyors. To attain the status of a chartered engineer, this degree is followed by structured postgraduate training leading to the Professional Review or examination of the professional institution.

Minimum entry requirements for a degree course are two A levels/three H grades and three other subjects at GCSE/S grade (A-C/1-3). The A levels/H grades should include maths and physics. A BTEC/SCOTVEC national award in engineering or construction may be acceptable as an alternative to A levels/H grades, as may a relevant Advanced GNVQ/GSVQ III, eg Engineering, Construction and the Built Environment, or Construction.

Applicants with A levels that do not include maths and science may be accepted onto a foundation year preceding the first year of a civil engineering degree course in some institutions.

Incorporated engineer

Incorporated engineers need an accredited Higher National Diploma or Certificate in Civil Engineering Studies, or a degree accredited by the Joint Accreditation Panel or equivalent, followed by training at work, leading to the Professional Review or examination of a professional institution.

Minimum entry requirements for higher national certificate/diploma are either: BTEC/SCOTVEC national award in an appropriate subject; or four GCSEs/S grades (A-C/1-3) and the study of two A levels/H grades with a pass in at least one; or a relevant Advanced GNVQ/GSVQ III, eg Engineering, Construction and the Built Environment, or Construction.

Applicants with A levels/H grades that do not include maths and science may be accepted onto a foundation year preceding the first year of a civil engineering higher national diploma course in some institutions.

Technician

Engineering technicians need either: a BTEC/SCOTVEC National Certificate in Civil Engineering Studies; or a National Diploma in Construction; or Advanced GNVQ in Construction and the Built Environment; or GSVQ Level III in Construction. They undertake further training at work in order to register as an engineering technician.

Minimum entry requirements for a national certificate, national diploma or Advanced GNVQ/GSVQ Level III are normally four GCSEs/S grades (A-C/1-3), preferably including maths, science and English, or Intermediate GNVQ/GSVQ Level II.

TRAINING

Chartered engineer

Degrees in civil and structural engineering include maths, materials, applied mechanics, computing, drawing and communication skills, with structural, water or geotechnical engineering in various proportions. To become a chartered engineer, further postgraduate training is required. This is arranged by the employer and approved by the professional institution.

Schemes run by the Institution of Civil Engineers lead to a Professional Review consisting of a presentation, an interview and two essays. Successful candidates can become members of the Institution. They are registered with the Engineering Council as chartered engineers, and may use the initials CEng, MICE after their name.

Those applying to the Institution of Structural Engineers complete a Record of Practical Training and sit a Part 3 exam. Success leads to registration as a chartered engineer, membership of the Institution, and the title CEng, MIStructE.

Incorporated engineer

Higher national certificate/diploma courses include: science, maths, technical studies, structural theory and design, contractual administration, soil mechanics, an individual project and options such as highways, water treatment or structural design.

Further training at work leads to the Incorporated Professional Review of the ICE or the Institute of Highway Incorporated Engineers (IHIE) or the associate membership examination of the IStructE. Successful candidates are registered with the Engineering Council as Incorporated Engineers, gain associate membership of the ICE or IStructE or Fellowship of the IHIE, and are entitled to use the letters IEng, AMICE, AMIStructE or FIHIE after their name.

Technician

BTEC/SCOTVEC National Certificate in Civil Engineering Studies and BTEC National Diploma in Construction include construction, drawing, applied sciences, surveying and maths.

To become an engineering technician, further training at work is required, leading to the Technician Professional Review. Successful candidates are registered with the Engineering Council and become technician members of the ICE or the IHIE.

Most technicians go on to study for a higher national certificate or diploma.

LATE ENTRY

The minimum age for registration as a chartered civil engineer is 25 years. In practice most candidates are in their mid/late twenties by the time they are ready for the Professional Review that leads to registration. There is no maximum age for registration.

Most universities and colleges welcome applications from adults. There may be some flexibility over entry requirements for applicants who lack the normal academic qualifications but have relevant work experience.

Access courses for adults who wish to study for a degree but do not have the necessary qualifications are offered at many colleges throughout the UK. They are usually one year full-time or one/two years part-time with daytime and/or evening attendance.

The Institution of Civil Engineers and the Institution of Structural Engineers have a mature candidate scheme for adults who wish to become chartered engineers, incorporated engineers or engineering technicians but who lack the normal academic qualifications. Applicants should be over 35 with at least 15 years' experience in construction, including responsibility for initiating and managing projects. The scheme entails submitting essays and project reports and attending an interview.

OPPORTUNITIES

The three main areas of work for civil and structural engineers are with consulting engineers, contractors, or client organizations such as local authorities.

Consulting engineers

Firms usually specialize in certain types of project, such as roads, power stations or docks and harbours. They may work for many different clients, including overseas governments. Working with a team of technicians and quantity surveyors, consulting engineers undertake design and feasibility studies. They appoint contractors to carry out the project but supervise the work themselves.

Contractors

Contractors may undertake all types of construction, or specialize in either building or civil engineering. Civil engineers work at head office and on site. At head office they are employed as designers, estimators, planners or general administrators. On site they work as construction managers, site managers, site engineers or section heads.

Client organizations

In the public sector, local authorities are major employers of civil engineers. They work as county or municipal engineers, in technical administration or in planning departments. For water authorities they build dams and reservoirs and design water supply and sewerage systems. For dock and harbour boards they build quays, jetties, etc. Civil engineers work in various departments of the Civil Service, principally the Department of the Environment, and in research establishments.

Gas and electricity supply companies employ civil engineers to design storage, generating and distribution systems.

For transport authorities they design and construct lines and stations and plan the services.

In manufacturing industry, civil engineers are employed on the construction and maintenance of industrial plant. Oil companies use them as drilling or field engineers. In the quarrying, cement, brick and tiling industries they work as research and production engineers.

There are also some opportunities in the Armed Forces, and as teachers in universities and colleges.

Overseas there are good opportunities with British firms of consulting or contracting engineers working for foreign governments, or with international oil and mining companies.

There are about 100,000 professional civil and structural engineers in Britain. Demand fluctuates to some extent with the state of the economy. The Construction Careers Service issues a list of firms willing to sponsor students onto degree courses and the professional institutions provide lists of firms with approved training schemes. Journals advertising vacancies include: *Construction News, Contract Journal, New Civil Engineer, Offshore Engineer, Structural Engineer.*

PAY AND CONDITIONS

Salaries depend on experience and the type of employer. They range from about £12,000 for a newly qualified graduate to £30,000 or more. A 16-year-old trainee technician might start at about £7,000.

A 37-hour week is normal in design offices, local government and public service. On site, hours are often irregular and can include evening and weekend work with up to and in excess of 50 hours worked. Site engineers and managers may be on 24-hour call in case problems arise.

PROSPECTS

Progression depends very much on ability, experience and ambition. Civil engineers commonly change their jobs many times in order to gain experience and responsibility, and switch between the public and private sectors. The promotion ladder can lead to posts as chief engineer, associate or partner.

The ICE, IStructE and IHIE run mid-career education courses for continuing professional development.

An NVQ/SVQ in Construction Project Management Level 5 has been introduced, and other relevant NVQs/SVQs are being developed.

Higher degrees in specialized aspects of civil engineering are available and may be of advantage in applying for some senior posts. Chartered engineers with at least four years' work experience can apply for the status of European Engineer (Eur Ing).

RELATED OCCUPATIONS

Professional engineer, architect, building services engineer, building surveyor, planning and development surveyor, town planner.

FURTHER INFORMATION

The Civil Engineering Careers Service*, The Institution of Civil Engineers, 1-7 Great George Street, London SW1P 3AA, 0171 222 7722

The Institution of Structural Engineers, 11 Upper Belgrave Street, London SW1X 8BH, 0171 235 4535

Construction Careers Service*, CITB, Bircham Newton, King's Lynn, Norfolk PE3 1RH, 01553 776677 ext 2424

FURTHER READING

Leaflets/booklets are available from the addresses marked*.

Job Outlines – Professional Engineering – COIC

Periodicals: New Civil Engineer (ICE), The Structural Engineer (IStructE), Highway and Transportation (IHIE)

In the careers library, classified under UN.

1. TOWN PLANNER CLCI:US
2. TOWN PLANNING TECHNICIAN CLCI:US

BACKGROUND INFORMATION

Planning is a major tool for influencing the environment. Land is in limited supply, and the population is increasingly aware of environmental concerns. Planners have the task of balancing conflicting demands: protecting both countryside and urban areas from unsightly development, while providing for increased requirements for housing, industry, recreation and transport.

Consideration must be given to social and economic factors, for example: population drift from the countryside to towns and vice versa; the need to locate new industries in areas of high unemployment; requirement for transport networks in order to get people to work; the need to undertake urban renewal projects; the rise in car ownership. All these factors bring demands for roads, housing, schools, shops, factories and leisure facilities. These must be balanced, wherever they occur, with protection of the landscape, preservation of historic buildings, wildlife conservation and minimum increase in pollution. Planners must consider the future, forecasting likely needs and developments, rather than simply aiming to solve today's problems.

Planning cannot be carried out patchily, with each region or area acting solely on its own concerns. A comprehensive town and country planning system has therefore been established, regulated by Acts of Parliament. Strategic planning sets out the broad framework of policies on development over a given period. Local planning translates these broad proposals into much more detailed plans for specific areas.

Planning decisions are taken ultimately by politicians at either national or local level. Professionally qualified planners prepare and co-ordinate plans for the development of particular areas and advise councillors or ministers on the benefits and drawbacks of various possible solutions. They are assisted by town planning technicians, differently qualified, but working in an important support role.

1. TOWN PLANNER (US)

THE WORK

A town planner's prime task is to find and evaluate information in order to make judgements. They conduct research, carry out surveys and analyse information, before presenting reports giving the different options and likely effects of these to the people ultimately responsible for taking planning decisions. Some information may already be available in the form of published reports or from censuses; some is obtained from other departments within their own councils, from health authorities, transport organizations or from the Department of the Environment; but in many cases town planners have to devise questionnaires, take advice from other professionals such as architects, engineers and surveyors, or go out on site to assess situations themselves. They frequently make use of computers, feeding in data to construct different models.

Typical problems on which they might work include: assessing the number of people likely to move into an area over a ten-year period, their ages, and consequent demand for houses, schools, sheltered accommodation and leisure facilities; the changing nature of employment, with resulting need for different amounts of industrial or office premises; assessing the impact of a proposed new road system or industrial development on the community, examining environmental factors like noise, pollution and increased traffic; deciding whether a new housing development or shopping centre would put strain on existing transport services or adversely affect existing residents.

In all cases, planners must work within the constraints of existing legislation, national and regional plans – and finance – aiming to reach the best compromise solution.

Public consultation is an important part of the planning process. Planners try to involve residents in the early stages of preparing plans, by organizing displays in public places such as town halls and libraries and holding public meetings at which they speak and answer questions. Since people take an active interest in plans affecting their areas, and it is often difficult to accommodate the conflicting views of different interest groups, meetings are often lively affairs and planners must be able to explain the reasons behind certain proposals convincingly.

As one method of ascertaining people's opinions and of explaining planning policies and constraints, planners increasingly talk to interested groups in the community and may take part in school environmental education classes.

Their exact duties vary according to whether they are engaged in strategic or local planning.

Strategic planning is carried out at county level in England and Wales, and at regional level in Scotland.

County and regional planning departments prepare structure plans or policy statements, detailing the amount of industrial development envisaged for an area: what type it should be and where it should be located; the number of houses to be built and in which areas; changes necessary to transportation systems, such as the construction of major roads and bypasses; proposals for new hospitals; protection of scenic areas; the consequences of major projects like power stations and mines; policies on waste disposal; and control of mineral extraction.

A structure plan with appropriate diagrams is produced, usually for a ten-year period, and, once approved by councillors is presented to the Secretary of State for the Environment. If the Secretary of State is satisfied that adequate public consultation has taken place, approval is given, but any individual or company has the right to appeal to the Secretary of State against any part of the plan they wish.

Local planning is done by district councils. Planners working for these authorities working closely with county planners and with colleagues in adjoining districts, convert the structure plan into a detailed local plan which shows exactly how any proposed changes in land use would be made and how individual properties would be affected. An important part of their work is development control or assessing applications to change the use of individual buildings or pieces of land, then granting or withholding planning permission. Again, individuals have the right of appeal against decisions, in this case to an independent planning inspector (planning reporter in Scotland).

Planners in private sector consultancy work on a variety of projects. They may do projects for planning departments that sometimes contract out part of their work, or may work for groups or individuals wishing to appeal against planning decisions or proposals. In this case they investigate all the likely implications of the local authority's/central government's proposals and write a report.

WORK ENVIRONMENT

Planners spend most of their time in offices, although they make site visits from time to time. When out on site they can be working in all weathers. They may spend considerable amounts of time in travelling to attend meetings or conduct surveys. A driving licence is useful.

SKILLS AND INTERESTS

Planners need an interest in the environment and its effect on people's lives.

They must be aware of the needs of all sections of the community, yet be capable of working realistically within environmental, legal and financial constraints.

They must be able to communicate with a wide range of people, from fellow professionals – they often work in teams with architects, landscape architects, civil engineers and surveyors – to elected politicians and members of the public.

It is important to be able to write clear reports in language that is non-technical and is easily understood. As they become more senior they need to develop public speaking skills in order to present reports at council meetings, address public meetings and conduct or defend planning application appeals.

The work involves researching and analysing a wide range of subjects including law, housing and economics. Much of the information is technical or in chart, graph or statistical form, and increasing use is made of computers.

They need administrative and managerial skills in order to be able to organize their own workloads and supervise the work of junior staff.

ENTRY REQUIREMENTS

Minimum entry requirements to degree courses are normally: five GCSEs/S grades (A-C/1-3) plus two A levels/ three H grades (useful subjects are English, maths and history, or geography or a foreign language); or a relevant BTEC/SCOTVEC national certificate or diploma; or equivalent.

Full details of entry requirements can be obtained from individual institutions.

TRAINING

There are three possible routes to qualification as a planner.

1. By following one of the four-year full-time or five-year sandwich degree courses that are accredited by the Royal Town Planning Institute (RTPI) as fulfilling the academic requirements for membership. These are available at a number of universities and, at some, may be studied on a part-time basis while in employment.

2. By taking a postgraduate degree or diploma that also fulfils the academic requirements for RTPI membership. Courses last for two years full-time or three years part-time. In order to gain entry to one of these courses it is normally necessary to have a relevant first degree in a subject such as geography, geology, ecology, economics, architecture, statistics, landscape architecture or transportation.

3. The Joint Distance Learning Diploma in Town Planning course is also available. This comprises eight courses, five provided by the Open University and three jointly by a consortium of four Planning Schools (at the University of the West of England at Bristol, Dundee University, Leeds Metropolitan University, and South Bank University, London). This permits people to qualify at their own pace through home study. No formal entry requirements are stipulated although a graduate entry route is available which comprises two Open University courses plus three planning courses.

In order to become a member of the RTPI, it is necessary, in addition to passing the academic stage, to complete: *either* two years' experience in professional work directly related to town planning (one year if a sandwich course was taken); *or* the part-time equivalent if work and study are combined. Normally, one year must have been completed after passing all the relevant examinations. Applicants for membership must provide a brief summary of the work undertaken and a statement of experience countersigned by two chartered town planners.

LATE ENTRY

Mature entrants over the age of 25 years who can demonstrate that they are capable of postgraduate level study and who have relevant qualifications or experience may be admitted to the postgraduate courses through a special entry scheme.

OPPORTUNITIES

Planning is a comparatively small but growing profession. The RTPI has over 17,000 full and student members.

Around 60 per cent of qualified planners work in the public sector – for a total of over 500 separate organizations.

Those working for local authorities are employed by county, regional or district councils. A small number work for central government departments – for the Department of the Environment or Scottish or Welsh Offices – where their role is to co-ordinate local planning policies to ensure that they are in line with national and regional policies.

Others may be employed by urban development corporations, which have been established by the Government to develop inner city areas.

There are increasing openings in private practice. There are now over 1,250 planning consultancies that may conduct work for people making planning appeals or carry out projects on a fee-paying basis for central and local government departments. As a result, there are many more opportunities to move between the public and private sectors during the course of a planning career. It is common practice to gain experience in local government before moving to the private sector, although this is not always the case. People with previous experience in architecture, engineering or transport, for example, may start work in consultancies.

Other opportunities exist with tourist boards, water companies, health authorities, construction companies and environmental organizations.

RTPI qualifications are recognized internationally. A small number of British planners are employed in over 70 countries. There are increasing opportunities in the EU for qualified planners able to speak another European language.

PAY AND CONDITIONS

Salaries vary with different employers. Local authorities no longer offer standard pay scales. However, many planners are on a pay-scale from £12,243 to £18,250, with planners who already possess the RTPI qualification being appointed well above the minimum. Senior planners might expect a salary between £19,562 to £23,150, and those in very senior jobs, considerably more.

Planners employed in central and local government usually work a 37-hour week. Many departments operate a flexi-time system. Senior staff often have to attend evening meetings. Hours worked in consultancies are more variable, depending on the flow of work. Periods of long hours worked to meet a deadline may be balanced by quieter times in slack periods.

Job sharing and flexible work patterns are becoming more common.

PROSPECTS

Formal career and promotion structures exist within local government, although the number of very senior posts is limited. Mobility is usually required to gain promotion, and many young planners choose in any case to move several times during the early stages of their careers in order to gain breadth of experience in different areas and different sectors of employment.

In the private sector it is possible to become self-employed or to open one's own consultancy business after suitable experience.

RELATED OCCUPATIONS

Architect, landscape architect, civil engineer, surveyor, housing manager, town planning technician.

FURTHER INFORMATION AND READING

Please see article 2. TOWN PLANNING TECHNICIAN.

2. TOWN PLANNING TECHNICIAN (US)

THE WORK

Planning technicians, sometimes known as technical assistants or technical officers, are important members of the planning team, providing essential support to professional staff and carrying out many of the tasks connected with planning work.

Although they are less concerned with policy, they have greater technical skills in some areas of planning work, notably analysis of data, collection of information and use of computers.

Planning departments have to store large quantities of records – plans, photographs, maps, reports and notes on listed buildings. Technicians help to organize, index and store these; make limited revisions to maps; and produce extracts, enlargements or reductions from maps and charts when required.

They help to collect and analyse planning information required by the professional planners. Some of the information is already available from published reports – the census and statistics on, for example, population and employment trends – but some has to be acquired. Technicians do this by helping to conduct surveys – first devising questions and identifying the right people to ask and in some cases conducting the survey. Analysing the collected information, usually with the help of the computer, is the next stage. Finally, they write a report and may produce costings.

They assist with much of the administration connected with development control by recording and checking on the progress of planning permission applications. They may be required to deal with written or verbal enquiries in connection with these from members of the public or councillors on the planning committee.

Meeting and dealing with the public is often an important part of their work. They are heavily involved in the process of public consultation, setting up exhibitions, writing leaflets and making available relevant maps, charts and drawings.

WORK ENVIRONMENT

Planning technicians spend most of their time in the office, but they may do some outdoor work, accompanying planners on site visits. They also travel to various venues when arranging exhibitions, and may carry out field surveys, which involves interviewing the public.

It is useful to hold a driving licence.

SKILLS AND INTERESTS

Technicians must be able to work accurately and neatly. They should be numerate, since they spend much of their time working with statistics.

They must enjoy working as part of a team, but also be able to work on their own. Sometimes they have to work under pressure when figures, statistics or a report are required urgently.

They need the ability to write clear reports and need good verbal communication skills as they frequently interview, or answer enquiries from, members of the public.

ENTRY REQUIREMENTS

Minimum requirements in England and Wales are four GCSEs (A-C) including maths and a subject testing the use of written English such as English, history or geography. In Scotland four S grades (1-3) are required in subjects including maths; one from science, geography or statistics; and one from English, history, geography, economic organization or modern studies.

Advanced GNVQ in Construction and Built Environment or GSVQ at Level III in Land-based Industries may be regarded as alternative qualifications.

Some entrants have BTEC/SCOTVEC National or Higher Certificates/Diplomas in Planning or Land Administration. Some enter with specialist degrees, eg in geology.

TRAINING

Planning technicians are trained largely on the job and take BTEC/SCOTVEC national certificate qualifications by part-time study over two years. (SCOTVEC modules are available in Planning, Landscape and Townscape; BTEC has a national certificate qualification in Land Administration, devised in consultation with the RTPI.)

The national certificates include the study of: computing, construction, economics, elements of planning, environmental planning, legal and communication studies, map studies, maths, statistics, public administration, and property valuation.

After obtaining the national certificate, it is possible to proceed to a higher certificate via a further two-year part-time course. This includes more advanced subjects such as data management, administrative law, development control, planning law, and social surveys.

Some local authorities and private sector employers give technicians day release.

BTEC/SCOTVEC qualifications may be replaced or augmented soon by NVQs/SVQs at Levels 3 and 4. These will also be relevant for planning enforcement staff and planning administrators.

While training, technicians are eligible to join the Society of Town Planning Technicians as a student member, and, once trained, as a full member. With two years' experience, including at least one after qualifying, or four years experience before qualifying, they may be able to join the Royal Town Planning Institute as a Technical Member.

LATE ENTRY

There are no upper age limits, although some employers may give preference to school-leavers. Those with relevant national certificate, higher national certificate or degree qualifications gained on full-time courses or specialist skills, eg in graphic design, survey work or information systems, are welcomed for some posts.

OPPORTUNITIES

The majority of posts are with county, regional and district council planning departments. A very small number of planning technicians work for central government, mainly in the Department of the Environment.

Some opportunities exist with private sector employers, although planning consultancies often recruit only experienced technicians.

Vacancies occur occasionally with environmental and conservation organizations such as the National Park Authorities and the Countryside Commission.

It is usually necessary to contact a wide range of employers and consider travelling some distance, or moving, in order to find a trainee position.

PAY AND CONDITIONS

Salaries for planning technicians employed by local authorities are paid on nationally agreed scales, but vary since authorities may fix different entry points according to age and qualifications. Salaries tend to commence in the range from £6,500 to £10,300, depending on age and qualifications. Senior technicians may earn up to £15,000 or more.

Local and central government planning departments usually work a 37-hour week, many of them operating a flexi-time system.

Salaries vary widely in the private sector. Hours vary according to need. When a project deadline has to be met, some overtime may be necessary.

PROSPECTS

There is a clearly defined promotion structure in local authority planning departments, with opportunities for promotion to senior technician, responsible for the work of several staff.

Promotion to supervisory level work is also possible in planning consultancies and other organizations.

In all cases, it may be necessary to move in order to gain promotion.

It is possible for a planning technician who has obtained the BTEC/SCOTVEC national-level qualification to become a professional planner by following one of the training routes described in article 1. TOWN PLANNER. It must be emphasized, however, that this is not a recommended route for entering the profession.

RELATED OCCUPATIONS

Architectural technologist, surveying technician, surveyor, town planner.

FURTHER INFORMATION

The Royal Town Planning Institute*, 26 Portland Place, London W1N 4BE

Society of Town Planning Technicians* (address as RTPI)

FURTHER READING

Leaflets/booklets are available from the addresses marked*.

Environmental Planning, Conservation and Management – AGCAS

In the careers library, classified under US.

1. FARM MANAGER CLCI:WAB
2. FARM WORKER CLCI:WAB
3. FISH FARMER CLCI:WAG

BACKGROUND INFORMATION

Agriculture may be defined as the large-scale raising of animals and crops to provide food. Its importance can be seen by the fact that it occupies over three-quarters of the total area of Britain and produces 60 per cent of all the food needed in Britain. Agriculture has undergone great change, brought about by technological developments, increased mechanization and greater EC and government influence.

Farming can be divided into three main types:

Livestock – the raising of dairy and beef cattle, sheep, pigs, poultry, goats, deer, etc.

Arable – the growing of cereals (wheat, barley and oats), root crops (potatoes, sugar beet, etc), oil seed rape, and large-scale vegetable production.

Mixed – combines both livestock and arable farming.

1. FARM MANAGER (WAB)

THE WORK

Farm managers are responsible for the forward planning and day-to-day running of a farm on behalf of a tenant farmer, owner occupier or commercial organization.

Farm managers have to agree policy with the farm owner or tenant. Some owners and tenants set clear guidelines while others delegate some responsibility for deciding farm policy to the manager. This may include planning the farm's budget and production targets for the following twelve months.

Record-keeping – both financial and of livestock and crop development – is an important part of a farm manager's work. Computers are increasingly used for this purpose. Paperwork can take a lot of a manager's time, although some receive help from clerical or secretarial staff.

Only on the largest of farms are managers engaged solely on administrative work. Most managers contribute to the day-to-day practical work of the farm. With livestock, this may include feeding and watering animals, supervising births, nursing sick animals and milking cows. Arable work involves driving a tractor for a variety of purposes. Work is likely to include using other machinery – such as combine harvesters and straw balers – and driving lorries.

Managers are responsible for making decisions affecting the farm, such as planning livestock breeding and crop planting schedules. They are also responsible for decisions relating to buying, for example of feed, fertilizer and machinery, and for marketing the farm's produce.

Managers recruit and dismiss staff. They organize and supervise the work of staff, although on large farms they may delegate this to supervisory staff. There are some posts with less responsibility, such as assistant farm managers and unit managers – responsible for a pig, poultry or arable unit. Managers arrange for the repair and maintenance of the farm's buildings, machinery and equipment.

On many farms it has been necessary to diversify into other activities, such as recreation and the provision of accommodation. Farm managers oversee these developments.

WORK ENVIRONMENT

All farm managers spend time indoors carrying out administration, which involves sitting for long periods of time. The proportion of time spent on administration depends on the size of the farm. Managers of large farms spend more of their time carrying out administrative duties (though they may be assisted in this by assistant farm managers and farm secretaries). Managers of small farms are likely to spend a greater proportion of their time outdoors in all weathers on practical work, which can be dirty and, with livestock, smelly. The work can also be heavy and involve standing, bending and carrying. Work usually involves driving, both on and off the farm.

SKILLS AND INTERESTS

Farming is a business, and owners employ managers to maximize profits from the farm. Ability with figures is essential. Managers must be able to prepare production targets and budgets and monitor progress towards meeting those targets within budget. Commercial sense is essential in making decisions on buying materials and equipment for the farm and in selling the farm's produce. It is also needed when considering diversifying into non-farming activities, such as providing bed and breakfast accommodation.

Farm managers should have an interest in science, as agriculture is subject to constant scientific and technological developments. They need to keep abreast of developments that can be used to benefit the farm.

They must be able to communicate effectively with staff, the farm owner and specialists such as veterinary surgeons and accountants.

Factors such as weather conditions make precise planning difficult. Farm managers, therefore, need to be good problem solvers and good organizers, and need to have the ability to make decisions.

It is important that farm managers are fit and healthy and capable of the day-to-day physical work on the farm.

ENTRY REQUIREMENTS

Most managers hold a higher national certificate/diploma or degree and have considerable practical agricultural experience. Some also hold a postgraduate qualification in farm business organization and management.

Degrees in agricultural subjects require: five GCSEs/S grades (A-C/1-3) with two A levels/three H grades, two of which should be sciences or equivalent. For most degree courses it is essential to have had at least one year's relevant pre-course experience.

BTEC higher national diploma in agricultural subjects requires: four GCSEs/five S grades (A-C/1-3), including English and two maths/science subjects, with one A level/ two H grades, including a science; or a relevant BTEC/ SCOTVEC national award; or equivalent. Applicants may be required to have practical agricultural experience before starting the course.

SCOTVEC higher national certificate/diploma in agricultural subjects has preferred entry requirements of: five S grades (1-3) including maths, chemistry and English and two H grades including a science or maths; or one A level in a science and four other GCSEs (A-C); or SCOTVEC national certificate or equivalent. For higher national certificate courses it is necessary to have had at least twelve months' practical experience and some formal agricultural training, eg national certificate.

For higher national diploma courses some evidence of practical agricultural experience is required.

Entry to supervisory-level posts may be with BTEC National Diploma in Agriculture, C&G National Certificate in Agriculture, or SCOTVEC National Certificate. Please see article 2. FARM WORKER for details.

TRAINING

Degrees. Courses last for three years full-time or four years on a sandwich basis and range from the general to the specialist. They are offered by a number of universities and by Harper Adams Agricultural College, the Royal Agricultural College, and the Scottish Agricultural College. Courses at universities concentrate on scientific, economic and management principles. Courses at the agricultural colleges combine general agriculture with practical experience and are more suited to intending farm managers.

BTEC Higher National Diploma in Agriculture. Courses are mostly for three years on a sandwich basis and prepare students for practical farming at supervisory level. They can be general or can allow specialization in, for example, arable, livestock or rural environment management. Courses are offered at several agricultural colleges in England and Wales.

SCOTVEC Higher National Certificate in Agriculture. Courses are one-year full-time and can be general or allow for specialization in crop husbandry, livestock husbandry, farm management, or poultry production. Courses are offered by the Scottish Agricultural College at its Aberdeen, Auchincruive and Edinburgh sites.

SCOTVEC Higher National Diploma in Agriculture. Courses are for two years full-time or three years on a sandwich basis, and are offered at the Scottish Agricultural College at the same sites as the Higher National Certificate in Agriculture. They offer a range of specializations including: crop and animal production; farm mechanization; farm management; and poultry production and management. The courses aim to prepare students for management posts in agriculture.

NVQs/SVQs in Agriculture at Level 3 are available in crop production and livestock production. In addition to units specific to crop or livestock production, each award includes: personal effectiveness; obtaining resources to maintain supplies; constructing and maintaining boundaries, drains and temporary buildings.

NVQs/SVQs in Agriculture at Level 4 are available in livestock management and in crop management (NVQ only). They include: personal effectiveness and organizing work; procuring resources to obtain services and supplies; obtaining and using information for problem solving; planning production; marketing produce.

LATE ENTRY

There is no upper age limit for entry to farm management but entry still requires considerable practical experience and high-level qualifications – see ENTRY REQUIREMENTS. It may be possible for adults without the normal academic entry qualifications to be accepted onto full-time courses.

OPPORTUNITIES

Farm managers are employed by commercial organizations that own farms, by tenants and by owner occupiers. There are regional variations in agricultural activity. Livestock farming takes place mainly in the uplands of Britain, with sheep farming mainly in Scotland, Wales and Northern England. Arable farming is concentrated in lowland areas, particularly in the East and South of England. Mixed farming takes place all over England, Scotland and Wales.

There are approximately 8,000 farm managers in the UK, a number that has been stable. Competition for vacancies is intense and most become farm managers only after considerable experience as a unit manager or supervisor. It is often necessary to move to secure a farm manager post. Vacancies may be advertised in *Farmers Weekly, The Scottish Farmer* and *Poultry World*. It is not possible for many who enter as unit managers or supervisors to become farm managers. They either continue in their posts or transfer to work supporting agriculture, with agricultural contractors or in technical sales, for example.

The chances of entry into specific sectors of agriculture, such as arable, beef or poultry production, upland sheep farming, and so on, depend on their current prosperity, which is influenced to some extent by EC and government policy.

PAY AND CONDITIONS

Salaries vary widely, depending on size of the farm or unit for which the manager is responsible. Salaries may range from £9,000 to £30,000. Managers are usually provided with a rent-free tied home and use of a vehicle. Bonuses and profit-sharing schemes boost income for some managers.

There are no set working hours in farm management. Workload can vary according to season and on the pressure of paperwork. Early morning, evening and weekend work may be necessary. A 60 to 70-hour week is normal.

PROSPECTS

A promotion structure for farm managers is only possible on the largest farms.

Self-employment is an option for very few. Land to lease is scarce and very expensive; the cost of buying land is prohibitively high.

It may be possible to work abroad, for example, in New Zealand and Australia. Opportunities in Europe are limited but developing – knowledge of the appropriate European language is necessary.

There are opportunities for experienced farm managers to enter: advisory work, for example, with the Agricultural Development and Advisory Service (ADAS) or the Scottish Agricultural College; the agricultural service industries, for example, with manufacturers of fertilizers, feedstuff and agricultural machinery and equipment; or farm management consultancy.

RELATED OCCUPATIONS

Horticultural manager, forest officer/manager, fish farm manager, estate manager, marketing manager, farm worker.

FURTHER INFORMATION AND READING

Please see article 2. FARM WORKER.

2. FARM WORKER (WAB)

THE WORK

Livestock and arable farms tend to employ specialist workers in those areas. Mixed farms may employ specialists in both livestock and arable work and/or farm workers with experience of both areas. In addition to their specialist tasks most farm workers are involved in farm maintenance work, such as fencing, hedging and building maintenance, although on large farms specialist staff may be employed for this work.

Many farm workers work under the supervision of a farm owner or manager. On large farms their work is overseen by forehands or supervisors. Farm workers may themselves supervise casual staff on occasions.

Livestock. There are some tasks common to all livestock workers whatever animals they work with – feeding and watering the animals, supervising births, giving vitamins and medication to the animals, checking on growth, maintaining hygienic conditions, nursing sick animals, and keeping records. Other activities vary according to the animals concerned, which are mainly: beef cattle, dairy cattle, sheep, pigs, and poultry.

Arable. Much of the work with arable farming involves driving a tractor with a variety of implements and attachments. Tasks include ploughing fields, breaking down furrows, making a tilth, sowing or drilling seeds, fertilizing, planting, spraying crops, digging ditches and trimming hedges. Other machinery is used, including combine harvesters, straw balers, mowers and forage harvesters.

Farm workers also operate fixed plant, such as grain-drying, storage machines and milking machines. They also maintain machinery, drive lorries, and prepare and pack crops for dispatch.

Mixed farms. On mixed farms, livestock and arable specialists carry out the tasks described above but are also expected on occasion to get involved in work outside their specialism. Mixed farms also employ general farm workers who are involved with both livestock and arable farming.

WORK ENVIRONMENT

Most farm workers spend the majority of their time outdoors in all weathers. Work can be dirty and, with livestock, smelly. It can be heavy and involve standing, bending and carrying. With some intensive livestock farming, such as poultry or pig production, much of the work is indoors. Many farm workers drive lorries on the farm and for collection and delivery purposes. Arable farming involves much tractor driving.

SKILLS AND INTERESTS

Farm workers should have an interest in science in order to understand the process of rearing livestock or growing crops.

Practical ability is important as is adaptability, as most farm workers have to carry out a variety of tasks. It is helpful if farm workers have an interest in mechanics and can cope with maintenance and simple repairs, as much farm work involves the use of machinery. All farm workers must work carefully and safely.

Numeracy is necessary for such tasks as weighing feed and calculating fertilizer use. Farm workers need to be able to keep written records, of livestock development, for example.

Livestock workers should enjoy working with animals but should not be sentimental about them.

Farm workers should be able to follow spoken and written instructions and carry them out accurately. Farm work can be routine but the well-being of livestock and the growth of crops can depend on that routine being followed closely. Workers should not mind working alone for long periods of time.

Farm workers must be fit, healthy and capable of physically demanding work. They should be prepared to work outside in all weather.

ENTRY REQUIREMENTS

There are no minimum qualifications required for entry to farm work.

School-leavers may enter direct or follow a full-time course. Most direct-entry school-leavers begin on work-based training.

Entry may also be possible through Modern Apprenticeships leading to NVQs/SVQs Levels 3 and 4. Check with your local careers office, TEC/LEC for details.

BTEC First Diploma in Agriculture. No particular qualifications are required for entry but good GCSEs/S grades are useful.

BTEC National Diploma in Agriculture. Requires: four GCSEs/S grades (A-C/1-3) including English and two maths/science subjects; or BTEC First Diploma in Agriculture, or equivalent. Applicants may be required to have practical experience of farm work before starting the course. Completion of work-based training or the BTEC first diploma satisfies this requirement.

C&G National Certificate in Agriculture (NCA). Needs a good general education with some GCSEs/S grades preferred. Entrants normally have to be at least 18 years and have a minimum of one year's practical farm-work experience. Work-based training can meet that requirement.

SCOTVEC National Certificate. Entry is with a good general education.

TRAINING

Young people on work-based training gain experience on a farm and have day or block release to local agricultural college. They work towards NVQ Level 2 or, in Scotland, SVQ Level 2 and SCOTVEC National Certificate modules.

School-leavers directly employed are trained by their employer. They may attend day or block release courses at a local college and work towards NVQ/SVQ qualifications.

BTEC First Diploma in Agriculture. Courses are offered at colleges of agriculture in England and Wales, for one year full-time. They provide a general introduction to agriculture and usually lead to entry to the national diploma. By the end of the course students may have gained credits towards NVQs Levels 1 and 2.

BTEC National Diploma in Agriculture. Courses are offered at colleges of agriculture in England and Wales. They last for two or three years depending on the practical experience of the student. Courses can be general or specialist and can lead to credits towards NVQs Levels 2 and 3.

C&G National Certificate in Agriculture. Courses are offered at colleges of agriculture in England and Wales, for one year full-time. They are general courses that provide basic training for those seeking to work in practical agriculture. Holders of the NCA may, after a further year's practical experience, take the **C&G Advanced National Certificate in Agriculture (ANCA)**, a one year full-time course, either in general agriculture or in a specialist area. By the end of the courses, credits towards NVQs Levels 2 and 3 may have been gained.

SCOTVEC National Certificate in Agriculture. Courses are offered (one year full-time) at the Scottish Agricultural College (Aberdeen and Auchincruive sites) and at Borders College, Oatridge Agricultural College, and Elmwood Agricultural and Technical College. They cover such areas as crop and livestock production, construction/maintenance of farm boundaries, and operation of farm transport. By the end of courses, credits towards SVQs Levels 2 and 3 may have been gained.

A number of **NVQs/SVQs in Agriculture** are available at Level 1. They include: crop and livestock production; livestock production; mechanized field crop production/intensive crop production. In addition to units specific to crop and/or livestock production, the awards include: personal effectiveness; maintaining services and structures; transporting mechanically. The NVQ/SVQ in Agriculture (livestock production) allows for specialization in dairying, beef, sheep, pigs, goats or poultry.

NVQs/SVQs in Agriculture at Level 2. These are available in similar areas, plus estate maintenance. For information on NVQ/SVQ awards at Levels 3 and 4 please see article 1. FARM MANAGER.

LATE ENTRY

There is no upper age limit for entry to farm work. Adults interested in agriculture must be capable of coping with the physical demands of the work.

There may be specific training opportunities directed at adults available in some areas for this type of work. Candidates may have to satisfy certain conditions to be eligible. Contact your local Jobcentre, careers office or TEC/LEC for details.

OPPORTUNITIES

There are opportunities for farm workers in livestock, arable and mixed farming. Please see article 1. FARM MANAGER for the distribution of British farms.

The number of farm workers has decreased steadily because of increased mechanization. That trend has accelerated in the 1990s as financial difficulties, particularly faced by large farms, have led to reduced employment.

Chances of finding work are considerably better for more skilled workers. The demand for casual, part-time and seasonal workers has decreased substantially. The prospect of finding work in different sectors of agriculture – arable, beef or poultry production, etc – varies and is influenced partly by current EC and government policy.

Vacancies for farm workers may be advertised in local newspapers.

PAY AND CONDITIONS

General farm workers earn approximately £78 a week at age 16 and £92 at age 17. The standard basic weekly wage is £113 at age 18, £127 at 19 years and £149 at age 20 and over. For those with craft status, the minimum wage rates (age 20 or over) are £171, and £176 for workers with an NVQ/SVQ Level 3. There is a standard 39-hour week. Overtime is frequently necessary and depends on the demands of the work. Overtime is payable at an enhanced rate.

Many farm workers have a rent-free (or low-rent) tied cottage. Some workers in lodgings receive a lodging allowance.

PROSPECTS

Promotion to supervisor or unit manager is possible only on larger farms. Competition for such vacancies is intense. Experience and qualifications are important when seeking advancement, as is the willingness to move to another area.

It is difficult for farm workers to find work overseas. Self-employment is rarely possible.

RELATED OCCUPATIONS

Forest worker, gamekeeper, groundsman/woman, horticultural worker, farm manager.

FURTHER INFORMATION

Careers in Landbased Industries (formerly CETAC)*, 10 Northgate Street, Warwick CV34 4SR (written enquiries only, accompanied by sae)

The Association of Colleges in the Eastern Region (ACER)*, Merlin Place, Milton Road, Cambridge CB4 4DP, 01223 424022

Principals of local agricultural colleges – addresses and telephone numbers available from telephone directories or from a list held by the Careers in Landbased Industries.

FURTHER READING

Leaflets/booklets are available from the addresses marked*.

Agriculture, Horticulture, Forestry and Fisheries – AGCAS

Careers Working with Animals – Kogan Page

In the careers library classified under WAB.

3. FISH FARMER (WAG)

BACKGROUND INFORMATION

Fish farming is concerned with producing fish for food, for angling and, to a lesser extent, for ornamental pools. As the traditional sea fishing industry has declined, cultivating fish for food purposes has grown. There is also a continuing demand from anglers for fish to restock rivers and ponds. Most fish farming is concerned with producing fin fish, particularly rainbow trout and salmon, although some fish farmers specialize in shellfish, such as oysters, mussels and scallops. Some ornamental fish, such as golden orfe, are also bred in this way.

THE WORK

Fish farmers breed and rear fish for sale mainly for food and for angling. Some specialize in hatching eggs and raising fry, while others buy in young fish and rear them until they are ready to be sold. Some are involved in both. Tasks include:

Feeding. Fish are kept in ponds, tanks, cages, pens or concrete raceways. They are fed with specially prepared food. Feeding may be automatic or by hand. Daily feed rations are based on the total weight of stock and water temperature.

Grading. Fish are frequently graded by size and moved to larger tanks. Grading may be done by hand, involving catching fish in hand nets, then sorting them by weight, or it may be done automatically. On some farms without catwalks across the tanks workers wear chest waders and work in the water.

Treatment of disease. Fish farmers keep constant watch for any evidence of disease or infection and apply appropriate treatment. They may add chemicals to the water to safeguard against disease.

Maintaining water quality. Fish farmers use automatic equipment to monitor the oxygen content of water and frequently take the water temperature. Workers keep clean the grills or screens that are used to prevent leaves and weeds entering the water and contaminating it and periodically drain the tanks and hose them down.

Maintenance. Workers carry out any routine maintenance work that may be needed, such as simple plumbing, carpentry and brickwork.

Harvesting. Fish grown for food are killed, gutted and placed in ice for transportation.

Management. Managers have additional duties, including keeping records of fish numbers and average weight, ordering feed and chemicals, marketing, keeping financial records and staff supervision.

Farming salmon is slightly different. Salmon breed in fresh water and mature at sea. After salmon have been reared in fresh water for a year or two they are transferred to pens in the sea, where they are matured until marketable. Salmon farm workers move between the pens by boat.

WORK ENVIRONMENT

Fish farmers work outdoors in all weathers, including the cold and the wet. For some, work includes working in water while wearing chest waders. Salmon farming involves some work in boats at sea.

The job involves much standing, bending and carrying and some heavy lifting.

Many fish farms are in remote and isolated areas.

SKILLS AND INTERESTS

Fish farmers need an interest in science in order to understand the conditions that are necessary for fast, healthy growth of fish.

Good practical skills are required, such as building skills, and workers must be prepared and able to tackle whatever needs doing. Workers should be fit and strong as the work is active and involves heavy lifting.

Workers on fish farms often work alone, so the ability to use initiative is important. They must be conscientious when checking, for example, water temperature and oxygen content, as fish are susceptible to disease if conditions are unsuitable. Good powers of observation are required to spot possible evidence of disease or infection before it can spread.

All fish farm workers should be able to swim. Those working on salmon farms should be capable of learning basic seamanship, as they spend some time in boats at sea moving between salmon pens.

Fish farming is a business, so fish farm managers or owners need commercial skills for budgeting, marketing their fish and keeping financial and other records.

ENTRY REQUIREMENTS

No formal academic qualifications are required for entry to fish farming. An aptitude for science – particularly biology and chemistry – and practical subjects is helpful.

SCOTVEC National Certificate in Fish Farming. No specific qualifications are required but it is an advantage to have some GCSEs/S grades (A-C/1-3), particularly in English, maths and science.

BTEC First Diploma in Fishery Studies. Requires a good general education and enthusiasm for the career.

BTEC National Diploma in Fishery Studies. Requires a merit or distinction pass in the first diploma; four GCSEs/S grades (A-C/1-3) or equivalent. It also requires a minimum of twelve months' full-time experience of fishery work. Candidates must be at least aged 17 on entry.

BTEC Higher National Diploma in Fishery Studies. Requires one A level/3 H grades including a science and four GCSEs/S grades (A-C/1-3) or equivalent. A minimum of twelve months' full-time experience of fishery work is necessary.

Degrees with relevance to fish farming usually require: a good pass in a relevant BTEC national diploma; or SCOTVEC national certificate with appropriate modules; or at least two A levels/three H grades, usually in science subjects, and a further three GCSEs/two S grades (A-C/1-3) in different subjects.

Postgraduate courses relevant to fish farming require a relevant degree for entry.

Institute of Fisheries Management Certificate in Fish Farming. No particular qualifications are needed but students must be members of the Institute.

Entrants to fish farming should be physically fit. A driving licence is usually essential.

TRAINING

Pre-entry

SCOTVEC National Certificate in Fish Farming (one year full-time) is offered by The Barony College and Inverness College. Both courses include a short placement on a commercial fish farm. BTEC courses are offered at Sparsholt College, Hampshire. All include practical experience of fish farming.

BTEC First Diploma in Fishery Studies (one year, full-time) provides an introduction to fish farming, fishery management and aquatics.

BTEC National Diploma in Fishery Studies (two years, full-time) is a scientifically based practical training course.

BTEC Higher National Diploma in Fishery Studies (three years, sandwich) covers fish farming, fishery management, fish science, business management, engineering and estate maintenance.

Degree courses. A number of universities offer degree courses (three or four years, full-time) with some relevance to fish farming, such as marine and freshwater biology, and aquatic biology. The Scottish Agricultural College offers a BTechnol course in Aquaculture, based at its Aberdeen site.

Postgraduate courses available include aquaculture, applied fish biology, fisheries science and fisheries management.

Institute of Fisheries Management Certificate in Fish Farming can be studied by correspondence course either before or after entry to fish farming.

On entry

Specific training schemes for young people are run by The Barony College, Lews Castle College, and North Atlantic Fisheries College. Training combines practical experience on a fish farm with some time at college working towards SCOTVEC modules.

All entrants to fish farming receive on-the-job training from experienced staff. That may be supplemented by short part-time courses in, for example, fish health and smolt production.

There may be some opportunity to work towards NVQs in Fish Husbandry at Level 2, specializing in either cyprinids, salmon, shellfish or trout, or SVQs in Fish Husbandry at Level 2 in fin fish or shellfish. They include: first aid; assisting operations in a hatchery; routine estate work and maintenance; maintaining fish in a holding unit; operating safely in the workplace; optimizing water conditions in a fish holding unit. Those concerned with shellfish include operating small boats and managing shellfish stock and equipment on shore or sea sites, while the others include: operating and maintaining agricultural tractors; maintaining feeding programmes on a fish farm; selecting and preparing fish for sale or transfer.

LATE ENTRY

There is no upper age limit for entry to fish farming. Mature applicants may be accepted onto the full-time courses described in TRAINING without the usual academic entry requirements, particularly if they have relevant experience.

There may be specific training opportunities directed at adults available in some areas for this type of work. Candidates may have to satisfy certain conditions to be eligible. Contact your local Jobcentre, careers office or TEC/LEC for details.

OPPORTUNITIES

Commercial fish farms are the major employers but fish farms are also run by water authorities, government departments, industrial firms, private estates and angling organizations.

There are approximately 870 fish farms throughout England and Wales, with some concentration in Hampshire, Yorkshire, Wiltshire, South West England and the Lake District. They employ just under 900 full-time and almost 1,000 part-time workers.

There are approximately 1,000 fish farms in Scotland, the majority concerned with salmon and concentrated along the west coast and in the islands. They employ approximately 1,500 full-time and 700 part-time workers.

Although fish farming has expanded, opportunities for employment are scarce, as most farms operate with minimal staffing. It is often necessary to move to get a job. Vacancies may be advertised in local newspapers, the angling press, *Fish Farmer* and *Fish Farming International.*

PAY AND CONDITIONS

There are no standard rates of pay in fish farming. Some employers pay weekly rates similar to those of general farm workers – £70 at 16 years, £85 at 17 years, £105 at 18 years and £138 at 20 years and over. Some employers pay less than these rates. Overtime may be payable. Technicians with large organizations may earn between £10,000 and £13,000 at age 18. Hatchery managers may earn between £13,000 and £16,500.

Self-employed fish farmers' earnings are related to profit and vary considerably.

Working hours are long and irregular. Early morning and evening work may be necessary.

Many fish farms are in remote areas, and tied accommodation may be included in the terms of employment.

PROSPECTS

On small fish farms there is little or no opportunity for promotion. On larger farms there can be a structure that allows promotion to supervisory or management posts.

There are some opportunities for working abroad as many countries have a well-developed fish-farming industry. Trout cultivation, for example, is well developed in France, Germany and Italy, salmon in Norway, carp in Northern Europe, and both salmon and trout in North America.

It is possible to become self-employed by owning and managing a fish farm, although it involves considerable financial investment.

RELATED OCCUPATIONS

Waterkeeper/bailiff, gamekeeper, forest officer, farm manager, farm worker, countryside ranger/warden, scientist/technician, fisherman/woman.

FURTHER INFORMATION

The Barony College*, Parkgate, Dumfries DG1 3NE, 01387 860251

Careers in Landbased Industries (formerly CETAC)*, 10 Northgate Street, Warwick CV34 4SR (written enquiries only, accompanied by sae)

Institute of Fisheries Management*, 22 Rushworth Avenue, West Bridgeford, Nottingham NG2 7LF, 0115 945 5722

Inverness College*, 3 Longman Road, Inverness IV1 1SA, 01463 236681

Lews Castle College*, Stornoway, Isle of Lewis PA86 0XR, 01851 703311

North Atlantic Fisheries College*, Port Arthur, Scalloway, Shetland ZE1 0UN, 01595 880328

Sparsholt College Hampshire*, Sparsholt, Winchester, Hampshire SO21 2NF, 01962 776441

FURTHER READING

Leaflets/booklets are available from the addresses marked*.

In the careers library classified under WAG.

1. HORTICULTURAL MANAGER CLCI:WAD
2. HORTICULTURAL WORKER CLCI:WAD

BACKGROUND INFORMATION

There are two main areas of horticultural work, with a wide range of opportunities in related areas.

Commercial horticulture involves the cultivation of salad crops, soft and 'top' fruit (such as apples and pears), vegetables, flowers for cutting, trees, shrubs, bulbs, and plants for sale through shops and garden centres or for use in parks, planting schemes, etc.

Many horticultural businesses specialize in just one or two activities, such as large-scale production of field vegetables or ornamental plants, or raising seedlings, in controlled conditions, for sale to commercial growers.

Some activities are concentrated in particular areas of the country. Orchards are found mainly in the South East, where the climate is more favourable for fruit growing. Lincolnshire is an important region for field cultivation of vegetables, such as celery, onions and cauliflower, whereas Bedfordshire is traditionally known for its Brussels sprouts.

Protected cropping nurseries, where crops such as tomatoes, lettuce, flowers for cutting, bedding plants and pot plants are grown under glass or plastic, are found in many places, although West Sussex, Lancashire and East Yorkshire are important centres. Tree and shrub nurseries are found in most parts of the country, as are garden centres.

Amenity (or environmental) horticulture includes the initial design, and subsequent maintenance and management, of parks, open spaces, sports grounds, roadside areas, public gardens, the gardens of private estates and countryside recreation areas. It also includes landscape design, construction and maintenance.

Traditionally, much of amenity horticulture has been the responsibility of local authorities. However, local authorities are now required to invite competitive tenders for the upkeep of their parks, gardens, recreation areas, etc.

Amenity horticulture also includes maintenance of the gardens of large estates, many of which are now owned by organizations, such as the National Trust, and of specialist gardens such as the Royal Botanic Gardens at Kew or the Royal Horticultural Society's Garden at Wisley.

Developing areas of amenity horticulture include 'interior landscaping' – designing and maintaining indoor plant areas in shopping centres and commercial premises; and horticultural therapy – the provision of gardens and horticultural training for people suffering from mental or physical illness or disability.

The maintenance of sports grounds, which is a specialized branch of amenity horticulture, is covered in the separate article GROUNDSMAN/WOMAN.

1. HORTICULTURAL MANAGER (WAD)

THE WORK

Horticultural managers in both commercial and amenity sectors may be responsible for all, or some, of the following:

Planning, which includes overall strategic planning deciding on the general direction of the business or organization, and crop planning – deciding on the crops and/or plants to be grown, and when, where and how to grow them.

Managing staff, including hiring and firing, directing, organizing and co-ordinating, either personally or via a team of supervisors, depending on the size of the organization.

Financial management, which involves monitoring costs and being responsible for maintaining profits. Managers may tender for contracts (in amenity horticulture).

Ordering supplies of seed, plants, fertilizer, equipment, etc.

Marketing produce, and arranging for its transport and distribution.

Maintenance and repair, including arranging for maintenance and repair work to be carried out on buildings, machinery and equipment.

Day-to-day duties, involving dealing with problems such as staff disputes or the non-arrival of materials, as they arise.

Managers are increasingly likely to use computers for tasks such as planning, scheduling and financial management.

Managers need to be in close touch with work outside and may carry out practical tasks.

WORK ENVIRONMENT

The work is partly office-based, sometimes with travel to several different production sites.

SKILLS AND INTERESTS

Horticultural managers need business and organizational skills, as well as a thorough knowledge of good horticultural practice. Numerical ability is required to analyse computerized data and deal with accounts, budgets, costings and other financial matters.

Good communication skills, both spoken and written, are required. Horticultural managers need to be capable of dealing confidently with staff, customers and suppliers. Good negotiating and marketing skills are needed when dealing with retail outlets, growers and distributors.

Managers need technical knowledge of plant stock and a scientific understanding of environmental conditions, crop pests, soil chemistry, plant physiology, etc.

ENTRY REQUIREMENTS

Degree courses in horticulture. Entry qualifications for degree courses in horticulture are: two or three A levels or three or four H grades, usually including chemistry and a biological science, with supporting GCSEs (A-C/1-3) including maths and chemistry, if this is not obtained at A level/H grade, or equivalent. Check detailed requirements with prospectuses.

BTEC higher national diploma in horticultural subjects. Candidates should have: four GCSEs/S grades (A-C/1-3) in appropriate subjects plus at least one A level (preferably in a science subject), having studied a second subject to A level or two H grades; or a BTEC/SCOTVEC national certificate or diploma; or equivalent. Twelve months' practical experience in horticulture may be required.

BTEC national diploma in horticultural subjects. Entry requires: four GCSEs/S grades (A-C/1-3), including English or a subject testing command of English and two maths or science subjects, or equivalent. Practical experience in horticulture may be needed. Candidates with a credit or distinction in the National Certificate in Horticulture (please see article 2. HORTICULTURAL

WORKER) may enter the second year of a BTEC national diploma course.

Kew Diploma in Horticulture. Candidates need two A levels/H grades at grade C or above, preferably in science subjects, two years' practical experience, and associated horticultural training (such as NVQ/SVQ Level 2 in Horticulture, BTEC/SCOTVEC national or higher national diploma). There is a special entry scheme for sixth-formers, for which previous practical experience is not required.

Royal Botanic Garden, Edinburgh. Candidates for the SCOTVEC HND Horticulture with Plantsmanship run jointly with the Scottish Agricultural College (SAC) need GCSEs/SCEs in five subjects, two of which should be at H grade, or one at A Level. These requirements may be relaxed at the discretion of the Principal at SAC and the Regius Keeper at the Garden.

TRAINING

The following qualifications are suitable for intending managers. In their first appointments, graduates and diplomates may be expected to gain general experience, including working at supervisory level, before they have sufficient expertise to be appointed to managerial-level posts.

Degree courses in horticulture. Three-year courses are offered at the Universities of London (Wye College), Nottingham, and Reading; four-year sandwich courses are offered at Hadlow College (in conjunction with the University of Greenwich), Hertfordshire University (in association with Writtle College), Myerscough College (in conjunction with the University of Central Lancashire), Pershore College (validated by Coventry University), Writtle College (in conjunction with Anglia Polytechnic University), and the University of Strathclyde (in conjunction with the Scottish Agricultural College).

BTEC higher national diploma courses in horticultural subjects. They are offered on a three-year sandwich basis at a number of horticultural colleges. Some courses concentrate on amenity horticulture options, some on commercial horticulture.

The Scottish Agricultural College Higher National Diploma. This is a one-year course validated by the Scottish Education Department.

BTEC national diploma in horticultural subjects. Courses lasting two years or three years (sandwich) are available at a number of colleges in England and Wales.

For further information about courses, consult the Institute of Horticulture or *Courses in Land-Based Industries* published by the Association of Colleges in the Eastern Region (ACER).

The Kew Diploma in Horticulture. This is a degree-equivalent course at the Royal Botanic Gardens, Kew. The course lasts for three years, except for sixth-form entrants without previous experience, who take a four-year sandwich course.

Royal Botanic Garden, Edinburgh. A two-year SCOTVEC HND course in Horticulture with Plantsmanship is run jointly with the Scottish Agricultural College. Students spend year one in Edinburgh and year two at SAC's Ayr campus at Auchincruive. Students who achieve the necessary credits may proceed to the third year of the BSc Horticulture offered through Strathclyde University.

NVQs/SVQs in Commercial Horticulture at Level 3. These are available in: mechanized field crop production; fruit crop production; intensive crop production; nursery stock production. NVQ Level 3 awards are also available in mushroom crop production, while SVQ Level 3 awards are also offered in garden centre operation and general practice. An NVQ/SVQ at Level 4 is available in crop management.

NVQs/SVQs in Amenity Horticulture at Level 3. These are available in: constructing and restoring landscapes; designing and specifying landscape designs; managing trees and woodlands; sports-turf maintenance. Level 4 awards are available in: designing landscapes and planning their management; managing landscape construction and maintenance.

Horticultural workers with craft qualifications may enter management posts, sometimes after taking further qualifications. Please see article 2. HORTICULTURAL WORKER.

LATE ENTRY

The usual requirement of twelve months' practical experience in horticulture may be waived or reduced to three months for students of 19 years or over.

OPPORTUNITIES

In the commercial sector there are opportunities with plant, tree and shrub nurseries, vegetable growers and fruit growers. Managers may specialize in areas such as crop production or marketing, or may have overall responsibility for all aspects of commercial production.

Garden centres and garden departments in other retail organizations recruit horticulturists as management trainees.

Supermarkets that sell large quantities of fruit and vegetables employ horticulturists to purchase and monitor the quality of supplies. There are also similar opportunities with importers and wholesalers.

There are also opportunities with co-operative marketing associations, which sell produce on behalf of commercial growers.

In amenity horticulture, managers are employed by local authorities and contractors; the work may involve liaising with and monitoring the progress of private contractors, or managing a direct labour force employed by the council or private contractors. There is also a limited number of openings with private estates, national parks and botanic gardens.

Vacancies are advertised in specialist magazines such as *Grower* and *Horticulture Week.*

PAY AND CONDITIONS

Starting salaries for managers with the qualifications outlined under TRAINING vary considerably, ranging from around £8,000 up to £14,000. Senior managers – for example, in charge of large nurseries or garden centres – can earn in the region of £15,000 to £30,000. Similarly, there is a very wide range of salaries for experienced managers. A company car may be provided.

Working hours are around 40 a week, sometimes with additional weekend and evening work.

PROSPECTS

Career prospects may be improved by taking the Royal Horticultural Society's Master of Horticulture award

MHort(RHS), an advanced qualification in practical horticulture at degree-equivalent level. Five years' full-time experience (or three years' experience and two years spent in horticultural education) is required. Minimum academic entry requirements are two A levels, including one science subject, or equivalent qualifications. Advanced horticultural qualifications give exemption from parts of the course and examination. Courses are available (mainly on a part-time basis) at a number of colleges throughout the country, or by correspondence.

The MHort(RHS) or postgraduate qualifications (MSc, MPhil, PhD), may lead to academic or research posts.

There tends to be a more defined career structure in amenity horticulture (particularly in local authorities). In commercial horticulture, where there are very varied employment opportunities, prospects depend very much on the policy of the individual employer.

Back-up services to the horticultural industry offer many opportunities, including the following.

ADAS – the Government's Agricultural Development and Advisory Service – employs graduates or people with equivalent qualifications in horticulture as advisory officers. They provide a service to growers, and also work at experimental horticultural stations, developing new techniques and practices for the industry.

Advisory and consultancy work is available for the self-employed and with private firms.

Research– the Agricultural and Food Research Council runs three research stations covering horticultural crops. There are also several research stations run by commercial firms, and ADAS experimental horticultural stations.

Teaching, training and lecturing in horticultural subjects.

Horticultural journalism including publishing.

Horticultural therapy in settings such as hospitals and residential homes.

Trained horticulturists are recruited for posts abroad by organizations such as the Overseas Development Administration. Short-term overseas posts are offered by VSO. Horticulturists are also employed overseas by the Commonwealth War Graves Commission.

RELATED OCCUPATIONS

Farm manager, forest officer, retail manager, landscape architect, scientific officer (nature conservation).

FURTHER INFORMATION AND READING

Please see article 2. HORTICULTURAL WORKER.

2. HORTICULTURAL WORKER (WAD)

THE WORK

There are two main areas of work common to both commercial and amenity horticulture.

Propagation includes sowing seeds, in trays or outdoors; raising plants from cuttings; pricking out and potting up seedlings, then 'potting on' (transferring growing plants to larger pots); budding and grafting (techniques used for propagating roses and trees).

Crop husbandry is looking after crops whilst they are growing and involves watering, feeding, and trimming plants. Horticultural workers apply fertilizers, pesticides and herbicides, and maintain a controlled environment for protected crops, with the right levels of temperature and humidity.

In commercial horticulture, harvesting is an important aspect of the work. Workers pick crops and place them in containers. They grade produce by size and quality, and package it, ready for market. Harvest is the busiest time of the horticultural year, and casual workers are often taken on for the picking season. Permanent horticultural staff may be responsible for supervising the casual workforce.

In amenity horticulture, propagation and plant husbandry involve similar duties to those required in the commercial sector but there is no harvesting. Amenity horticulture also involves tasks such as mowing lawns, pruning shrubs, applying mulches to protect plant roots, staking plants, keeping edges of beds and lawns tidy, and removing autumn leaves.

In both sectors of horticulture, many tasks are mechanized; digging of large areas, for instance, is usually done with a Rotavator, rather than by hand, and ride-on mowers are used for cutting grass. There is, however, a considerable amount of hard manual work, with the use of hand tools such as trowels, spades and forks.

In garden centres and other retail outlets such as farm shops, workers act as sales assistants, and give advice to customers, as well as looking after plants.

For working outdoors horticultural workers may wear overalls, boots, or waterproof clothing.

WORK ENVIRONMENT

Horticultural workers spend much of their time outdoors, unless they are working with protected crops or in retailing.

The work is physically demanding, involving a lot of walking, standing and bending, and some lifting/carrying, for instance of sacks of compost, pots, or trays of plants. Disability, however, is no bar to employment in horticulture, although it may restrict the choice of work available. Working conditions can be cold, wet and muddy.

Horticultural workers often work in small groups of three or four; they may work in larger teams, or alone.

SKILLS AND INTERESTS

It is important to be interested in plants and nature and to understand scientific and technical information relating to plant growth, and control of pests and diseases.

In glasshouse crop production, an understanding is needed of bed rotation and technical information, such as humidity levels and temperature settings.

To be capable of the full range of horticultural tasks, workers need a reasonable standard of physical fitness. Manual dexterity is required for jobs such as grafting, budding and potting.

It is important to get on well with others and to be able to work as a member of a team. Horticultural workers in garden centres work closely with the public, so they need good communication skills and a wide knowledge of plants and chemicals used for the control of pests and diseases.

ENTRY REQUIREMENTS

There are no formal entry requirements for direct entry to employment or training schemes for young people, but some GCSEs/S grades, especially in science subjects, are an advantage.

C&G National Certificate in Horticulture. Applicants must be at least 17 years old and have one year's suitable pre-course practical experience. This requirement may be modified for mature applicants. There are no set academic requirements, although these may be specified by individual colleges.

TRAINING

Many young people enter horticulture via training schemes for young people. This provides practical training at the workplace and off-the-job courses, usually at local colleges, on day or block release. College training normally leads to NVQ/SVQ Level 1 and 2 awards, specializing either in amenity or commercial horticulture. Modern Apprenticeships may also be available leading to at least an NVQ/SVQ Level 3. For details of training schemes for young people contact your local careers office, TEC/LEC.

Trainees may also take National Proficiency Tests.

Alternatively, in England and Wales it is possible to take a one-year full-time course for the National Certificate in Horticulture, awarded by City and Guilds. In Scotland, one-year full-time programmes of SCOTVEC modules are available. Young people must preferably have one year of suitable pre-course experience.

C&G National Certificate in Horticulture. The curriculum for these courses is set by individual colleges, and relates to local horticultural needs. Various options are available at different colleges, including: amenity horticulture; commercial horticulture; garden centre practices; horticultural contractors' operations; nursery practices; and nursery stock production. Similarly, in Scotland there is a flexibility over the modules taken on a one-year course.

The Royal Horticultural Society's General Examination in Horticulture. This is a further nationally recognized qualification, with open access. Courses for the examination are available on a part-time basis, usually over one or two years, at about 80 centres. Correspondence courses are also available. The standard of knowledge required is equivalent to GCSE level in science. The more advanced RHS Diploma in Horticulture is also available; this qualification is recognized for associate membership of the Institute of Horticulture.

NVQs/SVQs are available in both Amenity Horticulture and Commercial Horticulture at Levels 1 and 2.

Courses for people with disabilities are offered at various specialist centres. Further details are available from disablement resettlement officers or from the Royal Agricultural Society of England's Careers, Education and Training Advice Centre.

LATE ENTRY

There are no upper age limits on entry. Adult applicants for one-year National Certificate in Horticulture courses may be accepted with less than one year's pre-course experience.

Adults may be able to gain certification of horticultural skills without taking a formal training course, via Accreditation of Prior Learning.

There may be specific training opportunities directed at adults available in some areas for this type of work. Candidates may have to satisfy certain conditions to be eligible. Contact your local Jobcentre, careers office or TEC/LEC for details.

OPPORTUNITIES

Horticultural workers are employed in the commercial sector by fruit and vegetable growers, protected cropping and tree/shrub nurseries. There are many opportunities in garden centres and garden departments of other retail organizations.

In amenity horticulture, there are opportunities both for direct employment with local authorities and for work with private contracting firms.

There are opportunities for trained staff to work overseas.

Self-employment is possible; the most likely areas are those requiring little capital investment, such as interior landscaping (looking after plants in shops and offices), or professional gardening and landscaping.

PAY AND CONDITIONS

Commercial horticulture. Wages depend on age, experience and type of employment. General workers aged 16 to 19 years receive basic wages of around £67 to £133 a week. Workers aged over 20 years earn basic salaries of between £129 and £174 a week. Overtime payments can increase wages.

Hours of work in England and Wales are 40 a week; in Scotland, they are either 40 a week throughout the year or 41½ in summer and 36½ in winter. Weekend work may be required, particularly in summer. Some jobs are available on a seasonal basis.

Amenity horticulture. In local authority employment, pay rates for gardeners (aged 18 years or over) range from about £110 to £130 a week for 39 hours. Overtime and bonus payments may be available. Pay rates for staff employed by private contractors vary with different employers.

PROSPECTS

Horticultural workers with the National Certificate in Horticulture or NVQ/SVQ Level 2, and several years' experience in practical horticulture, may be appointed to supervisory posts. Supervisory work involves directing staff engaged in practical operations, ensuring that production targets are achieved and deadlines met. Supervisors may also be responsible for ordering supplies, stock control, administration of staff timesheets, and bonus payments. In retail operations they may be responsible for dealing with customer complaints.

It may be possible for supervisors with further qualifications to gain management posts.

RELATED OCCUPATIONS

Farm worker, groundsman/woman, gardener, forest worker, fish farmer.

FURTHER INFORMATION

Careers in Landbased Industries (formerly CETAC)*, c/o Warwickshire Careers Service, 10 Northgate Street, Warwick CV34 4SR (written enquiries only, accompanied by sae)

The Association of Colleges in the Eastern Region (ACER)*, 2 Looms Lane, Bury St Edmunds IP33 1HE, 01284 764977

The Institute of Horticulture*, 14-15 Belgrave Square, London SW1X 8PS, 0171 245 6943

The Royal Botanic Gardens, Personnel Section, Kew, Richmond, Surrey TW9 3AB, 0181 332 5127/5141

The Royal Botanic Garden, 20A Inverleith Row, Edinburgh EH3 5LR, 0131 552 7171

Royal Horticultural Society's Garden*, Supervisor of Studies and Training, Wisley, Woking, Surrey GU23 6QB, 01483 224234

FURTHER READING

Leaflets/booklets are available from the addresses marked*.

Job Outlines – Horticulture – COIC

Agriculture, Horticulture, Forestry and Fisheries – AGCAS

In the careers library classified under WAD.

GROUNDSMAN/WOMAN CLCI:WAD

BACKGROUND INFORMATION

The Institute of Groundsmanship (IoG) defines the work as managing land for sport and recreation and keeping the soil in the right condition for any given activity'. Soil, and the grass that grows on it to form turf, is the groundsman/woman's basic concern. Very different types of ground are required for different kinds of sport; compare, for example, the fine turf of a cricket pitch with the rougher surface of a football pitch.

Groundsmen/women are responsible for making sure that playing facilities are kept in the best possible condition for any given sport. They also maintain other areas, such as lawns, grass verges and flower beds.

In a broader sense groundsmanship, as a specialist branch of amenity horticulture, is part of the sport and recreation industry. Promotion is likely to lead away from the maintenance of sports grounds into the more general area of leisure facility management.

THE WORK

Groundsmen/women usually organize their own day-to-day work in order to prepare and maintain the sports facilities for which they are responsible. The work varies with different types of ground. Some facilities, such as school playing fields, are used on a year-round basis and are constantly maintained to a given standard. Groundsmen/women working at Wimbledon concentrate their efforts on providing a top quality playing surface for special competitions and also for club play throughout the season.

In both cases, groundsmen/women plan a regular maintenance schedule, but for Wimbledon or any facility used for major events there is additional work to prepare the ground for specific fixtures.

The work involves the following aspects:

Groundsmen/women regularly mow the grass during the growing season (generally from March to September, but this varies with the weather – during a warm winter, the grass does not stop growing). Other tasks include: scarification (removal of dead grass); sowing seeds or replacing turf in worn areas; application of fertilizers and pesticides; rolling where necessary, for a smooth surface.

They also mark out lines, to a high degree of accuracy, for playing areas, and generally maintain the surrounding area, including borders and flower beds, to provide an attractive environment.

Groundsmen/women use a variety of mowers for different jobs. For large areas they use ride-on mowers or sets of 'gang mowers' fitted behind tractors. Whereas for smaller areas or fine surfaces they use small pedestrian mowers.

Other tools and equipment include fertilizer distributors, sprayers, rollers, irrigation equipment and a wide range of hand tools, including shears, spades, hoes and other general gardening tools. Groundsmen/women are responsible for maintaining their tools and machinery.

Groundsmen/women may also manage facilities made of synthetic turf, concrete and tarmac. They may be responsible for seating and for setting out and removing protective coverings over pitches. In local authorities, they may take care of verges along highways and in parks, as well as at sports grounds. Some groundsmen/women order their own supplies of seed, fertilizer, and so on, calculate costings, and manage a team of staff.

WORK ENVIRONMENT

Almost all the time is spent outdoors.

Groundsmen/women are usually based at one site, but some jobs, particularly at supervisory and management level, involve travel to several sites – for instance, to all the football pitches in the local area.

Groundsmen/women employed by private clubs are likely to spend much of their time working alone; in local authority employment, it is more common for them to work in pairs, or small teams.

SKILLS AND INTERESTS

An interest in gardening is useful. Manual dexterity is required for using hand tools and for work on fine turf areas.

It is important to be physically fit, although slight disability is no bar to employment in groundsmanship, provided applicants are capable of a lot of walking, some bending and lifting, and occasional strenuous effort.

Numeracy is required for calculating quantities (of fertilizer, for instance). Groundsmen/women in supervisory posts need to be capable of tasks such as processing staff timesheets and calculating bonus payments.

Groundsmen/women need reasonable spoken communication skills, particularly in private sports clubs where they may have to deal with members' complaints and liaise with a committee. Tact and diplomacy may sometimes be required.

It is necessary to be self-motivated and capable of organizing one's own work.

ENTRY REQUIREMENTS

There are no formal entry requirements but individual employers may specify their own.

TRAINING

Practical experience is supplemented by on-the-job training from senior staff.

Qualifications in groundsmanship are not essential, but are advantageous, and may be required for the more responsible posts.

A number of NVQs/SVQs in Amenity Horticulture are available at Levels 1, 2, 3 and 4.

The Institute of Groundsmanship (IoG) offers the National Practical Certificate, the National Technical Certificate, the National Intermediate Diploma and the National Diploma in Turfculture

The National Practical Certificate is based on practical groundsmanship skills. Attendance at a formal course of study is not essential (although courses are available). Successful completion of the Certificate gives accreditation towards part of the NVQ/SVQ in Amenity Horticulture at Level 1.

The National Technical Certificate is based on the NVQ/SVQ in Amenity Horticulture (Greenkeeping – Sports Turf – Sports Ground Maintenance) at Level 2. It is now being offered in the majority of horticulture colleges in the UK, either as a full-time or day release programme.

Specific training schemes for young people may be available. Contact your local careers office, TEC/LEC for details.

LATE ENTRY

There are no formal age limits, and maturity can be an asset for this type of work. Experience in a related occupation, such as farming, is an advantage. Adults may improve their chances of finding employment by studying for the Institute of Groundsmanship qualifications.

There may be specific training opportunities directed at adults available in some areas for this type of work. Candidates may have to satisfy certain conditions to be eligible. Contact your local Jobcentre, careers office or TEC/LEC for details.

OPPORTUNITIES

The main employers are: private sports clubs – for example, football clubs, tennis clubs, and cricket clubs; local authority parks or leisure and recreation departments; horticultural contractors, which provide services for local authorities and other organizations such as sports clubs; universities or hotels with sports facilities.

Groundsmen/women are employed throughout the country, although there are more jobs available in the major centres of population. The number of opportunities is increasing slightly.

Vacancies are advertised in *The Groundsman* and *Horticulture Week*. Self-employment, as a horticultural contractor, is possible. There is considerable demand from employers overseas for trained groundsmen/women.

PAY AND CONDITIONS

Pay varies for groundsmen/women. The Institute of Groundsmanship recommends minimum salary scales of £6,460 to £7,000 for juniors. Groundsmen/women can expect from £9,000 to £10,701 depending on skill level. A head groundsman/woman would earn in the region of £15,000 plus. The IoG recommends additional increments for those with qualifications.

Pay in the private sector varies with individual employers. Some private sports clubs provide accommodation.

Hours of work are usually 37½ to 40 a week, but flexibility over work schedules is needed because the spring and summer growing season is busier than autumn and winter. Some jobs are offered on a seasonal basis. A lot of part-time work is available. Weekend work may be required to prepare the ground for specific events.

PROSPECTS

Promotion prospects are improved by the possession of formal qualifications (see TRAINING). Qualifications can lead to the post of head groundsman/woman responsible for managing a small team of staff.

There are opportunities to progress into general sports and leisure management, particularly with local authorities. Qualifications suitable for intending supervisors and managers include the following:

Institute of Groundsmanship Intermediate Diploma – candidates need at least four years' relevant experience and should hold the IoG National Technical Certificate or an equivalent qualification;

Institute of Groundsmanship National Diploma – for candidates with the Intermediate Diploma and at least six years' experience;

BTEC National Diploma in Horticulture (specializing in Turf Science and Sports Ground Management Amenity Horticulture) – courses are normally available on a three-year sandwich basis, with the second year spent on a work placement;

City & Guilds National Certificate in Horticulture (C&G 0350) – this is a one-year full-time course offered at a number of agricultural colleges. Specialist options (at certain colleges) include groundsmanship, greenkeeping and sportsground management.

NVQs/SVQs in Amenity Horticulture are also available at Levels 3 and 4.

RELATED OCCUPATIONS

Horticultural worker, horticultural manager, sports/leisure centre assistant, gardener, golf greenkeeper, farm worker, forest worker.

FURTHER INFORMATION

The Institute of Groundsmanship*, 19-23 Church Street, The Agora, Wolverton, Milton Keynes MK12 5LG, 01908 312511

FURTHER READING

Leaflets/booklets are available from the address marked*.

In the careers library classified under WAD.

FORESTRY: WAF

1. FOREST OFFICER CLCI:WAF
2. FOREST WORKER/RANGER CLCI:WAF

BACKGROUND INFORMATION

A major force in modern forestry during the past 60 to 80 years has been the development of industries based on wood (such as wrapping and writing papers, cardboard packaging, insulating boards, and plywood). These require a large and regular supply of wood of uniform quality.

Another factor has been the increasing recognition of the role played by trees in stabilizing soil and regulating the flow of water into streams and rivers. Forests also provide a source of shelter for houses, buildings, crops, wild and domestic animals, and many plants. Not least in terms of importance is the aesthetic appeal of wooded areas, with their peace and tranquillity being enjoyed and appreciated by many.

So, although forestry is primarily to do with the production of timber for sale, it is also closely connected with enhancement of landscape, conservation of wildlife, and public recreation.

Growing commercially useful timber on the land available has meant an emphasis on softwoods (such as conifers), which grow on the more exacting upland soils in Scotland, Northern England and Wales. Now, however, the Government is encouraging the planting of broad-leaved trees (such as oak, ash, beech) with the use of goats. These more traditional hardwoods usually require good soil and milder climatic conditions, generally found in the lowlands.

The forestry industry in Great Britain is small, employing approximately 20,000 people. Another 11,000 are employed in related wood-processing industries.

The state-owned Forestry Commission manages about 40 per cent of the forests in Britain. The Commission is divided into two main sub-divisions:

– Forest Enterprise is the operational arm responsible for the Forestry Commission's forests and woodlands. It markets timber, provides recreational opportunities and safeguards forest flora and fauna.

– The Forestry Authority administers grants, provides control functions such as felling licensing, carries out research, advises private woodland owners and liaises with local authorities and countryside groups on land uses.

The remainder of the forestry industry is managed by private estate owners (especially in Scotland), co-operative forestry societies, commercial firms (particularly contractors who provide tree-care services), local authorities and some timber merchants. Private woodlands vary greatly in size and organization, although work tends to be broken down into three groups – managerial staff, foresters and forest workers.

Like forestry companies, the co-operatives provide management and marketing services, including specialist areas. They employ forest officers (also known as woodland managers) and foresters who either engage forest workers directly or put work out to contract.

1. FOREST OFFICER (WAF)

THE WORK

Forestry Commission

Forest officers, working for Forest Enterprise, are technical managers responsible for the annual planning and day-to-day organization of a particular area of forest/woodland. Forest officers plan the annual work programme to ensure cultivation and harvesting take place at the correct times. The work involves decisions concerning seed collection, preparation of land for tree planting, raising and planting trees for afforestation and replanting, tree thinning including organization of marking, sometimes felling, and transportation of timber. General day-to-day care of woodland areas includes the checking of trees for pests and disease, ensuring problems are rectified by administering proper treatment.

Forest officers are also responsible for fire protection arrangements within their area.

Forest Enterprise provides and supervises recreational and leisure facilities for the general public. Forest officers are becoming increasingly involved with recreational aspects of forest and woodland areas. This may include organizing the layout of nature trails and provision of caravan sites and information centres. Conservation aspects also have priority and can involve anything from the management and provision for deer and other wildlife, to landscaping motorways and derelict sites.

Forest officers working for Forest Enterprise are responsible for staff, organizing them according to annual and daily management plans. This includes supervising forest workers, organizing the training of existing staff or new entrants, and becoming directly involved with new forest officer training. The forest officer is responsible for safety standards, estimating costs, setting piecework rates, and measuring and controlling work programmes.

Forest officers working for the Forestry Authority act as advisers for private estates in the area, administer grants and liaise with local authorities and countryside groups.

Experienced forest officers may have specialist duties, such as research, education and training, or technical development (work study). These are normally undertaken on a five-year tour of duty.

The private sector

Within the private sector the work is similar, with emphasis on tree crops and timber, management of woodlands, land evaluation, marketing of timber, and provision of contract services.

In both public and private sectors a further area of responsibility is the control of financial affairs. This may range from simple accounts and book-keeping to controlling capital assets, including sophisticated machinery, amounting to thousands of pounds depending on size and scope of the employing organization.

WORK ENVIRONMENT

Forest officers are office-based, but work outdoors for part of the day dealing with the practicalities of the work. Approximately three-fifths of forest officers' time is spent outdoors whatever the season or weather conditions. Although forest officers are likely to work in the most beautiful parts of the country, locations are generally remote, away from towns and cities. The larger forests are mostly in the upland areas, particularly Scotland, Northern England and Wales.

SKILLS AND INTERESTS

Forest officers need to be able to plan, organize and supervise the work of others. Ability to plan ahead for the long-term is essential; the forest officer may have the satisfaction of creating a lasting resource for future generations, but must be aware that mistakes are also long-lasting.

The work involves careful collection and analysis of facts and figures, so numeracy is essential.

Written and spoken communication skills are required for negotiating, answering enquiries, liaising with outside organizations, managing and supervising staff, writing reports and correspondence.

Some scientific knowledge and an interest in the environment are also required.

Physical fitness is important; the work involves a lot of walking, often over rough terrain.

ENTRY REQUIREMENTS

Entry to the Forestry Commission is with one of the following:

BSc in Forestry. Minimum entry requirements for degree courses are five GCSEs/S grades (A-C/1-3) including maths, with two A levels or three H grades (usually three/four A levels/H grades in science subjects are preferred or required, depending on the course). It is helpful to gain some practical experience in forestry before starting on a course.

BTEC/SCOTVEC Higher National Diploma in Forestry. Minimum entry requirements are normally: one A level or two H grades and supporting GCSEs/S grades (A-C/1-3); or a BTEC/SCOTVEC national award; or equivalent.

BTEC National Diploma in Forestry or SCOTVEC equivalent. Entry is normally with: four GCSEs/S grades (A-C/1-3) including maths, English and a science subject; or a relevant BTEC first diploma, or equivalent.

City and Guilds Phase IV Certificate in Forestry or SCOTVEC equivalent. There are no minimum entry requirements, but practical experience is a condition of entry to courses.

Possession of a full driving licence is essential.

Private sector employers' requirements vary.

Candidates should check with universities and colleges for details of specific entry requirements.

TRAINING

Degree courses

First degree courses in forestry or forestry-related subjects are available at the following universities:

Aberdeen University: three-year ordinary and four-year honours degree in Forestry, with two parallel programmes, one in Forest Management and one in Arboriculture and Amenity Forestry.

Edinburgh University: four-year honours course leading to BSc in Ecological Science and Forestry. A four-year joint honours degree in Agriculture, Forestry and Rural Economy is also available.

University College of North Wales, Bangor: three-year honours degrees in Agroforestry, Forestry, Soil and Forest Science, Forestry and Wood Science, or Wood Science. (Wood science courses are primarily for those who wish to work in timber-using industries.)

BTEC/SCOTVEC higher national diplomas

Newton Rigg College: a three-year course, including one year's work experience, leading to the BTEC Higher National Diploma in Forestry and NVQ Level 4.

Inverness College: a three-year programme, including a year's practical experience, leading to the SCOTVEC Higher National Diploma in Forestry.

BTEC/SCOTVEC national certificate/diplomas

Courses usually last two years full-time, or three years including a year's practical experience. Colleges running courses include: Newton Rigg, Inverness, De Montfort University, Askham Bryan College, Barony College, Herefordshire College of Agriculture, and Sparsholt College.

City and Guilds courses are for those already employed in the industry, and are taken on a part-time basis. The existing City and Guilds Phases I-IV are being replaced by courses leading to National Vocational Qualifications.

NVQs/SVQs in Forestry at Levels 3 and 4 are being developed. Once the NVQ/SVQ Level 3 has been accredited, trainees will be able to enrol on a forestry Modern Apprenticeship scheme.

The Institute of Chartered Foresters' examinations are for those in employment in the industry. Possession of other forestry qualifications may grant exemption from part of the examinations. Alternatively, the Central Forestry Examinations Board offers a National Diploma in Forestry (NDF) by examination for those who wish to obtain a management level qualification through private study.

Once in a post, forest officers may take short technical courses organized by the Forestry and Arboriculture Safety and Training Council (FASTCO).

LATE ENTRY

Competition for the limited number of available vacancies is keen. It is, therefore, unlikely that adults looking for a change of career, without any previous forestry qualifications or experience, will be successful. Mature student applications are considered by those universities offering forestry degree courses, but, again, relevant forestry experience is likely to be essential.

OPPORTUNITIES

Despite an increase in resources available to forestry, the introduction of mechanization and improved methods has meant a significant reduction in the number of jobs. Competition is intense, with more people training than can be absorbed. Even finding a job or practical experience before college or university can be difficult.

The Forestry Commission is the largest employer overall and covers the whole of Great Britain. The concentration of forestry, however, tends to be in Scotland, Northern England and Wales – with corresponding employment opportunities often in remote, outlying areas. Research work is mostly based at Alice Holt Lodge, near Farnham, Surrey, with another main research station at Bush Estate, near Edinburgh.

Other employers include private landowners, local authorities, national companies, co-operative forestry societies and contracting companies.

Vacancies for forest officer posts within the Forestry Commission are filled by competitive interviews, which are normally held annually.

The following journals may carry advertisements for vacancies in the private sector: *Quarterly Journal of Forestry, Forestry, British Timber, Timber Grower, Scottish Forestry.*

PAY AND CONDITIONS

Wages and salaries in the Forestry Commission are as follows: Forest officer III – £14,019 to £23,114; forest officer II – £14,303 to £25,815; forest officer I – £19,549 to £31,246.

No average pay scales are available for the private sector. Pay is generally less for comparable positions except at the higher end of the scale. A vehicle may be provided.

In the Forestry Commission and local authorities a 42-hour week is standard. Overtime is worked when required. Forestry Commission salaries include an element for 'all hours worked' and no additional overtime payments are made. In the private sector, especially in the larger commercial companies, supervisory staff must be willing to work hours as required by the employer, including evening and weekend work. More often than not, extra time worked is balanced by time off in lieu.

PROSPECTS

Management of private forests is likely to be the growth area for future forestry employment with promotion opportunities being reflected accordingly. There is, however, no formal structure for promotion; prospects vary according to size and structure of individual organizations.

For higher-level posts, many employers require full membership of the Institute of Chartered Foresters.

Promotion within the Forestry Commission depends on merit, ability and the number of vacancies that arise.

There are opportunities for self-employment, for instance as a forestry consultant.

There may be opportunities for forestry graduates to work overseas, as requests from foreign countries arise. These are usually on limited term appointments and candidates may be required to have specialist experience.

RELATED OCCUPATIONS

Arboriculturalist, horticultural manager, farm manager, landscape architect, land agent/agricultural surveyor, forest worker/ranger.

FURTHER INFORMATION AND READING

Please see article 2. FOREST WORKER/RANGER.

2. FOREST WORKER/RANGER (WAF)

THE WORK

The duties of a forest worker are all practical, concerning the general upkeep of forest and woodland areas. This includes clearing scrub to promote the healthy growth of young and established trees, helping to control harmful diseases, pests or forms of wildlife, planting and tending young trees, pruning and felling trees, and the general upkeep of boundary fences, ditches and drainage systems.

The work is fairly mechanized, with skilled forest workers using tractors and chain saws. Such jobs as ploughing and drain making are all mechanized. Hand tools such as bill hooks, hand saws and portable power saws are also used. Although the forest worker is likely to work out in all weathers, maintenance of forest machinery and sharpening of hand tools is likely to be carried out on cold and rainy days.

Firefighting is also part of the forest worker's duties. A constant look-out is kept for fire hazards. Where an area of forest or woodland is close to industry or houses, fires can be frequent. Duties also include maintaining firefighting equipment.

Forest workers may specialize in cutting tree lengths, tractor driving, and lorry driving to move wood stacks to transportation points.

Depending on the type of employer, it may be possible for some forestry workers to specialize in nursery work. Many plants are raised from seeds carefully collected from trees in this country or obtained from North America, Japan and Europe. A variety of native and exotic species are raised for replanting in such places as city streets and open spaces, along motorways, etc.

Some forest workers within the Forestry Commission (Forest Enterprise), may work as forest rangers. Forest rangers deal with wildlife control and conservation. They protect animals and birds by creating and maintaining habitats, control pests and conserve the forest environment. They are also responsible for protecting forests from misuse by the general public. This includes reminding people about fire risks, supervising, and generally taking care of, public facilities such as car parks, picnic sites, and caravan areas.

WORK ENVIRONMENT

Forest workers work mostly outside in all weathers, whatever the season. Only when the conditions are very bad or wet do they work indoors on machine and tool maintenance, gate making, etc.

The work is dirty and can be dangerous. Special protective clothing is supplied although this may be restrictive. Chemical spraying, which has to be carried out in warm weather, can be uncomfortable because it involves wearing plastic protective clothing, which can be hot.

Larger forests and woodland areas are mostly in the upland parts of Britain, particularly Scotland, Northern England and Wales. Workers must be prepared to live and work in isolated places. Accommodation may sometimes be provided by the employer.

SKILLS AND INTERESTS

Forest workers need to be fit, as the work is physically demanding. They should be capable of sustained hard work – moving around in undergrowth and branches, carrying and using a chain saw, etc is physically demanding. Felling trees is strenuous work and may involve working at heights.

Forest workers must be good at manual work and able to use machinery and hand tools safely with skill and speed. Common sense is required because of the hazardous nature of the work. They should be observant – able to detect changes in drainage and soil features which may affect the performance of machinery and general standard of work.

Forest workers need the ability to work on their own initiative as well as forming part of a team. Even when working in pairs for safety, it can be a solitary job as workers may be isolated by protective clothing, machinery may be noisy, and they may be working at a fast pace.

The forest ranger and warden must be able to deal with visitors tactfully, but firmly if needed. Rangers should be interested in animals and birds.

Respiratory and skin allergies (including asthma, hay fever, chilblains, and eczema) may cause difficulties.

ENTRY REQUIREMENTS

No minimum formal educational qualifications are required. Those with GCSEs/S grades (A-C/1-3) may have an advantage because of the intense competition for places.

A driving licence is an advantage, although not essential.

TRAINING

Specific training schemes for young people are available within the forestry industry. They include work experience and college training. Trainees work towards NVQs/SVQs at Levels 1 and 2, and may take City and Guilds qualifications. The schemes are available through a number of colleges of agriculture/forestry and other training organizations.

It is also possible to enter forestry after taking a one-year full-time BTEC first diploma. Colleges running courses for this qualification include Newton Rigg College, Sparsholt College, Llysfasi College of Agriculture, and De Montfort University. In Scotland, one or two-year SCOTVEC national certificate courses are available at Inverness and Barony Colleges.

Courses for the National Certificate in Forestry, awarded by City and Guilds are available at a number of colleges, either full-time or part-time, over a period of at least one year.

All forest workers, including those who do not follow any formal college training, are expected to do in-service training, to gain considerable skill with forest tools and machinery. Safe handling of equipment is essential.

NVQs/SVQs in Forestry are available at Levels 1 and 2, and cover skills such as planting, fencing, draining, pruning, timber harvesting and nursery work. The NVQ/SVQ at Level 2 includes supervisory skills and monitoring contract work to ensure that standards are maintained.

The Forestry and Arboriculture Safety and Training Council (FASTCO) runs skill courses in various areas according to local demand. Courses vary from basic forestry techniques, chain-saw basic handling and maintenance, to advanced chain-saw and tree-climbing courses, lasting between one and five days. Details from FASTCO or individual colleges.

LATE ENTRY

There is no upper age limit but applicants should consider the physical demands of the job. Health and fitness determine suitability. Those with a farming background and knowledge of the machinery and tools used, may have an advantage.

There may be specific training opportunities directed at adults available in some areas for this type of work. Candidates may have to satisfy certain conditions to be eligible. Contact your local Jobcentre, careers office or TEC/LEC for details.

OPPORTUNITIES

There are few direct openings, either with the Forestry Commission or private sector employers. However, there are good opportunities for those who are prepared to undertake contract work on a self-employed basis – increasingly, the Forestry Commission and other organizations use the services of contractors, rather than directly employed labour.

The following journals may carry advertisements for vacancies in forestry work: *Quarterly Journal of Forestry, Forestry, British Timber, Timber Grower, Scottish Forestry.*

PAY AND CONDITIONS

There are wage agreements for forestry workers. Unskilled workers aged 18 years and over earn minimum wages of £138.83. Wages for other workers vary according to experience, type of work and seniority. Ranger trainees – £138.83 a week; rangers – £157.75 a week.

Skilled workers, including foremen/women, receive a higher basic wage of around £134.87 to £182 a week. Pieceworkers are usually able to earn substantially more than the basic rate. Overtime may be available.

A 42-hour week, inclusive of meal breaks, is standard for forest workers, although some overtime and weekend work may be necessary. Starting and finishing times often depend on the season.

PROSPECTS

Forest workers with suitable experience and personal qualities may be promoted to foreman/woman.

The duties and responsibilities of a foreman/woman include supervising the work of a group of forest workers or contractors, to maintain standards, output and safety measures. Foremen/women are also responsible for the timing of work and keeping accurate timesheets. They are involved with on-the-job training and generally keeping a watch for hazards such as damage by fire, insects, wild animals, disease and trespass.

Forest workers who show suitability may become wardens or rangers, although vacancies are few and sought after.

Within the private sector, it may be possible to progress to supervisory and even managerial posts by experience only. Absence of a clear hierarchy of responsibility, however, may mean comparatively fewer opportunities occur.

The Forestry Commission and many private sector employers encourage employees in the development of their full potential by providing the opportunity for further training and education.

RELATED OCCUPATIONS

Farm worker, horticultural worker, wood mill worker, gamekeeper, fish farmer, countryside ranger/warden, forest officer.

FURTHER INFORMATION

Forestry and Arboriculture Safety and Training Council*, 231 Corstorphine Road, Edinburgh EH12 7AT, 0131 334 8083

Forestry Commission*, 231 Corstorphine Road, Edinburgh EH12 7AT, 0131 334 8083

Institute of Chartered Foresters, 7A St Colme Street, Edinburgh, EH3 6AA, 0131 225 2705

Enquiries about employment with Forest Enterprise as a forest worker can be made to Local Forest District Offices; the address and telephone number can be found in local telephone directories.

FURTHER READING

Leaflets/booklets are available from the addresses marked*.

Job Outlines – Forestry and Arboriculture – COIC
Working in Outdoor Jobs – COIC

In the careers library classified under WAF.

1. VETERINARY SURGEON CLCI:WAL
2. VETERINARY NURSE CLCI:WAL

BACKGROUND INFORMATION

Veterinary surgeons (vets) work mainly in general practice, where they treat a variety of animals. Much of the work, particularly in urban areas, is with domestic pets, but some vets treat farm animals, poultry, horses and ponies. There are also specialist areas, such as public health and research and investigation into animal disease, in which vets are employed. Just as surgeons treating human patients are assisted by hospital nurses, so veterinary surgeons are assisted by veterinary nurses (VNs). VNs help during treatment and operations, and also assist with the general running of veterinary practices.

1. VETERINARY SURGEON (WAL)

THE WORK

Around three-quarters of all vets in the UK work in general practice; others hold appointments in the State Veterinary Service, universities, research establishments, pharmaceutical companies and other organizations. The work varies considerably in these different settings.

General practice

The main emphasis in general practice is on diagnosis and treatment of disease and injury. Vets also inoculate animals against disease, carry out neutering to prevent unwanted breeding, and advise owners on matters such as food intake and breeding.

A substantial proportion of the work is with domestic pets such as dogs, cats, rabbits, hamsters and caged birds. Many vets may also treat horses and ponies.

Some practices in rural areas work mainly with farm animals or horses, others with 'small animals' (mainly pets); mixed practices deal with the whole range of species.

Vets working with farm animals are concerned with matters such as animal health and welfare, improvements in productivity, artificial insemination, and disease control programmes. Modern farming demands a high standard of veterinary service – this may include providing written reports.

A considerable amount of practice time may be spent on 'part-time' appointments. Many vets in farm practice are local veterinary inspectors for the Ministry of Agriculture; their duties include testing cattle for disease, inspecting cattle markets, and working in abattoirs to ensure welfare and hygiene standards are met. Vets may also inspect conditions at greyhound race tracks, riding establishments, zoos, dog breeding and boarding kennels, and pet shops, on behalf of local authorities. They may advise on the welfare of laboratory animals used in scientific experiments.

Other appointments

Vets employed by the animal welfare societies or the Royal Army Veterinary Corps are engaged in similar duties to those in general practice, whereas those working for organizations such as research institutes and pharmaceutical companies may concentrate entirely on research. In university veterinary schools, vets teach and carry out research.

In the State Veterinary Service, investigation and field officers are involved in matters such as the control of disease, special investigations, general advisory work and the improvement of farm animal welfare. There is no clear distinction between investigation and field officers, although the former provide most diagnostic services, the latter statutory work, carried out where there are legal obligations – for instance, after a notifiable disease, such as foot-and-mouth, has been reported.

WORK ENVIRONMENT

Vets in small animal practices spend much of their time in the surgery. In mixed practices and practices dealing with farm animals or horses, a lot of the time is spent travelling – 100 miles a day is not uncommon.

Vets in general practice have a great deal of contact with people from a variety of social backgrounds, and also with practice staff, who include other vets, veterinary nurses and other workers, such as receptionists.

Research and investigatory work is carried out in both laboratory and clinical areas. Most research jobs involve some contact with people from within the organization and outside.

All vets must be prepared to work in smelly and messy conditions; they need to wear appropriate protective clothing for the job they are tackling.

SKILLS AND INTERESTS

Vets need to be dedicated to animals and their welfare. Veterinary practice is not a 9 to 5 job, and the training is lengthy; commitment and a sense of vocation are essential.

Dealing with people is an important part of the work; vets should be tactful, patient and sympathetic, with good communication skills. They often need to help owners to make difficult decisions, such as whether to have an elderly and much-loved pet put down.

Good powers of observation are required – animals cannot, of course, describe their symptoms, and to make a diagnosis, the vet must be aware of small and important changes in an animal's appearance and behaviour.

Manual dexterity is needed for animal handling and performing surgical procedures. The work can be physically demanding, particularly when it involves horses or farm animals, and vets often work in cold, wet, dirty and smelly conditions. It is important not to be squeamish about messy tasks, such as making internal examinations.

Veterinary practice is unsuitable for people who are allergic to fur or hair.

Vets in private practice need to develop all the skills associated with running a business. In public appointments, vets carry considerable responsibility and require strong personalities to enforce hygiene regulations which may affect the livelihood of other people.

ENTRY REQUIREMENTS

Entry is via a veterinary degree. This is extremely competitive; it is harder to obtain a university place to study veterinary science than to enter any other course.

The minimum academic requirements for university entry are two A levels/three H grades and three other subjects at GCSE/S grade (A-C/1-3). In practice, however, applicants for places at university veterinary schools need three A levels/five H grades, with high grades. The most usual subjects are chemistry, biology and either physics or maths, but other subject combinations (which must include chemistry) may be accepted, for instance, chemistry, physics and zoology. At GCSE/S grade, preferred subjects include English, chemistry, physics, biology and maths or another numerate subject. Intending students should check detailed entry requirements with university veterinary schools. Advanced GNVQ/GSVQ Level III in Science is not yet accepted as equivalent to A levels/H grades.

Before applying for a place, it is important to spend a week or preferably more helping out in a veterinary practice. This helps intending students to decide whether they are really suited to the work, and to make sure that they do not suffer from allergic reactions when handling animals. All university veterinary schools now insist on applicants having had experience in a practice and/or experience with healthy animals including livestock – for instance on a farm, in kennels, catteries or riding stables – to prove interest and commitment.

TRAINING

The university veterinary schools in Great Britain have been allowed to increase their intake to a 'core' of about 400 students, with the schools free to admit additional numbers, if they wish.

Six university veterinary schools offer degrees in veterinary science, veterinary medicine or veterinary medicine and surgery. They are: Bristol, Cambridge, Edinburgh, Glasgow, Liverpool, and London. The length of the course is five years, except at Cambridge, which runs a six-year course.

Degrees from the six university veterinary schools confer on holders the right to membership of the Royal College of Veterinary Surgeons (RCVS) and the right to practise as a vet in the UK and other European Union countries (provided they are citizens of the UK or another EU country). No one can practise as a vet in the UK without being a member of the RCVS.

The way subjects are spread through the veterinary degree course varies from university to university; there is no uniform pattern. All, however, cover: scientific disciplines dealing with animal structure and functions (for example, anatomy, physiology and biochemistry); pharmacology, pathology, microbiology, parasitology and bacteriology; animal health and husbandry; clinical medicine and surgery; reproduction; and veterinary public health.

Courses cover all the main domestic and agricultural species. Students learn to handle and examine animals from the first year onwards. They also receive instruction in matters such as legal requirements, meat inspection and food hygiene.

In the vacations, all students are required to obtain specific experience in farm and veterinary work. This includes 26 weeks' 'extra-mural tuition' during the later years of the course, spent mainly in veterinary practices, but also at laboratories, investigation centres and abattoirs.

After graduation, those who enter general practice start as assistants. They usually remain assistants for several years, until they have the experience to be accepted as partners. To acquire a partnership, it is necessary to make a financial investment in the practice.

LATE ENTRY

The university veterinary schools consider the selection of a few mature students each year; the majority of those who are accepted are graduates with first or upper second class honours degrees in related subjects such as biochemistry or zoology.

Mature applicants are advised to write to the university veterinary schools for advice on their individual cases.

OPPORTUNITIES

There are some 10,300 active vets in the UK – including general practitioners and those employed in other fields. The Royal College of Veterinary Surgeons has over 16,000 members, but this figure includes retired and overseas members.

At present, the demand for veterinary surgeons exceeds supply.

Private practice

About 8,500 vets work in private practice. On average, there are three or four vets in a practice, but there are variations: some practices are single-handed, whereas others are staffed by as many as 15 vets.

Vets in private practice are self-employed. However, newly qualified vets are employed by practices, as assistants, on a salaried basis. Once they have gained experience, they may be able to purchase a share in a practice; alternatively, they may set up a new practice.

The State Veterinary Service – part of ADAS (Agricultural Development and Advisory Service of the Ministry of Agriculture, Fisheries and Food – MAFF). The State Veterinary Service has three parts: the Veterinary Investigation Service, the Central Veterinary Laboratory and the Veterinary Field Service. Veterinary Investigation Centres provide diagnostic services for practising vets and laboratory support for the Veterinary Field Service; they also carry out disease surveillance. The Central Veterinary Laboratory carries out research, develops diagnostic tests for animal diseases and provides services for the veterinary profession, and agricultural and pharmaceutical industries. The Veterinary Field Service has centres throughout Great Britain, and takes action to control outbreaks of notifiable disease. Veterinary Field Service staff are also involved in monitoring animal welfare and in public health matters. In addition two new agencies have been established recently under the aegis of the MAFF: the Meat Hygiene Service and the Veterinary Investigation Service. These employ some staff full-time and contract others either from practices or as freelances via specialist employment agencies.

University veterinary schools– six universities offer veterinary courses. The work includes research, undergraduate and postgraduate teaching, and the provision of clinical and pathological services.

Research institutes– include the Agricultural and Food Research Council, the Medical Research Council and the charitable Animal Health Trust.

In **pharmaceutical companies, industry and commerce** the work includes investigations into medical or veterinary problems, biomedical research and technical advice on the development of drugs, vaccines and food additives. There may be opportunities for overseas travel.

In **local government** some veterinary surgeons are employed on a full-time basis to advise on animal-related matters and to supervise the enforcement of public health and animal welfare legislation. Some of these have transferred to the new Meat Hygiene Service. This work is also carried out on a part-time basis by vets in private practice.

Animal welfare societies employ about 230 vets, and include the People's Dispensary for Sick Animals (PDSA), the Royal Society for the Prevention of Cruelty to Animals

(RSPCA) and the Blue Cross. The main employer is the PDSA.

In the **Royal Army Veterinary Corps** the work mainly involves looking after the Army's horses and dogs. Vets normally enter on short service commissions, although regular commissions are available. There are opportunities to serve in every country in which the British Army is stationed.

Overseas Development Administration– contract appointments in developing countries are available.

Apart from the opportunities to work abroad described above, it is also possible for vets from the UK to practise in other European countries, as their qualifications are recognized throughout the European Union.

PAY AND CONDITIONS

Veterinary assistants in general practice (the majority of vets start their careers in such posts) usually earn between £12,000 and £21,000. In addition, most veterinary assistants are paid housing and car allowances. Earnings of principals and partners depend very much on the success of the practice.

Vets in government service, the universities, research institutes and commercial organizations usually work office hours, but may still be called upon to work extra hours as necessary.

There are some opportunities for part-time work.

Running a veterinary practice is a 24-hour-a-day, 365-day-a-year responsibility. Every practitioner has an obligation to deal with emergencies. In a single-handed practice, the vet can only take time off if a member of a neighbouring practice agrees to provide cover or if a locum is employed. Even in practices with several vets, someone has to be on-call at all times.

PROSPECTS

The majority of newly qualified vets start their careers as assistants in general practice; they may move into other branches of the profession later on.

In general practice, vets generally become senior assistants after two or three years. After gaining further experience, they may become partners or set up their own practices. Both options require a substantial financial investment.

In the State Veterinary Service, there is a clear promotion structure; the same applies to university work (candidates for promotion are usually expected to hold a postgraduate degree or diploma). In industry, promotion opportunities depend on the size of the company; progression may mean moving out of veterinary work into a more general management role.

The contracting policy of the government agencies means there may be opportunities for freelance work as a vet, either direct or via a specialist employment agency, but, due to the shortage of vets in the UK, there is an inflow of vets from other European countries for these posts.

Prospects for promotion in animal welfare societies are limited.

RELATED OCCUPATIONS

Zoologist, biologist, doctor (GP), doctor (hospital), veterinary nurse, RSPCA/SSPCA inspector.

FURTHER INFORMATION AND READING

Please see article 2. VETERINARY NURSE.

2. VETERINARY NURSE (WAL)

THE WORK

Veterinary nurses (VNs) assist vets with the care and treatment of animal patients. They work mainly with dogs, cats, small mammals such as hamsters and rabbits, and caged birds, although in some practices they may also work with farm animals and horses, or with exotic species such as snakes, which are increasingly popular as pets.

The nursing duties of a VN involve generally assisting the vet in the practice. VNs hold animals whilst vets carry out examinations and treatment. They collect specimens, make simple laboratory tests, and, when specimens require more extensive testing, prepare samples for posting to commercial laboratories.

Assisting vets during operations is an important aspect of the work. VNs prepare animal patients for surgery, for instance by shaving the operation site. They assist with administering and monitoring anaesthesia, and hand instruments and dressings to the vet during the operation. They monitor the animal's condition during surgery and after the operation.

VNs also maintain the equipment used for anaesthesia, radiography and laboratory testing. They keep stocks of drugs, and may dispense drugs, under the direct supervision of the veterinary surgeon.

Other nursing duties include developing X-rays, assisting with the preparation and positioning of animals for X-rays, and preparing and administering drugs (this includes giving injections under the supervision of the veterinary surgeon). VNs deal with emergencies and may give first aid in the vet's absence. Occasionally they accompany vets on their rounds.

Veterinary nurses also carry out other practice duties. They prepare the consulting room and diagnostic equipment. Before operations, they get the theatre ready, and sterilize and lay out surgical instruments. They may have general cleaning duties.

In practices that have hospitalization quarters, VNs are involved in general daily care of the animals. They clean pens or cages, provide fresh bedding, feed the animals and ensure that a supply of fresh drinking water is available. They also exercise and groom animals in their charge.

VNs may also have reception and clerical duties, including answering the telephone, keeping an appointments book, maintaining and filing case records and other documents such as laboratory reports, and dealing with correspondence. They also advise owners on matters such as vaccinations, neutering, house-training and nutrition.

Uniforms (green and white striped for trainees, bottle green for qualified VNs) are provided by employers.

WORK ENVIRONMENT

The work takes place in the practice premises and animal quarters. In mixed practices, veterinary nurses may sometimes work out of doors, helping with the treatment of large animals.

Working conditions, particularly in the animal quarters, are noisy, sometimes cramped, and, on occasion, smelly.

Veterinary nurses spend much of their working day with vets, often on a one-to-one basis. They also have a great deal of contact with animal owners.

SKILLS AND INTERESTS

Veterinary nurses need a strong interest in animals, but without over-sentimentality. An interest in science, particularly biology, is also important.

VNs need to be able to receive and transmit information accurately; during training, they learn the technical vocabulary used by vets, and are expected to have a good command of the correct terminology by the time they qualify. It is also important to be able to communicate well with other members of the practice staff and with animal owners. A good telephone manner is required. Tolerance and patience are needed for dealing with owners who are anxious or upset about their pets.

Manual dexterity is required for animal handling and delicate tasks such as giving injections.

A sense of responsibility is important, to ensure that the animals are properly cared for and treatment routines followed precisely.

VNs need neat, legible handwriting for keeping records. Keyboard skills are an advantage.

Willingness to carry out messy jobs such as cleaning up blood and vomit is essential.

ENTRY REQUIREMENTS

For the Royal College of Veterinary Surgeons (RCVS) Veterinary Nursing Scheme, entry requirements are as follows:

1. Four GCSEs/S grades (A-C/1-3), including English language and either a science subject or maths, or equivalent/higher qualifications, eg Intermediate GNVQ/ GSVQ Level II in Science.

2. Applicants must be 17 years or over. (Consent of a parent or guardian must be obtained for applicants under 18 years.)

3. Applicants must have obtained paid employment at an approved training centre (ATC), or have the promise of such employment, in writing. An approved training centre is a veterinary practice or similar establishment approved by the RCVS for training veterinary nurses; not all practices are ATCs. A list of ATCs is available from the British Veterinary Nursing Association (BVNA). The BVNA's employment register may help with finding a position.

Application for enrolment application forms to become a student is made to the BVNA with a statement showing you can meet these requirements. Fees are charged for enrolment and for each examination.

Applicants who cannot meet the educational requirements can take a Pre-Veterinary Nursing exam which qualifies for entry. The Pre-VN is a four-year course, and the only entry requirement is being currently employed in a veterinary practice, not necessarily an ATC.

Employment in a nursing auxiliary role in veterinary practices may be obtainable without qualifications.

TRAINING

RCVS Veterinary Nursing scheme

Training lasts for a minimum of two years and includes the study of: anatomy; physiology; first aid and nursing; husbandry and dietary requirements; theatre practice; kennel and hospital management; quarantine procedures; laboratory techniques; anaesthesia; dispensing; radiography and dark room techniques.

Students gain practical experience, with tuition from employers and colleagues, by working in an ATC. Theoretical knowledge may be gained by attending full-time, part-time, day release or evening courses at colleges, by correspondence course or by private study. Although a few colleges offer full-time residential courses (of varying length), it is not possible to attend these without having completed a period of training at an ATC. Details of all courses are available from the British Veterinary Nursing Association.

Two examinations must be passed before a trainee qualifies as a veterinary nurse and becomes eligible for entry to the List of Veterinary Nurses maintained by the BVNA. The Part I examination is usually taken one year after enrolment with BVNA, and the Part II examination following two years' training.

Entry may be possible via training schemes for young people, for those who fulfil the RCVS entry requirements. Contact your local careers office or TEC/LEC for further information.

Other training

A few veterinary surgeons prefer to train their own nurses, though this is discouraged. The training received will be specific to that particular practice, may be narrow in scope, and will not necessarily be recognized by other employers; it may be difficult to change jobs.

LATE ENTRY

There are no fixed upper age limits. Adults must have the qualifications described in ENTRY REQUIREMENTS, and their training is the same as for young people. Rates of pay are also likely to be the same as for younger entrants, and this may be a deterrent.

OPPORTUNITIES

There are about 3,000 qualified VNs in the UK. The majority work with vets in general practice. Some work in veterinary hospitals, which are veterinary practices fulfilling certain RCVS requirements. There are also a number of VNs employed by animal welfare societies. Over 180 are employed by the People's Dispensary for Sick Animals (PDSA), at its 57 veterinary centres throughout Britain. All PDSA entrants train for the VN qualification. Other animal welfare societies like the RSPCA and the Blue Cross also train and employ VNs.

Some veterinary nurses work in university veterinary schools, and in research establishments. There are a few opportunities in zoos and animal laboratories. Breeding and boarding kennels may employ VNs as managers. Some move into jobs as representatives for companies in veterinary medicine or insurance fields.

The British Veterinary Nursing Association runs an employment register that puts prospective students and qualified VNs in touch with potential employers. Vacancies are also advertised in Veterinary Nursing and Veterinary Record.

There are opportunities to work abroad; a number of VNs are employed in Australia and New Zealand.

Temporary locum work is available, particularly during peak holiday periods.

PAY AND CONDITIONS

There are no nationally agreed rates of pay for veterinary nurses. Salaries vary according to employer, geographical location and the individual nurse's experience.

The PDSA pays students from starting salaries of £5,437 to £5,601 depending on age and qualifications, to £5,927. On passing the Part II examinations, nurses are paid on a scale ranging from £8,561 to £10,359. The scale for head nurses extends from £10,875 to £13,159.

Hours of work depend on the individual employer, but will generally be at least 35 hours a week and often 37 to 40. Hours are likely to be variable, with on-call duties. Weekend work is often required. There are some opportunities for part-time work.

PROSPECTS

Until recently, prospects for promotion have been rather limited, but they are now improving. In general practice, VNs may become head nurse or practice manager; duties include organizing staff rotas, interviewing prospective staff, assisting with training, dealing with banking and carrying out basic book-keeping.

Further qualifications may improve prospects. Qualified veterinary nurses working in approved training centres may study for the two-year Diploma in Advanced Veterinary Nursing (Surgical). Nutritional certificates are also available.

VNs are also moving into related careers such as product management with pharmaceutical companies, lecturing and training.

RELATED OCCUPATIONS

Zoo keeper, kennel worker, horse groom, RSPCA/SSPCA inspector, dog groomer, guide dog trainer/mobility instructor.

FURTHER INFORMATION

The Blue Cross*, Shilton Road, Burford, Oxon OX18 4PF, 01993 822651

British Veterinary Nursing Association*, Unit D12, The Seedbed Centre, Coldharbour Road, Harlow, Essex 01279 450567 (please enclose a large sae)

The Royal College of Veterinary Surgeons (RCVS)*, 32 Belgrave Square, London SW1X 8QP, 0171 235 4971/2 (sae required)

People's Dispensary for Sick Animals (PDSA)*, Whitechapel Way, Priorslee, Telford, Shropshire TF2 9PQ, 01952 290999

RSPCA*, Causeway, Horsham, West Sussex RH12 1HG, 01403 264181

FURTHER READING

Leaflets/booklets are available from the addresses marked*.

Job Outlines – Work with Animals – COIC
Working in Work with Animals – COIC
A Career as a Veterinary Surgeon – Royal College of Veterinary Surgeons
Careers Working with Animals – Kogan Page

In the careers library classified under WAL.

RSPCA/SSPCA INSPECTOR CLCI:WAL

THE WORK

Inspectors aim to prevent cruelty to animals and to encourage kindness and humanity in their treatment.

Inspectors spend most of their time working independently, dealing directly with animals and with the owners/people concerned. They perform a variety of different tasks each day, travelling around in a specially equipped van containing ropes, rescue equipment, overalls, drugs (for the humane destruction of animals, etc), and a radio/mobile telephone allowing speedy contact in cases of emergency.

An inspector's work can be roughly divided into three parts:

Law enforcement and investigatory work: inspectors carry out the policing function of the Society, attempting to enforce the legislation affecting animals. The principal laws are the Protection of Animals Act 1911 and the Protection of Animals (Scotland) Act 1912; other laws concern such things as the transit of animals, the protection of birds and pets, and animal welfare. There are also a large number of specific regulations concerning different species.

The majority of complaints come from the public. All are investigated, logged and reported, even though around three-quarters are unfounded. Inspectors visit premises and try to gain access to the animal suspected of suffering. They may give advice, take statements and ask the police to assist by obtaining search warrants in suspicious circumstances. They have no powers to force entry or to remove animals (unless the owner agrees), however bad the conditions. The inspector decides on what action to take, for instance educating an owner or attempting to remove the animal.

Court proceedings are taken against people suspected of wilful cruelty or neglect. If investigations lead the inspector to believe that court action may be possible, details are sent to the headquarters so that proceedings can begin. The inspector's evidence to the court must be accurate and detailed, strictly following the requirements of the Police and Criminal Evidence Act 1984, if a case is to be successful.

Other duties include detecting the occurrence of illegal acts, for instance dog-fighting, cock-fighting or badger-baiting.

Inspection: inspectors are responsible for the general patrol, observation and routine inspection of a designated area, to try and ensure that all establishments selling or dealing with animals (for example, pet shops, boarding kennels, riding stables, zoos, circuses, farms and slaughter houses) maintain proper standards. An important aspect of the work is attending local events such as cattle-markets and race meetings.

Inspectors are concerned with the transportation of live animals, by road, sea or air. They may check the conditions in which animals are transported – calling at railway stations when a consignment of animals is expected, or inspecting a wagon transporting animals.

Welfare work: on receiving a victim of cruelty, or an abandoned or unwanted pet, the inspector calls the veterinary surgeon, if necessary, and then attempts to secure accommodation for the animal. The Society runs its own kennels and homes, and maintains lists of volunteers willing to accept animals either temporarily or permanently. A good many animals, although kept as long as possible, are not found homes and must be destroyed.

The inspector is required to slaughter animals humanely at times.

Some animals become injured as a result of accidents, for example, road accidents or oiled birds that are victims of spillages. The inspector attempts to alleviate their suffering, in whatever way is possible. The inspector is also involved in rescue work. This can cover anything from rounding up strays, to complex and difficult operations involving animals stranded on cliffs, or sinking in mud. In some cases expert assistance is sought from, for instance, climbers or coastguards.

Inspectors receive large numbers of telephone enquiries, usually from members of the public seeking advice about animal welfare. If they are unable to advise individuals directly, they usually know to whom to refer them. They sometimes have to respond to emergency calls after normal hours.

WORK ENVIRONMENT

Inspectors usually control an area of between 50 and 2,000 square miles, depending on location. Much of their time is taken up investigating complaints. A major problem in urban areas may be abandoned animals; while, in rural areas, much time may be spent visiting farms and livestock markets. Coastal regions have particular problems relating to the effects of pollution on wildlife.

Inspectors spend about half of their time on the road between visits. Outdoor work can involve cold, wet and dirty conditions, and rescue work may be dangerous. They may be called out at any time, day or night, though there is normally a rostering system for out-of-hours work.

Inspectors work largely alone, keeping in regular contact with their chief inspector. They liaise closely with other specialists, such as veterinary surgeons, the police, the fire brigade and rescue workers.

SKILLS AND INTERESTS

Inspectors should be dedicated and caring, with a genuine concern for animals and an ability to cope dispassionately and calmly in emergency situations. They should not be squeamish, and must be prepared to slaughter animals humanely if necessary to prevent suffering.

Inspectors must be tactful, diplomatic, confident and level-headed, since people suspected of cruelty may be resentful, obstructive or even aggressive. The work can be frustrating at times, since inspectors' powers are limited and they may be unable to act in every situation seeming to demand it. They should be able to plan their own work and should have good standards of verbal or written communication. They must be prepared to work long hours, spending a lot of time outdoors, often in adverse weather conditions.

ENTRY REQUIREMENTS

Applicants for the RSPCA and the SSPCA need a good general education and a full, clean, current driving licence. They must pass a medical. The RSPCA requires applicants to be able to swim 50 metres fully clothed, be fit and able to take part in physical training, have animal-handling experience, and be prepared to relocate to any part of England and Wales after training. They must also have good inter-personal skills.

The SSPCA requires applicants to have had previous experience working with animals, preferably from a farm or veterinary background.

The minimum age for entry is 22 years for the RSPCA, or 25 years for the SSPCA.

TRAINING

RSPCA training lasts approximately six months. The course comprises an initial twelve to thirteen weeks' training at the Society's headquarters in Horsham, followed by six weeks' field training under the supervision of an experienced officer and a final five weeks' study at headquarters in Horsham.

Theoretical training covers such subjects as the law relating to animal welfare, animal injury and disease; investigative and interview techniques; court procedure; rescue techniques; humane slaughter; the work of animal clinics, hospitals and homes; report writing; and animal first aid, care and welfare instruction. Trainees must pass written exams. After training there is a one-year probationary period.

Training with the SSPCA usually lasts six months. Part of this is spent at the Society's headquarters in Edinburgh, part gaining field experience. As with the RSPCA, a final examination is necessary.

Successful trainees may be posted anywhere, and become permanent members of staff at the rank of inspector.

LATE ENTRY

All entrants are adults. The maximum age for entry to the RSPCA is normally 40 years, although applicants leaving HM Forces may be admitted up to the age of 42 years. The upper age limit for the SSPCA is 45 years. The SSPCA requires practical experience of work with animals, preferably farm animals. The RSPCA gives preference to applicants who have had experience working with the public. Experience of working with animals is not essential for the RSPCA, although it may be an advantage. Experience may be gained in veterinary practices, farming, kennels, etc.

OPPORTUNITIES

The RSPCA employs around 300 inspectors; the SSPCA employs around 45 inspectors who cover the whole of Scotland apart from the city of Aberdeen and county of Aberdeenshire (which are the responsibility of a small, local society).

Competition for available posts is severe. The RSPCA receives several hundred applications every year for around 24 vacancies. The SSPCA has about two vacancies a year and receives 20 to 30 applicants a week.

PAY AND CONDITIONS

Trainee inspectors with the RSPCA receive a basic salary of £9,441. Experienced inspectors are paid on a scale from £11,328 to £13,304. Field chief inspectors earn from £14,081 to £15,283. Trainees with the SSPCA receive a basic salary of £10,944, rising to £15,408.

Inspectors also receive allowances for unsocial hours, overtime payments, accommodation allowances, uniforms and shoe allowances where applicable. RSPCA Inspectors working in or around London receive an additional supplement.

Inspectors work Monday to Friday, 9am to 6pm (RSPCA) or 8.30am to 5pm (SSPCA) with weekends, plus emergency call-out duties. Working hours can, therefore, be very long and irregular.

PROSPECTS

Inspectors may receive promotion to higher grades. Some RSPCA inspectors move into specialist work at the headquarters in Horsham, investigating matters such as the transport and slaughter of livestock in the UK and EU, or illegal blood sports.

RELATED OCCUPATIONS

Veterinary nurse, kennel worker, zoo keeper, countryside ranger/warden, guide dog trainer/mobility instructor.

FURTHER INFORMATION

The Royal Society for the Prevention of Cruelty to Animals*, Causeway, Horsham, West Sussex RH12 1HG, 01403 264181

The Scottish Society for the Prevention of Cruelty to Animals*, Braehead Mains, 603 Queensferry Road, Edinburgh EH4 6EA, 0131 339 0222

FURTHER READING

Leaflets/booklets are available from the addresses marked*.

Job Outlines – Work with Animals – COIC
Working in Work with Animals – COIC
Careers Working with Animals – Kogan Page

In the careers library classified under WAL.

1. **GUIDE DOG TRAINER/MOBILITY INSTRUCTOR CLCI:WAM**
2. **KENNEL WORKER CLCI:WAM**
3. **DOG GROOMER CLCI:WAM**
4. **HORSE GROOM CLCI:WAM**
5. **RIDING INSTRUCTOR CLCI:WAM**
6. **ZOO KEEPER CLCI:WAM**

BACKGROUND INFORMATION

Many people are very keen to work with animals. This leads to great competition for jobs. Every employer, from zoos to kennels to riding schools, is inundated with applications from young people.

Looking after animals all day is very different from caring for family pets. The work is hard, often dirty, with long, unsocial hours. Some jobs can be very lonely, with only the companionship of animals for much of the day. However, there will usually be some contact with people – owners, customers, the general public – and, in several jobs outlined in these articles, skills in dealing with people are important.

In addition, jobs with animals are rarely well paid. Careers with the animal organizations, or in research, offer salaries that compare favourably with those in some other jobs, and some of the larger commercial establishments pay reasonable wages, but rates of pay with the small privately owned concerns can be very low indeed. Profits in the animal care business are not large, and employers cannot afford high wages.

The jobs described here are all different, but they all have certain similar requirements. Anyone interested in a career with animals must be fit, healthy, unsentimental and not allergic to fur and fluff. There is always some risk of picking up an infection from the animals. The most popular jobs are those with dogs and horses.

1. GUIDE DOG TRAINER/MOBILITY INSTRUCTOR (WAM)

BACKGROUND INFORMATION

The Guide Dogs for the Blind Association was formed in 1931 to train guide dogs and their new owners to work together. Most guide dog owners regard their dogs as an extension of themselves, enabling them to do all the everyday things sighted people take for granted: shopping, walking to work, crossing roads and using public transport. Owners and dogs are matched very carefully, and are helped to form a good working partnership.

About half of the guide dogs currently used are crosses between labradors and golden retrievers, although other breeds are also used.

Young puppies are placed with families, known as puppy walkers, who take care of them for a year, getting them accustomed to home life, public transport and busy streets. Young adult dogs then go to one of the Association's regional centres where they are placed with guide dog trainers for training. During their training at the centre, the dogs live in kennels. When the dogs are ready, usually after about six months, they are handed over to guide dog mobility instructors who carry out advanced training, and then train dogs and owners together for four weeks.

THE WORK

Guide dog trainers begin to work with the dogs when they leave their puppy walkers and come to the regional centre. At first they help the dogs to settle in, spending the first few weeks taking them for pleasure walks and assessing their suitability for training. After about three weeks, proper training begins.

Dogs are first taught to walk in the centre of the pavement and to obey simple commands – 'Forward', 'Left', 'Back', etc. They then learn to sit at every kerb and not to cross if traffic is approaching. Next they are introduced to wearing a harness and begin more specialized training, learning obstacle avoidance. Dogs learn that when they are in harness they are working; when not in harness they are as free as any other family dog.

All the time the trainer is building up close communication with the dog – praising it and teaching it to respond to voice and hand. Before handing the dog on to the mobility instructor, the trainer spends some time wearing a blindfold whilst working with the dog.

The **guide dog mobility instructor** takes over the training in the last few months before the dog meets its owner. More advanced guiding skills are taught, such as shoulder work – helping the person handling it to get through a crowd without bumping into people. Dogs are then carefully matched with their new owners. An elderly retired person for example, has different requirements from a younger person still at work with a more active social life. Visually impaired people spend a month at the centre and are taught, in groups of four owners and dogs to an instructor, how to get to know and work with their animal. Instructors encourage the owners to have confidence in their dogs, and to work in gradually more complicated situations. They teach owners how to handle their animals correctly, without damaging the training that has already been given.

After the owners and dogs have gone home they are visited by a guide dog mobility instructor. The instructor makes further visits periodically to provide support and help with any problems.

WORK ENVIRONMENT

Both trainers and instructors spend most of their working hours outdoors, in all weathers.

SKILLS AND INTERESTS

Instructors and trainers need to be physically fit and prepared to work for long hours at a time. They need good physical co-ordination, a great deal of patience and, of course, a love of animals.

Instructors need to be good with people too. They must be able to sympathize with the fears of a visually impaired person about to receive a guide dog, and to sort-out any worries and apprehensions. They must be able to establish good relationships with people and, as teachers, know when to be firm. A sense of humour often helps.

ENTRY REQUIREMENTS

Guide dog trainers – entry requirements are three GCSEs/S grades (A-C/1-3) including English and maths and a science subject or equivalent. The minimum age is 18 years.

Guide dog mobility instructors – entry requirements are five GCSEs/S grades (A-C/1-3) including English, maths, a science subject and preferably a social science subject. Minimum age is 18 years.

A full driving licence is essential for both types of work.

Experience of handling dogs or other animals is also required, as is work or social experience with adults from various backgrounds.

TRAINING

Guide dog trainers join the Association as training entrants, spending two months learning basic dog care skills, in kennels. They then spend eleven months working towards the guide dog trainer qualification. All training is carried out by qualified Association staff at the regional centres, and all trainees are paid. Guide dog trainers work towards a City and Guilds qualification (guide dog trainer).

Guide dog mobility instructors serve a three-year apprenticeship. This is modular, and culminates in the Guide Dogs for the Blind Association's guide dog mobility qualification.

LATE ENTRY

Applications from older candidates are encouraged, since previous work experience is often valuable, especially if in a caring role or one working with animals. This experience may have been gained in either a paid or voluntary capacity.

OPPORTUNITIES

Between 16 and 20 apprentice guide dog mobility instructors are engaged each year. Guide dog trainers are engaged on an ongoing basis; however, there tend to be waiting lists for such positions. The Association receives around 100 enquiries every week from people interested in a career with guide dogs.

Employment is at The Guide Dogs for the Blind regional training centres at Middlesborough, Bolton, Leamington Spa, Redbridge, Wokingham, Exeter, Forfar in Scotland, and the breeding centre at Tollgate, Warwickshire. There are also smaller support centres at Maidstone, Nottingham, Southampton, Liverpool, Sheffield, Cardiff, Belfast and Larkhall, Scotland.

PAY AND CONDITIONS

Guide dog trainers commence on £8,340, rising to £11,120 on qualifying (after a minimum of 13 months). The maximum salary is £13,676 reached by annual increments. Hours of work are 35 a week.

Apprentice guide dog mobility instructors commence on £12,247 rising to £16,330 on qualifying (after a minimum of 37 months). The maximum salary is £19,499. Guide dog mobility instructors work an average of 35 hours a week, but this includes weekends and bank holidays whilst training students with dogs. However, time off in lieu is given.

A six-month 'living in' period is compulsory for all new guide dog trainers and instructors, during which time food and accommodation are provided free of charge at the centre. After this period, accommodation is sometimes available, subject to appropriate charges and availability.

PROSPECTS

There are opportunities for dog trainers to be promoted to senior guide dog trainer or puppy walking supervisor. Guide dog mobility instructors may be promoted to supervisory and managerial posts.

RELATED OCCUPATIONS

Veterinary nurse, horse riding instructor, animal technician, dog groomer, kennel worker, farm worker, RSPCA/SSPCA inspector, zoo keeper.

FURTHER INFORMATION

Please see article 2. KENNEL WORKER.

FURTHER READING

Please see article 6. ZOO KEEPER.

2. KENNEL WORKER (WAM)

BACKGROUND INFORMATION

Kennels vary in size, some employing very few staff and others having several hundred dogs to look after. The latter are more likely to have managers, experienced kennel workers and trainees on the staff.

THE WORK

The work is hard and often dirty. Typical daily duties in all kennels include: cleaning out the kennels and changing bedding; exercising the dogs; checking for illness – dealing with minor ailments personally, or sending for the vet; preparing meals; mixing special diets; and cleaning and grooming the dogs. From time to time kennel staff may also have to stay up all night with a bitch about to produce a litter. Those with hunt kennels may act as 'whippers-in', learning to train and control hounds.

Dogs may be in kennels for very short periods, in which case there is little chance to get to know them. But in various charities' kennels, staff may have cared for a dog for several months and come to know it well before it is handed over to a new owner. There will also be some contact with people.

Staff in some kennels meet prospective buyers and show them round; in others they may also have to advise customers on animal care. Kennel staff employed at training centres of the Guide Dogs for the Blind Association are expected to talk to and get to know the visually impaired who have come to train with their dogs.

WORK ENVIRONMENT

This is largely outdoor work, exercising and feeding the animals, often in the cold and wet. Conditions can be dirty and smelly.

SKILLS AND INTERESTS

Kennel workers must love and care for dogs. They need to be hard-working and dedicated to the job.

An unsentimental love of animals is needed, and, because of the nature of some of the duties, staff should not be squeamish.

Kennel workers require a firm but gentle manner and need to be able to handle all sizes and types of dogs. They need patience and the ability to encourage and calm nervous dogs.

The work requires a sense of responsibility and the ability to work without supervision and as part of a team.

Good health and physical fitness are essential; the work is physically demanding and active.

ENTRY REQUIREMENTS

Entry is possible without formal qualifications, although GCSEs/S grades (A-C/1-3) are an advantage.

There are no set entry requirements for BTEC first diploma courses, although colleges may require one to two GCSEs/S grades (A-C/1-3). For BTEC national certificate/diploma courses entry requirements are four GCSEs/S grades (A-C/1-3) or equivalent, preferably including maths and a science subject.

Some private schools ask for GCSEs/S grades (A-C/1-3) in English, biology and maths.

The Guide Dogs for the Blind Association requires applicants for kennel work to be over 18 years old, with GCSEs/S grades (A-C/1-3) in English and maths, or equivalent.

TRAINING

Training is generally given on the job, but there are also some full-time and part-time courses at colleges of further education and private training schools.

On-the-job training in private kennels involves practical experience, supervised by the owner or manager. Young people often enter work in private kennels via training schemes for young people (contact your local careers office, TEC/LEC for details). Trainees may be able to take part-time courses at local colleges, leading to NVQs/SVQs in Animal Care at Levels 1 and 2. Alternatively, they may take an open learning course, run by the Animal Care College and Canine Studies Institute.

Animal Care NVQs/SVQs at Levels 3 and 4 are currently being developed. Level 3 may be available from autumn 1996.

BTEC First Certificate/Diploma in Animal Care (generally one year, full-time, although some part-time courses are available) are offered by a number of colleges including Bishop Burton College of Agriculture, North East Surrey College of Technology, Cambridgeshire College of Agriculture and Horticulture, Carmarthenshire College of Technology and Art, Sparsholt College, Rodbaston College, Lancashire College of Agriculture and Horticulture, Pencoed College, Reaseheath College, Derbyshire College of Agriculture and Horticulture, Bicton College of Agriculture, Dorset College of Agriculture and Horticulture, Gloucestershire College of Agriculture, West Sussex College of Agriculture and Horticulture (Brinsbury College), and the College of Animal Welfare (Godmanchester, Cambridge).

BTEC National Diploma in Animal Care (usually two years, full-time) are available at Bicton College of Agriculture, Gloucestershire College of Agriculture, Sparsholt College, Bishop Burton College of Agriculture, Lancashire College of Agriculture and Horticulture, Pencoed College, and Rodbaston College, Staffordshire.

Training is also provided by private training schools attached to boarding kennels. Private training schools, which operate on a fee-paying basis, should be chosen with care.

Charitable and voluntary organizations, such as the Guide Dogs for the Blind Association, usually provide full-time training for their own staff.

The Animal Care College/Canine Studies Institute offers a variety of open learning courses covering various aspects of the care of dogs and other small animals.

LATE ENTRY

Late entry is unusual. The rates of pay for a trainee are not attractive, and unless capital is available to staff one's own kennels, prospects are limited. However, there is no formal upper age limit provided that one is keen and physically fit.

OPPORTUNITIES

There are several different types of kennel:

Breeding kennels are often fairly small family businesses specializing in the breeding of one or two types of dog.

Boarding kennels are where owners leave their pets for any period from a weekend to several weeks whilst they are away on holiday or business.

Quarantine kennels– dogs brought into this country must spend six months in a kennel approved by the Ministry of Agriculture, Fisheries and Food to ensure that they are free from disease, particularly rabies.

Hunt kennels– hunting stables keep their own hounds and employ staff who act as kennel workers and 'whippers-in', training and controlling the hounds.

Racing kennels– greyhound kennels may be quite large with a trainer looking after groups of dogs and supervising one or two handlers.

Kennels maintained by animal welfare organizations– such as the RSPCA or the National Canine Defence League (NCDL). The RSPCA and NCDL care for strays and unwanted animals until they can be found a home.

There are also some opportunities in the **Armed Forces**.

Competition for vacancies with any of the above is very intense, with hundreds of people applying for very few posts. Vacancies are sometimes advertised in the specialist dog magazines. Preference is often given to those with experience of kennel work on a voluntary basis.

PAY AND CONDITIONS

Pay is variable, but can be up to £100 a week plus a bonus. In some establishments both pay and conditions can be very poor. Generally speaking, larger private establishments and charitable organizations tend to offer the best conditions, with set pay scales. Anyone applying for a job in kennels, particularly a training post, should try to choose an employer with a good reputation, and insist on a proper contract.

Kennel staff work unsocial hours including weekends and holidays. Boarding kennels are particularly busy in the summer holiday season and at Christmas and Easter.

PROSPECTS

Prospects for advancement are not good except in some of the larger establishments, where kennel staff may progress to kennel supervisor, assistant kennel manager or kennel manager. Many entrants aspire eventually to run their own kennels; this requires a lot of capital, experience and a head for business.

RELATED OCCUPATIONS

Guide dog trainer/mobility instructor, dog groomer, RSPCA/SSPCA inspector, farm worker, veterinary nurse, zoo keeper.

FURTHER INFORMATION

Animal Care College and Canine Studies Institute*, Ascot House, High Street, Ascot, Berkshire SL5 7JG, 01344 28269

College of Animal Welfare*, Woodgreen Animal Shelter, Kingsbush Farm, London Road, Godmanchester, Cambridge PE18 8LJ, 01480 831177

Guide Dogs for the Blind Association*, Hillfields, Burghfield Common, Reading, Berkshire RG7 3YG, 01734 835555

National Canine Defence League, 17-26 Wakley Street, London EC1V 7LT, 0171 837 0006

Royal Society for the Prevention of Cruelty to Animals (RSPCA)*, Causeway, Horsham, West Sussex RH12 1HG, 01403 264181

FURTHER READING

Please see article 6. ZOO KEEPER.

3. DOG GROOMER (WAM)

THE WORK

Dog groomers are concerned with dog trimming. They may also be known as dog or canine beauticians.

Many long and short-haired breeds of dog require the attention of dog groomers; poodles may be the best known but others include spaniels, terriers, Old English sheepdogs and Afghan hounds. Some dogs need trimming every six weeks, to keep their coats manageable.

The first task is clipping, for which the dog is usually placed on a table. Careful attention must be given when clipping delicate areas, particularly around the face, between the pads and over the paws. Clipping involves using electric clippers, though a stripping knife (similar to a razor) may be used for those breeds with an inner protective coat of thick hairs (such as West Highland White Terriers), which could be damaged by clippers.

The dog is then shampooed and rinsed, usually in a bath. Most are dried with a special stand electric hairdryer. The animal's coat is brushed or combed and a final trim with scissors completes the grooming.

In addition to trimming and bathing dogs, groomers provide other services which include nail clipping, teeth cleaning, ear cleaning and treatments for parasites. A dog groomer might expect to deal with around four to six dogs a day, depending on the attention the dogs require.

Some dog groomers prepare dogs for shows and competitions.

WORK ENVIRONMENT

Dog groomers work inside, usually based in a shop of some type. This may be a room adjoining a pet shop, part of a boarding kennel or breeder's premises, or a dog grooming salon. Some groomers work from their own homes and travel to owner's homes to give grooming services.

Working areas usually comprise a working table or bench, baths, sinks and kennels or places for dogs to wait between each stage of the process.

Much of the working day is spent standing. The atmosphere may be warm and humid.

SKILLS AND INTERESTS

In addition to liking animals, dog groomers must be able to handle dogs of all types. Talking to the animals while grooming can help to calm those that are nervous or agitated. Dog groomers should handle dogs with care and in a gentle manner. Manual dexterity is required for handling the equipment used in trimming and clipping. Accuracy when using clipping equipment is essential and great care is necessary to avoid injury to the animal.

Groomers should be able to work alone or as part of a team. The work may be considered creative to some extent; an eye for detail and good eye-to-hand co-ordination are important.

ENTRY REQUIREMENTS

There are no minimum educational requirements. Personal characteristics and practical ability are often considered more important than academic qualifications.

TRAINING

It is useful to have had some sort of experience in handling, bathing and grooming dogs before beginning training, though these skills can be learned during training. There are two main methods for training as a dog groomer: fee-paying course or traineeship. Training varies in quality and length.

Private fee-paying courses are available at a number of private training establishments and last anything from three months to one year, depending on the content of the course. The longer courses tend to include other aspects of dog care and give the student experience of different breeds of dog and types of cut and style. On completion of the course a certificate or diploma is usually awarded. A list of approved schools is available from the British Dog Groomers' Association.

Traineeships: many dog groomers learn their craft by joining established parlours or experienced groomers as juniors, or by learning the trade as part of general kennel work. Training is given on the job, although it may include off-the-job training, and lasts for around one to two years.

It is also possible to learn basic grooming as part of a full-time course in animal care – see article 2. KENNEL WORKER.

There may be opportunities for school-leavers to obtain places in salons via specific training schemes for young people. Contact your local careers offices, TECs/LECs for details.

Dog groomers may take the Dog Grooming Certificate 7750, which is a written paper and a series of skills tests developed by City and Guilds and the British Dog Groomers Association. It is recommended that entrants to the exam have had 18 months' to two years' experience.

LATE ENTRY

Entry on to fee-paying courses is equally open to adults and school-leavers. Mature candidates may find difficulty entering employment as trainees, since employers may tend to favour younger applicants.

There may be specific training opportunities directed at adults available in some areas for this type of work. Candidates may have to satisfy certain conditions to be eligible. Contact your local Jobcentre, careers office or TEC/LEC for details.

OPPORTUNITIES

There has been an increase in demand for the services of dog groomers in recent years. Many of the establishments traditionally providing services for or with animals, such as pet shops and boarding kennels, are offering grooming facilities as additional services.

However, the opportunities to work as a full-time dog groomer are limited and vary according to area, local demand and competition.

Demand for services may vary seasonally, as owners often let their dogs' coats grow in cold weather.

It may be difficult to find traineeship places and competition may be high for those that are available.

Vacancies may be advertised in *Our Dogs* and *Dog World*.

PAY AND CONDITIONS

Hours vary. In a shop, groomers usually work Monday to Saturday. Some groomers work weekends. Part-time work is possible.

It is not possible to give the wages of trainees or experienced dog groomers, since there are no national standards and most groomers are self-employed. Work with animals is sometimes poorly paid.

PROSPECTS

Having completed their training most dog groomers become self-employed, although some may continue to work for the employer that trained them. There are few, if any, opportunities for promotion for dog groomers.

RELATED OCCUPATIONS

Kennel worker, riding instructor, horse groom, horse breeding stud assistant/groom, jockey/stablehand, guide dog trainer/mobility instructor, RSPCA/SSPCA inspector, veterinary nurse.

FURTHER INFORMATION

British Dog Groomers' Association/Pet Care Trust*, 170 Mile Road, Bedford MK42 9TW, 01234 273933

FURTHER READING

Please see article 6. ZOO KEEPER

4. HORSE GROOM (WAM)

THE WORK

The daily routine for grooms varies according to the type and size of stable and level of the groom's skill. The basic tasks, however, are mucking out, quartering, sometimes exercising, grooming, rugging, watering, feeding and bedding down.

First thing in the morning the groom inspects the horses, making sure they have suffered no injury during the night, have finished their late night feed, hay and water. They are then usually given fresh water and a small feed, are mucked out and given a day bed. When this is done, the horse is brushed over quickly and stable stains removed with a water brush. The mane is laid – brushed out and set on the correct side and dampened with the water brush. A tail bandage is usually applied, the feet oiled and the horse is then ready for either its owner or the stable staff to exercise it.

Grooms exercise horses mainly by riding at a brisk walk, trot or canter, and they may also lead a second horse at the same time. Daily exercise rides last for around an hour.

After exercise, the horse is fully groomed – sometimes called strapping. This is done while the horse is still warm and the pores are open. It takes 30-45 minutes to groom a horse properly.

Other duties usually include tacking up, fitting riding tack, which includes a variety of bridles, head collars, halters, saddles, etc. Grooms must be able to fit this equipment correctly, avoiding any risk of injury to the horse (or rider). In addition, tack is regularly cleaned to maintain a good condition, preventing mould and perishing, and checked for wear, especially in the stitching.

Grooms may use a variety of tools to clip and trim the horse's coat or hair. Clipping machines are used on the main body, and different types of clip are used according to how the horse is to be worked. Trimming can be with scissors and comb.

Additional duties include attending to sick or injured animals. Grooms may treat minor wounds and keep basic health records. When the veterinary surgeon is called the groom must closely follow directions and provide relevant information about the horse's condition. The nursing that follows may include taking and recording temperature, pulse and respiration, administering medicines, etc.

General knowledge about horse shoeing is essential, such as the fact that special shoes are used in particular cases. Grooms must know shoeing procedure and how to remove broken or twisted shoes.

WORK ENVIRONMENT

Duties involve working outdoors in all weather. Horses must be attended to every day, all the year round, and this can mean working in extremely cold and wet conditions. In addition, mucking out and cleaning the yard are often dirty/smelly jobs. Physical fitness is required and there can be much bending, climbing, lifting and carrying involved in the work. Some duties, such as grooming, are quite strenuous.

Due to the nature of the work, and because stables are often in remote areas, grooms often live-in and may share meals, household chores, etc. Working with horses, in many respects, is more a way of life than a job.

Grooms may travel, to competitions, for example, and spend time away from home.

SKILLS AND INTERESTS

Grooms must genuinely love and care for horses. It is essential that grooms are fit and have the stamina to endure long hours of hard physical work for modest rewards in terms of pay. A degree of strength is also required for some of the duties, such as lifting bales of hay and grooming.

Practical hand skills are necessary and great care must be taken when performing some of the more delicate tasks, such as trimming and bandaging. Grooms should be observant and notice any changes in a horse's condition. A responsible attitude is required. Intricately plaiting manes and grooming for competitions, shows, and so on, requires patience and attention to detail. The groom must also be able to work quickly and remain calm when under pressure, particularly on competition days.

Clear spoken communication skills are important for speaking to customers, vets, etc. Legible handwriting is required for record-keeping and writing messages. Grooms need basic arithmetic for tasks such as measuring feeds.

It is not necessary that grooms are exceptional riders but they should be confident and competent.

ENTRY REQUIREMENTS

Formal educational qualifications are not required for entry to work as a groom. Employers, the organizations offering formal qualifications for grooms, ie the British Horse Society (BHS) and Association of British Riding Schools (ABRS), and colleges do not ask for academic qualifications. However, candidates should have a good basic education.

Some knowledge of biology is essential, to understand how the horse's body functions and how to keep the animal in a healthy condition. Experience of working with horses is useful, and may be required.

Entrants for British Horse Society (BHS) exams must be BHS members. The minimum age for BHS Horse Knowledge and Riding exams including the BHS Grooms Certificate is 16 years, 17 years for the third stage, and 20 years for the fourth stage.

The minimum age for the ABRS Preliminary Horse Care and Riding Certificate Levels 1 and 2 is 16 years. It is open to candidates who are in full-time training or employment with horses. The ABRS Grooms Certificate is open to those with practical experience in the handling and care of a variety of horses. The ABRS Grooms Diploma is open to holders of the ABRS Grooms Certificate and a current First Aid Certificate, and who are 18 years or over. They must also have a wide knowledge and experience of a great variety of horses, and be capable of organizing and supervising other staff.

Individuals normally provide their own riding clothing/ protective headgear.

A driving licence is useful/required for some jobs.

TRAINING

There are a number of recognized qualifications for grooms and, although qualification is not necessarily required, those with awards may have improved chances of employment.

Qualifications include:

– NVQs/SVQs in Horse Care at Levels 1 and 2 and Level 3 in Horse Care and Management.

– NVQs/SVQs are also available in Racehorse Care at Level 2 and Race Horse Care and Management at Level 3.

British Horse Society (BHS)

BHS offers exams in Horse Knowledge and Care in four stages:

Stage I: students are tested on their understanding of the basic principles of horse care. They must show, working under supervision, knowledge and practice of caring for a horse in the stable and at grass.

Stage II: entrants must have passed Stage I and the BHS Riding Road Safety Test. They must understand the general management and requirements of horses and should be able to work under regular but not constant supervision. Candidates need to show a higher standard of efficiency in knowledge and practical ability.

Stage III: applicants must have passed Stages I and II Horse Knowledge and Care. Candidates must show that they are able to care for up to four horses in stables and at grass, and pass a written test. Success in Stage III leads to the award of Groom's Certificate.

Stage IV: candidates are of a more advanced level and must be capable of taking charge, without supervision, of a group of horses of various types. Success in Stage IV leads to the award of Intermediate Stable Manager's Certificate.

An advanced qualification – BHS Stable Manager – is available for experienced candidates aged 22 years and over who possess the Intermediate Stable Manager's Certificate. The senior BHS qualification is The BHS Fellowship Examination, the minimum age for entry to which is 25 years.

Association of British Riding Schools

Preliminary Horse Care and Riding Certificate Levels 1 and 2: this exam is designed to show that a young groom is competent in the basic skills but must work under supervision.

ABRS Grooms Certificate: this exam is designed to show the practical ability of grooms working basically on their own, but with some supervision.

ABRS Grooms Diploma: those holding this qualification have wide knowledge and experience with horses, and are able to work without supervision, and, if required, supervise the work of other staff.

No written papers are required for any of the ABRS examinations, and there is no requirement that candidates must be members of the Association. All exams are a day in duration, and are of a practical nature.

Formal training methods for grooms

Training schemes for young people: school-leavers may gain work experience and training as grooms via specific training schemes. Most training is on employers' premises, with an element of off-the-job training. Some courses are based at colleges of agriculture; these include work placements. There is no guarantee of a full-time job on completion of training; however, trainees are generally preferred by employers to those without experience. Candidates may have the opportunity to enter for BHS or ABRS exams.

Working pupils: training is offered to young people by employers and in return the trainee works at the school/ centre. There may be opportunities for taking recognized BHS/ABRS qualifications. Terms and conditions vary and the BHS and ABRS advise that employers and pupils should agree a contract covering aspects such as duties, hours, rules, holidays, training, approximate date of exams and financial arrangements. Pupils do not usually receive a wage and may have to pay contributions towards accommodation and meals.

Fee-paying students: riding schools run courses to train students for examinations. These can be fairly intensive, of three to twelve months' duration. However, fees can be very high and, although pass rates are also fairly good, they are not guaranteed.

Private study: individuals may prepare for BHS/ABRS exams in their own time. The difficulty is in gaining the required practical or work experience, and achieving a sufficiently high standard without coaching.

LATE ENTRY

Individuals of any age may become grooms. Traditionally, it has been a career pursued by young people of 16-18 years. However, this is changing, and employers are now looking towards employing more mature people.

Part-time employment with horses is common for older people.

OPPORTUNITIES

Grooms are employed at all types of stable/equestrian centre:

Riding schools – there are many schools situated throughout the country. Most employ grooms, although smaller stables may use instructors to perform the groom's duties.

Polo stables – polo is an amateur sport played in the summer season from April to September. Grooms are employed to prepare ponies for games – grooming, plaiting manes, bandaging/booting legs, etc. During the game they ensure a change of mount is ready and attend to ponies coming off the field – take tack off, rub down, etc. They also attend to minor injuries. Many grooms are employed on a seasonal basis although a skeleton staff may be kept on during the winter. Some polo players tour overseas and grooms accompany them.

Hunting stables – grooms may be known as 'strappers' and can be employed during the hunting season which runs from October to March. Horses spend the summer out in paddocks, but a small number of grooms are employed all year round to exercise horses and ensure fitness for the season. During a hunt, grooms may prepare fresh horses to change to at a given rendezvous, and deal with tired horses.

Competition stables – individuals keeping horses for showjumping, dressage, showing, eventing, and so on, employ grooms at their stables to care for and exercise their horses. The work can involve travelling overseas with the top riders and teams.

Livery stables – look after horses for those owners who do not have their own stables. Riding schools often accept a number of livery horses.

Private stables – private individuals who keep horses in their own stables usually employ at least one groom.

Trekking centres and riding holiday hotels – seasonal work is available for grooms during summer months to care for horses, lead treks, etc.

Other opportunities – a limited number of grooms may be employed in circuses, zoos (pony departments) and in stud and breeding establishments.

Vacancies may be held by local careers offices and Jobcentres. Vacancies may also be advertised in the local newspapers. Yellow Pages should provide a list of local employers.

Vacancies for jobs and training courses are advertised in the equestrian magazines – *Horse and Hound, Pony, Riding*. There are also a number of employment agencies that deal solely with vacancies for stable staff.

There are a number of opportunities to work overseas, for which a second language can be an advantage.

PAY AND CONDITIONS

Rates of pay vary enormously, making it difficult to give meaningful figures. Accommodation, meals and training received are usually taken into account when calculating wages.

A 40-hour week is usual, but extra hours may be required on competition or event days. Hours may be spread over seven days, sometimes involving early starts, but in general a five-and-a-half day week is a planned target.

Working with horses involves a certain amount of risk of injury. Grooms should ensure in their contract that they are covered by employers' liability insurance. They are also advised to take out personal accident insurance.

PROSPECTS

Grooms may improve their qualifications by taking ABRS and British Horse Society qualifications up to stable-manager standard. Minimum age for entry to the BHS Stable Manager examination is 22 years. This is an advanced qualification for those experienced in all aspects of horse care. Holders will also be capable of organizing and running a stable – planning, staffing, construction, stocking, purchasing, book-keeping, etc. Additional qualifications may help the groom achieve senior and/or better jobs.

Some employers have a hierarchy that allows progression to head groom for the experienced and capable. Other grooms may improve their position by changing employers.

RELATED OCCUPATIONS

Horse breeding stud assistant/groom, riding instructor, jockey/stablehand, kennel worker, veterinary nurse, zoo keeper, farrier, farm worker.

FURTHER INFORMATION

Please see article 5. RIDING INSTRUCTOR.

FURTHER READING

Please see article 6. ZOO KEEPER.

5. RIDING INSTRUCTOR (WAM)

THE WORK

Instructors teach skills and techniques to a wide range of people, from beginners to experts, and help them to develop their performance techniques and abilities. They may work with highly skilled professional riders or solely with beginners. The qualification level of instructors, such as British Horse Society Assistant, Intermediate or Full Instructor standard, affects the type of work they carry out. Only very experienced and exceptionally skilled trainers work with top-level riders.

Instructing professionals: an instructor may be responsible for coaching a team of riders. This involves ensuring that individual talents are used to greatest effect and appropriate team tactics are employed. Individuals must be moulded and encouraged into a unit, co-operating as a team. It also involves assessing the strengths and weaknesses of opposing competitors and planning strategies with their riders. The instructor works closely with the team manager determining who will ride in particular events, etc.

Instructing amateurs: instruction is given in rudimentary techniques – mounting the horse correctly, riding with good seat and position, etc. Many pursue the sport as a recreation; others want to develop their abilities seriously and get involved in high-level competitions. Much of the work is concerned with children, including children with disabilities, and good teaching skills are essential. One of the most important aspects is to ensure that participants are trained safely. Bad techniques can result in injury, and great care must be taken to make certain that riders know their own capabilities.

Instructors must take command, particularly in cases of emergency.

Developing a training programme, aiming for the highest possible level of mental and physical fitness for competition riders, can prove difficult when riding is a part-time activity and there are other demands on riders' time. Instructors must be prepared to pass their trainees on to other instructors more able to help them fulfil their potential.

Instructing involves giving trainees oral directions and also giving practical demonstrations. Instructors should observe performances, identify problems and organize training to overcome weaknesses. They must also provide interesting and varied ways of practising the same activity time after time. It is important that a participant's skills are developed gradually, with progression from one level of competition to the next at their own pace.

In addition to preparing riders for showjumping, dressage, eventing, and so on, the instructor must also be fully conversant with the rules and regulations of competitions.

Horse schooling and care. As well as instructing people, the riding instructor is responsible for schooling horses. Similar skills are required. A training programme of practice and exercises must be devised to organize the breaking and obedience of the horse to a rider's command. The instructor prepares a fitness programme according to the condition of the horse. When training or exercising, the instructor may lunge the horse using a rein designed for the purpose, and as with any equipment/tack, safe use is essential to avoid injury to the horse. Observation, leading to early detection of problems, can benefit both horse and rider; the instructor can then prepare practice that concentrates on the areas needing attention.

Instructors, at all grades, often have responsibility for a number of horses and/or ponies. This involves making sure that they are watered, fed and groomed each day, exercised regularly, and that bedding/stables are kept clean. Tack – saddles, bridles, harnesses, and so on – must also be checked and cleaned to ensure a good condition is maintained.

Pupils are taught how to care for the horse, as well as riding skills.

WORK ENVIRONMENT

Instructors may be involved in work inside at times – large centres may have facilities for indoor training during winter months – but most of their duties are undertaken outdoors, and in all weathers.

Mucking out, stable and yard duties can be dirty and smelly jobs. There may be a significant amount of travelling involved, accompanying pupils to gymkhanas, showjumping competitions and other events. Some freelance instructors travel to work at different schools and centres. Travelling can require short and long stays away from home. At top levels, instructors may go abroad with competitors.

Due to the nature of the work, early morning starts and stables located in remote areas, instructors often live in and to some extent become part of the family, sharing meals, household chores, etc.

Instructors often work alone with their pupils; however, it is also necessary to liaise with other people, such as vets and farriers.

SKILLS AND INTERESTS

The work is both physically and mentally demanding and requires the stamina to endure long hours of hard work. Physical fitness is essential for carrying out many of the daily tasks and a degree of strength is also necessary, for grooming horses and lifting bales of hay, for example.

Instructors teach people of all ages from a variety of backgrounds. Much of the work is often with children. Patience and good communication skills are required. They should be able to give oral instructions clearly.

Instructors should be able to assess and motivate people: some may respond best to encouragement and gentle persuasion; with others, a firm approach may bring results. The difficult task of getting riders to persevere during the bad times is as important as being able to motivate a good performer to continue to work to maintain form or strive to improve.

Instructors are also concerned with schooling horses and must apply similar skills to teaching the animals, as to teaching the riders. Patience, tolerance and self-control are essential. The horse must be kept physically fit and healthy, and trained to a high standard. Some understanding and appreciation of horse psychology is demanded.

It is important that instructors can establish discipline and keep control of situations. They may need to act quickly without panic in a crisis, and should be able to anticipate the actions of both horse and rider.

Instructors need not be exceptional performers but must have enough riding expertise to inspire confidence.

Self-employed instructors need knowledge of business management. A knowledge of book-keeping, accounting and secretarial skills would be advantageous.

ENTRY REQUIREMENTS

Riding instructors do not necessarily have to be qualified and, therefore, formal academic qualifications are not required. However, most instructors are qualified and hold British Horse Society qualifications at Assistant, Intermediate, Instructor or Fellow standard. Entry, for candidates under 18 years, to the Assistant Instructor's Preliminary Teaching Test examinations is with a minimum of four GCSEs/S grades (A-C/1-3), or equivalent. Subjects must include English. To enter the test, candidates must have passed the BHS Stage II examination.

Entry requirements for college courses vary, but there are no set minimum academic requirements for BTEC first certificate/diploma courses. Some riding experience is normally required. For BTEC national diploma courses, the usual requirement is four GCSEs/S grades (A-C/1-3) or equivalent.

For the BHS Assistant Instructor award, candidates must be aged at least 17 years 6 months, and for the Intermediate Instructor award 20 years. The minimum age of entry to the BHS Instructor's exam is 22 years. For the Fellowship exam candidates must be at least 25 years.

There is no minimum age for the ABRS Initial Teaching Award. For the ABRS Teaching Certificate, the minimum age at which the exam may be taken is 19 years.

Individuals are normally expected to provide their own riding clothing and protective headgear.

A driving licence is useful.

TRAINING

Although riding instructors are not required to be qualified, most are, and those with awards have far higher prospects for employment and promotion.

The British Horse Society (BHS) runs examinations leading to nationally recognized qualifications. Professional qualifications for riding instructors are as follows:

BHS Assistant Instructor: there are four examinations

leading to this qualification – Stages I to III of the BHS Horse Knowledge and Riding examinations (please see article 4. HORSE GROOM) and the BHS Preliminary Teaching Test. Assistant instructors are qualified to work in a stable yard and teach basic riding and stable management.

BHS Intermediate Instructor: this is achieved by passing the BHS Horse Knowledge and Riding examination Stage IV and the BHS Intermediate Teaching examination. Candidates must also hold a British Red Cross, St John's Ambulance or recognized equivalent First Aid Certificate. The Intermediate Instructor's award requires a high standard of horsemanship and teaching, and the instructor should be able to work without supervision.

BHS Instructor's Certificate: this is awarded to candidates who hold the Intermediate Instructor's Certificate and pass two examinations: the BHS Stable Manager's Examination and the BHS Equitation and Teaching Examination. The Instructor's Certificate is the main BHS professional qualification.

BHS Fellowship Certificate: this is a senior qualification, for which candidates must demonstrate an advanced knowledge of equitation and horsemanship.

The Association of British Riding Schools (ABRS) offers two teaching qualifications: the ABRS Initial Teaching Award and the ABRS Teaching Certificate. The ABRS Initial Teaching Award is a foundation qualification for those who are capable of teaching at a basic level in a riding school. The ABRS Teaching Certificate is a more advanced qualification for teachers with greater experience. Both examinations are of a practical nature, and no written papers are required. An ABRS Teacher's Helper Certificate and Advanced Teaching Diploma are being developed.

NVQs/SVQs Levels 1 and 2 in Horse Care, and Level 3 in Horse Care and Management, are available, although there are no NVQs/SVQs specifically for riding instructors.

Training for BHS/ABRS examinations

The main routes for training for BHS/ABRS qualifications include:

Working pupils: training is offered to young people by employers, riding schools and stable proprietors. In return the trainee works at the school or centre. This is a popular and economical way to train. Training for Assistant Instructor exams usually lasts for around one year depending on previous experience.

Fee-paying students: riding schools run courses to train students for exams and these can be fairly intensive, of three to twelve months' duration. However, fees can be very high and, although pass rates are also fairly good, there is no guarantee of passing the examinations.

Training schemes for young people: in many areas school-leavers have the opportunity to start a career with horses through these schemes.

Full-time college courses: a number of colleges offer courses leading to BHS awards, usually in the context of a BTEC first certificate/diploma or national diploma. They include: Cambridgeshire College of Agriculture and Horticulture, Sparsholt College, Bishop Burton College, Lancashire College of Agriculture and Horticulture, Brooksby College, Pencoed College, Askham Bryan College, Writtle College, Duchy College of Agriculture and Horticulture, Bicton College, Gloucestershire College of Agriculture, Coleg Glynllifon, Otley College of Agriculture and Horticulture, Craven College, Moulton College, Myerscough College, West Oxfordshire College, Walford College of Agriculture, Cannington College, Hartpury College, and Warwickshire College. In Scotland, colleges offering full-time courses leading to BHS awards and SCOTVEC national certificate modules in subjects such as equitation and horse care include: Oatridge Agricultural College, Aberdeen College, Thurso and Borders.

Private study: individuals may study and prepare for BHS exams in their own time. The BHS will provide their syllabuses (priced).

LATE ENTRY

People of any age can become riding instructors. Most instructors are qualified and the BHS may waive the academic qualifications required for entry to exams for older applicants. There are no upper age restrictions for entry to BHS or ABRS exams.

Employers tend to favour young applicants/school-leavers for this type of work. Mature candidates should be active and outdoor people, with the physical fitness and stamina required for the work.

OPPORTUNITIES

Horse riding is becoming increasingly popular, and the number of riding schools is growing. There is a reasonable number of jobs for qualified instructors of all standards. However, there are more candidates for suitable jobs than there are vacancies.

Some of the work is seasonal and employers often require experienced instructors who can work without supervision. This is particularly the case with those employed by private stables, and so on, and they are also often required to undertake groom duties. In addition, instructors employed by trekking centres are usually qualified or pass a company training course.

There are very few jobs for work with top-level competitors; the competition for any vacancies is extremely intense.

Riding instructors are employed at all the following types of stable/equestrian centre:

Riding schools: many qualified instructors work at schools that are situated throughout the country. Some small schools employ an instructor to work as an instructor/groom. Opportunities for qualified instructors are good.

Competition stables: individuals keeping horses for showjumping, dressage, showing, eventing, and so on, may employ instructors as grooms and to exercise their horses. The work can involve travelling overseas with the top riders and teams. Very few instructors, and only those who are highly successful, train horses and riders at the top levels.

Private stables: private individuals who keep horses in their own stables may employ an instructor, often to carry out grooming duties. Instructors may be preferred, for example, when there are children in the family to be instructed in riding.

Pony trekking centres and riding holiday hotels: seasonal work is available during summer months for instructors, as trek leaders. Experienced instructors may be employed, or some work freelance and provide services for a number of riding establishments.

For self-employment, individuals need to be established and should have had a degree of success with riders, as well as having business skills. Some instructors buy and run their own riding schools; however, this requires a large capital investment.

Employment opportunities with commercial stables – using horses to show and/or make deliveries – and with the uniformed forces are extremely limited. The police may employ instructors who have been trained outside the force, at the discretion of the Chief Constable; however, this is very uncommon. Most instructors in mounted police sections are trained police officers who have specialized – progressing from work as a mounted police rider to instruction.

Vacancies for jobs and training courses are advertised in *Horse and Hound, Pony, Riding*. There are also a number of employment agencies that deal solely with vacancies for stable staff and instructors.

There are a number of opportunities to work and teach overseas. A second language can be helpful here.

PAY AND CONDITIONS

The British Horse Society issues guidelines to pay rates for people holding BHS qualifications. However, rates of pay vary enormously, making it very difficult to give any meaningful figures. In addition, instructors may receive accommodation, meals and further training at the employer's expense. Such provisions are usually taken into account in the payment of wages.

The guidelines suggest the following rates: Fellows of the Society (FBHS) – £20,000 to £25,000; BHS Instructor (BHSI) – £18,000 to £20,000; BHS Intermediate Instructor (BHII) – £9,000 to £15,000; BHS Assistant Instructor (BHSAI) – £6,000 to £9,000.

Wages for self-employed instructors depend on their experience, skill, success in attracting business, etc. Some can charge fairly high fees.

Working with horses involves a certain amount of risk of injury. Trainees and instructors should ensure that they are covered by employers' or their own insurance.

Many people want to take riding lessons outside usual working hours, in the evenings and at weekends. Instructors therefore tend to work unsocial hours. In addition, horses need regular attention – feeding, watering, etc – which may mean early morning and late evening duties.

Some schools have rotas for days off and for late night stable duties. In general, many instructors work long hours – up to 60 each week. Part-time work may be possible, especially for freelance instructors who find work with local riding establishments. In some types of work there are seasonal variations – pony trekking holidays offer opportunities for instructors during the summer months.

PROSPECTS

Once fully qualified, an instructor may find opportunities, with employers of large riding centres, to advance within the hierarchy to head or senior instructor.

Many instructors work freelance, dividing their time between a number of schools and clubs. It is possible – and an ultimate aim of some instructors – to open and run a riding school. As well as requiring a good deal of expertise and business knowledge, this demands a substantial capital investment to buy and equip the stables and horses.

There are other opportunities for good riding instructors; for example, they may become judges for showjumping or dressage competitions run by the British Show Jumping Association or British Horse Society. There is a small number of jobs in designing and setting up courses for different sorts of horseriding competition. Some instructors may be selected to become British Horse Society examiners.

An employer may allow an instructor to ride in shows and other events, and provide training and practice facilities. However, for even those with outstanding ability and use of the facilities of a school or stable, it is very difficult and also expensive to become a successful professional competitive rider.

RELATED OCCUPATIONS

Sports coach/instructor, guide dog trainer/mobility instructor, groom, horse racing jockey/stablehand, kennel worker, veterinary nurse, zoo keeper.

FURTHER INFORMATION

The Association of British Riding Schools*, Queen's Chambers, 38-40 Queen Street, Penzance, Cornwall TR18 4BH, 01736 69440

The British Horse Society, Training Office, Stoneleigh Park, Kenilworth, Warwickshire CV8 2LR, 01203 696697

FURTHER READING

Please see article 6. ZOO KEEPER.

6. ZOO KEEPER (WAM)

BACKGROUND INFORMATION

In Great Britain there are about 250 zoos, safari parks, bird collections and aquariums. The major collections, in terms of numbers of visitors, are at London, Whipsnade, Chester, Bristol, Edinburgh, and Paignton.

Smaller zoos tend to specialize.

Many zoos are involved in educational projects and in scientific research. They also help to ensure the survival of rare species by planning breeding programmes; indeed, it is often a matter of pride amongst zoo staff that most of the collection has been bred in captivity.

Zoos are run by zoological societies, charitable trusts, local authorities or private businesses.

THE WORK

An important part of the work is providing routine daily care for the zoo's animals. Keepers muck out and clean pens and cages. They prepare food which may involve, for instance, chopping up vegetables and adding vitamins. Some animals require hand feeding. Keepers also ensure that fresh water and clean bedding are available, and that animal houses are kept at the right level of temperature and humidity.

Keepers are responsible for checking the general health and condition of the animals in their care. They observe animals for signs of illness and injury, keep records of health, diet and behaviour, and assist vets when animals need treatment. If animals display aggression towards each other, keepers may try to intervene and separate them.

To ensure the safety of both animals and visitors, keepers make regular checks of fences and barriers for signs of wear or damage. They also prevent the public from feeding the animals or climbing the barriers. Other responsibilities include removing harmful or poisonous weeds from animal enclosures and, in smaller zoos, keeping paths and flowerbeds clean and tidy. At the end of each day, keepers check that animal quarters and public gates are securely locked.

Keepers usually come into contact with visitors and answer questions about the zoo and its collection. In some zoos they give talks or lectures, and participate in special events organized for schools and other groups.

In safari parks, the animals roam about in large enclosures and an important part of the keepers' work involves patrolling, in jeeps, to make sure that visitors are safe and do not behave irresponsibly – for instance, getting out of their cars and approaching animals, or even picnicking close to groups of lions or tigers. Keepers also deal with any accidents or vehicle breakdowns that occur.

An area of increasing importance in keepers' work is environmental enrichment – that is to say, making the conditions for the animals as near-natural as possible, combating the boredom of captivity, and enhancing their quality of life. This can involve such measures as varying feeding times and places (to prevent the animals becoming inured to a stereotyped routine), and providing toys, shelter from the public's gaze, and so on.

WORK ENVIRONMENT

Depending on the type of animals they care for, keepers may work indoors or may spend much of their time out of doors, in all weathers. Conditions can be wet, cold, dirty, muddy and smelly. Indoors, the atmosphere may be humid.

Keepers wear uniforms or overalls, provided by employers.

They may work alone, in pairs or in small teams, depending on the job in hand. Food preparation may be carried out as a group activity. Keepers work in pairs when entering enclosures containing dangerous animals.

SKILLS AND INTERESTS

Keepers need to be enthusiastic about animals, and able to convey their enthusiasm to visitors. A pleasant manner and good spoken communication skills are required for answering enquiries about the animals' background, habits, etc. An interest in geography is useful, to understand and convey information about animals' natural habitats.

It is important to be prepared to carry out hard physical work cleaning and mucking out pens and cages – in all weathers.

Keepers need to be patient with both animals and public. Reliability and punctuality are necessary; animals rely on a consistent routine.

Working with wild animals can be hazardous and it is essential for keepers to have a responsible attitude towards safety, and to adhere to codes governing safe working practices.

Physical fitness is required. The work is unsuitable for people with allergies to fur or hair, and for those with certain disabilities. Walking, standing, bending and some lifting (of sacks of animal feed, for instance) are required. Keepers must be prepared to be inoculated against various animal diseases.

ENTRY REQUIREMENTS

There are no set minimum educational entry requirements, but employers often prefer applicants with three to five GCSEs/S grades (A-C/1-3), including maths, English and a science subject. Geography, a foreign language and subjects indicating practical abilities are also useful.

Because entry is highly competitive, it is an advantage to

have had experience of voluntary work with animals. Experience in a zoo volunteer scheme is valuable for those who are interested in working in a zoo or in other jobs involving the care of animals. If voluntary zoo work is not available, then experience with animals in other settings, such as farms, kennels or stables, is also helpful.

Entry as a trainee is possible at 16 years, but some employers prefer more mature applicants and set a minimum age of 19 or 21 years (especially for work with large animals such as elephants).

In safari parks, a driving licence is essential.

TRAINING

Training on entry to zoo work involves practical experience in different departments, to enable trainee keepers to gain experience with a range of animals.

They receive on-the-job training from other members of staff and study for the City and Guilds Certificate in Zoo Animal Management (C&G 7630), which is available as a correspondence course run by the National Extension College, Cambridge. The course consists of study units, assignments and a project. It takes about two years to complete, on a part-time basis. Employers may pay tuition fees and allow for some study to take place during working hours.

The course has the following four elements:

1. Introduction: reasons for the existence of zoos; record-keeping, finance and management; housing and zoo design; nutrition and diet; safety, hygiene, restraint and transport; breeding; and animal behaviour.

2. The study of particular animal groups such as amphibians and reptiles, primates, mammals living in water, elephants and other large mammals.

3. The study of children's zoos, endangered species and the supply of animals to zoos.

4. Completing a project.

Students take a written examination, and their practical work is assessed by a representative of the zoo's management.

NVQs/SVQs in Animal Care are available at Levels 1 and 2. They are not specifically for zoos but cover the whole animal-care industry. Level 3 and 4 awards are being developed, with Level 3 having one unit specifically related to zoo work; it will be at approximately the same level as the City and Guilds Zoo Animal Management Certificate.

Opportunities may be available through training schemes for young people. Contact local careers offices, TECs/LECs for further details.

LATE ENTRY

Zoos tend to prefer applicants under the age of about 30 years, and it may be difficult for older people to become zoo keepers unless they have closely related experience.

OPPORTUNITIES

Only about 700-800 people work in zoos and wildlife collections in Britain.

Entry is highly competitive and there are many more applicants than vacancies. Many employers keep waiting lists of applicants. The best way of finding work is to write to local zoos (always enclose a stamped addressed envelope). Employers usually prefer handwritten letters, addressed to a named individual.

It may be possible to start on a voluntary basis, perhaps at weekends, for example, in order to gain experience and to be known to the zoo when a full-time vacancy arises. Many zoos have special volunteer schemes. Another possibility is to find other work in a zoo – as a car park attendant or gardener, for instance – on the understanding that a keeper's post may later be available.

Jobs are advertised in *Cage and Aviary Birds, International Zoo News* and the Association of British Wild Animal Keepers' (ABWAK) Journal, *RATEL*.

PAY AND CONDITIONS

Rates of pay vary with different employers. Wages are often comparatively low but in some establishments subsidized accommodation – often a single room with shared facilities – may be provided.

Both zoo opening hours and hours of work are longer in the spring and summer season – which lasts from April to September or October – than in the autumn and winter. During the season, there may be a staggered shift system, for instance one shift of 7.45am to 5pm and a second of 9.45am to 7pm. Hours of work are shorter in winter.

Smaller zoos sometimes close during the winter, but keepers are employed on a year-round basis to provide animal care.

Keepers work a five, five-and-a-half, or six-day week. Weekend and bank holiday work (on a rota) is required, as these are the busiest times.

PROSPECTS

The promotion structure varies in different zoos. Generally, however, keepers are responsible to senior keepers or section leaders, who in turn report to the head keeper.

Head keeper is a managerial role, with responsibility for all practical matters related to animal care. Promotion prospects beyond head keeper level are extremely limited, and even becoming head keeper can be very much a case of waiting until the current post-holder reaches retirement age. Frequently, finding more responsible work is likely to involve moving to another zoo.

Some keepers move into related areas of work such as the RSPCA inspectorate, kennels or stables.

RELATED OCCUPATIONS

RSPCA/SSPCA inspector, horse groom, kennel worker, dog groomer, veterinary nurse.

FURTHER INFORMATION

Association of British Wild Animal Keepers (ABWAK)*, 12 Tackley Road, Eastville, Bristol BS5 6UQ (sae required)

National Extension College*, 18 Brooklands Avenue, Cambridge CB2 2HN, 01223 316644

Federation of Zoological Gardens of Great Britain and Ireland*, Zoological Gardens, Regent's Park, London NW1 4RY, 0171 586 0230 (sae required)

FURTHER READING

Leaflets/booklets are available from the addresses marked*.

Job Outlines – Work with Animals – COIC
Working in Work with Animals – COIC
Working in Outdoor Jobs – COIC
Careers Working with Animals – Kogan Page

In the careers library classified under WAM.

1. COUNTRYSIDE/CONSERVATION OFFICER CLCI:WAR
2. COUNTRYSIDE RANGER/WARDEN CLCI:WAR

BACKGROUND INFORMATION

In Britain several statutory organizations have responsibility for conservation of the natural environment.

The Countryside Commission is an advisory body aiming to preserve the English natural heritage and make it more accessible to the public. Its tasks include designating national parks, providing grant aid for conservation projects, and sponsoring training for countryside staff. Each national park authority is responsible for developing and managing its area.

English Nature promotes nature conservation in England. It advises government on conservation issues, conducts research, runs 150 national nature reserves and identifies Sites of Special Scientific Interest (SSSIs).

Scottish Natural Heritage and the Countryside Council for Wales undertake both the administrative and practical aspects of conservation in Scotland and Wales respectively. They are responsible for protecting the countryside so that people can use and enjoy it in a sustainable manner. They have an advisory and educational role, conduct research and provide grant aid for conservation work. They also develop and manage Natural Heritage Areas, SSSIs and national nature reserves.

Forest Enterprise is concerned with timber production, but also with conserving forest wildlife and providing recreational facilities.

Local authority countryside and recreation departments run country parks, regional parks and other outdoor recreation sites. Planning for urban and rural development also involves conservation issues.

In addition, many voluntary and charitable organizations promote the interests of wildlife and conservation. They include the National Trust and National Trust for Scotland, the Royal Society for the Protection of Birds and national and local wildlife trusts, whose work is co-ordinated by the Royal Society for Nature Conservation.

Work in countryside conservation is diverse but not plentiful. Long-term planning, policy-making and research is generally the province of countryside or conservation officers. Day-to-day management of sites is the responsibility of rangers and wardens.

1. COUNTRYSIDE/CONSERVATION OFFICER (WAR)

THE WORK

Countryside and conservation officers are responsible for the scientific planning and management of areas of land. They aim to protect the countryside and help people to value and enjoy it without harming it or inconveniencing its inhabitants. Many posts carry a strong public relations role – not only encouraging people to learn about their natural heritage but influencing policy at local and national level, so that roads are built or industrial sites planned with conservation in mind.

The range of duties varies from one place to another but in differing proportions most include ecological surveys, practical land management and educational or advisory work. In general, the title of conservation officer implies greater concern with protecting wildlife; countryside officer with managing public access.

Surveys involve identifying plant and animal species, mapping their habitat and drawing up plans to preserve it, for example, by checking the spread of bracken or erecting deer fences. Surveys to identify SSSIs and national nature reserves are organized by conservation officers and scientists with English Nature and Scottish Natural Heritage. In liaison with local planning authorities and conservation organizations, they establish the sites and explain to land owners how they are affected. They also carry out environmental assessments on proposed new developments – for example, predicting the effect of a new airport or motorway on wildlife and landscape. They may represent their authority at public inquiries.

Land management involves forward planning and immediate action. For example, a long-term plan to regenerate woodland entails organizing and supervising a series of conservation projects such as scrub clearance, drainage and tree-planting. Officers may be in charge of full and part-time wardens and rangers, trainees and volunteers. Explaining the job to staff and showing them how to do it can involve a good deal of practical work.

Developing a project involves working closely with agencies such as Forest Enterprise, the Countryside Commission, local wildlife trusts, other conservation organizations, planning officers and local councillors. Officers meet farmers and land owners to explain what is going on, enlist their co-operation, and negotiate access or other problems.

Providing information to the public is an important part of the work. This can include setting up displays at information centres, writing leaflets and talking to local groups and to the press. Some are appointed as education officers to run courses at study centres and to involve schools or other groups in conservation projects of their own.

Being in charge of any group involves administrative work – the management of staff, resources and finance. Officers take part in the recruitment and training of staff, allocate money and equipment between sites, and plan the budget for future developments.

WORK ENVIRONMENT

Many posts combine indoor and outdoor work. Much of the planning and administration is done in an office and in meetings, but site surveys, instruction and maintenance go on outdoors in all weather conditions. Most jobs entail driving to different sites.

SKILLS AND INTERESTS

An enthusiastic commitment to nature conservation is essential, together with the ability to convince others of its importance.

Countryside/conservation officers need to combine scientific interest in the natural environment with a practical outlook on its day-to-day management. Keen powers of observation, an enquiring mind and a methodical approach are required for assessing a site.

Officers should be able to talk to a variety of people from experts to amateurs. In the course of a week they could help a primary school plant trees, negotiate access with a land owner, instruct volunteers on fencing and ditching, and put the case for preserving ancient woodland at a public inquiry into road building.

Officers should be efficient, well-organized managers, able to set goals and organize people and resources to achieve them. Team work is important as they work in liaison with land agents, scientists, planners, statutory and voluntary agencies.

For most jobs it is necessary to be fit and active and prepared to join in with the heavy work.

ENTRY REQUIREMENTS

Most countryside/conservation officers hold a degree or BTEC/SCOTVEC higher national diploma. Appropriate degree subjects include life sciences, ecology, environmental science, geography or geology. BTEC/SCOTVEC higher national diploma courses are available in subjects such as environmental planning and management, conservation management, landscape or amenity horticulture, and leisure studies.

The usual minimum requirements for a degree course are five GCSEs/S grades (A-C/1-3) and two A levels/three H grades; or a relevant BTEC/SCOTVEC national award, or equivalent, such as Advanced GNVQ/GSVQ Level III. For higher national diploma courses they are one A level/two H grades with four GCSEs/S grades (A-C/1-3); or a relevant BTEC/SCOTVEC national award, or equivalent.

It may be possible to work for voluntary bodies and charitable organizations with A levels/H grades and evidence of both commitment and experience.

Competition for posts is extremely fierce. It can be an advantage to hold a postgraduate diploma or higher degree in conservation, ecology, land management or related subject. In all cases practical experience is essential. There are some opportunities to gain paid experience as a part-time or seasonal ranger or warden, and many more to do voluntary work with agencies such as the British Trust for Conservation Volunteers (BTCV), the National Trust or local groups.

An alternative entry route is to gain professional qualifications and experience in a related field such as planning, landscape management, leisure management or teaching.

A driving licence is required.

TRAINING

In-service training is provided by employers in health and safety and management skills, often using distance learning packages. Short courses in a range of management and ecological topics are offered at many colleges and field study centres. Many are sponsored by the Countryside Commission. Training across the UK is co-ordinated by the Environmental Training Organization (ETO.)

Full-time and part-time courses leading to a **higher degree** or **postgraduate diploma** are offered at many institutions. A wide range of subjects is available in the field of ecology, nature conservation and environmental or leisure management.

Open learning and correspondence courses in these subjects are run by the Open University, Open Business School, Institute of Leisure and Amenity Management (ILAM) and other institutions.

NVQs/SVQs in Environmental Conservation (Landscapes and Ecosystems) are available at Levels 2, 3 and 4, for people working in a range of conservation or countryside management jobs. Standards are set by COSQUEC (Council for Occupational Standards and Qualifications in Environmental Conservation). The awards are based on competence at work and may also involve short or part-time courses at a college or training centre. The awarding bodies are BTEC, SCOTVEC and C&G/NPTC (National Proficiency Tests Council).

LATE ENTRY

Maximum age limits are not usually stated. Previous experience in related fields such as planning, leisure management or teaching may be helpful, and it is essential to have extensive experience and knowledge of conservation and natural history.

OPPORTUNITIES

Conservation and countryside management is a small but slowly increasing profession, with 2-3,000 posts at present at officer grade. In many areas, similar or related work goes under different job titles, such as field officer, scientific officer or adviser.

In the public sector, conservation and countryside officers work for English Nature, national parks, the National Rivers Authority and local authority countryside, recreation or planning departments. Scottish Natural Heritage employs area and research officers, who do similar work. The Countryside Commission and the Countryside Council for Wales employ professional staff, mostly in an advisory or administrative capacity, but do not directly manage any land. Other government bodies such as the Natural Environment Research Council offer opportunities for scientists in environmental research.

In the voluntary sector, many organizations provide opportunities for management, scientific research, advice, education and interpretation in the field of countryside conservation. The National Trust employs advisers, with technical and support staff, as well as estate wardens and a range of administrative and marketing staff. The National Trust for Scotland employs a small number of rangers, naturalists and specialist advisers, all science graduates. There are also a few openings with local and regional wildlife or nature conservation trusts, the RSPB, Council for Protection of Rural England and other voluntary and charitable organizations.

There are a few opportunities with private companies and consultancies for conservation officers and advisers.

PAY AND CONDITIONS

Starting salaries range from £10,000 to £14,000 and may rise to over £20,000. In theory most officers work a 37 to 40-hour week, Monday to Friday, but a good deal of flexibility is expected and there may be frequent evening meetings.

PROSPECTS

The statutory bodies provide a career structure leading up through senior scientific or administrative grades. Charitable and voluntary organizations offer less structured career prospects. It is often necessary to move around the country to gain experience and promotion.

Qualified and experienced conservation officers may become advisers with the National Trust, wildlife or conservation trusts, or other organizations such as the Farming and Wildlife Advisory Group.

RELATED OCCUPATIONS

Forest officer, horticultural scientist, landscape architect, town planner, estate manager, land agent, research scientist, leisure centre manager.

FURTHER INFORMATION AND READING

Please see article 2. COUNTRYSIDE RANGER/ WARDEN.

2. COUNTRYSIDE RANGER/WARDEN (WAR)

THE WORK

Rangers and wardens look after the countryside for the benefit of its wildlife and of the people who visit and use it. The main elements in the work are advice and information, liaison, conservation and day-to-day maintenance. The duties vary from one place to another, and the job titles may be interchangeable, but in general rangers have more dealings with the public, wardens with practical conservation.

Rangers help people to enjoy the countryside and to respect and care for it without causing damage or inconveniencing other users. They advise visitors where to go and what to look for and answer their questions about the area and its wildlife. They may talk to school or community groups and organize guided walks. At weekends and holiday times they may be based at an information centre or car park. They also patrol the area looking for signs of damage and, in a firm but tactful manner, try to prevent people causing it. The aim is prevention by persuasion but, if necessary, they may need to report problems to the police.

Rangers are the link between the land-owning authority, visitors and the local community. They sort out disputes over rights of access and put up stiles and signposts to help walkers keep to the paths. They talk to farmers about conservation on their land – preserving hedgerows or stone barns, for example – and may suggest sources of grant aid to help with this.

Rangers also pass information back to their authority on their area's special needs. They monitor the number of cars, mountain bikers and others, the state of the footpaths and the need to repair damage, combat erosion or improve facilities. They also help with ecological surveys, recording animal and plant species, numbers of nesting birds, and so on, and the need for special measures to protect them. Surveys can be a major part of the work for wardens on estates and nature reserves.

Both wardens and rangers carry out practical maintenance work. This includes fencing, drainage, litter picking, path repair and the management of woodland by pruning, scrub clearance and tree planting. They usually carry out a good deal of the heavy work themselves and may also supervise estate workers and volunteers.

Wildlife rangers in the Forestry Commission are responsible for protecting plantations, creating areas for wildlife conservation, supervising sporting activities and assisting visitors.

Keeping records and reporting incidents entails a varying amount of paperwork. Some rangers and wardens are responsible for part of a budget; planning and costing products such as footpath maintenance or tree planting, and choosing equipment and materials for the job.

Rangers and wardens are trained in first aid, and they help to deal with emergencies such as fire, flood or mountain rescue.

WORK ENVIRONMENT

Rangers and wardens work outdoors most of the time, whatever the weather. Their areas vary widely – a stretch of long-distance footpath, a patch of woodland or wetland, a country park, a regional park or a range of hills.

SKILLS AND INTERESTS

Rangers and wardens need a good understanding of the needs of the countryside and of its users. The work calls for commitment to the interests of nature conservation and the ability to communicate this commitment to others.

They should be able to explain matters clearly and simply to all sorts of groups and individuals, ranging from school-children and picnickers to ecologists, birdwatchers and farmers. Tact and diplomacy are required in preventing trouble and solving disputes.

Rangers and wardens should be fit and strong and keen to work outdoors in all weathers. Practical skills such as hedge-laying or chain-saw operation are useful. In watching and caring for wildlife, patience and good powers of observation are required.

Rangers and wardens should be responsible, self-reliant and able to work on their own initiative, often alone though sometimes in teams of two or three. They should also feel confident to lead groups of walkers or naturalists and to take charge of voluntary workers.

ENTRY REQUIREMENTS

Formal academic qualifications are not always required for the job of ranger or warden. However, an increasing number of applicants hold qualifications ranging from an appropriate BTEC/SCOTVEC diploma or NVQ/SVQ Level 3 award, to a degree.

Experience in related employment such as estate work or forestry is a great advantage. Commitment to nature conservation is essential; as evidence, employers look for voluntary work, or experience as a part-time ranger or warden.

For many posts there is a minimum age of 21 years.

A countryside management course can provide a good background for work as a ranger or warden. Courses leading to nationally recognized qualifications at all levels are available at many institutions. They may be studied full-time, part-time or by distance learning.

Suitable courses include:

GNVQ in Land and Environment and **City and Guilds in Recreation; Care and Conservation.** No formal academic qualifications are needed, although individual institutions may set entry requirements.

BTEC/SCOTVEC National Diploma/Certificate in Conservation; Land Use and Recreation; Countryside Skills; Countryside Management. No formal academic qualifications are required for SCOTVEC national courses. For BTEC national awards the normal entry requirements are: four GCSEs/S grades (A-C/1-3); or Intermediate GNVQ/GSVQ Level II; or equivalent.

BTEC/SCOTVEC Higher National Diploma/Certificate in Countryside Recreation; Conservation Management; Rural Resources Management; Leisure Management.

Entry is usually with one A level/two H grades with four GCSEs/S grades; or a relevant BTEC national award; or equivalent.

The National Trust runs a three-year careership scheme for young people in Countryside Management or Amenity Horticulture, combining work experience with study for NVQ Level 3.

TRAINING

In-service training is organized by employers. A typical training programme for rangers covers: the role of the ranger; map-reading and moorland navigation; countryside safety including rescue, fire-fighting and first aid; the role of volunteers in conservation; local knowledge; radio communication; law in the countryside.

Short external courses are also provided. These are organized by the Countryside Management Association, the Scottish Countryside Rangers' Association, the National Parks' Staff Association and colleges of agriculture and horticulture. Many of the courses are sponsored by the Countryside Commission and are held at colleges and field study centres throughout the UK. Topics range from dry-stone walling to countryside interpretation and staff management.

The British Trust for Conservation Volunteers (BTCV) and the Scottish Conservation Projects Trust (SCPT) run six/twelve-month training courses in conservation skills, as well as short courses for trainees and volunteers.

NVQs/SVQs in Environmental Conservation (Landscapes and Ecosystems) are available at Levels 2, 3 and 4.

LATE ENTRY

Most full-time rangers and wardens are appointed in their mid-twenties or later, after experience of related jobs. Upper age limits are not usually imposed, provided applicants are fit and strong.

There may be specific training opportunities directed at adults available in some areas for this type of work. Candidates may have to satisfy certain conditions to be eligible. Contact your local Jobcentre, careers service or TEC/LEC for details.

OPPORTUNITIES

Numbers of full-time rangers and wardens are small – under 1,000 – and growing only slowly. They are supplemented by many more part-time and seasonal assistants and by volunteers. Vacancies everywhere are few and over-subscribed and are usually filled by those with part-time or voluntary experience.

The largest employers of rangers are the countryside, planning and leisure departments of local authorities, and the national and regional parks. The Forestry Commission employs about 300 wildlife rangers, who are recruited from its own forest workers.

English Nature and Scottish Natural Heritage employ site managers and wardens in small numbers to run their National Nature Reserves. There are a few opportunities for wardens on private estates. The National Trust, Royal Society for the Protection of Birds, wildlife trusts and other charitable organizations occasionally offer paid work for wardens, as well as opportunities for volunteers.

The British Trust for Conservation Volunteers and many local groups also organize voluntary work in countryside conservation. This provides valuable experience and helps applicants test the depth of their own commitment to the work.

Vacancies are advertised in the national and local press and journals such as *New Scientist*.

PAY AND CONDITIONS

Pay varies widely, starting from between £7,158 to £10,000, rising with experience to £18,800 or more.

In the National Trust, local government and other statutory bodies the hours are officially 37 to 40 a week, but in practice they are often long and irregular and involve some weekend work.

Part-time or seasonal work is often available.

PROSPECTS

The statutory authorities and major charitable organizations such as the National Trust provide a career structure with promotion through senior grades to area, chief and district ranger or head warden. In smaller charitable and voluntary organizations, there is less scope for advancement. Promotion depends mainly on experience and opportunity.

For those seeking to become conservation officers or countryside managers, it can be helpful to gain qualifications such as an advanced diploma or a masters' degree. These are available by full-time, part-time or distance study in a range of environmental and management subjects, such as ecology, environmental management or countryside recreation management. Gaining NVQs/SVQs is helpful in seeking advancement.

RELATED OCCUPATIONS

Forester, estate worker, gamekeeper, fish farm manager, farm worker, landscape gardener.

FURTHER INFORMATION

British Trust for Conservation Volunteers*, 36 Saint Mary's Street, Wallingford, Oxfordshire OX10 0EU, 01491 839766

The Countryside Commission*, John Dower House, Crescent Place, Cheltenham, Gloucestershire GL50 3RA, 01242 521381

Countryside Management Association*, c/o Centre for Environmental Interpretation, Manchester Metropolitan University, St Augustines, Lower Chatham Street, Manchester M15 6BY, 0161 247 1067

English Nature*, Northminster House, Peterborough PE1 1UA, 01733 340345

The Environment Council*, 21 Elizabeth Street, London SW1W 9RP, 0171 824 8411

Wildlife Trusts National Office*, The Green, Witham Park, Waterside South, Lincoln LN2 7JR, 01522 544400

Scottish Conservation Projects Trust*, Freepost, Stirling FK8 2BR, 01786 479697

Scottish Natural Heritage*, Battleby, Redgorton, Perth PH1 3EW, 01738 627921

COSQUEC, The Red House, Pillows Green, Staunton, Glos. GL19 3NU. 01452 840825

Environmental Training Organization (ETO), (address as COSQUEC)

FURTHER READING

Leaflets/booklets are available from the addresses marked*.

Job Outlines – Nature Conservation – COIC
Working in the Environment – COIC

Careers in Environmental Conservation – Kogan Page
The Environmental Careers Handbook – Institution of Environmental Scientists
Careers in Conservation – RSPB
Careers in the Environment – The Environment Council
Council Directory of Environmental Courses – The Environment Council

In the careers library classified under WAR.

GROUP Y – TRANSPORT

1. AIRLINE PILOT CLCI:YAB
2. AIR CABIN CREW CLCI:YAB
3. AIRCRAFT MAINTENANCE ENGINEER
CLCI:RAB
4. AIR TRAFFIC CONTROLLER CLCI:YAB

BACKGROUND INFORMATION

The articles in this section refer essentially to employment in UK airlines. There are around 30 of these companies flying aircraft in and out of the UK. Other employment is with smaller firms such as air taxi companies or, in the case of maintenance engineers, with aircraft and component manufacturers.

Airlines or their agents employ many other types of staff than the ones described in the following articles – in airline security, airline lounges, in baggage handling, check-in facilities and passenger services, flight catering, and 'slot' allocation at Heathrow and Gatwick.

The industry has been adversely affected by recession, meaning that competition is even greater for employment than in normal years and some airlines are not recruiting for certain jobs.

A great number of other jobs at airports are provided by employers other than airlines. These employers include BAA plc, HM Customs and Excise, Home Office Immigration officials, airport police forces, Department of Transport and concessionaires appointed by BAA plc for car hire, parking, catering, etc.

Air traffic controllers, employed by National Air Traffic Services (a joint Civil Aviation Authority (CAA) and Ministry of Defence organization) work at main control centres and at airports in the UK.

1. AIRLINE PILOT (YAB)

THE WORK

Pilots fly aircraft on long and short-haul flights. Duties begin one hour before take-off when pilots check pre-flight plans. These define the route to be taken and height maintained, and include meteorological information. Pilots do complex calculations of take-off and landing weights and they have to work out the fuel needed from distance travelled and height and weight to be maintained. Pilots also check that equipment and instruments are functioning properly and that noise regulations for take-off and landing are observed. Their work includes briefing the crew and supervising loading and refuelling. Initial contact is then made with air traffic control, who advise the pilot on take-off.

Pilots need to be able to understand and interpret the data presented to them on instruments and controls and they use computers in their calculations. Take-off and landing are the most complicated aspects of a flight, but pilots may have to make adjustments as necessary during flights and have to use their skills continuously, checking instruments for malfunction even while the plane is on automatic pilot.

They maintain contact with air traffic controls and cabin crew throughout the flight and speak at intervals to passengers, giving them information over the public address system on cruising speed and height and details of ground areas they are flying over, as well as warnings of turbulence and difficult weather conditions. They may also leave the flight deck to speak to passengers.

Duties are shared usually with one co-pilot, occasionally two on long-haul, but responsibility for the aircraft and its safety rests finally with the pilot.

After landing, when the aircraft has been taxied to its final position, the pilot shuts down the engines and writes a flight report, noting any problems or instrument difficulties.

WORK ENVIRONMENT

Flight decks, where pilots spend long hours in a seated position, are typically very confined spaces.

Flight delays because of weather or other difficulties, along with 24-hour schedules, mean irregular working hours and periods spent overseas in a hotel or airport. There are strict rules over the number of hours pilots may work without a rest period, but because they are flying 'unsocial' hours they can experience jet lag, particularly on long-haul schedules, and may return on scheduled flights as passengers.

SKILLS AND INTERESTS

The work of pilots involves great responsibility both for aircraft and for the safety of passengers and crew. They need to be self-confident and at ease working with other people.

Pilots have to be reliable, calm and level-headed, able to take charge in an emergency and have good clear communication skills both within the team on board and with air traffic control. The ability to inspire confidence in both passengers and air crew is very important.

Good practical and co-ordination skills are needed along with technical skills and understanding. Written English must be of a good standard for report writing.

Good health and fitness are vital and tested on application and at regular intervals throughout a pilot's career.

ENTRY REQUIREMENTS

A commercial pilot's licence (CPL) with instrument rating (IR), awarded by the Civil Aviation Authority (CAA), is needed to fly aircraft registered in the UK 'for hire or reward'. To become the commander of an airliner requires an Airline Transport Pilot's Licence (Aeroplane) – ATPL (A).

There are currently moves to have a common European licensing structure and it is likely that all members of an airliner's flight deck crew will be required to pass the ATPL ground exams. For this reason, few UK airlines now accept the CPL with IR, without passes in the ATPL ground exams.

There are a number of different ways of obtaining the standard to acquire the CPL and ATPL, and entry requirements depend on the method used:

1. Full or partial sponsorship and training by airlines normally requires a minimum of five GCSEs/S grades (A-C/1-3) (seven for British Airways) including English, maths and a science with two A levels/three H grades preferably in maths and physics. Advanced GNVQ/GSVQ Level III and BTEC/SCOTVEC national awards are also acceptable, preferably in a relevant area, such as science or engineering.

2. Private residential training schools use entry standards that are recommended by the CAA. These are five GCSEs/S grades (A-C/1-3) including English, maths and a science that includes a substantial content of physics. Applicants with alternative qualifications, eg GNVQ/GSVQ and BTEC/SCOTVEC awards, are considered on their merits and will need to satisfy the training schools that they have a sufficient level of English, maths and science to

benefit from training. This is a very expensive method of training, costing upwards of £50,000.

3. Training as a pilot with one of the Armed Forces (entry requirements similar to above) and taking a conversion, or abridged, course for qualification for commercial pilot.

4. Gaining a private pilot's licence (PPL) and 700 hours' flying experience, perhaps by working as an instructor, to be eligible to sit the written and practical tests for the CPL and ATPL ground exams. This also is an expensive route though it can be taken over a little longer period. The expense can be reduced by a 'self-improver' route that combines a series of training courses with flying experience of approximately 250 hours. The PPL route may be affected by the introduction of a European licensing system.

Individual airlines have additional requirements which vary but all of them include good eyesight (that may include glasses but must reach a certain standard), normal colour vision, good hearing and physical fitness.

Age requirements are usually between 18 and 24 years for training (26 for graduates). For previously experienced pilots, age requirements vary and entry depends on individual qualifications and experience.

Airlines have height restrictions – for British Airways, for example, it is between 1.58m (5 feet 2 inches) and 1.91m (6 feet 3 inches).

British airlines also require that applicants have the unrestricted right to live and work in the UK and be able to obtain a passport allowing unrestricted access world-wide.

TRAINING

Training may take place full-time on a residential basis at a college of air training, or part-time via approved flying schools.

Would-be pilots have to obtain one or more levels and categories of licence that permit them to fly aircraft – from command of smaller aircraft (or as co-pilot in larger ones) to the highest category, which is the ATPL, allowing pilots to be in charge of the wide-bodied jets – but see notes under ENTRY REQUIREMENTS for likely changes.

1. Residential courses are available at Air Service Training College (Perth Airport), Oxford Air Training School (Oxford Airport), British Aerospace Flying College Ltd, (Prestwick Airport), Cabair College of Air Training (Cranfield Aerodrome, Bedford) and South East College of Air Training (Kent International Airport).

Training lasts up to 15 months and provides training to full ATPL standard for sponsored and private students. Students finish with a CPL/IR with 'frozen' ATPL, which means that, when they reach the minimum age (21) and hours (1,500) requirements, their licence is automatically upgraded to ATPL. Students also achieve an NVQ/SVQ in Piloting Transport Aircraft at Level 4.

Practical training includes flying in single and twin-engined aircraft and in simulators. There is a high technical subject content including avionics, aerodynamics navigation, meteorology, aircraft design and aviation law.

For people who already have some flying experience, shorter courses are available. They first need to be assessed by the CAA (who charge a fee), which gives details of the requirements that need to be met by doing an abridged course.

After completing training via one of the above methods, pilots with full ATPL standard train as co-pilots with an airline before being eligible for promotion to pilot.

2. The slightly cheaper method of training privately via a PPL, outlined under ENTRY REQUIREMENTS above, can be followed by short courses to obtain the ATPL. Some pilots gain flying experience at schools in the USA, where fees are cheaper, but CAA standards must still be met on return to the UK to be eligible to fly aircraft here (preference is usually given to UK-trained pilots).

3. Conversion courses are open to ex-Armed Forces pilots to train to ATPL standard.

Training continues throughout the career of a pilot as new aircraft and instruments are introduced and new type and instrument ratings need to be added to their licence. They also take regular refresher courses.

LATE ENTRY

Trainee pilots are normally aged between 18 and 24 years (26 for graduates). British Airways recruits trainees between 18 and 28. For conversion courses, pilots may be aged up to 35 years.

OPPORTUNITIES

The majority of civil airline pilots are employed by British Airways. British Airways employs around 3,000 pilots. The airline recruits a small number of cadet pilots but competition is intense, with about 40 applicants for each vacancy. Recruitment depends to a great extent on expansion of business and the purchase of more aircraft.

The fact that larger aircraft are being used, though, means fewer pilots for more passengers, and this also affects expansion of recruitment.

PAY AND CONDITIONS

The basic salary range for commercial pilots is around £30,000. A new captain begins at £48,700. Average captain's pay is between £55,000 and £61,000. All salary scales increase each year. In addition, expenses are paid and travel permits are granted.

PROSPECTS

Pilots usually begin as co-pilots or second officers, though military-trained pilots may well begin as first officers. Promotion is often based on the types of aircraft that the pilot flies, with the highest pay going to captains of wide-bodied jets, but some airlines accord promotion, regardless of aircraft type, from second officer to first officer to captain.

After captain, promotion is to chief pilot, or some may move into management or training, some combining chief pilot with training duties and/or administrative positions.

Pilots tend to stay with the airline that employs them, though at times airlines may take experienced pilots from small companies. This is because moving from one company to another means starting at the bottom again, before being able to gain promotion to higher posts and higher pay.

RELATED OCCUPATIONS

Pilot: Armed Forces, pilot: air taxi company, RAF officer, RN officer, merchant navy officer, air traffic controller.

FURTHER INFORMATION AND READING

Please see article 4. AIR TRAFFIC CONTROLLER.

2. AIR CABIN CREW (YAB)

THE WORK

Air cabin crew look after the welfare, comfort and safety of passengers travelling in aircraft. They attend a pre-flight briefing at the report centre at least one hour before take-off, which deals with the special needs of passengers, business information and matters of safety. They board at least half an hour before take-off and check the emergency equipment is in order, the aircraft and cloakrooms are tidy, and seat pocket information is in place. They also check that sufficient meals and drinks are available for the number of passengers and put away the catering trays.

Having welcomed passengers on board and shown them to their seats, they check that doors are closed and seat belts fastened. Before take-off they demonstrate the use of emergency equipment and point out exit doors, and notify the pilot when they are ready for take-off.

During the flight they serve meals and drinks. Meals are usually pre-packed and may need heating. On some flights cabin crew sell duty-free goods such as alcohol, perfume and tobacco. This work is usually done in pairs in certain sections of the cabin, the work being allocated by the chief stewardess or steward. They make announcements on behalf of the pilot and again check that safety belts are fastened.

During their work they may have to deal with emergencies, such as the ill-health of passengers, and must be able to administer first aid. In case of flight emergencies they have to immediately apply the safety drills they learned in training and help passengers from the aircraft before leaving themselves.

When the flight is over they check stocks of duty-free goods and complete account sheets showing balance of cash and stock so that new stock can be ordered.

WORK ENVIRONMENT

The working environment is cramped and often very warm. Cabin crew spend a lot of time on their feet. Long-haul flights involve spending periods away from home and some involve crossing time zones with the possibility of jet lag.

SKILLS AND INTERESTS

Cabin crew require a neat appearance. They need to be in good health and have stamina. Agility and a good sense of balance are needed, both for working in confined spaces and also for emergency procedure practice.

This work suits responsible, confident people who are good at dealing with all types of passengers. They require a polite, pleasant and tactful manner with the ability to put people at ease.

Common sense and calmness, together with the ability to react quickly in the case of emergencies, is needed.

Crew members need to be able to work in a team. A clear speaking voice is essential and good written English is required for writing reports.

They need to be numerate since they have to balance accounts and deal with a variety of currencies on a flight.

Punctuality is very important.

ENTRY REQUIREMENTS

Each airline has different requirements. They all, though, expect a good standard of education, usually some GCSEs/S grades (A-C/1-3), often including English and maths. Airlines do not necessarily require a qualification in a foreign language but most insist on applicants being able to hold a conversation in a foreign language related to the routes the airline flies. British Airways, for example, requires applicants to be skilled in one of 26 specified languages.

The most essential requirements are the right personality, a good standard of health and smart personal appearance – applications need to be supported by a recent full-length photograph. Weight is expected to be in proportion to height and minimum height requirement is usually 1.57m (5 feet 2 inches) to 1.62m (5 feet 4 inches). Minimum age for entry to employment varies between airlines, but is usually 20 years.

Experience of working with members of the public or in the caring field is important, for example, nursing, teaching, catering, travel agency or airport work. Applicants are normally required to be able to swim.

Some companies permit glasses or contact lenses to be worn up to an unaided vision standard. Some companies require good colour vision. A medical certificate of fitness is required to fly world-wide.

Female staff have to wear a hairstyle suitable for the uniform hat. Males are not normally permitted to wear beards, although moustaches may be allowed.

Applicants must be in possession of a British passport or be able to obtain one before employment. Passports should allow applicants unrestricted access to the areas serviced by the particular airline.

Living within easy travelling distance of the airport with reliable transport is also a requirement.

TRAINING

Individual airlines provide their own training which normally takes between three to six weeks. It is usually held in an airline environment which includes a mock-up aircraft cabin. Practical and written tests are taken at various stages of the training, which includes study of food and drink service and galley management, currency exchange, customs and immigration regulations and documentation, first aid and medical training, safety and survival, care of special passengers, personal hygiene and grooming.

Methods of training include lectures, visits, demonstrations, discussions, films, slides and energetic emergency procedure practice.

On completion of initial training, entrants have a probationary period of between six months and a year. This consists of on-the-job training under the supervision of experienced cabin crew.

Crew also re-train in safety and emergency procedures for each type of aircraft they work in.

NVQs/SVQs in Air Cabin Crewing are available at Levels 2 and 3.

LATE ENTRY

The upper age limit for entry is usually 28 to 35 years.

OPPORTUNITIES

Competition for employment is intense, with some airlines receiving as many as 30,000 or more enquiries each year. As a result, airlines rarely have to advertise. Recruitment has been at a low level in recent years.

Airlines that do a lot of charter work to holiday destinations may recruit people on a seasonal basis in a temporary capacity initially. They may then be offered permanent work if suitable positions arise. British Airways employs support cabin crew who work part-time.

Opportunities for work with foreign airlines is usually dependent on being able to converse fluently in the language of the country and being able to conduct an interview and training in that language. Some countries, such as the Gulf states, recruit British nationals.

Some airlines run training schemes for young people that include cabin services department training. Places available are, however, extremely limited. Trainees may gain permanent employment with the airline afterwards, or be helped to find alternative employment in the travel industry.

PAY AND CONDITIONS

These varies according to the employing airline.

Basic salaries are usually between £7,000 and £8,500. These are increased by payments of allowances for unsocial hours or for overseas work, bringing the total to over £10,000. There are additional allowances, eg for being able to speak foreign languages, and commission may be paid on the sale of duty-free goods.

Shift patterns can be very irregular as airlines fly 24 hours a day. Within Europe duties have a typical pattern of four to six days on duty with two to four days off, and each day's duty may include several short-haul flights. On long-haul flights, the system is different and may include rest periods abroad and time off on return. In addition standbys are worked.

Subsidized travel is available and subsidized payments for periods spent away from home.

PROSPECTS

These vary according to the employing airline. In some, promotion is automatic through seniority grades, while with others it is dependent on a more senior member of staff leaving. Promotion is also to senior steward/stewardess, called the 'Number One', who decides which sections of the plane the others work in. Promotion can also entail moving on to work in the first-class section of the plane.

Employment as air cabin crew is not as short term as it once was, with staff staying longer, into their late fifties on some airlines.

Opportunities may exist to move to another airline or into other work such as ground duties, administration and training and recruitment.

RELATED OCCUPATIONS

Ship steward/stewardess, waiter/waitress, hotel receptionist, resort representative, travel courier, travel agency consultant/clerk.

FURTHER INFORMATION AND READING

Please see article 4. AIR TRAFFIC CONTROLLER.

3. AIRCRAFT MAINTENANCE ENGINEER (RAB)

THE WORK

Aircraft maintenance engineers in civil aviation work normally specialize in mechanical or avionic engineering. Mechanical engineers service and overhaul engines and airframes. Avionics engineers specialize in the maintenance of instruments, electrical and electronic equipment, automatic pilot, navigation, radar and radio communication.

Both types of engineer carry out routine maintenance on the ground during aircraft turnaround at airports, and respond to reports from air crew of any difficulties experienced during flights, repairing and making corrections. They also do maintenance and overhaul of aircraft in hangars and workshops when an aircraft is due for its regular inspection and checks.

The work involves using hand and power tools for replacement of parts and the treatment of corrosion, checking of tyres, brakes, instruments, wheel flaps, etc – any parts affecting the safety of the aircraft. Safety equipment is also checked. They complete worksheets for checks made and these are certified by themselves if they are licensed to do so, or by a qualified supervisor.

Engineers work as part of a very organized and highly efficient team and, particularly during turnarounds, they work at speed and under pressure. Work is normally carried out under supervision, though this depends on the categories of licence the engineer is qualified in.

Flight engineers are still carried in a few aircraft, such as the DC10, Tristar and some B747 models. They work on the flight deck during long-hauls and are responsible for the correct functioning of systems and equipment, liaising with ground staff when on the ground. Developments with the newer wide-bodied aircraft, though, have meant the use of computers in flight decks allowing only two-person crews of pilot and co-pilot, so the job of flight engineer is gradually disappearing.

WORK ENVIRONMENT

Aircraft maintenance engineers work in airports on the apron during turnaround, working in all types of weather conditions and at height in exposed conditions. On routine overhauls and checks they work indoors in workshops and hangars.

Work is normally carried out at the home airport. Aircraft maintenance engineers with seniority and experience sometimes work overseas, supervising the work of contracted foreign crew who do checks on the employing airline's aircraft.

Inside the aircraft, the work is carried out in often cramped and confined conditions, requiring bending in awkward positions.

Flight engineers work in the confined spaces of flight decks.

Maintenance engineers normally wear overalls and safety equipment such as eye protectors, harnesses and ear defenders as necessary. Flight engineers wear a uniform similar to that of pilots.

SKILLS AND INTERESTS

All aircraft maintenance engineers must have a strong sense of responsibility since the safety of the aircraft and passengers depends on them to a large degree. All aircraft engineers need manual, technical and mechanical aptitude. Different areas of work require varying degrees of fine manual skills, good powers of analysis and the ability to read drawings.

Since aircraft have to be serviced in a short time, engineers have to be able to work at speed yet still be accurate. They must work well as members of a team.

They must have normal colour vision and a good head for heights. Physical fitness and agility for working in confined and cramped conditions are also required.

ENTRY REQUIREMENTS

Apprenticeships

Major airlines and independent aircraft maintenance organizations usually offer a number of apprenticeships each year, some in engines and airframe engineering only.

Craft apprentices normally require GCSEs/S grades (A-C/1-3 desirable) in English, maths and a science (preferably physics or combined science that includes physics) and a technology subject.

Technician apprentices usually need four GCSEs/S grades (A-C/1-3) in the same subjects required for craft apprentices. That gives them the minimum requirements to enter a BTEC national certificate course.

Applicants for both craft and technician apprenticeships with alternative qualifications, eg BTEC first award, SCOTVEC national certificate modules or Intermediate GNVQ/GSVQ Level II are also considered.

Whatever their qualifications, applicants for both craft and technician apprenticeships usually have to pass practical and written tests. They must have normal colour vision and may be expected to pass a medical examination.

Age limits on entry vary but are usually between 16 and 21 years.

Modern Apprenticeships are being introduced for some young people. The recommended entry requirement is a minimum of three GCSEs/S grades (A-C/1-3) including English, maths and physics or combined science that includes physics. A practical subject such as CDT is very useful.

Full-time college courses

City and Guilds 2590 Aeronautical Engineering Competencies courses have varying entry requirements. They range from no specific qualifications but aptitude for science and calculations, to two GCSEs/S grades (A-C/1-3) including maths or a science subject.

Brunel College of Art and Technology's Foundation Certificate in Aeronautical Maintenance Engineering requires a minimum of either: three GCSEs/S grades (A-C/1-3) including English, maths and physics or combined science that includes physics; or BTEC First Diploma in Engineering; or a BTEC national diploma; or Intermediate GNVQ/GSVQ Level II in Engineering.

BTEC National Diploma in Engineering (Aerospace) or Aeronautical Maintenance Engineering or Aerospace Studies usually requires a minimum of either: four GCSEs/S grades (A-C/1-3) including English, maths and a science that includes physics; or a BTEC first award in engineering; or appropriate SCOTVEC national certificate modules; or Intermediate GNVQ/GSVQ Level II in Engineering.

Oxford Air Training School, a fee-paying college, requires a good secondary education standard with a minimum age of 17-and-a-half on entry, for its aircraft maintenance engineering course.

The above outlines entry requirements for training places. It is possible to work in aircraft engineering without these qualifications and gain experience on the job, but employers usually require the minimum qualifications described above or experience in other areas of engineering.

TRAINING

Training for aircraft maintenance engineers is normally via industry-recognized apprenticeships and college courses. This is because of the need for engineers to reach certain licence standards to be able to certify their own and others' work. The courses bring students to the level needed to take the necessary examinations for licences.

Training other than that outlined under ENTRY REQUIREMENTS is obtained via employment and experience on the job, and licences can be applied for after gaining experience and technical knowledge at work.

Pre-entry

City and Guilds 2590 Aeronautical Competencies courses are offered full-time for two years by several colleges and provide a basis of knowledge required for an NVQ Aircraft in Maintenance Engineering at Level 3.

Brunel College of Art and Technology's one year full-time Foundation Certificate in Aeronautical Maintenance Engineering can lead to entry to the BTEC Higher National Diploma in Aeroplanes and Engines Maintenance Engineering; or Avionics Maintenance, and/or to the CAA maintenance engineering programme.

BTEC national diploma courses (two years full-time) may be attended as a student or as an employee sponsored by an employer. Courses are designed to meet the educational and technical requirements for aircraft maintenance engineers. They are offered at several colleges and can lead to entry into work and further study at higher national certificate level or to entry into higher education for a higher national diploma or degree. These courses also provide a basis of knowledge required for the NVQ in Aircraft Maintenance Engineering at Level 3. It is possible that these courses will be phased out when Advanced GNVQ in Engineering and additional specialist aeronautical units are introduced.

Oxford Air Training School offers a twelve-month course leading to basic mechanic standard, then several courses that take between two-and-a-half to three years to complete for the CAA Aircraft Maintenance Engineer Licence.

On entry

Basic engineering training is usually carried out by employers in the aeronautical industry supported by release to an air training college or specialist aeronautical training provider.

The course of study followed depends on GCSE/S grade results. Entrants with four GCSEs/S grades (A-C/1-3) usually follow a BTEC National Certificate in Aerospace Engineering, while others follow the City and Guilds 2590 course.

NVQs/SVQs in Aircraft Maintenance Engineering (Mechanical and Avionic) are available at Level 3. Levels 2 and 4 are being developed.

Those on Modern Apprenticeships work towards one of several NVQs/SVQs at Level 3. There is no set length of time for Modern Apprenticeship training but it is likely to be at least three years. Contact your local careers office or TEC/LEC for details.

Licences are issued in various categories, such as Airframe, Engine, Avionic and Radio, and are divided into two parts: Licence Without Type Rating (LWTR), which shows basic knowledge but does not grant certification privileges, and Type Ratings (TR), which include certification privileges in respect of certain light aircraft and their systems.

In addition to having experience and/or formal training, applicants must be at least 20 years before applying for LWTR and at least 21 years for TR. It is general practice that trainees follow an initial two years' training, then a further two years' experience is required to reach licence application standard. Applicants for licences have to show at least three years' experience relating to the maintenance of operating aircraft and pay appropriate fees.

Maintenance of large aircraft is undertaken by CAA-approved organizations who confer on their own engineers certain certification privileges. Those engineers must successfully complete a CAA-approved course (appropriate to Type) and be holders of an appropriate LWTR before being granted a Company Approval certificate that allows them to certify work.

The Aviation Training Association publishes Open Tech materials that enable aircraft maintenance engineers to prepare through distance learning for the LWTR, the Aeronautical Maintenance Certificate (AMC), and acquire the technical knowledge necessary for an NVQ/SVQ in Aircraft Maintenance Engineering (Mechanical and Avionic) at Level 3.

Part-time and short courses are available for people with a basic mechanical or electrical/electronic engineering background with little or no experience of civil aviation maintenance. There are also revision courses for those with experience but little or no training.

NB: The existing licence system is due to change to a European licence system some time from 1999. That will affect the information in this section on licensing.

LATE ENTRY

Upper age limits for apprenticeships are set by individual employers but college courses are available at all ages.

Employment opportunities may be available to those with a basic mechanical or electrical/electronic background.

OPPORTUNITIES

Most aircraft maintenance engineers are employed by airlines or independent aircraft maintenance engineering companies. Competition for training places is quite intense. Companies restrict entrants to those living within a certain radius of where they are based.

Other opportunities are in work for companies that do contract work for airlines, in air taxi companies, and flying clubs. Aircraft manufacturers who do work on the maintenance of aircraft also employ aircraft maintenance engineers, as do component workshops, where licences are not needed.

The possibilities of finding work abroad are diminishing as countries increasingly show preference for their own nationals, but the UK Maintenance Engineers' Licence is accepted by all countries signatory to the International Civil Aviation Authority. It is occasionally possible to work overseas for the home airline overseeing foreign contract workers on aircraft turnaround overseas.

Flight engineers are usually now recruited from ground engineering trades or the RAF, as demand for their services has diminished. Developments with newer wide-bodied jets have resulted in two-person air crews of pilot and co-pilot only.

PAY AND CONDITIONS

Aircraft maintenance engineers without licences earn between £15,000 and £19,500. Licensed technicians earn around £18,500 to £19,500. There are additional payments for the possession of CAA licences as well as overtime, shift and unsocial hours allowances. Salaries are set to amounts agreed with the engineering unions.

PROSPECTS

Promotion for aircraft maintenance engineers is to supervisory positions. Engineers holding a Licence with Type Rating or a Company Approval Certificate are at an advantage in seeking promotion.

Exams are available to qualify for flight engineer work but, as the need for this work has decreased, so have the opportunities for promotion via this route.

Work in aircraft design work and aeronautical engineering is confined to those who are able to extend their qualifications to a Higher National Diploma in Aeronautical Engineering.

RELATED OCCUPATIONS

Aircraft maintenance engineer: Armed Forces, motor vehicle mechanic, auto electrician, engineer.

FURTHER INFORMATION AND READING

Please see article 4. AIR TRAFFIC CONTROLLER.

4. AIR TRAFFIC CONTROLLER (YAB)

THE WORK

Air traffic controllers (ATCOs) are responsible for keeping the aircraft under their control separated safely from each other, both in the air and on the ground. They work either at en-route centres (area control) or airports (aerodrome/ approach control). They use VHF radio to issue instructions, advice and information to pilots in order to maintain a safe, orderly and rapid flow of air traffic. ATCOs keep close watch over the aircraft either visually (aerodrome) or by radar (approach/area control). Sophisticated computers are used to keep up-to-date information and help the overall air traffic situation.

Area control

This is provided at the two Area Control Centres (ACC), based at West Drayton, near Heathrow, and at the Scottish and Oceanic Control Centre at Prestwick. There is a further sub-centre based at Manchester Airport. These centres provide air traffic services within their designated area to all aircraft flying in controlled airspace in the UK and across the North Atlantic. (Not all airspace is controlled, to allow for such as pleasure and military flying.)

Control is maintained by taking into account vertical and horizontal distances between aircraft and using such factors as aircraft performance, requested routings and the effects of weather (for example, strong winds) on airspeed, aircraft headings etc.

Approach control

Approach controllers guide aircraft and organize the order in which they take off or land. They keep moving aircraft separate, either by using radar, or, if radar is not available, by a procedural control based on aircraft estimates and performance. They organize aircraft into the most rapid order for landing, or, if there are delays, place aircraft into a holding pattern clear of the departure path.

Aerodrome control

Controllers at aerodromes ensure that aircraft taxi safely, taking their turn in an orderly manner from their parking stands to the runways, and keep vehicles clear. The controllers are responsible for separating aircraft and instructing them to take-off or land as rapidly and efficiently as possible. At major airports, this task is divided into air control and ground movement control.

WORK ENVIRONMENT

In area and approach control, ATCOs work in rooms with low levels of lighting to enable them to see clearly the information relayed to them on radar screens. Daylight-viewing radar, however, is increasingly being used. They do not have visual contact with the aircraft themselves.

Aerodrome controllers work in a control tower which has a 360 degree view of the surrounding area, thereby allowing them visual contact with aircraft.

Most ATCOs work in a seated position and wear headphones. Work, particularly at peak periods, can be intense, with aircraft at Heathrow, for example, landing and taking off at a rate of two a minute.

SKILLS AND INTERESTS

The work requires the capacity for intense concentration and a very strong sense of responsibility. ATCOs need to be able to respond quickly and efficiently at all times, particularly in emergencies. They need to be decisive and have a calm, unruffled method of working. A high standard of physical fitness is required, including good colour vision, eyesight and hearing and a clear speaking voice.

As controllers normally work in the same team, gaining rapport with each other, ability in and liking for team work is very important. Technical aptitude is also important, because of the complex radar and computer systems used. The ability to deal with figure work and calculations is also important.

ENTRY REQUIREMENTS

Entry requirements for the necessary training depend on the employer. Most ATCOs are employed by National Air Traffic Services (NATS) whose requirements for student entry are as follows:

– aged at least 18 and under 27 years on the date of application;

– GCSEs/S grades (A-C/1-3) including English and maths. As further evidence of academic ability, applicants should have completed a period of post-GCSE/S grade education, such as two A levels/three H grades; or a BTEC/SCOTVEC national course; or Advanced GNVQ/GSVQ Level III.

– candidates with previous relevant aviation radar experience are required to have English and maths GCSEs/S grades (A-C/1-3), but may be accepted without further examination passes.

ATCOs employed by NATS must be eligible to work in the UK and need security clearance before starting work.

The other employers of ATCOs in civil aviation vary in their requirements, some only employing experienced personnel. Others usually recruit entrants aged between 18 and 21 years and expect five GCSEs/S grades (A-C/1-3) including English, maths and a science. Applicants with alternative qualifications, eg GNVQ/GSVQ, are considered on their merits.

A good standard of fitness is necessary, with normal colour vision, good eyesight and hearing and no speech defects. ATCOs need to pass regular medical tests.

All ATCOs have to obtain Civil Aviation Authority (CAA) licences to do their work.

TRAINING

NATS Student Air Traffic Controller Scheme

The training consists of courses of study followed by practical training lasting 74 weeks. Most of the courses are run at Bournemouth International Airport at the Civil Aviation Authority's College of Air Traffic Control. Practical training is on simulators at the college followed by live training at operational units throughout the UK. The courses include subjects such as: aviation studies; telecommunications; navigation; meteorology; and radar and non-radar elements of aerodrome approach and area control. Examinations have to be passed at various stages in order to continue training.

Trainees study for the award of CAA licences, three of which are needed to qualify and are normally obtained during the course. The type of licence obtained depends on whether the student is due to go to an area centre or an airport.

Licences have to be validated for the place of work by completing a period of supervised duty before the ATCO is permitted to control aircraft solo. Other courses are available to experienced ATCOs, such as automatic data processing, technical appreciation and instructor training.

Other airports and local authority entry

Training is through courses at the College of Air Traffic Control at Bournemouth International Airport or other approved air traffic control training establishment. This is supplemented by on-the-job training, before beginning operational work.

NVQs/SVQs in air traffic control are being developed.

LATE ENTRY

The age restrictions outlined under ENTRY REQUIREMENTS apply.

OPPORTUNITIES

The majority of UK air traffic controllers are employed by NATS, which is a joint CAA and Ministry of Defence organization and employs some 1,500 ATCOs. They work at BAA airports and certain other airports, and at the main area centres at West Drayton and Prestwick. The airport air traffic services are at Aberdeen, Belfast, Birmingham, Cardiff, Edinburgh, Farnborough, Gatwick, Glasgow, Heathrow, London City, Manchester, Stansted and Sumburgh. Although a preference can be expressed, ATCOs may be posted wherever needed.

Currently more ATCOs are needed as air traffic increases and new ATC systems are introduced. Recruitment is likely to be at a rate of over 90 student entrants a year over the next few years at least.

Air traffic controllers are also employed at private and local authority owned airports and at private airfields.

There are some opportunities in Commonwealth and other English-speaking countries, but these countries have their own licensing requirements and are increasingly employing their own nationals.

PAY AND CONDITIONS

Student air traffic controllers with NATS earn £14,202 on appointment and £14,921 on successful completion of radar rating, and are also paid an accommodation allowance. On appointment as ATCO the annual salary is £24,000 rising to over £37,000. Those in the most responsible positions can earn over £48,000. These figures include an unsocial hours payment of £3,536 for those working shifts.

Air traffic control services operate 24 hours a day and most ATCOs do a 40-hour week with eight-hour shift periods, spending two hours maximum sitting at a radar screen followed by half-hour breaks (longer at busy periods). The week usually includes night, early morning and late afternoon shifts, as well as bank holidays and weekends.

PROSPECTS

Promotion after training in NATS is by a grade system from ATCO 3 to ATCO 2 and then to ATCO 1, depending on the units at which ATCOs are stationed and level of responsibility. Beyond grade 1, promotion is to management and planning. Additional training is provided at the College of Air Training for specific posts such as instructing.

RELATED OCCUPATIONS

Air traffic control officer (Armed Forces), airline pilot, airline flight operations assistant, coastguard, merchant navy officer.

FURTHER INFORMATION

The Aeronautical Training Group, Prospect Way, London Luton Airport, Luton, Bedfordshire LU2 9QH, 01582 418668

Aviation Training Association*, 125 London Road, High Wycombe, Bucks HP11 1BT, 01494 445262.

Recruitment and Selection*, Meadowbank, British Airways, PO Box 59, Hounslow, Middlesex TW5 2QX

Oxford Air Training School, CSE Aviation Ltd, Oxford Airport, Kidlington, Oxford OX5 1RA, 01865 841234

Civil Aviation Authority*, Recruitment Services, Room T820, CAA House, 45-59 Kingsway, London WC2B 6TE, 0171 832 6696

General Aviation Manufacturers and Trades Association Ltd, 19 Church Street, Brill, Aylesbury, Bucks HP18 9TG, 01844 238020

National Air Traffic Services*, CAA House, 45-49 Kingsway, London WC2B 6TE

FURTHER READING

Leaflets/booklets are available from the addresses marked*.

Flight International Directory Part 1 UK and Ireland – Flight International Directories

Periodicals: Flight International – Reed Business Publishing

In the careers library classified under YAB/RAB.

1. ROAD TRANSPORT MANAGER CLCI:YAD
2. BUS/COACH DRIVER CLCI:YAD
3. BUS CONDUCTOR CLCI:YAD
4. TAXI/PRIVATE HIRE VEHICLE DRIVER CLCI:YAD
5. LGV DRIVER CLCI:YAD
6. CAR/VAN DRIVER CLCI:YAD
7. DRIVING INSTRUCTOR CLCI:YAD

BACKGROUND INFORMATION

As many people in large cities rely on public transport to reach their places of work, most industries and businesses in the UK are dependent on a smoothly flowing passenger transport system. **Road passenger traffic** consists largely of local public transport, coach companies running scheduled services between major towns and cities, holiday tour operators, and companies offering private coach hire. **Road haulage and delivery** are carried out by operators which may be single-vehicle businesses or companies owning fleets of 1,000 vehicles. The road haulage industry is one of the most important service industries in the country: over 85 to 90 per cent of the nation's goods are carried by road in about 450,000 large goods vehicles.

1. ROAD TRANSPORT MANAGER (YAD)

THE WORK

The road transport manager's job is to maximize the use of resources, both people and vehicles. In some small firms the transport manager is also a driver, and in solo operations is owner-driver or, effectively, driver-manager.

There are two sectors of the road goods transport industry: the 'own account' sector, firms that transport their own goods; and the 'hire or reward' sector, firms that exist in order to transport goods for other people. A similar division exists in the bus and coach sector.

The main responsibility of transport managers is to plan the work schedules of drivers and vehicles. In road haulage, they arrange a vehicle, driver and delivery date for each load, make sure that every vehicle travels full, and try to find a load for the return journey as it is not economic to have lorries travelling empty. Plans are entered on large diary sheets. Transport managers calculate whether a load will fit into a vehicle without breaking the weight regulations, and whether it can be delivered on time without breaking laws either on drivers' working hours or on the distance travelled by a vehicle since its last service. Large firms use computers for such calculations.

Costing is an important part of the work; prices have to be competitive enough to attract customers but high enough to cover costs and make a profit. When customers ask for an estimate over the phone, the transport manager has to think quickly.

Route planning calls for knowledge of the geography of the firm's area, shipping, docks, tipping sites, overnight parking, and drivers' accommodation facilities, etc. The transport manager works out the safest and shortest route to the destination, taking into account such hazards as low bridges and extensive road works.

They also ensure that maintenance and repairs are carried out effectively at the scheduled times.

There is a considerable amount of paperwork: invoices, delivery notes, shipping documents, etc. In addition the transport manager must follow up customers' complaints and cope with emergencies, such as accidents and breakdowns. There is also an element of personnel work; the transport manager must brief drivers, answer their questions, handle their complaints, delegate work and make sure the office runs smoothly.

There are a great many laws and regulations relating to the road haulage industry, and it is the transport manager's responsibility to see that none of these is broken, and at the same time that the best use is made of drivers and vehicles. In particular, they must ensure their drivers are aware of the current regulations regarding tachographs, drivers' hours and over-loading. They are responsible for preventing and removing any malpractices.

While all this falls within the responsibility of the transport manager, in larger firms the detailed work is carried out by clerical staff or junior managers whom the transport manager supervises.

WORK ENVIRONMENT

The transport manager spends most of the day in the traffic office, part of it in the yard with the drivers, and part in the workshop with maintenance staff.

SKILLS AND INTERESTS

Transport managers come into contact with all sorts of people: lorry drivers, mechanics, maintenance staff and customers. They will have some dealings with the police, the Department of Transport, the Licensing Authority, trade unions and employers' associations, and they have to be able to communicate with all these people, on the telephone, face to face and in writing.

Excellent organizational skills are required for planning and scheduling work. Computer literacy and mathematical ability are needed for route scheduling, expenditure control, etc. An understanding of relevant legislation is essential. Foreign languages may be an advantage.

Transport managers should be sociable, practical and tough but flexible in outlook and not given to worrying. They must be able to think and act quickly and work under pressure. Tolerance and a sense of humour are needed to deal with disgruntled drivers, complaining customers and difficult situations. Transport managers must be accurate when doing cost calculations as mistakes can prove expensive. They have to take responsibility for their own actions; when anything goes wrong they are in the front line.

ENTRY REQUIREMENTS

Transport managers are normally required to hold a driving licence for the class of vehicle for which they are responsible. EU legislation requires all transport managers from both national and international firms to hold a Certificate of Professional Competence (CPC) which can be acquired during training.

Many transport managers start their careers as drivers or clerks and work their way up, but direct entry to a one to two-year management training scheme normally requires a minimum of five GCSEs/S grades (A-C/1-3), including English and maths, with two A level/three H grades. The Chartered Institute of Transport recommends that A level/H grade subjects include economics or geography. Many management trainees have degrees or BTEC/ SCOTVEC higher national certificates/diplomas.

TRAINING

Management training is primarily on the job, working alongside and assisting experienced managers in a series of different departments, possibly with short courses at training centres in specialist aspects.

Training may include assessment for NVQ/SVQ in Supervisory Management at Level 3 and/or in Management at Level 4, to standards set by the Confederation of Passenger Transport UK (CPT UK) and the Road Haulage and Distribution Training Council (RHDTC).

In addition, practising managers of 'hire or reward' and passenger transport firms require a Certificate of Professional Competence (CPC). This can be achieved by becoming a corporate member of a recognized professional body such as the Chartered Institute of Transport (CIT) or the Institute of Transport Administration (IoTA), or by passing an examination administered by the Royal Society of Arts (RSA) or IoTA, or by obtaining the CIT Certificate in Transport.

Membership of the professional bodies is achieved by passing or gaining exemption from their examinations. Holders of relevant degrees or BTEC/SCOTVEC higher national certificates or diplomas (in Transport Management, Transport Operations, for example) may gain full or part exemption. Further details are available from the CIT or IoTA.

Courses for the CPC are available via correspondence, at local colleges or other training establishments – a list of centres is available from the RSA or IoTA.

Postgraduate qualifications in transport are also available.

LATE ENTRY

There is no age limit for entry, though entry to management trainee schemes is normally after university or college. Entry may be possible from driving and clerical jobs into supervisory or junior manager posts. A relevant BTEC/SCOTVEC award or degree may assist promotion prospects.

OPPORTUNITIES

Most firms in the contract haulage sector have a transport manager. Only the larger firms in the 'own account' sector do so; in smaller companies these duties will be handled by a manager who also has other responsibilities.

Contract haulage has increased in recent years while own-account operators have declined, as large companies have come to realize that it is more economic to contract out these services.

PAY AND CONDITIONS

Pay is negotiated by individuals and therefore varies from firm to firm. Rates of pay are likely to be higher in the 'own account' sector. Transport managers earn salaries broadly equivalent to other managerial posts demanding similar qualifications or experience. Most earn in the region of £12,000 to £20,000. Many transport managers earn additional payments for unsocial hours. These shift allowances can often be considerable.

Shift work and long/irregular hours are common.

PROSPECTS

In small firms promotion is unlikely but in large organizations it is possible to progress to responsibility for several branches or depots in an area or region, and from there to national transport manager. A move into general management may then be possible.

Experienced staff may move into related areas, such as local authority highways and planning departments, transport consultancy or teaching in further or higher education.

RELATED OCCUPATIONS

Distribution manager, warehouse manager, freight forwarder, LGV driver, travel agent.

FURTHER INFORMATION

Chartered Institute of Transport*, 80 Portland Place, London W1N 4DP, 0171 636 9952

Institute of Transport Administration*, 32 Palmerston Road, Southampton SO14 1LL, 01703 631380

Road Haulage and Distribution Training Council (RHDTC)*, Suite C, Shenley Hall, Rectory Lane, Shenley, Radlett, Hertfordshire WD7 9AN, 01923 858461

RSA Examination Board, Westwood Way, Coventry CV4 9HS, 01203 470033

DFURTHER READING

Leaflets/booklets are available from the addresses marked*.

IPC Transport Press Journals: Motor Transport, Commercial Transport Magazine

The Transport Manager's and Operators' Handbook – Kogan Page

Transport and Distribution – AGCAS

Careers on the Move – CIT

Transport Management (the IoTA bi-monthly journal)

In the careers library classified under YAD.

2. BUS/COACH DRIVER (YAD)

THE WORK

The duties carried out by the bus or coach driver depend on the type of service being offered.

Local bus services are the most common type of bus driving. London services and a few other companies offer a crewed service, but most now favour one-person operation (OPO), ie one person driving and collecting fares.

Long-distance and excursion services: there are four different areas of work, and individual drivers may be involved in all four:

Long-distance express services. This type of driving has longer distances between stops and may include some motorway driving. Drivers have to move passengers' suitcases into and out of the boot of the coach when passengers embark or leave at a main stopping point. There is a network of these routes across the country. There may be shorter, express inter-city services between large towns and cities within an area.

Day excursions include trips to the countryside, exhibitions, sports events, the seaside, etc. The driver has to start at a particular time and location and arrive at a particular time at the destination. Full-day excursions are likely to involve day and evening work. Drivers must be careful not to exceed the legal number of hours they may drive without a break. Long periods of waiting may occur on reaching their destination.

Regular contract bookings. The coach and driver are hired by an organization to follow the same route, usually both morning and evening, picking up and setting down particular passengers (as opposed to the general public). These may be school-children, factory workers, nurses, and similar.

Holiday tours. During a holiday tour, a driver may be away from home for up to three weeks at a time. The driver follows the main routes that the organization or employer has planned out but, within this, has some authority to make minor changes due to traffic hold-ups, unexpected hazards, and so on. This work involves responsibilities that are in addition to the usual ones of passenger (and pedestrian) safety. A serious mechanical breakdown could involve having the coach repaired, hiring another coach, or arranging for alternative accommodation for the passengers if it is not possible to get them to the planned destination.

WORK ENVIRONMENT

Driving in a large town or city, with heavy traffic and many pedestrians, is very different from the slower pace of country routes. The driver of a crewed bus has a very different environment from the driver of an OPO bus who has to deal much more with passengers. All drivers must cope with driving safely under varying light conditions and in all types of weather.

Local bus services. Town and city bus drivers, whose routes include the majority of local bus services, negotiate a route through heavy traffic and the pollution caused by traffic exhaust fumes.

Private hire and excursion services may involve driving in the city, countryside, or to the seaside. It is often necessary to wait around for several hours for passengers to return to the vehicle.

Holiday tours require much more involvement with the passengers. If the tour is to a foreign country, a driver has to cope with a foreign language and any problems that occur. Changes of route, due to road conditions or hazards, also pose more problems if the country is not well-known to the driver. They may spend long or short periods away from home.

The wearing of a uniform is usually compulsory. Much of the time is spent sitting at the controls. In modern or luxury coaches there may be specially designed seats for maximum comfort.

SKILLS AND INTERESTS

Bus and coach drivers need to be skilled at driving in all sorts of conditions, including bad weather, busy traffic, and so on, on all types of roads. They need to be patient and calm with the ability to maintain concentration. Bus and coach drivers need to be honest and reliable. They should be punctual and able to work unsupervised. Good communication skills are required, as is a pleasant manner when working with the public. Numeracy is needed for those taking fares and giving change. Coach drivers require good map-reading skills, and, for those working with tourists, historical and general knowledge is useful.

Drivers must be in good health and have a reasonable standard of fitness. For safety reasons, drivers should not have heart trouble.

ENTRY REQUIREMENTS

Most bus or coach operators do not require any formal academic qualifications. Organizations may give arithmetic tests to applicants, to check that would-be employees would have no problems giving change or adding up the day's takings. Some also assess driving skills. A full clean car driving licence is essential. Employers may also look for a few years' experience of driving and of working with people, eg as a shop assistant.

Some firms lay down minimum and maximum height requirements. Drivers may also be expected to pass a medical examination; drivers over 45 who are applying for or renewing a PCV licence require a medical certificate. Wearers of contact lenses and those suffering from certain medical conditions may not be accepted.

All bus and coach drivers must hold a Passenger Carrying Vehicle (PCV) licence; some firms prefer entrants who hold a PCV licence already. The minimum age for the PCV test is 21 years, so this is effectively the minimum age for entry, though some firms may accept people under this age as trainee drivers.

Some bus operators do not take on new employees as trainee drivers. They take on trainee bus conductors and give them driver training later if a vacancy occurs and they are thought to be suitable for the job. Would-be drivers undergo a great deal of on-the-job training as bus conductors. This includes learning bus routes, and practice in dealing with the public, working out fares and giving change. It also enables them to get used to the shift system.

TRAINING

A bus driver is required, by law, to have a PCV (Passenger Carrying Vehicle) licence. Private training and examination are available; it is also possible to be trained by the employing firm. Consult *Yellow Pages* for private training organizations running courses for the PCV licence and approach local bus/coach companies for their requirements.

If accepted for driver training, an employee spends some time in a training school, receiving tuition in a classroom, and on and off the road. For firms running one-person operated buses or coaches, training in handling passengers, dealing with fares and tickets, etc may precede or accompany driver training.

Initial practice in manoeuvring takes place off the road but this is followed by a period spent practising manoeuvring on a variety of actual routes, accompanied by a trainer. The period of time spent on driving training depends on the quickness and ability of the trainee but is usually around ten to fifteen days. When trainees are considered ready they take a PCV test. They may practise in a skid pan, learning to control buses in dangerous situations, though buses are exceptionally stable vehicles.

When they have obtained a PCV licence, bus drivers are given a period of route learning.

NVQs/SVQs in Bus and Coach Driving and Customer Care are available at Level 2. A Level 3 qualification is planned for long-distance coach drivers who have the additional responsibilities of dealing with hotels, tourist attractions, etc.

LATE ENTRY

There is effectively a minimum age limit of 21 years for bus and coach driving jobs. Some companies specify an upper age limit of between 50 and 60 years, but many employers accept people up to retirement age as long as they are fit enough to cope with the demands of the job and pass a medical. Experience of driving a minibus or van helps when applying for jobs.

OPPORTUNITIES

Bus and coach drivers can work for local authorities, passenger transport executives, private coach hire or charter firms, express services and tour operators. Openings vary from region to region. Overall, jobs have declined in recent years. However, there are still opportunities in large towns and cities, and for drivers who are prepared to work on tours and travel all over this country and/or abroad.

Self-employment is possible for those with the necessary experience and available capital required to buy a coach or bus. For this they need to hold a Certificate of Professional Competence, obtained by exam or by becoming a member of a professional body such as the Institute of Transport Administration or the Chartered Institute of Transport.

PAY AND CONDITIONS

Wages vary from company to company and depending on the location and type of driving involved.

Basic weekly wages are for five-day weekly rotas, and include Saturday and Sunday premium rates and any overtime that is built into the basic duties. Rates also vary for minibus drivers and big bus drivers, coach drivers generally receiving allowances for staying away from home.

Shift work is often necessary. Drivers are usually expected to work from 35 to 42 hours a week, Monday to Sunday. Shifts last for approximately eight hours (though some may involve four hours on duty, four hours off and four hours back on). Some large bus companies have a small permanent nightshift. The dayshift can run from 4.15am to 12.00 midnight, and drivers can be expected to work any shifts between these times. Shifts are usually arranged on a rota basis.

Saturday and Sunday work is built into the basic schedule, and overtime work is available.

PROSPECTS

A possible career progression for a bus driver is to gain promotion to an inspector. There are various grades of inspector. Some work on general traffic duties, whilst others are part of the garage supervisory staff. Others work in radio-control rooms. Prospects for promotion vary, however; in many companies avenues for promotion do not exist.

Bus drivers may take a sideways step and join the ranks of the clerical staff, progressing from there to managerial and administrative positions within a bus organization. Most large bus companies give vacancy information to all their employees, and preference is sometimes given to employees who can prove that they are capable of other types of work. It may also be possible to train to become a bus and coach driving instructor. An NVQ/SVQ in Bus and Coach Driving Instruction is available at Level 3.

Some drivers move from public transport into driving for day trips or holiday tour groups.

RELATED OCCUPATIONS

LGV driver, car/van driver, roundsman/woman, removal man/woman, taxi/private hire vehicle driver.

FURTHER INFORMATION AND READING

Please see article 3. BUS CONDUCTOR.

3. BUS CONDUCTOR (YAD)

THE WORK

Bus conductors collect fares, issue tickets and check bus passes. They deal with passengers' questions, advising them when they have reached their destination and directing them around the district. They also provide help with customers' baggage, such as loading and unloading pushchairs and heavy shopping onto the bus.

Conductors must ensure the safety of their passengers at all times by limiting the numbers allowed standing, controlling children, etc. They check the bus does not pull away when passengers get on and off; the conductor signals to the driver to start off from bus stops.

Paperwork includes noting the number and types of passenger, recording the fares, referring to tables to check fares and times of buses, logging the length of journey and any incidents, such as writing brief accident reports when necessary. They count, bag and balance the money taken, with the number of tickets issued.

WORK ENVIRONMENT

Buses and coaches are fairly comfortable, but can be very cold on winter mornings or uncomfortably hot in summer. Conductors may have to cope with the smell of fumes from traffic.

Periods of very hectic work (such as rush hours) are often interspersed with periods of relative quiet. Conductors may have to wait to change buses and routes in all weathers.

SKILLS AND INTERESTS

Conductors need to be reliable and punctual, neat and tidy in appearance and willing to wear a uniform. They require good communication skills and must be polite and patient when dealing with all members of the public. A friendly and cheerful nature is helpful. They should be able to do basic arithmetic, to take fares and give change. Conductors need to be able to work well without supervision and work as part of a team with the driver. The job involves a large amount of standing, walking and, on some buses, climbing stairs, so conductors must be fit and active.

ENTRY REQUIREMENTS

Applicants should normally be over 18 years, although younger people may be accepted by companies running special training schemes. No minimum academic qualifications are required. Most bus companies set tests, including spoken English and arithmetic/cash handling. Some firms prefer applicants to live near the garage where they are based. It is sometimes in the candidate's favour to have a driving licence or be learning to drive. Experience in work dealing with the public such as waiter/waitress or shop assistant may help as well.

Some bus companies specify a maximum height of 1.83m (six feet). Wearers of contact lenses and those with certain medical conditions may not be accepted for entry. All bus companies require candidates to pass a medical.

TRAINING

Conductors usually train for two to four weeks but this varies from company to company.

Training covers all conductor duties, for example: reading fare tables; operating ticket machines; keeping records of tickets issued; cashing up; company regulations; safety; and customer care. A period of time is usually spent on route-learning and working with a crew under the supervision of an experienced conductor. Some companies give trainees a test at the end of their training; others rely on an assessment by the supervisor.

Some companies run training schemes for young people where they may gain experience in clerical and garage maintenance departments before becoming conductors as soon as they are 18 years old.

LATE ENTRY

There is usually no upper age limit for entry, though some companies refuse applicants over 50 or 55 years. Most companies accept or prefer mature applicants, providing they are fit, healthy and have the required personal qualities such as self-confidence and good communication skills.

OPPORTUNITIES

Opportunities exist with bus companies. Many companies have now switched to one-person operated (driver-only) buses, so opportunities may be limited.

Demand for bus conductors varies from region to region. They are mostly employed on buses in cities and large towns.

PAY AND CONDITIONS

Pay varies according to the employer and the shifts worked. As well as statutory overtime, there is extra pay for working unsocial hours, weekends, and for the four-hour wait between split shifts. There is a very small number of conductors employed throughout the country with pay varying depending on location.

Conductors work a 38 to 40-hour week. Overtime is available in some companies; some expect crews to work six days, although this is not compulsory. The working week starts on Monday and rest days are rotated to give three or four every five to six weeks. Crews work eight-hour shifts: very early morning (3 or 4am) to early afternoon; early afternoon to early evening; and early evening to late at night. Some companies work split shifts: four-hour turns in the morning and afternoon rush hours with a gap of four hours in between. Routines change weekly following rest days; as bus services start and finish at different times, so shift times vary from day to day. Crews must get to and from work when public transport is not running; most garages operate a staff bus along a limited route.

PROSPECTS

Many conductors enter training to become Passenger Carrying Vehicle (PCV) drivers, once they are familiar with their company's services, routes and fare system. Those with experience as drivers can be promoted to inspector, depending on ability.

Some conductors, who are promoted to supervisory or inspector level, work on schedules or routes. A few people move to work for private coach companies as stewards and stewardesses.

RELATED OCCUPATIONS

Train driver, taxi/private hire vehicle driver, station assistant, bus/coach driver.

FURTHER INFORMATION

See local telephone directories and *Yellow Pages* for addresses of local bus and coach companies.

Bus and Coach Training Limited*, Regency House, 43 High Street, Rickmansworth, Hertfordshire WD3 1ET, 01923 896607

FURTHER READING

Leaflets/booklets are available from the address marked*.
Job Outlines – Driving – COIC
In the careers library classified under YAD.

4. TAXI/PRIVATE HIRE VEHICLE DRIVER (YAD)

THE WORK

Taxi and private hire drivers carry passengers to their destinations in return for payment.

Taxi drivers must hold a special licence (see TRAINING). They may stand at a designated taxi rank, or ply for hire, ie drive around looking for passengers.

Most drivers assist passengers and load luggage, then start the sealed fare meter (rented and maintained by large companies) to show the cost of the journey. They are responsible for driving the customer by the most direct or convenient route – this can be enforced by law.

They collect the fare from the customer when the journey is over, and change is given if appropriate.

All drivers perform minor emergency repairs and keep their taxis clean, inside and out. They are responsible for the car being in a roadworthy condition.

Private hire vehicles carry out similar duties but are not allowed to stand at taxi ranks or ply for hire.

Customers contact taxi hire agencies who contact drivers using two-way radios.

Private hire drivers may make longer trips – to airports, bus and rail stations, for example; they may also be hired for functions such as weddings and funerals.

WORK ENVIRONMENT

Most time is spent in the cab or car, with limited space and long periods of sitting. Helping customers with luggage involves bending, lifting and carrying. There may be fumes from traffic.

SKILLS AND INTERESTS

Taxi/private hire drivers must be competent drivers, who remain alert and are able to concentrate. They need to be able to drive carefully in all conditions – bad weather, heavy traffic, etc. They must be honest and trustworthy. Patience and the ability to deal with people tactfully are needed. Some mechanical knowledge is useful to undertake emergency repairs, though most use garage services. Basic numeracy is needed to give correct change to customers and complete tax returns.

Good health and eyesight are essential: taxi drivers are expected to go for regular health checks.

ENTRY REQUIREMENTS

Taxi drivers: no formal educational qualifications are required but a full, clean driving licence is needed. Applicants must obtain a special licence from their local authority, or, in London, from the Public Carriage Office (PCO). To hold this, they must be over 21 years but applications may be considered from those over 20 years and 3 months. They must also pass a medical. All applicants need a good knowledge of their area and may have to take a test.

In London, candidates must pass the 'Knowledge of London' test before they are issued with a licence.

Recent criminal convictions or serious traffic convictions are a bar to obtaining a cab driver's licence, although this may not apply if a reasonable number of years has elapsed without further incident.

Private hire vehicle drivers: do not require a special licence in all local authorities. However, some impose their own regulations, such as set tests and medicals. These may be the same as for taxi drivers and the licence may allow them to drive both types of car.

TRAINING

Taxi drivers must undertake training to gain their licence. This is most difficult in **London** where they must do 'the Knowledge'. For those aiming to work as a taxi driver in central London or at Heathrow Airport, they must do the 'All London' test. Suitable candidates are issued with a Blue Book which lists 400 'runs' within a six-mile radius of Charing Cross, which they must learn. This is usually done by riding a moped or cycling round London making notes. This can take up to four years but is possible in 12 to 24 months. Some private schools offer coaching in preparing for the test; students working in small groups can learn faster. When learner taxi drivers are sure that they know all routes, street names and places of interest required, they must pass: the Knowledge of London test – a number of 15-minute oral examinations conducted by a Knowledge of London Examiner at the PCO, and a driving test.

If successful, they receive a licence and the green badge allowing them to ply or stand for hire anywhere within the Metropolitan and City of London police areas (a total of 786 square miles).

Another option is to study for a suburban licence covering one of 16 'sectors' outside the central London area. For a licence and a 'yellow badge', drivers must learn 30 runs and pass a knowledge test. This is possible in six to twelve months. Yellow badge drivers can ply for hire within their licensed area and are allowed to take passengers outside the area. However, they are not allowed to pick up passengers outside their sector.

Outside London, most local authorities set their own tests of local knowledge, usually with a stringent driving test, before awarding licences.

Private hire drivers do not need a special licence in all local authorities. Some, however, have the same requirements as for taxi drivers.

NVQ/SVQs at Levels 1, 2 and 3 should be available soon, suitable for new entrants, experienced drivers and for those planning to become taxi/private hire operators.

LATE ENTRY

There is no upper age limit for entry and adult entry is common for taxi and private hire driving. Previous experience of driving work can be helpful.

OPPORTUNITIES

Licensed taxi drivers and private hire vehicle drivers are self-employed. They may be an owner-driver, a journeyman/woman (hires the cab from a fleet operator) or a flat operator (rents the cab from the owner).

The largest number of taxi drivers work in London and are governed by the Public Carriage Office. Other taxi drivers are granted their licence by the local authority. Opportunities occur throughout the country, but there is likely to be more demand in towns and cities.

PAY AND CONDITIONS

Earnings are entirely dependent on fares taken; owner-drivers generally earn more than journeymen/women. Licensing authorities control the maximum fares charged by taxi drivers, except in London where the tariff is set by the Government. Most private hire agencies use the same rates, to be competitive.

Taxi drivers can work long and irregular hours; there is no legal limit on the time they spend driving. They are only restricted when, as journeymen/women, they are working a double shift with another driver and must return to change over. Peak periods are morning and evening, between which drivers may be out for 18 hours, although not all of this will be spent driving.

PROSPECTS

There is no promotion ladder; journeymen/women often work towards becoming owner-drivers, possibly with the long-term aim of owning a fleet of vehicles.

RELATED OCCUPATIONS

LGV driver, chauffeur/chauffeuse, car/van driver, bus/coach driver, roundsman/woman.

FURTHER INFORMATION

Licensed Taxi Drivers Association, 9-11 Woodfield Road, London W9 2BA, 0171 286 1046/7

Metropolitan Police Service, Public Carriage Office*, 15 Penton Street, London N1 9PU, 0171 230 1631

Private Hire, Hackney Carriage and Chauffeur ITO, c/o 14 Widdrington Terrace, North Shields, Tyne and Wear NE29 0BZ, 0191 258 1955

FURTHER READING

Leaflets/booklets are available from the address marked*.

Job Outlines – Driving – COIC

In the careers library classified under YAD.

5. LGV DRIVER (YAD)

THE WORK

Large goods vehicle (LGV) drivers (formerly heavy goods vehicle drivers) collect, transport and deliver goods. LGVs are divided into two categories, according to the weight and the type of vehicle: an LGV licence with category C entitlement qualifies the holder to drive rigid vehicles over 7.5 tonnes; an LGV licence with category C and E qualifies the holder to drive articulated lorries and lorries pulling a trailer.

Drivers may have to clean, refuel, load and unload their

lorries; the load has to be secured with ropes and covered with special sheets. This can be heavy, dirty, and wet work, and protective clothing is usually provided. Drivers are solely responsible for the safety of their loads; they must be able to deal with leakages, accidents and mechanical faults. Some drivers specialize in transporting dangerous loads, such as petrol, chemicals, nuclear waste.

Drivers may plan their own routes, aiming for the quickest and most economical. Those who work for small firms or are self-employed may have to find their own loads for the return journey.

Drivers must know, understand and obey the many regulations relating to their vehicles, eg weight and load-distribution rules, special speed limits. A tachograph in the lorry cab records the number of hours spent driving, resting, doing other work such as loading and unloading, the speed of the vehicle and the distance travelled.

Drivers are also likely to deal with documents such as customers' invoices and delivery notes.

WORK ENVIRONMENT

Modern lorry cabs can be very comfortable, with insulation, heating and air-conditioning. Some lorries have sleeping bunks, and even cookers and fridges, for long-distance trips. Some LGV drivers travel to overseas destinations. Much time is spent alone. Loading and unloading usually takes place out of doors.

SKILLS AND INTERESTS

LGV drivers must enjoy driving and have good driving ability. They require patience and a tolerant attitude to other road users. It is also important to be able to maintain concentration for long periods while driving. Drivers must be happy to spend most of their working hours alone. They need a responsible attitude and must be able to work without supervision. They should be careful and security conscious; the loads lorries carry are valuable and some can be potentially dangerous. Loading and unloading can involve lifting and carrying heavy items. Drivers need to be polite to customers and must be able to complete the necessary paperwork.

ENTRY REQUIREMENTS

Drivers must be literate and numerate; they must hold the appropriate LGV licence (see TRAINING), and possess a good driving record. Some firms recruit only drivers over the age of 25 for insurance reasons. The LGV test includes a medical: good eyesight and good colour vision are necessary. Candidates must normally be at least 21 years of age.

However, the LGV Young Driver Scheme has been re-introduced. Entry to this can be at 16-19 years, though employers are more likely to take 16-17 year olds. There are no educational requirements, but successful applicants are likely to have a few GCSEs/S grades (C/3 or above), preferably including maths and English, to indicate they can cope with NVQ/SVQ Level 2. They have to meet the same medical requirements as older drivers.

Modern Apprenticeships are also available, which may include LGV driver training. Applicants should have three GCSEs/S grades (C/3 or above) in maths, English and one other subject, or Intermediate GNVQ/GSVQ Level II, or equivalent, in order to display ability to complete the Apprenticeship and achieve NVQ/SVQ Level 3.

TRAINING

The LGV licence is divided into two categories: category C entitles the holder to drive rigid vehicles over 7.5 tonnes, and category C and E, which also entitles the holder to drive articulated lorries and lorries pulling a trailer. Firms may train their own drivers; join together in a training association and combine to employ an instructor; use the group training associations; or use the LGV sections of private driving schools. Courses last one to three weeks, depending on the category of vehicle. In addition to driving skills and knowledge, they may also cover simple mechanics, loading, and securing loads. The test consists of manoeuvring the vehicle in a confined space, 25 miles of road driving, and answering questions on the Highway Code and LGV regulations.

Trainees on the Young Driver's Scheme will normally obtain a car/van driving (Category B) licence at 17 years and gain an LGV rigid vehicle licence at 18 years. This allows them to work as a driver unaccompanied on revenue-earning activities for their employer. After two years of satisfactory monitored experience, they may start training to drive an articulated lorry on a provisional C and E licence. They are assessed towards NVQ/SVQ in Transporting Goods by Road at Level 2. On completing the scheme at 21 years, they receive a Young Large Goods Vehicle Driver Certificate.

Modern apprentices specializing in driving are expected to undertake NVQ/SVQ Level 2 units in Transporting Goods by Road, plus some units from the Storage and Organizing Road Transport Operations. They go on to units in Supervisory Management at Level 3. On completion, an Apprenticeship Certificate is awarded by the Road Haulage and Distribution Training Council (RHDTC). Apprenticeships are expected to take three to four years.

Experienced drivers and trainee drivers may also be assessed for NVQ/SVQ qualifications.

It is possible to train for an LGV licence privately, at a specialist driving school, and take the test independently.

LATE ENTRY

Opportunities are available for adults in this type of work. Entrants must hold the appropriate LGV licence, and possess a good driving record. The majority of LGV drivers are over 25 years. Some insurance companies demand drivers are over 30 years, for example those driving hazardous chemicals.

Some people enter LGV driving work or training for it from employment in other jobs in the road haulage and distribution industries such as warehouse worker.

OPPORTUNITIES

Opportunities are available throughout the country; however, competition for work is keen. Many LGV drivers are self-employed, owning and driving one vehicle. Some firms operate lorries to carry their own goods, but the main employers of LGV drivers are independent road haulage firms. Some firms specialize in transporting certain goods, such as livestock and chemicals.

PAY AND CONDITIONS

Wages vary according to the carrying capacity of the vehicle and the nature of its load. Average earnings based on a standard 40-hour week range from £9,000 to £12,000, depending on the area and class of driver.

LGV drivers work a basic 40-hour week that is governed by strict legal requirements. A driver must not drive for more than nine hours in a day. After four-and-a-half hours driving, whether continuous or accumulated, drivers must take a break of 45 minutes. A driver must have a minimum daily rest of eleven consecutive hours. This may be reduced to nine hours not more than three times a week as long as the reduction is compensated by an equivalent rest before the end of the following week.

A subsistence allowance for reimbursement of any overnight expenses incurred is paid tax-free.

PROSPECTS

Drivers who show management potential may become supervisors or move into managerial positions in larger firms. Many aspire to having their own vehicle, becoming self-employed and ultimately owning their own haulage firm. Some firms in the international haulage business offer good prospects.

RELATED OCCUPATIONS, FURTHER INFORMATION AND READING

Please see article 6. CAR/VAN DRIVER.

6. CAR/VAN DRIVER (YAD)

THE WORK

A tremendous variety of work is available; a detailed job description depends on the employer and the goods. The majority of van drivers deliver goods from one destination to another. Distribution begins with a manufacturer delivering bulk goods to a warehouse or wholesaler by rail and/or LGV. From there, smaller amounts of mixed goods are transported to retail outlets by light commercial delivery van drivers (vehicles between 3.5 and 7.5 tonnes). A tachograph in these vehicles records the numbers of hours spent driving, resting, carrying out other work such as loading and unloading, the speed of the vehicle and the distance travelled.

Delivery van drivers may load their vans following order sheets, plan their routes, unload the correct goods and obtain a receipt from the customer. They may be expected to help set up the goods (furniture, for example) to the customer's requirements. They may be known as **merchandisers**. The size and weight of goods can vary enormously, from bouquets of flowers to grand pianos. Some drivers may be expected to contact their employer at least once a day. Some work in a small familiar area – within a 15-mile radius of base, for example – others go much further afield. Drivers in private security firms are given unarmed (and sometimes armed) combat training.

Van sales drivers are responsible for sales as well as delivery. Those in the wholesale trade usually have an area in which they visit all customers and potential customers, taking orders and delivering goods. In many cases they are responsible for deciding how much of a certain item they need to carry. They may also be expected to canvass for new customers and advise both them and existing customers on new lines and special promotions. Milk, bread, fish, grocery, butchery and greengrocery are the major areas in which light commercial van sales drivers work. They also work in fast food: vans carrying fish and chips, hot dogs, baked potatoes, ice-cream, and so on, travel round certain areas, stopping frequently to sell, for example in housing estates, or the lay-bys of large trunk roads.

Many drivers in door-to-door retail sales are self-employed; others start by buying a franchise from a company which then trains them, sells them the necessary equipment (ice-cream making equipment, for example) and advertises for them.

Chauffeurs/chauffeuses are employed by private households or by large companies to drive people rather than goods. In private households, they may drive their employer to and from work, to social functions, and their employers' children to school. In companies they are used to take senior managers to meetings, rail stations and airports, etc.

WORK ENVIRONMENT

The main workplace is the van's cab; drivers must drive safely in changing traffic and road conditions, in varying light conditions and in all weathers. There is often variety in the premises visited and the routes taken during deliveries.

SKILLS AND INTERESTS

Drivers require good driving skills and the ability to concentrate for long periods. They must be able to work to a schedule and cope with delays, emergencies, etc. It is useful for drivers to be able to carry out minor repairs on their vehicles. Drivers must be honest, reliable and punctual. They should be able to work alone and unsupervised, although some drivers have assistants. Drivers require a good knowledge of the local area and those making longer trips should be able to follow a map.

Good communication skills are needed for dealing with customers. Van drivers selling goods require sales ability and numerical skills for handling cash. Those who load and unload goods need to be physically fit.

ENTRY REQUIREMENTS

Formal academic qualifications are not normally required. Employers look for reasonable reading, writing and arithmetic, and may set simple tests. A clean car driving licence is necessary. People of 21 years or, in come cases, over 25 years are preferred for insurance reasons. Some employers look for several years driving experience, and value applicants whose previous work has involved dealing with people.

Employers operating light goods vehicles in category C1 on distribution work may offer Modern Apprenticeships that include driver training. Applicants may require three GCSEs/S grades (C/3) in maths, English and one other subject, or Intermediate GNVQ/GSVQ Level II, or equivalent, in order to display ability to complete the apprenticeship and achieve NVQ/SVQ Level 3.

TRAINING

Until recently the category B car driving licence covered vehicles up to 7.5 tonnes. Now it is necessary to pass an additional test for a category C1 licence in order to drive light goods vehicles between 3.5 and 7.5 tonnes gross. Applicants must be 18 years.

For driving work involving cars and small vans, there is little, if any, formal training. Any prior experience of distribution work is therefore useful for younger applicants. Drivers are taught the job and the route by experienced drivers or supervisors in anything from two days to a few weeks. Classroom sessions may teach routines of completing report forms, dealing with cash payments, and company policy. Drivers of vans and light goods vehicles can be assessed for NVQs/SVQs in Road Haulage and Distribution at Levels 1 and 2.

Modern Apprenticeships incorporate training and work experience in non-driving aspects of distribution as well as driving tuition. These apprentices are expected to undertake NVQ/SVQ units in Storage and in Organizing Road Transport Operations at Level 2, before completing units in Transporting Goods by Road. They go on to take units in Supervisory Management at Level 3. On completion, a Modern Apprenticeship Certificate is awarded by the Road Haulage and Distribution Training Council (RHDTC). Apprenticeships are expected to take three to four years.

Experienced drivers and trainee drivers may also be assessed for NVQ/SVQ qualifications.

It is possible to train for a C1 licence privately, at a specialist driving school, and take the test independently.

Chauffeurs/chauffeuses may receive special training in the care and maintenance of cars such as Rolls Royces and Bentleys. They may also be trained in anti-terrorist driving techniques.

LATE ENTRY

Many van driving jobs are open only to adults with the appropriate licence, and adult entry is usual. Almost any sort of driving and/or retail experience is useful. See ENTRY REQUIREMENTS.

Some people enter delivery/distribution driving work or training for it from employment in other jobs in these companies, such as warehouse worker or lift truck driver.

OPPORTUNITIES

Many manufacturing and service companies have their own delivery vans and employ their own drivers – dairies, bakers, private security companies, large department stores, large retail operations and wholesale suppliers, for example. Some companies specialize in delivery work for other businesses, individuals, etc. The Post Office employs van drivers to transport parcels and mail. There are opportunities for self-employment and for operation on a franchise basis.

Work is usually centred in and around large towns and cities. The distribution of goods is a major industry, and job prospects are fair.

Chauffeurs/chauffeuses are employed by private individuals, companies and government departments. Posts with private individuals may require additional skills such as gardening or valeting. Sometimes joint posts are available for couples.

It is possible, though rare, to be a self-employed chauffeur/chauffeuse.

PAY AND CONDITIONS

Wages vary from around £135 to £235 a week, depending on the work and the responsibility involved.

Hours vary, but a 40 to 48-hour week is average. Some firms operate a piecework system, allowing employees to finish work when they have completed the jobs allocated to them. Overtime is often available; weekend deliveries may be necessary. Some companies offer part-time work. Some jobs, such as milk delivery, mean a very early start and weekend work.

Chauffeurs/chauffeuses with private households often live in. They are usually expected to wear uniform and may have to work unsocial hours including evenings and weekends.

PROSPECTS

There is no direct promotion ladder; drivers may transfer to clerical jobs within the same company, or become transport supervisors in larger companies.

RELATED OCCUPATIONS

Taxi/private hire vehicle driver, bus/coach driver, large goods vehicle (LGV) driver.

FURTHER INFORMATION

Consult the *Yellow Pages* for addresses of possible employers.

Road Haulage and Distribution Training Council (RHDTC)*, Suite C, Shenley Hall, Rectory Lane, Shenley, Radlett, Hertfordshire WD7 9AN, 01923 858461

Road Haulage Association Ltd, 35 Monument Hill, Weybridge, Surrey KT13 8RN, 01932 841515

FURTHER READING

Leaflets/booklets are available from the address marked*.

Working in Outdoor Jobs – COIC

In the careers library classified under YAD.

7. DRIVING INSTRUCTOR (YAD)

BACKGROUND INFORMATION

The road transport industry, with some 24 million motor vehicles (almost 20 million private cars), offers a vast field of work for professional instructors. Most start off by working for driving schools but eventually run their own businesses. There are also jobs training passenger carrying or large goods vehicle drivers mainly with the larger transport firms. There are approximately 33,000 approved driving instructors, and nearly 36,400,000 licence holders in the UK.

THE WORK

Driving instructors are responsible for training people in vehicle handling and knowledge of the highway code to a sufficiently high standard to pass the driving test and theory test, and beyond. This is usually done by giving the learner driver a series of driving lessons, each lasting for about an hour. The average person requires about 35 lessons before taking the 'L' driving test, depending on age and learning ability of the pupil. One driving instructor may coach from six to nine clients a day. Other instructors teach by using intensive methods, such as a five to ten-day full-time courses, not only for the basic licence, but also to advanced levels.

A lesson usually consists of practical instruction in the car with the instructor sitting beside the pupil.

Instructors explain to the pupil how to use each control correctly. They often demonstrate the skills or procedures. As the pupil's skills improve, instructors give fewer instructions, leaving the pupil to make decisions.

Instructors use dual controls as a safety aid, to prevent danger or damage.

Instructors need to pre-plan routes for each lesson in order to avoid or incorporate specific road conditions according to the student's ability and progress. Instructors are fully responsible for the safety of their pupil, vehicle and other road users during the period of the lesson.

In addition to practical driving skills, instruction is also given in road craft, including a knowledge of the Highway Code. This can be done by discussing with the pupil specific situations and how to react to them.

Sketch maps and diagrams are used as illustration. The pupil's knowledge is continually checked by the instructor, who must keep a close watch on the pupil's response and reactions while driving. Gradually the pupil learns to read and react properly to the signals and movements of other road users.

Some instructors also provide classroom instruction, for groups of pupils, with the help of visual aids, for the separate theory test.

Instructors need a basic knowledge of car mechanics in order to explain the working of car systems: the gears, for example.

When the pupil is sufficiently trained, an application for a test date is made. The driving test itself is conducted by a driving examiner.

Instructors have to carry out a certain amount of paperwork, although some franchise driving schools employ clerical staff to deal with most of the administrative functions. Most self-employed instructors have some form of office support to answer the telephone and book lessons.

Driving instructors keep a daily record showing payments received and lessons given and receipts issued, etc. They also keep records on the progress of each student, noting down strengths and weaknesses, progress, routes used, etc.

Specialist instruction. Some driving schools also offer other forms of instruction, depending on the experience and ability of their instructors, such as tuition for experienced drivers in advanced and high-performance driving. Other schools offer private tuition for passenger carrying vehicle and commercial or large goods vehicle driving (though large passenger and commercial transport organizations have their own PCV/LGV instructors). Some companies may ask driving schools to 'assess' commercial drivers before taking them on as employees. An increasing number of driver training centres also offer NVQ/SVQ assessment services.

WORK ENVIRONMENT

The majority of a driving instructor's time is spent on the road, in the tuition vehicle. Lessons take place in all but the most severe weather conditions. Hot weather can cause discomfort to both instructor and pupil, particularly when driving in cities and in heavy traffic.

SKILLS AND INTERESTS

As driving can be stressful, it is important to be both patient and even-tempered when teaching pupils with different levels of skill and temperament. Instructors need to be able to gain and build up the confidence of their pupils. They need to give clear and concise instructions to the learner.

The ability to explain procedures and techniques in straightforward and understandable terms is also important. Skills in assessment are required as the instructor needs to identify the pupil's strengths and weaknesses. The safety of the pupil, vehicle and other road users during the lesson is the instructor's responsibility, so it is important to be alert and act responsibly. Some knowledge of the mechanics of a motor vehicle is useful.

ENTRY REQUIREMENTS

No academic qualifications are required. To give driving instruction (for money) in a car, a candidate must be registered with the Driving Standards Agency (an agency of the Department of Transport) as an Approved Driving Instructor (ADI) or licensed trainee. Applicants must: have held a full British car driving licence for at least four years out of the six years preceding the date of application; have no motoring convictions of any kind (five or more penalty points can debar you but the Registrar may disregard offences that happened a long time ago); have no criminal convictions of any kind; provide two referees to attest to your good behaviour and suitability; pass the 'Register' qualifying examinations.

The minimum age is 21 years. Many driving schools prefer people over 25 years, as the insurance premiums are lower.

Specialist driving instructors are normally recruited by driving schools after individuals obtain professional qualifications. Some employers in the road haulage or bus and coach sectors select their instructors from among their experienced drivers and give them appropriate training either within the company or at a specialist training establishment.

TRAINING

The Register of Approved Driving Instructors and the licensing scheme for trainee instructors are administered by the Driving Standards Agency of the Department of Transport.

In order to be registered as an ADI, it is necessary to pass the Register Qualifying Examination. This is in three parts: a written test; a practical test of driving ability; and a practical test of ability to instruct. Each part must be passed before the next can be taken. Qualification must be achieved within two years, following the successful completion of the Part 1 written test.

Applicants may sit the exam independently, but many take training, normally at their own expense. Courses are run by specialist training establishments or by driving schools. Intensive courses last between one and three weeks. The exact nature, content, and standards of courses vary, so details should be carefully checked. The Driving Instructors Association's *Recommended Training Establishment Directory*, created by the industry and the DSA, lists approved training establishments.

Of 18,000 people who take the exams each year only about 3,000 are successful. For those who pass each exam first time, the fees, plus registration, total £415.

The trainee licensing scheme is open to those who have passed the first two parts of the Register Qualifying Examination (the written test and the practical test of driving ability). The trainee licence, which is valid for six months, allows the holder to instruct for payment without being registered as an ADI. Trainee licence holders are usually employed by a driving school, which must provide at least 40 hours' practical instruction, given by a qualified ADI. During the first three months that the licence is held, trainees must be under the direct personal supervision of an ADI for at least 20 per cent of the time they spend instructing pupils.

It is not necessary to participate in the trainee licensing

scheme in order to pass Part 3 of the Register Qualifying Examination.

ADI registration. On successfully passing all parts of the Register Qualifying Examination, the name of the applicant is entered on the ADI register and an official certificate of registration is issued. This must be displayed on the tutor's car. The registration must be renewed every four years. When required by the ADI Registrar, instructors must undergo a test of continued ability and fitness to give instruction. An instructor's name can be removed from the register if the required standards are not met.

Professional qualification. The Associated Examining Board in conjunction with the Driving Instructors' Association have developed a professional qualification for all driving instructors entitled the Diploma in Driving Instruction, aimed at improving the status and standard of professional instruction. There are no formal entry qualifications. The DIA have also developed a BSc/BA degree in Driver Education, which is offered by Middlesex University, for which the Diploma constitutes the entry qualification. Further details are available from the DIA.

Specialist instruction. There is no compulsory registration for these instructors, though, for the LGV field, RTITB Services does hold a register of approved instructors which is recognized by the industry. Employers send experienced lorry or bus/coach drivers on driving instructor training courses at specialist training establishments or train them internally.

NVQ/SVQ. NVQ/SVQ in Driving Instruction at Level 3 is available for instructors in all licence categories – car, motor-cycle, bus/coach and road haulage.

LATE ENTRY

All entrants are adults; it is very rare for anyone under 23 years to enter this field.

OPPORTUNITIES

There are currently some 33,000 approved driving instructors and about 1,500 licensed trainees in Great Britain, although not all ADIs operate. There are no restrictions on how many driving instructors can operate in an area and competition for business may be intense.

Many instructors begin by working with a franchised car driving school – there are many schools in each town and city throughout Great Britain. Some schools, such as **The British School of Motoring**, offer a franchise system for their instructors – the instructors are self-employed, but pupils and their cars are provided by the school in return for payment of a franchise fee. They may also provide help in the form of initial training, documentation and administration services.

Some specialist instructors, such as passenger carrying and large goods vehicle instructors, are employed by large transport and passenger vehicle companies in their own training schools, or work for training associations. The police, fire brigade, ambulance service and the Armed Forces also have their own driving instructors.

PAY AND CONDITIONS

A well-established instructor can currently expect to earn about £9,500 to £15,000. Out of this they must pay their car costs and business running expenses. Their net income is usually between £5,000 and £12,500.

Instructors need to work whenever clients are available; at any time during the week including weekends.

Most instructors are self-employed. It is possible, by only having a small number of pupils, to work part-time, but the actual hours worked are still dictated by the pupils' needs and tend to be in the evenings or at weekends.

PROSPECTS

The main progression is into self-employment, after having saved up enough capital to buy a dual control car and other initial expenses. The chances of becoming self-employed and successful vary from area to area. Some areas are over-subscribed with instructors, making it sometimes necessary to move home to become established. Initially there may be a loss of earnings before a reputation is built up.

It is estimated that there is only enough business for half of the 33,000 driving instructors on the Register if they all work full-time. However, many work part-time, and 2,000 to 3,000 ADIs leave the Register each year as 3,000 more come on.

Some instructors progress to become senior instructors, assistant managers and managers with their employing school. If there is a shortage of instructors, managers may continue to take pupil drivers as well as administer the office.

The Driving Standards Agency occasionally recruit experienced driving instructors as driving examiners. Examiners must be at least 26 years, with experience of working with the public in a position of authority. They must have held a licence for six years without a serious motoring conviction, and have wide experience of driving in the last three years including knowledge of motoring and road traffic problems and trends, elementary knowledge of transport law, and some experience of large goods or passenger carrying vehicle driving and/or motorcycles. Acceptance is by competitive examination, interview and driving test, plus a four-week course followed by a special test. Full details are available from the Driving Standards Agency.

RELATED OCCUPATIONS

Driving examiner, training officer, motorcycle instructor.

FURTHER INFORMATION

Driving Instructors' Association (DIA)*, Safety House, Beddington Farm Road, Croydon, Surrey CR0 4XZ, 0181 665 5151

Driving Standards Agency (DSA)*, Stanley House, Talbot Street, Nottingham NG1 5GU, 0115 955 7600

Bus and Coach Training Ltd*, Regency House, 43 High Street, Rickmansworth, Hertfordshire WD3 1ET, 01923 896607

Road Haulage and Distribution Training Council (RHDTC)*, Suite C, Shenley Hall, Rectory Lane, Shenley, Radlett, Hertfordshire WD7 9AN, 01923 858461

RTITB Services Ltd*, CENTREX Training and Conference Centre, High Ercall, Shropshire TF6 6RB, 01923 777777

British Motorcycle Federation, 129 Seaforth Avenue, Motspur Park, New Malden, Surrey KT3 6JU, 0181 942 7914

FURTHER READING

Leaflets/booklets are available from the addresses marked*.

The Driving Instructor's Manual – DIA

So You Want to be A Driving Instructor – DIA

Your Road to Becoming an Approved Driving Instructor – DSA

In the careers library classified under YAD.

1. TRAIN DRIVER CLCI:YAF
2. STATION ASSISTANT CLCI:YAF
3. TRACK/OVERHEAD LINE WORKER CLCI:YAF
4. SIGNALS/TELECOMS TECHNICIAN CLCI:YAF/RAL
5. RAILWAY FITTER/ELECTRICIAN CLCI:YAF/RAK

BACKGROUND INFORMATION

Railtrack is responsible for track and infrastructure and controls day-to-day operations through the signalling system. Its responsibilities are: timetabling, operation of the signalling systems, plus investment in track and its maintenance. Revenue is raised by charging operating companies for use of the track.

Twenty-five operational units – such as South West Trains, Inter-City West Coast and Great Eastern Railways are responsible for operating passenger train services in the UK, and five companies for transporting freight. Passenger services through the Channel Tunnel to Brussels and Paris are operated by Eurostar, a tri-national Belgian, British and French company.

Infrastructure Maintenance Companies (IMCs) which work from regional centres, maintain signals, track and overhead lines on behalf of Railtrack while Racal-BRT is responsible for telecommunications. Drivers, guards/conductors and station assistants are employed by the Train Operating Companies (TOCs). TOCs are also responsible for on-train catering services, which are contracted out to different catering companies.

The various companies also employ computer, property and legal specialists and managers – there is a graduate entry training scheme which provides one route to senior management – and all the administrative, personnel, marketing and purchasing officers found in any large company. This article covers only some of the specialist work that is done only for rail companies.

1. TRAIN DRIVER (YAF)

THE WORK

Train drivers drive diesel or electric trains. They control the speed of the train, driving it carefully on gradients and bends. They obey speed limits, signals and set procedures for stopping and starting trains. They have a detailed knowledge of their usual routes, including track layout, speed limits, gradients, of the whereabouts of signal boxes, stations and level crossings, and of what conditions to expect on the track in different weather conditions. They learn and obey signalling rules.

Drivers are responsible for keeping to a timetable but cannot ignore driving conditions or disobey signallers' instructions even if obeying them is likely to make the train late. Often they work with a guard/conductor, but on driver-only trains they are responsible for operating the doors, in some cases for making announcements, and for passenger safety.

They keep a record of each journey and report any engine defects. If they observe an incident on the track they stop the train and get out in order to investigate. They are responsible for assessing the seriousness of any engine or track fault and for deciding whether to continue the journey.

Some drivers regularly travel long distances: others drive trains on suburban services.

Drivers of Eurostar trains have to obey three or four regulatory and signalling systems: British, French and/or Belgian, plus a different set when in the Tunnel itself. The driver is in radio communication with control centres in each country and speaks to them in their own language.

WORK ENVIRONMENT

Drivers spend most of their working shift seated. Their cabs are small, relatively comfortable, but noisy. Some outdoor work is required from time to time. When checking the safety of the train or track they may work in all kinds of weather conditions.

They may work alone for long periods of time.

They wear a uniform which is provided by the employing Train Operating Company (TOC).

Drivers may not drink any alcohol while on duty or immediately before their shift.

Eurostar drivers occasionally have to spend the night in a hotel in Paris or Brussels.

SKILLS AND INTERESTS

Train drivers must be very safety conscious and prepared to obey safety regulations at all times in order to avoid accidents. They must have quick reactions and be capable of making instant decisions in emergencies. They must be able to stay calm and not panic when problems or accidents do occur. They also need powers of concentration since stretches of some journeys can be routine and monotonous.

Drivers must be capable of working on their own without direct supervision.

It is helpful to have some mechanical ability in order to understand how the engine and the cab equipment work and to identify and repair minor faults.

They should be pleasant and courteous when dealing with customers. A smart appearance is essential.

ENTRY REQUIREMENTS

There are no minimum entry requirements but a good standard of general education is required. TOCs expect a basic knowledge of English and maths. Most companies set an aptitude test.

Drivers must be physically fit and able to pass a medical examination – which includes tests for alcohol and drug abuse.

Good hearing, eyesight and colour vision are required. The wearing of glasses is not normally permitted unless these are worn to correct only a slight vision defect.

There is a minimum age of 18. School-leavers may join training schemes for young people.

Eurostar drivers are recruited from BR drivers with at least five years' experience of driving high-speed main line trains. They have to pass aptitude and personality tests, a strict medical, and assessments of their ability to learn complex signalling rules and French.

TRAINING

Entrants join as trainee trainman/women and are then selected for training as drivers or conductors according to requirements. It is possible to transfer from conductor duties to train driving.

Initial training for drivers takes between six and eight weeks. Further training courses, each one including aptitude tests and assessments, are necessary if a driver successfully applies to drive a higher speed train.

Eurostar drivers follow a one-year course of classroom training, which includes training on a simulator. They also learn French to a high level and spend a period during their training staying with French families.

Train Operating Companies run training schemes for young people in general traffic operations. Trainees may receive off-the-job training leading to qualifications validated by BTEC, SCOTVEC or City and Guilds. They receive practical experience at stations, freight terminals, carriage servicing depots, and with guards and conductors on trains. They may apply for trainman/woman positions when they reach the age of 18.

NVQs/SVQs in Rail Transport Driving are available at Level 2.

LATE ENTRY

There are good opportunities for adult entry. However, applicants for training as drivers must be under 46 years.

A return to work scheme is available, to enable parents of either gender, who leave work to care for young children, to return to work at a later date.

OPPORTUNITIES

The rail industry employs about 17,000 drivers. Many opportunities are in heavily populated areas, particularly in London and the South East.

PAY AND CONDITIONS

The basic working week varies but is around 39 hours. Shifts which are rostered in advance include bank holidays, weekends and nights.

The basic wage for a driver is approximately £225 a week. Overtime and allowances for work in London and the South East supplement this.

Contributory pension schemes are available. Uniforms are provided free.

PROSPECTS

Drivers may apply to drive higher speed trains (which brings an increase in responsibility and salary) or move to companies whose trains are driven at greater speeds. There are also prospects of transfer to supervisory and management levels of work.

RELATED OCCUPATIONS

Bus/coach driver, LGV driver, station assistant, bus conductor, signals technician.

FURTHER INFORMATION AND READING

Please see article 5. RAILWAY FITTER/ ELECTRICIAN.

2. STATION ASSISTANT (YAF)

THE WORK

Station assistants are based at railway stations or at yards. Their duties vary according to where they work, but include

the following: ensuring that trains depart on time, and that all passengers are securely aboard before closing the doors and signalling to the conductor that the train may depart; assisting customers with luggage; helping disabled passengers to board trains and find their seats; answering queries about train arrivals and departures; checking tickets as customers arrive at platforms; operating information boards; making announcements over the public address system; and loading and unloading parcels and freight.

Some station assistants clean and tidy platforms and waiting rooms, or use carriage cleaning equipment in yards. They may drive small trucks to take parcels and goods to and from trains, or drive passengers who find difficulty in walking in special courtesy vehicles.

WORK ENVIRONMENT

The work may be indoors or outdoors and in all weathers. Uniforms are provided and protective clothing is worn for cleaning duties.

SKILLS AND INTERESTS

Station assistants should enjoy providing a service to the public. They should have a smart appearance and should be pleasant and polite, even when dealing with difficult people.

They may be the only people employed by Train Operating Companies (TOCs) who meet most customers, and they are expected to give a good impression of their employing company.

They must be able to communicate with all kinds of people and speak clearly. They must be able to remember information and be capable of looking up and understanding timetables. They must learn safety and emergency procedures and be ready to put these into operation and evacuate stations if necessary.

They should be capable of working on their own initiative and making decisions, even though they normally work as part of a small team.

Station assistants should be physically fit since they are usually expected to do some lifting.

ENTRY REQUIREMENTS

There are no minimum entry requirements but a good general education is required. TOCs set literacy and numeracy tests.

Applicants must be physically fit with good hearing, eyesight and normal colour vision. They have to pass a medical examination.

The minimum age of entry is 18 years. School-leavers may enter through training schemes for young people.

TRAINING

TOCs run short introductory training courses at their own training centres or others. Training is then continued on the job under the supervision of experienced station assistants and station managers.

NVQs/SVQs in Rail Transport (Passenger Services) are available at Level 2. Some train operators also offer NVQs/ SVQs in Customer Service at Level 2. These cover staff employed in on-train and on-station operations, ticket office, travel centre and telephone enquiry bureaux.

LATE ENTRY

There are no fixed upper age limits and consequently good opportunities for adult entrants.

OPPORTUNITIES

There are opportunities in all parts of the country, although the largest concentration of jobs is in London and the South East.

PAY AND CONDITIONS

The basic working week is about 39 hours. Shifts which are rostered in advance include bank holidays, weekends and nights.

The basic wage for a station assistant is approximately £158 a week. Overtime and various allowances including for work in London and the South East supplement this.

Contributory pension schemes are available. Uniforms are provided free.

PROSPECTS

Station assistants may re-train as drivers or conductors. They also have the opportunity to be promoted to supervisory or managerial positions.

RELATED OCCUPATIONS

Train driver, conductor, bus/coach driver, bus conductor, hotel porter, airport baggage handler, track and overhead line worker.

FURTHER INFORMATION AND READING

Please see article 5. RAILWAY FITTER/ELECTRICIAN.

3. TRACK/OVERHEAD LINE WORKER (YAF)

THE WORK

Track workers maintain the railway track and the area surrounding it. Their work is essential to maintain safe operating conditions for trains. It is heavy outdoor work, which involves lifting rails, checking rail fastenings, shovelling ballast and using machinery to pack the track and make it level.

Overhead line workers install and maintain electrical power lines above the track. Teams of workers erect structures and install wires. They are also responsible for the general maintenance and repair of the overhead line and ancillary equipment.

WORK ENVIRONMENT

Track and overhead line staff work out of doors in all weathers. Track workers work in gangs ranging in size from two to over 30 people. They often have to travel, both locally and further afield.

Overhead line workers are based at depots, which cover wide geographical areas.

Working conditions may be cold, wet and dirty. The work involves lifting, carrying and exerting strenuous effort.

Protective clothing, headgear and footwear are provided.

SKILLS AND INTERESTS

Track and overhead line workers must be strong and physically fit. They should have manual dexterity and some mechanical aptitude. It is important to be able to work in a team.

Overhead line workers need a good head for heights. They may work up to twelve metres above the ground.

ENTRY REQUIREMENTS

The minimum age of entry is normally 18 years. A small number of junior trainees aged 16 to 17 years are recruited for work on the overhead line, but in general, older applicants are preferred.

Applicants need a good standard of general education, good hearing, eyesight and normal colour vision. They must pass a medical examination.

TRAINING

BR infrastructure companies provide a one-week induction course, followed by training in specific skills as appropriate. Courses vary from maintenance company to renewal company, and amongst both types of company NVQs/SVQs are available at Levels 2 and 3 in Rail Transport Engineering for the following maintenance disciplines: plant, electrification, track signals, telecommunications, traction and rolling stock.

LATE ENTRY

There is no maximum upper age limit.

OPPORTUNITIES

Track workers are employed throughout Britain. Overhead line workers are employed in most areas of the country but not in certain parts, for example Wales, the West Country or the North of Scotland, where lines are not electrified.

PAY AND CONDITIONS

The basic working week is around 39 hours. Shifts which are rostered in advance include bank holidays, weekends and nights. A large amount of weekend work is involved since as much maintenance as possible is carried out then, to minimize disruption to train services.

The basic wage for a track and overhead line worker is approximately £160 a week. Overtime and various allowances including for work in London and the South East supplement this.

Contributory pension schemes are available. Protective clothing is provided free.

PROSPECTS

Promotion prospects are linked to skill levels. As workers learn new skills, such as welding, they are promoted to higher grades with pay increases.

There are also possibilities of promotion to supervisory and managerial work.

RELATED OCCUPATIONS

Road worker, construction operative, civil engineering operative, gas distribution worker, electricity distribution worker, telephone technician.

FURTHER INFORMATION AND READING

Please see article 5. RAILWAY FITTER/ENGINEER.

4. SIGNALS/TELECOMS TECHNICIAN (YAF/RAL)

THE WORK

Technicians install, maintain and replace the signalling and telecommunication equipment that is used to control train movements and to pass on information to members of staff and to customers. Occasionally, they work in project offices, assisting engineers with the specification and design of new or replacement signalling or telecommunications systems.

They may specialize in either:

Signalling. This involves electronic, light-current and mechanical engineering. Signalling technicians construct and fit new signalling equipment and cables. They service, check and adjust equipment used in: railway signals; control systems that operate track equipment; control panels – equipment used to control train movements; track circuits, which detect the position of each train on the line; and the point machines that switch trains from one line to the other. They diagnose and repair faults on all the equipment. They may control a section of the track.

Telecommunications. This includes work on: telephones and telephone networks; data handling networks – which transfer messages between computers, teleprinters and fax machines; radio systems; security and surveillance systems; and passenger information systems, such as TV monitors and indicator boards.

Technicians are responsible for installing and maintaining the equipment, diagnosing faults and carrying out repairs.

WORK ENVIRONMENT

Most communication apparatus runs alongside the railway track, so signals technicians spend most of their time out of doors where they can work in all kinds of weather conditions. Telecommunications technicians work indoors in telephone exchanges, outdoors, and also underground. Overalls and protective clothing are provided.

Technicians sometimes work alone but, more often, in small teams.

The work involves travel to different sites. Some technicians travel large distances, particularly in rural areas.

SKILLS AND INTERESTS

Technicians must be able to work quickly and concentrate for long periods. Manual dexterity, accuracy and attention to detail are important. They should be interested in technology and able to understand technical diagrams and drawings. They must be able to do simple calculations. They need to be fit and able to work in confined spaces and at heights. They should be able to react quickly in emergencies and use their initiative.

ENTRY REQUIREMENTS

Entrants are accepted up to the age of 18. IMCs set their own entry requirements, which are likely to be four GCSEs (A-C) or equivalent, including maths and a science subject. In Scotland the minimum requirements are likely to be four S grades (1-3) including maths, a science and English.

Normal colour vision and good hearing are essential. Eyesight should be good. Glasses may be worn. It is necessary to pass an entrance test and a medical examination.

TRAINING

Off-the-job training is carried out in Racal-BRT own training centres and in colleges. Trainee technicians receive on-the-job training on site, working with experienced staff.

They take courses leading to BTEC, SCOTVEC or City and Guilds qualifications in telecommunications or electronic engineering.

Training normally takes three or four years.

NVQs/SVQs in Rail Transport and also in Signal Operation are available at Level 2. Telecommunications and Signal Engineering and Maintenance and Fault Finding are available at Levels 2 and 3.

LATE ENTRY

Adults are not normally recruited unless they have previous, relevant experience.

OPPORTUNITIES

Many technicians are employed by Racal-BRT and infrastructure maintenance companies. There are some opportunities to work with other companies that carry out varying levels of telecommunications-related work.

Openings for signalling technicians have been increasing as old mechanical signalling systems have been gradually replaced with electronic equipment. In telecommunications also, opportunities have increased with the introduction of computers and modern information systems such as train indicator boards.

PAY AND CONDITIONS

Trainees start on a minimum of approximately £150 a week. They are paid allowances, bonus, and overtime.

Technicians work a basic 37-hour week in shifts, which include evening and weekend working. The basic working week is 39 hours. Shifts, which are rostered in advance, include bank holidays, weekends and nights.

Contributory pension schemes are available. Uniforms are provided free.

PROSPECTS

There are prospects of promotion to supervisory and management positions.

RELATED OCCUPATIONS

Telephone technician, electronics technician, electrician, computer service engineer.

FURTHER INFORMATION AND READING

Please see article 5. RAILWAY FITTER/ ELECTRICIAN.

5. RAILWAY FITTER/ELECTRICIAN (YAF/ RAK)

THE WORK

Railway fitters and electricians maintain and repair locomotives, passenger coaches and wagons. They also maintain, service and repair equipment such as boilers, pumps, cranes and lifts together with power supplies. They are assisted by unskilled staff, who undertake more routine work such as cleaning, labouring and heavy lifting.

They are employed by train operating companies (TOCs).

Please see article AUTO-ELECTRICIAN (RAE) for information on the work of an electrician.

WORK ENVIRONMENT

Fitters and electricians normally work indoors in workshops where coaches and locomotives are brought for servicing. The work can be oily and dirty. Some fitters/electricians work out of doors in sidings.

SKILLS AND INTERESTS

Fitters and electricians should be physically fit and capable of heavy lifting. They should be able to work as members of a team but also on their own with a minimum of supervision.

They should be numerate as they have to make calculations and should have manual dexterity for using tools and equipment.

ENTRY REQUIREMENTS

Training is by means of an apprenticeship for which applicants should be under 17 years. Individual TOCs set their own entry requirements. These are likely however, to include GCSEs/S grades (A-C/1-3) in English, maths and science.

Applicants must have good eyesight with normal colour vision and good hearing.

Unskilled workshop assistants are recruited over the age of 18 years.

Qualified fitters and electricians who have served recognized apprenticeships with other employers are also recruited.

TRAINING

Apprenticeships last four years and include both on-the-job training and college courses leading to City and Guilds, BTEC or SCOTVEC qualifications.

LATE ENTRY

Entry to an apprenticeship is not possible over the age of 17 years. There is no upper age limit for qualified fitters and electricians.

OPPORTUNITIES

There are opportunities with all the Train Operating Companies throughout the country.

PAY AND CONDITIONS

The basic working week is 39 hours. Evening and weekend work may be required.
Fully trained fitters and electricians are paid approximately £185 a week. There are possibilities for overtime work. A bonus is paid.

Contributory pension schemes are available. Overalls and protective clothing are provided free.

PROSPECTS

There are opportunities for promotion to supervisory and management positions.

RELATED OCCUPATIONS

Maintenance fitter, welder, auto-electrician, heating and ventilating fitter, telephone technician, mechanical engineering worker.

FURTHER INFORMATION

Contact regional infrastructure maintenance companies or Racal-BRT offices.

BR infrastructure companies notify vacancies to careers offices and Jobcentres.

FURTHER READING

Working In Passenger Transport – COIC

In the careers library classified under YAF/RAL.

1. MERCHANT NAVY DECK OFFICER CLCI:YAL
2. MERCHANT NAVY ENGINEERING OFFICER CLCI:YAL
3. MERCHANT NAVY DUAL CERTIFICATE OFFICER CLCI:YAL
4. MERCHANT NAVY RATING CLCI:YAL

BACKGROUND INFORMATION

The majority of merchant ships today either transport various types of cargo or provide support services to the Royal Navy and to drilling platforms and rigs. The Merchant Navy also includes tugs and many other specialist vessels. Apart from ferries and around 30 luxury cruise liners, a very few merchant ships carry passengers.

Patterns of work vary widely. Coastal companies tend to undertake short voyages, the longest lasting about twelve weeks at a time. Longer voyages are made by ocean-going carriers, such as container ships going to Australia and New Zealand or tankers that transport cargo to ports in every corner of the world.

The Merchant Navy fleet has become smaller in recent years, due mainly to the introduction of larger ships staffed by smaller crews. In the 1970s it is estimated that for every giant container ship which was launched, seven conventional ships were scrapped. For some years job opportunities were poor, but this is changing. The Chamber of Shipping states that great opportunities are opening up for British shipping.

These articles describe the work of deck, dual certificate and engineering officers and ratings – the ship's workforce. Crew opportunities may not be as good as for officers, as many UK shipping companies have traditionally employed foreign crews. However, this situation is now changing, and in many areas the ratio of British to overseas ratings is becoming more even.

At one time the Merchant Navy was exclusively male, but women are now recruited at all levels and compete on equal terms with men. Women currently form around two to three per cent of the total workforce.

1. MERCHANT NAVY DECK OFFICER (YAL)

THE WORK

Deck officers are responsible for the safe navigation of the vessel while at sea and, when in port, for the safe and efficient loading or discharging of the cargo. Very often the cargo is stowed in large containers, which are lifted onto and off the deck by crane. If the cargo is in bulk, it is stowed in tanks or holds and discharged through pipelines and hose, or by other mechanical means.

Deck officers supervise the crew when they are engaged in such tasks as general maintenance work, cargo tank or hold cleaning and preparation work and mooring operations. If supplying a platform or a rig, the vessel does not tie up but is manoeuvred to keep it close alongside.

At sea, each officer usually takes responsibility for two 'watches' – four-hour periods of bridge duty – in every 24 hours. Watch-keeping officers navigate a course (previously decided by the captain), check the vessel's position periodically, and alter course to allow for the effects of tides and currents. They must, while on watch, remain aware of other ships, of weather conditions, and of any hazards to navigation. Although there are sophisticated navigational aids, deck officers must be able to navigate without them in case systems fail.

When not on the bridge, deck officers have other duties, such as checking safety and firefighting equipment, and making sure that all deck gear is working properly. In addition, there is always a certain amount of paperwork, including the correction of navigational charts. Most of the ship's legal and commercial business is looked after by senior deck officers.

WORK ENVIRONMENT

Deck officers, as their title implies, spend much of their time on deck, though on a modern ship the bridge itself, with all the navigational equipment, is protected from the elements.

On all ships, except some ferries, the ship is the crew's home as well as workplace. On large ships officers have their own cabins with bathroom facilities and, when off duty, they usually have the use of a swimming pool, a library, videos, table tennis, darts and a bar for socializing. On smaller ships facilities are more limited.

A cruise ship gives officers a chance to mix with many different people, and the social facilities and meals are those of a first-class hotel. But there are only about 30 cruise ships out of a total trading fleet of more than 600.

SKILLS AND INTERESTS

Shipping companies look for self-reliant people who have demonstrated some capacity for leadership. They must be prepared to work long and unsocial hours, often with little or no time ashore.

Deck officers need mathematical ability for navigation. They also must have an understanding of engineering and scientific principles to enable them to cope with cargo handling, ship stability requirements and high-technology bridge equipment. They must be people who enjoy responsibility, and are capable of responding quickly to any emergency that may arise.

Except on ferries, they work and live in close proximity to the same people, perhaps for months on end, so they must be tolerant and sociable. A sense of humour is a great help.

ENTRY REQUIREMENTS

The normal entry age range is 16 to 19½ years at the time of joining, though there is more flexibility than in the past. Anyone planning a degree course before applying for training should consider this age range carefully as they may find themselves too old on graduation. Older applicants, up to the age of 25, are occasionally considered.

Candidates must be of good general health and physique and have to pass a stringent medical. Deck officers must have near perfect eyesight without glasses, and no defects of colour vision, in order to pass the Department of Transport's eyesight test.

Suitable candidates are normally employed as cadets by a shipping company or training group capable of organizing all aspects of training, both at college and at sea.

People with three GCSEs/S grades (A-C/1-3) including maths and physics with, preferably, a language, can apply for training for the Short Sea Restricted Licence that is operated within the European trading area.

The minimum educational requirements laid down by most

shipping companies operating ships world-wide are GCSEs/S grades (A-C/1-3), or equivalent, in at least five subjects, including physics, maths and a subject involving the use of English. It should be noted that entry is highly competitive, and applicants with better qualifications than the minimum will enjoy an advantage.

Holders of A levels/H grades or equivalent qualifications may enter accelerated training schemes, which can be completed within three years.

TRAINING

For a 16 to 19-year-old with the required GCSEs/S grades, a cadetship is split between time at sea and time at college, and lasts three to four years, sitting the professional and ancillary examinations required for a Class 4 or Class 3 Certificate of Competency. Those with A levels/H grades may complete the course in three years, gaining a Class 3 Certificate of Competency.

Patterns of training vary according to the specific programme being followed. The following is fairly typical. Training begins with a four-week residential induction course held at a nautical college. This course prepares cadets for life at sea and covers safety, shipboard familiarization, the organization of a ship's company, health, hygiene and an outline of the structure of the Merchant Navy. Cadets also receive a record book which incorporates tasks and projects to be carried out throughout training.

The first period at sea usually lasts about ten months, normally in two voyages, with leave in between. During this time cadets learn basic seamanship and carry out practical tasks, helping the workforce. They also follow a correspondence course set by the college to which they are attached for the duration of the training period.

The next phase of training, at college, is mainly academic, introducing the cadet to professional subjects such as chart work and meteorology. During the second period at sea, cadets take on more responsibility and, towards the end, keep four-hour watches on the bridge under supervision.

After the examinations they return to sea to complete outstanding sea-time, and understudy the officer of the watch both at sea and in port. The training period finishes on completion of the sea-time required for the issue of the Class 3 Certificate. Cadets can then be considered for promotion to third officer.

The programme for deck officer trainees with slightly lower academic qualifications lasts about three to three-and-a-half years. It comprises periods at college and at sea, broadly covering the same areas of training as described above for cadets. A minimum of 20 months' sea-time must be completed and sea service is often performed in a rating capacity. The programme leads to a Class 4 or Class 3 Certificate of Competency in exactly the same way as above.

Much of the training organized by the Merchant Navy Training Board is carried out at colleges based in Gravesend, South Shields, Southampton, Glasgow and Fleetwood.

Over the next five years the Merchant Navy is introducing a system of qualifications based on NVQs/SVQs. It is envisaged that this system of training and assessment, in combination with oral examinations, will become the only route to gaining Certificates of Competency. NVQs/SVQs in Merchant Vessel Operations are currently available at Levels 2, 3 and 4.

LATE ENTRY

Adult entry as a deck officer is very rare except for former Royal Navy officers. In addition, some shipping companies sponsor deck ratings with the relevant academic qualifications on the Class 4 supplementary training scheme. The scheme includes extra studies in navigation and chartwork, a correspondence course and college modules, and leads to a Class 4 or Class 3 Certificate. Successful ratings can then qualify as watch-keeping officers.

OPPORTUNITIES

Britain's Merchant Fleet provides employment for about 18,000 deck and engineering officers and there is recruitment at present.

Employers vary tremendously and so do the ships they own and operate. There are 47 shipping companies currently recruiting. Their fleets range from a fleet of owned and chartered tankers to specialized vessels that support offshore exploration and production activities. The latest ships in container transportation are some 37,200 tonnes dead weight and carry cargo all around the world.

In contrast, there are vessels operating mainly in the European trading area, accounting for nearly one-third of the British Merchant Navy. The vessels include a variety of sizes and types but are generally smaller than ships sailing world-wide. Some can pass beneath road and rail bridges, and sail up rivers and canals to ports up to 200 miles from the sea.

PAY AND CONDITIONS

Pay for deck officers varies with the company and the type of trade in which it engages. Officers may work about five months and then take a couple of months leave. Over a couple of years, the annual salary could then average out at around the following figures: third officer – £12,000 to £16,000; second officer – £16,000 to £20,000; chief officer – £24,000 plus; master – £30,000 plus.

Cadets earn from £4,000, depending on the employing company. Food and accommodation are provided, and travel expenses are also met by the employer.

A ship operates 24 hours a day, seven days a week. On a large ship, deck officers are normally on watch for four hours, with eight hours off before the next watch. Watch systems may be different on smaller ships. Tours of duty vary between several months and a few weeks, and are followed by leave periods which also vary depending on how long someone has been away. Crews do not stay together, or necessarily return to the same ship, although the captain and the chief engineer may be attached to a particular ship for about two years.

PROSPECTS

Present prospects are excellent, with all opportunities being open to both men and women.

Promotion depends on a combination of length of service and merit. To reach the most senior positions, drive and determination are essential. Officers must also obtain the relevant Certificate of Competency awarded by the Maritime Safety Agency.

Class 3 and 4 Certificates equip someone as a watch-keeping officer on any ship anywhere in the world. Class 5 is the watch-keeping certificate for a ship of limited size in the European trading area. The Class 2 Certificate is the minimum qualification for a chief officer (most hold Class 1), and the Class 1 Certificate is for a master of any ship, anywhere in the world. Holders of any of the Certificates 2, 3, 4 and 5 may obtain a command endorsement enabling them to take command of a smaller ship in the European trading area.

Deck officers can also study for the Extra-Master's Certificate or a degree in nautical studies.

Experienced officers often find their skills in demand ashore, in administrative posts with shipping and oil companies, with dock and harbour boards, and in other posts where sea experience is relevant. Some master mariners go on to become pilots.

RELATED OCCUPATIONS

Coastguard, harbourmaster, marine engineer, Royal Navy officer, Royal Navy rating, telecommunications engineer, electronics engineer, ship's pilot.

FURTHER INFORMATION AND READING

Please see article 4. MERCHANT NAVY RATING.

2. MERCHANT NAVY ENGINEERING OFFICER (YAL)

THE WORK

The ship's engineers have responsibility for the care and maintenance of the entire ship, and the operation of the ship's engine room. This holds the main engine, boilers, pumps, fuel systems, hydraulic systems, and the ship's electrical generating plant and distribution system.

Power requirements vary according to whether the ship is in port or at sea. However, a tanker may need as much power to drive the pumps as it does to move through the sea. This power must be available whenever it is needed. Some ships are powered by diesel engines, while others have turbines.

The latest ships have a good deal of electronic control and automation. On such ships the engine room is not continuously staffed; a panel of alarm and monitoring systems is connected up to the engineers' accommodation and to the bridge. As a result, engineers can often work a fairly normal day, from 9am to 5pm, but if there is an emergency they must turn out at a moment's notice.

The job is still a very practical one, and engineers spend most of the day in boiler suits. Junior officers up to the level of third engineer are mainly working with their hands, and to some extent supervising engine-room ratings. Even chief engineers spend about a quarter of their time in practical tasks. If any part of a ship's systems fails, it must be dismantled, assessed, repaired, reassembled and put back into operation. Sometimes spare parts have to be manufactured on board. In general, however, crews today are too small to execute major repairs, and all modern ships now have back-up systems, which can be switched in if one of the main systems fails.

WORK ENVIRONMENT

Engineering officers share the same facilities as deck officers and the general environment is the same. However, the main workplace for engineers is the engine room, which can be hot, noisy and, to some extent, dirty. Engineers are also involved in the maintenance of deck machinery, whatever the weather. The environment in which they work has improved considerably in recent years with the increase in automation. However, their job is demanding and they often have to work in far from ideal locations – for instance, maintaining and repairing equipment in confined spaces or in refrigerated areas.

SKILLS AND INTERESTS

Engineering officers must be practical and resourceful people with an aptitude for maths and physics – they must acquire a thorough knowledge of diesel engines, steam turbines, boilers, electrical power generation and circuits, electronics and systems engineering. Manual dexterity is necessary; much of the work involves the servicing and repair of equipment. They must enjoy solving problems, and be flexible enough to adapt to advances in technology and working practices.

Like deck officers, they need to be able to get on well with others, having qualities of leadership and communication skills.

ENTRY REQUIREMENTS

For normal age of entry, please see article 1. MERCHANT NAVY DECK OFFICER.

Candidates must be of good general health and physique and pass a thorough medical. They must have a reasonable standard of sight in both eyes, with or without spectacles.

The minimum educational requirements are normally four GCSEs/S grades (A-C/1-3), or equivalent. These must include maths, physics and a subject involving the use of English.

An alternative method of entry is to have completed at least three years' Department of Transport approved engineering craft practice training, or the Engineering Training Authority's modular system of training for engineering craft workers.

TRAINING

The training takes three to four years (three years for A level/H grade entrants, where the length of sea service is the same but the college time shorter). Patterns of training vary somewhat according to the specific programme being followed. The programme outlined below is typical.

The first year is spent in a residential marine college, concentrating mainly on the academic side of engineering. Subjects include applied mechanics, applied heat, engineering drawing and marine electrotechnology. Cadets also receive practical training in fitting, machining and welding. Towards the end of the year they complete the standard Merchant Navy sea-survival course and a basic firefighting course.

The second year is spent at sea – usually in two voyages with a period of leave in between – gaining shipboard experience under instruction from the ship's engineer officers. Cadets have to carry out a number of operational and maintenance tasks and projects set in their record book. They also follow a correspondence course.

The final phase of training involves a further two years at college (one year for A level/H grade entrants). The course leads to the BTEC Higher National Diploma or SCOTVEC Higher National Certificate in Marine Engineering, and a Department of Transport Class 4 (Engineering) Certificate of Competency. These complete the cadetship and qualify the students as watch-keeping officers. (Success in the higher national diploma will give students maximum exemptions in the Department of Transport's examinations for Class 2 and Class 1 Certificates.)

The programme for engineer officer trainees entering with lower academic qualifications lasts three years, at college and sea, leading to a Class 4 Certificate of Competency and the written part of Class 3.

The programme for people with previous craft experience lasts about nine months, during which a minimum of six months' sea-time must be completed. Trainees are employed in the capacity of assistant engineer while training, and may obtain the Class 4 Certificate of Competency.

Over the next five years the Merchant Navy is introducing a system of qualifications based on NVQs/SVQs. It is envisaged that this system of training and assessment, in combination with oral examinations, will become the only route to gaining Certificates of Competency. NVQs/SVQs in Merchant Vessel Operations are currently available at Levels 2, 3 and 4.

LATE ENTRY

As described in ENTRY REQUIREMENTS, it is possible for people who have trained in engineering skills to join the Merchant Navy. No age requirements are specified. It is also possible, though unusual, for candidates with relevant qualifications to take a degree in marine engineering, and then go to sea and obtain their Certificates of Competency.

OPPORTUNITIES

Opportunities for both men and women to train as engineer officers are good, provided they meet the required standards. Please see article 1. MERCHANT NAVY DECK OFFICER, for details.

PAY AND CONDITIONS

Pay varies with the company and the type of trade. Officers may work for around five months and then take a couple of months leave. Over a couple of years the annual salary could then average out at: junior or fourth engineer – £12,000 to £15,000; third engineer – £18,000; second engineer – £24,000; and chief engineer – £30,000 to £40,000.

Cadets earn from £4,000, depending on the employing company. Food and accommodation are provided, and travel expenses are also met by the employer.

On some ships engineer officers work watch systems in the engine space, and have other duties to perform when off watch. On modern ships with highly automated engine rooms, engineers may be on duty during daytime hours only. However, the ship has to be maintained 24 hours a day, seven days a week, and engineers are always on-call for emergencies. They may revert to watch-keeping duties when the vessel is approaching land or is in a crowded seaway.

The length of time they spend on board depends on the type of ship on which they work. Leave varies, according to company and rank. Chief engineers can spend three months on and three months off; other engineer officers do up to five months on and have two or three months off. Officers rarely return to the same ship's company or indeed to the same ship, apart from the chief engineer, who may be appointed to a particular ship for about two years.

PROSPECTS

Present prospects are excellent. On obtaining the Department of Transport's Class 4 (Engineering) Certificate of Competency, cadets are ready to take up an appointment as a watch-keeping engineer officer. Promotion usually follows success in further professional examinations.

Engineering officers interested in obtaining higher academic qualifications can enter for the Department of Transport Extra First Class Certificate of Competency, or study for degrees in marine engineering at higher education institutions.

After some years at sea, the training and experience of engineer officers is so wide ranging that they are welcome in both offshore and shore-based industries. They may expect to achieve managerial posts in production and process plants or in work with local authorities, hospitals, hotels or large industrial complexes. There is also the opportunity to become an engineer or fleet manager with a shipping company.

RELATED OCCUPATIONS

Please see article 1. MERCHANT NAVY DECK OFFICER.

FURTHER INFORMATION AND READING

Please see article 4. MERCHANT NAVY RATING.

3. MERCHANT NAVY DUAL CERTIFICATE OFFICER (YAL)

THE WORK

Traditional dividing lines between the deck and engineering branches are becoming less easily defined, and the role of the ship's officer is changing. This is a consequence of the increasing sophistication of navigational and mechanical equipment, together with the use of computers and electronic control and automation in modern ships. This process of change is expected to continue.

In response, the dual certification cadetship has been devised. Cadets who successfully complete the course gain qualifications as both deck and engineer officers. The duties of both have been described in the previous articles in this section.

WORK ENVIRONMENT

Please see article 1. MERCHANT NAVY DECK OFFICER and article 2. MERCHANT NAVY ENGINEERING OFFICER.

SKILLS AND INTERESTS

People wanting to study for this dual qualification need to be good all-rounders with an interest in the use of machinery and an aptitude for understanding mechanical and electronic principles. Flexibility is one of the prime requirements, for their responsibilities are wide-ranging.

Like any ship's officer, they must be prepared to accept responsibility at an early age and be able to supervise and direct the work of others. For other desirable personal qualities, see article 1. MERCHANT NAVY DECK OFFICER and article 2. MERCHANT NAVY ENGINEERING OFFICER.

ENTRY REQUIREMENTS

The preferred age of entry is up to a maximum of 19½ years. Applicants must be of good general health and physique, and have to pass a stringent medical examination. They must have near-perfect eyesight without glasses and no defects of colour vision, in order to pass the Department of Transport's eyesight test.

The course is a demanding one. Candidates must have a minimum of five GCSEs/S grades (A-C/1-3), including maths, physics and a subject involving the use of English.

TRAINING

The training is almost equally divided between college and sea. It lasts about 18 months longer than the training for either deck or engineering cadetships. Patterns of training vary somewhat according to the specific programme being followed. The programme below is typical.

The first year is spent in a residential marine college, concentrating mainly on the academic side of deck officer and engineering work; subjects include applied mechanics, applied heat, engineering drawing and marine electrotechnology. Cadets also receive practical training in fitting, machining and welding. In addition, they take the standard Merchant Navy sea-survival course and a basic firefighting course. At the beginning of the summer holiday they have a six-week block of workshop practice.

The second year is spent at sea – normally on two voyages with a period of leave in between – gaining shipboard experience under instruction from the ship's deck and engineer officers.

Time is equally divided between deck and engine-room duties. Cadets are issued with two record books (one deck and one engine) in which are set out a number of operational and maintenance tasks and projects which must be completed. They also follow a correspondence course set by the college. Eight hours of study time is given each week, but cadets are expected to spend at least an equal amount of their own time in studying.

The third phase involves returning to college for 30 weeks for further study. This includes both engineering and deck subjects, such as chartwork, meteorology, stability, cargo work, etc. At the end of the college phase, cadets should have completed all the academic work for their engineering qualifications, but they require more practical experience before they are eligible to hold a Class 4 (Engineering) Certificate of Competency.

For the fourth phase, cadets return to sea for about nine months, again working in both engine room and deck departments. During this time, however, they undertake duties with more responsibility, and their involvement with bridge watch-keeping steadily increases, under the supervision of one of the deck officers. Cadets also have further correspondence course exercises and more complex record-book tasks and reports to complete.

Returning to college for two terms, they sit the various examinations required for a Class 3 (Deck) Certificate of Competency.

The final phase of training consists of a further three or four months at sea, to complete the statutory minimum sea-time needed to validate the certificate.

On successful completion of the courses, candidates are also awarded a Higher National Diploma in Marine Technology. Having passed the examinations and fulfilled the statutory sea-time requirements, they are ready to take

up an appointment as a watch-keeping deck or engineer officer.

Over the next five years the Merchant Navy is introducing a system of qualifications based on NVQs/SVQs. It is envisaged that this system of training and assessment, in combination with oral examinations, will become the only route to gaining Certificates of Competency.

NVQs/SVQs in Merchant Vessel Operations are currently available at Levels 2, 3 and 4.

LATE ENTRY

The scheme is only available to people up to 19½ years of age. There is no late entry.

OPPORTUNITIES

A number of the larger shipping companies recruit men and women to train for this dual qualification. The number of vacancies is limited, however, and competition for places is intense. For general opportunities, please see article 1. MERCHANT NAVY DECK OFFICER.

PAY AND CONDITIONS

Please see article 1. MERCHANT NAVY DECK OFFICER and article 2. MERCHANT NAVY ENGINEERING OFFICER.

PROSPECTS

Once qualified, the dual-certificated officer may decide to specialize in one department or to progress up the ladder in both. Whichever course is chosen, qualification gives exemptions from some of the professional examinations in both departments. Openings ashore are as in article 1. MERCHANT NAVY DECK OFFICER.

RELATED OCCUPATIONS

Please see article 1. MERCHANT NAVY DECK OFFICER.

FURTHER INFORMATION AND READING

Please see article 4. MERCHANT NAVY RATING.

4. MERCHANT NAVY RATING (YAL)

THE WORK

There are three kinds of ratings – deck, engine room and catering. Some ships operate with general-purpose crews, and such ratings spend some time working in the engine room as well as on deck. Today, crews are smaller than they used to be, and equipment is far more sophisticated. As a result, ratings take on more responsibility than in the past and work with less supervision, and there are fewer job and training opportunities.

1. Deck rating

Work at sea varies very much with the type of ship, but is predominantly manual – cleaning, sweeping, chipping off rust, polishing, etc. With a big company like P & O Containers, the emphasis is on general shipboard maintenance, along with stacking and manoeuvring containers, checking their contents, taking fire prevention measures, and so on. On the other hand, in the Royal Fleet Auxiliary (RFA) there is probably a larger content of traditional seamanship – wire splicing, rope work, and operating lifting gear. RFA ratings form flight parties during helicopter operations; they are also trained to assist in the operation and maintenance of sophisticated replenishment equipment, and in nuclear, biological and chemical defence.

Whatever the ship, time may have to be spent preparing and painting the steelwork. When a ship carries cargo, tanks or holds have to be cleaned and inspected. Ratings also act as look-outs and helmsmen on the bridge. In port, they assist in the mooring of the ship, in the preparations for cargo operations and taking on board of stores, as well as in fire and security patrols.

2. Engine room rating

Engine-room ratings are responsible for the day-to-day cleanliness of the engine room and for routine oiling, greasing and servicing of machinery. As they gain experience, they help officers to monitor and ensure the safe running of main plant and ancillary equipment. They also help to repair and maintain other machinery on board.

In some companies, the work of deck and engine-room ratings is combined into that of 'general purpose' ratings, allowing more flexibility in the tasks that they can undertake.

3. Catering rating

The duties of junior catering ratings are normally: to clean accommodation areas and public rooms; to help the cook in the preparation of food, to clean galleys and cooking utensils, and to help in the maintenance of fridges, freezers and hygiene in all food preparation and serving areas; to serve meals to officers and crew; and to load and stow the ship's consumable stores.

WORK ENVIRONMENT

For deck and engine-room ratings, please see article 1. MERCHANT NAVY DECK OFFICER. Catering ratings work under cover except when loading stores or taking part in safety drills. Galleys can be hot. On most ships ratings have single cabins with adjacent toilet facilities, and off-duty facilities are good.

SKILLS AND INTERESTS

Shipping companies look primarily for some indication of an interest in a seafaring career, perhaps as a member of the sea cadets. Applicants need to be mature people, with a sense of responsibility, a willingness to leave home for long periods, and an ability to get on with others.

With the reduced size of crews, everyone's contribution matters and they must be able to work without constant supervision on what are often quite technical tasks. For most tasks a high degree of manual dexterity is necessary. Flexibility is required, too, particularly on smaller ships where divisions between the different jobs are sometimes blurred.

ENTRY REQUIREMENTS

All trainee ratings must be sponsored by a shipping company or training group. There are no specific age or qualification requirements for entry; these are determined by individual shipping companies. However, most applicants are between 16 and 19, and GCSEs/S grades (A-E/1-5) in maths and English are preferred.

To join a company as a Supplementary Scheme trainee,

candidates must have, or expect to get, a minimum of three GCSEs/S grades (A-C/1-3) or equivalent, in maths, physics and a subject showing the use of English.

All candidates must be of good physique and health. Eyesight requirements are the same as for MERCHANT NAVY DECK OFFICER (please see article 1), though perfect colour vision is not required.

TRAINING

Rating training takes place at the nautical colleges at Glasgow, Gravesend, South Shields, Fleetwood and Southampton. There are three separate fully residential courses for junior ratings, all of which include a significant emphasis on health and safety. Every trainee rating takes the Merchant Navy Training Board Stage I Firefighting course, a first aid course, the Department of Transport Personal (Wet Drill) Survival Course, and a recognized course leading to the Department of Transport examination for the Certificate of Proficiency in Survival Craft. Successful trainees receive a Test Certificate at the end of all courses. All trainees – deck, engine-room and catering – spend a week at sea on board a training vessel. Formal instruction is limited to Monday to Friday, and a variety of extracurricular activities is available.

1. Deck and general purpose rating

This 13-week course includes the Department of Transport Efficient Deck Hand Certificate examination. It includes instruction in: the use of hand and power tools; shipboard maintenance; bridge familiarization; engine-room machinery familiarization; rope and wire work; derricks and lifting gear; tanker safety; and general ship knowledge. Successful trainees gain remission of sea services, and are required to serve at sea as junior deck ratings for only two months before promotion.

2. Junior engine room rating

Again, this is a 13-week course. Junior engine room ratings complete much of the work undertaken by the deck trainee, but also receive instruction in a ship's main propulsion machinery and basic electrical equipment. Most of the instruction and work is of a practical nature and includes instruction on the safety precautions to be taken when using machinery. The course also includes an introduction to workshop practice.

3. Catering rating

This eleven-week course is designed to prepare ratings for work in either the main galley or as stewards. In addition to the safety training already described, there is instruction in basic cookery, food service and housekeeping, nutrition, personal hygiene and food hygiene.

4. The Supplementary Scheme

Supplementary Scheme trainees attend a nautical training college and follow the same course as that taken by junior deck ratings. They also have additional classes to revise basic educational subjects such as maths, and to introduce them to chartwork and navigation.

Two periods of seagoing training follow, usually with leave between. During this sea phase, trainees must follow a correspondence course and gain practical experience.

The third phase – one academic term – is college-based, studying a range of academic subjects, and this is followed by another seagoing phase. A further correspondence course and record book work are undertaken, and trainees are given instruction about officers' duties and bridge watch-keeping. After a minimum of 26 months at sea, trainees return to college for two academic terms, leading to the examination for the Department of Transport Class 4 Certificate of Competency (or Class 3, depending on progress). Ratings may then apply for a vacancy as a third officer.

Over the next five years the Merchant Navy is introducing a system of qualifications based on NVQs/SVQs. It is envisaged that this system of training and assessment, in combination with oral examinations, will become the only route to gaining Certificates of Competency. NVQs/SVQs in Merchant Vessel Operations are currently available at Levels 2, 3 and 4.

LATE ENTRY

Late entry is unusual, except for engine-room ratings with recognized engineering qualifications in maritime-related subjects obtained ashore.

OPPORTUNITIES

Individual shipping companies recruit their own ratings. Some companies employ British officers but use foreign crew to man the ship, so job opportunities for trainee ratings do not arise as frequently as for cadets. Some school-leavers who join as ratings have a chance to train as officers while working as part of the crew; this is known as the Supplementary Scheme. For details, please see ENTRY REQUIREMENTS and TRAINING.

For a description of different types of employer, please see article 1. MERCHANT NAVY DECK OFFICER.

PAY AND CONDITIONS

The weekly rate is based on a 40-hour week, but the average overtime worked by a seaman grade 1A on a foreign-going ship is over 25 hours a week. The basic rate is about £115 a week; the average weekly pay may work out at about £270. Many shipping companies pay a salary that consolidates the average overtime worked.

For conditions, please see article 1. MERCHANT NAVY DECK OFFICER.

PROSPECTS

During the first six to twelve months of sea service, promotion depends on length of service and age. After that, it depends on qualifications held, on service, and on ability. Deck ratings and engine-room ratings can advance to petty officer and chief petty officer. After about a year at sea, catering ratings can opt to become stewards, and ultimately advance to chief steward; or, with study for additional qualifications, they may become cook, then chief cook. Catering officers on passenger carrying vessels are usually promoted from catering ratings, though there are very few such posts.

RELATED OCCUPATIONS

Royal Navy rating, chef/cook, motor vehicle mechanic, maintenance fitter, Merchant Navy deck officer, Merchant Navy engineering officer.

FURTHER INFORMATION

Chamber of Shipping, Merchant Navy Training Board, Carthusian Court, Carthusian Street, London EC1M 6EB, 0171 417 8400

The National Sea Training Centre (NSTC)*, Denton, Gravesend, Kent DA12 2HR, 01474 363656

Ship Safe Training Group Ltd*, 2nd Floor, 135 High Street, Rochester, Kent ME1 1EW, 01634 405252

FURTHER READING

Leaflets/booklets are available from the addresses marked*.

In the careers library classified under YAL.

1. WAREHOUSE WORKER CLCI:YAT
2. LIFT TRUCK OPERATOR CLCI:YAT

1. WAREHOUSE WORKER (YAT)

BACKGROUND INFORMATION

Warehouses receive, store and send out all kinds of raw materials and manufactured goods. Items may pass through several different warehouses before sale or export, moving around in bulk or singly. The types of work and the numbers of people employed depend on the goods stored and the size of the warehouse; one or two people may do all the tasks described below, or there may be several employees, each with a specialized job.

THE WORK

Warehouse workers are involved in receiving, storing and sending out goods from warehouses.

Checking goods in and out. Goods arrive either from another department, as finished goods for dispatch, or from outside, as parts to be stored and used within the firm, such as fresh foods or component parts for engineering. The warehouse worker carefully checks everything that comes in and signs the delivery forms when everything is accounted for. This can be a long job, causing congestion if more than one lorry arrives at the same time. Warehouse workers may unload and stack goods by hand or may use trolleys and lift trucks (some warehouses employ full-time lift truck drivers to move heavy goods). It may be necessary to check dates for the use of goods and stack them accordingly. Supervisors and department managers arrange storage locations.

Order picking/assembling. Items that have been ordered, either by customers or by other departments of the firm, must be picked out. Order pickers/assemblers work from order sheets given out at the beginning of the day. Paperwork is involved in noting inconsistencies in orders, checking the state of stocks and re-ordering if necessary. To reach goods, workers often have to walk, stretch, bend and use ladders.

Packing. Assembled orders are prepared for posting or transporting in the smallest, safest, lightest packages possible. Goods may have to be checked for faults before dispatch.

Storekeeping. This may include counter work – selling parts to customers or to people in the trade – which involves taking money, dealing with cheques and debit and credit cards, and giving advice on a wide range of items of stock. Most store departments have computerized record systems; store staff may use computer terminals or refer to print-outs to check availability of parts.

WORK ENVIRONMENT

Warehouses are found throughout the UK, eg in mail-order firms, hospitals, supermarkets and manufacturing industries of all kinds. Warehouses are often large and airy; they can be cold in winter. Some (for perishable foods, for example) are refrigerated and staff must wear protective clothing. Warehouse workers are exposed to all weathers when accepting deliveries or loading lorries.

SKILLS AND INTERESTS

Warehouse workers need to be able to carry out basic figure work to check deliveries. They also require neat handwriting for marking orders.

Computers may be used in some warehouses, to check goods in and out and to monitor stock levels. Workers should be adaptable and willing to learn how to use new technology.

Honesty is essential; a good memory is an asset. Warehouse workers should also be neat, tidy and safety-conscious, especially when stacking and storing goods and moving them from heights. Stacking and storing goods requires the ability to judge space.

Some workers operate lift trucks to move large or heavy goods.

ENTRY REQUIREMENTS

No academic entry qualifications are usually required; however, entrants must be able to read and write clearly and carry out basic figure work.

The physical ability to lift and carry goods is necessary. Some employers use colour-coded stock control systems; applicants may have to pass a colour vision test.

Entry may be via specific training schemes for young people.

TRAINING

Training is usually given on the job, given by experienced warehouse workers.

Training schemes for young people offer a combination of off-the-job training and work experience.

NVQs/SVQs in Wholesaling, Warehousing and Stores are available at Levels 1 and 2.

LATE ENTRY

There is no upper age limit for entry; many employers prefer adult entrants.

There may be specific training opportunities directed at adults available in some areas for this type of work. Candidates may have to satisfy certain conditions to be eligible. Contact your local Jobcentre, careers office or TEC/LEC for details.

OPPORTUNITIES

There are vacancies in many types of warehouses throughout the UK. Employers include supermarkets, hospitals, engineering and textile firms, colleges, offices, garages and DIY stores. They are located both in towns and on industrial estates. In large warehouses, workers are more likely to specialize in tasks such as store keeping and order picking.

PAY AND CONDITIONS

Wages vary and there are often bonus schemes on top of the basic pay which ranges from around £190 to £260 a week. Overtime rates can also increase wages.

Warehouse staff work around 40 hours a week. Some do shifts, involving early morning, late night or Saturday work. Overtime work is often available and it may also be possible to work part-time.

PROSPECTS

There may be opportunities for promotion with some employers. Warehouse workers may move into different types of warehouse work such as full-time lift truck driving.

Those with ability and experience may progress to supervisory posts, in charge of a number of workers. It is possible to move into warehouse management. NVQs/ SVQs are available for managers in Wholesaling, Warehousing and Stores at Levels 3 and 4.

RELATED OCCUPATIONS

Lift truck operator, storekeeper, packer, warehouse manager, motor vehicle parts.

FURTHER INFORMATION

Institute of Logistics, Douglas House, Queen's Square, Corby, Northamptonshire NN17 1PL, 01536 205500

United Kingdom Warehousing Association, Walter House, 418-422 Strand, London WC2R 0PT, 0171 836 5522

FURTHER READING

In the careers library classified under YAT.

2. LIFT TRUCK OPERATOR (YAT)

BACKGROUND INFORMATION

Most factories and warehouses dealing with goods employ at least one person to operate a lift truck. There are many different types of lift truck, from small conventional front and side-loading lift and reach trucks to large industrial tractors, rough terrain and platform trucks, pedestrian-controlled and straddle-carriers. This article concentrates on the operation of conventional reach and counter-balanced lift trucks, operated by hand levers and foot controls, and powered by electricity, petrol, diesel or bottled gas.

On a standard counter-balanced lift truck the load is raised, carried and lowered outside the wheelbase of the truck with the weight of the load forward of the front axle. Reach trucks work the same way, but the load is carried within, or partially within, the wheelbase of the truck. A reach mast is extended to pick up the load and retracted to transport the load. The two projecting forks or lifting attachments used on both these types of lift truck are operated hydraulically.

THE WORK

Lift trucks are operated by one person and allow quick and easy transportation of heavy goods. Goods are loaded and unloaded from lorries, aircraft or vans and stacked on a level or at heights.

Loading, unloading and stacking. Before lifting the load, operators must know the rated capacity of the load and then make sure the truck is not overloaded or the load unstable.

Operators stack loose items or goods on pallet boards – open-sided platforms which hold the goods above the ground leaving space for the forks underneath. Storage space is costly and limited, so goods are often stored in high stacks. To stack, the operator approaches a stack with a load at ground level, then elevates the load to the required height, moves the truck slowly forward to position the load as required, and lowers the load onto the stack. Operators have to make sure they do not dislodge adjacent stacks or catch the load on any overhead obstacles. Having stacked the load safely the forks are lowered until free of the load, and the truck is reversed clear.

Transporting. Operators have to drive accurately; space is limited in warehouses and factories, gangways are often only just wide enough for a truck's movements. Operators must be able to operate the truck in reverse, for example, when transporting a load down a slope or when travelling up inclines unladen. They must know the layout of the workplace, and be aware of any obstacles, such as lights, cables and support columns, and must remove any obstructions.

Safety. The operator must drive carefully, load the truck correctly, and make sure that the stack is secure. They have to give signals, warning horns, etc.

Maintenance. Operators may be responsible for carrying out simple inspection and maintenance work on the truck, for example, charging the battery or refuelling. Routine daily checks must be made, and any defects must be reported to the service engineer.

Miscellaneous duties. Operators usually have to keep simple records, and must be able to follow worksheet instructions. They may also help load and unload trucks manually and perform other warehouse duties such as packing.

WORK ENVIRONMENT

Operators work both indoors, in a warehouse, and outside, in a goods yard or transporting goods to other sites. Some trucks have enclosed cabs which provide some protection against adverse weather, but outdoor work can still be cold and wet.

Operating lift trucks involves sitting for most of the day.

SKILLS AND INTERESTS

Lift truck operators must have a responsible attitude, and a patient and steady approach to their work; loading, unloading and stacking can take a long time. They must be able to follow safety rules and understand the importance of safe and careful operating.

Operators require good physical co-ordination to operate a truck and to be able to assess weights, distances, etc. It may be necessary to follow written instructions, complete worksheets and keep records.

Lift truck operators must be able to co-operate with other members of staff.

ENTRY REQUIREMENTS

No formal educational qualifications are needed but there are recommended minimum age limits in some sectors of industry. In road haulage and distribution, the recommended minimum age is 17 years, and this is in line with the requirements of the Health and Safety Executive. There is an approved code of practice covering operation and training. Applicants may have to pass a medical and an assessment test to determine their suitability for training. A driving licence is not required if a truck is used on works property only, but many employers may prefer candidates to hold one.

TRAINING

The Road Transport Industry Training and Business (RTITB) Services recommends that basic training should be provided for all lift truck operators, either by an RTITB-accredited in-house training scheme or a training scheme run by an RTITB-accredited commercial organization. Those run by commercial organizations – for example, lift truck manufacturers or specialist training companies – may take place in a training centre or on the employer's premises. Basic training courses usually last from one to five days, and involve theoretical and practical instruction and exercises. Subjects include: an introduction to the truck; mounting and dismounting; steering techniques; using the controls; lifting and depositing; stacking and de-stacking; transporting; and working in confined areas. Trainees are also taught safe operating practices, engineering principles (counter-balance, stability, and so on), and truck maintenance procedures (inspection, re-fuelling, etc). A certificate of basic training is awarded on successful completion of some courses. RTITB Services recommendations specify that all basic training should be carried out off the job by an RTITB-accredited training provider.

Basic training is usually followed by specific job and familiarization training, provided by the employer. Operators work under supervision after basic training until fully competent.

NVQs/SVQs in Lift Truck Operations at Level 2 are available and may be combined with Assisting in Road Haulage and Distribution Operations at Level 1 and Storing Goods for Distribution by Road at Level 2.

LATE ENTRY

Prospects for adult entry are quite good; employers often prefer adult applicants and look for a mature and responsible attitude. Some experience of work in warehouses or stores may be an advantage.

There may be specific training opportunities directed at adults available in some areas for this type of work. Candidates may have to satisfy certain conditions to be eligible. Contact your local Jobcentre, careers office or TEC/LEC for details.

OPPORTUNITIES

Lift truck operators work in factories, stores, warehouses, goods yards or heavy haulage depots. They may be employed in any industry dealing with heavy or bulky goods.

It is estimated that there are around 750,000 lift trucks in operation in Britain, with 1,250,000 people operating them.

PAY AND CONDITIONS

Pay varies according to employer and hours worked. Generally operators can expect to receive wages ranging from around £140 to £260 a week. Additional payments may be made for shift and night work. Some employers have productivity bonus schemes which can raise earnings. Overtime rates are paid for extra hours.

Operators work hours to suit their employers. This can involve: standard day hours, Monday to Friday; shifts covering 24 hours; double day shifts; or permanent nights. Overtime may be available and may be required by some employers.

PROSPECTS

Promotion prospects are limited. Suitable and experienced operators may be selected to train as instructors; a number of companies are accredited by RTITB Services to offer specialist instructor training courses. Courses feature an independently conducted test and examination, success in which leads to registration on the National Register of Approved Instructors/Examiners maintained by Road Transport Industry Training and Business Services, and the award of a RTITB certificate of registration. The registration is valid for five years and may be renewed after re-examination of the instructor. Some operators progress by moving to other related jobs – for example, as supervisors in warehousing or dispatch.

RELATED OCCUPATIONS

Warehouse worker, car/van driver, LGV driver, construction plant operator.

FURTHER INFORMATION

RTITB Services*, CENTREX Training and Conference Centre, High Ercall, Telford, Shropshire TF6 6RB, 01952 770441

FURTHER READING

Leaflets/booklets are available from the address marked*.

In the careers library classified under YAT.

DIVER CLCI:YAZ

BACKGROUND INFORMATION

Diving in itself is not a career, it should instead be considered as a vehicle to enable a person to carry out a job underwater instead of on land. Some divers dive full-time, others such as marine scientists may dive as part of their work. There are a number of different types of divers: commercial divers who work inland, inshore and offshore; police underwater search divers; Royal Navy divers; recreational diving instructors; and some marine scientists and nautical archaeologists. Occasionally divers are needed for film and television work.

THE WORK

Commercial diving –this is divided into two areas:

Inshore diving – this covers up to twelve miles from the coastline plus inland diving in reservoirs, rivers, canals, fish farms and lakes. Inshore and inland work is basically civil and structural engineering but underwater. Divers can be involved in port, harbour, reservoir and bridge inspection, construction and repair, construction of new sewage outfalls and lock gate inspection. They also carry out remedial work in lakes, rivers, reservoirs, canals, etc. Where existing structures are to be removed they may demolish them with explosives. Divers build the structures and inspect them during and after construction for any faults. After structures are completed they regularly inspect and maintain them. Fish farms are another area needing divers, and here their work could include, for instance, sorting out nets or recovering dead fish. In ports, divers may also be used for such tasks as untangling ropes from a ship's propeller.

Offshore diving includes the exploration and exploitation of sub-sea oil and gas resources all over the world. Divers work from ships or oil platforms and their work includes laying and maintaining pipelines and lines for communication systems. This may involve digging trenches on the sea bed using specialized equipment and laying and connecting the pipes, which may involve welding. They carry out construction and maintenance work on oil platforms and rigs and inspect the structures for corrosion either by eye, underwater cameras or non-destructive testing equipment such as ultrasonics. They clear marine growth from the parts of rigs and platforms under the sea and carry out repairs.

Police underwater search divers search for stolen property both in and out of the water. They also search for and recover bodies from lakes, canals, reservoirs, rivers, sewers, drains and cesspits. In many cases there is little or no visibility and divers carry out their searches purely by feeling. They also deal with corpses on land where decomposition has taken place and breathing apparatus has to be worn. In the case of VIPs visiting an area, they carry out underwater security searches for explosives. Another part of their work is assisting customs and excise officers by searching the hulls of ships for drugs. There is not usually enough work for underwater search teams to dive full-time, so they also work in support groups carrying out general police duties.

Royal Navy divers – there are three types of divers in the Royal Navy, but all begin their careers in another specialization. Ship's divers or diving officers are based on board every ship in the Fleet and, although not full-time divers, they may be called upon at any time to check the ship's hull for limpet mines, carry out simple underwater maintenance tasks, or search for equipment lost over the side in harbour. Ship's divers in the Fleet Air Arm may volunteer to become search and rescue (SAR) divers. Usually working from helicopters, they are trained to rescue people trapped in capsized vessels or crashed aircraft, or from coastal cliff faces.

Ship's divers and diving officers in the Fleet may volunteer to become full-time clearance divers. These divers are trained in all aspects of air and mixed-gas diving, some becoming saturation qualified. They are also trained to use all underwater tools and camera equipment and carry out bomb and mine disposal, search open water, for lost aircraft, for instance, and carry out underwater engineering and battle damage repair. Clearance divers are based either on mine countermeasures vessels or in specialized teams ashore.

Marine scientists – divers may be from any discipline needing to research underwater, including biologists, chemists, geologists and geographers. Their work is concerned with scientific data collection and observation. Depending on their discipline they could be testing oceanographic equipment or studying sea life – both plants and fish, looking at distribution patterns of various forms of sea life and examining the effects of pollution.

Nautical archaeologists – like the marine scientists, most nautical archaeologists do not dive full-time, although a small number do. Their work includes surveying vessels that have sunk. Normally they gather data and then protect the vessel from any threat. In exceptional cases, such as the *Mary Rose* they are involved in recovering the vessel and bringing it on to land. They also survey any settlements that are now underwater.

All of these divers work in teams of about four or five. One diver is underwater, the others are on the surface. One of the team looks after that diver and communicates with them – this may be through a series of pulls on a rope attached to the diver or by voice through a communication line. Another diver is ready as a standby in case of emergency, and the fourth is preparing to dive. In addition there is a diving supervisor who controls the diving operation.

Recreational diving instructors – teach snorkelling and scuba diving to both children and adults. They teach both the theory and practice of scuba diving – diving in pairs, sharing an airline, using and caring for equipment, the theory of tides, underwater navigation, how to swim underwater, and how to prevent problems and get out of trouble.

Film and television work – very occasionally divers are needed for this type of work. Camera work is done by experienced camera crews who also have the relevant diving qualifications. The underwater actors may be stunt-men/women who are qualified divers, or in some cases commercial divers may be used.

All divers wear specialized equipment, which varies depending on the type of diving. It includes protective suits – these may be dry suits or, in the case of offshore diving, they may wear suits through which warm water is pumped. They wear fins, or in some cases weighted boots. Some have full face masks; others wear helmets. Their breathing supply may be from cylinders strapped to their backs, or in many cases it is supplied by pipe from the surface.

WORK ENVIRONMENT

Commercial divers – offshore diving contractors are mainly based in Aberdeen and Great Yarmouth. Offshore divers, when diving, live on board ships and on oil platforms, in Britain and abroad. They are often required to take up a job at very short notice, and may be away from home for considerable periods of time. Inshore divers travel from their homes to wherever in the country they are needed, and stay there for the duration of the contract which is often only a couple of days.

The waters they dive in are usually dark and, in some cases, can be cold in spite of protective clothing. Although divers are part of a team, once underwater they are often on their own. Some offshore divers work from diving bells, which can be cramped. Divers involved in deep work may be required to live in compression chambers for up to four weeks at a time.

Police underwater search divers dive in lakes, rivers, canals, reservoirs, drains and cesspits. They are based with one police authority and have to travel to anywhere within their area. They may also have to travel to neighbouring authorities who do not have an underwater search unit.

Recreational diving instructors usually work in a rather more pleasant environment, in swimming pools and suitable diving waters in the UK and abroad.

Marine scientists and archaeologists' environment depends on where they are working. Some of their work may be in warm clear waters. Their work can involve travel both in Britain and abroad.

Royal Navy divers are based at inshore establishments, here and abroad, and on board ship. They may be required to dive in any conditions at any time of the day or night.

SKILLS AND INTERESTS

Firstly, divers must be comfortable and confident in the water. It is vital that they can work as part of a team – the lives of divers depend on others in their team. They also have to be comfortable working on their own underwater with just a communication line to divers on the surface. They should be physically fit. All divers need to be very safety conscious; they also have to be able to keep calm and act quickly in emergencies. Police divers in particular need to be very painstaking and methodical to carry out searches.

ENTRY REQUIREMENTS

Commercial divers –divers must have the appropriate Health and Safety Executive (HSE) qualifications for the job they wish to do. There are no specific academic entry requirements for diving schools, although those who have no previous relevant qualifications or experience such as engineering or construction work, welding, photography, mechanics fitting, plumbing or electrical work, may find it extremely difficult to get work. All applicants for diving schools undergo a medical and need to be medically fit and able swim. Also, most have a commercial diving aptitude test which includes checks in maths and English, a swimming test, manual dexterity, and a shallow recompression chamber dive.

Police underwater search divers – join as police constables; after two years' probation, they can then apply to join an underwater search unit. Applicants must be physically fit and be able to swim. All applicants are interviewed to determine their suitability for this work. Please see the article POLICE CONSTABLE (MAB).

Royal Navy divers – there is no direct entry into this specialization – divers transfer from other branches. Please see Royal Navy articles (BAB).

Recreational diving instructors – all paid recreational diving instructors in the UK must hold a certificate of training recognized by the Health and Safety Executive, such as the HSE part 4 (restricted). There are a number of good training schools and lists of addresses can be obtained from the Health and Safety Executive.

To start an instructors' course applicants have to be able to swim and to hold relevant diving qualifications, such as BSAC's sports diver and dive leader qualifications, or PADI's open water diver, advanced open water diver, rescue diver and dive master qualifications. There may also be some medical restrictions.

Marine scientists and archaeologists require a degree, often a PhD in the appropriate discipline, plus appropriate HSE diving qualifications. Many take up diving whilst at university and already have a relevant sports diving qualification.

TRAINING

The main qualifications for professional divers are those issued by the Health and Safety Executive. With the exception of police and Armed Forces divers, others usually have to finance their own training.

Most courses leading to HSE qualifications cost between £1,200 and £7,500 plus accommodation for the duration of the course. A small number of academic institutions may finance marine scientists through their diving training. Recreational instructors also finance their own training, although this is more in the region of a couple of hundred pounds.

There are five UK diving training standards:

– HSE Part 4 (professional scuba diver). This is a three-and-a-half-week to four-week course which costs about £1,200. Holders are qualified to use underwater breathing apparatus, breathing air to a maximum depth of 50 metres.

– HSE Part 4 (restricted). Courses for this vary in length – contact diving schools for information. Holders are restricted to the instruction of amateur divers.

– HSE Part 3 (inshore air diver). This is a four to six-week course costing about £2,000. Holders are qualified to use scuba and surface supplied equipment, breathing air to a maximum depth of 50 metres, for operations not connected with offshore installations.

– HSE Part 2 (mixed gas diver). Before taking this course divers must first have held HSE Part 1 for twelve months and had considerable commercial experience. Divers are qualified to operate from closed diving bells using gas mixtures other than air, to depths over 50 metres. The course lasts three weeks and costs about £7,500.

– HSE Part 1. This is a ten-week course costing about £4,000. Scuba divers are qualified to use surface supplied equipment, a wet bell and certain tools, breathing air to a maximum of 50 metres.

These four courses vary but most cover diving medicine and physics, elementary seamanship and small boat handling, use of diving equipment, operation and maintenance of hand tools and legislation.

Police underwater search diversare trained at one of the two police diving schools in Glasgow or Newcastle. They undergo an eight-week course leading to HSE Part 3.

Royal Navy divers. All Royal Navy divers must start as ship's divers. Training involves a four-week course using compressed air equipment and learning how to perform elementary underwater tasks. They may then expect to spend at least two years on a ship or submarine as part of a team, honing their skills and gaining experience.

A ship's diver in the Fleet Air Arm may then volunteer to become an SAR diver. This involves further training to become familiar with the operation of helicopters and additional diving training to acquire SAR skills.

Other ship's divers, if they enjoy diving and would like to become one of the RN's professional divers, may then apply to become clearance divers. If they are officers they do an intensive course (of approximately nine months), specializing in both mine warfare and clearance diving. Ratings do a basic course to qualify as able seaman (divers) and further advancement courses at each stage of their careers. Many RN qualifications are recognized by the HSE.

Recreational diving instructors – courses cover all aspects of diving instruction both theory and practical and include an examination. Some instructors also take HSE courses. For jobs abroad they usually go on to a further advanced instructing course, also followed by an examination.

Marine scientists – usually have to finance their own training, and most go up to HSE Part 4.

LATE ENTRY

There are no maximum age limits for divers, although they must be physically fit and undergo a medical examination every year. Entry and training are as described above.

OPPORTUNITIES

Most commercial divers work for firms of diving contractors, on short-term contracts. The need for divers has been decreasing over recent years – one of the reasons being the use of Remotely Operated Vehicles (ROVs) which can do some of the tasks previously done by divers. Both offshore and inshore divers live anywhere in the country but must be prepared to travel anywhere in the world.

Police underwater search divers are usually based with one police authority; however, not all authorities have an underwater search unit and they may have to travel to neighbouring areas without one. There are not many police divers – an underwater search unit covering a large geographical area may have as few as nine divers.

Recreational diving instructors – this is the one area where opportunities are increasing, as more people today are interested in learning to dive. In particular, there are increasing opportunities abroad in diving holiday centres. Entry into this work is extremely competitive and would-be divers are advised to get as much relevant experience and training as possible.

PAY AND CONDITIONS

Inshore divers earn between £35 and £100 a day. Offshore divers may earn from £130 to £210 a day. All commercial divers work on contracts. Offshore contracts may last about two to four weeks. If it is a long-term contract then there may be teams of divers working one month on and one month off; however, during their time off they are not paid. Inshore divers tend to do small contracts of as little as one or two days each.

Hours vary depending on the type of diving – offshore divers usually work shifts of twelve hours on, twelve hours off. Police and Royal Navy divers work shifts but are on-call 24 hours a day, seven days a week.

PROSPECTS

Commercial diving – as divers gain experience they can achieve more pay. The normal promotion route is from diver to diving supervisor in charge of a team of divers. Divers wanting promotion or the better paid jobs usually take further courses to qualify them as: underwater inspectors, trained to carry out underwater visual inspections and operate video and still cameras; or diver medics – trained to give emergency assistance to a casualty and carry out first aid action under medical guidance. Divers with considerable experience may also take HSE Part 2 which opens up the possibility of deep and saturation diving at considerably more pay.

For those with the necessary qualifications and experience it may be possible to work as a HM Inspector of Health and Safety.

RELATED OCCUPATIONS

Training instructor, sports coach, teacher, RN rating.

FURTHER INFORMATION

Health and Safety Executive*, Rose Court, 2 Southwark Bridge, London SE1 9HS, 0171 717 6000/6307

Society for Underwater Technology*, 76 Mark Lane, London EC3R 7JN, 0171 481 0750

Nautical Archaeological Society, c/o 19 College Road, HM Naval Base, Portsmouth PO1 3LJ, 01705 818419

From individual diving schools – addresses from HSE.

FURTHER READING

Leaflets/booklets are available from the addresses marked*.

In the careers library classified under YAZ.

INDEX

INDEX

INDEX

INDEX